(continued from front flap)

Interspersed with the company profiles are numerous short articles and fillers that give inside information on the business world, and many photographs, drawings, cartoons, and charts. Of unique value is the only published index to link all the major brand names with the companies that produce them.

An unparalleled reference work, essential for both consumer and executive, *Everybody's Business* is the one eye-opening and indispensable guide to the people, products, and profits of corporate America.

Milton Moskowitz, a longtime "corporation watcher," has been writing about business for over twenty-five years. For the last twelve years he has written a popular column appearing in newspapers nationwide through The Los Angeles Times syndicate.

EVERYBODY'S BUSINESS

EVERYBODY'S BUSINESS

AN ALMANAC

The Irreverent Guide to Corporate America

EDITED BY

Milton Moskowitz
Michael Katz
Robert Levering

Harper & Row, Publishers, San Francisco
Cambridge, Hagerstown, Philadelphia, New York,
London, Mexico City, São Paulo, Sydney

1817

ACKNOWLEDGMENTS

Everybody's Business reflects the perceptions of its three editors, but it involved a team effort of writers, editors, researchers, fact checkers, administrative whizzes, typists, messengers, and assorted tipsters: our masthead (page v) lists the principal contributors by name. We are indebted to a number of other people and organizations, above all the Data Center, a remarkable research arm located at 464 19th Street, Oakland, California 94612, (415) 835-4692. A nonprofit, user-supported library with a vast collection of newspaper and periodical clippings on labor, corporate, and industry topics, they also offer an information search service on subjects related to U.S. corporations and their influence around the world.

Two other nonprofit research outfits were important sources of information. One was the Council on Economic Priorities, who publish regular reports on topics related to the social and political impact of American corporations, such as equal employment, environmental quality, military production, consumer practices, and foreign activities. The Council is headquartered at 84 Fifth Avenue, New York, New York 10011, (212) 691-8550. The other important resource was the Corporate Data Exchange. Their manuals, available from their office at 198 Broadway, Room 706, New York, New York 10038, (212) 962-2980, give a picture of the major owners of U.S. corporations.

Among others we want to acknowledge are Theodore L. Cross, editor and publisher of *Business and Society Review*, whose suggestions were always on target; Robert Kahn, management consultant and publisher of *Retailing Today*, whose fund of knowledge matches the modern computerized information banks; and Mary Jane Kaplan, who injected her organizational skills into a sprawling editorial operation at precisely the time they were needed.

Finally, we are especially grateful for the support we got from Harper & Row's San Francisco office. Despite the almost overwhelming demands of the schedule and the sheer volume of manuscript, our friends at Harper & Row continued to provide invaluable help toward the successful completion of the book. Thank you Dessa Brashear, Marie Cantlon, Clayton Carlson, Tom Dorsaneo, Jim Fox (in New York), Joanne Farness, Catherine Hopkins, Lucia Kelly (in New York), Richard Lucas, Kathy Reigstad, and Eva Marie Strock.

We would also like to express our appreciation to the following people who made valuable contributions to the book: Paul Cohen, Barbara Curcio, Mildred Howie, Bob Johnson, Alice Tepper Marlin, Francis Moriarty, Jane Radcliff, Dick Raymond, Lawrence Schulz, Gordon Sherman, JoAnn Sonn, Janet Stock, Lee Townsend, Charles Varon, and Beclee Wilson.

Acknowledgments for materials used with permission appear on page 916.

Library of Congress Cataloging in Publication Data
Main entry under title:

Everybody's business.

Includes indexes.
1. Corporations—United States—Handbooks, manuals, etc. 2. United States—Commerce—Handbooks, manuals, etc. 3. United States—Industries—Handbooks, manuals, etc. 4. Big business—United States—Handbooks, manuals, etc. I. Moskowitz, Milton. II. Katz, Michael. III. Levering, Robert.
HD2785.E88   338.7'4'0973   80-7336
ISBN 0-06-250620-X
ISBN 0-06-250621-8 (pbk)

80 81 82 83 84   10 9 8 7 6 5 4 3 2

Staff writers: Linda Hess, Judith Landy, Michael E. Miller, Mark Paul, Susan Shepard, W. A. Van Winkle

Researchers/Fact checkers: Wendy Batson, Eileen Murray, Katy O'Connell, Paulette Long

Administrative coordinator: Haruko Smith

Contributing writers: Adele Framer, Georgia Smith, Valerie Blalock, Paul Hawken, Katherine Hughes, Leslie Goldberg, Carol Townsend

Contributors: Susan Benson, Tom DeVries, Paul Gillette, Betty Killich, Steve Koppman, Herb Lawson, Tim Miller, Kirk Nicewonger, Elizabeth Tuomi, Carol Williams

Research assistants: Camille Cusumano, Susan Mesner, Mary Ellen Farwell, Cres Fraley, Gary Kamiya, Wil Kirkland, Sandra Leatherman, Gita Macmillan, Mitch Paradise, Ann Robertson

Indexers: Margaretta Northrop Kamiya, Michael E. Miller

Copy editor: Susan Weisberg

Proofreaders: Katherine Lee, Patricia Reilly

Illustrator: Tom Durfee

Design and art direction: Bruce Kortebein/ Design Office

Typography: Haddon Craftsmen (Com Com, Inc.), Turner, Brown & Yeoman, Inc., Petrographics/Typeworld, Mercury Typography

Page make-up: Nanci Chin, Donna Davis, Leslie Yee

CONTENTS

INTRODUCTION

Big corporations do much to shape how we live, yet there has been no book in which to look up such central players in American life as Exxon, Kellogg, Sears, ITT, and RCA. Most of the published information about them is written in a special language and documented with statistical tables that mean little to many of us.

Everybody's Business answers a wide range of questions about 317 large companies—without jargon or technical language. We have tried to fashion a work that is more than a mere collection of facts. We have attempted to penetrate the reclusiveness that characterizes most corporations, not so much to muckrake as to discover what is really distinctive about each company. Even the largest corporations have their own style and personality. Because we see corporations in human terms, as groups of people who make decisions and act in comprehensible ways, we use a grammatical construction that some may find offensive: we refer to companies as "they" and avoid the impersonal or inanimate "it."

In pursuing the differences between corporate personalities, we made a particular effort to track down and relate the histories of companies. Corporations, like people, are often better understood by looking at their past. In the business world, where eyes are usually fixed firmly on the road ahead, this exercise is seldom performed.

There are other useful keys to the corporate personality: sales figures tell you one thing, the presence (or absence) of minorities and women on the board of directors tells you something else. The number of brand names or companies they own gives you one picture of the corporation, the amount of time the company spends in courtrooms reveals still another.

How did we decide which companies to include? The first criterion was size: most of the largest companies in the country can be found in these pages. Nearly all those profiled take in more than $1 billion every year; well over half take in more than $2 billion. But size was not our only standard. Selection was biased in favor of companies whose products and/or services are household names. We also included some sub–$1 billion companies because they seemed to us to be important or just plain interesting.

Sprinkled among the company descriptions are numerous short essays and background facts that provide a behind-the-scenes look at the business world—fragments of forgotten history, tidbits about how certain industries operate, rankings and lists that tie together the information in the corporation profiles.

We hope the almanac we have assembled will be read with interest and amusement by friends, foes, and neutral observers of American business. We welcome responses from our readers, especially those who work for the companies included in this edition. Send your comments to: *Everybody's Business*, 1537 Franklin Street, San Francisco, California 94109.

Milton Moskowitz
Michael Katz
Robert Levering

GUIDE TO CORPORATION PROFILES

To make our profiles easier to read, we've adopted the format explained below. The reader will find that we have not rigidly adhered to our own format, however, often adding other kinds of material, sometimes omitting categories altogether.

Sales and Profits: The 1979 figures as reported by the company. Where companies do not disclose their figures (private companies such as Gallo or S. C. Johnson), we've used informed estimates from other sources.

Forbes 500 rank: The sales rankings taken from the May 12, 1980, issue of *Forbes*. We've used *Forbes* rather than the Fortune 500 listing because *Forbes* includes service companies (banks, insurance companies, airlines, utilities) as well as manufacturers.

Other rankings: These come from the company, from trade industry sources, and from articles about the company.

Founded: The starting year of that company which has an unbroken line to the corporation being profiled.

Employees: The company's own figures.

What they do: What they make or sell and how they do it.

History: Where they come from.

Reputation: How they're perceived by others.

What they own: Mostly physical properties (or other companies). The prime source is the company's 10-K report to the Securities and Exchange Commission.

Who owns and runs the company: The chief honchos—top officers, members of the board of directors. As for ownership, we mention only the holders of significantly large blocks of stock. The data comes generally from either the company's proxy statement to shareholders (which must disclose any ownership interest of more than five percent and usually reports the holdings of directors) or the ownership manuals issued by the Corporate Data Exchange. Where we have offered a dollar figure for the worth of an individual's stock holdings, it is based on that stock's price in early 1980.

In the public eye: Occasions that brought the company into the limelight. Among these could be lawsuits, studies done by public interest organizations, and charitable contributions made by the company.

Where they're going: An educated guess.

Access: The address and phone number of the home office. Information about plant tours, people to contact, and hot lines comes from the company.

Stock performance: These were calculated for us by Chase/Interactive Data. The two points of comparison are the price the stock was selling for on the first trading day of 1970 and the price it was selling for on January 2, 1980.

Consumer brands: The names of the products or services the company offers to consumers. Our principal sources were the companies themselves and the annual 100 Leading Advertisers issue of *Advertising Age*.

1

FOOD, GLORIOUS FOOD

Butchers, Bakers, and Canned-Food Makers

Beatrice

Sales: $7.5 billion
Profits: $261 million
Forbes 500 rank: 47
Rank in food processing: 1
Rank in dairy products: 2
Rank in yogurt: 1
Rank in ready-to-drink orange juice: 1
Rank in nuts: 2
Rank in Oriental foods: 2
Founded: 1894
Employees: 88,000
Headquarters: Chicago, Illinois

What they do. Beatrice Foods is the best-disguised conglomerate in the United States. They're the largest food company in the nation, but not many people outside the business world have heard of them. And Beatrice likes it that way. They don't make a lot of noise; they never promote the Beatrice name. What they do is move around and buy up other companies the way Monopoly players do when they land on property squares. Since 1943 they have landed on more than 400 companies. Twenty-five

years ago Beatrice was a $200 million dairy company. Today they're an $8 billion giant, unrecognized by the public, although virtually everyone in the country has probably bought something made by a Beatrice-owned company at one time or another.

When Beatrice swallows another company, its identity is never obliterated. On the contrary, they want the acquisition to continue under the same name, with its old brands, and usually with the same management. The only changes are that Beatrice owns most of the stock, the profits go to Chicago, and the company is watched carefully to see that it performs—in other words, increases sales and profits *every year*. As a corporation, Beatrice has done that for 28 consecutive years.

Beatrice owns dairies all over the country, producing milk, cream, cheese, butter, yogurt, and ice cream under a variety of brand names. Meadow Gold, Dannon, and Louis Sherry are a few of them. Food lines include La Choy (Oriental) and Rosarita (Mexican). Tropicana juices and Brookside wines belong to the stable, as do Swiss Miss chocolate mixes. Beatrice is one of the largest suppliers of food to restaurants under

Here's the Randy Carter family of San Jose, California, surrounded by what the average American family eats in a year: 2½ tons of food.

the John Sexton institutional label. They also own half a dozen soft drink bottling plants.

While food is the breading that holds this conglomerate together, the people at Beatrice have spiced their mix by acquiring companies in other fields: they also own the companies that make Samsonite luggage, Charmglow barbecues, Hekman furniture, Buxton wallets, Melnor sprinklers, Airstream motor homes, and Bonanza trailers.

Finally, since going overseas in 1961 with a condensed milk plant in Malaysia, Beatrice has gone around the world board enough times to own 185 plants in 28 countries, among them the giant Lacsoons dairy in Belgium, the leading ice cream maker in Denmark (Premier), and the Kaugummi chewing gum company in West Germany. Beatrice now makes dairy products or candy on every continent except Africa. Their international sales are $1.6 billion, eight times Beatrice's total sales 25 years ago.

All told, Beatrice companies market an estimated 9,000 different products, although it's unlikely that anyone has ever stopped to count them up.

History. Beatrice demonstrated very early on a knack for making money out of food. The enterprise was started in 1894 by two "butter and egg" men, George E. Haskell and William W. Bosworth, who formed a partnership in Beatrice, Nebraska. They bought butter, eggs, and poultry from farmers, graded them, and shipped them. Then they bought a churn to produce their own butter from milk provided by local farmers. The butter was churned, of course, from the cream skimmed off the milk. There was never enough cream, so Haskell and Bosworth established skimming stations where farmers could deliver their milk to have the cream separated off. There still wasn't enough cream, so Haskell and Bosworth supplied the farmers with hand cream separators. This enabled the farmers to separate the cream on the farm and keep the skim milk for animal feeding. The separators were not exactly given to the farmers; they were supplied on credit. The farmers paid for the separators from the proceeds of their sales of cream. The Beatrice Creamery Company did so well with this scheme that they sold 50,000 separators in Nebraska between 1895 and 1905. It was ingenious. First Beatrice made money selling cream separators to farmers. Then they made more money selling the butter which they churned from the cream skimmed off by the farmers.

By 1899 Beatrice was churning 940,000 pounds of butter a year. They pushed into other states, using the same system, and by

1904 the company was churning 10 million pounds of butter. They developed a brand name for their butter—Meadow Gold. It was trademarked in 1901 and became the first butter to be advertised in a national magazine in 1912. Later the name was used on other dairy products. (Meadow Gold dairy products can be found today in 46 out of the 50 states.)

The ice cream cone made its debut in 1904 at the St. Louis Exposition—and three years later Beatrice began making ice cream at Topeka, Kansas. A second ice cream plant was opened a few years later in Beatrice, and by 1910 Beatrice was operating nine creameries and had sales branches dotting the nation. To keep a watchful eye on this expanding business, Beatrice moved their headquarters to Chicago in 1913.

After George Haskell died in 1919, the next major thrust of the company was masterminded by his nephew, Clinton H. Has-

---

WHERE OUR FOOD COMES FROM

Top Livestock Producers
1. IOWA $4.3 billion
2. TEXAS $3.5 billion
3. CALIFORNIA $2.9 billion
4. WISCONSIN $2.6 billion
5. NEBRASKA $2.3 billion

Top Fruit, Vegetable, and Grain Producers
1. CALIFORNIA $6.5 billion
2. ILLINOIS $3.9 billion
3. TEXAS $3.4 billion
4. IOWA $2.8 billion
5. MINNESOTA $2.1 billion

Top Producers of Cattle and Calves
1. TEXAS $2.5 billion
2. IOWA $1.8 billion
3. KANSAS $1.7 billion
4. NEBRASKA $1.7 billion
5. COLORADO $1.2 billion

Top Pig Producers
1. IOWA $2.0 billion
2. ILLINOIS $941 million
3. INDIANA $555 million
4. MISSOURI $514 million
5. MINNESOTA $509 million

Top Dairy Producers
1. WISCONSIN $1.9 billion
2. CALIFORNIA $1.2 billion
3. NEW YORK $983 million
4. MINNESOTA $817 million
5. PENNSYLVANIA $809 million

Top Chicken Producers
1. ARKANSAS $489 million
2. GEORGIA $430 million
3. ALABAMA $353 million
4. NORTH CAROLINA $322 million
5. MISSISSIPPI $240 million

Top Egg Producers
1. CALIFORNIA $344 million
2. GEORGIA $287 million
3. ARKANSAS $176 million
4. NORTH CAROLINA $162 million
5. ALABAMA $158 million

Top Corn Growers
1. ILLINOIS $1.9 billion
2. IOWA $1.2 billion
3. INDIANA $1.0 billion
4. NEBRASKA $965 million
5. MINNESOTA $567 million

Top Wheat Growers
1. KANSAS $907 million
2. NORTH DAKOTA $532 million
3. OKLAHOMA $466 million
4. MINNESOTA $390 million
5. TEXAS $315 million

Top Potato Growers
1. IDAHO $229 million
2. WASHINGTON $148 million
3. CALIFORNIA $119 million
4. MAINE $115 million
5. OREGON $67 million

Top Rice Growers
1. ARKANSAS $368 million
2. TEXAS $211 million
3. LOUISIANA $171 million
4. CALIFORNIA $163 million
5. MISSISSIPPI $38 million

Top Tomato Growers
1. CALIFORNIA $579 million
2. FLORIDA $156 million
3. OHIO $46 million
4. NEW JERSEY $21 million
5. INDIANA $16 million

Top Peanut Growers
1. GEORGIA $315 million
2. ALABAMA $131 million
3. NORTH CAROLINA $90 million
4. TEXAS $81 million
5. OKLAHOMA $58 million

Top Orange Growers
1. FLORIDA $523 million
2. CALIFORNIA $140 million
3. TEXAS $18 million
4. ARIZONA $9 million
5. LOUISIANA $3 million

Top Apple Growers
1. WASHINGTON $199 million
2. NEW YORK $73 million
3. MICHIGAN $52 million
4. PENNSYLVANIA $37 million
5. NORTH CAROLINA $29 million

Source: U.S. Department of Agriculture, 1978.

kell, elected president in 1928. Beatrice then had four milk plants. By 1932 Beatrice had milk plants in 32 cities and was selling 27 million gallons a year. Beatrice became, along with Kraft and Borden, a powerful processor of dairy products. Indeed, they bought so many local dairy operations that the government stepped in and gained a court order putting a freeze on further acquisitions of milk plants.

In 1943, during World War II, Beatrice bought their first nondairy business: La Choy Food Products. Soon they were picking up companies all over the place, in foods and nonfoods, in the United States and other countries. By 1972 they were big enough to buy Eckrich meats, which already had sales of more than $200 million, as did Tropicana Foods, acquired in 1978. Beatrice has avoided companies that require major capital investments, looking instead for producers of "foods that grow in popularity at a greater rate than the population, such as candy, pickles, olives, specialty, and snack foods." Beatrice also has never taken over a company against the wishes of its management.

Reputation. Beatrice is known as a faceless conglomerate that doesn't make many mistakes. And if made, mistakes are not tolerated: companies and managers are eliminated if they don't measure up. Wallace Rasmussen, who ran Beatrice from 1976 to 1979, once said: "You don't dance with a skeleton very long."

What they own. The following plants, branches, warehouses, depots, distribution centers, and other facilities (both leased and owned) in the United States and overseas.

Food and related services:

Dairy and soft drinks	520
Grocery	190
Food distribution and warehousing	150
Specialty meats	60
Confectionery and snack	70
Agriproducts	60
	1,050

Manufactured and chemical products:

Institutional and industrial	120
Travel and recreational	100
Housing and home environment	130
Chemical and allied products	100
	450

Who owns and runs the company. Beatrice has been run by a series of tough-minded managers, most of them from the dairy business. Working for Beatrice is a little like serving in the army. At the bottom are 430 so-called profit centers—the companies that make and sell products and employ people. They report up to 81 groups. The 81 groups report up to 22 divisions. And the 22 divisions report up to corporate headquarters in Chicago where 250 people, including the top officers of the company, work. Chicago is where the scores are kept, where the major decisions are made. A worker in the Dannon yogurt plant in Long Island City is likely to know as much about what's going on in Chicago as a private in Fort Benning, Georgia, is likely to know about operations in the Pentagon.

Despite efforts to maintain a low profile, Beatrice top management occupied page one of the *Wall Street Journal* in 1979 because of a brief but intense power struggle. The issue was who should replace Rasmussen, who was retiring as chairman and chief executive officer. Press reports conflicted, but what seems to have happened is that certain newer directors tried to gain a majority on the Beatrice board after reports of bribes and payoffs to customers exceeding $20 million over a six-year period. The outsiders' motion was squashed by the Beatrice old hands who put in their own man, James L. Dutt, to succeed Rasmussen.

One of three directors who then resigned was Durward B. Varner, former president of the University of Nebraska (the state where Beatrice was born). Dr. Varner disclosed that the board had offered him a post of director emeritus for life at an annual salary of $12,000. He rejected the offer, making an emotional speech to the board in which he stated: "I can ill afford to give up the prospect of $12,000 or more for life for my family. Yet the issue is one of fundamentals. I simply couldn't in good conscience serve on this board or be paid for not serving and remaining silent. There is the basic question of my integrity, my honor, my sense of responsibility—and they aren't for sale at any price nor at any time."

In the public eye. To aid youth in a proper understanding of the free enterprise system, Beatrice invited 48 high school students from Los Angeles to attend the company's 80th annual meeting in 1977. Out of this exercise came two student essays, which won Beatrice-awarded prizes of $350 and $250. George G. Robinson, the winner of the top prize, wrote at the end of his essay: "My personal encounter with Mr. Rasmussen was short but will always be remembered. While we were shaking hands, one of the photographers took a picture. I was told personally by Mr. Rasmussen that the photo would probably be included in next year's annual report." It wasn't.

Where they're going. Rasmussen, a crusty executive, was once asked how long Beatrice could keep up its growth spurt. He said: "For eternity."

Stock performance. Beatrice stock bought for $1,000 in 1970 sold for $1,131 on January 2, 1980.

Access. 2 North LaSalle Street, Chicago, Illinois 60602; (312) 782-3820.

Major employment centers. Denver; Fort Wayne, Indiana; and Winston-Salem, North Carolina.

Consumer brands.

Dairy products: Meadow Gold and Viva; Dannon, Danny-Yo, Viva-Yo, and Yomix yogurt; Louis Sherry and Sanson ice cream; County Line cheese; Hotel Bar butter; Swiss Miss and Sanna hot chocolate.

Bakery products: Martha White bread & muffin mix; Mother's cookies; Little Brownie; Murray Biscuit; Krispy Kreme doughnuts; Country Hearth; Tatum Bakers and ButterKrust breads.

Specialty foods: La Choy Oriental foods, Gebhardt and Rosarita Mexican foods; Aunt Nellie's glass packed vegetables; Mario's olive products; Brown-Miller pickles; Shedd's peanut butter and margarine; Tropicana fruit drinks; Brookside wines; Peter Eckrich, Kneip, Lowrey's, Boizet, Campofrio and Rudolph meat and specialty meat products.

Confectionery and snacks: Switzer licorice; Richardsons after-dinner mints; Clark, ZagNut, The Jolly Rancher, Holloway Milk Duds, Phoenix Now & Later, Red Tulip, Savoy and Slo-Poke candies and chocolates; Fireside and Doumak marshmallows; Jubilee fruit toppings and Fisher Nuts.

Travel-related products: Airstream and Bonanza motor home; Mark Fore luggage carrier, Buxton leather goods; and Samsonite luggage.

Outdoor & sports clothing: Allison and Velva Sheen

T-shirts; Campus Casuals; Swingster caps and clothes; E. R. Moore jogging suits; Sportsline slumberbags.

Home furnishings: Samsonite, Hekman and John Hancock furniture; Beneke bathroom accessories; Liken, Max Kahn and Del Mar window coverings; Stiffel lamps; ArtistOKraft cabinets; Culligan water purifiers; Melnor water sprinklers; Charmglow Bar-B-Q grills; and Rid-O-Ray insect controller.

Sales: $4.3 billion
Profits: $134 million
Forbes 500 rank: 98
Rank in food processing: 12
Rank in dairy industry products: 3
Rank in cheeses: 2
Founded: 1857
Employees: 39,600
Headquarters: New York, New York

What they do. Borden is a chemical giant wrapped in a food package. They turn out a long line of food products, but for 30 years chemicals have been their explosive gainer. Borden ranks today as one of the nation's 15 largest chemical producers, and Borden chemicals yield greater profits than Borden foods. And since 1968 top officers have been coming from the chemical side of the business.

> **Food ranks as America's biggest industry, by any measure that is applied. Americans spend $250 billion a year on food—$1,000 for every man, woman, and child in the country.**
>
> **Food puts more people to work than any other business. Some 4 million people work on farms. Another 1.6 million are employed in the food processing industry, 2 million work in food stores, and another 4 million are employed at places that serve food.**

Borden grew up in the dairy business and remains one of the major producers of milk, ice cream, and cheeses. They're second only to Kraft in cheeses, and first in soft ripened cheeses (Liederkranz, camembert, brie, gruyere). Other food lines became Borden properties when the companies that make them were acquired. These include Wyler's drink mixes, Sacramento tomato juice, Snow's clam chowder, ReaLemon reconstituted lemon juice, Colonial sugar, Creamettes pastas, and Cracker Jack. (Borden sells 500 million boxes of Cracker Jack a year.) They still make their original product, Eagle condensed milk.

Borden also makes basic chemicals such as formaldehyde, methanol, acetic acid, urea, vinyl acetate, and vinyl chloride—and Borden's plants take nearly all of this output to produce a wide variety of intermediate and end products: fertilizers, plastic film, adhesives, printing inks, wall coverings, glues, tapes, spray paints. Elmer's glue and Mystik tape are two of their end products. Borden is believed to be the largest producer of formaldehyde, the basic building block in adhesive resins. Borden's plastic film, Resinite, is the leading brand of transparent film for the wrapping of meats and produce.

Gail Borden: the great compressor.

History. Returning in 1851 from England, where he had received a gold medal from Queen Victoria for his invention of a dehydrated meat biscuit, Gail Borden was anguished by the cries of hungry babies aboard ship. Four died from drinking contaminated milk. That experience impelled Borden, an inveterate tinkerer, to experiment until he came up with a vacuum process to remove water from milk and make it safe for use over a long period of time. He called his product condensed milk, received a patent for it in 1856, and started a company to make it in 1857.

Borden was already 56 years old when he launched his company in New York City. He had previously been a surveyor, school teacher, newspaper man, land owner, cattle raiser, and customs collector at the Port of Galveston. As editor of the *Telegraph and Texas Register*, the first permanent newspaper in Texas, he wrote a headline that became a famous rallying cry: "Remember the Alamo."

The Civil War brought Borden huge government orders for condensed milk, and the fledgling company netted $145,000 in 1864.

Gail Borden died in 1874. A year later his company, then called New York Condensed Milk, began selling fluid milk in New York City, delivering it by horse and wagon. In 1885 they became the first to sell fresh milk in bottles. By the end of the century they had facilities in 17 towns and cities, plus a Canadian subsidiary.

Their dairy business expanded so rapidly that by 1929 Borden was the largest food company in the nation, except for the big meat packers, Swift and Armour. 1929 also marked Borden's entry into chemicals with the acquisition of the Casein Company of America. It was a logical move: casein is a milk and cheese protein used to make adhesives.

By the time Borden celebrated their 100th birthday, in 1957, sales were nearing $1 billion, and the company had embarked on a program to become less dependent on dairy products, which represented only 28% of sales by 1978.

The Early Misadventures of Gail Borden

"Condense your sermons," Gail Borden urged his pastor; "The world is changing. Even lovers write no poetry, nor any other stuff and nonsense, now. They condense all they have to say, I suppose, into a kiss."

Borden was also obsessed by the idea that food could be preserved by condensing, but his early experiments were unsuccessful, to put it mildly. A condensed meat "biscuit" he invented for Texans headed for California during the 1850s Gold Rush proved to be nutritious but tasted awful. New York's Central Park architect Frederick Law Olmsted tried Borden's meat biscuits on a journey in Texas but threw the evil-tasting lumps to the birds long before he reached his destination.

Undeterred, Borden continued his experiments with dehydrating and concentrating foods. "I mean to put a potato into a pillbox, a pumpkin into a tablespoon, the biggest sort of watermelon into a saucer," he declared emphatically. He once subjected friends to a dinner party consisting entirely of the products of his experiments: condensed and concentrated soups, main course, fruits, and extracts. While Borden ate heartily and discoursed enthusiastically on the fine flavors of his concoctions, his guests toyed unhappily with their food. All firmly refused second helpings.

Afterward the unfortunate diners were lured onto another of Borden's inventions, the "land schooner," a contraption that used wind power to move on land. Its sails raised, the schooner moved down the beach, gaining speed at an alarming rate. Borden's passengers yelled for him to stop, at which point it was discovered that the braking mechanism was ineffective. As panic broke out amidships, Borden swung the rudder the wrong way, and the schooner splashed into the waves, capsizing and dumping all hands into the sea. Unhurt, the group scrambled ashore. "Where's Gail?" inquired one of Borden's dripping guests. The reply, doubtless influenced by both dampness and indigestion, came swiftly: "Drowned, I do sincerely hope!"

Neither drowned nor discouraged, Borden went on to further experiments—and to found what later became a giant corporation built on his 1853 discovery of a process for making condensed milk. As he rode the train to work in New York City each day, he passed a cemetery where he had built his own tombstone—in the shape of a condensed milk can.

Reputation. Borden is regarded in the business world as a plodding giant, solid but unimaginative. But Borden does have one of the best-known brand names in the grocery field. For many years they used the slogan, "If it's Borden, it's got to be good."

What they own. Thirty-one food plants, 64 dairy facilities, and 71 chemical plants in the United States; 48 food and dairy plants and 49 chemical facilities overseas. The Pepsi-Cola bottling plant in Indianapolis. Among their major facilities are cheese plants in Wisconsin, a potato chip factory in Pennsylvania, and a huge petrochemical complex on the Louisiana Gulf Coast. Overseas Borden owns the largest commercial baker in West Germany, Weber, and Denmark's Cocio chocolate milk company. Today 20% of Borden's business is done outside the United States.

Who owns and runs the company. Family influences are gone. Gail Borden's son, Henry Lee, retired as president in 1902. Albert G. Milbank died in 1948, after serving as chairman for 30 years. (His granduncle, Jeremiah Milbank, had staked Gail Borden.) Augustine R. Marusi became the first nondairy man to head the company when he was named chairman and chief executive officer in 1968. An engineering graduate, Marusi was a chemical salesman in North Carolina during the early 1950s, when an opportunity to go to Brazil for Borden presented itself. He took it and built a thriving chemical operation there, returning to New York to leapfrog over all the dairymen. Marusi was succeeded in 1979 by his longtime deputy, Eugene J. Sullivan. Top management at Borden has a strong Irish Catholic flavor. The board is an elderly bunch, including several retirees. It also includes a woman, Patricia Carry Stewart, and a black, Franklin H. Williams.

In the public eye. Under Marusi's leadership Borden tried to be in the vanguard of socially sensitive corporations. Borden pioneered in a program to buy goods and services from minority-owned companies, and Marusi himself played an important role in the launching of the National Minority Purchasing Council. However, there was resistance in the ranks to many of the social pronouncements that emanated from New York headquarters.

Where they're going. Borden is looking for snappy, new products that can be sold nationally. In 1979 they were pushing ahead with Cracker Jack ice cream bars and Borden's Yogurt Shakes.

Stock performance. Borden stock bought for $1,000 in 1970 sold for $1,038 on January 2, 1980.

Major employment centers. Columbus, Ohio; Chicago; and Tampa, Florida.

Access. 277 Park Avenue, New York, New York 10017; (212) 573-4000.

Consumer brands.

Dairy products: Borden; Lady Borden ice cream; Eagle condensed milk; Lite-line; Liederkranz cheese.

Other food products: Sacramento tomato juice products; Cracker Jack; Country Store dehydrated potatoes; Campfire marshmallows; Wyler's soup and soft drink mixes; ReaLemon; Cheez Kisses; Snow's chowders; Bama jams, jellies, and fruit drinks; Flavor House nuts; Kava instant coffee; Cremora; Old London melba toast; Wise potato chips; Colonial sugar; Creamettes pasta; None Such mincemeat; Deran candies; Chicago Almond; Drake's cakes (Ring

---

CHOW, CHOW, CHOW

Annual Sales in Millions

Canned Dog Food
1. ALPO (*Liggett*) $155
2. KAL KAN (*Mars*) $110
3. KEN-L-RATION (*Quaker Oats*) $80
4. FRISKIES (*Carnation*) $54
5. MIGHTY DOG (*Carnation*) $52

Dry Dog Food
1. DOG CHOW (*Ralston Purina*) $320
2. PUPPY CHOW (*Ralston Purina*) $110
3. CHUCK WAGON (*Ralston Purina*) $90
4. GRAVY TRAIN (*General Foods*) $75
5. HIGH PROTEIN DOG MEAL (*Ralston Purina*) $65

Moist Dog Food
1. KEN-L-RATION BURGERS (*Quaker Oats*) $81
2. TOP CHOICE (*General Foods*) $80
3. GAINES BURGERS (*General Foods*) $70
4. KEN-L-RATION SPECIAL CUTS (*Quaker Oats*) $31
5. GAINES VARIETY (*General Foods*) $22

Canned Cat Food
1. 9 LIVES (*Heinz*) $140
2. FRISKIES (*Carnation*) $111
3. KAL KAN (*Mars*) $53
4. PURINA VARIETY MENU (*Ralston Purina*) $41
5. PUSS 'N BOOTS (*Quaker Oats*) $33

Dry Cat Food
1. CAT CHOW (*Ralston Purina*) $104
2. FRISKIES (*Carnation*) $70
3. MEOW MIX (*Ralston Purina*) $62
4. SPECIAL DINNERS (*Ralston Purina*) $35
5. KITTEN CHOW (*Ralston Purina*) $12

Moist Cat Food
1. TENDER VITTLES (*Ralston Purina*) $95
2. 9 LIVES SQUARE MEAL (*Heinz*) $18
3. MOIST MEALS (*Quaker Oats*) $17
4. WHISKER LICKINS (*Ralston Purina*) $15

Source: John C. Maxwell, Lehman Brothers Kuhn Loeb Research, in *Advertising Age*, June 18, 1979.

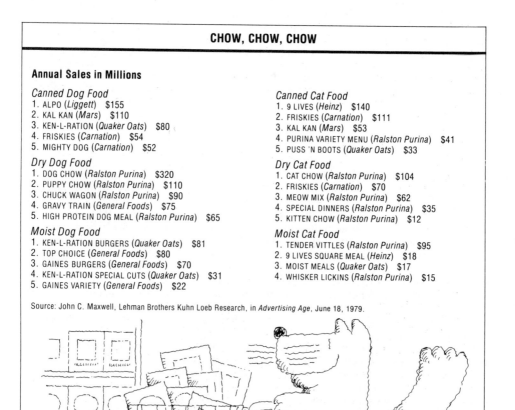

Ding, Devil Dogs, Yodels); Calo pet foods.
Clothing: Alex Colman women's sportswear and dresses.
Cosmetics: Jean Patou fragrances (Joy, Caline, and Moment Supreme perfumes).
Home and office accessories: Elmer's glues; Mystik tapes; Wonder Bond adhesive; Krylon spray paints; Wall-Tex vinyl wall coverings; Sterling office accessories.

Campbell's

Sales: $2.2 billion
Profits: $132 million
Forbes 500 rank: 236
Rank in food processing: 17
Rank in soups: 1
Rank in frozen dinners: 1
Rank in canned spaghetti: 1
Founded: 1869
Employees: 34,500
Headquarters: Camden, New Jersey

What they do. Campbell Soup marches to a tune of their own. One of the oldest companies in America, Campbell is a cautiously managed enterprise that emphasizes old-fashioned virtues, one of which is frugality. In an age where corporations routinely go into debt to finance their growth, Campbell sticks resolutely to a pay-as-you-go basis. They owe little money to anyone and could pay that off tomorrow if they wanted to.

Campbell cans, freezes, and bakes food products—more than 600 of them. They are by far the leading manufacturer of soups, holding an estimated 80% of this $1 billion market. Campbell packs 54 varieties of condensed soup to which water has to be added. The number 1 seller in the line, for as long as anyone can remember, is tomato, followed by chicken noodle and cream of mushroom. Since 1970 Campbell has also marketed Chunky ready-to-serve soups which, in addition to water, carry higher prices and greater profit margins than traditional condensed soups.

History. Joseph Campbell, a fruit merchant, and Abram Anderson, an ice box manufacturer, formed a partnership in 1869 to can and preserve fruits and vegetables.

They operated from Camden, New Jersey, across the Delaware River from Philadelphia; Campbell's headquarters have never moved. Anderson left the business in 1876. Campbell retired in 1894. Arthur Dorrance replaced Anderson in 1876 as Campbell's partner, and the Dorrances became the dominant family influence in the company.

Arthur Dorrance's nephew, Dr. John Thompson Dorrance, was a brilliant chemist who joined the company in 1897. He invented condensed soup, which is simply soup from which the water has been removed. At that time three companies canned soup in America, but they couldn't achieve wide distribution because they shipped bulky, water-logged cans. Campbell's condensed product swept the nation. The company began advertising, on New York City streetcars, in 1899. By 1904 they were selling 16 million cans of soup a year. Campbell's first national ad ran in *Good Housekeeping* in 1905. By 1911 they had entered the California market and reached national distribution, one of the first American companies to sell a brand-name food product from coast to coast.

The establishment of Campbell's soup as a staple in American kitchens enriched the Dorrances, who became fixtures in Philadelphia's "Main Line" society. When Dr. Dorrance died in 1930, after having served as president of Campbell since 1914, he left the third-highest estate recorded up to then: $115 million. His son, John T. Dorrance, Jr., is chairman of Campbell today.

Campbell proceeded with typical circumspection in buying other companies. Franco-American, the first company in America to pack soup, was acquired in 1915. The next major purchase wasn't made until 1955, when Omaha's C. A. Swanson, a frozen dinner packer, came aboard. Campbell entered the baked goods business in 1961, with the acquisition of Pepperidge Farm, a Norwalk, Connecticut, quality baker whose sales now approach $300 million.

Campbell turned friskier in the 1970s

Americans spend $3.8 billion a year on snack foods. This includes $1.7 billion for potato chips, $1 billion for nuts, $485 million for corn chips, $170 million for pretzels, and $95 million for prepopped popcorn.

when they entered the dog food, restaurant, garden, chocolate, and pickle businesses, mostly by buying other companies. They did start their own dog food business from scratch (a move prompted by many years of sponsoring "Lassie" on television), but Recipe dog food has not met expectations: it ranks 10th in the market.

Campbell entered the pickle business in 1978 by using a million of its shares (worth roughly $35 million) to acquire Vlasic Foods, a Michigan packer of pickles, relishes, peppers, and sauerkraut. The result was to make Campbell the nation's largest pickle packer, further irritant to longtime rival H. J. Heinz.

Reputation. Campbell's isn't flamboyant. They do not concoct products in the laboratory. They're not a profligate user of addi- tives. Although soups now represent less than half their business, they're still called Campbell Soup. Smoking is still not allowed in the company's headquarters offices (except in the dining room), even though they are now separated from the canning plant. To make the most use of space—and to cut down on personal telephone calls—all Campbell executives except the chairman and the president share offices with their secretaries.

What they own. Fourteen canned food plants—from Chicago to King's Lynn, England, and Yaizu, Japan. Nine frozen food plants—from Sumter, South Carolina, to Modesto, California. Twelve bakery product plants—from Burbank, California, to Nieppe, France. Three candy plants. Six pickle plants. Fifty-four retail bakery thrift

The Evolution of Foodless Food

People have tampered with food at least since the American Indians discovered they could preserve their meat by drying and pulverizing it, then mixing it with melted fat. To anyone not used to it, the Indians' pemmican tasted terrible, but it was nourishing, compact enough to carry on long journeys, and resistant to spoilage.

It was not until the nineteenth century that food processing became an industry. The scientific spirit of the age held that anything in nature could be analyzed, understood, and probably improved upon. No longer were people content to eat only what was in season and grown locally. Inventors experimented feverishly to find ways of preserving perishables. In 1809 a confectioner named Nicholas Appert—"the father of modern canning"—achieved a breakthrough when he found a way to preserve meat, fruit, and vegetables indefinitely by cooking them in sealed jars. The tin can was invented the following year, and by 1819

the first commercial canning plant was cranking out its product.

The canning revolution freed the American diet from the constraints of time and distance. The techniques of mass production could be applied to food: a single canning factory could efficiently turn out a supply of food able to survive long-distance shipping all over the country and to remain edible for months or years on grocers' shelves. For the first time, industry began to see food as a manufactured product. By the late 1920s food processing had become big business. Food itself began to be tailored for efficient shipping, packaging, and display.

From the start, though, there were problems with the new, altered foods. Whether they were canned, dried, or condensed, they just didn't taste or look like what Americans were used to. Processing dulled the bright hues of fruit, turned meat gray, blunted subtle flavors. The public was wary, and food

processors sought ways to restore to their product the lost look, taste, and texture of freshness. At first, they added touches of sugar, salt, vegetable color, and flavoring extracts. As the industry grew more scientifically sophisticated, chemists devised a host of preservatives, flavoring agents, stabilizers, thickeners, and emulsifiers to resist spoilage and re-create or sustain the qualities associated with fresh foods.

After World War II "convenience" foods became the rage. A generation of women who had gone to work during the war were unwilling in peacetime to stay home fussing over meals. Exotic processing and packaging technologies, developed during the war to feed G.I.'s, were adapted to produce the "instant," ready-mix, heat-and-serve foods that began to appear on nearly every table. The public mood favored technological bravado and novelty. Consumers would try anything once, and if the new convenience foods (notably

shops. Although Campbell uses prodigious amounts of vegetables and fruits, except for mushrooms and lima beans they do not grow ingredients, but contract with farmers in advance of growing seasons for the bulk of their commodity needs. Campbell does own eight mushroom farms. And they manufacture virtually all their containers, enough to rank as the nation's third largest can manufacturer. In Australia Campbell sells soups and other packaged items (such exotics as pineapple cordial and ravioli in beef sauce) under the Kai-ora label. In Belgium they own the cookie and cake manufacturer Delacre.

Who owns and runs the company. Campbell did not sell stock to the public until 1954, and Dorrance family members and Dorrance family trusts still control 37% of the stock, a holding worth in the neighborhood of $400 million. The next largest single block is held by Robert J. Vlasic, who sold his pickle company to Campbell; he owns 480,000 shares. John Dorrance has been chairman of Campbell since 1962, but virtually nothing has ever been written about what he does. He never grants interviews. No photograph of him has ever graced an annual report.

In many large food companies the emphasis is on marketing skills. At Campbell, where obsession with food quality and plant efficiency are hallmarks, the emphasis is on production skills. *Forbes* noted with incredulity in 1979 that Campbell didn't have a single marketing professional among its top two dozen managers.

Until 1978 Campbell didn't have a female or minority group member on the board;

TV dinners) didn't taste anything like what mother used to make, no matter. The consumer of the fifties was ready to sacrifice nearly anything to save time.

With shoppers eager for convenience meals, processors looked for ways to make every imaginable dish an instant one. Some real foods flunked the test. Frozen cream pies thawed into hopeless glop—until some imaginative chemists developed a coconut oil–based, nondairy product with a creamy texture that could withstand freezing and thawing. Cream was eliminated from the formulas of most cream pies, and soon fruit and eggs disappeared from others. Synthetic substitutes were cheaper, less subject to fluctuations of price and supply— and consumers accepted them.

Pream, an instant powdered coffee "cream," made its appearance in 1952. Prepared with dehydrated cream, lactose (milk sugar), and nonfat milk solids, it had most of the advantages that the processing industry and the public had come to associate with convenience foods: virtually immune to spoilage, it needed no refrigeration, and it was light, compact, and handy. But, like the early processed foods, it didn't taste like what consumers expected to put in their coffee. Its natural dairy ingredients were altered by their processing, giving it a flavor something like condensed milk.

Food technologists set to work to improve on nature. In 1961 Carnation marketed Coffee-Mate, a powdered coffee "creamer" that heralded a wave of nondairy coffee "lighteners." Though it contained no cream, Coffee-Mate tasted to many people more like cream than its powdered predecessor did. Not really "nondairy," it contains sodium caseinate, a form of milk protein, along with corn syrup solids, partially hydrogenated vegetable oil, mono- and diglycerides, dipotassium phosphate, sodium silocoaluminate, artificial flavor, and artificial color.

Spurred by the success of Coffee-Mate and other fabricated foods, in the sixties and seventies the food industry devised ingenious simulations for the whole range of foods: synthetic meringues and creams made from cellulose derivatives; artificial meat made of textured vegetable protein infused with artificial flavors to mimic beef, pork, bacon, or ham (such as Baco*s); and fruit-flavored drinks innocent of fruit. Tang, for example, contains sugar, citric acid (provides tartness), malto dextrin (provides body), calcium phosphates (regulates tartness and prevents caking), potassium citrate (regulates tartness), natural orange flavor, vitamin C, artificial color, vitamin A palmitate, and BHA and alpha-tocopherol (preservatives).

The revolution was complete.

they accomplished both by electing Claudine B. Malone, a black associate professor of business administration at Harvard Business School. At 42 she is the youngest member of the board. The average age of Campbell Soup directors is 62. Members of minority groups represent 28% of Campbell's U.S. work force.

Employment opportunities at Campbell have not kept pace with the company's growth. In 1969, when they celebrated their 100th birthday, Campbell had 30,000 employees. Ten years later, by which time their business had more than doubled, the employee force was 34,000. At the Camden plant alone automation enabled the company to chop the production payroll from 6,300 in 1960 to 2,300 today.

In the public eye. Campbell gives little to charity—well under 1% of pretax profits. But they have demonstrated a high measure of devotion to Camden, maintaining their headquarters there although many businesses have deserted this gray, rundown city that was once a shipbuilding center. Campbell has been under attack in California and Ohio for pressuring farmers to mechanize their harvesting of tomatoes—and in Ohio the Toledo-based Farm Labor Organizing Committee (FLOC) called for a boycott of Campbell products in 1979 as part of their efforts to secure higher wages and better working conditions for the migrant workers in the fields.

Where they're going. Campbell is not about to change a winning formula. While other food companies were getting into toys and taco stands, Campbell was buying an old-fashioned pickle packer.

Stock performance. Campbell stock bought for $1,000 in 1970 sold for $842 on January 2, 1980.

Major employment centers. Camden; Napoleon, Ohio; Paris, Texas; and Sacramento, California.

Access. Campbell Place, Camden, New Jersey 09101; (609) 964-4000. Campbell will arrange tours of canned food plants as long as they do not interfere with production routines. Make arrangements with the plant managers at Camden, Napoleon, Chicago, Paris, and Sacramento. At the Camden site Campbell maintains a museum of

antique soup tureens. More than 200,000 visitors went through the museum in 1978. Admission is free.

Consumer brands.

Grocery products: Campbell soups, tomato juice, and canned beans; Swanson frozen and canned foods; V-8 vegetable juice; Godiva chocolates; Franco-American canned pasta; Vlasic pickles, relishes, and sauerkraut; Recipe pet foods; Pepperidge Farm bread, rolls, stuffing, cookies, and cakes.

Restaurants: Hanover Trail steak house; Herfy's hamburger house; Pietro's Gold Coast pizza.

Retail outlets: Lexington Gardens garden centers.

Sales: $2.8 billion
Profits: $138 million
Forbes 500 rank: 171
Rank in evaporated milk: 1
Rank in pet foods: 2
Rank in diet meal bars: 2
Founded: 1899
Employees: 22,600
Headquarters: Los Angeles, California

What they do. Carnation began in evaporated milk, and milk products are still their mainstay. Under the Carnation name they market milk, ice cream, yogurt, cottage cheese, instant nonfat dry milk, and instant breakfast. They also make an array of other brand-name food products, including Coffee-Mate nondairy creamer, Contadina tomato sauce, and Friskies dog and cat food. In addition, they produce boats, trailers, tin cans, contour maps, school rings, diplomas, and hand tools. They have subsidiaries in some two dozen foreign countries, from Malaysia to the Ivory Coast, and they sell their products in more than 130 lands.

History. Elbridge Amos Stuart had started several retail and wholesale grocery businesses in El Paso and Los Angeles before he joined Thomas Yerxa in 1899, bought a bankrupt milk-condensing plant in Kent, Washington, and started the Pacific Coast Condensed Milk Company. As production began, Stuart had decided the label would be red and white, but he was not sure what name to put on it. Walking in downtown Seattle, he glanced in the window of a tobacco shop, saw a box of cigars labeled Carnation, and adopted the name. From the beginning the cans bore the slogan, "Milk from contented cows." In 1954 Carnation developed a way to make instant dry milk that dissolves quickly in water. From this research followed Coffee-Mate, the first nondairy creamer, and instant breakfast.

Reputation. Carnation used to be notorious for their highhandedness with reporters (they wouldn't see them), stockholders (they told them as little as required), and even customers (their lockhold on the evaporated milk market enabled them to be indifferent towards grocers). They're softening up in their old age. In early 1980 they even permitted their shares to be listed on the New York Stock Exchange, a move that will require them to issue information they have always kept to their bosom.

What they own. Twenty-two dairy product plants, 3 plants for processing tomatoes and potatoes, and six pet food plants in the United States. Forty-six other food product plants in other countries. Twenty-seven can factories, 15 animal feed mills, and a raft of subsidiaries, including Herff Jones (school rings and yearbooks), Camera Art School Photographers, and the Dayton Reliable Tool & Mfg. Co.

Who owns and runs the company. The heirs of Elbridge Stuart own 50.2% of the stock. H. E. Olson, an accountant who started with Carnation in 1931, became the first nonfamily member to head the company, when the founder's son died in 1972. The founder's grandson, D. L. Stuart, is president now, and his brother R. F. Stuart is vice-president. The Stuarts plan to reduce their holdings.

In the public eye. It is illegal for a corporation to give money to a presidential campaign, but Carnation did. Chairman H. E. Olson had to repay $16,000 to the company for a contribution Carnation made to the Nixon campaign in 1972. He was also fined $1,000.

Where they're going. Into potatoes. Carnation now makes 14 varieties of frozen processed potatoes, and they are determined to make inroads on Ore-Ida, the company that controls nearly half the $400 million market.

Stock performance. Carnation stock bought for $1,000 in 1970 sold for $1,172 on January 2, 1980.

Access. 5045 Wilshire Boulevard, Los Angeles, California 90036; (213) 931-1911.

Consumer brands.

Food products: Carnation dairy and dairy-based products and instant breakfast; Slender diet foods; Coffee-Mate creamer; Contadina tomato products; Alber's corn meal and grits.
Pet food: Friskies; Bright Eyes; Mighty Dog; Buffet; Chef's Blend.

Castle & Cooke

Sales: $1.6 billion
Profits: $31 million
Forbes 500 rank: 317
Rank in bananas: 1
Rank in tuna: 3
Rank in lettuce: 1
Rank in pineapples: 1
Founded: 1851
Employees: 40,600
Headquarters: Honolulu, Hawaii

What they do. Founded by missionaries who came to bring Christ to Hawaii, Castle & Cooke has become a global farmer under attack by church groups and labor unions for their treatment of workers. Today they grow pineapples in four countries, bananas in six; lettuce, mushrooms, and sugar in the United States. They're the fourth-largest landholder in Hawaii, and they control a network of businesses throughout the Pacific.

Castle & Cooke's best known brand name is Dole. Dole pineapples account for 50% and Dole bananas 39% of the U.S. market, the two crops together making up nearly two-thirds of C & C's sales and half the profits. Under the Bud Antle label Castle & Cooke is the largest U.S. marketer of iceberg lettuce. Bud Antle also produces the celery that consumers add to the Bumble Bee tuna packed by C & C in the Northwest. C & C owns another farmer of the sea, Pan-Alaska Fisheries, a leading U.S. producer of shrimp and crab. In 1973 C & C entered the mushroom business by buying West Foods of Salem, Oregon. Now they're producing 50 million pounds a year, making them second to Ralston Purina. The mushrooms also carry the Dole label.

History. There's an old Hawaiian saying that "when the missionaries came, the Hawaiians had all the land and the missionaries had all the Bibles. Now the Hawaiians have the Bibles and the missionaries have all the land." When Messrs. Samuel Castle and Amos Cooke sailed from Boston harbor in 1836, they took brides and bibles "on their way to the heathen." After months of disease and racking seasickness, they arrived in Hawaii. When they saw the native Hawaiians who greeted them clad only in scanty breechclothes, Sisters Castle and Cooke returned to the hold of the ship and wept the rest of the day.

The partnership of Castle & Cooke was formed in 1851 to take over the failing depository that supplied the missionaries with flour, tombstones, and calico. The modest store soon expanded into codfish, whiffletrees, guttapercha, and Jenny Lind cakes. The business flourished, and soon Castle & Cooke were buying land, first at 50¢ an acre, later at $1. In 1858 the two men teamed up with a Rev. Elias Bond to form the Kohala Sugar Company. Kohala began with 3,280 acres of land, $40,000 in capital, and a sugar mill shipped around Cape Horn from Scotland. When native Hawaiians would not work in the mill, contract laborers, mainly Chinese, were imported.

By 1875 Kohala was earning its initial cost two or three times a year, and Castle and Cooke were firmly established as suppliers and marketers for the big plantations. They began to buy and control shipping and banking interests as well. In 1894 Castle & Cooke was incorporated, and Castle's son-in-law, J. B. Atherton, became the first president. In 1908 Castle & Cooke invested in Matson shipping lines, and later they built the Royal Hawaiian Hotel to serve the growing tourist trade. Matson grew by buying out competitors until they virtually controlled the flow of goods to and from the Islands.

In 1932 Castle & Cooke acquired 21% of

Amos Starr Cooke: he came to Hawaii to convert the heathen.

Samuel Northrup Castle: he did too.

Jim Dole: founder of the pineapple industry.

the trouble-plagued Hawaiian Pineapple Company, which had been started and operated by Jim Dole, another Bostonian who originally came to Hawaii to start a coffee plantation. Instead, in 1901 he began to plant pineapples, then a little known fruit, and two years later he began to can them. In 1911 Dole commissioned Henry Ginaca, an engineer, to develop a machine that could remove the pineapples' tough outer shell. The Ginaca machine not only cut away the shell but cored up to 96 pineapples per hour, making possible the mass production of canned pineapple. Dole's consumer ads carried the slogan: "It Cuts with a Spoon—Like a Peach." By the mid-1920s 80,000 cases a year were sold.

When the Depression arrived, it hit Dole hard. He had bought the whole island of Lanai for pineapple production. Housewives could no longer afford the Hawaiian fruit, and Dole was stuck with 230 million plants and millions of unwanted cans of pineapple. Castle & Cooke reorganized the company, sending Jim Dole away for a "well-earned rest." Dole finally quit, embittered and angry at being squeezed out, but by that time *Dole* was printed on every pineapple label.

After World War II the unions so far successfully resisted by C & C moved to organize Hawaiian labor. The struggle climaxed in 1949, when Harry Bridges' International Longshoremen's and Warehousemen's Union called a strike that shut Hawaii down for 179 days and left Matson Lines severely weakened. Wages were improved, and C & C began to lose the advantages of being geographically isolated and economically powerful. They responded by buying other companies, beginning in 1961 with Columbia River Packers.

Reputation. Castle & Cooke is known for high-quality foods and a low-paid work force. In 1973 *Forbes* magazine reported that the company "pushed to transfer pineapple production from Hawaii, where the lowest-paid worker makes $3 an hour, to the Philippines, where he makes 20¢, and to Thailand, where he makes maybe 10¢."

What they own. Castle & Cooke's biggest asset is probably land, grossly undervalued on the company's books at $37.3 million. They own 149,000 acres in Hawaii, including virtually the entire island of Lanai, 60 miles from Honolulu. They also own 7,600

Brand name lettuce being packed in the field by Castle & Cooke's Bud Antle.

acres in California, 165,000 acres in Honduras, and 4,800 acres in Costa Rica. In addition, Castle & Cooke owns California's Arenson Products, maker of an automatic pool cleaner; a pipe foundry in Thailand; rock quarries in Malaysia; and beverage bottling plants in Honduras and Belize; and a fleet of refrigerated cargo vessels.

Who owns and runs the company. The largest block of stock (8%) is wielded by the Hawaii Trust Company for the benefit of the Castle and Cooke family interests. One family member, A. S. Atherton, is still on the board, but the commander of the ship today is Donald J. Kirchoff, an abrasive Harvard Business School graduate who made his mark in the banana business at Standard Fruit before it was scooped up by Castle & Cooke in 1964.

In the public eye. Kirchoff has given the back of his hand to church groups who have criticized Castle & Cooke's labor policies in Third World countries. He has described these critics as a "pseudo elite" who sing the "siren songs of Marxist ideologues."

Brazil is the largest supplier of food products to the United States, with about $1.4 billion worth of coffee, cocoa beans, and various fruits and vegetables. The other large food exporters to the United States include Mexico ($1 billion), Canada ($672 million), Indonesia ($628 million), and the Philippines ($599 million).

Where they're going. Under Kirchoff's leadership Castle & Cooke has been adept at borrowing money and expanding into many food areas. They still seem intent on farming, however, and Kirchoff has vowed that the company founded by missionaries will not "forfeit its principles to guerillas of any political stripe."

Stock performance. Castle & Cooke stock bought for $1,000 in 1970 sold for $916 on January 2, 1980.

Access. 130 Merchant Street, Honolulu, Hawaii 96813; (808) 548-6611.

Consumer brands.

Bud of California lettuce, celery, and cauliflower; Dole pineapple, bananas, and fresh mushrooms; Bumble Bee and Royal Alaskan seafoods; Pool Sweep swimming pool cleaner.

Sales: $5.0 billion
Profits: $420 million
Forbes 500 rank: 79
Rank in soft drinks: 1
Rank in citrus drinks: 1
Rank in wine: 5
Founded: 1886
Employees: 36,100
Headquarters: Atlanta, Georgia

What they do. If all the Coca-Cola ever consumed by the human race were poured over Niagara Falls, "the Falls would flow at their normal rate for 8 hours and 57 minutes," according to one of the "gee-whizzers" collected by the Coca-Cola Company. The world's best-selling product is 99.8% water and sugar. Caffeine is present, and so is caramel coloring. What else it contains, and in what proportions, has always been a matter of curiosity. The so-called "secret" ingredient is believed to be a flavoring mixture derived from coca leaves (with the cocaine removed) and cola nuts. Other ingredients different chemists have identified at different times are: cinnamon, nutmeg, lime juice, vanilla, fluid extract of guarana

(the roasted seed of a Brazilian tree), various citrus oils, and glycerin. Whatever the formula is, the Coca-Cola Company is not telling. Nor are they required to.

The Coca-Cola Company doesn't actually sell the soft drink to consumers at all. What they do is buy sugar (10% of all sugar sold in the U.S.), mix it with their secret concentrate, and then sell the syrup to bottlers. The other half of what they do is advertise —on a vast scale—to support their brand.

The franchise bottling system is what allows Coca-Cola to reach around the world to 1,450 bottlers, 550 of them in the United States, but only 17 of these company-owned. These independent bottlers have circumscribed areas in which to sell. In New York and Los Angeles, the Coca-Cola bottlers have become major companies in their own rights.

Coca-Cola is no longer a one-product company. Their other soft-drink brands include TAB, Sprite, Fresca, Fanta, and Mr. Pibb. They bought the Minute Maid orange juice business. They market teas and coffees under the Maryland Club and Butter-nut names. They have entered the wine business by purchasing New York's Taylor wine company and California's Monterey and Sterling vineyards.

But the original product remains the bellwether. Coca-Cola accounts for 70% of the company's soft drink sales, both in the United States and overseas. In short, it's a $2.3 billion product. (And that's just the volume done by the syrup supplier. The amount spent by the imbibers is ten times more.) Coke is sold in 135 countries. In 1978 sales outside the United States accounted for 46% of revenues and 61% of profits.

A drink this popular couldn't fail to attract defamers. E. J. Kahn detailed many in his book *The Big Drink.* For example, a left-wing Italian newspaper reported that "only a few people succeed, when first drinking Coca-Cola, in getting rid of that unpleasant impression of sucking the leg of a recently massaged athlete." A neo-Fascist paper in Milan described Coke as "half-way between the sweetish taste of coconut and the taste of a damp rag for cleaning floors."

In the United States Coca-Cola had one of its most ferocious enemies in Dr. Harvey W. Wiley, the father of the Food and Drug Administration. At the turn of the century he called the sellers of the drink "dope peddlers" and took the company to court on charges of product adulteration.

Women of fashion at the soda fountain, all healthy and happy, and all drinking Coca-Cola. Why? Because of its delightful flavor and beneficial results.

Coca-Cola soda fountain, circa 1905.

History. Coca-Cola was invented in 1886 by John Styth Pemberton, an Atlanta pharmacist who fooled around with patent medicines. Some of his concoctions were Triplex liver pills, Globe of Flower cough syrup, Indian Queen hair dye, Gingerine, Extract of Styllinger (a blood medicine), and French Wine Coca. Precisely how he came up with the syrup that his bookkeeper, Frank Robinson, called Coca-Cola is not clear, except that it was a modification of French Wine Coca, and it too claimed to cure what-ails-you: headaches, sluggishness, indigestion, and throbbing temples resulting from overindulgence. Less than a year after he first blended Coca-Cola in an iron pot in his backyard, Pemberton's own health failed. In 1887 he sold two-thirds of his business for $1,200, and on his deathbed in 1888 he sold the remaining third for $550. The Pemberton business quickly changed hands again, and by 1891 it was in the possession of another Atlanta pharmacist, Asa Briggs Candler, who knew about Coca-Cola because he'd taken it for his headaches and dyspepsia. Candler bought it for $2,000.

Asa Candler laid the foundations of the Coca-Cola business. At first, he too promoted the drink as a nostrum, but soon he realized the potential this miraculous syrup had as a simple soda fountain drink. He sent salesmen across the country instructing druggists what to do with a keg of Coca-Cola. Considerable sums were invested in advertising. Painted Coca-Cola signs went up on barns everywhere. Trays, Japanese fans, bookmarks, and glasses all bore the Coca-Cola legend. By 1895 Coke was sold in every state and territory in the country. The syrup was produced in satellite plants in Chicago, Dallas, and Los Angeles. By 1898 they had moved into Canada, Hawaii, and Mexico. Although the Coca-Cola trademark was registered with the U.S. Patent Office in 1893, there were many imitators, scolded by Candler as "unscrupulous pirates."

In those early years Coca-Cola found converts who liked the drink so much that they became salesmen for the product (and very rich in the process). Asa Candler was content to make and sell his syrup, remaining skeptical of the idea of bottling it. In 1899 he signed a contract giving two Chattanooga lawyers the rights to bottle Coca-Cola in virtually the entire United States for one dollar. The Chattanooga group set themselves up as middlemen who bought the syrup from the Coca-Cola Company and resold it to local bottlers across the country. Thus was born the franchise system that is the basis of the Coca-Cola business today.

Coca-Cola's close involvement with the city of Atlanta began with Asa Candler. In 1907, when a real estate panic threatened, he bought $1 million worth of homes and resold them to people of moderate incomes for 10% down and 100 payments at low interest. He also gave Emory University its land and a large part of its endowment. In

1916 he stepped down as Coca-Cola president and was elected mayor of Atlanta, running on a reform ticket for a job that paid $4,000 a year. At the same time, he gave all but 1% of his stock in Coca-Cola to members of his family. Three years later, without consulting him, the Candlers sold the company to a group headed by Georgia financier Ernest Woodruff. The price: $25 million. It was the largest financial transaction that had ever taken place in the South.

In 1923, when Woodruff brought in his 33-year-old son, Robert Winship Woodruff, to run Coca-Cola, the company was well-established but had lost its sense of direction. The younger Woodruff, a taciturn man who has never sought the limelight, has been described by associates as fairly inarticulate. Exactly how he did it remains a mystery, but no one doubts that he gave this company its wings. Part of the secret was certainly advertising, massive doses of it, that elevated a 5¢ soft drink into a symbol as resonant of America as baseball and hot dogs. Artful advertising was crafted by a North Carolina–born copywriter, Archie Lee, who remained a "country boy" even after going to work at the D'Arcy Advertising Agency in St. Louis. Lee hired great illustrators for Coca-Cola: Fred Mizen, Hayden Hayden, Haddon Sunbloom, Norman Rockwell, and N. C. Wyeth. Lee penned Coke's famous advertising slogan, "The pause that refreshes." And Woodruff, back in Atlanta, was ready to back Lee with millions of dollars.

At one point shortly after he assumed the helm, Woodruff called in the entire sales force and informed them that the sales department was being abolished and that they were jobless. However, he said, he would have something further to tell them the next morning. The former sales people retired uneasily to their hotels. When they reassembled the next day, Woodruff announced that the company was forming a service department and would welcome their applications for jobs in it. The message Woodruff delivered was that their job was not so much selling Coca-Cola as catering to the needs of their customers. The message goes to the heart of this business. As Woodruff explained to writer E. J. Kahn: "We've tried to show Coca-Cola as a pleasant, unassuming social amenity. I guess that's what they now call the soft sell. We've never made claims. We've tried to do with our advertising what we always try to do with everybody inside and outside the company—to be liked. We've tried to practice what Archie [Lee] preached."

Coca-Cola's syrup production has never employed very many people. But a large number of employees do market research

According to *Food Engineering*, a 12-ounce can of Coca-Cola contains 65 milligrams of caffeine, while a 12-ounce can of its main competitor, Pepsi-Cola, yields only 43 mg. By comparison, 5-ounce cups of the following types of coffees and teas have these amounts of caffeine: drip-grind coffee from an automatic coffee maker—150 mg; drip-grind coffee from an electric percolator—104 mg; instant or freeze-dried coffee—66 mg; black tea brewed for five minutes—50 mg; and black tea brewed for one minute—33 mg.

into why people drink the beverages they do, more work on the advertising that exploits these findings, and still more carry out the sales support programs that help bottlers and retailers increase gallonage. Bob Hall, a Southern writer, described this effort in 1977 as "the most incredible mobilization of human energy for trivial purposes since the construction of the pyramids."

Delony Sledge, longtime advertising director of Coca-Cola, tried to explain the old Coca-Cola spirit to writer Pat Watters. "It has been said that this wasn't a business," Sledge said; "it was a religion. And during those days, by God, it was a religion. . . . You don't get that out of a General Motors. You don't get that out of an IBM. . . . The product has some kind of strange characteristic. . . . I think it's symbolism. I don't know why, I've spent up to 50 years now trying to figure it out." A minister once told a gathering of Coca-Cola bottlers: "I see a strange connection between your slogan, 'The pause that refreshes,' and Christ's own words, 'Come unto me, all ye that travail, and I will refresh you.'"

E. J. Kahn quotes a more blunt explanation given by a Coca-Cola man: "You want to know what makes Coke so romantic to so many people? Well, maybe that starry-eyed kid who lives next door to you was sitting in a drugstore booth with his girl one night, and maybe they were drinking Coke, and maybe while they were drinking that Coke was the first time that girl let the boy put his hand on her leg."

Coca-Cola's place in American life reached a peak during World War II. Immediately after Pearl Harbor Robert Woodruff struck back with the words: "We will see that every man in uniform gets a bottle of Coca-Cola for 5¢ wherever he is and whatever it costs." General Dwight D. Eisenhower, a Coke fancier, agreed. While competing soft-drink companies watched helplessly, Coca-Cola bottling plants were set up near all battle fronts. When the war was over, Coca-Cola had 64 overseas bottling plants in place, most of them ferried over at the expense of U.S. taxpayers.

During the Cold War Coca-Cola as a symbol of American life had to face fierce attacks by Communists. Efforts were also made to keep it out of France: "The moral landscape of France is at stake," said the respected French daily *Le Monde*. In the end, Coca-Cola won most of those fights.

A Nation of Furtive Snackers

Americans, a psychological researcher finds, no longer eat meals; we eat snacks. Instead of three squares a day the average American family engages in 20 "food contacts," Dr. Paul A. Fine reported to the American Medical Association. On the basis of interviews with housewives and their "diaries" of actual food consumption, Dr. Fine found that the diet of the "American mainstream" is "Oreos, peanut butter, Crisco, T.V. dinners, cake mix, macaroni and cheese, Pepsi and Coke, pizzas, Jell-O, hamburgers, Rice-a-Roni, Spaghetti-O's, pork and beans, Heinz ketchup and instant coffee."

These facts were not easy to come by, Dr. Fine reports. "So deep is the strength of the ideal 'shoulds' with regard to food and eating that the topic engenders much social lying—sheer refusal to talk in a group, to let others know the truth about what really goes on in one's family with regard to eating. . . . It may be easier to get people to talk with complete frankness about their sex life than about the eating patterns of the family they are supposed to be in control of and toward which they feel an enormous sense of responsibility."

Source: John L. Hess and Karen Hess, *The Taste of America* (Penguin Books, 1977).

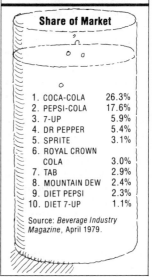

THE 10 MOST DRUNK SOFT DRINKS IN AMERICA

Share of Market

1. COCA-COLA	26.3%
2. PEPSI-COLA	17.6%
3. 7-UP	5.9%
4. DR PEPPER	5.4%
5. SPRITE	3.1%
6. ROYAL CROWN COLA	3.0%
7. TAB	2.9%
8. MOUNTAIN DEW	2.4%
9. DIET PEPSI	2.3%
10. DIET 7-UP	1.1%

Source: *Beverage Industry Magazine*, April 1979.

Their sales are strong in France now. Once on the Arab boycott list because of a franchised bottler in Israel, Coca-Cola is now being bottled in Egypt. And in a final, well-publicized irony, Coke is moving into the People's Republic of China.

Reputation. The role of Coca-Cola in the economy of the South is not unlike that of oil in the Arab world. "This drink is one of the few things that the South developed itself, and that the North hasn't taken over," noted John Gunther in his book *Inside USA.* Coca-Cola's friend is Jimmy Carter (Pepsi's is Richard Nixon). Consumption of Coke in the South (especially Georgia) is double its consumption anywhere else.

What they own. A key to the vault at the Trust Company of Georgia, where the secret formula for Coca-Cola is kept. On the company's books the "formula, trademarks, goodwill and contract rights" are carried at the grossly underestimated value of $101 million. Coca-Cola makes their precious nectar in 16 plants across the country.

Who owns and runs the company. The Woodruffs remain the biggest shareholders, controlling perhaps 5% of the shares, although Robert Woodruff has given away an enormous amount. Toward the end of 1979 he gave Emory University three million shares of Coca-Cola stock, then worth about $100 million. It was called the largest single donation in the history of American philanthropy and brought to $210 million the money he has given to that institution. Emory, with five million shares of stock, became one of the largest shareholders in the Coca-Cola Company.

Robert Woodruff stepped down as chairman in 1955, but he was still around the company as 1980 dawned. He was 90 years old, serving as chairman of the finance committee.

Coca-Cola has a better record than most Southern-based companies in employing blacks. Members of minority groups made up 31% of the company's employee force at the end of 1978, and minorities held 17% of all managerial positions. One of the highest-ranking blacks in U.S. business is William Sharp, vice-president of Coca-Cola USA in charge of advertising.

In the public eye. When William B. Hartsfield, mayor of Atlanta since 1937, stepped down in 1962, he told Pat Watters that he had never taken an action without considering the effect it would have on the Coca-Cola Company and "my good friend Bob Woodruff." Maynard Jackson, Atlanta's first black mayor, said: "The Coca-Cola Company has been a superb citizen, both corporate and personal, of Atlanta."

One of the worst moments in Coca-Cola's experience occurred in 1970, when NBC aired a documentary exposing the wretched housing and working conditions in the Minute Maid orange groves in Florida. Coca-Cola had owned Minute Maid for 10 years and claimed that they were just about to put into operation a plan to upgrade the conditions in the groves. The plan they did implement was later hailed as a model program. In 1972 Cesar Chavez organized the Minute Maid farm workers, securing what he said was the best first contract he had gotten anywhere.

Coca-Cola's 1979 annual meeting saw the first nonmanagement resolution ever submitted: a proposal that bottlers be asked to observe a "code of minimum labor standards." The demand followed reports of brutality at the Coca-Cola bottling plant in Guatemala. A Guatemalan labor leader who came to the meeting reported that "Coca-Cola's image in Guatemala couldn't be worse. In Guatemala crime is referred to as Coca-Cola." The resolution was overwhelmingly defeated at urging of Coca-Cola managment, who maintained they had no right to interfere in the affairs of independent bottlers.

Where they're going. Coca-Cola is poised on the edge of three almost virgin territories: the Soviet Union, China, and the Arab world. Meanwhile, they're very serious about the wine business, and they're also into inland shrimp farming.

Stock performance. Coca-Cola stock bought for $1,000 in 1970 sold for $839 on January 2, 1980.

Access. 310 North Avenue, N.W., Atlanta, Georgia 30313; (404) 898-2121.

Consumer brands.

Coca-Cola; Coke; TAB; Sprite; Fanta; Mr. Pibb; Mello Yello; Fresca; Minute Maid; Hi-C; Snow Crop; Butter-nut; Maryland Club; Taylor; Great Western; The Monterey; Taylor California Cellars; Sterling.

CONSOLIDATED
FOODS CORPORATION

Sales: $4.7 billion
Profits: $111 million
Forbes 500 rank: 84
Rank in food processing: 8
Rank in vacuum cleaners: 1
Rank in frozen pastries: 1
Rank in pantyhose: 1
Founded: 1939
Employees: 80,900
Headquarters: Chicago, Illinois

What they do. Consolidated Foods, a casserole cooked up originally by Nathan Cummings, a crusty, autocratic Chicago industrialist and art collector, is in the business of buying and selling companies. In the 1970s alone they bought at least 70 companies and sold as many—sometimes the same ones. This potpourri is held together by a corporate staff operating from the heart of Chicago's financial district, just up the block from another hungry accumulator of companies, Beatrice Foods.

From Chicago stretch lines of control to companies throughout the nation: Popsicle in Englewood, New Jersey; Lyon's restaurant chain in California; Fuller Brush of Great Bend, Kansas; Electrolux of Stamford, Connecticut, the door-to-door seller of vacuum cleaners; California-based Shasta Beverages, the nation's seventh-largest soft drink bottler; Lawson Milk, an Ohio-based chain of 722 convenience stores; a clutch of regional meat packers, mostly pork processors, with combined sales of $600 million; and Hanes hosiery of Winston-Salem, North Carolina, developer of L'eggs pantyhose.

Closer to headquarters are two major food processors: Chicago-based Booth Fisheries, a leading packer of frozen seafood, and Kitchens of Sara Lee, the nation's number 1 baker of frozen pastries, in Deerfield, Illinois. Both are susceptible to quick unannounced visits by Consolidated's founder Nate Cummings, who likes to confront secretaries with paper clips he digs out of wastebaskets.

History. Nate Cummings had little formal education. He started out in the shoe business in the 1920s and later bought a candy and biscuit company, which he sold for a handsome profit. Then in 1939, when he

was 43 years old, he borrowed $5.2 million to acquire a large Chicago wholesaler, which he renamed Consolidated Foods in 1954. Cummings was a restless acquirer. By the time he relinquished the president's title in 1970, he had bought more than 90 companies.

Reputation. They'll buy you today and sell you tomorrow.

What they own. Approximately 135 plants in 35 states and 12 foreign countries.

Consolidated Foods did not have a major presence overseas until 1978, when they acquired a 60% stake in Douwe Egberts, a Dutch marketer of tea, coffee, and tobacco. They have a 20% slice of the European coffee market, and their Amphora brand is the top imported pipe tobacco in the United States.

Who owns and runs the company. Although ostensibly retired, 84-year-old Nate Cummings remains the largest stockholder, with 1 million shares worth about $25 million. The *Wall Street Journal* noted in 1976 that when "Consolidated hit $1 billion in sales, the company had the simplest organization chart you ever saw. It was Nate." The first president to succeed Cummings, William Howlett, didn't understand that and was fired after two years. His transgressions included not inviting Cummings to speak at the annual meeting and neglecting to put the founder's picture in the annual report. The next president, William A. Buzick, Jr., was forced out in 1975, after earnings faltered. Now at the helm is John H.

The two richest U.S. Senators owe their fortunes to food families. When government officials had to disclose their finances in 1979, the U.S. Senate turned up with 25 millionaires. Heading the list was Senator H. J. Heinz, III, from Pennsylvania, whose net worth was declared as $20 million, stemming mainly from the Pittsburgh food processor founded by his great-grandfather in 1857. In second place was Senator John Danforth from Missouri, with a net worth of $17 million derived from the Ralston-Purina business founded in St. Louis by his grandfather in 1894. Both Heinz and Danforth are Republicans.

Bryan, Jr., whose family business, Bryan Brothers Packing of West Point, Mississippi, was acquired by Consolidated in 1967. After taking over, Bryan sold off about 50 companies, most of them small firms that had been acquired by Buzick.

Cummings bought companies whose owners wanted to sell, but the new management is not averse to forcible takeovers. In 1978 they raised $250 million to scoop up Hanes over the objections of the founding Hanes family. Bryan accumulated enough stock in 10 days to give the Hanes management no option. After the deed was done, Gordon Hanes said: "It was hard for me to believe that there were people who didn't give a damn about anything except money —the lawyers, the bankers. The Hanes family spent three generations building this business, and it was taken away from us in 10 days."

Where they're going. The objective now is to buy only big companies. In 1979 John Bryan told a *Fortune* reporter: "It's utter foolishness to have a $10-million company in a $4-billion or $5-billion corporation."

Stock performance. Consolidated Foods stock bought for $1,000 in 1970 sold for $632 on January 2, 1980.

Access. 135 South LaSalle Street, Chicago, Illinois 60603; (312) 726-6414.

Consumer brands.

Grocery products: Shasta soft drinks; Hollywood candy bars; Bloch & Guggenheimer pickles, relishes, and sauerkraut; Delson candies; Union sugar; Douwe Egberts coffee; Amphora pipe tobacco.

Frozen foods: Booth's seafood; Chef Pierre pies; Sara Lee baked goods; Popsicle; Fudgsicle.

Meat products: Hillshire Farms sausages; Kahn's packaged meats; Rudy's Farm country sausage; Lauderdale sausages; Bryan processed and canned meat.

Restaurants: Lyon's.

Household products: Electrolux vacuum cleaners; Fuller Brush.

Clothing and personal care products: Sirena swimwear; Aris gloves; Robert Bruce men's and boys' sportswear; Hanes underwear; L'eggs hosiery; Bali & Canadelle intimate apparel; L'erin cosmetics.

Hobbycraft: Tyco model railroad and road racing sets.

Continental Baking

Sales: $1.27 billion
Profits: $24.8 million
Rank in baking industry: 1
Founded: 1911
Employees: 29,000
Headquarters: Rye, New York

What they do. Continental Baking became the largest baker in the United States by marketing a national bread and automating so that local bakeries could not compete. Wonder, the bulwark of Continental's business, is the largest-selling brand of bread in the world. They crank it out of 42 plants across the country from computerized mixing and baking machines. To make the most of the equipment, Continental tries to bake seven days a week, three shifts on weekdays and two on weekends, providing a constant flow of many products: Hostess Twinkies and Sno-balls, Love's Biscuits, and bread sold under various names, including Wonder and Profile. Continental also produces potato chips in Memphis, bulk candy in Minneapolis, chemicals in Kansas, and Morton's frozen foods in Gloucester, Massachusetts.

History. Continental was formed in 1924 by the merging of formerly independent bakeries into one holding company. In the early years of this century, bakeries were locally owned. But in 1911 Max Oscher, an investment banker, brought together bakeries from New York, Massachusetts, Rhode Island, Ohio, Washington, D.C., New Jersey, Michigan, and Louisiana under one roof, the General Baking Company. General's success touched off a wave of similar mergers, including the Ward Baking Company, the Purity Bakeries Corporation, the Southern Bakeries Corporation, and Continental, which was by far the largest, employing 10,000 people and operating 106 bakeries in 1925.

Continental's rapid acquisition of competitors brought Senate attention. In 1924 they were charged with monopolistic practices by the FTC, which wanted to break up the company. These charges had not been settled when the nation's three largest bakeries—General, Ward, and Continental—announced plans to combine into an entity that would have controlled 10% of the nation's baking output. The merger was coined the "bread trust." William B. Ward, who was to head the operation, publicly stated that the new corporation would have a "soul." In the corporate charter was a specific provision stating that the corporation might donate some of its profits to charity. Ward spoke glowingly of recreation and community centers that would spring up across the land under Continental's benevolence.

The linking of philanthropy with an apparent monopoly caused opponents to claim foul. The bread trust got a chance to bare its soul when the Justice Department sued for antitrust violations. It chose not to and quickly signed a consent decree that broke up the trust. Continental, left alone, went back to the old ways, buying several bakeries a year. In 1968 Continental was acquired itself by International Telephone & Telegraph for stock worth $279 million.

Reputation. Continental is probably the most efficient of the cardboard bread manufacturers. To nutritionists Twinkies represent the nadir of American food, the largest single ingredient being sugar.

What they own. Headquartered in the Westchester County suburb of Rye, New York, Continental occupies a 151,000-square-foot building. To deliver the baked goods from their 61 plants to stores, Continental operates a vast fleet of owned and leased vehicles: 8,000 route and support trucks, 1,100 passenger cars and vans, 700 tractors, and 800 trailers.

Who owns and runs the company. ITT, the 11th-largest industrial corporation in America.

In the public eye. In 1971 television viewers were greeted by actress Julia Meade delivering this Federal Trade Commission-mandated *mea culpa* on behalf of Profile bread (which had been promoted by Continental as an aid to dieters): "I'd like to clear up any misunderstanding you may have about Profile bread from its advertising or even its name. Does Profile have fewer calories than other breads? No, Profile has about the same per ounce as other breads. To be exact, Profile has seven fewer calories per slice. That's because it's sliced thinner. But eating Profile will not cause you to lose weight. A reduction of 7 calories is insig-

---

AMERICA'S DIET SHAPERS

Annual Spending on Advertising

1. GENERAL FOODS $340 *million*
2. GENERAL MILLS $170 *million*
3. PEPSICO $156 *million*
4. BEATRICE FOODS $150 *million*
5. NORTON SIMON $145 *million*
6. ESMARK $141 *million*
7. COCA-COLA $139 *million*
8. McDONALD'S $137 *million*
9. KRAFT $114 *million*
10. PILLSBURY $104 *million*
11. CONSOLIDATED FOODS $92 *million*
12. RALSTON PURINA $91 *million*
13. NABISCO $91 *million*
14. KELLOGG $80 *million*
15. NESTLÉ $78 *million*
16. H. J. HEINZ $74 *million*
17. QUAKER OATS $69 *million*
18. MARS $60 *million*
19. CAMPBELL SOUP $56 *million*
20. BORDEN $50 *million*
21. STANDARD BRANDS $34 *million*
22. CARNATION $29 *million*

Source: *Advertising Age*, September 6, 1979.

---

nificant." The commercial ran for a year with no visible effect on sales.

In 1979 a defense attorney in San Francisco found an unusual new use for Continental's highly-sugared product, Twinkies. Defending Dan White on charges of killing Mayor George Moscone and Supervisor Harvey Milk of San Francisco, attorney Douglas Schmidt told the jury that White's mental capacity was diminished by his wolfing down junk food—Coke, Twinkies, doughnuts, candy bars. White was acquitted on the murder charge and found guilty of voluntary manslaughter.

Where they're going. Continental hopes to sell 1 billion Twinkies a year.

Access. Halsted Avenue, Rye, New York 10580; (914) 967-4747.

Consumer brands.

Breads: Wonder; Profile; Daffodil Farm; Fresh Horizons; Home Pride; County Fair; Sunrise; Proclaim; Braun; Fresh and Natural; Staff; Omar Pride; Hall Pride; Cain's English muffins.

Other bakery products: Hostess snack cakes (Twinkies, Cup Cakes, Finer Donuts); Sno-balls; Love's biscuits, cakes, and breads; Wonder snack foods; Ding-Dongs; Ho-Ho's.

Other food products: Morton frozen dinners and desserts; Seven-Up candy bars; Foot-Long franks.

Sales: $1.6 billion
Profits: $51 million
Rank in canning: 1
Rank in pineapples: 2
Rank in bananas: 3
Founded: 1916
Employees: 43,000
Headquarters: San Francisco, California

What they do. Based in a state that produces more than 40% of the fruits and vegetables grown in the United States, Del Monte is easily the nation's largest fruit and vegetable canner. From 46 processing plants in the United States and 22 in other countries, Del Monte turns out 250 canned, dried, snack, frozen, and refrigerated foods in a variety of styles and sizes—more than 90 million cases a year. In most categories the Del Monte brand ranks number 1 or number 2 in sales. The average supermarket will carry anywhere from 70 to 100 Del Monte products.

Del Monte is also in the fresh fruit business—bananas and pineapples—and through two subsidiaries has a small stake in the food-away-from-home market, managing several hundred cafeterias, providing vending services, and supplying airline meals.

The Del Monte canneries generally go full blast from June through November. During this period there's a sharp increase in short-term borrowing to finance the costs of seasonal labor (this can add 33,000 extra persons to Del Monte's payroll) and purchase of farm-fresh produce. Inventories will build to a peak in these six months and then slope down to a low point by the end of May (assuming the packer is not stuck with a lot of unsold goods).

Del Monte grows very little of the raw product. On the other end, however, they make their own cans, print their own labels (more than two billion a year), pack only for the Del Monte label, and distribute through their own sales force.

History. Fruit and vegetable farming began in California during the 1870s and 1880s, many of the field workers being Chi-nese who had come to build the railroads. The numerous canneries that sprang up in the state's Central Valley had trouble coping with boom-and-bust cycles, so they opted for the course then being followed by manufacturers in the Midwest and East: consolidation. In 1889, 11 of the biggest canneries formed a new combine: the California Fruit Canners Association (CFCA). In 1916 the company known today as Del Monte was organized by the merger of CFCA with two other canners and a large food wholesaler, J. K. Armsby. The company took the prosaic but accurate name of California Packing Corporation and began life with more than 60 canneries. They also began with a brand name, Del Monte, which had been used by a predecessor company for 25 years.

Calpak was not responsible for any technological advances in canning. They were responsible, however, for making Americans brand conscious. In 1917 their first national advertisement in the *Saturday Evening Post* said simply: "California's finest canned fruits and vegetables are packed under the Del Monte brand." It was the start of a campaign that succeeded in establishing Del Monte as one of the best-known brand names in America. McCann-Erickson, the agency that prepared the initial ad, continues to handle Del Monte's advertising today. It was not until 1967 that Calpak got

Here's how it began: Del Monte's first national ad, 1917, in the Saturday Evening Post.

around to changing their name to Del Monte.

In the 1970s bananas became a major profit maker for Del Monte, but this is a business they backed—or lucked—into. In the late 1960s United Brands, a conglomerate that owns United Fruit, got the idea of acquiring Del Monte. But United Fruit was then bound by an antitrust decree to sell off at least 10% of their banana operations. Del Monte, with uncharacteristic agility, bought a small banana importer, thus making themselves invulnerable to takeover by United Brands. A few years later Del Monte helped United Brands satisfy the antitrust obligation by buying their Guatemalan plantations for $20 million.

In 1978 Del Monte was helpless before a new assault. RJR Industries, the nation's largest cigarette maker, offered to buy Del Monte for a price negotiated up to $48 a share, or $580 million. Del Monte shares had never traded at such a lofty level and, in the opinion of most Wall Streeters, never would have done so under their own steam. So Del Monte's two cigarette-smoking leaders—chairman Alfred W. Eames, Jr., and president Richard G. Landis—sold out the company to the maker of Winston, Camel, Vantage, Salem, and Now cigarettes.

Reputation. Del Monte is known as an oldline canner. According to the head of a San Francisco personnel agency, "if you stay at Del Monte too long, you may be unemployable anywhere else."

What they own. Fifty-nine food processing plants, 14 can manufacturing plants, 7 ocean-going fishing vessels, 11 refrigerated vessels to haul bananas from Central America to U.S. ports, 80,000 acres of banana plantations in Guatemala and Costa Rica.

Who owns and runs the company. RJR Industries, 100%.

In the public eye. Del Monte has been notably unresponsive to outside pressures. They had a bloody labor history in the 1930s, fighting off union organizing drives until they signed what some consider a sweetheart contract with the Teamsters. Church groups have charged the company with exploiting low-cost labor in Third World countries. Del Monte has been packing pineapples in the Philippines since 1926. A report prepared by a church-backed organization said: "After decades of exploiting the country's natural resources, Del Monte has left behind little of the wealth created by its operations." When Del Monte's proposed purchase of United Fruit's Guatemalan plantations was held up in 1970 and 1971, the company sought advice from the U.S. ambassador to Guatemala, Nathaniel Davis, who advised

Peaches en route to Del Monte cans.

Del Monte to retain a Guatemalan consultant. A year later the deal went through. A subsequent investigation by the Securities and Exchange Commission revealed that Del Monte paid a $500,000 commission to their Guatemalan consultant.

Del Monte was the first of the big canners to put nutritional labels on cans.

Where they're going. After completing the purchase of Del Monte in early 1979, RJR announced that the present management of Del Monte would remain in place and that the company would continue to operate from San Francisco without interference.

Major employment centers. San Francisco Bay Area; Rochelle, Illinois; and Hawaii.

Access. One Market Plaza, San Francisco, California 94119; (415) 442-4000.

Consumer brands.

Del Monte canned foods; Granny Goose snack foods; Perky turnovers; Award frozen entrees.

Sales: $6.7 billion
Profits: $92.4 million
Forbes 500 rank: 55
Rank in food processing: 5
Rank in meat packing: 2
Rank in peanut butter: 3
Rank in car stereo speakers: 1
Rank in brassieres: 1
Founded: 1875
Employees: 46,000
Headquarters: Chicago, Illinois

What they do. Many people do not recognize Esmark as the old familiar Swift & Co., once the nation's largest beef packer. The switch came in 1973, when Swift decided their time-honored name was too closely associated with the meat business to represent the new conglomerate, which includes such diverse lines as insect spray, gasoline, bras, and car stereo speakers. The *Es* in the

new name, they explained, signified the "S" of Swift, and *mark*, they thought, conveyed a "strong connotation of worth, ownership, and excellence."

Swift is now merely Esmark's food division, and though it generates by far the most revenue of all the company's sectors, it's the least profitable. In 1978 the food business accounted for more than two-thirds of Esmark's gross income but only one-fifth of the profits. Swift provides fresh meat to supermarkets and butchers, and also markets an array of consumer products: packaged bacon and hot dogs; canned ham; Butterball turkeys; Brown 'N Serve sausage; Peter Pan peanut butter; Allsweet margarine; Strongheart dog food; and various types of cheese, salami, and cold cuts.

Much more profitable for Esmark is International Playtex. When the meat packers took over the Living Bra makers in 1975, the humorists had a field day, but Esmark can laugh all the way to Fort Knox. Playtex now produces more than one-fourth of the company's profits. Besides its established line of bras, girdles, pantyhose, and rubber gloves, Playtex is challenging Tampax in the tampon field.

Most home gardeners are acquainted with Vigoro fertilizer, plant foods, weed killers, bug dust, potting soil, and the like, made by Estech, the company's chemicals division, which also makes such items as wax, adhesives, and dental supplies (including Pro-Tek toothbrushes). Esmark owns an oil company, too: Vickers, which runs more than 400 gas stations in the Midwest, operates a refinery in Oklahoma, and has its own supply company, TransOcean Oil.

Esmark branched out further in 1978 to buy STP, the maker of STP Oil Treatment and a raft of other car products, and Pemcor, maker of Jensen car stereo speakers, the industry leader.

History. Gustavson Swift was a butcher and slaughterer from Massachusetts who perceived a way around the practice of shipping livestock from the grazing lands of the Midwest to the urban centers of the East on railroad cars. In 1875 he started his own meat-packing company in Chicago, which he built up into the mammoth slaughtering operation that inspired *The Jungle*, Upton Sinclair's muckraking novel of the Chicago stockyards.

To begin with, Swift perfected the refrigerated railroad car, which worked by sending fresh air across blocks of ice, and which made it feasible to ship slaughtered meat to the East. But he still faced several obstacles. Eastern butchers saw the Chicago meatpackers as threats, and railroads that reaped hefty profits by shipping live cattle reacted by levying excessive charges on Swift's cars. His solution was to build his own cars, convince the Grand Trunk Railroad (the only road that did not ship livestock or maintain stockyards) to carry them, and form partnerships with New England butchers who agreed to sell only his meat.

By 1908 Gustavson Swift's sons were managing a company that occupied 200 acres in Chicago, slaughtered 8 million animals a year, and had extensive markets in meat by-products such as soaps, hides, and glue. The company became so big and powerful that the federal government brought an antitrust suit against Swift and fellow meatpackers Armour, Wilson, and Cudahy, charging them with monopoly and price fixing. Under a consent decree reached in 1920 these companies were forbidden to go into more than 100 different businesses, including the restaurant business.

Swift was a latecomer to the diversification sweepstakes, not venturing from the meat business until 1968, with the acquisition of Vickers Petroleum. By then they were already taking a beating from a couple of upstarts, Iowa Beef Processors and Missouri Beef Packers (now MBPXL). These companies had taken Gustavson Swift's original idea one step further and set up modern, efficient slaughterhouses in small midwestern towns closer to where cattle are raised. Swift was stuck in Chicago with fifty-year-old slaughterhouses and big-city labor costs.

Rather than stand and fight, Swift chose to trim back the meat business and diversify. Since 1969 they have closed fifty meatpacking plants and laid off or retired 18,000 workers. Swift now has more people on pensions than on payroll.

Reputation. The investment community still doesn't know what to make of Esmark, despite company ads in the business press which try to explain what they are up to. Consumers may be even more confused as Swift, the old red meat company, comes at them with Sizzlean, a processed pork strip 50% leaner than bacon.

What they own. Six businesses: Swift, Estech, Vickers, Playtex, STP, and Pemcor.

Who owns and runs the company. The

The President versus The Pork Sausage

In the early 1900s adulteration of processed foods brought a public clamor for pure-food laws, but Congress consistently managed to direct its attention elsewhere. Upton Sinclair's muckraking novel *The Jungle* unmasked grisly conditions in the meatpacking industry, but still the government failed to act.

Finally, in 1905, President Theodore Roosevelt forced a favorable congressional vote on the first Pure Food and Drugs Bill. A popular cartoon character of the day, Finley Peter Dunne's Mister Dooley, explained in his inimitable Irish brogue how the President happened to conclude he must push the bill. Said Mister Dooley:

Tiddy was toying with a light breakfast an' idly turnin' over th' pages iv th' new book [Sinclair's exposé] with both hands. Suddenly he rose fr'm th' table, an' cryin' "I'm pizened," begun throwin' sausages out iv th' window. Th' ninth wan sthruck Sinitor Biv'ridge on th' head an' made him a blond. It bounced off, exploded, an' blew a leg off a secret-service man, an' th' scatthred fragmints desthroyed a handsome row iv ol' oak-trees. Sinitor Biv'ridge rushed in, thinkin' that th' Prisidint was bein' assassynated

be his devoted followers in th' Sinit, an' discovered Tiddy engaged in a hand-to-hand conflict with a potted ham. Th' Sinitor fr'm Injyanny, with a few well-directed wurruds, put out th' fuse an' rendered th' missile harmless. Since thin th' Prisidint, like th' rest iv us, has become a viggy-taryan . . .

On June 30, 1906, Roosevelt signed into law the bill to "regulate interstate commerce in misbranded and adulterated food, drinks and drugs."

Source: *Great Stories of American Businessmen* (American Heritage, 1972).

Jack A. Vickers family owns the biggest bloc of Esmark stock (3.8%), which they got when Esmark took over their oil company. Donald P. Kelly, Esmark's president and chief executive, was the main architect of the company's diversification program that started in the late 1960s. He joined Swift in 1953 and took over the top job in 1977 from Robert Reneker, whose father was once Swift's chief hog buyer.

In the public eye. Playtex's drive to take over the tampon market from Tampax suffered a setback in 1978 when *Consumer Reports* published a poll of its readers showing that 8% of those who had tried Playtex deodorant tampons would not use them again because of "medical problems, rash or infection." Deodorant tampons account for five-sevenths of Playtex's tampon sales. The year before Playtex had sued Tampax for $100 million over a Tampax ad that reprinted a warning from the Playtex carton, cautioning that the deodorant tampons might be irritating to some users. Tampax agreed to stop using the ad, and Playtex dropped the suit.

STP Oil Treatment was advertised in such a misleading way during the 1970s that a Federal Trade Commission complaint resulted in the company having to run $200,000 worth of humiliating ads to announce they had been fined $500,000 for "certain allegedly inaccurate past advertisements." No sooner had they agreed to eat this humble pie than Esmark paid $117 million to acquire the company.

Where they're going. Swift remains a question mark. In October 1978 Kelly said: "We haven't anything that isn't for sale. Swift must either perform, or it won't be there." A few months later he amended that to say: "Swift isn't for sale." But if a buyer comes around . . .

Stock performance. Esmark (Swift) stock bought for $1,000 in 1970 sold for $1,145 on January 2, 1980.

Access. 55 East Monroe Street, Chicago, Illinois 60603; (312) 431-3725.

Consumer brands.

Swift: Brown 'N Serve sausage and ham patties; Sizzlean and Firebrand breakfast strips; Strongheart and Rival dog foods; Pour'n fry shortening; Homemade Soup Starter; Butter-ball turkeys; Swift Premium International Entree prepared dinners; Cremol Plus cake and icing shortening; Trophy margarine; Tem-Cote butter coating; Mr. Host, Sugar Plum, and Joyner's hams; Lazy Maple bacon.

Estech: Vigoro plant- and vegetable-care products; Par Ex professional lawn-care products; Harvest King.

Vickers: Vickers automotive products.

Playtex: Playtex and Playtex Plus tampons; Cross Your Heart, Free Spirit, Instead, and Super Look bras; Tek toothbrushes; Playtex baby-care products; Playtex gloves for household use; Givenchy body smoothers; Round-The-Clock pantyhose.

STP: STP motor oil, oil filter, gas treatment, oil treatment, and other car-care products; Son of a Gun! vinyl and leather restorer.

Pemcor: Jensen audio and high-fidelity equipment.

General Foods

Sales: $5.5 billion
Profits: $232 million
Forbes 500 rank: 67
Rank in food processing: 3
Rank in coffee: 1
Rank in gelatin desserts: 1
Rank in table syrup: 1
Rank in rice: 2
Rank in cereals: 3
Rank in dog food: 4
Founded: 1929
Employees: 50,000
Headquarters: White Plains, New York

What they do. General Foods set the mold for the modern food corporation. They are themselves the product of 50 years of merging by smaller companies. Their 1,600 researchers cook up substances in laboratories which win acceptance as foods (with the help of a $300 million-a-year advertising budget) and become number 1 in markets which never existed before. Pop Rocks, Shake'n Bake, Tang, Dream Whip, Stove Top stuffing mix, and so forth, are all General Foods products.

General Foods also is the nation's largest coffee roaster (40% of their total business). Whether you buy Maxwell House, Yuban, Sanka, Brim, Maxim, Mellow Roast, or General Foods International Coffees, you're buying General Foods. (In the case of the last two, however, there's a question of whether they should be called coffee. Mellow Roast is a grain-extended product; International Coffees have sugar as a principal ingredient.) Coffee consumption has been declining steadily in the United States since 1962, when more than 100 companies were roasting coffee; by 1978 their ranks had dwindled to 40. However, the main casualties have been small local companies. General Foods and Procter & Gamble (Folgers) now sell 60% of the ground coffee in the country, and General Foods brands account for nearly 50% of the instant coffee business.

Markets outside the United States generate about a quarter of General Foods' sales (but only 5% of profits). They make Bird's desserts and Master McGrath dog food in Britain, Hollywood chewing gum and Krema candies in France, Kockens spices in Sweden, Cafe Monky in Spain, Kibon ice cream in Brazil, Rosa Blanca soups in Mexico, Rumic sauces in Japan, and Cottee's cordials in Australia.

History. The world's largest coffee seller traces their roots to a health food zealot, Charles William Post, who tried to wean Americans away from coffee and tea. A businessman who had suffered a series of reverses in both his business and health, Post arrived in 1891 as a patient at the famous Battle Creek Sanitarium run by the Kelloggs. Only 37, he was so emaciated he had to be pushed about in a wheelchair by his wife. Post recovered his health at the sanitarium, and after leaving, he began to make a cereal beverage that had been served there as a coffee substitute. He originally called it Monk's Brew, but in 1896 the name was changed to Postum—and sales took off under the impact of a strong ad campaign depicting the beverage as a builder of "red blood." In 1898 C. W. Post marketed another product similar to the granola that had been served at the sanitarium, calling it Grape-Nuts. In 1904 came a corn flakes product that Post proudly called Elijah's Manna. A flop under that name (not all Americans were as religious as C. W. Post), it became a winner after it was renamed Post Toasties.

The series of mergers that created today's General Foods began in 1925, when the Postum Cereal Company combined with the Jell-O Company. Here's the rest of the

---

TOP COFFEE ROASTERS

Share of Market

Regular Coffee
1. FOLGERS (*Procter & Gamble*)   26.5%
2. MAXWELL HOUSE (*General Foods*)   22.3%
3. HILLS BROTHERS   6.9%
4. MAX-PAX and BRIM (*General Foods*)   3.5%
5. BUTTERNUT (*Coca-Cola*)   2.7%
6. SANKA (*General Foods*)   2.0%
7. YUBAN (*General Foods*)   2.0%
8. MELLOW ROAST (*General Foods*)   1.8%
9. CHASE & SANBORN (*Standard Brands*)   1.6%
10. MARYLAND CLUB (*Coca-Cola*)   1.4%

Instant Coffee
1. MAXWELL HOUSE (*General Foods*)   24.0%
2. TASTER'S CHOICE (*Nestlé*)   12.5%
3. NESCAFÉ (*Nestlé*)   10.5%
4. SANKA (*General Foods*)   10.0%
5. FOLGERS (*Procter & Gamble*))   8.0%
6. TASTER'S CHOICE DECAFFEINATED (*Nestlé*)   5.1%
7. MAXIM (*General Foods*)   4.0%
8. MELLOW ROAST (*General Foods*)   3.5%
9. BRIM (*General Foods*)   3.0%
10. SUNRISE (*Nestlé*)   3.0%
11. FREEZE DRIED SANKA (*General Foods*)   2.5%
12. YUBAN (*General Foods*)   1.3%
13. DECAF (*Nestlé*)   1.0%
14. KAVA (*Borden*)   1.0%

Source: *Advertising Age*, April 30, 1979.

---

recipe: add Ingleheart Brothers (Swans Down cake flour) and Minute tapioca (1926); absorb Franklin Baker (coconut), Walter Baker (chocolate), and Log Cabin (syrup) (1927); throw in Clarence Birdseye's frozen food company (here, in 1929, you get all the quick-freezing patents and a new name: General Foods). Stir the following slowly into the mixture: Gaines dog food (1943), Kool-Aid (1953), Good Seasons salad dressing (1954), Open Pit barbecue sauces (1960).

Strange as it may seem, nothing went sour until recent times. The FTC made General Foods give up SOS scouring pads (a 1957 acquisition) on grounds of unfair competition. The Burger Chef fast-food business has lost money steadily ever since General Foods paid $16 million for it in 1968. Three nonfood companies purchased by General Foods after 1970 were sold off later: Viviane Woodward (door-to-door cosmetics), Khoner Brothers (toys), and W. Atlee Burpee (the nation's largest seed company).

Reputation. No other food company talks as much about technology as General Foods does. They search constantly for technologies that will give them a significant advantage over competitors. Here is their own description of how products come about: "Sometimes General Foods' marketing people bring an idea to research and production people saying: 'We think we can sell this product if you can make it.' Other times . . . researchers in the laboratory . . . may say to the marketing people: 'We think we can make this product if you can sell it.'"

What they own. Thirty-six plants in the United States, including the world's largest coffee processing facility at Hoboken, New Jersey. Research kennels housing some 500 dogs near the Gaines plant at Kankakee, Illinois. Eight hundred Burger Chef restaurants (one-quarter of the units in the system). Five plants and 4 restaurant chains (Crock & Block, 1867, Ernie's Fine Foods, White Spot) in Canada. Eleven plants in eight European countries and 30 plants in six other countries.

Who owns and runs the company. Institutions, as opposed to individuals, own 75% of General Foods stock. All the officers and directors combined own less than 1%. Professional managers call the shots. Marilyn Bender, a former *New York Times* reporter, once called the company's relationship with the Harvard Business School "intimate." General Foods' organizational style is not unlike Procter & Gamble's. Both companies give early responsibility to young business school graduates, and both rely heavily on new products, extensive consumer research, and blockbuster adver-

The Frozen Inventor

"I have taken all knowledge to be my province," pronounced Sir Francis Bacon, the seventeenth-century philosopher-scientist-politician. But Bacon met a sudden end when he tried to invent food. Riding from London to Highgate one snowy winter day in 1626, Bacon decided to test his theory that flesh could be preserved by freezing. He stopped at a cottage, bought a fowl, killed it on the spot, and stuffed it with snow. He had time to report that his experiment was a success before he died of the exposure he suffered while performing it.

No one succeeded in freezing food on a commercial scale until three centuries later. The inspiration then came from caribou steak.

Charles Birdseye was a Brooklyn-born explorer-adventurer-inventor who spent most of his life in out-of-the-way places. While on a fur trapping expedition in Labrador, he noticed that when the Eskimos froze caribou meat in the dry Arctic air, it was still flavorsome and tender when thawed and cooked months later. Efforts to freeze meat in the United States by methods then available had so far all failed to produce a palatable result.

Birdseye reasoned that the Eskimos could succeed where technologically more advanced societies had failed because the extremely low Arctic temperatures froze the meat much faster than any process tried elsewhere. As it turned out, he was right. Slow freezing meat and other foods forms large ice crystals, which destroy cell walls and let natural juices leak out when the food is thawed. The faster the freezing, the smaller the ice crystals, the more thawed food retains its original taste and texture.

Returning to the United States with his discovery in 1917, Birdseye formed a company called General Seafoods. Birdseye's laboratory in Gloucester, Massachusetts was devoted to finding a commercial way of imitating the Eskimos, and the inventor froze everything he could get from the local fishermen: sharks, small whales, even an alligator. After much research he developed equipment and procedures that became the basis of today's frozen-food industry.

In 1924 Birdseye founded the General Foods Company, which began quick-freezing foods on a large scale. Five years later the Postum Cereal Company bought his company for $22 million and soon adopted the name General Foods Corporation. Birdseye got a job as head of the General Foods laboratory in Gloucester, where he developed a new method for dehydrating food.

Like Francis Bacon, Birdseye died from the effects of a research expedition. Sent to Peru on an assignment to develop paper out of a local plant called agave, he suffered a heart attack from the high altitudes. He died in October 1956, after returning to the United States.

tising. C. W. Cook, chairman of General Foods from 1966 to 1974, was recruited from Procter & Gamble, as was the present chairman, James L. Ferguson, a Harvard Business School graduate. Of the 35 top corporate officers, only one is a woman: Marguerite C. Kohl, vice-president for consumer affairs.

In the public eye. General Foods tries to respond quickly to social pressures. After the civil rights protests of the early 1960s, the number of minority employees doubled within five years. The Federal Trade Commission has two complaints pending against General Foods: a monopoly action brought against the top four cereal makers, and an action charging that General Foods used their dominant position in coffee to undercut competitors when Folgers started to expand across the country. General Foods was one of the first corporations to leave New York City, having pulled out in 1954 for suburban White Plains. Now they are planning another move—to Rye, New York, four miles away.

Where they're going. Although a lot of people are unhappy with chemical additives, General Foods is not about to give up on laboratory development of foods. They will also try to build overall consumption of their biggest product, coffee, to reverse the decline that has taken place. And they will try to expand their restaurant operations.

Stock performance. General Foods stock bought for $1,000 in 1970 sold for $809 on January 2, 1980.

Major employment centers. Westchester County, New York (corporate headquarters and research center); Battle Creek, Michigan; and Dover, Delaware.

Access. 250 North Street, White Plains, New York 10625; (914) 683-2500.

Consumer brands.

Coffees: Maxwell House; Yuban; Sanka; Brim; Max-Pax; Maxim; General Foods International Coffees.
Desserts: Jell-O; D-Zerta; Cool Whip; Dream Whip; Minute tapioca.
Baking and canning products: Calumet; Baker's; Swans Down; Certo; Sure-Jell.
Pet foods: Gaines; Gravy Train; Prime; Top Choice; Cycle.

> **Frozen-food consumption nearly doubled between 1963 (when it was 6.1 billion pounds) and 1976 (11.5 billion pounds). Keeping pace was output of aluminum foil trays, up from 1.9 billion to 4.4 billion in the same period.**

Other foods: Birds Eye frozen vegetables; Minute rice; Stove Top stuffing mixes.
Seasonings and condiments: Shake 'n Bake; Butter 'n Bake; Good Seasons; Open Pit.
Beverages: Kool-Aid; Kool-Pops; Awake; Orange Plus; Tang; Start; Country Time; Postum.
Breakfast foods: Log Cabin; Country Kitchen; Post cereals (Post Toasties, Grape-Nuts, Raisin Bran, 40% Bran Flakes, Fortified Oat Flakes, Alpha-Bits, Super Sugar Crisp, Frosted Rice Krinkels, Honeycomb, Pebbles, Post-Tens, Treat-Pak).
Restaurants: Burger Chef.
In a class by itself: Pop Rocks.

THREE'S COMPANY

Share of Market Held by Top 3 Brands

GELATIN DESSERTS	98.4%
MARSHMALLOWS	98.2%
FROSTINGS	97.7%
FROZEN DINNERS	92.8%
TABLE SALT	91.7%
CORN AND TORTILLA CHIPS	86.7%
KETCHUP	86.1%
SPAGHETTI SAUCE	85.9%
PRETZELS	85.6%
SALAD AND COOKING OIL	85.5%
VINEGAR	84.1%
HONEY	82.2%
SHORTENING	81.0%
NUTS	80.7%
FLOUR	80.4%
PEANUT BUTTER	78.6%
MUSTARD	76.2%
JAMS AND JELLIES	75.2%

Source: *Progressive Grocer,* July 1978.

> **Coffee is the largest single food item imported into the United States (nearly $4 billion a year), followed by fish ($2 billion), meat ($1.2 billion), and sugar ($1 billion).**

General Mills

Sales: $3.7 billion
Profits: $147 million
Forbes 500 rank: 123
Rank in food processing: 23
Rank in family flour for home use: 1
Rank in baking mixes: 1
Rank in toys: 1
Rank in cereals: 2
Founded: 1928
Employees: 66,600
Headquarters: Minneapolis, Minnesota

What they do. General Mills is the world's largest toy maker (Monopoly, Lionel trains). They sell stamps and coins to collectors. They're one of the largest costume jewelry makers (Monet). They produce furniture, clothes (David Crystal, Ship 'n Shore), golf shoes (Foot-Joy), and luggage. Through mail order and more than 100 of their own stores, they sell art and needlework supplies (LeeWards), women's apparel (Talbots), outerwear (Eddie Bauer), and wall coverings. They operate more than 300 restaurants (Red Lobster, York Steak House). And all of these acquired businesses lie outside General Mills' main line of endeavor: food processing. General Mills is a $2 billion-a-year food manufacturer, a ranking producer of ready-to-eat cereals (Cheerios is number 1 in dollar sales), mixes (Bisquick and Betty Crocker), flour (Gold Medal), frozen seafoods, snacks, imitation bacon chips, and a bagful of other packaged foods.

History. General Mills was put together in 1928 by James Ford Bell, who was president of a Minneapolis miller, Crosby-Washburn, longtime rival of the other big Minneapolis miller, Pillsbury. Bell got half a dozen big milling companies around the country to combine forces. The new company had a toehold in the cereal market with a four-year-old brand, Wheaties, that became one of the most widely advertised products during the Depression years. They also had Betty Crocker, who was invented in 1921 by Crosby-Washburn's advertising manager. General Mills forged ahead in break-

fast cereals but remained closely tied to the flour business. Charles Bell, James Ford Bell's son, loosened that tie. After World War II he hired his former Air Force commanding officer, Gen. Edwin Rawlings, who closed down half the company's flour mills and embarked on a diversification program that continues today. In 1964 General Mills reached to Dallas to buy Morton Foods, a corn chip, potato chip, and pork skin producer (not related to Continental Baking's Morton frozen foods). In 1966 they went to Georgia to acquire the Tom Huston Peanut Company, a prime supplier of peanut butter sandwiches and marshmallow pies to vending machines. Then, in 1967 and 1968, they pulled off a four-part parlay that brought into the "Big G" fold Kenner Products, the Play-Doh manufacturer; Craft Master, maker of paint-by-number sets; Model Products, maker of model toys; and Parker Bros., maker of Monopoly and other board games. Since that time General Mills has never stopped acquiring.

Reputation. General Mills grows by scooping up other companies, especially small operations that can be infused with capital to expand.

What they own. One hundred fifteen production facilities, including 27 toy and game plants, 8 cereal factories, and 1 synthetic sponge plant. The Super Bubble gum business. The Slim Jim jerky business. The Nerf soccer ball business.

Who owns and runs the company. General Mills got their chairman, E. Robert Kinney, by acquisition: he was formerly president of Gorton's. General Mills has a heavy Twin Cities (Minneapolis/St. Paul) establishment on their board of directors: Kenneth Dayton (Dayton's department store), Stephen Keating (Honeywell), Lewis W. Lehr (3M), Louis W. Menk (Burlington Northern), John W. Morrison (Northwestern National Bank), and Waverly G. Smith (St. Paul Companies). Also on the board are two women, Betsy Ancker-Johnson, vice-president for environmental activities at General Motors, and Gwendolyn A. Newkirk, a black who is chair of the department of education and family resources at the University of Nebraska.

In the public eye. In 1972 and 1973 Gen-

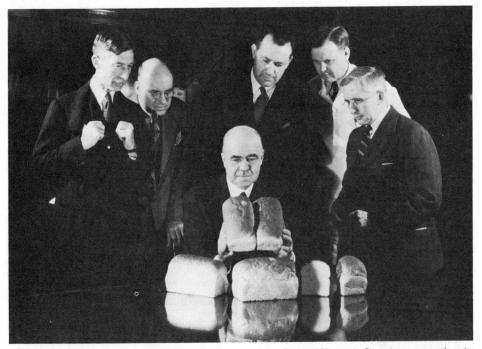

Pioneers of General Mills in days when it was easier to know what General Mills made. Seated is company founder James F. Bell.

eral Mills was the target of a boycott instituted by the National Urban League and the National Organization of Women over employment of minorities and women. It was then that they recruited a black, Cyrus E. Johnson, from Illinois Bell. Johnson is now vice-president and director of corporate personnel. Minority group members today represent nearly 19% of General Mills' U. S. work force. General Mills has also sharply increased their philanthropic contributions. Grants totaled $4.7 million in 1979, nearly 2% of pretax profits, and the company proudly noted that while they ranked 86 on the Fortune 500 list, they were the 27th largest corporate giver.

Where they're going. General Mills will continue to look for companies to buy. They've joined the Italian wave (pizza), and they hope to be in on the Mexican wave (restaurants). If inflation makes it more difficult for people to buy meats and fish, General Mills has high hopes for Hamburger Helper. (The ingredients which are supposed to help your hamburger are starch, bouillon, sugar, hydrolized vegetable protein, vegetable shortening, dehydrated vegetables, monosodium glutamate, lactic acid, caramel coloring, citric acid, ar-

tificial color, disodium inosinate, and disodium guanylate.)

Stock performance. General Mills stock bought for $1,000 in 1970 sold for $1,429 on January 2, 1980.

Major employment centers. Boston, Minneapolis, and Chicago.

Access. 9200 Wayzata Boulevard, Minneapolis, Minnesota 55440; (612) 540-2311. Inquiries and complaints should go to the Consumer Response Department, Box 1113, Minneapolis 55440. The Betty Crocker Kitchens at corporate headquarters can be toured Monday through Friday at 10 A.M., 11 A.M., 1 P.M., 2 P.M., and 3 P.M.

11% of the potatoes grown in the United States are consumed in the form of potato chips.

Consumer brands.

Breakfast products: Cheerios; Golden Grahams; Crazy Cow; Corn Total; Wheaties; Cocoa Puffs; Kix; Fun Pack; Total; Nature Valley Granola; Franken Berry; Country Corn Flakes; Lucky Charms; Buc Wheats; BooBerry; Fruit Brute; Trix; Count Chocula; Kaboom; Frosty's; Nature Valley Granola Bars; Breakfast Squares.

Snack products: Tom's snack products, Slim Jim sausage products and beef jerky; Penrose pickled meat products; Andy Capp's potato snacks; Pemmican beef jerky.

Mixes and convenience foods: Betty Crocker, Bisquick baking mixes; Hamburger Helper and Tuna Helper prepared dinner mixes; Mug-O-Lunch; Potato Buds; Betty Crocker potato casseroles.

Family flour: Gold Medal; La Pina; Red Band; Gold Medal Wondra; Complete Pancake Mix.

Frozen foods: Gorton's frozen seafood products; Saluto frozen pizza and Italian frozen entrees; Louise's Home Style Ravioli Co.

Other foods: Jesse Jones breakfast sausages, frankfurters, and luncheon meats; Bac Os imitation bacon chips; Yoplait yogurt; Pioneer Products cake decorations, candles, and party novelties; O-Cel-O sponges.

Restaurants: Red Lobster Inns; York Steak Houses; Casa Gallardo; Hannahan's; Fennimore's; Betty Crocker Pie Shops.

Toys and games: Parker Brothers board games: Monopoly, Ouija, Clue, Sorry, Happy Days, Pay Day; family games: Bonkers, Boogle; foam products: Nerf; electronic games: Merlin, Sector, P.E.G.S. Kenner: Star Wars toys; SSP racers; Easy Bake ovens; Spirograph design toys; Give-A-Show projectors; Play-Doh modeling compound; Baby Alive Doll; Darci Cover Girl Fashion Doll; Discovery Time preschool toys. Fundimensions: Craft Master paint-by-number painting system; MPC plastic model kits; Lionel trains; other craft and hobby items.

Stamps and coins: H. E. Harris: stamps; albums; and philatelic supplies. R & R Stamps: first-day covers to stamp collectors. Bowers and Ruddy Galleries coins.

Clothing and accessories: David Crystal men's, women's, and children's apparel; Izod, Chemise Lacoste, Haymaker, Crystal Sunflowers, Equations, Lord Jeff men's apparel; Ship'n Shore (Inner Visions) women's apparel; Foot-Joy golf shoes; Monet costume jewelry; Ciani precious metal jewelry.

Specialty retailing and other: LeeWards Creative Crafts hobby craft, art supplies, and needlework; Eddie Bauer hunting, camping, and general outdoor clothing and equipment; The Talbots women's retail apparel; Wallpapers to Go self-service wallpaper stores; Pennsylvania House traditional American furniture; Kittinger eighteenth-century English furniture reproductions; Dunbar contemporary furniture.

DOES IT PAY TO BE SWEET?

Market Share By Percentage of Sales		Total Sugar Content
CHEERIOS (*General Mills*)	6.1%	3%
SUGAR FROSTED FLAKES (*Kellogg*)	5.0%	56%
KELLOGG'S CORN FLAKES	4.9%	5%
RICE KRISPIES (*Kellogg*)	4.6%	8%
KELLOGG'S RAISIN BRAN	4.4%	29%
CHEX (*Ralston Purina*)	3.5%	32%
CAP'N CRUNCH (*Quaker Oats*)	3.5%	32%
POST RAISIN BRAN (*General Foods*)	3.5%	29%
SHREDDED WHEAT (*Nabisco*)	3.2%	1%
FRUIT LOOPS (*Kellogg*)	3.1%	48%
SPECIAL "K" (*Kellogg*)	2.7%	5%
LIFE (*Quaker Oats*)	2.4%	21%
POST GRAPE-NUTS (*General Foods*)	2.4%	7%
WHEATIES (*General Mills*)	2.4%	8%
POST SUGAR CRISPS (*General Foods*)	2.0%	46%

Source: *Advertising Age*, July 9, 1979; U.S. Department of Agriculture, 1979.

In 1950 Americans spent 22% of their disposable incomes on food. In 1978, this figure was down to 17%. Families earning less than $5,000 a year spend 40% of their incomes on food, families earning more than $20,000 spend less than 10%.

An October 1978 editorial in *Food Engineering* warned readers, "Health foods and 'organic' foods made a comeback [in the 1970s], and some of these were as dangerous as eating berries in the jungle."

Gerber

Sales: $564.7 million
Profits: $28.3 million
Rank in baby foods: 1
Founded: 1901
Employees: 9,000
Headquarters: Fremont, Michigan

What they do. Gerber invented commercial baby foods. They pack 150 varieties in five U.S. plants, and they hold 70% of the U.S. market.

History. Frank Gerber began canning peas in Fremont, Michigan, in 1901. In 1927 his daughter-in-law, Mrs. Dan Gerber, complained to her husband about the chore of straining peas for their newborn baby. So Dan had the cannery do it—and it wasn't long before Fremont's biggest business was baby foods. The original five items were strained peas, spinach, prunes, carrots, and vegetable soup. Gerber used to snipe at competitors Heinz and Beech-Nut with the slogan: "Babies are our business— our *only* business," but they had to drop that after buying into insurance, toys, clothing, day-care, and trucking. They also make Dri-Pride incontinent pads (diapers for the elderly).

Mrs. Dan Gerber with her daughter in 1928: the inspiration for Gerber's strained baby foods.

Reputation. They are known for benevolence in their hometown of Fremont, where Gerber is the economic mainstay.

Who owns and runs the company. Gerbers are no longer active in the day-to-day management of the company, but they control more than 20% of the stock. Two women and a black hold board seats.

Snapping and Stretching

If chewing gum had a patron saint, it would probably be General Antonio Lopez de Santa Anna, the Mexican general better known as Sam Houston's opponent in the Battle of Jacinto in 1836. Luckily for gum lovers, Santa Anna came out of the war with his life, a ticket to New York, and a large chunk of chicle (the dried sap of the sapodilla tree found in the Mexican jungle).

Santa Anna had great expectations that a yankee inventor could turn his chicle into a rubber substitute and thereby make both their for-

tunes. It never happened. Santa Anna's great yankee hope, Thomas Adams of Jersey City, struck out on his rubber/chicle experiments, and Santa Anna returned to Mexico, without the worthless chicle.

But Adams's yankee ingenuity turned up a use for the chicle. Adams had noticed that both his son and Santa Anna chewed the stuff. Why not sell the chicle in place of the inferior paraffin/resin chew then available?

The "Adams New York Gum—Snapping and Stretching" had no flavor or sugar,

but kids loved it, despite the vociferous opposition of ministers, teachers, parents, and the press.

The modern stick of Doublemint or Juicy Fruit gum bears little resemblance to the chew from the jungles of Mexico. What we buy today is a sweetened, flavored stick of polyvinyl acetate, a substance straight from the labs of DuPont. Americans chew their way through 10 million pounds of the stuff every year.

In the public eye. Gerber used to add MSG, salt, and sugar to their baby foods to make them more palatable (to mothers). All these ingredients have now been eliminated or sharply reduced, after much pressure from consumer groups.

Where they're going. The big question is: will some other company scoop up Gerber? Anderson, Clayton, the big Texas oil processor, tried in 1977 but had to retreat when the whole town of Fremont rose up in Gerber's defense. The Texans said, "We've been pictured as Attila the Hun coming to lay waste to Michigan." Management's refusal to accept the Anderson, Clayton offer resulted in a class action suit by some Gerber stockholders who felt the company wasn't doing right by them. Anderson, Clayton was ready to pay $40 a share, while Gerber's stock entered 1980 at $25 a share.

Stock performance. Gerber stock bought for $1,000 in 1970 sold for $634 on January 2, 1980.

Austin cars were bought by Gerber Foods to tour the country promoting their baby foods in 1931 and 1932. The car horns played "Rock-a-Bye-Baby."

43 new Chevrolets were delivered to the fleet department of Gerber Foods in 1940.

Major employment centers. Fremont; Ephrata, Pennsylvania; and Asheville, North Carolina.

Access. 445 State Street, Fremont, Michigan 49412; (616) 928-2000. Inquiries to: Mrs. Verabelle Willis, R.N., consumer relations manager at the Fremont headquarters. The Fremont plant welcomes visitors. Tours are also given at the four other baby food plants in Rochester, New York; Asheville, North Carolina; Ft. Smith, Arkansas; and Oakland, California.

Consumer brands.

Gerber baby foods, baby-care items, sneakers, and toys; Hankscraft humidifiers and nursers; Dri-Pride incontinent pant system; Babygro infant garments.

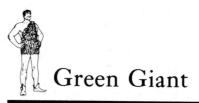

Green Giant

Sales: $486 million
Profits: $10.4 million
Rank in canned peas: 1
Rank in canned corn: 1
Rank in canned asparagus: 1
Rank in canned mushrooms: 1
Rank in frozen prepared vegetables: 1
Founded: 1903
Employees: 7,700
Headquarters: Chaska, Minnesota

What they do. The world's largest packer of peas and corn ceased to be an independent entity in the early days of 1979, when shareholders agreed to sell their company to a Minnesota neighbor: Pillsbury. The sale came shortly after Green Giant had celebrated their 75th birthday, proclaiming: "We are excited about the years before us. We are grateful for the chance to explore new valleys and to do so with the hand of a wise and well-loved Giant on our shoulder." But the "giant" whose hand came to rest on this shoulder turned out to be the little Pillsbury doughboy. Pillsbury paid $150 million to tuck Green Giant into their corporate folds.

What Green Giant packs is more often than not the sales leader. They hold more than 20% of the market for canned peas, corn, and asparagus. Their 13% share of the canned mushroom market tops all other brands. In green beans they're second only to Del Monte. Green Giant is the only major canner to have made the transition to freezing food. Their major thrust has been in frozen prepared vegetables, where they enjoy 50% of the market. What's the difference between frozen vegetables and frozen *prepared* vegetables? Plenty. Frozen broccoli is a frozen vegetable; frozen broccoli with a cheese sauce is a frozen prepared vegetable, carrying a considerably higher price—and profit margin—than the plain variety.

Most of the vegetables used by Green Giant are grown and processed during a three-month summer period, when the company hires some 20,000 temporary employees every year.

History. Green Giant was founded as the Minnesota Valley Canning Company by 14 merchants who met one evening in 1903 in the back of James A. Cosgrove's harness shop in Le Sueur, a town in southwestern Minnesota. (The town was named for a French explorer, Pierre Charles Le Sueur, whose name was later to go on millions of cans of very young, small "Early Peas" packed by Green Giant.) The chairman of this first meeting was Carson Nesbitt Cosgrove, elder brother of the harness maker. Cosgrove was a 5'3" dynamo who had come to Le Sueur in 1872 when he was 19. C. N., as he was called, introduced the first herd of registered Herefords to Minnesota, served as a state senator, and was one of the principal organizers of the Minnesota state fair. His son, Ward Cosgrove, headed Green Giant for 40 years. His grandson, Robert Cosgrove, was chairman in 1979 when the company was sold to Pillsbury.

The first product of Minnesota Valley Canning was canned white cream-style corn, packed from corn grown in the Minnesota valley where Le Sueur is located. They shipped 11,750 cases in their first year under the labels Artesian and Minnesota Valley. Americans of that time had a strong color prejudice, preferring white corn and dismissing the yellow variety as "horse corn." Minnesota Valley changed that habit. In 1924 they began packing yellow corn that was sweeter than white and easier to grow. Today U.S. corn eaters overwhelmingly favor yellow.

Minnesota Valley first packed peas in 1907. There, too, Americans had strong prejudices, preferring Early June peas, which are small, smooth, and round. In the early 1920s Ward Cosgrove returned from Europe with an English variety pea called Prince of Wales, which was wrinkled, oblong, and much larger than Early Junes, and also sweeter and more tender. So strange was this variety to the American palate that Minnesota Valley's private label customers—wholesalers and stores that put their own names on product supplied by processors—refused to stock them. So Minnesota Valley marketed the big peas under their own label, and bragged about their size by calling them "green giant." When the company tried to trademark the green giant name, they were advised that product descriptions cannot be trademarked. This rejection prompted the invention of the "giant" as a symbol that could be trademarked. The first giant appeared on a label in 1925. He looked more like a dwarf, and he was white. He wore a scruffy bearskin. He scowled. Later he became green, and when a young copywriter, Leo Burnett, opened his own advertising agency in Chicago in the 1930s, with Minnesota Valley as a charter client, the Giant underwent further sprucing up. He became taller; he smiled; he traded in his bearskin for a leafy suit. And one day, as Burnett was going over an ad, he penciled in the word *Jolly* in front of the Giant's name.

In 1950 Minnesota Valley Canning became the Green Giant Company.

Reputation. Green Giant has one of the best reputations in the food industry for quality products and fair dealing. They lost money in only one year: 1932.

What they own. Green Giant operates 19 processing plants in 11 states. Property, plants, and equipment were valued at $130 million prior to the acquisition by Pillsbury.

Who owns and runs the company. Pillsbury is now the sole owner. Executives of Green Giant were usually home-grown, but in 1975 Thomas H. Wyman was recruited from Polaroid to become president and chief executive officer. Wyman was then 45 and left Polaroid for the opportunity of running his own show at Green Giant. He is now vice-chairman of Pillsbury, with responsibility for all consumer products. Wyman had a contract stipulating that he would be paid three years salary if Green Giant was acquired by another company. When it was, he received a check for $490,695.

Where they're going. With Pillsbury's weight behind them, Green Giant can be expected to become a more aggressive competitor, producing more convenience foods backed with heavy advertising. Reflecting on the benefits of being part of the Pillsbury family, Wyman said Green Giant no longer has to make "trips to different banks with our kneepads on."

Major employment centers. Chaska, Glencoe, and Le Sueur, Minnesota.

Access. Hazeltine Gates, Chaska, Minnesota 55318; (612) 448-2828. Green Giant's processing plants are open to tours by appointment only. The Glencoe, Minnesota plant is the largest sweet corn processing facility in the world. The Le Sueur facility is the original plant, located in the "Valley of the Jolly Green Giant." Questions or complaints about Green Giant products should be addressed to: Candy Christeinsen Jenks, director of consumer affairs. General inquiries about the company should be directed to: A. B. Fiskett, director of corporate communications. Both are at the Chaska headquarters.

Consumer brands.

Green Giant, Jolly Green Giant, Le Sueur vegetables.

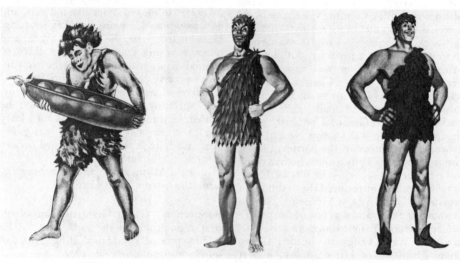

| 1926 | 1960 | 1970 |

Evolution of the Jolly Green Giant.

The Green Eavesdropper

In an official company history Green Giant owned up to the fact that in the early days their own management didn't know how canning worked. Small canneries of that time hired plant superintendents who kept canning methods a secret from the company as a form of job insurance. "George F. Winter solved this problem in 1916," says the company history, "by hiding in the rafters of the plant, watching the superintendent at work, and taking notes on his procedures. Winter's feat enabled the company to learn the actual canning process for the first time. George went on to become superintendent of production and a member of the board of directors until his retirement in 1954."

Heinz

Sales: $2.5 billion
Profits: $110 million
Forbes 500 rank: 207
Rank in food processing: 15
Rank in ketchup: 1
Rank in frozen potatoes: 1
Rank in vinegar: 1
Rank in baby foods: 2
Founded: 1869
Employees: 34,000
Headquarters: Pittsburgh, Pennsylvania

What they do. Most people link Heinz and ketchup in the same breath, and with good reason. Ketchup is the most widely used condiment on American tables, and Heinz has been packing it for more than 100 years. Their market position is awesome: the Heinz brand captures 40% of ketchup sales in grocery stores and 60% in restaurants.

Heinz is, of course, more than ketchup. Today, they make hundreds of food products on four continents. Their British subsidiary is so strong and well entrenched that most people there regarded it as an English company (the source of such English delicacies as "beans on toast" and "spaghetti on toast"). British sales represent one-sixth of Heinz's total volume. Another big chunk, more than 20%, is contributed by Star-Kist, the California tuna packer acquired by Heinz in 1963.

Heinz does well overseas, in some cases better than in the United States. They may get trounced by Campbell in the United States, but they hold something like 65% of the British soup market. Heinz used to be embarrassed because they made twice as much money overseas as they did here. Wall Street people accused the company of letting the American business slide. When R. Burt Gookin took over as chief executive officer in 1969, becoming the first non-Heinz family member to hold the top position, he vowed to change that relationship —and he did: Heinz now does about two-thirds of their business inside the United States.

History. The man who gave this company its name, and whose great-grandson is now a U.S. Senator from Pennsylvania, was depicted as follows by biographer Robert C. Alberts in *The Good Provider:*

H. J. Heinz was a small man with prodigious energy and drive. His blue eyes sparkled, his reddish muttonchop whiskers bristled, and he seemed always to move along at a half trot. He carried a pocket diary, a notebook, and a steel tape measure that he whipped out on any occasion to record interesting dimensions —the width of a doorway, the thickness of a sill, the circumference of a column. He was a cheerful man who greeted you, in the words of a contemporary, "with the old-fashioned courtesy of the last generation." He had overpowering enthusiasms: for work and success, for travel, for his family, for religious pursuits and kind deeds, for good horses and bad paintings. He liked others to enjoy what he enjoyed; so far as is known, he is the only American industrial magnate who ever returned from Florida (in 1898) with an 800-pound, 14½-foot, 150-year-old live alligator and installed it in a glass tank atop one of his factory buildings so that his employees might share his pleasure in the sight.

The first of nine children born to two German immigrants, Henry J. Heinz grew up near Pittsburgh in a strict Lutheran household where children who missed church were required to sit down and listen to their mother retell the minister's sermon. At age 8 he was already selling produce from the family garden to other households. By 10 he had a wheelbarrow; by 12 a horse and cart.

In 1869, when he was 25, Henry formed a partnership with a friend to sell food in bottles. Their first product was horseradish; then came sauerkraut, pickles, and vinegar. It was a business that went under in the panic of 1875, but Henry Heinz started over again the following year, carrying in his pocket a notebook marked "M.O.," which stood for moral obligations and contained a list of all the people he owed money from the bankruptcy of the previous company. These debts were all paid as Henry Heinz's second company succeeded and he became known throughout the land as the pickle king. The Heinz company bottled and sold pickles, relishes, sauces, and condiments to spice up what was then a monotonous American diet. They made tomato soup and then beans in tomato sauce. In 1893, when the World's Columbian Exposition was staged in Chicago, Heinz had the largest exhibit of any American food company.

Heinz entered the twentieth century as one of the nation's premier businesses. They were the number 1 producer of pickles, vinegar, and ketchup; the largest grower and processor of mustard; and the fourth-largest packer of olives. In all, they made more than 200 products, giving the lie to the "57 Varieties" slogan that Henry Heinz had coined in 1892. Actually, it wasn't even accurate then—Heinz had more than 60 products in 1892—but he liked the poetic cadence of that number, and he put it on all his labels and in all his advertising. In 1900 it went up in lights in New York's first large electric sign, at Fifth Avenue and 23rd Street. The sign was six stories high, used 1,200 bulbs, and cost $90 to illuminate each night. It had a green pickle 40 feet long and at first advertised the "57 Varieties Exhibited at Heinz Pier, Atlantic City," a reference to the 900-foot pier that Heinz built at Atlantic City in 1898, which remained a tourist attraction until 1944. Henry Heinz was considered an advertising and merchandising genius, but he gave orders never to run any Heinz advertising in Sunday newspapers so as not to disturb the Sabbath.

Henry Heinz was known as one of the five Pittsburgh millionaires (the others being Carnegie, Frick, Westinghouse, and Mellon). On the Allegheny River across from downtown Pittsburgh he had constructed an ornate Romanesque complex of plants that became a mecca for tourists who visited the facilities to watch white-frocked girls pack his products. Heinz received many awards for his model factories, including the ultimate accolade from Harry W. Sherman, Grand Secretary of the National Brotherhood of Electrical Workers of America, who visited the Heinz plant and called it "a utopia for working men."

When he went to England in 1886, Henry

Heinz had a sample case with him. He came home with orders for seven products, and by 1905 Heinz was manufacturing in England. In 1906, following the publication of Upton Sinclair's *The Jungle*, a searing novel about the Chicago stockyards, the United States was the scene of a hotly debated move to establish a Pure Food Act to regulate conditions in food processing facilities. Most of the U.S. food industry was bitterly opposed to the legislation, but not Henry Heinz, who supported it and sent his son to Washington to campaign for it. Henry Heinz died in 1919 at age 75, leaving an estate of $4 million. The largest bequest, aside from those to his family, was $300,000 to Sunday school associations.

Reputation. They're an old-fashioned company out to demonstrate they can be just as aggressive as the next guy.

What they own. Sixteen processing plants in the United States and 24 abroad (12 of them in the United Kingdom). The Hubinger Company, an Iowa corn processor. And the Weight Watchers business—both the frozen-food products sold under that name and the weight-reduction programs.

Who owns and runs the company. When Henry Heinz died in 1919, he was succeeded by his son Howard, who died in 1941 and was succeeded by his son, H. J. Heinz II, now chairman of the board. H. J. II's son, H. J. Heinz III, worked for the company from 1965 to 1970. He was elected to Congress in 1971, representing the Pittsburgh suburban district (in the 1974 election he received a phenomenal 72% of the vote), and to the U.S. Senate in 1976. Heinz family members still control about 20% of the company's stock (worth some $175 million).

In 1976, 43-year-old Anthony J. F. O'Reilly was elected to succeed R. B. Gookin as chief executive officer. O'Reilly is not a cookie-mold business executive. A native of Ireland, he has been, among other things, a world-class rugby player and a professional singer. He first joined Heinz in Britain.

Where they're going. In 1978 Heinz spent $10 million on new product development and $120 million on advertising. Asked about new product development at a security analysts' meeting in late 1978, O'Reilly said: "In many ways the best way to get into

The market for cat food in the U.S. is "two-and-a-half to three times the size of the baby food market," Anthony J. F. O'Reilly, president of H. J. Heinz Co., a major producer of both products, told the *Wall Street Journal*. "That will tell you something about our changing tastes."

new product development is to take over some other guy's idea by buying the company."

Stock performance. Heinz stock bought for $1,000 in 1970 sold for $1,876 on January 2, 1980.

Access. P.O. Box 57, Pittsburgh, Pennsylvania 15230; (412) 237-5757. Plant tours were discontinued in 1972. Automated plants are not as interesting as the old ones were.

Consumer brands.

Heinz; Star-Kist tuna; Great American soups; Ore-Ida potatoes; La Pizzeria; Mrs. Goodcookie; 9-Lives cat food; Weight Watchers.

 **Hershey**

Sales: $1.2 billion
Profits: $53.5 million
Forbes 500 rank: 406
Rank in candy: 2
Rank in chocolate: 1
Founded: 1900
Employees: 25,800
Headquarters: Hershey, Pennsylvania

What they do. Hershey is, perhaps more than any other company besides Coca-Cola, an American institution. Their main product, the chocolate candy bar, comes from a town in Pennsylvania named Hershey, after the company's founder, where, for 58 years, visitors have trooped through the largest chocolate factory in the world. Hershey bars are sold in tens of thousands of places across the country: movie theaters, groceries, drugstores, five-and-dimes, tobacco shops, candy stores, vending machines.

The price of the Hershey bar has been a barometer of inflation. The 5¢ Hershey bar was introduced in 1921. It didn't move up to 10¢ until 1969. Today it's 25¢. Not too many companies will find, as Hershey did, that a price increase will land them on the front pages of newspapers.

The company became famous for a peculiarity: they refused to advertise. "Give them quality," said founder Milton S. Hershey. "That's the best kind of advertising." For many years critics of advertising would cry triumphantly, "Look at Hershey, they don't advertise and they're number 1 in their field."

Hershey didn't change, but the world did. After World War II candy stores and tobacco shops disappeared, engulfed by the wave of supermarkets whose shelves were stocked with products presold by advertising. Movie theaters also dwindled, routed by television. A whole generation grew up on the tube. And sitting there before the video screen, munching potato chips, Americans began to worry about the excess weight they were carting about. Candy consumption nosedived. Bowing to the inevitable, Hershey appointed an advertising agency. On July 19, 1970, their first consumer ad—a full page for Hershey's syrup—appeared in 114 newspapers. Two months later their ads were on radio and TV. Today they mount an advertising barrage of $25 million a year, not enough yet to enable Hershey to regain the first-place position they lost to Mars. Recent market reports show Mars holding 35% of the candy bar market, Hershey 30%.

The most important raw material in Hershey's life is the cocoa bean, which makes the company highly dependent on West Africa, the source of two-thirds of the world crop. Beans arriving at Hershey are cleaned, roasted in hot-air currents, and shattered to extract from the husks dry nibs which hold the natural fat of the cocoa bean: cocoa butter.

To make their milk chocolate, Hershey also buys milk from 1,000 farms, which need 50,000 cows to supply Hershey's needs. Every day they use enough milk to supply all the people in a city the size of Salt Lake City. Hershey is the nation's largest single user of almonds.

Hershey candies are widely distributed, to put it mildly. The company sells directly to more than 20,000 customers, and Hershey products are on sale at more than 1 million retail outlets.

In addition to the Hershey brand chocolates, the company markets Reese's Peanut Butter Cups (as a result of a 1963 acquisition), the Kit Kat wafer bar and Rolo chocolate-covered caramels (through a 1970 licensing agreement with Britain's Rowntree Mackintosh), and Y & S licorice products (through a 1977 acquisition).

Hershey has succumbed to another mod-

BEST SELLING CANDY BARS

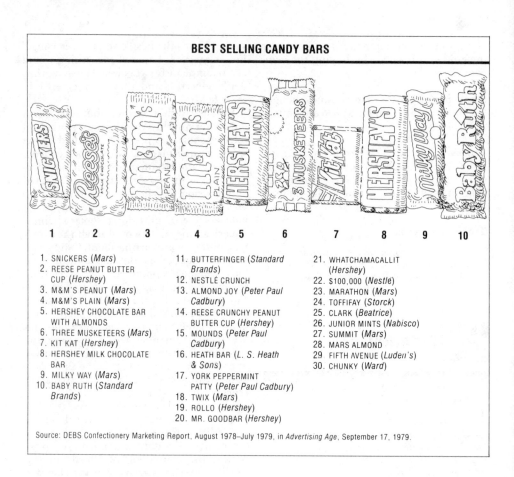

1   2   3   4   5   6   7   8   9   10

1. SNICKERS (*Mars*)
2. REESE PEANUT BUTTER CUP (*Hershey*)
3. M&M'S PEANUT (*Mars*)
4. M&M'S PLAIN (*Mars*)
5. HERSHEY CHOCOLATE BAR WITH ALMONDS
6. THREE MUSKETEERS (*Mars*)
7. KIT KAT (*Hershey*)
8. HERSHEY MILK CHOCOLATE BAR
9. MILKY WAY (*Mars*)
10. BABY RUTH (*Standard Brands*)

11. BUTTERFINGER (*Standard Brands*)
12. NESTLÉ CRUNCH
13. ALMOND JOY (*Peter Paul Cadbury*)
14. REESE CRUNCHY PEANUT BUTTER CUP (*Hershey*)
15. MOUNDS (*Peter Paul Cadbury*)
16. HEATH BAR (*L. S. Heath & Sons*)
17. YORK PEPPERMINT PATTY (*Peter Paul Cadbury*)
18. TWIX (*Mars*)
19. ROLLO (*Hershey*)
20. MR. GOODBAR (*Hershey*)

21. WHATCHAMACALLIT (*Hershey*)
22. $100,000 (*Nestlé*)
23. MARATHON (*Mars*)
24. TOFFIFAY (*Storck*)
25. CLARK (*Beatrice*)
26. JUNIOR MINTS (*Nabisco*)
27. SUMMIT (*Mars*)
28. MARS ALMOND
29. FIFTH AVENUE (*Luden's*)
30. CHUNKY (*Ward*)

Source: DEBS Confectionery Marketing Report, August 1978–July 1979, in *Advertising Age*, September 17, 1979.

ern affliction: diversification. They make pasta products under four different regional brand names: Skinner, San Giorgio, Delmonico, and P & R. They operate the Cory coffee-service plan for offices. In 1979 they entered the fast-food business by acquiring the 600-unit Friendly Ice Cream chain.

History. Hershey Foods is the legacy of one man, Milton Snavely Hershey, who grew up in the Pennsylvania Dutch country of Mennonite farmers, where the highest virtues were hard work, religious devotion, and simplicity. He was apprenticed to a candy maker in Lancaster at age 15. At 19 he was off—first to Philadelphia, then to Denver, Chicago, New Orleans, and New York, all the while practicing the candy trade. Before he was 30 years old, he was back in Lancaster, penniless. He started making caramels there, using a fresh milk formula he had learned in Denver. A super salesman, Hershey built a major business

that made him a very rich man. According to an official company biography, Milton Hershey had never had time to think about marriage while he was building his business. "He lived in small drab houses and worked in bleak basement kitchens for long hours each day." All of Lancaster, including his mother, was surprised then when he came home with a bride, the beautiful Catherine Sweeney of Jamestown, New York, whom he had met in a candy shop where she was employed. They were married in the rectory of New York's St. Patrick's Cathedral in 1898, when Hershey was 41 years old.

Two years later, at the dawn of the new century, Hershey sold the Lancaster Caramel Company for $1 million. He could have retired in comfort at that point, but this was not his plan. He expressed his feeling about what he wanted to do with the rest of his life thus: "What I want to do is to find a practical use for what I have and put it to work in a way that will benefit others."

That practical use turned out to be a chocolate factory in the countryside at Derry Church in Dauphin County, Pennsylvania, 30 miles from Lancaster. Why there? Because Milton Hershey had been born there. The factory was completed in 1905, and Derry Church was renamed Hershey in 1906. By 1911 Milton Hershey's new company was selling $5 million of chocolate a year.

But it was more than a chocolate company that Milton Hershey was interested in creating. He had been reared on the Mennonite precept that money was not to be used for personal gratification. In 1909 he and Mrs. Hershey, who were never to have children, founded and personally financed the Milton Hershey School for orphaned boys. The first classes were held in the farmhouse where Hershey had been born. ("Every time I see these boys playing on the lawn," Milton Hershey once said, "I think of the time when I roamed these fields as a barefoot boy.")

In 1918 the prosperous chocolate company was donated to a trust for the school. In effect, the orphanage owned the Hershey company (and it is still the largest shareholder). Meanwhile, the town of Hershey grew under the benevolent prodding of its founder. Homes were built and rented or sold to Hershey workers. A water company and electric utility were chartered. Stores were opened. A bank was established. Milton Hershey built a planned community before that term was invented. In the early years the affairs of the company, the school, and the town were commingled, but in 1927 a tripartite division separated the three. As part of that reorganization 20% of the Hershey company's stock was sold to the public, and the Hershey shares were listed on the New York Stock Exchange.

In 1927 Milton Hershey was 70 years old. His wife had died 12 years earlier, but he wasn't through building. The Great Depression was a motivator for Milton Hershey. While his business associates were concerned about conserving assets, Hershey wanted to put unemployed people to work. On a hill overlooking the town a grand luxury hotel, patterned after a Mediterranean resort, went up. Near the hotel an extensive rose garden was planted; today it covers more than 23 acres. Five golf courses were created, making Hershey the "golf capital of Pennsylvania." A Romanesque community center building was erected; it houses the Hershey Public Library and two theaters. The Hershey Museum of American Life was opened, featuring collections of native American, Eskimo, and Pennsylvania German artifacts. A sports arena with a seating capacity of 10,000 was built; the Hershey Bears, a professional hockey team, play there, and the Ice Capades were born on the Hershey rink in 1940. Finally, in 1939 the Hersheypark Stadium was completed as a setting for college football games, concerts, rodeos, and other outdoor shows; it has a seating capacity of 16,000, well above the total population of Hershey (then or now).

Milton Hershey died on October 13, 1945, exactly one month after his 88th birthday.

Reputation. Hershey is an old-fashioned company that makes quality chocolate products and still lives in the shadow of its benevolent founder. Although they advertise today, they're careful about the kind of promotion directed to children. They are an industry leader in providing nutritional information on labels.

What they own. The chocolate plant at Hershey covers 2 million square feet of floor space. Hershey also owns 20% of the voting shares of Marabou, the largest chocolate and confectionery company in Scandinavia. At the end of 1978, prior to the acquisition of Friendly Ice Cream, Hershey had assets (land, buildings, and equipment) valued at more than $250 million. Their debt is so small that they could pay it off tomorrow if necessary.

Who owns and runs the company. The Milton Hershey School and School Trust own 56% of Hershey Foods. True to a script that could have been written in Hollywood, the present chief executive officer of Hershey Foods, William E. Dearden, is a graduate of the Milton Hershey School. He was placed there by his widowed father in 1935, when he was 12 and Milton Hershey was 78. In 1978 Hershey's corporate headquarters moved to Highpoint Mansion, the restored home of Milton Hershey.

Girls were admitted to the Milton Hershey School in 1976. Two years later Hershey Foods elected their first female board member: Francine I. Neff, an Albuquerque banker who served as the 35th treasurer of the United States.

In the public eye. Good citizenship is something Milton Hershey built into the core of this company. Here's a description of how it works from the official company biography, *Hershey:*

> In March 1963, Samuel Hinkle, then president and chairman of Hershey and a manager of the charitable trust, the M. S. Hershey Foundation, called Dr. Eric A. Walker, president of Penn State University.
>
> "Eric," said Sam, "we've been wondering if Penn State is interested in starting a medical school."
>
> Walker replied, "Sam, you might as well stop and save my time and yours. There's not a nickel in Harrisburg for that purpose."
>
> Hinkle: "How much would it take?"
>
> Walker: "Oh, about $50 million."
>
> Hinkle: "What would you say if we told you we had $50 million to start with."
>
> Walker: "That might be different."

And that was the start of the Milton S. Hershey Medical Center of Pennsylvania State University, located on a former Milton Hershey School farm.

Where they're going. Hershey has responded to declining consumption of candy by launching an advertising program and buying noncandy companies (pasta, restaurants). There's no turning back the clock. Hershey will continue to advertise and, with a strong cash position, will be looking for other acquisitions. The Friendly Ice Cream addition has already brought a fundamental change, virtually tripling the number of people on the payroll. Hershey also hopes to reduce dependence on the cocoa bean by using a substitute cocoa butter developed in the laboratories of Procter & Gamble.

Stock performance. Hershey stock bought for $1,000 in 1970 sold for $995 on January 2, 1980.

Major employment centers. Hershey; Oakdale, California; and Wilbraham, Massachusetts.

Access. 19 East Chocolate Avenue, Hershey, Pennsylvania 17033; (717) 534-4200. Hershey's chocolate plant has been open to visitors since 1915. From 1927, when records were first kept, until the middle of 1973, more than 10 million visitors were recorded. In fact, traffic got so heavy that Hershey had to discontinue the tours of the plant itself, and in 1973 they opened a Chocolate World exhibition hall. Chocolate World is open Monday through Saturday from 9 A.M. to 4:45 P.M. Admission is free. Free tours are also offered at the Oakdale, California plant and the Canadian plant at Smith Falls, Ontario.

Consumer brands.

Chocolate and candy products: Hershey's; Reese's; Krackel; Kit Kat; Mr. Goodbar; Whatchamacallit; After Eight; NibNax; Y & S licorice; Marabou, Rolo.

Pasta: San Giorgio; Delmonico; Skinner; P & R (Procino-Rossi).

Other: Friendly Ice Cream restaurants; Cory Food Service.

Sales: $1.4 billion
Profits: $30.6 million
Forbes 500 rank: 353
Rank in meat packing: 6
Founded: 1891
Employees: 8,300
Headquarters: Austin, Minnesota

This is one of the last of the Mohicans: an independent meat packer. Hormel traffics mainly in pigs, slaughtering and processing them in 20 plants across the country and marketing the meats under such well-known brand names as Hormel, Spam, Dinty Moore, and Mary Kitchen. Hormel was the first packer to can ham—in 1926. Spam, introduced in 1937, is (believe it or not) the world's largest selling brand of canned meat. Their Dinty Moore stew is the best selling canned stew, and they also claim first place for Hormel's canned chili. George A. Hormel founded this company in 1891. Today directors and officers hold less than 2% of the stock; the Hormel family holds more than half of the shares. In 1978 Richard L. Knowlton was elected president of Hormel, the first Austin native to hold that position since Jay C. Hormel, son of the founder, became president in 1929. Nearly 10% of the people who live in Austin work for Hormel. One-third of the 4,600 shareholders live in Austin, and the Hormel annual meeting is a big social event for the town, attended by some 1,000 folks. At the 1980 meeting they gave away a $4 package of Hormel meats to each attendee.

Access. 501 16th Avenue N.E. (P.O. Box 800), Austin, Minnesota 55912; (507) 437-5663.

Consumer brands.

Hormel, Spam, Dinty Moore, and Mary Kitchen meats.

IFF International Flavors and Fragrances

Sales: $409 million
Profits: $61.5 million
Rank in artificial flavors: 1
Rank in artificial fragrances: 1
Founded: 1909
Employees: 3,480

What they do. The next time you walk by a bakery and catch a whiff of freshly baked bread, sniff again. You might actually be smelling a spray-on aroma manufactured by International Flavors and Fragrances.

IFF keeps more than 80,000 secret formulas for flavors and scents in their corporate vaults—formulas to flavor your morning coffee, orange juice, and bacon; or to scent your soap, shaving cream, deodorant —even toilet paper. If there is a taste or smell, IFF can reproduce it and peddle it to the food, cosmetics, or personal products industries. IFF employs 30 flavorists in their laboratories who work with thousands of chemical flavors. The best flavorists remember them all. They work at desk-sized "consoles" where each individual taste (called a *note* in flavor jargon) can be combined to produce the perfect strawberry, cherry, or Baco-bit. Says chief flavorist Alfred Glossens, "We've done meat loaf. We do bubble gum, yogurt, chicken, cookies. We do mouthwash, detergents, toilet bowl cleaners, the finest French perfumes. We've done a lot of fantasy flavors and scents. For instance, there is no such flavor as tutti-frutti in nature. We've done it." IFF estimates that 75% of the products on your supermarket shelf contain either artificial flavors or scents. More than 5,000 scents and 2,000 flavors emerge from IFF's labs every year.

History. International Flavors and Fragrances traces their roots to Dutch immigrant A. L. van Ameringen, who brought his old world perfume expertise to the United States and, with William Haebler, founded van Ameringen-Haebler, Inc., in New York. But the post–World War II boom in air fresheners, after-shave lotions,

What's in a Smell?

The creators of artificial odors and flavors have a terminology all their own. An individual flavor is referred to as a *note*. When a flavorist decides to create, let's say, an artificial strawberry flavor, he keeps in mind the notes of real strawberries. These are, among others, straw or hay notes, sour notes, sweet notes, sweet green notes, ester notes, green butter notes, rose effects, and, in some cases, what flavorists call "decidedly balsamic character."

Flavorists would say that ordinary cow's milk has "a minute note of the body odor of the cow" and a "slightly feedy note." Beer and honey both share "horsey notes," apples have "pip notes," and mint and anise, obviously, have "tingle notes." "Oily Tonka-bean undertones" find their way into nuts, cheese, vanilla, and caramel flavors; and "sweet-like notes" appear in rum, chocolate, and butterscotch flavors. "Tarry-repulsive" and "choking" notes are used in some cheeses, coffees, and nut flavors, while "grassy notes" pop up in wine and brandy. Some cheeses even have the "fecal note"—commonly called Skatole, from the Greek word for excrement.

Source: *New Times,* June 1976.

International Flavors and Fragrances flavors dog food, using up to 150 canine panelists to find out exactly what they like. Each is served two bowls of food—one with flavoring, one without. What remains in each bowl (and on the ground nearby) after the meal is carefully gathered, bagged, tagged, and sent back for analysis. The greatest pitfall in the tests, the flavorists say, is "paw prejudice." Most dogs are right- or left-pawed and tend to go for whichever bowl appears on their "good" side.

All breeds, with one exception, have sophisticated taste-buds. The exception is the lowly beagle. "They'll eat whatever is put in front of them," one researcher says. "You can't learn anything from a beagle."

Source: *New Times,* June 1976.

and the like quickly transformed the business. In 1958 van Ameringen bought the Dutch firm of Polak & Schwarz and formed International Flavors and Fragrances.

In 1963 van Ameringen's hand-picked successor, company counsel Henry G. Walter, began to expand IFF's influence in the food industry. Before 1960 the only synthetic flavors were fruit, vanilla, maple, and certain spices. But under Walter's management IFF began to experiment with flavors for meats, vegetables, and all manner of seafoods. Today IFF is the world's largest maker of scents and flavors, controlling 28% of the world market. Board chairman Walter, a colorful sort who bicycles to work in Manhattan and wears custom-made suspenders decorated with skunks, attributes IFF's success to their appeal to basics. "Primitive society," he says, "tells us where it's at. Our business is basically sex and hunger."

Reputation. One of the leanest companies around. IFF has only 50 salespeople in the entire world, 20 of them in the United States. Altogether IFF generates more than $100,000 in sales for each of their 3,480 employees—a ratio few manufacturing companies can match.

What they own. Although most of the experimenting with new flavors and scents occurs at the main Research and Development Center in Union Beach, New Jersey, International Flavors and Fragrances also has labs in 22 foreign countries.

Who owns and runs the company. The Haebler and van Ameringen families hold a combined total of 27.3% of IFF's stock. Chairman Henry G. Walter owns 13.3%.

Where they're going. Walter plans to put more effort into foreign sales, which currently account for 67% of IFF's business. His theory is that even relatively poor developing nations will spend money on soft drinks, soap, cigarettes, and certain cosmetics. But IFF plans to keep a low profile overseas. "We are no Coca-Cola or ITT," Walter says. "Why, we even sell a lot of fragrance to Colonel Quaddaffi's country!" He means Libya, of course.

Stock performance. International Flavors and Fragrances' stock bought for $1,000 in 1970 sold for $950 on January 2, 1980.

Access. 521 West 57th Street, New York, New York 10019; (212) 765-5500.

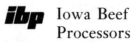 Iowa Beef Processors

Sales: $4.2 billion
Profits: $42.7 million
Forbes 500 rank: 103
Rank in meat packing: 1
Rank in food processing: 17
Founded: 1960
Employees: 9,400
Headquarters: Dakota City, Nebraska

What they do. Iowa Beef revolutionized the meat packing industry 20 years ago when they set up slaughterhouses in small towns in the heart of America's beef country. Before that cattle were usually shipped live to stockyards in major urban centers such as Chicago. Iowa Beef sidestepped the problems of shipping live animals and paying much higher big-city wages by putting their plants in places like Denison, Iowa; West Point, Nebraska; and Emporia, Kansas.

Iowa Beef is not nearly as well known as Swift, Wilson, Armour, Morrell, or Cudahy. But in 1978 Iowa made more money than these five packers combined, and their share of the market is at least twice that of any other beef packer. They have a private radio network to coordinate cattle purchases from ranchers and feeders in the Midwest and Northwest and delivery to the nearby slaughterhouses. On a day when all nine of their beef abattoirs are operating at capacity, 16,788 cattle come in alive and leave as packaged meat and bulk by-products. Their slaughterhouses are highly mechanized steak factories. After an animal is slaughtered, its carcass moves through the plant on conveyor belts while laborers perform specialized tasks that reduce it to boxed, plastic-wrapped cuts of beef. The meat is then shipped to some 2,500 regular customers—supermarket chains, meat brokers, wholesalers, and restaurant and hotel chains. Only 54% of what Iowa Beef calls "the beef animal" can be sold as meat; much of the remainder is sold to other manufacturers for use in shoe leather, dog food, laundry detergent, cosmetics, and even chewing gum.

Iowa Beef holds about 12% of the fresh beef market. Cries of "monopoly" have been raised by competitors, but Iowa Beef officials like to point out that their company holds only 6.1% of the total U.S. meat protein market (beef, pork, poultry, and fish). "We don't consider ourselves big," Robert L. Peterson, president, told the *Wall Street Journal.* "I fail to understand how such a small percentage can be considered a monopoly."

History. The late Currier J. Holman, a former Swift slaughterhouse butcher turned independent cattle dealer, founded the company in 1960 with Andy Anderson. Holman managed the firm while Anderson came up with the innovative meat-packing system that propelled Iowa Beef to national leadership. Anderson left in 1969 and later started Madison Foods, which processed hogs for Armour the same way Iowa Beef processes cattle. In 1976 Iowa Beef bought Madison Foods in a deal that the *Wall Street Journal* described as providing "staggering" profits to Madison stockholders—at least three of whom were high-ranking officers of Iowa Beef.

Reputation. "Business as we pursue it here at IBP is very much like waging war," Currier Holman has said. Holman and Iowa Beef were convicted in 1974 of conspiring with a Mafia figure to bribe their way into New York City, the world's largest meat market, by paying off butcher's union officials and supermarket executives. The *Wall Street Journal* reported that Iowa Beef's "history is laced with criminals, gangland figures, civil wrongdoers, brazen conflicts of interest and possible violations of antitrust and labor law. Floating in and out of the scene are people engaged in vicious beatings, shooting and fire-bombings."

In 1974 *Forbes* characterized the company as follows: "At Iowa Beef, getting into trouble is a way of life. So is making money."

What they own. Nine beef slaughterhouses (one kosher) in Iowa, Minnesota, Nebraska, Kansas, Texas, Idaho, and Washington. One pork plant in Nebraska. Two trucking companies to fill in where common carriers cannot deliver the products.

Who owns and runs the company. The largest portion of Iowa Beef—about 18%— is owned by the Pacific Holding Corporation, which belongs to David H. Murdock, a Los Angeles businessman. Iowa Beef's directors are all white males, many of whom have worked in the meat industry all their lives. Vice-chairman Dale Tinstman, a former securities dealer, was sued by the SEC in 1974 for misleading the public in a large bond sale. He agreed to a court order barring him from any supervisory role in the securities industry for two years, whereupon Iowa Beef hired him as its financial advisor. He later became president of the company.

In the public eye. In the 1978 annual report Iowa Beef said: "Some of the media manipulator organizations that seem to be burgeoning these days have hit upon the phrase, 'Food for people—not for profit,' as a rallying cry. To that we reply: 'If there is no profit in producing food, then soon there will be no food and no jobs in the food industry.' "

Where they're going. As more and more of the food dollar winds up in cash registers of fast-food establishments, Iowa Beef is banking on "a move toward portion control products—individual servings, fresh or frozen—produced at processing plants and delivered to the store. The long-range outlook is for complete factory prepared meals, pre-cooked and ready for home use." They also foresee the day when they will be able to channel some of the less desirable meat by-products away from the dog food can and onto the dinner table. "Some of these by-product based foods may not be acceptable for consumption by populations in highly developed nations such as the United States," they admit, but they predict that "some of the less fortunate nations of the world will welcome these newly developed products as an effective way of combating malnutrition and mass starvation."

Stock performance. Iowa Beef stock bought for $1,000 in 1970 sold for $2,431 on January 2, 1980.

Access. Dakota City, Nebraska 68731; (402) 494-2061.

Kellogg's

Sales: $1.8 billion
Profits: $162.6 million
Forbes 500 rank: 284
Rank in food processing: 29
Rank in cereals: 1
Founded: 1906
Employees: 21,000
Headquarters: Battle Creek, Michigan

What they do. Kellogg makes ready-to-eat cereals—and a lot of money. They turn a dollar of sales into much more profit than any other food company. Kellogg earns such high returns by dominating the marketplace: They produce the leading breakfast cereal in America (in terms of pounds sold per year), Kellogg's Corn Flakes, and hold a 42% share of the ready-to-eat cereal market. From 49 plants in 22 countries Kellogg produces 80 freight cars of Corn Flakes every day, and a total of 2½ billion boxes of all their cereals a year. Rice Krispies have made Kellogg the world's largest purchaser of rice. Other cereals require daily purchases of 48,000 bushels of corn and 300,000 pounds of wheat bran. In a year the company buys 150 railroad cars of waxed paper to keep it all fresh.

Kellogg also owns several subsidiaries that make other kinds of foods. At Mrs. Smith's Pie Company they make frozen

The Electrified Steak

Beef is aged to make it more tender. Traditional aging can take three weeks to produce high-quality steaks. Now this process is being speeded up by subjecting carcasses to electric shock treatments.

The treatments began at a Texas slaughterhouse in 1978. As the carcasses go through the production line, they are jolted with 565 volts of electricity 16 times within

a minute. These jolts break up tough, sinewy muscles and also trigger a chemical reaction, releasing natural enzymes that enhance flavor and tenderness (that's what normally takes place during the aging process).

Electrically stimulated beef is said to be 30% more tender than conventional beef. In addition, the aging time for steak supposedly is cut from

21 to 7 days.

The application of electricity to beef was developed by animal scientists at Texas A & M University. The electrodes installed at meatpacking plants to electrify beef were designed by Le Fiell Company, a San Francisco company that manufacturers slaughterhouse equipment.

pies and Eggo frozen waffles; at Fearn International they make LeGout canned dinners; at Pure Packed Foods they make nondairy toppings and creamers; at Salada Foods they make tea and drink mixes. About one-third of Kellogg's business is done outside the United States, in Europe, Australia, Japan, and South America, where they manufacture and market their whole range of cereals as well as other products such as potato chips, soups, frozen pizza, and nonprescription cold remedies.

History.   Kellogg's rise to the top of the cereal market came through the efforts of founder William Keith Kellogg. W. K. Kellogg worked for years as the business manager of the world-famous Battle Creek Sanitarium in Michigan, where his brother, Dr. John Harvey Kellogg, was chief surgeon and superintendent. Dr. Kellogg was a Seventh Day Adventist, and he and his patients observed a strict vegetarian diet. To make the meatless fare more palatable, the brothers began experimenting with various foods in the sanitarium kitchens. During one such experiment in 1894 they placed some boiled wheat on a baking tin when Dr. Kellogg was called away by an emergency operation. When they returned the next day, they ran the wheat through a roller, expecting it to come out in sheets. What emerged instead were individual flakes, the forerunner of ready-to-eat cereals. This accidental discovery was welcomed by the patients, who loved the new foods coming from the sanitarium kitchens. Former patients would write to the company requesting that the flakes be sent to them by mail.

To meet the demand, Dr. Kellogg started the Sanitas Food Company, which produced wheat flakes, rice flakes, and corn flakes using the same process. The corn flakes were not popular at first because the kernels were so tough, so W. K. Kellogg

William K. Kellogg, a successful broom salesman at age 14.

developed a tastier flake using only the grits, or heart, of the corn and adding malt. He then bought the commercial rights from his brother (who was more interested in the sanitarium anyway), and in 1906 he started his own business, the Battle Creek Toasted Corn Flake Company. In the beginning,

Get Out Your Magnets

Kellogg Co. recently reduced the iron content of its Frosted Rice cereal to 10% of the government's "recommended daily allowance" from 25% after consumers discovered they could move flakes of the cereal around with magnets.

As a company spokesman explains it, "We had problems evenly distributing the product's sugar coating," which contained microscopic ground particles of pure iron, a common additive in flour and baked goods. Now, the

spokesman avers, Frosted Rice can't be moved with magnets unless "they are very, very strong."

Reprinted from the *Wall Street Journal,* June 21, 1977.

Kellogg had to compete with 42 other cereal companies in Battle Creek alone, all of which were trying to capitalize on the popularity of the brothers' inventions. One of them was run by an ex-patient of the sanitarium, C. W. Post.

The new company began production at the rate of 33 cases a day. Three months later they placed their first full-page ad in the *Ladies' Home Journal.* It was a masterpiece. It began by saying the advertisement "violates all the rules of advertising" because the company had paid $4,000 for an ad to stimulate demand for a product that most readers couldn't purchase, since the plant was producing to capacity and couldn't fill the orders it already had. Nevertheless, at the bottom was a handy coupon for the reader to take to her local grocer if he did not already carry Toasted Corn Flakes. If the grocer agreed to buy one case of 36 boxes, the customer would receive one free box, plus another for each additional case the grocer ordered throughout the summer. It worked.

By 1909 the company was selling more than 1 million cases a year. Two years later the advertising budget had reached $1 million, part of which was spent to erect the world's largest electric sign on the Mecca Building at Times Square in New York, with the "K" in Kellogg 66 feet tall. The company started a plant in Canada in 1924, one in Australia in 1928, and one in England in 1938. During the Depression W. K. Kellogg doubled his advertising budget.

Reputation. Kellogg has such a sure touch in the cereal business, from both the manufacturing and the marketing sides, that it seems nothing short of an antitrust action can upend this company. They are "evangelistic" in their efforts to persuade children to have breakfast. And they're good at this preaching: between 1972 and 1979 per capita consumption of ready-to-eat cereals in the United States went up 40%.

What they own. Plant and equipment valued at $725 million, at cost. Kellogg's cereals are produced at five U.S. plants. Their valuable brand name, which the Federal Trade Commission would like to eviscerate, is not carried at all as an asset on the company's books.

Who owns and runs the company. Kellogg is nearly half-owned and controlled by the W. K. Kellogg Foundation, which the company's founder established in 1930, when he was 70 years old. Although Kellogg was known to be tough and frugal in business, he gave the greatest portion of his fortune, valued then at $50 million (and now at over $750 million), to his foundation. The purpose of the foundation was "the promotion of the health, education and welfare of mankind." The company is run by longtime insiders. Board chairman Joseph E. Lonning joined Kellogg in 1941, and president William E. LaMothe in 1950. Since 1976 Kellogg has had a black and a woman on the board in the sole person of Dolores Wharton, author and lecturer.

In the public eye. A company that began as a producer of health foods finds itself today in the ironic position of defending cereals like Kellogg's Sugar Smacks, which contain 56% sugar. In 1977 Kellogg ran a two-page advertisement in seven big-city newspapers to refute charges that presweetened cereals are not nutritious. Kellogg argued that ready-to-eat cereals account for only 2% of sugar consumption in the United States and that research has shown "no relationship between the amount of cereals consumed . . . and the incidence of tooth decay in children." When the American Dental Association attacked the ad as "seriously misleading," Kellogg's president LaMothe said the company was thinking of taking legal action against the ADA and other groups "who make false statements" about Kellogg and its products.

Kellogg is under fire from the Federal Trade Commission on two different fronts. The FTC has under consideration a rule that would sharply restrict television advertising directed at children. Kellogg says such a rule "may result in a deterioration in breakfast habits in the United States." The FTC also has brought an action (still pending) against the three top cereal makers (Kellogg, General Mills, and General Foods), alleging that they constitute a "shared monopoly." If the FTC has its way, Kellogg would be divided into five different companies. LaMothe's rebuttal: "To try to punish success in the free enterprise system is a terrible direction for our country to be taking."

Where they're going. Wall Street people, who often regard Kellogg as a hick from Battle Creek, keep advising the company to diversify as the other big food companies have. When *Business Week* posed that idea to LaMothe in 1979, he said: "There are companies who will pay an outrageous price for an acquisition, and it may be good for them. Fortunately, we don't have to panic into something."

Stock performance. Kellogg stock bought for $1,000 in 1970 sold for $1,841 on January 2, 1980.

Major employment centers. Battle Creek, Omaha, and Memphis.

Access. 235 Porter Street, Battle Creek, Michigan 49016; (616) 966-2000. Kellogg's home plant in Battle Creek offers one-hour tours every weekday from 9 A.M. to 4 P.M. For information call (616) 966-2304. Questions or complaints should be directed to the consumer services department: (616) 966-2275. They won't take a collect call, but you can leave your number and they will call you back.

Consumer brands.

Ready-to-eat cereals: Kellogg's Corn Flakes; Rice Krispies; Raisin Bran; Special K; Sugar Frosted Flakes; Sugar Smacks; Apple Jacks; Froot Loops; Sugar Corn Pops; Corny Snaps; Cocoa Krispies; Frosted Rice; Cracklin' Bran; Concentrate; All-Bran; 40% Bran Flakes; Bran Buds; Most; Graham Crackos.
Other grocery products: Mrs. Smith's frozen pies; Pop-Tarts; Salada teas; Eggo frozen waffles.

> "Fresh foods spoil too fast," says Glenn Stelzer, sales director of the food and fragrance development department at Hercules, Inc., a chemical company. "You just can't move them to the consumer fast enough."
> —Reprinted from the *Wall Street Journal*, June 31, 1977.

⬡ Kraft

Sales: $6.4 billion
Profits: $188.1 million
Forbes 500 rank: 59
Rank in food processing: 2
Rank in dairy products: 1
Rank in cheese: 1
Rank in salad dressings: 1
Founded: 1903
Employees: 48,000
Headquarters: Glenview, Illinois

What they do. To appreciate the scale of Kraft's operations would require a trip around the world, to the 130 countries where Kraft products are sold. There's probably not a single grocery in the United States that does not carry some of their products, and a customer would be hard pressed to eat in an American restaurant and *not* consume one of their products.

One hundred and seventy plants on five continents turn out thousands of products for Kraft under some 850 trademarks. The largest facility, built in Champaign, Illinois, in 1963, covers 1.2 million square feet, or 28 acres, all under one roof, and produces 406 different items, including margarine, salad dressings, mustard, pasta, vinegar, and cheese.

Their well-known brand names include Kraft, Velveeta, Parkay, Miracle Whip, Philadelphia, Cracker Barrel, Sealtest, Light n' Lively, Breyer's, and Breakstone's.

To sell these products to stores and restaurants, Kraft deploys an army of 5,000 salespeople. So strong is Kraft's capability as a distributor that they also handle the products of others; for example, they distribute all of Pillsbury's refrigerated doughs. In selling to restaurants, they sup-

Why They Named Fig Newtons

James Henry Mitchell, a Philadelphia inventor, devised a machine that could simultaneously make a cookie and fill it with preserves or jam. It was tried out for the first time in 1892 at the Kennedy Biscuit Works in Cambridgeport,

Massachusetts. This bakery followed the practice of naming cookies and crackers after towns around Boston: Beacon Hill, Shrewsbury, Brighton, Melrose. The cookie filled with jam was called the Newton, after the town of

Newton. As figs became the most commonly used filling, the cookies were rechristened Fig Newtons.

ply not only 600 Kraft products, but 1,200 food items packed by other companies. Kraft also makes food products for supermarket chains that put their own names on them.

Kraft invented processed cheese. Before refrigeration cheese was sold in wheels which spoiled quickly when cut. Kraft perfected a pasteurized cheese made from milk solids; this cheese did not spoil and could be canned. Kraft patented the process in 1916 and, during World War I, proceeded to sell 6 million pounds of the cheese to the U.S. Army. Kraft has been the cheese king of America ever since. Their share of the market is estimated at 50%.

Kraft is currently marketing an "imitation" or "engineered" cheese—a cheese analog (or imitation) made with vegetable oil instead of butterfat. Since processed cheese is an imitation cheese, what do you call an imitation of an imitation? The National Cheese Institute suggested that the category be identified as Golana because "it is pleasant sounding . . . and is analog spelled backwards." Kraft is selling it under the brand name Golden Image.

History. There are two strands to the Kraft corporate history.

One goes back to James L. Kraft, whose father was a Mennonite farmer in Canada. James Kraft came to Chicago in 1903, rented a horse and wagon, and began wholesaling cheese. Arriving at Chicago's South Water Street market early in the morning, Kraft would buy rounds and resell them to grocers later in the day. His four brothers—Fred, Charles, Norman, and John—joined the business, which did so well that by 1914 they were selling 31 varieties of cheese in many parts of the country under the brand names Kraft and Elkhorn. After World War I the Krafts introduced a five-pound cheese loaf wrapped in foil and set inside a rectangular wooden box. Within a month Kraft was producing 15,000 boxes a day to satisfy demand. In 1928 Kraft merged with a rival company, Phenix Cheese. Kraft-Phenix was a major company, accounting for 40% of the nation's annual cheese consumption. They also had operations in Canada, Australia, Britain, and Germany.

The other strand goes back to Thomas H. McInnerney, a Chicago pharmacist who went into the ice cream business in 1914 by purchasing the Hydrox company. In 1923 McInnerney merged Hydrox with Pittsburgh's Rieck-McJunkin dairy to form the National Dairy Products Corporation. They added other ice cream and milk companies, including New York's Sheffield Farms, Philadelphia's Supplee-Wills-Jones (the nation's oldest dairy), and Cleveland's Telling-Belle-Vernon. National Dairy had sales of $213 million in 1928.

The two strands were roped together in 1930 when National Dairy acquired Kraft-Phenix. With sales of $375 million, the new company ranked as one of America's largest.

It was a bifurcated corporation for the next four decades. In Chicago Kraft functioned virtually as a separate entity, fighting the Great Depression with such processed specialities as Velveeta, Miracle Whip, Parkay margarine, and Kraft caramels. James L. Kraft was still in charge, and other Krafts were also prominent in the management. Meanwhile, the parent company, National Dairy, was headquartered in New York, close to the canyons of Wall Street, functioning primarily as a holding company for the entities that had been acquired.

James L. Kraft died in 1953 at age 78. His brother John reportedly was squeezed out by the New York financial overseers and left to establish the John Kraft Sesame Corporation of Paris, Texas. He was bitter, alleging that his brother's purpose to supply high-quality, low-priced, nutritious foods was being subverted by a New York management interested mainly in profits. Kraft Sesame developed more than 100 sesame-based vegetarian products, but the company didn't succeed and ended up selling most of its sesame seeds to McDonald's for hamburger buns.

In 1969 National Dairy adopted the corporate title of Kraftco, after their most famous brand, and in 1972 transferred their corporate headquarters from New York to the Chicago suburb of Glenview. In 1973 they celebrated the company's 50th birthday, thereby dating their founding to 1923, when National Dairy was formed. But in 1976 they decided to change their name again—this time to Kraft, Inc.—and in 1978 they celebrated the 75th birthday of the company, thereby dating the founding to J. L. Kraft and getting the public relations advantage of two birthdays.

Reputation. Although Kraft still markets

some natural cheeses, they are becoming known as masters of ersatz products: Velveeta, Miracle Whip, Kraft imitation mayonnaise, Golden Image. In his book *The Chemical Feast* James Turner said: "Kraft has been responsible for the decline of the quality of cheese made in the U.S."

What they own. Subsidiaries all over the world in addition to their extensive manufacturing facilities in the United States, where they have seven multiproduct plants. Kraft does 30% of their business outside the United States.

Who owns and runs the company. All the directors and all the officers combined own less than one-half of 1% of Kraft stock. In 1978 the five top officers received total compensation of $2.5 million. Of the 31,000 U.S. employees, nearly 15% are minorities. However, minorities hold less than 4% of Kraft positions designated as "officials and managers."

In the public eye. Kraft has been almost invisible in the cultural affairs of Chicago and New York. However, they are known for their sponsorship of quality programs in broadcasting. In 1978 Terrence O'Flaherty, longtime radio-TV critic for the *San Francisco Chronicle*, said that Kraft was one of the few sponsors who have earned the right to have their name in the title of a show.

Where they're going. Kraft is that rarity: a big company that has not diversified widely. Some observers feel that will change in the 1980s, however. Kraft defines their target as follows: "to participate in all meals, wherever consumed."

Stock performance. Kraft stock bought for $1,000 in 1970 sold for $1,213 on January 2, 1980.

Access. Kraft Court, Glenview, Illinois 60025; (312) 998-2000.

Consumer brands.

Dairy products: Kraft; Sealtest; Breakstone's; Light n' Lively; Parkay; Velveeta; Philadelphia Brand; Cracker Barrel; Breyer's.
Other grocery products: Miracle Whip salad dressing; Kraft dinners, snacks, peanut butter, salad dressing, and condiments; Cheez 'n Crackers.
Housewares: Chilton; Slick-Kote; Globe.
Toys: Fun Trend.

Libby's

Sales: $600 million (estimated)
Rank in food canning: 2
Founded: 1868
Employees: 9,500 (full-time and seasonal)
Headquarters: Chicago, Illinois

What they do. Libby, for many years second to Del Monte in the canned food business, packs ketchup and cans vegetables, fruits, meats, juices, and fruit drinks at 15 plants scattered across the country. Their product line has been reduced from 135 to 97 items since they were acquired by Nestlé in 1976. The first company to pack tomato juice, they remain the brand leader, holding 22% of the market. They're also first in canned beets, sauerkraut, and pumpkin (10% of America's beets and 60% of the world's pumpkin end up in Libby cans). They maintain a canned meat line of 19 items, including pork brains with gravy, corned beef hash, Sloppy Joe, and tripe.

History. Libby grew up in the shadow of the Chicago stockyards, packing meat in tins. They were founded in 1868 by Archibald McNeil and two brothers, Arthur and Charles Libby, none of whom survived the century. Their descendants did not follow them into the business, and the company passed into the hands of the nation's largest meat packer, Swift & Co., which had to divest itself of Libby in 1920 under the terms of a decree breaking up the "meat trust." Libby then proceeded under their own steam until Nestlé, in a series of gulps, swallowed the entire enterprise by 1976.

Reputation. They have a touch of yesteryear about them. In 1978, 183 employees celebrated their 10th anniversary with the company; 143 marked their 15th; 44 their 20th; 68 their 25th; 61 their 30th; 11 their 35th; 4 their 40th; 2 their 45th; and 1 his 50th.

Who owns and runs the company. Nestlé, a Swiss firm. Libby's former president, David E. Guerrant, now heads all Nestlé operations in the United States.

Major employment centers. Chicago; Sacramento and Sunnyvale, California.

Access. 200 South Michigan Avenue, Chicago, Illinois 60604; (312) 341-4111. Write Mary Hale Martin, a pseudonym invented in 1924. (Libby was one of the first companies to hire a home economist to deal with the public.) The Libby plant at Morton, Illinois, offers tours during September at Pumpkin Festival Time.

Consumer brands.

Libby's foods.

On February 10, 1884, a *Chicago Tribune* correspondent covering the Zulu wars reported: "After the battles in the land of the Zulus, and later when the last gun was fired on the banks of the Nile, the battlefields were strewn with empty cans bearing the well-known brand of Libby, McNeil & Libby."

Sales: $1.4 billion
Profits: $42.3 million
Forbes 500 rank: 357
Rank in hot dogs: 1
Founded: 1883
Employees: 13,000
Headquarters: Madison, Wisconsin

What they do. In the faceless world of the hot dog, Oscar Mayer invented, in 1944, a machine that would put a little piece of paper around each of their hot dogs identifying it as an Oscar Mayer wiener. (Engineers said the hot dogs resembled machine gun cartridges, which became the inspiration for the name of Oscar Mayer's packing subsidiary, Kartridg-Pak.) Besides individually banded wieners, Oscar Mayer also pioneered the Chub machine to put liver sausage in durable saran tubes; the slice-pack—vacuum-sealed cold cuts in a clear package

with a metal disc for a base; vacuum-sealed hot dogs in twin-packs; and vacuum-sealed bacon with a back window so that the consumer could see a representative slice. Though these may seem minor breakthroughs in the course of human events, for Oscar Mayer they were keys to the successful marketing and promotional strategies which stress the company's products as tastier, fresher, and of higher quality.

While 70% of their sales come from processing, Oscar Mayer also sells fresh meats, lard, by-products, and, more recently, pickles and sauerkraut from their latest acquisition, the Claussen Pickle Company.

History. Oscar Mayer was a German immigrant who spent several years in the meat-packing industry before setting out on his own. He persuaded his two brothers, Max and Gottfried, to join him in 1883 in establishing a small sausage shop on Chicago's north side. (Gottfried had spent several years apprenticed to Nuremberg's famous *wurstmachers*.) The Bavarian-type sausages were widely accepted, so five years later, with borrowed money, the brothers bought property at Sedgwick and Beethoven in Chicago and erected a two-story market. It is now the site of their Chicago plant.

Reputation. Oscar Mayer has the best reputation in the meat business, not only for quality, but for honesty and integrity. They were one of the first companies to accept 100% government inspection of their meats. They became a union shop in 1934 (a year before the Wagner Act was passed) and have never had a major work stoppage. The investment community gives Oscar Mayer top marks for a meat company. The company sincerely believes that their business is dedicated to serving the American people wholesome, fresh food and was "stunned" when the first mention of the possible carcinogenic properties of nitrites was published in the media.

What they own. A 25% share of Prima Meat Packers, Ltd., in Tokyo, a company which manufactures and markets a line of meats similar to Oscar Mayer's. They also own a controlling interest in Ven-Packers, a meat company in Venezuela, and a 40% interest in Oscar Mayer of Spain. The Kartridg-Pak Company, co-owned with Dow Chemical, manufactures food-processing

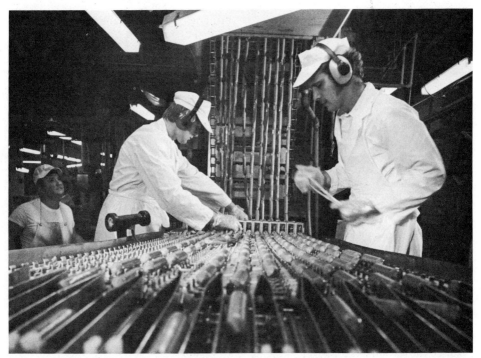
Oscar Mayer's "hot dog highway" turns out 36,000 hot dogs per hour.

machinery for the meat industry, packaging equipment, and machinery for the aerosol business. Oscar Mayer also owns Quality Control Spice Company and Scientific Protein Laboratories; the latter makes biochemical meat by-products for the pharmaceutical, food, and chemical industries.

Who owns and runs the company. Oscar Mayer family trusts own over 50% of the shares. The company had been managed by Mayers for three generations, until P. Goff Beach was appointed chief executive officer in 1965. Recently the company announced that Beach would be succeeded by Harold Mayer as chairman and Jerry Hiegel as president. Asked what he would do as new president, Hiegel said that "I wish I were an Oscar Mayer wiener" would continue to be the company's main advertising thrust. "We're very much entrenched in Americana," he said.

In the public eye. A 1978 study showed that sodium nitrites caused cancer in test animals, though some subsequent studies conflict with that finding. If, however, nitrites are proved to be carcinogenic, meat packers will have to eliminate them from their products. Nitrite preserves meat and prevents botulism organisms from growing. It also gives processed meats their characteristic flavor and color—a hot dog without nitrites looks embalmed. Oscar Mayer opposes the possible ban and maintains that nitrites are safe.

Where they're going. Oscar Mayer is exactly where they want to be—in the consumer food business selling convenience foods to a rushed world.

Stock performance. Oscar Mayer stock bought for $1,000 in 1970 sold for $1,556 on January 1, 1980.

Major employment centers. Chicago; Madison; and Davenport, Iowa.

Access. 910 Mayer Avenue, Madison, Wisconsin 53707; (608) 241-3311. Address inquiries to G. Frank Kauffman.

Consumer brands.

Oscar Mayer meats; Claussen pickles.

Sales: $2.4 billion
Profits: $99.8 million
Forbes 500 rank: 224
Rank in baking industry: 2
Rank in cookies: 1
Rank in crackers: 1
Founded: 1898
Employees: 39,000
Headquarters: East Hanover, New Jersey

What they do. Nabisco is the company that took crackers out of the barrel. While they have bought various nonbakery companies and expanded to other countries, they remain primarily what they were at birth: an American baker of high-quality cookies and crackers. Ten U.S. plants turn out 1 billion pounds of cookies and crackers a year, making Nabisco by far the dominant producer of those items. It also makes Nabisco the second-largest baker in the nation (after ITT's Continental Baking unit). Sales of cookies and crackers account for 60% of Nabisco's total volume. Among their well-known brand names: Ritz, Oreo, Fig Newtons, Lorna Doone, Chips Ahoy, Uneeda, Wheat Thins, Triscuit.

Nabisco also makes pretzels (Mister Salty), snacks, ice cream cones, cheese spreads, cake mixes, dates, hot and cold cereals (Cream of Wheat, Shredded Wheat), candy, pet foods (Milk-Bone), frozen meat entrees, toiletries (Aqua Velva), drugs and health aids, draperies, and shower curtains.

To produce baked goods, Nabisco buys large amounts of commodities: wheat, sugar, shortening, cocoa, and corn and soybean products. Nearly all their flour needs are supplied by three company-owned mills, and such are these needs that Nabisco ranks as the nation's eighth-largest flour miller.

Nabisco has always relied heavily on advertising. In 1978 they spent $11 million on research and development, and $95 million on advertising. They are the nation's 31st-largest advertiser.

History. Nabisco was born of strife. On February 3, 1898, two giant bakery groups, New York Biscuit and American Biscuit, called a truce to eight years of bitter confrontation. They agreed to combine forces,

bringing with them another large group, United States Baking, and a number of independents, to form the National Biscuit Company. They commanded 114 bakeries with 400 ovens in a territory stretching from New York to Salt Lake City and from Portland, Maine, to New Orleans. The leader of the new company was a Chicago lawyer, Adolphus W. Green, the last of 11 children, who said: "We should all fight together, not fight each other."

It was Green who realized the importance of having a package that keeps biscuits fresh. His law partner, Frank Peters, came up with one: a cardboard carton lined with waxed paper that enveloped and protected the crackers. Previously crackers were shipped in—and sold out of—barrels that were placed on the floor of the general store.

Green also sensed the importance of developing a brand-name cracker that could be produced and sold throughout the country. His first candidate was the soda cracker. And the brand name he selected: Uneeda.

Finally, it was Green who recognized the importance of advertising. He appointed N. W. Ayer to handle Uneeda's advertising, giving the agency an unprecedented budget. Uneeda was advertised for the first time in 1899. Within the next decade Ayer was to place $7 million of advertising for Uneeda and other National Biscuit Company products.

Green turned what was a loose collection of regional bakeries into a national network of bakeries making the same products in the same way. Binding the network together was advertising, which built consumer demand and in turn made grocers happy to see the National Biscuit salesman when he arrived. In 1900 Uneeda was already selling at the rate of 10 million packages a month. It was followed by Fig Newtons, Jinjer Wayfers, ZuZu ginger snaps, Nabisco Sugar Wafers, Nabisco Graham Crackers, Premium Saltines, Oyster crackers, Animal Crackers, Social Tea biscuits, Oreo cookies, and Mallomars. Green, never noted for his modesty, said, "We do not aim to sell all the biscuits consumed in this country. . . . So far as we have any monopoly in this business, it is one that the people have voluntarily conferred upon us." Many years later *Fortune* was to say that National Biscuit "did almost as much as the introduction of canned foods before it, and the invention of electric refrigeration after, to change the techniques of modern merchandising."

This cookie and cracker maker thus became one of the major industrial corporations of the early twentieth century. They hired thousands to work in their plants; most were women, many were newly arrived immigrants. In 1906 Green moved the company's headquarters from Chicago to New York, where National Biscuit was the largest manufacturing establishment in the city. The National Biscuit complex on Manhattan's lower west side—running from 14th to 16th Streets and from 10th to 11th Avenues—was the largest baking center in the world. Green had a visitors' gallery put up on the 10th floor of one of the buildings. In *Out of the Cracker Barrel*, a 1969 history of the company commissioned by Nabisco, author William Cahn described the scene:

When the wind was right, seamen and stevedores coming off the North River docks could sniff appetizing smells of Vanilla Wafers and Marshmallow Fancies.

On other days, the aroma of Animal Crackers and Fig Newton Cakes contrasted sharply with the smells emanating from taverns along Ninth Avenue. "An air of innocence," one writer put it, "clings to the National Biscuit Company, as it must to any business where grown men concern themselves with a ginger snap named Zuzu."

The red-brick bakery buildings in New York served Nabisco for more than half a century. In 1958 production was shifted to a sleek new plant occupying 40 acres at Fair Lawn, New Jersey, 20 miles northwest of New York City. The corporate headquarters remained in New York, though it moved uptown from 14th Street to Park Avenue. In 1975 the headquarters was again relocated, this time on a 120-acre golf course at East Hanover, New Jersey.

Nabisco has used profits from cookies and crackers to buy other businesses. Shredded Wheat came aboard in 1929, Milk-Bone in 1931, Dromedary in 1954, Cream of Wheat in 1961. In 1963 Nabisco

By This Name, Ye Shall Know Me...

Every Nabisco package carries a corporate seal. The first example was the "In-er Seal," to advertise the air-tight package for crackers invented by Nabisco. In 1918 the packages carried the logo NBC, which stood for National Biscuit Company. The one feature present in all versions is the replica of a printer's mark used in the fifteenth century by the Society of Printers in Venice. The cross with two bars and an oval represents the triumph of the moral and spiritual over evil and the material.

1900

1941

1918

1952

1923

1958

Evolution of the Nabisco symbol.

acquired the New England candy manufacturer James O. Welch Co., maker of Chuckles, Junior Mints, and Sugar Daddy sticks. (Profits from this enterprise enabled Robert O. Welch to found the ultra-right-wing John Birch Society in 1958.) In 1970 Freezer Queen Foods became part of Nabisco. The most remarkable addition was J. B. Williams, a toiletries and drug producer acquired on the last day of 1971. Nabisco was at first a little shy about admitting that the maker of Oreo cookies was now selling Geritol, Sominex, and Serutan, and they neglected to mention these products in the 1972 and 1973 annual reports. Associated Products, acquired in 1973, brought Nabisco into drapery and curtain manufacturing. Nabisco entered the toy business in 1971 by acquiring the plastic model builder Aurora Products, which was sold in 1977 after producing mainly losses.

Foreign expansion, beginning with the acquisition of Canada's Christie, Brown & Co. in 1928, was accomplished in the same manner: local firms were bought up. Between 1960 and 1967 Nabisco acquired biscuit makers in nine different countries. One of them, Harry Trueller of West Germany, invented zwieback. They acquired another German biscuit maker, XOX, in 1970—and sold it off in 1977.

Reputation. They bake quality goods, but they're stodgy and slow to react. They keep to themselves. A strong streak of paternalism has always run through Nabisco. In 1905, when wagon makers in Chicago walked out in a wage dispute, Green fired all of them. In 1914, when National Biscuit was at the height of their powers, every employee—and there were then 30,000 of them (almost as many as today)—received a $5 gold piece as a Christmas present. During the Great Depression, however, Nabisco cut the payroll and slashed the wages of plant workers, while increasing the dividends to shareholders. In the 1978 annual report the management stressed that "each and every employee has the responsibility to contribute to the final sales and earnings goals of the Company."

What they own. Thirty-eight plants in the United States, including a boxboard mill and two carton printing plants, and a machine shop that builds about 20% of Nabisco's manufacturing and packaging machinery. Overseas Nabisco has 24 plants in 13 countries, including the Frears biscuit operation in England, Belin biscuits in France (Pepito), and the Sprengel chocolate factories in West Germany.

Who owns and runs the company. The chairman and chief executive officer of Nabisco today is Robert M. Schaeberle, who came up through the financial side. A Dartmouth graduate, he joined Nabisco in 1946, having never worked for another company. It was not until 1975 that a woman—Dr. Helen Guthrie, professor of nutrition at Pennsylvania State University—was elected to the board. In 1979 Carol S. Tutundgy was named vice-president of industrial relations, Nabisco's first female officer.

The largest owners of Nabisco stock are people who sold companies to Nabisco. They are Matthew B. Rosenhaus (J.B. Williams), with 4.5%, and Morris L. Levinson (Associated Products), with 1.3%. The one link to the early days of the company is William H. Moore, a board member who is the grandson of Judge William H. Moore, founder of the New York Biscuit Company.

In the public eye. In 1972 the Federal Trade Commission obtained a consent order that banned Nabisco's J. B. Williams unit from making misleading claims for Vivarin, a stimulant made mainly of caffeine and sugar. In 1973 J. B. Williams was slapped with an $812,000 fine for violating a cease-and-desist order on advertising claims made for Geritol. In 1975 J. B. Williams was ordered to recall from the marketplace all stocks of Sominex 2, a sleeping aid containing an antihistamine whose use is restricted by the Food & Drug Administration to the prescription market.

Where they're going. Nabisco expects to do what they have always set out to do: sell more cookies and crackers in the American market. Although they have expanded overseas, they still derive 87% of their profits from the U.S. market. And although they have diversified into other lines, they still derive 92% of their profits from food. Given their fat cash position, they can be expected to buy other companies, even though this tactic has occasionally boomeranged.

Stock performance. Nabisco stock bought for $1,000 in 1970 sold for $902 on January 2, 1980.

Access. East Hanover, New Jersey 07936; (201) 884-0500.

Consumer brands.

Cookies and crackers: Oreo, Fig Newton, Chips Ahoy, Peanut Brittle, and Apple Crisp, Premium Saltines, Wheat Thins, Ritz, Chippers, Dixies, Nabisco Graham, Nabisco Cheese Peanut Butter, Swiss Cheese Snack, and Country Cheddar'n Sesame Snack crackers; Lorna Doone shortbread; Uneeda biscuits.
Cereals: Nabisco Shredded Wheat; Team; Cream of Wheat; Morning Power; Nabisco 100% Bran.
Snack foods: Chipsters; Diggers; Korkers; Flings Curls; Mister Salty pretzels.
Candies: Chuckles; Sugar Daddy; Junior Mints.
Dog food: Milk-Bone; Blue Mountain.
Other food products: Dromedary cake mixes, dates, and pimientos; Freezer Queen frozen meat entrees.
Pharmaceuticals: Geritol vitamins; Sominex sleep aid; Serutan laxative; Acu-Test in-home pregnancy test kit; P.V.M. protein powder meal replacement.
Toiletries: Rose Milk skin-care products; Aqua Velva men's toiletries; 'Lectric Shave preshave lotion; Ace combs.
Household accessories: Hygiene and Drylon shower curtains; Everlon draperies.

Sales: $11.5 billion
Profits: $435 million
Rank in world manufacturing: 30
Rank among non-U.S. manufacturers: 15
Rank in Switzerland: 1
Rank in food processing: 27
Rank in chocolate: 1
Rank in coffee: 2
Rank in infant formulas: 1
Founded: 1866
Employees: 146,000 (including 26,000 in North America)
Headquarters: Vevey, Switzerland
U.S. Headquarters: White Plains, New York

What they do. Nestlé is the colossus of the world food industry. Like Swiss bankers, they don't talk a lot, but they reach into most corners of the world. They are perhaps the only company doing 96% of their business outside their home country: at the end of 1978 they had 308 factories in 52 countries. So huge is Nestlé that their sales are double those of either Kraft or General Foods, two huge U.S. food processors. Nestlé's U.S. sales alone—generated by Nescafe, Taster's Choice, Nestea, Nestlé candy bars, Quik, Libby's canned foods, Stouffer's frozen dinners, and many other products—are now crowding the $3 billion mark, which would rank them among the top 10 American food processors. They added to their American larder in 1978 by acquiring Alcon Laboratories, a Fort Worth drug company that is the world's largest producer of medical preparations and instruments for eye treatment, and in 1979 by acquiring the Beech-Nut baby food business. Nestlé's own list of what they call "important brands" runs to more than 650 names. You're a customer of Nestlé if you dine at one of the 24 Rusty Scupper restaurants in America. In Norway the Nestlé-Findus company is the largest food business. In Japan Nestlé has an 860,000-square-foot plant turning out 10,000 tons of Nescafe a year. In Saudi Arabia, Nestlé negotiated a contract with the government to feed 300,000 school children a daily meal. One of Nestlé's first products, infant milk formula, is now an enormous seller in Third World countries, which has led church organizations and other groups to mount a worldwide boycott of all Nestlé products on the grounds that the milk food discourages mothers from breast feeding and thus leads to malnutrition and infant mortality.

History. Although Nestlé was founded in Switzerland, an American link was present from the start. After the Civil War Charles A. Page was posted to Zurich as the American consul. He hit upon the idea of making condensed milk in Switzerland (Gail Borden had been making it in America for 10 years). So in 1866 Page and his brother George, who came out from America, organized the Anglo-Swiss Condensed Milk Company (so named because they expected Britain to be their big market) at Cham, a small town on Lake Zug in central Switzerland. That was one root of what was to become Nestlé.

The other root was forming at virtually the same time 120 miles away in the town of Vevey. Henri Nestlé, a German-born merchant, artisan, and inventor who came to live in Vevey in 1843, hit upon the idea of making a milk product that could substitute for mother's milk. His interest was spurred by high infant mortality rates: in Switzerland one out of five babies died in the first year of life. In 1867 Nestlé tried out his new product, which was milk mixed with meal that had been baked by a new process. It was given to a prematurely born baby who had refused his mother's milk and was suffering from convulsions. The 15-day-old infant thrived on the milk food, and Nestlé then began to make it in large quantities.

For the rest of the century these two milk-based Swiss companies built up sizable businesses—and inevitably became bitter rivals. Anglo-Swiss challenged Nestlé by making an infant milk food, and Nestlé countered by fielding a condensed milk. Both marketed their products all over the world. Anglo-Swiss put up plants in England and the United States and developed a famous brand name, Milkmaid. The Nestlé products were sold under the Nestlé name, even after Henri Nestlé sold his company to three well-to-do Swiss burghers in 1875 for 1 million Swiss francs.

Talk surfaced as early as 1881 about the two Swiss firms combining, but it didn't happen until after George Page died in 1899. Page's son Fred sold all the American plants of Anglo-Swiss to the Borden company, and in 1905, with the help of the ubiquitous Swiss bankers, the two Swiss companies joined on an equal basis to form the Nestlé and Anglo-Swiss Condensed Milk Company. The new company kept registered offices at both Cham and Vevey, a practice still followed today. Even in 1905 Nestlé was big, with 7 factories in Switzerland and 11 more in five other countries.

Most Americans recognize Nestlé only as a chocolate company. But Nestlé didn't get into the chocolate business until 1904, when they arranged with the Swiss General Chocolate Company to market all their chocolate products outside Switzerland. In return Swiss General Chocolate agreed to produce a line of Nestlé milk chocolate, and Nestlé got a small part of the chocolate firm. At the time Swiss General Chocolate was a combination of two large Swiss chocolate makers. In 1911 a third producer came into the company, and in 1929 Nestlé bought the whole operation.

The 1930s were rocky times for Nestlé, as for the rest of the world. They were forced to close plants in various countries, and when the worldwide depression dried up Swiss exports, they had to shut down their two oldest factories—at Cham and Vevey. Still, by 1938 Nestlé had 105 plants operating all over the world, from South Africa to Panama to Japan.

The year 1938 was also a Nestlé milestone: the introduction of Nescafe instant coffee, their first non-milk-related product. In 1930 Brazil was experiencing such huge coffee surpluses that they were destroying beans to keep prices from falling lower than they already had, and the Brazilian Coffee Institute asked Nestlé to explore new uses for coffee beans. In 1937 Nestlé came up with a coffee-flavored powder. Nescafe went on sale in Switzerland on April 1, 1938. In 1939 manufacturing began in France, Britain, and the United States.

In the United States, the world's biggest coffee market, Nestlé opened a campaign for Nescafe in July 1940, just after the Nazis had marched through France. They looked to sell 100,000 cases a year; soon they were selling a million cases a year. World War II turned out to be a great marketer of instant coffee. Soluble coffee became a staple beverage as a result of its use by the U.S. Army, and then through distribution to the civilian populations of liberated Europe and Asia. By the time the war was over, instant coffee was on the threshold of a mighty advance, and Nescafe was to become the most important product in the Nestlé stable.

Since World War II Nestlé has moved into many other nonmilk businesses, mostly by buying other food companies. Among these acquisitions are the Swiss Maggi soups and spices (1947); the English Crosse & Blackwell (1960); the Italian Locatelli (1961); the Norwegian Findus (1962); and two U.S. companies, Libby, McNeil & Libby (1970) and Stouffer (1973). They also bought a minority interest in the French cosmetics firm L'Oreal in 1974.

Reputation. Nestlé is admired in the international business community for having written the book on the rules, procedures, and philosophy of operating a multinational business. Their effectiveness is shown by the profits they squeeze from sales: Nestlé consistently earns 4% on the sales dollar, one of the highest rates of profit of any major food company. Nestlé's philosophy is to build quality into their products. "If we have a definite superiority of quality," a Nestlé executive once said, "the consumer will accept a higher price."

What they own. At the end of 1978 the fire insurance value of Nestlé's buildings, machinery, tools, furniture, and vehicles was $6.2 billion. The company had on hand $2.1 billion in cash.

Who owns and runs the company. Nestlé paid dearly for their 49% stake in L'Oreal. Liliane Bettencourt, daughter of L'Oreal's founder, came away the biggest individual shareholder in Nestlé: she is believed to have 4% of the shares. Nestlé management is proud to be an international group. The current chairman is French, one of his predecessors was Italian, and 40% of the headquarters staff is non-Swiss. Of the five executive vice-presidents one is French, another Italian. The chief legal counsel, Franklin Gurley, is American. Nestlé people rarely leave once they join up. Pierre Liotard-Vogt, now chairman, explained: "People get stable employment unless they turn mad or steal."

In the public eye. Nestlé has conceded that "breast milk is the best food infants can possibly receive," but they have strongly defended their sale of infant formula in Third World countries. That market is one that Nestlé developed through advertising and promotion over many years, and Nestlé's share is estimated between one-third and one-half. They maintain their milk food is a safe product that contributes to the health of babies who for one reason or another cannot be fed by their mothers. But church groups all over the world, including the National Council of Churches in the United States, are supporting the Nestlé boycott. They contend that promotion by Nestlé and other companies has weaned mothers away from breast feeding their babies and has induced Third World families to spend major portions of their income on an unnecessary product in the belief they are doing what's best for their babies. Nestlé argues that the Third World has problems much more pressing than this one, and they dispute the evidence that bottle feeding has led to malnutrition. The antiformula people have been zealous in their attacks on Nestlé. When a Swiss group published a pamphlet with the title "Nestlé Kills Babies," Nestlé was so furious they went to court and were able to win a libel suit.

Where they're going. Nestlé is beginning to diversify outside the food business. After they bought L'Oreal, one company leader said, "We found out that research on cosmetics is very close to research that we are doing for aromas of food."

Access. 1800 Vevey, Switzerland; (021) 510112. In the United States: 100 Bloomingdale Road, White Plains, New York 10605; (914) 682-6000.

Consumer brands.

Candy bars, cookie mixes, cocoa mixes, other chocolate products: Nestlé; Quik.
Instant coffees and teas: Nescafe; Taster's Choice; Decaf; Sunrise; Nestea.
Soups and seasonings: Maggi; Crosse & Blackwell; Souptime; Lunchtime.
Frozen vegetables and frozen dinners: Libby's; Stouffer.
Other grocery products: Wispride cheese; Deer Park bottled water; Pride's dips and spreads; Choco-Chill cold chocolate.
Hotels and restaurants: Stouffer.
Cosmetics: L'Oreal; Lancôme; Guy LaRoche; Biotherm; Ted Lapidus.

NORTON SIMON INC

Sales: $2.7 billion
Profits: $124.2 million
Forbes 500 rank: 184
Rank in tomato processing: 1
Rank in salad and cooking oil: 1
Rank in popcorn: 1
Rank in Scotch whiskey: 1
Rank in ginger ale: 1
Rank in imported gin: 2
Rank in car rental: 2
Rank in sewing patterns: 2
Rank in cosmetics: 3
Founded: 1968
Employees: 35,000
Headquarters: New York, New York

What they do. Norton Simon is a food-based conglomerate, the offspring of two restless acquisitors: Norton W. Simon and David J. Mahoney. Operating from the West Coast, Simon laid the foundation with 29 years of patient building—and gave his name to the enterprise. Operating from the East Coast, Mahoney added the superstructure that today houses a large and incongruous family of brand-name products. Norton Simon fills supermarket shelves with Hunt's tomato sauce and Wesson oil, bottles Canada Dry mixers, owns the Old Fitzgerald bourbon distillery, peddles Max Factor cosmetics, imports wine from France (the Alexis Lichine selection), makes wine in California (San Martin), and rents cars under the Avis sign. Hence the claim: "At least one of our brands is used in nine out of every 10 American households."

History. Cigarette smokers used to wonder why so many matchbook covers carried recipes featuring Hunt's canned tomato products. Norton W. Simon was the reason. He controlled Ohio Match and he controlled Hunt Foods—and he believed in one hand washing the other. That's also why Hunt was a big advertiser in *McCall's* and *Redbook* magazines, which Simon also controlled. He paid attention to such details.

Born in Portland, Oregon, Simon was 14 when his father's department store was wiped out in the financial panic of 1921. It was a disaster he was not to forget. Young Simon peddled bags, towels, and tissues to local merchants after school and put $3,000 he saved into the stock market rather than toward college. He got out with $35,000 before the 1929 crash, and then, in a move that was to become characteristic, he bought a bankrupt orange juice company, renamed it Val Vita, revived it, and began canning tomatoes. Simon's tactic, in the midst of the Depression, was lower prices. He did so well that Hunt Bros. of Fullerton, California, bought Val Vita for $4 million. Armed with these proceeds, Simon began buying into Hunt, and by 1943 he had enough stock to control the company. Simon then invested in a slew of other companies, among them Wesson oil, which was based in the South; Canada Dry, a soft drink bottler and liquor importer based in New York: and McCall, a New York-headquartered company that published and printed magazines and marketed sewing patterns. None could complain about Simon's motives. He made them all stronger than he found them.

In 1968 Simon combined all his enterprises into a new corporation that carried his name—and then, in a not uncharacteristic move, walked away from it all to devote himself to his art collection, politics (he

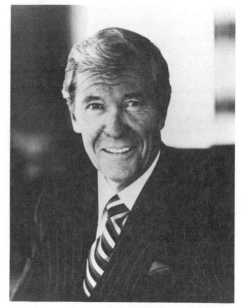

David Mahoney: boy from the Bronx makes good.

spent $2 million in 1970 trying vainly to win the Republican nomination for the U.S. Senate in California), and his new wife (in 1971 he divorced his wife of 37 years and married actress Jennifer Jones).

Today he owns very little stock in the company bearing his name. He doesn't even hold a seat on the board of directors. "I felt possessed rather than possessing," said Simon explaining recently why he left. Various observers have tried to figure out Norton Simon. Marilyn Bender, writing in the *New York Times* in 1974, called him "a brooding figure on the American business scene, a would-be messiah of industry and the arts who moves circuitously and always draws a controversy with one grandiose gesture or another." Phyllis Berman, writing in *Forbes* in 1979, depicted him as a "classic pessimist" who "seems more like an embittered intellectual than a builder of corporate empires."

When Simon stepped down in 1968 from the leadership of the corporate empire he had created, the company was run for a year by a troika. The chairman was William E. McKenna, the chairman of the finance committee was Harold M. Williams, and, three thousand miles away in New York, David Mahoney was named president. Simon had recruited Mahoney to become president of Canada Dry in 1966. In August

1969 Mahoney emerged as number 1. He was obviously Simon's choice. Corporate headquarters of Norton Simon, Inc., were switched from Fullerton to New York.

Norton Simon and David Mahoney are a study in contrasts. If Simon is a contentious loner, Mahoney is a gregarious New Yorker once described as having grown up in the bar of the restaurant 21, where he would nurse a drink all night while he made important contacts. Mahoney actually grew up in the Throgs Neck section of the East Bronx, the son of a union crane operator. His first job was in the mailroom of the old Ruthrauff & Ryan advertising agency. He was a vice-president and account executive by the time he was 25. He married a Powers model, and a few months later, when he was 28, he left to set up his own advertising agency, taking with him a client: Virginia Dare Wine. Mahoney always had the facility for making friends—and money. Contacts enabled him to land the Good Humor ice cream account. He got along so well with the client that he was offered the presidency of the company, which he took, selling his fledgling advertising agency. When Good Humor was sold to Thomas J. Lipton in 1961, Mahoney made a bundle on his stock and moved to Colgate-Palmolive as heir apparent. But he couldn't wait around. When Norton Simon offered him Canada Dry to run, he accepted. Irwin Ross, who interviewed Mahoney for *Fortune* magazine in 1972, said his operating principle was "to get on well with everybody. It is still hard to find an enemy of David Mahoney."

Mahoney is comfortable with companies that depend on extensive advertising, and he has acted accordingly in restructuring Norton Simon, Inc. He sold off more than 20 businesses—all the publishing properties, printing plants, Ohio Match, and soft drink bottling facilities. In their places have come Max Factor, Old Fitzgerald bourbon, Tanqueray gin, Halston, Orlane, and Avis. Since taking over, Mahoney has more than doubled sales, tripled profits, and put his stamp on Norton Simon, Inc.

Reputation. Under David Mahoney, Norton Simon is an aggressive marketer of consumer goods and services, intent on winning in any field they enter.

What they own. Norton Simon has assets of $2 billion, but Mahoney has pointed out that "our brand names are perhaps our most valuable asset," and they're not reflected on the books.

Who owns and runs the company. The Firestein family, the previous owners of Max Factor, have more than 6% of the common shares. The second largest owner is the Norton Simon Profit Sharing Trust, with nearly 3% of the shares. David Mahoney is clearly in charge. For his efforts he received total compensation of $2 million in 1978, making him one of the highest-paid executives in U.S. business. Simon once compared himself to his successor as follows: "I owned only 10% or 20% of the company but I always acted like I owned 100%—and people assumed it was true. That meant I never had to socialize with the business establishment like Mahoney does." On his 56th birthday, in 1979, David Mahoney told a group of his top executives: "I believe that things can be made to happen, and that belief was tested in the Bronx during the Depression and on the beaches of Okinawa. I didn't get here by playing polo."

In the public eye. Norton Simon, Inc., was saluted by the *New York Times* in 1979 for pledging to hire 250 unemployed, disadvantaged youths, which will be 1% of the company's domestic work force. In place is a strong equal-employment effort that has resulted in women making up 41% of the work force, minorities 29%. Two women hold board seats. Another director is Luther H. Foster, the black president of Tuskegee Institute.

Where they're going. *Forbes* magazine asked Norton Simon in 1979 what he thought of the future. He said: "I think we're in for long-term serious economic trouble," adding: "Everybody is performing a service that nobody wants." A few months later David Mahoney told Norton Simon stockholders: "I am confident that Americans can get their act together and not only survive but thrive. I'm equally confident that NSI will prosper and grow in the years ahead."

Stock performance. Norton Simon stock bought for $1,000 in 1970 sold for $868 on January 2, 1980.

Access. 277 Park Avenue, New York, New York 10017; (212) 832-1000.

Consumer brands.

Food products: Hunt's tomato products; Wesson oil; Reddi-whip whipped cream; Manwich sandwich sauces; Snack Pack puddings; Sunlite sunflower oil; Orville Redenbacher's Gourmet Popping Corn; Prima Salsa spaghetti sauce; Pfeiffer salad dressings.

Cosmetics: Max Factor; Orlane; Halston; Jean D'Albert.

Liquors and wines: Johnnie Walker Scotch whiskey; Tanqueray gin; Aalborg Akvavit; Mandarine Napoleon; Pimm's Cup; Weller Reserve; Weller 107; Old Fitzgerald; and Alexis Lichine wines. Producer of San Martin wines.

Soft drinks: Canada Dry; Barrelhead.

Other businesses: McCalls's sewing patterns; Avis rent-a-car.

Sales: $5.1 billion
Profits: $264.9 million
Forbes 500 rank: 75
Rank in soft drinks: 2
Rank in snack foods: 1
Rank in fast foods: 4
Rank in sporting goods: 1
Founded: 1896
Employees: 95,000
Headquarters: Purchase, New York

What they do. "We sell lifestyle," says John Sculley, head of Pepsi-Cola operations for the world's second-largest soft drink maker. The recipe for Pepsi's lifestyle consists of sugar, potatoes, corn, fat, flour, tomatoes, cheese, meat, saccharin, and seasonings—all purchased in huge quantities and served up in Pepsi soft drinks, Frito-Lay snack foods, and Pizza Hut and Taco Bell fast-food outlets.

Pepsi-Cola has been trying, it seems almost for this entire century, to displace Coca-Cola as the number 1 soft drink in the gullets of Americans. They've made progress, but they're still second. The Coca-Cola brands hold at least one-third of the U.S. market, while the Pepsi brands have a little less than one-quarter. Those brands, in addition to Pepsi-Cola, include Diet Pepsi, Mountain Dew, Pepsi Light, Teem, Patio, and Aspen. They are bottled in 416 plants

across the United States. PepsiCo itself owns the 19 bottlers in Dallas, Houston, Los Angeles, Milwaukee, New York, Philadelphia, Phoenix, and Pittsburgh; the others are owned and operated by independent bottlers who buy a cola concentrate from Pepsi, add sugar or another sweetener to make a syrup, and then make the drink by adding carbonated water.

Outside the United States Pepsi's soft drinks are bottled or canned in 600 plants located in 126 countries and territories. PepsiCo owns 34 of these facilities. Twenty years ago Coca-Cola outsold Pepsi 20 to 1 in overseas markets. That lead has now been cut to 2 to 1. In much of the Arab world and in all of the Soviet Union Pepsi has the cola market all to itself.

If your town doesn't have a Pepsi-Cola bottling plant, it may very well have a factory turning out Lay's potato chips or Fritos corn chips. Pepsi bought Frito-Lay in 1965 and is now the largest snack food producer. They're the first company on earth to have reached annual sales of $1 billion in these delicacies. The Frito-Lay snacks are produced in 38 plants and are delivered to thousands of retail outlets by a sales force of 7,200 persons who make 700,-000 calls a week on customers.

PepsiCo is the nation's fourth-largest fast-food server, with Pizza Hut (more than 4,000 outlets) and Taco Bell (more than 1,-000). There's a Pizza Hut in every state except Delaware. From the West Taco Bell has fanned out to cover 41 states.

Also part of PepsiCo are two large motor carriers, North American Van Lines and Lee Way Motor Freight, and the nation's largest maker of sporting goods, Wilson.

History. Back in the 1890s, inspired by an Atlanta pharmacist's success with Coca-Cola, imitators popped up everywhere, keeping the patent lawyers busy. In New Bern, North Carolina, another pharmacist, Caleb D. Bradham, concocted a cola syrup which he called Pepsi-Cola. He dropped the drugstore business entirely by 1902, and a year later he registered the Pepsi-Cola name. By 1909 there were 250 bottlers in 24 states; such was the American thirst for cola drinks. Bradham advertised: "Pepsi-Cola is the Original Pure Food Drink—guaranteed under the U.S. Gov't. Serial No. 3813. At all soda fountains, 5¢ a glass—at your grocer's, 5¢ a bottle. Beware of imitations." Bradham went broke after World War I. Lawrence

Dietz, in his book *Soda Pop*, explained why: "When a man sits with a warehouse full of 22¢ sugar in a 3¢ market, he inevitably is sitting with corporate books that are written in blood-red ink."

Pepsi-Cola was bounced around like a basketball for a couple of decades. Wall Street lawyers got into the act, the company changed hands twice, and finally, during the 1930s, it ended up in New York City as an appendage of the Loft candy shop chain. What kept the brand alive was a Depression-born idea to sell Pepsi in 12-ounce bottles (versus Coke's classic 6-ounce size) and advertise it with lyrics written to an old English hunting song, "D'ye Ken John Peel":

Pepsi-Cola hits the spot
Twelve full ounces, that's a lot
Twice as much for a nickel, too
Pepsi-Cola is the drink for you.

That jingle kept Pepsi alive during World War II when the Coca-Cola-fed troops of the United States were defeating the Nazis and the Japanese. After the war the troops came home to Coca-Cola, and Pepsi had to regroup again, this time under Alfred Steele, a supersalesman who left a Coca-Cola vice-presidency in 1949, took 15 men with him, and revitalized the Pepsi brand. Steele told the bottlers: "You can conserve your way to bankruptcy or you can spend your way to prosperity." In other words: advertise. Pepsi abandoned the Depression tactic of selling itself as a cheap drink and adopted the premise that it was the beverage for "those who think young": the Pepsi Generation. Steele's wife, actress Joan Crawford, accompanied him on many promotional trips, and after

Steele died in 1959, she was elected to the board and remained a Pepsi cheerleader.

The company was run for a while by a lawyer, but the next strong man was Donald M. Kendall, an ex–Golden Gloves fighter who came aboard in 1947 as a fountain syrup salesman and by 1957 was head of Pepsi-Cola's international division. It was Kendall who staged the famous kitchen debate between Nikita Khruschev and Richard Nixon at the 1959 Moscow Trade Fair, getting the Soviet premier to knock back nine bottles of Pepsi. Back in the United States, Kendall rose to the number 1 spot at Pepsi in 1963 and then engineered the 1965 merger with Frito-Lay that resulted in PepsiCo. In that same year he married for the second time. His bride was Baroness Ruedt Von Collenberg, who had been introduced to Kendall by a Pepsi bottler in Germany.

Kendall remained close friends with Richard M. Nixon, becoming one of his staunchest supporters, even after Watergate. It was during the Nixon administration that Kendall went back to Moscow and cracked the Soviet market for Pepsi-Cola in exchange for distributing Stolichnaya vodka in the U.S. He said: "If we can get the Soviet people to enjoy good consumer goods, they'll never be able to do without them again."

Reputation. There's a much more aggressive stance to PepsiCo than Coca-Cola, perhaps because they're an underdog, perhaps because their style has been fashioned in urban concrete settings, or perhaps because of Donald Kendall, an abrasive, white-haired, pugnacious executive who, according to *Forbes*, reorganized the company so

Soviet Pepsi Generation

In 1978 PepsiCo renewed and expanded their bilateral pact with the Soviet Union whereby PepsiCo imports Stolichnaya vodka into the United States in return for Pepsi-Cola plants in Russia. It was the occasion for this exchange of toasts:

Donald M. Kendall, chairman

of PepsiCo: "Improved ties help create a network of interlocking relations of mutual value and reduce the antagonism and suspicion which, in the past, permeated virtually all East–West contacts after decades of mutual hostility."

Juri B. Zhizhin, Soviet vodka

czar: "Let there be a Pepsi bottle on the table of every Soviet family, and let every American family adorn its table with a bottle of Stolichnaya."

ruthlessly that he earned the nickname White Fang. Michael Jensen of the *New York Times* wrote that Kendall "has scaled the corporate ladder not so much by virtue of cerebral accomplishment as by sheer drive and ambition."

What they own. Pepsi owns more bottling plants than Coca-Cola. They also operate more fast-food establishments than McDonald's does. More than half the Pizza Huts and Taco Bells are company operated.

Who owns and runs the company. PepsiCo has been a management-dominated company for many years. The largest indi-vidual stockholders are people who sold out to PepsiCo: Herman Lay, who has 1 million shares, and Frank Carney, the Pizza Hut founder, who has 600,000 shares. The board is all white and all male. The vice-president for corporate affairs (and occasional spar-ring partner for Kendall) is Cartha De-Loach, who was J. Edgar Hoover's right-hand man at the FBI.

In the public eye. The Department of Ag-riculture wants to prohibit students from buying soft drinks and snacks from school vending machines until after lunch is served. "We believe," responded PepsiCo in 1979, "it is unwise to deprive children of

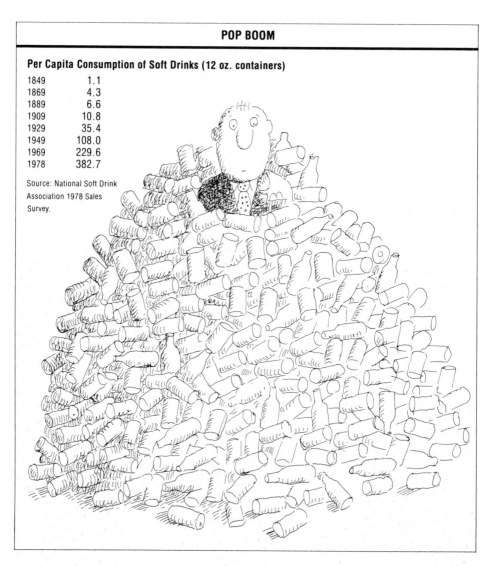

POP BOOM

Per Capita Consumption of Soft Drinks (12 oz. containers)

Year	Containers
1849	1.1
1869	4.3
1889	6.6
1909	10.8
1929	35.4
1949	108.0
1969	229.6
1978	382.7

Source: National Soft Drink
Association 1978 Sales
Survey.

products they desire on the basis of competition with other foods. We also believe that freedom of choice is a fundamental concept of our society."

However, the freedom of blacks to find jobs at PepsiCo's Lee Way trucking subsidiary was apparently restricted, according to a suit brought by the Justice Department in 1972. The complaint said that of 820 long-distance drivers at Lee Way, there were only five blacks and eight Hispanics. In 1980 PepsiCo settled the suit by agreeing to pay a total of $2.7 million in back pay to 82 blacks who were denied jobs. It was the largest settlement ever achieved by the government in an antidiscrimination case.

Fed up with New York City, Kendall had the PepsiCo headquarters removed to suburban Purchase, New York, not far from his Greenwich, Connecticut, home.

Where they're going. Here's how PepsiCo looks at the world: per capita consumption of soft drinks in the non–U.S. world has a long way to go to catch up to the American standard of gulping; more and more people are eating meals away from home; and at home the traditional three-meals-a-day pattern is changing to "more frequent mini-meals." That leaves a wide open berth for Pepsi-Cola, Pizza Hut, Taco Bell, and Frito-Lay.

Stock performance. PepsiCo stock bought for $1,000 in 1970 sold for $1,493 on January 2, 1980.

Access. Purchase, New York 10577; (914) 253-3027. Inquiries for Pepsi-Cola should be addressed to Mary Ellen Gowin, Manager Consumer Affairs, Pepsi-Cola's Purchase office; Snack Foods: Gay Thomason, Manager Consumer Services, Frito-Lay Tower, Dallas, Texas 75235.

Consumer brands.

Beverages: Pepsi-Cola; Pepsi Light; Diet Pepsi; Mountain Dew; Teem; Aspen.
Snack foods: Fritos; Chee-tos; Doritos; Ruffles; Tostitos; Go-B-Tweens; Lay's; Fantastix.
Restaurants: Taco Bell; Pizza Hut.
Transportation: North American Van Lines; Lee Way Motor Freight.
Sporting goods: Wilson, Staff, Walter Hagen, X-31, Wilson 1200, Ultradyne II, Blue Ridge, Sam Snead, Billy Casper, Laura Baugh, Patty Berg, Carol Mann golf clubs; Pro Staff golf balls; Match Point, Extra, Advantage, Jack Kramer, Chris Evert Autograph tennis rackets.

PET

Sales: $1.3 billion
Profits: $33 million
Founded: 1885
Employees: 18,200
Headquarters: St. Louis, Missouri

Another company whose lease on life was canned milk (Borden, Carnation and Nestlé are three others), Pet disappeared as an independent corporate entity in 1978 when they were acquired for $400 million by IC Industries, a Chicago conglomerate with a railroad base. A group of Swiss immigrants founded Pet in 1885 as the Helvetia Milk Condensing Company. In 1961 milk products were still accounting for virtually all of their sales. They then went on a merger-and-acquisition binge and after passing the $1 billion mark in 1975 were swallowed themselves. They make the best-selling box of candy in the world: Whitman's Sampler. They own the world's largest processor of pecans: Funsten. They're the leading retailer of wine and liquor in Missouri.

Access. 400 South Fourth Street, St. Louis, Missouri 63166; (314) 621-5400.

Consumer brands.

Foods: Pet milk; Golden Key evaporated milk; Laura Scudder snack foods; Whitman's candies; Aunt Fanny's bakery goods; Downy Flake waffles; Sego liquid diet; Spoon-Up diet pudding; Funsten nuts; Heartland cereals and syrup; Musselman's fruits; Gulf Belle and Orleans canned shrimp and oysters; Reese Finer Foods; Old El Paso Mexican foods; Compliment sauces; Pet-Ritz frozen pie crusts.
Stores and stands: "905" convenience stores, Stuckey's pecans and roadside stands.

The Pizza Hut system, with 3,000 outlets, reports this annual shopping list: 65 million pounds of flour, 40 million pounds of cheese, 356 million pounds of meat, 1.5 million cases of tomato products, 210,000 cases of mushrooms, and 70,000 cases of olives.

Sales: $2.2 billion
Profits: $83.5 million
Forbes 500 rank: 245
Rank in flour for home use: 2
Rank in frozen pizza: 1
Rank in pancake mixes: 2
Rank in refrigerated doughs: 1
Rank in dehydrated mashed potatoes: 1
Rank in restaurants: 3
Founded: 1869
Employees: 58,100
Headquarters: Minneapolis, Minnesota

What they do. Mention Pillsbury and most people think of flour. Flour milling was the original business, and that's the product they're most strongly identified with. But now, following a ten-year acquisition binge, Pillsbury bakes pizza, bottles apple juice and vinegar, produces spaghetti and other pastas, packs dehydrated potatoes, makes artificial sweeteners and diet bars, sells refrigerated ready-to-bake doughs and cake-decorating products, cans peas and corn, freezes vegetables in rich sauces, mills rice, stores and merchandises grain, sells feed ingredients—and on top of all that operates one of the largest restaurant businesses in the nation.

Pillsbury became a hydra-headed giant by design. The decision was made to grow, so they went out and bought a passel of companies: Burger King, Totino's, Steak & Ale, American Beauty Macaroni, Speas, Pioneer Food, and Green Giant.

Pillsbury's refrigerated doughs (rolls, biscuits, cookies, etc.) are distributed to grocers by Kraft, one of the industry giants. So big is this business that sales to Kraft account for 10% of Pillsbury's entire sales.

The major change at Pillsbury has been their emergence as a restaurateur. Pillsbury has followed Americans out of the supermarket to serve them where they dine away from home. Other food processors have moved in this direction, but none as extensively as Pillsbury. With restaurant sales approaching $1 billion a year, Pillsbury ranks third behind McDonald's and Kentucky Fried Chicken in the eating out market.

Restaurants including Burger King, Steak & Ale, and Poppin Fresh Pie Restau-

rants generate 40% of Pillsbury's profits. Pillsbury's strong push in the restaurant field has also changed the company in one other important respect: they have become more labor-intensive. Pillsbury has 12,800 persons working in U.S. food processing operations. On the restaurant payrolls are 42,000 employees.

History. Pillsbury's turbulent history has been intertwined with the development of the city of Minneapolis and the state of Minnesota. The business dates from 1869, the year Charles A. Pillsbury, then 27 years old, paid $10,000 for a one-third interest in a five-year-old Minneapolis flour mill. He was staked by his father, George A. Pillsbury, and his uncle, John S. Pillsbury, who was later to serve three terms as governor of Minnesota and was regarded as the "father of the University of Minnesota" (he once saved the fledgling school from a mortgage foreclosure). Charles himself was to be elected to the state senate for five successive two-year terms, and he was called "the most influential man" in that body. By investing in new machinery that was able to process hard spring wheat into fine white flour, the Pillsburys built a prosperous business. Minneapolis became the center of the flour milling industry, and by 1886 the company called C. A. Pillsbury was doing $15 million of business a year and may well have been the largest milling company in the world.

In 1889 the 20-year-old Pillsbury firm passed into the hands of an English financial syndicate, which merged it with other American firms to form Pillsbury-Washburn Flour Mills. Charles Pillsbury stayed on as managing director but died in 1899 at age 57. In 1907 Pillsbury-Washburn floundered after bad weather caused extensive crop damage. Unable to meet its bills, the company went into receivership. A year later a leasing company was organized to operate the flour mills. It was called Pillsbury Flour Mills. Active in the management were three Pillsburys: Alfred F., son of Governor John Pillsbury; and Charles S. and John S., twin sons of founder Charles Pillsbury. In 1923 Pillsbury-Washburn disposed of all assets to the leasing company, and in effect the Pillsburys regained control of the company founded by their fathers.

Pillsbury family members still maintain a presence in the company bearing their name, but they are no longer active in day-to-day management.

Reputation. Most people still have a warm feeling about Pillsbury, the flour miller. Some of this feeling has been engendered by the annual "Bake-Off" Pillsbury has sponsored since 1949. Since then, more than $2 million in cash prizes have been awarded to contestants in this recipe competition, which concludes with finalists preparing their recipes twice for a panel of judges. Inside the company, though, they know it's a new ball game. Pillsbury is bent on growing. Products—and people—who don't measure up are axed. In 1976 a middle-level executive who didn't want his name used told the *Wall Street Journal:* "People aren't exactly trembling, but everybody is keeping a scorecard. They know who has come and who has gone, and they know there's a pressure to perform in this company like there never has been before."

What they own. Pillsbury has well over 100 food processing and food warehousing facilities in the United States, including 8 flour mills, 17 apple juice and vinegar plants, 5 spaghetti plants, and 76 grain elevators.

Who owns and runs the company. Two Pillsbury brothers—George S. and John S.—hold seats on the board but together own less than 2% of the stock. Their holdings are outweighed by those of Norman Brinker, founder of the Steak & Ale restaurant chain, who owns some 450,000 shares (worth about $14 million), or nearly 3% of the stock. The man running Pillsbury since 1973 is tough-minded William H. Spoor, architect of the current expansion program and holder of 20,000 shares. He has brought in people from the outside, saying, "We were too inbred." (Spoor himself never worked for another company.) He hired Raymond F. Good from H. J. Heinz to run Pillsbury's consumer products division, but Good left after the Green Giant leader, Thomas Wyman, was slotted above him as vice-chairman.

Spoor didn't hesitate to take Pillsbury out of the chicken, flower, housing, and publishing businesses when they failed to produce the kind of growth and profit he was looking for. Pillsbury may be the only food company to have a function called vice-president of mergers and acquisitions. It was filled by Jerry W. Levin, who was promoted in 1979 to vice-president of corporate strategy and acquisitions. Spoor, the son of a flour salesman, thought of becoming a minister when he was young. He went to Dartmouth and ran the hurdles. A former employee calls him "an ex-track star who's still running the big race."

In the public eye. Pillsbury is one of the pillars of the Minneapolis community, a major supporter of cultural and civic improvement programs. Their charitable contributions budget, including that of Green Giant, is now over $2 million a year. While their rival, General Mills, relocated its headquarters to a Minneapolis suburb, Pillsbury elected to stay downtown, not far from the banks of the Mississippi River where they began in 1869. A twin tower complex called Pillsbury Center will be ready for occupancy in 1981. The company said the decision to stay in Minneapolis was prompted "from a conviction that the company, its employees and stockholders will benefit from a continuing involvement and participation in the center city." Pillsbury says women hold 16% and minorities 9% of its corporate-wide managerial and professional positions. Pillsbury asks managers to set goals for utilization of minority and female personnel and tells them that they will be measured on the results.

Where they're going. William Spoor is out to build a great big company.

Stock performance. Pillsbury stock bought for $1,000 in 1970 sold for $1,085 on January 2, 1980.

Access. 608 Second Avenue South, Minneapolis, Minnesota 55402; (612) 230-4966.

Consumer brands.

Baking products: Pillsbury line of baking mixes and frostings (Pillsbury PLUS, Bundt, Streusel Swirl, Rich 'N Easy, No Bakes), Best flour, Hungry Jack dehydrated potatoes and refrigerated dough, Ballard refrigerated dough, Wilton cake decorating products.
Frozen and canned foods: Totino's and Fox frozen pizza, Green Giant, Kounty Kist, LeSueur, Holloway House, Clark, Dawn Fresh, Niblets.
Other groceries: Funny Face soft drink mix, Sprinkle Sweet and Swift 10 food sweetener, Figurines diet bars, Farina hot cereal, Food Sticks, Wheat Nuts, Speas apple juice and vinegar products, Dawn Fresh gravy and sauce, American Beauty pasta products.
Restaurants: Burger King, Steak & Ale, Poppin Fresh Pie Shop.

Sales: $2.0 billion
Profits: $84.5 million
Forbes 500 rank: 270
Rank in food processing: 20
Rank in hot cereal: 1
Rank in ready-to-eat cereal: 4
Rank in pet foods: 4
Rank in toys: 3
Founded: 1891
Employees: 29,000
Headquarters: Chicago, Illinois

What they do. Quaker Oats is a cereal-based company that has expanded into pancakes and cookies, pet foods, frozen pizza, restaurants, toys, needlecraft yarns, and chemicals. Headed by a founder's grandson, this old-fashioned company sometimes seems out of place in the modern world. Their largest-selling product is the one they started with more than 100 years ago: oatmeal. They bake cookies for the Girl Scouts.

Quaker is king of the hot cereals, holding more than 50% of this market, or more than $100 million in annual sales for the company. But the market is not expanding and is only about one-tenth the size of the ready-to-eat cold cereal business, in which Quaker ranks fourth, with 9% of the market.

Quaker owns two of America's oldest brands. The Quaker Man trademark was registered in 1877. Aunt Jemima dates from the 1893 Chicago exposition, where a black woman who went by that name demonstrated a pancake flour. Quaker bought the Aunt Jemima Mills of St. Joseph, Missouri, in 1925. Aunt Jemima is still the leading pancake mix today—and the name also goes on syrup, frozen waffles, frozen French toast, and frozen pancake batter.

Quaker was one of the early leaders of the pet food business, with Ken-L-Ration and Puss'n Boots brands. They rank third today, with 12% of the market. Quaker became the leading supplier of Girl Scout cookies when they acquired Burry Biscuit in 1962.

Quaker got into chemicals in 1921 by recycling waste materials. The more oatmeal people ate, the more oat hulls piled up at Quaker plants. A Quaker chemist, Harold Brownlee, found a way to make furfural from the hulls. Furfural is a chemical discovered by a German scientist 100 years earlier, but it remained a laboratory curiosity until Quaker's development of a commercial process. Furfural and its derivatives were later found to have many applications, especially as a solvent in oil refining. Today Quaker is the largest producer of furfural, and it's a bigger business than oatmeal: $125 million a year.

History. The company we know today as Quaker Oats was organized at the end of the nineteenth century by oatmeal millers who decided that instead of fighting one another they would do better to band together and divide up the market. In 1891 seven of the oldest and largest millers formed a stock company, the American Cereal Company, which was powerful enough to be labeled the "oatmeal trust." In 1901 it changed its name to the Quaker Oats Company, taking the name of a predecessor company, Quaker Mill of Ravenna, Ohio, which had registered the Quaker Man trademark in 1877.

The early leaders of the Quaker Oats Company were Henry P. Crowell, who had headed the Quaker Mill in Ohio, and Canadian-born Robert Stuart, who had followed in the footsteps of his Scottish father, John Stuart, an oatmeal miller. In 1873 the Stuarts, along with another Scottish Presbyterian, George Douglas, built a gigantic oatmeal mill at Cedar Rapids, Iowa. Robert Stuart married a niece of Mrs. George Douglas, and from that union came the Stuarts who were to lead Quaker Oats through most of the twentieth century.

The Scottish connection with oatmeal is strong. Samuel Johnson, in his admirable dictionary, defined oats as "a grain, which in England is generally given to horses, but in Scotland supports the people." At one point, oats occupied one-third of the Scottish land that was in crops. It's from oatmeal that the Scots make porridge. Oatmeal was also popular in Ireland, but it never caught on in England except as gruel served to invalids. It was this strong English prejudice that the oatmeal sellers of America had to overcome. A cartoon in a 1910 issue of *Cosmopolitan* showed a Yankee farmer who, after eating oatmeal, would prance around his barnyard and drink from the horses' trough.

It's a tribute to the marketing skills of the early Quaker Oats management that this prejudice was overcome, and Americans began to substitute grain cereals for meats at breakfast.

To accomplish the turnaround, Quaker Oats began selling rolled oats in packages instead of in bulk, making oatmeal one of the first foods to be packaged. And along with that change came a vigorous advertising campaign on behalf of Quaker Oats, including the placing of premiums, such as pieces of china, inside the packages. Early Quaker Oats advertising contained lines like "Quaker Oats give you strength—strength of mind—strength of body. Then you are healthy and happy. Then you are honestly thankful." It was the old American appeal to eat what's good for you. By 1918 Quaker Oats had reached an annual sales level of $123 million, which made it one of the largest companies in the nation.

Fifty years later Quaker's sales had advanced only just past the $500 million mark.

In 1969 the company went on an acquisition spree, buying Fisher-Price, the nation's largest maker of preschool toys; Magic Pan, a San Francisco restaurant specializing in crepes; and Celeste, a small Chicago pizza maker. In 1972 they added Needlecraft Corporation of America, maker of needlecraft kits and yarns.

Reputation. Oatmeal has a stick-to-the-ribs quality, connoting all the homespun virtues. Quaker is known for those qualities too. Solid and dependable. The Fisher-Price toy subsidiary enjoys much the same reputation.

What they own. Twelve food plants and 5 toy plants in the United States. The Burry bakery at Elizabeth, New Jersey. Ten Needlecraft plants. Eighty Magic Pan restaurants. Five chemical plants in the United States, 3 in Europe. The John Stuart

The Quaker Man

The Quaker Man was one of the first trademarks for packaged foods when the Quaker Oats Company had him registered on September 4, 1877. In 1915 the Religious Society of Friends (Quakers) tried to stop the company from using the Quaker name. They failed in their effort to get Congress to prohibit manufacturers from using the name of a religious denomination on a product. The Quakers then sought action in a number of states, but Quaker Oats used all the resources they could summon to beat back this attack, and the Friends succeeded in only one state: Indiana.

The Quaker Man became a little jollier in 1946 at the end of World War II and even warmer and friendlier in the 1957 painted version that still appears on Quaker Oats oatmeal tubes. He became quite stylized in the corporate symbol adopted in 1970.

1877   1946

1957   1970

Evolution of the Quaker Oats symbol.

Research Laboratories at Barrington, Illinois, outside Chicago, staffed by more than 450 scientists and technicians and housing some 400 dogs and 600 cats. Subsidiaries in 14 other countries (Quaker does 26% of its sales outside the U.S.).

Who owns and runs the company. Family influences are still strong at Quaker. Robert D. Stuart, Jr., heads the company, just as his father did before him. Stuart's brother-in-law, Augustin S. Hart, Jr., is vice-chairman. All the Stuarts went to Princeton. Most have been active in Republican Party politics.

The Stuart family owns a little more than 1% of Quaker stock (worth about $7.5 million). The Quaker Oats profit-sharing plan is one of the largest holders, owning 3.2% of the outstanding shares. 63% of Quaker's U.S. employees are shareholders.

In the public eye. Ten years ago Quaker issued a credo that committed the company to "the highest ethical and moral standards." One out of every six employees is a minority group member. Some 15 years ago, when the city of Danville, Illinois, was being considered for a new plant, Quaker told the city that if Danville had an open housing ordinance, barring discrimination, it would impress Quaker "as an indication of the city's intent for social progress." The ordinance passed—and two days later Quaker approved the location of a new plant in Danville.

Quaker was pained in 1978 when protesters in San Francisco attacked the company and runner James Fixx for sponsoring a run under the flag of Quaker's 100% Natural cereal, which has a 21% sugar content. In his best-selling book *The Complete Book of Running,* Fixx had written that sugar "may do considerable harm." Blasted for becoming a Quaker spokesman, Fixx said: "It's a commercial country. We're all trying to make a living any way we can."

Where they're going. A new management team is in place, and it appears certain that the next chief executive officer of Quaker will not be a Stuart or the descendant of a founder. Quaker does not enjoy the same following on Wall Street that other companies do. But that may be one of their perverse strengths. They have not chased fads as much as other food processors have.

Stock performance. Quaker Oats stock bought for $1,000 in 1970 sold for $925 on January 2, 1980.

Access. Merchandise Mart Plaza, Chicago, Illinois 60654; (312) 222-7111.

Consumer Brands.

Cereals: Cap'n Crunch; 100% Natural; Life; Quaker Shredded Wheat; Quaker Puffed Wheat; Quaker Puffed Rice; Quaker Oatmeal.
Other grocery products: Aunt Jemima pancake mixes, waffles, and syrups; Celeste frozen pizza; Ken-L Ration and Puss'n Boots pet foods; Mr. Chips, Gaucho, Fudgetown, Scooter Pie, and Burry's Best cookies; Euphrates crackers.
Toys: Fisher-Price.
Needlecraft products: Wonder Art; Gold Bell; Needle Queen.
Retail outlets: Magic Pan restaurants; Badger Mills and Fixler Brothers needlecraft stores.

▓ Ralston Purina

Sales: $4.6 billion
Profits: $128 million
Forbes 500 rank: 87
Rank in food processing: 6
Rank in animal feeds: 1
Rank in dog food: 1
Rank in cat food: 1
Founded: 1894
Employees: 70,000
Headquarters: St. Louis, Missouri

What they do. Based in a state where hogs and cattle far outnumber people, Ralston Purina is primarily a feeder of animals rather than humans. Strip away animal products and Ralston Purina dwindles to a small company. Agricultural products, which include a line of 350 basic animal and poultry feeds (products that bear such names as Purina High Octane Baby Pig Chow and Purina Horse Chow Checkers), account for one-half of Ralston's total sales. Another 20% comes from pet foods. Most of the rest is contributed by restaurants and a grocery products line that includes Chicken of the Sea tuna, Chex cereals, Country Stand mushrooms, and RyKrisp and Bremner crackers and cookies.

Ralston, the world's largest producer of commercial feeds for livestock and poultry, became king of the pet food market only recently. Over the past 15 years, while the human birth rate went down, the cat and dog population soared—and pet owners were made to feel guilty about feeding their animals table scraps. Soon 50-pound bags were being wheeled into supermarkets, and pet foods occupied more space than any other food category (they were also the most profitable). At the same time, the market shifted strongly from moist items packed in cans toward dry foods—and beating the drum for this shift was Ralston Purina. For Ralston it was a bonanza. It's one thing selling feeds to farmers—the profit margins there are narrow. It's quite another thing selling pet foods in the great big consumer arena, where the margins are wide. Purina Dog Chow and Purina Cat Chow are both world market leaders.

Chow profits allowed Ralston some self-indulgence. They bought Keystone, a Rocky Mountain resort in Colorado, and a hockey team, the St. Louis Blues (more out of civic pride than anything else). They entered the floriculture business. They bought and expanded the Jack-in-the-Box hamburger chain. They opened 60 "theme" restaurants bearing such snappy names as Tortilla Flats, London Opera House, and Boar's Head. From the standpoint of stockholders who were looking for a fancy return, these were not memorable experiences. In 1979 Jack-in-the-Box conceded the entire eastern part of the country to the other hamburger chains, and the floriculture business was abandoned.

History. William H. Danforth, born in 1870 in a small town in southeast Missouri, was told by his father to "get into a business that fills a need for lots of people, something they need all year around in good times and bad." Danforth heeded that advice by opening a feed business near the St. Louis levee in 1894. He bought grains from farmers, mixed them into 175-pound sacks, and sold them back to farmers as feed for their horses and mules. Waldemar A. Nielsen, in his book *The Big Foundations*, described Danforth as "such a stereotype of the Victorian virtues of hard work, clean living, and positive thinking that he would have been a comic figure had he not been so obviously

sincere—and so successful." In the early years of the company Danforth used to lead his employees in prayer, and calisthenics, every day. He was proud of never having missed a day of work because of illness.

Danforth was deeply religious. He always carried a pocket Bible with him, and he taught Sunday school at his local church. He also happened to be a promotional genius. The *Purina* in the company's name was coined from an early Danforth slogan, "Where Purity is Paramount." Another early Danforth slogan was: "If Chicken Chowder won't make your hens lay, they must be roosters." The *Ralston* in the company's name came from a Dr. Ralston, who headed a prominent health club at the turn of the century. Danforth got him to endorse a wheat cereal. The famous *Chow* brand name was originated by Danforth after he returned from service in World War I. (He had gone to France to minister to the spiritual needs of the troops, serving as a representative of the Young Men's Christian Association, a nonmilitary role that did not prevent him from coming home with four battle stars.) He had noted the enthusiasm with which the doughboys responded to "chow call," so back in St. Louis, he replaced the word *feed* with *chow*.

The company's checkerboard symbol also came from Danforth's personal experience. He grew up near a family, the Browns, whose children always wore clothes their mother had made from distinctive red-and-white checkerboard cloth. Danforth reasoned that the checkerboard would identify his products as clearly as it had the Brown kids. So eventually it went on everything, even becoming the company's address. A man of unbounded enthusiasm, Danforth sometimes wore a red checkerboard jacket and matching socks to the office.

Danforth retired from the company in 1932—turning over the reins to his son Donald—and for the next 20 years devoted himself to the Danforth Foundation, which he and his wife had established in 1927. William Danforth died in 1952. He had also helped form the Christian Carolers Association in St. Louis in 1911 and had served as its president for 40 years. He died on Christmas eve while waiting for the singers to arrive at his home.

At that juncture, 1952, Ralston Purina was 58 years old—and its great growth was still ahead of it.

Reputation. Although they're a great big corporation today, Ralston Purina retains a preachiness inherited from their founder. There's a link to that heritage since the Danforth Foundation is the company's largest share-owner. They say they have tried "to maintain the intimacy and camaraderie often lost in a large enterprise."

What they own. A long string of feed plants throughout the United States, Canada, Latin America, and Western Europe. Eighteen pet food plants, 5 cereal plants. Nine hundred restaurants. Twelve fishing vessels and an equity interest in 25 tuna seiners. The WARF Institute, a Madison, Wisconsin, life-sciences laboratory staffed by 250 scientists, technicians, and support personnel.

Who owns and runs the company. Although Danforth family members are no longer active in the day-to-day management of the company, they still have the largest number of votes through their personal holdings and through their control of the Danforth Foundation, the company's largest shareholder. On the board are two grandsons of the founder: Donald Danforth, Jr., who is president of Danforth Agri-Resources, Inc. (a family investment company); and William H. Danforth, chancellor of Washington University in St. Louis, a major beneficiary of Danforth Foundation grants. Another grandson, John, is the junior U.S. senator from Missouri; his holdings of Ralston Purina stock, valued between $7 and $17 million (depending on the price of the stock), make him one of the wealthiest members of the Senate. Like other Danforths, he is described as somber and deeply religious. He was trained as both a minister and a lawyer.

Ralston Purina has a tradition of growing their own people. R. Hal Dean, chairman and chief executive officer since 1968, is a 40-year veteran. The top people have more than 25 years service with the company. Two former agriculture secretaries—Earl Butz and Clifford Hardin—have been directors of the company. Hardin returned to the company as vice-chairman after leaving government service. Of 60,000 U.S. employees, nearly one out of every four is a member of a minority group. The lone woman on the board is Mary Wells Law-

Food Engineering's Hall of Fame

In 1978 *Food Engineering* magazine published the 50th anniversary issue, in which they announced the Food Engineering Hall of Fame, a gallery of people who deserved recognition for advancements in food technology that have touched millions of lives. These little-known pioneers, selected by companies and trade associations, included people both active and dead. Here are 6 of the 44 tributes from *Food Engineering:*

Adolph S. Clausi, General Foods: One of Clausi's toughest assignments came in the early 1950s. In an attempt to put more enjoyment into breakfast, Clausi collaborated with another GFer, Raymond G. Mohlie, and developed "shaped" cereals. Up until then, all cereals were flaked or rounded. There wasn't any equipment capable of producing shapes—the flaking rolls flattened everything. Clausi, working with extrusion technology and a special puffing process, developed Post Brand Alpha-Bits, a cereal containing letters of the alphabet. The success of this product led the way to a whole series of different shaped cereals. Also, in the early 1950s Clausi came up with the concept for Jell-O Brand Instant Pudding, which has been a leader in its category since it was introduced nationally in 1953.

Dr. John Fogelberg, R. T. French Company: Dr. Fogelberg's employment at R. T. French spanned 39 years, beginning in 1932 and ending with his retirement in 1971. He helped to refine and develop the dehydrated potato concept into the first instant potato ever marketed anywhere in the world. He also perfected a patented method for the nitrogen packing of dehydrated potato granules in flexible pouches. This latter development in 1953 resulted in an immediate expansion of the market, laying the groundwork for the gradual national acceptance of instant potatoes as a food staple. Dr. Fogelberg also pioneered the development of dry packaged seasoning mixes such as spaghetti sauce mix, brown gravy mix, and many others. Dr. Fogelberg also holds a patent on a shark repellent which he developed for the U. S. Navy during World War II.

rence, head of an advertising agency (Wells, Rich, Green) that handled $23 million of Ralston Purina advertising in 1978.

In the public eye. The Danforth Foundation won high marks in Waldemar Nielsen's book for the caliber of its giving, which he called "creative, socially pertinent, and professionally competent." In its early years the foundation gave a lot of money to religious education; more recently it has been a major supporter of black colleges. In their home town Ralston Purina took the lead role in the LaSalle Park redevelopment project near company headquarters. During 1978 the company funded the nation's first economic education workshop for secondary level teachers of American Indians in the Southwest and also awarded grants to 28 nonprofit agencies to provide salaries for 525 summer workers. There are signs, though, that the company is beginning to chafe in this role. In a recent statement R. Hal Dean said: "We've gone for two decades on a constant trend of increasing our social concerns to the point that we are going to have to get back to economic reality. . . . How far can you go with the producers supporting the nonproducers? We're just about there."

In 1977 Ralston introduced a new presweetened cereal called Cookie-Crisp, which did so well in the marketplace that the company called it "the most successful new children's cereal introduced in the past 13 years." Cookie-Crisp was pitched to children watching TV by showing a package inside a cookie jar, a commercial that provoked the fury of the public-interest group Action for Children's Television.

Stock performance. Ralston Purina stock bought for $1,000 in 1970 sold for $1,239 on January 2, 1980.

Major employment centers. St. Louis and San Diego.

Access. Checkerboard Square, St. Louis, Missouri 63188; (314) 982-0111.

Felix Germino, Quaker Oats Company: Mr. Germino directed the development of the technology resulting in the product Tender Chunks. This dog food is widely recognized by those familiar with the field as a unique, breakthrough product. It embodies many innovations which have not previously been incorporated in a product. It is expanded, yet retains moist characteristics, remains soft over extended periods of time, and is shelf stable.

Paul Holton, Holton Food Products Company: Since the middle 50s, millions of pounds of Scrambled Egg Mix (also known as "Egg Mix, Dehydrated") have been produced by egg companies for both Military and Civilian feedings. A spray-dried powder, this scrambled egg mix has been manufactured by essentially the same process described by Paul Holton in a 1947 patent which covered the spray-drying of a homogenized blend of fresh eggs, milk, and vegetable oil to produce a fine-tasting, long-lasting product. A commercial item recently developed by Holton is an egg white product which whips up to a freeze-stable meringue topping for use by large volume pie bakeries.

John de Jonge, Banquet Foods Corporation: Some of the highlights of Mr. de Jonge's career with Banquet are the development of the past and present coatings for fried chicken, the refinement of the process by which all cuts and size ranges of chicken may be fried in the same system, and the development of proper continuous filtering systems for the frying fat.

R. E. (Bud) Miller, Kraft, Inc.: Mr. Miller has devoted his entire adult lifetime to the food industry. His greatest contribution was in the development of a system to produce individually wrapped slices of process cheese. In this endeavor, he was instrumental in the development, design, and installation of a high speed system that has become the standard for producing Kraft individually wrapped process slices worldwide.

Reprinted from *Food Engineering,* October, 1978.

Consumer brands.

Pet foods: Purina Dog, Puppy, Cat, and Kitten Chow; Chuck Wagon; Fit & Trim; Moist & Chunky; Bonz; Variety Menu; Tender Vittles; Lovin' Spoonfuls; Meow Mix; Whisker Lickins; Country Blend; Good Mews; High Protein Dog Meal.

Cereals and crackers: Rice, Wheat, Corn, and Bran Chex; Hot Ralston; Instant Ralston; Cookie-Crisp; RyKrisp.

Seafoods: Chicken of the Sea tuna and oyster stew; Van Camp's tuna.

Restaurants: Jack-in-the-Box; Boar's Head; Hungry Hunter; Stag & Hound; The Dry Dock; Barclay Jack's; Monterey Jack's; The Boat House; Tortilla Flats; London Opera House; J. W. Wheeler's; The Dock; Monterey Whaling Village; Mountain Jack's; J. Ross Browne's Whaling Station.

Hockey: St. Louis Blues.

B *Standard Brands*
INCORPORATED

Sales: $2.6 billion
Profits: $86.4 million
Forbes 500 rank: 193
Rank in food processing: 16
Rank in margarine: 1
Rank in nuts: 1
Rank in yeast: 1
Founded: 1929
Employees: 23,000
Headquarters: New York, New York

What they do. This is a curious company that has competed in the food and liquor industries by finding niches unoccupied by others. When challenged, their instinctive reaction is to give up. They have managed to do quite well over the years without being a frontrunner or registering their name with the public. They are living proof that being number 1 is not everything. A perfect example of the Standard Brands operating procedure is Chase & Sanborn coffee, one of the oldest coffee brands in America and for many years the leading brand. After World War II General Foods moved their Maxwell House brand into the ring with Chase & Sanborn. Standard Brands said "Why fight?"—and let General Foods have the market by gradually reducing the advertising support behind Chase & Sanborn. However, they continued to "milk" the brand by selling it to restaurants, where it remains a strong seller.

Standard Brands does have a long line of packaged foods and liquor products. Their most versatile brand name is Fleischmann's —it goes on yeast, margarine, bourbon, gin, vodka, and blended whiskey. They own the Planters nut business. They're the source of Baby Ruth and Butterfinger candy bars. They import Dry Sack sherry and Benedictine and B & B liqueurs. They market two California wines, Souverain and Weibel. They do a third of their business outside the United States (they own Droste Dutch chocolate), and they are especially strong in Canada, where their sales now exceed $300 million a year. Outside the consumer foods field, they own Clinton Corn Processing in Clinton, Iowa, maker of corn syrups used as sugar substitutes.

Refugees from General Electric assumed command of Standard Brands in the late 1970s. The chairman is F. Russ Johnson, ex-GE marketing executive. General Electric symbolizes everything Standard Brands was not: professional management. The new team paid $20 million to acquire a Mexican foods company; it turned out to be a loser. They introduced a line of pretzels, potato chips, corn chips, and cheese curls under the Planters label; it didn't keep Frito-Lay awake at night. And they introduced Smooth & Easy, a margarinelike stick that turns into a gravy when heated; it flopped. Standard Brands hasn't introduced a successful new product since their 1972 launch of Egg Beaters, a cholesterol-free substitute for eggs.

History. Standard Brands has roots in three companies that go back more than 100 years.

One was established in Cincinnati in 1868 by Charles Fleischmann, a Hungarian-Jewish immigrant. He joined with a distiller, James M. Gaff, to organize a company that was the first to make compressed yeast in the United States, thereby laying the groundwork for the nation's baking industry. In 1870 they also became the first company to distill gin in America. A Fleischmann descendant, Julius, later became mayor of Cincinnati. Another, Raoul, put up much of the money to launch the *New Yorker* magazine in 1925.

A second was begun in 1863 in Fort

Wayne, Indiana, where two druggists began to mix baking soda and cream of tartar to save home bakers the trouble of making their own leavening. They called their product Royal baking powder.

The third company was also started in 1863, in Boston, where two coffee and tea merchants; Caleb Chase and James Sanborn, combined their enterprises. In 1879 they became the first American company to pack roasted coffee in sealed cans.

Fleischmann, the Royal Baking Power Co., and Chase & Sanborn consolidated their forces into Standard Brands on June 28, 1929.

Fleischmann's yeast, Chase & Sanborn coffee, and Royal desserts and puddings made the company a leading food supplier to the nation during the 1930s. They sponsored one of the most popular programs in the early history of radio: the Chase & Sanborn hour starring Edgar Bergen and Charlie McCarthy.

Much of their recent growth was fueled by acquisitions: Standard Margarine (1942), Clinton Corn Processing (1956), Planters nuts (1961), and Julius Wile (1972). They recently bought all the liquor brands of American Distilling.

Reputation. Standard Brands used to be known as dull. Now they're just regarded as confused.

Who owns and runs the company. The major stockholders are banks, insurance companies, and other institutions.

In the public eye. Standard Brands withdrew their Saf-T-Pops candy from the market in 1977, citing public concern over children's consumption of refined sugar. At the same time, they introduced their new Reggie! chocolate-covered caramel-and-peanut candy bar.

Where they're going. No one knows. Perhaps you can figure out where by deciphering this statement from one of the GE alumni: "Our thesis is that Standard Brands will be able to outperform its peer companies by a rigorous discipline of differentiated allocation of resources to high potential product-market and competitive opportunities." As 1979 drew to a close, Standard Brands bought their way into a clutch of new businesses: Inver House Scotch, Bourbon Supreme, Guckenheimer blended whiskey, Tvarski vodka, El Toro tequila.

During the 1920s Curtiss (acquired by Standard Brands in 1964) promoted their Baby Ruth candy bars by using barnstorming biplanes which dropped bars on cities and towns by parachute. The bar was named not for the famous baseball player, Babe Ruth, but for President Grover Cleveland's daughter, Ruth, who was born in the White House.

Stock performance. Standard Brands stock bought for $1,000 in 1970 sold for $1,044 on January 2, 1980.

Access. 625 Madison Avenue, New York, New York 10022; (212) 759-4400.

Consumer brands.

Grocery products: Planters and Southern Bell nuts and nuts products; Blue Bonnet and Fleischmann's margarines; Royal gelatins and puddings; Pinata; Latolteca and Chapala Mexican foods; No-Bake cheese cake; Chase & Sanborn coffee; Tender Leaf tea; Egg Beaters egg substitute.

Pet foods: Hunt Club; Burger Bits; Walter Kendall; and Fives.

Candies: Curtiss; Baby Ruth; Butterfinger; Reggie!; Droste; Coconut Grove; Saf-T-Pops; Melville; Pearson; and Wayne Bun.

Spirits: Fleischmann's Preferred whisky; Fleischmann's Gin and Royal vodka; Canadian Ltd Canadian whisky; Capercaillie and Churchill scotch whiskies; Garnier cordials and brandy; Gaston de Lagrange cognacs; Amaretto di Amore; Fonda Blanca White and Gold tequilas; Trigo White and Gold rums; White Tavern vodka, gin and whisky; Duval vermouths; Benedictine D.O.M.; Cafe Benedictine; Comandon and Delamain cognacs; Lemon Hart rums; Montesquiou armagnac; Montgommery calvados; Get Pippermint and Suze aperitif; Pernod liqueur; Inver House scotch whisky; Burbon Supreme; Guckenheimer branded whisky; Tvarski vodka; Burton's gin; El Toro tequila; Piping Rock cordials; Droste chocolate liqueur; and Cockspur rum.

Wines: Weibel; French Kiss; William Alsatian; Antinori; Bollinger; Chanson; Deinhard; Langlois-Chateau; Leacock Madeiras; Prats Freres; Robertson's port; St. Raphael; Ste. Roseline; Souverain; Dry Sack; Lily Marlene Liebfraumilch; Cherry Elsinore; and Williams & Humbert.

Beer: Moosehead Ale; Pilsner Urguell; Dos Equis; Superior; Whitbread Ale; Mackeson Stout; Skol Beer; and Foster's Lager Beer.

> The average American chomped his or her way through 15.4 pounds of candy last year. The figure sent waves of alarm through the candy industry: it was the lowest per capita consumption since 1938 and more than five pounds below consumption in 1968.

UB United Brands

Sales: $3.5 billion
Profits: $21.4 million
Forbes 500 rank: 135
Rank in food processing: 7
Rank in bananas: 2
Rank in meat packing: 3
Founded: 1871
Employees: 48,000
Headquarters: New York, New York

What they do. When Wallace Booth took over as president of United Brands in 1975, he said, "It's important that I don't get too knowledgeable about the past." If ever there was a company with good reason to keep its skeletons in the closet, United Brands is it. As the United Fruit Company, they were the largest private landowner in several countries and a major economic and political force in Latin America for decades. Their habit of overthrowing unfriendly governments and installing regimes more to their liking gave rise to the term *banana republics.* If storms or disease battered one area, United Fruit would pick up and move to another spot on the several million acres they controlled, taking with them all their telephone lines, bridges, and workers' houses.

For United Fruit it was all part of the job of producing four out of every five bananas sold in the United States. United Brands is no longer the top banana seller in America (Castle & Cooke's Dole is), but they are still first worldwide. Their Chiquita brand is a household word in Europe as well as the United States. They grow their own bananas on plantations in Panama, Honduras, and Costa Rica, and buy them from other growers in Colombia, Ecuador, Mexico, and the Philippines.

Though bananas account for some 70% of the company's profits, they make up only about one-third of their sales. United Brands also grows oil palms in Central America, lettuce in California and Arizona (Sun Harvest), melons in Honduras, and house plants in Florida. Since 1966 they have owned A & W, the root-beer maker that pioneered the drive-in restaurant concept. They also own John Morrell & Co., which markets a wide line of processed meats under its own label as well as regional brands like Chicago's Scott Peterson-

Saratoga and San Francisco's Bob Ostrow. In Central America they make margarine and salad oil for the Latin American market, as well as plastic film to keep bugs off the banana plants. Their TRT Telecommunications, which started in Latin America as Tropical Radio Telegraph, now carries telex messages between the United States and Europe, Asia, and Central America.

History. Bananas were a strange and exotic fruit in America in 1870, when Captain Lorenzo Baker first steered a shipload of them into Boston harbor and a merchant named Robert Preston sold them to the town's more adventurous citizens. Preston and Baker formed the Boston Fruit Company in 1885, buying bananas in Jamaica for 25¢ a stem and selling them up and down the East Coast for $2 to $4 from a group of 11 company ships called the Great White Fleet (white to reflect the sun and keep the fruit cool). In 1899 Boston Fruit merged with three banana companies controlled by Minor C. Keith, an insolvent railroad tycoon who had set up three banana plantations along his railroad line in Costa Rica. Under the new business, United Fruit Company, the Great White Fleet grew to 95 ships, and Keith laid down a vast railway network across Central America (at the eventual cost of thousands of workers' lives).

United Fruit solidified their hold on the U.S. and European banana markets in 1930, when they bought their main competitor, the Cuyamel Fruit Company, from Samuel Zemurry, known as Sam the Banana Man. Twenty years earlier Zemurry had helped overthrow the government of Honduras, which had made the mistake of trying to impose duties on his banana operations there. Now he became United Fruit's largest stockholder. In 1932, when the price of the stock dropped, Zemurry protested to the Brahmin board of directors, whose ranks included representatives of such old-guard Boston families as the Coolidges, Jeffersons, and Channings. Daniel G. Wing, chairman of the First National Bank of Boston, replied disdainfully that he could not understand Zemurry's thick Russian accent. Sam the Banana Man stormed out, returned later with a fistful of proxies, and voted himself president. By the time he stepped down in 1950, United Fruit owned more than 3 million acres of land in Latin

America. In Cuba Angel Castro and his sons Raoul and Fidel worked on a United Fruit Company sugar plantation.

United Fruit helped to engineer the overthrow of the government of Guatemala in 1954, after the leftist leader Jacobo Arbenz Guzman began to make noises about expropriating their plantations. The company launched a public relations barrage to persuade the American press the Kremlin was on the march in Guatemala, and the CIA sponsored a "revolution" in which the invaders used United Fruit Company boats to transport troops and ammunition. United Fruit also supplied two ships for the less successful Bay of Pigs invasion in 1961.

Once the pride of Boston, United Fruit fell in 1969 into the hands of a lonely crusader, Eli Black, a former rabbinical student who used his knowledge of balance sheets to build a comglomerate with a social conscience. Black started with a small bottle-cap company, American Seal-Kap, from which base he took over the much larger Morrell meat business, naming his new holding company AMK. Then, borrowing heavily on his newly acquired assets, Black gained control of United Fruit, renaming his holding company United Brands. As leader of United Brands, Black built houses for banana plantation workers and sold them at half cost, set up schools and hospitals, doled out interest-free loans and free medical care, and raised wages to twice what his workers could get elsewhere. On his visits to the banana realms he often lectured local leaders on their social responsibilities. In California Black's Sun Harvest subsidiary became one of the first growers to sign with Cesar Chavez's United Farm Workers.

Then, in 1975, Eli Black smashed the plate glass window in his office on the 44th floor of New York's Pan Am building, threw out his briefcase, and leaped to his death. At the time it seemed as if Black was despondent that his company had lost $44 million the previous year, after Hurricane Fifi had wiped out two-thirds of their banana crop in Honduras. One week later, however, the story broke that Black had paid $1.25 million to a Swiss bank account on behalf of the president of Honduras in exchange for getting a $1-a-box banana export tax reduced to 25¢. By extending the bribe, United Brands had driven a wedge into the newly formed OPEC-style alliance among Honduras, Costa Rica, Panama,

I'm Chiquita Banana

The United Fruit Company's introduction of the Chiquita banana was one of the century's major marketing coups. It seems no one had ever thought of putting a brand name on each individual banana. [When United Fruit did it, they became the world's largest user of pressure-sensitive labels.] Following the Chiquita brand came the Chiquita song ("I'm Chiquita Banana, and I'm here to reveal . . ."), a vaguely Calypso-style ditty that made the hit parade and found its way onto most of the country's juke boxes.

Flushed with success, the Madison Avenue wizards went on to play up the obvious sexual inferences with scenes like Miss Chiquita dancing with a giant banana. In the 1950s they came up with an ad that showed a banana standing on end, with a red circle drawn around its base and a vertical vector indicating eight inches. "What does a banana have to be to be a Chiquita?" read the copy. "It's sort of like passing the physical to become a Marine . . . right height . . . a good 8 inches along the outer curve . . . at least 1¼ inches across the middle . . . plump . . . the peel has to fit tightly. The banana has to be sleek, and firm." The ad ran in several women's magazines before *Life* magazine caught on and refused insertion.

Guatemala, and Colombia, who had joined together in declaring the $1 tax. Two weeks after the story surfaced the government of Honduras toppled in a military coup, and United Brands stock fell to its lowest level of the century.

Reputation. United Brands is seen as still trying to sort out the disarray and get their house in order.

What they own. 110,000 acres of banana and oil palm plantations, primarily in Costa Rica and Honduras. Forty banana boats. Nine meat slaughtering and processing plants in the Midwest.

Who owns and runs the company. Two brothers, Seymour and Paul Milstein, are in charge of the rescue operation. They own 14% of the stock and have backing from a group that controls another 36%. In that group are the reclusive Cincinnati financier Carl Lindner, the Detroit industrialist Max M. Fisher, and the Detroit real estate baron Alfred Taubman.

In the public eye. Hastened by threats of expropriation from local governments, United Brands follows a more responsible course today in Latin America. In Panama, they sold 100,000 acres to the government for $1.50 an acre, leasing back 39,000 acres for $2 million a year. (This deal moved General Omar Torrijos, the Panamanian chief of state, to toast company president Wallace Booth as a "good gringo.") They made similar deals in Honduras and Costa Rica—and they sold all their banana plantations in Guatemala to Del Monte to satisfy a long-standing antitrust action.

Where they're going. The best bet is that the Milsteins will move United Brands into other businesses—probably by acquisition.

Stock performance. United Brands stock bought for $1,000 in 1970 sold for $473 on January 2, 1980.

Major employment centers. Morrell plants in Sioux Falls, South Dakota; East St. Louis, Illinois; and Arkansas City, Kansas.

Access. 1271 Avenue of the Americas, New York, New York 10020; (212) 397-4000.

Consumer brands.

Bananas: Chiquita; Fyffes; Amigos.
Meat and meat products: John Morrell; Broadcast; Tom Sawyer; Bob Ostrow; Scott Peterson-Saratoga; Peyton; Hunter, Partridge; Rodeo; E-Z Beef.
Foliage plants: Full-O-Life.
Restaurant and root beer: A & W.

Consumption of bottled water has tripled since 1968. 75% of domestic bottled water is reprocessed tap water.

Wilson Foods

Sales: $2.3 billion
Pretax profit: $23.7 million
Rank in meat packing: 4
Founded: 1853
Employees: 10,000
Headquarters: Oklahoma City, Oklahoma

What they do. Wilson puts more pork on American tables than any other company. Lamb, too (but Americans are not big lamb eaters). Wilson also packs beef and veal. Their main raw material is livestock. Animals are slaughtered and processed at 15 plants and sold as fresh meats or as packaged specialties—ham, bacon, frankfurters, sausages, and luncheon meats sold nationally under the Wilson Certified and Wilson Corn King labels. Wilson meats are sold regionally under the Fischer's label in Kentucky, the Briggs label in the Washington-Baltimore area, and the Nepco (New England Provision Company) label in New England. In 1978 they began supplying precooked pork sausages to McDonald's.

Fresh meats represent 70% of Wilson's $2 billion business—and that's the trouble. Selling commodities is not as profitable as selling brand-name packaged goods as is the case for a meat packer like Oscar Mayer. Wilson has been a major meat supplier to America for more than a century and has little to show for it—in profitability (zero in 1978), public recognition (Wilson is not a well-known brand name), or independence (since 1967 they have been a subsidiary of LTV Corporation).

In the meat-packing industry Wilson ranks behind Iowa Beef Processors, Swift (now part of Esmark), and Armour (now part of Greyhound).

History. Wilson was one of the early Chicago meat packers, ranking third in the infamous "big four"—Swift, Armour, Wilson, and Cudahy—that came to be known as the "meat trust." They all operated out of the sprawling, odorous Union Stockyards built by the railroads to receive the hogs and cattle grown on Midwest farms. Wilson was the first of the big packers to close down their ancient slaughterhouses in Chicago and move them closer to the sources of supply. In 1917 Wilson's meat business was large enough to place it among the 50 largest industrial corporations in the land. Wilson had also developed two profitable sidelines: sporting goods and pharmaceuticals, both of them by-products of meat packing (footballs made of pigskins, tennis rackets made of guts, hormones and steroid drugs derived from animal organs). As they used to say in the Chicago stockyards, to make out you had to process everything but the squeal. It was this tripartite package that attracted entrepreneur Jim Ling as he was building his Ling-Temco-Vought (LTV) conglomerate in the mid-1960s. Ling decided to move on Wilson in 1966. Stanley Brown described in his 1972 biography, *Ling*, what happened when Clyde Skeen, president of Ling-Temco-Vought, flew to Chicago and met on December 21, 1966, with Roscoe Haynie, president of Wilson:

> Haynie had no idea why Skeen wanted to see him, and for the first few minutes of their brief first encounter it seemed as though Skeen had come to discuss Wilson golf clubs with him. Then Skeen told him why he had asked for the meeting and Haynie was furious, as any man would be when first told a plan was in the works to take over his company.

Unbeknown to Haynie, the plan was already far advanced before Skeen got to his office. Ling and his cohorts had spent the previous two days in New York lining up the money. They were prepared to offer $62.50 a share for Wilson stock that was then selling for $49.50, and had never sold higher than $57.87. Wilson's management held little of the stock. The visit to Haynie was mostly a courtesy call. By January 5, 1967, Wilson was bagged. Haynie, swallowing his pride, moved to Dallas and became Ling's chief lieutenant, overseeing the Wilson operations.

Ling's first move after the acquisition was to split Wilson into three parts—Wilson & Co. (meat), Wilson Sporting Goods, and Wilson Pharmaceutical & Chemical—and sell pieces of each to the public. On Wall Street they were nicknamed Meatball, Golfball, and Goofball. It was a case of the parts being worth more than the whole. Before long LTV's majority interest in these three companies had a market value much greater than what Ling had paid for the whole Wilson shebang.

Reputation. By 1970 the bubble burst: Ling-Temco-Vought almost collapsed under a mountain of debts. It was eventually restructured minus Jim Ling and minus the Wilson sporting goods and drug operations. Still there—some say like an albatross—is the Wilson meat business, grinding out lots of sales dollars and puny, if any, profits.

What they own. Wilson has meat-packing plants in Colorado, Georgia, Illinois, Indiana, Iowa, Kentucky, Minnesota, Missouri, and Oklahoma. They also own 2 meat plants in New Zealand. The Wilson-owned buildings cover 2.4 million square feet.

Who owns and runs the company. LTV now owns all the stock of Wilson Foods. Kenneth J. Griggy has been president and chief executive officer of Wilson since 1975. He had previously been president of a Texas rice company, Riviana Foods, and before that was with Ralston Purina.

In the public eye. Wilson modified their bacon processing procedures in 1978 to make sure not to exceed the nitrite levels—no more than 120 parts per million—specified by the U.S. Department of Agriculture.

Where they're going. Wilson wants to become more consumer-oriented, so they're emphasizing brand-name products. They recently introduced a line of Continental Deli products, 38 meat specialties representing the cuisines of 14 different countries (French cervelat, Italian pepperoni, German braunschweiger, etc.). Each item is packaged with a label bearing the colors of the flag of the country it represents, a move that brings to mind Jimmy Carter's 1979 comment that the United States is not so much a "melting pot as minestrone."

Access. 4545 North Lincoln Boulevard, Oklahoma City, Oklahoma 73126; (405) 525-4545.

Consumer brands.

Wilson, Certified, Corn King, Western Style, Briggs, Fischer, Nepco, Continental Deli, and Thomas E. Wilson Masterpiece meats.

TOP 50 CORPORATE COOKS

Annual Food Sales

1. KRAFT $5.44 *billion*
2. BEATRICE FOODS $5.37 *billion*
3. GENERAL FOODS $4.74 *billion*
4. COCA-COLA $4.12 *billion*
5. ESMARK $4.05 *billion*
6. RALSTON PURINA $3.57 *billion*
7. UNITED BRANDS $3.47 *billion*
8. CONSOLIDATED FOODS $3.25 *billion*
9. CPC INTERNATIONAL $3.02 *billion*
10. IOWA BEEF $2.97 *billion*
11. PEPSICO $2.93 *billion*
12. GREYHOUND (*Armour meats*) $2.75 *billion*
13. ANHEUSER-BUSCH $2.40 *billion*
14. H. J. HEINZ $2.40 *billion*
15. SEAGRAMS $2.36 *billion*
16. STANDARD BRANDS $2.36 *billion*
17. CAMPBELL SOUP $2.20 *billion*
18. LTV (*Wilson Foods*) $2.19 *billion*
19. CARNATION $2.19 *billion*
20. PHILIP MORRIS (*Miller Brewing, 7-up*) $2.14 *billion*
21. BORDEN $2.13 *billion*
22. PROCTER & GAMBLE (*Folger's, Duncan Hines*) $2.06 *billion*
23. GENERAL MILLS $2.06 *billion*
24. ARCHER-DANIELS-MIDLAND $2.02 *billion*
25. NABISCO $1.97 *billion*
26. RJR INDUSTRIES (*Del Monte*) $1.92 *billion*
27. NESTLÉ (*Libby*) $1.77 *billion*
28. ITT (*Continental Baking, Morton Frozen Foods*) $1.70 *billion*
29. KELLOGG $1.69 *billion*
30. HEUBLEIN $1.49 *billion*
31. ASSOCIATED MILK PRODUCERS $1.48 *billion*
32. ANDERSON, CLAYTON $1.46 *billion*
33. CENTRAL SOYA $1.36 *billion*
34. NORTON SIMON $1.35 *billion*
35. OSCAR MAYER $1.34 *billion*
36. GEORGE A. HORMEL $1.20 *billion*
37. CASTLE & COOKE $1.13 *billion*
38. JOS. SCHLITZ BREWING $1.08 *billion*
39. PILLSBURY $993 *million*
40. QUAKER OATS $985 *million*
41. A.E. STALEY $983 *million*
42. IC INDUSTRIES (*Pet*) $959 *million*
43. KANE-MILLER $959 *million*
44. LAND O'LAKES $920 *million*
45. INTERNATIONAL MULTIFOODS $916 *million*
46. CAMPBELL TAGGART $885 *million*
47. AMSTAR $879 *million*
48. FEDERAL $857 *million*
49. FOREMOST-McKESSON $821 *million*
50. ADOLPH COORS $747 *million*

Source: *Food Processing*, December 1979.

Farmers and Food Brokers

Anderson Clayton

Sales: $1.5 billion
Profits: $48.8 million
Forbes 500 rank: 339
Rank in food processing: 32
Founded: 1904
Employees: 15,000
Headquarters: Houston, Texas

What they do. When cotton was king, William Lockhart Clayton, who had been born to a cotton farmer, raised in poverty, and schooled in the backwoods, was emperor. His company, Anderson, Clayton & Co., was for decades the largest cotton company in the world, known in the trade as the "big store." In 1951 the "store" did over $1 billion dollars business in cotton alone, a record never to be surpassed, as natural fibers came to be largely replaced by synthetics.

Today Anderson, Clayton makes many different kinds of food products, emphasizing vegetable oils and related items. After a banner year in 1951 Anderson, Clayton bought Mrs. Tucker's foods and started making margarine and shortening. From there they launched Seven Seas salad dressings, imitation cheeses, and Chiffon soft margarine, the original and best-selling soft margarine. Anderson, Clayton's moves from commodities tied to cyclical swings in the market toward consumer foods was explained by former executive Claude Fuqua: "Food profits rise as you come closer to the table." Besides the table, Anderson, Clayton serves in other areas: insurance (Ranger/Pan American Insurance and Ameri-

can Founders Life Insurance), warehousing (Gulf Atlantic Distribution Services), and materials handling (Long Reach). They are the largest crusher of cottonseed oil in the United States. Meal from the crushed seeds are processed into animal and poultry feeds. In 1967 they purchased Tomco Genetic Giant, expanding their original business of hybrid corn to include sorghum and cotton.

History. In the company history of Anderson, Clayton the only reference to William Clayton's youth is that he won the Tennessee state shorthand writing contest in 1895. Nine years after that signal event Clayton joined with his brother-in-law, Frank E. Anderson, and with Frank's brother Monroe to form Anderson, Clayton & Co., a cotton merchant partnership based in Oklahoma City. Before World War I cotton was a European industry tightly controlled by monied interests that maintained bulging warehouses close to the textile mills in England, France, and Germany. The United States was simply a source of raw materials, and Anderson, Clayton sold directly to the Europeans. When war threatened Europe, it was Clayton who realized the long-term implications for American cotton. He moved his warehouses to Houston, the front door of the cotton market, and obtained loans to build warehouses, compresses, and shipping terminals. The plan paid off handsomely. As the United States moved from a debtor to a creditor nation, and as banking moved from London to New York, the well-financed Clayton began selling directly to the European textile mills, by-passing the old trading houses, and made tremendous profits in the bull market that followed the war. It was a lesson Will Clayton would not forget.

Flush with cash, Anderson, Clayton expanded across the Southwest, buying cotton gins and oil crushing plants. In 1921 they began similar operations in Mexico, and in 1934 they began pressing cotton in Brazil. The move to Brazil was prompted by the protective tariffs adopted by the Roosevelt administration during the Depression. European nations, angered by the duties, began buying cotton from other countries. By switching operations to Brazil, Anderson, Clayton avoided the de facto boycott and continued to market cotton. From 1935 to 1940 Brazil enjoyed a cotton boom, and Anderson, Clayton made enormous profits. During World War II cotton sales to Europe stopped, however, and the Brazilian government stepped in to buy the unsold cotton at support prices. By the time the war ended, the Brazilian government was selling cotton to governmental agencies in Europe, and Anderson, Clayton was left without any market to be a middleman in.

The problem began to be solved in 1944, when Clayton was appointed undersecretary of state for economic affairs under Roosevelt. William Lockhart Clayton is credited with creating the Marshall Plan, a windfall for his company. During the New Deal cotton had become a subsidized crop, pricing U.S. cotton out of world markets. Without their Brazilian supplies on the one hand, and strapped by expensive American cotton on the other, Anderson, Clayton needed a way out. The Marshall Plan supplied the countries of Western Europe with the credit they needed to buy goods. And the Plan gave American business an overwhelming advantage in Europe since credits could be spent only on U.S. products. Cotton was given a high priority because textile mills provided both clothing and jobs.

As the world's largest supplier of cotton, Anderson, Clayton benefited enormously. Meanwhile, Brazil could not sell its cotton, and the industry faltered and slowly shrank. As cotton was waning in Brazil, Anderson, Clayton invested in vegetable oils, consumer products, and finally, in 1958, coffee, becoming one of the world's leading exporters of green coffee. (They sell more than 40% of their green coffee to one customer: General Foods.)

By the mid-sixties cotton was no longer a growth industry, and Anderson, Clayton began phasing out of it. They sold 300 of 450 cotton gins and disposed of their steamship company, terminals, and warehouses. They discontinued about $45 million dollars of loans to cotton farmers and, to add to their kitty, sold equity in some of the Mexican and Brazilian food companies. As the cash piled up, they purchased 15 companies in eight years. Two they sought to acquire resisted, however—Stokely-Van Camp and Gerber's both fought Anderson, Clayton's takeover bids and won. It is assumed that Anderson, Clayton is still looking for a major acquisition to add to the nest.

Reputation. The company has put forth a strongly worded philosophy: "In all [the company's] business relationships conformance to the highest standard of ethics is a requirement so firmly established and well-recognized that alternatives are not seriously considered or discussed. . . . Likewise, in governmental relationships, whether in the legislative or regulatory area, the company seeks no special privileges or favors. . . ." In 1976 the *Wall Street Journal* reported that Anderson, Clayton made $2.1 million in "questionable payments" to foreign nations.

What they own. In the United States Anderson, Clayton owns 9 oilseed crushing plants, 3 vegetable oil refineries, 94 cotton gins, 4 cotton compresses, 6 edible food processing plants, 3 commercial farms, 1 hatchery, 6 animal feed mills, 9 seed processing plants, and 21 commodity warehouses. Most of their plants are in the South and the Southwest.

Who owns and runs the company. The Clayton family owns 29% of the outstanding shares (worth about $85 million), controlled by directors S. M. McAshan, Jr., William Garwood, W. St. John Garwood, Jr., Dr. Benjamin M. Baker, Jr., and Burke Baker, Jr., all of whom are related by marriage to the founder. Another director is Leon Jaworski, the Watergate special prosecutor.

Where they're going. As Anderson, Clayton gradually got out of the cotton business, they preferred a new company philosophy that they would not be involved with a business that was outside the control of management, based on the weather, or subject to government edict. What does that leave? Imitation dairy products. "The cow is very inefficient," says Robert McDonald, president of Anderson, Clayton's food division. He is supported by T. J. Barlow, the chief executive officer, who says: "Everything the cow makes can be made from vegetable oil and vegetable protein, and that's what we want to do."

Stock performance. Anderson, Clayton stock bought for $1,000 in 1970 sold for $2,353 on January 2, 1980.

Access. 1010 Milam, Houston, Texas 77002; (713) 651-0641.

Consumer brands.

Margarines: Chiffon; Meadolake; Grayson; Hollandale; Log Cabin; Velvet; Flair; Golden Mist; Accolade.
Shortenings and salad dressings: Seven Seas; Mrs. Tucker's; Jaxmor; Capri; Unique; Velvet; Gleam; Flair; E-Z Flo; Lik-Wid; Fryo; Liquifry; Kerba; Meva; Southern Queen; Nylene.
Cheese and cheese substitutes: Hoffman's; Purity Maybud; Woody's; Unique Loaf.

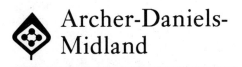

Archer-Daniels-Midland

Sales: $2.3 billion
Profits: $56.4 million
Forbes 500 rank: 231
Rank in flour milling: 3
Rank in soybean processing: 2
Founded: 1902
Employees: 5,254
Headquarters: Decatur, Illinois

What they do. Archer-Daniels-Midland sits in the middle of the Midwest farm belt, headquartered in the same central Illinois city as competitor A. E. Staley. They buy crops, chiefly soybeans, wheat, and corn, and convert them into ingredients used in animal and human foods. But hardly any of ADM's several hundred agricultural products are marketed directly to consumers, either human or animal: the company sells to

food processors, animal feed manufacturers, and commercial bakers.

ADM's biggest business is the pale yellow soybean, one of America's principal farm crops. Soybean oil is used in margarine, shortening, salad oil, and other food products. It was ADM that first developed edible soy protein in 1930, and the company is now the leading marketer of textured vegetable protein, which is used as a meat extender and meat substitute. ADM also mills wheat into flour and refines corn into syrups, starches, high-fructose sweeteners, and the alcohol used in gasohol.

History. ADM descended from a clutch of small midwestern companies that processed farm products. The earliest was Daniels Linseed, founded in 1902 to make flax seed into linseed oil, the yellowish drying oil that is used in paints, varnishes, and castor oil (and that ADM still manufactures). But they were a sleepy, little-noticed company until they recruited a free-wheeling Minnesota farmer-businessman named Dwayne Andreas to take over in 1965. Andreas stepped up ADM's soybean crushing operations, sold off a money-losing chemical business to Ashland Oil, and bought a number of companies: Fleischman Malting (1967), the National City Bank of Minneapolis (1969), Corn Sweeteners (1971), Supreme Sugar (1973), and Tabor & Co., a grain merchant (1975).

Reputation. ADM is a secretive company that releases information only with great reluctance. When Andreas took over, he eliminated a 27-person public relations department.

What they own. ADM has 60 plants in the United States, including 11 flour mills, 10 soybean processing plants, 4 corn milling plants, and a number of grain elevators.

Who owns and runs the company.
Dwayne Andreas and his family own more than 11% of ADM's stock; another 13% is held by other directors. ADM's 13-man board includes three members of the Andreas family, one Archer, one Daniels, and a Tabor. ADM's processing operations are highly automated, thus requiring only a small work force. *Fortune* has observed that "all ADM executives are fanatic about keeping down labor costs." No new salaried position can be created without written authorization of the president.

In the public eye. A friend of the late Senator Hubert Humphrey, Andreas was in charge of the "blind trust" set up for Humphrey when he became vice-president in 1965. Some ADM stock was later transferred from the trust to Humphrey's 1972 presidential campaign, according to a 1974 Senate Watergate Committee report. Andreas also contributed to President Nixon's reelection effort, including a $25,000 cash gift that was, unbeknownst to Andreas, funneled to a Watergate burglar. Andreas is not a stereotypical conservative corporate executive. He has also contributed to Martin Luther King, Jr.'s Southern Christian Leadership Conference, the Americans for Democratic Action, and the American Civil Liberties Union, and has been known to advocate increases in the corporate income tax rate.

Where they're going. With beef prices rising steadily, ADM can be expected to benefit from the company's strong position in soybeans, which are increasingly being used as a major source of protein. Also potentially very profitable is gasohol, a motor fuel containing alcohol derived from agricultural crops and gasoline. ADM was the first of the corn refiners to move into any substantial production of gasohol. In the banking business they're going nowhere,

however. Since Andreas bought the Minneapolis bank, the ownership laws have been changed, and the company must divest itself of the bank by 1981.

Stock performance. ADM stock bought for $1,000 in 1970 sold for $8,425 on January 2, 1980.

Access. 4666 Faries Parkway, Decatur, Illinois 62525; (217) 424-5200.

Consumer brand.

Gooch Foods pastas.

Cargill

Sales $11.3 billion
Profits: $121 million
Rank in grain trading: 1
Rank in soybean processing: 4
Founded: 1865
Employees: 24,000
Headquarters: Minnetonka, Minnesota

What they do. Hardly anyone has heard of Cargill, though it is the world's biggest agribusiness company and one of the largest companies in the nation. They do not make well-known consumer products or operate stores. None of their stock is held by the public, which means zero visibility on Wall Street. What they do is buy grains —corn and wheat—from farmers and sell them on world markets. And in this business they're number 1. Cargill has a profound effect on what farmers get for crops and what consumers pay for bread and meat.

As a privately owned company, Cargill is not ranked by *Forbes* or *Fortune* with other big corporations. If they were, they would place 18th in sales among all U.S. companies. Cargill's sales are larger than those of any U.S. food processor. Through their hands go as much as a quarter of the corn and wheat exported from the United States, making Cargill the biggest single contributor to the plus side of the U.S. balance of trade ledger. Cargill operates on an enormous scale. They have access to $1 billion of prime-rate credit to finance grain pur-

> Texas has the most farms in the U.S. (197,000) and the most farmland (140.6 million acres). Missouri has the next highest number of farms (133,000), followed by Iowa (128,000), Illinois (117,000), and Kentucky (117,000). There are a total of about 2.7 million farms in the United States.

chases. Their 140 foreign subsidiaries and affiliates run plants and offices in 38 countries. They own and lease 5,000 rail cars, 500 river barges, and 14 ocean-going ships. Each of their 345 storage elevators can hold enough grain to make six loaves of bread for every person in the United States; together they hold a total of 300 million bushels of grain.

Until 1948 Cargill's only business was grain. But today grain represents less than 40% of their business. Cargill processes soybeans, refines corn, mills flour, produces animal feeds, mines salt, makes steel, sells fertilizers, processes poultry and other meats, trades commodities for clients, manufactures chemicals, builds their own ships, makes vegetable oils, and underwrites insurance. In 1978 they put $75 million on the table to outbid a public company, Omaha's ConAgra, and acquire MBPXL, the nation's second-largest meat packer. Now, as Dan Morgan points out in his book *Merchants of Grain*, Americans "eat steak cut from animals fattened on Cargill grain in Cargill feedlots and slaughtered in a Cargill packing house." And it can be seasoned with Leslie salt, another business Cargill bought in 1978 for $30 million.

History. The company started in 1865 with one grain warehouse in Conover, Iowa, operated by William Cargill, the son of a retired Scottish sea captain who had settled his family on a Wisconsin farm. As the western wheat fields opened up with the coming of rail lines after the Civil War, William Cargill and his brothers were there with the right product: grain elevators or warehouses to store the crops. They opened elevators in the Iowa, Wisconsin, and Minnesota farm fields. William Cargill made his headquarters in La Crosse, Wisconsin, where he lived across the street from another Scottish Presbyterian family, the MacMillans. His eldest daughter married John High MacMillan in 1895, and his eldest son also married a MacMillan. The Cargills and the MacMillans have ruled this grain company ever since.

History was on their side. The need to store crops became crucial as farm population declined while farm output, spurred by technology, soared. It was a situation made to order for the middleman, and Cargill grew to be the biggest middleman of them all.

Reputation. Cargill is secretive but they are not regarded as speculators. Although they operate in a field where gambling on price fluctuations is rampant, they play it safe: they seek a middleman's, not a speculator's, profit.

What they own. Cargill's assets exceed $3.25 billion. In addition to their agribusiness holdings, they own a life insurance company, Summit National, and a commodity brokerage house, Cargill Investor Services (where customers are free to speculate).

Who owns and runs the company. 85% of the stock is owned by 33 members of the Cargill and MacMillan families and the Cargill Foundation; the rest by Cargill executives.

There are no directors from outside the company. The chairman is Whitney MacMillan, grandson of John H. MacMillan.

Cargill is headquartered in a 63-room replica of a French chateau on a 250-acre estate 12 miles from downtown Minneapolis. About 130 persons work in the chateau, which still has 13 working fireplaces. Another 1,000 more employees work in an adjoining building. One large drawing room of the chateau serves as a Cargill nerve center, where more than two dozen traders watch an electronic board spew out the latest commodity price quotations. Nearby teletype machines clatter away, receiving information from Cargill offices around the world. The traders are constantly on the phone, buying and selling commodities that mean food for a hungry world.

The *Wall Street Journal* visited the chateau and found that senior executives keep their doors open and "mingle easily with other employees." *Forbes* magazine visited and said, "For all its growth, the company has maintained an informal—almost a family company—style."

In the public eye. Minneapolis has one of the most progressive business communities in America, but Cargill is invisible there. The MacMillans and Cargills have been called "clannish Scotsmen." As author Dan Morgan said, "They have long been considered standoffish by the gregarious, civic-minded citizens of Minneapolis."

Secrecy is a way of life in the grain trade,

where information is the key to buying and selling decisions. But Cargill has had difficulty maintaining that tradition lately. In 1972, when a large portion of the U.S. wheat crop was sold to the Russians and bread prices in the supermarkets leapt high, Cargill came under sharp fire from farmers who felt they didn't get the best price for their crops. Calling their first press conference ever, Cargill announced that they had actually lost money on the Russian deal. The few details that are known about Cargill's operations and finances were squeezed out of the company in recent years by a Senate committee investigating multinational corporations and by the Securities and Exchange Commission, which looked into Cargill's acquisition of MBPXL.

Where they're going. The question is how big Cargill can get and still remain a privately owned, family-run corporation. Some financial observers are betting that Cargill will emerge from the 1980s as a publicly held firm.

Major employment center. Minneapolis.

Access. 15407 West McGinty Road, Minnetonka, Minnesota 55343; (612) 475-7575.

Consumer brands:

Nutrena animal feed; Paramount, Honeysuckle, Riverside, and Medallion poultry; Light Crust flour; Leslie salt.

Central Soya

Sales: $2.4 billion
Profits: $33.6 million
Forbes 500 rank: 209
Rank in lecithin: 1
Founded: 1934
Employees: 9,100
Headquarters: Fort Wayne, Indiana

What they do. Central Soya crushes soybeans, merchandises grain, produces animal feeds, and turns out over 100 million chickens and turkeys a year. Annually, they produce 3.5 million tons of feed, and store 75 million bushels of grain. Though their operations are central to the food business, the only products they sell directly to consumers are Mrs. Filberts margarines and salad dressings. Central Soya products are common in lists of ingredients, especially lecithin, a widely used emulsifier.

History. Dale W. McMillen, who operated a grain elevator in Fort Wayne, founded Central Soya in 1934. McMillen pioneered the processing of soybeans in America with a German solvent process that extracted 95% of the oil in the soybean. It took five years to get the machine working properly, but when it did, Central Soya was ready to participate in the forthcoming soybean boom. McMillen died in 1978 at age 91.

Reputation. Central Soya remains the middleman between the farmer and the rest of the food chain. They own no land, and they do not engage in commodity speculation. They have registered for themselves the trademark, "The Foodpower People."

What they own. Eight soybean processing plants in the Midwest. Thirty-four feed plants across the country. One hundred seventy seven river barges.

Who owns and runs the company. Solid midwestern folk. Dale W. McMillen, Jr., is chairman of the executive committee. The McMillens remain the largest individual stockholders with more than 3% of the stock.

In the public eye. Fort Wayne is dotted with McMillen gifts, including a park and a library at the Indiana Institute of Technology.

Stock performance. Central Soya stock bought for $1,000 in 1970 sold for $970 on January 2, 1980.

Major employment centers. Athens, Georgia; Fort Wayne and Decatur, Indiana.

Access. 1300 Fort Wayne National Bank Building, Fort Wayne, Indiana 46802; (219) 425-5100.

Consumer brands.

Mrs. Filberts margarines and salad dressings.

Do You Know What You're Eating?

Match the labels with the product. 15 to 20 correct answers: chemical guru. 10 to 14 correct answers: good taste buds. 5 to 9 correct answers: you might as well be eating paste. 0 to 4 correct answers: better see your doctor.

A COOL WHIP TOPPING (*General Foods*)

B COUNTRY TIME LEMON-ADE DRINK (*General Foods*)

C LISTERINE MOUTHWASH (*Warner Lambert*)

D DOVE SOAP (*Lever Bros.*)

E GAINES BURGERS (*General Foods*)

F CARNATION INSTANT BREAKFAST (*Carnation*)

G MASSENGIL DISPOSABLE DOUCHE (*Beecham*)

H HERSHEY'S SYRUP (*Hershey*)

I KELLOGG'S FROSTED FLAKES (*Kellogg*)

J HARTZ HAMSTER & GERBIL MUNCH (*Hartz*)

K COFFEE-MATE NON-DAIRY CREAMER (*Carnation*)

L SURE ANTI-PERSPIRANT ROLL-ON (*Procter & Gamble*)

M FARMER JOHN LIVERWURST (*Clougherty Packing Co.*)

N FRESH HORIZONS WHITE BREAD (*Continental Baking*)

O d-CON RODENT POISON (*Sterling Drug*)

P SCHILLING IMITATION BACON BITS (*McCormick*)

Q HERB-OX BEEF BOUILLON CUBES (*Pure Food Co.*)

R PEPSODENT TOOTH-PASTE (*Lever Bros.*)

S ORANGE JUICE

T PREPARATION H OINTMENT (*American Home Products*)

Source: *Mother Jones*, September/October 1979.

1 Meat By-Products, Soybean Grits, Sucrose, Soybean Meal, Propylene Glycol, Wheat Flour, Corn Syrup, Soybean Hulls, Chicken Digest, Salt, Dried Whey Product, Calcium Carbonate, Water, Beef, Vegetable Oil, Mono Calcium Phosphate, Iron Oxide, Potassium Sorbate, Animal Fat (with BHA), Ethoxyquin, Zinc Oxide, Ammoniated Glycrrhizin, Vitamins, Calcium Pantothenate, Ethylenediamine Dihydriodide.

2 Corn Sirup (sic), Water, Sugar, Cocoa, Salt, Mono and Diglycerides from Vegetable Oil, Xanthan Gum, Polysorbate 60, Vanillin.

3 Water, Sugar Syrup, Citric Acid, Sodium Citrate, Vegetable Gum, Natural Flavors, Potassium Sorbate, Sodium Benzoate, Vitamin C, Glyceryl Abietate, Artificial Color, BHA.

4 Sodium Cocoyl Isethionate, Stearic Acid, Sodium Tallowate, Water, Sodium Isethionate, Coconut Acid, Sodium Stearate, Sodium Dodecylbenzenesulfonate, Sodium Cocoate, Fragrance, Salt, Titanium Dioxide.

5 Live Yeast Cell Derivative, Shark Liver Oil, Phenylmercuric Nitrate.

6 Soy Flour, Vegetable Oil, Salt, Natural and Artificial Flavors, Caramel, FD&C Red No. 3, BHA, BHT.

7 Milled Corn, Sugar, Salt, Malt Flavoring, Vitamins, BHA.

8 Hydrolyzed Vegetable Protein, Salt, Sugar, Onion, Autolyzed Yeast, Beef Fat, Malto-Dextrin, Celery, Caramel, Beef Extract, Disodium Inosinate, Disodium Guanylate.

9 Zirconium-Aluminum-Glycine-Hydroxychloride Complex, Water, PEG-40 Stearate, Glyceryl Stearate, Glycerin, Refined Paraffin, Isopropyl Palmitate, Magnesium Aluminum Silicate, Fragrance.

10 Non-Fat Dry Milk, Sugar, Cocoa, Corn Syrup Solids, Lactose, Isolated Soy Protein, Sodium Caseinate, Lecithin, Magnesium Hydroxide, Ammonium Carrageenan, Artificial Flavors, Sodium Ascorbate, Ferric Orthophosphate, Vitamin E Acetate, Vitamin A Palmitate, Niacinamide, Copper Gluconate, Zinc Oxide, Calcium Pantothenate, Thiamine Mononitrate, Pyridoxine Hydrochloride, Folic Acid.

11 Water, Hydrogenated Coconut and Palm Kernel Oils, Sugar, Corn Syrup, Sodium Caseinate, Dextrose, Natural and Artificial Flavors, Polysorbate 60, Sorbitan Monostearate, Xanthan Gum, GUAR Gum, Artificial Color.

12 Pork, Pork Livers, Pork Snouts, Bacon (cured with Water, Salt, Sodium Phosphate, Soy Sauce, Flavoring, Sodium Erythorbate, Sodium Nitrate), Salt, Corn Syrup, Spices, Flavoring, Hydrolyzed Vegetable Protein, Monosodium Glutamate, Sodium Nitrate.

13 Corn Meal, Vegetable Oil, Artificial Meat Flavors, Salt, Artificial Coloring.

14 Water, Alcohol, Thymol, Eucalyptol, Methyl Salicylate, Menthol, Benzoic Acid, Poloxamer 407, Caramel.

15 Corn Syrup Solids, Partially Hydrogenated Vegetable Oil, Sodium Caseinate, Mono and Diglycerides, Dipotassium Phosphate, Artificial Flavorings and Colors.

16 Orange Juice.

17 Water, SD Alcohol 40, Lactic Acid, Sodium Lactate, Oxtoxynol-9, Cetylpyridinium Chloride, Sorbic Acid, Disodium EDTA, Fragrance, D&C Red No. 19.

18 Homogeneous Mixture of Cereals (Corn, Wheat, Rice), Wafarin.

19 Sorbitol, Water, Alumina, Hydrated Silica, Glycerin, PEG 32, Sodium Lauryl Sulfate, Dicalcium Phosphate, Cellulose Gum, Flavor, Titanium Dioxide, Sodium Saccharin, Sodium Benzoate.

20 Water, Flour, Powdered Wood Cellulose, Wheat Gluten, Brown Sugar, Salt, Sugar, Yeast, Lactalbumin, Calcium Sulfate, Sodium Stearoyl-2-Lactylate, Mono and Diglycerides, Polyglycerate 60, Polysorbate 60, Potassium Bromate, Artificial Flavor, Vitamins and Calcium Propionate.

Answers: 1-E; 2-H; 3-B; 4-D; 5-T; 6-P; 7-I; 8-O; 9-L; 10-F; 11-A; 12-M; 13-J; 14-C; 15-K; 16-S; 17-G; 18-O; 19-R; 20-N.

—*Richard Kirschman*

Continental Grain

Sales: $10 billion (estimated)
Rank in grain trading: 2
Founded: 1813
Employees: 18,000
Headquarters: New York, New York

What they do. Continental Grain is a privately owned grain trader that was founded in Europe, moved to the United States after World War II, and is at home any place in the world where sellers and buyers of grains can be brought together.

Continental ranks second in this business to Cargill and, by some estimates, handles a quarter of U.S. grain exports. Like Cargill, they function as a middleman, buying grain from farmers and other dealers and selling it to customers around the world, including governments. In the grain business, the main assets are not physical plants, but bank credits needed to buy grain, and consequently Continental is one of the biggest users of short-term credit in the world. In the words of a retired Continental trader, "I used to go to the bank and say, 'Can I have a hundred million dollars?' The answer was always 'yes.' " Cargill is based in Minneapolis, near the source of supply; Continental is based in New York, near the source of credit.

The key to success in grain dealing is information. The traders monitor political, economic, and climatic conditions all over the world to gauge who will want—or need —to buy grain and at what price. Such information is golden, not to be shared with outsiders. For example, American farmers complain that Continental bought their crops in 1972 knowing that the huge Russian wheat deal was in the works, while the farmers themselves were unaware of the deal and sold for a lower price than they would have otherwise. But that's precisely how profits are made in grain trading—and how the price of bread is determined.

Continental has used profits from trading to buy out other companies that make products from grain. Today, Continental makes animal feeds, processes poultry, bakes bread (Oroweat in the West, Arnold in the East), produces pet foods and frozen dinners. They also mill soybean oil, and run a

What Happened to Levy's?

You don't have to be Jewish

to love Levy's
real Jewish Rye

Classic ad from Doyle Dane Bernbach agency helped a Brooklyn bakery to gain some time before being swallowed.

Local bakeries throughout the country have died or been absorbed during the past 30 years. One of the most recent to fold was the Levy's bakery of Brooklyn, founded in 1888. They are remembered by many New Yorkers—and by advertising aficionados everywhere—for the dramatic campaign, "You don't have to be Jewish to love Levy's." Posters executing that theme featured pictures of an American Indian, an Irish policeman, a Japanese boy, a red-cassocked choir boy, and other non-Jewish ethnics, each munching on a sandwich made with Levy's real Jewish rye bread.

The campaign started in 1961 and saved the bakery, which had been in financial difficulties for many years.

Requests for the posters arrived from all over the world. In addition to helping the bakery, the campaign was a great boon to the advertising agency that created it— Doyle Dane Bernbach, reinforcing the "creative revolution" in the advertising business.

In 1979 the Brooklyn bakery, still beset with financial troubles, closed and sold their assets (the Levy name and the sour starter for the rye bread) to Arnold Bakers of Greenwich, Connecticut, a subsidiary of one of the world's giant grain traders, Continental Grain.

Like many other New Yorkers, Levy's real Jewish rye has moved to Connecticut.

commodity brokerage house (Conti-Commodity Services).

History. Continental Grain is the creation and property of the Fribourgs, a Belgian-Jewish family. The business was founded by Simon Fribourg, great-great-grandfather of current president Michel Fribourg. Their first major international deal came in 1848, during a drought in Belgium, when Simon's son traded several sacks of gold for large stocks of Ukranian wheat. The Fribourg brothers became influential during the latter half of the nineteenth century as Europe began to change from a rural to an industrial economy, with people increasingly working at a distance from their food sources. By 1900 England was growing only a fraction of the wheat it consumed, and the Fribourgs filled the gap. The Fribourgs reorganized their business as Continental Grain after World War I, establishing a U.S. subsidiary in Chicago. In 1940, when German armies overran Belgium and France, the Fribourgs fled, regrouping in New York after World War II.

Reputation. Continental maintains a secrecy described by *Forbes* as "no less fanatical that that displayed by the late Howard Hughes." As a privately owned company, Continental is not required to disclose much information about operations, and they don't. Dan Morgan, author of *Merchants of Grain*, was granted an hour-long interview with Michel Fribourg. He hoped for more time, but several months later he received a letter from Continental saying, "It has been decided that we choose not to participate in further interviews with you." Morgan explained why the Russian leaders liked to deal with Continental: "The mysterious, aristocratic Michel Fribourg was just the kind of archetypal capitalist who perfectly fitted the old Communist stereotype and had the same strong personal authority as did the people at the top of the Soviet bureaucratic hierarchy."

What they own. Information on who's growing, and who's likely to be buying, grain. A lot of important telephone and telex numbers around the world.

Who owns and runs the company. Michel Fribourg. He is assumed to own 90% of Continental Grain, and he is not known for

In 1850 more than 80% of America's people lived on farms. Each farmer produced enough food for himself and three other people. Official estimates are that only 2 to 4% of the population lives on farms today. But each farm worker today feeds 58 other Americans, most of whom live in cities.

sharing power. His family's wealth has been estimated at half a billion dollars. The *New York Times* reported that the Fribourgs live "as the storybook aristocrats did." They have half a dozen homes: a townhouse on Manhattan's Upper East Side (with a 1,500-bottle wine cellar), a ski lodge in upstate New York, a "spring home" in Connecticut, a Paris apartment, a summer house on the French Riviera, and a hideaway in the Alps.

In the public eye. Wheat-growing farmers, grain-buying Turks (who reneged on a huge contract), bread-buying consumers, and information-seeking reporters all had it in for Continental during the 1970s. In 1976 Continental pleaded no contest to 50 federal charges of manipulating the scale at its grain elevator at Westwego, Louisiana, and paid a half-million-dollar fine. By coincidence, in December 1977 that same elevator exploded, killing 36 persons, in the worst disaster of its kind in U.S. history.

Where they're going. Continental is accustomed to performing its economic function in a world torn by political strife.

Access. 277 Park Avenue, New York, New York 10017; (212) 826-5100.

Consumer brands.

Oroweat and Arnold Bakers bread; Polo Food frozen dinners; Hilbun chickens; Ful-o-Pep pet food; Wayne animal feeds.

In 1920 there were 6.5 million farms in the United States. Today only 2.8 million farms remain, but wheat and beef production has tripled and corn production has increased by 75%.

International Inc.

Sales: $3.7 billion
Profits: $178.7 million
Forbes 500 rank: 126
Rank in corn oil: 1
Rank in corn syrup: 1
Rank in mayonnaise: 1
Rank in peanut butter: 1
Rank in tints and dyes: 1
Rank in spray and corn starches: 1
Founded: 1906
Employees: 42,500
Headquarters: Englewood Cliffs, New Jersey

What they do. Corn is a crop discovered by American Indians. This company, whose name was originally Corn Products Refining, found so many uses for it that they expanded into a leading multinational operator whose work force is two-thirds non-American. CPC is still headquartered in the U.S. but overseas businesses earn two-thirds of their profits.

CPC sells corn products to a wide variety of industries—starches to paper companies, dextrose to brewers, and fructose sweeteners to food and beverage companies, for example. However, unlike other corn processors, CPC has some strong consumer brands. They're the nation's leading producer of mayonnaise—selling it in the East under the Hellmann's name, in the West under the Best Foods name. They're also number 1 in peanut butter, selling it everywhere under the Skippy label.

The big CPC brand in Europe is Knorr, a line of dehydrated soups that dates from 1838 and sells on the order of 15 billion servings a year. CPC once invested a ton of money to bring Knorr to America to challenge Campbell Soup. It turned out to be one of the most notable flops of modern business history.

History. In 1842 Thomas Kingsford, an English immigrant to the United States, developed a wet milling process by which starch could be isolated from corn. Subsequently, various companies were organized to make corn starch and corn syrup, and by the end of the century they had formed what was pejoratively called the "glucose trust." But the monopoly was too inefficient to withstand the assaults of Edward T. Bedford and his associates, who formed the New York Glucose Company in 1901. Bedford's company so aggressively took over the market that in 5 years they merged the principal companies in the industry into a new monopoly called Corn Products Refining Company, which accounted for virtually all the corn refined in the country for the next 10 years. An antitrust action broke up the monopoly in 1916, but Corn Products Refining Company continued as the dominant force in the industry. They built their corn milling plants in the Midwest, close to the source of supply (Argo corn starch comes from Argo, Illinois), but control was always in the hands of New York financiers. The rest of the story is largely one of acquisition after acquisition. They bought a German starch plant after World War I and then spread across the globe: South Africa, Brazil, India. After World War II they bought the big German soup maker, Knorr. In 1958 they greatly expanded their consumer goods business by acquiring Best Foods (Hellmann's and Skippy). One of their latest acquisitions is S. B. Thomas, the English muffin producer, whose sales they more than quadrupled during the 1970s.

WHAT THE FARMER REAPS

When you Buy a Dollar's Worth of:	The Farmer Gets:
BAKERY AND CEREAL PRODUCTS	13¢
FRUITS AND VEGETABLES	25¢
FATS AND OILS	38¢
DAIRY PRODUCTS	50¢
MEAT	55¢
POULTRY AND EGGS	60¢

Source: United States Department of Agriculture, 1978.

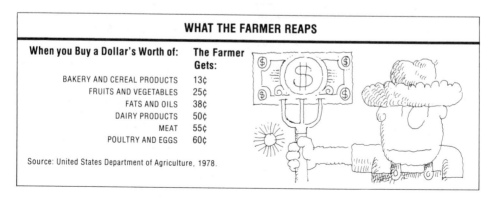

Reputation. They rely on old processes and old brands. "Here is no fad-chasing outfit," concluded *Forbes* in a 1980 appraisal. The corporate name was changed in 1969 to CPC International but even in business circles the company is still often referred to as "Corn Products."

What they own. One hundred fifteen plants in 45 countries.

Who owns and runs the company. There are no dominant stockholders. The route to the top is illustrated by the path taken by chairman James W. McKee: cost accountant with CPC's Italian affiliate, financial manager with the Brazilian company, head of the old Cuban subsidiary, financial officer in New York headquarters, comptroller, chairman.

In the public eye. During the late 1960s CPC made a major move into the educational field, adding four different companies. The best known of these acquisitions was Methods for Intellectual Development (MIND), a remedial education and training system hailed at the time as a miraculous way to improve the skills of workers and bring the unemployed and disadvantaged into the labor force. Management predicted at the time that this new division would one day be an important contributor to earnings; today not one of these companies is left at CPC. CPC reports that 25% of the U.S. employees are minority group members and 31% are women, but no officers are members of either group. Native Americans have been portrayed in a patronizing manner in CPC's television pitches for Mazola margarine.

Where they're going. Syrup derived from corn is now being used to sweeten Coca-Cola. Ethanol derived from corn is now being mixed with gasoline to produce gasohol. CPC is the world's largest refiner of corn. Why should they go anyplace else?

Stock performance. CPC stock bought for $1,000 in 1970 sold for $2,000 on January 2, 1980.

Major employment centers. Englewood Cliffs, New Jersey; Brussels, Belgium; Buenos Aires, Argentina; Hong Kong.

Access. International Plaza, Englewood Cliffs, New Jersey 07632; (201) 894-4000.

Consumer brands.

Food products: Fanning's Bread and Butter Pickles; Argo corn starch; Golden Griddle pancake syrup; Hellmann's/Best Foods mayonnaise and sandwich spread; Karo syrups; Mazola corn oil, margarine, and No Stick shortening; Nucoa margarine; Skippy peanut butter; Spin Blend salad dressing; Thomas' English muffins; Knorr soups; Bosco milk amplifier; H-O cereals; Presto cake flour.
Laundry aids: Argo, Linit and Niagara starch; NuSoft fabric softener; Rit tints and dyes.
Restaurants: Dutch Pantry.

Sales: $498 million
Profits: $41.6 million
Founded: 1912
Employees: 3,600
Headquarters: DeKalb, Illinois

Produces hybrids, high-yield seeds which do not reproduce and therefore have to be repurchased by farmers every year. They're believed to be second in the hybrid business to the Iowa-based Pioneer Hi-Bred International. DEKALB's hybrids are sold through a network of 7,500 farmer-dealers, which is why you see those DEKALB winged corn signs as you drive through the Midwest. DEKALB's other businesses include oil and gas (exploration and production), breeding stock for hybrid egg-laying chickens (they're no. 1 in this field), commodity brokerage (Heinhold), irrigation equipment (Lindsay), and a controlling interest in Dynapol, a California company trying to develop long-chain molecules to prevent certain food additives from being absorbed by the body. Descendants of founder Thomas Roberts own almost 40% of the company and hold the top management positions.

Access. Sycamore Road, DeKalb, Illinois 60115; (815) 758-3461.

THE FEDERAL COMPANY

Sales: $930.9 million
Profits: $22.4 million
Rank in chickens: 1
Rank in flour milling: 8
Founded: 1925
Employees: 9,000
Headquarters: Memphis, Tennessee

What they do. Federal is the nation's largest supplier of chickens, selling under the Holly Farms name, primarily in the South. The Holly Farms unit at Wilkesboro, North Carolina, maintains an army of 1.5 million breeder hens, who lay 5.5 million eggs a week. The eggs go to 13 Holly Farms hatcheries, where chicks emerge after 21 days of incubation. The chicks are then delivered to "growout" farms owned and operated by independent farmers who are paid to raise chickens for Holly. Holly provides the farmers with all the feed, veterinary care, and other support services needed. After two months, by which time the broilers should weigh four pounds, they

---

WHO'S GOING TO SEED?

Seed Company	Owner
BURPEE SEEDS	ITT
COKER'S PEDIGREED SEED CO.	KLEINWANZIEBERER SWATZUCHT AG
DORMAN SEEDS	CARGILL
FERRY-MORSE SEEDS	PUREX
FUNK SEEDS	CIBA-GEIGY
NORTHROP-KING	SANDOZ
O'S GOLD SEED CO.	CENTRAL SOYA
WARWICK SEEDS	PFIZER

Source: *CoEvolution Quarterly*, Winter 1979/80, from a chart prepared by Graham Center Seed Directory.

An Assembly-line Chicken in Every Pot

Fluffy yellow, yeeping in frail voices, the 100,000 baby chicks ride a conveyor belt through the fluorescent-lit world of factory farming. Only minutes out of the incubator, they will never see a barnyard. There will be no scratching in the dust for tasty bugs, no strutting in the sun, no crowing to announce the dawn. These babies will spend their brief eight weeks of life crammed by the tens of thousands into automated chicken houses equipped with a futuristic array of electronically controlled feeding, watering, and ventilating devices. In this synthetic environment automatic alarm systems ring if anything goes wrong. Otherwise, these broilers-to-be will grow, almost untouched by human hands, until their final conveyor belt ride to the automatic killing knife.

If they were laying hens rather than meat chickens, they would spend their lives huddled nearly immobile in cramped wire cages arrayed in windowless chambers where there is neither day nor night, only a twilight gloom that science has found makes hens lay eggs around the clock. In the near-darkness hens use less energy, while producing record numbers of eggs: 250–300 per hen each year. Some 280 million American hens live this way, producing eggs so efficiently that an egg today sells for less than it did in 1920. Each year the average American eats 275 of these ovoid protein packages, little dreaming of the hen's travail. But the assembly-line hen expires in a year or two; her barnyard ancestor, by contrast, lived 10 years or more.

In a way, the laboratory-calibrated mass production of chickens and eggs is a triumph over the limits of nature. As recently as 1957 it took 16 weeks and 10 pounds of feed to rear a 4-pound broiler. Now it takes half the time and less than 8 pounds of computer-formulated feed. Chicken, once a costly Sunday treat, is now plentiful and costs little more than it did 30 years

are picked up and delivered to nine Holly processing plants in North Carolina, Virginia, and Texas. There the chickens are slaughtered, cut, packed, and labeled. Then they are off to the marketplace in Holly's refrigerated trucks, which deliver them to 6,000 supermarkets. The life span of a Holly Farms chicken is about three months.

Hazards of Chicken Inspecting

At the modern, highly mechanized poultry-processing plant owned by Gold Kist, a farmers' cooperative that kills, plucks, cleans and chills 230 million chickens a year, the mirror inspectors have to watch the birds whizzing by at the rate of 70 a minute, four birds a minute faster than before. The plant now turns out 128,000 chickens a day, 9,200 more than before, with one-fourth fewer inspectors.

The mirror inspectors see the chickens after they have been through the rubber "fingers" of the plucking machine. As the chickens pass by upside-down over-head, a stainless-steel trough to catch the drippings moves below in the opposite direction. The inspectors complain that this two-way movement "hypnotizes" them, producing a sort of dazed condition.

Ester "Rosie" Rosenbaum, one of the 14 inspectors at Gold Kist, sniffs in disgust at the new system. And just to think, she says, she became a chicken inspector back in the 1960s because President Kennedy said "to do something for my country." . . .

Reprinted from the *Wall Street Journal*, October 12, 1979.

ago. The price of chicken rose only 17 percent between 1950 and 1979, while beef and pork prices tripled. As red meat consumption drops, chicken consumption grows, and the mechanized broiler industry cranks out 13 billion pounds of chicken a year, live weight, or 60 pounds of processed broilers for every man, woman, and child in the nation.

But assembly-line chicken farming has its casualties. One is the small farmer. In 1910 there were 5.5 million farms in America, with an average of 80 chickens apiece. Today a handful of conglomerate businesses dominate chicken and egg production, each with millions of chickens. Some run an egg-to-market operation, with their own hatcheries, breeder houses, and feed mills. Others contract out the chick-rearing process to farmers, but under strict controls: company supervisors are often on 24-hour, radio-call alert in case of trouble in the henhouse. The huge capital outlay required for an automated chicken operation has completely eliminated most small farmers from this curious version of the pastoral dream.

The other casualty of chicken mass production may be the product itself. Inoculated, dosed with antibiotics to ward off disease and boost growth, injected with dye to turn meat a healthy-looking yellow, the modern chicken makes bland eating compared to its robust, free-roaming barnyard ancestor.

Finally, the modern chicken is genetically programmed to specialize in meat or eggs. Gone is the brood hen who clucked protectively over her chicks and gathered them to her ample feathered bosom at night. Today's laying hen is an egg-making mechanism with all the maternal instincts of a pocket calculator, bred to scatter her eggs to the conveyer belt and lay, lay, lay.

In the year ending June 2, 1979, Holly sold 779 million pounds of chicken—about 200 million broilers. That was enough to give them 7.5% of the total U.S. market, and first place in the industry.

To feed all these chickens, Holly operates feed mills that turn out more than 1 million tons of feed a year.

Poultry represents 55% of Federal's business. Another quarter comes from their flour and bakery products, whose main customers are commercial bakeries. Federal also makes animal feeds and pet foods, and owns National By-Products of Des Moines, a company that buys animal parts considered inedible for humans—60% of the animal, including excess fat, bones, viscera, and hides—and renders them into products that can be marketed (mainly animal fats and proteins sold to manufacturers of pet foods and animal feeds).

History. Federai's roots go back to the Grenada Cotton Compress Company, founded in 1887 in Grenada, Mississippi, to warehouse and compress cotton grown in the Mississippi Delta. In 1925 Grenada merged with several other southern cotton companies to form Federal Compress and Warehouse. Cotton was their only business until 1959, when they bought Dixie Port-

> In California, the nation's most productive agricultural state, farmers sold their 1979 crops for $11 billion and netted $3 billion after expenses. By comparison, Du Pont, the nation's largest chemical company, sold $11 billion worth of products but cleared only $1.5 billion.

land Flour Mills. Two years later they bought a small animal feed producer, Cosby Hodges Milling of Birmingham, Alabama. And in 1968 they said goodbye to cotton and hello to chickens. For $33 million they sold their entire cotton-compressing operation and acquired Wilkesboro's Holly Farms Poultry Industries, one of the first of the chicken "factories." It was a propitious change. Cotton was going nowhere, but mass-produced chicken was coming into its own.

Reputation. Federal has the down-home flavor of the Old South. It's possible to call the company and within seconds, without identifying oneself, be speaking to the executive vice-president. Federal illustrated the 1978 annual report with Norman Rockwell–type pictures of vintage Americana: a dog jumping through a car window to chase a cat, a white-frocked girl discovered gorging herself on chocolate cake under a table at a church bake sale.

What they own. Holly Farms Poultry Industries, Wilkesboro; National By-Products, Des Moines; Dixie Portland Mills, Memphis; White Lily Foods, Knoxville; Globe Products, Clifton, New Jersey; Rustco Sales, Denver; Diana Fruit Preserving, Santa Clara, California; Cosby-Hodges Milling, Birmingham, Alabama; Crescent Food, Los Angeles; 107 Holly Farms Fried Chicken Restaurants (47 of which are owned jointly with Safeway) in Washington, D.C., Virginia, North Carolina, and Arkansas.

Who owns and runs the company. One-third of Federal's stock is owned by persons who are or have been officers, directors, or employees of the company. Nearly half the shares are held by residents of North Carolina, Tennessee, Iowa, and Texas, where Federal's largest facilities are found. Fed-

DECLINE OF THE FAMILY FARM

Number of Farms in the U.S.

Year	Farms	Year	Farms
1930	6.5 million	1964	3.5 million
1935	6.8 million	1965	3.4 million
1945	6.3 million	1966	3.3 million
1950	5.9 million	1967	3.2 million
1951	5.6 million	1968	3.1 million
1952	5.4 million	1969	3.0 million
1953	5.1 million	1970	3.0 million
1954	4.9 million	1971	2.9 million
1955	4.7 million	1972	2.9 million
1956	4.6 million	1973	2.8 million
1957	4.5 million	1974	2.7 million
1958	4.3 million	1975	2.7 million
1959	4.2 million	1976	2.7 million
1960	4.1 million	1977	2.7 million
1961	3.9 million	1978	2.6 million
1962	3.8 million	1979	2.3 million
1963	3.6 million		

eral does not pay the kind of salaries common at other companies; in 1978 no executive earned more than $100,000. Seven of the 12 board members are Federal executives. One of the outsiders is L. M. Clymer, who resigned as president of Holiday Inns in 1978 because of his religious objections to the company's entry into gambling. There are no women on the board.

Stock performance. Federal stock bought for $1,000 in 1970 sold for $1,480 on January 2, 1980.

Major employment center. Wilkesboro, North Carolina.

Access. 1755-D Lynnfield Road, Memphis, Tennesse; (901) 761-3610.

Consumer brands.

Grocery products: Holly Farms broilers, chicken franks, and bolognas; White Lily flour and baking mixes; Field & Show, Jazz, and Town & Country pet foods; Rustco baking mixes, jams, and jellies.
Restaurant: Holly Farms Fried Chicken.

The Greener Pastures of Cow No. 598

Calf No. 598 first opened her wide brown eyes on a spring afternoon in 1974. She had a brief glimpse of her mother, No. 411. It was her first and last contact with the big black-and-white spotted Holstein. Her sire, the champion bull named Dauntless, No. 598 would never meet. No matter; her mother had never met Dauntless either. He was selected for her by a computer crammed with data on dairy cow genetics. Conception was by artificial insemination.

Taken from her mother, No. 598 spent her first weeks alone in a calf pen, in a row of such narrow, roofed enclosures designed to shelter newborn calves. A human attendant fed her milk from No. 411, but 411, after her moment of maternity, was back in the herd. Milking machines have her valuable product twice each 24 hours. Between milkings and during them she ate incessantly to sustain the vast flow.

No. 598 grew fast and progressed to a bigger calf pen, then to a corral. Like her mother, she never roamed green pastures in search of tender grass and clover. Her feed, laboratory-tested, came to her in the troughs of a feeding corral. Energy that might be squandered in wan-

dering, according to modern dairy science, can better be converted into milk.

When 598 was old enough to be inseminated, the dairy computer selected her mate from a program containing lineage data on bulls and their daughters. The goal: dairy cows that stay healthy and give birth easily while producing unprecedented tonnages of quality milk, converting each ounce of costly feed into milk with optimal efficiency. Years of human effort had produced the computer bank of genetic information that had doubled milk yield per cow per year to an undreamed of 20,000 pounds.

After an uneventful pregnancy No. 598 gave birth to a bull calf. Useless for dairy purposes, the calf was sold to be fattened for beef. Few dairies keep bulls these days, since a handful of prize sires, their prowess in begetting milk-machine daughters recorded in the all-knowing computer, supply the nation with frozen semen.

With the birth of her calf No. 598 began the endless cycle of pregnancies, births, and lactations that would be her life until her milk output dropped below a profitable level. Monthly computer entries recorded her milk

yield, quality, and other critical data. As her production tapered off at the end of each lactation, a computer reminder alerted the dairyman to her earliest likely breeding date. Rest periods between lactations were short, since "dry" cows consume feed without producing profit.

Twice each 24 hours No. 598 trotted from corral to milking barn, so cluttered with gleaming metal machinery and plastic tubing that there was barely room for the cows and the laborers who, working at frenzied speed, washed udders, attached and detached milking suction cups, regulated machinery, and dispensed feed via devices calibrated to give each cow the optimal ration for her maximum output.

When the computer at last showed No. 598's yearly milk output dropping, she was culled from the herd. She could still be giving enough to satisfy the dairyman of two decades ago but no matter, the inexorable logic of cost-profit ratios dictated No. 598's end. Although cows can live into their twenties, No. 598 was only six years old when she made her final contribution to the nation's food supply, as dairy beef.

Land O' Lakes

Sales: $2 billion
Profits: $32 million
Rank among farmers' cooperatives: 2
Rank in butter: 1
Founded: 1921
Employees: 7,850
Headquarters: Minneapolis, Minnesota

What they do. Land O' Lakes is a cooperative that markets the products of member farmers and also buys products to supply the member farmers. In 1978 they marketed 6.7 billion pounds of dairy products, 79 million pounds of turkeys, 28 million pounds of margarine, 15 million dozen eggs, and 16 million bushels of soybeans. They sold their members 589,000 tons of feed, 1 million tons of fertilizer, $66 million worth of chemicals, 44 million pounds of seeds, and 165 million gallons of fuel.

In short, this co-op is a big business. So strong are they that in 1978 they acquired, for $12.7 million, Spencer Foods, one of the nation's 10 largest meat packers. Spencer was the largest privately owned company ever acquired by a farm co-op.

Land O' Lakes has become a powerful brand name. Originally the brand name went only on butter, and Land O' Lakes is the leader in that field, butter being one of its few products with national distribution. But the brand goes on some 400 products today, including milk, cheese, turkey, eggs, and canned and frozen foods. Land O' Lakes also operates a chain of Bridgeman Restaurant and Ice Cream Parlours, primarily in Minnesota.

The most startling departure from tradition was the introduction of a margarine under the Land O' Lakes name. The company was so closely associated with butter —and with historic enmity toward margarine—that this move was considered heresy by some dairy people. But Land O' Lakes moved into markets across the country with the message: "It takes a butter company to give you the taste you really want in margarine."

History. Land O' Lakes was organized in 1921 to give farmers in the upper Midwest economic clout. The argument was that by banding together the farmers could get a better price for their products, and they could also buy in bulk to get their supplies at lower prices. Butter was their point of departure.

Reputation. They may be farmers, but increasingly they talk like a big, sophisticated food company. For example, in one of their promotional brochures, they say, "Naturally, branded foods bring a better price than bulk commodities. Processing adds utility and appeal that customers are willing to pay for," And: "Whole, eviscerated turkeys are good business for Land O' Lakes turkey growers. But they're even better business after they've been further processed into turkey parts, roasts, slabs, slices, rolls, cubes, patties, and other products."

What they own. Land O' Lakes has plants and equipment worth about $170 million, at cost.

Who owns and runs the co-op. 175,000 farmers in six states: North Dakota, South Dakota, Nebraska, Minnesota, Iowa, and Wisconsin. The membership area is made up of 17 districts, each of which elects two members to a board of directors that functions much like the board of directors of a corporation. As a cooperative, Land O' Lakes returns to members the bulk of profits from operations.

In the public eye. Land O' Lakes represents itself as a bastion for farmers to ward off control by government and by large private corporations.

Where they're going. The goal is to become "a total food company." Moving into margarine was one step, Spencer Foods another. Now they are beginning to expand in the restaurant field.

Major employment centers. Minneapolis; Albert Lea, Minnesota; and Fort Dodge, Iowa.

Access. 614 McKinley Place, Minneapolis, Minnesota 55413; (612) 331-6330.

Consumer brands.

Food products: Land O' Lakes.
Restaurants: Bridgeman's and Bridget's.

Staley

Sales: $1.4 billion
Profits: $23.6 million
Forbes 500 rank: 350
Rank in corn processing: 2
Founded: 1898
Employees: 4,200
Headquarters: Decatur, Illinois

What they do. In 1979 the Coca-Cola Company began using a corn sweetener instead of sugar in their soft drinks. That was good news for Staley, who came on stream that year with a new plant in Lafayette, Indiana, which makes the specific sweetener—55% high-fructose corn syrup—specified by Coke. Making products from corn —starches, syrups, dextrose, oils, animal feeds, adhesives, coatings—is what Staley is all about. They're the nation's second-largest refiner of corn (after CPC International). They're also one of the five largest processors of soybeans.

Staley is logically located in the midst of the source of supply: Decatur, in the center of Illinois, is at the heart of the Midwest corn belt.

History. Staley wasn't always in Illinois. August Eugene Staley, a North Carolina farm boy, began making cream corn starch —a product used to thicken desserts and gravies—in a Baltimore loft in 1898. In 1906, just as Corn Products Refining was being formed in New York, Staley moved closer to the raw material he was using. He bought two buildings and 40 acres left by a defunct corn milling firm in Decatur and started grinding corn. He soon went bankrupt, but he started over again and made it work the second time, developing corn syrups for the food industry. In 1922 he opened the first U.S. plant for the processing of protein-rich soybeans.

A better known product of Staley's early history was the company's football team, Decatur's Staley, which became the Chicago Bears under the ownership and coaching of George Halas, a Staley engineer. In 1929 Staley built a 14-story headquarters building that became known as the Castle in the Cornfield. It's often mistaken for the Illinois state capital building (which is, of course, in Springfield, not far from Decatur).

Reputation. Staley sticks to what they know best. *Business Week* called them "stodgy." *Forbes* said they were "quiet" and "low key." In 1975 H. J. Heinz offered $260 million for Staley, but the Staley family turned it down (so Heinz went off and bought another corn processor, Iowa's Hubinger).

What they own. Staley has three corn milling plants, five soybean processing facilities, three starch processing plants, eight consumer products plants, and at least nine elevators, or grain warehouses, in Illinois.

Who owns and runs the company. The Staleys still own 40% of the stock. Top executives own another 10%. Henry Staley, a vice president, is the only family member still active in the business. Corn milling relies on expensive machinery instead of labor. Although sales are over $1 billion, Staley needs fewer than 5,000 employees.

Where they're going. Staley looks for high-fructose syrups to take more markets away from sugar. And they expect the once-lowly soybean to become a greater and greater source of protein, displacing meat.

Stock performance. Staley stock bought for $1,000 in 1970 sold for $3,316 on January 2, 1980.

Major employment centers. Decatur, Illinois; Lafayette, Indiana; and Morrisville, Pennsylvania.

Access. 2200 Eldorado Street, Decatur, Illinois 62525; (217) 423-4411.

Consumer brands.

Food products: Wagner fruit drinks; Gold 'n Soft margarine; Staley waffle and pancake syrups; Cream corn starch.

Other: Sta-Puf, Sta-Flo starches and fabric finisher; Sno-Bol bathroom bowl cleaner; Rain Drops water softener; Diaper Sweet.

> There are 123 million cattle, 55 million pigs, and 13 million sheep in the United States.

I. J. Stoneback

Sales: $94,000
Profits: $4,000
Employees: 1
Location: Lawrence, Kansas

What he does. On a typical summer day I. J. Stoneback gets up at the break of dawn, eats a hearty breakfast of ham and eggs, walks out of his suburban-style ranch house to the nearby cattle lot where he feeds his livestock some hay and grain pellets, then climbs onto his John Deere tractor and heads for a full day in his wheat and soybean fields.

Stoneback farms a thousand acres of lush U.S. heartland. About one-third of his acreage is cropland, on which he grows soybeans, or a combination of wheat and milo (a grass to feed the cattle). The wheat goes to local elevators—middlemen who resell to the large flour mills. Local processors buy the soybeans as raw material for livestock feed. Stoneback used to raise sheep and hogs, but now cattle are his only livestock, grazing on the pastureland which makes up the remainder of his property. In 1964 he started with 10 heifer calves; now he has 145 head.

History. Stoneback grew up on a 160-acre farm settled by his great-grandfather, who came to Kansas from Pennsylvania Dutch country in the mid-nineteenth century. One of the state's original pioneers, he was granted a 160-acre plot in north-central Kansas to live on and farm under the Homestead Act of 1862.

Ninety years later, in 1941, I. J. left his father's farm and bought another 160-acre homestead farm, paying $50 an acre. Five years later, at the age of 29, he married Mabel Green, whose folks ran a hardware store in Lawrence. The Stonebacks have three children and two grandchildren, none of whom farms.

In 1973 the U.S. Army Corps of Engineers condemned most of Stoneback's property for a federal reservoir. He used the proceeds from the condemnation, plus some cash he borrowed from the bank, to buy 940 acres of nearby farmland; he continues to live on the 2 dozen acres left him of the original land.

Stoneback hired a man to help him farm his expanded acreage and to share the heavy work of improving the new land with ponds and terraces. The employee lives in a farmhouse on the newer property with his wife and three children.

The business of farming. Stoneback ekes out a living between the whims of weather, an ever-changing marketplace, and the rising price of fuel and oil. In 1977 torrential rains wiped out his wheat crop at harvest time. The next year drought took out half the soybeans; Stoneback got a $17,000 federal disaster loan at 3% interest.

His luck seemed to change in 1979, when he harvested a full crop of 8,000 bushels of soybeans, but the market price sank and Stoneback sold only half the crop for about $28,000. He is storing the rest until the price goes up again.

In the same year Stoneback took 50 steer calves to the stockyards in Kansas City and sold them to slaughterhouses. His total sales of grain and livestock in 1979 amounted to $94,000; his expenses came to $90,000. Stoneback's costs include about $8,000 he pays his farm hand (who also receives a rent-free farmhouse and one slaughtered steer a year); payments on the mortgage and other loans; and other farming expenses like fuel, feed, fertilizer, agricultural chemicals, new machinery, and maintenance. Expenses have risen prodigiously in the last few years because of his dependence on gas (fuel for the tractors and other equipment) and other petroleum-based products (fertilizers and many agricultural chemicals).

Because the $4,000 profit in 1979 was not enough to live on, Stoneback borrowed about $10,000 from a bank with which he has a close relationship. Near the end of each year Stoneback meets with a financial consultant from the bank who advises him on whether to increase his expense for the coming year by purchasing fuel, chemicals, and other materials for future use, or to increase his income by selling grain or cattle. The bank is more than willing to offer such advice; Stoneback owes more than a quarter of a million dollars in various loans on his property, and the yearly increase in his land value makes him a good risk for small personal loans.

Faced with rising costs and an uncertain market, Stoneback feels squeezed. He says, "The chemical companies and the oil companies fix expenses, and the grain companies and slaughterhouses fix prices. If it weren't for the increase in the land values every year, farmers throughout the Midwest would be bankrupt. I think family farming is threatened."

Reputation. Stoneback denies that there is any such person as a "typical farmer," but he has the virtues normally associated with the term. He's hard-working (dawn-to-dusk labor in the fields) and honest in his business dealings, and he has an almost mystical attachment to the land.

What he owns. Stoneback owns 723 acres plus a half-interest in another 240 acres (his brother-in-law owns the other half but leaves the farming to Stoneback). For the purpose of U.S. Department of Agriculture programs, he lists his property (including his two houses, several barns, sheds, and grain bins) as worth $719,000, though its actual market value is probably higher. He also has a sizable investment in machinery, including three tractors, three pickup trucks, a gleaner combine, a hay baler, and other equipment. He values all this at $58,-600, though its replacement value may be three or four times that figure.

Figuring in his 145 head of cattle at $98,-200, Stoneback's assets of property, machinery, and livestock come to $984,800. Subtracting loans (mostly long-term real estate morgages) of $268,350, he calculates his net worth at $716,450.

"Because the assets of a farm like this are so large and the amount of money that can be made each year is so small," Stoneback says, "virtually no one can afford to buy a farm today. You can't borrow to buy one."

Public affairs. Stoneback has been active for years in a variety of farmers' organizations, including the American Agriculture Movement, which organized "tractor-cades" in favor of stronger government price supports. "Farmers have very little influence in this country since politicians don't pay much attention to them," he says. "All my life I have believed that the only way to do anything about that is for farmers to unite and speak with one voice."

In 1972 he won a seat on the Douglas County Commission, but he was defeated in his reelection bid four years later. Though he enjoyed his work as a county commissioner, Stoneback says he is happy to be farming full time again.

Where he's going. Big changes aren't part of Stoneback's dreams. "I plan to just keep things going as they are," he says. "I enjoy working on the land and improving it, and I will keep at it for as long as I can."

He notes that large corporations have bought some of the land in his part of the state and moved their employees in to run the farms. Stoneback was not surprised when one of those enterprises recently folded. "Corporations have a real problem because they lose the personal touch," he says. "We farmers have an involvement with what we are doing and a love of the land. That's the most important ingredient in farming."

Farm of the Future

A caption under a drawing in the February 1970 *National Geographic* read:

Farm of the Future: Grainfields stretch like fairways and cattle pens resemble high-rise apartments in a farm of the early 21st century. . . .

Attached to a modernistic farm house, a bubble-topped control tower hums with a computer, weather reports, and a farm-price ticker tape. A remote-controlled tiller-combine glides across a 10-mile-long wheat field on tracks that keep the heavy machine from compacting the soil. Threshed grain, funneled into a pneumatic tube beside the field, flows into storage elevators rising close to a distant city. The same machine that cuts the grain prepares the land for another crop. A similar device waters neighboring strips of soybeans as a jet-powered helicopter sprays insecticides.

Across a service road, conical mills blend feed for beef cattle fattening in multilevel pens that conserve ground space. Tubes carry the feed to be mechanically distributed. A central elevator transports the cattle up and down, while a tubular side drain flushes wastes to be broken down for fertilizer. Beside the farther pen, a processing plant packs beef into cylinders for shipment to market by helicopter and monorail. Illuminated plastic domes provide controlled environments for growing high-value crops such as strawberries, tomatoes, and celery. Near a distant lake and recreation area, a pumping plant supplies water for the vast operation.

Grocers and Supergrocers

The Great Atlantic and Pacific Tea Company

Sales: $6.7 billion
Loss: $3.8 million
Forbes 500 rank: 56
Rank in food retailing: 3
Rank in retailing: 6
Founded: 1869
Employees: 72,000
Headquarters: Montvale, New Jersey

What they do. A & P, now controlled by Tengelmann Corporation of West Germany, operates the third-largest food retailing corporation in the United States. Centered primarily in the East, with stores as far west as Chicago, A & P also operates diversified support facilities for their stores, including warehouses, bakeries, coffee roasters, dairies, a cheese factory, frozen-food plants, a nut processing company, a laundry, a printing plant, and 12 fresh produce sheds.

History. George Huntington Hartford was born in Augusta, Maine, in 1833, the son of a farmer and merchant. At the age of 25 he quit a clerking job in Boston and journeyed to St. Louis, where he set up a shop that represented George Francis Gilman's New York leather business. The flow of imported hides proved to be irregular, so the industrious Hartford installed a retail selection of coffee, teas, and spices in his shop. When Hartford moved to New York two

years later, Gilman was established in the grocery business. Hartford, now a junior partner, began buying tea and coffee on the waterfront docks, using Gilman's import connections. The two of them slashed the prevailing price of tea from $1 per pound to 30¢ and advertised that they had eliminated six to seven middlemen.

In 1869 the partners opened a series of stores with the pompous name of Great Atlantic and Pacific Tea Company. The stores were designed by Gilman, who indulged himself in the ornate facades and interiors. The front of the first store, on Vesey Street in New York, was painted with "real vermillion imported from China," with touches of gold leaf which reflected the light of the capital "T" illuminated in gas over the doorway. The windows were festooned with red, white, and blue globes. Inside tea bins copied the facade in bright reds and gold. The cashier's cages were built to resemble miniature Chinese pagodas. In the center of the store a large cockatoo squawked "welcome," and on Saturday nights a band played free.

A & P undersold all the competition and had mushroomed to 100 stores when Hartford's son, Geroge, Jr., joined the business in 1880 at age 15. By this time the flamboyant Gilman had retired to Connecticut, boasting to friends that he would live as a rich man if each store sent him only a dollar a day. The stores did. In Connecticut Gilman designed a large luxurious estate that combined New England and Moorish styles. He had 60 servants, 40 horses, and a race track that was roofed over to trot them on. He was seen disporting down the country lanes in a six-horsed tallyho coach preceded by liveried trumpeters announcing his eminence. If he should meet a funeral procession on the road, he would immediately turn back. His fear of death was so strong that he refused to make a will, and he died intestate in 1901. After much legal wrangling Huntington Hartford's "oral partnership" with Gilman was deemed valid, and the Hartfords got the stock. They now owned A & P 100%.

While Gilman had been playing, the Hartfords were busy. Red-and-gold A & P carts traveled the back roads delivering tea, baking powder, and silver polish. Continuing a tradition started at the original Vesey Street store, "premiums" were given with each purchase, including lacquer tea trays, the "Little Bright Eyes Story Book" for children, fancy ceramics, and chromos ("indistinguishable from genuine oil paintings"). Soon they introduced trading stamps so that housewives could collect them for special premiums—marble-topped tables, mantle clocks, and Morris chairs.

In New York George Hartford, Jr., sat in the Vesey Street pagoda and counted the receipts from all the stores as they were brought in. When he asked a chemist friend what was in baking powder and learned that the expensive powder was made of alum and carbonate, George screened off a corner of the store and had the chemist manufacture the first A & P brand of merchandise.

George's careful frugal ways were borrowed from his father, who managed to get himself elected to 12 terms as mayor of Orange, New Jersey, during this period. George, Sr., quietly presided over his stores, town, and family, wearing a flowing beard and speaking in a slow drawl. In 1888 his son John joined the business. Like his brother Geroge, Jr., John had very little schooling when he started work with A & P. But unlike the shy and retiring George, Jr., John had a charming and easygoing manner. While George, Jr., counted, John sold.

By 1900 A & P had 200 stores and was grossing about $5.5 million in tea, coffee, spices, and basic groceries. After the panic of 1907 a somber mood descended on the country. A & P was still giving away premiums and trading stamps, taking phone orders, and making free deliveries against charge accounts, but people were beginning to worry about the "high cost of living."

A & P founder George Hartford looking over his two sons, John A. and George Ludlum Hartford.

By 1912 John had tired of the expense of the premiums, and he wanted to drop them from all 400 stores. He heard that there was a store in New Jersey that gave nothing away and didn't deliver or offer charge accounts, but instead offered the lowest prices in town. The store was booming. John's request to try out such a plan was rejected by both his brother and his father, who called his "economy" store idea "crack-brained." John finally won sway, and with $3,000 opened the first "cash-and-carry" store right around the corner from A & P's biggest money-maker in New Jersey. Within six months he put the bigger store out of business and launched A & P on the greatest retail expansion that the world has ever seen, before or since. Within three years they opened up 7,500 economy stores, usually small, one-person operations which had the same goods in the same location in every store. It was said at the time that John could walk blindfolded into any store and find the beans.

Between 1912 and 1915 the company opened an average of eight stores a day. John ran about the country, personally choosing sites, hiring managers, selecting stock, and supervising alterations. A store could open within five days, but George, the cautious brother, would close it if it lost money for even a week. By 1917, when the elder Hartford died, A & P had become a national institution, grossing $125 million a year. It had permanently changed American food retailing from a labor-intensive service industry with high margins to volume-oriented, low-cost, low-profit, standardized chains that insisted on uniformity and consistent standards of quality.

When their father died, the brothers, then known as Mr. John and Mr. George, divided up the executive tasks. Mr. George became chairman and remained reclusively attached to company headquarters, keeping his frugal and conservative eyes on the finances. Mr. George did not go into stores. Every morning at exactly eight o'clock he arrived at the Graybar Building in New York, where he retired to a drab office whose sole decoration was an old carafe. He never went out for lunch.

Mr. John became president, and it was his duty to be the gregarious face of A & P. He attended most store openings, dressed in tailored grays and fedora. He greeted visitors in a paneled office with a portrait of the "old man" over the mantelpiece.

A & P rode out the Depression with little noticeable disturbance. The company could not lower prices fast enough during the deflationary period that followed the crash and made more money than Mr. John thought it should. Such concerns did not bother Mr. George, who kept A & P's surplus cash in short-term government bonds, $47 million all due within one year, because the U.S. budget was "unbalanced."

Despite their differences, the two Hartfords presided over what was the largest merchandising empire in the world, controlling salmon fishing fleets in the Northwest and canneries across the country, and buying more coffee from Brazil than any other corporation. By 1934 A & P had reached a peak of 15,000 stores—and the supermarket concept began seriously affecting their operations. Started as cut-rate discount stores in used warehouses, these new food emporiums operated under the names of King Cullen and Big Bear seemed distasteful to both George and John Hartford. But by 1936 Mr. John realized that, distasteful as they may have seemed, the new independents with their large range of foods, self-service systems, and low prices were the way of the future. George was violently opposed to the horrific expenses entailed in such a change-over, but John thought it was change or perish.

A & P opened 500 supermarkets in 1938 and 1,000 more in 1939. Within three years 70% of the old stores had been closed, and A & P once again attained the market share they had in 1929. This buoyancy was short-lived, as the company came under government attack for antitrust practices.

Congressman Wright Patman from Texas called the chains monopoly practices. When a proposal to tax chains was put forth earlier in the 1930s, the brothers were unimpressed: "If the people of the United States like our stores so little that they are willing to tax us out of business, that is their affair. We will shut up our shop. We have not spent, nor will we spend, a single penny to fight chain-store taxation." Patman was responding not only to industry pressure, but also to the fears of local neighborhoods. Every time an A & P cash-and-carry store would open, at least one "mom and pop" store would disappear. Despite A & P's low prices, it was often considered disloyal to shop at an A & P because the local grocery was operated by a relative or a friend.

In the end A & P spent more than a single penny to fight their political battles. They hired the public relations firm of Carl Byoir to represent them to the public and the government. In 1937 A & P ran an advertisement in 1,400 newspapers across the country to answer Wright Patman. Mr. John and Mr. George said that they didn't personally need A & P because they already had enough money for life. But they pointed out that A & P's 90,000 employees did need the company, especially since A & P paid higher wages for shorter hours than the industry average. To charges of profiteering A & P countered with the fact that they netted only 1% after taxes.

In 1949 Mr. John appointed David Bofinger president and retired to the board. Bofinger died a year later, and another longtime A & P employee, Ralph Burger, who had started as an $11-a-week clerk in 1911, assumed the job. Burger was as austere as Mr. George and refused to move into Mr. John's more refined offices after John's death in 1951. (The 79-year-old Mr. John had been attending a board meeting of the Chrysler Corporation, listening to a discussion about how the company needed younger blood. He got up, saying, "Then you won't be needing me any more," and walked to the elevator, where he collapsed from heart failure.)

In 1957, when Mr. George was dying at the age of 92, Burger was at his bedside as

George whispered his last instructions: "Ralph, take care of the organization." It was widely understood that George meant: "Ralph, run it the way we would." And Ralph did, running the company in the 1950s as he saw the brothers do it in 1930. Both Mr. John and Mr. George left their stock to the Hartford Foundation, a medical research charity, and named Burger president of the foundation.

In 1958 the company was reorganized and sold stock to the public for the first time, but the foundation, which Burger headed, held the controlling shares. Burger continued to operate the way he thought the brothers would want him to. He fended off repeated challenges by Hartford family members and ran A & P with a quirky, secretive, and covetous air, loyally retaining and promoting curmudgeons who had labored as he had from clerks to officers. He spoke not at all to the press and grudgingly to stockholders. The Hartford heirs and heiresses were incensed, especially playboy Huntington Hartford, Jr., but none of them showed any inclination to work in the business. Furthermore, since they disagreed among themselves, Burger was free to run things as he saw fit. And he did until his death in 1969.

When Burger died, A & P was the biggest retailer in the United States. The nearest competitor was Safeway, whose $2.5 billion sales were less than half of A & P's $5.4 billion. In that year *Fortune* wrote: "Nobody expects that a single competitor is going to knock A & P off the pinnacle in the near future."

But the A & P stores began to lose ground rapidly in 1970. Kroger, Jewel, Winn-Dixie, and Acme were all competing vigorously for market shares. Safeway, by far the largest in the West, was nipping at A & P's heels for the number 1 spot in food retailing. Although A & P commanded a vast number of company-owned factories and canneries, their stores were small, spartan, and poorly maintained. Instead of building new stores in the suburbs like its competitors, A & P spent money on its manufacturing facili-

THE DECLINE OF MOM AND POP STORES

Year and Number of Independent (Non-Chain) Stores

Year	Number of stores
1940	446,350 stores
1950	400,700 stores
1960	260,050 stores
1970	208,300 stores
1978	169,500 stores

Source: *Progressive Grocer*, April 1979.

ties, which had grown to include 23 bakeries; 6 coffee roasting plants; 3 milk processors; 3 ice cream companies; and factories for jams, jellies, hosiery, delicatessen products, fish, poultry, and even ketchup.

To counter eroding sales, A & P introduced their "WEO" (Where Economy Originates) campaign: the stores cut prices drastically in a desperate effort to regain customers. But the maneuver didn't work. Most of A & P's stores were poorly located, inner-city operations too small to support a discount operation. Furthermore, A & P was met head-on by competitors in pricing, advertising, and marketing. In 1973, after A & P reported losses of $51 million, WEO was quietly dropped, and Safeway became the nation's largest food retailer. That year, for the first time in their history, A & P went outside their ranks and selected Jonathan L. Scott, former head of the Albertson's chain, to revive the ailing giant.

The 44-year-old Scott, who had been the "wunderkind" of the Idaho-based chain, arrived to high praise and hopes. He immediately began a drastic curtailment of stores, cutting outlets from 3,500 to 1,800, which resulted in a $157 million loss in fiscal 1975. He instigated a "Price and Pride" program, retrained employees to bolster sagging morale, opened new 55,000-square foot stores, and decentralized management into eight regional offices. In 1978 the company sank into the red again, and *Fortune* called Scott's performance "the most disappointing management failure of recent years." Scott's attempts to cut labor costs backfired. By closing half the stores, he was forced by union contracts to retain those with seniority, letting go his younger, more vigorous workers on lower pay scales. When staff in the larger stores were cut down, customers found themselves waiting in long lines and walked out, abandoning their shopping carts in the aisles. Managers reported finding 20 to 30 such carts at the end of the day. Stores became dirty. One manager said that, "while the crud kept mounting, . . . it got to the point where we not only had dirt, we had dirty dirt." The stock which had once hit a high of $70 was now selling at $6. One analyst said that Scott's activities were like "rearranging the deck chairs on the Titanic." In 1978 Kroger overtook A & P— and the onetime king was now third in the grocery industry.

In 1979 the German supermarket giant Tengelmann bought 44% of the outstanding shares of A & P for $79 million. The Hartford Foundation, which had refused an offer of $40 per share a decade earlier, settled for $7. Most other family members also sold out. Tengelmann, a $3 billion company with 2,000 store outlets in Germany, picked up balance sheet assets worth about $600 million. Some analysts say the purchase is the first hopeful sign since the Hartfords died. Another analyst, highly doubtful of A & P's future, asked: "Do you think maybe we finally put one over on the Germans?"

Reputation. The A & P supermarket chain is widely regarded as a relic of yesteryear, running stores which are old-fashioned in both appearance and operations.

Who owns and runs the company. What was once the largest family-controlled enterprise in retailing is now almost completely devoid of Hartford stockholders. With the German corporation owning almost half of the outstanding shares, control rests with Tengelmann's chairman Erivan Haub.

Jonathan Scott remains as chairman and chief executive officer. Joining him as president in 1977 was his colleague at Albertson's, David Morrow.

Where they're going. Tengelmann owns a chain of stores in Germany called PLUS, a German acronym for *prima leben und sparen* which translates as "quality living and saving." A & P has begun to open PLUS units in the United States. A PLUS store carries only 850 nonperishable food and general merchandise items, about one-fourth of which are private label or generic items manufactured by A & P. The remaining items are brand-name products. There is no service; goods are sold from cartons on pallets and from shelves, customers must bring their own bags or pay for them, and they bag their own purchases. Payment is cash only.

Stock performance: A & P stock bought for $1,000 in 1970 sold for $321 on January 2, 1980.

Access. 2 Paragon Drive, Montvale, New Jersey 07645; (201) 573-9700.

Consumer brands.

A & P; Ann Page; Our Own teas; Warwick and Crestwood candies; Bokar, Red Circle, and Eight O'clock coffees; Jane Parker bakery goods; Marvel.

Sales: $2.7 billion
Profits: $38.3 million
Forbes 500 rank: 188
Rank in food retailing: 9
Founded: 1939
Employees: 24,400
Headquarters: Boise, Idaho

Albertson's is widely recognized as one of the best-managed companies in the supermarket industry. They operate 365 supermarkets in 15 western and southern states, most of them in the Far West: California, Oregon, Washington, and Idaho. They're known as a chain that pays attention to consumer needs and that breeds topnotch managers. Jonathan L. Scott married the boss's daughter and rose to the presidency of Albertson's. When the Scotts were divorced, founder Joe Albertson retained his ex-son-in-law as president. Scott now runs the A & P chain. A. J. "Joe" Albertson, formerly a district manager of Safeway, opened his first store in Boise in 1939. He was one of the pioneers of the complete one-stop, self-service concept of supermarketing. Albertson, who was 73 in 1979, serves now as chairman of the executive committee, controlling 25% of the stock. He and his wife and their daughter, Barbara Rasmussen, sit on the board.

Access. 250 Parkcenter Boulevard, Boise, Idaho 83726; (208) 344-7441.

> Food stores rang up $190 billion in sales in 1978, more than one-quarter of all retail sales in the United States.

American Stores

Sales: $3.8 billion
Profits: $44.4 million
Forbes 500 rank: 119
Rank in retailing: 8
Rank in food retailing: 6
Rank in drug retailing: 3
Founded: 1891
Employees: 48,000
Headquarters: Wilmington, Delaware

One of the largest mergers in the history of U.S. retailing was accomplished in 1979, when American Stores combined with the Skaggs Companies of Salt Lake City. The result was a new retail giant whose operations span the country under a variety of names:

370 Acme and Super Saver supermarkets in seven eastern states: Delaware, Maryland, New Jersey, New York, Pennsylvania, Virginia, and West Virginia.

319 Alpha Beta supermarkets in Arizona and California.

238 Skaggs drug stores and combination drug/supermarkets in 21 states stretching from California to Illinois and from Texas to the Canadian border.

132 Rea & Derick and Hy-Lo stores in Pennsylvania, New York, and Maryland.

41 family restaurants (most of them Alphy's) in California, and 12 Hardee's fast-food outlets in Pennsylvania, Delaware, and New Jersey.

Although American Stores was the larger unit, it was Skaggs that did the acquiring—and L. S. Skaggs emerged as the largest stockholder. The merger agreement provided that the new company would be named American Stores and that it would at first be headquartered in Wilmington, Delaware, but one of the first orders of business would be the construction of a new corporate headquarters building in Salt Lake City. The ostensible reason for the merger was to combine the drug skills of Skaggs with the supermarket skills of American. However, shortly after the wedding, Value Line Investment Survey said "the honeymoon period is apparently over," with profits not living up to expectations.

Stock performance. American Stores stock bought for $1,000 in 1970 sold for $1,564 on January 2, 1980.

Access. One Rollins Plaza, Wilmington, Delaware 19803; (303) 571-8733.

 Dillon

Sales: $1.8 billion
Profits: $33.6 million
Forbes 500 rank: 291
Employees: 20,000
Headquarters: Hutchinson, Kansas

Dillon operates a bunch of supermarket chains under a bunch of names. They have 65 Dillon Stores in Kansas, Oklahoma, Missouri, and Arkansas, 53 Fry's in Arizona and California, 50 King Soopers in Colorado, and 24 City Markets in Colorado, Wyoming, and Utah. In addition, they run three different convenience store chains: 91 Quik Stops in Northern California, 113 Kwik Shops in Kansas, Nebraska, and Iowa, and 101 Time Savers in Louisiana. To round it out, there are 18 D.G. Calhoun's department stores in Kansas. Dillon has one of the highest profit margins in the supermarket industry. The Dillons are very much in control. Ray E. Dillon is chairman and his son, Ray E. Dillon, Jr., is president.

Access. 700 East 30th Street, Hutchinson, Kansas 67501; (316) 663-6801.

Sales: $1.3 billion
Loss: $7.0 million
Forbes 500 rank: 370
Founded: 1965
Employees: 16,000
Headquarters: Bedford Heights, Ohio

One of the top 15 supermarket operators, Fisher is a major contender in two big cities: Cleveland, where Fisher-owned Fazio's goes head-to-head with Pick-N-Pay for market leadership; and Chicago, where their Dominick's has done so well it ranks number 2 now, behind Jewel. Fisher operates 158 supermarkets and leased food departments. They invaded the Southern California market and then retreated, selling their stores to Albertson's. Fisher Foods was formed in 1965 by the merger of companies controlled by the Fazio and the Costa families. Carl Fazio is chairman, and the Fazio family controls 25% of the stock.

Access. 5300 Richmond Road, Bedford Heights, Ohio 44146; (216) 292-7000.

Fleming Companies Inc.

Sales: $2.5 billion
Profits: $16.4 million
Forbes 500 rank: 201
Rank in food wholesaling: 2
Founded: 1915
Employees: 7,500
Headquarters: Oklahoma City, Oklahoma

Fleming buys grocery products and resells them to 2,300 stores in 21 states. It's an enormous business shielded from public view, but if you've ever shopped in a food store bearing the banners IGA, Minimax, Thriftway, United Super, or Dixie Dandy, you may well have been buying goods supplied by Fleming. Like other wholesalers, they have edged into the retail sector. They own 45 Piggly Wiggly stores in Alabama, Mississippi, Georgia, and Florida, and they have a network of 48 gasoline stations in the Midwest.

Access. 6601 North Broadway, Box 26647, Oklahoma City, Oklahoma 73126; (405) 848-7721.

The selling area of U.S. supermarkets totaled 11,050 acres in 1977. Stretched out into a single aisle, this area would reach from New York to Los Angeles and back again.

About one-sixth of the world's agricultural exports are shipped from the United States, making this country the top food exporter.

Sales: $1.2 billion
Profits: $17.9 million
Forbes 500 rank: 388
Founded: 1935
Employees: 12,100
Headquarters: Landover, Maryland

Giant operates 117 supermarkets in the Baltimore–Washington–Richmond corridor, where they go head-to-head with the nation's largest supermarket operator, Safeway Stores. The battle is often a standoff, although latest figures show Giant in the number 1 spot. Giant made news in the grocery industry in 1970 when they hired as consumer advisor Esther Peterson, who had previously been consumer affairs advisor in the White House. Under her leadership Giant supermarkets pioneered many programs, including unit pricing, open dating, nutritional labeling, and the promulgation of a "Consumer's Bill of Rights." All of the voting shares are held by members of the founding Cohen and Lehrman families.

Access. 6300 Sheriff Road, Landover, Maryland 20785; (301) 341-4100.

> The average supermarket shopping trip takes 30.77 minutes. Women shoppers spend an average of $1.07 for each shopping minute.

What Ever Happened to the Milkman?

Fifty years ago America had 12,000 home-delivery dairies that employed 70,000 "routemen"—milkmen on delivery routes. By the late 1970s there were only 600 distributors left who delivered to homes, and they employed about 4,000 routemen.

The old milkman was a many-sided figure. To live up to expectations, he had to be alert, punctual, dependable, courteous, good at record keeping, friendly, and attractive. Good eyesight and patience were also important, since he was expected, while delivering before sunrise, to read hastily scribbled notes left in empty bottles. He might be asked to put the trashcan on the curb for pickup or to pour milk in a nearby saucer for the customer's cat.

Until 1900 most milk was carried "loose" in ten-gallon cans. The milkman had quart- and pint-sized tin dippers, and customers came out to his wagon with their pitchers. Milk was delivered twice daily. Milk held overnight in old-time ice boxes often soured by morning. The milk was kept chilled in the wagon by ice-filled burlap bags placed on top of the milk containers.

In the 1890s a New York glass company started promoting milk bottles. The bottle held a little less than the quart it advertised, making money for everyone but the customer. These costly and complicated early bottles resembled home-canning jars, with glass cap, rubber seal, and wire hold-down clamp. They were replaced by the long-necked bottle, which was built to exaggerate the depth of the cream-line—in America considered a main criterion of value—and thus promote sales. In 1936 American Can brought out the first flat-top, rectangular paper containers. Later came gable-top Pure-Pak containers and plastic containers.

Although in the 1920s a specialized four-cylinder-engine milk truck was put on the market, horse-drawn milk wagons were in common use until the mid-1930s. A horse, unlike a truck, would learn a route and often stop automatically at appropriate houses. A horse could be bought for a mere $100, far less than any truck, and had an average life of a dozen years—at least as long as a truck.

After World War II distributors found the home-delivery system increasingly less economical. The cost of sending a man and a truck to a house and delivering low-cost items was too great. The supermarkets that were knocking out small grocers could sell milk cheaper, usually pricing it at a minimum markup, often as a loss leader to draw in customers for more profit-making items. One old-time milkman, his services no longer required, sat down and wrote his recollections in a small book, which is the source for this article. *Old-Time Milkmen: Their Labors and Loves*, written and published by Hank Morse, is available from its author at 402 West Washington Blvd., Montebello, California 90640.

Health and Natural Food Stores

Number of stores nationwide: 6,600
Sales: $1.56 billion
Profits: $163 million
Sales of a typical store: $236,000
Profits of typical store: $24,800
Employees in the industry: 37,000
Employees per store: 5.6
Average wages per hour: $3.26

What they do. The typical health or natural food store stocks $28,000 worth of merchandise, ranging from bulk food grains to $25 bottles of shampoo or vitamins. Less than half the items in stock are food products, but food accounts for about three-fifths of sales. The food items consist largely of staples such as rice, beans, pasta, oil, and honey, but the stores also carry dairy products, herbs, teas, snacks, and baked goods. Of the nonfood items the largest single category is vitamins, followed by health and beauty aids, books, and appliances.

History. Health food stores began in the 1930s when small shops in America's larger cities began selling specialty foods, catering largely to people on restricted diets and those who wanted to buy vitamins, which were not widely sold at that time.

It wasn't until the mid-sixties that the natural foods business began, as dozens of alternative businesses cropped up to service the growing counterculture. Natural foods stores sold primarily food—bulk grains, seeds, nuts, dried fruit, sprouting beans, and fresh produce and juices—and some did not carry vitamins at all. The distinction between these two types of stores has gradually blurred, and each type now has characteristics of the other.

What they own and rent. Most proprietors rent their buildings, partly because the industry is so new. Two-thirds of the stores today have been in business less than five years, and while 600 new stores started business in 1978, 400 also went out of business. The average store rents from anywhere between $400 and $2,000 a month, depending on the location. Most stores buy or lease their refrigeration equipment, which is usually their biggest asset after their inventories.

Who owns them. Stores in most cases are owned by two people. Two-thirds of the owners are also store managers and work full time. In many cases the store is their first business. If the store succeeds, it is usually only because the owners work long hours or the employees earn close to minimum wage. Owners are predominantly white, middle-class, college educated, and in their late twenties or early thirties, though there are now a few chains, such as the General Nutrition Centers, whose stores are generally located in malls and managed by older women.

Where they're going. The natural foods business has been called the only major marketing innovation in food to emerge in the past decade, and one that has led a transformation of American eating habits toward fresh and unprocessed foods. Some people in the business think the industry as a whole is in the process of establishing an alternative food supply and marketing system. They may also be doing research and development for the major food companies who wait for foods to prove popular in health food stores and then introduce their own nationally advertised brands, such as Quaker 100% Natural, a corporate version of granola. In 1979 General Mills bought Celestial Seasonings, an herbal tea company that began in Boulder, Colorado, ten years earlier. San Diego now has a 27,000-square-foot health food supermarket with nine checkout stands. They expect to gross $4 million in their first year.

FOOD COOPERATIVES IN THE MARKETPLACE		
Percentage sold by coops:	1950	1975
COTTON AND COTTON PRODUCTS	12%	26%
DAIRY PRODUCTS	53%	75%
FRUITS AND VEGETABLES	20%	25%
GRAINS AND SOYBEANS	29%	40%
LIVESTOCK AND PRODUCTS	16%	10%
POULTRY PRODUCTS	7%	9%
Source: Corporate Data Exchange.		

JEWEL

Sales: $3.8 billion
Profits: $50.7 million
Forbes 500 rank: 121
Rank in retailing: 13
Rank in food retailing: 7
Founded: 1899
Employees: 33,000
Headquarters: Chicago, Illinois

What they do. Jewel sells more foodstuffs to Chicagoans than any other retail chain. From this strong base in the nation's third-largest market, they have expanded to other regions and other kinds of retail business. They operate more than 400 stores under the Jewel, Jewel T Discount, Eisner, Star, and Buttrey names; 261 Osco drugstores; 94 Brigham's ice cream shops; and 222 White Hen Pantry convenience stores. Most of the Brigham's and White Hen stores are franchised. There are only a few states left where Jewel does not have a retailing presence. Many of the new supermarkets are superstores built in tandem with Osco drugstores. Jewel's original business was a home-delivery shopping service, and they still operate it, with 1,200 routes in 40 states. Jewel is also a formidable manufacturer of the products they sell. Their manufacturing volume alone is $320 million.

History. Before we went to stores in cars, stores came to our doors in horse-drawn carts. One of those "stores" was the Jewel Tea Company, started in Chicago at the turn of the century by Frank Vernon Skiff and his brother-in-law Frank Ross, who sold coffee, tea, spices, and extracts off their wagons. By 1905 Jewel was roasting their own coffee. By 1915 the business had grown to 850 routes and annual sales of $8 million.

Jewel went through a number of management and ownership changes (founders Skiff and Ross were forced out in 1919), but the company survived all of them, including the arrival of the automobile. Jewel's routes were motorized by 1926. What almost sunk them was the "Green River Ordinance" of 1932, under which the town of Green River, Wyoming, prohibited salesmen from making uninvited calls on homes. This "public nuisance" law spread, as Jewel says in the company history, "like an epidemic throughout the Midwest." So in self-defense Jewel went into the retail grocery business in their home city. In 1934 they set forth a set of principles for their food store operations. These were called Jewel's "Ten Commandments": (1) Clean and white stores; (2) friendliness; (3) self-service; (4) true quality; (5) freshness; (6) low prices; (7) honest weight; (8) variety of foods; (9) fair dealings; (10) the Jewel guarantee—complete satisfaction or money back with a smile.

Reputation. Jewel was the first major chain to date perishable items, list prices of prescription drugs, and sell generic grocery items.

What they own. Jewel owns 228 real estate affiliates, which own the properties where Jewel stores are located. They have a 42% interest in Aurrera, Mexico's largest publicly owned retailer. Aurrera recently opened one of the world's first "hypermarkets," a 188,000 square foot Gran Bazar in Mexico City.

Who owns and runs the company. In 1979 Lord, Abbett & Co., an investment advisor, reported ownership of 7.4% of Jewel stock. All the directors and officers together hold 3% of the shares. On Jewel's board are two women—New York attorney Barbara S. Preiskel and Iowa nutritionist Helen LeB. Hilton—and a Jesuit priest, Raymond S. Baumhart, president of Chicago's Loyola University. Weston R. Christopherson became chief executive officer in 1980. A lawyer, he grew up in North Dakota, where his father was a tenant farmer.

In the public eye. Jewel maintains a Consumers Advisory Council with a department that advises customers, for example, to boycott meat when prices get too high. They are also one of the few big chains that have returned to depressed minority-population neighborhoods. They have built new stores in Chicago's inner-city areas and taken customers away from A & P.

Where they're going. In the first hookup between a Japanese and a U.S. firm, Jewel has signed on as a supermarket consultant to Seiyu Stores, Japan's third-largest grocery chain.

Stock performance. Jewel stock bought for $1,000 in 1970 sold for $895 on January 2, 1980.

Access. 5725 N. East River Road, Chicago, Illinois 60631; (312) 693-6000.

Sales: $9 billion
Profits: $85.7 million
Forbes 500 rank: 36
Rank in retailing: 5
Rank in food retailing: 2
Founded: 1883
Employees: 63,539
Headquarters: Cincinnati, Ohio

What they do. Kroger runs a mean, tough show. They became number 2 in the supermarket industry in 1979, passing A & P, by keeping their stores up to date, making them bigger, concentrating their efforts in areas where they are strong, and building up a strong cadre of hard-nosed grocery managers. During the 1970s Kroger spent close to $1 billion to open new stores and upgrade old ones.

Kroger's 1,200 food stores are located primarily in a 21-state band that stretches from the Great Lakes to the Gulf of Mexico. They also operate the 70-unit Market Basket chain in Southern California. Kroger's share of the market can be considerable: 50% in Cincinnati, 38% in Columbus, for example. But they won't battle Fazio's and Pick-N-Pay in Cleveland, nor will they confront Jewel in Chicago. Kroger is also in the drugstore business—and they're big there, too. They have 487 SupeRx stores, half of them next to Kroger Supermarkets. Other retail operations fielded by Kroger include the BiLo stores, 10,000-square-foot discount houses carrying 450 items; Sav-On drugstores; and Barney's Food Warehouses, named after founder Barney Kroger.

History. Bernard H. Kroger was the son of immigrant German shopkeepers who were wiped out in the panic of 1873. Setting out on his own at the age of 16, Barney sold coffee and tea door-to-door. He took orders one day and delivered them the next by horse and cart. After several years of selling from tea wagons, the owners of the Impe-

rial Tea Co. of Cincinnati offered their 21-year-old salesman $12 a week and a 10% share of the profits if he would manage their failing enterprise. He accepted, fired everyone except the delivery boy, and began to work 16-hour days, with the help of a new cash register and cashier (innovations at that time). Peevish, cranky, and irascible, Kroger was known as a particular and demanding buyer, weeding out merchandise until the store's inventory was up to his quality standard. His customers became devoted. At the end of the first year Imperial Tea had made a $3,000 profit. Kroger asked for a one-third share of the company, was refused and stalked out to form his own company.

Kroger's Great Western Tea Co. in Cincinnati was ruined by the flooding Ohio River soon after it opened in 1883. He borrowed and opened again, and the store flourished. By 1885 Kroger had four stores, and he began placing what were the first grocery ads in daily newpapers. His wagons and stores were painted fire-engine red, and while his competitors laughed, the customers flocked in. The competitors stopped laughing when Kroger began purchasing by the carload and underselling them with loss leaders, another Kroger first. At the time Kroger figured the overhead in his original store to be 4%: $4 for himself, $1 for rent, and $1 for expenses on sales of $150 a day. In 1899 his wife and son died from diseases, and Kroger plunged ever more deeply into his business life, becoming obsessed with success. Kroger was loud and erratic, with a temper that could explode at the slightest transgression. Managers would be fired on the spot for a dirty store.

Kroger expanded into mail order and manufacturing. In 1902 Great Western Tea was renamed Kroger Grocery and Baking, and 40 stores were flying the Kroger name. Kroger was the first grocer to operate his own bakery, selling his bread for 2½¢ a loaf. He was also the first grocer to bring a meat department into a grocery store—and he fought a long battle with his butchers to prevent them from shortweighting and stealing. As Kroger expanded across the Ohio countryside, he steadily bought out his competition. In 1928, at age 68, he sold all his holdings just before the crash, retired to Palm Beach, Florida, and took up golf.

Reputation. Kroger is known as a street

fighter. Several of their competitors have filed lawsuits charging them with price-cutting—slashing prices to increase business and drive the competition to the wall. A Kroger competitor quoted in *Supermarket News* said: "Kroger is good. It's tough. What it does to gain business is not illegal. It is business . . . good business for Kroger, rough business for us." Kroger went head-to-head with A & P in Ohio and drove them out of the state.

What they own. Besides their retail outlets, manufacturing facilities that produce a quarter of their food sales: bakery products, peanut butter, dairy products, jams and jellies, sausages, salad dressings, coffee and tea, and candies. They have a 50% interest in three amusement parks: King's Dominion in Virginia, Carowinds Theme Park in North Carolina, and the Hanna-Barbera Marineland near Los Angeles.

Who owns and runs the company. The largest stake, 5%, belongs to Cincinnati's American Financial Corp., controlled by Carl H. Lindner, a financier who also owns the biggest share of United Brands. Kroger is considered the university of the retail food industry. They hire more people than they need for key positions, then let them fight it out for advancement. As a result, ex-Kroger people can be found all over the supermarket industry. At one time there were so many that a Kroger Alumni Group published a newsletter and held annual meetings.

In the public eye. Kroger has traditionally been considered a prounion company. A Retail Clerks' Union official gave *Supermarket News* this assessment of his dealings with Kroger: "Tough negotiations in a frank and trusting fashion." Said a Kroger vice-president in charge of labor relations: "There's nothing wrong with us. The trouble is with business executives who have never even sat down with their opposite numbers in labor."

Where they're going. Kroger is now a strong number 2 in the supermarket industry and is growing more rapidly than Safeway, the industry leader.

Stock performance. Kroger stock bought for $1,000 in 1970 sold for $1,345 on January 2, 1980.

Access. 1014 Vine Street, Cincinnati, Ohio 45201; (513) 762-4000.

Consumer brands.

Retail outlets: Kroger's; SupeRx drugstores; BiLo stores; Sav-on drugstores; Barney's Food Warehouse; Kroger Family Center.
House brands: Kroger; SupeRx.

Lucky

Sales: $5.8 billion
Profits: $98 million
Forbes 500 rank: 65
Rank in food retailing: 5
Rank in retailing: 10
Founded: 1931
Employees: 58,000
Headquarters: Dublin, California

What they do. Lucky is a three-part retailer. They operate food stores (the original business), department stores, and a large number of specialty stores, primarily in the western and southwestern parts of the country. Food stores account for two-thirds of sales but only one-third of profits. The Lucky units break down as follows:

Food stores—428 units, of which 179 are conventional supermarkets and 249 are discount centers, larger outlets which also feature apparel, liquor, and drugs. Lucky's food outlets boast the highest average sales per store in the industry: $6.7 million in 1978. The food stores fly these flags: Lucky and Food Basket (in the Far West), Eagle (Southwest and Midwest), Kash N' Karry (Florida).

Department stores—Lucky moved into this field in 1960 with the purchase of two Southern California membership stores: Gemco and Memco. These 77 stores (52 of them in California) now make Lucky the nation's fifth-largest mass-merchandise retailer. The stores each average $20 million a year.

Specialty stores—Lucky operates a number of stores in single product categories: Pic-A-Dilly (low-cost women's apparel), Yellow Front (everything from sporting goods to imported baskets), L & G (sporting goods), and Mays and Stacy (drugs).

Fabrics—159 retail fabric outlets under the Hancock's name.

Restaurants—160 Sirloin Stockade restaurants in the West and Midwest; Fred's Gang dinner restaurants in Oklahoma City and Memphis.

Automotive—209 auto parts stores in 10 western states under the Kragen, Dorman's, and Checker names.

History. In 1931 the Depression prompted six stores located near San Francisco to team up and form a company called Peninsula Stores. Four years later they added a store in nearby Berkeley, and by 1947, the chain had 29 outlets and had changed their name to Lucky. They're still based in the San Francisco Bay Area.

Reputation. Tagged the "butcher, baker, and candlestick maker" (Lucky does them all), Lucky is considered an astute marketer to the middle- to lower-middle-class shopper. Lucky's profits run higher than the industry average, while their prices tend to run lower. They avoid gimmicks like trading stamps and games.

What they own. Close to a third of a billion dollars in real estate at market prices, although it is carried on the books at less than half of that due to depreciation. Lucky owns a real estate subsidiary which is able to secure 100% financing on its new properties. So when Lucky puts up a new store, it puts nothing down.

Who owns and runs the company. The two largest shareholders are the Rubenstein-Freidman family interests, which own 3% of the outstanding shares, worth $17 million at market value; and the California Employees Retirement Systems, which owns a similar amount. Chairman Wayne Fisher has headed the company since 1974 and owns over $1 million worth of stock, along with options for more.

In the public eye. Lucky is not known for civic involvement.

Where they're going. To stay in the food business, but diversify further into nonfood retailing, where the margins are higher.

> Grapes and cotton grown in California each generated cash receipts of more than $1 billion in 1979, marking the first time any California crop exceeded that level.

Stock performance. Lucky stock bought for $1,000 in 1970 sold for $1,269 on January 2, 1980.

Access. 6300 Clark Avenue, Dublin, California 94566; (415) 828-1000.

Consumer brands.

Harvest Day, Lady Lee grocery products.

Malone & Hyde

Sales: $1.6 billion
Profits: $21.3 million
Forbes 500 rank: 316
Rank in food wholesaling: 3
Founded: 1907
Employees: 6,000
Headquarters: Memphis, Tennessee

The largest food wholesaler in the South, Malone & Hyde supplies a full line of groceries to 2,500 independent supermarkets in 16 states from Florida to Texas and north to Indiana. Most of their customers are family-owned supermarkets competing against the big chains. Malone & Hyde has also drifted into the retail side. They have a 150-unit drugstore chain operating under the names Super D, Sommers, and Petty; a 24-unit sporting goods chain, Sunset Sport Centers, based in Salt Lake City; a new auto parts chain, Hyde's Auto Shack; and 44 supermarkets. The Hyde family owns 25% of the stock. Joseph R. Hyde, III, chairman and president, started attending directors' meetings when he was 14.

Access. 1451 Union Avenue, Memphis, Tennessee 38104; (901) 345-4200.

Safeway

Sales: $13.7 billion
Profits: $143.3 million
Forbes 500 rank: 17
Rank in retailing: 2
Rank in food retailing: 1
Founded: 1915
Employees: 144,000
Headquarters: Oakland, California

What they do. The world's largest super-market chain is headquartered in an ancient, nondescript Oakland warehouse which carries no identifying sign. Safeway considers this image to be in keeping with a business where profits are measured by a penny on a dollar of sales.

Safeway sells more grocery products than any other company, through 2,425 supermarkets, 1,971 of them in the United States. In 1,036 cities and towns they have only one store, and that unit is usually the market leader.

They operate primarily in 22 states west of the Mississippi River. One strong outpost on the eastern seaboard consists of 250 supermarkets fanning out from Washington, D.C., north to Baltimore and Wilmington and south to Richmond.

For many years Safeway ran second behind the A & P chain, whose strength was in the big cities of the East, but when A & P began to falter in the late 1960s, Safeway continued to accelerate, overtaking A & P's sales in 1973 and presently outselling them two to one. Unlike A & P, Safeway continually upgrades and enlarges their units. They closed more than 1,000 stores during the past ten years and opened 1,270 new ones. The average Safeway store now rings up sales of $5 million a year ($13,700 a day).

Safeway's only business is retailing. However, more than a quarter of their sales is now from products bearing their own brand names, which they manufacture themselves, process, or buy from others. Their private label line extends to 5,600 different items. Safeway has never lost money, although since 1931 they have never

Safeway's first store, 18 x 32 feet, in American Falls, Idaho.

earned more than 2¢ on the sales dollar. The average over the past 10 years has been 1.22¢.

One of the few U.S. food retailers to have moved overseas, Safeway has 277 stores in Canada, 88 in England and Scotland, 63 in Australia, and 26 in West Germany.

History. Two families helped build Safeway, one from a fundamentalist background, the other from Wall Street. It was an odd combination—but it worked. S. M. Skaggs, a Baptist minister, built an 18 by 32 foot grocery store in American Falls, Idaho, prompted by a messianic zeal to help his flock and his neighbors, mostly hard-pressed grain farmers who had to pay high prices for their foods. The Skaggs credo was: "He who serves best, profits most." From its start in the summer of 1915 the Skaggs store was dedicated to building sales volume by taking only a small profit on the merchandise sold. This operating philosophy was to be followed by the six sons of S. M. Skaggs, who put their stamp on American retailing as few families have. (In addition to Safeway, four other major U.S. retailing organizations can trace their roots to the Skaggs family: the Osco, Longs, Skaggs (now merged with American Stores) drug chains, and the Pay-less drug chains. The eldest son, M. B. Skaggs, extended the original grocery store to a western chain that by 1926 encompassed 428 units in 10 states: the Skaggs United Stores.

Skaggs merged in 1926 with a Southern California chain of 322 stores originally known as the Sam Seelig stores that had adopted the Safeway name in 1925. The New York investment house Merrill Lynch, which had financed chain-store developments in the East, now came into the picture: the Skaggs-Safeway merger was negotiated by Charles Merrill and M. B. Skaggs.

The Safeway chain coined big profits from its inception. In 1927, with 915 stores, they earned $1.9 million on sales of $69 million. Expansion was so rapid that by 1931 they had 3,527 stores, the high point in store population. Thereafter the number of stores went down, but store size went up. Safeway was one of the first chains to embrace self-service, to establish huge warehouse distribution centers, and to build the giant supermarkets that became the workhorses of the grocery industry.

When Safeway Stores was incorporated in 1926, there were four Skaggs brothers in the organization. M. B. Skaggs ran the company until 1934, when he passed the reins to Lingan A. Warren, a remarkable grocery

Brave New Supermarket

Soft music spins a mood of detached serenity as the shopper strolls lightly along carpeted aisles carrying a paper bag about the size of a business envelope. She has no shopping cart, and she needs none. There is nothing in this futuristic supermarket to put in a cart—no cans of beans, no packaged cake mix, boxes of detergent, or cartons of milk. The shopper never sees or touches most of the items she will eventually take home. Each of the store's 4,500 grocery items is represented by a single dummy specimen—a dummy can or package exactly like the real thing, ranged on gleaming glass shelves alongside sleek lucite boxes of computer-coded cards. Choosing what she wants from the dummy items, the shopper collects a three-by-five-inch card for each one. Moving smoothly along the ranks of shelves, she puts in her envelope cards for green peas, prune Danish, frozen haddock, scouring powder, and cat food.

Finishing quickly with the compact grocery section, the shopper moves to the perishables, where reality reasserts itself in the form of fresh vegetables, meat, and delicatessen items. But instead of the traditional shopping cart, she propels a plastic tub along a waist-high, U-shaped conveyor belt. A produce manager weighs and bags her carrots, butter lettuce, fresh mushrooms. She hadn't meant to buy meat today, but the conveyor belt guides her inexorably through all the perishables departments, in what the store's designers call "structured traffic flow." This means that the shopper can't avoid some sections at will; here the decisions are made by the machinery.

At the end of the conveyor belt the shopper arrives at the Control Center, a series of square holes in the wall, each with its computer terminal and control operator. Emptying the shopper's bag of

man often described as crusty and autocratic, but known throughout the industry as a crusader who would never bend his principles. Lingan Warren ran an unusual company. His contract specified that he was to receive no salary if the company didn't make money. He fought repeated battles on behalf of his customers: waging war against trading stamps, trying to break the dairy/government agreements that fixed the price of milk, urging brand-name manufacturers to cut prices rather than distribute cents-off coupons. In one celebrated case in Colorado he personally paid a fine levied because of Safeway's price-cutting.

Warren's 21-year reign at Safeway was marked by an enormous expansion in volume, but his policies did not yield high profits. As a result, on October 3, 1955, Lingan Warren resigned. From Merrill Lynch, Pierce, Fenner & Beane in New York came Robert A. Magowan, who had married Charles Merrill's daughter, Doris, in 1925.

In 1956 Safeway's profits virtually doubled. They doubled again in the next ten years and then nearly tripled by 1975.

M. B. Skaggs, the company chairman, retired in 1941. There are no longer any Skaggs family members in Safeway.

Reputation. Safeway is a tough competitor. They run big, modern, clean stores that stock a cornucopia of goods, but they're not flashy. While they are no longer pioneers, they are quick to spot new trends and latch onto them.

Robert Kahn, a retail management consultant, says that since Lingan Warren left the company, it's the profit consideration that prevails.

What they own. Safeway owns a network of 30 distribution-warehousing centers and 28 freestanding warehouses; a fleet of 2,600 tractor-trailer trucks plus 2,200 additional trailers (the largest private trucking fleet in the world); 21 meat-cutting plants; 16 bakeries; 20 fluid milk and ice cream plants; 5 soft drink bottling plants; 4 meat processing plants; 6 egg candling plants; 3 coffee roasting plants; 3 fruit and vegetable canning plants; 2 jam and jelly plants; an edible oil refinery; and a dressing and salad oil plant.

Who owns and runs the company. The largest shareholder, with nearly 7% of the stock, is the Republic National Bank of Dallas, trustee of Safeway's profit-sharing plan. The largest single family holding—about 1.5% of the total stock—is in the hands of Magowan family members. It's an influen-

---

product cards, the operator waves a wand over them, which scans the codes on each card; a display screen instantly posts the price and description of each coded item. Perishables are punched into a keyboard. In seconds two computers at the back of the store, connected to the terminals, produce a printout invoice in duplicate. The shopper gets a copy, while the other copy goes to the backroom.

In the vast backroom the real groceries repose on shelves in letter-coded aisles. A team of two pickers assembles the order, moving up and down the aisles in a sequence dictated, for maximum

efficiency, by the computer printout. In less than eight minutes a picker wheels the bagged order to the waiting shopper's car.

No Buck Rogers dream, this operation, called The Shopping Machine, is open for business in Valley, California, a town some 50 miles north of Oakland. Duplicate stores are planned for other locations in the state. Consumer response has been enthusiastic, bolstered by Shopping Machine innovations that include discounting prices and accepting credit cards for purchases.

The Shopping Machine's inventors say their creation eliminates the waste of a con-

ventional supermarket operation, with its endless price-stamping on thousands of individual items and restocking of huge arrays of merchandise on the selling floor. The new setup also eliminates pilferage, since few people will bother to steal dummy groceries. The miniaturized display area cuts down on investments for equipment and fixtures.

Whether or not The Shopping Machine becomes the supermarket of the future may depend on the consumer's willingness to exchange speed and economy for the furtive pleasure of squeezing a roll of Charmin.

tial holding. Two Magowans—Merrill L. and Peter A., sons of Robert A. Magowan —hold seats on Safeway's board, and at the end of 1978 Peter Magowan was promoted over a number of officers to succeed William S. Mitchell as chairman and chief executive officer. The selection of another Magowan to head the company came after four years of stagnant earnings. Safeway has two women on its board—Mary Gardiner Jones, a former member of the Federal Trade Commission with close links to the consumer movement, and Marjorie S. Kinney, a Los Angeles businesswoman who heads her own company.

Of Safeway's 144,000 employees 79,000 are food clerks who stock the shelves and operate the cash registers. In 1978 the average Safeway store manager made $25,000. One out of every five employees is a member of a minority group, one out of every three is a woman. However, as of 1979 there were no women or minorities in officer ranks.

In the public eye. Safeway was one of the first chains to adopt unit pricing, showing the total price and the price per pound. Some Safeway brands have carried nutritional labels for 10 years. And Safeway has an open dating policy which marks packages with a "freshness date," after which the item will not be sold. All products bought at Safeway have a money-back guarantee.

On the other hand, Safeway has been cited by the Federal Trade Commission for selling advertised items above the advertised prices. Safeway is the largest buyer of grapes in the nation but offered no support to the United Farm Workers' effort to organize grape pickers. In 1978 Safeway truck drivers and warehouse workers, represented by the Teamsters, went on a bitter strike to protest the use of a computerized time-and-motion system that the union said was a speedup. The system allowed workers 4½ minutes a day to use the bathroom. Clerks in the Bay Area struck the chain for similar reasons in 1980.

Where they're going. Safeway's recent expansion to North Carolina suggests they are ready to reach beyond their traditional trading area. Wherever they go, they may be expected to continue closing small stores and opening more giant-sized units, both here and abroad.

Stock performance. Safeway stock bought for $1,000 in 1970 sold for $1,419 on January 2, 1980.

Access. Fourth and Jackson Streets, Oakland, California 94660; (415) 891-3000.

THE SOUTHLAND CORPORATION

Sales: $3.9 billion
Profits: $67.5 million
Forbes 500 rank: 115
Rank in convenience stores: 1
Rank in food retailing: 6
Founded: 1927
Employees: 37,000
Headquarters: Dallas, Texas

What they do. Southland both operates and franchises the vast 7-Eleven chain: 6,600 convenience stores in 42 states, plus another 634 in Japan. In terms of number of units they are the nation's largest food chain. 7-Elevens are not grocery stores in the conventional sense. They don't sell any fresh meats, fruits, or vegetables. Instead, they offer such things as money orders (they sell more than anyone except the post office), comic books, beach picnic paraphernalia, flashlight batteries, pantyhose, and *Playboy* magazine (they sell more copies than any other retailer), as well as grocery items like bread, milk, packaged meats, canned goods, cereal, doughnuts, beer, cigarettes, and soft drinks. They also do a brisk business in prepared food and drink, notably sandwiches, coffee, hot chocolate, and Slurpees, a frozen syrup concoction available only at 7-Eleven.

The 7-Eleven store is the modern world's version of the corner mom and pop grocery, where people who need a few items between time-consuming trips to the supermarket are willing to pay higher prices for the convenience of shopping there. They are almost always open: originally they stayed open from 7 A.M. to 11 P.M., but four-fifths of them are now open 24 hours a day, every day except Christmas. The average customer spends 3½ minutes in the store and leaves only about $1.50 behind. But 7-Eleven stores attract more than 5 million customers a day, so those little purchases add up. About one-quarter of the stores sell gasoline at self-service pumps.

Southland makes it just as convenient for 7-Eleven store managers to keep their shelves stocked as it is for their customers to stop in for a six-pack. Often the managers don't even have to bother to order supplies; a Southland agent comes around to each store twice a month to take inventory. A company computer relays the replacement orders to Southland warehouses in Texas, Florida, Virginia, and Illinois, where the goods are loaded onto trucks and shipped to the stores.

History. When Joe C. Thompson was a high school student in Dallas at the time of the First World War, he spent his summers loading blocks of ice onto horse-drawn wagons for the Consumers Ice Company. Later he joined the ice firm and came up with the idea of chilling watermelons and selling them off the ice docks. The first ice-cold watermelons sold in Texas, they became an immediate success.

In 1927 Consumers joined with four other Texas ice companies to form the Southland Ice Company, based in Dallas. Thompson became a director of the new firm. That summer a Southland ice dock manager named "Uncle Johnny" Green was doing a bustling business keeping his ice dock open 16 hours a day, seven days a week. At the suggestion of his customers, he added a sideline of bread, milk, and eggs, which continued to sell briskly even after the summer ice business dropped off. The next spring he called on Joe Thompson and presented him with $1,000 in cash—Southland's share of the grocery profits. The convenience store business was born.

Soon the company was running a string of convenience stores from their ice docks. Called Tote'm Stores, their trademark was an Alaskan Indian totem pole displayed outside. Thompson became president of the company in 1931, at age 30; one week later he was elected to the Dallas City Council. The company expanded steadily, boosted by the repeal of prohibition in 1933, which allowed the Tote'm stores to sell cold beer. In 1946 they changed the name of the stores to 7-Eleven, and by the end of 1947 there were 74 of them. At the time Joe Thompson died in 1961 there were nearly 600 stores, but the real growth spurt came under his sons, who took over the business. The older brother, John, became president, and Jere became a vice-president. The 1,000th store opened in 1963. There were 1,500 in 1965, 3,500 by 1970, and more than 6,500 by 1980.

Reputation. It's the company that realized you don't want to stand in a supermarket line for a pack of cigarettes or a can of beer.

What they own. Southland owns and runs about 4,000 of the nation's 7-Eleven stores and franchises the rest to independent operators. The person who leases a 7-Eleven franchise gets a fully stocked store and must then "invest" an amount equal to the value of the inventory (about $20,000). Southland pays the utilities and property taxes and takes about half the profits. The franchisee foots the operating expenses, including the store's payroll.

Southland also runs a string of dairies that produce milk, ice cream, yogurt, and the like under 11 regional labels such as Adohr Farms, Oak Farms, and Cabell's. In 1968 the company that gave the world Slurpees took over the prestigious Gristede Bros. grocery chain of New York City, which carries a variety of up-scale merchandise such as croissants and caviar. Southland also owns the Chief Auto Parts chain of more than 100 stores in Southern California.

Who owns and runs the company. The three sons of Joe C. Thompson control the company, with 15% of the stock (worth about $70 million). John is chairman and chief executive, Jere is president, and Joe, Jr., is a vice-president. The company's employees' savings and profit-sharing plan holds about 3% of the stock and owns more than 1,000 of the 7-Eleven stores.

In the public eye. Each year the 7-Eleven stores raise some $4 million for Jerry Lewis's Labor Day Telethon for the Muscular Dystrophy Association. A major part of their effort comes from displays in each store near the cash register urging customers to "Let Jerry Keep the Change for his Kids."

Since 7-Eleven stores are open all night and are frequently subject to armed robber-

ies, Southland is particularly concerned with fighting crime. They have sponsored television showings of "Scared Straight," a documentary aimed at setting juvenile delinquents on the straight and narrow. In 1977 they prevailed upon California country rock musician Commander Cody to change the lyrics of a song he had recorded, "7-Eleven," which they felt encouraged shoplifting. (Original version: "At the 7-Eleven, choices are two: steal from them, or let them steal from you." Amended version: "Steal from them, they'll throw the book at you.")

President Jere Thompson was an early fund-raising leader in John Connally's 1980 presidential campaign. In 1977 he announced that the 7-Eleven stores owned by Southland would no longer sell cigarette papers. "I don't think we ought to be encouraging people to smoke marijuana when it's against the law," he said.

Where they're going. Having conquered suburban America, Southland began in 1977 to put a few stores in central cities—Boston, New York, San Francisco—where they depend more on neighborhood foot traffic than on customers who arrive in their cars. "Why, the Northeast is a great area," chairman John Thompson told the *Washington Star*. "We haven't really saturated that market at all. And the Midwest? Well, we've hardly gotten started there. And California? Sure, we have 900 stores in California, but you can build forever in that state."

Stock performance. Southland stock bought for $1,000 in 1970 sold for $1,729 on January 2, 1980.

Access. 2828 North Haskell Avenue, Dallas, Texas 75204; (214) 828-7011.

Consumer brands.

House brands: Adohr Farms, Bancroft, Briggs, Cabell's, Embassy, Harbisons, Horten's Midwest Farms, Oak Farm, Velda Farms, Cooper Farms, Big Deal, Gram Daddy, Big Wheel, Reddy Ice, Lilly Ice Cream, 7-Eleven, and Slurpee frozen carbonated drink.

Retail outlets: 7-Eleven, Gristede's, Charles & Co., Barricini Candy Stores, Chief Auto Parts stores, Hudgins Truck Rental.

Retail Sales / Share of U.S. Market

1. SAFEWAY
   Oakland, CA / $10,946 *million* / 6.00%
2. KROGER
   Cincinnati, OH / $8,706 *million* / 4.77%
3. A&P
   Montvale, NJ / $6,283 *million* / 3.44%
4. SUPER VALU STORES•
   Hopkins, MN / $5,491 *million* / 3.01%
5. WINN DIXIE
   Jacksonville, FL / $5,247 *million* / 2.87%
6. AMERICAN STORES
   Philadelphia, PA / $5,100 *million* / 2.79%
7. FLEMING COMPANIES•
   Topeka, KS / $4,751 *million* / 2.60%
8. LUCKY STORES
   Dublin, CA / $3,699 *million* / 2.02%
9. SOUTHLAND (*7-Eleven*)
   Dallas, TX / $3,456 *million* / 1.89%
10. WAKEFERN FOOD•
    Elizabeth, NJ / $3,110 *million* / 1.70%
11. GRAND UNION
    East Paterson, NJ / $3,060 *million* / 1.67%
12. MALONE & HYDE•
    Memphis, TN / $2,950 *million* / 1.61%
13. JEWEL
    Chicago, IL / $2,812 *million* / 1.54%
14. CERTIFIED GROCERS OF CALIFORNIA•
    Los Angeles, CA / $2,617 *million* / 1.43%
15. SUPERMARKETS GENERAL
    Woodbridge, NJ / $2,064 *million* / 1.13%
16. WETTERAU FOODS•
    Hazelwood, MO / $2,058 *million* / 1.12%
17. DILLON
    Hutchinson, KS / $1,965 *million* / 1.07%
18. PUBLIX SUPER MARKETS
    Lakeland, FL / $1,934 *million* / 1.06%
19. SUPER FOOD SERVICES•
    Dayton, OH / $1,678 *million* / 0.92%
20. ASSOCIATED WHOLESALE GROCERS•
    Kansas City, KS / $1,650 *million* / 0.90%
21. S. M. FLICKINGER•
    Buffalo, NY / $1,629 *million* / 0.89%
22. UNITED GROCERS•
    Richmond, CA / $1,489 *million* / 0.81%
23. VON'S GROCERY
    El Monte, CA / $1,473 *million* / 0.80%
24. SPARTAN STORES•
    Grand Rapids, MI / $1,432 *million* / 0.78%
25. SCOT LAD FOODS•
    Lansing, IL / $1,404 *million* / 0.76%
26. FIRST NATIONAL STORES
    Somerville, MA / $1,365 *million* / 0.74%
27. FISHER FOODS
    Bedford Heights, OH / $1,327 *million* / 0.72%
28. NASH FINCH•
    Minneapolis, MN / $1,263 *million* / 0.69%
29. CERTIFIED GROCERS OF ILLINOIS
    Chicago, IL / $1,261 *million* / 0.69%
30. STOP & SHOP
    Boston, MA / $1,225 *million* / 0.67%
31. WALDBAUM
    Central Islip, NY / $1,128 *million* / 0.61%
32. AMERICAN STREVELL•
    Salt Lake City, UT / $1,119 *million* / 0.61%
33. NATIONAL TEA
    Rosemont, IL / $1,096 *million* / 0.60%

Top Supergrocers?

34. WAPLES PLATTER*
Fort Worth, TX / $1,091 million / 0.59%
35. WEST COAST GROCERY*
Tacoma, WA / $1,053 million / 0.57%
36. PACIFIC GAMBLE ROBINSON*
Seattle, WA / $1,022 million / 0.56%
37. FOOD FAIR
Philadelphia, PA / $1,005 million / 0.55%
38. GIANT FOOD
Landover, MD / $994 million / 0.54%
39. RICHFOOD*
Mechanicsville, VA / $977 million / 0.53%
40. ALBERTSON'S
Boise, ID / $963 million / 0.52%
41. TWIN COUNTY GROCERS*
Edison, NJ / $958 million / 0.52%
42. ALFRED M. LEWIS*
Riverside, CA / $956 million / 0.52%
43. ASSOCIATED GROCER*
Seattle, WA / $948 million / 0.51%
44. FOX GROCERY*
Belle Vernon, PA / $948 million / 0.51%
45. RALPH'S GROCERY*
Compton, CA / $877 million / 0.48%
46. SCRIVNER*
Oklahoma City, OK / $859 million / 0.47%
47. SPRINGFIELD SUGAR &PRODUCTS*
Suffield, CT / $844 million / 0.46%
48. WHITE ROSE FOOD*
Farmingdale, NY / $844 million / 0.46%
49. BORMAN'S
Detroit, MI / $839 million / 0.46%
50. FARM HOUSE FOODS*
Milwaukee, WI / $835 million / 0.45%
51. UNITED GROCERS*
Portland, OR / $815 million / 0.44%
52. RED OWL STORES
Hopkins, MN / $801 million / 0.43%
53. ASSOCIATED FOOD STORES*
Salt Lake City, UT / $797 million / 0.43%
54. CULLUM
Dallas, TX / $791 million / 0.43%
55. ASSOCIATED GROCERS*
Phoenix, AZ / $740 million / 0.40%
56. AFFILIATED FOODS*
Dallas, TX / $740 million / 0.40%
57. KEY FOOD STORES COOPERATIVE
Brooklyn, NY / $721 million / 0.39%
58. ASSOCIATED GROCERS OF COLORADO*
Denver, CO / $711 million / 0.38%
59. HY-VEE FOOD STORES
Chariton, IA / $683 million / 0.37%
60. H. E. BUTT GROCERY
Corpus Christi, TX / $650 million / 0.35%
61. ALLIED SUPERMARKETS
Livonia, MI / $648 million / 0.35%
62. WEIS MARKETS
Sunbury, PA / $622 million / 0.34%
63. SMITH MANAGEMENT
Salt Lake City, UT / $621 million / 0.34%
64. PETER J. SCHMIDT*
Buffalo, NY / $598 million / 0.32%
65. PNEUMO
Boston, MA / $594 million / 0.32%
66. FED MART
San Diego, CA / $580 million / 0.31%

67. NIAGARA FRONTIER SERVICES*
Buffalo, NY / $571 million / 0.31%
68. ROUNDY'S*
Milwaukee, WI / $559 million / 0.30%
69. PIGGLY WIGGLY CAROLINA*
Charleston, SC / $559 million / 0.30%
70. FRANKFORD-QUAKER GROCERY*
Philadelphia, PA / $550 million / 0.30%
71. FURR'S
Lubbock, TX / $550 million / 0.30%
72. BI-LO
Mauldin, SC / $547 million / 0.29%
73. U R M STORES*
Spokane, WA / $531 million / 0.29%
74. ARDEN GROUP
City of Commerce, CA / $524 million / 0.28%
75. McLAIN GROCERY*
Massillon, OH / $522 million / 0.28%
76. ALTERMAN FOODS
Atlanta, GA / $512 million / 0.28%
77. KOHL'S FOOD STORES
Milwaukee, WI / $500 million / 0.27%
78. SCHNUCK MARKETS
Bridgeton, MO / $500 million / 0.27%
79. CHATHAM COMPLETE FOOD CENTERS
Warren, MI / $482 million / 0.26%
80. HANNAFORD BROTHERS*
South Portland, ME / $478 million / 0.26%
81. GODFREY
Waukesha, WI / $471 million / 0.25%
82. B. GREEN & COMPANY*
Baltimore, MD / $465 million / 0.25%
83. PRICE CHOPPER DISCOUNT FOODS
Schenectady, NY / $450 million / 0.24%
84. BIG BEAR STORES
Columbus, OH / $450 million / 0.24%
85. MARSH SUPERMARKETS
Yorkstown, IN / $447 million / 0.24%
86. CERTIFIED OF FLORIDA*
Ocala, FL / $446 million / 0.24%
87. FOOD TOWN STORES
Salisbury, NC / $445 million / 0.24%
88. THRIFTMART
Los Angeles, CA / $432 million / 0.23%
89. NATIONAL CONVENIENCE STORES
Houston, TX / $426 million / 0.23%
90. GENERAL GROCER COMPANY*
St. Louis, MO / $417 million / 0.22%
91. GIANT EAGLE
Pittsburgh, PA / $400 million / 0.21%
92. SYSCO*
Houston, TX / $398 million / 0.21%

* The asterisked companies are food wholesalers rather than food chains. The wholesalers sell to independent grocers, whom the American Institute of Food Distribution defines as those who do not operate their own warehouses (and thus buy from wholesalers). The figures for the wholesalers listed above represent the retail sales of the food purchased from the wholesalers and sold to the public by the independent grocers. According to the Institute, 52% of retail food sales in the United States are made through independent grocers.

Source: The American Institute of Food Distribution, Inc., Fair Lawn, New Jersey. Most of the figures are for the 12 months ending March 31, 1980, and represent only domestic sales of these companies.

⠿ Stop & Shop

Sales: $1.9 billion
Profits: $14.9 million
Forbes 500 rank: 280
Rank in food retailing: 16
Founded: 1914
Employees: 27,000
Headquarters: Boston, Massachusetts

Stop & Shop operates 157 supermarkets, nearly half of them in the state of Massachusetts. They're Boston's number 1 food supplier. From food they have branched into other retail businesses: 76 Bradlees discount stores, 44 Medi Mart discount drug stores, 47 Charles. B. Perkins tobacco shops, and 12 Off the Rax women's apparel stores. All these businesses are also located primarily in the Northeast. This food chain maintains consumer panels in the communities they serve, thereby giving customers a direct channel to store management. The Rabb family that built this retailing organization holds 20% of the stock.

Access. P.O. Box 369, Boston, Massachusetts 02101; (617) 463-7000.

Supermarkets General

Sales: $2.4 billion
Profits: $23.5 million
Forbes 500 rank: 222
Rank in food retailing: 17
Employees: 27,000
Headquarters: Woodbridge, New Jersey

Operating in one of the most competitive grocery markets in the nation, this company's Pathmark chain blasted its way into first place in the New York metropolitan market with an aggressive pricing strategy, a private label line of drugs and food products that now extends to more than 2,000 items, and the building of huge combination food and drug stores (their Super Centers each cover 50,000 square feet). They operate 111 Pathmark supermarkets in New Jersey, New York, Pennsylvania, Delaware, and Connecticut. Their market share in New York City is 15% and they are taking close to 10% of the grocery dollars in Philadelphia. Supermarkets General grew out of a cooperative organization formed by small grocers to compete against the big chains. They operated under the Shop-Rite name. The two largest members of the cooperative combined in 1966, and in 1968 the Pathmark name went up on all the stores. Founders Alex Aidekman and Herbert Brody hold 15% of the stock.

Access. 301 Blair Road, Woodbridge, New Jersey 07095; (201) 499-3000.

Sales: $3.5 billion
Profits: $43.3 million
Forbes 500 rank: 134
Rank in food wholesaling: 1
Founded: 1870
Employees: 13,500
Headquarters: Hopkins, Minnesota

The nation's largest wholesale grocer supplies some 1,900 independently owned and operated supermarkets, most of them in the Midwest and the South. Their customers are stores belonging to these independent groups: IGA, Super Dollar, Sunflower, U-Save, Sure-Save, Banner, Mr. Quick. They also operate a growing retail business: more than 100 groceries (most of them under the Super Valu name); the Shopko discount department store chain in Wisconsin, South Dakota, Michigan, and Minnesota; and the 34-state County Seat jeans chain. It was County Seat that initiated price-cutting in the jeans market in 1978, a move that had nationwide repercussions: stores all over the country slashed the price of jeans.

Access. 101 Jefferson Avenue South, Hopkins, Minnesota 55343; (612) 932-4444.

Sales: $4.9 billion
Profits: $94.5 million
Forbes 500 rank: 81
Rank in food retailing: 4
Rank in retailing: 11
Founded: 1925
Employees: 55,500
Headquarters: Jacksonville, Florida

What they do. Winn-Dixie sells food to the South through 1,170 supermarkets in 14 states. They reject the superstore concept of mixing clothes and hardware with food; they sell food. And their traditional approach has tripled sales in the last 10 years —Winn-Dixie makes more money per checkout dollar than any other supermarket chain. Critics say it's because Winn-Dixie pays low wages; Winn-Dixie says it's because they run a better show. In addition to selling they make their own baked goods, milk, ice cream, salad, jams and jellies, mayonnaise, detergents, and soda, besides packaging coffee, tea, and spices.

History. W. M. Davis borrowed $10,000 in 1925 to open his first grocery store in Lemon City, Florida. His four sons took over nine years later, and they're still running things.

The Davis brothers believed in growth through acquisition, a theory they practiced so successfully that the FTC halted their store buying from 1966 to 1976 for antitrust reasons. Winn-Dixie celebrated the end of the 10-year moratorium with the acquisition of Kimbell Stores of Texas.

Winn-Dixie operates as far north as Indiana and as far west as Texas. They have 66 stores which carry the Buddies name and 33 Foodway stores.

Reputation. The *Dixie* in Winn-Dixie's name is the key to this company's outlook. They're solidly southern, paternalistic, and antiunion.

What they own. Distribution and manufacturing facilities, including bakeries, bot-

tling plants, box plants, and food processing facilities, in 17 southern cities.

Who owns and runs the company. The Davis brothers, joined by Vice Chairman A. D. Davis's son, Robert, are all board members. The Davis family owns 28% of the stock. On the all-male, all-white board are only three outside directors: Dr. Richard V. Moore, honorary chancellor of Bethune-Cookman College in Daytona Beach, Florida; G. Keith Funston, former head of the New York Stock Exchange; and George A. Smathers, former U.S. Senator from Florida. Many Winn-Dixie employees participate in the earnings through their ownership of stock, a point the company always makes to confound their critics. Half of all full-time employees are stockholders, and in every Winn-Dixie store there's an average of 14 employee shareholders. In 1978, when 165 employees retired, they went out with a total of $5.3 million from their profit-sharing accounts—an average of nearly $32,000 per person.

In the public eye. The stock-ownership figures do not impress labor leaders incensed at Winn-Dixie's refusal to accept unions. The United Food & Commercial Workers International Union, the largest union in the AFL-CIO, called for a consumer boycott of Winn-Dixie, receiving support from Dr. Joseph E. Lowrey, president of the Southern Christian Leadership Conference, who told a rally in 1979: "We're gonna make old Winn-Dixie free at last—or it will be last to ever be free."

Winn-Dixie's management would not be moved from their position. In 1979 they abandoned the state of New Mexico rather than deal with a union that represented workers at 23 supermarkets. When a boycott was organized, Winn-Dixie simply sold off the stores.

Where they're going. Winn-Dixie shows no interest in buying anything but food stores in the southern states.

Stock performance. Winn-Dixie stock bought for $1,000 in 1970 sold for $1,616 on January 2, 1980.

Access. 5050 Edgewood Court, Jacksonville, Florida 32203; (904) 783-1800.

Fast-Food Folks

ARA
SERVICES

Sales: $2 billion
Profits: $52.6 million
Forbes 500 rank: 265
Rank in food service: 1
Rank in vending machines: 1
Rank in magazine distribution: 1
Rank in school busing: 1
Rank in nursing homes: 1
Founded: 1959
Employees: 100,000
Headquarters: Philadelphia, Pennsylvania

What they do. ARA services 8 million customers a day. They feed people *en masse* —in airplanes, company cafeterias, college dormitories, public schools, hospitals, national parks, football stadiums, racetracks, and golf courses. They do it with vending machines (ARA owns 115,000 of them), coffee-service systems, and restaurant operations. They operate food systems in 12,000 offices and factories, 50 airlines, 350 colleges, and 1,200 schools. They feed the New York Jets as well as employees of Ford, Xerox, IBM, and the Pentagon. You're eating in an ARA restaurant when you dine atop the John Hancock building in Chicago or the Bank of America building in San Francisco. In addition, ARA distributes magazines to 22,000 outlets (380 million copies a year); transports 550,000 children to and from school; administers 314 hospitals on a contract basis; runs 209 nursing homes under their subsidiaries, National Living Centers and Geriatrics; picks up, cleans, and delivers 70 million uniforms a year—and has recently added to this panoply of services a trucking outfit, Smith's

Transfer, whose routes cover most of the eastern part of the United States.

History. The company was formed in 1959 by the merger of two small vending companies, one in Chicago and one in Los Angeles. Their first name was Davidson Automatic Merchandising, after one of the founders, Davre J. Davidson. They soon changed to Automatic Retailers of America, later abbreviated to ARA. They entered the food-service field in 1961 by acquiring Slater Systems of Philadelphia.

Reputation. ARA is known as a tough and aggressive company that strives for market dominance. They will go head-to-head with competitors and be prepared to lose money for years in order to win ultimately. The people who have to eat ARA fare often complain about the quality and stingy portions. An employee of a West Coast electronics firm said: "When ARA took over the cafeteria, I started brown-bagging."

What they own. ARA owns, at cost, $210 million in vending machines, $90 million in buses, and $60 million in nursing home facilities.

Who owns and runs the company. The top 20 shareholders, who control nearly half of the common shares, consist largely of insurance companies, banks, pension funds, and the like. ARA's chairman and cofounder, William Fishman, is the largest individual shareholder but ranks 36th in ownership. To carry out their service operations, the company requires an enormous work force—one of the largest in American business. A third of their U.S. employees are represented by unions.

In the public eye. ARA's hungry acquisition program has brought frequent scrapes with the Federal Trade Commission. They were barred in 1973 from buying any more large vending machine companies or magazine distributors for 10 years. In 1979 they had to pay a $300,000 Justice Department fine after they bought four more magazine wholesalers in violation of a consent decree.

Where they're going. With the service sector the most dynamic part of the U.S. economy, ARA feels they're sitting pretty. They look to do more of the same.

Stock performance. ARA stock bought for $1,000 in 1970 sold for $429 on January 2, 1980.

Access. Independence Square West, Philadelphia, Pennsylvania 19106; (215) 574-5000.

Sales: $414 million
Pretax profits: $38 million
Rank in restaurants: 2
Founded: 1955
Employees: 11,500
Headquarters: Louisville, Kentucky

What they do. Kentucky Fried Chicken may be finger-lickin' good, but Heublein, the fast-food chain's latest owner, is still trying to wipe red ink off their hands. They're number 2 in the fast-food business, well behind McDonald's, so they're trying harder.

Kentucky has a few more fast-food restaurants than McDonald's (5,355 to 5,185), but not nearly as many customers. The average KFC restaurant sells $325,000 worth of food a year, one-third of what the average McDonald's does. One reason for the gap may be that hamburgers are more popular with Americans than chicken. Another reason is that Kentucky Fried Chicken outlets were originally conceived as takeout places rather than restaurants.

KFC's third owner, vodka distiller Heu-

blein, believes they have moved KFC onto the right track. Restaurants are being remodeled to provide additional seating and drive-through windows. Inspectors are sent out to grade the restaurants on 37 different areas of performance. For example, "If as many as 5 customers are in line, customer must receive order within 2 minutes per customer in line," 5 points. A score of 90 or better may bring the store manager a bonus; a score below 60 may bring a pink slip.

KFC is in the franchise business, which means they license others to operate Kentucky Fried Chicken restaurants at specific locations. With the franchise come precise instructions on how to prepare the chicken, right down to seasonings, temperature, and cooking time. Franchisees pay KFC an initial fee of $4,000 and monthly fees amounting to 4% of gross sales. In addition, franchise holders are expected to contribute 1½% of their gross sales to a national advertising kitty, and most are also obligated to allocate another 3% of gross sales for location promotion and advertising. Total sales of the KFC system, including franchises, is $1.2 billion.

WHO MAKES THE MOST PROFIT ON A DOLLAR OF SALES?	
KELLOGG	16.1¢
CAMPBELL SOUP	11.7¢
NABISCO	9.5¢
CARNATION	9.4¢
GENERAL FOODS	8.3¢
PILLSBURY	8.3¢
CPC INTERNATIONAL	8.2¢
NORTON SIMON	8.1¢
QUAKER OATS	8.1¢
H.J. HEINZ	7.8¢
GENERAL MILLS	7.6¢
RALSTON PURINA	7.1¢
BEATRICE FOODS	7.0¢
CONSOLIDATED FOODS	6.6¢
KRAFT	6.2¢
BORDEN	5.8¢
STANDARD BRANDS	5.5¢

Source: Based on 1978 annual reports.

Food represents 37% of fast-food operators' expenses; labor costs 23%.

History. Kentucky Fried Chicken was started in 1955 by Colonel Harland Sanders, a seventh-grade dropout who had been in many businesses, including motels and restaurants, before coming up with a special seasoning for fried chicken that was to make him famous—and wealthy. He was already 66 years old when he started to franchise his chicken recipe. In 1964 another Kentuckian, flamboyant John Y. Brown, bought the business from Sanders for $2 million. He built KFC into a $250 million enterprise before unloading it on Heublein in 1971. The gold mine Heublein thought they had bought turned out to be a greasy trap that caused them to spend Smirnoff profit dollars chasing after Kentucky Fried Chicken losses. John Brown, who sold them the business, had this to say about Heublein in a *Forbes* interview: "Heublein turned it into a cold, insensitive business. For our people, it was like going into the Army."

Interestingly enough, when KFC was spurting red ink in 1976, it was the company-owned units that were doing the worst, not the franchised ones. Heublein was sim-

Popcorn

The crunch of buttered popcorn resounds strongly through recent American life. Popcorn is symbolic of and indispensable to the nation's mainstream amusements, its wholesome exuberance inextricably linked to baseball, circuses, and the movies. Americans eat some 400 million pounds of popcorn annually, and the industry supports a Popcorn Institute

Early ad for Jolly Time popcorn offered prompt shipments, packed in heavy jute bags—any quantity.

that tests poppers and offers tips on popcorn safety. Popcorn advertising has depicted Ozzie and Harriet, Danny Kaye, and Arthur Godfrey as eating popcorn. Popcorn is most popular in the Midwest, least popular in Manhattan. The American Dental Association endorsed it as a snack in preference to sugared treats.

Yet at the beginning of the twentieth century, popcorn was a rarity in American grocery stores. Popping machines were invented in 1885 and gaily painted, mobile popcorn wagons sold popcorn on town and city street corners. Corn for home popping could be bought only in bulk, however. The 1897 Sears, Roebuck catalog advertised a 25-pound sack of it, still on the cob, for $1.00.

American Indians had used popcorn for millennia: archaeologists have used radiocarbon dating to prove that ears of popcorn found in a New Mexico cave were 5,600 years old. An Indian is supposed to have presented a deerskin sack of popped corn to the Pilgrims at the first Thanksgiving. Whatever the reason, popcorn did not easily catch on in the United States. Farmers in the Midwest grew and popped small quantities for their families, but it took an Iowa farmer's son named

Cloid H. Smith to make it a national institution.

Smith reasoned that the detonating corn would be popular for home use if it was attractively packaged and vigorously promoted, with brand-name identity. In 1914 Smith formed the American Pop Corn Company and packaged his first 1-pound packages of popcorn, after shelling, grading, and cleaning it by hand with the help of his mother. The family coined the name Jolly Time to evoke associations of festivity, and their cardboard packages showed laughing urchins delightedly wolfing handfuls from a huge bowl. Advertising placards promised "fine popping quality . . . Just fine for Halloween parties."

The brand-name popcorn was an instant success. By the end of the first year Smith's company had sold more than 75,000 pounds of popcorn. Smith moved his operations into bigger quarters, and in 1926 the American Pop Corn Company incorporated in Iowa.

Jolly Time popcorn promised its customers reliable popping, but the cardboard packages posed problems. The reason popcorn pops is a peculiarity of its structure: an extraordinarily hard outside kernel surrounds a soft, moist

ply not giving KFC managers incentives to perform well. Hicks B. Waldron, president of Heublein, conceded in an interview with *Forbes* that the company did not know what it had gotten itself into: "We had actually bought a chain of 5,000 little factories all over the world, and we simply didn't have experience in handling that kind of operation."

Reputation. Millions of Americans swear by the colonel's recipe, but when *Consumer Reports* checked out a KFC place in 1979, they found that the chicken "had a rather limp and oily coating," actually necessitating considerable finger licking. Still, most observers of the fast-food scene believe KFC has made a comeback from the time in 1976 when Colonel Sanders, who is still retained by Heublein as a $200,000-a-year goodwill ambassador, walked into a New York City KFC accompanied by a *New York Times* reporter, tasted the chicken, and snapped: "That's the worst fried chicken I've ever seen."

---

inner nugget of starch. When the corn is heated, the moisture in the starch turns to steam, which expands, exploding the kernel and turning it inside out. Smith's high-quality corn lost its pop because it dried out when left too long in the cardboard boxes, the result being those terrors of the popcorn trade called "old maids": kernels that lurk unpopped as charred morsels after their companions have exploded.

American Can Co. bailed Jolly Time out of its trouble in 1925, designing an airtight metal can that turned out to be the forerunner of today's beer can. The cheerful red, white, and blue can carried the motto "Guaranteed to Pop."

Smith strenuously promoted the wholesomeness, quality, and fun of his popcorn. Popular magazines of the day, including *The Farmer's Wife, The Saturday Evening Post, Good Housekeeping,* and *Liberty* showed fresh-faced children, mothers, even Santa Claus enjoying Jolly Time. People were encouraged not only to pop corn but to make things out of it afterward, such as popcorn balls and Christmas decorations. Popcorn ads were heard on radio starting in 1930.

When movies became pop-ular, theater managers at first barred popcorn from their lobbies after moviegoers complained that the scent and noise of popcorn broke the spell of on-screen drama. Popcorn vendors with portable poppers mounted on Ford or Stanley Steamer chassis took up positions outside the theaters. Many of the vendors were "plants," working in teams to show theater owners how popular and how profitable popcorn could be. During the Depression the moviehouse managers relented, largely because they needed cash. Popcorn sold in theater lobbies turned out to be, in some cases, almost as profitable as admission tickets. By 1947, 85% of the nation's theaters sold popcorn. The saying current among theater managers was: "Find a good popcorn location and build a theater around it." Popcorn became synonymous with the movies.

Sales boomed. In 1948, 300,000 acres of midwestern farmland were planted in popcorn—an increase from 20,000 acres in 1900.

Then came television. Starting in 1949 moviegoing dwindled, and with it, popcorn consumption. Movie theaters folded, and second-hand commercial poppers flooded the market. The Pop-corn Institute met in plenary session amid gloom. The Institute recognized that the American public had come to associate popcorn exclusively with movies. The industry now had the peculiar task of finding a way to revive the nearly extinct custom of home popping.

At home or at the movies, the popcorn planners noticed, Americans drank a lot of Coca-Cola. The Institute approached the Coca-Cola Company with the proposal that Coke could be promoted even more effectively in tandem with a dry, salted snack that led, inevitably, to thirst. Coke-popcorn ads strove to persuade American TV watchers that Coke was best when accompanied by popcorn.

By late 1951 a survey of Chicago TV owners proved the success of the Coke-corn promotions. Fully 63% of TV watchers munched popcorn from one to four nights a week, and another 10% ate popcorn five or six nights each week. Sales of electric home poppers began to boom.

Today two-thirds of all the popcorn produced in the world is consumed in American homes, much of it in front of the TV.

What they own. Kentucky Fried Chicken owns 743 restaurants in the United States. 3,511 more are franchised. An additional 1,047 KFC restaurants are outside the United States, mostly in Australia, Britain and Japan. KFC used to grow their own chickens but abandoned that business. They also used to produce equipment for the store but gave that up, too.

Who owns and runs the company. Heublein, Inc., of Hartford, Connecticut, is the sole owner, but Kentucky Fried Chicken still maintains headquarters in Louisville. Running KFC for Heublein is Michael Miles, who had great success managing the international KFC operation. When Miles took over in 1977, he called a meeting of the operating people and told them: "Okay, fellas, if you want to play, you're welcome to stay. If not, you ought to leave now because you won't like it around here." Many of them did leave.

Where they're going. Heublein has two options: (1) continue to upgrade KFC outlets and grab a bigger share of the eating-out dollar, or (2) get rid of the business and stick to vodka.

Access. 1441 Gardiner Lane, Louisville, Kentucky 40232; (502) 459-8600. Inquiries or complaints should be sent to: Shirley Topmiller, manager–consumer affairs, Kentucky Fried Chicken, P. O. Box 32070, Louisville 40232. The Louisville headquarters houses a Colonel Harland Sanders Museum where you can see historic artifacts from the career of the founder. It's open from 8:30 A.M. to 5:00 P.M. every weekday. Admission is free, and no appointment is needed.

THE FAST FOOD POPULATION

1.	KENTUCKY FRIED CHICKEN	5,355 *restaurants*
2.	McDONALD'S	5,185 *restaurants*
3.	INTERNATIONAL DAIRY QUEEN	4,820 *restaurants*
4.	PIZZA HUT	3,710 *restaurants*
5.	BURGER KING	2,153 *restaurants*
6.	TASTEE FREEZ	2,022 *restaurants*
7.	A & W	1,500 *restaurants*
8.	WENDY'S	1,407 *restaurants*
9.	HARDEE'S	1,125 *restaurants*
10.	SONIC DRIVE-INS	1,061 *restaurants*

Source: *Restaurant Business*, March 1, 1979.

Sales: $1.9 billion
Profits: $188.6 million
Forbes 500 rank: 276
Rank in restaurants: 1
Rank in franchising: 1
Rank in retailing: 31
Founded: 1955
Employees: 98,000
Headquarters: Oak Brook, Illinois

What they do. McDonald's is as American as apple turnovers. The stars and stripes wave daily outside most of their 4,500 restaurants in all 50 states (they have another 700 in foreign countries, 200 of them in Japan). You can walk into a McDonald's and get a hamburger, french fries, and a shake inside of 50 seconds, and the meal will taste just the same in Tallahassee as it does in Tacoma—or, for that matter, Tokyo. The hamburger patty will weigh exactly 1.6 ounces and will arrive on a bun exactly 3½ inches across, garnished with precisely one-fourth of an ounce of minced onions. The french fries will have been cooked within the past seven minutes, the hamburger in the last ten. What's more, the bathroom will be clean and the parking lot free of teenage troublemakers.

Over the past 25 years McDonald's has done to restaurant food what Henry Ford did to automobiles a generation earlier. Ray Kroc, the driving force behind McDonald's, didn't invent the product—he just figured out how to mass-produce it uniformly in truly astounding quantities and convince millions of Americans they needed to buy one (and another, and another). There are now far more McDonald's outlets alone in the United States than there were fast-food restaurants 30 years ago, and the chain has more than twice as many outlets as its nearest competitor, Burger King. Out of every fast-food dollar Americans spend, McDonald's gets 20¢.

Each year half a million head of cattle are raised, slaughtered, and frozen into patties to satisfy America's appetite for McDonald's hamburgers. Every three months the company sells another billion burgers. Each morning they serve $1 million worth of Egg McMuffins. McDonald's is the country's biggest buyer of processed potatoes (for their french fries) and fish (for Filet-O-Fish). Keeping them supplied with paper packaging requires the sustained yield of more than 300 square miles of forest. McDonald's restaurants are also the nation's leading employer of young people, with some 150,000 high school–age workers behind the counters.

Most McDonald's restaurants are run by franchisees. It takes an individual operator about a quarter of a million dollars up front to get started selling McDonald's hamburgers, and each franchise runs for only 20 years, after which it reverts to the company. The company takes a total of 11½% of the gross for both royalties on the McDonald's name and for rent on the building. Even though the franchisees don't own their buildings, they still have to pay the property taxes, insurance, and maintenance. They also buy all their own food (from independent suppliers approved by the company) and pay their own employees. Still, with the average annual gross

for a McDonald's franchise running close to $1 million, a hard-working franchisee can turn a profit of $50,000 to $70,000 a year for overseeing a crew of high school kids perform simple tasks for the minimum wage. To learn the ins and outs of running a McDonald's franchise, the would-be operator takes a two-week course in "hamburgerology" at the company's Hamburger University in suburban Chicago, not far from the gleaming white corporate headquarters called Hamburger Central, where McDonald's executives lie on a waterbed in the company's "think tank" and dream up new delicacies like Chicken Nuggets and Triple Ripple Ice Cream.

History. Ray Kroc was a 52-year-old all-purpose salesman when he met Maurice and Richard McDonald in 1954. The McDonald brothers ran a hamburger stand in San Bernardino, the California terminus of transcontinental Route 66, on the eastern edge of sprawling greater Los Angeles. At the time Kroc was selling the Prince Castle

Watch Out, Big Mac!

Fleer Corporation, the small Philadelphia company that in 1928 invented the pink, stretchy chewing stuff called bubblegum, has recently begun selling a new gum called Bubble Burger. It comes in a small plastic container that resembles a miniature fast food take-out box, and the gum itself looks just like a hamburger—shrunk to about two inches in diameter.

Fleer's president told a *Forbes* reporter, "Actually, it's very complicated to make. The secret is in the color, and in learning how to handle three layers so that they stay together and don't slip!"

Other recent Fleer contributions to the marketplace include Gatorgum (with time-release lemon-lime flavor to help quench the thirst of the junior jogger), and Razzles (bubblegum in a pill form, made by drying the gum into a powder).

Source: *Forbes*, October 29, 1979.

TOP 25 INDEPENDENT RESTAURANTS

	Sales (1979)	Seats	Average Check per Customer
1. WINDOWS ON THE WORLD *New York City*	$15.8 *million*	910	—
2. TAVERN ON THE GREEN *New York City*	$11.0 *million*	1,000	$18.00
3. SPENGER'S FISH GROTTO *Berkeley, CA*	$ 9.2 *million*	700	$ 5.50
4. "21" CLUB, INC. *New York City*	$ 8.6 *million*	450	—
5. MAI-KAI RESTAURANT *Ft. Lauderdale*	$ 7.4 *million*	600	$19.00
6. ZEHNDER'S *Frankenmuth, MI*	$ 6.6 *million*	1,200	$ 5.91
7. RAINBOW ROOM *New York City*	$ 6.5 *million*	700	—
8. FRANKENMUTH BAVARIAN INN *Frankenmuth, MI*	$ 6.5 *million*	1,000	$ 5.92
9. RASCAL HOUSE *Miami Beach*	$ 6.1 *million*	425	$ 3.88
10. MAXWELL'S PLUM *New York City*	$ 5.8 *million*	235	$15.50
11. TANGIER RESTAURANT & CABERET, *Akron*	$ 5.6 *million*	2,000	$11.00
12. CARSON CITY NUGGET *Carson City, NV*	$ 5.4 *million*	650	$ 4.85
13. PAM PAM EAST *San Francisco*	$ 5.1 *million*	315	—
14. GRAND CONCOURSE *Pittsburgh*	$ 5.0 *million*	412	$14.85
15. JOE'S PIER 52 SEAFOOD *New York City*	$ 5.0 *million*	183	$16.00
16. LEGAL SEA FOODS *Chestnut Hill, MA*	$ 5.0 *million*	210	—
17. WEBERS, INC. *Ann Arbor, MI*	$ 4.6 *million*	1,300	$ 9.65
18. COLUMBIA *Sarasota, FL*	$ 4.5 *million*	390	$14.75
19. COLUMBIA *Tampa, FL*	$ 4.3 *million*	1,660	$16.00
20. PEA SOUP ANDERSEN'S *Buellton, CA*	$ 4.2 *million*	680	$ 5.50
21. NICK'S FISHMARKET *Chicago*	$ 4.1 *million*	185	$30.00
22. DAPHNE'S *Elizabeth, NJ*	$ 4.0 *million*	275	$ 9.10
23. DAPHNE'S *Miami*	$ 4.0 *million*	300	$ 9.30
24. BISHOP'S *Lawrence, MA*	$ 4.0 *million*	530	$ 9.75
25. ANDERSON'S CAJUN'S WHARF *Nashville*	$ 3.0 *million*	650	$ 8.20

Source: *Restaurant Hospitality*, June 1980.

Multi-Mixer, a contraption that could make six milk shakes simultaneously. The McDonalds ordered eight of them. As Max Boas and Steve Chain report in their book *Big Mac*, "Ray Kroc showed up there one day after deciding that he wanted a firsthand look at an operation that found it necessary to make forty-eight milkshakes at the same time."

Kroc was amazed. He hung around the McDonald's hamburger stand for two or three days, watching customers line up at the window under a pair of garish golden arches to order ready-made hamburgers and french fries that were kept warm under heat lamps. He estimated that the stand was doing $250,000 worth of business a year. On the second day he approached the brothers about franchising the operation. They were leery of this fast-talking salesman from Chicago, with his bow tie, roomy suit, and brilliantined hair. They had already sold six franchises in California and didn't think they wanted to get any bigger. But Kroc was persistent, and the brothers finally gave in. Kroc headed back to Illinois and opened his first McDonald's in Des Plaines, near Chicago. He hasn't stopped to this day.

By 1960, when Kroc bought out the McDonald brothers for $2.7 million, there were some 250 McDonald's stands across the United States. Kroc is now worth at least a quarter of a billion dollars. In 1974 he used some of his spare cash to buy the San Diego Padres baseball team.

Reputation. McDonald's divides Americans down the middle: are they a menacing, junk-food monoculture? Or are they familiar, reliable places to take the family when there's nothing much to eat at home? The discussion doesn't disturb McDonald's sales—it's likely to take place in the line at one of their hamburger stands.

What they own. The company itself owns and operates about 1,600 McDonald's restaurants, or just under one-third of the total. They also own the land and buildings of most of the McDonald's stands operated by franchisees. But probably their most valuable property is the magic McDonald's name, which they spent $215 million to advertise in 1978.

Who owns and runs the company. Ray Kroc, now senior chairman of the board, is by far the biggest McDonald's stockholder,

with more than 16%. Fred Turner, who became president in 1968 at age 35, is board chairman and chief executive. "Fred didn't finish college," Kroc has said of Turner. "He has what we need: spirit and guts and dedication and integrity. Forget the brains. Fred is a multimillionaire, but it hasn't slowed him down." Turner gets $325,000 a year to run the company.

In the public eye. McDonald's tries hard to project an image as almost a charitable organization. Local outlets sponsor campaigns on fire prevention, bicycle safety, and litter cleanup, with advice from Hamburger Central on how to extract the most publicity for their efforts. Each year McDonald's sponsors the All-American Band, in which two high school students from each state are chosen to march in Macy's Thanksgiving Day parade in New York City and the Rose Bowl parade in Pasadena. Franchisees are urged to join their local Chamber of Commerce, United Way, American Legion, and other bastions of All-Americana.

Still, several communities have said "no, thanks" to attempts to bring in the Big Macs. When McDonald's tried to open a stand at Lexington Avenue and 66th Street on New York's posh Upper East Side in 1974, such prominent citizens as Theodore White and Mrs. McGeorge Bundy joined the battle to drive them off. In 1979 the gentry of Martha's Vineyard in Massachusetts, including summer residents like John Updike, Carly Simon, and Mia Farrow, kept Ronald McDonald at bay, at least temporarily, through a petition campaign that persuaded the local board of health to deny the company a septic tank permit. The editor of the weekly Vineyard Gazette led the fight. McDonald's, he said, is "a symbol of the asphalt and chrome culture that we do

> The restaurant industry, with sales of more than $70 billion, is the third-largest U.S. industry and the nation's largest employer—with almost 4 million employees.
>
> There are 360,000 eating establishments in the United States, about 70,000 of which are fast-food places. Total sales for all America's eateries amount to $80 billion a year.

not have here, and its coming means that we will have succumbed at last to the megalopolis which we have dreaded." In San Francisco an alliance of unions, community groups, and restaurant owners fought bitterly—but unsuccessfully—to stave off a McDonald's onslaught in the early 1970s.

When Richard Nixon's campaign agents were twisting arms of the big guns of American business for the 1972 election, Ray Kroc kicked in $225,000. The next year Nixon supported Kroc in his efforts to have the federal minimum wage law amended to provide for a "youth differential" so that employers could hire 16- and 17-year-olds and full-time students at 80% of the minimum wage.

The company had to contend with a new and mysterious enemy in 1978, when a rumor made the rounds in several states that McDonald's used ground worms in their hamburgers. Nobody ever figured out how it got started, but the story gained such wide circulation that McDonald's held a press conference in Atlanta to refute it, and even solicited a letter from Secretary of Agriculture Bob Bergland attesting to the pure beef content of the burgers.

Where they're going. McDonald's has managed to stay independent while conglomerates have absorbed all their major competitors. Pillsbury owns Burger King, Heublein owns Kentucky Fried Chicken, General Foods owns Burger Chef, Ralston-Purina owns Jack-in-the-Box, but Ray Kroc still controls McDonald's. The fast-food industry has showed signs of tapering off in recent years, partly because of gasoline shortages and rising beef prices, but McDonald's, with its enormous promotional clout, seems to be in better shape to weather rough times than any of the competition. Hamburger Central is essentially inflation-proof: as menu prices go up, so does the company's take from the gross receipts. They say they have no interest in diversifying. "McDonald's is single-minded," Fred Turner has said. "We have a great business with tremendous growth and our mind is set on McDonald's—period." For the foreseeable future they plan to keep adding about 500 restaurants each year—350 in the United States and 150 abroad.

Stock performance. McDonald's stock

bought for $1,000 in 1970 sold for $3,051 on January 2, 1980.

Access. McDonald's Plaza, Oak Brook, Illinois 60521; (312) 887-3679. Hamburger Central is open for tours, and local McDonald's stands will generally accommodate community groups that want to tour the place. Complaints should be sent to the Consumer Affairs Department, McDonald's Corporation, One McDonald's Plaza, Oak Brook, Illinois 60521; (312) 887-3200.

> **Meals away from home represent 35% of food spending by Americans.**

THE FASTEST BUCK ON THE BLOCK

Average Daily Sales per Restaurant

1. McDONALD'S $2,416
2. BIG BOY $1,707
3. PONDEROSA $1,701
4. PERKINS $1,602
5. WENDY'S $1,553
6. BURGER KING $1,487
7. SIZZLER STEAK HOUSE $1,474
8. BONANZA $1,384
9. HARDEE'S $1,375
10. ARBY'S $1,184

Source: *Restaurant Business*, March, 1, 1979

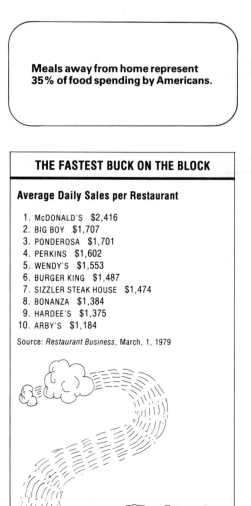

2

CLOTHING AND SHELTER

Textile Weavers

 Burlington Industries

Sales: $2.7 billion
Profits: $76.2 million
Forbes 500 rank: 187
Rank in textiles: 1
Founded: 1923
Employees: 66,000
Headquarters: Greensboro, North Carolina

What they do. The world's largest maker of textiles has discovered—as the food processing companies have—that the closer they can get to the consumer, the more profitable the business is. So Burlington has been deemphasizing basic textile production in favor of products that sell under their own brand names.

Not that Burlington doesn't continue to make a lot of fabrics. Their fabric sales are double those of the number 2 producer, J. P. Stevens, and stitched into all kinds of garments—suits, shirts, dresses, jeans. Most of their business comes from the sale of fabrics

to other companies, but Burlington is now concentrating more on their own fabric and home furnishings brands—Vera, Anne Klein, Oleg Cassini, Lees, Monticello, John Weitz, and Levi's (under whose name they are licensed to make socks). Their strategy seems to be paying off, especially with rugs, carpets, sheets, towels, draperies, and furniture. In 1978, for instance, home furnishings accounted for only 35% of Burlington's sales but a whopping 60% of their profits.

To supply their mills, Burlington buys virtually every type of fiber, man-made and natural, though man-made fibers such as rayon make up most of their raw materials.

History. In 1919, when he was in his early twenties, J. Spencer Love went to work for his uncle in a Gastonia, North Carolina cotton mill. Four years later he became principal owner of the mill. He persuaded the citizens of Burlington, North Carolina to sell stock to help him finance a new mill there, and on November 6, 1923, the new company, Burlington Mills, was born. It was almost a stillbirth because the mill produced cotton products that were going out of style. Love turned to a new man-made fiber called rayon. The public loved the shiny new fabric. By 1927 Love had two mills in Burlington, and sales topped $1 million.

While the New England textile industry was foundering in the Great Depression, Burlington was in a position to capitalize on the low costs (especially the cheaper labor) of the South. They gobbled up mills that others were forced to close, and by 1937 sales were $25 million from 19 plants. Three years later sales had more than doubled again. Burlington entered the hosiery business the same year. The 1950s brought even greater growth through acquisitions of well-known textile companies such as Pacific Mills and Klopman Mills, and in 1955 Burlington Mills became Burlington Industries. In 1960 James Lees & Co., a Philadelphia carpet maker founded in 1854, was acquired.

Spencer Love was the architect of the company's growth. Charles F. Myers, who succeeded Love, described him as follows: "He utilized his time with care. He had secretaries in his office and secretaries at home. When he came off the tennis court, he had a secretary waiting and he would go right to work dictating." In 1962, when he was 65, Love died of a heart attack after playing tennis. (His son, James Spencer Love, Jr., had a somewhat less illustrious career, though not with Burlington. In 1976 the New York Supreme Court barred him for life from engaging in the securities business in that state after commodities options companies he headed allegedly defrauded customers of hundreds of thousands of dollars.)

Burlington entered the furniture busi-

Modern weavers in a Burlington plant use air jets (rather than shuttles) to carry the yarn across the warp of the fabric.

ness in 1966 with the acquisition of Globe Furniture of High Point, North Carolina. Other acquisitions in the home furnishings industry followed rapidly.

Reputation. Although J. P. Stevens is labor's target number 1 in the textile industry, Burlington's record appears to be not much better. Of their 98 plants, only four have unions—and they were unionized prior to their acquisition by Burlington.

What they own. Burlington is constantly closing old mills and plants and opening new facilities. In the past five years 51 U.S. plants were closed or sold. That still leaves them with 98 manufacturing facilities in the United States, 60 of them in North Carolina.

Who owns and runs the company. William Klopman, chief executive officer since 1976, became a Burlington manager when the company founded by his father was acquired. And Burlington's current number 2 man, Frank Greenberg, joined in 1959 when Charm Tred Mills, the scatter-rug company owned by his father, was acquired. There have been stormy times in the Burlington executive suite. When Klopman was named head of the company, seven top executives walked out. Klopman was described in the *New York Times* as "tough as old leather" and "ruthless in dealing with executives he felt did not measure up to his standards." *Business Week* said Klopman's aggressive style bothers people at Burlington; one former manager has said: "They fear he might put the Klopman 'K' before the Burlington 'B.'"

Burlington has, in effect, dual headquarters—Greensboro, heart of the manufacturing operations, and New York City, where the merchandising offices are. Executives commute between the two points in a company plane. Klopman is based in Greensboro; Greenberg in New York. Gulf & Western, the conglomerate, reported in early 1980 that it owned 6.4% of Burlington's stock.

In the public eye. Burlington was in the limelight in the late 1960s when the Federal Trade Commission investigated their powerful role in the textile industry. The company consented in 1969 to a decree barring them from any acquisition in the textile industry for 10 years without prior FTC approval. More recently Burlington's management has mounted a public campaign to block new cotton dust standards set by the Occupational Safety and Health Administration. The government believes the standards are necessary for worker protection, but Burlington claims they are more comprehensive than medically necessary and technically impossible. In another arena, Burlington has led the textile industry's battle to restrict imports of foreign textiles. They warn that these imports threaten 2.3 million jobs, 23% filled by minorities and 65% by women.

Burlington has placed on the board a woman, Ernesta D. Ballard, president of the Pennsylvania Horticultural Society, and a black, Frank S. Jones, professor of urban affairs at the Massachusetts Institute of Technology.

Where they're going. As long as people wear clothes, Burlington should have a bright future, especially since they now have some of the most efficient plants in the industry. They have put nearly $1 billion into plant improvements in the past 5 years.

Stock performance. Burlington stock bought for $1,000 in 1970 sold for $495 on January 2, 1980.

Access. 3330 West Friendly Avenue, Greensboro, North Carolina 27420; (919) 379-2000. Burlington's New York City office [1345 Avenue of the Americas; (212) 333-5000] has a simulated textile plant that visitors can tour, on a moving walkway, from Tuesdays through Saturdays.

Consumer brands.

Domestics: Vera, Anne Klein, Oleg Cassini, Lees, Monticello, John Weitz, Burlington.
Carpets: Lees, Monticello, Burlington.
Fabrics and yarn: Burlington, Klapman Mills.
Furniture and home accessories: Burlington, Globe, Westwood.
Clothing: Burlington.

> **15,000 companies make clothing in the United States. The average manufacturer has 90 employees and grosses $2.3 million annually.**

Sales: $828 million
Profits: $35 million
Rank in textiles: 6
Founded: 1888
Employees: 22,500
Headquarters: Fort Mill, South Carolina

What they do. Springs Mills is a 92-year-old, well-established maker of bed linens. In spite of some branching out, their principal business is still the weaving and fabricating of cotton and cotton-synthetic blend textiles. Springs Mills is best known for white goods: sheets, pillow cases, and bedspreads marketed under such brand names as Springmaid and Pequot and such designer labels as Bill Blass. They sell sheets with art designs from the Metropolitan and Guggenheim Museums and even have a bed set designed for them by Princess Grace of Monaco from a pressed flower motif. Besides finished items, Springs Mills also manufactures fabrics for home sewing; distributes Ultrasuede, the Japanese-made leatherlike fabric; and wholesales finished fabrics to other manufacturers, who turn them into shirts, blouses, dresses and sleepwear.

In 1973, to counter the ups and downs of the textile business, Springs Mills went into frozen foods, paying $35 million for Georgia-based Seabrook Foods; they later picked up several other food processing operations. Ironically, the frozen food business has turned out to be weaker than textiles. Troubles began in 1974, when the recession encouraged consumers to buy, and even grow, fresh foods and leave the more expensive frozen stuff in the case. Nevertheless, Springs Mills now has nine food processing plants from California to New York, selling frozen vegetables, fruits, and seafood under such names as Seabrook Farms, Snow Crop, and Carnation Seafood. True to their southern roots, Seabrook packs such regional specialties as collard greens.

History. The company draws its name from Leroy Springs, who became president early in this century when his father-in-law resigned rather than obey a summons to New York City to meet with bankers. The story is that old Captain Samuel White told his board of directors that he had gone North of the Mason-Dixon line only to chase Yankees, not to take orders from them. Captain White and others had organized the original Fort Mill plant in 1887, a time when, the company history says, "many similar Southern communities shook off the paralysis of Reconstruction by building small plants to spin and weave the cotton ginned from their lands." Both the looms and the weavers for the venture had to be imported from the North, and none of the Fort Mill founders had any experience with cotton manufacturing or corporate finance.

While many of these southern cotton operations floundered, the Fort Mill business survived. It was their particular luck, according to the company history, to have support from the community, while elsewhere "mill managers kept to lighted streets. . . . For years the [other] mills needed as many lawyers to defend damage suits as workers to weave cloth."

In more modern times Springs Mills was blessed with a president who not only built the company into one of the largest textile firms in the nation, but also turned the advertising world on its ear with his promotional campaigns for Springmaid fabrics in

Coal, Water, and Cheesecake

The giant leg jutted into the air, 35 feet high. A woman's leg, clad in a silky-looking nylon stocking, it appeared in Los Angeles soon after World War II. Crowds gathered to gape at the display, but the man whose invention it publicized would have blushed. Wallace Hume Carothers, inventor of nylon, was a shy, bespectacled organic chemist who might well have spent his life in academia had not Du Pont been hungry for new products.

In 1927, when E. I. du Pont de Nemours & Company hired Carothers away from his teaching job at Yale, the explosives firm was taking the then-revolutionary step of starting its own "pure" research laboratory to develop new consumer products. Carothers's scientific breakthrough cost Du Pont a reputed $27 million and required 11 years of research. Thirty years earlier Carothers would have become a national hero, along with Eli Whitney, Thomas Edison, and Alexander Graham Bell. Instead, his name is commemorated on a plaque on a laboratory wall, his patents belong to the corporation, and the name people remember when they

think of nylon is Du Pont.

When Carothers went to work for Du Pont, there was no such thing as a truly synthetic textile fiber. The closest approximation was rayon, first marketed some 40 years earlier. But rayon was not really synthetic: it was a laboratory product derived from cellulose, a natural component of plants. Furthermore, rayon could not approach silk's quality. Carothers's discoveries produced a whole family of entirely synthetic, high-quality fibers from inorganic materials that, at the time, were cheap and plentiful: coal tar, petroleum by-products, water, and air.

Carothers did what no one had done before: he created in a laboratory giant molecules, or polymers, linked in long, strong chains much like the protein chains in silk and wool. His first efforts produced a glutinous substance that could be pulled into long threads. Stretched, the threads surprisingly became stronger, as the molecules "locked" firmly into one another. The filaments were shiny and pliable like silk, but they had one fatal drawback: they melted at relatively low temperatures. Over the next four years Carothers and his

assistants produced thousands of chemical combinations and hundreds of fibers, none of them good enough for commercial marketing. Gloom settled over the lab in Wilmington, Delaware.

Then in 1934 Carothers squeezed a viscous substance through a hypodermic needle, producing a long filament that was lustrous, silky, and far more elastic than silk. It survived every test Carothers could devise for it. The stuff, christened Polymer 66, was like nothing ever seen in the world before.

Du Pont kept its triumph under wraps while a crew of applied scientists and engineers figured out ways to economically manufacture and use the new fiber. In 1938 the company unveiled its "new artificial silk, superior to natural silk or any synthetic rayon in its fineness, strength and elasticity." Du Pont carefully avoided stigmatizing its miracle fiber by marketing it as a lowly substitute for something else. From the start, they ballyhooed it as a premium product, worthy of premium prices.

In 1940, renamed nylon, Du Pont's breakthrough went on sale nationwide in the form of women's hosiery.

the prudish years following World War II. Elliott Springs cranked out ads featuring risqué young women and outrageous copy using words like *ham hamper* and *lung lifter* to describe undergarments. One ad for women's panties was captioned "You put up a good front and we'll bring up the rear." The daring language and illustrations got Springs Mills a lot of publicity—and also kept the ads out of a number of publications.

Elliott Springs ran the business with a whimsical hand. He carried on a hilarious correspondence with business associates and hapless enemies. He also wrote short stories which were published in national magazines and at least eight books, including a delightful history of the company, *Clothes Make the Man.*

After Springs died in 1959, his son-in-law, H. William Close, became president. Close is a more conventional business type. "We're not a bunch of clowns," he said one day, perhaps a bit defensively. His 10-year reign was marked by expansion and by such a sharp decline in profits that in 1969 Springs Mills had to break tradition and go outside the family to bring in Peter Scotese from Federated Department Stores as president. According to *Business Week,* Scotese

New York stores got an initial allotment of 72,000 pairs of "nylons"; they sold out in eight hours, despite the limit of 2 pairs per customer. Long queues formed around stores known to have received consignments. In the first year of production Du Pont sold 64 million pairs.

Then came World War II. Silk, a Japanese monopoly, vanished from U.S. markets—and nylon filled the gap. U.S. forces were outfitted with almost 4 million nylon parachutes, not to mention innumerable nylon-corded airplane tires, netting, jungle hammocks, and the like. To boost the war effort, movie sex goddess Betty Grable auctioned off her once-worn nylons for as much as $40,000 each.

It was a sensational triumph for the early corporate research system. The chemistry that produced nylon gave rise to a host of other successful synthetics—Orlon, Dacron, Lycra. Du Pont's shrewd investment in basic research made fortunes for the company many times over.

But Wallace Carothers knew nothing of all this. In 1937, two days after his forty-first birthday, he died by his own hand.

Wallace Carothers in his lab at Du Pont.

PROTECT YOUR ASSETS

SPRINGMAID FABRICS

SPRINGS MILLS, Inc.

Colonel Elliott Springs was an irrepressible madcap who ran the Springs Mills textile company after World War II and who had a weakness for risque, *double entendre* jokes and illustrations which he used freely in advertising Springmaid fabrics. Many magazines of the day turned them down.

was "recruited to rescue the company." Profits are now at record high levels.

Reputation. The playful days of Elliott Springs are gone. Scotese is on record as ready to fire any manager who does not perform.

What they own. Twenty-two textile plants, most of them within 125 miles of the original Fort Mill headquarters.

Who owns and runs the company. Close took the company public in 1966, but he and other family members control 60% of the stock. It's clear that Scotese is in charge. He even runs the company from New York rather than Fort Mill, where Close remains as board chairman. In 1980 Scotese, getting ready to exit the company, brought in another outsider as president: Walter Y. Elisha, former vice chairman of the Jewel Companies. In 1979 absenteeism at Spring Mills textile plants was 8.3%. Employee turnover was 30.7%: of their 15,960 textile workers, more than 5,000 left during the year. While that may seem high, the company points out that the average in the textile industry is nearly double that rate.

Where they're going. During 1979 they acquired Lawtex, a Dalton, Georgia, producer of bedspreads, draperies and comforters, and Graber Industries, a Middletown, Wisconsin, maker of window decorating products, explaining: "Acquisitions remain a continuing objective for Springs."

Stock performance. Springs Mills stock bought for $1,000 in 1970 sold for $1,172 on January 2, 1980.

Access. Post Office Box 70, Fort Mill, South Carolina 29715; (803) 547-2901.

Consumer brands.

Linens: Springmaid; Skinner; Pequot; Morgan Jones.
Home-furnishing textiles: Graber; Conso; Lawtex; Regent.
Fabrics: Ultrasuede; Springmaid.
Frozen foods: Carnation; Seabrook Farms; Snowcrop; Chill Ripe; Brookfarms; Gold King.
Other foods: McKenzie's southern specialty vegetables and fruit.

J. P. Stevens

Sales: $1.8 billion
Profits: $47.7 million
Forbes 500 rank: 285
Rank in textiles: 2
Founded: 1813
Employees: 43,400
Headquarters: New York, New York

What they do. Few people recognize J. P. Stevens products by name, but just about everyone knows the company by reputation as organized labor's number 1 enemy in the United States. Anyone who saw the 1979 Hollywood movie *Norma Rae* knows the story. That film is based on the struggle of Crystal Lee Sutton, a union organizer who was fired from a J. P. Stevens textile mill in Roanoke Rapids, North Carolina. Since the Textile Workers Union started organizing their mills in the South in 1963, J. P. Stevens has been fighting like General Beauregard to keep the union out.

Besieged by consumer boycotts and adverse court decisions, J. P. Stevens nevertheless remains nonunion and a vigorous number 2 in the textile industry. They weave and knit fabrics from cotton, polyester, and wool, and they sell them to clothing manufacturers and fabric retailers. They also make home furnishings—sheets, pillowcases, towels, bedspreads—and industrial fabrics, such as insect screening and automobile floor carpeting. As Stevens Graphics and Foote & Davies, they turn out phone books, catalogs, and other printed matter.

The boycott of Stevens products, led by the Amalgamated Clothing and Textile Workers Union, has been endorsed by the AFL-CIO and the National Council of Churches. It's hard to make a dent in a company like Stevens through a boycott, however, as only about one-third of their sales come from items sold directly to consumers, and these have so many different brand names that it's hard to keep them straight. Stevens claims the boycott has not hurt them one bit. Profits were up 31% in 1979.

History. The origins of J. P. Stevens go back to the War of 1812, when Nathaniel ("Captain Nat") Stevens was running a general store in Andover, Massachusetts. Convinced that the war with England, the great textile exporter of the time, presented a splendid opportunity for American makers of wool cloth, Stevens turned his father's grist mill into a woolen mill in 1813. After the war British woolen goods returned to the American market and put many New England mills out of business, but Captain Nat survived by becoming the first American producer of flannel. He called his firm the Factory Company but changed the name to the Stevens Company when he bought out his last partner in 1832. After his death in 1865 his son Moses took over the company, which he renamed M. T. Stevens & Sons. During 40 years at the helm, Moses found time to serve in the U.S. House of Representatives, where, as a member of the Ways and Means Committee, he helped push through wool tariff legislation favorable to the textile industry. M. T. Stevens was the largest and richest wool manufacturer in America until 1899, when American Woolen was formed. That same year Moses's nephew, John Peters Stevens, Sr., opened J. P. Stevens & Co. in New York —a textile-selling house to market his uncle's mill goods.

J. P. Stevens, Sr., was one of the first barons of the textile industry to see the potential of the South, where new, efficient mills proliferated after World War I. These mills, as described by M. A. McLaurin in *Paternalism and Protest*, had the flavor of the Old South: "The mill president replaced the plantation owner; the mill village replaced the slave quarters and the tenant's weatherbeaten shack.... Like the planter, the entrepreneur looked after the social and moral, as well as economic, well-being of his work force." J. P. Stevens and his cousin Nat (Moses's son) traveled through the South, lining up new accounts for the Stevens selling house and investing in the mills themselves.

Meanwhile, the CIO, trying to organize northern textile mills in the 1940s, focused on M. T. Stevens & Sons. By 1945 they had organized five of the company's 10 plants, and the South, with its time-honored distrust of unions, looked more and more attractive to the Stevens family. In 1946 the two branches of the family business merged with eight other southern textile companies and started closing down their unionized New England mills, taking the machinery with them to the South, laying off more than 10,000 workers over a 25-year period, and setting the stage for the showdown with organized labor that rages today.

The new company was called J. P. Stevens & Co. At its head were two sons of J. P. Stevens, Sr.: Robert Stevens as chairman and J. P. Stevens, Jr., as president.

During World War II, when Robert Stevens was a colonel in charge of the Army's textile purchases, the company got more than $50 million worth of government contracts. Stevens later became secretary of the army and emerged with the image of a persecuted hero after a nationally televised 35-

Four-fifths of all American clothing workers are women—a total of 1 million, or one-fifth of all women who work in manufacturing.

The amount of clothing imported into the United States more than doubled between 1968 and 1977.

day browbeating by Senator Joseph McCarthy who was holding hearings in his search for communists in government.

Reputation. Few companies have ever received such consistently bad press as J. P. Stevens. The Textile Workers Union has managed to keep them in the spotlight as "the nation's number 1 scofflaw," and the company conceded the public relations battle from the start. James D. Finley, head of Stevens from 1969 through 1979, rarely talked to the press and never argued publicly in support of his company, except at the annual stockholder's meetings. "I give them a chance once a year to work me over, and that's enough," he told *Fortune*'s Walter Guzzardi, Jr. Stevens's image had sunk so low by 1978 that *Fortune* called the company an "embarrassment to the business community."

What they own. Eighty-one manufacturing plants in the United States (61 of them in North and South Carolina, 14 more in Georgia and Virginia). Subsidiaries in Mexico, New Zealand, Canada, Britain, and France.

Who owns and runs the company. Former chairman Finley was the force behind the company's resolve to fight the union down to the end. *Fortune* described him as a "Georgian of iron character and rigid bearing." In June 1979, Finley told *Fortune*, "I wouldn't change anything if I could do it all over again," and added, "We don't have any problem, the union has a problem." But, the magazine observed, "In his resolve he stands alone, a man isolated in an isolated corporation." When Finley stepped down at the end of 1979, he was succeeded by Whitney Stevens, the oldest son of Robert Stevens. The Stevens family still owns a large block of the stock.

Despite their image as a southern company, Stevens is run from New York City and has close financial ties with Manufacturers Hanover Trust, Goldman Sachs, J. P. Morgan, and other titans of Wall Street. Nevertheless they have taken to holding their annual meetings in Greenville, South Carolina, in a futile attempt to escape union pickets.

In the public eye. Organized labor has made few inroads into the southern textile mills: only 10% of the 700,000 workers are unionized. After losing at Cannon Mills, Burlington Industries, and other companies, the union focused on J. P. Stevens. Since beginning a drive in 1963, the union has won only three of more than a dozen elections at Stevens mills. The union has downplayed the significance of these defeats, claiming that company pressure made fair elections impossible at most plants. Shortly before one election, they charge, the company "paraded a one-legged man on crutches around the facilities to tell the workers he had lost the leg because of a strike."

Where the union has won elections, no contract has yet been negotiated with Stevens. Where they have lost, they have challenged the results and managed to have some of them set aside. They have barraged the company with charges of unfair labor practices. The National Labor Relations Board (NLRB) has generally ruled in favor of the union, finding the company guilty in several instances of illegally discharging or intimidating workers and of refusing to bargain in good faith. Stevens has repeatedly lost appeals of these decisions in the federal courts. They argue that "the law is prounion," but they insist that their "determination to comply" with it is "unqualified."

Where they're going. The union has recently come up with a new tactic: trying to isolate J. P. Stevens from the business community by zeroing in on interlocking directorships. In 1978 the union brought enough pressure on New York Life Insurance to force their chairman and the Stevens chairman off each other's boards. By pressuring Avon Products they got the Avon chairman to resign from Stevens's board. The company replaced the two fallen directors with southerners not affiliated with other corporations.

Some observers detect a glimmer of conciliation at headquarters, but at the annual meeting on March 4, 1980, newly installed chairman Whitney Stevens said: "We in the management of the company do not believe that a union has anything constructive to offer the company or its employees."

Stock performance. J. P. Stevens stock bought for $1,000 in 1970 sold for $915 on January 2, 1980.

Access. Stevens Tower, 1185 Avenue of

the Americas, New York, New York 10036;
(212) 575-2000.

Consumer brands.

Sheets and pillowcases: Beauti-Blend; Beauticale;
Fine Arts; Peanuts; Tastemaker; Meadow-
brook; Utica; Utica & Mohawk; and the de-
signer labels Yves St. Laurent, Angelo
Donghia, Suzanne Pleshette, Dinah Shore,
Ava Bergmann.
Towels: Fine Arts; Tastemaker; Utica.
Table linen: Simtex.
Blankets: Forstmann; Utica.
Draperies: J. P. Stevens.
Carpets: Contender; Gulistan; Merryweather;
Tastemaker.
Hosiery: Big Mama; Finesse; Hip-Lets; Spirit.

West Point Pepperell

Sales: $1 billion
Profits: $27.4 million
Forbes 500 rank: 453
Rank in textiles: 3
Founded: 1844
Employees: 24,000
Headquarters: West Point, Georgia

West Point–Pepperell, the company that
brings you Martex towels, operates 37 mills
in seven states, nearly all of them in the
South. Their "bed and bath" products—
sheets, towels, blankets, bedspreads—produce about one-quarter of their sales. Carpets and rugs account for another quarter;
and fabrics for clothing, such as denim, corduroy, and blends of polyester and cotton

---

TOP 10 SEWING STATES

State/Number of Clothing Workers

1. NEW YORK 204,688
2. PENNSYLVANIA 141,012
3. CALIFORNIA 104,160
4. NORTH CAROLINA 77,216
5. TEXAS 77,196
6. GEORGIA 71,904
7. TENNESSEE 67,863
8. NEW JERSEY 59,139
9. ALABAMA 51,553
10. SOUTH CAROLINA 46,744

Source: American Apparel Manufacturers Association, 1979.

---

blends generate another third, and the rest
comes from industrial fabrics that end up as
awnings, sails, tents, and so on.

West Point–Pepperell was formed in
1963 by the merger of two textile compa-
nies whose roots go back to the last century.
Pepperell began in 1850 at Biddeford,
Maine. The West Point mill was started in
Georgia after the Civil War by two broth-
ers, LaFayette and Ward Crockett Lanier,
both Confederate Army veterans. Joseph L.
Lanier, Jr., grandson of founder LaFayette
Lanier, is chairman and chief executive of
West Point–Pepperell. He holds 20,324
shares (worth about $600,000).

Access. 400 West 10th Street, West Point,
Georgia 31833; (205) 756-7111.

Consumer brands.

Bed and bath products: Martex, Lady Pepperell,
Vellux.
Carpets: Cabin Crafts, Georgian, Walter.

Sewers and Cobblers

Sales: $1 billion
Profits: $67.3 million
Forbes 500 rank: 445
Rank in jeans: 2
Rank in women's jeans: 1
Founded: 1916
Employees: 30,000
Headquarters: Greensboro, North Carolina

What they do. For every five pairs of jeans sold by Levi Strauss, Blue Bell sells three. And in such places as Italy and the United Kingdom, Blue Bell is number 1. They do 40% of their sales abroad. For all that, they remain a strictly down-home company in management, policy, and plant location.

Blue Bell makes a broad line of clothing for men, women, and children. Though they are best known for their Wrangler jeans, their line also includes Maverick and Sedgewick sportswear; Big Ben and Red Kap work clothing; and an array of products labeled by Sears, Roebuck, Penney, and Montgomery Ward. They also franchise Wrangler Wranch clothing stores. Two-thirds of their sales are from clothes other than jeans; western wear (excluding jeans) and sportswear bring in about half their money. Blue Bell recently bought Jantzen, the Portland, Oregon, swimwear manufacturer.

History. Blue Bell began life as Jellico Manufacturing Company in Jellico, Tennessee, where, with 35 sewing machines, they made suspender-bib overalls favored by field workers. By 1930, after some mergers, they had become the Blue Bell Overall Company, the world's largest producer of work clothes, and moved to Greensboro. Things progressed rather sleepily until after World War II, when Blue Bell made the key decision to follow Levi Strauss into snug, western-cut jeans.

The trouble was, Levi's was already established in most department stores before Blue Bell got there, so Blue Bell was forced to sell in lower-priced department store budget basements, chains, and discounters. Nearly 90% of Blue Bell's business was channeled into such customers as Sears, Penney, and Ward.

Though there was certainly enough money to go around in that booming era of denim, Blue Bell was uneasy with their bargain-basement image. They began using cowboy stars to promote their Wrangler brand and expanded into ladies' sportswear, men's shirts, slacks, leisure suits, boots, and shoes. And finally, to establish a foothold in the upstairs departments, Blue Bell introduced the "Wrangler Wroom," a special selling area in large stores for their broadened line of products.

The mix paid off well. By 1979 Blue Bell had racked up their first billion-dollar year. Not bad for a company whose strategies still originate amid the tobacco fields of North Carolina.

Reputation. For all their growth, Blue Bell remains deeply rooted in the South. According to *Forbes*, "Headquartered in a modest four-story red brick building in downtown Greensboro, North Carolina, Blue Bell's white-shirted executives seem faceless. . . . Levi Strauss makes much of social consciousness. . . . Blue Bell runs a determinedly nonunion shop, and its executives make no bones about their conservatism."

What they own. Blue Bell has 108 plants, 81 of them in the United States. Of these 25 are in North Carolina alone, with another 45 located in other states of the Confederacy.

They also own one hot-air balloon with "Wrangler" printed on the side of the bag. The balloon recently set a new altitude record of 27,000 feet.

Who owns and runs the company. Blue Bell's officers and board of directors collectively owns 4% of the company.

In the public eye. Blue Bell is resolutely in favor of import restrictions and tariffs. Their vice-president of marketing, Edwin F. Lucas, has told *Forbes* in 1979, "We would like to see our government take some steps to protect the employment of textile and apparel people in this country . . . whose jobs are in serious jeopardy."

Where they're going. Blue Bell's Wrangler is determined to wrest more of the jeans market away from what is referred to by one executive as "that San Francisco jeans company." Wrangler Wranch franchises will be increased by about 30 units per year. Their pitch: "Wrangler doesn't just mean cowboy anymore."

Stock performance. Blue Bell stock bought for $1,000 in 1970 sold for $3,918 on January 2, 1980.

Access. 335 Church Court, Greensboro, North Carolina 27401; (919) 373-3400.

Major employment centers. Greensboro; Tupelo, Mississippi; and Luray, Virginia.

Consumer brands.

Big Ben; Jantzen; Long Time Friend; Lucchese; Maverick; Red Kap; Rustler; Sedgefield; Wrangler; Wrapid Transit apparel.

Brown Group, Inc.

Sales: $1.1 billion
Profits: $41.8 million
Forbes 500 rank: 413
Founded: 1878
Employees: 26,000
Headquarters: St. Louis, Missouri

This 102-year-old company is known to generations of mothers and their children for the Buster Brown shoe line. Their 45 plants, located mostly in small towns in the South and Midwest, can turn out 120,000 pairs of shoes a day—6% of all shoes manufactured in the United States. Two-thirds of their output is women's shoes. Brown owns the 200-unit Regal shoe chain, and they operate more than 750 shoe departments housed in such leading department stores as Macy's, Ivey's, Famous-Barr, and Joske's. Their 225-store Cloth World operation is the nation's largest chain of retail fabrics. They also run several clothing store chains and manufacture Hedstrom juvenile furniture and toys and Eagle sports equipment. Incidental intelligence: Brown licenses Nippon Shoe to make Regal shoes—and Regal is now the number 1 shoe brand in Japan.

Access. 8400 Maryland Avenue, St. Louis, Missouri 63105; (314) 997-7500.

Consumer brands.

Shoes: Air Step, Buskens, Connie, Corelli, DeLiso, Fanfares, Footworks, Jacqueline, Larks, Life Stride, Marquise, Naturalizer, Palter, Risque and Tempos for women; Italia, Levi's for Feet, Pedwin, Regal, and Roblee for men; Buster Brown and The Wikler Shoe for children.
Recreational products: Hedstrom; Oakhill; Eagle; Itza; Kent; Vittert; Court Casuals; Gerry; Kenyon, Redfield; Tempco.
Clothing stores: Meis family fashion stores; Cloth World fabric stores; and BottomHalf pants stores.

> About half of all American feet are now covered with imported shoes, according to *Leather & Shoes*, an industry publication.

> American consumers spend about 6% of their income on clothes.

Cluett

Sales: $671.6 million
Profits: $17.4 million
Rank in men's shirts: 1
Founded: 1851
Employees: 21,908
Headquarters: New York, New York

What they do. Cluett, a company that started out making collars, was transformed into one of the country's largest clothing firms with the help of World War I and a celebrated advertising campaign.

Cluett's most famous product is the Arrow shirt. But you can also buy their shirts at Sears, Roebuck and J. C. Penney, their biggest customers. Other clothing labels in the Cluett stable include Halston suits, Gold Toe Socks, and Duofold underwear.

Cluett sells their own products (and those of others) in their 28 retail specialty stores: The Metropolitan in Dayton, Lytton's in Chicago, Young Quinlan in Minneapolis, and Boyd's in St. Louis.

History. For 70 years after the company's founding in 1851, Cluett made only one thing: starched collars, which they produced in Troy, New York. George B. Cluett bought the business in 1885 and gave it his name. Four years later he merged with another collar maker who had two invaluable resources: the trademark Arrow and a brilliant salesman named Frederick F. Peabody, who bought into the company.

Peabody expanded the Arrow line to no fewer than 400 different models of collars. To sell them, he collaborated with J. C. Leyendecker, an artist, and created the "Arrow Collar Man"—lofty browed, clear eyed, square jawed. By the end of World War I Arrow's sales exceeded $32 million a year, and the company employed 6,000 workers.

Returning American soldiers had become accustomed to a new type of garment they wore in the service: a shirt with an attached soft collar that didn't chafe—so in 1921 the company began making shirts with attached collars. The Arrow Collar Man's new slogan was: "Only Arrow Shirts Have the Arrow Collar." There was one problem: the shirts kept shrinking.

Enter Sanford Cluett, nephew of George B. Cluett. An inventor with 200 patents in his name, he devised a way to compress cotton fabric under tension to the same extent that it would shrink after washing. Shirts treated under this revolutionary process were labeled Sanforized. For the first time men could buy shirts to fit exactly. Cluett, Peabody now makes $9 million a year by licensing the process.

Cluett, Peabody ran into problems when they decided to expand in the late 1960s. After they added 57 retail stores, they had to sell or close 30 of them. They also had to sell Atlantic luggage.

Reputation. Despite heavy competition from Manhattan, Phillips-Van Heusen and Levi Strauss, Cluett hangs on as the world's largest shirt maker.

What they own. Twenty-nine manufacturing plants in the United States and 2 in other countries.

Where they're going. In 1978 Arrow was making four dress shirts to one sports shirt. Their aim now is to make more sports shirts, which account for 70% of shirt sales. In 1979 they introduced Arrow Cotton-Ease shirts, which are made entirely of cotton but don't need ironing.

Stock performance. Cluett, Peabody stock bought for $1,000 in 1970 sold for $316 on January 2, 1980.

Access. 510 Fifth Avenue, New York, New York 10036; (212) 930-3000.

Consumer brands.

Clothing: Arrow shirts; Glentex scarves and accessories; Gold Toe socks; Donmoor boys' wear; Duofold winter underwear; Halston suits; RPM and Dobie Originals sportswear; Van Roalte gloves.
Retail stores: Boyd's; Young Quinlan; Lytton's; The Metropolitan.

Before Arrow made shirts they made collars — and that's all they made.

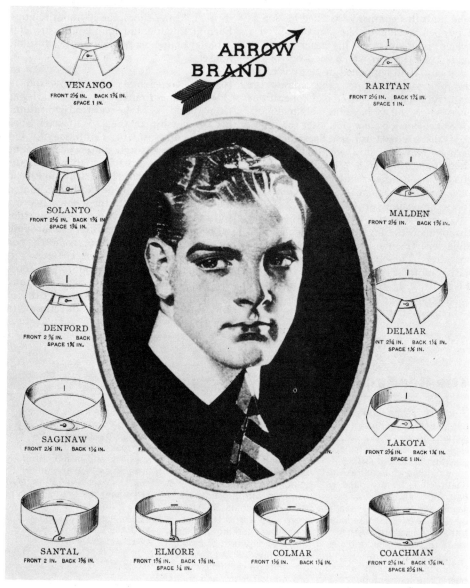

GENESCO

Sales: $993 million
Loss: $6.3 million
Forbes 500 rank: 460
Founded: 1924
Employees: 36,000
Headquarters: Nashville, Tennessee

What they do. Genesco, manufacturer of shoes and men's clothing, is trying to survive the wounds left by a family battle that almost tore the company apart. A father who built this company installed his son as a puppet president. The son organized a palace revolt and threw his father out. Four years later the son was booted out of the company. It all happened in Nashville, but the blows reverberated throughout the country. Genesco once had operations everywhere; many have been sloughed off. One of the major pieces left after the shooting is the original business: shoes, including Jarman and Johnston & Murphy men's shoes. Genesco also supplies shoes to Sears, Roebuck and other retailers who put their own names on them (13% of Genesco's footwear business in 1978).

Genesco sells 16% of the shoes they make through stores they own or through leased shoe departments they run in stores owned by others. These Genesco-operated outlets carry another troop of names, including Flagg Bros., Hardy, and Jarman.

Some big men's clothing brands belong to Genesco (Lanvin and Chaps suits, for example), but half their clothing business comes from private-label customers (stores that put their own names on clothes supplied by Genesco).

Genesco also limps along in the men's clothing store field. They own eight different local chains, ranging in size from the 2-store Gilbert's operation in South Bend, Indiana, to the 33-store Roos/Atkins network in Northern California. In addition, they own 150 Kress variety stores.

They have succeeded in disposing of a lot of other acquired businesses, some of them —Bonwit Teller stores, Charles Jourdan shoes, I. Miller shoes, the Plymouth Shops, Formfit lingerie and foundation garments —better known names than those left in the house.

History. Genesco was created by God.

When James Franklin Jarman came home from World War I, he was ready to resume his partnership in the J. W. Carter Shoe Company in Nashville, Tennessee. But Jarman grew increasingly uneasy over what he saw as the collapse of Christian mores in the company. One Saturday he drove to Franklin, a small town outside Nashville, rented a hotel room, and spent the whole day praying and thinking. "Be ye not yoked together with unbelievers," the Bible he brought along advised. "Wherefore come ye out from among them and be ye separate." Jarman later related: "I went out of that room feeling absolutely sure in my heart and mind that God wanted me to go all the way and thus entirely sever my connection with

The Ready-Made Blues

Crude, shapeless, and cheap, the first ready-made clothing earned the well-deserved scorn of Americans when they first appeared in the early nineteenth century. The unattractive, factory-made garb found favor only with sailors and laborers. Those who could afford it continued to have their attire custom made to their measure by tailors, dressmakers, milliners, and shoemakers, as had been done for centuries. Poorer people made their own clothes at home.

Over the next half-century the ready-made industry improved its techniques. Overcoats were the first factory-made garments able to achieve respectability and compete with prestigious tailor-made coats. By 1860 more than 4,000 U.S. factories were turning out nearly $80 million worth of clothing. During the Civil War military demands on the industry proved that factories could be set up to mass-produce cloth-

ing with the newly invented sewing machine's 125 stitches per minute. After the war ready-mades became big business, and fashion itself became an industry rather than the exclusive prerogative of the wealthy few.

Source: Robert Atwan, Donald McQuade, and John W. Wright, *Edsels, Luckies, & Frigidaires* (Dell, 1979).

the company." By 1924 he had saved up enough to found the Jarman Shoe Company.

It was a quick success, due largely to the Jarman Friendly Fives, a $5 shoe that took a great shine. In 1932 the company's name was changed to General Shoe. When Jarman died in 1938, his son, Walton Maxey Jarman, succeeded him. Sales were then $13 million a year.

Maxey Jarman was, like his father, a God-fearing Baptist. And like his father, he had a vision, although it may not have been inspired by the scriptures. He was intent on making General Shoe grow. Described by *Fortune* as "the cold-blooded dreamer of Nashville," Maxey became a deacon of the First Baptist Church of Nashville, conducted Bible classes in his home on Sunday afternoons, befriended evangelist Billy Graham—and meanwhile bagged other companies. He bought so many shoe makers that in 1956 he had to promise the Federal Trade Commission, in a consent decree, to go easy. So he began to buy apparel companies and stores instead—95 of them in the next 16 years. He shortened the company's name to Genesco in 1959.

By 1968 Genesco had become the first apparel company to do $1 billion a year in sales. And at the confluence of Fifth Avenue and 57th Street in New York City, the fashion corner of the world, this Bible-belt company was represented by a prestigious phalanx of stores selling high-priced clothes and shoes to men and women: Bonwit Teller, Henri Bendel, I. Miller, Delman, Charles Jourdan, Frank Brothers, Whitehouse & Hardy, and Johnston & Murphy.

In 1969, content with what he had wrought, Maxey Jarman, then 65, stepped down, ostensibly succeeded by his son Franklin. Not at all like his father or grandfather, Frank Jarman didn't read the Bible and never went to church, and he was married and divorced twice. Maxey actually continued to run Genesco from his position as chairman of the finance committee. In 1972 his son Frank made a bid for control. He failed to get a majority of the board, but a year later he came back and won, unceremoniously forcing his father Maxey out of the company he had created.

Genesco was then a company already beginning to creak under the weight of aimless acquisitions—and it had the red ink to prove it. Reflecting on what his father had bought, Frank Jarman said: "We went on a billion-dollar ego trip, a 10-year binge, and we are living through one hell of a hangover now." It was a hangover Frank Jarman was never able to get over. He shucked a lot of things his father had bought, closing down some 200 stores and firing 10,000 people. Even so he wasn't able to get Genesco on an even keel. The company made money one year and lost the next year. In 1977 Genesco's two vice-chairman teamed up with board members who were not on the company payroll to strip Frank Jarman of his power. A few months later 66-year-old John L. Hanigan, who had revitalized Brunswick Corp., was enticed out of retirement with the assignment to right Genesco. The first non-Jarman to run the company, Hanigan unloaded a string of unprofitable properties including all the women's and children's apparel companies. He fired the chairman of Bonwit Teller because he had used store employees to help decorate his Park Avenue apartment, according to a rumor reported by the *New York Times.* Hanigan later sold off all the Bonwit Teller stores. The Kress stores have been more of a problem: no one wants them.

There are no Jarmans on Genesco's board today.

Reputation. They're known as the country boy who fell flat on his face when he hit Fifth Avenue.

What they own. Less and less each year.

Who owns and runs the company. John Hanigan and the board members who brought him in. The ringleader is considered Harold K. Johnson, a retired U.S. Army general who has been on the board since 1968. Hanigan has a strong incentive.

Sneakers account for about half of all shoe sales in the United States, according to Samuel Americus Walker, *Sneakers* (Workman, 1978). Every year Americans buy more than 200 million pairs of sneakers, over half of them imported. Taiwan sends 65 million pairs, 3 million arrive from Japan, 1.3 million come from Hong Kong, and 31.4 million make their way here from South Korea.

When he was hired, Genesco's stock was selling at $6.38 a share. He has a contract running to May 1, 1981, at which time he collects $125,000 for every dollar over $6.38 that the stock is selling for. In other words, if Genesco common stock is then trading at $14.38, Hanigan receives a bonus of $1 million in addition to an annual salary of $325,000. In early 1980 Genesco was selling at less than $4 a share.

Where they're going. Right back where they started from: making and selling shoes.

Stock performance. Genesco stock bought for $1,000 in 1970 sold for $147 on January 2, 1980.

Access. 111 Seventh Avenue North, Nashville, Tennessee 37202; (615) 367-7000.

Consumer brands.

Men's shoes: Cedar Crest; Fortune; Jarman; John Ritchie; Johnson & Murphy; Wrangler Shoes for Jeans.
Women's and children's shoes: Charm Step; Cover Girl; Easy Street; Storybrook; Vogue.
Private-label shoes: Dominion; Republic; Sentry.
Tailored clothing: Chaps by Ralph Lauren; Churchill; Donald Brooks; Guy LaRoche; Hardy Amies; Lanvin; Tom Weiskopf.
Jeans, work pants: Contur; Hayes; MALE.
Hoisery: Camp; D'Orsay; John Weitz.
Pajamas, underwear: Pleetway; Rogue.
Private-label apparel: Aimsbrooke; Bacon/Baker-Cammock; Grief & Company; Harpeth; Haywood; Phoenix.

Sales: $630.8 million
Profits: $21.0 million
Rank in men's clothing: 1
Founded: 1872
Employees: 20,000
Headquarters: Chicago, Illinois

What they do. Men's suits are linked in the minds of most consumers with Hart Schaffner & Marx. They make suits ranging in price from $100 to more than $350 under the Hickey-Freeman name. They also manufacture women's suits, sport coats, slacks, outerwear, rainwear, and sportswear.

H S & M not only makes clothes, but sells them through 274 stores in 67 metropolitan areas. Among the better known retail units are Wallachs (New York and New England), Baskin (Chicago), Silverwoods (Los Angeles), Hastings (San Francisco), Charles A. Stevens (Chicago), and Leopold Price and Rolle (Houston). The stores account for nearly two-thirds of the company's total sales, but supplying them takes only about one-fifth of their manufacturing output. The stores stock clothing from other suppliers, though they choose to buy most of their men's tailored clothing from Hart Shaffner & Marx.

History. In 1872, six months after the great Chicago fire, Harry Hart, 21, and his brother Max, 18, opened a clothing store on State Street called, logically enough, Harry Hart and Brother. Two brothers-in-law, Levi Abt and Marcus Marx, joined the business, which was renamed none too melodiously Hart, Abt & Marx. In 1887 Joseph Schaffner replaced Abt, and the present name was adopted.

After a merchant from out of town bought several garments to resell himself, the partners decided to go after more such orders. Their search was so successful that the wholesale business soon outstripped the retail, and Hart Schaffner & Marx as we know them were on their way: building factories; sending out salesmen dressed in silk toppers, spats, and walking sticks; showing finished garments from as many as 20 wardrobe trunks; employing such unheard-of sales techniques as selling from fabric samples; and running the first national clothing advertising.

In 1954 H S & M acquired Society Brand Clothes. Ten years later they picked up Hickey-Freeman, followed by Jaymar-Ruby and Gleneagles in 1967. Meanwhile they bought up locally owned retailers across the country until the Justice Department stepped in. Under a 1970 consent decree H S & M agreed not to acquire any more men's wear stores for 10 years and to sell off 30 of their existing stores. They promptly proceeded to expand abroad, acquiring a half-interest in Robert's, a large Mexican retailer and manufacturer, and an 11% stake in Britain's Austin Reed, also a manufacturer and retailer of men's wear.

Reputation. An old-fashioned company, in good standing with labor, Hart Schaffner & Marx connotes quality garments. They were the first to tailor a tropical-weight suit and the first to blend wool and the new synthetics in men's suits.

What they own. Hart Schaffner & Marx has more than 20 major manufacturing plants in the United States, the biggest ones being in their headquarters city, Chicago. All of their retail stores occupy leased space (annual rent: nearly $20 million). H S & M also "owns" technical manufacturing know-how that they license to companies abroad. Their income from licensing tops $1 million annually.

Who owns and runs the company. The founding families departed the scene 30 years ago. The president and chief executive officer today is Jerome S. Gore, who joined the company in 1941 and rose through the ranks. Gore owns 40,000 shares, one-half of 1% of the total. Employees of H S & M, through a savings-investment plan, own about 5%.

In the public eye. In the closing years of the last century, terrible working conditions and low wages resulted in a four-month industry-wide garment workers strike in Chicago. Joseph Schaffner was among the first to come to an agreement with the new union—and that agreement served as a model for later clothing industry contracts. Hart Schaffner & Marx didn't have another strike or lockout until 1974, when the Amalgamated Clothing Workers called a clothing industry walkout that lasted nine days. In 1964 the Labor Department named H S & M and the Amalgamated Clothing Workers to its Hall of Honor, the first two organizations admitted.

H S & M has been working with other clothing manufacturers to stem the tide of imports from the Far East.

Where they're going. In the case of Hart Schaffner & Marx, it seems to be more a matter of where the times are going. In 1970 they had sales of $360 million, while jeans maker Levi Strauss had sales of $325 million. Today, Levi Strauss has a $2 billion volume compared to H S & M's $600 million. Although H S & M is banking that kids who buy jeans will turn to suits as they

Chicago's Hart, Schaffner & Marx, the nation's largest men's suit maker as long as anyone can remember, featured this strikingly attired gentleman in 1897.

grow older, they bought a small jeans manufacturer in 1972.

Stock performance. Hart, Schaffner & Marx stock bought for $1,000 in 1970 sold for $382 on January 2, 1980.

Major employment centers. Chicago, New York, and Buffalo.

Access. 36 South Franklin Street, Chicago, Illinois 60606; (312) 372-6300.

Consumer brands.

Hart Schaffner & Marx; Christian Dior; Austin Reed; Society Brand; Jack Nicklaus; Johnny Carson; Nino Cerruti; Jaymar; Gleaneagles; Sterling & Hunt; Graham & Gunn; Fashionaire; Hickey-Freeman; Walter-Morton; Cary Middlecoff; Allyn St. George; Ridingate; Great Western.

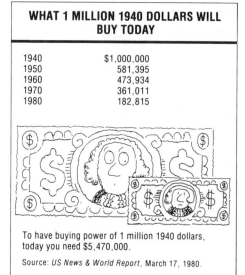

WHAT 1 MILLION 1940 DOLLARS WILL BUY TODAY

1940	$1,000,000
1950	581,395
1960	473,934
1970	361,011
1980	182,815

To have buying power of 1 million 1940 dollars, today you need $5,470,000.

Source: *US News & World Report*, March 17, 1980.

INTERCO
INCORPORATED

Sales: $2.0 billion
Profits: $106.7 million
Forbes 500 rank: 260
Founded: 1911
Employees: 43,000
Headquarters: St. Louis, Missouri

What they do. Interco, formerly known as the International Shoe Company, decided that making shoes is not enough. They are still based in the shoe capital of St. Louis, Missouri, and they still make shoes—Florsheim and Thayer McNeil, for example—but almost half their sales and earnings are now derived from making clothes and operating various kinds of retail chains.

Interco began stuffing their boots with other companies in 1964. Today they own more than 10 clothing manufacturers and more than 800 stores. Among their many clothing brands are London Fog, Clipper Mist, Queen Casuals, Big Yank, and Stuffed Jeans. Their retail group includes junior department stores (P. N. Hirsch, Kent's, Miller's), convenience discount stores (Sky City, Eagle Family), home improvement centers (Central Hardware), and apparel

shops (Fine's, Alberts, Alcove). They added the Ethan Allen furniture company to the stable in 1979.

History. In 1911 two shoe manufacturers in St. Louis merged to form the International Shoe Company. The shoe firm thrived for 40 years under the Fine and Rand families, but by 1953, when they bought Florsheim, a successful quality men's shoe retailer, International had run out of steam. The Florsheim addition alone could not save International as their attempt to enter the retail shoe business failed miserably. In 1962 *Forbes* called the company "down at the heels."

Interco's unlikely savior turned out to be Maurice R. ("Dude") Chambers, a "shoe-dog" (as he calls salesman) who dropped out of school at age 16 and worked his way up from shoe salesman to become president in 1962. Chambers streamlined the operations by closing unprofitable stores, modernizing others, and cutting inventory. In selecting companies to buy, he looked out for effective managers; after acquisition, Chambers would leave them alone to continue their winning ways. In the 13 major acquisitions he made between 1964–74, the old management stayed on.

Instead of buying stores in big cities, Interco bought discount department stores in towns too small for the big retailers. Chambers described his plan: "We make money by watching our pennies on the volume. And these small towns are as plentiful as porgies." As *Forbes* pointed out in 1971, "Maybe an MBA [a business school graduate] would have been too smart to buy unpromising little stores in nowhere little towns," but under Chambers's guidance, Interco tripled sales in the decade 1962–72.

Reputation: The business press that once called Interco a footdragger, now claims that they're "making big strides." Interco is so steady and successful that some smaller companies like Big Yank clothing have asked Interco to please buy them.

What they own: Besides their retail outlets, Interco owns or leases 24 shoe plants and 61 clothing plants across the United States.

Who owns and runs the company. This remains a strong St. Louis company. The statement sent to shareholders for the 1979 annual meeting showed that two St. Louis banks—First Union and Mercantile—were holding shares representing 12.5% of the outstanding stock (some of it undoubtedly in trust for descendants of the founding families). Henry Rand, who died in 1962, was the last member of a founding family to head the company. Chambers, who succeeded Rand, relinquished the chief executive's post in 1976 to William L. Edwards, Jr., who came up through the financial side of the business. He is director of another St. Louis bank: Boatmen's.

Where they're going. Interco plans to continue to buy other companies.

Stock performance. Interco stock bought for $1,000 in 1970 sold for $1,465 on January 2, 1980.

Access. Ten Broadway, St. Louis, Missouri 63102; (314) 231-1100.

Consumer brands.

Women's clothing: Clipper Mist; College-Town; Devon; Gateway Casuals; It's Pure Gould; Lady Devon; Lady Queen; London Fog; Panther; Queen Casuals; REJOICE!; Stuffed Jeans; Stuffed Shirt.

Men's clothing: Big Yank; Biltwell; Campus, Concept II, Easy Life, Esprit, Pro-action, Rugged Country, and Studio One by Campus; Clipper Mist; Cowden; Gateway Casuals; John Alexander; Leonard Macy; London Fog; Mr. Golf, Mr. Tennis; Startown; Tailor's Bench; Tour de France.

Retail stores: Alberts; Albert K; Alcove; Central Hardware; Carithers; Eagle Family Discount Stores; Fine's; Golde's; Hirsch Value Center; Idaho Department Store; Jeans Galore; Keith O'Brien; Kent's; Miller's; P. N. Hirsch; Shainberg's; Sky City Discount Center; Standard Sportswear; Thornton's; United Shirt; Wigwam.

Retail shoe stores: Florsheim Shoe Shops, Florsheim Thayer McNeil Shops, Thayer McNeil Shoes; Duane's; Miller Taylor; Phelp's; Thompson; Boland & Lee.

Men's shoes: Ambassador; City Club; Florsheim, Florsheim Imperial, Royal Imperial by Florsheim, Idlers by Florsheim, Weeds from Florsheim; Grizzlies; Hy-Test; Julius Marlow; Patriot; Rand; Roberts; Winthrop; Worthmore.

Women's shoes: Crawdads; diVina; Miss Wonderful; Patriot; Personality; Thayer McNeil; Thomas Wallace; Vitality.

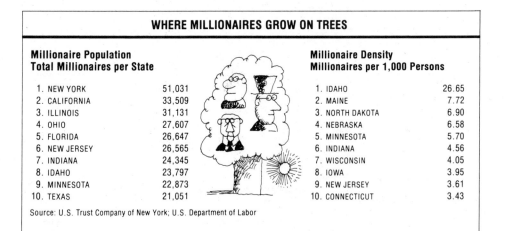

WHERE MILLIONAIRES GROW ON TREES

Millionaire Population Total Millionaires per State			Millionaire Density Millionaires per 1,000 Persons	
1.	NEW YORK	51,031	1. IDAHO	26.65
2.	CALIFORNIA	33,509	2. MAINE	7.72
3.	ILLINOIS	31,131	3. NORTH DAKOTA	6.90
4.	OHIO	27,607	4. NEBRASKA	6.58
5.	FLORIDA	26,647	5. MINNESOTA	5.70
6.	NEW JERSEY	26,565	6. INDIANA	4.56
7.	INDIANA	24,345	7. WISCONSIN	4.05
8.	IDAHO	23,797	8. IOWA	3.95
9.	MINNESOTA	22,873	9. NEW JERSEY	3.61
10.	TEXAS	21,051	10. CONNECTICUT	3.43

Source: U.S. Trust Company of New York; U.S. Department of Labor

Sales: $2.1 billion
Profits: $191.5 million
Forbes 500 rank: 248
Rank in apparel: 1
Rank in pants: 1
Founded: 1850
Employees: 44,700
Headquarters: San Francisco, California

What they do. "An event without precedent in the history of human attire" is how *New Yorker* writer John Brooks described it when youths all over the world adopted bluejeans as their uniform in the 1970s. Sparked by James Dean and Marlon Brando in the '50s, the bluejeans habit marched through the protest movements of the '60s, embraced Jimmy Carter ("I am one of their best customers") in the '70s, and landed on the drawing boards of chic fashion designers like Oscar de la Renta and Yves Saint Laurent. For Levi Strauss, a private company that had been quietly making the garment for a hundred years, it was like being kicked in the rear by a mule; they found themselves catapulted into the ranks of publicly held multinational corporations. Other people made bluejeans, but Levi's sold the classic.

In 1979 Levi's made 143 million garments, enough to put one—a pair of pants or a shirt or a jacket or a vest—on more than half the people living in the country. Of those garments, 127 million were pants. Levi produces one out of every three pairs of jeans sold in the U.S. They're now the third or fourth largest shirt maker. They have become the largest maker of brand-name boys' wear and one of the leading producers of women's sportswear. All these garments bear one brand name: Levi's. The socks and shoes that bear the Levi's name are made by Burlington Mills and the Brown Group, respectively, under license from Levi Strauss.

To make their clothes in 1979, Levi Strauss bought 41 billion yards of thread and 305 million yards of fabric, enough, as author Ed Cray pointed out (in his book *Levi's*), "to wrap a cummerbund of cloth six times around the equator." They are the world's largest consumer of denim, corduroy, and hopsacking supplied by textile mills in the United States and overseas.

STATUS SYMBOLS HIT BY INFLATION

1940 Price		1980 Price
$25,000	FULL-LENGTH SABLE COAT	$75,000
$15	RUSSIAN CAVIAR (14-OZ. TIN)	$300
$55,000	TOWNHOUSE ON NEW YORK'S FIFTH AVENUE	$2,500,000
$2,500	STEINWAY BABY GRAND PIANO	$10,900
$20,000	YACHT (40 FOOT)	$200,000
$9	PLACE SETTING OF STIEFF ROSE SILVER (4 PIECE)	$810
$450	TUITION AT PRINCETON UNIVERSITY (PER YEAR)	$5,585
$2,000	PAINTING BY JAN BRUEGHEL	$560,000
$3	TATTINGER'S VINTAGE CHAMPAGNE	$30
$4	COGNAC (FIFTH)	$13
$3,800	GEM-QUALITY EMERALD (3½ CARAT)	$90,000
$3,000	FLAWLESS DIAMOND (3 CARAT)	$75,000

Source: *US News & World Report*, March 17, 1980.

These fabrics—plus millions of rivets, buttons, and zippers—are dispatched to 100 sewing plants, many of them in the South, where the Levi's garments are turned out. From there they go to huge distribution centers prior to shipping to stores.

Levi Strauss supplies retailers directly through a sales force of 800 people. Their garments have the widest distribution ever achieved in the clothing industry, with 24,000 retail accounts. One pants chain, The Gap, accounts for 6% of Levi's U.S. sales, and The County Seat, another pants chain, is not far behind. Since 1978, when Levi settled an action brought by the Federal Trade Commission, the company no longer suggests retail prices, and retailers are free to mark up Levi's products as they see fit. The FTC had also charged that the company unfairly refused to sell to certain dealers, especially wholesalers or discount chains, such as K mart. Levi's still denies their goods to these outlets, as the FTC settlement allows them to control their distribution channels.

Levi Strauss now does 35% of their sales outside the United States. They manufacture in Australia, Argentina, Belgium, Canada, Brazil, France, Mexico, Britain, Hong Kong, and the Philippines. A Hungarian plant is also producing Levi's under license. Virtually none of the garments produced overseas are imported to the United States, and the company's plants do not supply garments for sale under any label except Levi's.

History. The brand and the company are named for Levi Strauss, a German-Jewish immigrant who came out to San Francisco from New York in 1850, when he was 20 years old, with the idea of selling dry goods, especially tent canvas, to the goldminers in California. It turned out there was not a great market for tents, so Levi Strauss used the canvas to make pants, which the miners called Levi's, after the supplier. The pants were durable—and they became even more durable when Jacob Davis, a Nevada tailor who was a Russian-Jewish immigrant, discovered a new way to repair the ripped pockets on the pants of customers. In 1872, with the help of the town druggist, Davis drafted a letter to the "Gents" of the Levi

Zip'er Up!

In 1893 armies of buttons, layers of laces, and bumpy ranks of hooks and eyes locked people into their clothes. Dressing and undressing was a wearisome chore; seduction, an almost unthinkable one.

In that year a Chicago inventor named Whitcomb L. Judson patented a device he called a "cheap locker or unlocker." Designed on a hook-and-eye principle, it could be opened or closed only by many painstaking turns of a "slider" that pulled together hooks on one side, eyes on the other. Nevertheless, a lawyer-entrepreneur from the Westinghouse Electric Co., Colonel Lewis Walker, thought the gizmo looked promising. For the next two decades Judson and Walker's Automatic Hook and

Eye Company made enticing claims ("A Pull and It's Done"), but the embarrassing fact was that the fasteners, installed in women's skirts, shredded underwear and popped open at all the worst possible moments.

His company teetered on the edge of bankruptcy, but, with the visionary stubbornness that characterized the era, Colonel Walker refused to give up. In 1906 he recruited a young engineer, Gideon Sundback, to the cause, and in 1913 Sundback came up with the first reliable, simple slide fastener. It was the zipper as we know it—hookless and eyeless—although it was years before it got its popular name.

Forming a new firm, the Hookless Fastener Co., Walker set about selling the

reinvented device. At first he had little luck: housewives and garment manufacturers, mindful of the flaws of the zipper's predecessors, refused to buy. The device survived only by the grace of the Navy, which tried it out in flying suits. When the grueling tests were over, all that was left of the suits were the zippers. The Navy ordered thousands.

In 1923 the B. F. Goodrich Co. introduced rubber galoshes with the hookless fasteners. A Goodrich executive, delighted with the boots, zipped the fasteners up and down, declaring, "Zip 'er up!" The name not only stuck but entered the English language as a generic term for the device.

Strauss Company, offering for $68 (the cost of a patent application) a half-share in the rights to sell his pants. This document (reproduced by Ed Cray in *Levi's*) contained the prophetic words, "The secratt of them Pents is the Rivits that I put in those Pockets."

The "Gents" were soon convinced, Davis moved to San Francisco, and within a few years the company was turning out a model that has remained virtually unchanged until the present day: the "501 Double X blue denim waist overall"—501 being the lot number, Double X the term for heavyweight denim. The jeans were "guaranteed to shrink, wrinkle and fade." According to legend, miners, farmers, and cowboys who wore them made each pair fit perfectly by putting them on when they were new and jumping into a watering trough. When the pants dried, they fit.

Levi Strauss built a prosperous business and became a prominent citizen of San

Not a jeans-looking person at all, Levi Strauss looked like this when he arrived in California during the Gold Rush of the 1850s. His name now goes on more than 200 million new garments a year.

Francisco. He was a bachelor, and when he died in 1902, he left the bulk of his $6 million estate to four nephews: Jacob, Sigmund, Louis, and Abraham Stern. For the first half of the twentieth century, the business of Levi Strauss advanced steadily, with no great change. They continued to make bluejeans in San Francisco. However, the greater part of the business was really quite close to peddling: they took blankets, underwear, shirts, and other goods made by other companies and wholesaled them to retailers in the West. The descendants of Levi Strauss continued to be active in the business—and they ran it in ways that were to become distinctive characteristics of the company. When the great 1906 earthquake leveled San Francisco, destroying the Levi Strauss facilities, the company took out ads in the city's newspapers to inform their 350 employees that their salaries would be continued until further notice. At the same time, Levi Strauss informed retail merchants whose stores had been wiped out that they could apply to Levi's for low- or no-interest loans.

Jacob Stern ran Levi Strauss until 1927, succeeded by his brother Sigmund, who died the following year. Into the top position then came Walter Haas, Sr., who had married Sigmund Stern's daughter, Elise. Helping him to manage the business was his brother-in-law, Daniel Koshland. The Haas-Koshland team was to run Levi Strauss through the Depression and World War II, by which time annual sales had reached the $8 million mark. The 501 waist overall was growing in popularity, but most of the business was still in wholesaling goods made by others. Not too many people in the East had heard of Levi Strauss & Co.

The fourth generation of the Levi Strauss family entered the business after World War II: the brothers Walter Haas, Jr., and Peter Haas. It was Wally Haas, Jr., who made a crucial decision in 1948 to discontinue the wholesale business and concentrate on manufacturing Levi's brand-name garments. Hindsight makes it look like a brilliant move. At the time its brilliance was not so easy to see: clothing they made themselves accounted for only one-fourth of Levi's business.

The changes then came very rapidly. In 1950, when the company's centennial was celebrated, sales were $12 million. By the end of the 1950s Levi Strauss was making 20 million garments a year, half of them the

Double X overalls, and sales were nearly $50 million. The company began to make all kinds of garments, eventually even suits to be worn by office workers. As their productive capacity expanded through the South, Levi Strauss continued to do things out of the ordinary: they began integrating their plants before the equal employment laws of the 1960s were passed.

Large-scale success brought an inevitable consequence: the need for outside financing. The decision to sell stock to the public for the first time was made in 1970. Walter Haas, Sr., was not comfortable with the move, and his son, Walter, Jr., made the announcement to company stockholders at a tense meeting held in a large auditorium near the company's San Francisco headquarters. In the room were 29 employee stockholders, not counting the members of the Haas family, who were to become instant millionaires. Levi Strauss went public in April 1971 with the sale of 1,396,000 shares at $47 a share. That represented 13% of the stock in the company, but it was one of the largest public stock offerings ever made. The offering sold out within a day.

Walter Haas, Sr., died in his sleep at his Pacific Heights home in San Francisco in December 1979, at the age of 90. He had lived to see the company achieve their first $2 billion year. A few days later Daniel Koshland died at 89.

Reputation. Beyond offering a reliable product in a shaky world, Levi Strauss has become widely known for assuming responsibility for the well-being of their employees and of the communities in which they have a presence. And they do this with a minimum of fanfare.

What they own. Sixty-one factories and distribution centers, the biggest concentration being in Texas, where there are 13 manufacturing facilities. Another 57 facilities (11 of them in Texas) are leased. Of incalculable value is the Levi's brand name, which is registered as a trademark in more than 150 countries.

Who owns and runs the company. Members of the Haas and Koshland families own nearly half the stock; the Haases (Walter and Peter) hold the two top positions in the company; and Walter's son, Robert, an executive vice-president, joined the board of directors in 1980. Franklin A. Thomas, a

Why Levi's Changed the 501

Picture a scene from the Old West, sometime in the 1870s. Weary cowboys in dusty Levi's gather around a blazing campfire, resting after a day of riding and roping on the open range. The lonely howl of a distant coyote counterpoints the notes of a guitar as the moon floats serenely overhead in an unpolluted sky afire with stars.

Suddenly a bellow of pain shatters the night, as a cowpoke leaps away from the fire, dancing in agony. Hot Rivet Syndrome has claimed another victim.

In those days Levi's were made, as they had been from the first days of Levi Strauss, with copper rivets at stress points to provide extra

strength. On these original Levi's—model 501—there were rivets on the pockets, and there was a lone rivet at the crotch. The crotch rivet was the critical one: when cowboys crouched too long beside the campfire, the rivet grew uncomfortably hot.

For years the brave men of the West suffered from this curious occupational hazard. But nothing was done about it until 1933, when Walter Haas, Sr., president of Levi Strauss, chanced to go camping in his Levi's 501s. Haas was crouched contentedly by a crackling campfire in the high Sierras, drinking in the pure mountain air, when he fell prey to Hot Rivet Syndrome. He consulted with professional wranglers in his

party. Had they ever suffered the same mishap? An impassioned *yes* was the reply.

Haas vowed that the offending rivet must go, and the board of directors voted it into extinction at their next meeting.

Except for eliminating the crotch rivet, the company has made only one other stylistic change in its 501s since they were first marketed in 1873. Responding to schools' complaints that Levi's pocket rivets scratched school furniture, the company moved the rivets to the front pockets. Otherwise the Levi's 501 shrink-to-fit jeans on the market today are identical to the pants that won the West.

trustee of the Ford Foundation, is a director, as is Mary Lothrop Bundy, an educator and wife of the former president of the Ford Foundation, McGeorge Bundy.

In 1975, when Levi first achieved sales of $1 billion, they shared that accomplishment with employees by passing out awards of stock or cash. Four years later, when they crossed the $2 billion mark, all 42,000 employees received awards ranging from $50 (for those newly hired) up to $350. At the same time, retirees were each sent $100 checks.

80% of all U.S. employees are women, and women hold 24% of jobs classified as "officials and managers." Women now comprise 16.4% of the sales force. 49% of the people on the U.S. payrolls are members of minority groups, and at the end of 1979 minorities held 14% of the "officials and managers" positions in the company. Of the 64 plants in the United States, 29 are unionized. 57% of all employees are covered by union contracts.

In the public eye. Levi Strauss believes in having social programs keep pace with profit growth. In 1979, when earnings increased by one-third, charitable contributions were nearly doubled, to reach about $7 million. The company's giving approximates 1.5% of pretax profits, which puts them well above the average. In place at the company is a 22-person staff that operates the Levi Strauss Foundation and community affairs programs. This constitutes one of the largest staffs of its kind in American business. The foundation funds early child development programs and services for elderly citizens, among other projects.

Where they're going. There's an old saying in the business world that "no one remains small by choice," and Levi Strauss is now locked into an inexorable growth pattern. It took 125 years to reach $1 billion, only 4 years to add on another billion. Some feel this careening expansion is changing the company into a more impersonal organization. Ernest Griffes, manager of employee benefits, told writer Ed Cray: "Levi Strauss is a classic example of the old-line, paternalistic company coming of age in the impersonal, modern world. The family's desire to relate to the good old days is like two people trying to pull a horse through a knothole."

Stock performance. Levi Strauss stock bought for $1,000 in 1971 sold for nearly $3,000 on January 2, 1980.

Access. Two Embarcadero Center, San Francisco, California 94106; (415) 544-6000.

Consumer brands.

Levi's.

MELVILLE CORPORATION

Sales: $2.0 billion
Profits: $101.2 million
Forbes 500 rank: 261
Rank in shoe retailing: 1
Founded: 1892
Employees: 43,472
Headquarters: Harrison, New York

What they do. It's not unusual for Melville to open as many as seven stores in the same suburban shopping mall, each with a different name, selling different goods to a different set of customers. The Chess King shops lure teenage boys with blaring rock music, trendy shirts, and jeans. The teenage girl on an allowance can shop at Foxmoor Casuals, while her mother may buy discount name-brand clothing at Clothes Bin, Fashion Action, or Marshalls.

Melville's shoe stores, Thom McAn and Vanguard, cater to every age group. And if you'd rather buy your sneakers at the self-service shoe department in the shopping mall's K mart, you're still getting Melville shoes. Making 14 million pairs of shoes a year, Melville needs a lot of outlets.

Melville also owns the CVS (Consumer Value Stores) chain of discount drugstores, operating mainly in the Northeast. That

> According to the Oxford English Dictionary, the word *jean* derives from *Genoese* and originally meant twilled cloth made in Genoa. *Denim* got its name from the city of Nimes, in southern France, where the cotton fabric was traditionally produced. It was originally called *serge de Nimes*, which the British corrupted to *denim*.

brings the total of Melville retail outlets to almost 4,000 across the country.

History. Frank Melville's prospective bride didn't care for his former occupations as cowboy, sailor, and stagecoach driver. So in 1882 Frank got a job as a shoe clerk for $11 for working a 92-hour week. Soon he managed to establish himself as a traveling wholesaler, and when one of his customers skipped town without paying for a shipment of shoes, Frank got his big break. He took over the man's three shoe stores in New York and started the Melville Shoe Company in 1892.

Frank's son, Ward, became the real force behind the company's success. He made two excellent decisions: enter the shoemaking business by merging his company with the manufacturing firm of his World War I commanding officer, and create what became the famous Thom McAn brand of shoes (by shortening a Scottish golf pro's name). The first Thom McAn store opened in New York in 1922, offering black or brown men's shoes for $3.99. Five years later they had 370 Thom McAn stores across the country.

But the sensible black shoe didn't wear well into the fashion-conscious 1950s. Despite a merger with Miles Shoes, Melville ran into trouble. The company's savior turned out to be a shoe designer named Francis C. Rooney, whose father had also been in the shoe business. He succeeded Ward Melville in 1964. Rooney moved Melville out of the cities and into the suburban shopping malls, where they became a trendy, youth-conscious fashion chain.

Reputation. This company knows how to milk a fad for all it's worth. Rooney recruited Chubby Checker, Ravi Shankar, and the Monkees to plug products. In the late 1960s Melville started a chain of psychedelic stores called Now Shops, selling posters, incense, and other "things for your pad," as Rooney put it. Phyllis Berman of *Forbes* calls Rooney "one of the smartest retailers in the U.S." Rooney continues to think big. "We don't sell shoes," he claims, "we sell excitement. You might say we compete with General Motors, because they get people to spend money on exciting cars instead of exciting shoes."

Who owns and runs the company. Many of the directors of Melville came along when their companies were bought by Melville. The directors and officers are all white males, three of whom are over 80 years of age. Directors and officers own about 20% of the stock, Frank Melville owns 8%, and director Murray Rosenberg, founder of Miles, owns about 9%.

In the public eye. Ward Melville acted as the patron saint of Stony Brook, New York. Not only did he donate the land for the State University of New York at Stony Brook, but he also contributed to the historic restoration of the town into "Long Island's Little Williamsburg." On the Miles side of Melville, Murray Rosenberg donated over $1 million to Mount Sinai Hospital in New York.

Where they're going. Melville's decision to close up shop in the downtowns and move to the suburbs may have saved them in the 1950s, but may come back to haunt them. Suburban growth and mall development are leveling off now. Melville is responding with free-standing buildings (many of them converted supermarkets) not located in shopping centers.

Stock performance. Melville stock bought for $1,000 in 1970 sold for $1,571 on January 2, 1980.

Access. 3000 Westchester Avenue, Harrison, New York 10528; (914) 253-8000.

Consumer brands.

Shoe labels and stores: Thom McAn; Vanguard.
Clothing shops: Chess King (young men's); Foxmoor, Clothes Bin, Fashion Action (young women's); Marshalls (discount stores).
Clothing: Metro pants.
Drug, health, and beauty aid stores: CVS.

Why Keds Aren't Peds

Back in 1917 the National India Rubber Company felt they needed a snappier name to help sell their sneakers. After mulling over 300 suggestions, they settled on *Peds*. Research disclosed, however, that the name *Peds* was already taken, so the company substituted a "K" (for kids).

—Samuel Americus Walker, *Sneakers* (Workman, 1978).

Housing People

American Standard Inc.

Sales: $2.4 billion
Profits: $132 million
Forbes 500 rank: 214
Rank in plumbing: 1
Founded: 1881
Employees: 49,000
Headquarters: New York, New York

What they do. American Standard's advertisements often use semi-clad women to supply the excitement their fixtures may lack. Looking for excitement is nothing new at American Standard. During the late 1960s the man in charge of the faucets was William D. Eberle, a Boise Cascade alumnus whose simple prescription for progress (learned at Boise) was: buy, buy, buy. From 1967 to 1971 he doubled American Standard's sales by scooping up companies here, there, and everywhere. Unfortunately, he also managed to depress profits by 90%—and in late 1971 American Standard had to flush down the drain one-fifth of their assets, finishing the year $84 million in the red. Fortunately, one of the companies they bought was Mosler Safe, headed by William A. Marquard, who took over what the business press bluntly labeled a "mess" and restored American Standard to a gushing profit maker. He sharply reduced the debt, shed real estate and housing businesses, shut down seven building products plants in France, and cut the number of employees from 65,000 to 49,000. By 1979 he was able to boast: "None of our businesses is losing money." Plumbing fixtures now represent less than a third of American Standard's sales. Their biggest business is transportation products, notably brakes and heavy off-highway trucks (used in mining and construction) made by Westinghouse Air Brake, one of Eberle's luckier acquisitions (he had to fight Crane to get it).

History. It's rich with mergers and acquisitions.

American Radiator was founded in Buffalo in 1881 to make equipment for steam and hot water heating of buildings. In 1899 the ubiquitous J. P. Morgan consolidated under that name just about every heating equipment company in the United States. American Radiator was selling all over the world by 1910.

Two plumbing supply companies—Ahrens & Ott of Louisville and Standard Manufacturing of Pittsburgh—joined forces in 1899 to form Standard Sanitary. Their most important product was enameled cast iron plumbing fixtures. They pioneered such advances as the one-piece lavatory, claw-foot and built-in bathtubs, and the single tap for hot and cold water.

Along the way both companies made a steady practice of buying out other companies in their respective fields. Then, in 1929, these two companies combined to form the American Radiator & Standard Sanitary Corporation. In that same year they bought C. F. Church, the nation's leading maker of toilet seats (thereby consolidating their hold on the bathroom).

Eberle came along in the 1960s and took the company out of the bathroom, although in the 1970s they were still running ads that described the bathroom as "the most important room in your home . . . It's the only room where a guest can lock the door and judge so much about you—your taste, your character, and your life style. And can do it without fear of interruption or embarrassment."

Reputation. American Standard is known as a old-line company run by a hardnosed manager. An oil painting of a bathtub decorates Marquard's office. "That bathtub reminds me from where we came," he told *Financial World* in 1976. "And it is also an excellent reminder of what can happen if you don't manage to deal with change." Translation: drain the losers?

Who owns and runs the company. Described by *Forbes* as the man who put "Humpty Dumpty together again," Marquard was still at the helm as 1980 dawned. His titles: chairman and president.

In the public eye. The company paid out $9.1 million in a 1971 price-fixing court case, which also involved 15 other major plumbing fixtures companies. An American Standard executive received the harshest sentence: one year in jail (suspended after 60 days) and a $40,000 fine.

Where they're going. To the rest of the world. They're already doing nearly half their business outside the U.S.

Stock performance. American Standard stock bought for $1,000 in 1970 sold for $1,593 on January 2, 1980.

Access. 40 West 40th Street, New York, New York 10018; (212) 840-5100.

Consumer brands.

American-Standard, Ideal-Standard, Standard plumbing fixtures; Majestic fireplaces; Modernfold walls; Steelcraft doors.
Security and graphic products: Mosler safes, locks, alarms; American Bank stationery.

> The average American family must earn twice what it earned in 1970 to maintain the same standard of living.

Armstrong

Sales: $1.3 billion
Profits: $66.0 million
Forbes 500 rank: 368
Rank in flooring: 1
Rank in carpets: 4
Rank in ceilings: 1
Founded: 1860
Employees: 24,400
Headquarters: Lancaster, Pennsylvania

What they do. They used to be known as Armstrong Cork, after the product that was their original business. Although cork had long been only a small part of their business, they continued to honor the old name until early in 1980. Then they followed the lead of others and renamed themselves Armstrong World Industries. Not even being in the heart of the Pennsylvania Dutch country insulated them from the trendy soothsayers of New York. Armstrong's chief enterprise these days is making and selling interior furnishings—flooring, ceilings, and furniture—in coordinated designs, creating what they call "The Indoor World." More than half their total sales come from "resilient flooring" (tiles and linoleum) and carpets. They also make industrial products such as gaskets, fiberboard, and acoustical wall panels.

Although they have 13 plants in six foreign countries from England to India (including a champagne and wine bottle cork plant in Spain), more than 80% of their sales come from the United States.

History. In 1860 Thomas Morton Armstrong used $300 he had saved from his salary as a shipping clerk to join John D. Glass in buying a cork business in Pittsburgh. When the inventions of the screw-top Mason jar and the spring stopper for soda water bottles threatened the cork business, Armstrong Cork set out to find other uses for cork, and in 1902 they started making cork insulation for cold-storage rooms. In 1907 Thomas Armstrong's son Charles thought Prohibition might wipe out what was left of the cork stopper business and steered the company into linoleum, which in those days was made with finely ground cork powder. That was how Armstrong got into flooring and interior furnishings, where they've stayed ever since. In 1967 they added E & B Carpet Mills of Arlington, Texas, and in 1968 they picked up Thomasville Furniture Industries of Thomasville, North Carolina.

Reputation. In the nineteenth century the prevailing business ethic was "Let the buyer beware." Tom Armstrong's slogan, however, was "Let the buyer have faith." He was one of the first manufacturers to put his own name on his products, and he guaranteed everything he sold. As a result, products could be shipped to distant places and customers could buy them without fear of being taken in. The simple act of taking responsibility for their products did wonders for Armstrong's sales volume, and the company could easily absorb the few items that were actually returned by dissatisfied customers.

They still pride themselves on their in-

THE 50 RICHEST U.S. COLLEGES & UNIVERSITIES

Market Value of Investments on June 30, 1979

1. HARVARD	$1.45 billion	26. U. OF VIRGINIA	118 million
2. U. OF TEXAS	1.05 billion	27. CARNEGIE-MELLON	113 million
3. YALE	578 million	28. WESLEYAN	107 million
4. COLUMBIA	504 million	29. BROWN	107 million
5. PRINCETON	474 million	30. U. OF MICHIGAN	100 million
6. U. OF CALIFORNIA	385 million	31. U. OF MINNESOTA	95 million
7. MASSACHUSETTS INSTITUTE OF TECHNOLOGY	374 million	32. SMITH	92 million
8. U. OF ROCHESTER	324 million	33. U. OF PITTSBURGH	92 million
9. U. OF CHICAGO	311 million	34. U. OF CINCINNATI	88 million
10. CORNELL	288 million	35. RENSSELAER POLYTECHNIC INSTITUTE	87 million
11. NEW YORK U.	273 million*	36. OBERLIN	85 million
12. RICE U.	271 million	37. WILLIAMS	85 million
13. NORTHWESTERN	257 million*	38. SOUTHERN METHODIST U.	79 million**
14. WASHINGTON U.	221 million	39. AMHERST	77 million
15. ROCKEFELLER U.	202 million	40. BEREA	77 million
16. DARTMOUTH	174 million	41. SWARTHMORE	76 million
17. U. OF PENNSYLVANIA	168 million	42. VASSAR	75 million
18. JOHNS HOPKINS	165 million	43. U. OF RICHMOND	71 million
19. CALIFORNIA INSTITUTE OF TECHNOLOGY	164 million	44. OHIO STATE	68 million
20. U. OF NOTRE DAME	138 million	45. BRANDEIS	60 million
21. U. OF SOUTHERN CAL.	130 million	46. ROCHESTER INSTITUTE OF TECHNOLOGY	58 million
22. U. OF DELAWARE	128 million	47. WAKE FOREST U.	57 million
23. WELLESLEY	126 million	48. LEHIGH	56 million
24. DUKE	123 million	49. SUNY, BUFFALO	53 million†
25. CASE WESTERN RESERVE	119 million	50. LAFAYETTE	53 million

*As of August 31, 1979.
**As of May 31, 1979.
†As of March 31, 1979.

Source: Chronicle of Higher Education, March 3, 1980.

---

tegrity. On their centennial in 1960 they distributed copies of the company's principles to all their employees. Among them: "To respect the dignity and inherent rights of the individual human being in all dealings."

What they own. Twenty-two flooring and 6 ceiling plants, six of them in Pennsylvania, most of the others in the East. Six carpet plants and 22 furniture plants, thirteen of which are located at Thomasville, North Carolina. Thirteen plants in Canada, England, Spain, West Germany, India, and Australia.

Who owns and runs the company. Since 1860 Armstrong has had only eight presidents, each trained by his predecessor. The two largest blocks of stock are controlled by J. P. Morgan (9%) and the National Bank of Detroit (7%). The board of directors includes two women: Naomi Albanese, dean of the University of North Carolina's School of Home Economics, and Mary Joan Glynn, a former advertising agency executive. An ex-Armstrong advertising manager, Cameron Hawley, went on to write some fairly successful novels, including *Executive Suite.*

In the public eye. Armstrong was the first company to provide free dental care for their employees (1909), and they were also pioneers in extra pay for overtime (1913), shop committees to consult with management (1919), paid vacations for all employees (1924), and group life insurance (1931). They criticized Franklin Roosevelt's New Deal, feeling that employee benefits should come voluntarily from employers rather than through government compulsion.

As public awareness of the link between asbestos and cancer grew during the late 1970s, Armstrong became a defendant, along with several other companies, in nearly a thousand lawsuits filed on behalf of cancer victims who had been exposed to asbestos fibers. Armstrong stopped selling asbestos insulation in 1969, but they still make some vinyl asbestos tiles.

Where they're going. Not ones to lurch wildly in new directions, they will probably keep doing essentially what they have been doing most of this century: making indoor products and adapting to the times. One such adaptation is a new energy-saving system for large buildings called Thermalon, which consists of panels to insulate windows from the inside and reduce heat loss.

Stock performance. Armstrong stock bought for $1,000 in 1970 sold for $466 January 2, 1980.

Access. Liberty and Charlotte Streets, Lancaster, Pennsylvania 17604; (717) 397-0611. Questions or complaints should be addressed to Mr. A. J. Armstrong or Mrs. Jane Deibler, Customer Response Center, Armstrong Cork Company, Armstrong House, Lancaster Square, Lancaster, PA 17604.

Consumer brands.

Flooring: Armstrong; Solarian; Tredway; Sandoval; Imperial Excelon; Stylistik Tile; Castilian.
Carpets: Trustmark; Footsteps; Radiant Shadows; Fox Ridge; Grand Junction; Sun Star; Sculptured Touch; Evans-Black.
Ceilings: Headliner; Stratford; Colonial Sampler; Stockbridge.
Furniture: Thomasville's Founders; From the Four Corners; Camille; Huntley.

CRANE ®

Sales: $1.6 billion
Profits: $55.0 million
Forbes 500 rank: 324
Rank in plumbing: 4
Rank in industrial valves: 1
Founded: 1855
Employees: 19,686
Headquarters: New York, New York

What they do. Under the leadership of Thomas Mellon Evans, Crane has become more interested in buying and selling companies than they are in their original business of plumbing fixtures. In the 1930s and 1940s American bathrooms sported more Crane sinks, toilets, and tubs than those of any other company, but today plumbing and building products account for less than 3% of the company's sales.

Crane has spread into the manufacture of

pollution-control devices, brakes and pumps for aircraft and rockets, industrial valves, and vending machines (whose major customers are Coca Cola bottlers). The company's collection of subsidiaries includes Medusa cement (ranked fourth in cement) and CF & I Steel.

History. R. T. Crane and his brother Charles started casting lightening rod tips in a small iron foundry in Chicago on the fourth of July, 1855. The Crane Company got a boost in the 1890s from architect Louis Sullivan's new skyscrapers, which demanded large amounts of cast pipe for central heating. The Crane brothers met the challenge and quickly jumped into another building innovation: enameled cast iron for indoor bathrooms.

R. T. died in 1912, at the age of 79, but his son, R. T. Crane, Jr., decided to make America want a better bathroom. Crane conceived of the idea of the modern bathroom and created the first practical decorative bathroom fixtures. He pushed the idea with an advertising budget of more than $1 million a year when the largest consumer advertisers were only averaging $300,000. He even built a million-dollar showroom on the Atlantic City boardwalk in 1926 to show off the company's bathtubs.

In 1959, when entrepreneur Thomas Mellon Evans bought control of the firm, Crane was known as a leading producer of quality bathroom fixtures. Despite his benign Santa Claus looks, Evans was a recognized takeover artist, the "corporate embodiment of Jaws, the great white shark," as Representative Frank Thompson of New Jersey put it to *Business Week* in 1976. His strategy for expansion is simple: quietly buy up 5% of an ailing business, offer to buy the business for a song, and when the company refuses to sell (as they often do), go to court. Crane's 10-K contains nine pages of litigation proceedings. As Evans says, "I have to keep the lawyers happy."

In 1960 Evans decided to use the Crane name for his collection of companies, and since then Crane has not been just a plumbing fixtures and valve company. Evans's tactics have paid off in profits for Crane, with the acquisition of over 80 companies.

Reputation. They'll make you an offer you can't refuse, at least as long as Evans is in charge.

What they own. Crane owns plants scattered around the United States, Canada, Europe, Australia, and Mexico. They also own the Medusa Cement Corporation, 96.3% of CF & I Steel Corporation of Colorado (which includes 350,000 acres and raw materials for steelmaking), and 95.6% of Huttig Sash & Door Company of St. Louis, Missouri.

Who owns and runs the company. Thomas Mellon Evans (who is a distant relative of the Pittsburgh Mellons). He owns about 12% of the stock. The Crane Fund owns about 9%, Hershey Trust owns about 23%, and Connecticut Mutual Life holds a 14.7% interest. The all-male board of directors includes Thomas Evans's son.

As for life at the top at Crane, *Forbes* repeats the company definition of an optimist as a Crane executive who brings his lunch to work.

In the public eye. "Evans is a very tough operator. If you don't make money, regardless of what it does to employees or the community, he closes you down," a former plant officer told *Business Week* in 1974. Crane has closed four steel plants, throwing 4,000 people out of work. Evans claims that he tries to find buyers for the plants, but a plant is often worth more as scrap than as a functioning business, so he doesn't try hard. As Frank Thompson points out, "Evans has a long history of acquiring shaky companies and then dissolving them for the tax write-off."

Where they're going. Sluggish companies with in-ground natural resources are next on the Evans hit list. Crane has a lot of cash available for acquisitions, but no one knows what company Crane will go for. Evans told an inquisitive *New Yorker* reporter, "What the hell, you have no right digging into what other people are buying and selling."

Stock performance. Crane stock bought for $1,000 in 1970 sold for $4,014 on January 2, 1980.

Access. 300 Park Avenue, New York, New York 10022; (212) 980-3600.

Consumer brands.

Crane plumbing fixtures and Huttig doors and sashes.

Sales: $2.3 billion
Profits: $114.6 million
Forbes 500 rank: 234
Rank in asbestos: 1
Rank in fiberglass: 2
Founded: 1858
Employees: 32,900
Headquarters: Denver, Colorado

What they do. For years Johns-Manville could be proud that they were the nation's largest manufacturer of asbestos products. Now they must wish the stuff would go away and take its grim consequences with it. They face thousands of lawsuits from victims of deadly diseases caused by asbestos.

J-M still produces insulation galore, using fiberglass, asbestos, and other minerals, mingled with paper, cement, brick, cloth, and plastic, to regulate temperatures in roofs, walls, spaceships, dishwashers, refrigerators, furnaces, catalytic converters, and brakes. They also make a miscellany of other products, including roofing shingles, plastic pipe, city street lights, swimming pool filters, irrigation systems, and soundproofing. In 1979 they took over Olinkraft, a wood and paper company with three-quarters of a million acres of timberland in Louisiana, Arkansas, Texas, and Brazil.

History. For most of this century J-M was as bland as their insulated roofing, though the company grew steadily. Everything changed in the 1970s, the transformation symbolized by the move of their corporate headquarters from a dreary old brick building in New York (characterized by one

Wall Street observer as a place with "no signs of life. It was like somebody had just died up there.") to a 10,000-acre ranch amid breathtaking Rocky Mountain scenery, setting off a marvel of modern architecture in aluminum and glass. The man who engineered this change—W. Richard Goodwin, Johns-Manville's president from 1970 to 1976—wasn't around to enjoy it: two weeks before he was to move into his brand new office, he was summarily fired by the directors, who were pleased with the ranch and the company's impressive growth under Goodwin's administration, but they didn't appreciate his management style. It was the spirit of J-M's conservative past rising to reassert itself.

That past began in 1858 when Henry Ward Johns started a roofing business in West Stockbridge, Massachusetts. From the beginning he was fascinated with asbestos, and in 1868 he got his first patent for an asbestos compound to make roofing fire resistant. In the next decade he developed asbestos for pipe insulation. His business grew. In 1880 the H. W. Johns Manufacturing Company began making asbestos-containing paints and opened a second factory.

The other half of J-M goes back to 1886, when Charles B. Manville started the Manville Covering Company in Milwaukee. He and his three sons made pipe coverings and other nonasbestos insulations. For asbestos supplies they relied on H. W. Johns, and Manville became Johns' western distributor.

Johns died in 1898. Three years later the two companies were merged as Johns-Manville under the presidency of Charles Manville's son Thomas, who set the company's conservative tone. According to a 1934 *Fortune* article, Manville "took little advice; borrowed no money; and dickered with no competitor," and disdained research, boast-

Asbestos: Deadly Substance

Asbestos is a mineral consisting of white waxy fibers that look a little like dental floss. It has the strength of steel, the durability of marble, and has no equal as an insulator.

Asbestos is extracted from a green-colored magnesium silicate rock, the biggest deposits being in Canada, the Soviet Union, South Africa, and China. Very little is found in the United States. The Jeffrey Mine in Asbestos, Canada, the largest asbestos mine in the world, is owned and operated by Johns-Manville. In 1978 the Jeffrey Mine yielded 10,341,800 tons of asbestos-bearing rock, from which J-M was able to extract 629,500 tons of asbestos.

ing once that he had "never spent a nickel on laboratories or chemists." But he was an expert salesman, diversifying the J-M line and increasing sales to an annual $40 million. The most significant acquisition of this period was the world's largest asbestos mine, in Quebec.

After Thomas Manville's death in 1925, another family member, H.E. Manville, ruled briefly. But in 1927 he sold his family's controlling interest in the company to J. P. Morgan & Co., and the influence of the Morgan banking organization remains strong to this day. The story of the next 30 years is mainly a catalog of acquisitions and expansions. (So is the story of Tommy Manville, grandson of the founder, who, before he died in 1967, married 11 women 13 times.)

By the late 1960s the directors were aware that their drab and slow-growing, no-debt, no-planning company was in danger of falling behind. They urged their president to find someone to rejuvenate the old nag. He brought in Dick Goodwin—systems consultant, Ph.D. in psychology, and New York University professor of business—who proceeded to do exactly what had been asked of him as a consultant: he set up planning systems for all 12 of the company's divisions. The directors were so pleased that at their urging he became J-M's senior vice-president for planning in April 1969. Twenty months later he was president and chief executive officer.

Then Goodwin really began streamlining and restyling. He made major acquisitions and divestitures. Profits rose 115% between 1970 and 1974; sales rose 91% by 1975. Most spectacular of all was the move to Colorado, the debut of an absolutely new corporate image.

But as Goodwin's boldness grew, the old-school directors quietly began to chafe. Two issues pushed them over the edge: an attempt by Goodwin to break the company's historic ties with the Morgan banking interests, and his plan to expand the number of directors from 12 to 20. In September 1976, the night before a board meeting in New York, three outside directors informed Goodwin that they and six colleagues wanted him to resign, that under the bylaws they weren't required to tell him why, and that was that. Next morning senior vice-president and director John A. McKinney (who hadn't been in on the firing decision) was made president; he is still in charge, holding the titles of chief executive officer and chairman of the board.

Reputation. Johns-Manville today is synonymous with the deadly asbestos. It may take years, if ever, for them to achieve a different identity.

What they own. Fifty-seven plants in 26 states, 7 in Canada, and 21 overseas, from Belgium to Singapore. Their principal mine is located in Asbestos, Canada.

Who owns and runs the company. The all-white, all-male board of directors includes one French Canadian (president of a Canadian mining company), the chairmen of American Can Company and Phelps Dodge (copper and uranium mining), John A. Love, a former governor of Colorado, and the dean of Princeton University's School of Architecture and Urban Planning, along with the traditional representative of Morgan Guaranty Trust.

In the public eye. In 1898 H. W. Johns, the great asbestos enthusiast, died of a chronic lung disease. His death was prophetic of millions more. Only recently has it come to light how grim the harvest will be. Asbestosis—incapacitating and eventually fatal scarring of lung tissues. Mesothelioma—cancer of the chest and abdominal linings. Lung cancer. Gastrointestinal cancer. These are the diseases known to be associated with the inhalation of asbestos fiber. The first two are caused simply by exposure to asbestos.

Only a small fraction of those who have been exposed to asbestos were directly involved in asbestos production. The rest include garment workers who make coats combining wool, nylon, and asbestos; auto mechanics who install asbestos on brake linings; painters who mix it with their paints; demolition workers who shake free millions of particles while destroying buildings; and shipyard workers who applied paints mixed with asbestos. Former HEW Secretary Joseph Califano guessed that 8 to 11 million workers have been so exposed.

Statistics vary on the number of asbestos-related deaths that have occurred and will occur. HEW's Califano stated that "the roughest kind of estimate" indicates 1.5 to 2 million persons already have died. Dr. Irving Selikoff of the Mt. Sinai School of Medicine in New York, the most prominent researcher on the problem, says that 18% of all cancer deaths in the next 25 years will be linked to asbestos.

A rush of articles tell stories of men who have to walk backwards upstairs, or live with oxygen tubes up their noses, whose wives won't sleep in the same room because they cough all night; of families decimated after several generations of employment at "the plant"; of whole towns (like Manville, New Jersey, and Tyler, Texas) under the pall of fibrous white dust that brings workers both their bread and butter and their deaths.

And the lawsuits multiply.

At the center of the vortex is the world's largest asbestos miner and manufacturer of asbestos products—Johns-Manville. The first asbestos lawsuit against J-M was filed in 1967. Ten years later about 400 were pending; by December 1979, close to 10,000. The stakes are rapidly getting higher. Although J-M kept their average settlement down to $16,000 through 1979, continuing investigation by lawyers for the many plaintiffs has uncovered evidence that may be very damaging in future cases. Records have been produced suggesting that the company knew of serious health hazards since the 1930s. Some press accounts suggest that until the early 1970s, they had a policy of not telling employees that their medical examinations showed signs of asbestos-related diseases. Courts have begun admitting class action suits, one of which (not involving J-M) was recently settled for $20 million. Among suits currently at issue against J-M, one is asking half a billion dollars for each plaintiff.

J-M has moved vigorously to defend themselves, devoting six pages of their 1978 annual report to "The Asbestos Issue." They charge flagrant sensationalism and falsehood on the part of the media and "some officials." J-M points out that long before the current spate of lawsuits, the company led the industry in research on asbestos hazards, voluntary control of dust levels in plants, and free physical examinations for employees. Adversaries reply that J-M did not publish the results of their research, did not warn employees of dangers, denied them access to their medical records, and sometimes missed the most blatant cases in their cursory exams.

A large part of J-M's strategy involves shifting the responsibility to government and to other industries they hold equally at fault. They are pointing a finger at the tobacco industry since studies show that risk of lung cancer is multiplied by a factor of 60 or more if the asbestos worker smokes. J-M refuses to hire smokers. While "willing to pay our share, and even more than our share," J-M insists the federal government, which controlled the wartime shipyards where a great number of asbestos workers were exposed, and which has recommended "safe" exposure levels all along, should bear a large part of the burden. J-M has drafted and promoted legislation to shift worker redress from the courts to a government compensation program modeled on, but much larger than, that instituted for coal miners' black lung disease. The legislation is sponsored by Representative Millicent Fenwick of New Jersey, whose district happens to include J-M's largest plant, which employs thousands of her constituents.

Where they're going. Aside from the financial threat posed by the asbestos litigation, J-M appears to be healthy. Fiberglass now contributes close to one-third of their sales, and asbestos accounts for only 19% of profits (down from 37% in 1976). McKinney says "unless the courts start to hold us liable for punitive damages, we will survive."

Stock performance. Johns-Manville stock bought for $1,000 in 1970 sold for $804 on January 2, 1980.

Major employment centers. Manville, New Jersey (shingle and pipe factory); Defiance, Ohio (fiberglass factory); Denver, Colorado (corporate headquarters).

Access. Ken-Caryl Ranch, Denver, Colorado 80217; (303) 979-1000. The policy on public tours varies from plant to plant. For questions or complaints, write to the company's Product Information at their world headquarters in Denver, or call (303) 979-1000, extension 4636.

Mobile homes now make up over half of all new housing sold in the U.S. to people with $15,000 or less.

Kaufman △ Broad

Sales: $495.5 million
Profits: $19.2 million
Founded: 1957
Employees: 4,300
Headquarters: Los Angeles, California

What they do. Over 100,000 families live in homes built by Kaufman & Broad—even though Eli Broad, the chairman and co-founder, doesn't know anything about building homes. Broad is a certified public accountant by trade. Under his guidance Kaufman & Broad concentrated on the business end of building and farmed out the actual hammer-and-nail work to subcontractors. Their standard procedure is to acquire a tract of land, subdivide it, put up model homes, and then construct individual houses only after they are sold. They concentrate on low- and moderately priced homes.

In 1971 Kaufman & Broad decided to take out insurance against the usual boom-and-bust cycles that plague the rest of the housing industry. They bought Sun Life, one of the nation's top 60 life insurance companies; by the end of the decade they had added two more smaller life insurance companies. Whenever the housing market stumbles, the steady insurance companies continue to pour greenbacks into Kaufman & Broad's coffers; life insurance provided almost half their income in 1979.

History. Eli Broad and Donald Kaufman started out in 1957 with $25,000 and a few small lots on the outskirts of Detroit. Thanks to Broad's able and shrewd financial management, Kaufman & Broad grew rapidly thereafter. By 1969 they were second only to Levitt (as in Levittown) in home building. They now have developments in the United States, Canada, France, Germany, and Belgium. In 1964 the corporate offices were moved from Detroit to Los Angeles.

Reputation. A 1973 *Barron's* article accused Kaufman & Broad of hiding much of their profit and avoiding taxes through "liberal accounting ploys." Although Broad hotly disputed the charge, ensuing rumors caused K & B stock to fall from a 1972 high of $51 a share to only $2.25 in 1975.

Who owns and runs the company. Broad, with 13% of the stock, continues to control Kaufman & Broad. Kaufman, his partner, still owns 8.3%.

In the public eye. In 1978, following complaints from homeowners, the Federal Trade Commission ordered Kaufman & Broad to repair structural defects in more than 20,000 homes they had built in suburban Chicago. As a result of the order K & B must now give homebuyers a detailed warranty. They have handled 3 urban redevelopment projects in the Los Angeles area.

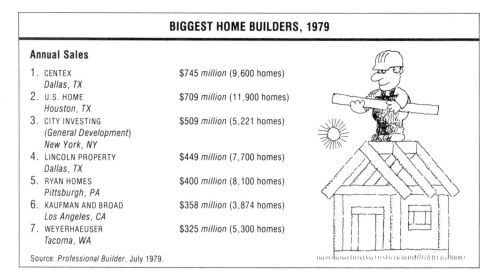

BIGGEST HOME BUILDERS, 1979

Annual Sales

1. CENTEX — $745 *million* (9,600 homes)
   Dallas, TX
2. U.S. HOME — $709 *million* (11,900 homes)
   Houston, TX
3. CITY INVESTING — $509 *million* (5,221 homes)
   (General Development)
   New York, NY
4. LINCOLN PROPERTY — $449 *million* (7,700 homes)
   Dallas, TX
5. RYAN HOMES — $400 *million* (8,100 homes)
   Pittsburgh, PA
6. KAUFMAN AND BROAD — $358 *million* (3,874 homes)
   Los Angeles, CA
7. WEYERHAEUSER — $325 *million* (5,300 homes)
   Tacoma, WA

Source: *Professional Builder*, July 1979.

Where they're going. Eli Broad describes Kaufman & Broad as "marathon runners, not sprinters." He says his company has "absolutely no desire to be the fastest growing home builder over the next 10 years."

Stock performance. Kaufman & Broad stock bought for $1,000 in 1970 sold for $592 on January 2, 1980.

Major employment centers. Los Angeles and San Francisco.

Access. 10801 National Boulevard, Los Angeles, California 90064; (213) 475-6711.

KOHLER

Sales: $365 million
Profits: $24.5 million
Rank in plumbing: 2
Founded: 1873
Employees: 5,000
Headquarters: Kohler, Wisconsin

What they do. Kohler used to be known more for labor problems than bathtubs. Today Kohler and the company town the Kohlers built outside Sheboygan, Wisconsin, are booming. They are challenging American Standard for first place in the manufacture of enameled cast-iron, vitreous china, and fiberglass plumbing fixtures.

Kohler also makes electric generators for standby power systems, yachts, motor homes, and recreational vehicles. Admiral Byrd used Kohler generators on his Antarctic expeditions of 1926 and 1933. Kohler two- and four-cycle engines power lawn and garden tractors, snowmobiles, farm machinery, and industrial equipment. The company famous for sinks is now the country's largest manufacturer of air-cooled, cast-iron engines.

History. John Michael Kohler set up his iron foundry in Wisconsin in 1873, with ideas of company paternalism and high-quality craftsmanship that were legacies of his native Austria. He passed on these old-country attitudes to his sons, who took over the business at the turn of the century.

Walter J. Kohler, the elder son, dreamed of a planned company town on Lake Michigan. With Frederick Law Olmsted, of Central Park fame, Walter organized his community for "greater industry and happier workers." He built and sold houses with limitations on colors and styles "to maintain a high-class residential community."

Kohler began manufacturing plumbing fixtures when the process for enamel-coated cast iron was developed in the late 1800s. They later added other processes for plumbing fixtures: vitreous china and fiberglass. Kohler craftsmen today make the china in much the same way their grandfathers did, in special sand molds at the pottery in Kohler, Wisconsin.

The company began to grow along with the building trades. After World War I the planned village never housed more than 10% of Kohler's white-collar employees. Most of the line workers lived in Sheboygan. They chafed under what Walter's nephew called "enlightened paternalism" until the local union called a strike on July 16, 1934. Kohler village police shot and killed two pickets and wounded 47 others before the governor sent out the National Guard to "disarm the Kohler blackshirts." The strike continued until World War II brought the workers back into the plant, which had been operating with scabs and nonstriking employees.

Walter's equally unyielding half-brother, Herbert V., became Kohler president in 1937 and chairman in 1940. An immense man with a jutting jaw, Herbert believed "union leaders who convince the workman that his employer is his natural enemy serve only the Marxian doctrine." Herbert contended that each worker should decide whether or not to join a union. Kohler workers walked out again on April 5, 1954, in a bitter strike that dragged on until September 1, 1960. The *New York Times* called it the "longest major strike in the history of U.S. labor."

Herbert stuck to his right-to-work stance, for which he won the National Association of Manufacturers' "Man of the Year" award in 1958. He thought outside agitators caused the strike, particularly United Auto Workers president Walter Reuther, whom he called a "Moscow-trained socialist." Reuther classified Herbert Kohler as the "most reactionary antilabor, immoral employer in America."

Bathtubs were never like this: Kohler's "Environment," a teak-and-cypress enclosure in which, the Kohler people point out, "the occupant selects the elements of nature she desires to experience and a time limit for each cycle. Completely in control, she can sunbathe in Baja Sun, refresh in Tropic Rain, and enjoy Jungle Steam, Spring Showers, and Chinook Winds. Heat lamps, sun lamps, 'rain' nozzles and stereo speakers are located in the enclosure's ceiling." The cost: about $12,500 (including installation).

Herbert even turned down an appeal for arbitration from his nephew, Walter J. Kohler, Jr. Like his father Walter J. Kohler, Sr., who served as Republican governor of Wisconsin from 1929–31, the younger Kohler held the office from 1951–57. (Ironically, the Kohlers share the distinction of father-son governorships in Wisconsin with progressives Robert LaFollette and his son Philip.)

A U.S. Senate committee investigation discovered that the Kohler Company had bought riot guns, tear gas, and machine guns before the strike began in 1954. Strikers recalled Herbert striding through the pickets with a club in his hand saying, "I am the law here!" On the other hand, the committee found that strikers committed hundreds of acts of vandalism against the company and scabs.

Finally the National Labor Relations Board ruled in 1960 that the company prolonged the strike through unfair labor practices. After a few more appeals, Kohler reinstated almost all of the strikers and paid out $4.5 million in back pay. Although labor relations with Kohler are said to be good today, workers in the foundry erected a sign along the path of the visitor tour which reads, "Please do not feed or tease the workers. Thank you. The Management."

Kohler's conservativism never extended to their plumbing design. They are known for producing colorful, bold, and unusual fixtures. Their "Environment" system simulates rain forests, cold breezes, or desert heat at the touch of a dial, all in the privacy of your bathroom. Since the Environment costs about $12,500, only two were sold last year.

Reputation. Kohler, guided today by chairman Herbert V. Kohler, Jr., keeps financial details secret. *Fortune* magazine related how, in 1979, Kohler sidestepped the Securities and Exchange Commission requirements for public filing of financial information by reducing the number of shareholders from 423 to 250, a safe margin from the 500 shareholders required for public disclosure.

What they own. Besides plants in Wisconsin, Kohler also owns plants in South Carolina, Texas, and Ohio, as well as subsidiaries in Toronto and Mexico City.

Who owns and runs the company. Kohler is a private corporation. The Kohler family owns 90% of the stock. Two Kohlers sit on the board of directors, which has no members who are not company officials. Kohler's first nonfamily president, James L. Kuplic, was elected in 1962.

In the public eye. Nine years after the last Kohler strike ended, a federal court found Kohler, American-Standard, and Borg-Warner (along with some smaller companies) guilty of conspiring to fix prices on $1 billion worth of plumbing fixtures. The court fined Kohler $4.3 million.

Where they're going. It's a secret.

Access. Kohler, Wisconsin 53044; (414) 475-4441. Visitors may tour the Kohler, Wisconsin plant weekdays at 9 A.M.

Consumer brands.

Kohler plumbing fixtures.

Sales: $904.7 million
Profits: $25.0 million
Forbes 500 rank: 499
Founded: 1946
Employees: 5,809
Headquarters: North Wilkesboro, North Carolina

What they do. Unless you live in the Southeast, odds are you've never heard of Lowe's. They run a chain of 199 large lumber and building materials stores, almost all of which are south of the Mason-Dixon line in towns with names like Zebulon, North Carolina, and Warner Robins, Georgia.

A Lowe's customer could, in a single stop, buy everything needed to build a house: concrete, lumber, roofing, gypsum wall-board, siding, paint, doors and windows, bathtub, shower stall, furnace, fireplace, all the electrical wiring and fixtures, and, of course, the kitchen sink. When the house was finished, Lowe's could supply the refrigerator, range, and microwave oven; power lawn mower and garden tools; go-carts and bicycles for the kids—even a color television set. And if all that seemed like too big a project, Lowe's might be able to talk the customer into one of the mobile homes for sale in the parking lot.

History. Lowe's began in 1945 when two ex-GI's, Jim Lowe and his brother-in-law, Carl Buchan, opened a hardware store in North Wilkesboro, North Carolina. Sales were brisk enough for them to buy a small lumber yard in nearby Sparta in 1949, but that was as far as they went until 1952, when Lowe sold out to his partner. Buchan liked the company's slogan, "Lowes's Low Prices," enough that he decided not to change the name.

At the time, most building supplies were sold through specialized retailers—a plumbing supply store here, an electrical supply store there, and various hardware, heating, and lumber outlets scattered among the smaller cities in the South. Buchan predicted (accurately) that housing construction in the South would boom in the 1950s, and he decided to combine his hardware store and his lumber yard complex into a single operation. In 1952 his sales were slightly more than $4 million. By 1958, with 12 stores in other North Carolina cities and additional outlets in Virginia, Tennessee, and South Carolina, Lowe's total was $22 million and climbing.

Today more than half of Lowe's business consists of selling to professional home builders.

Reputation. Lowe's retains their homespun, family feeling, largely as a result of their decision to locate most stores in small and medium-sized southern cities and in rural areas—although they have 21 stores in Georgia, for example, there are none in Atlanta. And Lowe's corporate headquarters is still located in tiny North Wilkesboro—population 4,197.

What they own. Most of Lowe's 199 stores are supplied directly by wholesalers, but in the last few years the company has opened two central warehouses, mostly to supply their stores with consumer items. They also have a huge central lumber yard in Thomasville, North Carolina, and several smaller yards throughout the South.

Who owns and runs the company. When Charles Valentine retired after 17 years with Lowe's, he had a nest egg of more than a half-million dollars. The oddity was that Valentine was a 51-year-old laborer with a sixth-grade education who worked on the company's loading dock, never earning more than $125 a week.

The reason for this apparent oddity is Lowe's incredible profit-sharing plan—the best in the nation, according to the Profit Sharing Research Foundation. Lowe's forks over a sum equal to 15% of each employee's earnings at the end of each year and invests it in the employee's name—about 90% of it in Lowe's stock. Upon retirement (or earlier, if the employee requests), Lowe's puts the proceeds into the employee's savings account. A few years ago more than 50 of Lowe's 3,000-odd employees had more than $400,000 each socked away in stock; and one, a former Lowe's manager named Cecil Murray, retired with $3.5 million in profit-sharing benefits.

Lowe's employee stock ownership plan accounts for about 17% of the stock ownership. All 12 of the directors are Lowe's officers or employees.

In the public eye. Lowe's doesn't make many headlines, mostly because they have stayed away from major media markets. Their main contact with the world outside their customers is Lowe's annual report—a shimmering, glossy, information-packed, four-color gem in a group of usually lifeless publications. *Financial World* gave Lowe's their "Oscar" in 1971 for the best annual report in the country.

Where they're going. The profit-sharing plan, plus a few other benefits, has given Lowe's employees a feeling the company describes as "evangelistic zeal." Lowe's firmly believes that keeping their employees happy keeps sales and profits high. That's the reason, they say, for their rapid expansion. Lowe's now opens an average of about 20 new stores every year. They are now in 19 states, as far north as Ohio and Indiana and as far west as Indiana.

Stock performance. Lowe's stock bought for $1,000 in 1970 sold for $1,767 on January 2, 1980.

Access. P. O. Box 1111, North Wilkesboro, North Carolina 28656; (919) 667-3111.

UNITED STATES GYPSUM //
BUILDING AMERICA

Sales: $1.5 billion
Profits: $123.5 million
Forbes 500 rank: 332
Rank in gypsum: 1
Founded: 1901
Employees: 20,700
Headquarters: Chicago, Illinois

The pasty white stuff we called plaster of Paris in our arts and crafts days is no kiddie industry to U.S. Gypsum. Almost three-quarters of the company's profits come from wallboard and building products made from plaster of Paris, or gypsum as it's officially called. All U.S. Gypsum's businesses involve a resource from the earth: wood and mineral fibers for insulation, metals for drywall systems, and clay.

The company put their building materials to good use in the 1960s, when they rehabilitated six Chicago slums, five Cleveland tenements, and six buildings in New York's Harlem. They then sold the fixed-up buildings for less than their true value to nonprofit housing agencies. In 1975 U.S. Gypsum and three other gypsum makers (National Gypsum, Georgia-Pacific, and Jim Walter) were convicted of engaging in a conspiracy to fix prices on $4.8 billion of gypsum products over a 14-year period. They appealed to the U.S. Supreme Court, which ordered a new trial. In 1980 the Justice Department, instead of retrying the charges, settled the case with an agreement that the four companies pay extra income taxes. U.S. Gypsum's part of the settlement cost them $2.6 million. Claude Huckleberry, who was the government's chief witness in the case, called the settlement a "sellout."

Access. 101 South Wacker Drive, Chicago, Illinois 60606; (312) 321-4000.

US·HOME®

Sales: $935.3 million
Profits: $41 million
Forbes 500 rank: 484
Founded: 1954
Employees: 3,100
Headquarters: Houston, Texas

What they do. Homebuilding is one industry where small operators still dominate. The average builder is a local operator who puts up eight or ten houses a year and sells them for a total of perhaps $500,000. By contrast, U.S. Home, the nation's largest builder of single-family houses, built 14,000 of them in 1979 but so fragmented is the industry that this represented only 0.8% of the market. They operate in two dozen metropolitan areas in 11 states. Most of their developments lie in the sunbelt, from Florida to Arizona, but they also have divisions in such outposts as New Jersey, Minnesota, and Colorado. In 1980 they penetrated California for the first time when they bought a Bakersfield builder. More than 100,000 families live in houses built by U.S. Home. The company's motto is: "America calls us home." Their average house price in 1978 was $49,500—some $12,000 below the national average.

U.S. Home encourages the entrepreneurial spirit. They have 32 homebuilding divisions with more or less independent presidents who find the sites to develop, decide what kinds of houses to build, pick local contractors to do the construction, and sell them through their own sales force (they rarely go through real estate agents). Sometimes they have to compete with several other U.S. Home divisions in the same city. If they're good, they can win bonuses of several hundred thousand dollars a year. In any year there may be half a dozen division presidents who make more than U.S. Home chairman Guy Odom's $225,000 salary.

History. Turbulence and high drama have marked U.S. Home's brief existence. Robert Winnerman, a New Jersey developer, started the earliest branch of the company in 1954. He merged with Charles Rutenberg, a Florida builder, in 1969. Over the next three years they bought nearly 20 other companies, including one run by Guy Odom of Texas, a self-taught devotee of "management science." The top two officers clashed over business strategy, and when Rutenberg bought out Winnerman in 1973, Odom left, too. The company soon went into a tailspin. Odom, meanwhile, had started his own company, which he built into a $55 million business in three years. To get him back, Rutenberg bought Odom's new company in 1977 and made him president of U.S. Home. A few months later, the directors gave Rutenberg a surprise: they installed Odom as chairman and handed Rutenberg his hat.

Under Odom white shirts and conservative suits replaced the casual garb of the Florida development company. He was the first to apply the management policies of large industrial corporations to a homebuilding company. Psychological and intelligence testing became the chief factor in hiring and promotion—even the officers of potential acquisitions are expected to submit to the tests. In his first year as chairman Odom boosted revenues 92%. "I've never been associated with a loss," he has said. "I don't know what it feels like, and I don't want to find out."

Reputation. U.S. Home is one of the few homebuilders to have succeeded on more than a regional scale. To develop the right kind of division presidents, U.S. Home has a "great books" program. One evening every two weeks small groups of aspiring executives get together to discuss some of Odom's favorite books, including Ayn Rand's *The Virtue of Selfishness*, Alfred P. Sloan's *My Years with General Motors*, and Machiavelli's *The Prince*.

What they own. U.S. Home owns or controls 50,000 lots in 15 states.

Who owns and runs the company. In January 1980 France's largest homebuilder, Societe des Maisons Phenix, acquired a 16% stake in U.S. Home. The next largest shareholder, with 7% of the stock, is Guy Odom.

In the public eye. U.S. Home has been a good place for women to get ahead. L. Rita Osfield is senior vice president of management development (the "great books" program), and the company's top salesperson of 1978 was a woman: Pat Cox of Phoenix, who rang up $5.7 million in sales. There are no women directors, however.

Where they're going. U.S. Home is positively buoyant about their future. "The postwar baby boom has now reached the prime homebuying age group," they point out. According to *Fortune,* the company's officers "see no reason why U.S. Home can't build in all" 172 of the nation's major metropolitan areas. On the other hand, if a recession combines with record high mortgage rates, they may find themselves with a lot of houses nobody can afford to buy.

Stock performance. U.S. Home stock bought for $1,000 in 1970 sold for $923 on January 2, 1980.

Major employment centers. Tampa/Clearwater, Florida; Houston, Texas; Minneapolis, Minnesota.

Access. 1177 West Loop South, Houston, Texas 77027; (713) 877-2311. You can tour a "model home" at most of their new developments.

Sales: $1.9 billion
Profits: $98.0 million
Forbes 500 rank: 273
Rank in building materials: 3
Founded: 1946
Employees: 25,200
Headquarters: Tampa, Florida

Jim Walter recognized the potential market for prefabricated house shells when a passer-by offered a high price for Walter's own unfinished house in Tampa, Florida. On his first day of business, back in 1946, he sold 27 of the shells. Postwar landowners put up their lots as collateral, bought Jim Walter shells for them, and finished the interiors themselves. Before long the Jim Walter Corporation was producing a whole slew of accessory building materials, from pipes and plumbing to concrete and insulation.

The company's record earnings from 1970 to 1979 made a dozen Walter executives into millionaires (one executive's card reads simply "Eugene R. Katz. Millionaire"). Jim Walter, a former truckdriver, owns 3% of the stock, enough to pay for his brown Rolls-Royce and African safaris. Despite the southern informality of the company, everyone knows Jim's the boss. A sign in his office reads, "He who got the gold makes the rules."

Access. 1500 North Dale Mabry, Tampa, Florida 33607; (813) 871-4811.

Wickes

Sales: $2.1 billion
Profits: $39.7 million
Forbes 500 rank: 249
Rank in retail lumber: 1
Rank in retail furniture: 2
Founded: 1854
Employees: 16,815
Headquarters: San Diego, California

What they do. Walking into a Wickes store for the first time, you might think you had stumbled into the local A & P by mistake. But instead of canned beans and boxes of breakfast cereal, Wickes's customers fill their carts with things like building tools, molding strips, and shelving brackets.

Wickes introduced their first supermarket-style lumber and building materials store in 1954, and now they have more than 300 home improvement marts (including 38 in Europe)—selling everything from raw lumber to shower nozzles and bags of peat moss. In the early 1960s Wickes decided the supermarket idea might work with furniture, too. Since then they've opened 23 enormous furniture warehouse/showrooms, most of which are in the Midwest. Wickes also makes much of the furniture they sell.

Although these businesses account for more than half their sales, Wickes is more than just do-it-yourself supermarkets. They moved into agriculture after World War II and now have a midwestern network of grain and bean elevators, mostly in Minnesota, North Dakota, and Michigan. A subsidiary, the Sequoia Supply Company, wholesales lumber to industrial accounts and retail lumber yards. And a separate manufacturing group produces everything from forest products like paneling and particleboard to carbon graphite (for paints and pencil leads) and lathes for making automotive crankshafts.

History. The two Wickes brothers, Henry and Edward, opened their Saginaw, Michigan, machine shop in 1854 to manufacture gang-saws for the local lumber industry. Twenty years later, as Michigan's timber stands began to thin out, they started making steam boilers for sawmills and later for ships. In 1890 they bought a graphite mine in northern Mexico and began selling graphite to paint and pencil manufacturers. The brothers' descendants ran the machinery, graphite, and boiler-making businesses as separate entities for more than 50 years.

In 1947, following a wartime boom in the boiler industry, the three companies merged to form The Wickes Corporation. Their new president, Daniel Fitz-Gerald, looked around for something to spend the boiler profits on and ended up buying two grain and bean elevator companies that were near the Saginaw home office. One of Wickes elevator managers noticed that local farmers spent much of the money Wickes paid them for beans on lumber and tools, and suggested that the company open lumber and hardware outlets at their elevator sites. Fitz-Gerald did just that—creating the first of the Wickes "supermarkets" in 1954.

The supermarket idea made Wickes so much money that they began buying other companies in the 1960s. They picked up a machine manufacturer in 1963, two building-supply companies in 1964, a particleboard maker in 1965, and a number of lumber and furniture companies later in the decade. They even bought an Elkhart, Indiana, mobile home manufacturer in 1969 and opened a chain of "Wanderland" recreational vehicle lots, but the project proved to be a disaster. When the bottom fell out of the mobile home market in the mid-1970s, Wickes pulled out.

In 1972 Wickes moved their corporate headquarters to San Diego. The company claimed that they wanted to be closer to the lucrative West Coast lumber market, but anyone who has ever wintered in Saginaw might suspect other motives.

Reputation. Unlike other acquisitors, Wickes buys companies to run them, not to sell them off a few years later for a quick profit. Wickes chief financial officer David J. Primuth was quoted in a 1978 *Los Angeles Times* story as saying, "We intend to operate every company we acquire. Forever."

What they own. Although they finally sold the boiler division in 1966 to Combustion Engineering, Wickes still runs their grain elevator and machinery businesses. In 1979 they picked up MacGregor Golf Company, which makes a full line of golf equipment.

Who owns and runs the company. Descendants of the Wickes brothers continue to own a significant minority of the stock, but the last family member involved in the actual management of the company was H. Randall Wickes, who retired as president in 1964. Wickes has been publicly owned and listed on the New York Stock Exchange since 1961.

In the public eye. Wickes likes to keep a very low profile. Chairman McNeely told the *Los Angeles Times* that they were "not very flamboyant people" and added that Wickes was probably "the least-known big company around." Their only press clippings come from business publications.

Where they're going. Wickes will continue buying other companies. According to McNeely, "If we don't grow, we perish." As 1980 opened, they were trying to scoop up Gamble-Skogmo, a $2 billion Minneapolis-based retailer, mail order seller, and financial services supplier.

Stock performance. Wickes stock bought for $1,000 in 1970 sold for $474 on January 2, 1980.

Access. 1010 Second Avenue, San Diego, California 92101; (714) 238-0304.

Consumer brands.

Wickes lumber and furniture; Builders Emporium lumber and building materials; Farmaster fences and gates; Yorktowne kitchen cabinets; MacGregor golf equipment.

> The decade of the 1970s saw 17.8 million new houses and apartments and 3.6 million new mobile homes in the United States.

Appliance Makers

Sales: $1.2 billion
Profits: $94.4 million
Forbes 500 rank: 399
Rank in power tools: 1
Founded: 1910
Employees: 18,500
Headquarters: Towson, Maryland

What they do. Black & Decker's "basic product is new products," according to *Forbes.* Once a do-it-yourselfer buys a drill, saw, sander, or grinder, he will never need another one. But he might want the latest jigsaw, or a hand-held battery-operated vacuum cleaner—which happen to be made by Black & Decker. About 40% of Black & Decker's sales come from products that didn't exist five years ago. As one analyst points out, "The idea is to keep churning out new items regularly so Black & Decker is never dependent on any one blockbuster." They have certainly succeeded in the portable power tool market, ranking first in power tool sales here and overseas. The company got a jump on the foreign market when they sent representatives to Russia and Japan in 1918. They now do about 60% of their business abroad.

History. S. Duncan Black and Alonzo G. Decker first turned out such items as milk bottle cap machines, vest pocket adding machines, and a currency-cutting machine for the U.S. Mint before they hit the big time in 1916 with the first portable electric drill. They moved their machine shop from downtown Baltimore to rural (now suburban) Towson, Maryland, where they parlayed a $1,200 loan from Decker's father-in-law into the power tool giant Black & Decker is today.

In 1936 Black & Decker developed the first power hammer. In 1946 they entered the consumer market with the world's first line of electric drills for home use and they made the first finishing sanders and jigsaws for do-it-yourselfers in 1953. They responded to the surge in suburban living in 1957 by making their first outdoor products —hedge trimmers and lawn edgers. In the early 1960s they were the first to make battery-powered drills and hedge trimmers. In 1971 a Black & Decker gizmo powered the Apollo lunar surface drill, which the Apollo 15 astronauts used to remove moon samples.

Reputation. Black & Decker is one of the few American companies to beat the Japanese at the game of price-cutting: they claim to undersell the giants of Japanese power tools, Makita and Hitachi, by more than 20%. In this country consumers benefit from the Black & Decker practice of cutting the price of a product 25% when its sales double. A quarter-inch drill that sold for $25 in 1959, for example, sold for $8 in 1979. *Forbes* calls Black & Decker "one of the toughest competitors in U.S. business."

What they own. Black & Decker has come a long way from Baltimore. They originally moved to Towson because they thought that country people were more honest and dependable than city folk and made better employees, and they have been locating their plants in rural areas ever since. They now own 31 plants in North Carolina, Ohio, Wisconsin, New York, Arizona, California, Canada, Japan, Europe, Australia, and Argentina. Two-thirds of their 304 product service centers are overseas.

Who owns and runs the company. When Francis Lucier became chief executive officer in 1975, his promotion marked the first time Black & Decker was headed by neither a Black nor a Decker. The company's founders died in the 1950s, and Robert Black, the brother of the original Black, took over the presidency. He was succeeded by Alonzo Decker, Jr., in 1960. Robert Black, who, in his eighties, still sits on the board of directors, told the *New York Times,* "We've never had a genius in our organization."

In the public eye. Black & Decker have managed to avoid unions in almost all their plants. (The one exception, DeWalt Radial-Arm in Lancaster, Pennsylvania, was already unionized when Black & Decker bought them in 1960.) Vice-president Gerald Seidl told the *New York Times,* "Our benefits are better than any union could offer." The company maintains a store that sells Black & Decker products to employees at a discount, and the company offers courses for workers at the plant and at nearby colleges.

During the tenure of Alonzo Decker, Jr., from 1960–72, employees could go directly to Decker with their problems. Lawrence Freeny of the *New York Times* wrote that "Decker made a practice of talking with workers in all departments and greeting as many of them as possible by name"; he would not hear of an executive dining room. Perhaps Alonzo Decker adopted a down-to-earth attitude after he was laid off from Black & Decker for a year and a half during the Depression.

Black & Decker's 1978 annual report included a pitch for a group called Citizen's Choice, which they described as "an alternative to other so-called grass-root organizations which encourage more and more government spending and regulation." For $15 in yearly dues Citizen's Choice will keep you posted on "legislation and other federal government activities which are seriously eroding individual freedoms."

Stock performance. Black & Decker stock bought for $1,000 in 1970 sold for $1,489 on January 2, 1980.

Major employment centers. Hampstead, Maryland; Lake Havasu, Arizona; and Fayetteville, North Carolina.

Access. 701 East Joppa Road, Towson, Maryland 21204; (301) 828-3900. Consumer inquiries should be addressed to Ms. Betty Neal at the company's headquarters. Arrangements for tours of Black & Decker plants should be made at the local level.

Black & Decker became the first power tool manufacturer to test the outerspace market when their battery-operated drill went along the Apollo 15 mission in 1971.

Consumer brands.

Black & Decker power tools.

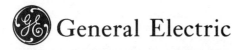# General Electric

Sales: $22.5 billion
Profits: $1.4 billion
Forbes 500 rank: 11
Rank in light bulbs: 1
Rank in home appliances: 1
Rank in nuclear reactors: 2
Rank in jet engines: 2
Founded: 1878
Employees: 401,000
Headquarters: Fairfield, Connecticut

What they do. Little did Thomas Alva Edison realize when he invented the light bulb in 1879 that his device would give rise to a world-class industrial superpower. He might not have sold his General Electric stock in 1894 to pursue an ill-fated iron ore mining venture in New Jersey. That stock would now be worth at least half a billion dollars. Edison's mine collapsed but today GE owns 49% of Samarco Mineracao, a Brazilian company which extracts iron ore from the interior of that country, transporting it in slurry form by pipeline to coastal points. The investment in the Brazilian company exceeds $600 million, but GE operates on such a vast scale that the mine is just a nice little sideline, hardly worth mentioning to the company's stockholders, who now number more than half a million.

For consumers GE makes, markets, and services a long line of appliances, from toasters to washing machines. These are sold under two brand names: GE and Hotpoint. In most of these product categories, the GE brand is either number 1 or number 2. GE is still the largest maker of light bulbs, by some estimates accounting for more than 50% of the market. They are the only American company that still assembles all their black-and-white television receivers in this country—at Portsmouth, Virginia. Most of the others are imported.

GE manufactures a wide variety of equipment used by utility companies in the generation and transmission of electricity. These include giant steam turbine generators, nuclear reactors, transformers, circuit breakers, switchgears, and meters.

Their customer list is long. GE sells to, among others, aircraft companies (jet engines); hospitals (X-ray machines, cat-scanners); railroads (diesel locomotives); automobile manufacturers (headlamps); steel mills (electric motors); machine tool manufacturers (metal cutters); and the Defense Department (missile launch systems). They make tough plastics (Lexan and Noryl) and silicone chemicals. They own a mining company, Utah International, that extracts Australian coking coal to feed the steel mills of Japan. They own and operate a clutch of radio and TV stations plus a bunch of cablevision systems. And since they are such a prodigious cash machine, they also field a finance company, General Electric Credit Corporation, that has enough money out on loan—more than $6 billion—to produce annual profits of $80 million. So on top of everything else, they make money on money.

No other manufacturer has the national presence GE has. They operate 218 manufacturing plants in 34 states and Puerto Rico. In city after city—Louisville, Kentucky; Schenectady, New York; Pittsfield, Massachusetts; Columbia, Maryland; Cleveland and Philadelphia—they rank among the largest employers. Only four companies—AT&T, General Motors, Ford, and Sears, Roebuck—have larger U.S. payrolls than General Electric.

To run this vast array of businesses, GE pioneered a decentralized form of management that has become a textbook study. Managers are given authority to operate businesses that, if broken out, would rank as huge enterprises in their own rights. At the same time, all sectors retain a "GE look": this is one company, no matter how sprawling. Planning is methodical. Goals are set, and managers are measured on how closely they meet them.

Edison's legacy also made GE a technology-based company. General Electric has frequently been termed an "engineer's company." On the payroll today are 15,000 people with technical degrees, 1,500 of them holding Ph.D.'s. GE's annual research budget tops $1 billion. They have been awarded 50,000 patents, the most ever received by a company.

GE is also first in another area: exporting equipment out of the United States. They logged export sales of nearly $2.7 billion in 1979. In addition, they have 127 manufacturing plants in 24 other countries.

History. In October 1878 the Edison Electric Light Company organized to back Thomas Edison's experiments at Menlo Park to develop an incandescent lamp—experims crowned with success a year later. Present at the birth of the company, along with Edison and his friend Grosvenor P. Lowrey, were representatives of John Pierpont Morgan, who had his fingers in so many industrial pies that the process of combining companies into one entity, such as U.S. Steel, came to be known as "Morganizing" industry. It was the power of the Morgan banking house that fueled the growth of General Electric.

When they marked their 100th birthday in 1978, GE had this to say about Thomas Edison: "Had he wished, he might have become an important corporate executive or an entrepreneur amassing great fortunes. Instead, he chose to remain in his laboratory, exploring nature's secrets and there found wealth of another and perhaps more enduring kind."

That's not the way Edison saw it. When Morgan combined the Edison company with a competing firm, Thomson-Houston, in 1892, the resulting entity was called General Electric. Edison was named to the board but was miffed because his name did not adorn the new company. According to Edison's biographer Robert Conot, author of *A Streak of Luck,* Edison went to his first and last board meeting in August 1892. "I will not go on the board of a company that I don't control," he said. Two years later he sold all his GE shares, though he remained tied to the company as a consultant and collector of royalties on patents he held.

The avenues that opened for Edison's successors were broad, fast moving, and seemingly never ending. In 1885 a skyscraper using electric elevators went up in Chicago. In 1890 the electric chair was introduced to execute prisoners. Electric trolleys were built in every big American city.

The Evolution of the Toaster

The first toaster consisted of a long-handled fork with the bread at one end and a human at the other kneeling in the soot and ashes of an open fireplace. Toast, not surprisingly, failed to become a breakfast staple. In the nineteenth century, after wood and coal stoves replaced the fireplace for cooking, tin and wire toasters designed to sit atop the stove and use its heat appeared on the market. One popular type looked like a small tin tower, tapering toward the top so a slice of bread could lean against each of its four sides. Such toasters had to be closely watched since they lacked any form of heat control, and bread had to be turned by hand.

Electric toasters appeared soon after the turn of the twentieth century—skeletal, intricate structures of naked wire, without covers or shells. General Electric's first came out in 1905. Westinghouse followed with the "toaster-stove" in 1910. Later versions had doors that enclosed the heating elements and pulled down to admit the bread. Some strange variants appeared, like The Estate Stove Company's four-slice model, with revolving toast holders projecting from its sides like the wings of a mutant dragonfly.

But making toast still required moment-to-moment human attention. During World War I Charles Strite, a master mechanic, could no longer endure the burnt toast served in his company's lunchroom in Stillwater, Minnesota. In his home shop he set to work to devise a toaster that would not depend for successful toasting on the vagaries of human attention. Strite's invention was the first successful pop-up toaster. He patented it in 1919 and formed a company to produce it commercially for restaurants. But production and sales were slow, and the company floundered.

In 1926 the firm marketed an improved home model called the Toastmaster. It had clock-type timing adjustable for desired degrees of doneness, and when the toast reached perfection, the current shut off and the toast was ejected. The same year Max McGraw, founder of the McGraw Electric Company (later McGraw-Edison), bought Strite's firm. Backed by an infusion of working capital and marketing experience, Toastmaster became a household word, and the minds of breakfasting Americans were freed to wander at will.

Toastmaster's success prompted imitators, including Thomas A. Edison, Inc., and General Electric. Small refinements have continued to increase the toaster's autonomy. Yet, strangely enough, the Bromwell Wire Goods Company of Michigan City, Indiana, founded in 1819, still cranks out its original tin and wire models, designed for use on wood or coal stoves.

Electric motors made factories more productive. And everywhere homes were being lit up.

To consolidate their position at the forefront of this revolution, GE established a corporate research laboratory at Schenectady, New York in 1900. One of the first scientists to work there was Charles Steinmetz, the brilliant hunchbacked immigrant from Germany, who was nicknamed "the wizard of electricity." Meanwhile, the Morgan financiers in control of GE pushed ahead with one combination after another. GE and Westinghouse were bitter enemies at first, but they entered into a patent pool in 1896. In 1903 GE absorbed Stanley Electric, a transformer manufacturer based in Pittsfield, Massachusetts. Not content with simply supplying the equipment that could generate electricity, GE sought to operate the local utilities that provided it and formed Electric Bond & Share as a holding company for their utilities. After federal antitrust hackles were raised, GE left the utility business in 1924.

Antitrust seems to have been a problem for GE during most of their corporate life. After World War I they joined with their ostensible competitor, Westinghouse, to launch the Radio Corporation of America in the broadcasting field. (GE themselves opened one of the first radio stations, WGY, Schnectady, in 1922.) GE owned 60% of RCA, Westinghouse 40%. This combination was actually promoted by government officials in Washington, D.C., who wanted to prevent Guglielmo Marconi from getting a foothold in the American market. In 1930, after the government saw the antitrust implications of this patent pool, they

changed their minds—and GE sold off their RCA holdings. Another action, settled in 1949, found that GE had effective control of 85% of the light bulb business—55% from their own output and 30% from that of licensees. The court forced them to open up their patents to other companies. However, GE's dominant position in the lamp market financed their entry into the appliance business. Between 1911 and 1967 GE was a defendant in 65 antitrust actions.

GE grew steadily during the 1920s and 1930s; on the eve of World War II the company was depicted as follows in *Fortune*: "Profits have been consistently large, dividends consecutively generous, and stock a perennial blue chip. . . . GE engineers have merged their erratic tendencies, if any, into the corporate personality. Their minds work with the accuracy and uniformity of slide rules. . . ." Heavily involved in industry's war effort, GE entered World War II doing $340 million of business a year and emerged doing $1.3 billion. When union leaders came in after the war asking for a $2-a-day increase, the company's offer was 10¢ an hour—"take it or leave it." This ushered in the period of "Boulwarism," a concept of employee relations developed at GE by Lemuel P. Boulware and admired by other corporate executives for its toughness.

While GE was giving short shrift to unions, their managers were being pushed to produce high profits. One way they accomplished that mission was by sitting in hotel rooms with competitors and rigging prices on a wide range of electrical equipment sold to utilities. The tipoff on this conspiracy came from the Tennessee Valley Authority, which complained that it was being forced to invite bids from foreign electrical manufacturers because U.S. firms had raised prices 50% with no variation at all from company to company. The Justice Department soon indicted 29 corporations and 45 individuals. The evidence of price-fixing on everything from $2 insulators to multimillion-dollar turbine generators was so well documented that all the defendants pleaded guilty or no contest to the charges. When sentences and fines were levied in 1961, GE, whose market share in the price-fixed products was the largest, was socked with the largest fine: $437,500. But they had to pay much more to settle the damage suits filed by customers who bought the price-fixed equipment. The settlement with the

Six-pack: the Fukishima station of Tokyo Electric Power in Japan is the world's largest nuclear power installation: it has six General Electric boiling water reactors.

The Turning Point

The first known sale of an electric iron was in 1896, when the Ward Leonard Electric Company of Wisconsin marketed electrically heated flatirons with replaceable heating units. But the electric iron business was hampered for years by two factors: the heavy, cumbersome design of the irons themselves, and the lack of electric power. Power companies generally supplied electricity only at night for lighting; few electrified homes had power during daylight, when most women did their ironing.

In 1903 Earl H. Richardson, plant superintendent of an Ontario, California, power company, resolved to change matters. He reasoned that if electric irons came into widespread use, demand for electricity would increase and the power companies could operate around the clock. "Load building," as it came to be called, was a startling idea to his superiors, who paid it no heed.

After long experimentation, Richardson produced a small, light iron heated by a glowing resistance wire wrapped around a brass core that conducted heat to the base of the iron. Samples distributed to power company customers were an instant hit. Richardson even persuaded management to generate electricity all day on Tuesdays—ironing day in most households.

Demand grew, encouraging Richardson to form his own manufacturing firm, the Pacific Electric Heating Company. But sales were less brisk than Richardson anticipated, and complaints were many. The new irons were better than others on the market, customers conceded, but they had one serious flaw: they overheated in the center.

Richardson conferred with his wife, who urged him to make irons with more heat in the point, where it was needed to press around buttonholes, ruffles, and pleats.

In 1905 Richardson gave samples of his improved iron to customers. A week later all refused to part with "the iron with the hot point."

It was the turning point for electric irons. Under the Hotpoint trademark, Richardson's company sold more electric irons than any other company in the United States. Hotpoint is now owned by General Electric.

U.S. government alone came to $7.3 million. Payments to utilities were well over $50 million. Three GE officials were given 30-day jail sentences, and other GE executives were forced to leave the company.

It was a dark moment for General Electric, but they managed to survive.

In the 1970s, instead of fixing prices or engaging in antitrust conspiracies, they bought other entities. In 1976 they made the biggest acquisition in U.S. corporate history up to that time, paying $2.2 billion for Utah International, which put GE in the natural resources business: mining coal, copper, uranium, and iron ore, and producing natural gas and oil.

Reputation. General Electric is widely regarded in business circles as one of the best-managed companies in America. This assessment is not exactly shared by labor leaders, who have long resented GE's "papa-knows-best" approach to dealing with their work force. Some 110,000 GE employees are represented by unions.

What they own. Property, plant, and equipment that cost $8.3 billion to build and acquire. At the close of 1978 GE had $2 billion in cash. On the Navajo Indian reservation in New Mexico, GE's Utah International subsidiary produces steam coal that constitutes the entire fuel requirement for the 2,085-megawatt Four Corners Plant owned by six utilities. This mine is operated under a long-term lease with the Navajo Tribe.

Who owns and runs the company. Although there are more than half a million shareholders, institutions such as bank trust departments, insurance companies, pension funds, and investment companies control more than 20% of GE's stock. The largest of these institutional investors, providing a continuity with GE's past, is Morgan Guaranty (they hold 1.3%), whose president, Lewis T. Preston, sits on the GE board of directors. The largest individual stockholder is Edmund W. Littlefield, who came by his 439,818 shares as a result of the Utah International acquisition. GE's top officers and division general managers and all the directors, including Littlefield—a

The all-GE kitchen of the 1930s had a General Electric "Monitor Top" refrigerator, a Hotpoint range, a GE clothes washer and other GE housewares — hardly leaving any room for people.

total of 124 people—own altogether about three-tenths of 1% of all the stock. In short, GE is run by professional managers rather than owners. GE has been a training ground for many other corporations. Managers impatient at making it to the top of the GE maze frequently leave to get their shot at running other companies. In 1979 three senior vice-presidents—Thomas A. Vanderslice, Stanley C. Gault, and Alva O. Way—all left, to join General Telephone, Rubbermaid, and American Express, respectively. The presidents of Heublein, CBS, and Northrop are all ex-GEers. Another distinguished alumnus: novelist Kurt Vonnegut, Jr., who worked in public relations.

GE moved during the late 1960s and early 1970s to alter the all-white, predominantly male cast of their employee force. They have made significant progress—women now account for 29% of total GE employment, minorities nearly 11%. Because they are so dependent on scientific personnel, GE has been a leader in encouraging high school–age minority students to consider engineering as a career;

they have also been the number 1 recruiter of black graduate engineers. In 1978 GE signed a settlement with the Equal Employment Opportunity Commission, agreeing to set aside $32 million to "accelerate" advancement of women and minorities in the company. Father Theodore V. Purcell of Georgetown University, who has made extensive studies of minority employment in industry, gives GE high marks for developing a system that rewards managers for performance and penalizes them for nonperformance in this area.

In the public eye. In the late 1970s GE chairman Reginald H. Jones emerged as the leading spokesman for the business community. He was reportedly offered two cabinet posts by President Jimmy Carter, and in 1979 an article in the *New York Times Magazine* saluted him as "a new breed of businessman that may be good for General Electric—and for the country." Stuart Eizenstat, President Carter's domestic affairs adviser, called Jones "one of the wisest, most intelligent, most informed people on policy issues that I have ever met."

As the controversy over nuclear power swirled, GE held to their position that the United States must "exercise *all* its domestic energy options to keep from going into a serious economic decline." Between 1975 and early 1980 GE did not receive a single order for a reactor. However, they entered 1980 with a nuclear business backlog of $5.2 billion, representing fuel and service contracts and old orders. According to trade journals, GE's worldwide nuclear installations looked like this at the start of 1980:

	Operating	Uncompleted
United States	25	33
Overseas	16	12
Licensees	10	11
	51	56

The total of 107 was only eight behind the number credited to Westinghouse. GE has claimed that their training procedures for personnel are superior to those of their competitors. They also claim that their reactors have a better performance record than the competition. The nuclear installation that failed at Three Mile Island was Babcock & Wilcox's.

Where they're going. GE's massive research commitment places them on the frontier of many new businesses, so they feel confident they will win, no matter which way the technology ball bounces. They claim, for example, that they have "the nation's largest industrial solar development program," and they point out that "practically every other conventional and unconventional energy source under development is almost exclusively for the production of *electric* power." But GE is moving off their traditional base. In 1979 electrical equipment provided only 47% of their profits.

Stock performance. General Electric stock bought for $1,000 in 1970 sold for $1,306 on January 2, 1980.

> General Electric marketed their first electric range in 1906: a wooden table with 30 plugs and switches powering 13 appliances, including an oven, double boilers, pots, a frying pan, a coffeemaker, a toaster, and a waffle iron.

Major employment centers. Schenectady, New York (motors, generators, turbines), 23,000; Louisville, Kentucky (major appliances), 18,000; Evendale, Ohio (jet engines), 12,000; and Lynn, Massachusetts (turbines, generators, small jet engines), 10,000.

Access. 3135 Easton Turnpike, Fairfield, Connecticut 06431.

Consumer brands.

General Electric; Hotpoint.

Scovill

Sales: $941.6 million
Profits: $32.0 million
Forbes 500 rank: 481
Rank in sewing notions: 1
Rank in tire valves: 1
Rank in blenders: 1
Rank in electric knives: 1
Rank in corn poppers: 1
Rank in snap fasteners: 1
Rank in door chimes: 1
Rank in lighting fixtures: 3
Founded: 1804
Employees: 18,928
Headquarters: Waterbury, Connecticut

What they do. It took a lot of brass for Scovill to do what they did in 1976. In fact, as Scovill punned in a full-page ad they placed in the *Wall Street Journal*, it "took all of it": they sold off the brass business that had been part of the company for more than 100 years. The decision, in the end, came down to this: Would you rather be known as an operator of a brass mill or as a manufacturer of such jazzy items as Hamilton Beach corn poppers and Nu Tone door chimes? You might say, "Why not do both?" Scovill tried exactly that. Under the leadership of their chairman, Malcolm Baldrige, they had expanded into a bunch of new businesses, mostly by buying other companies. By 1976 they had reduced brass to a quarter of their total sales. The problem was that the people on Wall Street were so thick they refused to recognize this transformation. Scovill was still reviewed where

Malcolm Baldridge adjusts the stirrup of his saddle. A regular participant in rodeos as a roper, Baldridge is chairman of Scovill.

it always had been—in the metals industry. So Baldrige threw out the brass works. At least *that* got their attention.

Today, Scovill's companies make products falling into four broad categories: housing—Nu Tone intercom systems, Yale locks, Ajax cabinet hardware; housewares—the Hamilton Beach and Dominion lines; automotive—Schrader tire valves; and sewing notions—the Dritz and Clinton lines, and zippers and fasteners sold under the names Gripper and Nyguard.

History. Scovill, one of the oldest companies in America, started out as a button manufacturer in the industrial mill town of Waterbury, Connecticut. Abel Porter founded the Abel Porter & Company button business in 1804 and was the first American to make gilt buttons. His successors, the Scovill brothers, bought the company and moved it into heavier brass casting and rolling.

It was in the mid-1960s that Scovill set about exploring realms beyond brass. They proved to be nimble in scooping up other companies. One of their biggest buys was the small-appliance business of Westinghouse. The big Pittsburgh electronics company found it difficult to make money in appliances. Scovill annexed the business to their Hamilton Beach unit—and had no trouble making money. Scovill is now one of the three companies making a full line of small appliances (the other two are General Electric and Sunbeam).

While Baldrige has succeeded in taking Scovill out of brass, the change has not done much to lift the price of Scovill's stock. In early 1980 it was trading on the New York Stock Exchange in the same range it was trading in 1976.

Reputation. You can take a company out of New England but it's hard to take New England out of a company. Although they have little to do anymore in their native Waterbury, they maintain a commitment to that tired old mill town. In 1979 they put up a new headquarters building near the site of Abel Porter's original button plant. Scovill has paid cash dividends to their stockholders for 123 consecutive years—the longest record of any company on the New York Stock Exchange. The company points out it would have been 129 years had not a heavy snowstorm in 1855 kept directors from meeting to approve the annual dividend.

What they own. Through acquisitions, Scovill now owns plants all over the United States as well as in Mexico, Australia, Germany, Canada, England, France, Brazil, South Africa, India, and Japan.

Who owns and runs the company. Chairman Malcolm Baldrige is the major influence at Scovill. While other executives relax with a sedate game of golf, Baldrige rides rodeo and ropes steers for fun—not exactly standard behavior for a Yale University stalwart.

Baldrige owns about 1.5% of Scovill's stock. The all-white, all-male directors and officers own another 1%. (Baldrige's sister, Tish, is the successor to Emily Post, arbiter of manners and social conduct in America.)

In the public eye. Scovill has made great strides in minority employment. Minorities, as a percentage of total employment, increased from 6% in 1963 to 23% in 1979.

Where they're going. They've achieved the balance they were looking for in their operations. Now they're planning to grow in these designated areas by buying other companies.

Stock performance. Scovill stock bought for $1,000 in 1970 sold for $796 on January 2, 1980.

Major employment centers. Cincinnati, Ohio; Lenoir and Dickson, Tennessee.

Access. Scovill Plaza, Waterbury, Connecticut 06720; (203) 757-6061. The NuTone Division (doorbells) has a toll-free number for complaints and inquiries: (800) 543-8687.

Consumer brands.

Housing Products: NuTone doorbells and intercoms; Lightcraft, Sterling, and Artolier light fixtures; Ajax hardware; Markel heaters.

Housewares: Hamilton Beach and Dominion appliances.

Automotive: Schrader tire valves and gauges.

Sewing notions: Dritz; Clinton; Hero knitting needles; StayLastic/Smith tapes; Gripper snaps; and Nyguard zippers.

Locks: Yale, Norton, BKS, and FAS.

SINGER

Sales: $2.6 billion
Loss: $92.3 million
Forbes 500 rank: 194
Rank in sewing machines: 1
Rank in power tools: 2
Rank in dining room and bedroom furniture: 2
Founded: 1851
Employees: 81,000
Headquarters: Stamford, Connecticut

What they do. Singer, like Pepsi and Coca-Cola, is one of the few brand names known from Topeka to Timbuktu. Singer began sending salesmen and sewing machines overseas in the mid-1800s, and today there are Singer sewing machines in nearly every nation on earth, with instruction manuals printed in 54 different languages. But lately the bobbin has turned. Facing stiff competition from Japanese manufacturers, Singer's sales have slipped from 3 million sewing machines a year in the early 1970s to only 2 million today; and Singer, America's first multinational company, has seen their once-lucrative U.S. market eroded by cheap foreign imports.

Not that Singer is about to fold. They still sell plenty of machines in the developing countries of the Third World, where their vast market position is strong. And Singer's other businesses are doing well. Sewing machines and related products account for about half their sales. The rest comes from other consumer products and government contracts. Singer sells many of their products through their own retail stores—3,200 of them around the world. They do 42% of their business outside the United States.

Sears, Roebuck is their biggest customer, buying 8% of Singer's total output, which includes power tools (which Sears markets under their Craftsman trademark), vacuum cleaners, and a line of bedroom and dining room furniture (also sold by the Levitz and J. C. Penney chains). Oddly, Sears is also one of Singer's biggest competitors, stocking many of the Japanese sewing machines which have given Singer such a tough time lately.

Singer also makes air-conditioning and heating equipment; gas meters; thermostats; and a number of valves, electrical switches, and other components used in everything from dishwashers to auto dashboards. Most of their government work is done for either the military or NASA. They make the guidance system for the Trident missile, as well as navigation systems for several planes and ships. Apollo lunar modules have carried Singer instruments to the moon and back.

History. While imprisoned in an Indian jail, Mahatma Gandhi learned to sew on a Singer machine, which he called "one of the few useful things ever invented." Gandhi probably didn't know that its nineteenth-century inventor was a notorious profligate.

Isaac Merritt Singer was born in Oswego, New York to poor German immi-

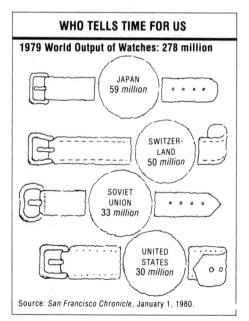

WHO TELLS TIME FOR US

1979 World Output of Watches: 278 million

JAPAN
59 *million*

SWITZER-LAND
50 *million*

SOVIET UNION
33 *million*

UNITED STATES
30 *million*

Source: *San Francisco Chronicle,* January 1, 1980.

grant parents in 1811. At the age of 12 he ran away and joined a troupe of traveling actors, memorizing huge chunks of Shakespeare and several temperance plays in spite of his almost complete illiteracy.

Although actor's pay was miniscule, Singer managed to avoid a regular job until 1835. After that he worked as a pressman, a ditchdigger, a sawmill worker, and—in his spare time—an inventor. By 1850 Singer had invented a rock-drill and a mechanical device for carving wood-block type. After patenting the carving device, Singer set off for Boston to sell it to type manufacturers. It was there that he took an interest in one of his prospective client's other businesses —a sewing machine repair shop.

The sewing machine was not a new idea. The first patent had been issued in England in 1790, and several other machines had come and gone since then. But none was reliable or convenient enough to be commercially successful. The most promising, with the first eye-pointed needle, had been invented by an American, Elias Howe, Jr., in 1846; it could sew only a few stitches at a time and spent most of its life in repair shops. When a friend told Singer he could make more money in a year with a practical sewing machine than he could in 50 with his wood-carver, Singer began to tinker. He later told the friend, "I don't care a damn for the invention. The dimes are what I'm after."

The Invention of the Vacuum Cleaner

In 1901 an Englishman named H. C. Booth, seized by inspiration, turned around in his seat in a Victoria Street restaurant and sucked vigorously on the plush upholstery. He nearly died of dust inhalation, but he had proved his point: suction was the best way to get dust out of furniture. At the time, homes, factories, and railroad cars were cleaned either with brooms, carpet sweepers, or with compressed air devices that blew the dust away in gusts.

The British consider Booth to be the father of the vacuum cleaner, but two Americans duplicated his insight the same year. Corrine Dufour invented a device that used an electric motor to suck dust onto a wet sponge. Her invention disappeared into the labyrinths of history.

Not so David E. Kenney's cleaner, which had a vacuum pump connected by tubing to a long nozzle. Kenney's device, like Booth's in England, was a huge roaring monster powered by a heavy motor and a big fan. Only by a great stretch of the imagination could it be called portable. Installed in the basements of homes, the power center of these early suction cleaners was connected by

pipelines to outlets in each room, where a cleaning nozzle could be attached whenever anyone wanted to vacuum. Some such systems actually transported household grime into sewer lines rather than into bags and advertised that "you never see it again."

In another adaptation the power plant was mounted on a large wheeled cart, pulled from house to house by teams of cleaning men, who operated long nozzles that ran from the cart parked in the street into the interiors of the homes.

Meanwhile, in 1907 an aging inventor named Murray Spangler, down on his luck, was working as janitor in a Canton, Ohio, department store. He developed a chronic cough from the clouds of dust stirred up by the carpet sweeper the store issued him to clean its vast expanses of carpet, so he fiddled with inventions for dustless cleaning. His first successful vacuum cleaner used an old motor from an electric fan placed on top of a soap box with its cracks sealed by adhesive tape and stapled to a piece of broom handle. A pillow case was attached for a dust bag. The contraption worked so well he decided to

refine and market it.

Spangler patented his invention in 1908 and formed the Electric Suction Sweeper Company. But his finances were shaky until he sold one of his cleaners to his cousin, whose husband was William H. Hoover, a saddlery maker. Hoover figured that vacuum cleaners had a brighter future than saddles. Late in 1908 he became president of the newly formed Hoover Company, with Spangler as superintendent.

The original Hoover Model O looked like a bagpipe attached to a cake box, but it embodied the basic principles of modern-day vacuum cleaners, sucking dust and grit into a cloth bag via power provided by a compact electric motor, with a swivel handle attached to the motor casing. The user could expect to hear "only the soft purr of the little motor," promised a 1909 Hoover ad in the *Saturday Evening Post*.

Sold in hardware stores, the new machines found few buyers at first. But when Hoover visited the stores and demonstrated the cleaners to housewives, their indifference changed to enthusiasm, and Hoover, who had the business acumen Spangler lacked,

Singer finished his machine in 1850. In principle, it was the same machine Singer makes today—complete with Howe's eye-pointed needle, a presser-foot, lock-stitching, a two-spool thread-feeder, and straight or curved-line sewing—and it made Singer a fortune almost overnight. Howe and two other manufacturers filed suit against Singer, claiming that parts of his machine infringed on their previous patents. To defend his new invention, Singer found a prim young lawyer named Edward Clark, who agreed to take the case in exchange for a share of the business.

Clark hurled as many patent infringement lawsuits at Howe and the others as they had thrown at Singer. Finally he brought them all together for a peace parlay, and from the meeting emerged the Sewing Machine Combination, America's first patent pool, which would jointly license sewing machine manufacturers for $15 per machine. Singer and Howe were to receive $5 each from the sale of any machine in the United States, with the other two manufacturers sharing the other $5. Satisfied, Clark went back to running the company.

Because of the exorbitant price—$125 at a time when the average American household earned only $500 annually—sewing machines had been available only to industries and professional tailors. Clark changed all that in the late 1850s by intro-

soon spotted the opportunities for selling his portable machines house-to-house. The company developed a high-powered direct sales organization for door-to-door trade, which flourished until after World War II, when vacuum cleaners became over-the-counter items in retail stores.

Rival companies were soon turning out vacuum cleaners that modified and refined the basic upright. In 1914 the Premier Vacuum Cleaner Co. of Cleveland was able to admonish women to buy by asking rhetorically, "Why sigh for the freedom from sweeping and dusting that 85,000 other housewives enjoy?" Premier's "dirt devourer" sold for a measly $25.

In 1924 an oddly-shaped vacuum cleaner, unlike any seen in the United States, arrived in America with a salesman named Gustaf Sahlin. Made by a Swedish company called Aktiebolaget Elektrolux, it was the first canister, or tank-type, vacuum cleaner to be sold in the United States. Marketed door-to-door, the cylinder-shaped Electrolux soon rivaled sales of its upright American cousins.

APPLIANCES ON THE MARCH INTO AMERICAN HOMES

	1968 (61.3 million homes)	1973 (69.4 million homes)	1978 (77.8 million homes)
AIR CONDITIONERS, ROOM	33.5%	48.9%	55.4%
CALCULATORS	—	26.2%	98.4%
COFFEEMAKERS, DRIP-TYPE	—	1.6%	30.0%
CORNPOPPERS	21.7%	36.3%	43.0%
DIGITAL WATCHES	—	0.5%	36.7%
DISHWASHERS	20.8%	34.3%	41.9%
DISPOSERS, FOOD WASTE	20.5%	35.3%	42.9%
DRYERS, CLOTHES (electric and gas)	38.8%	53.9%	60.3%
FREEZERS	28.5%	37.9%	44.9%
HAIRDRYERS, HAND-HELD	—	9.1%	35.8%
HAMBURGER MAKERS	—	—	15.5%
IRONS	99.5%	99.9%	99.9%
KNIVES, ELECTRIC	32.4%	39.4%	41.7%
MICROWAVE OVENS	—	1.2%	7.1%
MIXERS, FOOD	80.5%	87.3%	92.2%
RANGES, ELECTRIC, FREE-STANDING	36.2%	46.4%	50.8%
SLOW COOKERS	—	4.6%	34.2%
TELEVISIONS, COLOR	35.7%	67.1%	85.2%
TOASTERS	89.3%	96.5%	99.9%
WASHERS, CLOTHES	60.8%	67.8%	75.2%

Source: *Merchandising*, March 1979.

The first gas range was demonstrated at the London Crystal Palace Exposition in 1851.

ducing the first consumer installment plan in history. For $5 down and $3 a month, every American household could now afford a Singer machine. Clark's installment plan, coupled with an aggressive promotional campaign, gave the Singer company a decisive advantage over competitors.

Meanwhile, Clark's partner was involved in some private business of his own. By 1852, when he and Clark formed their partnership, Isaac Singer had already secretly fathered 11 of his eventual brood of 24 children by four different women, only one of whom he had bothered to marry. Through a series of complicated ruses, Singer managed to keep the women apart until 1860, when one of his consorts noticed him out for a ride with another woman. Putting two and two together, she set off in hot pursuit—screaming the sordid details of their relationship for all to hear. The police were called in to break up the violent argument that ensued. Newspaper stories followed, and within a few days the entire nation knew all about the sewing machine tycoon's sex life. Singer took the younger sister of one of his mistresses and fled to Europe.

The Pecksniffian Clark, along with the rest of New York society, was outraged; three years later the two men dissolved their partnership, each retaining some of the stock and selling the rest to their employees. Clark continued to have a hand in Singer operations and was largely responsible for building the company's first overseas plant in Glasgow, Scotland in 1867.

Singer died at his mansion in Devonshire, England in 1875; Clark died 7 years later. But the Singer machine continued to make new friends all over the world. South Pacific islanders once ranked the three basic essentials of life as food, shelter, and a Singer sewing machine. Singer was in Africa before Stanley ever set off in search of Livingstone. The Wright Brothers used a Singer to stitch the canvas wings of their airplane. And Admiral Richard Byrd took six Singer machines with him to Antarctica.

By the end of World War II the sewing machine market in America had matured. Most American households already had one of the durable machines and were reluctant to buy another. So Singer expanded their sewing operations overseas while diversifying into other businesses at home. They also spruced up their machines and began a campaign to convince Americans that home sewing was a fashionable leisure-time activity rather than a harsh necessity. The architect of this post–World War II transformation was an austere lawyer, Donald P. Kircher, who ruled Singer singlehandedly from 1958 to 1975, buying other companies (and selling them when they didn't work out) and hiring people from other companies (and firing them when they didn't work out). The Friden business machines company he bought in 1963 turned out to be a disaster, leading in 1974 to a $10 million loss, Singer's first deficit since 1917 when their Russian properties were seized. In 1975, Kircher came down with a series of illnesses and while he was on his hospital bed the directors looked for a successor. They found one at Xerox: Joseph B. Flavin, who was given a fancy contract and a mandate to turn the company around. He started by sloughing off the business machines operation, taking one of the largest losses in corporate history: $371 million. Flavin is still plugging leaks.

In 1978, in a tragic footnote to this era, Donald Kircher was shot to death at his summer home in Kingwood Township, New Jersey. The assailant was his brother-in-law, Charles J. Moeller, Jr., who had been evicted a few weeks earlier from a guest house on the Kircher estate.

Reputation. Although Singer machines retain their reputation for reliability, the company as a whole seems to be sewing in circles.

What they own. The recent decline in sales has caused Singer to either close or cut back production of industrial sewing machine plants in Clydebank, Scotland, and St. Jean, Canada, as well as the main plant in Elizabeth, New Jersey. In addition, they've closed 150 of their American stores and now have only 800 outlets in the United States, compared to 1,400 in Canada and Europe and 900 throughout the rest of the world.

Who owns and runs the company. Only 3 of Singer's 13 directors are company officers; 8 others are outside business executives, and the remaining director is actress Polly Bergen, who also does some advertising and promotional work for the company. The directors and officers together hold about 2% of Singer's stock.

One of Sunbeam's original products was this dog-driven sheep shearing device used in the late 1890s.

In the public eye. Singer came forward in 1977 to disclose to the Justice Department that two managers had held unauthorized meetings with a competitor about the pricing of gas meters. As a result, Singer gained lenient treatment when an antitrust action was brought in 1978: they were named in a civil complaint along with two other gas meter manufacturers, Rockwell International and Textron, but were excluded from the criminal suit filed against Rockwell and Textron.

Where they're going. A 1978 *Wall Street Journal* article concluded that Singer may have to worry about a takeover attempt. An unnamed analyst was quoted as saying, "[Singer] doesn't have a balance sheet to write home about, but Flavin can't stand there and not look over his shoulder." Flavin, however, thinks the sewing machine business will frighten away any suitor. "Who would want to solve that one?" he asked in 1980.

Stock performance. Singer stock bought for $1,000 in 1970 sold for $109 on January 2, 1980.

Access. 8 Stamford Forum, Stamford, Connecticut 06904; (203) 356-4200.

Consumer brands.

Singer sewing machines; Manor House furniture; and Caramate sound/slide projectors.

Sunbeam

Sales: $1.3 billion
Profits: $47.8 million
Forbes 500 rank: 374
Rank in small appliances: 1
Founded: 1893
Employees: 29,000
Headquarters: Chicago, Illinois

What they do: Looking for a bathroom scale with digital readout? An electronic desk-top cigarette lighter? Or perhaps a talking barometer with miniradio tuned to continuous U.S. Weather Service broadcasts? With a keen sense of the American consumer's taste for novelty and convenience, Sunbeam has successfully designed and marketed scores of such exotic and unusual items, as well as standard household equipment like irons, toasters, mixers, and coffeemakers. Four-fifths of their sales come from consumer products, which they make under their own name and brands like Oster, Mixmaster, and Northern. They sell almost as many of these household gadgets overseas as they do in the United States. The rest of their business comes from industrial and commercial products such as furnaces for the aluminum industry, frying machines for fast-food restaurants, and reach-in refrigerators for 7-Eleven stores.

History. Sunbeam goes back to the Chicago of the 1890s, where John K. Stewart and Thomas J. Clark made mechanical horse clippers. By 1897 they had expanded into sheep-shearing machines and flexible shafts for grinders and drills, and they incorporated as the Chicago Flexible Shaft Company. Soon they were making industrial furnaces and heaters for horse-drawn carriages as well.

In 1910, to offset the seasonal demand for livestock barbering equipment, they made their first appliance: an electric iron. This product did so well that the company plunged enthusiastically into the appliance business, marketing electric mixers (1930), pop-up toasters (1935), coffeemakers (1938), and waffle bakers (1940).

They started calling their appliances Sunbeam in their ads in 1921, but it wasn't until 1946 that the name was given to the company. Then, catering to the postwar demand for consumer products, they came out with a flurry of convenience devices. In 1950 they made an egg cooker and the next year a baby bottle warmer. Sunbeam was the first on the market with an electric frying pan (1953), an electric razor for women (1955), and a portable hair dryer (1956). Then came electric can openers, knife sharpeners, blenders, rotisseries, and snow throwers. Now they make hundreds of different products, with new ones coming

along all the time. "Our distributors don't like it; our dealers don't like it; and we don't like it either," chairman Robert P. Gwinn has said. "But new products are our lifeblood. We introduce them to keep our consumers happy."

In 1968 Sunbeam took the first steps out of the consumer product field in 50 years, picking up the Illinois Water Treatment Company (water softeners) and Thermco Products (industrial furnaces). In 1972 they added the John Zink Company (burners and air conditioning) and Bally Case & Cooler (commercial refrigerators).

Reputation. By "thinking small" and paying close attention to product quality, Sunbeam has been able to survive, even flourish, in a business that has brought down giants like Westinghouse, Frigidaire, Admiral, and Philco.

What they own. Forty-six plants in the United States (many of them in the South) and 31 plants in foreign countries, from Australia (where they first established a subsidiary in 1914) to West Germany.

Who owns and runs the company. Robert Gwinn, who turned 70 in 1978, has been on the board since 1952 and still runs the company. In 1971 he moved from president to chairman to sidestep Sunbeam's mandatory retirement rule of 65, which doesn't apply to the chairman. Gwinn's older brother, H. C. Gwinn, also sits on the board. The biggest block of stock (6.3%) is controlled by the First National Bank of Chicago. Jacqueline Zink of Tulsa controls the second biggest block (5.5%), which her family got when Sunbeam traded more than 1 million shares of stock for the John Zink subsidiary.

In the public eye. Sunbeam turned the gadgets on their own employees in the 1950s when they noticed that a lot of electric razor parts were disappearing from the factory. The machinists' union balked when Sunbeam tried to make all their shaver department workers take lie detector tests.

Where they're going. In the past, *Forbes* has observed, electrical gadget companies have "found out that Americans can get along very nicely without them when a recession squeezes the family budget." Sunbeam has come through past recessions better than most of their competitors, but their industrial and commercial divisions now provide them with an anchor in economic storms.

Stock performance. Sunbeam stock bought for $1,000 in 1970 sold for $688 on January 2, 1980.

Access. 5400 West Roosevelt Road, Chicago, Illinois 60650; (312) 854-3500. Address questions or complaints to Wayne R. Smith, Director, Consumer Affairs, Sunbeam Corporation, 2001 South York Road, Oak Brook, Illinois 60521.

Consumer brands.

Sunbeam, Mixmaster, Le Chef, Oster, and Northern appliances; Hanson scales; Springfield thermometers and barometers; Neosho barbecue grills; Aircap mowers; Bennett-Ireland fireplace equipment.

Whirlpool
CORPORATION

Sales: $2.3 billion
Profits: $110.9 million
Forbes 500 rank: 235
Rank in laundry appliances: 1
Founded: 1911
Employees: 22,200
Headquarters: Benton Harbor, Michigan

What they do. Whirlpool ranks second to General Electric in the appliance business. But unlike GE, Whirlpool's life begins and ends with appliances. Their principal customer is Sears, Roebuck, the nation's largest retailer. Sears sells appliances made by Whirlpool under the Kenmore name. This interdependence began when the appliance maker was five years old and has been lessened as Whirlpool sold more and more of their products under their own name. Sears now accounts for half of Whirlpool's sales, compared to two-thirds 10 years ago. Under their own brand name Whirlpool now sells a full line of household appliances: washing machines, dryers, freezers, refrigerators, air conditioners, ranges, trash compactors, microwave ovens, and food waste disposers.

History. It was in St. Joseph, on the shore of Lake Michigan, that two brothers, Fred and Lou Upton, and their uncle, Emory Upton, set up the Upton Machine Company in 1911 to make a hand-operated washing machine. They also made air rifles, Boy Scout camp kits, and toys. In 1916 they made their first sale to Sears, Roebuck, across the lake in Chicago. By 1925 the only washing machines sold by Sears came from the Uptons. In 1929 the Uptons merged their operations with the Nineteen Hundred Washer Company, losing their name but becoming part of the world's largest laundry appliance company.

The old relationship continued; Sears, Roebuck was still the mainstay of Nineteen Hundred in 1947, when the decision was made to market a washing machine under a new name: Whirlpool. By 1950 the product had done well enough to prompt the company to adopt its name. The move to sell under their own name did not jeopardize the bread-and-butter Sears business. Elisha Gray, II, who was then president of Whirlpool, had begun his career with Sears and was able to convince his old employer that the greater efficiencies achieved by increased production would also benefit the giant retailer.

Here's the early Whirlpool—an electric washing machine made in 1911 by Upton Machine Company, predecessor of today's Whirlpool Corporation. The company says to pay no heed to the reference to Chicago on the front of the machine—"nobody really knows why it's there." The machine was built in St. Joseph, Michigan, twin city of Benton Harbor, still the Whirlpool headquarters.

"Take Courage, Great Army of Washers"

"Mothers, Wives, Daughters, and all the great army of Washers, take courage," exclaimed an 1870 ad for a primitive washing machine designed to replace the scrubbing board. The ad claimed that the "Little Joker" would save "labor, doctor's bills, soap, fuel, cross babies, blue Mondays, cold dinners, cross women, sour men, weary aching limbs, sickness, suffering, and death caused by over-work, exposure, and colds."

If these seem extravagant claims for a device that was no more than a hand-pumped agitator clamped to the side of a wooden washtub, consider what washday had been like before. One housewife of the early nineteenth century wrote instructions for laundering that detail a grim Monday struggle: hauling water in buckets; heating huge cauldrons over outdoor wood fires; and hand scrubbing, bleaching, and bluing, culminating in hand wringing. Ending on a note of heroic virtue, the writer advised the sufferer to brew herself a cup of tea, sit on the front porch, "rock a spell, and count your Blessings."

Efforts to liberate mothers, wives, and daughters from this weekly ordeal produced a series of weird contraptions, starting with the first washing machine patent in 1805. Many early washers were no real improvement over the scrubbing board. An 1846 version, for example, looked like a small derrick atop a basin, was hand-cranked, and worked by scrunching the clothes to and fro over a bed of rollers.

Around 1900 various hand-cranked machines began to displace the scrubbing board, and by 1916 the Pittsburgh Gage and Supply Co. was able to advertise its Gainaday electric washing machine as a replacement for unreliable washerwomen. The Gainaday had a revolving cylinder and needed no cranking, but it was far from automatic. Not until 1939 did the long line of washer experiments produce a practical automatic machine with timing devices to change speeds and expel water without human intervention. At that point, the great army of washers could be said to be freed from the perils of cross babies, cold dinners, and weary aching limbs.

Gray soon decided to make Whirlpool a full-line appliance manufacturer. He accomplished this in 1955 by acquiring other companies, the key ones being Seeger Refrigeration and the appliance businesses (air conditioning and ranges) of RCA. In 1966 Whirlpool purchased a majority interest in Warwick Electronics, Sears's major supplier of TV sets. But Sears turned increasingly to Japanese suppliers, and in 1976 Whirlpool sold the TV business to Japan's Sanyo Electric. The Japanese quickly turned Warwick's Arkansas plant from a money-loser into a profitable operation.

Reputation. Whirlpool is known for making top-quality products and for being responsive to consumer needs and complaints. "We try to operate with the heart and sensitivity of a small company and the brains of a big one," said one Whirlpool executive.

Who owns and runs the company. The largest single shareholder is Robert C. Upton, 64-year-old son of founder Lou Upton. Steve Upton, the son of founder Fred Upton, is vice-president of consumer affairs at Whirlpool. Two Sears officials sit on the board.

In the public eye. Whirlpool has a corporate code of ethics that states: "No employee of this company will ever be called upon to do anything that is morally, ethically or legally wrong." Yet in 1980 the Supreme Court ruled against Whirlpool in a case that upheld the right of workers to refuse to perform tasks they believe pose a danger of threat or serious injury. The Labor Department had sued Whirlpool after two maintenance workers at the company's Marion, Ohio, plant refused to step onto a wire mesh screen 20 feet above the factory floor. Earlier several employees had fallen through the screen, one to his death.

Where they're going. They appear to be content with their double life as a major seller of brand-name appliances and a major supplier to Sears, Roebuck.

Stock performance. Whirlpool stock bought for $1,000 in 1970 sold for $957 on January 2, 1980.

Major employment centers. Evansville, Indiana; Fort Smith, Arkansas; and Marion, Ohio.

Access. Benton Harbor, Michigan 49022; (616) 926-5000. Whirlpool was the first company in the industry to install a nationwide toll-free number for consumers: the Cool-Line. According to the company, they received 170,000 calls on this line in 1979. The numbers are (800) 632-2243 for Michigan residents, (800) 253-1121 for residents of Alaska and Hawaii, and (800) 253-1301 for the rest of the country.

Consumer brands.

Whirlpool appliances; Thomas and Vox electronic organs.

White Consolidated Industries, Inc.

Sales: $2.0 billion
Profits: $62.9 million
Forbes 500 rank: 263
Rank in home appliances: 3
Founded: 1866
Employees: 31,000
Headquarters: Cleveland, Ohio

What they do. Millions of Americans use one or more of their home appliances every day, but White Consolidated Industries is hardly a household word. This low-profile but aggressive conglomerate has specialized in taking over ailing companies and erasing all traces of red ink through relentless cost cutting.

White Consolidated has absorbed and resuscitated an appliance hall of fame, including such names as Kelvinator, Gibson, Westinghouse, Bendix, Philco, Hamilton, Cold-Guard, Perfection, Vesta, Crosely, and most recently Frigidaire. And besides the famous brands they've salvaged, they sell almost as many appliances under the private labels of mass-merchandisers such as Sears, J. C. Penney, Montgomery Ward, Gambles, and Western Auto. They also make sewing machines under five of their own brand names.

White Consolidated has picked up 20 companies that produce a wide range of equipment for heavy industry, accounting for more than one-quarter of their total sales. They make printing presses and duplicating machines under the names ATF, Davidson, Ditto, and King Press; commercial laundry washers under the White-Westinghouse brand; and Typhoon centralized air-conditioning units.

History. Originally established in 1866 to manufacture and market the sewing machine that Thomas H. White had successfully developed, the Cleveland company branched into automatic lathes, screw machines, roller skates, and bicycles. Six years after Thomas's three sons created their first White Steamer, a water-powered automobile, the auto manufacturing became a separate business; it still exists today as White Motor Corp. and makes heavy duty trucks and tractors.

Tensor's Annual Meeting Hits Snag—Nobody Came

Tensor Corp. officials stood poised to shed some light on the company's operations at its annual meeting, but nobody came.

Well, at least not enough for a quorum. There was only one shareholder there who wasn't an officer, director or broker, Jay Monroe, president of the lamp maker, said. "He was in the neighborhood; he came for the danish," Mr. Monroe said with a moan.

"Nobody cares."

It isn't that Tensor didn't want anybody. The company spent $850 waxing the floor, washing and painting the walls and even installing an air conditioner. "Everybody in the place got all dressed up," Mr. Monroe said.

Still, the meeting Tuesday was held in the company's Brooklyn factory, which Mr. Monroe conceded isn't the lushest location. The company came up short, by about 20,000 votes, of the required quorum of 50% of its 475,463 shares outstanding. "We're just going to forget the whole thing," Mr. Monroe said. The nine incumbent directors will serve for another year.

Reprinted from the *Wall Street Journal*, May 17, 1979.

The White Sewing Machine Co. was still relatively small (about $20 million in annual sales) when Ed Reddig became chairman in 1957. In short order, the former accountant closed down all of the company's U.S. manufacturing operations, throwing 5,000 employees out of work, and started making White sewing machines in the Far East with cheaper labor.

For the next decade Reddig warmed up by buying 18 small industrial manufacturing concerns. In 1966 he took over Whitin Machine Works, a troubled textile machinery maker with sales almost double those of White at the time. Then came Hupp's Gibson appliances (1967), Studebaker's Franklin appliances (1967), American Motors' Kelvinator appliances (1968), Bendix's refrigerator products (1971), Athens Stove Works (1973), and Westinghouse's major appliances (1976, now called White-Westinghouse).

In a matter of days after White Consolidated takes over a company, heads begin to roll. 70% of Kelvinator's administrative staff was thrown out within a month; nearly 40% of Westinghouse's workers at three big plants in the Midwest were shown the door in the first weeks.

Reddig's brutal tactics sometimes backfired. Three companies fought successfully to prevent becoming part of the White Consolidated family—Mack Trucks (1967), Allis-Chalmers (1969), and White Motor Corp. (1971 and again in 1976). Mack Trucks president Zenon C. R. Hanson explained to the Wall Street Journal that he resisted Reddig's overtures because, "If we're going to get into bed with someone, it's going to be a mature Park Avenue glamour girl, not a Times Square streetwalker." (Mack Trucks now belongs to the Signal Companies.)

In terms of dollars and cents in the corporate coffers, however, Reddig's tough methods paid off. Every one of the failing companies turned a profit soon after White acquired it. Westinghouse's appliance division, for instance, was losing $2 million a

month before their takeover. In three months White-Westinghouse was making a handsome profit.

By the time Reddig retired in 1976, White Consolidated had passed the $1 billion mark in annual sales. Reddig's hand-picked successors followed his lead by buying Ford's appliance division, including part of Philco, in 1977, and two years later by taking over General Motors' Frigidaire.

Reputation. Ed Reddig died in 1979, but what the Wall Street Journal refers to as "the Reddig shakeout" lives on to send shivers through the appliance industry. In Reddig's words, "Hell, we look at a company with a problem the same way a surgeon looks at a patient with cancer. The earlier you get the damned thing, the less it's going to spread."

What they own. Most of White's 15 home appliance manufacturing plants are located in the Midwest and the South.

Who owns and runs the company. A White board member says that "Reddig was a one-man management. He made every decision." Though no one man has emerged to fill his shoes, the three top officers spent a combined total of more than 50 years "suffering, bleeding, and dying under Ed Reddig," and are committed to his business practices.

Most of White's board of directors do not work for the company. In fact, these outside directors cast the deciding votes in 1976 against Reddig's proposed merger with White Motor Corp. Reddig was seriously ill at the time, and several accounts of the board meeting contend that Reddig could have swung the meeting for the merger had he been there.

In the public eye. Although 19,900 of their 31,000 employees are covered by union contracts, White Consolidated takes a hard line in labor negotiations. They are more than willing to withstand strikes to get their way. Not long after White took over Westinghouse's appliances, the new owners absorbed a three-month strike of workers at six White-Westinghouse plants. White officials had tried to force workers at each plant to negotiate separately for new contracts instead of accepting a common national one. According to Reddig's successor as

American manufacturers exported 371,000 refrigerators, 883,000 room air conditioners, 1.1 million electric clocks, 750,000 vacuum cleaners, and 136,000 microwave ovens in 1978.

chairman, Roy H. Holdt, "Without some strikes, we might not have been able to compete in the marketplace." Because of their labor stance one union organizer says, "White is red; White is bloody."

Where they're going. Any appliance company that begins to falter had better watch out. White is still interested in gobbling up more brand names.

Stock performance. White Consolidated stock bought for $1,000 in 1970 sold for $1,247 on January 2, 1980.

Access. 11770 Berea Road, Cleveland, Ohio 44111; (216) 252-3700.

Consumer brands.

Home appliances: Kelvinator; Gibson; White-Westinghouse; Bendix; Philco; Hamilton; Cold-Guard; Perfection; Vesta; Crosely; Frigidaire; Leonard; Roy.
Sewing machines: White; Domestic; Elna; Universal; Hilton.

Sales: $1.1 billion
Profits: $19 million
Forbes 500 rank: 431
Rank in color television: 2
Founded: 1918
Employees: 23,004
Headquarters: Glenview, Illinois

What they do. Zenith is an anomaly in an age of conglomerates. They make and sell television sets and radios, and that's about it. The company managed to maintain the leading position in the color television set market from 1972 to 1978, a remarkable feat in a cutthroat industry. But RCA, Zenith's longtime rival, took over the number 1 spot in 1979. Now that electronic manufacturing is based in Taiwan, Korea, and Japan, no radios are made in the United States anymore. All Zenith's radios, stereos, and video player-recorders are produced abroad.

History. Zenith's history mirrors the history of radio and television. It began with

an amateur radio station that Karl Hassel and R. H. G. Mathews ran in Chicago in 1918. Five years later the Zenith Radio Corporation began making and selling radio equipment. They built the first portable radio in 1924 and introduced pushbutton tuning (1927).

Zenith pioneered television and FM radio just before World War II, then produced radar and communications equipment for the war effort. Their greatest contribution to postwar culture came in 1948, when they introduced their first line of black-and-white television receivers and bought the Rauland Corporation of Chicago, which made picture tubes. By 1959 Zenith sold more black-and-white televisions than anyone else and have retained that position for 20 consecutive years. In 1961 they entered the color TV market and developed the FM broadcasting system approved by the FCC.

Zenith's story in the 1970s, however, is a fight for life against the huge influx of cheaper Japanese televisions. John Nevin, former chairman of Zenith (and now president of Firestone), filed antitrust suits against the Japanese companies, testified against them in Congress, nagged the U.S. Treasury and Justice departments, and sang the praises of American-made products. His aim was to stop what he called "the predatory pricing" and "dumping" practices of Japanese companies (by which they would sell a product in the United States for less than it was worth in their own country). As American television companies suffered layoffs, losses, mergers, and takeovers (often by Japanese companies), Nevin demanded that the federal government enforce its 1971 antidumping laws.

Nevin's crusading bore fruit. The Japanese were adjudged to be dumping their sets here—and after negotiation they agreed to put a ceiling on their exports to the United States. But this action may have come too late for Zenith.

The United States imported 6 million black-and-white TV sets, 2.8 million color sets, 530,000 videotape recorders, 22.7 million calculators, 3 million CB radios, 18.5 million hairdryers, and 3.9 million electric shavers in 1978.

In 1978 Zenith's profits were lower than they were in 1968, on about the same amount of sales. The all-American company laid off one-quarter of their American employees and started making some of their color TV sets in Mexico and Taiwan.

Reputation. With big American companies like RCA and GE on one side, and the Japanese manufacturers on the other, Zenith seems like a small, embattled business trying to grope through a field of giants.

What they own. Ten plants in the Chicago area; others in Missouri, Indiana, Pennsylvania, Texas, Mexico, Canada, and Taiwan. They also have Zenith's image as a solid, established, American company, which chairman Joseph Wright calls "an asset that doesn't show on the balance sheet, [but] the strongest thing the company has."

Who owns and runs the company. The all-male board includes John Johnson, former publisher of *Ebony* magazine. Zenith was the first national company to advertise in *Ebony*.

In the public eye. Zenith is aggressively Chicagoan. Former chairman Nevin once joked to the *New York Times*, "When we built a plant in Missouri, some of our people considered it an overseas assignment." They have the highest percentage of black workers of any major company in Chicago.

Where they're going. Zenith recently branched out by acquiring Heath, makers of do-it-yourself electronics kits and personal microcomputers. But they're still essentially a one-product company, and right now they look like a sitting duck for takeover by another company—possibly Japanese.

Stock performance. Zenith stock bought for $1,000 in 1970 sold for $295 on January 2, 1980.

Access. 1000 Milwaukee Avenue, Glenview, Illinois 60025; (312) 391-7000.

Consumer brands.

Zenith and Heathkit home entertainment.

TOP 20 UTILITIES

Sales/Profits

1. PACIFIC GAS & ELECTRIC (*San Francisco*) $4.3 *billion* / $458 *million*
2. CONSOLIDATED EDISON (*New York*) $3.3 *billion* / $324 *million*
3. SOUTHERN COMPANY (*Atlanta*) $3.1 *billion* / $219 *million*
4. COLUMBIA GAS SYSTEM (*Wilmington*) $2.9 *billion* / $153 *million*
5. AMERICAN ELECTRIC POWER (*New York*) $2.8 *billion* / $260 *million*
6. COMMONWEALTH EDISON (*Chicago*) $2.7 *billion* / $297 *million*
7. SOUTHERN CALIFORNIA EDISON (*Rosemead, California*) $2.6 *billion* / $346 *million*
8. AMERICAN NATURAL RESOURCES (*Detroit*) $2.5 *billion* / $149 *million*
9. INTERNORTH (*Omaha*) $2.5 *billion* / $186 *million*
10. PEOPLES GAS (*Chicago*) $2.4 *billion* / $140 *million*
11. PUBLIC SERVICE ELECTRIC & GAS (*Newark*) $2.5 *billion* / $233 *million*
12. PACIFIC LIGHTING (*Los Angeles*) $2.2 *billion* / $98 *million*
13. CONSOLIDATED NATURAL GAS (*Pittsburgh*) $2.0 *billion* / $128 *million*
14. CONSUMERS POWER (*Jackson, Michigan*) $2.0 *billion* / $204 *million*
15. FLORIDA POWER & LIGHT (*Miami*) $1.9 *billion* / $205 *million*
16. HOUSTON INDUSTRIES $1.8 *billion* / $162 *million*
17. MIDDLE SOUTH UTILITIES (*New Orleans*) $1.8 *billion* / $182 *million*
18. TEXAS UTILITIES (*Dallas*) $1.8 *billion* / $211 *million*
19. VIRGINIA ELECTRIC & POWER (*Richmond*) $1.7 *billion* / $196 *million*
20. DETROIT EDISON $1.7 *billion* / $176 *million*

Based on 1979 sales and profits figures.

3

ALCHEMY: LOOKING, FEELING, AND SMELLING GOOD

Beauty Sellers

AVON

Sales: $2.4 billion
Profits: $251 million
Forbes 500 rank: 221
Rank in cosmetics: 1
Rank in costume jewelry: 1
Founded: 1886
Employees: 31,000
Headquarters: New York, New York

What they do. The Avon Lady may be the most ubiquitous sales figure of all time. There are a million of her (most of whom are housewives) selling 700 kinds of cosmetics, fragrances, toiletries, and costume jewelry in 26 countries. She plies her wares everywhere, from a boat in the canals of Bangkok, to the door of a farmhouse in North Dakota, to the most distant reaches of New Zealand.

Avon relies exclusively on a legion of Avon Ladies, rather than on any stores, to sell their products, all manufactured in Avon plants. To become an Avon Lady, a woman must pay a one-time franchise fee of $10, for which she receives a starter kit of products and an exclusive territory of some 150 households. She sells door to door within her territory from catalogs and samples, writes up her orders, and sends them to an Avon distribution center. When Avon delivers the order to the saleswoman, she delivers it to the customer and collects payment on the spot. The Avon Lady receives no salary or stipend from the company, only a commission—40% if she sells at least $100 worth of goods every two weeks, otherwise, only 25%.

It's an enormously lucrative system for Avon, which has consistently been one of the most profitable companies in the land. However, the average Avon representative takes home less than $1,900 a year. Not surprisingly, the annual turnover rate of Avon Ladies is somewhere between 100% and 150%.

Avon is so big that, just by adding costume jewelry to the line, the company quickly became that product's number 1 distributor.

The total line carried by Avon representatives includes perfumes, colognes, sachets, lotions, soaps, powders, lipsticks, eye shadows and mascaras, skin-care products, nail- and hand-care products, sham-

Mrs. P.F.E. Albee was the first Avon Lady. She began selling the Little Dot Perfume Set in 1886 in New York. She also recruited others to sell at the same time, enabling Avon to bypass the retailer. To this day Avon products have never been sold in stores.

History. In the 1880s David H. McConnell was a door-to-door book salesman in New York. To get his foot in the door, he filled small vials with perfume, which he gave to housewives who let him pitch his books. In a very short time he figured out that perfume was a bigger hit than books, and in 1886 McConnell, then 28, founded the California Perfume Company, a name he chose to evoke an image of clean, fresh air.

The first Avon Lady in fact, if not in name, was Mrs. P. F. E. Albee, who sold McConnell's Little Dot Perfume Set door to door and recruited other women to join her. It was she who developed for McConnell the selling network that is the fiber of Avon today, as well as the Avon representative image as a friendly neighbor rather than an itinerant peddler. She died in obscurity in 1914.

In 1928 the company introduced the Avon line of products, including a toothbrush and talc. The company responded to the Depression by telling representatives to canvas their territory every three weeks rather than monthly. The result was a sales increase of 70% while America went broke.

In 1935 Avon ventured into the media, sponsoring a national radio program, "Friends," a twice-weekly show of "music and chatter." In the mid-fifties Avon expanded overseas, where today they net more than 40% of their sales.

In 1954 Avon launched an intensive TV ad campaign, "Avon Calling," using an unforgettable ding-dong chime. The mastermind behind this classic was Monroe Dreher, whose ad agency got the account after he and company president David McConnell, Jr., the founder's son, had developed a golfing friendship at the Montclair Golf Club in New Jersey.

Avon prospered for the next two decades, but in the early seventies their sales were off for the first time. According to some observers, the company was partially a victim of women's liberation, which raised the level of expectations of Avon's principal market—the suburban housewife. Many former customers were no longer home when the Avon Lady came calling because they were now at work themselves. What's more, the company was having problems attracting and keeping saleswomen, who were often referred to contemptuously as ding-dong ladies.

Avon responded by reshaping their product line, cutting territory size for more in-

poo, hair conditioners, brushes, after-shave lotions, shaving creams, deodorants, oral hygiene products, room sprays, baby products, rings, earrings, bracelets, and necklaces.

In addition to these products, Avon sells men's and women's clothing (Family Fashions) by mail order—and Geni tableware. Geni goods are sold like Tupperware: an Avon sales representative throws a party to sell Geni to her friends and neighbors. Geni is the one Avon enterprise operating in the red.

In 1979 Avon bought the prestigious Tiffany & Company, seller of precious jewelry, sterling silverware, goldware, watches, china, glassware, stationery, clocks, and other fine things. Tiffany's famous main store is on New York's Fifth Avenue, and it has branches in Atlanta, Beverly Hills, Chicago, Houston, and San Francisco.

> **Alberto-Culver of Melrose Park, Illinois, brings you VO5 hair products, the Sugar Twin sugar substitute, Milani salad dressings, and Frye boots.**

tensive selling, and nearly tripling their U.S. advertising. In the course of one 1979 campaign Avon estimated that a typical U.S. woman would see or hear Avon plugs at least 19 times.

Reputation. Avon is as cautious and conservative as the mature, middle-American image they cultivate for their Avon Ladies. They let others introduce new products and only market their own versions when they've been tried and tested. Avon marketing chief James E. Clitter explains, "What does mid-America, average everybody, want? What's comfortable at the PTA? The average American is not the New York City swinger."

What they own. Avon has four U.S. manufacturing plants. Their Springdale, Ohio, cosmetic plant is the largest of its kind in the world: 23 football games could be played simultaneously under its one roof. They own seven U.S. distribution branches, where offices are located and merchandise is received, warehoused, and shipped to Avon representatives. The company also owns 16 international factories.

Who owns and runs the company. 9½ %

of Avon's stock is owned by brothers Hays and W. Van Alan Clark, grandsons of founder David McConnell. Both Clarks sit on the Avon board.

In the public eye. A brochure for new Avon recruits proclaims, "It's your own piece of the great American dream."

Avon's critics contend that piece can turn out to be small, indeed. The *Wall Street Journal* figured out that in 1977 Avon ambassadors' "average take-home income is probably around $1.20 an hour"—far below the then-minimum wage of $2.30 an hour. Two years later *Forbes* offered a similar portrait of the typical Avon Lady: "The average representative is about 35, married, and sells roughly $4,900, at retail prices, per year. She takes home some $1,912, and out of that . . . she pays her taxes, for her samples, sales books, travel expenses, and telephone calls." *Forbes* estimated that the turnover rate of Avon representatives is more than 100% a year, though, it added, "Some cosmetics industry analysts . . . estimate it runs closer to 150%."

Despite Avon's dependence on the good will of women, it was not until 1972 that any woman sat on their board of directors. They were in the process of negotiating a

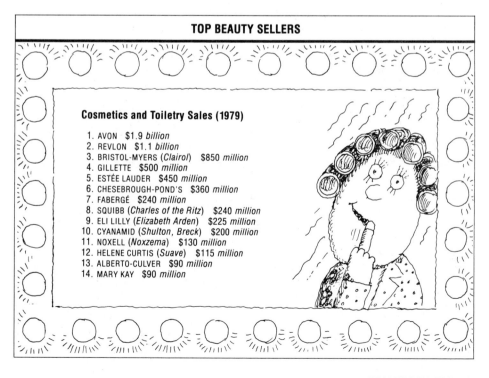

TOP BEAUTY SELLERS

Cosmetics and Toiletry Sales (1979)

1. AVON $1.9 *billion*
2. REVLON $1.1 *billion*
3. BRISTOL-MYERS (*Clairol*) $850 *million*
4. GILLETTE $500 *million*
5. ESTÉE LAUDER $450 *million*
6. CHESEBROUGH-POND'S $360 *million*
7. FABERGÉ $240 *million*
8. SQUIBB (*Charles of the Ritz*) $240 *million*
9. ELI LILLY (*Elizabeth Arden*) $225 *million*
10. CYANAMID (*Shulton, Breck*) $200 *million*
11. NOXELL (*Noxzema*) $130 *million*
12. HELENE CURTIS (*Suave*) $115 *million*
13. ALBERTO-CULVER $90 *million*
14. MARY KAY $90 *million*

sex discrimination suit at the time. Today there are two women on the 14-member board.

Avon also ran afoul of the Food and Drug Administration, which forced recall of seven products between 1968 and 1971, including Avon baby powder for contamination that could cause respiratory infection.

Avon chairman David Mitchell got some headlines in 1978 when he resigned from the board of J. P. Stevens under heavy pressure from the Amalgamated Clothing and Textile Workers Union. In his departing statement Mitchell expressed his "highest regard" for the Stevens management in their struggle to avoid unionization.

Where they're going. Avon's purchase of Tiffany's marks a sharp break with the past and may augur a twin-sided movement into higher-priced, high-fashion merchandise and the retail over-the-counter business. But the Value Line Investment Survey believes "foreign markets are the key to the company's growth." Avon now does 41% of their sales overseas.

Stock performance. Avon stock bought for $1,000 in 1970 sold for $459 on January 2, 1980.

Access. 9 West 57th Street, New York, New York 10019; (212) 593-4017.

Consumer brands.

Fragrances: Zany, Tempo, Ariane, Candid, Emprise, Timeless, Unspoken, Sweet Honesty, Come Summer, Sonnet, Honeysuckle, Hawaiian White Ginger, Apple Blossom, Unforgettable, Bird of Paradise, Moonwind, Field Flowers, Charisma, Occur!, Topaze, Cotillion, Here's My Heart, and Roses.
Men's toiletries: Trazarra, Clint, Everest, Wild Country, Deep Woods.
Other products: Family Fashions by Avon, Geni; Avon jewelry and cosmetics.
Jewelry store: Tiffany's.

Chesebrough-Pond's Inc.

Sales: $1.2 billion
Profits: $82.6 million
Forbes 500 rank: 404
Rank in cold cream: 1
Rank in spaghetti sauce: 1
Rank in petroleum jelly: 1
Rank in nail polish remover: 1
Rank in hand-care lotion: 1
Rank in cotton swabs: 1
Rank in bath beads: 1
Rank in home permanents: 1
Founded: 1846
Employees: 18,500
Headquarters: Greenwich, Connecticut

What they do. It's a triumph of modern corporate alchemy: Ragu spaghetti sauce combined with Vaseline petroleum jelly, Adolph's seasonings, Wind Song perfume, Cutex nail polish, Health-tex children's

Trout and Movie Tears: The Versatility of Vaseline

Robert A. Chesebrough was a 22-year-old chemist in 1859 when he accidentally discovered the waxy substance that oilmen called rod wax because it collected on the rods of oil pumps. Chesebrough refined a sample of this petroleum residue, tested it on himself and acquaintances, and decided he had discovered a wonder cure for scrapes, cuts, and burns. When the medical establishment of the day proved cool to his breakthrough, he took to the roads of upper New York state with horse and wagon, handing out thousands of jars of his "Vaseline" to everyone who would try it.

Public demand for Chesebrough's product grew phenomenally as people found that Vaseline soothed their minor wounds far better than most nineteenth-century nostrums. Chesebrough deployed a dozen horse-and-buggy hawkers to peddle his balm through New Jersey and Connecticut, and soon Vaseline was selling at the rate of a jar a minute.

As the Chesebrough Manufacturing Company grew from horse-and-buggy enterprise into corporate giant, letters sent to the company by Vaseline users revealed that Chesebrough's translucent jelly possessed a versatility

garments, Q-tips, and Weejuns loafers. Chesebrough-Pond's makes these and other products in 25 countries and sells them in 140. Chesebrough-Pond's breaks down their sales dollar like this: health and beauty products, 20%; packaged foods, 19%; Health-tex (children's clothes), 16%; Prince Matchabelli (fragrances, cosmetics), 10%; Bass (shoes), 3%; hospital products (thermometers, wound dressings), 3%; international, 29%.

Chesebrough-Pond's boasts that 90% of American families use their products, which, they say, "work, like the competitive free-enterprise system which produced them."

History. Companies, unlike people, can often decide when they were born. So Chesebrough-Pond's celebrated their 100th birthday in 1980 even though their roots go back much farther. The year they used to claim for their founding was 1846, when Theron T. Pond, a chemist in Utica, New York, brewed a new kind of witch hazel, an extract from the bark of the witch hazel tree, in his laboratory. Pond called his witch hazel Pond's Extract. Later he moved his distillery to Connecticut—first to Chester and then to nearby Clinton, where Chesebrough-Pond's still has a plant—and began to make other toiletries and cosmetics. The J. Walter Thompson advertising agency made Pond's a famous name during the 1920s, when socially prominent women including European royalty, endorsed Pond's skin cream in a series of ads.

That's the Pond's branch of the family tree. The other branch grew from another chemist, Robert A. Chesebrough, who at age 22 had a kerosene business in Brooklyn, New York. One day in 1859 Chesebrough heard about a fabulous oil strike in Pennsylvania, so he invested some of his savings in a railroad ticket to Titusville, the heart of the oil boom. He returned to Brooklyn not with oil, but with a paraffinlike residue left on the rods of the oil pumps; workers in the field raved about the substance as a salve for cuts and burns. Back in his laboratory, Chesebrough worked for months to find a process that could extract this residue from petroleum. He turned himself into a human guinea pig to test the product, inflicting scores of cuts and scratches on his body and searing his fingers with flame. The translucent jelly he applied to his wounds seemed to work, and by 1870 Chesebrough was turning out the balm in quantity. He called it Vaseline Petroleum Jelly (from the German *wasser*, water, and the Greek *elaion*, olive oil). Chesebrough incorporated his company in 1880 (Chesebrough-Pond's new birthday), and a year later he sold out to his source of supply: the Standard Oil Company. In 1911, when the Standard Oil trust was dissolved, Chesebrough was set loose as an independent company.

Pond's and Chesebrough continued on their separate courses until 1955, when they merged. The link was Clifford M. Baker, Pond's chairman who was also a director of Chesebrough. Chesebrough-Pond's then bagged Pertussin cough syrup (1956), Prince Matchabelli (1958), Aziza (1959), Q-Tips (1962), Erno Laszlo Institute (1966),

beyond its discoverer's wildest dreams. Gobs of Vaseline have, inexplicably, lured trout to fishermen's hooks. Dabs of it on the famous faces of movie stars have simulated tears of cinematic grief. Commander Peary's intrepid arctic explorers took it with them because it resists freezing even at 40 degrees below zero. Reports reaching the Chesebrough company from remote jungle regions indicated that natives used jars of Vaseline as money after finding that not even blazing tropical suns would turn it rancid.

Still, a novice Chesebrough employee cringed when the company got a report that people in India were using Vaseline to butter their bread. Chesebrough assured the young man that it could do them only good; he himself ate a spoonful every day as a general panacea.

When, in his late fifties, Chesebrough was seriously ill with pleurisy, he prevailed upon his nurse to rub him from head to foot with Vaseline. He recovered, surviving to the age of 96. On his deathbed, in 1933, he attributed his longevity to Vaseline.

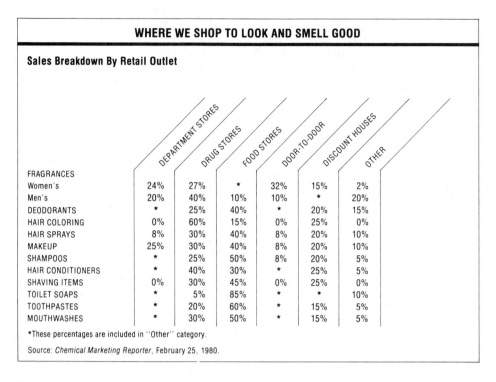

WHERE WE SHOP TO LOOK AND SMELL GOOD

Sales Breakdown By Retail Outlet

	DEPARTMENT STORES	DRUG STORES	FOOD STORES	DOOR-TO-DOOR	DISCOUNT HOUSES	OTHER
FRAGRANCES						
Women's	24%	27%	*	32%	15%	2%
Men's	20%	40%	10%	10%	*	20%
DEODORANTS	*	25%	40%	*	20%	15%
HAIR COLORING	0%	60%	15%	0%	25%	0%
HAIR SPRAYS	8%	30%	40%	8%	20%	10%
MAKEUP	25%	30%	40%	8%	20%	10%
SHAMPOOS	*	25%	50%	8%	20%	5%
HAIR CONDITIONERS	*	40%	30%	*	25%	5%
SHAVING ITEMS	0%	30%	45%	0%	25%	0%
TOILET SOAPS	*	5%	85%	*	*	10%
TOOTHPASTES	*	20%	60%	*	15%	5%
MOUTHWASHES	*	30%	50%	*	15%	5%

*These percentages are included in "Other" category.

Source: *Chemical Marketing Reporter*, February 25, 1980.

Ragu (1969), Health-tex (1973), Adolph's (1974), and Bass (1978).

Reputation. They're shrewd marketers, expert at what's called line extension: Vaseline petroleum jelly gave birth to Vaseline Intensive Care lotion; Ragu spaghetti sauce spawned Ragu Classic Combinations and Ragu Extra Thick and Zesty Sauce; and so on.

What they own. Fifty-seven subsidiaries all over the world, from Zambia to Singapore.

Who owns and runs the company. The only person with as much as 1% of Chesebrough-Pond's stock is Louis Russek, retired chairman of Health-tex. The company's 20 officers are all men. There's one female director: Jane Cahill Pfeiffer, chairwoman of the National Broadcasting Company.

In the public eye. Chesebrough-Pond's is one of the few large companies that had no legal entanglements to report in their 1979 reports to shareholders and the Securities and Exchange Commission. In 1973 the U.S. Food and Drug Administration ordered them to recall their Pertussin medicated vaporizer spray because of 18 deaths associated with its use. The FDA said 17 of the deaths occurred when people sniffed the chemical product compressed in a container trying to get a drug high.

Where they're going. They have money in the bank, little debt—and a yen to buy.

Stock performance. Chesebrough-Pond's stock bought for $1,000 in 1970 sold for $871 on January 2, 1980.

Access. 33 Benedict Place, Greenwich, Connecticut 06830; (203) 661-2000.

Consumer brands.

Cosmetics/toiletries: Vaseline Petroleum Jelly; Vaseline Hair Tonic; Vaseline Intensive Care lotions and baby products; Pond's Angel Face Makeup; Pond's creams and powders; Aziza eye makeup; Cutex nail polish, lipstick and polish remover; Erno Laszlo skin care preparations; Groom & Clean hair products; Odorono deodorant.

Health aids: Q-tips cotton swabs and cotton balls; Pertussin cough and cold products.

Fragrances: Prince Matchabelli's Aviance, Cachet, Wind Song, Golden Autumn and Prophecy.

Clothing: Health-tex children's clothing.

Food: Adolph's meat tenderizer, salt and sugar substitutes; Ragu spaghetti sauces.

# Colgate-Palmolive

Sales: $4.5 billion
Profits: $13 million
Forbes 500 rank: 92
Rank in toothpaste: 2
Rank in soap and detergent: 2
Rank in shaving cream: 2
Rank in rice: 1
Rank in adhesive bandages: 2
Founded: 1806
Employees: 56,600
Headquarters: New York, New York

What they do. Colgate-Palmolive used to get kicked around with such impunity by Procter & Gamble that 10 years ago they moved into new businesses to avoid meeting the P & G powerhouse head on. Lacking the initiative to develop new products on their own, they bought other companies with superprofits from overseas markets where P & G had yet to catch up. Colgate's buying spree in the 1970s captured 21 companies with combined sales of more than $1 billion. They soon owned the outfits that made Carolina rice, Hebrew National hot dogs, Ram golf clubs, Etonic jogging shoes, Curad bandages, Pangburn chocolates, and Helena Rubinstein cosmetics.

This strategy, initiated by David R. Foster, who had grown up in Colgate (his father headed the British company), was widely chronicled in the business press. In 1977 the *Wall Street Journal* said Foster had put "once-stuffy Colgate on a bold new course," and noted, "When Mr. Foster wants something, Colgate goes after it." Take, for example, the Mission Hills golf course outside Palm Springs, California, site of the annual Dinah Shore women's golf tournament sponsored by Colgate. One year the greens did not play well, so Foster had Colgate buy the property for $5.5 million to insure proper upkeep. Later Foster built a home for himself at Mission Hills.

As the decade came to a close, however, sales dropped, and Colgate reversed gears. Out the door again went Ram golf clubs, Leach racquets, Hebrew National meats, the Lum's and Ranch House restaurants, and Maui Divers coral jewelry. The worst disaster was Helena Rubinstein. Bought in 1973 for stock worth $142 million, it never made any money for Colgate—and no one

has been willing to take it off their hands, even at knockdown prices. David Foster's resignation was demanded by the board of directors in 1979 and he retired to Mission Hills on a pension of $211,000 a year.

Colgate's traditional second place in both the toothpaste and soap-and-detergent markets remains intact. They try harder with brand names like Ultra-Brite, Ajax, Palmolive, Fab, and Cold Power. They also have a winner in their 1972 acquisition, Boston-based Kendall, maker of baby products (Curity), bandages (Curad and Bauer & Black), athletic supports (Bike), and hospital products. Still in place is Colgate's powerful international operation, especially in Latin countries. They do more than half their business outside the United States, and that business generates three-quarters of the company's profits.

History. Colgate has been making soap since 1806, when 23-year-old William Colgate opened a "Soap, Mould & Dipt Candles" factory and shop two blocks from where New York's World Trade Center stands today. Colgate began selling toothpaste, in jars, in 1877. Toothpaste in a tube —Colgate Ribbon Dental Cream—make its debut in 1908.

In 1864 another soap manufacturer, B. J. Johnson, started up in Milwaukee. He introduced Palmolive toilet soap in 1898, naming it for the oils it contained. In the early years of this century it was the best-selling soap in the world.

In 1872 still another soap company was started, this time in Kansas City by the Peet brothers. They subsequently opened a plant in Berkeley, California, to make soap for people west of the Rockies.

All three of these soap makers joined forces after World War I, forming Colgate-Palmolive-Peet; the name was shortened to Colgate-Palmolive in 1953. Headquarters of the company for many years was Jersey City, where William Colgate had moved his factory in 1820. In 1956 Colgate moved back across the Hudson River to a new nondescript building on Park Avenue.

Colgate was an early multinational. Between 1914 and 1933 they established 16 foreign subsidiaries. They moved into Canada, Australia, Europe, and Latin America, setting up manufacturing plants and also buying out local companies. Today Colgate boasts of marketing directly to 1.5 billion people in 58 countries and exporting to another 641 million persons in 70 more countries.

Meanwhile, Colgate took a beating from the Procter & Gamble machine at home. When detergents replaced soap after World War II, P & G grabbed a lead they were never to relinquish. Next P & G came up with the fluoride ingredient in Crest toothpaste, winning the endorsement of the American Dental Association and knocking Colgate Dental Cream off a perch it had held for 80 years. Colgate knew they were in trouble. It took them years to learn how to make a fluoride toothpaste, and they never did get back to first place.

Reputation. The term *professional management* has never been applied to Colgate-Palmolive. They were long known as a "one-man-rule" company: Edward H. Little took command in 1938; then George H. Lesch, who succeeded him in 1960; then Foster in 1971.

What they own. Two hundred factories around the world, including the sprawling complex that still functions in Jersey City, where virtually every household and personal-care product on the roster is made. They have a 75-acre research center at Piscataway, New Jersey, from which cynics say nothing of worth has ever emerged.

Who owns and runs the company. Colgate's new boss is Keith Crane, who rose through the international ranks. Crane joined Colgate in 1937 as a 16-year-old office boy with the New Zealand company. He became sales and advertising manager, helping to make Colgate-New Zealand profitable; his reward was the general manager's post in South Africa. In 1965 he was placed in charge of Colgate's Australian operations. By 1972 Colgate-Australia was earning $3.5 million in profits on sales of $47 million—and Crane was summoned to the big trouble spot: the United States. He is now one of the few foreigners running an American corporation (if Colgate can be considered American).

Although Colgate has invested a lot of money and energy in women's sports events, there are no women on the board and only one female officer: Tina Santi, vice-president for public relations.

In the public eye. During the 1970s Colgate ran a "Help Young America" campaign inviting consumers to send in box-

Keith Crane, one of few aliens to head a major U.S. corporation, has the imposing task of creating clarity from Colgate-Palmolive chaos. Crane is a native of New Zealand and made his mark running Colgate's Australian operations.

tops from Colgate products along with their votes on which of the following youth groups should receive Colgate more than a third of a million charity dollars: Boy Scouts, Boys Club of America, Girls Club of America, Camp Fire Girls, and National 4-H Clubs.

Where they're going. Any place where Procter & Gamble can't find them.

Stock performance. Colgate-Palmolive stock bought for $1,000 in 1970 sold for $969 on January 2, 1980.

Access. 300 Park Avenue, New York, New York 10022; (212) 751-1200.

Consumer brands.

Toiletries and cosmetics: Colgate Dental Cream and other dental products; Ultra-Brite toothpaste; Respond shampoo; Palmolive toiletries; Hand-i-Wipes; Mersene denture cleanser; Curity, Curad, Bauer & Black, and Telfa first-aid products; Helena Rubinstein cosmetics; Irish Spring, Cashmere Bouquet, Spree Bar, Palmolive, and Palmolive Gold soaps; Hair Defense hair protector; Challenge dandruff shampoo; Lustre-Creme lotion and shampoo; Moment of Truth deodorant; Palmolive, Rapid Shave, and Colgate Instant Shave shaving creams; Dermassage soap and lotion; Fluorigard anticavity rinse.

Household products: Fab, Fresh Start, Dynamo, and Cold Power laundry detergents; Ajax all-purpose cleaner; Baggies plastic bags; Wash 'n' Dry; Florient air freshener; Galaxy floor cleaner; Pritt glue stick; Dermassage dishwashing liquid; Axion presoak.

Food products: River, Carolina, Mahatma, Success, Water Maid, and Bake-It-Easy rice and rice products; Hills pet foods; MBT broth.

Sports and recreational products: Tretorn sneakers; Etonic golf and running shoes; Bike athletic supports.

The Gillette Company

Sales: $2 billion
Profits: $11 million
Forbes 500 rank: 266
Rank in razors and blades: 1
Rank in deodorant: 2
Rank in ballpoint pens: 2
Rank in disposable lighters: 2
Founded: 1901
Employees: 31,700
Headquarters: Boston, Massachusetts

What they do. Were it not for Gillette's diligent research and development department, modern science might not know that the average man's beard is composed of 15,500 whiskers and covers one-third of a square foot of face area, that these whiskers are as tough as copper wire of the same thickness, that they grow at the rate of 5½ inches per year (or 27½ feet in a lifetime), and that the average man will spend 3,350 hours of his life scraping them away. Numbers like these make Gillette happy. They also make razor blades a big business.

In the 80-year-span since King C. Gillette changed the faces of the earth with his first safety razor, Gillette's R & D department has kept them one scrape ahead of the competition. Their achievements—just for starters—include the first adjustable razor, the first twin-blade razor and cartridge, and the Atra pivoting-head razor. Gillette still sells all three, as well as their well-known Super Blue, stainless steel, and Platinum Plus blades; but only Gillette's twin-blade "shaving systems" (Atra, Trac II, and Good News! disposable razors) receive their much-ballyhooed Microsmooth ultrasonic honing.

Although razors and blades account for almost 75% of Gillette's profits, they also make a wide line of toiletries and grooming aids. Right Guard deodorant, second only to Ban, is a Gillette product, as are Soft & Dri and Dry Idea nonaerosol deodorants (their personal-care division president once boasted that "this company knows more about armpits" than any of their competitors). Gillette also markets such hair care products as Toni home permanent kits, Tame and Earth Born creme rinses, The Dry Look aerosol hair groom for men, Silkience hair conditioner, Ultra Max blow-driers, and Easy Roller curling irons.

Gillette bought the Paper Mate pen company in 1955 and now puts out Flair porous-tip and Write Bros. stick pens, as well as Paper Mate ballpoints. In 1979 they introduced EraserMate, the first refillable pen with erasable ink. They own the German Braun company, maker of deluxe electric shavers, coffee grinders, and other small appliances, and the French S. T. DuPont group, which manufactures cigarette lighters and leather goods. They created the Cricket disposable lighter in 1972, now sold throughout the world.

History. While the name Gillette is today synonymous with the scraping of faces, to 1895 America it meant socialism. King C. Gillette, the practical inventor of the first safety razor, was best known for his idealistic 1894 book, *The Human Drift,* which set forth a sweeping plan for a worldwide utopia under a single enormous corporation, that would end all competition. Gillette even went so far as to set up The Twentieth Century Corporation, but the idea fizzled.

Then in 1895 the 40-year-old bottle cap salesman had a flash of inspiration. After trying repeatedly to put an edge on his straight razor with a leather strop, Gillette came up with the idea of a rigid-handled safety razor with replaceable blades. He carved a rough prototype out of a block of wood and showed it to friends, but it was not until 1901 that the idea finally became a metal reality—thanks to a Boston inventor and machinist named William Nickerson. The two men formed the American Safety Razor Company that same year and convinced a number of wealthy Bostonians to back them.

The company quickly established a reputation for marketing brilliance by peddling "Service Set" shaving kits (3.5 million razors and 36 million blades) to departing doughboys during World War I. When the soldiers returned, they were confirmed Gillette customers. During the 1920s Gillette embarked on a series of promotional campaigns that sealed the fate of the straight razor. Under the motto "Shave and Save" banks across the country gave away Gillette razors to every new depositor. Hotels, restaurants, and service stations gave away razors at their opening day ceremonies. And one enterprising merchant sold 100,000 boxes of marshmallows by packing a free Gillette razor in each one.

Gillette became a major radio sports sponsor in the 1930s and later carried that tradition over to television. They sponsored the 1939 baseball World Series for a total of $100,000 (they now pay that for a single minute of World Series time), and quickly followed with the Orange and Sugar Bowl football games and the 1940 Kentucky Derby. In 1941 the company began sponsoring dozens of different sporting events, all of which were advertised as part of Gillette's "Cavalcade of Sports." In 1941 they initiated their long association with professional boxing—and its overwhelmingly male audience—by sponsoring the Joe Louis–Billy Conn heavyweight championship fight. Today Gillette spends $155 million a year on advertising plus another $84 million on such sales promotions as baseball's All-Star Game ballot cards.

Gillette had no serious competition for male faces until the early 1960s, when Wilkinson Sword introduced the first stainless steel blade and temporarily stole a big share of the market. (Gillette subsequently released their own stainless version and won much of it back.) But the major nick in Gillette's throat is the Bic Pen Company, the American branch of France's Société Bic. When Bic introduced the first of its cheap (19¢) ballpoints in 1961, Gillette's Paper Mate dominated the market. Bic soon passed them and now controls 60% of the ballpoint business. Then came the battle over disposable lighters, and Bic won that one, too. Their "Flick Your Bic" ad campaign has gained them 52% of that market, while Gillette's Cricket places second with 30%.

But the hardest slap yet to Gillette's clean-shaven face has been Bic's 1975 introduction of the disposable razor. Gillette quickly countered with their Good News! razor, which has two blades to Bic's one, and now appears to be leading the fight—but the jury is still out. Gillette's biggest problem here is that the Good News! is basically a Trac II cartridge with a plastic handle. Trac II cartridges sell for as much as 36¢; but because of Bic's Shaver the Good News! had to sell for under 20¢—and Gillette feels as if they're slowly cutting their own throats.

Reputation. Properly Bostonian. A former insider claimed in a 1976 *Forbes* story that Gillette is "a supergentlemanly club." *Forbes* said that Edward Gelsthorpe, a brilliant marketer who lasted only one year as Gillette's president, was "rejected by the organization like a foreign body" for innovative promotional ideas that made old-liners nervous. They quoted Gelsthorpe as saying Gillette "didn't want anyone to rock the boat."

What they own. 60% of the world's wet-shaving market. Gillette's 1967 purchase of Braun, the German electric shaver manufacturer, and their subsequent attempt to market Braun shavers in the United States, is one of the oddest antitrust stories in Justice Department annals. In 1975, after a seven-year antitrust suit, Gillette agreed to settle by setting up a separate company, Cambridge Shavers, to import the Braun razors into the United States and investing $2.5 million in their new competitor. Now although Gillette owns and runs Braun's foreign operations, the Braun razor is sold here by another company of Gillette's creation. That was the price they had to pay to keep Braun.

Who owns and runs the company. Of the eight members of Gillette's board of directors, only two (chairman Coleman Mockler and president Stephen Griffin) are officers of the corporation. The board also includes one woman—Rita Ricardo Campbell, an economist at the West Coast "think tank," the Hoover Institution (where her husband is the director).

In the public eye. Gillette has an unusual division called Product Integrity. Its head, vice-president Robert Giovacchini, is empowered to yank any Gillette product off the market at any time, even if it means overruling executives far senior to him. One of Giovacchini's more controversial decisions was the $1.5 million recall of two new Gillette antiperspirants in 1973: he claimed there might be a danger to consumers who inhaled the zirconium in the formula. The recall publicly embarrassed Gillette and enraged Procter & Gamble, which sold a similar zirconium deodorant that they claimed was safe. But Giovacchini is still on the job.

Stock performance. Gillette stock bought for $1,000 in 1970 sold for $502 on January 2, 1980.

Access. Prudential Tower Building, Boston, Massachusetts 02199; (617) 421-7000.

Consumer brands.

Razors and blades: Trac II, Atra, Good News!, Super Stainless, Platinum Plus, and Super Blue.
Hair products: The Dry Look, Max Hold men's hair spray; Toni home permanent kits; Earth Born shampoos and creme rinses; Adorn and Adorn Firm & Free hair sprays; Promax and Super Max hair blow-driers; Easy Roller curling irons.
Deodorants: Right Guard; Soft & Dri; Dry Idea.
Pens: Write Bros.; Flair; Paper Mate; Erasermate.
Other products and services: Foamy shaving cream; DuPont lighters; Cricket disposable butane lighters; Sunoroid sunglasses; Braun appliances; Liquid Paper.

JOHNSON PRODUCTS CO., INC.

Sales: $33 million
Profits: $321,000
Rank in black-owned businesses: 4
Founded: 1954
Employees: 500
Headquarters: Chicago, Illinois

What they do. Black Americans spend an estimated $800 million a year on hair-care products and cosmetics—and that's the market this black-owned company serves. They were moving along sensationally until the mid-1970s, when they were caught in a pincers movement. On one flank companies like Revlon and Avon went after the black market (Revlon introduced their Polished Amber line in 1975). On the other flank Johnson Publishing, publisher of *Ebony* and *Jet,* wheeled their Fashion Fair cosmetics line into prestige department stores across the country. And up the middle their profitable market in Nigeria collapsed because of political turmoil in that African nation. Johnson Products has yet to fully recover.

At their only factory, on Chicago's south side, Johnson produces a line of personal grooming aids—hair dressings, hair relaxers, conditioners, shampoos, and cosmetics—that are designed for black consumers. Their two primary brands are Ultra Sheen and Afro Sheen. Drugstores are the company's most important retail outlet, followed by groceries. They spend $6 million a year (18% of sales) on advertising and promotion. The advertising mainstay for seven years has been "Soul Train," a television show oriented to young blacks.

History. The practice of blacks straightening their hair so that it would look more like the hair of whites has been going on for more than 100 years. The original method was a hot comb; later chemicals were used. George E. Johnson had been a door-to-door salesman in Chicago for Fuller Products, a black cosmetics firm, before he left in 1954 to manufacture and sell a new straightener called Ultra Wave. He was encouraged to make that move by Dr. Herbert A. Martini, a German-born chemist who ran the laboratory at Fuller. It was Martini who helped develop Ultra Wave and later the other major products in the Johnson line.

The most important of Johnson's products was the Ultra Sheen line, introduced in 1957, which enabled Johnson Products to get into the beauty shop market. Ultra Sheen was a breakthrough in that the line included a cream press permanent that could be used to straighten hair rather than the grease-and-smoke treatment of the hot comb. In addition, the Ultra Sheen relaxers could be used by women at home between visits to beauty parlors. Before that, hair had to be greased and hot-combed frequently—as often as once a week—and the grease was bad for the hair.

The straightener market was threatened in the late 1960s, when the civil rights movement gave rise to "black is beautiful" and the Afro hair style. Martini responded by coming up with the Afro Sheen line for natural hair. There are now 10 different products under the Afro Sheen label; however, their sales have tapered off following a decline in the popularity of the Afro.

In 1969 George Johnson took his company public, selling 300,000 shares on the American Stock Exchange. Johnson Products is the only black-owned company in the nation whose shares can be bought by the public.

Reputation. The unanswered question is: can Johnson Products compete against the big boys in the cosmetics and toiletries business? Since 1976, when they began to face tough competitors, Johnson's sales have declined from $40 million to $33 million, and their profits from $4 million to $321,000.

What they own. Johnson owns Debbie's School of Beauty Culture, which operates eight schools (five in Chicago, and one each in Detroit; East St. Louis, Illinois; and Montgomery, Alabama) that train beauticians. They own 40% of a Nigerian company that produces the Johnson line in a factory outside the capital city of Lagos. Nigeria has the largest black population in the world.

Who owns and runs the company. George Johnson, president, and his wife, Joan, who serves as treasurer, control more than 65% of the shares. Of the six directors only John T. Shriver, the stockbroker who took them public, is white. Johnson Products has been a revolving door for marketing and research people. Through the door have come people from Gallo, Clairol, Avon, Revlon, Estée Lauder, and Gillette.

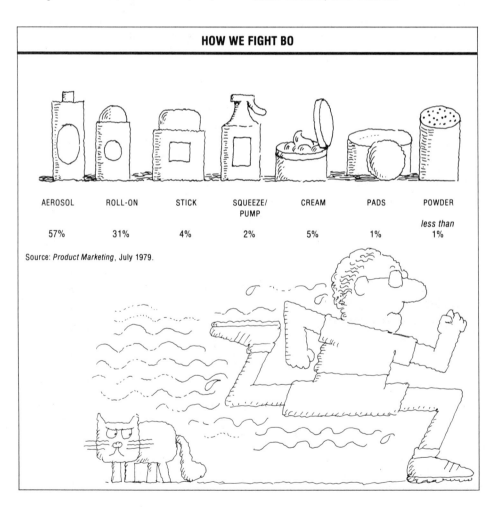

HOW WE FIGHT BO

AEROSOL	ROLL-ON	STICK	SQUEEZE/ PUMP	CREAM	PADS	POWDER
57%	31%	4%	2%	5%	1%	*less than* 1%

Source: *Product Marketing*, July 1979.

In the public eye. In August 1975 the Federal Trade Commission required the company to include a warning on Ultra Sheen hair straighteners that the chemicals used in the products might be hazardous. Johnson charged that the FTC move damaged them considerably since their main competitor, Revlon, was not required to include a similar warning on their competing product for another 20 months.

Where they're going. "We expect we've passed the bottom of the trough," George Johnson told *Advertising Age* late in 1979. "Our business is going to pick up. I expect to go back to being number 1 in the industry."

Stock performance. Johnson Products stock bought for $1,000 in 1970 sold for $330 on January 2, 1980.

Access. 8522 South Lafayette Avenue, Chicago, Illinois 60620; (312) 483-4100.

Consumer brands.

Ultra Sheen, Afro Sheen, Ultra Wave, Bantu, Precise, Moisture Formula.

REVLON

Sales: $1.7 billion
Profits: $153 million
Forbes 500 rank: 304
Rank in cosmetics: 2
Employees: 29,000
Founded: 1932
Headquarters: New York, New York

What they do. Revlon sells hope in a jar. Or as their leader, Michel Bergerac, says: "What we are selling are hopes and dreams, not frozen peas." You can see this high gloss selling all over the place; Revlon's ad budget is about $100 million a year. Anyone who reads magazines or watches television has seen Revlon models Lauren Hutton and Shelley Hack (of "Charlie's Angels" fame) pushing Revlon eye make-up, foundation, perfumes, skin treatments, nail polish, and lipstick. Revlon and Avon run neck-and-neck in cosmetics. Two of Revlon's fragrances, Charlie and Jontue, are the top-selling perfumes in the world.

But Revlon isn't just powder puffs and shampoo. In recent years they've branched out into men's cosmetics, prescription and over-the-counter drugs, diagnostic clinics, and optical equipment. In fact, health services and products now account for about a third of Revlon's business.

History. The history of the American cosmetics industry is dominated by strong-willed, tyrannical leaders like Helena Rubinstein, Elizabeth Arden, Max Factor, and Estée Lauder. Revlon's founder may have been the most eccentric megalomaniac of them all.

Charles Revson founded the Revlon nail enamel company with $300 in 1932. Although he had two partners (his older brother Joseph, and the source of the letter "L" in Revlon, Charles Lachman), Revlon was Revson's baby right from the start. Until he died at age 68 in 1975, Revson lived only for Revlon. He thought nothing of holding meetings until two in the morning or calling his chemist late Sunday night for three hours. And why not? For years he pushed his nail polish salon by salon, until he had a near monopoly on beauty parlor sales in 1941. He expected the same dedication from his employees.

Revson expanded into the lipstick market with the famous slogan "Matching Lips and Fingertips," and created a style women just had to have. His infallible eye for color, packaging, and advertising produced such landmark ad campaigns as "Fatal Apple" and "Fire and Ice." Revson did make an occasional blunder, however, such as his idea for a male genitalia deodorant called Private.

But to make Revlon into the cosmetics empire it became he "chewed up executives the way some people chew vitamins," as one former employee reported. Revson himself said, "All I demand is perfection," according to Andrew Tobias' biography of

> In terms of marketing, you've got to have the will to win. You've got to see the blood running down the street. You've got to be able to take it. You've got to be able to shove it. If you're not, you're nobody. You never will be.
>
> —Charles Revson, president of Revlon, as quoted in Andrew Tobias's *Fire and Ice: The Story of Charles Revson, the Man Who Built the Revlon Empire*, (William Morrow & Co., 1976).

Revson, *Fire and Ice.* His brother Martin, who quit the company in 1958, sued Charles for fraud and misrepresentation over the amount paid to him for his share of Revlon. During the trial he stated "The rate of turnover of Revlon executives became a subject for ribald humor."

Charles Revson hired and fired receptionists to go with the changing decor of his offices, humiliated employees with obscene verbal assaults and pretended to sleep during presentations. Revson did pay his terrorized employees very well, however.

Revlon's profits led to their reputation for being well managed, but the beauty industry traditionally has had fat profit margins that covered a lot of Revson's creative excesses like re-packaging products after he already approved the first package (a recent *Time* article computed the cost of ingredients in a tube of lipstick at 8% of the sales price). Toward the end of his life Revson became obsessed with the success of Estée Lauder, and he spent huge amounts of money to compete with her high-priced cosmetics. Not only did Estée Lauder still outsell Revlon's expensive line, but Revson neglected his cheaper cosmetic group, losing business to Maybelline and Cover Girl.

By the 1970s Revlon needed a "numbers man" in order to continue as a profitable, independent company. Revson chose Michel Bergerac, president of ITT-Europe. Revson paid Bergerac an unheard of $1.5 million just to sign the contract in 1974. Bergerac is obviously worth it: he's doubled sales and profits.

The big change in Revlon's image is from the erratic creativity of Revson to the balanced business school approach of Bergerac, who feels, "The most important thing is to seize a trend, and when we come in with our might it won't matter that we weren't the first. Everyone will think we were."

Reputation. Charles Revson claimed, "I don't ship shit," and the company is still known as producers of quality cosmetics. Revson arranged the cosmetics into seven "houses," or lines, from inexpensive all the way up to the ritz, a system that earned Revlon the title of "the General Motors of Beauty."

What they own. Plants in 15 states and 19 countries.

Who owns and runs the company. In the years since Revson's death Bergerac has persuaded most of the old regime's officers to leave the firm, including Revson's sons. It's very obvious who is in control of Revlon now, although some old Revson cronies still sit on the board of directors. Aileen Mehle, better known as gossip columnist Suzy Knickerbocker, is one such holdover. Directors own about 5% of Revlon's stock.

In the public eye. Although Charles Revson didn't care much for unions, the Distributive Workers of America organized Revlon in the 1940s. As biographer Andrew Tobias relates, "It was worth the money to get those workers to stop slipping little 'fuck you' notes into the compacts."

Revson's generosity extended to endowments for New York colleges, Brandeis University, and the Salk Institute. But Revson's favorite charity was himself. He bought and refurbished the third-largest private yacht in the world (only Onassis and Niarchos, the Greek shipping magnates, had bigger boats) for $3.5 million. He averaged about $5,000 a day in expenditures; even his custom-made undershorts cost him $26.50 a pair.

Where they're going. Revlon is certainly not planning to forsake cosmetics, but they are expanding into the health and drug market. Now that they're tops in the United States, they'll step up marketing overseas. A move in that direction was Revlon's recent acquisition of the French cosmetics company Institut Jeanne Gatineau.

Stock performance. Revlon stock bought for $1,000 in 1970 sold for $1,295 on January 2, 1980.

Access. 767 Fifth Avenue, New York, New York 10022; (212) 572-5000.

Consumer brands.

Cosmetics: Revlon; Moon Drops; Natural Wonder; Ultima II; CHR; Princess Marcella Borg-

---

"Creative people are like a wet towel. You wring them out and pick up another one," said Charles Revson, president of Revlon, after changing advertising agencies seven times in three years.

hese; Formula 2; Etherea; Catalyste; Eterna 27; Polished Amber.

Hair products: Flex; Milk Plus 6; Colorsilk and Roux haircolor.

Perfumes: Charlie; Jontue; Norell; Ciara; Cerissa; Intimate; Miss Balmain; Ecco; Fiamma; Andiamo; Bill Blass for Women; DiBorghese.

Antiperspirant: Mitchum.

Men's products: Braggi; Chaz.

Over-the-counter products: Oxy line of antiacne preparations; Pretty Feet & Hands rough skin remover; Orafix dental adhesive; Esoterica skin treatment; Tums antacid; Barnes-Hind wetting and soaking solution, Comfort Drops, One Solution, Titan, and Soft Mate solutions for contact lenses.

TAMPAX

Sales: $170.5 million
Profits: $33.6 million
Rank in tampons: 1
Employees: 2,600
Founded: 1936
Headquarters: Lake Success, New York

What they do. Tampax has virtually become the generic name for the only product the company makes. They sell more tampons than any other company, and they've done so for 44 years. They now rank third among menstrual protection companies after Kimberly-Clark (Kotex) and Johnson & Johnson (Modess, Carefree, Stayfree, and o.b.).

History. Tampax chairman Thomas Casey co-founded the company with the late Ellery Mann and the late Earle Griswold in New York in 1936. They manufactured cotton and paper tampons for internal menstrual protection—the first company to do so. Introducing the new product wasn't easy. British Roman Catholics opposed it; *Good Housekeeping* refused Tampax ads; doctors warned against using tampons. But Tampax honed in on the younger woman's desire for freedom of movement and developed what is now a $300 million-a-year business.

Tampax's success went unchallenged until recent years. Kimberly-Clark, John-son & Johnson, Esmark's Playtex, and Procter & Gamble are now battling for a piece of the market. Tampax controlled 75% of tampon sales through 1970. They're now down to 45% and running scared. They've upped their advertising budget from $13 million to $19 million, and they advertise on television (only after their competitors did). They also introduced two new sizes to challenge their rivals. But in spite of the competition Tampax still has no debt and $60 million in the bank.

Reputation. Casey once told *Forbes,* "We will tackle the giants and set them back because we have a better product and better know-how of the marketplace. Being a smaller company we will outmaneuver them."

What they own. Five plants in Massachusetts, Vermont, New Hampshire, Maine, and New York; plus facilities in Ontario, England, France, South Africa, and Ireland. Tampax is sold in 100 countries.

Who owns and runs the company. Casey, who was 72 in 1980, is the largest shareholder, with 3.4% of the stock. He was paid $120,000 in 1978—and his shares of stock netted him another $900,000 in dividends. Also on the board is Mary G. Kretschmar, whose mother, Gertrude Kendrick, was the original developer of the Tampax tampon

WHERE OUR HEALTH AND BEAUTY DOLLAR GOES	
PRESCRIPTIONS	41¢
OVER-THE-COUNTER-DRUGS	16¢
FOOT PRODUCTS	1¢
BABY NEEDS	4¢
DIET AIDS	1¢
FEMININE HYGIENE	2¢
ORAL HYGIENE	5¢
COSMETICS	7¢
WOMEN'S FRAGRANCES	5¢
WOMEN'S HAIR PREPARATIONS	6¢
MEN'S TOILETRIES	2¢
SKIN PREPARATIONS (*suntan products, cleaners, moisturizers, hand creams, masks, wrinkle removers*)	5¢
PERSONAL CLEANLINESS (*bath soaps, deodorants*)	5¢
Source: *Product Marketing,* July 1979.	

at a Denver company, Tampax Sales, bought out by Casey, Mann and Griswold.

In the public eye. Tampax was forced into advertising on television to defend their market position. Playtex was the first to promote tampons on TV in 1975, and they grabbed second place in the market by introducing a deodorant tampon. When Tampax reprinted in one of its ads a caution warning that Playtex uses on its packages of deodorant tampons, Playtex sued them for $100 million. The suit was settled out of court after Tampax agreed not to do that again, and Playtex said they wouldn't mention Tampax in their ads.

Where they're going. Thomas Casey knows that the tampon market is still growing and soon more American women will be using tampons than sanitary napkins, but the question is: can Tampax keep their share of the market in the face of so much high-powered competition? The second threat facing Tampax is the possibility of being bought by a bigger company. "I will listen to a legitimate inquiry but I won't talk to marriage brokers who are looking for a piece of the action," Casey told *Forbes.*

Stock performance. Tampax stock bought for $1,000 in 1970 sold for $564 on January 2, 1980.

Access. 5 Dakota Drive, Lake Success, New York 11042; (516) 437-8800.

Consumer brand.

Tampax.

THE CLEANEST HAIR IN THE WORLD

	Number Sold	Share of Market
HEAD & SHOULDERS	28.1 *million*	11.2%
PRELL	27.9 *million*	11.1%
SUAVE	25.3 *million*	10.1%
REVLON FLEX	17.9 *million*	7.1%
J & J BABY SHAMPOO	15.9 *million*	6.3%
AGREE	15.3 *million*	6.1%
BODY ON TAP	13.9 *million*	5.6%
BRECK	10.9 *million*	4.4%
CLAIROL HERBAL	8.7 *million*	3.5%
FABERGE ORGANICS	8.2 *million*	3.3%
ULTRA MAX	7.1 *million*	2.8%
MILK PLUS 6	5.8 *million*	2.3%
CLAIROL SHAMPOO COND	5.6 *million*	2.2%
YOUR HAIR SMELLS TERRIFIC	4.5 *million*	1.8%
WELLA BALSAM SHAMPOO	4.4 *million*	1.7%
SELSUN BLUE	3.9 *million*	1.6%
VIDAL SASSOON	3.8 *million*	1.5%
EARTH BORN	3.7 *million*	1.5%
TEGRIN	2.6 *million*	1.0%
CLAIROL SHORT & SASSY	2.5 *million*	1.0%
PRIVATE LABEL	14.4 *million*	5.8%
ALL OTHER	20.0 *million*	8.0%
TOTAL	250 *million*	100%

Source: *Private Label*, June-July 1979.

Health Hawkers

⊐ABBOTT

Sales: $1.7 billion
Profits: $179 million
Forbes 500 rank: 309
Rank in intravenous solutions: 2
Rank in eye drops: 2
Founded: 1888
Employees: 27,000
Headquarters: Chicago, Illinois

What they do. Falling behind in the white-coat race to make and market new drugs, Abbott has stepped up efforts to develop medical equipment such as blood-testing devices and machinery to pump intravenous fluids through the body. Since 1972 they have introduced 49 new products.

Prescription drugs now account for less than a quarter of Abbott's sales, and 40% of these sales come from the antibiotic erythromycin, sold under the brand names Erythrocin and E.E.S. Among Abbott's other drugs are the tranquilizer Tranxene, the anticonvulsant Depakene, and the sedatives Placidyl and Nembutal. Half of Abbott's pharmaceutical sales are outside the United States.

Abbott's Ross Laboratories make Similac, the largest-selling line of infant formulas—it has half the market. They produce adult formulas as well, under brand names like Vital and Ensure, for patients who have special dietary needs. Abbott's consumer products also include Murine eye-care preparations, Selsun Blue antidandruff shampoo, and the artificial sweetener Sucaryl.

History. Soon after starting out as a family doctor in Ravenswood, Illinois, Wallace Calvin Abbott discovered that he preferred

Dr. Wallace Calvin Abbott, founder of Abbott Laboratories, is shown surrounded by his original staff in front of the frame house on Chicago's Northside that served as his home, office and factory during the 1890s.

selling drugs to practicing medicine. An intense, hard-driving man, Abbott grew up on a Vermont farm and worked his way through school, taking his M.D. degree at the University of Michigan. Like his contemporary Teddy Roosevelt, Abbott was short, stocky, aggressive, and sported a walrus mustache.

It was not for lack of success as a doctor that Abbott turned to peddling nostrums: in 1890 he earned $8,000 on $2 house calls and $1 office visits. He bought a drugstore with the fees from his medical practice and advertised such products as Dr. Abbott's Tooth Ache Drops, Rock Candy Cough Syrup, Laxative Lozenges, Spring Blood Purifier, and Worm Medicine on his monthly bills.

Dr. Abbott became a convert to a new form of medication: alkaloid pills. Alkaloid extracts from plants (morphine, quinine, strychnine, and codeine, for example) had been used for fever reduction, but the crude liquid extracts were perishable, uneven, and nauseating. A Belgian surgeon, Dr. Adolphe Burggraeve, took a major step toward the era of modern pharmaceuticals when he precipitated the solid extracts and packaged them in granules that were "clean, compact, uniform, unspoilable and pleasant to take." Abbott began buying these granules from a Chicago company in 1887. But he was dissatisfied with their quality, and in 1888 began making alkaloid pills in his kitchen. Three years later he was advertising them to his fellow doctors.

Once launched as a drug manufacturer, Dr. Abbott showed his true mettle: he was a born salesman. From his printing press he issued brochures, advice, sales talks, maxims, and poetry—written nights, mornings, and in church on Sundays. One of his favorite headlines in medical journals was: "Doctor, we've a Nugget of Gold for you!" He also sold doctors shares in his growing business. An ad for his best-selling H.M.C. (hyoscine-morphine-cactin) tablets claimed that doctors who prescribed the pills were extinguishing the fear of childbirth, putting a stop to family quarrels, and as a result potentially increasing the national birth rate.

In 1900 he set up the Abbott Alkaloidal Company. That year's catalog offered more than 300 products and by 1905 sales had reached $200,000. Dr. Abbott was no longer practicing medicine. His uninhibited selling style brought down the wrath of the AMA, whose journal denounced Abbott as a charlatan and refused his advertisements for alkaloid pills. Not one to turn the other cheek, Wallace Abbott responded with a 48-page booklet, which he mailed to every doctor in the nation. He accused the AMA of conspiring to deny doctors the right to dispense drugs of their choosing, charged the journal editor with showing favoritism to a rival company, and prophesied that alkaloid drugs were the wave of the future. And he was right.

World War 1 opened new opportunities to U.S. drug firms as important pharmaceuticals previously supplied by German companies became unavailable. Abbott helped fill the void by devising ways to manufacture procaine (German novocaine)

and barbital (German veronal). Dr. Abbott died in 1921, shortly after ground was broken for new research laboratories in North Chicago. From those laboratories in the next three decades came the sedative Nembutal; the "truth serum" sodium pentothal; vitamins; Tridione, the first effective agent for treating *petit mal* seizures in epilepsy; Diasone, an oral drug for leprosy; various tranquilizers; and Sucaryl, a cyclamate discovered accidentally when a University of Illinois chemistry student put his cigarette down and found it sweet when he returned it to his mouth.

The aggressive sales style of Wallace Abbott remained a distinctive feature of Abbott Labs. Though the founder was a doctor, the company has most often been led by salesmen. During the 1933–1945 presidency of flamboyant DeWitt Clough, Abbott broke new marketing ground by bringing out an elegant promotional magazine, *What's New*, which was later copied by many competitors.

Reputation. Though the Abbott name has been well known to doctors for nearly a century, it no longer conjures up the image of imaginative research and product reliability that it once did. A major dent in the company's image was inflicted in 1971 by the largest product recall ever ordered by the Food and Drug Administration. Abbott had to recall from hospitals across the country 3.4 million bottles of intravenous solutions that were contaminated because they were improperly closed. According to the government, the contamination was associated with 350 cases of blood poisoning and 9 deaths. The Justice Department indicted Abbott and five of the company's executives on 60 counts, but after a government effort which was described in the *San Francisco Chronicle* as "wobbly," the case was dropped. Abbott ended up pleading no contest on one count of conspiracy and paying a fine of $1,000 for the misdemeanor, a denouement that the Public Citizens Health Research Group called "outrageous."

Americans over 65 years old consume 25% of all prescription drugs although they constitute only 10% of the population.

What they own. Abbott operates 18 plants in the United States and three in Puerto Rico. They have 77 foreign subsidiaries and manufacturing facilities in 28 countries.

Who owns and runs the company. Abbott boasts of a low employee turnover, but the present management team is not home-grown. President Robert A. Schoellhorn was recruited in 1973 from American Cyanamid; two other officers came from Texas Instruments. Abbott's board is devoid of blacks and women. By virtue of having raised the proportion of women and minorities in management and professional positions from 10% in 1973 to 20% in 1978, the company claims to have a strong affirmative action program (these groups constitute 65% of the U.S. population).

In the public eye. Their quarterly, *Commitment*, reports on Abbott's performance as corporate citizen and on health-care issues. The positions may be deduced from the names of some contributors: William E. Simon, Milton Friedman, William F. Buckley, and Senator S. I. Hayakawa. Abbott has tried repeatedly to get the FDA to rescind its 1969 ban on cyclamates (suspected of being cancer agents), claiming their research shows cyclamates to be safe.

On the other hand, Abbott has been more responsive than other companies to protests against promotion of infant formulas in Third World countries. They changed labels to stress the importance of breast feeding and to state clearly that an infant can become ill if the formula is improperly diluted or prepared with impure water.

Where they're going. Abbott is building an infant formula plant in the Soviet Union. They have also joined with Takeda Chemical, Japan's second-largest drug producer, to develop pharmaceutical compounds for the U.S. and Canadian markets.

Stock performance. Abbott stock bought for $1,000 at the start of 1970 sold for $2,150 on January 2, 1980.

> In the trade drugs that are available only by prescription are called "ethical." This does not mean that over-the-counter or "proprietary" drugs are "unethical."

Access. Abbott Park, Chicago, Illinois 60064; (312) 937-6100.

Consumer brands.

Over-the-counter products: Selsun Blue antidandruff shampoo; Faultless rubber products; Sucaryl sweeteners; Murine eye-care products.
Nutritionals: Similac and Isomil infant formulas; Ensure; Ensure Plus, Polycose, Vital™, adult nutritionals.

American Home Products

Sales: $3.4 billion
Profits: $396 million
Forbes 500 rank: 137
Rank in prescription drugs: 5
Rank in hemorrhoidal preparations: 1
Rank in wart medication: 1
Rank in insecticide: 2
Rank in canned spaghetti: 2
Rank in cold remedies: 3
Rank in pots and pans: 1
Founded: 1926
Employees: 49,619
Headquarters: New York, New York

What they do. When you call American Home Products in New York, the switchboard operator answers with the telephone number instead of the name of the company. That's peculiar behavior for a $3 billion corporation, but quite in keeping with AHP's operating style: they don't promote their corporate name. Although at least one of their products can probably be found in nearly every American home, the AHP name never appears on the package. Their long and varied lineup runs to hundreds, maybe thousands (AHP never lists how many), of products, including Preparation H hemorrhoid treatment, Chef-Boy-Ar-Dee canned spaghetti and meatballs, Compound W Wart remover, Primatene Mist respiratory spray, Black Flag Roach Motel traps, Sani-Flush bowl cleaner, and Anacin (to mention only a handful).

AHP's passion for anonymity springs both from their long-held conviction that corporate image making doesn't sell the product and from a desire to keep separate their prescription (promoted to doctors) and over-the-counter (promoted to anyone sitting before a TV set) drug operations. Why remind doctors who are prescribing Inderal to cardiac patients that the company supplying this important therapeutic agent is the same one screaming on the tube about Arthritis Pain Formula, Dristan cold tablets, and Easy-Off oven cleaner? The drugs they sell directly to the public are packed under the name Whitehall Laboratories. The prescription drugs are marketed by three different AHP units: Wyeth Laboratories, Ayerst Laboratories, and Ives Laboratories. A product like Easy-Off comes from their Boyle-Midway division, home base for Woolite cold-water wash, PAM cooking spray, Wizard charcoal lighter, the Black Flag insecticides, and Old English furniture polish (again to name only a handful of AHP's household products).

AHP may be the only major corporation in the land to do without a public relations department, but they are certainly not bashful about promoting their products, to consumers or to doctors. Their advertising expenditures run at a $200 million-a-year clip. Nevertheless, they are feared by Madison Avenue as demanding clients who always suspect that an agency is making too much money off them. One agency man said: "In dealing with American Home, the idea is to come in on your knees, not walk in tall and look clean. They prefer to work with grovelers." AHP even has an in-house groveler, the John F. Murray Advertising Agency, which they own. Murray is always ready to take AHP accounts resigned in frustration by independent agencies. The bulk of AHP's advertising money goes into television.

A spendthrift AHP is not. They don't go in for executive planes, fancy offices, or other corporate frills. They don't spend a lot of money on their annual report. Stories about their frugality are in constant circulation at the Madison Avenue gin mills. According to one that showed up in *Business Week*, Chairman William F. Laporte personally ordered that the width of the toilet tissue in the executive washrooms be reduced to save money. In search of confirmation *Business Week* got past AHP's security desk and discovered that the toilet paper "is indeed $9/16$ inch narrower than standard tissue."

AHP is one of the most profitable companies in American business, standing 46th among all companies in terms of profits after taxes. The AHP product mix breaks down as follows in terms of percentage of sales: prescription drugs, 39%; over-the-counter drugs, 14%; food products, 11%; candy, 9%; household products, 14%; housewares, 13%. But when it comes to profits, prescription drugs kick in 55%. Among AHP's major drugs are Ovral, Wyeth's oral contraceptive; Ayerst's Inderal (the third most prescribed drug in the United States); Premarin, an estrogen used in menopausal treatment; and Isordil, a coronary nitrate drug from Ives.

A third of AHP's sales are done outside the United States.

History. AHP's past is murky because that's the way the company would like it to be. There is no history of the company, authorized or unauthorized, and very few full-length newspaper or magazine stories have been written about them. American Home Products was incorporated in 1926 as a blend of nostrum makers. In at the beginning was a firm that had marketed Hill's Cascara Quinine, another that made a medicine called Petrolagar, and still another that made Freezone (still an AHP brand). Once AHP was formed, the strategy was to buy up small companies and add them to the corporate body. They bought and they bought, especially after Alvin George Brush, an accountant, took the helm in 1934. In his first eight years as chairman, while the country was mired for most of the time in a deep economic depression, Brush bought 34 drug and food companies for $7.6 million in cash and stock worth $18 million. Into the fold came Anacin, Black Flag, 3-in-One oil, BiSoDol, Kolynos toothpaste, G. Washington coffee, and Clapp's baby foods, among other products.

AHP's most important acquisition was a virtual gift. Wyeth, one of the oldest drug companies in America, was run by the Wyeth family until the business fell to Stuart Wyeth, an eccentric bachelor who spent a good part of his time cavorting in Paris. When he died there in 1929, he left John Wyeth & Co. to his alma mater, Harvard University. Harvard didn't have a clue what to do with the business and was pleased to get rid of it for virtually nothing in 1932. AHP, which scooped it up, knew what to do with it: Wyeth became the foundation of their prescription drug business and a well-known name to physicians. The division's operations are centered in the Philadelphia area.

Acquisitions continued to be a way of life for AHP. They moved into the housewares business with Ecko Products. They bought E. J. Brach, one of the largest of the packaged candy makers.

From the beginning it has been marketing prowess that made AHP's mixture work: when they took on Anacin, it was only a pain-killer promoted to dentists; when they took on Woolite, it was an insignificant product.

Reputation. *Business Week* summed it up 10 years ago: "One of the most common business platitudes is that a corporation's primary missions are to make money for its stockholders and to maximize profits by minimizing costs. At American Home, these ideas are a dogmatic way of life." AHP's advertising is not likely to win an award for creative excellence. As more than one observer has commented, "If you didn't have a headache before you saw or heard an Anacin commercial, you will after."

What they own. Because AHP functions as a holding company, they have an incredible number of operating subsidiaries. In their 1978 report to the Securities and Exchange Commission, they list 94 subsidiaries and add: "There have been omitted from the above list the names of eighty-four foreign subsidiaries and thirty domestic subsidiaries which, considered in the aggregate as a single subsidiary, would not constitute a significant subsidiary." AHP also owns 10% of the Wm. Wrigley Jr. chewing gum company stock.

Who owns and runs the company. There's very little turnover in the AHP executive suite. Alvin Brush was chairman from 1934 to 1965, when he was succeeded by William Laporte, the son of a Passaic, New Jersey, banker who was a friend of Brush's. Laporte, described as "intense, prim and dignified," went to Princeton and the Harvard Business School before joining AHP in 1938. Still running the company at the start of 1980, Laporte holds 127,156 shares, well under 1% of the total—but they are worth about $3 million, the dividends alone amounting to $200,000 a year. He also gets nearly a half-million dollars a year in salary.

Of AHP's 17 executive officers only one, Carol G. Emerling, secretary, is a woman. She joined the company in 1978 after four years as a regional director for the Federal Trade Commission.

In the public eye. AHP has gone head-to-

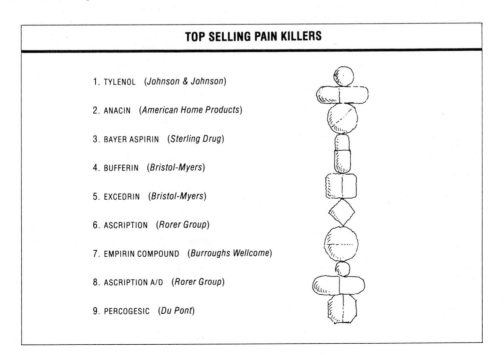

TOP SELLING PAIN KILLERS

1. TYLENOL   (*Johnson & Johnson*)

2. ANACIN   (*American Home Products*)

3. BAYER ASPIRIN   (*Sterling Drug*)

4. BUFFERIN   (*Bristol-Myers*)

5. EXCEDRIN   (*Bristol-Myers*)

6. ASCRIPTION   (*Rorer Group*)

7. EMPIRIN COMPOUND   (*Burroughs Wellcome*)

8. ASCRIPTION A/D   (*Rorer Group*)

9. PERCOGESIC   (*Du Pont*)

head with the Federal Trade Commission for many years over the claims made for a number of their products. The most recent dispute involves the advertising for Anacin. The FTC wants AHP to include in $24 million worth of advertising (the average budget for one year) the corrective statement that Anacin "is not a tension reliever." AHP has not claimed that Anacin relieved tension since 1973, but the FTC says consumers still believe it because of the many earlier Anacin pitches they were exposed to. AHP is fighting the decision to the bitter end.

Where they're going. AHP owes very little money and has plenty of cash on hand—$437 million at the end of 1978—to buy other companies.

Stock performance. AHP stock bought for $1,000 in 1970 sold for $1,137 on January 2, 1980.

Access. 685 Third Avenue, New York, New York 10017; (212) 986-1000.

Consumer brands.

Over-the-counter products: Anacin; Dristan cold tablets; Preparation H for hemorrhoids; Primatene Mist and Broniton for asthma; Anbesol antiseptic; Compound W for wart removal; Dry and Clear medicated cleanser; Semicid contraceptive; Predictor pregnancy test kit; Sleep-Eze; Arthritis Pain Formula; Denalen denture cleaner; Denorex medicated shampoo; Neet hair remover; Heet muscle ointment; Bisodol antacid; Outgro corn remover; Aero-Shave.
Oral contraceptive: Ovral.
Food products: Chef Boy-ar-dee; Dennison's; Gulden's mustard; G. Washington seasoning and broth; Jiffy and Crunch N Munch popcorn; Franklin nuts.
Candy: Brach's.
Household products: Woolite and Zero cold-water wash; Easy On starch; PAM cooking spray; Old English and Hawes furniture polish; Easy-Off oven and window cleaners; Wizard air fresheners and charcoal lighter; Black Flag insecticides; Depend-O bowl cleaner; Sani-foam all-purpose cleaner; HR2 rug shampoo; Griffin shoe polish; Antrol; Diaper-Pure; Snarol; Quick Dip; Aerowax; 3-in-One oil; Plastic Wood; Golden Touch; Dupli-color auto paint (Brush-In-Cap Touch Up, Auto-Panel, etc.); Pam.
Houseware: Ecko pots and pans; Baker's Secret bakeware; Top Drawer kitchen tools; Slaymaker locks.

⠿ American Hospital Supply

Sales: $2 billion
Profits: 109 million
Forbes 500 rank: 257
Rank in hospital supplies: 1
Founded: 1922
Employees: 29,800
Headquarters: Evanston, Illinois

With more than 1,500 peddlers hustling up business at hospitals around the world, American Hospital Supply dominates the medical supply business. About half of the 88,000 products sold by American Hospital are made in the company's own plants—products such as disposable plastic syringes, surgical gloves, bed pans, blood-typing serums, heart valves, and plastic lenses.

Still sitting on the board as honorary chairman is company founder Foster G. McGaw, who borrowed $30,000 in 1922 to start distributing hospital supplies and equipment in the Midwest. His name now graces Northwestern University's medical center in Chicago and that school's Big Ten fieldhouse. But while this supersalesman has seen laurels and honorary doctorates in his golden years, the company he founded has had its image tarnished. In 1978 Congress exposed the involvement of one of their international subsidiaries, American Health Facilities International, in a scheme to bribe South Korean officials with half a million dollars to obtain a health supply contract.

Access. One American Plaza, Evanston, Illinois 60201; (312) 866-4000.

BRISTOL-MYERS

Sales: $2.8 billion
Profits: $231.5 million
Forbes 500 rank: 178
Rank in hair coloring: 1
Rank in deodorant: 3
Rank in drain opener: 1
Rank in window cleaner: 1

THE DRUGMAKERS: WHERE THEY STAND

	1979 Sales	% in Prescription Drugs & other health care products (diagnostic aids, hospital supplies etc.)
1. JOHNSON & JOHNSON	$4.2 *billion*	18%
2. AMERICAN HOME PRODUCTS	$3.6 *billion*	39%
3. WARNER-LAMBERT	$3.2 *billion*	34%
4. BRISTOL-MYERS	$2.7 *billion*	34%
5. PFIZER	$2.7 *billion*	50%
6. MERCK	$2.3 *billion*	69%
7. ELI LILLY	$2.2 *billion*	50%
8. ABBOTT LABORATORIES	$1.6 *billion*	47%
9. UPJOHN	$1.5 *billion*	65%
10. STERLING DRUG	$1.5 *billion*	13%
11. SCHERING-PLOUGH	$1.4 *billion*	64%
12. SQUIBB	$1.4 *billion*	44%
13. SMITHKLINE	$1.3 *billion*	60%
14. RICHARDSON-MERRELL	$1.1 *billion*	25%

Source: *Business Week*, October 29, 1979, plus 1979 Annual Reports.

Founded: 1887
Employees: 32,600
Headquarters: New York, New York

What they do. "Headaches, hair, BO. They're what Bristol-Myers lives on." That's how *Forbes* characterizes this company. Bristol-Meyers turns out a slew of other products, including antibiotics, mops, laxatives, and infant formulas, but the preparations for headaches (Bufferin, Excedrin), hair (Clairol, Vitalis), and body odor (Ban) probably generate more than 40% of total sales.

Advertising space and time are Bristol-Myers's most important purchases. In 1978 the company spent $433 million on advertising and product promotion, more than a million dollars a day and almost one out of every five sales dollars. This is why you see Bristol-Myers commercials on the tube constantly; they are the nation's fourth-largest television advertiser.

The advertising is frequently surrounded by controversy. Bristol-Myers has gone to the mat more than once with the Federal Trade Commission over claims made for their headache remedies. On another front the agency that had been promoting the company's products for 44 years, Young & Rubicam, resigned $30 million of Bristol-Myers advertising in 1979 amidst considerable fanfare in the ad world, explaining that a "reasonable profit" could not be made under the conditions imposed by their client.

Bristol-Myers is nevertheless a big favorite on Wall Street: The market value of Bristol-Myers (what all of their stock sells for) is nearly triple that of Armco, a steel company, even though Armco and Bristol-Myers had almost identical 1978 profits (about $200 million each) and the steel company has assets valued at nearly double those of Bristol-Myers. On Wall Street fighting BO is viewed as healthier than making steel.

History. Bristol-Myers has been a familiar name to the public since the early days of radio, when the company's advertising head, Lee Bristol, regularly fielded comedian Fred Allen's wisecracks about network and advertising executives on a show sponsored by the company. Their advertising in those days had a one-two punch: "Ipana for the smile of beauty, Sal Hepatica for the smile of health." (For those too young to remember, Ipana, the company's original product, was a toothpaste, Sal Hepatica a laxative.)

The company goes back further, however. William McClaren Bristol and John R. Myers, graduates of Hamilton College in upstate New York, started the Clinton Pharmaceutical Company in 1887 to make bulk drugs for doctors. They adopted the Bristol-Myers name in 1900. William Bristol's three sons took over the company in 1928: Henry was president, William, Jr., headed manufacturing, and Lee advertising. During World War II, when the U.S.

government was looking for companies to make penicillin, the Bristols bought a company in Syracuse, New York, changed its name to Bristol Laboratories, and became one of the industry's leading antibiotic houses.

The Bristols can no longer be found in the company bearing their name. In their place are the Gelbs, Richard and Bruce, who came aboard in 1959, when Clairol was acquired. Lawrence Gelb, their father, was a chemist who pioneered the hair-coloring business at a time when its social standing was not too far from pornography. He sold the business to Bristol-Myers for $22 million four years after sales began to take off under the stimulus of a famous advertising campaign: "Does she . . . or doesn't she? Hair color so natural only her hairdresser knows for sure!" Richard and Bruce Gelb both graduated from the Harvard Business School and were very much at home in the world of advertising. Richard became president of Bristol-Meyers in 1967, by which time Clairol was the biggest product in the house.

Other acquisitions had meanwhile enlarged Bristol-Myers. The Drackett company of Cincinnati was purchased in 1965, bringing into the fold a clutch of household products, including Windex, O'Cedar mops, and Drano. Mead Johnson of Evansville, Indiana, was acquired in 1967, making Bristol-Myers a major maker of infant formula and children's vitamins.

The latest acquisition, in 1978, was Unitek, a California maker of orthodontic and dental supplies.

Reputation. Bristol-Myers is known not so much for imaginative product research as for marketing muscle, although they win some and lose some. Johnson & Johnson gave them a severe licking when Tylenol grabbed first place in the pain-killer market. But Bristol-Myers lucked out when the ban on flurocarbons crippled the aerosol deodorant market where they had never been strong, and their old Ban line came back strongly in roll-on and pump versions.

What they own. One hundred seventy-three subsidiaries in over 40 countries. They do about 30% of their business abroad.

Who owns and runs the company. The board is dominated by outside directors, one of whom is Martha Redfield Wallace,

How Clairol Brought Hair Dye Out of the Closet

In 1955 most Americans still associated tinted hair with shady ladies or, at best, aging actresses. Like lipstick, rouge, and mascara in the years before World War I, hair dye carried a moral stigma: "decent" women who colored their hair kept it a guilty secret. No more than 7% of all women dyed their hair.

These prejudices confronted Clairol at a time when the company believed they had perfected a line of hair colorings—Miss Clairol—good enough to find a huge market. The only barrier to success was the need to make dyed hair socially acceptable.

Clairol called in the mammoth advertising firm of Foote, Cone & Belding to reconstruct America's view of hair dye. According to Fairfax Cone's autobiography, *With All Its Faults,* a copywriter named Shirley Polykoff mas-

terminded the "Does She or Doesn't She" campaign, inventing not only the teaser line but the notion of putting a child in every ad. The child, she explained, added an aura of warmth and respectability, leading readers to see the woman model as "a mother, aunt, sister, teacher, or any other figure the viewer might choose for herself as a symbol of good moral character and good taste."

The sunwashed outdoor settings enhanced the image of naturalness, while the ad copy, "Hair Color So Natural Only Her Hairdresser Knows for Sure," reassured timid prospective customers that no garish, telltale hues would reveal their secret.

Clairol planned to invest their whole magazine ad budget for the new campaign in a family magazine like *Life,* reasoning that hair coloring

should become a family affair. But *Life* turned the ads down flat. The teaser line was too suggestive, said copy censors. Readers might ask themselves: "Does she or doesn't she *what?"*

Having already faced this objection from Clairol executives who worried about the ad's double entendre, Richard Gelb, son of Clairol founder Lawrence Gelb, challenged the all-male censor panel to research the ad's impact on *Life* 's women employees. The result: not a single woman claimed to see anything in the ad but the intended meanings.

Life relented, and soon dyed hair ceased to be shocking. By the late 1960s nearly 70% of American women were reported to use hair coloring, as well as an estimated 2 million men.

executive director of the Henry Luce Foundation. Clairol was bought for cash, and the Gelbs do not have huge blocks of stock. Bruce Gelb, executive vice-president of the company, does not have a board seat. His older brother, Richard, is chairman. Richard also serves as a director of the New York Times Company and New York's Lincoln Center for the Performing Arts. He is a charter trustee of Phillips Academy–Andover. Bristol-Myers is a Jewish-managed company in an industry with a tradition of antisemitism.

In the public eye. An administrative law judge of the Federal Trade Commission ruled in 1979 that Bristol-Myers had made unsubstantiated claims for the pain relievers Bufferin, Excedrin, and Excedrin P.M. When a newscaster for WCBS–New York reported that the FTC found the company's advertising claims for the painkillers to be "hogwash," Bristol-Myers filed a $25 million libel suit against CBS in late 1979, pointing out that an administrative law judge's ruling is not the final story.

Where they're going. With roughly $300 million cash on hand, Bristol-Myers is expected to be actively looking for other companies to buy. They're also making a strong run in the cold remedies market with Comtrex, which combines features of Contac, Dristan, and Nyquil.

Stock performance. Bristol-Myers stock bought for $1,000 in 1970 sold for $987 on January 2, 1980.

Access. 345 Park Avenue, New York, New York 10022; (212) 644-2100.

Consumer brands.

Toiletries and beauty aids: Clairol hair colorings; Clairol Herbal Essence, Body on Tap, and Condition shampoos; Final Net Clairmist hair sprays; Vitalis hair preparation; Ban and Tickle deodorants and antiperspirants; Son of a Gun and One for the Road hair driers; Kindness electric hairsetters.
Over-the-counter products: Bufferin and Excedrin analgesics; Colace and Peri-Colace anticonstipants; Keri Lotion moisturizer; Enfamil infant formula; Vi-Sols and Natalins vitamins; Sustagen nutritional supplement; Comtrex cold reliever.
Household products: Windex window cleaner; Vanish bowl cleaner; Drano drain opener; O-Cedar mops; Javex bleaches; Handle With Care clothes wash; Fleecy fabric softener.

Hoffmann-La Roche

Sales: $2.8 billion
Profits: $116 million
Rank among Swiss companies: 4
Rank in tranquilizers: 1
Rank in vitamins: 1
Founded: 1896
Employees: 40,000
Headquarters: Basel, Switzerland
U.S. headquarters: Nutley, New Jersey

What they do. Many jittery people would say that any company that makes the popular tranquilizers Valium and Librium can't be all bad. Every year an estimated 50 million prescriptions are written for Valium, the best-selling drug (that is, legal drug) of the nervous 1970s. Roche, as the company is called, also pioneered in the synthesis of vitamins. And Roche claims to be the world's largest producer of vitamin C, which has been trumpeted by some as the cure-all for everything from infections to the common cold.

But in recent years they have come under attack for a variety of alleged sins. Their effective promotion of Valium—Roche is recognized as one of most artful of drug promoters—was said to have caused an undue, some say addictive, reliance on this drug. "Thousands of Americans are hooked [on Valium] and don't know it," said Senator Edward M. Kennedy during 1979 Senate hearings on the prescribing of Valium.

Earlier, several European nations had demanded that Roche roll back the prices of Librium and Valium, charging that the company was reaping unconscionable profits on those two drugs. And the company was blamed for Italy's worst ecological disaster when its chemical plant in a suburb of Milan blew up in 1976.

The profiteering charges induced Roche, a Swiss firm, to lift slightly the veil that has traditionally shrouded the company. As a family-controlled enterprise with little stock in the hands of the public, Roche is under no obligation to disclose significant financial information to the outside world. But the furor in Europe led the company in 1974 to issue their first annual report covering the combined results of worldwide operations. Since then it has continued to issue annual reports, although, as the *Wall Street Journal* noted, "analysts consider

Roche's financial reporting skimpy even by Swiss standards."

Roche's U.S. affiliate is much more than a small outpost. In its own right the company is one of the oldest and largest in the American drug industry and is a major source of research (Librium and Valium were developed in Nutley, New Jersey, not Basel). The United States accounts for a third of Roche's worldwide sales volume. The U.S. prescription drug arm, Roche Laboratories, markets more than 40 products for physicians, employing an army of 700 sales representatives to call on doctors and hospitals. Roche is one of the largest advertisers in U.S. medical journals.

In addition to the two famous tranquilizers, the product lineup includes the sulfa drug, Gantrisin, and the most effective drug yet developed to treat Parkinson's disease, Larodopa. Also marketed in the United States are the Pantene hair products line, a by-product of Roche's vitamin research.

History. Research has been a hallmark of the Roche company since it was founded in 1896 by 28-year-old Fritz Hoffmann, a member of an old Basel merchant family. Following Swiss custom, Hoffmann had added his wife's maiden name to his when he married Adele La Roche. Hoffmann's idea from the start was to replace the crude mixtures compounded by pharmacists with standardized, packaged drugs. One of his first employees was an aggressive 21-year-old chemist, Emil C. Barell. In 1898 Barell produced the company's first specialty drug, a cough remedy called Thiocal, and in 1904, Digalen, the first injectable digitalis (used by heart patients); both are still in use today. Barell initiated programs by which Hoffmann-La Roche also funded scientists' research at universities and cultivated the medical profession. He once noted, "Not the man in the street, but the doctor is my customer."

The fledgling firm was quick to realize the world was its market, and before the First World War Hoffmann-La Roche had plants in a dozen countries. One of the largest, in Russia, was confiscated after the 1917 revolution. The U.S. branch was estab-

---

THE MOST POPPED PILLS

Annual World Wide Sales/Major Use

1. VALIUM   (*Hoffmann-La Roche*) $600 *million/Tranquilizer*
2. TAGAMET   (*SmithKline*) $500 *million/Ulcers*
3. ALDOMET   (*Merck*) $300 *million/High blood pressure*
4. CLINORIL   (*Merck*) $250 *million/Arthritis*
5. GARAMYCIN   (*Schering Plough*) $240 *million/Infection*
6. INDOCIN   (*Merck*) $200 *million/Arthritis*
7. LASIX   (*Hoechst*) $200 *million/High blood pressure*
8. INDERAL   (*American Home Products*) $200 *million/High blood pressure*
9. VIBRAMYCIN   (*Pfizer*) $200 *million/Infection*
10. KEFLEX   (*Eli Lilly*) $200 *million/Infection*
11. KEFLIN-N   (*Eli Lilly*) $150 *million/Infection*
12. MOTRIN   (*Upjohn*) $150 *million/Arthritis*
13. OVRAL   (*American Home Products*) $150 *million/Birth control*

Source: *Advertising Age*, April 2, 1979.

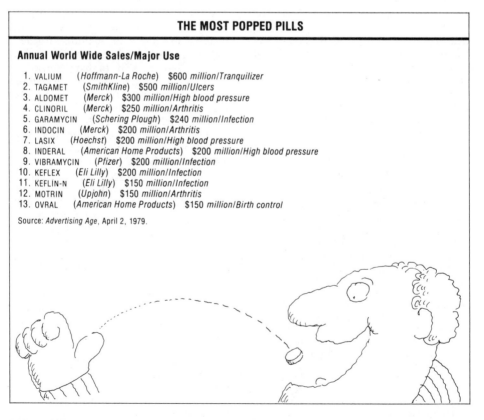

lished in lower Manhattan, near Wall Street (where Roche shares were never to trade), in 1905.

Roche's mold was thus set very early: heavy expenditures on research, lavish attention to doctors, multinational operations.

Roche has been research oriented on both sides of the Atlantic. In the thirties Swiss scientists did work that resulted in the synthesizing of vitamins C, E, and A. By building plants to mass-produce them, Roche sharply reduced vitamin prices. In Nutley, where Roche bought an abandoned farm and built its new U.S. headquarters in 1929, researchers were also productive. Among their discoveries have been Gantrisin, a sulfonamide introduced in 1949; Librium (1960); Valium (1963) and Rimifon (1951), a tuberculosis drug developed in a Roche chemotherapy department headed by Dr. Robert J. Schnitzer, who escaped from the Buchenwald concentration camp in 1939.

The U.S. company became particularly important to the Swiss parent during the Second World War. After France fell to the Germans in 1940, Dr. Barell himself moved to Nutley to direct Hoffmann-La Roche's worldwide operations from there for the balance of the war. Barell had become the head of the company in 1920 when Fritz Hoffmann died, and he continued to lead the company until his death in 1953 at the age of 79.

In the same year Barell assumed the leadership of the parent company, a supersalesman named Elmer H. Bobst became president of the American affiliate. Nine years earlier, in 1911, Bobst had been hired as a $30-a-week salesman. Son of a poor clergyman, Bobst was a pharmacist hired for the job mainly because his handwriting impressed the Roche personnel people, who believed in graphology. It turned out that Bobst's application had been written by his wife.

After becoming president of the American branch, Bobst worked on a contract

Drug Dealing, Swiss-style

Do the drugs made by legitimate pharmaceutical companies—narcotics, for example—sometimes end up in illegal street traffic? In his autobiography, *Bobst*, published by David McKay & Co. in 1973, drug industry pioneer Elmer H. Bobst described two run-ins he had on this question with the Swiss managers of Hoffmann-La Roche.

The first came in 1923 when Bobst, then head of U.S. operations for Roche, made his first trip to the company headquarters in Basle. Prior to going he had been informed by the U.S. Commissioner of Narcotics that Roche had been shipping illegal opiates to Mexico, Canada, and the United States. Bobst, the son of a Lutheran minister, told the Swiss that they must stop these shipments or else the U.S. government would stop all imports from Roche. According to Bobst, Dr. Emil Barell of

Roche replied: "Mr. Bobst, you did not know this, but we make $200,000 or more a year on those sales. We get a dollar, sometimes two dollars, more per ounce from those purchasers than through normal channels. Why must it stop? It's perfectly legal for us in Switzerland to fill any orders we receive."

Roche finally agreed to sign a statement saying they would not ship narcotics to illegal purchasers in Mexico, Canada, or the United States after Bobst told them: "If you attempt to carry on this trade that is degrading this company, there will be no Roche in America."

Twenty years later, when Dr. Barell had come to Nutley, New Jersey, to sit out World War II, Bobst was tipped off by Harry Anslinger, the U.S. narcotics commissioner, that Roche had planted acres of poppy plants in Argentina from which they

were planning to harvest the straw to produce morphine—all of which was contrary to the rules of the Geneva Convention on narcotics. Upon returning from Washington to Nutley, Bobst said he dressed down Dr. Barell and his brother-in-law, who also worked for the company, by declaring: "We have a fence around this plant and a guard on the gate. If either of you engage in any action of this sort again, I will instruct the guards to lock you out for good."

Barell, according to Bobst's account, was later hauled before the Alien Property Commission and told that if he didn't stop fooling around with narcotics he would either be thrown out of the country or interned.

Barell was head of Hoffmann-La Roche from 1920 to 1953.

that paid him $15,000 a year and 5% of profits before taxes, a deal that was eventually to make him one of the highest paid persons in the country. In his final year with Roche, 1944, Bobst outearned every business executive in the land, with the exception of the president of General Motors. Bobst loved to sell. He used to write "Dear Doctor" letters to physicians urging them to prescribe Roche drugs. In 1932, at the height of the Depression, he walked into a Lincoln automobile showroom in Montclair, New Jersey, and said to the salesman: "I'll take two. One of these and one of those. And I'll pay cash. I want to show my faith in the economy of this country."

Bobst was used to running his own show, and when Barell came to America during World War II, the two clashed. In his autobiography, published in 1973, Bobst told how he gave Barell a tongue-lashing when he learned that the Swiss had planted opium poppy plants in Argentina to extract morphine in violation of the rules of the Geneva convention on narcotics. In 1944, after repeated fights, Bobst quit, telling Barell: "The thing that's bothering you, Dr. Barell, is that you are not happy sitting in that chair you occupy. You want to sit in this chair [head of the American company], behind my desk. Well, you're not big enough to fill it."

To replace Bobst, who later went on to a second career with Warner-Lambert, Dr. Barell hired 6'5" Lawrence D. Barney, who had spent the previous 14 years as business manager of the Wisconsin Alumni Research Foundation, a research center that held valuable patents. Barney was president of Roche's American branch for the next 20 years.

Roche's commitment to research is exemplified in the Roche Institute of Molecular Biology, established at Nutley in 1967. Dedicated to basic research in the life sciences, the Institute, although clearly connected to a commercial enterprise, enjoys much of the academic freedom of an educational institution. It has a permanent staff of 120 scientists, who the company says are free to pursue projects "guided solely by the scientific importance of a problem." Leading scientists from all over the world are invited to spend a year or two at the Institute to pursue research of their own choosing.

The Nutley facility is matched by an Institute of Immunology that Roche main-tains in Basel. Roche has also started new research institutes in Japan and Australia, the latter specializing in marine pharmacology.

Reputation. Roche is recognized as a company that develops significant therapeutic agents. *Fortune* once depicted them as "a lucky company." They are known as a tough and aggressive competitor, not afraid to spend heavily on elaborate promotional materials to bedazzle the medical profession. Roche is also recognized as a good place to work; the U.S. company says it receives more than 60,000 applications for employment annually. And being Swiss owned they are very secretive.

What they own. Manufacturing facilities in 30 countries. In the United States Roche has facilities at 33 locations, the biggest concentration—16—being in the state of New Jersey, where the headquarters office is. At Belvidere, New Jersey, on the banks of the Delaware River, Roche operates the world's largest plant for the production of ascorbic acid (vitamin C), with an annual output of 10,000 tons. In 1963 the parent company acquired another Swiss firm, Givaudan SA, which is now the world's second-largest manufacturer, after International Flavors & Fragrances, of aromatics and flavors used in the food and cosmetic industries. Roche has been called a "marvel of self-financed growth." It has little or no debt and therefore finances research and new investments out of profits. With an annual research budget estimated at more than $300 million, that's a feat well beyond the capabilities or imagination of nearly all the companies in the world.

Who owns and runs the company. Fritz Hoffmann's family retains control, but the company is run by professional managers—in recent years, bankers in Switzerland and salesmen in the United States. Of the founding family's stock, 49% is voted by board member Paul Sacher, who conducts a chamber orchestra in Basel. His wife's

> Tranquilizers are a $2.3 billion-a-year business in the United States. Hoffmann-LaRoche, maker of Valium, Librium, and Dalmane, holds 80% of this market.

first husband, Emanuel Hoffmann (who was killed in a sports car accident in 1932), was a son of the founder. Head of the U.S. company is Irwin Lerner, who grew up in a Newark family too poor to send him to medical school. He rose to the top at Roche by being product manager on Librium and Valium.

In the public eye. In 1976 a Roche-owned chemical plant at Seveso, Italy, exploded, spreading a white cloud of deadly dioxin over 4,000 acres. A subsequent inquiry faulted Roche for unsafe conditions at the plant and for waiting 27 hours after the accident before notifying officials. More than 700 persons had to be evacuated from their homes; some 300 children later developed various skin diseases; others reported swollen livers; and nearly 40,000 animals (including rabbits, chickens, and dogs) died from eating dioxin-coated vegetables. Nearly 300 former residents of the town may never return to a fenced-off area of 215 acres still contaminated by a poison 1,000 times more toxic than strychnine. In early 1980 Roche agreed to pay Italian authorities $114 million in compensation, one of the largest amounts ever paid in a pollution claim case.

Even earlier than the Seveso explosion, the company felt harassed by politicians all over the world and has since been taking an increasingly combatative position. When various European governments challenged Roche on drug pricing in 1975, Adolf W. Jann, who was then chairman, retorted: "How can a government say a drug is too expensive? In England, the actual price for a daily dosage of Valium costs less than a single cigarette." Another company official put it this way: "If all the people who take Valium can work an extra two days a year, then British industry and the government would have regained all the extra profits it says we've earned."

In 1974 the directorate of the European Economic Community brought charges against Roche for abusing its dominant position in the vitamin market by giving rebates to large customers. The case was based on documents leaked by a disgruntled Roche manager, Stanley Adams. Roche was so furious at this transgression that when Adams entered Switzerland in 1975, the company had him arrested for industrial espionage and jailed in Basel. (Adams's wife committed suicide while he was in jail.) In

June 1976 Roche was found guilty of breaking the Common Market trade rules and fined $390,000. They appealed. In February 1979 the European Court of Justice upheld the conviction but reduced the fine to $260,000.

In the United States Roche has made a valiant effort to be a good company to work for by offering excellent fringe benefit programs to employees. In 1978 they had nearly 800 employees who had been with the company for more than 25 years.

Where they're going. Roche is moving into the production of xylitol, a crystalline fructose hailed as a healthful, low-calorie alternative to sugar. But their big bet is still in the research laboratories. For example, Roche is reported to be in the forefront of research on interferon, a protein believed by some medical researchers to have potential as an effective anticancer agent. Research has always paid off for Roche.

Access. Nutley, New Jersey 07110; (201) 235-5000.

Consumer brand.

Pantene hair products.

Johnson & Johnson

Sales $4.2 billion
Profits: $352.1 million
Forbes 500 rank: 105
Rank in adhesive bandages: 1
Rank in headache remedies: 1
Rank in contraceptives: 1
Rank in shampoo: 4
Rank in disposable diapers: 2
Founded: 1885
Employees: 67,000
Headquarters: New Brunswick, New Jersey

What they do. Try as you might, you just can't avoid Johnson & Johnson. At every stage of your life, they're waiting for you at the corner. The doctor who delivered you may have used J & J surgical gloves, hypodermic needles, or hemostats; and when your mother brought you home, she probably used some of J & J's baby products—oil, lotion, powder, shampoo, or disposable diapers. The time you fell off your bike and skinned your knee, you almost certainly wore a Johnson & Johnson Band-Aid.

As you approached puberty and learned the rudiments of feminine hygiene, you might have heard of Modess, Stayfree, or Carefree tampons and sanitary napkins— all of them J & J brand names. One night a few years later you probably came in contact with one of J & J's Ortho contraceptives—perhaps a birth-control pill or an intrauterine device, or maybe contraceptive foam or cream. On those nights when you had a headache and weren't in the mood, you might have resorted to a couple of J & J's Tylenol, the nation's most popular headache remedy.

When the infirmities of age take you back to the hospital, J & J will turn up again with surgical sutures, prescription and nonprescription drugs, even kidney dialysis machines. And as you draw your final breath, take one last look at the doctor's gown—and guess who made it.

History. In the 1870s medical science was just beginning to understand the need for proper hygiene in the operating room. British surgeon Sir Joseph Lister had accurately identified airborne germs as the principal cause of infection in hospitals. He recommended that all operating rooms, patients, and medical staff be frequently sprayed with a fine mist of carbolic acid, but his sterilization methods were too complex and cumbersome for most American hospitals. Robert Wood Johnson, who had been im-

pressed by a speech Lister gave in 1876, thought he had a better idea. In 1885 he formed a partnership with his two brothers, James Wood and Edward Mead Johnson, and, in a former wallpaper factory in New Brunswick, New Jersey, began making antiseptic, individually wrapped surgical dressings. Their first products were medicinal plasters mixed with an adhesive, but they soon developed an absorbent cotton-and-gauze dressing that could be mass-produced and shipped in quantity to large hospitals and podunk doctors alike. Their 1888 book on antiseptic procedures, *Modern Methods of Antiseptic Wound Treatment*, became the standard manual and won them a following among the medical profession. (Edward Mead Johnson left in 1897 to form his own drug company; Mead Johnson is now a subsidiary of Bristol-Myers.)

During the 1890s Johnson & Johnson began to experiment with dry heat and steam in an attempt to make a bandage which was not only antiseptic but sterile. They slowly evolved a process of repeated sterilization during production, and by 1897 they were beginning to use the new technique on catgut sutures.

Demand for the sterile bandages increased dramatically in the early twentieth century, and James Wood Johnson, who had succeeded his older brother as president in 1910, began to branch out into other products—the most famous being the Band-Aid, an adhesive bandage for consumer use. A newlywed J & J employee named Earl Dickson came up with the new bandage in 1920 because his wife, who was inexperienced in the kitchen, kept burning and cutting herself. Dickson showed the prototypes to his boss and, within the year, Johnson & Johnson was turning out Band-Aids. The product soon became standard issue in first-aid kits. One World War II bomber crew even credited Band-Aids with saving their lives: they had used them to patch leaks in the damaged plane's hydraulic system and were thus able to land safely.

Robert Wood Johnson, son of the founder, took over the company in 1932. Later known as "the General" because of his World War II career as a brigadier general, Johnson established policies which persist at the company today. Because he favored political involvement, some Johnson & Johnson executives took leaves of absence and went into state and local politics. Because he often said, "Make your top managers rich and they will make you richer," many J & J officers have retired as millionaires. And, because he believed in decentralization, J & J began buying companies and setting them up under virtually autonomous bosses. Today they own more than 100 different companies, each operating more or less independently.

Johnson & Johnson is known as a brilliant marketing company—a gold mine of profitable consumer products. They were among the first to capitalize on the postwar baby boom, and they have now expanded their product line to appeal to every age group in the population. Some companies are good at selling to doctors, others to consumers; J & J seems to be superb in both arenas. Their McNeil Laboratories division had a nonaspirin painreliever, Tylenol, that was sold for many years as a prescription drug, especially for children. J & J's marketing whizzes transformed it into a consumer drug pitted directly against Anacin, Bufferin, and Bayer. When Bristol-Myers moved in with a copycat product, Datril, in 1975, pricing it well below Tylenol, J & J fought back like a tiger, slashing prices on Tylenol and beefing up advertising. J & J whipped Bristol-Myers soundly—and in 1978 Tylenol became the best-selling product in the nation's drugstores.

J & J is not afraid to take on the big guys. They upgraded their baby shampoo into an adult product and took significant chunks of the market away from Procter & Gamble (Head & Shoulders, Prell). They have also been successful at selling their baby lotions and powders to adults. Altogether, J & J's consumer products account for about 45% of their sales.

They have, however, had their share of failures. A rat poison called Raticate went nowhere, and a hand lotion called Loving Hands also died on the shelves—possibly because its original name had been Pretty Paws. The company's Micrin mouthwash came on like gangbusters when it was introduced in 1961, and it rapidly acquired a 15% share of the market, second only to Warner-Lambert's Listerine. But by 1972 its share had fallen to a mere 4%, and in 1977 Micrin was quietly taken off the market. One advertising executive claimed the product failed because it was colored blue in order to differentiate it from competitors in that multihued marketplace. But a more likely reason is that J & J decided it was not going to put up the big bucks in this game

to fight Listerine and a new Procter & Gamble entry, Scope.

Reputation. Johnson & Johnson has a knack for selling products on television. Their campaign in the late 1970s for baby shampoo in the adult market—a perfect example—worked so well partly because they used popular athletes like Fran Tarkenton to promote it and partly because the slogan "gentle enough to use every day" convinced consumers.

What they own. Johnson & Johnson operates 20 different companies in the United States, all making products sold under J & J's brand names. They have affiliated companies in 41 foreign nations, and 168 manufacturing facilities worldwide.

Who owns and runs the company. Johnson & Johnson did not elect their first "outside" director (one who was not an officer of the company) until 1978. Of their 17 directors only 4 are now outsiders. As their former chairman, Philip Hofmann, once told the *New York Times*, "We have a board of directors meeting every day at lunch."

The Robert Wood Johnson Foundation, the second-largest foundation in the country, controls about 20% of the company's stock. Another 25% is held by the Johnson family itself, although the family no longer has any members on the board.

The company has a long history of secrecy and prefers to keep as low a profile as is humanly possible. In 1959 the General even considered delisting J & J stock from the New York Stock Exchange rather than be forced to file a revealing proxy statement. J & J loosened up somewhat after the General's death in 1968; but for a company with more than $4 billion in annual sales, it is astonishing that their business publication clippings wouldn't even fill a standard manila envelope.

In the public eye. The Robert Wood Johnson Foundation, created from a codicil in the General's will, grants an estimated $50 million annually to health and medical research. The country's second-largest foundation—behind the Ford but ahead of the Carnegie, Mellon, and Rockefeller foundations—after it received J & J stock worth more than $1 billion in 1971, the Johnson Foundation funds programs in health care, thereby giving money to institutions such as hospitals that are good J & J customers.

J & J has been praised for the decision to remain in New Brunswick, a town of only 40,000 people. New Jersey Governor Brendan Byrne told the *New York Times* in 1978 that the new J & J headquarters was "a major vote of confidence by one of our leading corporations in the future of a historic major city in our state."

On the negative side Johnson & Johnson has had a few problems with their birth-control pills. One oral contraceptive was recalled in 1975 when the company found unacceptably low levels of the female hormone estrogen in the pills. Two years later federal investigators documented cases of enlarged male breasts and vaginal bleeding among workers at the company's Puerto Rican Ortho plant. Once again the trouble was caused by estrogen, the main ingredient in Ortho's oral contraceptives. Several other makers of birth-control pills have had similar problems with the hormone.

Where they're going. Although J & J is loath to discuss their research and development in a highly competitive field, they have revealed several products now being tested. One of these, the Proximate disposable skin stapler, punches individual stitches into a wound—closing surgical incisions ten times faster than the conventional suturing method. And, in spite of management's insistence that J & J intends to remain in their basic businesses, they have recently begun manufacturing sausage casings for precooked institutional and consumer sausages.

Stock performance. Johnson & Johnson stock bought for $1,000 in 1970 sold for $1,-321 on January 2, 1980.

Access. 501 George Street, New Brunswick, New Jersey 08903; (201) 524-0400.

Consumer brands.

Baby products: Johnson & Johnson Baby Shampoo, Baby Oil, Baby Powder, Baby Lotion, and Disposable Diapers.
Feminine hygiene products: Modess sanitary napkins; Stayfree Mini-Pads and Maxi-Pads; Carefree Panty Shields; o.b. tampons.
Health aids: Tylenol analgesic; CoTylenol Cold Formula; Sine-Aid sinus reliever; Band-Aids.
Other products: Coets cosmetic squares; Shower-To-Shower body powder; Ortho contraceptive creams & foams.

Lilly

Sales: $2.2 billion
Profits: $329 million
Forbes 500 rank: 242
Rank in prescription drugs: 3
Rank in antibiotics: 1
Rank in insulin: 1
Rank in prescription painkillers: 1
Founded: 1876
Employees: 24,000
Headquarters: Indianapolis, Indiana

What they do. American doctors may have written Eli Lilly drugs on their prescription pads more often than those of any other company. Some critics think *too* often.

Lilly presents a contradictory picture. Regarded as one of the pillars of the U.S. drug establishment, they have long enjoyed the confidence of the medical profession. They developed some of the major lifesaving drugs of the century, most notably insulin and the Salk vaccine. On the other hand, there is evidence that Lilly has on occasion abused its respected position by producing addictive drugs. Around the turn of the century, Lilly was making cough syrups laced with heroin.

Lilly was an early experimenter with barbiturates. But they made their mark with insulin, a hormone extracted from the pancreas glands of animals. Insulin has extended the lives of hundreds of thousands of diabetics, victims of a mysterious disease that makes the body unable to handle sugar. Lilly made the first commercial batch of insulin in 1923, and they still held 85% of the market in 1979 when 1.6 million Americans were injecting it into their bloodstreams. Established firmly on their success with insulin, Lilly expanded until they were making more than 1,000 drug products. From 1930 to 1960 they were generally number 1 in the prescription drug business.

They still rank in the top tier, with sales of about $1 billion in "ethical drugs" (those sold only through the medical profession). More than half of that volume is in antibiotics. Lilly's antibiotic brands include Keflin, Mandol, Vi-Cillin K, and Ilosone. No Lilly

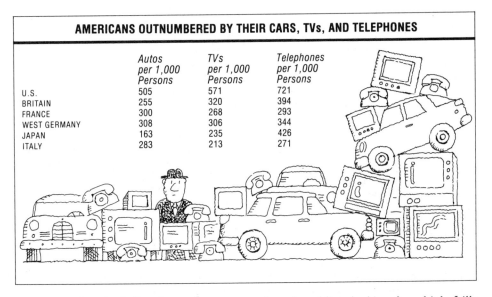

	Autos per 1,000 Persons	TVs per 1,000 Persons	Telephones per 1,000 Persons
U.S.	505	571	721
BRITAIN	255	320	394
FRANCE	300	268	293
WEST GERMANY	308	306	344
JAPAN	163	235	426
ITALY	283	213	271

AMERICANS OUTNUMBERED BY THEIR CARS, TVs, AND TELEPHONES

drugs are advertised directly to the user. Over-the-counter drugs are "not in keeping with our image," explains Chairman Richard D. Wood. "Let's face it," another top Lilly executive once said, "we make a product that nobody really wants to buy." To get doctors to prescribe their drugs Lilly maintains a formidable marketing apparatus. They're the only major drug company to distribute exclusively through wholesalers, thereby saving all their firepower for the medical profession. Lilly's detail force (the people who call on doctors and hospitals) numbers 1,150 persons, 80% of them registered pharmacists. It's the largest sales organization in the industry.

The joy and agony of Lilly are summed up in the drug Darvon. Introduced in 1957, it was billed as a nonnarcotic painkiller without the addictive properties of morphine and codeine. Lilly made it a winner with doctors: Darvon became the third most prescribed drug in the nation, with annual sales of nearly $100 million. In 1974 1.5 billion Darvon pills were dispensed. Then came a whiplash. As the *New York Times* reported, Lilly suddenly found themselves confronting charges that "Darvon was on the one hand even less effective than aspirin in killing pain and on the other, more common even than heroin in killing people." In 1978 Dr. Sidney M. Wolfe, director of the Nader-sponsored Health Research Group in Washington, D.C., demanded that Darvon be banned. He charged that it is addictive and associated with suicides, accidental overdoses, and

misuse by addicts looking for a high. Lilly researchers defended Darvon but, while the drug remained the leading prescription painkiller, the attack continued. In 1979 Health, Education, & Welfare Secretary Joseph Califano specifically asked doctors to avoid prescribing Darvon and urged patients not to ask for it. Lilly was also ordered to warn doctors about possible hazards associated with Darvon. In March 1980 the Food and Drug Administration sharply criticized Lilly for inadequate warnings, saying that Lilly's promise to contact 125,-000 doctors about Darvon's dangers had turned into "a standard promotional campaign." The active chemical in Darvon is propoxyphene, closely related to methadone, which was once hailed as a miraculous way to get addicts off heroin. Some medical authorities now believe methadone to be just as addictive as heroin. The largest maker of methadone also happens to be Eli Lilly.

History. Colonel Eli Lilly, a Civil War veteran (9th Indiana Cavalry), opened a small laboratory in downtown Indianapolis on May 10, 1876, and began making drugs of the time: pills, fluid extracts, elixirs. He was the first to develop gelatin-coated capsules to hold medicines, and to this day Lilly is one of the largest makers of empty capsules. He was also one of the first aggressive advertisers, promoting his products well beyond the Indianapolis area. As the company prospered he turned his attention to civic works. He donated a children's hospital to the city, and during the financial panic of 1893 he headed a committee to provide relief to the poor. Colonel Lilly died of cancer in 1898, succeeded by his son Josiah, a registered pharmacist. Josiah's two sons, Eli and Josiah, Jr., also became pharmacists in preparation for their careers in the family business. The founder's namesake became president in 1932; Josiah, Jr., succeeded his brother in 1948.

Lilly was a paternalistic company. In the Depression that followed the 1929 stock market crash, the Lillys fired no one, finding make-work jobs for employees rather than laying them off. Meanwhile the Lillys continued the family tradition of concern for Indianapolis. *Forbes* reported in 1971: "In Indianapolis their word is close to being law. Because the company did not want *Forbes* to do this story, the Indianapolis newspapers refused to sell pictures of the family or the company."

On the product development side not much is written about the company's drugs prior to 1923, when insulin was first made. There is a reference to a patent medicine called Succus Alterans, a compound recommended for everything from rheumatism to syphilis. Until 1919 Lilly's catalog also listed 4 kinds of heroin cough medicine. Their Glycerine Heroin Compound, containing one-eighth of a gram per pint of heroin hydrochloride, came in pint or gallon bottles. In the early part of this century heroin was touted as a cure for morphine addiction, just as methadone was to be touted as a cure for heroin addiction.

After launching insulin in 1923, Lilly synthesized more than 100 barbituric acids in their laboratories to produce Amytal and Amytal Sodium, drugs which became important in surgery and obstetrics. In 1928 they developed a liver extract to treat pernicious anemia. In 1936 they introduced the barbiturate Seconal as a sedative. Lilly be-

gan putting methadone in cough medicine after World War II. How did they get involved in methadone? Michael Smith, head of the largest drug detoxification program in South Bronx, New York, described it this way in his testimony before the National Hearings on the Heroin Epidemic in 1976:

Immediately after World War II in Europe, a Lilly research chemist named Dr. Ervin C. Kleiderer joined the Technical Industrial Intelligence Committee of the State Department, which was investigating Nazi drug companies. Kleiderer's team brought methadone to this country. Two years later Lilly marketed Dolophine cough medicine, retaining the Nazi brand name for methadone, which had been chosen to honor Adolph Hitler.

Lysergic acid, used in obstetrics (and the basic ingredient of LSD), was synthesized by Lilly in 1954. A year later Lilly played the leading role in manufacturing the Salk polio vaccine. Lilly turned out 60% of the Salk vaccine.

The Lilly Endowment, established by the family in 1937, became one of the major philanthropic organizations in the nation. Its overseers were the two sons of Josiah K. Lilly. Josiah, Jr., was an incredible collector. In 1956 he presented his collection of rare books, valued at more than $5 million and including some 20,000 first editions, to Indiana University. The Eli Lilly Library at Indiana instantly became one of the nation's great repositories of rare books. Josiah also had a collection of 6,000 gold coins —some dating from the early Mesopotamian empires—described by the Smithsonian Institution as one that "surpasses in scope any other collected by one man." He spent his later years reading the *Encyclopaedia Britannica*, and had reached the letter *G* at his death in 1966. His brother Eli was an active churchman and a student of history, especially Indiana history. He wrote a book, *Prehistoric Antiquities of Indiana*, and on his 84th birthday in 1969, Governor Edgar D. Whitcomb proclaimed April 1 "Mr. Eli Lilly Day." He died in 1977 at 91, outliving his wife and daughter.

Reputation. Even competitors acknowledge that Lilly has the premier marketing organization in the drug industry. An old industry saying has it that no matter who introduces a new drug, Lilly will manage to snare 6% to 8% of the market.

> According to *American Druggist*, marketers of over-the-counter drugs view with optimism the tremendous surge toward self-care, the result of a "growing desire among Americans to achieve greater physical well-being, vigor, and self-reliance in health matters." This trade journal also cites rising medical costs, "which encourages consumers to seek out low-cost remedies before visiting a doctor."

What they own. In addition to their pharmaceutical business, Lilly makes and sells $350 million worth of agricultural chemicals a year. Their main product is Treflan, a weed controller used on more than 50 crops. In 1970 they moved into cosmetics by outbidding American Cyanamid for the Elizabeth Arden business. Outsiders scoffed that a staid Indianapolis drug house would never make it in that field. But Arden now has sales of $200 million (triple what they had when Lilly bought it)—and is making money (which is more than some other acquired cosmetics houses are doing).

Who owns and runs the company. Lilly is a Hoosier company that doesn't cotton much to outsiders. Chairman Richard Wood was born and raised in Indiana. Other top people come from Indiana or nearby states. The board of directors—all-male and all-white in 1979—is dominated by company insiders. Wood is only the second non-Lilly family member to head the company. The Lilly Endowment owns 18% of the company's stock.

In the public eye. Under the direction of the Lillys, the Lilly Endowment concentrated their grants in the areas of education and religion, particularly in Indianapolis and Indiana. Indianapolis is dotted with the good works of the Lillys. In his book *The Big Foundations,* Waldemar Nielsen detailed how the foundation made a sharp turn to the right during the late 1950s and early 1960s when it was headed by John S. Lynn, a former Lilly executive who identified himself in *Who's Who* as chairman of the Indianapolis chapter of the Christian Anti-Communism Crusade. In 1962 the foundation identified its mission as one of contributing "to a better understanding of the anticommunist free enterprise limited government concept."

In addition to their problems with Darvon, Lilly, along with other drug companies, has been under fire for the marketing of the synthetic estrogen DES (diethylstilbestrol) to pregnant women. DES was prescribed to prevent miscarriages. It has since been linked to cancer, not just in the pregnant mothers who took the drug, but in their offspring. Lilly reported in 1979 that they were the defendants in about 95 suits based on DES use. An estimated 2 million women took DES between 1941 and 1971.

Lilly is believed to have been the largest manufacturer.

Where they're going. Lilly has a major research effort under way in the technology of DNA recombination, or gene-splicing. Insulin taken from human cells and transplanted to bacteria, where it grows, is expected to be one of the first products to come from this research. If so, this would be the first human insulin; the insulin now being used by diabetics comes from the pancreases of sheep and cattle.

Stock performance. Eli Lilly stock bought for $1,000 in 1970 sold for $1,165 on January 2, 1980.

Major employment centers. Lilly is Indianapolis's second largest employer; Lilly's other major labs are in Clinton and Lafayette, Indiana.

Access. 307 East McCarty Street, Indianapolis, Indiana 46225; (317) 261-2000. Inquiries about products should be sent to Consumer Technical Services, Eli Lilly, P.O. Box 618, Indianapolis, Indiana 46206. The Lilly Center at 893 South Delaware Street in Indianapolis contains an exhibit hall and rooms dedicated to the memory of the Lilly family. It's open for touring every weekday between 9 and 4, except Wednesday, when the hours are 11 to 4.

Sales: $2.4 billion
Profits: $381.8 million
Forbes 500 rank: 220
Rank in prescription drugs: 1
Rank in drugs for hypertension: 1
Founded: 1668
Employees: 28,700
Headquarters: Rahway, New Jersey

What they do. Sufferers of arthritis and high blood pressure swallow more than half a billion dollars worth a year of two Merck drugs—Indocin, the world's most pre-scribed drug for rheumatoid arthritis, and Aldomet, an antihypertensive agent that has the unfortunate side effect of producing impotence in some males. From this two-drug gold mine Merck minted 25% of their $2 billion in sales.

After the mid-sixties, when Aldomet and Indocin were introduced, Merck's research department hit a 10-year drought, during which time they didn't find one significant drug. To make matters worse, drug patents protect a discovery for only 17 years. Fac-ing the imminent loss of the monopoly on their top money-makers, Merck's managers have spent nearly a billion dollars on re-search since 1975—a gamble that paid off with the recent introduction of Clinoril, a painkiller for arthritis; Flexoril, which eases muscle spasms; Mefoxin, a general an-tibiotic; and Timoptic, a glaucoma treat-ment. Merck sells all of their drugs to doc-tors and hospitals rather than to the general public as over-the-counter medications.

To hedge their bets, Merck has recently followed the lead of other big pharmaceuti-cal companies and has begun to buy into other kinds of business; one of these, Hub-bard Farms, is the world's leading experi-mental breeder of chickens and turkeys with specific genetic traits—"superchick-ens."

Merck still relies on human and animal medicines for most of their income, how-ever. Among their more than one thousand health-related products, the 2,000-page *Merck Manual of Diagnosis and Therapy*, first published in 1899, remains the bible for doctors and nurses throughout the world.

History. Albert W. Merck, who sits on the board of directors today, descends directly from Friedrich Jacob Merck, who in 1668 bought an apothecary next to the castle moat in Darmstadt, Germany. His heirs continued to run the store and hobnobbed with some of Europe's intellectual giants, including the great German poet Goethe and the Italian physicist Count Alessandro Volta, after whom the unit of electrical en-ergy is named.

But it was Heinrich Emmanuel Merck's friendship with Justus von Liebig, who be-came known as the father of organic chem-istry, that led to the family's full-scale entry into drug manufacturing, according to Tom Mahoney's account in *Merchants of Life*. Merck took it upon himself to try Lie-big's theories in the marketplace. In a small house on the outskirts of Darmstadt he began manufacturing a series of drugs, starting with morphine in 1827.

By the time Heinrich Emmanuel Merck died in 1855, Merck's products were used all over the world, including the United States. To bolster sales in America, the company sent a German chemist, Theodore Weicker, to New York in 1887; four years later George Merck, Heinrich Emmanuel's grandson, followed. Weicker and the 24-year-old Merck formed a partnership, and in 1899 they bought land in Rahway, New Jersey, where they began manufacturing chemicals and drugs. Five years later the two men clashed; Weicker sold his interest in the company to George Merck and bought control of E. R. Squibb & Sons.

By the start of the First World War in 1914, George Merck's operation was selling $4 million in chemicals annually. When the United States entered the war, Merck was caught in the uneasy position of running a company that was largely owned by his relatives in the enemy country. So, on his own initiative, Merck gave the Alien Prop-erty Custodian 80% of Merck stock, the amount of the U.S. branch owned by his German cousins. He then patriotically ex-panded production of chemicals, doubling his sales during the war. In recognition of Merck's efforts the Alien Property Custo-dian sold the Merck shares, then worth $3 million, to an investment group which per-mitted George Merck to retain control of the corporation. When Merck died in 1926, control fell to his son, George W. Merck.

A Harvard chemistry graduate, the younger Merck established a large, modern research laboratory in Rahway in 1933. He recruited some of the nation's top chemists and biologists, who did pioneer research on several important vitamins (B_1, B_6, C, K, riboflavin, and niacin), which the company sold to food processors and packagers. To top off this work, in 1948 Merck scientists discovered vitamin B_{12}, which effectively stops pernicious anemia.

When the second World War began, George Merck was assumed to be enough of an American patriot to chair the United States Biological Warfare Committee, which sought ways to create deadly strains of diseases that could be used against the German and Japanese armies.

In 1943 a Merck-supported scientist iso-

"Take Off the Kid Gloves!"

"Tell 'em again, and again, and again," urges Merck's training guide for its salespeople on techniques for persuading doctors to prescribe the firm's arthritis drug. "Take off the kid gloves. . . . Now every extra bottle of 1,000 Indocin that you sell is worth an extra $2.80 in incentive payments. Go get it. Pile it in!!!"

Drug company salesmen or "detail men," who call on doctors to extol the virtues of their companies' products, are the cutting edge of the drug industry's $1 billion annual effort to influence physicians' prescribing habits. But the industry's hard sell is virtually invisible to the public. Manufacturers of brand-name prescription drugs, prohibited by law from advertising directly to the public or selling their products without a doctor's pre-scription, focus on selling to physicians, pharmacists, and hospital administrators. In the prescription drug business M.D.'s are the middlemen: their prescriptions determine industry sales—and profits.

Unlike most salespeople, the detail man takes no orders for products. His job is simply to convince doctors about his company's line of drugs.

Nationwide, the prescription drug industry supports some 20,000 full-time detail men. Each costs his employer more than $30,000 a year. A detail man, typically, is assigned to 100 to 150 doctors. He also makes calls on hospitals and drugstores in his territory, but his efforts focus on M.D.'s the industry has identified as "high prescribers."

Detail men provide doctors with prompt information about useful and even life-saving new drugs, but intense pressure from drug companies to generate drug sales can work against doctors' getting a balanced view of drug benefits and hazards or counterindications.

Not surprisingly, the more visits M.D.'s get from detail men, the more drugs they prescribe, according to a study by Hugh D. Walker, published by the Indiana University Press and reported on in Richard Hughes and Robert Brewin's *The Tranquilizing of America*. The Walker study also points out that the more the physicians habitually rely on drug industry information, the more drugs they prescribe. In an FDA study 61% of all doctors surveyed said they confer with detail men an average of 1.6 times a week—nearly as often as they consult with other doctors.

---

lated the wonder drug streptomycin; another later produced cortisone from ox bile. While these discoveries enhanced Merck's reputation, the company began to feel the intense postwar competition from their pharmaceutical customers, who began manufacturing their own drugs. In addition, some foreign firms began exporting vitamins at low prices. Consequently, Merck began looking for a powerful ally. In 1953 they formally merged with Sharp & Dohme, which began in 1845 as an apothecary shop in Baltimore operated by Alpheus Phineas Sharp and later expanded by selling drugs to the Union Army during the Civil War. The new company provided Merck with a line of sulfa drugs, vaccines, blood plasma products, and some well-known nonprescription drugs, such as Sucrets, Tracinets, and Tyrozets. But most important, Sharp & Dohme gave Merck marketing and distribution facilities—from now on Merck would market drugs under their own brand names instead of just selling to other pharmaceutical companies to sell.

Reputation. Merck has generally won high marks for the quality of their research. It's a company where scientists have been encouraged to explore. George W. Merck once said: "Medicine is for the patients. It is not for the profits. The profits follow, and if we have remembered that, they have never failed to appear. The better we have remembered it, the larger they have been."

What they own. Twenty-five plants in the United States and 45 in 28 other countries, 10 research laboratories, and 17 experimental farms. Merck does nearly half of their business outside the United States.

Who owns and runs the company. Merck has been publicly owned since 1919, when the U.S. government sold off the shares owned by the German branch of the Merck family. Merck descendents in the U.S. now own only a small fraction of the shares.

Since George Merck's death in 1957, the company has been run by professional managers. Henry W. Gadsen, who came to Merck from the Sharp & Dohme merger, was the chief executive from 1965 to 1976. He was known for his gruff, crude language. In a 1976 *Fortune* interview, he referred to certain blacks as "big bucks" because they were fearful of taking Aldomet. Gadsen was succeeded by John J. Horan, who was once Merck's director of public relations.

Half of Merck's employees work overseas. One-quarter of their U.S. labor force is represented by unions. On the board, which is dominated by outsiders, are a black—Dr. Lloyd C. Elam, president of Nashville's Meharry Medical College—and a woman—Marian S. Heiskell, a member of the founding family of the *New York Times*. Merck is in the midst of a $3.2 million program to expand opportunities for female and minority employees, an effort lauded by the Labor Department as being "creative and thorough."

In the public eye. Merck and several other drug companies are currently being sued by women who claim they developed vaginal cancer because their mothers took diethylstilbestrol (DES) during pregnancy; since 1974 more than 350 plaintiffs have filed suits seeking damages in excess of $3.5 billion.

Merck is fighting hard against proposed legislation that would substitute generic drugs for brand-name products in Medicare and Medicaid programs (which account for 25% of all prescription drug sales). Merck argues that not all generic drugs are as good as their brand equivalents and that doctors, druggists, and patients should have a choice in the matter.

Where they're going. In 1979 Merck told stockholders that the 1980s hold the possibility of medical advances "that will equal or surpass those of the 1940s." Merck chairman John Horan says: "Our aim now is to clearly establish Merck as the preeminent drug maker worldwide in the 1980s." Only West Germany's Hoechst is now bigger.

Stock performance. Merck stock bought for $1,000 sold for $1,280 on January 2, 1980.

Access. 126 East Lincoln, Rahway, New Jersey 07065; (201) 574-4000.

In 1978 $34 million was spent to advertise Anacin, $23 million plugged Dristan, and Alka-Seltzer went to market with $17 million behind it.

Sales: $537 million
Profits: $18 million
Forbes 500 rank: 399
Rank in hangover remedies: 1
Rank in children's vitamins: 1
Rank in scouring pads: 1
Founded: 1884
Employees: 8,500
Headquarters: Elkhart, Indiana

What they do. Miles, the maker of Alka-Seltzer, ceased to be American owned in early 1978, when they were acquired by the world's fourth-largest chemical producer, Bayer of West Germany. For $253 million Bayer got a company that makes medicines; vitamins (One-A-Day); soybean-based meat substitutes (Morningstar Farms); scouring pads (S.O.S.); chemical reagent strips to test urine and blood samples; and various ingredients, flavors, and enzymes used by food and beverage companies. The biggest seller, at $90 million a year, is Alka-Seltzer, a combination of aspirin, bicarbonate of soda, and citric acid. The Alka-Seltzer label is printed in 20 languages and sold in more than 100 countries.

History. Miles began in the dispensary of an Elkhart, Indiana, general practitioner, Dr. Franklin Miles. His first home remedy was a sedative he called Dr. Miles Nervine. The Dr. Miles Medical Company was formed in 1884, and by 1890 it had two other backers: George E. Compton and Albert R. Beardsley. The Miles, Compton, and Beardsley families were the builders of this company.

By their own admission Miles was "a small, rather static company" until Alka-Seltzer appeared on the scene. Its origin has been traced to the newsroom of the *Truth*, the Elkhart daily paper (and the only paper in the world to carry this name outside of Moscow's *Pravda*). Reporters there used to down a mixture of aspirin and bicarbonate of soda to ward off winter colds. Andrew Hubble Beardsley, the son of Albert Beardsley, was impressed that almost no one at the *Truth* was afflicted during the flu epidemics of 1918 and 1927. So he had a Miles chemist formulate a tablet made of the seemingly wonder-working mixture, and he launched it on the public in 1931. Somehow word got around that Alka-Seltzer was good for hangovers, and after the United States emerged from Prohibition in 1933, Miles's sales doubled every seven years.

Miles first sold stock to the public in 1955. The shares were selling for $24 in late 1977 when Bayer said they would pay "at least $40" for them. The German company ended up paying $47 a share, an offer Miles management found "most compelling." Bayer has no connection with Sterling Drug, the makers of Bayer aspirin in the United States.

Reputation. Miles showed they were far from being Hoosier hicks when they allowed imaginative people on Madison Avenue to develop a series of Alka-Seltzer TV commercials, beginning in 1964, that were hailed in the *New York Times* as "being among the most consistently brilliant show-stoppers ever created."

What they own. Seventeen manufacturing facilities in the United States; 20 plants in 15 other countries.

Who owns and runs the company. Bayer now owns a company which has never had a chief executive officer who wasn't a Miles, a Beardsley, or a Compton. Dr. Walter Ames Compton has been chief executive officer since 1964. Miles is the largest employer in Elkhart and lays claim to being an enlightened one; fringe benefits come to one-third of wage costs. Miles has more than 600 employees who have been with the company for 25 or more years.

In the public eye. Miles has had to defend their number 1 product from attacks in the mid-1970s by Ralph Nader and the Food and Drug Administration that Alka-Seltzer is an irrational product since it was promoted to relieve upset stomachs when it contains aspirin, suspected of being a stomach irritant. Miles heeded the criticism by reformulating their advertising to highlight both headache relief and help for queasy stomachs. And they brought out a nonaspirin Alka-Seltzer.

Where they're going. Bayer will make Elkhart the headquarters of their pharmaceutical operations in the United States. They have also agreed that Miles will retain its identity. Miles should benefit from

> **To persuade 200,000 U.S. doctors to prescribe their products, the drug companies spend approximately $7,500 on promotion for each doctor, every year, according to Richard Hughes and Robert Brewin in *The Tranquilizing of America: Pill Popping and the American Way of Life.***

Bayer's research capabilities: the German chemical giant has a research budget that almost equals the annual sales of Miles.

Major employment centers. Elkhart, Indiana; West Haven, Connecticut.; Bedford Park, Illinois.

Access. 1127 Myrtle Street, Elkhart, Indiana 46515; (219) 264-9398.

Consumer brands.

Over-the-counter products: Alka-Seltzer; Alka-2 antacid; One-A-Day, Flintstones, and Chocks–Bugs Bunny vitamins and minerals; Bactine antiseptic; Sunguard suntan lotion.
Household products: S.O.S. soap pads; Tuffy scouring aid.
Meat analogs: Morningstar Farms (Scramblers, Leanies, Grillers); Worthington Foods (Bolono, Saucettes, Super Links, Veja-Bits).

MortonNorwich

Sales: $732 million
Profits: $46 million
Rank in salt: 1
Rank in sore-throat remedies: 1
Rank in liquid spray cleaner: 1
Founded: 1890
Employees: 10,500
Headquarters: Chicago, Illinois

It's not known whether the Morton salt people had upset stomachs or whether the Pepto-Bismol crowd needed to spice up their bland diets. In any case, the two companies were married in 1969 and two years later adopted a child: the company that made the Fantastik spray cleaner. This mishmash tumbled forward until a deal was struck, in 1978, with Rhone-Poulenc, a French chemical-pharmaceutical giant, which is now in the driver's seat with 20%

of MortonNorwich.

The company mines salt, makes various drugs including remedies for athlete's foot and sunburn, turns out a bunch of household cleaners and insecticides. They claim that Pepto-Bismol now accounts for 11.7% of all stomach remedies sold. Morton table salt has more than half the U.S. market, and the company also makes Morton Salt Substitute and Morton Lite Salt. The French will be cheered up now whenever they hear of raging winters in the Midwest since MortonNorwich sells 15% of the company's salt for icy roads.

Stock performance. MortonNorwich stock bought for $1,000 in 1970 sold for $904 on Janaury 2, 1980.

Access. 110 North Wacker Drive, Chicago, Illinois 60606; (312) 621-5200.

Consumer brands.

Over-the-counter products: Pepto-Bismol upset stomach remedy; Chloraseptic sore throat spray; Norforms feminine hygiene products; Encare contraceptive; Norwich aspirin; Necta Sweet saccharin; NP-27 athlete's foot care; Norwich glycerin suppositories; Unguentine first aid ointment; Occusol eye drops.

Household products: Morton salt products; Spray 'n Wash soil remover; Fantastik spray cleaner; Glass *Plus glass cleaner; No-Pest strip insecticide; K2r spot-lifter; Pine Power disinfectant; Janitor In A Drum all-purpose cleaner; Grease Relief degreaser.

Sales: $2.7 billion
Profits: $237.9 million
Forbes 500 rank: 179
Rank in antibiotics: 2
Rank in eye drops: 1
Rank in liniment: 1
Founded: 1849
Employees: 40,700
Headquarters: New York, New York.

What they do. When the tiny Pfizer company decided to take on the drug industry giants in the mid-1950s battle for antibiotic supremacy, they not only achieved their goals, they made enemies of every big drug company in the United States. The drug business was genteel and introverted at that time, and Pfizer's aggressive promotional gimmicks—such as sending socks with the company's brand names printed on them to physicians—offended the industry's sense of dignity.

The established companies were even more offended when the gimmicks worked. Pfizer still holds a leading position in antibiotics, with 1978 sales of $475 million. Their best-selling antibiotic today is Vibramycin. They're still major promoters of their drugs to doctors—and now the rest of the industry copies their tactics.

Pfizer's attempt to branch out from the

HOW MUCH THE DRUGMAKERS SPENT FOR RESEARCH & DEVELOPMENT

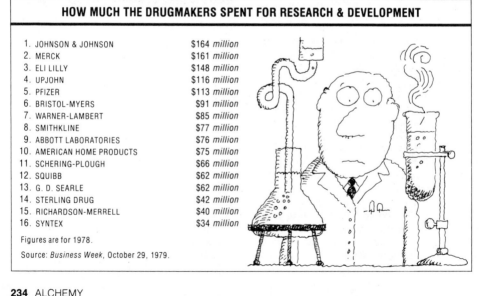

1. JOHNSON & JOHNSON	$164	*million*
2. MERCK	$161	*million*
3. ELI LILLY	$148	*million*
4. UPJOHN	$116	*million*
5. PFIZER	$113	*million*
6. BRISTOL-MYERS	$91	*million*
7. WARNER-LAMBERT	$85	*million*
8. SMITHKLINE	$77	*million*
9. ABBOTT LABORATORIES	$76	*million*
10. AMERICAN HOME PRODUCTS	$75	*million*
11. SCHERING-PLOUGH	$66	*million*
12. SQUIBB	$62	*million*
13. G. D. SEARLE	$62	*million*
14. STERLING DRUG	$42	*million*
15. RICHARDSON-MERRELL	$40	*million*
16. SYNTEX	$34	*million*

Figures are for 1978.

Source: *Business Week*, October 29, 1979.

"ethical" (prescription) market has met with indifferent success. Their entries in the cosmetic business—Coty fragrances, Imprevu perfume, and Black Belt and Hai Karate men's cologne—are only modest sellers. They have fared better with such over-the-counter remedies as Ben-Gay liniment and Visine eyedrops, each number 1 in its field, but Pfizer's business is still primarily prescription drugs.

Pfizer has been way ahead of the other drug companies in exploiting foreign markets. They get 56% of their sales and 65% of their profits overseas.

History. Unlike the other major drug companies, which were founded by physicians or scientists, Pfizer began as a chemical manufacturer and backed into the drug business almost by accident.

During the last half of the nineteenth century cofounders Charles Pfizer and Charles Erhart were content to produce in their Brooklyn laboratory iodine preparations, boric and tartaric acius, and the citric acid which Pfizer still makes and sells to soft drink companies. But in the 1920s Pfizer chemists discovered a new source of citric acid in black bread molds. Pfizer became so well-known for their mold fermentation processes that the federal government invited them to join in the search with other drug companies for a way to make penicillin on a large scale. They did better than anyone else; by the end of World War II Pfizer was making half the world's penicillin. However, heavy competition among the drug companies dropped the price of the new drug to such a low level that there was almost no profit in it by the end of 1948.

An energetic, fast-talking Brooklynite named John McKeen became president of Pfizer in 1949 and immediately began pushing company researchers to "come up with something." The "something" they came up with was oxytetracycline, a new antibiotic effective against more than 100 different diseases. The following year McKeen broke with the company's tradition of making drugs in bulk for drug distributing companies; McKeen sold the new drug directly to retailers and hospitals under the brand name of Terramycin.

Then in 1952 he began to advertise Terramycin to physicians by taking out enormous multipage ads in the *Journal of the American Medical Association.* The drug industry had never seen anything like it. In two years Pfizer spent $7.5 million to promote Terramycin.

The architect of this campaign was a psychiatrist-adman, Dr. Arthur M. Sackler, who was to become the undisputed king of medical advertising through his base at William Douglas McAdams Inc., an advertising agency specializing in prescription drug promotion. For years many of the important people in medical advertising came out of the McAdams shop.

Between 1952 and 1956 Pfizer remained the AMA journal's largest advertiser. But McKeen didn't stop there. He endeared Pfizer to doctors by hiring medical students for summer jobs as Pfizer salespeople (and augmented his tiny eight-man sales force in the process). It was his idea to send physicians bizarre promotional gifts, such as pillows and golf balls, all emblazoned with the names of Pfizer drugs.

When other drug makers criticized this hucksterism, McKeen simply ignored them. Pfizer's entry into the antibiotic field had put them in direct competition with two huge drug companies (American Cyanamid and Parke Davis) which had similar antibiotic products, a combined sales force of 1,300 people, and a total of 137 years in the retail drug trade. McKeen figured that his sales tactics were the only way Pfizer could carve out a slice of the market. Moreover, McKeen seemed to revel in his upstart image. Company legend has it that McKeen asked an assistant in 1961 what else he could do to keep the company growing. When the assistant timidly suggested that Pfizer buy another company, McKeen supposedly replied, "Fine. Which company?" Pfizer bought 14 companies in the next 4 years.

Reputation. Pfizer's image as the drug industry's huckster has faded since McKeen stepped down as president in 1965. Although the company is still seen as a new kid on the block, they have recently had a good record in getting new drugs approved by the FDA. Pfizer's drugs are seldom revolutionary since they usually follow other companies into new markets and then promote their way into competition. They also know how to make money; only Merck and Eli Lilly have higher profits.

What they own. Forty-seven production facilities in the United States and 49 plants overseas.

Who owns and runs the company. Directors own only 1% of the stock. Wall Streeters, who financed Pfizer's growth, are represented on the board by Felix G. Rohatyn, the Lazard Frères partner who helped to keep New York City afloat during its recent financial crises. Edmund T. Pratt, who sits on the General Motors board, was elected Pfizer's chief executive officer in 1972. Four doctors sit on the board, including Pfizer's research chief, Barry M. Bloom, and Gerald D. Laubach, an MIT Ph.D. who was elected president in 1972 after heading research and development. Also on the board is William J. Kennedy III, president of the nation's largest black-owned insurance company, North Carolina Mutual.

In the public eye. Pfizer has had a number of legal scrapes. In 1968 the U.S. Court of Appeals found that Pfizer and American Cyanamid had misrepresented and withheld information from the U.S. Patent Office in obtaining its tetracycline patent. Earlier a federal court in New York found them and two other drug companies (Cyanamid and Bristol-Meyers) guilty of antibiotic price fixing—and Pfizer agreed to pay $41 million to settle damage suits.

Where they're going. China, among other places. In late 1979 Pfizer announced that they would be selling and installing X-ray scanners in Chinese hospitals, and they hope to open China as a major market for antibiotics in the near future.

Stock performance. Pfizer stock bought for $1,000 in 1970 sold for $1,140 on January 2, 1980.

Major employment centers. Groton, Connecticut; Terre Haute, Indiana; Brooklyn, New York; and rural Wilmington County, North Carolina.

Access. 253 East 42nd Street, New York, New York 10017; (212) 573–2323.

Consumer brands.

Ben-Gay liniment; Pacquin hand cream; Visine eye drops; Hai Karate and Black Belt colognes; Desitin baby-care products; Coty perfumes (such as Imprevu, Elan, and Emeraude); Un-Burn sun-shield aerosols and lotions; and Swedish Tanning Secret suntan products.

The Prussian Gardener's Cabbage Cure

William Radam was a Prussian who emigrated to Austin, Texas, where he ran a nursery and seed store in the 1880s. Ailing with malaria and grieved by the loss of two of his children, he read of scientific discoveries proving that germs cause disease. The gardener pounced upon malevolent microbes as the cause of all his problems.

Convinced that millions of vicious germs were running loose inside him, Radam spent his days struggling with the invisible invaders. Driving to his store, he wrote, he could sit only on the very edge of his buggy seat; "the microbes would not let me sit any other way."

Radam then had a revelation: killing germs in people, he decided, must be like killing bugs on plants. If only he could find a substance capable of exterminating fungi, blight, and microbes on flowers and vegetables without harming the plants, he could use it to rid himself of his germs.

Radam offered a $1,000 prize to anyone who could kill cabbage blight without slaying the cabbages. Two military men tried for the prize, placing a kerosene can over an afflicted cabbage and igniting sulphur inside the can. The resulting fumes annihilated the blight but also sent the unfortunate cabbage to a heavenly garden patch. Undaunted, Radam tried dosing geraniums, strawberries, and grapes with agricultural remedies and patent medicines intended for human use. To his horror, compounds of both types killed more of his patients than they cured.

At last Radam came up with a potion that he claimed possessed the purifying powers of lightning. Made by burning chemicals inside a water-filled tank, it would kill "all fungus, germs, parasites," or anything else that caused people or plants to get sick. Radam christened his remedy Microbe Killer.

Whatever the flaws in his theories, the dauntless gardener believed in his brew and drank huge doses of it. He reported that before succumbing, his germs fought back so fiercely that he nearly went the way of his cabbage.

Radam patented his Microbe Killer in 1886 and began advertising it for sale. A credulous public, impressed by the scientific tone of Radam's ads and brochures, gulped the stuff by the gallon jug. (The average "cure" required 15 to 30 gallons, at

RICHARDSON-MERRELL INC.

Sales: $1.1 billion
Profits: $63 million
Forbes 500 rank: 426
Rank in cold remedies: 1
Rank in acne treatments: 1
Rank in denture adhesives: 1
Founded: 1828
Employees: 15,000
Headquarters: Wilton, Connecticut

What they do. Richardson-Merrell had trouble selling their Vicks cough drops in Japan because the word *cough* suggests a serious sickness to the Japanese. So Richardson-Merrell created an ailment called the "Ahems," the sound made by people clearing their throats, and their advertising zeroed in on the "Ahem bug." Result: Vicks now sells more than $10 million worth of cough drops a year in Japan.

This kind of marketing is typical of Richardson-Merrell, a company that spent $215 million on advertising and promotion in 1979—five times what they appropriated for research and development. Selling packaged drugs to consumers all over the world is this company's strong suit. Their well-advertised brands, such as Vicks cold remedies, Clearasil acne treatments, and Oil of Olay skin moisturizers, yield the bulk of Richardson-Merrell's profits.

Richardson-Merrell has had problems with their prescription drugs, however. They had the U.S. and Canadian distribution rights to the infamous sedative thalidomide, discovered to cause birth defects. And they were the company that developed and distributed the anticholesterol drug MER-29, which was withdrawn from the market in the mid-1960s after it was found to cause cataracts, baldness, and impotence. More recently they had to recall and reformulate their Sinex nasal spray in 1978, after Richardson-Merrell scientists found it to contain resistant bacteria.

These disasters notwithstanding, sales and profits have grown steadily in the past decade. Half their sales and two-thirds of their profits come from other countries.

History. The $1 billion enterprise that is

$3 per jug.)

By 1890 Radam was rich. He owned 17 factories around the country, all turning out jugs of his wine-tinted pink lightning. At his store on Broadway in New York, an agent handed out free glasses of the cure-all to passersby. Radam had abandoned his seed store in favor of a Fifth Avenue mansion overlooking Central Park, where, in frock coat and dignified beard, he penned scholarly treatises urging the sick to avoid doctors. Medical diagnosis, he argued, was a waste of time, since Microbe Killer could cure everything.

Radam's success was part of a curious phenomenon of the late nineteenth century. For the first time, scientists like Koch and Pasteur were identifying the real causes of disease. The public, reading dramatic newspaper reports of astounding research discoveries, found it difficult to distinguish between a Pasteur and a William Radam, whose ads ran alongside the news stories. The nostrum mongers, quick to make use of catchwords like *microbe* and *sanitary* in their sales pitches, made the age of scientific breakthrough into a golden age of patent medicines—and amassed great fortunes in the process.

Inevitably, Radam's Microbe Killer attracted the attention of both legitimate doctors and rival patent medicine men. A Dr. E. G. Eccles tested samples of Microbe Killer and published a report charging that it contained poisonous sulphuric and hydrochloric acids, along with traces of cheap chemicals of no known medicinal value.

Radam not only sued Eccles for libel, he also challenged the doctor to send him 50 incurable patients. In three months, Radam promised, his Microbe Killer would cure them all—unless, like rotten potatoes, they were simply too far gone. In the ensuing rounds of lawsuits and countersuits, Eccles came out ahead. Radam did, however, win cases against competitors who copied his patented trademark. But the legal furor revealed that, whatever else may have been in Microbe Killer, Radam's pink lightning was 99.38% water.

Source: James Harvey Young, *The Toadstool Millionaires.*

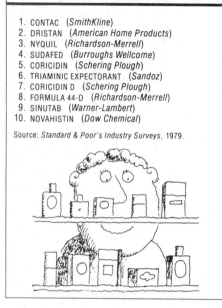
Richardson-Merrell grew from a mentholated ointment that people rubbed on their chests to form a sort of warm poultice or mustard plaster. Cold sufferers were advised to cover their chests with the Vicks VapoRub with a cloth and arrange their bedclothes like a funnel so that the vapors could be inhaled. The salve was developed by Lunsford Richardson, a druggist in the North Carolina Piedmont town of Greensboro. His inspiration was allegedly a "croupy baby," his older son Smith Richardson, who grew up to travel the unpaved roads of the Smokey Mountains and introduce folks to the small blue bottles of Vicks VapoRub. Before long the ointment was being rubbed on small chests with the lullaby litany, "Rub it on, sniff it in, it's good for you, it's made by Presbyterians." With a certain missionary zeal, spread first by horse and buggy and then with a fleet of spanking new Model T Fords, the Vick Chemical Company grew. (The Vick name was suggested to Lunsford Richardson by a magazine ad for Vick's seeds; Vick also happened to be his brother-in-law's name.) By 1910, when the enterprise was five years old, they were doing $50,000 in sales. They began moving out of the South in 1912, and by 1917 sales had reached $613,000—and there was still only one product.

It wasn't just Presbyterian zeal that won the day for Vicks VapoRub. The Richard-sons pioneered sales techniques that became the company's hallmark and were to be widely copied by other companies. Very early on Smith Richardson realized the potential in free samples. Whenever a new territory was opened, jars of Vicks VapoRub were passed out. They also developed the "spoon test" to sell storekeepers. If a merchant was a little dubious about this strange looking jar of ointment, the salesman would demonstrate the product's powers by placing a dab of VapoRub on a spoon and heating it with a match, and then having the merchant inhale the vapor.

Starting in 1912 the Richardsons used their own sales force to expand out of the South. They invaded the territory west of the Mississippi by taking advantage of a new post office regulation that allowed mail to be delivered to boxes without naming the residents. It was the birth of "occupant mailing." In a 50-day period Vick Chemical sent eight freight-car loads of VapoRub samples to 31 million people living in the western states.

When the Spanish influenza epidemic struck in 1918, Vick increased advertising, advising people on what to do if they came down with the flu and naturally getting in a plug for VapoRub. In two years sales increased by five times to nearly $3 million—and when Lunsford Richardson died in the summer of 1919 his Vicks trademark was a household word.

Vicks went into international markets well ahead of many American companies. They began exporting VapoRub to England, Mexico, Australia, and New Zealand during the 1920s, shipping their advertising techniques along with the product. By 1933 Vick Chemical's headquarters had shifted entirely from Greensboro to New York to take advantage of the advertising talent there. For many years Vick maintained their own house advertising agency.

New products began to be introduced in 1930, with Vicks Va-tro-nol Nose Drops and Vicks Medicated Cough Drops. Vicks Inhaler arrived on the scene in 1940. Today there are 17 products in the Vicks armada.

The Merrell roots of this company stretch back even farther—to 1828 when William Stanley Merrell, a chemist, started a company in Cincinnati to supply drugs to physicians in the west. Before that doctors had to get their medicines from Philadelphia. By 1858 the Merrell line included almost 1,000 products, boasting "the greatest

TOP TEN VITAMINS

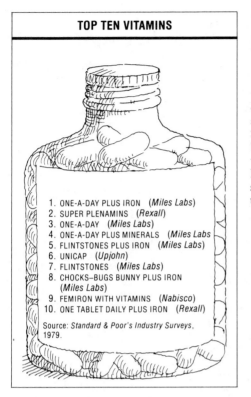

1. ONE-A-DAY PLUS IRON   (*Miles Labs*)
2. SUPER PLENAMINS   (*Rexall*)
3. ONE-A-DAY   (*Miles Labs*)
4. ONE-A-DAY PLUS MINERALS   (*Miles Labs*)
5. FLINTSTONES PLUS IRON   (*Miles Labs*)
6. UNICAP   (*Upjohn*)
7. FLINTSTONES   (*Miles Labs*)
8. CHOCKS–BUGS BUNNY PLUS IRON   (*Miles Labs*)
9. FEMIRON WITH VITAMINS   (*Nabisco*)
10. ONE TABLET DAILY PLUS IRON   (*Rexall*)

Source: *Standard & Poor's Industry Surveys*, 1979.

number of indigenous or botanic medicines of any house in the United States." Merrell is believed to be the oldest pharmaceutical manufacturer in the nation. They were acquired by Vick Chemical in 1938. The corporate name, Richardson-Merrell, was adopted in 1960.

More than two dozen other companies have been acquired during the past 40 years, among them National Drug, J. T. Baker Chemical, Lavoris, Milton Antiseptic in England, South Africa's Adams Group (Oil of Olay), Milwaukee's Lakeside Laboratories, and Formby's, in Olive Branch, Mississippi, maker of wood-care products.

Reputation. Richardson-Merrell still lives with the taint left by thalidomide. Particularly damaging also was the MER-29 debacle, in which evidence indicated clearly that lab tests had been faked and unfavorable results suppressed. Charged in federal court with making false statements and withholding information from the Food and Drug Administration, the company pleaded no contest and was fined a total of $80,000. Three Merrell executives were sentenced to six months of probation.

What they own. Eighteen manufacturing and research facilities in the United States and 35 facilities in 26 other countries.

Who owns and runs the company. The Richardson family interests control 27% of the stock. Of the 11 members of the board of directors, 3 are grandsons of the founder and a fourth is a relative by marriage. H. Smith Richardson, Jr., is chairman of the board. The Smith Richardson Foundation, which controls 7% of the company's stock, has a long record of contributing to conservative political causes. No blacks sit on the board, nor do any women.

In the public eye. The company took a tax deduction in 1978 when they donated vaccine research and production facilities, valued at $17 million, to the Salk Institute of Biological Studies—which turned around and sold the manufacturing plants to another company. Richardson-Merrell was the largest producer of the swine flu vaccine used in the ill-fated government mass inoculation program of 1976.

The thalidomide controversy still keeps Richardson-Merrell in the news. In late 1979 a California woman, grossly deformed because her mother took the tranquilizer thalidomide during pregnancy, filed a suit against the German manufacturer of the drug and its North American distributor, Richardson-Merrell. In 1975 the company settled suits by 28 Canadian children born with deformed limbs. The exact amounts of the settlements were not disclosed at the time but were said to be "the largest thalidomide settlements per individual child made anywhere in the world." More than 8,000 children worldwide were born with grave birth defects because of thalidomide between 1959 and 1962, but few were afflicted in the United States, where Richardson-Merrell had obtained the right to distribute the drug. There was limited distribution in the U. S. for testing but an alert federal Food and Drug Administration official succeeded in keeping the drug off the market.

On another front, Richardson-Merrell admitted in 1976 that during the previous 5 years they had made "a number of payments of questionable legality or propriety" overseas, totaling more than $1.2 million.

Where they're going. To court. In March 1980 a jury in Orlando, Florida, awarded a couple $20,000 in compensatory damages for birth defects suffered by their son, who was born with a malformed chest, right arm, and hand. The couple had charged that the defects were due to a Richardson-Merrell drug, Bendectin (prescribed for nausea during pregnancy), that has been taken by 30 million women (5 million in the United States). Richardson-Merrell interpreted the Florida decision as a victory; the couple had sued for $10 million in punitive damanges. Immediately after the verdict San Francisco attorney Melvin Belli said he would file 150 lawsuits on behalf of Bendectin users. Officials of the Food and Drug Administration testified on behalf of Richardson-Merrell, stating: "The association of risk is nowhere near the magnitude of thalidomide. We've been looking at Bendectin for years and we don't have any evidence at this time that we should take it off the market." Bendectin's worldwide sales in 1979: $15 million.

Stock performance. Richardson-Merrell stock bought for $1,000 in 1970 sold for $783 on January 2, 1980.

Major employment centers. Cincinnati; Phillipsburg, New Jersey; and Wilton.

Access. 10 Westport Road, Wilton, Connecticut 06897; (203) 762-2222. Complaints should be addressed to Consumer Affairs Department, Richardson-Merrell, 1375 Virginia Drive, Fort Washington, Pennsylvania 19034: consumers may also call collect to (215) 643-4000.

Consumer brands.

Over-the-counter drugs: Vicks (Formula 44, Ny-Quil, DayCare, Sinex, VapoRub, cough drops, throat lozenges, decongestant); Benzodent, Complete, Fasteeth, Fixodent, and Kleenite denture-care products; Clearasil and Topex for acne; Lavoris mouthwash; Demure douche; Lemon Jelvyn, Oil of Olay, and Night of Olay skin-care products; Bacimycin ointment; Cepacol and Cepastat mouthwash and lozenges; Consotuss cough syrup; Kolantyl antacid.
Other: Formby's wood-care products.

> **Americans swallow nearly 5 billion doses of prescription tranquilizers each year.**

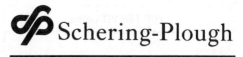
Schering-Plough

Sales: $1.4 billion
Profits: $222.3 million
Forbes 500 rank: 351
Founded: 1915
Employees: 17,900
Headquarters: Kenilworth, New Jersey

What they do. Schering-Plough unites two strains—one that goes back to Germany, the other to the streets of Memphis; one that specializes in ethical drugs available only with a doctor's prescription, the other in drugstore items hawked in every available medium including television and billboards. Their number 1 prescription product is Garamycin, an antibiotic used to treat serious infections. With worldwide annual sales in the quarter-billion dollar range, the importance of this drug can hardly be overstated. That's the Schering end of the business.

The Plough end sells many products well known in the consumer marketplace. Maybelline, the "beautiful eyes" product, accounts for more than half the eye cosmetics produced in the United States. Plough's sun-care lineup, including Coppertone and Solarcaine, does more than half the business in that market. Plough also pioneered and still dominates the children's aspirin market with the St. Joseph brand.

Between these two ends there's a middle ground where products are sold without a prescription but never advertised directly to the consumer. In this nether world are such Schering specialties as Coricidin, Afrin, and Chlor-Trimeton for colds and allergies, and Tinactin, a leading remedy for athlete's foot. Because these products aren't hawked on TV, they have an aura like prescribed drugs when doctors and pharmacists counsel, "I have just the thing for you."

History. The original Schering company began to export diphtheria antitoxin from Berlin to the United States in 1894; they established a branch in New York in 1929. After the United States entered World War II, Schering's U.S. assets were seized by the Alien Property Custodian, and a government lawyer, Francis Cabell Brown, was placed in charge. Brown recruited topnotch pharmacists, doctors, lawyers, and sales people, mostly from the government, to work for Schering, and within 10 years sales tripled, profits quadrupled, and 42 patents were received. When the company was put up for sale in 1952, it fetched $29 million—and the investors begged Brown to stay on. He did, leading Schering to the discovery of Meticorten, an important antiarthritic compound, and sales of $80 million by 1957. As author Tom Mahoney writes in *Merchants of Life*, this proves that "bureaucrats can become enterprisers."

Abe Plough is another story entirely. In 1908, as a teenager in Memphis, Tennessee, he borrowed $125 from his father, who was an auctioneer, mixed up a batch of cottonseed oil, carbolic acid, and camphor, and sold the potion to druggists as "antiseptic healing oil—the sure cure for any ill of man or beast." In 1915 he paid $900 for the inventory of the bankrupt Memphis Drug Company, mostly 5,000 cases of "Chill Tonic Oxidine," touted as a cure for chills and fever, or malaria. Plough sold the inventory for $34,000 in Louisiana and Texas. Five years later he bought the St. Joseph Company of Chattanooga, Tennessee, an aspirin maker, and rather than challenge the big companies in the adult field he went after—in fact, invented—the children's aspirin market. Plough went on to buy 27 other companies. He regularly spent 25% of sales on advertising—and became so impressed with the power of radio advertising that he bought several stations.

In January 1971 Plough merged his company into Schering. Now pushing 90 years of age, he is honorary chairman of the board.

The original Schering company, in Germany, is still very much in business and competes against Schering U.S.A. outside the United States. They're now both about the same size. About 45% of Schering-Plough's sales are done outside the United States.

Reputation. They're not regarded as one of the premier research houses of the pharmaceutical industry, but they're envied for their luck or ability in coming up with sales blockbusters like Meticorten and Garamycin.

What they own. In addition to manufacturing facilities, Schering-Plough owns five AM and five FM radio stations. At the beginning of 1979 they became the guru of sore feet by buying out the Dr. Scholl business, though the FTC forced the company to sell off the Dr. Scholl athlete's foot powder part of the business in May 1979.

Who owns and runs the company. A lawyer, Richard J. Bennett, was elected chief executive in 1978, succeeding Willibald Conzen, who moved up to chairman. Conzen has worked for both Scherings. He began his career with the German company when he was 17 and worked for them in South Africa during World War II. Then he came to the United States and joined the Schering company in New Jersey, rising to the top in 1966. Schering's board is all-white and all-male. The officers and directors together own less than one-half of 1% of the stock.

In the public eye. Testimony during the 1959–60 Kefauver hearings in the U.S. Senate disclosed that Schering's prednisolone (Meticorten) cost 1.6¢ per tablet to make and was sold to the pharmacist for 17.9¢ and to the patient for 28.8¢. Currently Schering is the defendant, along with other drug companies, in 22 suits brought by women charging they developed cancerous or precancerous lesions of the vagina and cervix as a result of their mothers' use of estrogen products during pregnancy.

Schering expresses concern about the trend toward the use of generic (unbranded) drugs, claiming that the Food and Drug Administration is not "capable of inspecting the 1,700 small pharmaceutical manufacturers with the same frequency and rigor that it does the major manufacturers that account for 90% of the pharmaceuticals sold in the U.S."

Where they're going. With the patents on Garamycin now beginning to run out, Schering-Plough is casting about for their next big winner. They have a lot of cash on hand and plan to buy other companies. But waiting in the wings might be a lifesaver: they own 16% of Biogen S.A., a Geneva-based company that recently reported it had found a way to produce human interferon in the laboratory through gene-splicing. Interferon is a natural virus-fighting substance that has potential use against a variety of diseases, including several types of cancer. Schering-Plough has the world-wide rights to market Biogen's interferon.

Stock performance. Schering-Plough stock bought for $1,000 in 1970 sold for $1,047 on January 2, 1980.

Access. 2000 Galloping Hill Road, Kenilworth, New Jersey 07033, (201) 931-2000.

Consumer brands.

Over-the-counter products: Chlor-Trimeton allergy tablets; St. Joseph children's aspirins; Afrin decongestant spray; Coricidin cold preparations; Tinactin antifungal; Emko contraceptive; Duration nasal spray; Di-Gel antacid; Correctol and Feen-a-Mint laxatives; Aspergum analgesics; Aftute antifungal; and Dr. Scholl foot care products.

Toiletries and cosmetics: Maybelline eye makeup; Coppertone, QT, Sudden Tan, Tropical Blend, Sun Gier and Solarcaine sun-care products; Artra skin cream; Sardo bath oil; Mexsana medicated powder; and PAAS Easter egg coloring kits.

Home products: Heart of American wood stains; Mitee plumbing compound; DAP caulking and sealant; Derusto specialty paint products; Duratite wood dough.

Radio stations: WVEE Atlanta; WXYV Baltimore; WHRK Memphis; WQXM Clearwater/St. Petersburg; WJEZ and WJJD Chicago; and WSUN Tampa/St. Petersburg.

Sales: $333.4 million
Profits: $21.2 million
Founded: 1956
Employees: 1,500
Headquarters: San Francisco, California

What they do. Shaklee is the Avon of health. Door-to-door representatives sell nutritional, household, and personal-care products with a heavy emphasis on the natural and the healthful. Nutritional supplements and foods make up 75% of their sales. Shaklee also employs the "Tupperware party" system of sales in which representatives (who are independent sellers supplied by Shaklee) invite people to their homes and sell Shaklee products in a festive setting. Shaklee spends no money on advertising. In 1979 they spent $9 million on sales conventions "to maintain the enthusiasm of the sales force."

History. Dr. Forrest Shaklee, who once worked with a traveling hypnotist and showman named "Professor" Santinelli, began Shaklee in 1956 in Oakland, California, to gain wider distribution for the food supplements he had developed and was dispensing from his chiropractic clinic. Shaklee insisted that his products work "in cooperation with nature." Early products included Pro-Lecin, a protein and lecithin supplement, and Vita-Lea, a formula of vegetable substances. The company started with $100,000 in orders and five distributors, with some business conducted from the doctor's basement.

Selling "natural health" products in California in the 1950s and 1960s proved only slightly less lucrative than selling lifejackets on the *Titanic* would have been. By 1973 Shaklee had grown to a $75 million business and began selling shares to the public—but 56% stayed securely in Dr. Shaklee's own family.

Shaklee grew too fast for their own management's capabilities, however. When they expanded into Europe they lost $6 million. They have since retreated to Britain, Canada, and Japan.

The glue that holds Shaklee together is an odd mixture of faith and mammon. The company depends on an independent sales force and treats them notably better than Avon does. Anyone who wants to take advantage of what the company calls "the opportunity to share Shaklee" must be recommended by someone already on the sales force (called "the Shaklee family") and buy a New Distributor's Kit for $12.50. Shaklee has devised a pyramiding system of recruitment, whereby the more salespeople you recruit for Shaklee and the better they do, the more you make. The company sells products to the salespeople at 30% below the suggested retail price. There is no sales quota, and the average yearly net for just a part-time selling schedule is $9,000. Shaklee provides the sales force with group life insurance and retirement benefits.

The company uses a variety of techniques to bolster staff faith in the healing properties of Shaklee products. Take the *Shaklee Survey:* this company monthly is filled with case histories of people whose lives have been changed by Shaklee products, along with articles on how to better sell those happiness-conveying items. And Shaklee's salespeople are good customers as well, perhaps heeding the founder's dictum to "be certain you have used the products before you sell them. You cannot successfully sell any products you do not believe in." Topped off with a healthy dose of Dr. Shaklee's positive-thinking philosophy, called thoughtsmanship ("What you think, you look; what you think, you do; what you think, you are"), Shaklee's representatives are evangelists, bringing good news to thousands of doors each day. There are even company songs to boost morale—"I Can, You Can, We Can the Shaklee Way," for example.

Reputation. Shaklee tries hard to distinguish themselves from pyramid sales organizations, such as "Holiday Magic," that have run afoul of the law. Part of their image-scrubbing is the formation of a board of directors whose members include Earl F. Cheit, dean of the business school at the University of California at Berkeley, former astronaut Alan B. Shepard, Lilyan H. Affinito, president of Simplicity Pattern, and newswoman and author Jeanne L. Parr. Also to this end was the 1980 headquarters move from Emeryville, a dreary town near Oakland, California, across the Bay to the financial district of San Francisco. Asked why, Raleigh Shaklee said, "Even in California, people say, 'Emeryville, where's that?' San Francisco has worldwide recognition."

What they own. Shaklee's most important resource is the zeal of its sales force.

Who owns and runs the company. Dr. Forrest Shaklee's family owns about half the company's stock.

Shaklee grew up at the turn of the century when Chautauqua shows and William Jennings Bryan were principal forms of entertainment, and young Shaklee saw and learned from both. *When Nature Speaks,* his autobiography, makes these claims for Shaklee: that he was one of the earliest film distributors and once fired Billy Rose; that he was the famous flying chiropractor who had a Davenport, Iowa, parade in his honor featuring a 50-foot replica of the human spine; and that he was an inventor who, with Henry Ford at his side, once egged on 82-year-old Thomas Edison and 61-year-old Harvey Firestone while they wrestled on the floor of Edison's lab.

While the Shaklees own the controlling shares, the company has been run since 1975 by a young former management consultant, J. Gary Shansby, who earned $500,000 in 1979, and who describes the Shaklee sales force as "just a happy bunch of people who are not primarily concerned about making money." Shansby is one of Shaklee's best customers: he downs 20 tablets a day.

In the public eye. Shaklee has had an occasionally uneasy relationship with the Federal Trade Commission. In 1973 the FTC undertook an investigation of alleged deceptive claims by Shaklee salespeople for an instant protein product. And the company has had to put a lid on some overenthusiastic salespeople who had claimed, according to the Food and Drug Administration, that Shaklee products could cure, among other things, cancer and diabetes.

In 1976 the FTC ordered that Shaklee could not restrain the sale of Shaklee products through retail stores. However, in May 1979 the commission came to the opposite conclusion in a similar case involving a competitor, Amway; Shaklee has petitioned the FTC for relief from the 1976 order.

Where they're going. Their stated aim is to become "the leading nutritional products company in the world."

Access. 444 Market Street, San Francisco, California 94111; (415) 954-2300.

Consumer brands.

Nutritional products: Herb-Lax; Instant Protein; Liqui-Lea; NPS, Pro-Lecin; Vita-Cal; Vita-Lea; Basic-D; Basic-H; Basic-G; Basic-I; Basic-L; Liquid-L.
Personal care products: Satin Sheen; Softer Than Soft; Desert Wind; Deux Vies; Golden Manner; Lady Shaklee; Lovue; New Concept; Rainsilk; Shaklee for Men.

SmithKline
CORPORATION

Sales: $1.4 billion
Profits: $233.8 million
Forbes 500 rank: 363
Rank in ulcer remedies: 1
Rank in cold remedies: 1
Rank in veterinary medicines: 1
Founded: 1830
Employees: 16,589
Headquarters: Philadelphia, Pennsylvania

What they do. Ten years ago, SmithKline was the senior citizen of the drug business —a tired, sleepy old Philadelphia gent going nowhere. Today they're born again. Thanks to their discovery of a new, effective antiulcer drug named Tagamet, Smith-Kline became the fastest-growing maker of prescription drugs in the world. Tagamet's sales in 1978 were $280 million; in 1979 they exceeded $450 million, becoming second only to Valium in prescription sales.

In addition to Tagamet, SmithKline makes Contac, the world's number 1 cold remedy, Sine-Off headache products, A.R.M. allergy medicine, and a full line of veterinary medicines for animal distemper and other diseases. They also market Sea & Ski suntan products.

History. SmithKline was one of a number of Philadelphia pharmaceutical houses that grew up to become full-line drug companies in the twentieth century. After World War II SmithKline decided to concentrate on such psychoactive drugs as benzedrine, dexedrine, and Thorazine—which they introduced in 1954. In 1956, for the first time in history, mental institutions began to discharge more patients than they admitted— a first made possible by Thorazine.

But then the new drug pipeline became clogged—at least for Smith Kline & French, as they called themselves in those days. With no new prescription winners in sight, they decided to go to consumers directly with over-the-counter medications. Contac cold capsules were their first entries in the consumer market—and they were successful from their introduction in 1960. Feeling they could then take the measure of Revlon, the Philadelphia Main Liners fielded Love cosmetics (a name appropriate to the 1960s). But in 1979 SmithKline in effect said to Revlon: "Okay, you can have the market." They folded the Love cosmetics business after a year in which factory sales totaled $9 million and $2 million was spent on advertising. With Tagamet, who needs a $9 million cosmetics business?

Reputation. As stuffy a company as you are likely to find—and quick to position themselves as saviors of the sick and infirm. After nearly doubling their profits in 1978, SmithKline preened themselves with this observation: "Tagamet is bringing relief from pain; is helping heal disease and save lives; reducing the need for hospitalization and surgery; and restoring normalcy to the life-styles of patients around the world. Truly a remarkable record."

What they own. In addition to their pharmaceutical operations, SmithKline has a $100 million business in ultrasonic technology (things like sonic welders and sonic cleaning) and a $50 million business in medical instruments.

Who owns and runs the company. Board chairman Robert F. Dee passes much of his time writing pamphlets called "Issues for Action" on subjects like federal taxation, which he likens to confiscation. Dee is also a vigorous supporter of tax credits for companies—like his own—which spend millions on research.

SmithKline's board is dominated by Philadelphians and includes one woman, Dr. Mary T. Kimpton, an economic consultant.

Where they're going. Tagamet sales should continue to climb but SmithKline is now looking for another blockbuster in auranofin, an antiarthritic compound now being tested. They had similar hopes for Selacryn, a drug used to treat hypertension, introduced in 1979. But Selacryn was recalled early in 1980 after reports of serious side effects such as liver damage.

Stock performance. SmithKline stock bought for $1,000 in 1970 sold for $5,030 on January 2, 1980.

Access. 1500 Spring Garden Street, Philadelphia, Pennsylvania 19101; (215) 854-5154.

Consumer brands.

Over-the-counter drugs: Contac; Sine-Off; A.R.M.; Contac Jr. (cold relief medicine for children); Fast-Aid skin anesthetic.
Other products: Sea & Ski tanning lotions.

SQUIBB

Sales: $1.5 billion
Profits: $123.7 million
Forbes 500 rank: 346

Rank in prescription drugs: 6
Rank in hard candy: 1
Rank in bubble gum: 1
Rank in sugarless gum: 2
Founded: 1858
Employees: 37,000
Headquarters: New York, New York

What they do. Squibb makes lifesaving drugs, bubble gum, and perfume. They used to make other things too: baby food, tea bags, coffee. But they sloughed those off in 1972. They also used to own the Lanvin perfume trademark. But they got rid of that in 1978. And they used to own Dobbs House, operator of a bunch of airport restaurants. They were in the process of selling those off as 1980 opened. The fact is: Squibb has never been able to make up its mind what to do. They were born in that quandary.

Squibb was feeling pretty healthy as they headed into the decade of the 1980s. Health-care products—mainly prescription drugs—accounted for half their sales. That's the company's oldest business, and they have in their research pipeline a product that some people tout as a winner capable of transforming Squibb into a pharmaceutical superpower. It's Capoten, a new treatment for control of high blood pressure.

Squibb was also doing well in the marketplace with their new Opium perfume, one of their Yves Saint Laurent brands. It registered sales of $3 million in its introductory year.

Squibb makes the top-selling bubble gum, Bubble Yum, the leading hard roll candy, Life Savers, the sugarless gum Care Free, Jean Naté bath oils, and a clutch of Charles of the Ritz fragrances.

They also compete in the vitamin market with Theragran.

History. Squibb has one of the oldest and best names in the American drug industry. They were established in Brooklyn in 1858 by Edward Robinson Squibb, a doctor who quit the Navy after he was told he could not be paid more than $150 a month. It was while he was a Navy doctor that he discovered how to make the first pure ether. His first product was chloroform. He built a substantial company, which he turned over to his sons, and they sold out in 1905 to Theodore Weicker, a German chemist, and his father-in-law, Lowell M. Palmer, a midwestern industrialist. (Weicker's grandson, Lowell Palmer Weicker, is now a U.S. senator from Connecticut.) In 1951 Squibb, still headed by a Weicker, was one of the largest companies in the U.S. drug industry, with annual sales of $100 million. It merged then with Mathieson Chemical—and that was the start of a tortured journey.

In 1953 Mathieson merged with Olin Industries, a gun maker, to form the Olin Mathieson Chemical Corporation. It was a huge company but gave all the appearance of not knowing what it was supposed to do. Things drifted along aimlessly until 1968, at which point Richard M. Furlaud, a graduate of Princeton and Harvard Law School, became head of the Squibb division. Furlaud felt that Squibb's merits were hidden in such a dull company, and he convinced the management to set Squibb adrift as an independent company. (At the time Wall Street was crazy for drug companies; chemical companies didn't excite their imagination.)

Furlaud was delighted to be running his own show. In 1968 he merged Squibb with Beech-Nut Life Savers, then he acquired Lanvin-Charles of the Ritz in 1971. The only chief executive officer the new Squibb has had, Furlaud was still running the company as 1980 dawned.

Reputation. A mixed bag. Squibb has always enjoyed a fine reputation as a purveyor of medicines, but they've had consistently poor luck with their marriages.

Who owns and runs the company. The largest single stockholder, with 3.9% of the stock, is Eugene F. Williams, Jr., chairman of the St. Louis Union Trust Company. He has worked for that bank since 1947. Four physicians sit on Squibb's board, one of them being Dr. Lewis Thomas, president of the Sloan-Kettering Memorial Cancer Center and a brilliant essayist. (His book, *The Lives of a Cell: Notes of a Biology Watcher*, won a National Book Award in 1975.)

Where they're going. David M. Paisley, a drug analyst for the brokerage house of Merrill Lynch, believes that Capoten, Squibb's new drug for controlling high blood pressure, is the most important product a drug company could come up with next to finding a cure for cancer. Paisley used to work for Squibb before switching to Wall Street.

Stock performance. Squibb stock bought for $1,000 in 1970 sold for $1,144 on January 2, 1980.

Access: 40 West 57th Street, New York, New York 10019; (212) 489-2000.

Consumer brands.

Over-the-counter products: Broxodent electric toothbrush; Spec-T cough and cold products; Sweeta sugar substitute; Squibb Golden Bounty; Theragran and Theragran-M high-potency vitamins; and Vigran vitamins.
Confectionery: Bubble Yum, Care Free, Beech-Nut, Beechies, and Fruit Stripe chewing gums; Pine Bros. cough drops; Life Savers; Breath Savers mints.
Fragrances: Enjoli; Opium; Rive Gauche; Yves Saint Laurent; Jean Naté.
Cosmetics: Charles of the Ritz; Country Cordovans; Revenescence; Alexandra de Markoff cosmetics; Bain de Soleil suntan lotion.

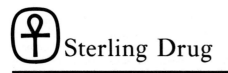 Sterling Drug

Sales: $1.5 billion
Profits: $111.6 million
Forbes 500 rank: 336
Rank in headache remedies: 3
Rank in household disinfectants: 1
Founded: 1901
Employees: 27,340
Headquarters: New York, New York

What they do. Sterling spends $20 million a year on advertising to convince skeptical consumers that Bayer aspirin is so superior to any other aspirin that they should pay double, triple and sometimes even quadruple the price of generic, unbranded aspirin. They have succeeded in making Bayer the leading American aspirin brand. That ain't hay in a country where people down 12,000 tons of aspirin a year, or 150 tablets per person.

Sterling didn't invent Bayer aspirin. They bought it at auction. In fact, Sterling's record as a developer of significant medicines is spotty. They got where they are today mainly by acquiring the ideas, processes and products of others, and by spending $80 million a year on advertising, considerably more than they spend on research. The result is a mixed bag of a company whose product lineup includes such prescription drugs as two potent pain-relievers Demerol and Talwin, and the anesthetics Marcaine, Carbocaine and Novocain; patented drugs like the Neo-Synephrine line of decongestants and the two old medicine chest standbys, Phillips' Milk of Magnesia and Haley's M-O; household chemicals like the Lysol disinfectants and d-Con rat killers; and cosmetics and toiletries like Dorothy Gray cosmetics and Givenchy perfumes.

Sterling derives half of their profits from operations outside the United States.

"Drunkards Cured Secretly" (Dope Fiends, Too)

In the balmy days before government regulation of the drug industry, patent medicines often contained alcohol, morphine, or opium. Normally the user had no idea what was in the potion, since panacea peddlers jealously guarded their secret formulas.

During and after the Civil War, when the popularity of patent medicines burgeoned, drug addiction grew prevalent, and was known as "the Army disease." Naturally, the nostrum mongers were eager to capitalize on this new and potentially profitable disease by offering "cures." Tear-jerking ads for these cures told of little girls who had

secretly cured their drunkard papas of the liquor habit by slipping the wonder cure, which arrived in a plain wrapper, into their coffee. "Drunkards Cured Secretly," advertised the makers of a tonic called Golden Specific. "Any Lady Can Do It At Home. It does its work so silently and surely that while the devoted wife, sister or daughter looks on, the drunkard is reclaimed even against his will."

So popular were drink-and-dope cures that Sears, Roebuck offered one in the catalog during the early 1900s. Both Sears' Cure for the Opium and Morphine Habit, and Sears' White Star

Liquor Cure were sent in plain, sealed packages to avoid alerting the patient.

Some such potions proved more pleasing to alcoholics than their doting families might have imagined. Parker's True Tonic, for instance, was "recommended for inebriates." But when the Massachusetts Board of Health tested the tonic, it proved to contain 41.6% alcohol.

Source: Gerald Carson, *One for a Man, Two for a Horse.*

History. Sterling specialized in painkillers —and advertising—from the start. In 1901 William Erhard Weiss, a pharmacist, joined with an old high school chum, Albert H. Diebold, to form the Neuralgyline Company in Wheeling, West Virginia. They made a pain reliever called Neuralgine, which they advertised on roadside signs in the Wheeling area. Sales in the first year were $10,000. In the second year, having found new investors to back them, they headed for Pittsburgh and launched a $10,000 advertising campaign. They made enough money to acquire another drug peddler, Sterling Remedy, in 1909. Sterling was adopted as the corporate name in 1917.

Aspirin, or acetylsalicylic acid, had been developed by Felix Hoffmann, a chemist working for the big German chemical firm Bayer just before the turn of the century— and Bayer had introduced this wonder drug, under its name, all over the world.

Bayer's U.S. business, having spent World War I in the hands of the Alien Property Custodian, was put up for sale at a public auction after the Armistice. Sterling outbid more than 100 American companies with an offer of $5.3 million. When a 1921 decision by Judge Learned Hand ruled that anyone selling acetylsalicylic acid could use the name "aspirin," Sterling had to fall back on the Bayer name which they alone had the right to use in the United States—and nowhere else in the world. They promoted Bayer aspirin heavily. And the magic of the name was such that Sterling held on to a major chunk of the U.S. market in the face of a host of competitors who made aspirin and aspirin combinations.

It was a different story in Latin America. There Sterling found themselves competing directly with the German Bayer company, which was selling the same goods under the same trademarks. To avoid further confusion and to ensure that both companies would not waste money, the German Bayer company and Sterling's William Weiss reached an understanding in 1923 under which the two agreed not to invade each other's territories. The agreement was modified 3 years later, after Bayer was swallowed by I. G. Farben, a big German industrial company. Under terms of the 1926 pact, I. G. Farben became half-owner of Winthrop Chemical, a subsidiary set up by Sterling to handle the Bayer products. In exchange I. G. Farben gave Sterling the U.S. rights to products and processes developed by Bayer research chemists in laboratories at Rensselaer, New York. So with no facilities or capabilities of their own, Sterling managed to have the Germans supply the research, and, as frosting on the cake, Weiss was even given an honorary doctorate from the University of Cologne. In 1941 "Dr." Weiss was forced to resign as chairman of Sterling as a result of a government antitrust suit that disclosed details of the Bayer-Sterling agreements of 1923 and 1926. (A few months after his ouster, Weiss was fatally injured in an automobile accident in Michigan.)

War once again proved profitable for Sterling. In 1945, after World War II was over, Sterling paid $9.5 million to acquire the German half-interest in Winthrop (which had again been seized by the U. S. government). During the war Sterling had mounted a major marketing offensive against the German Bayer brands in Mexico, Central and South America. While American troops were fighting all over the world, Sterling was fighting Bayer brand against brand with the largest advertising campaign ever seen in Latin America. Sterling emerged from the war with sales twice those of 1941.

Sterling's post-war growth has been fueled by buying other companies. They entered the dental field with the purchase of Cook-Waite Laboratories. They became leaders in decongestants (Neo-Synephrine) through buying Frederick Stearns & Co. They went into household products, cosmetics, and toiletries by acquiring Lehn & Fink. One very ambitious merger had gone awry much earlier. In 1928 Sterling banded together with Bristol-Myers, Vicks, and Life Savers to form an octopuslike company with the prosaic (but telling) name of Drug, Inc. However, they couldn't agree among themselves as to who should rule—and in 1933 the founding companies went their separate ways.

Reputation. Sterling deliberately maintains a low profile. They do nothing to promote a corporate image. (They have no public affairs or public relations officer.)

Who owns and runs the company. The top officers and directors—a group of 30 persons—hold among them about ½% of the stock. Dr. W. Clark Wescoe, Sterling's present chairman and chief executive officer, was recruited in 1969 from the University of Kansas, where he was Chancellor. Previously, he had been director of the university's medical center and dean of its medical school. To obtain Dr. Wescoe's services, Sterling agreed to make supplemental payments to him after his retirement at age 65 that would be equivalent to benefits he would have received if he had spent 30 years with the company. Sterling also sold him 9,000 shares of stock, taking his personal I.O.U. and allowing him to pay it off over 15 years with interest set at 2%.

In the public eye. Sterling is not known for their good works, nor do annual reports use any space reporting on such matters as equal employment opportunity, community relations or charitable contributions. In 1978, the Securities and Exchange Commission criticized Sterling for failing to disclose significant information to investors in their 1974 and 1975 financial statements. In the past the company has raised money among managers for a political fund to support congressional candidates "who have the best interest of our industry at heart."

In early 1980 Airwick, makers of Carpet Fresh, filed a suit charging Sterling Drug with patent infringement for Sterling's new rug and room deodorant and cleaner, Love My Carpet. Airwick's suit is based partly on remarks made by a Sterling executive named Steven W. Lapham before a group of marketing executives in November 1979. Lapham's theme was "Replicate, don't innovate," and he urged his audience to be copycats: "Someone else has gone and done your homework for you. They have taken the risk, the time, and spent the dollars." Lapham said that when Airwick first test-marketed Carpet Fresh in mid-1977,

Sterling thought the "whole idea had to be wrong." He said, "What housewife in her right mind would sprinkle white powder onto her carpeting before vacuuming?" But when Carpet Fresh showed promise, Sterling quickly began a crash project to duplicate it. In six months Sterling had their Love My Carpet on the supermarket shelves.

Unfortunately for Sterling, Lapham's speech was reported by *Advertising Age*, and Airwick's lawyers were off to the federal courthouse. As one marketing expert told the *Wall Street Journal* about the whole episode: "You don't win anything by shooting your mouth off in the marketplace."

Stock performance. Sterling stock bought for $1,000 in 1970 sold for $706 on January 2, 1980.

Major employment centers. New York City; Albany, New York; and Cincinnati.

Access. 90 Park Avenue, New York, New York 10016; (212) 972-4141.

Consumer brands.

Over-the-counter products: Neo-Synephrine nasal decongestants; pHisoDerm skin cleanser; Bayer aspirin; Diaparene baby wash cloths; Phillips' Milk of Magnesia; Midol, Cope and Vanquish pain relievers; Breacol; Bronkaid; Campho-Phenique; Fletcher's Castoria; Haley's M-O laxative-lubricant; Medi-Quik first aid spray; Stri-Dex medicated products for acne.
Household products: Lysol disinfectants; Wet Ones moist towelettes; Mop & Glo; d-Con insecticides & rodenticides; Minwax wood-finishing products; Beacon; Energine; Four/Gone; Rid-X.
Cosmetics and toiletries: Givenchy; Oglivie; Dorothy Gray; Tussy.

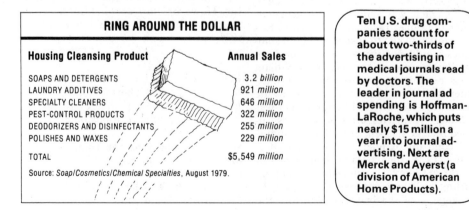

RING AROUND THE DOLLAR

Housing Cleansing Product	Annual Sales
SOAPS AND DETERGENTS	3.2 *billion*
LAUNDRY ADDITIVES	921 *million*
SPECIALTY CLEANERS	646 *million*
PEST-CONTROL PRODUCTS	322 *million*
DEODORIZERS AND DISINFECTANTS	255 *million*
POLISHES AND WAXES	229 *million*
TOTAL	$5,549 *million*

Source: *Soap/Cosmetics/Chemical Specialties*, August 1979.

Ten U.S. drug companies account for about two-thirds of the advertising in medical journals read by doctors. The leader in journal ad spending is Hoffman-LaRoche, which puts nearly $15 million a year into journal advertising. Next are Merck and Ayerst (a division of American Home Products).

Upjohn

Sales: $1.5 billion
Profits: $149.5 million
Forbes 500 rank: 334
Founded: 1886
Employees: 19,920
Headquarters: Kalamazoo, Michigan

What they do. The Upjohn family runs this huge multinational drug company from the improbable location of Kalamazoo, a small city situated midway between Chicago and Detroit, whose name was playfully mocked in the 1930s Glenn Miller hit of "I've gotta gal in Kalamazoo." *Kalamazoo* is an American Indian term meaning "boiling pot"—and the boiling pots of Upjohn churn out tens of millions of pills a year—primarily prescription drugs for heart disease, diabetes, fertility, arthritis, hypertension, cancer, and central nervous system diseases.

Upjohn's single most important drug at present is Motrin, used in treating arthritis. They also are leading producers of steroid hormones, used to treat allergies, inflammation, asthma, and hormone deficiencies.

Diabetics had to rely on insulin injections until 1957, when Upjohn introduced Orinase, followed in 1966 by Tolinase. These oral antidiabetics became sales powerhouses, but sales plummeted after questions about their safety were raised in 1970.

Upjohn also manufactures over-the-counter drugs, the best known being Cheracol cough syrup, Kaopectate (for diarrhea), and Unicap vitamins.

Since the early 1960s Upjohn has acquired half a dozen companies in various fields: insulating materials, engineering plastics, home health care, medical testing labs, agricultural seeds and chemicals, and poultry breeding.

History. In 1885 Dr. William Erastus Upjohn, the ninth of the 12 children of Dr. Uriah Upjohn, patented a process for making pills which dissolved readily within the body. This "friable" pill was a great step forward in medicine because it increased the accuracy of dosage. In 1886, with the backing of his older brother Henry, also a physician, he founded the Upjohn Pill and Granule Co. in Kalamazoo.

The company grew steadily. One early winner was a quinine pill; another was Phenolax Wafers, the first of the candy-type laxatives. A research laboratory started in 1913 led Upjohn into the modern pharmaceutical era: it produced the effervescent antacid Citrocarbonate, which reached sales of $1 million in 1926; Digitora, an oral digitalis tablet for heart patients; Kaopectate and the other nonprescription drugs; and, in 1935, the first cortical hormone, extracted from beef adrenals. To this day Upjohn is one of the industry's top spenders on research, exceeded only by Merck and Lilly.

The Upjohns, most of them physicians, went on passing the baton from one generation to the next. When founder William E. Upjohn died, in 1932, the city's flags all flew at half-mast. Dr. Lawrence Upjohn, William's nephew who had become president in 1930, headed the company until 1944, when he was succeeded by Donald S. Gilmore, scion of the family that owned Gilmore Brothers, Kalamazoo's largest department store. Gilmore's father was an early investor in Upjohn, and his mother was Dr. William Upjohn's second wife. In 1961 Ray T. Parfet became president and chief executive officer; Robert M. Boudeman took over the president's chair in 1970. Both had married into the family.

Upjohn didn't sell stock to the public until 1958. And it wasn't until 1968 that the company allowed anyone who was not a member of the family or the firm to sit on the board of directors.

Reputation. In the first small facility he opened, William Upjohn posted signs saying, "Keep the Quality Up." The signs are still there. In 1969 Wisconsin Senator Gaylord Nelson said Upjohn kept secret for a decade research reports casting doubt on the usefulness of Panalba, an antibiotic combination. In 1970 a research group sponsored by the National Institutes of Health linked Upjohn's oral antidiabetic Orinase with heart attacks and said the drug had "no place in the routine treatment of diabetes." That finding was confirmed by another study published in 1975. Dr. William Hubbard, Upjohn's president, said he wished the study "hadn't happened, but I think we face the future with as much equanimity as anyone."

What they own. In addition to more than 3 million square feet in the Kalamazoo facilities, Upjohn owns 66 research and manufacturing sites on six continents and maintains 47 subsidiaries in 34 countries. The Upjohn Research and Development Center, a new $43 million facility, was dedicated in Kalamazoo in 1976. They are virtually debt free.

Who owns and runs the company. The Upjohns. Members of the family still own 25% of the stock. The chairman, Ray Parfet, and the vice-chairman, Preston Parish, are both married to Upjohn daughters who are first cousins. Central to Upjohn's fortunes, though not a family member, is Dr. David Weisblat, head of research. There are neither women nor minorities on the board or in top management positions, although women make up one-third and minorities 12% of Upjohn's work force in the United States.

In the public eye. It's difficult to separate Upjohn from Kalamazoo. When William Upjohn died in 1932, he left half his estate of more than $1 million to local institutions. Of the $2.4 million of charitable contributions made by the company in 1978, $800,000 went to organizations in the Kalamazoo area. Between 1964 and 1977 Upjohn accounted for 48% of all industrial construction in the Kalamazoo area.

Upjohn's "good guy" reputation suffered when a major study showed that patients on Orinase were more likely to have heart attacks than other diabetics. In 1973 the British medical journal *Lancet* published an article linking Upjohn's two top antibiotics, Lincocin and Cleocin, with a high incidence of intestinal disorder, diarrhea, and occasional deaths. Sales of both drugs nosedived. Twice the Food and Drug Administration has ordered the Upjohn antibiotic, Panalba, off the market in the United States, but Upjohn reportedly continues to sell it in 33 other countries. They have been trying for more than 10 years to get U.S. government approval for Depo-Provera, a three-month injectable contraceptive.

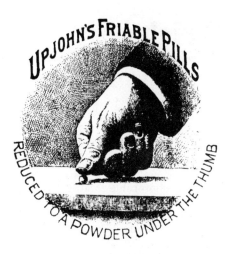

So that's how it started: Upjohn, back in the 1890s, developed a pill that would hold together but dissolve easily when swallowed—the friable pill.

Meanwhile, Upjohn continues to market the drug in over 60 foreign countries.

Where they're going. The biggest unknown in Upjohn's future is the result of 25 years of research into prostaglandins, a family of chemicals produced naturally in human cells under certain conditions and believed to be effective against a wide range of ills ranging from asthma to heart disease. In some laboratory tests cancerlike cells treated with prostaglandins have reverted to a near-normal state. Prostaglandins have the potential to sweep the pharmaceutical field as antibiotics did a generation ago—and Upjohn's lead in the field is undisputed. The only examples on the market so far are Prostin E2 and F2, an abortion agent and a labor inducer being sold in Britain. Applications to introduce them in the United States are pending with the FDA.

Stock performance. Upjohn stock bought for $1,000 in 1970 sold for $1,775 on January 2, 1980.

Access. 7000 Portage Road, Kalamazoo, Michigan 49001; (616) 323-4000.

Consumer brands.

Cheracol cough syrup; Unicap vitamin supplements; Kaopectate for diarrhea; Mycitracin antibiotic ointment.

Warner-Lambert
COMPANY

Sales: $3.2 billion
Profits: $123.3 million
Forbes 500 rank: 152
Rank in mouthwash: 1
Rank in razor blades: 2
Rank in cough drops: 1
Rank in antacids: 1
Rank in chewing gum: 1
Founded: 1856
Employees: 58,000
Headquarters: Morris Plains, New Jersey

What they do. A product of merger after merger, Warner-Lambert is such an artificial family that even their leader, Ward S. Hagan, conceded in 1979 that the people who work for the company "don't consider themselves Warner-Lambert people, they consider themselves Chicle people or Parke-Davis people." *Chicle* refers to gum manufacturer American Chicle, bought by Warner-Lambert in 1962. *Parke, Davis* refers to prescription drug maker Parke, Davis & Co., purchased in 1970. Those are only two of the numerous companies that have been spliced together to establish Warner-Lambert as a marketing powerhouse.

Their forte is selling. They took over the denture cleansing market in the mid-1960s with Efferdent's color-timing gimmick: when the water in the denture-cleaning glass loses its green color, it's time to take your dentures out. They introduced Fresh-en-up, a gum with a liquid center, whose sales soared to $70 million in 1978. Their genius for selling has put Warner-Lambert on top with Listerine mouthwash; Chiclets, Trident, and Dentyne gums; Gelusil and Rolaids antacids; and Hall's Mentho-Lyptus cough drops.

The crucial importance of selling can be seen in a breakdown of how Warner-Lambert spends their money. In 1978 they paid $1.3 billion for chemicals and other raw materials needed to make and package their products. They invested $85 million in research and development. Meanwhile, their total marketing costs were $881 million, of which $392 million represented expenditures for advertising and promotion. Warner-Lambert ranks as the seventh largest advertiser in the United States.

Warner-Lambert's sales can go up even if their own drug products falter. They are the world's largest supplier of the empty gelatin capsules in which many drugs are encased.

History. When Elmer Holmes Bobst took charge of the William R. Warner Company in 1945, he had already achieved success that would have satisfied most people. He was 61 years old and had recently quit as head of the American branch of Hoffmann-La Roche. He had built Roche into an important force in the U.S. drug industry, and thanks to a contract that gave him 5% of the profits, he had been one of the highest-paid persons in the country. At Warner it was almost like starting from the bottom again. He found a company choked by an obsolete inventory and highly erratic bookkeeping. Bobst was told that profits were $1.5 million on sales of $29 million, but a closer look showed that the company was losing money at the rate of $1.5 million a year. Bobst transformed the company, building a second career as illustrious as his first one. He was thus responsible for two major contenders in the U.S. pharmaceutical industry: Roche and Warner-Lambert.

The Warner company had roots in two cities: Philadelphia and St. Louis. William Warner was a Philadelphia pharmacist who, before the Civil War, invented the sugar-coated pill. It was to make him a fortune. Gustavus A. Pfeiffer & Co. was a St. Louis patent medicine company. In 1908 the Pfeiffers bought the Philadelphia company, retaining the Warner name. The Pfeiffers then bought the Hudnut and Du Barry cosmetics businesses—and they also moved the Warner headquarters to New York. And it was the Pfeiffers who invited Bobst to do his magic trick with the Warner company.

And magic it was. He brought people over from Roche to help him, he advertised Hudnut cosmetics on the Walter Winchell radio show, he changed the company's name to Warner-Hudnut, and then in 1951 he made the first of a series of acquisitions, buying Chilcott Pharmaceutical, a Morris Plains, New Jersey, drug maker. Soon Bobst was doing what he used to do at Roche: spending Sunday afternoons writing "Dear Doctor" letters, urging physicians to prescribe Chilcott's Peritrate for patients suffering from heart disease. (Peritrate is a blood vessel dilator, like nitroglycerine, and is still a good seller for the company.) After Chilcott there were many more acquisitions: Lambert Pharmacal (Listerine), Emerson Drug (Bromo-Seltzer), American Chicle, Smith Brothers (cough drops), American Optical, the Schick shaving business, and Parke, Davis. The company's name was changed to Warner-Lambert Pharmaceutical Company in 1955 and to Warner-Lambert in 1970.

When Listerine came into the house, the mouthwash had sales of $15 million a year. In 1957, hearing a warning about an impending Asian flu epidemic, Bobst took full-page ads in *Life* to advise readers: see your doctor for flu shots, avoid crowds, and gargle twice a day with Listerine. Warner-Lambert's advertising agency scoffed at the ad but Listerine did $26 million of business that year—and later went on to do much more. (The claim that Listerine helps people ward off colds was also to embroil Warner-Lambert in a long-standing fight with the Federal Trade Commission.)

In addition to building up Warner-Lambert, Bobst was a very active leader of the American Cancer Society—he turned down a merger with R. J. Reynolds Tobacco because of this association—and he was responsible for bringing his friend Richard Nixon to the New York law firm of Mudge, Stern, Baldwin & Todd in 1963. It was from there that Nixon launched his successful drive for the presidency. On Bobst's eighty-fifth birthday in 1971, President Nixon had a White House party for him. Elmer Bobst died in 1978, at the age of 93.

Reputation. Give Warner-Lambert a gimmick and an advertising budget and they'll give you a top-selling product.

What they own. Some of the best brand names in your local drugstore and supermarket. Not counting prescription drugs, Listerine is believed to be the largest selling drugstore product in the nation.

Who owns and runs the company. Warner-Lambert has a tradition of hiring people from the outside for the top jobs. In 1953 Bobst brought in a former governor of New Jersey, Alfred E. Driscoll, to be president. Stuart K. Hensley, from Gillette, succeeded Driscoll. Hensley was succeeded by E. Burke Giblin, who came from General Foods. And chairman Ward Hagan was recruited from Colgate-Palmolive. In 1977 Warner-Lambert put Irving Kristol, a New York University professor and a reigning intellectual guru of the conservative movement, on the board. Businessmen love him for his attacks on liberals.

In the public eye. In 1978 the Supreme Court upheld the Federal Trade Commission's order that Warner-Lambert be required to include in $10 million worth of advertising the disclaimer that their best-selling product "will not prevent colds or sore throats or lessen their severity."

In 1976 an explosion at the American Chicle gum plant in Long Island City, New York, killed six persons and injured other workers. Warner-Lambert was indicted by a grand jury for reckless manslaughter and criminally negligent homicide as a result of this accident. The company was accused of ignoring repeated warnings about the dangers of magnesium stearate at the plant. The New York Supreme Court dismissed the case in 1978, but in 1979 the Appellate Division reversed the Supreme Court and reinstated the indictment. Warner-Lambert called this ruling "outrageous." Magnesium stearate is a powdered lubricant used in the production of Freshen-up, the gum with the liquid center.

Where they're going. Warner-Lambert is still on the acquisition trail. They have bought more than 30 companies in the past 18 years. And now they're looking outside the drug field. In 1979 they paid $230 million—in cash—to acquire Entenmann's, a baker of quality cakes and cookies.

Stock performance. Warner-Lambert stock bought for $1,000 in 1970 sold for $567 on January 2, 1980.

Access. 201 Tabor Road, Morris Plains, New Jersey 07950; (201) 540-2000.

Consumer brands.

Health care: Lactona dental specialties; Gelusil, Rolaids, and Bromo-Seltzer antacids; Lubriderm, Sinutab, Anusol, Agoral, Halls, E.P.T., Caladryl, Tucks, Lavacol, Myadec, Abdec, Therapads, Saf-tip, Listerine, Listermint, Efferdent, Effergrip.

Gum and specialty foods: Dentyne, Trident, Freshen-Up, Chiclets, Clorets, Adams SourGums, and Bubblicious gum; Certs, Clorets, Dynamints, Rothchilds, Good & Plenty, Good & Fruity, Entenmann's.

Razors and blades: Schick; Plus Platinum; Super Chromium; Schick Super II; Ultrex; Lady Shick Super II; Personal Touch.

Other: Cool-Ray sunglasses.

Druggists

 Jack Eckerd

Sales: $1.3 billion
Profits: $59.3 million
Forbes 500 rank: 373
Rank in drugstore sales: 2
Founded: 1952
Employees: 24,000
Headquarters: Clearwater, Florida

What they do. "The nation's richest druggist" is what *Fortune* called Jack Eckerd in 1973. The retailing empire built on nearly 1,000 Eckerd drug stores in the sunbelt now includes 155 Eckerd Optical Centers, 36 JByrons department stores, and 80 casual clothing shops (Wrangler Wranch and The Junction). Stores range as far north as New Jersey, but most are in Florida, North Carolina, and Texas. And the man who built the empire has become a politician as well as a druggist.

History. Jack Eckerd began working during the Depression in the basement of his father's drugstore in Erie, Pennsylvania. His father, J. Milton Eckerd, told him: "Either you work harder and put in longer hours than anyone else, or you get into some other business." Eckerd stayed in the business. He bought three floundering drugstores in Tampa and Clearwater, Florida, in 1952, and attracted customers by challenging the state's fair-trade laws prohibiting price cutting. "Can you imagine us," said Eckerd, "selling the same products with little or no service as a drugstore that has help and delivery? So I went to court against Sterling Drug and Miles Labs." He was upheld by the Florida Supreme Court.

Starting in 1961 Eckerd went on to buy a series of southern-based drug chains, culminating in 1977 with his purchase of Eckerd Drugs of Charlotte, North Carolina. The name was not a coincidence. Milton Eckerd had started the North Carolina chain and sold the stores in the late 1930s to Edward M. O'Herron, his son-in-law. His

Testimonial from the Grave

A favorite advertising ploy of patent medicine companies was to print testimonial letters from grateful users who believed the wonder cure had saved them from the Grim Reaper. True believers had no idea that their heartfelt testimonials might also see duty under the trade names of a host of other nostrums. The industry's custom was to rent, sell, or exchange such letters, sometimes even advertising their stock with such offerings as "6,000 Nervous Debility, 300,000 all kinds of diseases (will sort)."

Occasionally there were slipups in this system, especially when the valuable letters had been in circulation so long that the writers expired. Such was the case with James R. Kimber, a labor leader who died on June 19, 1930, in Rochester, New York. Kimber's obituary ran in the *Rochester Democrat and Chronicle* on June 20, 1930. Five days later the same newspaper published an advertisement with his testimonial for a cure-all called Sargon, under the legend: "Labor Official Praises Sargon for New Health . . . Regained 18 Lbs. of Lost Weight and Troubles Disappeared, Says Kimber."

Source: Gerald Carson, *One for a Man, Two for a Horse.*

son, Edward M. O'Herron, Jr., sold the company in 1977 to Jack Eckerd, his half-uncle.

Eckerd ran in the 1970 Republican gubernatorial primary in Florida and lost. In 1974 he won the Republican nomination for U.S. Senator from Florida, but lost the election. Edward O'Herron, Jr., now a member of Jack Eckerd's board, ran for governor of North Carolina (as a Democrat) in 1976; he too lost.

Reputation. Jack Eckerd used to send out signed birthday cards to employees. In 1971 *Forbes* said of the company's style: "It may sound corny, but look at the results." *Fortune* reported in 1973 that Eckerd was selling drugs to the elderly practically at cost.

Who owns and runs the company. In 1975 Jack Eckerd became head of the General Services Administration under Gerald Ford, turning over the chairmanship of the company to longtime employee Stewart Turley. Eckerd returned to the board in March 1979. He still holds 13.7% of the company's stock—and his title now is chairman of the executive committee.

In the public eye. In 1971 Jack Eckerd gave over $10 million to Florida Presbyterian College, which promptly changed its name to Eckerd College.

Stock performance. Eckerd stock bought for $1,000 in 1970 sold for $1,601 on January 2, 1980.

Access. 2120 U.S. Highway 19 South, Clearwater, Florida 33518; (813) 531-8911.

Longs Drug Stores

Sales: $663 million
Profits: $24 million
Rank in drug store sales: 6
Founded: 1938
Employees: 6,500
Headquarters: Walnut Creek, California

What they do. Longs stores, a California phenomenon, don't look like drugstores.

Prescription medicines (accounting for only 8% of sales) tend to disappear among the appliances, food, cosmetics and toiletries, household supplies, photo equipment, liquor, tobacco, sporting goods, toys, and stationery. The company has apparently hit a winning combination, as it has a higher merchandise turnover and sales per store than any other drug chain. The average Longs does $5.8 million a year in standard items that can be ordered so quickly that warehousing is unnecessary. If an item doesn't sell, it doesn't stay around long.

History. Joseph M. Long's father-in-law was Marion Skaggs, founder of the grocery business that became the Safeway chain. In 1938 Skaggs lent Joseph and his brother Thomas $15,000 to start up a drugstore business. The Longs never needed another loan. "We don't borrow at all—not even one red penny," Joseph told the *San Francisco Examiner* in 1977 in one of his rare interviews. From 1938 to 1979 the Longs chain mushroomed from "a hole in the wall in Oakland" to 108 stores in California, a dozen in Hawaii, and one each in Alaska, Arizona, and Oregon.

Reputation. Longs is known as a place where the hired hands share in the rewards. A store manager hires, fires, buys, sets prices, and places advertising—in short, takes full charge. He can earn two to three times his salary in bonuses based on profit performance. Longs has a profit-sharing plan supported entirely by company contributions. "Some companies pay people with titles. We'd rather give them cash," Joseph Long says.

What they own. Longs owns more than half their stores. The rest are leased.

Who owns and runs the company. Skaggs money, through marriage, helped launch the Longs business in California. Founder Joe Long and his wife, Vera Skaggs, were divorced in 1979, but the Longs (including Joe Long's former wife) control more than half the stock. Their son, Robert M. Long, now runs the company.

Where they're going. In the past three years the company opened their first stores in Alaska, Oregon, Arizona, and Nevada. It's a big country . . .

Stock performance. Longs stock bought for $1,000 in 1970 sold for $1,965 on January 2, 1980.

Access. 141 North Civic Drive, Walnut Creek, California 94596; (415) 937-1170.

Sales: $927.5 million
Profits: $33.6 million
Forbes 500 rank: 488
Rank in drugstore sales: 4
Founded: 1947
Employees: 16,000
Headquarters: Twinsburg, Ohio

What they do. Revco stores do not bother with frills like lunch counters. The company believes prescriptions are essentially what bring people to drugstores—and they have parlayed that belief into a 24-state chain that has the largest number of drugstores in the nation: 1,200 at the start of 1980. An aggressive discounter, Revco beats the drums for low prices, especially on prescription drugs. They're now filling 40 million prescriptions a year, which account for 27% of their business, a ratio that is double the industry average. Of Revco's 16,000 employees more than 2,000 are pharmacists. Very different from a sprawling affair like a Longs or a Skaggs, the typical Revco packs some 8,000 items into an area of 8,500 square feet, usually leased space in a shopping center. They carry cosmetics, school supplies, cigarettes, and various household goods.

Revco runs a highly streamlined and centrally controlled operation out of Twinsburg, a town just south of Cleveland. All purchasing, pricing, advertising, merchandising, and accounting are directed from there. Merchandise is shipped weekly to all stores from seven distribution centers, keeping store inventory to a low level. Revco manufactures most of their store fixtures, and they have carpenter crews to put them in—they are ready to sell in 45 days after taking possession of a bare space. The company is so cost-conscious that trucks delivering to stores pick up merchandise from suppliers on the way back to the distribution centers.

Revco does 15% of their prescription business from third-party programs such as Medicare, Medicaid, and other health insurance plans. They benefit from these programs because while an average of 70% of all prescriptions written are filled, the figure rises to 95% when insurance pays. Sidney Dworkin, president of Revco, told stockholders toward the end of 1979: "Perhaps we don't like to be thought of as people who benefit from the misfortunes of others, but with inflation squeezing family budgets, our total discounting concept is more and more attractive to the consumer."

Like most drug chains, Revco buys drugs in large quantities and splits them into smaller packages to be shipped to their stores. In early 1980 the Food and Drug Administration shut down Revco's repackaging operations for 2 weeks after finding that some prescription medicines were being repacked without sufficient care; the FDA said Revco had failed to meet certain government regulations that require double-checking to ensure that drugs are in the right containers and correctly labeled.

History. Sidney Dworkin, described by the *New York Times* as "a mild-mannered certified public accountant from Detroit," is credited with building Revco. He was associated, as a stockholder and an officer but not an employee, with the original store—a conventional drugstore in Detroit operated by pharmacist Bernard Shulman. Shulman added a second store, and in 1956 converted both of them to a self-service, discount mode. The original name, Regal Drugs, was changed to Revco (after a Regal subsidiary, Registered Vitamin Company, that sold vitamins door to door). By 1961 the chain had 20 discount drugstores in the Detroit area. In that year they paid $2.2 million to acquire 40 Standard Drug stores in Cleveland. Dworkin became a fulltimer at Revco in 1963. In 1964, the year they went public, Revco's headquarters shifted to Cleveland. Dworkin took the president's chair in 1966 and rapidly expanded the company toward the East, the South, and the West through buyouts of more than 20 local drugstore operations. Once stores were bagged, Revco quickly converted all units to the self-service, discount way of life.

Revco today operates in a 24-state swath that extends from New York to Florida and from the eastern seaboard to Arizona.

Reputation. Every locally owned drugstore operation is on their shopping list.

What they own. They own the furniture and fixtures but not the stores. In Twinsburg they own their corporate headquarters building (on a 15-acre tract) plus 25 adjacent acres.

Who owns and runs the company. Dworkin and other company directors control 20% of the stock. Dworkin's two sons, Elliot and Marc, are both vice-presidents. The lone female on the board is Dr. Betty J. Diener, dean of the business school at Old Dominion University, Norfolk, Virginia.

In the public eye. Revco enrolls hundreds of thousands of senior citizens and families of newborn babies into a club which entitles them to a 10% discount on prescription drugs (and locks them in as steady customers). In 1977 Revco was fined $50,000 after pleading no contest to charges by Ohio officials that Medicaid bills submitted by the company had been falsified. They also had to turn back to the Ohio Welfare Department $521,000 that they had collected through Medicaid billing. Apparently frustrated at the long delay in state payments, Revco employees had fabricated new bills to substitute for the original ones. Revco, which prides itself on centralized management controls, said this maneuver was carried out "without Company knowledge or approval."

Where they're going. Revco is opening two stores a week and expects to hit $2 billion and 2,000 stores sometime in the 1980s. Meanwhile, they're also moving into manufacturing. They have bought four small drug companies (makers of vitamins, food supplements, cough syrups, liquid antibiotics and medicated shampoos); and they own 12% of a new drug, Prinar, an anti-inflammatory agent that is still being tested but has been hailed by some scientists as having an efficacy comparable to cortisone.

Stock performance. Revco stock bought for $1,000 in 1970 sold for $2,343 on January 2, 1980.

Access. 1925 Enterprise Parkway, Twinsburg, Ohio 44087; (216) 425-9811.

Consumer brands.

Revco.

Walgreens

Sales: $1.3 billion
Profits: 30.3 million
Forbes 500 rank: 366
Rank in drug retailing: 1
Founded: 1901
Employees: 28,000
Headquarters: Deerfield, Illinois

What they do. Walgreen, the company that invented the chocolate malted milk with ice cream, operates the nation's oldest and largest retail drug chain. They serve 1 million customers a day in 650 units located in 32 states and Puerto Rico. Chicago, where it all started, remains their strongest market, generating 21% of total sales. A high percentage of their stores are in the Midwest.

More than a retailer, Walgreen has three units manufacturing over 400 Walgreen brand products—drugs, cosmetics, toiletries, and household goods. These products are also wholesaled to some 1,400 independently owned drugstores known as "Walgreen Agency" units.

Walgreen is the nation's number 1 pharamacist, with an annual prescription business of more than $150 million. But they sell much more than pharmaceuticals. Where it's legal Walgreen sells liquor, which, together with cigarettes, brings in more than 20% of total revenues. Cosmetics and toiletries account for 13% of sales, and general merchandise (cameras, toys, school supplies, what-have-you) 29%.

Walgreen also runs nearly 300 restaurants, over 230 of them within or adjacent to Walgreen drugstores. Most of the free-standing restaurants are newly developed Wag's coffee shops. Walgreen's annual food-service sales are $100 million.

Retailing is a constantly changing scene. In the past five years Walgreen has opened

122 stores and closed 64. Many more were remodeled.

History. Walgreen's growth from a single store on Chicago's south side is a classic American success story minus the drama of vivid personalities, daring risks, or struggles for survival. Charles R. Walgreen, Sr., the son of a Swedish immigrant, had an innate sense of what it takes to succeed in retailing. He paid attention to details. From the very start Walgreen made some drug items so that he could charge low prices. According to his wife, Myrtle, "He always said that he wanted to make better products and sell them cheaper than anybody else, and he always based his prices on a percentage of profits. I used to say that it would be a world's wonder if the first words our children learned were not 'percent.'" Walgreen became a chain in 1909 with the purchase of a second Chicago store. Then came Charles Walgreen's own brand of "double-rich" ice cream served at a fountain connected to the store. The fountain survived the winter by becoming a soup-and-sandwich shop serving food prepared by Mrs. Walgreen. That was the start of Walgreen's restaurant business, and the origin of the drugstore soda fountain.

The third store came in 1911—and then the numbers just kept growing. Walgreen became a household word in Chicago during the 1920s. The first out-of-state store, in Hammond, Indiana, just outside Chicago, opened in 1924. By 1925 the chain had 65 links; in the next four years it exploded to 397 stores from coast to coast. In 1933, the depths of the Depression, Walgreen boosted their advertising budget to $1 million and paid their first stock dividend.

Mrs. Walgreen portrayed her husband as possessing a canny modesty: "He used to come home and remark, 'Well, today I hired another man who is smarter than I am.' I would comment that nobody in the drug business was smarter than he was. But Charles would say, 'The only really smart thing about me is that I know enough to hire men who are smarter than I am.'"

The founder died in 1939. His son, Charles R. Walgreen, Jr., followed in his father's footsteps. As a boy he worked in the stores, and he joined the company after graduating from pharmacy school. It was his task after World War II to convert the chain into a self-service operation. In the process the Walgreen stores became much bigger units, still emphasizing low drug prices. The soda fontains persisted. The big one in the Walgreen's at 1501 Broadway, New York, was replicated by Columbia Pictures for the 1955 film "My Sister Eileen."

In 1974 Walgreen became the first drug chain to top $1 billion in sales. Their latest expansion is a joint venture with Schnuck Supermarkets of St. Louis in combination food-and-drug stores. There are now four units in this chain.

The family tradition continues with Charles R. Walgreen, III, a registered pharmacist like his father and grandfather; he became president in 1969 and chairman of the board in 1976.

Reputation. The Walgreen chain was in the forefront of many changes in the retail drugstore field. They consistently stressed low prescription prices and supported the substitution of low-cost generic drugs for brand-name formulations. They were one of the first drug chains to provide customers with complete information about prescription drug prices, and they applauded the 1976 Supreme Court decision striking down state prohibitions against advertising prescription drug prices. They were the first drug chain to put prescription drugs in child-proof containers—long before it was required by law.

What they own. Six hundred eighty-eight drugstores; 37 separate restaurants; 50% interest in four Schnucks-Walgreens combination stores; 47% interest in Sanborns, a celebrated Mexican retailer and restaurateur; three plants which annually produce, among other things, 275,000 gallons of bubble bath, 180,000 dozen bottles of shampoo, a half-million cans of shaving cream, and a billion vitamin tablets; three photo processing studios that turn out more than 80 million color prints a year; and a Chicago-based travel agency, International Travel Service.

Who owns and runs the company. The Walgreen family is still in control. Charles R. Walgreen, III, has been chief executive officer since 1971. Although the company claims to provide an environment that fosters equal opportunity, it's not evident in the ranks of the officers. The board is dominated by management and Chicago-area business executives. No women. No blacks.

In the public eye. Walgreen appears to feel that they discharge their social responsibilities by running a drugstore chain that gives good value to customers.

Where they're going. They're just where they want to be (and where they've always been): running drugstores they call "appealing, convenient, pleasant to shop." They look forward to 1983, when 70% of the 200 most frequently prescribed drugs will no longer be under patent.

Stock performance. Walgreen stock bought for $1,000 in 1970 sold for $1,285 on January 2, 1980.

Access. 200 Wilmont Road, Deerfield, Illinois 60015; (312) 948-5000.

> The *American Druggist* reports that each woman, man, and child in the United States spent an average of $36.24 for prescription drugs in 1978. A total of 1.4 billion prescriptions were filled at a total cost of $7.9 billion.

THE CAR: PERSONAL MOBILITY

Auto Makers

American Motors

Sales: $3.2 billion
Profits: $68.1 million
Forbes 500 rank: 159
Rank in U.S. car production: 5
Rank in four-wheel-drive vehicles: 3
Founded: 1902
Employees: 28,400
Headquarters: Southfield, Michigan

What they do. The French, who came to America's aid in the war of independence, have now come to the aid of American Motors. A timely affiliation with Renault, the French government–owned auto maker, has whisked small but spunky AMC back from an ominous brink, where it has several times hovered but never gone over. "Nobody calls us just 'American Motors,'" AMC President W. Paul Tippett, Jr., once remarked. "It's 'Struggling American Motors,' 'Ailing American Motors,' or 'Moribund American Motors.'" Even in the best

of times the company has been known as "Tiny American Motors." A $3 billion corporation may seem pretty big, but not in the U.S. automobile industry. For every car American Motors sells, Detroit's Big Three car makers together sell 50. In the United States, Datsun outsells American 2 to 1; Toyota outsells them 3 to 1. Even Cadillac sells more.

American Motors Corporation makes three automobiles—the compact Concord, the subcompact Spirit, and the four-wheel-drive Eagle. The vehicle that has kept the company on the road for the last decade, however, is not a car, but the four-wheel-drive Jeep. In 1979 AMC sold about as many Jeeps as passenger cars (150,000 of each). AMC makes some components, such as bodies and axles, but they buy about 70% of their parts from other companies, including the Big Three. In 1978 they arranged to buy 100,000 four-cylinder engines a year from General Motors' Pontiac division, backing out of an earlier deal with Volkswagen.

After years of talks concerning possible mergers and bailouts, in 1979 the company announced an agreement with Renault. AMC now imports Renaults (chiefly Le

Car) and sells them through many of their auto dealers. AMC has over 1,600 dealers—more than any foreign car maker in the United States—and they hope to get 1,200 of them to sell Renaults. Renault sells AMC's Jeeps through their dealer network in Europe and South America. Further, Renault is investing $150 million in AMC, for which they will eventually receive nearly one-quarter of AMC's stock. In return, AMC plans to make front-wheel-drive Renault cars at their factory in Kenosha, Wisconsin, starting in 1982.

Although cars and Jeeps account for four-fifths of AMC's sales, the company also does a healthy business in heavy-duty military trucks and U.S. Postal Service delivery trucks, both made by their AM General subsidiary. Virtually all the trucks in the U.S. Army were made by AM General, and the company sells military trucks and Jeeps to some 90 foreign governments from Bolivia to Morocco as well. AMC also has small subsidiaries that make lawn and garden tractors, riding lawn mowers, and molded plastic parts for the auto industry.

A big part of the cost of making cars in America is retooling for the annual styling changes so dear to the hearts of Detroit. Without the resources of the Big Three, AMC has cut corners ingeniously while still coming out with new models each fall. The Eagle, which they unveiled in 1979, is essentially a Concord body and chassis that borrowed enough Jeep parts to make it the first four-wheel-drive passenger car in America. The Concord, in turn, is a remake of the Hornet, which AMC built from 1969 to 1977 and has recycled endlessly. The Gremlin, a big seller for AMC in the mid-1970s, was a chopped-down Hornet; the doors for the Spirit are the same as for the Hornet. And the AMX, the company's late-1960s fling at a two-seat sports car, was a truncated Javelin. "We just work with a tighter belt all the way around," AMC's vice-president in charge of styling explained to the *Wall Street Journal*.

History. Today's American Motors is the result of a 1954 merger of two losers, Nash and Hudson. Nash's origins go back to 1902, when the Thomas B. Jeffery Company of Kenosha, Wisconsin, built a one-cylinder Rambler automobile that sold for $750. Charles W. Nash, who had been head of Buick and later president of General Motors, bought the Jeffery company in 1916 and renamed it Nash Motors. In 1937 they merged with Kelvinator, a Detroit refrigerator maker, and became Nash-Kelvinator. Hudson was launched in Detroit in 1909 with money provided by Joseph L. Hudson, a local department store owner. Hudson turned out such memorable cars as the Essex, Terraplane, and Hudson Hornet.

The glory years for American Motors came in the late 1950s, when the Rambler, an obscure model that Nash had introduced earlier in the decade, caught the country's fancy. At a time when the Big Three's offerings were growing longer and wider and more baroque each year, AMC suddenly found themselves with a small, efficient "compact" car. George Romney, who became president of the company in 1954, touted the Rambler as the sensible alternative to what he called the "gas-guzzling dinosaurs." In their biggest year, 1960, AMC captured 7.5% of the domestic car market.

Romney left AMC in 1962 to run successfully for governor of Michigan. His politi-

---

U.S. TRUCK SALES

(based on registration of 3,467,910 trucks in 1979)

Maker / Percentage of Market

1. FORD   32%
2. CHEVROLET   31%
3. DODGE   10%
4. GMC   8%
5. JEEP   4%
6. INTERNATIONAL   3%
7. MACK   0.84%
8. PLYMOUTH   0.57%
9. KENWORTH   0.43%
10. FREIGHTLINER   0.39%
11. WHITE   0.26%
12. PETERBILT   0.25%
13. AUTOCAR   0.07%
14. WESTERN STAR   0.03%
MISCELLANEOUS (imports, Diamond Reo, Crane Carrier, Oshkosh, FWD, Hendrickson, etc.)   7.64%

Source: *Automotive News*, Market Data Book Issue 1980.

The world's population of 265 million cars and 70 million vans, trucks, and buses averages out to one motor vehicle for every 12 human beings.

cal career peaked and plummeted in 1968, when he lost the Republican presidential nomination. His loss was partly attributed to his remark during the campaign that he had been "brainwashed" by U.S. military officials in Vietnam while on a visit to the war zone.

AMC couldn't expect to keep the juicy compact car market to themselves for long. Soon the giants weighed in with compacts of their own—the Ford Falcon, for example. AMC tried making larger "luxury" cars, with dismal results. Between 1966 and 1971 the profits posted amounted to $27 million, and the losses to $145 million. In 1968 they sold Kelvinator to White Consolidated.

The move that saved AMC was their 1970 purchase of Kaiser-Jeep from Kaiser Industries, which had bought the company from Willys-Overland after World War II. AMC restyled and enlarged the Jeep, put in a V-8 engine, and promoted it as a recreational vehicle—a market that was just starting to boom. But by the mid-1970s they were back in the red, partly because of the gasoline shortages that cut deeply into recreational vehicle sales. Rumors flew that they were about to abandon cars and concentrate on Jeeps and trucks, but AMC decided to stick it out. By the end of the 1970s they were turning profits once more.

Reputation. AMC has many well-wishers; it seems nobody wants them to fail. They have sought and received waivers on exhaust emissions standards from the Environmental Protection Agency, claiming that compliance might push them over the cliff. The United Auto Workers union has consistently settled for less money from AMC than from the Big Three. Even their competitors seem to be rooting for them. Since 1970 AMC has arranged each year with General Motors to receive research data on emissions control. AMC has bought parts from GM, Ford, and Chrysler for years, and in 1977 *Forbes* reported that the Big Three "have been helpful, and unusually patient, creditors."

What they own. An automobile plant in Kenosha, Wisconsin. Jeep plants in Toledo, Ohio, and Brampton, Ontario. Four truck plants in Indiana and Texas. Twenty plants overseas, from Bangladesh to Venezuela. Assorted assembly and component plants in Michigan, Indiana, and Wisconsin.

Who owns and runs the company. By the end of 1979 Renault owned 4.7% of AMC's stock, and their share is scheduled to rise to 22.7% by the end of the century. Two Renault officers and one woman, a University of Michigan business professor, joined the board of directors in 1979 and 1980.

Gerald C. Meyers, chairman since 1978, came to the company in 1962 after stints at Ford and Chrysler. W. Paul Tippett, Jr., who took over from Meyers as president, has the unusual distinction among Detroit car executives of having worked outside the auto industry. He went from Procter & Gamble to Ford to STP to Singer before winding up at AMC. In 1978–79 Meyers performed the unheard-of feat of luring three high-ranking GM executives to AMC's marketing and public relations departments.

In the public eye. The California Air Resources Board levied a $4.2 million fine against AMC in 1976 for allegedly submitting "totally false" emissions test results and selling cars that exceeded the state's pollution control standards. But good will toward AMC evidently carried the day again: the company worked out a settlement of $1.1 million to be paid over five years.

Where they're going. Gerald Meyers has made no secret of his game plan. He predicts that the 30 companies now making cars will dwindle to about a dozen by the end of the century. He decided that the only way American Motors could be one of those survivors would be in association with a large manufacturer such as Renault.

Stock performance. American Motors stock bought for $1,000 in 1970 sold for $797 on January 2, 1980.

Major employment centers. Kenosha, Wisconsin; Toledo, Ohio; Brampton, Ontario.

Access. 27777 Franklin Road, Southfield, Michigan 48034; (313) 827-1000.

Consumer brands.

Cars: Eagle; Spirit; Concord; Le Car.
Jeeps: Laredo; Cherokee; Wagoneer.
Pickup trucks: Honcho.

CHRYSLER CORPORATION

Sales: $12.0 billion
Losses: $1.1 billion
Forbes 500 rank: 22
Rank in U.S. auto sales: 3
Founded: 1925
Employees: 157,958
Headquarters: Highland Park, Michigan

What they do. Chrysler is like one of those air-filled, sand-bottomed punching dummies that little boys are so fond of; they take a colossal punch, fall over, and then spring back up again to take another punch. Since the 1950s Chrysler has repeatedly guessed wrong and gotten knocked down for it. When America wants big cars, Chrysler is busy making small ones; and when America wants small cars, Chrysler makes big ones. In the 1970s they took the cruelest punches of all—declining sales and monumental losses that sent them down for the count of nine.

Chrysler always prided themselves on their engineering excellence, but those days are long gone. Chrysler gave the automotive industry the first high-compression engine, electronic ignition, torsion-bar suspension, unitized body construction, and power steering. But in times of spiraling gasoline prices, Chrysler's engineering prowess has not been equal to the task. It may not be fair, however, to blame the engineers for Chrysler's plight. For 25 years there have been stories in the press about one management after another coming in to rescue the company from previous mistakes. These stories are as current as today's newspaper.

Through all the turmoil of the past decade Chrysler remained the nation's third-largest auto maker. But their share of the American car market plunged from 16% in 1967 to 9% in 1979. To make matters worse, Chrysler kept turning out cars even when no one had ordered them, while other companies built cars only to fill orders from dealers. The result for Chrysler was a huge pileup of brand new cars that nobody wanted to buy.

In 1979 the manufacturer of Chryslers, Dodges, and Plymouths had a new management team in place and went to Washington, D.C. to plead poverty and ask for a $1.5 billion loan guarantee. Chrysler proposed to borrow the money from private parties who would lend it to them only if the government promised to pay it back if the auto firm couldn't. Chrysler also found a new explanation for their difficulties: government regulation. The story was that complying with government rules on fuel efficiency and antipollution devices adds $620 to the price of each Chrysler car, compared with $340 for each General Motors car. The disparity results, of course, because GM sells so many more cars than Chrysler and can spread the costs.

History. All this is a long way from the company Walter Chrysler created in the 1920s. Chrysler was the son of a Union Pacific Railroad engineer and was determined to become a machinist—so determined that he built his own tools prior to his apprenticeship with the Atchison, Topeka and Santa Fe Railroad in 1895. Between the ages of 18 and 33 Chrysler worked eight different jobs as a machinist in places like Trinidad, Colorado, and Oelwein, Iowa. In 1908, the same year he became a power superintendent for the Chicago Great Western Railroad, Chrysler took his entire $700 savings, borrowed another $4,300 from a

Giving a Horse an Even Break

Early automotive experiments had more to contend with than engineering problems. Those with financial interests in horse-drawn transportation and railroads both conspired against the new technology. In 1865 the British Parliament passed the Locomotives on Highways Act, otherwise known as the Red Flag Act, which limited the speed of "road locomotives" to 2 m.p.h. in towns and 4 m.p.h. on open highways. It also required every car to be attended by someone walking ahead waving a red flag; at night, a red lantern.

There was no such legislation enacted in the United States, although antispeeding societies were set up in many places, and restrictions to

banker friend, and bought his first motor-car—a Locomobile. Before driving it, Chrysler disassembled it and put it back together several times.

Four years later, having decided on a career in the auto industry, Chrysler became the works manager of Buick Motor Car, a division of General Motors in Flint, Michigan. Within five years he was president of Buick. In 1919 he became manufacturing vice-president of General Motors as well. Such was his expertise and reputation for building well-engineered cars that he could hold both jobs at the same time. Chrysler was earning well over $1 million a year at this point.

In 1920, after a brief stint at revitalizing sagging Willys-Overland, a car company in Toledo, Ohio, Chrysler took over as president of Maxwell Motor Car and began to build his dream car—a low-priced consumer model with a high-compression engine, which most engineers thought to be impossible for the moderate price range Chrysler aimed at. But by 1924 Chrysler had done the impossible: he created the six-cylinder Chrysler 50, the number indicating the speed his car could travel on a good highway. At a time when Ford's Model T was thought to have achieved the pinnacle of speed, at 35 miles per hour, Chrysler's new 50 astonished the nation. That year almost 32,000 Chryslers were built and sold, and Chrysler began work on three new models—the 60, the 70, and the 80, all numbers referring to the cars' top speeds. In 1925 Chrysler changed the company name to his own. The following year he moved from 27th place in the auto industry to 5th place, and the top four (Ford, GM, Dodge, and Nash) were looking over their shoulders.

With good reason. In 1928, the year Chrysler introduced the DeSoto and the Plymouth (named for the endurance and strength of the Pilgrims), Chrysler set about buying Dodge, a much larger company. After the death of the Dodge brothers, John and Horace, in 1925, the company had drifted and sales had declined. Chrysler, who needed their foundry to make parts he had previously bought from others, was able to buy the company for $225 million in Chrysler stock. Thus Chrysler became one of the Big Three with a stroke of the pen.

The company made a profit throughout the Depression, even making a run at Ford's second-place status prior to World War II. But after Walter Chrysler's death in 1940 the company began to flounder. In an attempt to cut costs Chrysler simply updated their 1942 model every year until 1953. As Ford's and GM's new models took more and more business away from Chrysler, the company finally—and reluctantly—brought out a totally new model that year. Then in 1960 Chrysler introduced the Valiant, a small, economical, low-priced model. But Chrysler had misread the public mood: America wanted luxury that year. Unfortunately, Chrysler had designed 75% of the assembly-line run as "stripped-down" (no costly extras) and made only 25% of the run "deluxe." They made a similar mistake in 1962, when they cut their Dodge and Chrysler models by nine inches in length and five inches in width; the cars flopped. Meanwhile, Chrysler, trying to be all things to all people, continued to make their Imperial luxury car in a suicidal attempt to compete with Cadillac and Lincoln.

Chrysler lost $8 million in 1970, but that merely foreshadowed what was to come. In 1974, stuck with a fleet of gas-guzzlers at the height of the Arab oil embargo, Chrysler took losses of $52 million. The next year losses skyrocketed to an unbelievable $260 million. After a brief two-year recovery

keep automobiles from frightening horses were hotly disputed. In 1904 Henry Hayes of Denver, Colorado, patented his answer to the problem: a mechanical model of a horse that could be attached to the front of an automobile. The model's front legs were supported by a wheel, and its hind legs fitted to the car's front axle. The eyes lit up like headlights and a storage area was provided in the rump, opened by lifting the tail. This metal creature, complete with a horn inside its head, was intended to make real horses feel at home with the vehicle that rattled along at its heels. It does not appear to have been a commercial success.

came another loss of $205 million in 1978; and Chrysler began to panic. Hearing that Lee Iacocca, president of Ford and creator of the popular Mustang, had been fired, Chrysler hired him to turn them around.

Essentially a salesman, Iacocca made his first big move: dismissing all the advertising agencies servicing Chrysler and consolidating the company's advertising with one agency, Kenyon & Eckhardt, which resigned their Ford business to take on the do-or-die assignment for Chrysler. It was the biggest account switch in the history of advertising. Kenyon & Eckhardt promptly put Lee Iacocca on television and prepared hard-hitting newspaper ads in which Iacocca argued Chrysler's case to the American public—and to the Congress. The government had to come to the aid of Chrysler, said Iacocca, because hundreds of thousands of jobs, and the welfare of the entire state of Michigan, were at stake. In August 1979 a cynic at another auto company said: "Other auto companies have a fall clearance, but Chrysler follows a different strategy: instead of trying to move customers into showrooms, it keeps trying to move part of the Treasury to Detroit."

At the start of 1980 Chrysler got the promise of a government guarantee of loans up to $1.5 billion provided they could raise another $2 billion on their own. Meanwhile, to get customers into the showrooms, Iacocca offered a revolutionary money-back guarantee if people bought Chrysler cars and returned them within 30 days because they didn't like them. In the first month the plan was in effect—February 1980—only 84 cars out of the nearly 3,500 sold were returned. But Chrysler's share of the market slid further to 9.2%. The government loan guarantee came through in May 1980.

Reputation. It depends on how you answer the question Chrysler asked in a 1979 advertisement: "Would America be better off without Chrysler?"

What they own. Chrysler has the most antiquated plant in the automotive industry. In 1979 they were operating seven factories that were more than 50 years old. In 1980, when they decided to stop making full-size cars, they closed their assembly plant in Hamtramck, Michigan, and their big Lynch Road assembly plant in Detroit. That left them with four car assembly

THE TOP TWENTY AMERICAN CARS

8.3 million domestically produced cars of 69 different models were sold in the United States in 1979. Here are the 20 best-sellers:

1.	CHEVROLET (*GM*)	449,001
2.	CUTLASS SUPREME (*GM*)	404,068
3.	CHEVETTE (*GM*)	375,724
4.	MALIBU (*GM*)	344,233
5.	FAIRMONT (*Ford*)	338,819
6.	CITATION/NOVA (*GM*)	308,437
7.	MUSTANG (*Ford*)	304,053
8.	MONTE CARLO (*GM*)	265,877
9.	REGAL (*GM*)	249,379
10.	FORD (*Ford*)	245,565
11.	OLDSMOBILE (*GM*)	223,699
12.	THUNDERBIRD (*Ford*)	215,698
13.	CADILLAC (*GM*)	206,164
14.	CAMARO (*GM*)	204,742
15.	PINTO (*Ford*)	187,708
16.	GRAND PRIX (*GM*)	175,573
17.	PONTIAC (*GM*)	171,301
18.	VOLARE (*Chrysler*)	167,091
19.	RABBIT (*Volkswagen*)	166,839
20.	FIREBIRD (*GM*)	149,211

Source: *Automotive News*, 1980 Market Data Book Issue.

plants in the United States. Chrysler has to buy a lot of their parts from suppliers. According to *New York Times* reporter Edwin McDowell, "Suppliers take an estimated 68¢ of every Chrysler revenue dollar, compared with 61¢ for Ford and 51¢ for General Motors, and there appears to be nothing the company can do about it."

Who owns and runs the company. Lee Iacocca and a bunch of his former underlings at Ford were in command of Chrysler as 1980 opened. Iacocca agreed to work for $1 a year until Chrysler was making money again. (But he was able to collect $1 million in 1979, part of the $1.5 million Chrysler promised him to make up the benefits he lost from Ford.) Among the people who were sitting on Chrysler's board as the company careened toward bankruptcy were: J. Richardson Dilworth, investment manager for the Rockefeller family; Gabriel Hague, chairman of Manufacturers Hanover Trust (a big lender to Chrysler); Tom Killefer, chairman of United States Trust Company; and John H. Coleman, retired deputy chairman of the Royal Bank of Canada. As the result of the difficult negotiations with the United Auto Workers to keep wage demands down during Chrysler's winter of discontent, the company agreed to put UAW president Donald Fraser on the board of directors. Fraser's clout with sena-

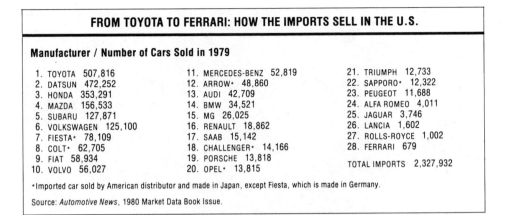

FROM TOYOTA TO FERRARI: HOW THE IMPORTS SELL IN THE U.S.

Manufacturer / Number of Cars Sold in 1979

1. TOYOTA 507,816	11. MERCEDES-BENZ 52,819	21. TRIUMPH 12,733
2. DATSUN 472,252	12. ARROW* 48,860	22. SAPPORO* 12,322
3. HONDA 353,291	13. AUDI 42,709	23. PEUGEOT 11,688
4. MAZDA 156,533	14. BMW 34,521	24. ALFA ROMEO 4,011
5. SUBARU 127,871	15. MG 26,025	25. JAGUAR 3,746
6. VOLKSWAGEN 125,100	16. RENAULT 18,862	26. LANCIA 1,602
7. FIESTA* 78,109	17. SAAB 15,142	27. ROLLS-ROYCE 1,002
8. COLT* 62,705	18. CHALLENGER* 14,166	28. FERRARI 679
9. FIAT 58,934	19. PORSCHE 13,818	
10. VOLVO 56,027	20. OPEL* 13,815	TOTAL IMPORTS 2,327,932

*Imported car sold by American distributor and made in Japan, except Fiesta, which is made in Germany.

Source: *Automotive News*, 1980 Market Data Book Issue.

---

tors was invaluable to Chrysler's successful lobbying effort.

Where they're going. It's tough to say. Chrysler brings in from Japan Mitsubishi-built models, which they sell under the names Colt, Challenger, Champ, Arrow, and Sapporo, as well as Dodge and Plymouth mini-pickup trucks. Chrysler owns 15% of Mitsubishi, but in March 1980 Iacocca called upon the U.S. government to curb imports from Japan. The Japanese companies, said Iacocca, should be required to have "some investment in the country," which raises the prospect that one of the big Japanese manufacturers might pick up Chrysler at a fire sale.

Stock performance. Chrysler stock bought for $1,000 in 1970 sold for $196 on January 2, 1980.

Major employment centers. Detroit, Michigan (74,500); St. Louis, Missouri (7,-500); and Kokomo, Indiana (5,800).

Access. 12000 Lynn Townsend Drive, Highland Park, Michigan 48288; (313) 956-5252. Consumer complaints and queries may be addressed to: Customer Relations, Chrysler Center, P.O. Box 857, Detroit, Michigan 48288; (313) 956-5970.

Consumer brands.

Chrysler: New Yorker; Cordoba; Newport; Le-Baron; Imperial.
Dodge: St. Regis; Colt; Omni; Challenger; Aspen; Diplomat; Mirada; Dodge pickups and vans; Sportsman; Ramcharger; D-50 Pick-Up.
Plymouth: Horizon; Champ; Sapporo; Arrow; Gran Fury.

Sales: $43.5 billion
Profits: $1.2 billion
Forbes 500 rank: 5
Rank in automobiles: 2
Rank in trucks: 1
Founded: 1903
Employees: 506,500
Headquarters: Dearborn, Michigan

What they do. If the United States had a royal family, it would probably be the Fords—they are the nearest thing to Plantagenets America has ever known. First came Henry Ford I, the conqueror, the empire builder who ruthlessly squeezed out the partners who helped him found his company in 1903, and who finally abdicated in favor of his son, Edsel I. After Edsel's untimely death in 1943, Henry returned to the throne until his grandson, Henry II ("Henry the Deuce"), had come of age. When Henry II himself abdicated in 1979, a 76-year dynasty appeared to be ended. But Phillip Caldwell, Henry's hand-picked successor, may be only a loyal lord protector for heir-apparent Edsel II, who was banished to Australia to learn the company ropes. Finally, completing the scenario is a usurper, Benson Ford II, who even now plots with his lawyers in California and New York, awaiting the perfect moment to step forward and seize the orb and scepter from his cousin Edsel.

Ford Motor dominions surpass any the Plantagenets dreamed of. They are the world's second-largest car company—lag-

Henry Ford is at the wheel of his first production car, the 1903 Model A Ford Runabout.

ging behind General Motors—with 4.5 million cars and trucks sold in 1978 in the United States alone, and another 2 million sold overseas. They rule over some half million serfs who assemble the company's parts in the massive River Rouge manufacturing complex near Dearborn, Michigan, and in smaller plants in Detroit, Kansas City, and throughout the country. Some work in such far-flung places as Germany, England, Canada, Spain, Brazil, Australia, Argentina, Mexico, or South Africa. Ford sells more cars overseas than General Motors. In Europe they rank third behind Volkswagen and Fiat.

Ford is also one of the world's largest tractor manufacturers. Their plants in the United States, Belgium, Brazil, France, and Great Britain make some 100,000 tractors a year. Ford Aerospace makes the control systems for several missiles and defense systems.

History. The son of a moderately successful farmer, Henry Ford was born in Dearborn Township, Michigan, in 1863. But he despised farming, preferring to tinker with the mechanical equipment in the barn in-

stead; and at 16 he apprenticed himself to a machinist and began repairing steam and gasoline engines on the Detroit waterfront. At 26 Ford took a job with Detroit's Edison Illuminating Company, the city's electric utility. Four years later, in 1892, Charles Duryea invented the first American automobile.

Ford was one of several dozen young American mechanics to be captivated by the news. In the 1890s the French were the masters of the motorcar (although the Ital-

Women buy nearly a quarter of all new cars and 14% of all used cars in the United States. According to auto makers, some models have more appeal than others for women. Of the principal drivers of Lincoln-Mercury's Versailles, 47% are women; 43% of Cadillac Seville drivers are women. Buick Regals and Ford Mustangs and Fairmont Futuras are also allegedly favored by female drivers.

ians and the English both had claims on the title), but no American had ever designed a practical model. Ford read every scrap he could find on Duryea's new invention and immediately decided to invent one himself. He worked for the next seven years—logging a full 10-hour day at Edison and then coming home to tinker in his garage at night—before he finally came up with one. It was a four-wheel "quadricycle"—a two-cylinder engine mounted on a light chassis supported by four bicycle wheels. It represented no great breakthroughs in design over Duryea's model, but it encouraged Ford to go ahead. By 1899, with two more models, Ford was a recognized pioneer in the development of the auto.

In 1903, with 12 investors and a total of $28,000 in capital, Ford launched his motor company. During the first 15 months he and his employees cranked out 1,700 Model As (not to be confused with the 1927 Ford Model A). The cars were simple, fast (by 1903 standards—about 20 miles per hour), and so dependable that at least 82 are still in running condition. During the next five years Ford and his engineers feverishly ran through 19 letters of the alphabet—from B to S—in an attempt to improve on the A. Some of these models were completely experimental and never reached the consumer. Of the ones that did the most successful was the Model N, a small, cheap, four-cylinder car that went on the market for $500. The biggest loser was the Model K, a $2,500 limousine.

The experience with the N and the K convinced Ford that the future of the auto industry lay in turning out inexpensive cars for a mass market. When one of his principal investors disagreed with him, Ford simply froze him out, buying up his shares and increasing his ownership of the company to about 58%. Then he turned to his next model—the T. Calling it the "universal car," Ford introduced it in 1908. Sturdy, cheap, and personable, the car rapidly captured the public's imagination and soon accounted for half the cars on the nation's highways.

By 1913 the demand for the Model T far exceeded the supply. Rather than raise prices—anathema to Ford's marketing philosophy—he decided to experiment. He assigned each workman in his shop a place in a line and gave each one a tool and a particular function to perform. Then he had a chassis dragged by rope and windlass along the line. When the experiment was through, the line had created a complete Model T in only a few minutes, compared to several hours using the standard techniques. Ford had created the mass-production assembly line, a process that soon had Model Ts rolling out the door at the rate of one every 10 seconds.

On January 5, 1914, Ford stunned the auto industry by announcing that, henceforth, his company's minimum wage would be $5 a day, more than double the existing minimum. Ford reasoned that he would sell more cars if his employees could afford to buy them; and his employees returned the favor by doing just that. "I can find methods of manufacturing that will make high wages," said Ford. "If you cut wages, you just cut the number of your customers." The move made Ford a hero to labor.

In the 19 years the Model T was produced, more than 15 million were sold. Ford Motor became the nation's leading car company; established plants in Highland Park, Michigan, Kansas City, Philadelphia, Minneapolis, Long Island, and Buffalo; expanded overseas (to Britain); bought Lincoln Motors; and began building airplane

Where the Car Money Went

In 1979 Americans spent $1,510 billion on personal consumption expenditures: food, clothing, housing, services—and transportation. Of the total, 13.5% ($203.4 billion) supported the automobiles of America. Here's where the auto money was spent:

	Amount
Auto Purchase	$69.1 billion
Gas and oil	$65.2 billion
Repairs, greasing, washing, parking, etc.	$34.2 billion
Interest on auto debt	$13.0 billion
Tires, accessories, and parts	$12.0 billion
Insurance	$ 8.9 billion
Tolls	$ 1.0 billion

Source: Automotive News, 1980 Market Data Book Issue; U.S. Dept. of Commerce, Survey of Current Business, March 1980.

engines. The success seemed unstoppable—but then Ford's personality threw an unexpected monkeywrench into the works.

By 1921 Ford had owned the *Dearborn Independent* newspaper for several years, using it mostly to promote his own ideal of free enterprise democracy. But in that year Ford began venting his own strange, vicious anti-Semitism. The paper ran, and then published as a pamphlet for mass consumption, the so-called "Protocols of the Elders of Zion," purportedly a plan by Jews for a takeover of the world and the destruction of the Aryan "race," but actually a defamatory forgery written by a czarist agent in Russia in 1905. Ford's newspaper blamed everything from chorus girls, cabarets, jazz, and alcohol to crime waves and pornography—even the 1919 "Black Sox" baseball scandal—on the Jews. Among the educated the ensuing publicity and lawsuits made Ford a laughingstock; among the ignorant they made him a hero.

Ford's public image continued to deteriorate, and he spent less and less time in the public eye. His final achievement came in 1932, when he helped develop the V-8 engine for a new Model A, which had finally replaced the Model T in 1927. After this Ford retired to his estate ("FairLane") and let his son Edsel run the company.

Edsel was more reflective than his father and was greatly troubled by the company's excessive reaction to the union organizing drives of the 1930s. His father's chief detective, Harry Bennett, shared Henry Ford's animosity toward labor and ruled a group of thugs who enforced his will. Edsel kept him on, nervously, partly because Bennett had been charged by Henry with the protection of Edsel's children after the Lindbergh kidnapping and Edsel owed him a favor. Meanwhile, Edsel had his hands full just worrying about the company's economic plight, for during the 1930s Ford had been surpassed by General Motors as the number 1 car company. Sales and profits were down sharply, and only the airplane engine division held firm. But World War II may have saved the company.

After Edsel died in 1943, Henry returned for two years and served as a caretaker until Henry Ford II completed his military service. Henry II, the oldest Ford grandson, quickly turned the losing company around by dumping Harry Bennett and bringing in a fresh new team of managers, a group of brilliant Air Force systems analysts who were looking for a peacetime challenge. What greater challenge than Ford Motor, then in a semimoribund state? Members of that famous group, called the "Whiz Kids," included Robert S. McNamara (later president of Ford, secretary of defense, and president of the World Bank), Arjay Miller (later president of Ford and dean of the Stanford Business School), and Charles B. Thornton (who left in 1953 to start Litton Industries, first of the postwar conglomerates). They had all worked together in the Air Force, and they all worked together to bring Ford back to life.

The company became a laughingstock in the 1950s when, under McNamara, they brought out the Edsel, which flopped dismally. But the Mustang, introduced in the 1960s, became one of Ford's hottest selling models of all time. Ford was never able to overtake General Motors, but they became a solid number 2, selling about one of every four cars sold in the United States.

Henry Ford II also moved on another front to dispel the illiberal anti-Semitic reputation the company had as a result of his grandfather's views and activities. He started the Ford Foundation, which many businessmen later thought was too liberal. Henry Ford himself cut his ties with the foundation in the late 1970s, despairing that it had apparently drifted into biting the hand that originally fed it.

Reputation. Everyone in the auto industry knows that Ford is nothing at all like General Motors. GM is known for their

> The word *taxicab* comes from the French *taximeter-cabriolet. Cabriolet,* from the Latin *capreolus,* a wild mountain goat, was what the French called their early horse-drawn passenger carriages because of their fast, jerky ride on rutted or cobbled streets—like a goat jumping from rock to rock down a mountainside. *Cabriolet* was shortened to *cab* in nineteenth-century London, and the word gained official use in the London Cab Act of 1896. The *taximeter* was added after cabs became motorized. It was, and is, the meter used to register the fare, or "tax," charged for the ride.

professional management, their efficiency, their imperturbability. Ford is known for "seat-of-the-pants" management, volatility, and horrendous mistakes. Not many people leave the GM upper ranks for other jobs; people at Ford are always doing that. John Neven left to run Zenith, and now he's at Firestone. Donald Frey left to run Bell & Howell. Lee Iacocca of Chrysler was kicked out as president of Ford, as was his predecessor, Semon Knudsen, whom Ford recruited from GM. The Cadillac is a GM image; the Mustang is Ford's image. GM people always look uncomfortable when they're called upon to meet the press. Henry Ford II loved to talk to the press. He always felt he could say what he wanted to because "my name is on the door."

What they own. Car and truck manufacturing and assembly plants in numerous American cities and in Windsor, Ontario, across the border from Detroit. The Rouge manufacturing complex in Dearborn accounts for one-seventh of their manufacturing capacity in the United States. Ford has subsidiaries around the globe, from Australia to Austria.

Who owns and runs the company. Ford Motor issues two kinds of stock: Class A, sold on the New York Stock Exchange and representing about 60% of the voting power; and Class B, owned almost entirely by the Ford family and representing the other 40% of control. Although it has never been tested, it is generally assumed that the family could work their will over the company in a showdown or proxy battle. But the Ford family is no longer the tightly knit group it once was. This point is made by the strange case of Benson Ford II, Henry II's nephew. Benson was so riled by the terms of his $7.5 million inheritance, which left effective control over his shares to his father and uncles, Benson I and William, that he filed suit to overthrow the inheritance conditions. As the final blow he hired Roy Cohn, a New York attorney with a tough-guy reputation (he was Senator Joe McCarthy's right-hand man during the 1950s witch hunts), to plead his case. The battle has been long and extraordinarily bitter.

In the public eye. Benson's court battle has kept the family in the news, just as Henry II's second divorce did earlier in the 1970s. But most damaging to company prestige has probably been the controversy surrounding the Pinto. *Mother Jones* magazine published an article by Mark Dowie in 1977 charging that 500 people had died in Pinto crashes in which the car's gas tank had burst into flames when the car was struck from behind. According to the magazine, Ford had rushed the car into production even though the company's engineers were aware that rear-end collisions could easily rupture the gas tank. The magazine charged further that Ford lobbied for eight years afterward against a federal standard that would have forced them to change the fire-prone gas tank. In 1979 the state of In-

Ford's Little Giant

Harry Bennett, Henry Ford's one-man union buster, became a legend in his own right during the 1930s. He obtained his job with Ford by accident. Small of stature, Bennett joined the Navy at the age of 17 and learned to box. After his discharge he practiced his new skills in barroom brawls. Following one especially bloody altercation in the Bowery, Bennett was saved from arrest only by the intervention of Hearst newspaper columnist Arthur Brisbane, who then took Bennett along to a lunch appointment with Ford.

"Can you shoot?" Ford asked Bennett, explaining that he needed a tough guy to deal with his workers.

Bennett took the job and quickly established a reputation with his "punch now, ask questions later" technique. He quickly became known in the industry as "the little giant." As the result of repeated threats on his life, Bennett began wearing only bow ties, fearing that if he wore a long tie someone would choke him with it.

Bennett was known to laborers and Dearborn, Michigan, locals as "the little man in Henry Ford's basement," an allusion to Bennett's basement office and to the questionable characters—reputed to be underworld mobsters— who visited him there.

Ford himself probably paid Bennett his highest compliment when he told a British visitor during World War II:

"Do you really want to get rid of Hitler? I'll send Harry over there with six of his men."

Source: *New York Times*, January 1, 1979.

diana charged Ford with three counts of reckless homicide in connection with the death of three young women in the fiery crash of a Pinto that was hit from behind. A jury in Elkhart, Indiana, found the company innocent in 1980, but the trial and surrounding publicity have done much to damage the company's image.

In June 1980 *Mother Jones* charged Ford with knowingly making cars whose automatic transmissions tend to slip from park to reverse when the car is idling. As of November 1979, the magazine reported, the National Highway Traffic Safety Administration had found the defect responsible for 60 deaths, 1,100 injuries, and 3,700 accidents. Ford knew about the problem as early as 1971, according to the magazine, and a Ford engineer proposed a solution, rejected by the company, that would have cost three cents per car.

On the other hand, Henry Ford II has probably done more than anyone else to rehabilitate downtown Detroit. The auto industry largely ignored the downtown area until the race riots of 1967. Ford was a prime mover in the creation of the Renaissance Center, a big hotel-and-office complex on the Detroit River.

Where they're going. *Time* reported in October 1979 that Ford might have a touch of "Chrysler Flu," meaning that GM's increasing dominance of the domestic market and the incursions of Japanese cars have resulted in multimillion dollar losses that could cripple the company. During the first quarter of 1980, Ford lost $164 million. They made $330 million overseas, but lost $494 million in North America. Ford may soon be joining Chrysler at the wailing wall.

Stock performance. Ford stock bought for $1,000 in 1970 sold for $972 on January 2, 1980.

Access. The American Road, Dearborn, Michigan 48121; (313) 322-3000.

Consumer brands.

Cars: Ford Fiesta, Fairmont, Granada, Thunderbird, Mustang, LTD, and Pinto; Mercury Marquis, Capri, Bobcat, Zephyr, Monarch, Cougar, Versailles; Lincoln Continental and Continental Mark V.
Trucks: Ford; Courier; Ranchero; F-series; Bronco; Econoline Van; Club Wagon.

During the 1970s 103 million bicycles were sold in the United States, compared with 102 million cars.

One out of ten service stations in the United States closed in 1979, leaving 153,200 in business, according to *Chain Store Age.*

DEATH ON THE WORLD'S HIGHWAYS

Country	Average Annual Death Rate per 100,000 Population	Number of Cars per 1,000 Population
AUSTRALIA	27.4	493
FRANCE	25.5	466
WEST GERMANY	24.1	354
CANADA	24.1	505
UNITED STATES	21.7	655
NETHERLANDS	17.4	411
ITALY	17.0	291
GREAT BRITAIN	11.6	303
JAPAN	9.2	339

Of about 205,000 deaths in traffic accidents throughout the world in 1976, some 47,000 (or 23%) occurred in the United States. In nearly all developed countries traffic accidents are the leading cause of death among adolescents and young adults.

Source: *Journal of American Insurance,* Summer 1979.

GM

Sales: $66.3 billion
Profits: $2.9 billion
Forbes 500 rank: 2
Rank in cars: 1
Rank in trucks: 2
Rank in buses: 1
Founded: 1908
Employees: 853,000
Headquarters: Detroit, Michigan and New York, New York

What they do. General Motors is the solid, faceless rock of American industry. Unlike Henry Ford II, who spoke for the auto industry for years, or Lee Iacocca, who popped up in television commercials after he took over Chrysler, GM's top executives are virtually unknown outside the company. They just go quietly about their business of running the world's largest automobile company with no more public personality than the lug nuts on a new Oldsmobile. John Z. DeLorean, who worked at GM for 17 years, said the company doesn't permit any individual to stand out. "When one does," added DeLorean, "he is rebuked, ordered to disappear into the wallpaper."

"General Motors is not in the business of making cars," GM chairman Thomas A. Murphy once said. "General Motors is in the business of making money." In the process they build three out of every five cars made in the United States, and about one-quarter of all the cars made in the world. Of all the cars sold in America, including imports, nearly half are made by GM. In 1979, through their 13,600 franchised dealers, they sold 2.2 million Chevrolets, 1 million Oldsmobiles, 730,000 Pontiacs, 790,000 Buicks, and 350,000 Cadillacs. They made another 1.5 million GMC trucks and buses.

Though GM has long dominated the U.S. car market, they have never done as well overseas as Ford. About 92% of GM's sales come from the United States and Canada. Most of their foreign sales come from Opel, Germany's number 2 car maker and a GM subsidiary since 1929; GM made nearly 1 million Opels in 1978. They also make Holdens in Australia, Vauxhalls in Britain, and Chevrolets in Brazil.

GM also makes airplane engines, diesel locomotives, navigation systems for guided missiles, and many other nonautomotive products. Their AC Spark Plug and Fisher Body divisions are well-known in their own right.

GM made refrigerators and other appliances under the famous name of Frigidaire until 1979, when they sold the division to White Consolidated Industries.

The company operates from two separate corporate headquarters: one on the 14th floor of a gray edifice in Detroit, near the automobile factories, and one on the 25th floor of an elegant building on New York's Fifth Avenue. Both are called the General Motors Building.

GM is the only company to own and operate an accredited college. The General Motors Institute in Flint, Michigan, is a five-year school that trains students to design and develop cars. It grants degrees in engineering and administration, and 95% of its graduates go to work for GM. The company's last two presidents graduated from the GM Institute.

History. In 1908, the same year that Henry Ford announced the Model T, William Crapo Durant formed General Motors in Flint, Michigan, to buy up the stock of several existing car companies. Durant was already the country's top carriage and wagon producer through his Durant-Dort Carriage company. He was also running Buick Motor Car, of Flint, which had been founded by David Buick in 1902. Within their first two years, General Motors bought two dozen other companies that made cars, electric lamps, and accessories. Olds Motor Vehicle, started in 1897 by Ransom E. Olds of Lansing, Michigan, became part of GM in 1908. In 1909 GM acquired the two-year-old Oakland Motor Car of Pontiac, Michigan (later renamed Pontiac), and the same year took over Cadillac Automobile, established in Detroit in 1902 and named after the French explorer who founded Detroit in 1701.

But Durant overextended himself financially, and in 1910 the company had to turn to a group of New York and Boston bankers to bail them out. Durant lost control of GM, but he soon devised an ingenious scheme to get it back. In 1911 he backed a race car driver named Louis Chevrolet in starting the Chevrolet Motor Company, which Durant rapidly built into a nationwide business. Then he started swapping Chevrolet stock for GM stock. By 1916 he had picked up enough shares of GM to oust the bankers and recover the company. With Durant back in the driver's seat, GM bought Chevrolet in 1918.

Two GM executives from the early years left to start their own automobile companies: Charles Nash, president of GM from 1912 to 1916, and Walter Chrysler, head of the company's Buick division around the same time.

Pierre S. du Pont, president of E. I. Du Pont de Nemours, bought some GM stock in 1914 as a personal investment, and a year later he became GM's chairman. His family's company then started investing heavily in GM, and by 1919 Du Pont owned more than 28% of GM's stock. One of the prime motivations for the Du Pont investment was to secure for themselves all the paint and varnish business of General Motors. But it was, of course, much more than that. In addition to providing the financial underpinning of the company, the du Ponts

Clear Days at General Motors

Many corporate bigwigs have written their memoirs, but few of them have used the occasion to tattle on the foibles, blunders, and hidden scandals of the companies they worked for. John Z. De Lorean, who spent 17 years at General Motors, was not your everyday executive. Known in the industry as a brilliant maverick, he rose from greenhorn engineer in the Pontiac Division to general manager of Pontiac, then general manager of Chevrolet, and finally became a $650,000-a-year executive on the hallowed Fourteenth Floor of GM's headquarters in Detroit, with a good shot at becoming president.

But De Lorean found life at the top crashingly dull, with none of the satisfactions he had experienced on the way up. His new job, he discovered, was a paper-shuffling stopover for men considered candidates for the presidency. He was now an "overseer" rather than a "doer." Each day 600 to 700 pages of paperwork arrived on his desk, some of it important, most of it trivial. His immediate boss started giving him make-work assignments involving things De Lorean thought should have been decided much lower in the organization.

In 1973, at age 48, De Lorean did what few top auto executives have ever done: he quit. Soon afterward he approached J. Patrick Wright, Detroit bureau chief of *Business Week* magazine, proposing that the two of them write the real story of GM, based on De Lorean's experience, and "open up the board room from the inside." The book, as De Lorean saw it, should be "a bible of what's wrong with the way business is done." Playboy Press outbid several other publishers, gave them a $45,000 advance, and suggested the title: *On a Clear Day You Can See General Motors.* Wright finished the book in 1975.

Then, according to Wright, De Lorean "embarked on a four-year pattern of vacillation," refusing to allow the book to be published. De Lorean was busy with plans to build a sports car called the DMC-12, and he feared that GM might try to block his car.

Wright, however, wasn't content to sit by while his work grew moldy in a drawer. In a surprise move in 1979 he went ahead and published the book on his own. He put up his life savings, took a second mortgage on his house, and had 20,000 copies privately printed and distributed to bookstores across the land. The book is written in the first person as De Lorean's

"own story," although Wright is listed as the author. The subtitle is: *John Z. De Lorean's Look Inside the Automotive Giant.*

A week after the book came out, De Lorean held a press conference in New York and acknowledged that it was authentic. He observed that the tone was a bit "harsher and more aggressive" than he might have liked, but he thought the book was "remarkably readable," and he praised Wright for publishing it himself: "That took a lot of guts and I admire him."

• • •

Following are three excerpts from *On a Clear Day You Can See General Motors.*

My introduction to "loyalty" was as assistant chief engineer at Pontiac. . . .

I was showering in a motel near San Francisco International Airport the morning of the first day [of a business trip] out there when the bathroom door flew open practically taking the hinges off in one jerk. I was shocked by the noise and I threw open the shower curtain and saw Estes who was chief engineer at Pontiac and my boss [Elliott M. "Pete" Estes, later president of GM]. The spitting image of Tennessee Ernie Ford, Estes was usually happy and pleasant. This time, however, he was red-faced

were to do at GM what they had done at their own company: set up a structure to enable managers to handle a large corporation. Durant, who managed by the seat of his pants, left GM in 1920—and the du Ponts were then in charge. Pierre du Pont, already chairman, took the president's title as well. In 1923 he relinquished the GM presidency to Alfred P. Sloan, Jr., but continued as chairman until 1929, when he was succeeded by his brother, Lammot du Pont,

who remained chairman until 1937. In their book, *Pierre S. du Pont and the Making of the Modern Corporation,* Alfred D. Chandler, Jr., and Stephen Salisbury said of Pierre du Pont: "He created two of the most successful modern large American business corporations, and he did so without losing legal and financial control of these enterprises." (The Du Pont company was forced to sell their GM stock by a U.S. Supreme Court decision in 1962, but members of the du

---

and mad. "Why the hell wasn't someone out to meet me at the airport this morning? You knew I was coming, but nobody was there. Goddamnit, I served my time picking up my bosses at the airport. Now you guys are going to do this for me," he barked.

• • •

Terrell [Richard L. Terrell, GM's vice chairman] was the master of the paraphrase, although he was by no means the only practitioner. He often parroted the views of Chairman [Richard C.] Gerstenberg with unabashed rapidity. So often did he do this that the practice became a joke. Divisional general managers and their staffs entertained each other over lunch with various impressions of Terrell paraphrasing Gerstenberg in an Administrative Committee meeting. The dialogue would go something like this: Gerstenberg: "Goddamnit. We can not afford any new models next year because of the cost of this federally mandated equipment. There is no goddamn money left for styling changes. That's the biggest problem we face."

Terrell, after waiting about 10 minutes: "Dick, goddamnit. We've just got to face up to the fact that our number one problem is the cost of

this federally mandated equipment. This stuff costs so much that we just don't have any money left for styling our new cars. That's our biggest problem."

Gerstenberg: "You're goddamn right, Dick. That's a good point."

• • •

The most embarrassing, and probably the most ridiculous, meeting I attended "upstairs" involved a presentation to the Industrial Relations Policy Group in the fall of 1972. A young guy from the labor relations staff was talking about an obscure personnel point which he proposed that we change. It was an insignificant matter by any corporate standard, having to do, as I remember, with adjusting a transferred employee's pay rate upward to correlate with the cost of living in his new locale. . . .

Looking around I counted up about $10 million worth of executive talent listening to and watching this presentation of cost-of-living graphs, color slides, industry analysis charts and company-by-company comparisons. The presentation finally ended. A couple of guys who were dozing in their seats blinked awake, and the room of executives looked toward the chairman for an indication of

what we were going to do, as usually happened. The chairman in this case was Richard C. Gerstenberg. . . . He snapped, "Goddamnit! I don't like to be surprised."

We were all stunned because the point of the meeting was so insignificant anyway. "What is Gerstenberg so surprised about?" I thought.

"We can't make a decision on this now," he continued. "I think we ought to form a task force to look into this and come back with a report in 90 to 120 days. Then we can make a decision."

He then rattled off the names of the members of the task force he was appointing. There was an eerie silence after the chairman spoke. It lasted for what seemed like half a day. The whole room was bewildered but no one had the courage to say why.

Finally, Harold G. Warner, the snow-white-haired, kindly executive-vice-president, who was soon to retire, broke the silence. "Dick, this presentation is the result of the task force that you appointed some time ago. Most of the people you just appointed to the new task force are on the old one."

Pont family are believed to hold shares worth about $1.2 billion.)

The du Ponts were responsible for reorganizing the company, but the man generally credited with shaping GM into a colossal global enterprise was Alfred Sloan, president of the company from 1923 to 1937 and then chairman until he retired in 1956 at age 80. Sloan's memoirs, *My Years with General Motors,* published in 1963, set forth his guiding philosophy for running the company: "decentralized operations and responsibilities, with coordinated control." In other words, he let the various division managers run their departments from day to day as they saw fit, and he encouraged them to show as much initiative as possible. "Give a man a clearcut job and let him do it," he said. At the same time, committees at the top of the corporate hierarchy set the company's policies and oversaw the long-range planning. Sloan's book has become a bible for business executives striving to manage organizations both large and small.

GM's motto in the 1920s was "a car for every purse and purpose." For those who had trouble keeping them all straight, there was a saying: "Chevrolet is for the hoi polloi, Pontiac for the poor but proud, Oldsmobile for the comfortable but discreet, Buick for the striving, and Cadillac for the rich." GM introduced many innovations in automotive technology, including the electric self-starter (Cadillac, 1911), the V-8 engine (Cadillac, 1914), and the automatic transmission (Oldsmobile, 1939).

In his book, Sloan recalled how GM passed Ford to become the nation's number 1 car maker. In 1921 Ford made 60% of all cars and trucks made in America, while GM made 12%. Ford's success rested on the Model T, a standard, mass-produced, low-priced car. Henry Ford saw the car market as "a mass market" that wanted basic transportation, Sloan wrote, while GM "worked out our competitive concept of the mass market served by better and better cars." What Ford failed to realize, Sloan observed, was that there were soon enough used cars to fill the demand for cheap transportation. "When first-car buyers returned to the market for the second round," he wrote, "with the old car as a first payment on the new car, they were selling basic transportation and demanding something more than that in the new car. Middle-income people, assisted by the trade-in and installment financing, thus created the demand not for basic transportation but for progress in new cars, for comfort, convenience, power, and style. This was the true trend of American life and those who adapted to it and met that need got the business." Comfort, convenience, power, style—GM has worshiped these gods ever since.

Model T sales began to drop, suggesting that GM was right. In 1927 Ford closed down his huge River Rouge manufacturing plant for six months to retool for the Model A, leaving the low-priced field wide open for GM's Chevrolet and Chrysler's Plymouth. "Mr. Ford regained the leadership again in 1929, 1930, and 1935," Sloan wrote, "but, speaking in terms of the generalities, he had lost the lead to General Motors."

One of the most famous lines about GM

STONEWALLING THE GASOLINE CRISIS

Domestic Passenger Car Use and Fuel Consumption

	Average Fuel Consumed per Car (Gallons)	Average Miles Traveled per Car	Average Miles per Gallon per Car
1967	684	9,531	13.9
1968	698	9,627	13.8
1969	718	9,782	13.6
1970	735	9,978	13.6
1971	746	10,121	13.6
1972	755	10,184	13.5
1973	763	9,992	13.1
1974	704	9,448	13.4
1975	712	9,634	13.5
1976	711	9,763	13.7
1977	706	9,839	13.9
1978	715	10,046	14.1

Source: Department of Energy's Monthly Energy Review, March 1980.

U.S. CAR MARKET SINCE WORLD WAR II

Percentage of All Car Sales

Year	GM	Ford	Chrysler	AMC*	Imports
1946	37.8	22.0	25.7	8.7	—
1947	41.9	21.1	21.8	5.9	—
1948	40.6	18.8	21.5	6.1	0.5
1949	42.9	21.3	21.4	5.7	0.3
1950	45.5	24.0	17.6	4.9	0.3
1951	42.8	22.2	21.8	4.7	0.4
1952	41.7	22.8	21.3	5.3	0.7
1953	45.1	25.2	20.3	3.6	0.5
1954	50.7	30.8	12.9	2.0	0.6
1955	50.8	27.6	16.8	1.8	0.8
1956	50.8	28.5	15.5	1.8	1.7
1957	44.9	30.4	18.3	1.8	3.5
1958	46.4	26.4	13.9	4.0	8.1
1959	42.1	28.1	11.3	6.0	10.2
1960	43.6	26.6	14.0	6.4	7.6
1961	46.5	28.5	10.8	6.3	6.5
1962	51.9	26.3	9.6	6.1	4.9
1963	51.0	24.9	12.4	5.7	5.1
1964	49.1	26.0	13.8	4.7	6.0
1965	50.1	25.5	14.7	3.5	6.1
1966	48.1	26.1	15.4	2.9	7.3
1967	49.5	22.2	16.1	2.9	9.3
1968	46.7	23.7	16.3	2.8	10.5
1969	46.8	24.3	15.1	2.5	11.2
1970	39.7	26.4	16.1	3.0	14.7
1971	45.2	23.5	13.7	2.5	15.1
1972	44.4	24.4	13.8	2.8	14.5
1973	44.3	23.5	13.3	3.5	15.2
1974	41.9	25.0	13.6	3.8	15.7
1975	43.3	23.1	11.7	3.7	18.2
1976	47.2	22.5	12.9	2.5	14.8
1977	46.7	22.7	11.0	1.7	18.3
1978	47.7	22.9	10.2	1.4	17.8
1979	46.5	20.3	9.0	1.5	22.6

*And predecessors

Source: *Automotive News*, 1980 Data Book Issue.

is actually a misquotation. Charles E. Wilson, president of GM from 1941 to 1953 and then President Eisenhower's secretary of defense, is popularly believed to have said, "What's good for General Motors is good for the country." What he really said was, "For years, I thought what was good for our country was good for General Motors, and vice versa."

In the 1960s GM propelled Ralph Nader to fame as the country's best-known consumer advocate. His book *Unsafe at Any Speed* blasted GM's rear-engine Corvair as a death trap. GM tried to discredit Nader personally and set private detectives on his tail. Nader sued GM for invasion of privacy, and the company was eventually forced to pay him $425,000. Ironically, while GM was publicly defending the Corvair as safe, former GM executive DeLorean disclosed in his book, *On a Clear Day*

You Can See General Motors, that the son of a top Cadillac executive was killed, the son of a GM executive vice-president suffered irreparable brain damage, the niece of another executive vice-president was severely injured, and the son of a Chevrolet dealer was killed—all in Corvairs.

Reputation. To some people GM symbolizes everything that's wrong with American mass culture: planned obsolescence, smog, gas guzzlers, suburban sprawl, freeways, the decline of public transportation. To others GM is the apex of efficiency, power, and profitability. GM is so central to the American economy that their stock is a bellwether of Wall Street: when GM stock goes up, the stock market goes up, and vice versa. The company's biggest worry over the years has been how to keep their share of the automobile market around 50%.

When it rises much higher, GM executives start to fret about possible antitrust action aimed at breaking the company up.

What they own. Car, truck, and bus factories in 22 cities in the United States and five in Canada. Major factories in Germany, Britain, Australia, Brazil, Mexico, and South Africa, and others in a host of countries from Chile to Malaysia.

Who owns and runs the company. General Motors cut their dividend almost in half in 1980—the first time that has happened in nearly a decade. That was bad news for their 1.2 million stockholders. Aside from A T & T, they have more shareholders than anyone else. They have three times as many stockholders as Ford, nearly twice as many as IBM. By cutting their dividend down from $1.15 a share every three months to 60¢, GM will save $158 million every quarter—or nearly $600 million for the year.

GM is such a big company, and its ownership so spread out, that it's hard to tell exactly who owns the company. But it seems likely that various members of the du Pont family still hold sizable chunks, even though the Du Pont Company had to get rid of their GM stock in the 1960s. As of 1968, Ferdinand Lundberg reported in his book *The Rich and the Super-Rich*, the du Pont family holdings still constituted "the largest identifiable block in General Motors stock." Stewart Mott, a New York philanthropist, bankrolls many liberal political causes with the income from GM stock he inherited from one of the company's early executives.

GM's leaders are among the most highly paid executives in the world. The chairman, president, and vice-chairman made close to $1 million apiece in salaries and bonuses in 1978. According to DeLorean, the lowliest GM vice-president makes well over $200,000 in a good year.

"General Motors is the kind of institution whose like doesn't exist elsewhere in Western civilization," said a Detroit executive to Joseph Kraft in the *New Yorker*. "It is America's Japan. It is a marvelous structure of committees . . . for administration, sales, engineering, merchandising, styling, and everything else. The committees are the company, and one of the ways you rise in the company is by being a committee man—preferably secretary of one of the committees. The people who succeed at GM generally come into the company very early, at low-level jobs. They don't have big ideas about rising to the top. They stick with the company, and eventually a few make it. To the outsider, they're not very impressive. They're not very interesting as people. They tend to talk in platitudes. All they know is the automobile industry. . . . They even tend to look alike. But on the inside it's very different. They're smart. They work hard."

In 1971 GM became one of the first big corporations to put a black on the board of directors. They chose the Rev. Leon H. Sullivan, pastor of the Zion Baptist Church in Philadelphia and founder of a self-help group, Opportunities Industrialization Centers. One of Sullivan's first acts as a director was to vote against the rest of the board in favor of an Episcopal Church resolution calling on GM to shut down their South African operations.

In 1977 GM appointed a black lawyer, Otis M. Smith, as their general counsel, the company's top legal post. Smith became "the highest ranking black in corporate America," the *New York Times* reported.

GM's first woman director, Catherine B. Cleary, came to the board in 1972 (there are two of them now), and in 1979 the company appointed two women vice-presidents, Betsy Ancker-Johnson in charge of environmental activities and Marina von Neumann Whitman as the company's chief economist.

GM purchases materials and services from 23,000 companies in the United States and Canada, including such industrial giants as U.S. Steel. But the largest supplier: the Blue Cross–Blue Shield health plans. In 1979 General Motors paid $1.4 billion to provide health-care coverage for their 468,000 U.S. employees. The average GM employee was paid $15.25 per hour (including benefits) in 1979. That wage will rise to $20 an hour by 1982 under a three-year contract with the United Auto Workers signed in 1979.

In the public eye. GM's annual meetings over the past 10 years have become sounding boards for stockholders' resolutions advanced by churches, minority groups, and others concerned with GM's record on such issues as air pollution, auto safety, South African investment, women executives, urban problems, and transit policy. GM now publishes a "public interest report" every year, outlining their progress and positions on these and other issues. At the end of 1979 minorities represented 19% of GM's work force. And the company is by far the nation's largest buyer of goods and services from minority-owned companies: $199 million worth in 1979.

Where they're going. Some critics say GM is too dinosaurlike to move quickly in response to changing conditions. Actually, the reverse could be true. GM may be so big and resourceful that they can do just about anything they set their mind to. GM was the first Detroit car maker to come out with a complete line of "downsized" big cars—smaller and lighter versions of their "full-size" and "intermediate" models such as the Chevrolet Caprice. GM's downsized line appeared in late 1977, two years ahead of Ford's and Chrysler's. *Business Week* surmised in 1979 that Ford and Chrysler had deliberately held back on downsizing to let GM take the risk of presenting "shrunken cars" to the American public. GM's gamble

has already paid off. In April 1979, just as gas lines were beginning to form throughout the United States, GM introduced the X-Car, their compact four-cylinder models with front-wheel drive, sold under the names of Chevrolet Citation, Pontiac Phoenix, Oldsmobile Omega, and Buick Skylark. Again, GM led the pack. By early 1980 GM's share of the market (excluding imports) jumped from about 60% to more than 65%, which "put Ford in trouble and sent Chrysler running to the government for help," according to Joseph Kraft in the *New Yorker*. GM invested a total of $20 billion in downsizing between 1974 and 1980, and according to Kraft, "They moved fast, and with a singleness of purpose that astonished all the [non-GM auto] executives I consulted."

The decision to build smaller cars was hotly debated inside GM. Old-line leaders of the Cadillac division were particularly opposed, and it took pressure from the board of directors (a rare event at GM) to force the move to make the Seville, a compact Cadillac that was soon outselling Mercedes-Benz in Beverly Hills.

How the Cadillac Got Its Fins

Those fanciful automobile tailfins of the 1950s were the culmination of sales policies begun in the 1930s by GM's Alfred Sloan. He introduced the annual model change, and its concomitant yearly price increase. "The primary object of the corporation was to make money, not just to make motor cars," Sloan said.

GM's Art and Color Department, later the Styling Division, was created in 1927. It grew and flourished even during the Depression, introducing The Sculptured Design, The Large Engine, and The Low, Lean Look. These changes were intended, Sloan said, "to create demand for the new value and, so to speak, create a certain amount of dissatisfaction with past models as compared with the new one." Great improvements were announced each year—

although innovations that would seriously damage the value of last year's models on the growing used-car market were avoided.

By the mid-'50s Detroit carmakers had brought the promotion of styling to such a peak that designers and engineers were sworn to secrecy, and industrial spies ran from shadow to shadow in the night. The November 4, 1957, issue of *Time* detailed the scene:

"Over all the styling studios hangs a curtain of near-nuclear-plant secrecy.

"Ford's fifteen studios have locks that can be changed in half an hour. A security force of twenty guards run by an ex-FBI agent checks every employee's badge (a different color for each division) to make sure that no one is where he should not be. Outside, the security patrol

has a sixty-power telescope to keep watch on a nearby grain elevator where rival spotters might lurk. All unused sketches are carefully burned; all experimental clay models smashed. Everywhere, posters exhort the stylists to keep mum about their work. Samples: 'No matter where, talk with care'; 'Don't foretell the future.'"

Still, the big companies always got each other's secrets. And in the end the best-remembered design gimmick of the '50s happened quite spontaneously. On a visit to a friend in the air force, GM's chief stylist Harley J. Earl saw some fighter planes with twin tailfins and was struck with inspiration. He slapped fins onto the 1948 Cadillac, and the auto industry didn't get over them for more than a decade.

William C. Durant
Founder of General Motors
President, 1916-1920

Pierre S. du Pont
Chairman, 1915-1929

Alfred P. Sloan, Jr.
President, 1923-1937
Chairman, 1937-1956

Working from his base at the Buick Motor Company, William C. Durant formed General Motors in 1908, the same year that Henry Ford announced the Model T. Durant was associated with GM for the next 12 years in various ways, often trying to raise money to keep the company together. His successor, Alfred P. Sloan Jr., was to characterize him as "a great man with a great weakness — he could create but not administrate."

Scion of the famous chemical family, Pierre du Pont provided the financial and management support that was crucial to the survival of General Motors in the post-World War I period. The eldest of 11 children, he assumed leadership of the family at age 14 when his father, Lammot du Pont, was killed in a nitroglycerin explosion.

An engineer, Alfred Sloan is generally credited with playing the most important role in establishing the mode of organization at GM. In 1963 the Society for the Advancement of Management named him "the most distinguished manager of the past 50 years." The eldest of five children, he grew up in Brooklyn. His father was a tea and coffee importer, his mother the daughter of a Methodist minister. He graduated from the Massachusetts Institute of Technology.

Stock performance. GM stock bought for $1,000 in 1970 sold for $723 on January 2, 1980.

Major employment centers. Flint, Detroit, and Pontiac, Michigan.

Access. 3044 West Grand Boulevard, Detroit, Michigan 48202; (313) 556-5000. 767 Fifth Avenue, New York, New York 10022; (212) 486-5000.

Most GM plants are open for tours, with advance notice and reservations necessary. Between mid-July and mid-November they shut down for yearly model changeovers.

Consumer brands.

Cars: Chevrolet Caprice, Chevette, Citation, Corvette, Impala, Malibu, Monza, Monte Carlo; Buick Century, Electra, Le Sabre, Regal, Riviera, Skyhawk; Oldsmobile Cutlass, Omega, Toronaco, Eighty-Eight, Ninety-Eight; Pontiac Bonneville, Catalina, Firebird, Grand Prix, LeMans, Phoenix, Sunbird; Cadillac Coupe de Ville, Eldorado, Fleetwood, Limousine, Seville.

Trucks: Chevrolet Luv, Silverado, Blazer, Cheyenne, Fleetside, Nomad, and Stepside; GMC Sierra Grande, Astro, Brigadier.

Spark plugs, filters, and other accessories: AC.

Radios, tape players, heater-air conditioning controls: Delco.

Batteries: Delco-Remy.

The fuel-related slump in the RV (recreational vehicle) industry has taken sales from a 1972 high of 747,500 units down to a mere 389,900 units in 1978.

About 22% of the 10,641,099 new cars sold in the United States in 1979 were imported, and 69.3% of the imports were from Japan.

Car Parts People

Sales: $3.9 billion
Profits: $162.6 million
Forbes 500 rank: 114
Rank in auto parts: 1
Rank in spark plugs: 3
Founded: 1924
Employees: 80,600
Headquarters: Southfield, Michigan

What they do. Without Bendix, much of the American economy would be unable to stop or go. Once a simple supplier of parts to the auto industry, the suburban Detroit company today boasts a roster that includes spark plugs, aluminum siding, and packing crates; missile guidance systems, instruments for spaceships, sonar for submarines; machine tools; and the electronic and mechanical components inside America's nuclear weapons.

Bendix's most visible consumer products are Autolite spark plugs and Fram filters; most of their products are sold to other manufacturers. To the auto and truck companies here and abroad Bendix supplies brakes, steering mechanisms, hydraulic systems, spark plugs, filters, and fuel-injection systems. Aerospace companies buy aircraft brakes and landing gear, gyroscopes, radar, navigation equipment, and sophisticated military weapons systems. For electric utilities Bendix makes generators, load sensors, and the piping for nuclear power plants. Their tool divisions make automated machinery and offshore oil rigs. Their forest products unit sells lumber and

other wood products, with 60% of their trees coming from government lands and the rest from 167,000 acres of timberland they own in California.

Bendix's largest customer (accounting for more than 10% of their sales in 1979) is Ford, which is bound by a Supreme Court decision to buy most of their spark plugs from Bendix until 1983. That proviso was part of a settlement in which they were forced to sell off the Autolite spark plug business they had bought in 1961. Another 12% of their sales comes from equipment sold to six other automotive makers: American Motors, Chrysler, General Motors, Peugeot, Renault, and Citröen.

History. Bendix owes much of their past success to two behemoths, one private, one public: General Motors and the Pentagon. The company was founded in 1924 by Vincent Bendix, producer of the first reliable four-wheel braking system for American cars and the inventor of the Bendix Starter Drive, the device that eliminated the automobile hand-crank starter. Soon afterward General Motors, the largest customer for Bendix's products, began a long but not always comfortable association with Vincent Bendix by lending him the money to buy the Eclipse Machinery Company, which had been making his Starter Drive under license. In the 1920s, while riding the auto boom, Bendix branched out into the new aviation industry by acquiring many small companies. He even changed his firm's name to Bendix Aviation. But the Depression severely battered the company, and in 1937 General Motors stepped in to straighten them out. Vincent Bendix was forced to resign, replaced by a GM vice-president.

Bendix benefited from GM's infusion of

management expertise, but the company's real savior was the Pentagon: during World War II military orders boosted their sales from $40 million to $900 million. The cutoff at the end of the war jolted Bendix, but the Korean War came to the rescue, and the Cold War insured their success.

In the last 20 years Bendix has diversified significantly, trying to even out the boom-and-bust cycle that comes from too heavy a dependence on the auto companies and the Pentagon. Sales to the government, which in the early '60s amounted to almost 80% of Bendix's business, are now only about 15% of the total. Their automotive divisions still account for about half their sales, but by acquiring Fram and Autolite Bendix has moved firmly into the replacement market, which is typically strong when new car sales lag.

Contrary to popular opinion, the Bendix Corporation has never made washing machines. The Bendix washing machine, on the market for many years, was a side interest of Vincent Bendix and was actually made by Philco.

Reputation. Under their former boss, W. Michael Blumenthal, Bendix was striving to build a reputation for social responsibility. Young William M. Agee, Blumenthal's successor, came to Bendix from Boise Cascade. You can take the boy out of Boise Cascade but you may not be able to take the Boise Cascade out of the boy. After acquiring a bunch of companies in 1979, Agee told a reporter: "We don't mind being called a conglomerate. We think diversity is a strength, not a weakness."

What they own. Sixty-six manufacturing plants in 25 states, and offices and factories in 20 countries on 5 continents.

Who owns and runs the company. General Motors sold their 25% interest in Bendix in 1948, and since then institutions such as bank trust departments and mutual funds have been big holders of the stock (as much as 40% of it in 1976). Agee arrived at Bendix in 1972 and took over in 1976 at the tender age of 38, when Blumenthal left to become Jimmy Carter's first treasury secretary. Articulate and aggressive, Agee is something of an iconoclast: one of his first acts was to banish the conference table from Bendix's boardroom, leaving the directors wondering where to put their elbows.

Where they're going. After other companies. In 1978 and 1979 they bought 20% of Asarco, the huge metals processor. In 1980 they swallowed Warner & Swasey, a Cleveland machine tool maker and a longtime promoter—in ads, posters, and other literature—of the free enterprise system, a campaign that has consistently denigrated the role of government.

Stock performance. Bendix stock bought for $1,000 in 1970 sold for $1,634 on January 2, 1980.

Access. Southfield, Michigan 48076; (313) 352-5000.

Consumer brands.

Automobile filters and wiper blades: Fram.
Spark plugs: Autolite.

For every 100 cars in use in the United States an average of 8 are junked every year and 11 new ones are registered.

Sales: $2.7 billion
Profits: $155.6 million
Forbes 500 rank: 182
Rank in fire-detection systems: 1
Rank in armored cars: 3
Founded: 1928
Employees: 54,800
Headquarters: Chicago, Illinois

What they do. Borg-Warner is an invisible giant. Virtually everything they make is sold to other companies. Formed by the merger of four auto parts companies, they still derive more than one-third of their sales from "transportation equipment," chiefly such automobile components as: clutches, transmissions, drive shafts, universal joints, differentials, axles, and the like. But they have broadened their original base to include chemicals and plastics (mainly Cycolac ABS, a tough, versatile plastic), air conditioning and refrigeration (York), pumps and oilfield equipment (Byron Jackson), armored cars, fire and burglar alarms, security guards (Baker Industries), and financial services including inventory financing for retailers of everything from musical instruments to snowmobiles (Borg-Warner Acceptance Corporation).

Borg-Warner systems have cooled nuclear power plants, banana boats, and an ice skating rink in Kuwait. The exterior of almost every telephone in the country is made from durable Borg-Warner plastics, which also go into suitcases, high heels, automobile grilles, and football helmets. They make a lot of the machinery used by American agribusiness, including tilling discs, irrigation pumps, and parts for farm machinery. Their security division runs a private police force that patrols the Bel Air section of Beverly Hills, California, home of show business superstars.

The four U.S. auto makers accounted for 22% of Borg-Warner's sales in 1978.

History. In 1928, when America's love affair with the automobile was in full bloom, the heads of four auto parts companies came together in Chicago as a defensive hedge against the growing power of the big car makers, who could make or break small parts suppliers. Each company had a specialty: Borg & Beck made clutches; Warner Gear made transmissions; Mechanics Universal Joint had pioneered the standard "U-joint"; and Marvel Carburetor was the country's leading carburetor maker. The new company was named Borg-Warner after the two major components. By the end of the next year they had expanded to include five more parts companies.

The man who headed the company for the first 22 years was Charles Davis, a Harvard graduate who for a time had been the yachting editor of the *New York Times.* Borg-Warner survived the 1930s in large part because of a division they had acquired almost accidentally—Norge, makers of "electric iceboxes." Borg-Warner had really been after Detroit Gear, a Norge subsidiary—but it turned out that the people who were fortunate enough to have jobs during the Depression flocked to buy refrigerators. (Borg-Warner finally sold Norge in the 1960s.)

After World War II Borg-Warner supplied automatic transmissions for almost the entire Ford line. (Ford is still Borg-Warner's largest single customer, accounting for about 10% of total sales in 1977.) In 1950 Davis, at age 73, turned the company over to a younger fellow: Roy Ingersoll, 64, head of the Ingersoll Steel and Disc Division. Borg-Warner's big plastics breakthrough came in 1953, when they developed Cycolac ABS. Soon RCA was using the tough plastic for their radio cabinets, and in 1959 Western Electric, A T & T's equipment subsidiary, selected it for their telephone housings. In 1955 Borg-Warner picked up Byron Jackson, the pump and oilfield tool makers, and the next year they bought York, one of the three largest makers of air conditioning and industrial refrigeration. Roy Ingersoll's son Robert, who took over in 1961, was appointed ambassador to Japan by President Nixon in 1972, and he served as a deputy secretary of state in the Ford administration.

Reputation. As a vast auto parts company, Borg-Warner became a model of organization that other companies studied. But they don't want to be known anymore as the giant of the auto parts business. Chairman James F. Beré puts it this way: "I don't care what category we are listed in—we are a complex company and labels are not important—just as long as people call us a good company."

What they own. Close to 100 plants worldwide—across the United States from Massachusetts to Southern California, and in 15 other countries on 6 continents. They also own a big chunk of stock in Hughes Tool, the world's largest maker of drilling bits (and the foundation of the Howard Hughes fortune).

Who owns and runs the company. The Chicago establishment bulks large in Borg-Warner's affairs. Among the all-white-male directors are the heads or former heads of Commonwealth Edison, Chicago's electric company; Illinois Bell Telephone; the First National Bank of Chicago; Jewel Companies, one of the nation's leading supermarket chains; Beatrice Foods, the nation's largest food processor; and R. R. Donnelley & Sons, the nation's largest printing firm. All these companies are headquartered in or near Chicago. Robert Ingersoll, who left the board when he joined the government, returned as a director in 1976; the same year he became deputy chairman of the University of Chicago's board of trustees. He's also a director of two big Western-based companies, Atlantic Richfield and Weyerhaeuser. Also on the board are two directors from Robert Bosch, the big German electronics firm that bought 10% of Borg-Warner's stock in 1977. The Federal Trade Commission has been trying since 1978 to knock the two off Borg-Warner's board on antitrust grounds, arguing that Borg-Warner and Bosch are competitors in some areas.

Jim Beré, a draftsman by training, has been running the company since 1972 and is credited with injecting some humanistic thinking into the company's affairs. He has particularly stressed "open communications" inside Borg-Warner. A consultant who has worked with many companies described the Beré influence as follows: "Borg-Warner used to be highly autocratic. Today, humanism permeates both strategy and day-to-day decisions. Somehow, I see less politics, less backbiting, less hassling than in a great many other companies."

Where they're going. More heavily into "service industries" like Baker and Borg-Warner Acceptance. They hope to get half their profits from service industries in the next decade. But that didn't stop them in 1978 from making a vain attempt to pick up the beleaguered Firestone Company at a bargain price.

Stock performance. Borg-Warner stock bought for $1,000 in 1970 sold for $1,442 on January 2, 1980.

Major employment centers: Chicago; Detroit; and Los Angeles.

Access. 200 South Michigan Avenue, Chicago, Illinois 60604; (312) 322-8500. They have a toll-free number with tape-recorded company information for calls from outside Illinois: (800) 621-5445.

Consumer brands.

Air conditioners: York.

Sales: $1.8 billion
Profits: $57.9 million
Forbes 500 rank: 297
Rank in truck diesel engines: 1
Founded: 1919
Employees: 23,300
Headquarters: Columbus, Indiana

What they do. The old Ku Klux Klan territory of southern Indiana seems an unlikely headquarters for one of the nation's most socially aware businesses, but Cummins Engine, which manufactures heavy diesel engines, breaks many stereotypes. They're not located in an area of high black population, but since 1965 blacks have held more management positions at Cummins than at some companies based in such urban areas as New York, Chicago, and Los Angeles. Most heavy industrial companies allocate something well below 1% of pretax profits for charitable contributions; Cummins allocates 5%, the maximum charitable deduction allowed by the Internal Revenue Service, *every year*. Since 1975 they have contributed an additional 1% of their international profits.

The company that behaves in this exemplar fashion is the world's largest independent maker of diesel engines, producing about a hundred different models. Managed by Ivy League whiz kids, Cummins sells about 80% of their engines for the boys who cruise the interstate highways in their eighteen-wheelers. Cummins engines are available as standard equipment from all major truck makers in the United States and from more than 125 truck manufacturers around the world. A David against the Goliaths, Cummins sells about 40% of all big-truck diesels every year, twice the market share of each of their two leading competitors, General Motors and Caterpillar Tractor. Cummins also makes diesel engines for off-road construction vehicles and for machinery used in logging, mining, agriculture, electric generation, and oil production.

History. In 1919 Clessie L. Cummins, a chauffeur, wheedled $27,400 out of his boss, a Columbus banker named W. G. Irwin. Cummins was convinced that Rudolph Diesel's "oil engine," then confined to stationary uses, could be redesigned so as to make it a flexible and cheap source of power. His first efforts were spectacularly unsuccessful, but with a little persistence and a lot more of Irwin's money, by the mid-1920s Cummins came up with a diesel that was both economical and dependable. To demonstrate its wonders, he staged a series of publicity stunts over the next decade. He entered a diesel-powered car in the 1931 Indianapolis 500, where it finished without a pit stop. He set land speed records for a diesel-driven automobile at Daytona Beach and endurance records by driving a diesel-powered truck from New York to Los Angeles in 97 hours and 52 minutes on only $11.22 worth of fuel. In 1937, after 18 years in business, Cummins Engine showed their first profit.

That same year J. Irwin Miller, W. G. Irwin's grandnephew, took over the reins of the company, which he continued to guide until 1977. Under his leadership the company invested heavily in research, and when the diesel engine proved its reliability during World War II when the famous "Red Ball Express" caravans moved supplies across Europe, Asia, and the Pacific islands, the diesel market, and Cummins, burgeoned. In the late 1960s and early 1970s they tried their hand at diversification— they bought an air-conditioner manufacturer, the K-2 ski makers, and a Swiss bank —but these ventures never worked out. Today Cummins Engine is back to doing what they have always done best: keeping the trucks rolling.

Reputation. Cummins is regarded as a company with a conscience.

What they own. Twenty-four manufacturing and assembly plants in the United States and six foreign countries. The major engine factories are in Columbus, Indiana; Charleston, South Carolina; Jamestown, New York; and Shotts, Scotland.

Who owns and runs the company. J. Irwin Miller, his wife, and his sister together control 24.7% of the stock. Miller remains on the board, but day-to-day control belongs to two men in their mid-forties, chairman Henry B. Schacht (Yale, Harvard Business School) and president James A. Henderson (Princeton, Harvard Business School). The Cummins board is not your everyday board of directors. On it are Franklin A. Thomas, president of the Ford Foundation (Irwin Miller is a trustee of the

Ford Foundation); Hanna H. Gray, president of the University of Chicago; and Sir William R. Hawthorne, professor of applied thermodynamics at Cambridge University in England. Henderson and Schacht live on the same street in Columbus, and John Lyst, business editor of the *Indianapolis Star*, reported in 1977 that "their families play tennis, volleyball and hockey together." Reporter Marilyn Bender of the *New York Times* noted that Columbus is a town where at parties they ask not what company you work for but what department. Determined to desegregate the management ranks at the company, Cummins recruited some 100 black managers and executive trainees to come to Columbus between 1965 and 1973. Results were mixed. Bender said that in Columbus the blacks found that "monotony is a more serious problem than racial adjustments." Two black managers left Cummins for high positions in government: James Joseph, appointed undersecretary of the Department of the Interior by Jimmy Carter, and Ulric St. Clair Haynes, Jr., appointed U.S. ambassador to Algeria by Carter.

In mid-1980 the conglomerate Gulf & Western owned 7.2% of Cummins stock.

In the public eye. Not many midwestern towns have a Christian Church shaped like a Star of David and capped with a soaring cross-topped spire. The North Christian Church in Columbus fits that description; the architect was Eero Saarinen. The Columbus Public Library was designed by architect I. M. Pei. Out front there's a Henry Moore sculpture. Columbus has more than 30 public buildings designed by illustrious architects. This attempt to make Columbus the "Athens of the prairie" didn't cost the city a dime—the tab was picked up by Cummins and their benevolent leader, J. Irwin Miller. A multimillionaire whose interests extend well beyond diesel engines, Miller is a liberal Republican, liberal enough to have made Richard Nixon's "enemies list." The major passion of Miller's public life has been promoting racial equality, and he has done that through numerous instruments —Cummins Engine, Cummins Engine Foundation, and a family foundation, the Irwin-Sweeney-Miller Foundation. Many of Cummins's corporate contributions have gone toward civil rights and minority economic development. Especially notable was the Delta Foundation they helped to establish in Mississippi to spur economic opportunities for blacks in that area. The company's total charitable contributions in 1978 were $3.6 million.

Where they're going. Cummins has recently increased investment in research to come up with fuel-efficient engines appropriate to an era of higher energy prices. One project their scientists are working on is a lightweight diesel to power automobiles of the future.

Stock performance. Cummins Engine Company stock bought for $1,000 in 1970 sold for $867 on January 2, 1980.

Major employment centers. Columbus, Indiana; Fostoria, Ohio; and Charleston, South Carolina.

Access. 432 Washington Street, Columbus, Indiana 47201; (812) 372-7211. Toll-free Customer Service Department number is (800) 457-5300. Many of their facilities are available for tour.

Sales: $5.3 billion
Profits: $77.7 million
Forbes 500 rank: 71
Rank in tires: 2
Founded: 1900
Employees: 107,000
Headquarters: Akron, Ohio

What they do. Few companies have had such bad press as Firestone Tire & Rubber. Defective tires, illegal political contributions, overseas bribery, tax fraud, allegations of unlawful gold trading—these are the stuff of the Akron-based tiremaker's recent press clippings. In the midst of their troubles they went right out and hired Jimmy Stewart, the nice-guy actor with the scratchy voice, to tell the TV audience what a swell company Firestone really is. They're reportedly paying him $750,000 over three years. Firestone needs all the credibility they can muster.

The nation's second-largest tire company, with 18% of the market, Firestone manufactures and sells tires and related products for cars, trucks, buses, tractors, and airplanes. Their tire operations go from A to Z. Firestone makes synthetic rubber from petroleum by-products at plants in Orange, Texas; Akron, Ohio; and Lake Charles, Louisiana. They turn out the fabric for tire castings at textile mills in Bowling Green, Kentucky; Gastonia, North Carolina; and Bennettsville, South Carolina. The tires themselves are made at factories in Pennsylvania, California, Ohio, Illinois, Iowa, Tennessee, Georgia, Oklahoma, and North Carolina, then sold to automakers and consumers through 2,100 Firestone stores and many independent dealers, including Montgomery Ward. And this is just in the United States. With tire plants in 25 countries on five continents, Firestone does about a quarter of their business overseas. Tire operations account for 80% of Firestone's sales; other divisions make plastics, rubber, and foam for industrial uses.

History. Firestone has a long and close association with Ford, and the pasts of the two companies are remarkably similar. Firestone was founded in Akron in 1900 by Harvey S. Firestone—like Henry Ford, a rebel against the restrictive patents and licensing arrangements that hampered the development of the early auto industry. The two men got together in 1906, when Ford ordered 2,000 sets of tires for his new cheap runabout. This was the beginning of Firestone's role as chief supplier for Ford. Ford and Firestone were both technical innovators and pioneers in mass-production, but both soon lost their industry's leadership to companies (General Motors and Goodyear) with superior marketing and management abilities. Like Ford, Firestone has remained a family-controlled business. And also like Ford, Firestone had, in the 1970s, a safety scandal.

In October 1978, under the threat of government action, Firestone agreed to recall 10 million Firestone 500 steel-belted radial tires which the National Highway Traffic Safety Administration had judged to have a safety defect. The controversy had begun in the spring of that year, when the government started investigating consumer complaints about bulges, cracks, and blowouts on Firestone 500s. Firestone executives, testifying before Congress, denied knowledge of any defects in their tires. They blamed the difficulties on poor maintenance by motorists and on misleading press reports, which by that time had attributed 27 accident deaths to the Firestone 500. However, as company documents made public by the National Highway Traffic Safety Administration revealed, Firestone executives had

Goin to Blazes

If you ever thought you could just go out and buy a fire truck, you might be surprised to learn that every one is custom made for the department that orders it—even the truck for the little village in Kansas with a population of 893. You might order a snorkel truck, a ladder truck, a pumper, a tanker, a grass-fire truck, a crash truck (heavily armored, used at airports), a rescue truck, or any of a hundred other specially designed vehicles meant for specific fire-fighting uses.

There is no standard equipment on a fire truck: every-thing is extra, and an options list of 8,000 possibilities adds up to a tab from $40,000 to well over $100,000. A truck committee from the fire company customer usually visits the truck manufacturer while their truck is being made, inspecting the work and making further changes and additions.

A few custom manufacturers—like Mack trucks, one of the largest in the industry—build their fire trucks from the bottom up, to specifications. Most companies buy the chassis from Dodge or International Harvester and build the rest of the equipment onto it.

Technology has made great changes in fire fighting, but tradition retains its grasp. In 1972 the Ward LaFrance company made and sold its first chartreuse-colored fire truck, claiming that chartreuse is the color best seen by the human eye, day or night. But the truck has not been popular with fire companies, who prefer the "fire engine red" trucks that most people associate with sirens and blazes.

In deep trouble because of the largest tire recall in history, Firestone hired veteran actor Jimmy Stewart to do commercials reassuring motorists that the company has today the same commitment to quality that founder Harvey S. Firestone (shown in inset at top) had.

been aware since 1972 of safety problems with the tire and had pinpointed much of the problem in 1975. But Firestone never conceded the tire was hazardous. Explained chairman Richard Riley: "We're agreeing to the recall because there has been so much publicity. The thought that there is a defect has been implanted so strongly that we have to convince our customers that we are interested in their welfare."

Reputation. The Richard Nixon of tire companies. *Fortune* said that the company, in trying to defend itself in the Firestone 500 hassle, "has often been its own worst enemy."

What they own. Firestone has rubber plantations in the Philippines, Brazil, Ghana, and Liberia. Their Liberian plantation at Harbel is the largest rubber plantation in the world. A reporter who visited there in 1975 found that Firestone's Liberian workers made between 8¢ and 23¢ an hour. In 1979 another reporter, Ste-

phen Talbot, visited the Firestone plantation and gave this picture in *The Nation*: ". . . the 220-square-mile plantation is reminiscent of the old American South—a company town complete with its own housing, church, stores, police force and jail. The white American president and managers dined in colonial style, served by impeccably dressed black waiters, and relaxed on their private nine-hole golf course. During a guided tour of the plantation, an angry worker took me aside to dispute what he had overheard of the company spokesperson's presentation. He said he earned only $180 a month after 20 years of service and revealed that the 12,000 Firestone employees were pressing management to recognize the union."

In the fall of 1979 Liberian president William R. Tolbert, Jr., visited the United States and asked Firestone in Akron to raise the wages of their Liberian workers to cap the discontent. In early 1980 the Liberian government was overthrown in a bloody coup that saw Tolbert assassinated.

Who owns and runs the company. The Firestone family still owns nearly a quarter of the company's stock but is no longer involved in management. A new president, John J. Nevin, was brought in from Zenith Radio in late 1979 to stop the company's skid.

In the public eye. Like the other Big Four tire companies, Firestone has had more than one brush with the law. Between 1970 and 1973 $330,000 worth of corporate funds from a slush fund maintained by Robert P. Beasley, vice-chairman and chief financial officer, were used for political contributions. But the Firestone story has an added twist. While Beasley was passing out cash to politicians, he was also tapping the illegal fund of $1 million for his own use. In 1978 Beasley was convicted in federal court of fraud and sentenced to four years in jail; he also faces a $625,000 civil suit by Firestone to recover some of the loot. Beasley, though, may have the last laugh. After his conviction he provided federal attorneys with documents that have led to a $62.1 million suit for illegal gold trading carried on for Firestone by a Swiss bank.

Where they're going. They're slimming down. Firestone announced early in 1980 that they were closing their tire plants in Dayton and Barberton, Ohio; Los Angeles and Salinas, California; and Pottstown, Pennsylvania. The closings threw 7,000 people out of work. Firestone conceded that these shutdowns would reduce their market share, but they explained: "Our interest is profitability."

Stock performance. Firestone stock bought for $1,000 in 1970 sold for $347 on January 2, 1980.

Access. 1200 Firestone Parkway, Akron, Ohio 44317; (216) 379-7000. For complaints contact Jack B. Scarcliff, (800) 321-9638.

Consumer brands.

Firestone, Dayton, Fidesta, Seiberling tires.

In 1979 Americans bought 10.7 million cars, 10 million bicycles, and 350,000 mopeds.

Sales: $2.5 billion
Profits: $88.7 million
Forbes 500 rank: 208
Rank in truck trailers: 1
Founded: 1899
Employees: 36,100
Headquarters: Detroit, Michigan

What they do. Fruehauf is the only corporation in America whose chairman and president had to report to probation officers. In November 1978 the U.S. Supreme Court refused to hear William E. Grace's and Robert D. Rowan's appeal of their conviction for having conspired to evade some of Fruehauf's federal tax liability. But the two felons are once again in their jobs with the world's largest manufacturer of truck trailers.

Fruehauf makes no motorized vehicles (or truck cabs or tractors), only the trailers that are hitched to the trucks. But Fruehauf makes a wide variety of trailers: from the familiar "semi" van (the enclosed trailer in which much of the country's freight is transported), to tank trailers (for carrying oil or other liquids), to flat-bed trailers (for lumber or long pieces of steel). In all, Fruehauf sells about a quarter of the nation's truck trailers. And the company is the only firm in the industry with local service centers throughout the United States and Canada to repair disabled trailers.

Although Fruehauf's trailer operations still yield more than half their sales, the company has branched out into other transportation areas in recent years. Fruehauf pioneered in making cargo containers for oceangoing ships, and they now have shipyards in Baltimore, Maryland, and Jacksonville, Florida, and a division that manufactures cranes and other equipment for unloading and loading containerized ships. In 1973 they bought Kelsey-Hayes, which supplies wheels, brake components, and axles for the big auto and truck companies. Kelsey-Hayes also has an aerospace division that builds helicopter transmissions, parts for jet engines, and hydraulic systems for the Pentagon's most sophisticated military aircraft.

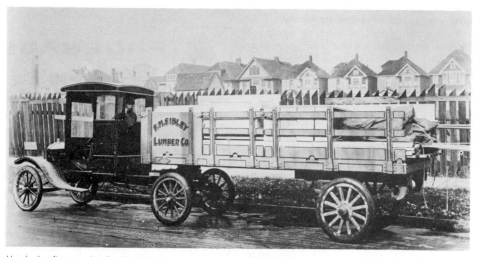

Here's the first semi-trailer, invented by Harvey Fruehauf in 1914. That's Harvey looking out from the cab.

History. August Fruehauf ran a large blacksmith shop (it could house 60 horses at a time) when, in 1914, a Detroit lumber manufacturer named Frederic M. Sibley, Sr., came to the shop for some help. Sibley had a boat that he needed to transport to his summer place in upper Michigan, but he didn't want to take it by horse and wagon since the trip would be too time consuming. Sibley wondered whether Fruehauf could make a contraption to hook to Sibley's Ford Model T roadster to haul the boat.

Sibley liked how the "semi-trailer," as Fruehauf called it, worked so well that he urged the blacksmith shop to make similar rigs for his lumber yard. Soon Fruehauf was soliciting business: he put a Fruehauf trailer ad in a national lumber journal in 1916, and he began using the slogan, "A horse can pull more than it can carry . . . so can a truck."

Before long Fruehauf forgot about fixing horseshoes and put all his energy into his successful truck trailer business. By the time August Fruehauf bowed out of the business in 1930, the company was making a wide variety of trailers, including tank trailers for oil and refrigerated trailers for ice cream.

August's son Harvey helped expand the business through the 1930s and 1940s, at the same time maintaining a hard line on unions. Fruehauf joined four other companies in fighting the Wagner Act, which had established the National Labor Relations Board in the early 1930s. In 1937, when the Supreme Court upheld the act, Fruehauf had to bargain with their employees.

When Harvey Fruehauf stepped aside as president in 1949, in favor of his younger brother Roy, the company ran into difficulties. Roy Fruehauf was a salesman, not an administrator, and operations were soon a shambles. The younger Fruehauf also was indicted, though later acquitted, on federal charges stemming from a 1954 Fruehauf loan to former Teamsters president Dave Beck. With the company floundering the Metropolitan Life Insurance Company and several of Fruehauf's bank creditors stepped in to force Roy Fruehauf out. His replacement in 1958 was William E. Grace, a blunt Texan who promised to cure everything that was wrong with the company. By reorganizing the corporation and vigorous cost-cutting, Grace soon had Fruehauf back on the road to financial success, if not rectitude.

Reputation. Fruehauf is as well known these days for scandals as for semis.

What they own. Fifty-one manufacturing plants and 115 sales, service, and rental branches in the United States and Canada. They also have operations in 12 countries overseas.

In the public eye. In 1970 the Fruehauf Corporation, chairman William Grace, and president Robert Rowan were indicted on federal charges of conspiring to evade more than $12.3 million in corporate excise taxes.

According to the prosecution, they had set up a phony wholesale price structure to evade the excise taxes and thereby gain a competitive advantage over other trailer companies. Manufacturers of truck trailers pay a 10% federal excise tax on the price they receive for each vehicle. Fruehauf concocted a scheme whereby they were able to bill their distributors at a lower price—58% of list instead of 61.7%—and thereby reduce the amount of taxes they had to pay the government. They later recovered that 3.7% difference by billing the distributors for certain services that were normally provided by Fruehauf (advertising, sales assistance, and things like that). So Fruehauf received the same money it always got—but its taxes were lowered. On a typical shipment, they invoiced at $268 less than formerly, thereby saving $26.80 in taxes.

In 1975 a federal judge in Michigan found the company and the two executives guilty, and he fined Grace and Rowan $10,000 each and sentenced them to six months in jail (later reduced to two years of probation). The defendants appealed the case, first to the U.S. Circuit Court of Appeals, later to the Supreme Court. All the while they kept their jobs, and Fruehauf paid their legal fees.

In November 1978, when the Supreme Court refused to hear their appeal, Grace and Rowan resigned. But Fruehauf had other plans. The company granted them unsalaried leaves of absence and kept open their seats on the board. Rowan was frequently called in as a $100-an-hour consultant. Five months later, on April 30, 1979, in their annual notice to stockholders, Fruehauf asked that Grace and Rowan be restored to their positions on the board and rehired. "While there is currently an increasing trend towards strict adherence to principles of public morality," the board's special counsel informed the stockholders, "it cannot yet be said that it must always override all other considerations."

Not all the stockholders agreed. One of the 350 stockholders who attended the annual meeting, Hope Brophy, who identified herself as a mother of five from Grosse Pointe, Michigan, stood up and declared that "the issue here is criminal behavior" and added: "What we're saying to young people today is that the American business system rewards criminal behavior." Brophy was overwhelmingly outvoted, and Grace and Rowan returned to run the company again.

Where they're going. Back to court. The IRS still has a civil action pending against Fruehauf to recover $50 million in back excise taxes and penalties. In addition, a stockholder has sued Fruehauf to force them to recover legal fees from Grace and Rowan.

Stock performance. Fruehauf stock bought for $1,000 in 1970 sold for $667 on January 2, 1980.

Access: Fruehauf Corporation, 10900 Harper Avenue, Detroit, Michigan 48213; (313) 267-1000.

GENERAL G TIRE ®

Sales: $2.3 billion
Profits: $81.7 million
Forbes 500 rank: 232
Rank in tires: 5
Rank in tennis balls: 1
Founded: 1915
Employees: 42,000
Headquarters: Akron, Ohio

Some sons learn their lessons too well. Take Thomas, Michael, and John O'Neil, the troika of brothers who run General Tire & Rubber and own 8% of the stock. They took over in 1960 from the founder, their father, William O'Neil, a freewheeling entrepreneur who built General from a simple tire company into a sprawling conglomerate by intuitive decision making. Father got General into radio and television, chemicals, plastics and tennis balls, airlines (Frontier), rocket propulsion and nuclear reactor parts (the last through acquisition of Aerojet, a big California aerospace and

A standard 1979 American car that sold new for $5,471 would cost $26,418 to replace all the parts if the car were totally demolished in a wreck.

engineering company). Though only fifth in the tire industry, General doesn't have to worry: 60% of their sales come from other sources. Detroit accounts for about a quarter of General Tire's business. They buy not only tires from General, but plastics and industrial products such as gaskets, windshield wipers, and valves. General sells to all four U.S. auto makers, which is why they feel they can advertise: "Sooner or later you'll own Generals." Their largest customer, generating more than 10% of their sales, is General Motors.

An iconoclast, William O'Neil was also something of a political curmudgeon: he thought every government intrusion into the economy—even in such basic matters as prohibiting price-fixing—was unwarranted meddling. Perhaps this attitude influenced the sons when General joined other tire companies and ignored the law by setting up slush funds to make illegal political contributions at home and bribes abroad.

Other companies did that too, but General's hanky-panky had some major consequences. Their RKO subsidiary operates 12 radio and 4 television stations in leading media markets. (RKO Pictures was bought from Howard Hughes in 1955.) One of the stations is WNAC-TV in Boston, long coveted by Boston supermarket heir David Mugar. For years, in proceedings before the Federal Communications Commission, Mugar had been challenging RKO General's license to operate WNAC. The FCC, charged with regulating broadcasting in the public interest, reconsiders licenses every three years, but it almost never fails to renew them. But in 1975, with the help of attorney Terry Lenzer, a former counsel to the Senate Watergate committee, Mugar found out about General's slush funds. He took the evidence to the FCC, telling how General had slipped a half-million to a Moroccan agent to keep Goodyear from doing business in that country; how General president Michael G. O'Neil had, from 1968 to 1973, paid out $350,000 in illegal political contributions from a "little tin box" of cash he kept in his office wall safe; how General had forked over $150,000 to Saudi businessman Adnan Khashoggi to get the company removed from the Arab blacklist. RKO General, Mugar said, was unqualified to hold the WNAC license, and challengers in Los Angeles and New York echoed the refrain.

This time the FCC listened and in January 1980 ruled that RKO General was unfit to hold the three television licenses. The O'Neils will appeal the ruling in federal court, where the case could be tied up for years. But if they lose, the FCC will cancel RKO's broadcast licenses. That could cost General some $600 million. In inflationary times even the wages of sin go up.

The unprecedented action by the FCC depressed the price of General Tire's stock. Sensing a bargain situation, the Gulf & Western conglomerate moved quickly in 1980 to buy 8.7% of General's stock for $30 million, just as earlier—in 1978 and 1979—they bought 6.1% of Uniroyal, another punctured tire maker.

Stock performance. General Tire stock bought for $1,000 in 1970 sold for $1,410 on January 2, 1980.

Access. One General Street, Akron, Ohio 44329; (216) 798-3000.

Consumer brands.

General tires; Penn tennis balls.

IMPORTED CARS SOLD IN THE U.S.	
Total *(all years through 1979)*	
1. VOLKSWAGEN*	3,637,413
2. TOYOTA	2,929,895
3. DATSUN	2,344,856
4. HONDA	1,149,027
5. FIAT	558,359
6. VOLVO	523,993
7. MAZDA	484,055
8. OPEL	474,450
9. MERCEDES-BENZ	453,406
10. SUBARU	449,561
11. COLT	372,153
12. CAPRI	358,896
13. AUDI	311,366
14. MG	292,389
15. TRIUMPH	209,268
16. BMW	196,019
17. FIESTA	191,813
18. PORSCHE	174,970
19. ARROW	150,316
20. RENAULT	140,108
21. SAAB	121,673
22. PEUGEOT	87,259
23. JAGUAR	64,733
24. AUSTIN	45,107
25. ALFA ROMEO	39,568
26. CHALLENGER	33,278
27. CRICKET	26,310
27. SAPPORO	26,225
28. ROLLS ROYCE	11,849
29. LANCIA	9,678
30. MISCELLANEOUS	181,417
TOTAL	**16,049,410**

*Volkswagen totals do not include cars assembled in the U.S.

Source: *Automotive News*, 1980 Market Data Book Issue.

BFGoodrich

Sales: $3 billion
Profits: $82.6 million
Forbes 500 rank: 163
Rank in tires: 4
Rank in polyvinyl chloride: 1
Founded: 1870
Employees: 42,213
Headquarters: Akron, Ohio

What they do. Goodrich is the brains of the rubber industry. They made the first cotton-covered rubber fire hose, the first pneumatic automobile tire, and the first commercial tubeless tire. Goodrich pioneered synthetic rubber. They made the first space suits worn by America's astronauts. They were the first to make radial tires in the United States. In the tire business at least, brains don't count for everything. The oldest and most technologically innovative of the Big Four rubber companies, Goodrich is nevertheless the smallest: their plants in Akron, Ohio; Miami, Oklahoma; Oaks, Pennsylvania; Fort Wayne, Indiana; and Tuscaloosa, Alabama account for 9% of U.S. tire production, less than a third of Goodyear's share.

With their long and distinguished list of "firsts" in research and invention, why don't they lead the industry? Perhaps it's because they didn't poke their heads out of the laboratory long enough to attend to selling their tires. And maybe they have been sluggish in modernizing their plants and organizing their distribution. Whatever the reasons, the business press has been asking for years when Goodrich was going to get their act together. Goodrich became so defensive about their position in the industry that in 1972 they began admitting in their ads that they're "the other guy."

Sometimes being the other guy does have advantages. You don't get hurt so badly in a downturn because you have less to lose. In 1979, when passenger tire shipments were down 9.3%, Goodrich's tire shipments declined only 6.1%. Whether sales go up or down, Goodrich is always lagging.

Goodrich has been channeling profits from tires into their industrial and chemical divisions. Goodrich is the oldest and largest U.S. producer of polyvinyl chloride resins and compounds—the raw chemical material for many plastics, particularly those used in construction. They also make a wide variety of synthetic rubbers and plastics, some of which they fabricate into hoses, conveyer belts, and vinyl fabrics for industry. In 1979 these nontire operations accounted for more than half of Goodrich's business—and 75% of their profits. Though their factories and rubber sources are spread across every continent except Antarctica, about three-fourths of their sales are made in the United States.

History. The first Akron rubber company, Goodrich was founded in 1870 by Dr. Benjamin Franklin Goodrich, a physician from upstate New York who served as a surgeon in the Civil War and then decided to go into business because he didn't think he could support his wife properly in the medical profession. They were on a train to Chicago to seek advice from a rich relative on relocating the Hudson River Rubber Company, a business he had bought into in 1869, when a stranger told him of the great possibilities in Akron, then served by two railroads, with another one coming. "Mary, get your bonnet on," cried the young entrepreneur. They got off at the next stop—considerably short of Chicago—and before the turn of the century Akron was the center of the world's rubber industry.

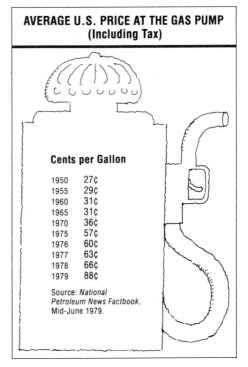

**AVERAGE U.S. PRICE AT THE GAS PUMP
(Including Tax)**

Cents per Gallon

1950	27¢
1955	29¢
1960	31¢
1965	31¢
1970	36¢
1975	57¢
1976	60¢
1977	63¢
1978	66¢
1979	88¢

Source: *National Petroleum News Factbook,* Mid-June 1979.

B. F. Goodrich died in 1888, when he was only 46. By that time his company was well established and had won a special reputation for solving problems related to the manufacture of rubber. In 1896, when a Cleveland bicycle manufacturer named Alexander Winton wanted tires for the "horseless carriage" he had just built, he came to Goodrich. They promptly turned out the first auto tires in America. Three years later, when a golfer complained to a Goodrich executive about the poor quality of golf balls, they came up with the rubber-wound ball, which revolutionized the game. Perhaps the company's most important technological contribution, though, came during the Second World War, when the Japanese cut the United States off from the Far East plantations that supplied 97% of the nation's rubber. Goodrich had been working on the problem of man-made rubber since 1926. Their first plant was producing two kinds of synthetic rubber by 1939 and had a 10,000-ton-a-year capacity at the time of Pearl Harbor. Goodrich then built and ran many of the government-owned plants supplying rubber for the war effort.

Reputation. The wags in Akron have it right: Goodrich develops it, Firestone takes credit for it, and Goodyear sells it.

What they own. Like the other rubber companies, Goodrich operates worldwide. They own tire factories in Colombia, Brazil, and the Philippines; chemical plants in Ireland, Holland, New Zealand, Belgium, Costa Rica, and Venezuela; and rubber plantations in Liberia and the Philippines.

Who owns and runs the company. In 1972 O. Pendleton Thomas was brought in as chairman after a long career at Sinclair Oil. He had a mandate to rejuvenate the sagging company. Thomas believed long-wearing radials would slow down Goodrich's domestic tire sales, and he saw the tire business primarily as a "cash cow" they could milk to finance ventures in chemicals, plastics, and industrial products. On his retirement in 1979 he was succeeded by president John D. Ong, an attorney who joined Goodrich in 1971. Thomas is the biggest single shareholder, with 1% of the stock. In 1980 Ong paid tribute to Thomas for transforming "a company that had substantial problems and poor prospects." (Goodrich people never tire of denigrating the company.)

In the public eye. Goodrich says they're the other guy, but they don't look much different from the rest of the industry when it comes to obeying the law. In 1979 Goodrich was fined $10,000 for having created a cash political slush fund by filing false deductions on their federal income tax returns. Between 1969 and 1975 Goodrich illegally reimbursed executives for about $127,000 in domestic political contributions and made $845,000 in illegal or questionable payments to foreign governments or go-betweens. Two of the executives responsible for these payments are still active in the company.

In 1969 the General Accounting Office, the watchdog agency of Congress, charged that Goodrich supplied a defective brake for an Air Force attack plane, falsifying tests to hide the defects. The incident later became the basis of a much-quoted article used in the Robert Heilbroner–edited book on corporate malfeasance, *In the Name of Profit.*

Where they're going. Polyvinyl chloride. And possibly a major new health and safety scandal. In the face of "tire-drag," Goodrich is heavily emphasizing chemicals, the most important being polyvinyl chloride

---

The Unsavory Henry J

In the 1950s, as major U.S. car companies mass-marketed cars that appealed to the prevailing public taste for chromium-plated spaciousness, a few independent automakers tried to counter by producing economy small cars, like Kaiser-Frazer's Henry J.

Although the smaller cars offered fuel economy and dependability, they failed to gratify the public's craving for images of swashbuckling power. Between 1950 and 1954 the Henry J sold fewer than 130,000 cars before the model was discontinued. The reason for its failure was best explained by a Georgia farmer, who said his 1951 Henry J was "like an unsavory gal ah once knew. She was really pretty great—but ah wouldn't associate mahself in public with 'er."

Source: Robert Atwan, Donald McQuade, and John W. Wright, *Edsels, Luckies and Frigidaires* (Dell, 1979).

(PVC), of which Goodrich is the largest U.S. producer. Their 1979 annual report announced that by 1985 they would double their output of PVC, a chemical used in plastic for dozens of house-building components such as floor and wall covering as well as for food packaging, bottles, dentures, pharmaceuticals, and other products.

But a 1974 report related the basic component of PVC, a fine white powder called vinyl chloride monomer, to a rare form of liver cancer. Ordinarily 25 people a year would contract the disease throughout the country, but six fatal cases were discovered among workers at a single Goodrich plant in Louisville, Kentucky. These workers had been exposed to the chemical over periods ranging from 14 to 27 years. Since vinyl chlorides have been in use for less than 30 years, it seemed possible that cases of the disease were just beginning to show up.

Stock performance. Goodrich stock bought for $1,000 in 1970 sold for $599 on January 2, 1980.

Access. 500 South Main Street, Akron, Ohio 44318; (216) 379-3985.

Consumer brands:

B. F. Goodrich; Diamond; Miller; Hood; Brunswick tires.

THE 50 MOST-PRODUCED CARS IN THE WORLD

Make and Model/1979 Production

1. TOYOTA COROLLA 637,816	26. CHEVROLET CAMARO• 257,873
2. VOLKSWAGEN RABBIT (*Golf*) 616,081	27. BUICK REGAL• 257,372
3. OLDSMOBILE CUTLASS• 507,542	28. OPEL REKORD 257,300
4. DATSUN 210 (*Sunny*) 506,242	29. DATSUN 310 (*Cherry*) 254,667
5. RENAULT R-5 488,855	30. BUICK• 252,220
6. FORD TAUNUS/CORTINA 457,900	31. MITSUBISHI MIRAGE/COLT 247,000
7. FORD FIESTA 449,200	32. PEUGEOT 305 245,700
8. CHEVROLET• 447,397	33. TOYOTA CELICA 245,468
9. CHEVROLET CHEVETTE• 413,627	34. TOYOTA CORONA 243,400
10. MERCEDES-BENZ W-123 400,440	35. PEUGEOT 504 238,300
11. RENAULT R-4 375,207	36. AUDI 80 236,901
12. RENAULT 18 366,861	37. CADILLAC• 230,958
13. FIAT/SEAT 127 366,150	38. MAZDA 626 229,760
14. FORD MUSTANG/MUSTANG II• 365,357	39. RENAULT R-12 227,306
15. OLDSMOBILE• 365,312	40. CHEVROLET MONTE CARLO• 227,043
16. TOYOTA/TERCEL/CORSA 357,018	41. TALBOT SIMCA HORIZON 222,296
17. FIAT RITMO 334,811	42. CITROEN GS 222,072
18. CHEVROLET MALIBU/CHEVELLE• 322,767	43. FORD FAIRMONT• 213,761
19. CHEVROLET NOVA/CITATION• 321,372	44. VOLVO 240 210,000
20. HONDA ACCORD 315,811	45. RENAULT R-14 197,607
21. FORD ESCORT 312,700	46. DATSUN 810 (*Bluebird*) 195,919
22. HONDA CIVIC 301,180	47. PONTIAC FIREBIRD• 194,033
23. OPEL ASCONA 284,691	48. NISSAN VIOLET 193,617
24. MAZDA 323 272,000	49. BMW 3-series 188,809
25. FORD THUNDERBIRD• 264,451	50. TOYOTA CRESSIDA 183,602

•U.S.–built cars. All others produced outside the U.S.

Source: *Automotive News*, 1980 Market Data Book Issue.

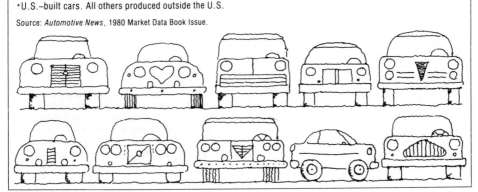

Sales: $8.2 billion
Profits: $146.2 million
Forbes 500 rank: 38
Rank in tires: 1
Founded: 1898
Employees: 154,000
Headquarters: Akron, Ohio

What they do. Throughout America Goodyear is known as the company with the blimp. In Akron they are called "The Brute." The nickname was coined by other members of the Big Four rubber companies to describe the marketing tactics that have kept Goodyear on top of the U.S. tire market for more than 60 years. The sobriquet catches the flavor of Goodyear's attitudes.

Just ask the tire workers of Akron. In 1978, when the United Rubber Workers would not make wage concessions the company wanted, Goodyear closed Akron's Plant 2, their last passenger car tire factory in the city once known as the tire capital of the world. (In 1929 Akron produced 75% of U.S. car tires; today it makes 1%.) Goodyear said the costs of converting the plant from bias-ply to radial tires was prohibitive, but they may have wanted to retaliate for the strikes that have hit the company like clockwork every three years. Now Goodyear makes their U.S. car tires in the South —they have big factories in Lawton, Oklahoma; Gadsen, Alabama; Union City, Tennessee; and Fayetteville, North Carolina, which are supplied with synthetic rubber by Goodyear's plants in Houston and Beaumont, Texas. Akron remains Goodyear's headquarters and home of several of their nontire operations, accounting for about 15% of their business, such as chemicals, wheels, industrial rubber products, flooring, and guidance systems for nuclear missiles.

Arrogance seems to be a way of life at Goodyear. While the rest of the world rode on radial tires, Goodyear stubbornly resisted, even though the radial was widely acknowledged to offer superior performance and a longer life than bias-ply tires. When B. F. Goodrich introduced radials to the United States, Goodyear still turned up their nose. Then in the early 1970s, as the radial tires began to make inroads, Goodyear deigned to enter the fray, announcing in a press release the dawning of the "Radial Age." The implication was clear that it's not the "Radial Age" until Goodyear says it is. Their success in selling has captured one-third of the U.S. tire market for Goodyear.

History. When Frank Seiberling and his brother Charles started their rubber company in Akron in 1898, they named it after the discoverer of vulcanized rubber, Charles Goodyear. With the Seiberlings selling and Paul Litchfield, an MIT graduate, introducing improved tire varieties, Goodyear by 1916 became the largest tire manufacturer in the United States, a position they have never relinquished. The Seiberlings' lack of financial acumen nearly brought the company to ruin in the brief depression that followed World War I, however. When Goodyear floundered, Dillon, Read & Co., the New York investment bankers, stepped in to reorganize the company, forcing out the Seiberlings in favor of their own man.

Since then Goodyear has maintained their position by selling harder than their competitors. During the Great Depression,

OFF TO THE RACES
U.S. New Car Prices (average)
1969	$3,400
1970	$3,430
1971	$3,730
1972	$3,690
1973	$3,930
1974	$4,390
1975	$4,750
1976	$5,470
1977	$6,120
1978	$6,470
1979	$6,940
Source: *Economist*, 1979; *Automotive News*, 1980 Market Data Book Issue.

In 1979 full-sized cars took only 4% of the U.S. new-car market, down from 40% in 1972, a year before gasoline prices rose sharply. Small cars took nearly 70% of the U.S. new-car market in 1979, compared to 37% in 1972.

Working on the skin of a Goodyear blimp in 1942 when the Akron tire maker built their airships for naval escort duty during World War II.

Goodyear's Flying Billboards

Even if, by some miracle, you had managed to get through life without having been exposed to a single commercial on television or radio or as much as one newspaper or magazine ad, there's one advertising campaign that would very likely have reached you anyway: the Goodyear blimp. Goodyear, the tire and rubber company based in Akron, Ohio, has kept their name in the skies over the cities and villages of America and Western Europe for more than 60 years.

Goodyear operates four different blimps: the Enterprise, the America, the Columbia, and the Europa (that one stays over there). The American airships hover over all parts of the country except for the Rocky Mountain states, where the air gets too thin (they can't rise much higher than 6,000 feet). When they have to cross the continent they take the southern route over the low desert, hugging the Mexican border. Top speed is only about 45 miles an hour, but a Goodyear blimp can operate eight hours a day for nearly a week on the amount of fuel a jumbo jet uses to taxi from ramp to runway before takeoff.

Each blimp is an inflatable bag made of rubber-coated polyester, 192 feet long, with no internal framework, and filled with $20,000 worth of helium. Slung underneath is a small gondola, about 25 feet long, equipped with two propeller engines and a rudder. In the daytime the gondola holds six passengers and a pilot. At night the passengers are cleared out and the space is filled up with computerized equipment that controls 7,500 colored lights on the sides of the airship. The lights spell out messages and enact animated dramas visible a mile away.

For the blimp aficionado who is dying to take a ride, about the only way to do it is to travel to Pompano Beach, Florida. That's where the Enterprise spends from roughly November to April, and where Goodyear operates half-hour excursions aboard the Enterprise. It's an extremely popular tourist attraction, so before you set out for Pompano Beach, phone (305) 946-4629 to make sure you can get on board the flying billboard.

when many dealers were wiped out, Goodyear opened their own company stores. Today they have about 1,600 retail stores. Later, when tires with off-brand names began to erode their profits, Goodyear went into that market, too. They now sell tires under the names of their subsidiaries, Kelly-Springfield and Lee Tire, and they make the Atlas brand tires sold by several oil companies. When the market for tires grew in other parts of the world, Goodyear went overseas. They now get 28% of their profits outside the United States.

Reputation. Goodyear is proud of having been led by men who grew up within sight of Akron's smokestacks. The problem with Goodyear is that those leaders have rarely been able to see much further.

What they own. Goodyear has 63 manufacturing facilities in 26 states, plus 49 plants in 30 foreign countries. They operate seven rubber plantations and numerous retread plants. In Arizona they have a 12,260-acre farm and a resort hotel (Goodyear Farms and Resort Hotel at Litchfield Park). But the plant they talk least about is the one they don't own. At their Portsmouth, Ohio, facility, owned by the U.S. Department of Energy, Goodyear turns out enriched uranium for nuclear power plants and weapons. They also own 4 Goodyear blimps.

Who owns and runs the company. The chairman and chief executive officer of Goodyear is Charles J. Pilliod, Jr., who started with the company as an Akron assembly-line worker. But Pilliod is not sentimental about his origins; he was the man who closed down Plant 2. In 1979 Goodyear's board was all white and all male.

One-Stop Chopping

A "chop shop" is an underworld auto garage that cuts up stolen cars and sells the parts separately at a huge profit, often totaling five times the original sticker price of the car. A chop shop can reduce an entire car to its salable parts in under an hour, making the stolen vehicle almost impossible to trace. Thieves often steal to order for these places, depending on the parts desired. (You could lose your whole car because somebody on the other side of town needed a carburetor.) According to one ex-thief (now in prison) who testified before the U.S. Senate in 1979, "A good car thief can make $150,000 to $200,000 in a year, working just a few hours a night" at this racket.

It is estimated that 55% of the 1 million-plus cars stolen in 1980 were destined to be taken apart in chop shops.

Source: *Newsweek*, December 10, 1979.

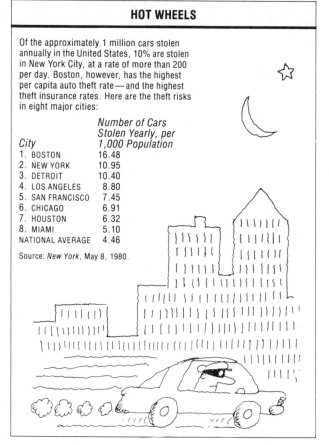

HOT WHEELS

Of the approximately 1 million cars stolen annually in the United States, 10% are stolen in New York City, at a rate of more than 200 per day. Boston, however, has the highest per capita auto theft rate—and the highest theft insurance rates. Here are the theft risks in eight major cities:

City	Number of Cars Stolen Yearly, per 1,000 Population
1. BOSTON	16.48
2. NEW YORK	10.95
3. DETROIT	10.40
4. LOS ANGELES	8.80
5. SAN FRANCISCO	7.45
6. CHICAGO	6.91
7. HOUSTON	6.32
8. MIAMI	5.10
NATIONAL AVERAGE	4.46

Source: *New York*, May 8, 1980.

COME FOR A SPIN IN MY ELECTROBAT!

Only the names remain of most of the more than 3,000 models of cars and trucks that have been manufactured in the United States. Here are some of them and the year(s) they were produced:

AMERICAN CHOCOLATE 1903–1906
AMERICAN UNDERSLUNG 1906–1914
AUTOHORSE 1917–1921
BOBBI-CAR 1947
BROWN'S TOURING CART 1898
BUCKEYE GAS BUGGY 1895
BUG 1914
BUGGYOUT 1909
BUGGYCAR 1907–1910
BUGMOBILE 1907–1909
BUZMOBILE 1917
CALORIE 1904
CLIMAX 1907
CROCK 1909
CROUCH 1900
CUCMOBILE 1907
DEPENDABLE 1919
DEWABOUT 1899
DOLLY MADISON 1915
ELECTROBAT 1895
EVERYBODY'S 1908–1909
FIELD STREAM 1887
FWICK 1912
GEARLESS STEAMER 1919–1922
GOETHEMOBILE 1902
HALL GASOLINE TRAP 1895
HOPPENSTAND 1948
HORSEY HORSELESS CARRIAGE 1899
HUPMOBILE 1908–1941
HUSTLER POWER CAR 1911
IMP 1913, 1915
IRVINGTON IZZER 1910
JETMOBILE (3 wheel) 1952
KEROSENE SURREY 1900
KLING 1907
KLINK 1907–1909
KLOCK 1900
KNOW 1922

K.C. 1921
LEACH 1899
LOCOMOBILE STEAMER 1899
OLD HICKORY 1915
OLD RELIABLE 1912
ONLY CAR 1911–1915
ORIENT-AUTO-GO 1900
O-WE-GO 1914
OWOSSO 1911
PACK-AGE-CAR 1925
PEOPLE'S 1901
PISCORSKI 1901
PLASS MOTOR SLEIGH 1895
PLAYBOY 1946–1949
PNEUMOBILE 1914–1915
POPPY CAR 1917
PUP 1948
QUEEN 1902–1906
QUICK 1899
RED BALL 1924
RED DEVIL STEAMER 1866
RIGS-THAT-RUN 1899
ROADABLE 1946
ROAMER 1916–1925
RUGGLES 1905
RUNABOUT 1902
RUSHMOBILE 1902
SEVEN-LITTLE-BUFFALOES 1908
SHAVERS STEAM BUGGY 1895
SILENT KNIGHT 1912
S. & M. 1913
STEP-N-DRIVE 1929
TALLY-HO 1914
TERWILLIGER STEAM 1904
VESTAL 1914
VIXEN CYCLECAR 1914–1916
ZIP 1913

In the public eye. Goodyear, which gives their blimps patriotic names like "America" and "Mayflower," was one of the companies which made illegal contributions to Richard Nixon's 1972 reelection campaign and was fined. Between 1964 and 1972 Goodyear gave out up to $242,000 in questionable donations to politicians from a slush fund in a foreign bank. But they do not appear to be particularly sorry about it. Russell DeYoung, the former chairman who was fined for the gifts to Nixon, is still on the board of directors. When asked during the Watergate hearings if he regretted his act, DeYoung said, "Not necessarily. We thought the reelection of the President was in the best interests of the country." Goodyear was also generous with foreign politicians: between 1970 and 1975 they gave out $845,000 in very questionable payments from slush funds maintained by foreign subsidiaries.

Goodyear has vigorously opposed federal standards for tire safety. And for years they resisted disclosing their record in hiring minorities and women. When Goodyear finally gave in, the reason for the obstinance became obvious: the proportion of women and minorities at Goodyear is well below the industry average.

Where they're going. The tire industry is in for hard times. At the same time that higher oil prices have pushed up the cost of making synthetic rubber, they have forced motorists to drive less, meaning fewer worn-out tires. Maybe "The Brute" has met its match in OPEC. But though other tire companies are diversifying, Goodyear is plowing straight ahead making a massive investment in tires. They unveiled a new corporate slogan in 1979: "Out front and pulling away."

Stock performance. Goodyear stock bought for $1,000 in 1970 sold for $419 on January 2, 1980.

Access. 1144 E. Market Street, Akron, Ohio 44316; (216) 794-2121.

Consumer brands.

Goodyear; Kelly-Springfield; Lee passenger car tires.

Sales: $2.6 billion
Losses: $120.5 million
Forbes 500 rank: 196
Rank in tires: 3
Founded: 1892
Employees: 49,000
Headquarters: Middlebury, Connecticut

What they do. Uniroyal is living proof that bigness alone is no guarantee of success. One of the nation's largest manufacturers of tires, they still manage to be one of the least successful. They lost a whopping $120 million in 1979. Saddled with some of the most outmoded tire plants in the industry, and half a billion dollars in debt to their own pension plan, Uniroyal spent most of the late 1970s selling off oper-

ations, including divisions that made golf balls, fire hoses, and Keds sneakers. The only reason they held on to the tire operation, many observers suspect, is that no one would be crazy enough to buy it.

Tires account for nearly three-fifths of their sales, and 70% of their tires go to a single customer—General Motors. Granted, the arrangement doesn't require an expensive marketing campaign, but neither does it make Uniroyal rich, since GM has tremendous bargaining clout. The real money in the tire business is in replacements for worn-out tires. Uniroyal, which controls 20% of the new tire market, sells only 10% of the replacement tires. That may be a sign that some GM customers don't think much of the tires that come with their cars. Indeed, in 1980 Uniroyal recalled 2 million steel-belted radial tires that the government found to have safety defects. It was the second-largest recall in industry history (after the 1978 recall of 10 million Firestone 500s).

What Uniroyal would really like to do is concentrate on plastics and chemicals. Their chemical division, which makes fungicides and herbicides for farmers as well as rubber and plastic for industry, produced 58% of their profits in 1978 on just 16% of total sales. They also make the vinyl-coated fabric Naugahyde, used in clothing and upholstery.

History. Uniroyal came to life in 1892 as the "rubber trust," a product of the great monopolistic era of American business. Put together by Charles R. Flint, the United States Rubber Company, as it was known then, combined nine of the leading U.S. manufacturers of rubber footwear. With a total of 70% of the market, the companies had little in common other than a desire to restrain competition. It took them 25 years to decide to market all their footwear under the brand name Keds. That same year, 1917, four tire companies that U.S. Rubber had bought began selling their products under the U.S. Royal brand, and by 1940 U.S. Royal controlled 30% of both the new and replacement tire markets. In 1939 U.S. Rubber bought Fisk Tire & Rubber of Chicopee Falls, Massachusetts, and picked up one of the most famous trademarks of the day: the Fisk boy, a yawning lad in pajamas with a candlestick, a tire, and the slogan "Time to Re-tire." In 1967 U.S. Rubber changed their name to Uniroyal.

Where Cars Are Built

American Motors

KENOSHA, WISCONSIN / AMX, Concord, Pacer, Spirit

Chrysler

BELVEDERE, ILLINOIS / Omni, Horizon
*HAMTRAMCK, MICHIGAN / Volare, Aspen
*LYNCH ROAD, DETROIT / Newport, New Yorker, St. Regis
NEWARK, DELAWARE / Volare, Aspen, Diplomat, LeBaron
ST. LOUIS / LeBaron, Diplomat, Caravelle
*MISSOURI / Voyager, Sportsman

Ford Motor

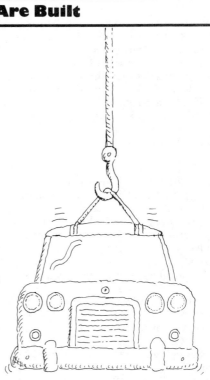

ATLANTA / Ford
CHICAGO / Thunderbird
DEARBORN, MICHIGAN / Mustang, Capri
KANSAS CITY / Fairmont, Zephyr
LORAIN, OHIO / LTD II, Cougar, XR-7, Club Wagon
LOS ANGELES / Ford, Thunderbird
LOUISVILLE, KENTUCKY / Ford
*MAHWAH, NEW JERSEY / Fairmont, Zephyr, Granada, Monarch
METUCHEN, NEW JERSEY / Pinto, Bobcat
ST. LOUIS / Mercury
SAN JOSE, CALIFORNIA / Mustang, Capri
WAYNE, MICHIGAN / Granada, Monarch, Versailles
WIXOM, MICHIGAN / Lincoln, Mark V

General Motors

ARLINGTON, TEXAS / Malibu, Monte Carlo, Cutlass
BALTIMORE / Malibu, Monte Carlo, LeMans
DETROIT / Cadillac, Seville
DORAVILLE, GEORGIA / Malibu, Monte Carlo, Cutlass
FAIRFAX, KANSAS / Buick, Oldsmobile, Pontiac
FLINT, MICHIGAN / LeSabre, Electra, Century, Regal
FRAMINGHAM, MASSACHUSETTS / Century, Cutlass, Regal
FREMONT, CALIFORNIA / Century, Malibu, Monte Carlo, Regal
JANESVILLE, WISCONSIN / Chevrolet
LAKEWOOD, GEORGIA / Chevette
LANSING, MICHIGAN / Cutlass, Oldsmobile
LEEDS, MISSOURI / Malibu, Monte Carlo
LINDEN, NEW JERSEY / Riviera, Toronado, Eldorado
LORDSTOWN, OHIO / Skyhawk, Monza, Starfire, Sunbird
NORWOOD, OHIO / Camaro, Firebird
OKLAHOMA CITY / Nova, Citation, Phoenix
PONTIAC, MICHIGAN / Pontiac, LeMans, Grand Prix
SOUTH GATE, CALIFORNIA / Chevrolet, Cadillac deVille
ST. LOUIS / Chevrolet, Corvette
TARRYTOWN, NEW YORK / Phoenix, Nova/Citation
VAN NUYS, CALIFORNIA / Camaro, Firebird
WILLOW RUN, MICHIGAN / Skylark, Omega, Nova/Citation
WILMINGTON, DELAWARE / Chevette, Acadian

Volkswagen of America

WESTMORELAND, PENNSYLVANIA / Rabbit

Checker Motors

KALAMAZOO, MICHIGAN / Checker

*These plants were shut down in 1980.

Source: *Automotive News*, 1979 Market Data Book.

Since World War II Uniroyal's share of the tire market has dramatically declined, and imported shoes have run Uniroyal out of the footwear business. They sold off the unprofitable Keds operations in 1979. In all, since 1975 Uniroyal has lopped off 28 plants with total sales of $1 billion and trimmed 25,000 employees from the payroll. But stuck with a marginally profitable tire operation, they're still struggling to survive.

Reputation. A giant that hasn't been able to manage their business.

What they own. Five major tire plants in the United States, three of which date back to the 1920s or earlier, and 25 other domestic plants, mostly in the East and the South. Rubber plantations in Indonesia, Malaysia, and Liberia—not for their tires (those are virtually all made from synthetics these days), but for other rubber products.

Who owns and runs the company. Gulf & Western, the New York conglomerate, owns the largest single block of Uniroyal stock (6.1%), which they picked up at the end of 1978 and the beginning of 1979 when the price sank to record lows. The all-white-male board of directors includes the president of General Foods and a former chairman of Colgate-Palmolive. Joseph Flannery, president since 1977, was made chief executive in 1980 and charged with finding a way out of Uniroyal's troubles.

In the public eye. In 1979, after the U.S. Labor Department barred them from federal contracts for allegedly discriminating against women workers, Uniroyal agreed to pay $5.2 million to more than 500 women who claimed they had been discriminated against at Uniroyal's Mishawaka, Indiana rubber-products plant.

Where they're going. With U.S. auto sales dwindling, Uniroyal, heavily dependent on the new-car market, is headed for more trouble. In the next few years Detroit is expected to stop selling new cars with spare tires, which would slash the original equipment business by 20%.

Stock performance. Uniroyal stock bought for $1,000 in 1970 sold for $214 on January 2, 1980.

Access. Middlebury, Connecticut 06749; (203) 573-2000. Uniroyal has a toll-free number for questions and complaints: (800) 221-3333; in New York call (212) 775-1395.

Consumer brands.

Uniroyal, Fisk, Gillette, and Peerless passenger tires.
Coated fabrics: Naugahyde-coated fabrics.

> The 800,000 tons of plastics used annually in U.S. automotive production represent 1/20 of the nation's plastic consumption.

5

HE CASH REGISTER: WHERE WE SHOP

Mass Merchandisers

Sales: $12.9 billion
Profits: $358 million
Forbes 500 rank: 19
Rank in nonfood retailing: 2
Founded: 1897
Employees: 208,500
Headquarters: Troy, Michigan

What they do. "We don't aspire to be a fashion leader," said a K mart official, "but we're fast followers." Fast enough to be this country's second-largest retailing chain, and running hot on the heels of first-place Sears. They operate some 1,500 K mart discount stores, over 300 Kresge variety stores, and 82 Jupiter discount stores in the United States, Canada, and Puerto Rico. The K mart decor has been described as "barren economical." But customers don't seem to mind, and K mart has made their fortune slashing overhead and offering their clientele bargains on everything from TV sets to motor oil to underwear. K mart doesn't issue their own credit cards, but they accept bank cards—which many chain retailers and department stores have resisted.

History. When Sebastian S. Kresge, founder of the S. S. Kresge chain, closed all his stores for an hour on the day Frank Woolworth died in 1919, he was acknowledging his indebtedness to the granddaddy of the five and dime. For Kresge was faithfully treading in Woolworth's footsteps when he took his life's savings and, with J. G. McCrory, bought a Memphis, Tennessee, store in 1897. The partners opened a second store in Detroit a year later. As aggressive then as now, the firm owned 150 dime stores with annual sales of over $12 million when they incorporated in Michigan in 1916 as S. S. Kresge.

Sebastian Kresge was a notorious penny-pincher. According to Waldemar A. Nielsen in *The Big Foundations,* Kresge was married three times, but "his first two wives divorced him, each citing his stinginess as a major complaint. He would wear a pair of shoes until they literally fell apart; when the soles got too thin, he would line them with newspaper. He gave up golf because he could not stand to lose the balls." He explained his hobby of bee-keeping: "My bees always remind me that hard work, thrift, sobriety, and an earnest struggle to live an upright Christian life are the first rungs of the ladder of success."

In the early days of dime stores, the top price was literally 10¢. But World War I inflation prompted Kresge to raise the limit to 15¢, then 25¢, and finally up to $1. The five-and-dime was dissolving into a variety store. But the company kept growing, and when Sebastian Kresge retired as president in 1929 (he remained for some time as chairman), his chain had almost 600 U.S. stores, a Canadian subsidiary, and annual sales of $156 million.

The man credited with creating the highly successful K mart concept is Harry B. Cunningham, who turned from newspaper reporting in Harrisburg, Pennsylvania, to become a Kresge store manager and ultimately president of the company in 1959. Cunningham built the first K mart in 1962 in a Detroit suburb, then proceeded to blitz the country, opening more than a hundred a year, usually as free-standing stores not associated with shopping centers. By the time the founder died in 1966 at age 99, Kresge's sales topped $1 billion, thanks mainly to K mart, which accounted for 162 of the company's 915 stores.

During 1976 Kresge launched an unprecedented 271 K marts—probably the first time in history that a company has opened 17 million square feet of retail space in a single year. The total number of Kresge stores had grown to 1,647, of which 1,206 were K marts. To acknowledge the fact that big discount houses had become the backbone of their business, Kresge's directors recommended to the 1977 annual meeting that the company's name be changed to K mart Corp. What ensued was an emotional debate. Stanley Kresge, the founder's son and a former chairman of the company, rose and told the meeting that he was "not pleased with the change," and he later explained to the *Wall Street Journal*, "We've been successful . . . with the Kresge name, and the company name should relate to the founder." But the directors won the vote in the meeting, 89.4 million shares to 11.3 million.

There's no question, considering the number of discounters who have toppled off the bandwagon in the last decade, that Cunningham's concept is working. In fact, his formula is so successful it has become virtually inviolate. With the exception of size, all K marts are identical: a customer who knows the layout of a store in Melrose Park, Illinois, won't have any trouble finding cameras, cosmetics, or corsets in the

K mart at Redwood City, California. A typical store has between 40,000 and 84,000 square feet, occupies one floor, stands by itself in a high-traffic suburban location, boasts plenty of parking, and is always clean and uncluttered.

Not one to lag behind in the computer age, the company has recently installed KIN, an acronym for K mart Information Network. This system allows stores to speed merchandise directly from distribution centers or suppliers by sending orders through store terminals via a central computer. KIN cuts several days off the order and delivery process, meaning fewer and briefer shortages, higher turnover, and blessedly higher profits.

Reputation. Seen one? You've seen them all. To the customer, they're standardized stores selling good values. It's not surprising if they are sometimes cited as lacking in social consciousness. K mart has no reason to be community-minded. With free-standing stores usually located on a highway between somewhere and somewhere else, K mart is not really part of any community.

What they own. Of the 1,782 stores operated at the beginning of 1978, 1,633 were leased and only 149 were partially or wholly owned, reflecting the company's principle that capital should not be tied up in real estate. There is a K mart chain in Canada and a K mart–owned insurance company, Planned Marketing Associates, based in Dallas. In 1980 the company bought the Texas-based Furr's Cafeterias, the nation's third largest cafeteria chain.

Who owns and runs the company. The largest stockholder is J. P. Morgan & Co., which owns 5.4% of the shares. Next comes the Kresge Foundation, with almost 4%. When Cunningham stepped down as chairman in 1972 (he remains a director and honorary chairman), the scepter was presented to Robert E. Dewar, who resigned in a surprise move in 1979 at age 57, though he remained on the board and became head of the National Retail Merchants Association. Dewar's successor was Bernard M. Fauber, who began as a Kresge trainee in 1941. K mart's 18 directors include one woman, former Congresswoman Martha Griffiths; and one black, banker David Harper, the only board member under 50.

The company sharply stepped up campus recruitment in the early 1970s until they were second only to the U.S. government as the country's largest recruiter of college graduates: at that time they were hiring 1,500 every year for a five- to six-year training program in which everyone started as a stock clerk and graduated as a manager.

Where they're going. K mart surged past J. C. Penney in 1977 to become the nation's second-largest retailer, and now they have a clear and simple goal: to knock off Sears as number 1. Former chairman Dewar predicted in 1979 that that glorious day would come "in the next few years." They aim to open a new store every two or three days in older high-growth suburban areas; they're also planning to go into smaller industrial and agricultural cities throughout the country, carefully fitting the size of the store to the size of the trading area.

Stock performance. K mart stock bought for $1,000 in 1970 sold for $1,310 on January 2, 1980.

Access. 3100 West Big Beaver Road, Troy, Michigan 48084; (313) 643-1000.

Consumer brands.

S. S. Kresge variety stores; K mart discount stores.

> Mail-order sales were nearly $22 billion in 1977. Clothing was the most popular category purchased through the mail, accounting for over $2 billion in sales; it was followed by insurance, at $1.5 billion; magazines at $1 billion; and records and tapes at $600 million.

JCPenney

Sales: $11.3 billion
Profits: $244.0 million
Forbes 500 rank: 24
Rank in retailing: 3
Rank in general merchandise retailing: 3
Founded: 1902
Employees: 206,000
Headquarters: New York, New York

What they do. These things win, said Jim Penney: preparation, hard work, honesty, confidence in people, spirit—and above all, practical application of the Golden Rule. He named his first shop the Golden Rule, and from the time it opened, when he was 27, until he died at 95, he never stopped trying to bring about a merger of profits and ethics. He was pretty good at both.

Penney's stores always emphasized low prices. About 80 years ago the first Golden Rule offered handkerchiefs at a penny each; children's dresses were 19¢; shoes, $1.49; and men's suits, $4.98 to $6.90. Sales that year were $28,898. Today, with sales running to about $30 million a day, Penney still calls attention to their low prices. (Nowadays that can mean $9 for a boy's shirt, $18 for a woman's blouse, or pillowcases at $6.99 a pair—prices mentioned in their 1979 annual report.)

Penney's is traditionally a seller of "soft goods"—mainly clothing and linens. They have long been the nation's largest seller of

James Cash Penney gave his name to one of the great retailing chains in America. A religious man, he made the Golden Rule a guiding principle at his company. He died in 1971 at age 95.

women's hosiery, sheets, blankets, cotton dresses, work clothes, and men's underwear. In 1976, by their own report, they sold enough sneakers to cover the feet of every man, woman, and child in New Jersey. For decades they were glad to be known as the store that sold affordable merchandise under the watchwords "Value, Quality, Service." In 1979 they lengthened that motto by one word: "Fashion." Profits had gone down the year before, and Penney's lost their long-held second position among the nation's retailers (after Sears) to a relative upstart, the K mart discount chain.

Besides the swing to fashion another big shift has been in the making. In 1963 Penney's opened their first "full-line" store, carrying about 70% soft goods (clothing and linens) and 30% items such as appliances, furniture, carpeting, tires, auto accessories, and sports equipment. By 1969 there were 1,441 Penney soft-line stores and 205 full-line. In 1979 the number of soft-line stores had gone down to 1,201, while the full-lines had increased to 482—and those 482 stores rang up 60% of the company's sales.

Penney's (unlike Sears) owns no interest in their suppliers and manufactures nothing. Ten thousand companies from Dallas to Taipei keep the stores filled with merchandise, and about 60% of the items carry the Penney label.

Today there are over 2,000 Penney stores in all 50 states and Puerto Rico. The company also has a few dozen Treasury discount stores, about 335 drug stores (Treasury and Thrift), and a big retail chain in Belgium. And they do a $1 billion mail-order business, still running a strong second to Sears in this department.

History. James Cash Penney was born September 16, 1875, on a farm near Hamilton, Missouri—the seventh of 12 children fathered by an unsalaried, unordained Primitive Baptist minister. Jim had a job as an errand runner by the time he was eight; at 10 he turned businessman. Having saved $2.50 from his errands, he bought some pigs —and got his first dose of how business ethics pays off. The pigs bothered the neighbors, his father said, so they'd have to be sold. They were—at a 2,300% profit. After graduating from high school, Jim Penney grew watermelons. He parked his wagon outside the county fair entrance to sell

them, but his father ordered him home: "Folks selling inside the fair *pay* for the privilege." Jim never forgot these early lessons, report Tom Mahoney and Leonard Sloane in their book *The Great Merchants.*

If the Reverend Penney sometimes questioned his son's methods, he could see the makings of a merchant and in 1895 got him a job at J. M. Hale & Brother dry goods store in Hamilton. Jim worked for $2.27 a month. Three years later his monthly salary was $25, and his father was pleased: "Jim will make it, I like the way he's started out."

Jim was making it, but his health was failing. The doctor ordered him to the drier climate of Denver, where he worked briefly in two stores. Then he moved to the small town of Longmont, Colorado, and opened a butcher shop that failed because he refused to bribe a chef with whisky to get the business of the Longmont Hotel. Flat broke, he went to work for T. M. Callahan and Guy Johnson, who owned several dry goods stores in the area. On the strength of his $50 a month salary, he married Berta Hess in 1899.

Within three years Penney, Callahan, and Johnson were partners in the first Golden Rule Store in Kemmerer, Wyoming. The store was off the main street. Penney insisted on cash-only sales. People said it couldn't work, but Penney was undaunted. He distributed handbills while Berta acted as clerk. They kept the store open from 7 A.M. until late at night. He slashed overhead and prices and gave a money-back guarantee. Impressed with first-year sales of almost $29,000, Callahan and Johnson made Penney a one-third partner in two more Golden Rule Stores, then sold out to him for $30,000 in 1907.

Now the father of two children, Penney revealed an even grander dream: a chain of six stores. "It's shooting for the moon," he told Berta; but he knew he could do it if he had the right men to work with—men of "responsibility . . . with indestructible loyalty" rooted in mutual confidence.

> The average regional shopping mall has at least one leading department store, occupies 30 to 50 acres, and needs a population of 150,000 customers to support its business, according to *Merchandising,* a trade journal.

After interviewing 50 candidates, he found one such man in Earl Corder Sams. Sams, like most top Penney executives, started at the bottom. He began as a clerk for Penney's store in Kemmerer in 1907 and eventually rose to president (in 1917) and chairman of the board (in 1946).

Jim Penney's goal leaped to 25 stores, and he had a novel plan to get them: help store managers to accumulate enough money from their earnings to buy a one-third partnership in a new store. By 1910 Penney had 14 Golden Rule Stores and eight partners (all of whom had started as clerks), and he had set up new headquarters in Salt Lake City.

When the structure appeared to be in place, he wrote in his autobiography, *Fifty Years with the Golden Rule,* "the thought crossed the minds of Mrs. Penney and myself that, eight years after buckling down in Kemmerer, we might with reason allow ourselves a belated wedding trip." They decided on Europe, and took a doctor's advice that Mrs. Penney should have her tonsils out prior to the sea voyage. Walking home from the hospital in the rain to save money, Berta Penney caught pneumonia; she died on December 26, 1910.

Beset by grief for years, Penney plunged even deeper into his work. He opened 20 additional stores in eight western states in rapid succession.

In 1913 Penney and his partners met in Salt Lake City and decided to incorporate under Utah law as the J. C. Penney Company. From the start the company resembled a fraternal organization as much as a corporation. J. C. drafted the "Penney Idea," a seven-point code of business ethics. He invented the Affirmation Ceremony for managers, who swore an Oath of Obligation (later changed to Oath of Affirmation), in which they not only pledged their loyalty to the company but also made a personal commitment to a life of "honesty, integrity, and moral leadership both within and outside the company." Penney would have no employees, only "Associates," trusted people who never had to be bonded. They would wear pins that said "Honesty, Confidence, Service, Cooperation." The J. C. Penney Company would be more than a place to earn money; profits and responsibility would be shared.

A phenomenal expansion ensued. By 1914 the chain had 48 stores and annual sales of $3.5 million. Headquarters moved to New York, the clothing and financial center of the nation. They began to buy whole chains of stores—54 from F. S. Jones and Company, 20 from the Johnson-Stevens Company, 113 from the J. B. Byars and J. N. McCracken companies. By the end of 1929 there were 1,395 Penney stores ringing up an annual $209 million. They listed themselves on the New York Stock Exchange six days before the crash, but even during the Depression expansion continued: in 1933 there were 1,466 stores; in 1941, 1,600. J. C. Penney and his Associates had opened an average of one new store every 10 days for 40 years.

But in the late 1950s the American market changed. William Batten, as assistant to president A. W. Hughes, presented a 150-page merchandising study that precipitated the shift from 96% soft goods to a complete range of personal and household items and an ever-increasing share of income from the hard goods.

Yet more changed than the stock. Salary policy, for one thing. Penney always liked to treat their managers as partners, paying them low salaries but giving them a share in the profits through year-end bonuses. Thus, until 1962 there was a pay ceiling of $10,000 a year, although store managers could usually expect to get at least as much in a year-end bonus. Many of them often had to borrow money to tide them over until the bonus came in. The salary scales have been lifted but incentives tied to profits were retained.

Penney entered the world of multinationals in 1968 by buying the 87-store Sarma chain in Belgium. They instituted credit operations in 1958 (against founder Penney's advice) and in 1962 opened up their nationwide catalog service. (They say their mail-order sales are growing at the rate of 20% a year.) They branched out to new enterprises in the mid-1960s, buying drug store chains and insurance companies, and moved from New York's tacky west side to the 45-story Penney Building (of which they occupy 36 floors) on the Avenue of the Americas. In early 1980 they opened a Wendy's hamburger stand in Brussels, Belgium. Penney has the Wendy's franchise for three other European countries—France, the Netherlands, and Luxembourg. Yet even with the changes the "Penney Idea" still rules, with store managers considered "partners" and employees "associates."

Alabama
WORTH RATLIFF (*Albertville*); LOVEMAN'S OF ALABAMA, THE PARISIAN, PIZITZ (*Birmingham*).

Arizona
JACOME'S, STEINFELD'S (*Tucson*).

Arkansas
THE BOSTON STORE, HUNT DRY GOODS (*Ft. Smith*); M. M. COHN, DILLARD'S (*Little Rock*).

California
MALCOLM BROCK (*Bakersfield*); GOTTSCHALK'S (*Fresno*); H. S. WEBB (*Glendale*); HARRIS'S (*San Bernardino*); WALKER SCOTT (*San Diego*); FORD'S (*Watsonville*); HINSHAW'S (*Whittier*).

Colorado
NEUSTETER'S (*Denver*).

Connecticut
SAGE-ALLEN (*Hartford*); DAVIDSON & LEVENTHAL (*New Britain*); WORTH'S (*Waterbury*).

Georgia
ASHER'S (*Savannah*).

Illinois
ROBESON'S (*Champaign*); CARSON, PIRIE, SCOTT, GOLDBLATT'S (*Chicago*); SPIESS (*Elgin*); BERGNER, SZOLD'S (*Peoria*); MYERS BROS. (*Springfield*).

Indiana
MINAS (*Hammond*); BALL'S (*Muncie*); MEIS BROTHERS (*Terre Haute*).

Iowa
ARMSTRONG'S, KILLIAN (*Cedar Rapids*).

Kentucky
BEN SNYDER (*Louisville*).

Louisiana
GOUDCHAUX'S (*Baton Rouge*); HOLMES, GODCHAUX'S, KRAUSS (*New Orleans*); RUBENSTEIN'S, SELBER BROS. (*Shreveport*).

Maine
PORTEOUS, MITCHELL & BRAUN (*Portland*).

Maryland
HUTZLER'S, BRAGER-GUTMAN (*Baltimore*).

Massachusetts
ENGLAND BROS. (*Pittsfield*); ALBERT STEIGER (*Springfield*); GROVER CRONIN (*Waltham*).

Michigan
CROWLEY, MILNER, HIMELHOCH'S (*Detroit*); STEKETEE'S (*Grand Rapids*); JACOBSON'S (*Jackson*); GILMORE BROS. (*Kalamazoo*); MILLIKEN'S (*Traverse City*).

Minnesota
FANDEL'S, HERBERGER'S (*St. Cloud*).

Mississippi
McRAE'S (*Jackson*).

Missouri
NEWMAN MERCANTILE (*Joplin*).

Montana
HART-ALBIN (*Billings*).

Nebraska
MILLER & PAINE (*Lincoln*); J. L. BRANDEIS & SONS (*Omaha*).

New Hampshire
MARLOW'S (*Manchester*).

New Jersey
MEYER'S (*Paterson*); S. P. DUNHAM (*Trenton*).

New York
MARTIN'S (*Brooklyn*); ADAM, MELDRUM, & ANDERSON, HENS & KELLY, SATTLER'S (*Buffalo*); ISZARD (*Elmira*); ROTHSCHILD BROS. (*Ithaca*); BIGELOW'S (*Jamestown*); MAYS, ALEXANDER'S, B. ALTMAN (*New York*); BRESEE'S (*Oneonta*); CARL CO. (*Schenectady*); ADDIS CO., CHAPPELL (*Syracuse*).

North Carolina
SPAINHOUR'S (*Elkin*); DAVIS (*Winston-Salem*); IVEY'S, BELK'S (*Charlotte*).

North Dakota
HERBST (*Fargo*).

Ohio
CARLISLE-ALLEN (*Ashtabula*); HIGBEE'S (*Cleveland*); SCHOTTENSTEIN'S (*Columbus*); ELDER-BEERMAN (*Dayton*); MARTING BROS. (*Portsmouth*); H. FREEDLANDER (*Wooster*).

Oklahoma
VANDEVER (*Tulsa*).

Oregon
THE HUB (*Coos Bay*).

Pennsylvania
WM. F. GABLE (*Altoona*); ORR'S (*Easton*); A. E. TROUTMAN (*Greensburg*); DEISROTH'S (*Hazleton*); GLOSSER'S, PENN TRAFFIC (*Johnstown*); WATT & SHAND (*Lancaster*); STRAWBRIDGE & CLOTHIER (*Philadelphia*); BOSCOV'S, C. K. WHITNER (*Reading*); OPPENHEIM'S (*Scranton*); HOUTS (*State College*); A. B. WYCKOFF (*Stroudsburg*); FOWLER, DICK, & WALKER (*Wilkes-Barre*); L. L. STEARNS (*Williamsport*); GRUMBACHER'S (*York*).

Department Stores

South Carolina
JAMES L. TAPP (*Columbia*); MEYERS ARNOLD (*Greenville*); AUG. W. SMITH (*Spartanburg*).

South Dakota
FANTLE BROS. (*Yankton*).

Tennessee
PROFFITT'S (*Alcoa*); IRA A. WATSON (*Knoxville*); HARVEY'S (*Nashville*).

Texas
SCARBROUGHS (*Austin*); THE FAIR (*Beaumont*); POPULAR DRY GOODS, THE WHITE HOUSE (*El Paso*); R. E. COX, MONNIG'S, STRIPLING'S (*Ft. Worth*); HEMPHILL-WELLS (*Lubbock*); SAKOWITZ (*Houston*); McCLURKAN'S (*Wichita Falls*).

Utah
AUERBACH'S, ZCMI (*Salt Lake City*).

Vermont
MANN'S (*Brattleboro*).

Virginia
W. S. PEEBLES & CO. (*Lawrenceville*); SMITH & WELTON (*Norfolk*); S. H. HEIRONIMUS (*Roanoke*).

Washington
GOLDEN RULE (*Bellingham*); GARDNER'S (*Walla Walla*).

Washington, D.C.
WOODWARD/LOTHROP.

West Virginia
A. W. COX (*Charleston*); PARSONS-SOUDERS, STONE & THOMAS (*Clarksburg*); ANDERSON NEWCOMB (*Huntington*); DILS BROTHERS(*Parkersburg*); STONE & THOMAS (*Wheeling*).

Wisconsin
SAMUELSON'S (*Eau Claire*); PRANGE'S (*Sheboygan*); T. A. CHAPMAN (*Milwaukee*); QUINLAN'S (*Reedsburg*).

Jim Penney resigned from the board in 1958 but stayed in close touch with the company until his death in 1971, at age 95. From his memento-filled office on the 45th floor of the Penney Building, he kept five full-time secretaries busy as he corresponded with Penney retirees, gave advice to young people, and managed his charitable and religious activities. The moral theme remained dominant to the end. Looking back on his company's long, successful history, he wrote, "Whatever I had to do with its beginning ... has come back to me a hundred-fold in the confidence—and I think I may say, humbly, the love—of my associates. All along the way they have strengthened me with their esteem; the desire to be worthy of them has made me a better man."

Reputation. J. C. Penney has a "good guy" image that may—or may not—stand them in good stead in the age of aggressive discount selling *à la* K mart. They may be the only company in America to employ a consumer advocate. He represents the consumer inside Penney's, checking both advertising and merchandising.

What they own. Besides the U.S. and Belgian stores, they own five catalog distribution centers, 10 insurance companies bearing variations of the Penney name, about $2 billion in merchandise, and $111 million in land. They sell more life insurance by mail than any other company, and they're putting insurance desks in their stores.

Who owns and runs the company. The largest shareholder is Penney's Savings and Profit-sharing Plan, which owns 12% of the stock. About 86,000 associates voluntarily deposit from 2 to 10% of their total earnings each year; the company matches up to 6% of an associate's earnings, depending on the year's profits. The board includes one black, Vernon E. Jordan, Jr., president of the National Urban League; and two women, Juanita M. Kreps, former secretary of Commerce, and Jane C. Pfeiffer, chairman of National Broadcasting Company. Penney's has a vice president in charge of Corporate Responsibility.

In the public eye. Contributions to charity in 1979 came to $4.8 million a year—1.2% of their pretax profits—four-fifths of which came from local stores rather than headquarters. The company sometimes "lends" paid employees to community or government projects. They have a good record on minority employment and economic development. Minorities make up 13% of Penney's work force and now hold more than 8% of management positions. Women fill about 40% of management slots in the company. In 1979 Penney bought $66 million of goods and services from more than 600 minority-owned suppliers, ranking them fifth in this area.

In 1976 three Penney executives were convicted on IRS charges stemming from charges of kickbacks. But Penney's still stands by the policy of trusting associates, pointing out that the total losses over the years have been less than what it would cost to bond employees.

Where they're going. Into fashion. Their Women's Fashion Program was scheduled to reach the racks of all full-line stores by the end of 1980, aimed at the working woman, whom Penney calls "a prime target customer" with a collective income of more than $250 billion. They'll also emphasize sports outfits and equipment and stock more fashionable menswear and home furnishings. They agreed in 1979 to honor Visa cards, to make it easier for you to buy their merchandise. In 1979, 43% of their sales were on credit—up from 37% in 1970.

Stock performance. J. C. Penney stock bought for $1,000 in 1970 sold for $530 on January 2, 1980.

Major employment centers. New York, New York; Milwaukee, Wisconsin; and Atlanta, Georgia.

Access. 1301 Avenue of the Americas, New York, New York 10019; (212) 957-4321.

The New York office regularly schedules tours. Consumers' questions may be sent to the Director of Consumer Affairs at the New York office.

Consumer brands.

J. C. Penney stores and merchandise.

> **Over 14 million people are employed behind counters or by companies that operate stores.**

Sears

Sales: $23.7 billion
Profits: $785.2 million
Forbes 500 rank: 9
Rank in retailing: 1
Rank in auto and homeowners insurance: 2
Founded: 1886
Employees: 424,000
Headquarters: Chicago, Illinois

What they do. The 110-story Sears Tower, the tallest building on earth, lords it over the Chicago skyline just as Sears, Roebuck towers above every other retailing organization in the world. Superlatives come easily when you're talking about Sears. They employ nearly half a million people—that means one of about every 200 employed people in the United States works for Sears. One in three American families has a Sears credit card. The famous Sears catalog, with a circulation of 50 million, has the most widespread distribution of any U.S. publication except the Bible. The Sears Tower alone has a population of 12,000.

But Sears has been hurting since the 1960s, losing big chunks of their markets to other chains, and suffering an identity crisis. After several years of soul searching, executive shuffling, and image shifting, the ailing mammoth has declared ardently and unequivocally that they are marching straight ahead—into the past.

During the 1970s Sears decided, "If you can't beat them, join them." After alternately raising prices to seem more fashionable and then slashing them like a discount house, Sears realized they weren't cut out to be Bloomingdale's or K mart. Sears reaffirmed their traditional commitment to middle-of-the-road merchandising in a five-year-plan unveiled at the end of 1978. "We are not a store for the whimsical or the affluent. We are not an exciting store. We are not a store that *anticipates*. We *reflect* the world of Middle America. And we must all look on what we are, and pronounce it good!"

Franklin D. Roosevelt once suggested that the best way to convince the Kremlin of the superiority of American life would be to dump thousands of Sears catalogs over Russia. He might not have been far off the

Sears, Roebuck was born in this railroad station in North Redwood, Minnesota, in 1886. Richard W. Sears was working there as a station agent. He moved the business to Chicago a year later.

mark. When Nikita Khrushchev and his wife were in San Francisco in 1959, Mrs. Khrushchev eagerly arrived at Sears before the store opened. Once in, she spent $100 on nylons, toys, and baby clothes to take back to the Soviet Union.

You can buy Sears-brand underwear, a Kenmore washing machine, a DieHard auto battery, or a do-it-yourself two-car garage kit at Sears, Roebuck. In fact, the more than 860 Sears stores in 50 states sell just about everything, as Americans know well, since three out of four adults visit Sears at least once a year. But for the first 20 years of their history there weren't any Sears stores: they were a mail-order business. The Sears catalog is still big business—$3½ billions in 1978. Actually there are five catalogs—the big ones (about 1,500 pages and five pounds each) that come out in fall and spring, and smaller ones for summer, winter, and Christmas, plus regional editions and updates. More than 350 million catalogs roll off the presses every year.

Even bigger than the mail-order business

is Allstate, the nation's second-largest insurer of homes and cars. The Allstate Group (which, besides insuring houses, cars, and lives, runs savings and loan associations and offers auto financing and other services) is pushing $5 billion in revenues, and in 1979 it produced 57% of Sears, Roebuck's profits.

International operations—wholly or partly owned retail stores in Canada, Mexico, Spain, and South America—account for 15% of sales. Sears also builds and runs shopping centers through Homart Development Co.

Sears stores carry only their own brands, bought from 12,000 suppliers. They own an interest in companies supplying 24% of their merchandise.

History. CHEAPEST SUPPLY HOUSE ON EARTH was the motto blazoned over a world globe on the cover of the 1894 Sears catalog. The same message was painted large across a five-story building in Chicago, rented by the growing mail-order company in 1895.

General Robert Elkington Wood was quartermaster for the U.S. Army during World War I and then went on to build the largest "quartermaster" organization in the world during three decades at the helm of Sears, Roebuck.

standing collar and black bow tie." Sears was superactive, a brilliant promoter and advertiser who worked from 7 A.M. to 11 P.M. and showed up nearly every morning "with all his pockets bulging with ideas he had scribbled down, advertisements he had written, plans he had outlined." Business boomed. From watches Sears expanded to diamonds (sold on the installment plan), then general jewelry. He opened a branch in Toronto. He published a catalog in 1887 giving the first version of what was to become Sears's famous money-back guarantee. And he based his business success and promotional enthusiasm on sensationally low prices.

In the next few years the business bounced between Chicago and Minneapolis. An 1892 catalog (still devoted almost totally to watches and jewelry) contained 55 pages of excerpts from letters testifying to the quality of Sears products. By September of 1893 the 196-page catalog had added sewing machines, furniture, dishes, clothing, harnesses, saddles, guns, wagons, buggies, bicycles, shoes, baby carriages, and musical instruments. And they had adopted the name that was to stick: Sears, Roebuck & Co. One year later the catalog had expanded to 507 pages, and the company had moved to the then-big Chicago building. Roebuck was intimidated by the deluge of orders, because only after they came in did the peripatetic Sears rush around Chicago finding the goods to fill them. The strain of 16-hour days, 7-day weeks, and wild financial commitments caused an unhealthy Roebuck to sell out to Sears for $25,000 in 1895. (It now takes Sears about 16 seconds to sell $25,000 worth of goods.) Roebuck returned in 1933 as a clerk.

Sears was tall and handsome, exuberant and charismatic, with black hair, a smartly curled moustache, bright, compelling eyes, and a flamboyant manner. But he needed a good manager, and he found one in Julius Rosenwald, a clothing supplier who became one of the key figures in the company's development. Low-profile but extremely effective, Rosenwald organized the business while Sears wrote spectacular ad copy for the catalog and for newspapers and magazines that reached all over rural America. A banker once said Sears could sell a breath of air. One of his famous early schemes became known as "Iowaization." In 1905 he wrote to his best customers in Iowa, asking them each to distribute 24 catalogs among their friends. If the friends

They were afraid the space would be too big for them, but within months it appeared too small. Sears, Roebuck's sales passed three-quarters of a million dollars that year.

The guiding genius was Richard Warren Sears, who in 1886 had been working as a stationmaster and telegraph agent in Redwood, Minnesota. A chance foray into watch peddling was so successful that Sears left his job at the railway station to start the R. W. Sears Watch Co. in Minneapolis. But that city was soon too small time for him, and in 1887 he headed for Chicago. He hired Alvah Roebuck from Indiana as a watch assembler and repairman. The quiet Roebuck is described in *Counters and Catalogues* by Boris Emmet and John E. Jeuck, a history of Sears, as looking like "a bank president or Methodist minister . . . tall . . . thin to emaciation, in a black suit, high

placed orders, Sears sent his original customers premiums—a bicycle, stove, or sewing machine. Catalog circulation, which had been 600,000 in 1902, passed 2 million in 1905. Iowaization spread to other states.

The company's main customers in those days were farmers across the Midwest. Local merchants attacked the catalog, calling the company "Rears and Soreback" or "Shears and Rawbuck," but farmers were won over by Sears's prices, selection, and promotion. By 1908 (the year Rosenwald became president) they had surpassed their nearest competitor—Montgomery Ward—by many millions in sales. And they had established an enormous base of good will, a unique emotional bond with their clientele. *Counters and Catalogues* reports how customers used to write Sears, Roebuck to ask advice on family matters, to report on crop and weather conditions, or just to let the firm know they were getting along all right ("recovered from the accident when the mule kicked me and broke my right arm, so I couldn't write sooner").

Richard Sears abruptly resigned as president in 1908, over a disagreement with Rosenwald, who continued to run the firm until his death in 1932. Rosenwald was remarkable not only for his business skills but also for his idealism. His philanthropies from the start of the century to the time of his death amounted to no less than $63 million, a figure that rose to $75 million by the time his heirs got finished fulfilling his last requests. In the early 1920s Rosenwald sensed that the rural to urban population shift spelled a new direction for Sears: a change in emphasis from mail-order business to retail stores for city dwellers. Stepping up to the chairmanship in 1924, he brought in new executives and in 1928 promoted General Robert Elkington Wood to the presidency to engineer and oversee the new era.

The General (as employees always called him) had been quartermaster for the construction of the Panama Canal, then quartermaster for the Army during World War I, and finally an executive at Montgomery Ward, before joining Sears. He was the single most dominant personality in the company's history. A reactionary (one writer called him a "political Neanderthal"), he headed the isolationist America First organization before World War II. In the 1950s, he was known as a prominent financial backer of Senator Joseph McCarthy. But Wood was a visionary when it came to busi-

The Sears Tower in Chicago—world's tallest building serves as headquarters for the world's largest retailer. At 1,454 feet the Sears Tower is 100 feet taller than New York City's World Trade Center.

ness. Seeing the enormous importance the automobile was gaining in American culture, he decided to locate Sears stores outside cities, in open spaces with plenty of room for parking. In the depths of the Depression he started Allstate to insure cars. With the opening of a retail store in Havana in 1942 Woods began Sears expansion into Latin America and built up chains of stores in the American South and West, where he rightly foresaw the population was going. His retirement in 1954 left a leadership vacuum that was still being felt in the 1970s.

Reputation. Sears had such a secure status as an American institution, and such a good image for serving the public, that when Senator Eugene Talmadge was running for reelection in Georgia, he told the voters they had only three real friends: Jesus Christ, Sears, Roebuck, and Gene Talmadge.

What they own. When Sears sneezes, their suppliers are likely to catch pneumonia. They have substantial investments in numerous companies that supply them with products. They hold between 20% and 50% of some 20 companies. Examples: Sears owns 31% of DeSoto, a Des Plaines, Illinois, manufacturer of paints, detergents, and furniture doing 70% of their $350 million business with Sears; Sears owns 22% of Kellwood, a St. Louis clothing manufacturer doing 74% of their $600 million business with Sears; and Sears owns 40% of Roper, a Kankakee, Illinois, maker of lawn mowers, gas and electric ranges, and chainsaws doing 68% of their $450 million business with Sears.

Who owns and runs the company. Sears has the largest profit-sharing plan in the country, with employees investing a small percentage of their salaries and the company contributing a percentage of profits. The plan invested heavily in Sears, Roebuck stock. As a result, the employee Profit Sharing Fund is the largest owner of Sears stock, holding 21% of all the shares. It used to function as a marvelous retirement benefit for employees, but that was when Sears, Roebuck stock advanced regularly on the New York Stock Exchange. For the last 15 years the stock has been going nowhere—and inflation has therefore eroded the value of the stock and the employee benefit.

Chicago magazine said in 1978 that the people who succeeded General Wood "were gray organization men running a gray organization—consolidators, not innovators." Edward R. Telling, who started with the company as a trainee and worked his way up through the store ranks, was the surprise choice for chairman in 1977. He had been in charge of bringing more centralized controls to Sears; as the *Wall Street Journal* put it, his mission had been "to help gain control of the company's undisciplined operations." In another surprise move, Edward A. Brennan, former head of the Southern territory, was named president in early 1980. At 46, he's the youngest person to hold that title since the 1920s.

In 1975, McKinsey & Co., a leading management consultant, was retained to do a thorough analysis of Sears operations. This study went on throughout 1976. In 1978 Sears hired the director of this study, Phillip J. Purcell, as vice-president in charge of planning. Purcell had been head of McKinsey's Chicago office. Purcell's the author of this statement: "Sears is so big. Until you've been in a huge institution like Sears—or, I suppose, General Motors, or the Defense Department—you cannot understand how big it is."

In the public eye. "I'm glad Sears is taking on someone its own size," joked a businessman when the company sued the U.S. government in January 1979. Sears has had an ongoing battle with the Equal Employment Opportunity Commission since 1973, when the EEOC charged them with discrimination on the basis of race, color, sex, and national origin in their hiring, pay, promotion, and other practices. Sears says they spent millions of dollars providing the commission with evidence that they weren't discriminating against anyone and in fact

"Please Rush..."

Mail-order catalogs, which were rural America's main link to civilization from the late 1800s through the early twentieth century, not only filled a unique social niche but inspired some of the strangest correspondence ever to travel via the U.S. mail.

"Dear Montgomery Ward," wrote a Minnesota woman at the turn of the century. "Do you still sell embalming fluid? I saw it in your old catalogue but not the new one. If you do, send enough for my husband, who is five foot eleven inches tall and weighs 165 pounds when in good health. Henry has been laying around the house looking mighty peaked lately and I expect him to kick off any time now. He liked to have gone last night. When you send the stuff please send instructions with it. Must I pour it down his throat just before he dies, or must I rub it on after he is dead? Please rush."

A Montana rancher actually ordered a wife from Sears, Roebuck. The item was not listed in the catalog, but Sears supplied her indirectly when a young order clerk quit her job and went west to marry the rancher.

More recently Sears got a letter asking: "Can you send me a 'love powder' from your

had a strong commitment to affirmative action and a laudable record of progress since the 1960s. But in 1977 the EEOC found "reasonable cause" to think Sears might be guilty on 74 counts of employment discrimination, including allegations that blacks and Hispanics got lower-paying and less-desirable jobs than whites, and that men were nine times more likely to become managers than women.

When negotiations with the EEOC broke down, amidst rumors that the government was about to file a massive discrimination suit against them, Sears pulled a tactical maneuver that *The Nation* called a legal fraud but a political masterstroke: they filed a class action suit against 10 federal agencies, on behalf of all retailers employing more than 15 people, charging that the laws under which the government was trying to stop discrimination were unfair, confused, and contradictory. Sears became the hero of every employer who feels plagued by government interference. A federal judge dismissed the suit, but later in 1979 the EEOC struck back with suits against Sears in Chicago, New York, Atlanta, Montgomery, and Memphis.

Sears has argued strongly—and publicly—that their record on minority and female employment is a good one. Sears is the second-largest employer of women (after A T & T) in the country, and they now have at least 10 female store managers. More than 30 stores have managers who are members of minority groups. Sears is particularly proud of the progress they have made since 1966. In that year minorities accounted for 8.7% of the total Sears work force; today they account for 20.6%. In 1966 blacks held four-tenths of 1% of the positions classified as "officials and managers"; today they hold 7.4%. Women hold 37% of the positions in the "officials and managers" category.

In 1980 Sears was indicted for conspiracy and filing of false papers with U.S. Customs over a nine-year period to conceal $1.1 million in rebates and kickbacks from Japanese television makers.

In 1978 community groups accused Allstate, the biggest insurer of homes in Chicago, of "redlining," cancelling or refusing to sell insurance to people in certain "poor" areas. The company decided to show their commitment to Chicago by contributing $1 million to the local branch of the Neighborhood Housing Services of America, a non-profit concern formed in 1974 to stimulate reinvestment in urban neighborhoods. Allstate's president called it "a serious investment in the cities where we have been doing business."

Where they're going. Sears isn't sure. Joseph T. Moran, their merchandising chief, said the job of redirecting Sears is comparable to "turning around a battleship in the middle of a river."

In a special report published by the trade magazine *Chain Store Age* in January 1980, Sears was depicted as having lost touch with the younger generation. The magazine interviewed residents of Redwood Falls, Minnesota, a farm town 100 miles from Minneapolis, and found that teenagers there do not shop at the Sears catalog store in town, and when their parents drive them to Minneapolis, where Sears anchors

---

drugstore? I can't keep my man home nights. I've tried everything from buying a television to hiding his pants. It's no use. Please help me. P.S. I do not want to buy in this town."

Mail-order houses have, among other things, sent a tombstone catalog to a lady who complained her husband had "kicked the bucket" due to a "snake oil" cure he purchased from the firm's cata-log; tracked down roaming husbands for customers through their orders; and located a runaway daughter who had "decamped for parts unknown with a low-down, no-account bum."

Although the larger mail-order houses became known for reliability, in the early years of mail-order selling many fly-by-night operators preyed upon a credulous rural populace. One Portland, Maine mail-order shyster advertised a guaranteed cure for slobbering horses. For 50 cents the unfortunate buyer received this advice: "Teach your horse to spit!"

Source: Robert Hendrickson, *The Grand Emporiums* (Stein and Day, 1979).

Woolworth

Sales: $6.8 billion
Profits: $180.0 million
Forbes 500 rank: 53
Rank in nonfood retailing: 4
Founded: 1879
Employees: 203,200
Headquarters: New York City

three malls, they still not do patronize Sears. "Assuming that what happened in Redwood Falls is characteristic," concluded *Chain Store Age*, "then Sears is losing a youth generation, leaving a gap between the child up to say, age 10, and the home-owning parent. The Sears gamble here is that when the teenagers of Redwood Falls form households they will once again patronize Sears."

Stock performance. Sears, Roebuck stock bought for $1,000 in 1970 sold for $529 on January 2, 1980.

Major employment centers. Headquarters Building (Sears Tower) and Catalog Merchandise Distribution Center in Chicago; catalog center in Philadelphia, Pennsylvania.

Access. Chicago, Illinois 60684; (312) 875-2500. Address inquiries and complaints to National Customer Relations, D/731A, Sears Tower.

Consumer brands.

Sears buys their products from many manufacturers, affixing their own brand names. These are the main Sears brands (available only in Sears stores):
Clothing: Junior Bazaar junior clothing; Roebucks western wear; Endurables hose; Cling-Alon leotards; Thumsup and Toughskins jeans; Winnie-the-Pooh children's apparel; Cushion-dri socks.
Automotive: DieHard batteries; Allstate and Roadhandler tires; Muzzler mufflers; Dashmate car radios.
Home appliances and furnishings: Kenmore; Silvertone TV and radio; Craftsman tools; Easy Living paint; Weatherbeater paint; Homart furnaces and plumbing; Open Hearth furniture; Ready-Stick floor tiles; Sears-O-Pedic mattresses; Heat Screen firescreens; Bagzilla trash bags.
Outdoor and entertainment products: Forecast and Courier luggage; Gamefisher fishing motors; Free Spirit bicycles; Ted Williams fishing tackle and guns; Video Arcade video games; Hillary outdoor equipment; Pak-A-Potti portable toilets.

What they do. Woolworth's is the first store many shoppers think of when they're in the market for a pocketbook, a bag of candy, a hair net, a house plant, or a girdle. In a year Woolworth stores sell $25 million worth of knitting yarn, $14 million worth of Timex watches, and $11 million worth of Maybelline eye makeup. They've generally been quick to pick up on fads. When the hula hoop craze swept the country in 1958, Woolworth sold 4 million of them in five months. They pulled off a similar coup with Beatles records and paraphernalia in 1964.

The problem for Woolworth is that the old variety store concept may have had its day. S. S. Kresge, for years a smaller competitor, started pulling out of the variety field in the early 1960s in favor of their discount K mart operation, and in 1970 they passed Woolworth and became the nation's third-largest retailer. W. T. Grant, another major variety store chain, went bankrupt in 1975.

Woolworth runs 1,800 of their traditional variety stores in the United States, but they have no intention of getting stuck with a dying business. Their answer to K mart is called Woolco, a chain of 400 discount stores in 45 cities. They own 2,200 Kinney Shoes stores, the nation's largest shoe chain under one name, which they picked up in 1963. Since 1969 they have owned Richman Brothers, a string of 300 men's and boys' clothing stores (they're called Anderson-Little on the East Coast). The Woolworth and Woolco stores operate 1,900 food outlets, from Woolworth lunch counters to Woolco Red Grille restaurants, serving 1 million customers a day.

Woolworth has 1,000 variety stores in Great Britain, where they have been an institution in working-class life for decades. The British operation produced nearly $2 billion in sales in 1978. They have a strong presence in Canada and Germany, and they have stores in Mexico, Spain, and Australia.

History. When 21-year-old Frank Winfield Woolworth left his parents' farm in 1873 and went to work in Watertown, New York, as an unpaid apprentice clerk in the Augsbury & Moore Corner Store, he couldn't seem to do anything right. He flubbed on filling out sales tickets and making change; he was sent home the first day to put on a white shirt and tie instead of the flannel shirt he'd come to work in; and he fumbled a bolt of cloth, flooding the aisles with calico.

Woolworth's first whiff of success came in 1878, when he helped launch the Corner Store's "5-cent counter," a promotional gimmick that was the inspiration for his own 5 and 10 cent empire. Frank persuaded his boss to lend him $315.41 worth of "Yankee notions," the staples of early American pack peddlers—thimbles, combs, buttonhooks, harmonicas, baby bibs, and the like. His first venture, The Great Five Cent Store, started in Utica, New York, in 1879, failed because of a poor location, but Woolworth opened a new store in Lancaster, Pennsylvania, just ten days later. There he sold toys, police whistles, kitchenware—all for 5 cents or less.

The Lancaster store caught on, and Woolworth upped his price limit to 10 cents. "As soon as we added 10-cent goods to the line," he later wrote, "we took away part of the 5-cent store's charm—the charm of finding only one price on a counter, and only one price in the store. But as long as we kept the 5-cent goods on one side of the store and 10-cent goods on the other, the charm was not entirely lost."

Frank changed the name to Woolworth's 5¢ and 10¢ Store. Branches at Harrisburg and New York folded, but a store opened in 1880 in Scranton, Pennsylvania, took hold, and the Woolworth chain was off. Frank Woolworth admired the red color of A&P grocery stores, and he painted his storefronts the same color, adding the firm's full name in gold letters: F. W. WOOLWORTH Co. By 1895 there were 28 stores,

Profit, Not Sales or Glory

Frank Woolworth believed in the effectiveness of window displays and personally made sure that store managers met his high standards. The following is the text of a letter addressed "To All Store Managers," dated January 14, 1891, and signed, simply, Frank W. Woolworth:

This is the time of year to push soaps, paper, envelopes, tinware, woodenware, music, notions, etc. I hope none of the stores will be foolish enough to place toys in the windows. You can make a handsome 5-cent window of soaps or stationery. A window of 10-cent tinware looks good if properly trimmed.

Glassware and crockery are holiday articles. I am convinced that some of the stores pay too much attention to these goods. Bear in mind, there is not so much profit in these as there is in some other lines. Profit is what we are working for, not sales or glory. I know of a store that does not like to put a line of woodenware in the window as it does not look as nice as crockery. This is not the way to make good profits. Don't be afraid to put goods in the window once in a while that pay a good profit.

We do not care to make a run on box paper that costs over 7 cents each, as it interferes with your line of paper and envelopes that you make a big profit on. Some of the stores have worked up a big trade on paper and envelopes, and some of the stores sell very little of them. This is a fault of yours, and not of the goods. In order to successfully get up a trade on paper and envelopes and hold it, you must make a nice display of them in the window. In the background display a large quantity of envelopes in their boxes neatly arranged with the price "5 cents per pack" marked on.

This is not all. Some time ago I was in one of the stores and their display of envelopes and paper looked awful. The envelopes had the bands broken, and there were some of them tied up with strings and some were loose. It was not necessary to ask if the goods sold well, as it was evident they did not. I asked just the same, and the reply was "No, they don't sell at all, I wish you would not buy any more for us." It was my time to talk then. I ordered all the rotten dirty stuff off the counter, and made a nice display of bright, clean goods. The result was this store has established a big trade on these items. I have done the same thing with the same result in several stores.

and sales were more than $1 million a year. Five years later there were 59 stores and annual sales of more than $5 million. Since the company first sold stock to the public in 1912, they have never failed to pay quarterly dividends to their shareholders.

Frank Woolworth opened his British stores—called Three and Sixpence stores—in 1909, and in 1912 he picked up five other five-and-ten chains in the United States.

The famous Woolworth Building in New York City was completed the next year; at the time it was the tallest in the world. President Woodrow Wilson pressed a telegraph key on April 24, 1913, to light the building for the first time. Called the "Cathedral of Commerce," the 792-foot skyscraper is still Woolworth's corporate headquarters. Frank Woolworth personally paid the $13.5 million construction costs in cash and installed himself in a 24th floor marble office that was a detailed replica of the Empire Room of Napoleon Bonaparte's palace in Compiegne, complete with an oil portrait and life-size bust of Napoleon. When he finished a day's work as the Napoleon of American commerce, he could go home to his 30-room mansion on Fifth Avenue, where he had installed an enormous pipe organ that played great works of music at the flick of a switch and displayed on the wall an illuminated portrait of the composer.

When Woolworth died in 1919, five days short of his 67th birthday, his empire encompassed 1,081 Woolworth stores, with annual sales of $119 million. He left a fortune worth $60 million. A granddaughter, Barbara Hutton, eventually inherited about one-third of the estate and made headlines by marrying Georgian Prince Alexis Mdivani, German Count Court Haugwitz Hardenberg Reventlow, movie star Cary Grant, Lithuanian Prince Igor Troubetzkoy, Dominican playboy Porfirio Rubirosa, German Baron Gottfried von Cramm, and Laotian Prince Doan Vinh Na Champassak.

Woolworth stores opened in Cuba and Germany during the 1920s. In 1932 price levels rose above 10 cents for the first time—after 53 years of business. For a few years 20 cents was the limit, but in 1935 they removed all arbitrary price limits.

In the wake of the great flight to the suburbs after World War II, Woolworth found their downtown stores less profitable and began opening stores in outlying shopping centers. But they were less able to adapt to the boom in discount stores that started in the early 1960s. Woolworth was considerably bigger than the Kresge variety store chain in 1962, but that year Kresge opened their first K mart, in a Detroit suburb. Kresge plunged into discounting, adding K marts at an astonishing clip and phasing out Kresge variety stores. Woolworth had their doubts about discounting, but they saw the need to do something. So they wavered for years between the two forms of retailing, cautiously opening a few Woolco discount stores while enlarging and upgrading their variety stores—which in turn were facing new competition from supermarkets, discounters, and other chain retailers. Woolworth watched helplessly as Kresge zoomed past. By 1975 there were 935 K marts with $6.3 billion in annual sales, while Woolworth had only 253 Woolco stores, with less than $2 billion in sales.

Reputation. Woolworth has the biggest identity crisis in American retailing. Aggressively wedded to the variety store concept at a time when many observers think the variety store is showing few vital signs, but still trying to move into the discount field, Woolworth has left customers wondering just what to expect in a Woolworth store these days. In public, at least, Woolworth remains doggedly optimistic about their main business. The variety store, chairman Edward F. Gibbons insisted to *Business Week* in 1978, is "alive, kicking, and getting better all the time."

What they own. Woolworth owns all the stock in their Canadian, German, Mexican, and Spanish subsidiaries, but they own only 53% of their British operation. They also own Kinney Shoe and the Richman Brothers clothing chain outright. Kinney also has two subdivisions: Susie's Casuals, a string of more than 200 clothing stores selling dresses to the college crowd, and Foot Locker, some 100 stores selling athletic shoes and assorted sporting goods.

Who owns and runs the company. Loews Corporation (whose business combines insurance, cigarettes, and real estate) controls about 2% of Woolworth's stock, and *Business Week* reported in mid-1979 that Loews was trying to raise that figure to 15%. Fred M. Kirby II, chairman of Investors Diversified Services, a Minneapolis-based investment company, owns nearly 2% of the stock in conjunction with his mother, Mrs. Allan P. Kirby. (Fred M. Kirby I owned one of the five-and-dime companies that Frank Woolworth bought in 1912.)

In 1979 Woolworth barely staved off a takeover attempt by Brascan, a Toronto-based holding company. Edward Gibbons, who became chairman in 1978, is the first person to head Woolworth who didn't come up through the stores. He was imported from United Brands in 1973.

In the public eye. Woolworth's has "one of the most systematic and effective affirmative action programs for . . . blacks, Puerto Ricans and other minority groups," according to Tom Mahoney and Leonard Sloane in their book *The Great Merchants.* In the late 1960s Woolworth moved to encourage black ownership of business property by selling their big store and land in Harlem to a community group, and then leasing them back. They also contracted to have the old store torn down and rebuilt by a black-owned construction firm.

Where they're going. Woolworth has been phasing out their smaller stores and concentrating on larger ones. Between 1968 and 1978 they closed down 734 little stores and opened 172 big ones with about the same amount of floor space. It's hard to see much difference between the newer, bigger variety stores and the Woolco discount stores. (On the new variety stores, the traditional red fronts have been replaced with more modern-looking blue ones.) Despite the company's stated support for variety stores, "most observers," according to *Business Week*, "think the company's future rests on its Woolco discount stores."

Stock performance. Woolworth stock bought for $1,000 in 1970 sold for $665 on January 2, 1980.

Major employment centers. New York, New York; Milwaukee, Wisconsin; and Denver, Pennsylvania.

Access. 233 Broadway, New York, New York 10007; (212) 227-1000. The Woolworth Building is open for public tours.

Consumer brands.

Woolworth (variety), Woolco (discount), Kinney Shoes, Susie's Casuals (women's wear), Foot Locker (athletic shoes), Richman Brothers (men's and boys' wear), and Anderson-Little (men's and boys' wear) stores.

Halt! In the Name of the Robot

One day in the not-too-distant future some luckless burglar robbing a store after hours is likely to hear an unearthly voice commanding: "Halt!" Should he try to flee, the thief will become the prey of a seven-foot-tall, 650-pound robot named Century I. Incorruptible, bulletproof, and absolutely dedicated to its mission of tracking down and immobilizing intruders, Century I is virtually impossible to elude. According to *The Grand Emporiums,* the robot is able to sense body heat, sound, or the slightest movement and can chase a suspect at speeds up to 20 miles an hour, disabling him with a jet of laughing gas, a powerful shock, a blinding strobe light, or high-frequency sound that causes intense ear pain. Its creators, Quasar Industries of Rutherford, New Jersey, claim Century I could even be programmed to kill, but the company says it will equip the robot only for "non-lethal restraint."

Except for its $75,000 price tag, Century I could be the answer to many a store manager's dream. As businesses try desperately to stem the $26 billion annual theft of merchandise from retail stores alone, the security industry grows almost as fast as crime does. One research firm predicts that annual sales of "protective services" like guards and electronic anticrime devices will reach $23 billion by 1990—more than triple the present market.

Meanwhile, clients of security services grumble about human guards who are given scant training and paid the minimum wage. Vincent Chisari, a onetime New York police inspector who is now vice-president for security at Republic National Bank of New York, complained to a *Wall Street Journal* reporter: "You tell a guard to watch that plant. 'Don't let it go out of the front door,' but he'll let it go out of the window because you didn't mention the window."

Now, would Century I ever make a mistake like that?

Department Store Operators

Associated Dry Goods

Sales: $1.8 billion
Profits: $44.0 million
Forbes 500 rank: 293
Rank in department stores: 6
Founded: 1826
Employees: 52,100
Headquarters: New York, New York

What they do. The name Associated Dry Goods seems a bit dry for the parent of such ritzy department stores as Lord & Taylor of New York, J. W. Robinson of California, and Goldwaters of Arizona. And Associated's stodginess may in fact be stifling some of the 16 department store groups the company owns.

The organization once characterized by *Forbes* as "the proudest department store chain in America" has gone steadily downhill since its profit-making peak in 1973. Still, the 163 stores that Associated operates rank among the nation's five largest chains. More than half their business is in women's fashions, sold through such stores as Joseph Horne in Pennsylvania, H. & S. Pogue in Ohio, Hahne & Co. in New Jersey, and Stix, Baer & Fuller in the Midwest.

History. Associated's beginnings go back to 1826 in lower Manhattan, where the sailing ships docked and the horse ferry arrived and departed for Brooklyn. This was the location chosen by Samuel Lord and George Washington Taylor for a dry goods store. New York's shopping districts flourished and died in various locations, and Lord & Taylor moved five times before arriving on Fifth Avenue in 1914. That same year Samuel W. Reyburn, a banker from Little Rock, Arkansas, formed Associated Dry Goods out of Lord & Taylor and sev-

eral other financially troubled stores. He became president in 1916, a position he held for 20 years.

But it was Dorothy Shaver who made Lord & Taylor, Associated's flagship, into a great fashion leader in the 1920s and '30s. Shaver came from Arkansas and joined Lord & Taylor in 1924. She always carried a delicate lace handkerchief, but ruled the store with an iron fist, and became the first woman president of a major department store in 1945. She brought American designers out of the obscurity of New York's garment district and into the international limelight. She is credited with innovating the boutique concept of merchandising, later practiced so successfully by Bloomingdale's; introducing the eye-catching Fifth Avenue Lord & Taylor store window; and promoting suburban expansion. She ran Lord & Taylor from behind her Chippendale desk until her death in 1959. In 1979 there were 33 Lord & Taylor stores, concentrated in the Northeast but scattered as far afield as Georgia, Texas, Illinois, and Michigan.

Unfortunately, Shaver's promotional genius did not extend to the parent company. When women went wild over pants, Associated's stores still featured dresses. The business was run like a loose federation of states' rights advocates. "They had a small office on Madison Avenue with maybe a dozen people," a former executive told *Forbes.* "They finally opened a central buying office—but it was 15 years after others did it." Lack of central control and antiquated merchandising techniques are blamed for Associated's steep slide in the 1970s.

Some of the stores have done better than others. In 1979 Associated identified their winners as Lord & Taylor, Sibley, Lindsay & Curr (Rochester, New York), Goldwaters (Arizona), and Pogue's; the losers were Stix,

Baer & Fuller (St. Louis), Joseph Horne (Pittsburgh), Stewart & Co. (Baltimore), and Denver Dry Goods (Denver).

Reputation. One good store (Lord & Taylor) does not a department store chain make.

What they own. Lord & Taylor and Robinson, which account for nearly half of Associated's profits. They also own 14 other department store groups that operate in 24 states and Washington, D.C., and one specialty store in the Midwest. The 189 stores contain 27 million square feet of selling space.

Who owns and runs the company. In 1975 the whole top management turned over. The new chairman was Richard Pivirotto (a former Princeton football player who married into a family that had owned a large chunk of Horne's stock), the new president William Arnold (described by *Forbes* as handsome and personable). Both were long-time Associated executives, and young (45 and 50, respectively) at the time. But the man most people are watching is Joseph Brooks, who in 1975 left Federated (where he was president of thriving Filene's of Boston) to become head of the crucial Lord & Taylor division. *Forbes* characterized Brooks as slick and egotistical. He used to walk into Filene's and hand his keys to the nearest employee to park his car.

The one woman director, Patricia Ann McFate, is the deputy chairman of the National Endowment for the Humanities.

Where they're going. Joe Brooks is hoping that computerized inventory, new staff, and new store branches can put Associated on top. If stores don't measure up, he's expected to axe them.

Stock performance. Associated stock bought for $1,000 in 1970 sold for $495 on January 2, 1980.

Access. 417 Fifth Avenue, New York, New York 10016; (212) 679-8700.

Consumer brands.

Stores: Lord & Taylor; Hahne & Company; William Hengerer; Powers Dry Goods; Stewart & Company; Stewart Dry Goods; J. W. Robinson; The Diamond; Sibley, Lindsey & Curr; Pogue's; Goldwaters; Stix, Baer & Fuller; The Denver Dry Goods; Joseph Horne; J. S. Ayres & Company; Robinson's of Florida; Sycamore Specialty Shops.

History of the Bon Marché — World's First Department Store

The French may dismiss the English as a nation of shopkeepers, but a Parisian couple is credited with the world's first department store.

In the Paris of the 1850s stores carried names like The Lame Devil, The Two Maggots, and The Beautiful Farmer's Wife. But Madame and Monsieur Boucicaut called theirs Bon Marché, actually meaning "cheap."

Everything about the Bon Marché was considered radical by mid-nineteenth-century shopkeepers. French law at one time had forbidden the sale of more than one kind of merchandise in a shop; the respected *Journal des Economistes* denounced the practice of selling stockings and handkerchiefs in the same place as "horrible." But worse than selling a variety of items, Monsieur Boucicaut encouraged browsing, thus tampering with the customer's long-understood moral obligation to buy. Boucicaut even lured customers into his emporium by giving away needles and thread. He did away with the time-honored tradition of haggling for price, and on occasion would put his merchandise on sale. Rather than sell an item for as much as possible, he tried to sell as many items as possible.

Upon Monsieur Boucicaut's death in 1877 his widow sold the business to the store's employees and guided its expansion until her own death 10 years later. After she died, Bon Marché was run cooperatively by its own employees; management was a team of three department heads elected by the store's employees.

Bon Marché remained the "greatest department store in the world" for many years, reaching over $30 million in sales by 1897 and inspiring the legions of retailers to come along next, R. H. Macy, Frank Woolworth, and John Wanamaker among them. The store has slipped somewhat from its world's-greatest position, but it is still in Paris in a much expanded version of its 1876 building designed by French engineer Gustave Eiffel.

Source: Nan Birmingham, *Store*.

Carter Hawley Hale Stores

Sales: $2.4 billion
Profits: $69.7 million
Forbes 500 rank: 218
Rank in department store chains: 4
Rank in booksellers: 2
Founded: 1896
Employees: 54,000
Headquarters: Los Angeles, California

What they do. Until the late 1960s Carter Hawley Hale ran a chain of middle-America-style department stores based mostly in California. But they apparently wanted more snob appeal than their Emporium, Capwell's, or Broadway stores provided, so they took over Bergdorf Goodman of New York, Neiman-Marcus of Texas, and Holt, Renfrew of Canada for a posh image in the late 1960s and early 1970s.

So badly did Carter Hawley Hale want Marshall Field of Chicago that they waited only one day after the sudden death of the store's chairman in 1977 to make an offer. "It was in poor taste," complained the new chairman of Field's, Angelo Arena (who had previously worked for Carter Hawley Hale). The company lost Marshall Field, but in 1978 they gained John Wanamaker's 16 department stores in the greater Philadelphia area and the 26 department stores operated by Thalhimers in southern Virginia and North Carolina.

History. Carter Hawley Hale, one of the largest retailers based west of the Mississippi, grew up in California. The first Hale Bros. department stores opened in 1876 in San Jose and Los Angeles. The first Broadway store was opened in Los Angeles in 1896 by Arthur Letts, an English immigrant. But the two had nothing to do with one another until the second half of the twentieth century. Letts ran The Broadway in Los Angeles. And the Hale brothers —Prentis, Sr., and Marshall—ran their stores in the northern part of the state: San Jose, San Francisco, Oakland, and Sacramento. (Los Angeles was given up early.) They might have continued as small regional stores if not for the arrival of Edward Carter at the helm of The Broadway in 1946. Then 34, he took over three stores

that had annual sales of $30 million as the representative of Blyth & Co., the investment banker that had bought The Broadway from the Letts' estate. Carter expanded first by moving Broadway branches into the Los Angeles suburbs (their 47 stores today constitute the largest department store group in the nation). In 1950 Carter expanded northward by merging with Hale Bros., whose operations included Weinstock's, the largest department store in Sacramento. It was one the ironies of this merger that although the Hale name survived in the corporate title, the stores which carried this name for so many years in the San Francisco Bay Area were not to survive. None is left today.

Carter and his first lieutenant, Philip Hawley, continued to expand (buying other stores) and upgrade (moving from dowdy stores to sleek high-fashion ones). By 1979 they had consolidated 117 department stores, 31 specialty shops, 520 Waldenbooks bookstores (second largest in the country after B. Dalton), and 38 Sunset House mail-order catalogue stores. Hawley likes to point out that they own no bargain stores. "We're probably the only one of the large-scale retailers that doesn't have at least one segment in discounting."

When the chain picked up Neiman-Marcus in 1968, they made only one stipulation: that Dallas-based Neiman-Marcus build more stores. At the time Neiman-Marcus was known throughout the country for the mink and sable coats, diamond-studded pipes, and 24-carat gold hard hats for Texas oil multimillionaires. Neiman-Marcus's first ad in 1907 stated that the store would "give buyers in Texas something out of the commonplace . . . exclusive lines which have never been offered to the buyers of Dallas." So it wasn't surprising when a Texas heiress named Electra Waggoner Wharton Bailey Gilmore once bought $20,000 worth of goods one day and returned the following day to spend another $20,000 for some items she'd forgotten to put on her shopping list. Under Carter Hawley Hale, Neiman-Marcus has opened nine branches from Bal Harbour, Florida, to Beverly Hills, and Chicago.

Bergdorf Goodman, on New York's Fifth Avenue, was considered the leading fashion store in the country when Carter Hawley Hale (still known, at that time, as Broadway-Hale) took it over in 1972. For years the Goodman family lived in a 16-room penthouse apartment above the main store at 58th Street. Under Carter Hawley Hale management, Bergdorf has failed to make a strong profit contribution. In the late 1970s, after extensive remodeling of the Fifth Avenue store to make room for new boutiques, Carter Hawley Hale complimented themselves by saying that the "overall effect of the redesigned second floor has been compared to that created by a stylish woman whose perfection derives from the coordination of beautiful parts that blend to become total elegance."

Reputation. Some analysts fault Carter Hawley Hale for mindless expansion. In 1980 *Forbes* characterized the company as having an "almost limitless fascination with buying up great old retailing names and trying to convert them into profitable businesses." The result has been a company that seems to be going in several different directions at once.

Who owns and runs the company. Hale Bros. Associates owns nearly 4% of the stock—and they're represented on the board by Prentis C. Hale, who was 69 in 1980. Another large stockholder by virtue of selling his company to Carter Hawley Hale is William B. Thalhimer, Jr., who holds 2.8% of all the shares. Edward Carter stepped down as chief executive officer in 1977 when he was 65 (he's still chairman) and was succeeded by Hawley, a former stockbroker who joined The Broadway in 1958. Hawley and Carter have the same academic pedigree: University of California and Harvard Business School.

The company changed their name from Broadway-Hale to Carter Hawley Hale in 1974. Asked why, Carter said the Broadway name, which stands for a "regional and medium-priced department store," was not appropriate for a company into stuff like Bergdorf Goodman and Neiman-Marcus. A competitor, apprised of the name change, said they should be called Ego, Inc.

Where they're going. The company launched an ambitious five-year plan in 1979 that called for $600 million in capital expenditures: roughly 60% for new stores and 40% for modernizing their cash registers and other equipment. They're one company that isn't making the massive move to the suburbs. They're also not actively looking for any more stores to buy,

but if something attractive comes along, they may consider it.

Access. 550 Flower Street, Los Angeles, California 90071; (213) 620-0150.

Consumer brands.

Department stores: The Broadway, Capwell's, The Emporium, Thalhimer's, John Wanamaker, Weinstock's, Bergdorf Goodman, Holt, Renfrew, Neiman-Marcus.
Bookstores: Waldenbooks.
Mail order house: Sunset.

Dayton Hudson Corporation

Sales: $3.4 billion
Profits: $192.1 million
Forbes 500 rank: 139
Rank in nonfood retailers: 7
Rank in booksellers: 1
Founded: 1881
Employees: 35,000
Headquarters: Minneapolis, Minnesota

What they do. Twiggy, the English supermodel of the 1960s, visited only one department store on her 1967 tour of the United States—and it wasn't in New York, Los Angeles, or even Chicago. Would you have guessed Dayton's of Minneapolis? Not many Americans know that the fashion-wise regard Minneapolis as a trend setter. Dayton's, the city's largest department store, was at the head of the pack with the Ivy League look in the '50s, Carnaby Street and Madras in the '60s, and Mao suits long before Nixon went to China. Dayton's is also responsible for building the first enclosed suburban mall in 1956, kicking off a tremendous change in both retailing and American lifestyle.

Dayton's has since merged with Hudson's, an old Detroit department store, to form an umbrella company of nine chains that operate in 44 states. Though not exactly a household name, except perhaps in

Minneapolis and Detroit, Dayton Hudson in 1978 sold quite a lot more for every square foot of store space than any other big retailer. The Dayton ability to spot a trend and capitalize on it now guides Dayton Hudson. Every one of the company's chains is a leader in its realm, a success credited to excellent management and systems like the "plannogram," a master blueprint that charts merchandise and stock location for hundreds of stores simultaneously. The Dayton-Minneapolis influence has spread to such Western stores as Diamond's of Arizona and Nevada, and John A. Brown of Arizona, as well as to the discount chains Lechmere (Massachusetts and New Hampshire) and Target (in the Midwest, Texas, and Rocky Mountain states). Dayton Hudson has bought their way into most of the chains they now own—for example, in 1978 they acquired Mervyn's, a spectacularly profitable medium-priced department store chain in California and the Southwest. But they have also originated two of the most successful chains: Target and B. Dalton bookstores. The hundreds of B. Daltons in 43 states sell more than any other bookseller in the country. B. Dalton, Target, and Mervyn's together account for over half of Dayton Hudson's business.

History. George Draper Dayton stood on a street corner in Minneapolis in 1900 and counted the cars as they went by. Apparently traffic was heavy enough to convince him to buy the land (now the most valuable in Minneapolis) where he started a department store in 1902. Dayton's profession had been banking, but he had a great feel for retailing and public relations. He promoted his new store with free food and slick newspaper ads; one of his masterstrokes was to pelt state fair-goers with a million blue feathers stamped "Dayton's," dropped from an airplane.

Meanwhile, in Ionia, Michigan, a more sober-minded Englishman had started his own department store. In *Old Masters of Retailing*, Philip J. Reilly relates how Joseph Lothian Hudson opened a small dry goods store in 1866 when he was 20, but the business went bankrupt in the crash of 1873. Though legally he could have cleared his debts for 60 cents on the dollar, Hudson eventually paid all his creditors in full, with interest. The virtually unlimited letter of credit he received for his integrity helped him start a store for boys and men in De-

troit in 1881. This time he succeeded, and by the turn of the century Hudson's was the "big store" in Detroit—known for quality and dignity (like the fine old passenger car named after Hudson when he lent money to a struggling young auto company in 1909). Hudson also started, in the early years of this century, the tradition of philanthropy and service that continues to distinguish Dayton Hudson today.

Back in Minneapolis George Dayton continued to run his department store with exuberant showmanship and good business sense until his death in 1938. His five grandsons, who had taken over by 1950, went on doing the same—only more so. They brought in superstars to entertain in the store (one "college night" that packed in 12,000 young people featured a door prize of a live horse). Quickly sensing the importance of the postwar move to the suburbs, they hired a Viennese architect, Victor Gruen, to build a shopping center in Southdale, Minnesota. Gruen enclosed the walkways to guard shoppers from frigid winters and searing summers—and the suburban mall was born. Dayton's branched out to other Minnesota towns. Their marketing philosophy: "everything to everyone," from bargain basement to high fashion.

Three of the grandsons served stints as chairman. Douglas Dayton saw the trend toward discount department stores, and he opened the first Target store in a St. Paul suburb in 1962. Today Dayton Hudson is one of the biggest discounters in the country. His brother Bruce changed the "y" in his last name to "l," and came up with the B. Dalton bookstores. By the late 1960s Kenneth Dayton realized that "family-owned department stores were a dying breed of cat," so the Daytons merged with Hudson's in 1969, getting ready to buy up other department stores instead of being bought themselves.

A melancholy note to this otherwise upbeat story: the venerable Hudson's department store, a Detroit landmark since 1881, has been deteriorating along with that city's downtown area. Though Detroiters can't quite believe it, the huge (2 million square feet) monument is scheduled to be closed by 1982. With its 49 acres of floor space, Hudson's long rivaled Macy's of New York as the world's largest store under one roof (although both have lost out to Marshall Field in recent years). Hudson's is the tallest department store in the world

(25 stories), has the largest flag anywhere (each star is 5½ feet high), and the tallest flagpole in Detroit. Hudson's, like Macy's, throws a huge Thanksgiving Day Parade, with 25 floats, 1,000 marchers, and over a dozen bands. Hudson's 500 trucks deliver 8 million packages a year.

Reputation. Dayton Hudson's corporate symbol is the amaranth, a flower that, according to Greek myth, never fades, only changes.

What they own. Fifteen Hudson's, 15 Dayton's, 9 Diamond's, 51 Mervyn's, and 5 John A. Brown department stores, as well as 67 Target and 6 Lechmere discount stores. The company also owns 357 B. Dalton and Pickwick bookstores; and 45 fine jewelry stores under the names Caldwell, J. B. Hudson, Jessop, Peacock, Shreve, and Warren.

Who owns and runs the company. The five Dayton brothers have owned 30% of the company since they sold stock to the public in 1966, but only Bruce and Kenneth Dayton now sit on the board. Kenneth Dayton stepped down from the chairmanship in 1977, while in his mid-fifties. The new leaders have been handpicked by the Daytons. Chairman William Andres started out selling budget bathrobes at Dayton's in 1958; by 1966 he was a vice-president. Stephen Pistner, who became president in 1977 at age 45, is known to work 65-hour weeks, flying around the country in the Dayton Hudson jet, visiting stores, snapping pictures, and tape recording talks with managers and customers. In 1978 the average age of the men who headed the company's 11 divisions was 48. B. Dalton's chairman was 40; the head of the $1.1 billion Target chain was 39.

Besides the brothers, the most significant stockholder is Mervyn Morris, founder of the Mervyn's chain; he owns 5% of the stock.

In the public eye. Dayton Hudson's commitment to public service led them to dispense $7.9 million to the arts and social welfare projects in 1978. They publish regular, comprehensive reports on "Community Giving." Projects supported in 1978 included a refurbishing of inner-city neighborhoods, a house for battered wives, bilingual legal assistance centers, wilderness summers for minority kids, and a wide vari-

THE TEN MOST SHOPLIFTED DEPARTMENTS

According to the FBI, retailers lost $8 billion from shoplifting in 1979. These are the most loss-prone departments in stores grossing over $1 million per year:

Losses as Percentage of Sales

SMALL LEATHER GOODS	6.5%
WOMEN'S AND MISSES SUITS	5.9%
COSTUME JEWELRY	5.4%
JUNIOR DRESSES	5.3%
MEN'S ACCESSORIES	5.1%
SPORTING GOODS	5.0%
JEWELRY AND WATCHES	4.5%
MISSES DRESSES	3.4%
SIX-FOOT SHOP	3.3%
FOUNDATIONS (*bras, girdles, etc.*)	3.2%

Source: *Chain Store Age Executive*, April 1980.

ety of artistic and cultural endeavors. They are one of the few big corporations to take the full 5% tax deduction allowed for charitable contributions. (By law, companies can contribute up to 5% of their pretax profits to charities and deduct that amount from their taxable income. Since the tax rate on corporate profits is close to 50%, this means that each dollar a company contributes really costs them only about 50¢.) Dayton Hudson has inspired a "5% Club" around Minneapolis, where Kenneth Dayton has enthusiastically convinced a number of companies to contribute the full 5% to worthy causes. He calls it the "5% solution" to social ills.

Where they're going "We're betting on our winners," says William Andres. In 1978 Dayton Hudson unveiled a five-year plan that involved roughly doubling the number of Mervyn's, B. Dalton, and Target stores. Department stores are growing too, though at a slower pace. The Daytons clearly chose their course when they merged with Hudson in 1969. They will probably pick up more department stores in the '80s.

Stock performance. Dayton Hudson stock bought for $1,000 in 1970 sold for $1,228 on January 2, 1980.

Major employment centers. Minneapolis, Minnesota; Detroit, Michigan; and Hayward, California.

Access: 777 Nicollet Mall, Minneapolis, Minnesota 55402; (612) 370-6948.

Consumer brands.

Department stores: Dayton's; Hudson's; Diamonds; John A. Brown; Mervyn's.
Discount stores: Target; Lechmere's.
Bookstores: B. Dalton; Pickwick.
Jewelry stores: J. E. Caldwell; J. B. Hudson; J. Jessop and Sons; C. D. Peacock; Shreve's; Charles W. Warren.

Federated Department Stores

Sales: $5.8 billion
Profits: $203.2 million
Forbes 500 rank: 66
Rank in department stores chains: 1
Founded: 1851
Employees: 117,151
Headquarters: Cincinnati, Ohio

What they do. Federated is the Jewish mother of American retailing. Like her stereotypical counterpart in the kitchen, she is content to bustle about in the corporate office, insisting only that her children keep control of their inventories as she offers advice on how to fatten up their bottom lines. She doesn't expect recognition for herself but does have a fierce interest in the success of her family.

And the 19 groups of Federated are successful. Each is usually a leader in its own geographical area, catering to middle- and upper-income customers across the country. Most of Federated's offspring are respected old department stores that date from before 1910: Abraham & Straus of Brooklyn, Bloomingdale's of New York, Boston Store of Milwaukee, Bullock's of

Los Angeles and Northern California, Burdine's of Miami, Filene's of Boston, I. Magnin of San Francisco, Foley's of Houston, Sanger-Harris of Dallas, Goldsmith's of Memphis, Lazarus of Ohio, Levy's of Tucson, Rich's of Atlanta, Rike's of Dayton, Shillito's of Cincinnati. There are also a few youngsters in the Federated family: Gold Circle discount stores of Ohio and Gold Triangle appliance and sporting goods of Florida. Ralphs, Federated's only food stores, claim to have more automated checkout stands than any of their competitors on the West Coast.

The 340 stores of Federated fill the equivalent of 22 Empire State Buildings with dresses, jewelry, underwear, Cuisinarts, track shoes, and thousands of items for work, relaxation, or an elegant night on the town.

Mother Federated encourages all her children to develop their own personality, style, and merchandise. She knows that the new wave sunglasses Bloomingdale's pushes in New York would be considered a poor joke at Rike's in Dayton. As long as the store sells well, Mama stays in the background, and the stores operate as if their own management was the ultimate authority.

History. It was actually a Jewish father who started the store that became the anchor of the Federated chain. Simon Lazarus emigrated from Germany in 1850 because of the Jewish segregation laws of 1848. He opened a one-room men's clothing store in Columbus, Ohio, in 1851, and from that base he and his family built the leading retail emporium in southern Ohio: the Lazarus department store. In 1928, when his grandsons were running the store, they bought an even older store, Shillito's of Cincinnati. Shillito's began selling dry goods in downtown Cincinnati in 1830, but according to the current biographers at Federated, by 1928 "the store had lost touch with its customers and had fallen from first to fourth in sales volume in the city." The Lazarus boys got Shillito's back in first place by 1937.

In 1929, they made an even bigger move. Fred Lazarus, Jr., went cruising on a yacht in Long Island Sound. His companions: the yacht's owner, S. F. Rothschild, president of Abraham & Straus in Brooklyn; Louis Kirstein, who ran Filene's of Boston; and Samuel Bloomingdale. Their alliance was sealed on that yacht, and Federated Department Stores was born.

The next store to join the team was Foley's, the biggest department store in Houston; they were purchased in 1945. Subsequent additions were rapid: Boston Store (1948), Burdine's and Goldsmith's (1957), Rike's (1959), Bullock's (1964), and Rich's, the largest department store in Atlanta (1976). All the stores that became part of Federated have histories of their own. Many were founded, as Lazarus was, by Jewish immigrants from Europe.

Morris Rich, a peddler who made his way from Hungary to Georgia in the 1860's, was one of those pioneer retailers. He had to put planks across the red clay mud to encourage customers into his first store in Atlanta which was still recovering from the Civil War (it had been leveled just two years before). Today Southerners are as chauvinistic about Rich's as they are about *Gone with the Wind*. During the Depression, when Atlanta could not pay its schoolteachers, Rich's cashed the city's worthless checks at full value for the teachers, no purchase necessary. Federated paid their entire 1975 earnings, $157 million, to acquire Rich's, the belle of southern retailing. It was the end of another family-owned operation.

Not to be left out of the early chronicles is the Golden Lady of the West, I. Magnin and Company. In 1870 Mary Ann Magnin, with eight children and an eye for *peau de soie* fabric, traveled with her husband and family from London around the Horn to San Francisco. Isaac took a job as a wood carver at Gump's, and Mary Ann, an accomplished seamstress, made fine baby clothes at home. At her insistence Isaac quit Gump's and sold clothes from a pack on his back. Mary Ann opened her first store in 1876 and named it after her husband. Her needlework soon included elegant blouses and bridal trousseaus. She did her own purchasing and supervised garment cutting, sewing, and alterations, while taking care of her family and teaching her sons accounting and the difference between *moire* and *pongee*.

Going Out of Business? Call Sam Nassi

Sam Nassi's business was bad. He'd spent the 1960s building one White Front discount store into a 37-store mini-empire, but by the early seventies his promotion wasn't working, and the stores were limping along. Nassi had to sell. He did the job himself, closing down store after store with the help of a professional, dismantling the business, and selling merchandise at a generous markdown. And surprise! His commission on the closeout sales—the work of a few weeks—was better than twice his annual salary as a White Front executive. Apparently closing stores was a business in itself. Nassi has been closing them ever since.

"I was 50 years old and faced with a situation where I had no job. Then I discovered that closing stores paid a lot better than opening stores," Nassi told the *New York Times*. Since 1971 he has bid for and taken more than $2 billion in unwanted retail goods off the hands of such merchandisers as Max Factor, Lehigh Valley Industries, W. T. Grant, and the Franklin Simon stores. The Sam Nassi Company, now a three-man partnership, reckons they do about 80% of the retail liquidations in the United States.

Nassi knows how to sell merchandise that a store can't move. His most noted success was the 1975 closeout of W. T. Grant, the biggest bankruptcy in retailing history. Nassi sold off the goods for $600 million. "I got Grant $400 million more than they had expected to get. They had figures that self-liquidation would get them about 18 cents to maybe 24 cents on the dollar. I said that until I got them 36 cents, I would get nothing as a commission. I got them over 50 cents on the dollar."

Nassi sold Grant's wares with a big advertising campaign and a well-publicized auction. The sale took five weeks, and Nassi took home a commission check for $7 million.

"There is some skill involved in doing a liquidation right," he says. "I need my people to see that the finishing touches are there, to keep the atmosphere right. My people know how to shrink the stores so that the goods have an appetizing look even on the last days of the sale."

Nassi's deals are usually made with ready cash. He says he likes to buy, get in and out and on to the next deal. A typical Nassi liquidation takes about four weeks.

But dealing with Nassi doesn't always mean going out of business. A chain store might liquidate some of its outlets in an effort to keep others prospering, as in the case of the 20 Globes Discount stores, which Nassi liquidated for Walgreen. "Wall Street heard we were negotiating with Walgreen's," says Nassi, "and the stock jumped."

By 1900 Mary Ann had practically retired, but kept an active role in policy decisions. I. Magnin was established as the provider of post–Gold Rush luxury. Even after retirement, however, she had her chauffeur drive her 2½ blocks from her home in the St. Francis Hotel to the store, where she made her daily rounds. In later years her maid pushed her up and down the aisles in a wheelchair, and she is reputed to have come to the store near the end of her life by ambulance and stretcher. I. Magnin was the first California store to see the selling potential of branches, and they opened their first one in Los Angeles in 1893. They were bought in 1944 by Bullock's, which became part of Federated in 1964.

Filene's, one of the charter members of Federated, operates what is probably the most famous bargain basement in all of retailing. Their store in downtown Boston puts goods in the basement and slashes prices 25% every 10 days until they are sold. What is unsold goes to charity.

Bloomingdale's, the trendiest store in the Federated family, had started out in 1872 as a good neighbor to the conservative middle-class families of Third Avenue and 59th Street in Manhattan. After World War II Bloomingdale's went after a chic image, and became a fashion pacesetter. It is now the store that Lee Radziwill, sister of Jackie Onassis and princess-by-marriage, describes as "the obvious place to go for everything." Anything that has made a splash in American department stores in the last 20 years was probably first tried out at Bloomingdale's. Bloomie's influence has been preserved on celluloid by a scene from *Annie Hall.* "Sometimes I wonder how I would stand up to torture," muses Diane Keaton. "You?" Woody Allen retorts. "The Gestapo would take away your Bloomingdale's charge card and you'd tell them everything."

Despite a tradition of autonomy for store divisions, the mother in Cincinnati knows how to lay down the law. In a 15-month period during 1978 and 1979 headquarters changed the managements of 10 store divisions. Abraham & Straus, with its big store in downtown Brooklyn (with 1.6 million square feet of floor space, it's the biggest store Federated has), is known to be one of the laggards, as are the Boston Store in Milwaukee, Rike's in Dayton, and the Bullock's stores in northern California. Federated measures their results by how much profit they make on a dollar of sales. In the early 1970s they were making 4¢ on each dollar. Now they're down to 3½ ¢.

Reputation. Both flexible and tough; known for decades, according to the *New York Times,* as "the best-managed retail chain in the country."

What they own. In 1979 Federated had 340 stores in 25 states, with almost 50 million square feet of selling space. The top-selling stores in 1979 were Ralphs ($882 million), Bloomingdale's ($518 million), and Abraham & Straus ($512 million).

TOP TEN DEPARTMENT STORES

Annual Sales

1. MACY'S (*New York*)	$650 *million*
2. HUDSON'S (*Detroit*)	$644 *million*
3. BROADWAY (*Los Angeles*)	$620 *million*
4. BAMBERGER'S (*New Jersey*)	$600 *million*
5. MAY CO. (*California*)	$575 *million*
6. MARSHALL FIELD (*Chicago*)	$490 *million*
7. BLOOMINGDALE'S (*New York City*)	$485 *million*
8. ABRAHAM & STRAUS (*Brooklyn*)	$475 *million*
9. BULLOCK'S (*Los Angeles*)	$460 *million*
10. MACY'S (*California*)	$425 *million*

Source: *Stores,* July 1979.

1979 RETAIL CLOTHING PRICES AND SALES

Type of Store/Average Cost of An Item of Women's Clothing/Total No. of Items

SPECIALTY STORES $19.86 / 631 *million*
DEPARTMENT STORES $18.71 / 867 *million*
SEARS, PENNEY & WARD (*mail order*) $12.26 / 133 *million*
SEARS, PENNEY & WARD (*retail*) $12.23 / 554 *million*
DISCOUNTERS (*Alexanders, Caldor, Korvettes, etc.*) $10.70 / 1.09 *billion*
VARIETY STORES $7.29 / 176 *million*

Source: *Chain Store Age,* General Merchandise Edition, March 1980.

Who owns and runs the company. Chairman Ralph Lazarus, whose father Fred started the Federated group in 1930, is described as the sort who will learn the first names of everyone in a store he is about to visit, down to third-level management. "You may not see him for a year," says a colleague, "but he'll call you by your first name. Which is not to say he isn't tough. He didn't get where he is by being a sweetheart." For most of the 1970s Lazarus worked in tandem with president Harold Krensky, who retired in early 1980. Howard Goldfeder, the new president, started as a Bloomingdale's trainee in 1947 (as did Krensky) and eventually became head of Bullock's of California (with a break during which he left Federated and served as president of the May Co.).

Two other members of the Lazarus family (Maurice and Charles) are on the board, which also includes Coca-Cola chairman J. Paul Austin and Dr. Jerome Heartwell Holland, the one black director and a former U.S. ambassador to Sweden. Kathryn Wriston, a lawyer, is the only woman on the board, although two other women serve as vice-presidents of the company.

In the public eye. Department stores have traditionally hired large numbers of women, whom they paid peanuts. In the past these women have put up with paternalism and exploitation. P. G. Winett, cofounder of Bullock's in 1903, was a "great fannypatter . . . always pinching the girls." Women now total 81% of Federated's salesclerks and 48% of the managers and professionals, although they don't seem to be promoted much into top executive levels. About 20% of Federated's employees are minorities, who work mostly as clerks, craftsmen, and technicians.

Stock performance. Federated stock bought for $1,000 in 1970 sold for $746 on January 2, 1980.

Access. 7 West Seventh Street, Cincinnati, Ohio 45202; (513) 579-7000.

Consumer brands.

Abraham and Straus, Bloomingdale's, Boston Store, Bullock's, Burdines, Filene's, Foley's, Goldsmith's, Lazarus, Levy's, I. Magnin, Rich's, Rike's, Sanger-Harris, Shillito's, Gold Circle, Gold Triangle, Richway, and Ralphs stores.

MACY∗S

Sales: $2.1 billion
Profits: $85.8 million
Forbes 500 rank: 243
Rank in department store chains: 5
Rank in store size: 2
Founded: 1858
Employees: 44,000
Headquarters: New York, New York

What they do. Where else but New York City could Jewish immigrants buy a department store founded by a Yankee Quaker that has sold silk to a harem, plumbing fixtures to the Liberian presidential palace, and cowboy suits to a chimpanzee named Kokomo? The store is R. H. Macy and Company, and if you can't find what you want on one of the store's eleven floors covering an entire city block on 34th Street at Herald Square, it may not exist.

Under five generations of the Straus family, Macy's has become the fifth-largest department store chain in the nation. Their 83 stores in ten states throughout the country are located in both downtown areas and suburban malls. Some of the branches, like the profitable California division, have taught their venerable parent a merchandising trick or two. But the heart of the Macy's empire is still New York.

The Herald Square store may no longer be, as they claimed for years, "the world's largest store under one roof" (Chicago's Marshall Field now holds that distinction), but they do ring up more sales than any other store in the world. Over 300,000 customers a day pass through the store at Christmastime; behind the counters they have had such salespeople as Burgess Meredith, Carol Channing, Butterfly McQueen, Garson Kanin, Shirley Jackson (who wrote a short story about the experience), and Jimmy Walker, once mayor of New York City.

Several babies have been born in the store, including one girl whose middle name became Macy. New Yorkers sprinkle their speech with such Macyisms as "Does Macy's tell Gimbel's?" (which means, you can trust me to keep a secret) and "I'd rather work in Macy's basement" (another way of saying I'd rather die), although the conversion of the basement to the cellar has

Where We Shop: The Top 100

Annual Sales

1. SEARS (864 stores) $17,514 *million*
2. K MART (2,069) $13,304 *million*
   K MART (1,688) $12,922 *million*
   KRESGE (381) $482 *million*
3. J. C.PENNEY (2,145) $11,274 *million*
   TREASURY (34) $418 *million*
4. F. W. WOOLWORTH (4,647) $6,785 *million*
   U.S. WOOLCO (312) $1,895 *million*
   U.S. WOOLWORTH (1,371) $1,645 *million*
5. MONTGOMERY WARD (419) $5,251 *million*
   JEFFERSON STORES (21) $248 *million*
6. FEDERATED DEPARTMENT
   STORES (245) $4,923 *million*
   BLOOMINGDALE'S (15) $518 *million*
   ABRAHAM & STRAUS (11) $512 *million*
   FOLEY'S (10) $412 *million*
   BURDINES (17) $407 *million*
   BULLOCK'S (*L.A.*) (22) $405 *million*
   GOLD CIRCLE (42) $388 *million*
   RICH'S (15) $329 *million*
   LAZARUS (16) $325 *million*
   FILENE'S (15) $268 *million*
   SANGER-HARRIS (11) $241 *million*
   SHILLITO'S (9) $212 *million*
   I. MAGNIN (24) $206 *million*
   RICHWAY (18) $205 *million*
   RIKE'S (5) $123 *million*
   GOLDSMITH'S (4) $112 *million*
   BOSTON STORES (6) $99 *million*
   BULLOCK'S (*North*) (5) $75 *million*
7. DAYTON HUDSON (661) $3,385 *million*
   TARGET (80) $1,121 *million*
   MERVYN'S (60) $656 *million*
   HUDSON'S (16) $652 *million*
   DAYTON'S (15) $357 *million*
   LECHMERE (6) $177 *million*
   DIAMONDS (9) $116 *million*
   JOHN A. BROWN (5) $49 *million*
8. MAY DEPARTMENT STORES (173) $2,957 *million*
   VENTURE (45) $536 *million*
   MAY CO. (*California*) (29) $501 *million*
   HECHT CO. (20) $316 *million*
   FAMOUS BARR (12) $303 *million*
   KAUFMANN'S (10) $254 *million*
   MAY CO. (*Cleveland*) (6) $207 *million*
   MEIER & FRANK (6) $148 *million*
   G. FOX (7) $145 *million*
   O'NEILL'S (10) $122 *million*
   MAY-DNF (9) $99 *million*
   STROUSS (9) $75 *million*
   MAY-COHENS (6) $42 *million*
9. CITY PRODUCTS (4,617) $2,445 *million*
   TG & Y (935) $1,486 *million*
   BEN FRANKLIN (1,920) $840 *million*
10. CARTER HAWLEY HALE (147) $2,408 *million*
    THE BROADWAY (49) $719 *million*
    EMPORIUM-CAPWELL (18) $398 *million*
    JOHN WANAMAKER (16) $328 *million*
    NEIMAN-MARCUS (12) $277 *million*
    THALHIMER (23) $166 *million*
    WEINSTOCK'S (10) $148 *million*
11. ALLIED STORES (216) $2,210 *million*
    JORDAN MARSH (*N. E.*) (14) $373 *million*
    JOSKE'S (27) $286 *million*
    BON MARCHE (27) $279 *million*
    MASS BROS. (18) $252 *million*
    JORDAN MARSH (*Florida*) (12) $176 *million*

POMEROY'S (14) $119 *million*
STERN'S (7) $112 *million*
DONALDSON'S (10) $98 *million*
GERTZ (5) $92 *million*
BONWIT TELLER (12) $84 *million*
BLOCK'S (8) $78 *million*
READ'S (5) $72 *million*
CAIN-SLOANE (4) $56 *million*
TROUTMAN'S (8) $39 *million*
DEY BROS. (4) $38 *million*
PLYMOUTH (31) $33 *million*
12. R.H. MACY (83) $2,058 *million*
    MACY'S (*New York*) (15) $717 *million*
    BAMBERGER'S (21) $577 *million*
    MACY'S (*California*) (17) $470 *million*
    DAVISON'S (11) $142 *million*
    MACY'S (*Kansas City*) (12) $105 *million*
    LaSALLE'S (7) $49 *million*
13. GAMBLE-SKOGME (3,283) $2,053 *million*
14. ASSOCIATED DRY GOODS (162) $1,783 *million*
    LORD & TAYLOR (34) $426 *million*
    J. W. ROBINSON (18) $250 *million*
    STIX BAER & FULLER (14) $199 *million*
    JOSEPH HORNE (13) $188 *million*
    L. S. AYER'S (12) $121 *million*
    SIBLEY'S (9) $114 *million*
    DENVER DRY GOODS (13) $99 *million*
    STEWART'S (*Maryland*) (5) $69 *million*
    POGUE'S (5) $56 *million*
    STEWART'S (*Kentucky*) (7) $53 *million*
    GOLDWATERS (6) $49 *million*
    ROBINSON'S (*Florida*) (7) $45 *million*
    POWER'S (7) $40 *million*
    HAHNE (7) $29 *million*
    WM. HENGERER (5) $24 *million*
15. WAL-MART (276) $1,248 *million*
16. GIMBEL-SAKS FIFTH AVENUE (69) $1,190 *million*
    SAKS (31) $532 *million*
    GIMBELS-NEW YORK (10) $228 *million*
    GIMBELS-MILWAUKEE (12) $154 *million*
    GIMBELS-PHILADELPHIA (10) $135 *million*
    GIMBELS-PITTSBURGH (6) $134 *million*
17. BELK STORES (380) $1,125 *million*
18. MERCANTILE STORES (84) $1,068 *million*
19. FRED MEYER (63) $1,060 *million*
20. MARSHALL FIELD (60) $904 *million*
    MARSHALL FIELD (*Chicago*) (17) $557 *million*
    FREDERICK & NELSON (13) $148 *million*
    HALLE'S (9) $76 *million*
21. G. C. MURPHY (467) $757 *million*
22. SCOA INDUSTRIES (*Hills*) (209) $623 *million*
23. McCRORY (715) $593 *million*
24. CARSON PIRIE SCOTT (26) $434 *million*
25. ROSE'S (227) $498 *million*
26. GARFINCKEL'S (207) $420 *million*
27. DILLARD'S (44) $391 *million*
28. STRAWBRIDGE & CLOTHIER (24) $365 *million*
    CLOVER (13) $115 *million*
29. NORDSTROM'S (29) $346 *million*
30. AMES DEPARTMENT STORES (135) $322 *million*
31. GOLDBLATT'S (45) $306 *million*
32. KUHN'S-BIG K (116) $298 *million*
33. WOODWARD & LOTHROP (14) $295 *million*
34. CITY STORES (70) $283 *million*
35. OUTLET CO. (167) $266 *million*
36. C. R. ANTHONY (310) $262 *million*
37. LIBERTY HOUSE (*AMFAC*) (45) $258 *million*

Reprinted with permission from *Chain Store Age*, General Merchandise edition, June 1980. Copyright
Lebhor-Friedman, Inc., 425 Park Avenue, New York, New York, June 1980.

retired that cliché. Millions of Americans watch the annual live or telecast version of the Macy's Thanksgiving Day Parade, a New York event since 1924. "The Miracle on 34th Street," a popular old film inspired by Macy's Christmas Santas, is shown on television year after year. And if you appreciate an Idaho baked potato, you can thank Macy's. They popularized Idaho as the spud state in 1926, and they've got a thank-you letter from the governor of Idaho to prove it.

Yet this Mecca of merchandising started out inauspiciously as the seventh attempt at retailing by a six-time loser.

History. Rowland Hussey Macy's family had lived on Nantucket Island, Massachusetts, for eight generations by the time he was born in 1822. At age 15 he shipped out to sea on a whaler, where he was tatooed with a red star that was later adopted as a trademark for Macy's. On his return Macy opened the first of his doomed dry goods stores in Boston; two years later he wrote the final entry in his account book: "I have worked two years for nothing. Damn, Damn, Damn, Damn." Macy tried his luck as a forty-niner in California, and in six other retail ventures that all failed. Why he made another attempt, and how he convinced someone to lend a man with his record $20,000, is a mystery. But the store he established in lower Manhattan (on 14th Street near Union Square) in 1858 took off.

Rowland Macy had an uncontrollable temper (later cured at a Moody and Sankey revival), an ulcer, and a severe case of stinginess; but he also had a flair for advertising and the ability to hire the right people.

Much of the store's success after 1860 must be credited to Margaret Getchell, a cousin of Rowland Macy who rose from cashier to store superintendent—the first woman executive of a large business. Getchell's motto was, "Be everywhere, do everything, and never fail to astonish the customer." She had a reputation for fixing anything with a hairpin. After her marriage to Abiel LaForge, she moved in over the store to mind it and her family at the same time. LaForge had been one of the presiding officers at the court-martial of Rowland Macy's son during the Civil War. At Rowland's request, LaForge had the son assigned to his company. LaForge's friendship with the father and son led to his meeting and marriage with Margaret Getchell, and a partnership with Rowland Macy.

The store continued to thrive under the Macy's four-point plan: 1) sell at fixed, marked prices; 2) sell for less; 3) buy and sell for cash only (credit cards were added in 1939); and 4) advertise heavily. By 1880 Rowland Macy, Margaret and Abiel La-Forge, and a third partner, Robert Macy Valentine, a nephew, had all died. Eight years later the store passed into the hands of three men who had run the china department at Macy's: Lazarus Straus and his two sons, Isidor and Nathan. The family moved the store uptown to the Herald Square location and started Macy's expansion. Isidor eventually became a U.S. congressman and a casualty on the *Titanic*. His son Jesse ran the firm until he became ambassador to France in 1930. The Straus family remained in control until 1968.

Under the leadership of Jesse, and later his son Jack, Macy's bought such department stores as LaSalle's of Toledo, Davison's of Atlanta, O'Connor Moffat of San Francisco, John Taylor Dry Goods of Kansas City (the latter two are now called Macy's), and the huge and successful Bamberger's of Newark, during the 1920s–1940s. Macy's was one of the first department stores to branch out from downtown with their Parkchester store in the Bronx. They now have 15 branch stores in the New York metropolitan area, as well as over 50 stores in six regional districts across the country.

The big event of the 1970s was bringing California to New York. This feat was accomplished by Edward Finkelstein, who had transformed Macy's California division into by far the biggest money-maker in the chain. Brought in to head the faltering New York stores in 1974, Finkelstein applied the same principles—make it more fashionable, airy, exciting—with excellent results. An example of his flair: he installed a replica of the famous Third Avenue saloon and restaurant P. J. Clarke's in Macy's on Herald Square. He is credited with transforming Macy's from a "grim warehouse" into "New York's ultimate loft."

Who owns and runs the company. Jack Straus, son of Jesse, stepped down from the chairmanship in 1968, but he and his son Kenneth still serve on the board of directors, and the Straus family still owns Macy's stock. Edward Finkelstein was recently elevated to the post of chief executive officer and is mentioned as heir apparent to chairman Donald Smiley.

Stock performance. R. H. Macy stock bought for $1,000 in 1970 sold for $1,500 on January 2, 1980.

Access. 151 West 34th Street, New York, New York 10001; (212) 695-4400. Address complaints and inquiries to the Public Relations Department and the Customer Relations Department at the 34th Street address.

Consumer brands.

Stores: Macy; Bamberger's; LaSalle's; Davison's.

Things a Body Can Get Along Without

Neiman-Marcus, the Dallas department store that caters to the very rich, is faced each Christmas with the problem of coming up with gift items the store can guarantee are unquestionably unique. In various years Neiman-Marcus has risen to the challenge by offering in the Christmas catalogue:

*His and hers volcanic craters, imported from Greece, at $5,000 each.

*A sterling silver "think tank" or privacy capsule, soundproof and equipped with options ranging from music to film projection, for $800,000.

*A pure gold omelette pan with a stainless steel core and rosewood handle, packed with four pounds of truffles, and four dozen double yolk eggs in a French oak box, for $30,000.

*A scientific expedition into Utah to look for remains of a giant carnivorous dinasour, *Allocarus*, at only $29,995 for each "Saurian Safari."

Should Neiman-Marcus customers still find themselves confounded for shopping ideas, the store offers a catalogue page describing "how to spend $1,000,000 at Neiman-Marcus."

A Texas cattleman who visited Neiman-Marcus summed up the store's merchandising emphasis when he remarked: "In all my time I never saw so many things a body kin get along without."

Source: Robert Hendrickson, *The Grand Emporiums* (Stein and Day, 1979).

An Electronics Gadgeteer

Tandy

Sales: $1.2 billion
Profits: $83.2 million
Forbes 500 rank: 392
Rank in home electronics: 1
Rank in microcomputers: 1
Founded: 1899
Employees: 20,700
Headquarters: Fort Worth, Texas

What they do. Tandy has grown like a Texas weed since buying a nearly bankrupt nine-store chain and mail-order electronics business called Radio Shack in 1963. Today it is nearly impossible to drive down a main street or past a shopping center without spotting the red and white Radio Shack signboard. Each of the more than 7,000 typically small stores is crammed with stereo equipment, radios, telephones, intercoms, tape recorders, magnetic tapes, and, of course, citizens-band radios. Tandy's biggest competitor, Lafayette Radio Electronics, is only one-eighth their size.

During 1976 and 1977, the heyday of citizens-band radio, CBs were Tandy's biggest-selling item. By the time the fad died down, Tandy had another "craze" in the works—a home computer, at an unbelievably low $599.95. For the first time, a customer could walk into a store and walk out with a computer small enough to sit on a desk top. Designed by Tandy, the TRS-80 was aimed at individuals who could use them to keep track of household finances and the like. More than 100,000 of the TRS-80s were sold between September 1, 1977 and June 1, 1979. When Tandy realized that the home computers were being scooped up by small businesses, they developed a second model,

the TRS-80 Model II—twice as fast as the first version and with a much larger memory. By late 1979, a few months after Model II was introduced, Tandy's computer sales were off and running, providing 8.2% of Radio Shack sales.

Since Radio Shack only stocks their own merchandise, executives must come up with 50 to 100 brand names, "because we don't want the store to look boring," one executive explained to *Advertising Age*. Radio Shack president Lewis Kornfeld described the process for naming the Archer line of electronic parts: "We named the line after Archer Avenue in Chicago. Every time we would fly to Chicago and land at Midway, we had to drive all the way down Archer to get into town. The line is named after the street."

History. "Mr. Lucky" was the name Charles Tandy used over the CB radio in his sleek black Lincoln. Lucky, indeed: in a few years in the early 1950s Tandy turned his family's business, a small Fort Worth leather store founded in 1899, into a nationwide chain of leathercraft and hobby stores. Of course, there was more to Tandy's success than luck. Under his simple-country-boy veneer lay a marketing genius.

Tandy tried oil wildcatting, real estate, and even a Texas department store in at-

> The buck—the ever-diminishing dollar—was a term originally used to refer simply to a deerskin, a common medium of exchange in frontier days.

tempts to branch out from his leathercraft business. Nothing seemed to click until 1963, when he bought Radio Shack. To just about everyone else the Boston-based chain of nine electronics stores, with a mail-order business that had nearly $800,000 in bills on which payments had not been made, looked like a dry well. Tandy's first move was to cut back Radio Shack's staff and move aggressively to get money back, eventually hiring a small army of collection lawyers— 900 of them—who managed to bring in a portion of those "noncollectible" funds. And he had other ideas in his back pocket.

Tandy cut inventory stock in half, carrying only items with a high turnover rate. He was a firm believer in leasing, rather than owning, retail space, and in advertising. ("If you want to catch a mouse, you have to make a noise like a cheese," Tandy said.) He plowed 8–9% of sales into advertising. From 1968–1973 the number of Radio Shack stores jumped from 172 to 2,294. In one year, 1973, Tandy opened over 594 stores—more than two stores per working day!

Tandy utilized the profit motive to grow. Everyone from store managers to executives, including Tandy himself, got relatively small salaries, and no pension plans or frills—but big bonus deals on results. For example in 1974 Tandy and his two highest-paid executives received $75,000 each in salary. But the two executives earned over $255,000 each in bonuses. Tandy's bonuses totaled $539,000.

Tandy also realized early on that a great way to keep the profits at home, was to "make your own." Today Tandy makes 43% of their own products at 20 domestic plants and 4 foreign ones. Fifty-five percent of Tandy's products are now made in Asia.

It was Charles Tandy's ideas and phenomenal energy that put Radio Shack on the map—or rather, all over the map. Despite his enormous success, Tandy remained, until he died peacefully in his sleep in 1978, the "good ole boy." He insisted on using his old office—the converted ground floor suite of a Fort Worth Christian Science reading room—even after the construction of Tandy Center, with two 19-story buildings in a complex occupying eight square blocks. He answered his own phone. His desk piled high with papers, Tandy's office resembled a three-ring cir-

The Honesty

In the 1880s a saloonkeeper fed up with losing his profits to thieving bartenders invented a device to guarantee honesty. James S. Ritty of Dayton, Ohio, was not alone in his problem. In those days storekeepers simply stuffed money into a cash drawer built into the sales counter, and dishonest employees could pilfer with ease. There was no effective way to keep track of sales and cash received.

Ritty and his mechanically gifted brother, John, devised a contraption to end such pilferage. The machine— ultimately to be known as the cash register—was christened "Ritty's Incorruptible Cashier"; it tabulated sales as they were made, announcing each transaction with a loud

cus, open to old friends and chance acquaintances as well as to Tandy executives. Gregarious almost to a fault, Charles Tandy was said never to have fired anyone. Instead, he would move the less capable from the front lines to less demanding positions.

When Tandy died in 1978 his boyhood friend and right-hand man Phil North temporarily filled the president and chief executive slots, although North confessed to *Fortune*, "All I know about electronics is that the funny end of the battery goes into the flashlight first." While not the nonstop talker that Charles Tandy was, the amiable North is following in his boss's footsteps, attempting to speed Tandy Corporation toward the $2 billion mark. "It's the one last thing I can do for him," North says.

Reputation. "We are a do-it-yourself company," says Lewis Kornfeld. Coming from a background in leathercraft kits, they have taught themselves electronics marketing so well that more outlets bear Tandy's Radio Shack name than any other in the world. In 1979 there were 7,353 Radio Shacks, 6,805 7-Elevens, and 5,530 McDonald's.

What they own. Since the 1975 spin off of Tandycrafts, the hobby and crafts chain, and of a printing operation and a chain of wall-and floor-covering stores, Tandy has plugged in exclusively to the electronics business. In a reversal of an earlier policy of never owning retail space, Tandy now owns about 60% of their stores, which are located in the United States, Canada, Europe, and Australia.

> "Saudi Arabian oil millionaires so miss Harrod's [a fashionable London department store] that they have raised $30 million to build a half-sized replica of Harrod's in Mecca, complete with canopies that shade the outside windows. They plan to stock their store with the best goods from around the world, just as the London Harrod's does. Unfortunately, they will not be able to use the name or the yellow logo (perhaps they will call it Dorrah's). . . . And finally, no sales ladies, just salesmen, as Moslem women are barred from working in stores." —*Retailing Today*, May 1980.

Machine

"bong" of a bell. To open the cash register and make change, clerks had to ring up each sale. There was no chance to pocket the money, since the Incorruptible Cashier recorded each sale, while its noisy bell shattered opportunities for stealth.

Installed at Ritty's watering hole, the mechanized guardian of staff morality caused a notable upswing in profits. Ritty set up a small factory to manufacture his device, but sales at first were slow. Retailers were reluctant to pay $50 for an unfamiliar contraption they had no idea how to use.

No more than a dozen cash registers were in use in 1882, when an intense, inventive man named John Henry Patterson discovered to his horror that his firm's company store was losing half its annual profits to thieving cashiers. Patterson promptly sent for two of Ritty's machines and installed them at the Southern Coal and Iron Company's store in Coalton, Ohio. So effective were the registers that Patterson was seized by a messianic vision of cash registers in every American retail business, sturdily foiling dishonest impulses.

In 1884 Patterson bought a controlling interest in Ritty's manufacturing operation, changing its name to National Cash Register, and mounted a fevered sales campaign to convince retailers that cash registers were indispensable. "I have called to interest you in a way to increase your profits," Patterson's salesmen would begin, in a polished sales pitch memorized from the company's training manual.

As National Cash Register salesmen advanced in an implacable wave, implanting cash registers in place of cash drawers in bars, cafes, and stores, indignation rose in the bosoms of bartenders and clerks deprived of their former unscheduled income supplements. So enraged were the bartenders that traveling salesmen for other, innocuous, products learned to protect themselves by announcing in loud tones whenever they entered a bar that they were *not* working for National Cash Register.

Source: Gerard Carson, "The Machine that Kept Them Honest."

Who owns and runs the company. Phil North "has been described as an interim chief executive officer, until a new successor can be found. He is vague about when he may leave," according to *Advertising Age.* Charles Tandy's wife, Anne Burnett Tandy, and the Charles D. Tandy Foundation own 6% of the company. Mrs. Tandy, an independently wealthy woman, sits on the board of the First National Bank of Fort Worth, raises quarter horses, and owns five ranches as well as one of the largest collections of modern art in the country. The next two biggest stockholders are Jesse L. Upchurch, chairman of Percival Tours, Inc., who owns 2.6% worth of Tandy stock, and James L. West, who owns 2.3%. West is also vice-chairman of the Tandy board.

In the public eye. The rambunctious company has gotten entangled in bitter and occasionally violent antitrust litigation, and one political scandal.

Recently Tandy was condemned by the Ontario Labor Relations Board for "persistent and flagrant unfair labor practices." In a sensitive labor dispute with the United Steelworkers, they seem to have moved like a Texas bull through a Canadian china shop. The board particularly deplored Tandy's anti-union tactics, including distribution to employees of bright red T-shirts bearing the inscription, "I'm a company fink," on the front, "and proud of it," on the back. According to the *Wall Street Journal,* "The panel also objected to the company's surveillance of its work force. Two former drug squad officers form a police department in the area and several of their underworld acquaintances were hired to spy on the union and infiltrate its ranks at the warehouse." Tandy was ordered to pay damages and sit down at the bargaining table. "If the steel-workers negotiate an agreement with Tandy, it will be the first union to do so in the U.S. or Canada."

California congressman Andrew J. Hinshaw was convicted on two felony counts of bribery in 1976. Hinshaw was found guilty of accepting $1,000 and stereo equipment from the Tandy corporation when he was Orange County assessor.

Where they're going. Europe and the Orient are a huge untapped market of electronic buffs and do-it-yourselfers. Having nearly saturated the United States with Radio Shacks, Tandy is opening outlets in Europe and in Japan at an impressive clip: 118 new Radio Shacks in Europe and 283 in Japan and other Far Eastern countries during 1978 and 1979.

Stock performance. Tandy stock bought for $1,000 in 1970 sold for $4,357 on January 2, 1980.

Access. 1800 One Tandy Center, Fort Worth, Texas 76102; (817) 390-3700.

Consumer brands.

Radio Shack stores. Realistic; Archer; Science Fair; Micronta; Patrolman; TRS-80 electronic products and parts.

Shoplifting losses, passed on by the retailer to the customer, account for about 3% of the average price tag. A shoplifter risks 1 chance in 35 of being caught and 1 chance in 1,200 of going to jail.

In one of the most famous photographs in the history of photojournalism, Sewell L. Avery, 70-year-old chairman of Montgomery Ward, is shown being carried out of his office at Ward headquarters in Chicago on April 27, 1944. President Franklin D. Roosevelt ordered him removed after Avery flatly refused to settle a labor dispute over union recognition. The dispute led to a strike, which the government said was delaying delivery of war-essential equipment. *Forbes* observed: "If a generation of Americans grew up thinking businessmen were Neanderthals, this picture of Sewell L. Avery convinced them."

6

ADVERTISING: AN AMERICAN ART FORM

Ad People

Interpublic

Sales: $374 million
Profits: $21.5 million
Rank in advertising agencies: 1
Founded: 1911
Employees: 8,880
Headquarters: New York

What they do. Interpublic has done in the advertising business what one of their main clients, General Motors, has accomplished in the automotive field. As GM makes cars through their divisions—Chevrolet, Buick, Oldsmobile, Pontiac, Cadillac—Interpublic makes ads through their divisions—McCann-Erickson, SSC&B, Marschalk, Campbell-Ewald.

Ads and commercials produced by these Interpublic agencies appear all over the world, from the "Mean Joe Greene" Coke commercials on U.S. television screens to Kentucky Fried Chicken ads in London newspapers to Nescafé banners in Kenya. They speak for 18,000 products made by 2,000 clients. The Interpublic agencies pro-

duce this advertising through 166 offices in 50 countries.

It adds up to quite a bundle of advertising. In 1979 the clients using Interpublic agencies spent a total of $2.57 billion. That's how much money passed through the hands of all these agencies on the way to buying time and space in various media (newspapers, magazines, radio and TV stations, outdoor billboards). The amount that clung to Interpublic is the sales figure posted above: $374 million, or roughly 15% of the advertising investment made by clients. That's the way the ad agency business works: an agency is compensated by a 15% commission on the advertising it handles, a commission that is paid by the media where the ads run.

Only four countries in the world—the United States, Japan, West Germany, and Britain—have advertising expenditures that top the total amount spent through the Interpublic agencies. Of every $100 spent on advertising in the world, $3 go through the Interpublic Group.

The McCann-Erickson agency is the "mother" of the Interpublic complex. From nine offices in the United States McCann converts ideas into printed advertisements and commercials that you see on the tube, hear on the radio, or read in newspapers and magazines for some very familiar products: Coca-Cola, Viceroy cigarettes, Inglenook wine, Early Times bourbon, Gillette's Atra razors, Don Q rum, Buick cars, the American Express Gold Card. Also in the McCann fold is Exxon, the world's largest petroleum pumper—and if McCann can be called the "mother" of Interpublic, Exxon has to be the "grandmother" (their histories are intertwined). But McCann is much more of an international agency than a U.S. one. Of their 5,860 employees, only 1,240 work in the U.S. offices; the rest are scattered around the world. McCann does 75% of their business abroad. In the United States they rank 11th in the advertising agency picture, but they rank among the top three agencies in 22 other countries. And McCann is number 1 in Germany, Finland, Italy, Nicaragua, Panama, and Hong Kong.

The next-largest Interpublic agency is SSC&B, purchased in September 1979 for $40 million ($30 million of it borrowed from Morgan Guaranty Trust). It constituted the largest acquisition in advertising agency history. You're looking at SSC&B's work when you see ads for Pall Mall and Lucky Strike cigarettes, Johnson & Johnson baby shampoo, Noxzema, Bayer aspirin, Lipton tea, and All detergent. SSC&B ranks 24th in terms of how much advertising they handle in the United States, but they too have an awesome international presence via an unusual arrangement with one of the world's consumer goods powerhouses—Unilever—that lifts them to 6th place among all U.S. agencies. SSC&B handles more than $1 billion of advertising a year around the world.

The third-largest Interpublic engine is Campbell-Ewald. They do the advertising for Chevrolet and Smirnoff vodka. And they too have a worldwide operation, with offices in Europe, Australia, Latin America, and South Africa.

The fourth Interpublic agency is Marschalk, with offices only in New York and Cleveland, ranking 30th in the U.S. agency business on the strength of advertising prepared for Standard Oil of Ohio, three Coca-Cola company brands—Minute Maid, Sprite and Mr. PiBB—and a couple of Heublein brands—A-1 steak sauce and Grey Poupon mustard. (Heublein's chairman,

Stuart Watson, came from Marschalk.)

While the Interpublic agencies are doing the advertising for thousands of products, five clients—two of them being General Motors and Coca-Cola—accounted for 36% of their total income in 1979. Coke advertising in the United States alone is pegged at $55 million a year.

History. Harrison King McCann was advertising manager for the Rockefeller Standard Oil Trust when it was dissolved by the Supreme Court in 1911 as a monopoly and split into 37 different companies. The largest of the divested companies was Standard Oil of New Jersey (now Exxon). McCann then set up his own advertising agency—H. K. McCann—with Jersey Standard as his first client. Another of his early clients was Chesebrough, maker of Vaseline, which also came out of the Standard Oil Trust. Handling the advertising for the largest oil company in the nation at the start of the automotive age was not a bad way to enter the agency business, and this founding account has remained with the same agency for nearly seven decades. But a large part of the history of this agency consists of combinations of various kinds. Embodied in the Interpublic Group of Companies are the vestiges of many pioneer advertising agencies of the United States. The chronology looks like this:

1901: Alfred W. Erickson, 25-year-old advertising manager of the James McCutcheon Co., forms his own advertising agency in New York. Erickson owns nearly all his

More advertising money is spent per person in the United States ($157 a year) than in any other country, according to *Advertising Age*. The next highest is spent in Bermuda and Switzerland ($110), followed by Canada ($103), Denmark ($99), Sweden ($92), Finland ($82), Australia ($82), Netherlands ($81), Norway ($73), Austria ($56), West Germany ($49), France ($47), Japan ($43), and the United Kingdom ($40).

The least amount of advertising money was spent in Ethiopia, where only 3 cents a year is spent for each person. The other countries where very little is spent on advertising are: Nepal (5 cents), Bangladesh (13 cents), Pakistan (20 cents), and India (23 cents).

clients, thereby becoming one of the richest people in the ad agency business. One of his early campaigns features baby chicks and the slogan, "Hasn't scratched yet," on behalf of Bon Ami cleanser.

1912: F. B. (Fritz) Ryan and Wilbur Ruthrauff establish the Ruthrauff & Ryan agency in New York. Two of their famous early accounts are Arthur Murray Dance Studios ("How I Became Popular Overnight") and the U.S. School of Music ("They Laughed When I Sat Down to Play the Piano").

1936: Six years after merging his company with H. K. McCann, Alfred Erickson dies, leaving an estate with art work valued at $5 million. The last great fortune he made was in a new film process: he invested $500,000 in Technicolor in 1932 and then persuaded Douglas Fairbanks, Jr., to shoot his next picture in Technicolor. In 1937 Erickson's widow gives $30,000 from his estate to the Harvard business school for an "exhaustive" study of the role of advertising. The result, five years later, is one of the landmark books in advertising theory, Neil H. Borden's *The Economic Effects of Advertising*.

1946: Three refugees from the Ruthrauff & Ryan agency—Raymond Sullivan, S. Heagan Bayles, and Donald Stauffer—and a veteran from the J. Walter Thompson agency, Robert T. Colwell, organize a new agency called Sullivan, Stauffer, Colwell & Bayles. Most of their early accounts—Noxzema, Smith Bros. cough drops, Lever's Lifebuoy and Silver Dust soaps—come from Ruthrauff & Ryan. Fifteen months after opening they are given the Pall Mall cigarette account—and they go on to advertise this brand into first place by 1960. Colwell returns to the more genteel surroundings of J. Walter Thompson in 1956, explaining to writer Martin Mayer: "When I was president of SSC&B, I was in the hospital four times, I had a heart attack, they took out my stomach, I almost lost my eyesight. My doctor said to me, 'Bob, I don't think this place agrees with you.' "

1955: McCann-Erickson buys Marschalk & Pratt, formed in 1923 by Harry C. Marschalk and Edward M. Pratt, but Marschalk is allowed to continue to operate under their own steam, soliciting and acquiring clients and doing their own advertising. It is the first move by Marion Harper, Jr., then president of McCann, to test his "holding company" concept. Up to then ad agency growth was inhibited by the predicament of "conflicting accounts": if you had one toothpaste account, for example, you couldn't very well take on another. But what if you had two different agencies . . . ? McCann now did.

Singing Their Hearts Out for Flea Collars

In the beginning was the jingle. Which one, nobody's quite sure. There are those who support the theory that General Mills was the first when they launched a little ditty called "Have You Tried Wheaties?" on the radio in the 1920s. Others argue for the "I'm Chiquita Banana" anthem. Still another faction roots for "J-E-L-L-O," written 30 years ago. The controversy will undoubtedly go on forever, but for now, $100 million a year goes into producing those musical tags you can't seem to forget.

In the rich but little-known jingle kingdom, there live composers and copywriters, music directors and engineers, studio musicians, and that most elusive, evasive quarry of all—jingle singers.

Jingle singers—the label sounds a little derogatory, doesn't it? As if they were insufficiently talented for real singing careers. As if they'd been helplessly marooned in this musical backwater, condemned forever to sing out their hearts for flea collars, candy bars, and cold remedies. . . . But you'd be wrong.

Anonymity, it turns out, is one of the jingle singer's major assets. "They avoid appearing on camera like the plague," says Roy Eaton, vice president and music director of Benton & Bowles, "because they want to appear on Miller *and* Löwenbräu *and* Schlitz *and* Pabst. . . . There's no competitive problem with that as long as they stay off camera."

Eaton estimates that 75 percent of the jingles that fill the airways are sung by no more than 30 people. And when you consider the incredible proliferation of jingles (today they comprise one-half of all top-40 radio programming), that comes out to a lot of singing by a very elite corps of singers. Eaton says the top ones easily make $200,000 to $300,000 a year. Another reason for privacy. As one of the singers explained (anonymously) in an interview with the *Wall Street Journal*, "How often do you think I'd get hired if the ad guys knew I'm making three

1970: SSC&B (the name has been reduced to initials because the telephone operators have became weary of saying "Sullivan, Stauffer, Colwell & Bayles" all day) enters into a worldwide partnership with Lintas (Lever International Advertising Service), advertising agency arm of the Anglo-Dutch giant Unilever, Ltd., a sort of combination of Procter & Gamble and General Foods.

1973: Campbell-Ewald becomes part of Interpublic, bringing the big Chevrolet account with them.

Interpublic's drive to become the General Motors of the advertising agency business was capped by the 1979 deal with SSC&B, which gave them three worldwide agency networks to offer advertisers. And two of these units by themselves—McCann-Erickson and SSC&B—rank among the 10 largest advertising agencies. Marion Harper is not around to savor the triumph of his concept. A research-minded adman who came to McCann-Erickson via his native Oklahoma and schooling at Yale, Harper put the foundation down but then had difficulty managing it; he was forced out in 1967.

In retrospect, there were two crucial developments during the 1950–60 decade when Harper was building up McCann-Erickson. One came in 1955, when the

SPENDING MONEY TO MAKE MONEY: THE COMPANIES THAT SPEND THE HIGHEST PERCENTAGE OF THEIR SALES ON ADVERTISING	
1978 Ad Expenditures as Percentage of Sales	
1. NOXELL	22%
2. ALBERTO-CULVER	19%
3. MILES LABORATORIES	12%
4. RICHARDSON-MERRELL	11%
5. STERLING DRUG	11%
6. A. H. ROBINS	10%
7. CHESEBROUGH-POND'S	9%
8. WM. WRIGLEY JR.	9%
9. SMITHKLINE	8%
Source: *Advertising Age*, September 6, 1979.	

Coca-Cola Company decided to end a 49-year-old relationship with D'Arcy Advertising of St. Louis. McCann offices overseas had already been handling Coke (D'Arcy didn't have any foreign offices), and that turned out to be a key factor in their appointment as the U.S. agency. The $15 million account switch was the largest agency change in the history of advertising up to that time. The second big event came in 1958, when the Buick division of General Motors decided to end a long relationship they had with the old Kudner Agency.

or four times what they are, and the chairman of the boards of some of the companies I work for knew I'm making more than they are?"

With this thick cloud of discretion gathered around their ranks, it's difficult to say who the reigning queen of the jingle singers really is. But the name that most persistently crops up in response to the question is Linda November. . . .

Her masterpiece, the one jingle that she herself selects as the apotheosis of her craft, was recorded two years ago for Meow Mix cat food. Although on most commercials the soundtrack is produced separately and then laid onto the film, the proce-

dure could not be followed here: The synchronization had to be too precise. So November studied the film until she had all the cat's mouth movements down pat. She knew when its mouth was open, when it licked its chops, what the expression on its face was. "I really believed in that little calico baby. And when I sang that line, 'Meow, meow, meow, meow,' I really felt like I'd created a character."

On one occasion, November had to sing like a person underwater, and on another, like a chicken underwater (for, you guessed it, Chicken of the Sea).

Len Dresslar, who's been ho, ho-ing for the Jolly Green Giant for sixteen years now,

has also had the privilege of playing a frog, a giraffe, and a trash can. Bill Dean remembers doing a session for an insect repellent. "The producer stopped us in mid-note and said, 'Wait a minute. You're not *happy* fireflies, you're *sad* fireflies.' We had to start all over and become sad fireflies."

Bill Marine, who refers to himself as the "Grand Old Man of Jingle Singers," recalls having played a wooden spoon for Wesson oil, chasing a fork and salad bowl down the street.

Reprinted from Robert Masella, "Linda, Queen of the Jingle—and Her Friends," *New York*, April 23, 1979.

McCann-Erickson was supposedly not eligible because they were doing the advertising for Chrysler. But Marion Harper at least knew his arithmetic. He looked at Chrysler and he looked at General Motors, and he asked: "From a long-term standpoint, which would be a more desirable client to have?" The self-evident answer led him to dump Chrysler and take on Buick, an act of disloyalty that brought him abuse in the advertising world. But no one ever faulted his arithmetic—which client would you like to have today?

This kind of movement still takes place in the agency world, even at Interpublic, where a strong attempt has been made to institutionalize what is a personal service business. In 1979 Carl Spielvogel, the vice-chairman of Interpublic, left the company, followed shortly afterward by William Backer, who had been the creative chief at McCann-Erickson, responsible for the Coca-Cola advertising. The two formed a new agency, Backer & Spielvogel. Shortly after that Miller beer, whose McCann-produced commercials have been amusing Americans for five years, moved their $85 million advertising account to the new agency. The move demonstrated an old adage that the agency business is the only business in the world where your inventory goes down in the elevator at the end of the day.

Reputation. In a fickle business, where accounts can come and go at the whim of a client, Interpublic has achieved some of the solidity of their big clients. They have a New York Stock Exchange listing. They're constantly merging. They also know how to fight back. When they lost Miller beer, they went out and got a dozen new accounts, including the $20 million Pabst beer business (when you see Pabst ads now, know that there's a special revenge motive working).

What they own. Advertising agencies are not big on properties. They pay out well over half their income to the people who work for them. At the end of 1979 Interpublic listed as one of their assets $276 million in "accounts receivable," the accounting term for what people owe you. That enormous sum is what their clients owed them for space and time already purchased—and that's enough to make an agency nervous because in this business the agency is legally liable to the media. Interpublic got an unwelcome Christmas present in 1979 when one of their clients, Marx toys, went bankrupt and couldn't pay $2 million for advertising that had been done by McCann-Erickson, leaving Interpublic to eat the bill. Most ad agencies are small enough to be destroyed by that kind of loss.

Who owns and runs the company. Interpublic has 2,600 stockholders, but the big one is media buff Warren Buffet, who made a lot of money in the stock market while sitting in Omaha and has since invested his gains in various enterprises, including the *Washington Post*, the Knight-Ridder newspaper chain, and another big ad agency, Ogilvy & Mather. Berkshire Hathaway, an insurance company 47% controlled by Buffet, holds 18% of Interpublic's stock; another 9% is held by Ruane Cunniff & Co., a Wall Street brokerage house with close ties to Buffet. The man in charge of Interpublic today is a hard-driving workaholic, Philip H. Geier, Jr., who took over the reins in 1979 at age 44. According to *Advertising Age* reporter Bernice Kanner, Geier "is the man who walked into the £6 ($14 million) McCann agency in Great Britain in 1969 and walked out four years later with that shop billing £40 ($92 million). Later, as head of McCann Europe, he breathed life into a concept that before only existed on paper, and made the agency the leader in that part of the world." Geier says he misses agency work but adds: "Acquisition and finance are also loves, and I'm consoling myself with them at Interpublic."

In the public eye. Their work is all over the television screen and the advertising pages of your favorite magazines and newspapers. But they let their clients take the bows.

Where they're going. Any place people use advertising. They made a deal with a big Hong Kong trading company, Jardine, Mathieson, to get into mainland China, and they are now doing the advertising for two government entities, the Civil Air Administration of China and the China International Travel Service.

Stock performance. Interpublic first sold stock to the public in 1971. Stock bought then for $1,000 was worth $3,300 on January 2, 1980.

Major employment centers. New York City and Detroit.

Access. Interpublic: 1271 Avenue of the Americas, New York, New York 10022; (212) 399-8000. McCann-Erickson, 485 Lexington Avenue, New York, New York; (212) 697-6000. Marschalk, 1345 Avenue of the Americas, New York, New York; (212) 974-7700. SSC&B 1 Dag Hammarskjold Plaza, New York, New York; (212) 644-5000. Campbell-Ewald, 1345 Avenue of the Americas, New York, New York; (212) 489-6200.

Sales: $265 million
Profits: $13.6 million
Rank in advertising agencies: one of top 3
Rank in public relations: 1
Founded: 1864
Employees: 6,300
Headquarters: New York, New York

What they do. Here's a company that knows a lot about you: what you buy, how you buy, where you buy and—most important—why you buy. They need to have this knowledge to shower you with the messages that persuade you to buy the products of their clients. In 1979 Thompson or JWT or J. Walter (they're called all three names in the ad business) turned out 53,000 ads and commercials on behalf of 800 clients all over the world. JWT has 67 offices in 32 countries. Over the years they have sold more goods in more countries than any other advertising agency. They are the oldest, and for many years were the largest, advertising agency in the world. Today, if you just count advertising placed in the United States, JWT ranks second to Young & Rubicam. If you count worldwide advertising, it's a three-cornered battle: JWT, Young & Rubicam, and McCann-Erickson, with very little separating them. Like most statistical exercises, it's confusing; suffice it to say that J. Walter Thompson is one of the "superagencies" of the advertising business. What's more, they're also the biggest

firm in the public relations field since their purchase of Hill & Knowlton in 1980.

Last year they handled the advertising of 4,068 different brands. You were watching a Thompson-crafted message if you saw a Ford Mustang commercial, a Burger King ad, an outdoor poster for Kodak film, a "Go for it!" magazine ad for Schlitz beer, an Aunt Jemima pancake mix ad, an animated cartoon commercial for Chevron (Standard Oil of California), a French's mustard ad in magazines, a Blue Cross–Blue Shield ad in New York City newspapers, an Oscar Mayer cold cuts commercial, a pitch for Kraft Cracker Barrel cheese, a Close-up toothpaste commercial, or one of those Samsonite commercials on TV—among many, many others. And that's just in the United States.

Overseas Thompson offices do Kellogg's cereal advertising, Nescafé instant coffee in Spain, DeBeers diamonds in Italy, Rowntree's After Eight mints in Britain, Labatt's beer in Canada, Clearasil acne treatment in West Germany. Thompson invariably ranks as one of the top 10 advertising agencies in any country in the world where advertising has become an important method of selling products and services. In Britain they are by far the largest advertising agency; they also place at or near the top in Canada, Argentina, Chile, Austria, Italy, the Netherlands, Spain, and West Germany. Of JWT's 6,300 employees 3,700 work outside the United States.

By Thompson's own count they're active in markets with a total population of 1.1 billion persons. To make sure they know what those people are thinking, they do considerable research. In 1979 they surveyed, interviewed, or contacted 1.2 million consumers. They own Basisresearch, the largest marketing research organization in West Germany. Their British Market Research Bureau is one of the largest research companies in the United Kingdom.

To produce all their ads, Thompson employs 1,316 writers, art directors, and TV producers—what the agency likes to call "one of the world's largest pools of creative talent." Big advertising agencies, JWT points out, "employ more creative people than any other social institution"—more than newspapers, magazines, broadcasting stations, or book publishers.

Thompson serves 800 client companies, but 20 of these advertisers bring in about half their total dollar volume of business. The largest is Ford Motor, accounting for 13% of Thompson's commissions and fees —which means that the Ford account is worth roughly $200 million a year. This explains why in the first moments of the 1965 blackout in New York, a voice in the creative department exclaimed: "Oh, no, we've lost the Ford account."

A word should be said about how an advertising agency makes its money. If you prepared your own ad and bought a full page in *The New Yorker* to carry it, it would set you back $8,300. If you used the services of an advertising agency to prepare the ad and buy the page in *The New Yorker*, it would still cost you $8,300. What happens, though, is that when the agency places the ad, *The New Yorker* grants them a commission of 15%. In this sense, the services of an advertising agency are free, like a travel agent's. The money a client spends through an agency is called billings. When they say an account is worth $20 million, it means the amount of money spent on advertising. The agency's compensation comes basically from the 15% commission granted by the media (newspapers, magazines, radio, and TV stations) where the ads run. There have been arguments in the industry for many years about the commission system (and some clients pay their ad agencies a fee instead), but it survives as the basic method of paying for agency service. How it came to be established goes back to the start of the advertising agency in the middle of the last century.

History. J. Walter Thompson certainly has tradition going for them. They grew up with advertising and helped to set its standards of practice. Very few agencies can

A Master Ad Man and His "Technique for

James Webb Young was the complete opposite of the Ivy Leaguer at J. Walter Thompson; he never even graduated from grammar school. Young was born in Covington, Kentucky, in 1886, and "in those days, in that part of the country," he said, "a boy was praised for his Horatio Alger Jr. ambition if he wanted to quit school and go to work at an early age." Young became a "cash boy" in a Cincinnati department store at age 12, after completing the fifth grade. The truant officer caught up with him and returned him to school, but after three months in the sixth grade he took a job with the Methodist Book Concern (the very outfit that had put William Carlton, the

founder of Thompson, in business) in Cincinnati, and "thereafter was never molested by the pedagogs." In 1912 Stanley Resor hired Young as a copywriter in J. Walter's Cincinnati office, and when Resor went off to New York in 1916, Young became manager of the office. Resor brought Jim Young to New York in 1917 and after a year dispatched him to Chicago, where he and Henry Stanton, an ex-Procter & Gamble sales manager, took over the western operation of Thompson, running it as a virtual independent satrapy. But Young's contribution was on what they call in the ad business the "creative" side—the business of writing ads. He was the Ernest Hemingway of

advertising copywriters. He wrote sparse but vivid copy that went unerringly to keys that rang up sales. For example, his 1919 ad for Odorono deodorant began, "Within the curve of a woman's arm: A frank discussion of a subject too often avoided . . ." Young was the advertising guru of Thompson for three decades, although he was never to be found in one place for too long. During the 1930s Robert M. Hutchins, the boy wonder chancellor of the University of Chicago, invited the self-educated Young to teach a course on advertising. Like Resor, Young was an advertising theorist: he was interested in how it worked. Unlike Resor, he wrote down his ideas. One of Young's

claim, as Thompson can, that they are older than most of the companies they represent. What is now J. Walter Thompson was born on December 5, 1864, at 171 Broadway in lower Manhattan, when William J. Carlton and Edmund A. Smith opened a business called Carlton & Smith. Smith dropped from sight a few years later, and the company's name was changed to William J. Carlton Co.

In those days ad agents functioned as middlemen between advertisers and media, but they were the agents of the publications, not the companies which advertised; that is, they contracted with newspapers and magazines to sell their advertising space, sometimes taking a commission, sometimes just buying the space outright and reselling it to advertisers. The specialty of the Carlton agency was space in religious publications, especially those put out by the Methodist Book Concern.

The most important move made by William Carlton was to hire a 20-year-old book-keeper named James Walter Thompson in 1868. Thompson, fresh from a two-year stint in the marine corps, was a fourth cousin of President Theodore Roosevelt. Thompson turned out to be a terrific salesman. He was one of the first to recognize

the importance of housewives as buyers of goods, saying later that his inspiration came from the following rhyme:

God bless our wives, they fill the hives
With little bees and honey,
They smooth life's shocks, they mend our socks,
But don't they spend the money!

Thompson was also one of the first to recognize that the most effective way to reach housewives was through magazines, especially the newly emerging women's magazines. He has been called "the father of magazine advertising in America." When Thompson made the rounds signing up magazines to represent, he found he had to do a sales job on publishers who had no great love for advertising. One of his first contracts was with *Harper's Magazine*, for whom he undertook to sell 100 pages of advertising a year. The editor threatened to resign, saying he didn't want his magazine turned into "a cheap circus magazine." In 1878, when Thompson sent *Peterson's Magazine* 25 pages of paid advertising for a single issue, the editor balked, saying he "wouldn't dare send the magazine out with so much advertising in it."

Under Thompson's spur the business

Producing Ideas"

famous lines is: "The best books about advertising are not about advertising." He wrote a remarkable book, a slim volume pragmatically called *A Technique for Producing Ideas.* Did Jim Young actually believe you could learn to have ideas? Yes! He explained that he had come to the conclusion that "the production of ideas is just as definite a process as the production of Fords; that the production of ideas, too, runs on an assemblyline; that in this production the mind follows an operative technique which can be learned and controlled; and that its effective use is just as much a matter of practice as is the effective use of any tool." And he added:

"If you ask me why I am willing to give away the valuable formula of this discovery, I will confide to you that experience has taught me two things about it:

"First, the formula is so simple to state that few who hear it really believe in it.

"Second, while simple to state, it actually requires the hardest kind of intellectual work to follow, so that not all who accept it use it.

"Thus I broadcast this formula with no real fear of flooding the market in which I make my living."

After this masterful "teaser" copy, Young's actual formula is something of a letdown. Here's how he summed up his five-step method in *A Technique for*

Producing Ideas:

"First, the gathering of raw material—both the materials of your immediate problem and the materials which come from a constant enrichment of your store of general knowledge.

"Second, the working over of these materials in your mind.

"Third, the incubating stage, where you let something beside the conscious mind do the work of synthesis.

"Fourth, the actual birth of the Idea—the 'Eureka! I have it!' stage.

"And fifth, the final shaping and development of the idea to practical usefulness."

thrived. But Carlton, a bookworm, was really not comfortable with advertising, so in 1878 Carlton became a bookseller and sold the advertising business to his bookkeeper. Thompson paid $500 for the business and $800 for the furniture in the office on the third floor of the old Times Building at 30 Park Row. He also renamed the agency after himself, deciding on the designation "J. Walter" to distinguish himself from the many J. W. Thompsons running around (his bank alone had 20 of them).

It was Thompson who established magazines as a medium where advertisers could register their brand names with people right across the country. By 1887 he was offering advertisers a catalog of 25 magazines, among them *Scribner's, The Century, American Magazine, Woman's Argosy, Godey's, Lippincott's,* and *The Forum.* By the end of the century this list expanded to 30, as Thompson secured a virtual monopoly on magazine advertising. If you wanted to run ads in those magazines, you *had* to go through J. Walter Thompson, who charged $10 a line. Between 1865 and 1900 advertising volume in the United States increased from $50 million to $540 million.

At the turn of the century advertising agents were gradually changing from sellers of space to representatives of advertisers, and Thompson was in the vanguard. He began putting out little blue books which were, in effect, attempts to educate companies on the role of advertising. They contained such homilies as: "Advertising has nothing to do with literature. It is salesmanship—but in advertising the salesman stands behind a printed page instead of a counter." By 1917, when the American Association of Advertising Agencies was formed by some 150 agencies, the function of the advertising agency as the representative of the advertiser was clearly established. However, one very important vestige of their days as space sellers remained, and it still does today: the system by which the media grants a 15% commission for advertising delivered to them by the agency.

For the first two decades of this century the J. Walter Thompson Company vied with N. W. Ayer of Philadelphia for leadership of the agency business. By 1916 the Thompson agency had 177 employees in five offices, serving some 300 clients who were spending a total of $3 million a year on advertising. James Walter Thompson, then 69, suspected the business may have peaked,

and in October 1916 he sold his agency for $500,000 to a group of Thompson employees headed by Stanley Burnet Resor, a 1901 graduate of Yale who had been hired in 1908 to run the newly opened office in Cincinnati. In 1917 Resor married Helen Landsdowne, a Thompson copywriter. (Copywriters compose the words used in ad messages or commercial scripts.) For the next 40 years this remarkable couple presided over a growth fed by the general expansion of advertising and also by some principles that became peculiar to the Thompson agency. Stanley Resor applied himself to the philosophy of advertising, often acting as if he were running a school. He was not a copywriter. He was not an artist. He was not a great salesman. He never gave speeches. *Advertising Age,* in summing up Resor's career, once said his great contribution came as a "predictor of human behavior."

One of Resor's first steps was to lop off 200 of the 300 advertising accounts the Thompson agency had been servicing. These were mostly small accounts, and the message was: we are going to be a great big agency serving great big advertisers. This action, taken in 1916, was propitious. During the Roaring Twenties advertising expenditures in the United States tripled— and Thompson was handling the big ones: Pond's cold cream, Libby's canned goods, Yuban coffee (they named this brand), Lux toilet soap, Fleischmann's yeast, Kraft cheese.

A second step was to collect around him an astonishing group of talented people in various disciplines. Resor didn't invent a style of advertising so much as an approach to it that said: to do effective advertising for a client, an agency had to know everything about the product and about the people to whom the product was being sold. Thompson was thus an early user of research. For one client, Red Cross shoes, which had haphazard distribution, the agency compiled a list of every town in the country with a population of more than 500. It became the start of a regularly updated volume, *Population and Distribution.* The Thompson people who developed it later helped the U.S. Census Bureau do its decennial survey. When John B. Watson, originator of the school of psychology known as behaviorism, was fired from Johns Hopkins University in the aftermath of a messy divorce case, Stanley Resor gave him a new home in Thompson's

10 TOP ADVERTISING AGENCIES

The following are the 10 largest U.S. advertising agencies ranked by the amount of advertising they prepared and placed for their clients in 1979. Billings are what the clients spent on advertising.

	Billings	*Major Brands*
1. YOUNG & RUBICAM	$1.2 *billion*	Kentucky Fried Chicken, Sanka brand coffee, Log Cabin syrup, Oil of Olay, Eastern Airlines, Band-Aids, Dash detergent, Early Times bourbon
2. J. WALTER THOMPSON	$788 *million*	Kraft, Kodak, Ford cars, Burger King, Listerine mouthwash, Close-Up toothpaste
3. OGILVY & MATHER	$712 *million*	Shake 'n Bake, Maxwell House coffee, Contac, Avon products, TWA, American Express
4. TED BATES	$653 *million*	Kool cigarettes, Colgate toothpaste, Rapid-Shave, Palmolive liquid, M&M's, Snickers, Kal Kan dog food, Maybelline, Visine
5. FOOTE, CONE & BELDING	$640 *million*	Kent cigarettes, Fritos, Clairol's Loving Care, Long & Silky, Miss Clairol, Mazda, Solarcaine, Raid, Off, Levi Strauss
6. LEO BURNETT	$640 *million*	United Air Lines, Kellogg's cornflakes, Marlboro cigarettes, Green Giant, Pillsbury cake mix, Oldsmobile
7. BBDO	$626 *million*	Pepsi, Campbell soups, General Electric, Wesson Oil, Viva towels, Right Guard deodorant, Hawaiian Punch, Life Cereal, General Electric, Du Pont, Old Milwaukee beer
8. GREY ADVERTISING	$498 *million*	American Motors, Canada Dry, Yuban Coffee, Minute Rice, Stove Top dressing, Downy fabric softener, Joy, Bold, Duncan Hines cake mix, Revlon's Flex shampoo, Eterna 27, Cremora, Cracker-jacks, Cycle dog food
9. DOYLE DANE BERNBACH	$492 *million*	Volkswagen, American Airlines, Hershey chocolate syrup, Mobil, Polaroid, Chivas Regal, Calvert Extra
10. McCANN-ERICSON	$463 *million*	Coca-Cola, Exxon, Buick, General Motors trucks, Viceroy cigarettes, Pabst beer, Inglenook wines

New York office, figuring his insights could help produce sales-effective advertising.

After World War I the Ivy League colleges began to send graduates into the advertising business, and Thompson took more of them than anyone else. The class of 1919 was said to be the first to send more graduates into advertising than banking. One of those 1919 recruits at J. Walter Thompson was novelist John P. Marquand, who struggled for two years writing copy for Rinso soap and U.S. Rubber tires before deciding that advertising was not for him. But by 1928 Stanley Resor was proud to report that of his 600 staffers, 150 were college graduates, 4 of them Ph.D.'s.

On the way to displacing N. W. Ayer as the nation's leading advertising agency, Thompson pioneered many avenues during the 1920s and 1930s. They didn't invent testimonial advertising, but under Helen Landsdowne Resor's influence they turned it into a powerful sales tool. They went to the high and mighty to secure testimonials for Pond's cream—would you believe, in 1926, the Queen of Spain? They introduced Lux toilet soap in 1925 and were soon using movie stars to establish it as a leading brand. They were the first—and this too was Helen Resor's influence—to use fine photography in advertisements. Up to then advertising art had been dominated by the illustrators—wash drawings and pen-and-ink sketches. Edward Steichen, the famous photographer, did his first work for Thompson in 1923: a close-up of hands peeling potatoes for a Jergens lotion ad ("Housework never yet spoiled the beauty of a woman's hands"). Helen Resor signed Steichen to an exclusive contract with J. Walter Thompson, under which he received $1,000 per photograph. Carl Sandburg, who was married to Steichen's sister, wrote in 1929 that his brother-in-law enjoyed the work for Thompson since it enabled a single photograph of his to "reach almost the entire literate population of the country" through ads in national magazines.

Thompson's business tripled during the 1920s, and one of the major factors in this growth was their entry into the international area. In 1923 they opened an office in London to handle a canned fruit campaign for their Chicago client, Libby, McNeil & Libby. They soon had another client: California's Sun Maid raisins. But the big breakthrough came in 1927, when General Motors suggested that Thompson open an office in every country where GM had a manufacturing or assembly operation. In the next six years 23 offices bearing the J. Walter Thompson name were planted in Europe, Africa, South America, Australia, New Zealand, India, and Southeast Asia.

A central figure in Thompson's rise during the 1920s was James Webb Young, whom Resor hired in 1912. Jim Young traveled to many of the overseas offices to inculcate the Thompson methodology, which was rooted in the concept that advertisements should concentrate not on being clever but on the specific benefits a product had for consumers. Thompson's normal procedure was to send Americans to head these offices and staff them entirely with local people. In 1927, when JWT offices were opened in Paris, Berlin, Copenhagen, Antwerp, Stockholm, Madrid, and Alexandria, Jim Young arrived in London with a contingent of "8 men, 3 wives, 1 baby and a cat."

Another Resor recruit, Samuel W. Meek, also a Yale graduate, was the great shaper of Thompson's international operations. He joined the agency in 1925 and was soon off to London as manager. Meek was notorious at Thompson for dashing around the world, buying things and leaving them for the next JWTer to bring home. Carroll Carroll, longtime radio writer for Thompson, said: "If you were planning a trip to any place on earth, the last person you'd tell had to be Sam unless you wanted to pick up a pair of pajamas that the Imperial Hotel in Tokyo was holding for him or a complete set of flatware from the Silver Vaults of London." Meek never considered the Thompson offices "branches." He was fond of saying: "We don't try to be a French or German or American agency. We're a professional company working throughout the world." Meek could be autocratic and impulsive. In 1942, when Pan American World Airways, a new client, wanted to inaugurate a high-level advertising campaign featuring inspirational messages for a world torn by war, Sam Meek said: "Get the Pope." They tried. Though they never did secure a testimonial from Pope Pius XII, they did manage to get messages (that ran in Pan Am ads) from Archbishop Samuel Stritch of Chicago, the Archbishop of Canterbury, philosopher John Dewey, and playwright George Bernard Shaw. But Meek was unhappy that they never got the Pope.

A marine captain during World War I, Meek had many connections with potentates in the Pentagon and the State Department. Thompson did recruitment advertising for the U.S. Navy during World War II, including the famous "Wings of Gold" campaign that said: "The Navy will invest $27,000 in each young man fine enough to qualify as a Navy flier. If you measure up you will wear the Navy Wings of Gold." In 1942 four ads appearing in national magazines drew 19,000 replies. Meek was responsible for Thompson's later being assigned the recruitment advertising for the U.S. Marine Corps, an assignment the agency still has.

The Great Depression, at its nadir, put 10 million Americans on the unemployment rolls, but many of the big advertising agencies rode it out in good shape because of the appearance of a new medium for their messages: radio. Under the direction of John Reber, Thompson became a leader in radio advertising. They not only produced the commercials but they had a hand in the shows as well. By 1929 there was a radio set in more than one-third of U.S. homes. In

1930 J. Walter Thompson had radio programs for 18 clients and they were accounting for 23 hours a week of network time. Among the performers Thompson put on radio were Al Jolson, Burns and Allen, Bert Lahr, W. C. Fields, Edgar Bergen and Charlie McCarthy, Nelson Eddy, Groucho Marx, and Lionel Barrymore. The "Lux Radio Theatre," produced from Thompson's Hollywood office, became a Monday night ritual for millions of Americans. Also produced from this office was the long-running "Kraft Music Hall," which introduced a host of stars, including a young singer called Bing Crosby. In his book of reminiscences, *None of Your Business*, Carroll Carroll reported: "After Bing had been on the air a couple of years for Kraft, memoranda started to dribble in from Chicago saying that certain members of the Kraft company (or their wives) thought the public was getting a little tired of Bing's singing style and that we ought to talk to him about changing it."

J. Walter Thompson entered World War II placing $40 million of advertising a year for their clients, who included Kodak, Shell Oil, Planters peanuts, Purolator, Kraft cheese, Libby's, Universal Pictures, the Lever Brothers soaps, and Scott Paper (where Stanley Resor was a director). During the war they gained two important accounts, Pan Am and Ford Motor (the General Motors overseas assignments disappeared with the advent of World War II). Thompson kept Ford's name alive during the war with the "There's a Ford in your future" campaign. In 1947 Thompson became the first agency anywhere to handle $100 million of advertising in a single year. The leaps then became geometric, in line with the tremendous post–World War II growth of the advertising business. JWT billed $200 million in 1954 and $300 million in 1957.

The Resors and their accomplices—Sam Meek, Jim Young, and others—ran quite a show. They had a way of doing business that was all their own. It was nondirective management: no tables of organization, no heads of departments, no list of rules handed out to newcomers. Someone once brought Resor a table of organization with neat boxes connected by lines. "Looks fine," Resor was supposed to have said, "but erase the lines." Resor felt that the best way to teach people anything was by example— if you stayed around Thompson long enough and watched carefully, you would, by osmosis, learn what to do and how to do it. This philosophy was carried to such an extreme that the bathrooms in the New York office were purposely not labeled "men" and "women," the idea being that you would soon find out which was which (although it sometimes played havoc with visitors).

There were other Thompson idiosyncrasies. For one, nepotism was a no-no; the agency didn't hire relatives of people working at Thompson or of people at client companies, and despite the example of the husband-and-wife team at the head of the agency, if there were marriages among staffers, one member was expected to leave. (Stanley and Helen Resor's son, Stanley R. Resor, was secretary of the army in the Nixon administration; their daughter, Helen, married Gabriel Hauge, longtime chairman of Manufacturers Hanover Trust.) For another, liquor accounts were forbidden. It wasn't that Resor was a teetotaler; he merely felt that alcohol could have a destructive effect on some people. He was reported to have said that if "we had a liquor account, we would go at it in such a way that a good many people would start drinking. The other agencies would not affect people so much."

The ambience of the Thompson offices was also distinctive. They moved into the Graybar Building adjoining Grand Central Station in 1927, and they created there (again under Helen Resor's influence) an atmosphere unlike that of any other advertising agency. Thompson executives were encouraged to decorate their offices with furniture and fixtures they found comfortable and pleasing, and to help them the agency collected fine period pieces. Going from one Thompson office to another then was like moving through a series of drawing rooms. Another of the Thompson rules was, no closed doors. When they moved into the Graybar Building, they installed on the 11th floor 26 wrought iron gates and grilles behind which the top people worked, visible to anyone passing by. The gates were forged by Samuel Yellin of Philadelphia, sometimes called "America's Cellini of wrought iron." In 1950, when Thompson expanded to the 12th floor, they ordered another 26 gates from Harvey Z. Yellin, who had succeeded his father at the forge. Tucked away on the 11th floor was a dining room reconstructed, plank by plank,

PR: What's All the Shouting About?

Public relations people have been called many names (some unmentionable). Inside the business world they fall under many titles or categories: publicists; press agents (a show business term); public affairs (more high-toned); corporate communications (lofty); public information (straight); corporate relations (covering a multitude of sins). A more derogatory name is "flack," dating from the days (not all gone) when a public relations representative was considered by newsmen as some form of low life, plugging any person or product, no matter what, simply because he was paid to do it. An estimated 115,000 people work in PR as of 1979.

Much of what you read in print or hear or see on radio and television originates in the head of a public relations person. No one is exactly sure how much. According to Ted Klein and Fred Danzig, authors of *How to Be Heard*, on some days between 50% and 75% of a newspaper's news columns can be traced to PR efforts. The proportion is probably much higher in such sections as business and entertainment. Whenever you see an author plugging his book on the Johnny Carson or Phil Donahue show, you can be sure the appearance is the work of a public relations person.

The basic difference between public relations and advertising is that advertising space and time are paid for, while publicity, if it works, ends up in news columns or on radio and TV programs as part of the normal coverage. Public relations is carried out in two basic ways: by companies themselves or by outside public relations firms retained by the companies. Huge corporations such as Kodak and Coca-Cola do both. They have large internal PR staffs, and they hire outside publicists.

General Motors has 200 people working in their public relations department, Ma Bell has 130. The Bank of America, whose corporate communications division reports to the vice chairman, has 105 people. Kraft, the big Chicago food company, has a 14-person public relations department headed by Mardie MacKimm. Public relations used to be considered a dead-end as far as rising any further in corporate ranks, but the *Wall Street Journal* reported in June 1980 that this attitude has changed and that PR is increasingly proving a fast track to top management. MacKimm is a case in point. She is not only a senior vice president at Kraft but a director of two big companies, Du Pont and F.W. Woolworth. There are other exceptions to the rule that PR people don't advance in corporate life. Herbert Schmertz, the detonator of Mobil Oil's aggressive public relations barrage, makes $300,000 a year and sits on the Mobil board of directors. Three chief executive officers who came up through the PR route are George Weissman, chairman of Philip Morris, John Horan, chairman of Merck, and Robert Heimann, chairman of American Brands.

The 1980 *O'Dwyer Directory of Public Relations Firms*, prepared by PR chronicler Jack O'Dwyer, lists 1,010 public relations companies. They are mostly small. Only 26 collected more than $1 million a year for their services. Only a dozen have more than 100 employees. As might be expected, the biggest concentration is in New York City— more than 400 of the PR firms listed in the O'Dwyer directory are headquartered there. Here are the top 10:

1. HILL & KNOWLTON
SALES: $28 million
EMPLOYEES: 754
HEADQUARTERS:
New York, New York
OWNED BY: J. Walter Thompson
Clients: The big guys. More Forbes and Fortune 500 companies than anybody else. Closest thing to a factory in the PR business. Trade associations, foreign government (Republic of Indonesia, Dutch Ministry of Economic Affairs), shoes to insurance, sugar to airlines. Counsels whiskey producers and the Calorie Control Council. Also trucking, steel, food, a Denver police union, and Dutch flower growers.

2. BURSON-MARSTELLER
SALES: $26 million
EMPLOYEES: 758
HEADQUARTERS:
New York, New York
OWNED BY: Young & Rubicam
Clients: Trade associations (kraut packers, macaroni institute and pro basketball), foreign governments (Argentina and the City of Berlin), banks, food, home furnishings, olives from Spain and apricots from California, the ITT-sponsored TV children's series and Babcock & Wilcox of Three Mile Island fame.

3. CARL BYOIR & ASSOCIATES
SALES: $14 million
EMPLOYEES: 441
HEADQUARTERS:
New York, New York
OWNED BY:
Foote, Cone & Belding
Clients: Not a big list. But a high-paying select few. They were *THE* Howard Hughes agency for whatever he needed; and they have long been A&P's outfit. They once represented I.G. Farben, the German company that used concentration camp labor for their chemical business. And Carl Byoir now handles the Friedrich Flick company, headed by the descendents of the convicted German war criminal. Other clients: Visa credit cards, ITT, Kraft, the Saudi Arabia International Airport project.

4. RUDER & FINN

SALES: $8 million
EMPLOYEES: 240
HEADQUARTERS:
New York, New York
Clients: The first big Jewish-owned PR firm that made it. They were not taken seriously until they got the Coca-Cola account. (Later resigned Coke because of conflict with client Philip Morris' 7-Up.) Big in arts programs, and in public service. Other clients run the gamut: clothes (J.C. Penney), books, oil, tires, recreation, publications, manufacturing, electronics (Japan's Fujitsu).

5. HARSHE-ROTMAN & DRUCK

SALES: $6 million
EMPLOYEES: 182
HEADQUARTERS:
Chicago, Illinois
Clients: They let the world know about Hollywood's Academy Awards every spring. They also pitch for avocados, pistachios, the annual Tournament of Roses, Marriott Hotels, Flower growers in the other Hollywood — Florida, a bit of banking, and the Kenya External Trade Authority.

6. DANIEL J. EDELMAN

SALES: $6 million
EMPLOYEES: 198
HEADQUARTERS:
Chicago, Illinois
Clients: Range from pets and foods to the Republics of Haiti and Turkey to sporting goods, candy bars, recreation, household goods — a good chunk of Gillette products, Toyota, and Pan American World Airways.

7. MANNING, SELVAGE & LEE

SALES: $5 million
EMPLOYEES: 125
HEADQUARTERS:
New York, New York
OWNED BY: Benton & Bowles
Clients: Some prestigious ones ranging from Aetna to Upjohn, Hoffman-La Roche, and Merck. The company also touts New York State tourism and features New York City's Radio City Music Hall's Rockettes on tour; furs, foods, and wines from France, Atlanta's botanical gardens, electronic manufacturers, steel, rice and greeting card publishers.

8. DOREMUS & CO.

SALES: $5 million
EMPLOYEES: 137
HEADQUARTERS:
New York, New York
Clients: Based in the Wall Street area, they're mainly a financial PR house with such prominent clients as Morgan Stanley, Dun & Bradstreet, American Re-Insurance, Bank of Tokyo Trust and Mortgage Insurance Companies; they also handle Casio, Aesthetic and Reconstructive Plastic Surgeons, Episcopal Church and the Harry S. Truman Scholarship Foundation.

9. BOOKE AND COMPANY

SALES: $4 million
EMPLOYEES: 94
HEADQUARTERS:
New York, New York
Clients: This shop represents plumbing equipment (American Standard), real estate (Century 21), pens (Bic); stuff for your linen closet (Cannon Mills), Swiss Bank Corp., Sea Containers, and an assortment of others ranging from home products to health services.

10. KETCHUM, MACLEOD & GROVE

SALES: $4 million
EMPLOYEES: 120
HEADQUARTERS:
Pittsburgh, Pennsylvania
Clients: Through their food public relations, West Coast arm, Botsford Ketchum, they handle almonds, prunes, raisins, strawberries, tree fruits, papayas, and potatoes. Pillars of Pittsburgh they serve Carnegie-Mellon University, Hershey, H.J. Heinz, Pennsylvania Gas, PPG Industries, Gulf Oil and Westinghouse Electric (all Quaker state companies).

from an old New England farmhouse. Many Thompson people lived in Connecticut's Fairfield County, and when they commuted to Grand Central Station, they could alight from their train, pad through the station dominated by an Eastman Kodak sign, and enter the Graybar Building directly without ever having to step outside on the pavements of New York City.

It was a genteel life, an ethos that suited Thompson in the first half of the twentieth century. They were leaders of the advertising industry, and they wore their crown regally. They were in the position of being able to select their clients. If they didn't like the kind of products a company made, they would not take the business.

The transition from that world to the explosive business that advertising became after World War II was not an easy one for Thompson—or the Resors—to make. The arrival of television coincided with an upsurge of what was called the "creative revolution" in the agency business. It was sparked by an influx of new people—not the Ivy League crew from which Thompson had drawn their sustenance, but Jewish copywriters (who were barred from many of the top agencies), Italian-American art directors, and fiery spirits like Mary Wells and Carl Ally. Their trademarks were humor (as in the Alka-Seltzer ads) and self-deprecation (such as the "think small" ads for Volkswagen). They turned the business on its ear while Thompson for the most part ignored the warning signs. Thompson put down the "creative" wave as a fad that would fade away, and they refused even to enter any of their ads in the numerous competitions that had popped up in the business. Thompson's position was that the products, not the advertisements, were to be celebrated, a position that did not endear them to hot-blooded artists and writers looking for recognition.

Stanley Resor, who had taken the helm of the agency in 1916, moved up to chairman in 1955 and selected as president the manager of the Thompson office in Detroit, Norman H. Strouse. It was Strouse who presided over the transition from the Resor era, and he turned out to be an inspired choice. Like Jim Young, Strouse was largely self-educated. A voracious reader, he collected anything and everything to do with Robert Louis Stevenson. He kept a hand printing press in his home. Strouse had great respect for the Thompson tradi-

tions, but he also sensed the complacency that had set in, especially in the area of television, where Thompson was not playing the role it had in radio. To shore up that position he brought in a show business type, Dan Seymour, from Young & Rubicam. The stage was then set for a dramatic conflict between the Seymour forces, who represented modernity, and the old-guard Thompsonites.

A turning point came in 1960, when Shell Oil, a client for three decades, fired Thompson. That was the year Resor, then 81, finally relinquished the chief executive's title. And Strouse, together with Seymour, began to dismantle some of the old structure. In 1964 Seymour became president. It was a wrenching period for J. Walter Thompson. A big computer was installed (it had to be RCA equipment because RCA was a client and was then making computers). "Men" and "women" signs did go up on the bathroom doors. In 1967 in came liquor assignments from the House of Seagram. In 1969 the company went public, and J. Walter Thompson was soon listed on the New York Stock Exchange.

In their first 100 years of existence J. Walter Thompson had only four presidents: William Carlton, James Walter Thompson, Stanley Resor, and Norman Strouse. They were to have four more in their next 10: Dan Seymour, Henry Schachte, Edward B. Wilson, and Don Johnston. One of the remarkable aspects of Thompson's first 100 years was that their growth was achieved without buying other established companies. Even overseas they preferred to start from scratch. The only companies they bought were ad agencies in the Philippines and Japan that had been started by an ex-Thompsoner. But it's a different story today, symbolized by the formation in May 1980 of a new holding company, the JWT Group, which will own a number of different entities. The company's direction was marked out in their 1980 annual report by this un-Resorlike pronouncement:

"We will enter any communications area that promises to contribute to overall growth and does not involve conflict of interest. We do this either by acquisition or by development from within."

Reputation. JWT used to be known as the "old lady" of the advertising agency business, a place where the account executives were tall (so they could tower over the clients), Brooks Brothers-clad, Ivy League graduates, and the receptionists were former Bonwit Teller saleswomen. For many people who worked there it was like a home (and it looked like one). That atmosphere is mostly dispelled by now under the new imperative that the "failure to innovate" can be their undoing. It's a business where past glories do not bring you new clients.

What they own. In a 1979 *New York Times* interview, chairman Don Johnston emphasized: "We're an advertising agency—only." The next year Thompson bought the world's largest public relations company, Hill & Knowlton, and set up the Interpubliclike JWT Group, whose holdings include Euro-Advertising, a network of six European advertising agencies; Lord, Geller, Federico, Einstein, a New York–based agency described by JWT as "noted for the quality of its creative work"; World Wide Agency, an employment advertising agency; and the old mother, the J. Walter Thompson advertising agency.

Who owns and runs the company. J. Walter Thompson first sold stock to the public in 1969, thereby enriching the relatively small group of top-level people who had been allowed to buy shares in the company. Annual meetings, which used to be held secretly in the theater that was part of the New York office, now take place at the Starlight Roof of the Waldorf-Astoria. In early 1980 the largest holder of Thompson stock was the employee retirement trust: it had 7% of the shares. Holding nearly another 7% was Marsh & McClennan, investment adviser and world's largest insurance broker.

Chairman Don Johnston is Thompson-trained to the core, having started out in 1950 in the mailroom of the Detroit office. His chief lieutenant, Wayne J. Fickinger, was a United Press newsman before entering the advertising business; he made his way to the Thompson presidency via the Chicago office, long an important stronghold for the company. Below Fickinger and Johnston is a small army of officers: 12 executive vice-presidents, 59 senior vice-presidents, and 246 vice-presidents. (The agency business is an anonymous business, and one of the psychological rewards is a title.) Gordon T. Wallis, chairman of New York's Irving Trust, sits on the board. Irving has been Thompson's banker for about 60 years, and those employees permitted to buy stock when the company was private were always able to get low-interest loans to finance their purchase by walking across 42nd Street to see the Irving loan officer. Once they left Thompson, however, their reception at Irving tended to be frosty.

In the public eye. J. Walter Thompson has never wanted to stand out under their own name. When the Graybar Building was being put up in 1927, they were scheduled to be the largest tenant and could have had the building named for themselves. Stanley Resor said no thank you, just as he steadfastly refused to affix to the Thompson stationery any indication of what the company did, pointing out that J. P. Morgan never needed to identify themselves either.

Perhaps the greatest public attention Thompson ever received was during the Richard Nixon administration and the Watergate scandal. Three ex-Thompsoners were prominent members of the Nixon team. One was H. R. "Bob" Haldeman, the White House chief of staff, who had been head of Thompson's Los Angeles office when he wasn't campaigning for Nixon. Another was Ron Ziegler, the White House press secretary who had been an account executive in the Los Angeles office, working on Douglas Aircraft and Walt Disney. And the third was Nixon's appointments secretary, Dwight Chapin, who had started at Thompson-Los Angeles before moving to the New York office. Both Haldeman and Chapin were convicted of lying under oath; both served jail sentences. J. Walter Thompson received a lot of notoriety as a result of the activities of their alumni, with some critics suggesting that Watergate reflected an "advertising morality" that infected the Nixon administration.

One other story flushed out in the aftermath of Watergate was a long-rumored Thompson connection to the Central Intelligence Agency. Philip Agee, a former CIA agent, revealed that the Washington, D.C.–based public relations firm Robert R. Mullen & Co. was a CIA front. One of Mullen's backers was Sam Meek, the organizer of Thompson's international operations. In his book on Watergate, *Nightmare*, J. Anthony Lukas said that Meek arranged to set up joint Mullen-Thompson offices in Paris, London, and Tokyo. Meek was at one point a major owner of the *Rome Daily American*, an English-language paper in Italy. Prior to the Bay of Pigs invasion in 1961, the CIA set up an organization called the Cuban Freedom Committee, which was funded by $2 million of secret CIA funds. Robert Mullen helped to set up the committee; Sam Meek sat on the board of directors.

Where they're going. To a new headquarters building, for one thing. In the spring of 1981 they are scheduled to leave the Graybar Building and take new offices a block away at 466 Lexington Avenue (where they will be paying annual rent of $6 million). It will mark the end of an era in many ways. Thompson is now committed to the superagency mode, a concept that would have been anathema to Stanley Resor, who believed that JWT became number 1 because of the excellence of their services. The new JWT is seeking to recapture first place by buying a lot of other companies.

Stock performance. J. Walter Thompson stock bought for $1,000 in 1970 sold for $867 on January 2, 1980.

Major employment centers. New York, Chicago, and London.

Access. 420 Lexington Avenue, New York, New York 10017; (212) 867-1000. Thompson is the only ad agency that has an archivist: Janet Swank.

TWO CENTURIES OF AMERICAN ADVERTISING

Total Advertising Expenditures (est.)

Year	Amount	Year	Amount
1776	$ 0.2 *million*	1930	$ 2,450 *million*
1780	$ 0.2 *million*	1935	$ 1,720 *million*
1790	$ 0.4 *million*	1940	$ 2,110 *million*
1800	$ 1 *million*	1945	$ 2,840 *million*
1830	$ 5 *million*	1950	$ 5,700 *million*
1840	$ 7 *million*	1955	$ 9,150 *million*
1850	$ 12 *million*	1960	$11,960 *million*
1860	$ 22 *million*	1965	$15,250 *million*
1867	$ 40 *million*	1970	$19,550 *million*
1876	$ 150 *million*	1971	$20,740 *million*
1880	$ 175 *million*	1972	$23,300 *million*
1890	$ 300 *million*	1973	$25,120 *million*
1900	$ 450 *million*	1974	$26,820 *million*
1904	$ 750 *million*	1975	$28,160 *million*
1909	$1,000 *million*	1976	$33,690 *million*
1914	$1,100 *million*	1977	$37,920 *million*
1920	$2,480 *million*	1978	$43,840 *million*
1925	$2,600 *million*	1979	$49,690 *million*
		1980	$56,800 *million**

*Projected.

Source: *Advertising Age.*

A Market Researcher

Nielsen

Sales: $398 million
Profits: $26 million
Rank in market research: 1
Rank in broadcast ratings services: 1
Founded: 1923
Employees: 17,060
Headquarters: Northbrook, Illinois

What they do. A critic once called them "the closest thing we have in modern times to a witch doctor," and *Newsweek* ascribed to them "literal life-and-death power over network programming through ratings." But the television rating surveys that have made A. C. Nielsen both famous and controversial comprise only about 10% of their sales. Most of their business (about 63%) is as mundane as shopping for groceries.

Every other month, hordes of Nielsen auditors pour into supermarkets, drug stores, liquor stores, department stores, camera shops, and the like, carrying their ubiquitous clipboards. There they count the number of a given item sold in that store during the previous two-month period and compile information on how well one brand of detergent did against another, whether it sold better in a special display, how well an ad campaign or other promotion affected sales, and so on. When the clipboard people finish, their information goes to a central computer in Northbrook, Illinois (north of Chicago), to be converted into printout data for Nielsen clients like Procter & Gamble to peruse. That's how the clients know whether it's worth their while to keep making the large economy size, or whether you're attracted to the lemon-freshened furniture polish they've spent

millions trying to sell you. Procter & Gamble alone forks out $1 million a year for Nielsen's services.

From these Nielsen audits come the brand shares you sometimes see quoted—Crest sells 24% of all the toothpaste bought, Maxwell House does 33% of the coffee business. These statistics are much in use in advertising agencies, where the account people await their results every bit as anxiously as TV program executives. To move a product up by one Nielsen point is a big marketing victory in the business. Nielsen is the company that keeps score for the big advertisers of consumer products. *Advertising Age*, in their obituary of A. C. Nielsen, who died in June 1980, credited him with the concept of market shares. "This turned marketing into a horse race, and only Mr. Nielsen had the scorecard. More marketing decisions, expenditures, and careers have been influenced by that single statistic, share of market, than any other."

Nielsen has built this ratings business into a $400 million statistical empire in 23 nations. They make more money than the next seven largest market research firms combined. But that's not all. Nielsen is also keeping track of how many and what kind of coupons you're clipping out of newspapers. Their clearinghouse operation employs 4,000 people to receive coupons that come back from supermarkets, count them up, and report on their success to the manufacturers. Another Nielsen division—Neodata Services in Boulder, Colorado—keeps track of the lists of subscribers to several national magazines; and yet another compiles data for the oil industry on the production of new wells and how much oil or gas is thought to be under them.

But most people know Nielsen only through their television rating system, which consists of 1,200 cigar box-sized audimeters hooked up to televisions in 1,-

200 carefully selected American homes. These audimeters—usually hidden in a closet so the family doesn't feel like so many laboratory rats—tell a computer in Dunedin, Florida, what's being watched on what channel and at what time. The information then goes back to the major television networks in the form of ratings, which indicate what percentage of American TVs were tuned to what program, and in turn help determine what programs the networks run. Everyone wants advertising time on the most popular shows, for which the networks charge their top rates. Since Nielsen determines which shows are the most popular—and since advertisers spend $3 billion on TV advertising every year—it's easy to see why A. C. Nielsen's TV rating service operates in a fishbowl of public controversy.

History. The man who started it all, Arthur C. Nielsen, was a bug for statistics, which was only natural because both his parents were accountants. He graduated from the University of Wisconsin with the highest scholastic average ever recorded in the college of engineering in 1919. Four years later he opened a statistical consulting firm with $45,000 borrowed from his fraternity brothers.

What Nielsen wanted to do was sell "performance surveys" to the manufacturers of industrial machinery, telling them what their customers thought about their products. But Nielsen had a hard time convincing hard-boiled machinery manufacturers that they actually needed his service: one even asked Nielsen, "Why don't you quit this business and get into something honest?" But at the request of a client he did his first consumer survey, opening the door to a whole new business. In the late 1930s Nielsen added a radio rating service to his operation, asking radio listeners to keep a "diary" of what they tuned into. But Nielsen soon discovered that they kept poor records and frequently even lied about their listening habits, usually in favor of snob-appeal programs. So Nielsen bought the rights to the audimeter invented by two professors at the Massachusetts Institute of Technology in 1936, and when television entered homes in the 1950s, he converted it to TV use. This was just one of the mechanical gadgets that Nielsen toyed with. He also came up with a Gas-Oil Recordimeter for automobile gasoline purchases and the House Recordimeter for housewives to keep track of home purchases.

Not everyone has been pleased with the Nielsen audimeters. Despite the fact that statisticians support the claim that 1,200 homes are a large enough sample to give a true report on American viewing habits, the ratings have been questioned (often by people who would like to see them come out differently). A 1963 congressional investigation revealed that some Nielsen families tuned in their TVs for babies and pets to watch. More recently, a Los Angeles columnist revealed that one Nielsen viewer unabashedly boosts the ratings of shows he respects—but doesn't watch—by leaving the TV on when he's not home. Because each Nielsen TV represents 63,000 non-Nielsen TVs, this particular viewer's habit could influence what you see and what advertisers pay for commercial time. In 1963, when he was Federal Communications Commission chairman, Newton Minow encouraged broadcasters to "cancel the ratings and keep the programs." Minow added, "I just don't think it [should be] the function of broadcasters simply to count eyeballs."

Although A. C. Nielsen's son had been running the day-to-day operations of the company for years, the elder Nielsen was a member of the board of directors until his death. *Advertising Age* recalled that "In his prime, Mr. Nielsen worked 60–70 hours a week, and his employees were used to being bombarded with his memos, which were long and detailed. Many were drafted in the back seat of his eight passenger blue Fleetwood Cadillac which—complete with blue shag rug—was equipped as a moving office."

Reputation. A. C. Nielsen is the official scorekeeper of business. Like a lot of scorekeepers, they get yelled at a lot, but they trust their computers.

What they own. By far their most valuable asset is their experience in measuring product movement through stores. In 1976 their bimonthly index sampled 1,350 grocery stores out of a total of nearly 200,000 across the country.

Who owns and runs the company. A. C. Nielsen, Jr., became chairman in 1975. The Nielsen family owns about 61% of the voting stock.

Where they're going. The biggest threat to Nielsen now is the Universal Product Code (UPC)—those little zebra-striped labels on supermarket products. Cash registers equipped with pen-sized scanners read the information contained in the stripes and lock it into a computer, which is then capable of performing the same task as Nielsen's audits. Although only a few hundred stores currently have the expensive equipment necessary to perform the scan,

Nielsen was worried enough to begin dabbling in the field themselves. They now augment their reports with information gleaned from UPC systems.

Stock performance. Nielsen stock bought for $1,000 in 1970 sold for $1,549 on January 2, 1980.

Access. Northbrook, Illinois 60062; (312) 498-6300.

The Biggest Advertiser

Procter & Gamble

Sales: $9.3 billion
Profits: $577 million
Forbes 500 rank: 32
Rank in advertisers: 1
Rank in bar soap: 1
Rank in cake mixes: 1
Rank in laundry detergent: 1
Rank in toilet tissue: 1
Rank in toothpaste: 1
Rank in mouthwash: 2
Rank in shampoo: 1
Rank in disposable diapers: 1
Rank in deodorants: 1
Rank in salad and cooking oil: 2
Rank in coffee: 2
Founded: 1837
Employees: 59,000
Headquarters: Cincinnati, Ohio

What they do. Mr. Clean gets rid of dirt and grime and grease in just a minute, Mr. Clean can clean your whole house and everything that's in it.

For the first time in your life, feel really clean; Get that Zest glow from head to toe!

Look Mom, no cavities!

Most Americans have dozens of Procter & Gamble advertising jingles tucked away in the nooks and crannies of their minds—and they have many actual P&G products on the shelves of their kitchens and bathrooms. Ivory soap, Crest toothpaste, Tide

> **"To analyze detergent performance, technicians in a P&G laboratory wash the laundry of five hundred employees every week. Some tests become a little bizarre. Employees sampling a new toothpaste or mouthwash, for example, enter a laboratory where they breathe through a hole in the wall. A researcher on the other side sniffs their breath to judge the product's effectiveness. A new deodorant is tested similarly, by a professional armpit sniffer."**
> —*Fortune*, July 1974.

William Procter (top) and James Gamble: they never knew what they were starting when they began to make soap and candles in Cincinnati in 1837.

detergent, Cascade in the dishwasher, Pampers on the baby, Crisco in the frying pan, Head & Shoulders to fight dandruff, green Prell for a regular hairwash, Spic and Span for walls and woodwork, Comet cleanser for those stubborn stains in the sink. It's hard to know whether the thoughts you have about these products are your own or the ones that have been folded into your mind (like the milk folded into Duncan Hines cake mix) after hundreds of TV commercials repeatedly watched over the years.

Veteran character actor Arthur O'Connell, whose performances in the films *Picnic* and *Anatomy of a Murder* won him Academy Award nominations, gained more lasting fame through his creation of "Mr. Goodwin," the kindly drugstore proprietor who switched customers to Crest toothpaste. "Nobody calls me by my right name anymore," O'Connell once said. "Everywhere I go I'm Mr. Goodwin, the old codger on the tube. But I don't mind. I've never had such adulation in my life, even when I was up for the Academy Awards."

The list of familiar Procter & Gamble brand names is perhaps the most eloquent statement of the company's penetration into the very grain of America's daily life. There are whole stables of laundry detergents (Bold, Cheer, Dash, Duz, Era, Gain, Oxydol); bar soaps (Camay, Coast, Ivory, Lava, Sateguard, Zest); and liquid dishwasher detergents (Dawn, Joy, Ivory). Crest is backed up by Gleem. And then there are Charmin toilet paper, Bounty paper towels, Jif peanut butter, Scope mouthwash, Folger's coffee, Downy fabric softener, Pringle's potato chips, Wondra skin cream.

It's no surprise if you feel that television has made you intimately familiar with these products and the dramatized family members, fix-it-men, genies, and authority figures who tout them on the home screen. P&G spends over half a billion dollars a year on advertising, 90% of it on TV. They are the nation's largest advertiser. And they are the reigning monarch over the world of soap operas, those daytime dramas aimed at women, heavily laced with commercials for things that lather or foam or will make your husband smile at the dinner table. They specialize in the slice-of-life skit—a dramatic moment over a washing machine, or a charged confrontation between parents and toothbrush-waving children. The soap operas themselves present dramas in a similar vein—endless cliff-hanging domestic crises that will hopefully jerk enough tears to keep you reaching for the Puffs facial tissues.

P&G owns and sponsors five vintage soaps: *As the World Turns, Edge of Night, Search for Tomorrow, Guiding Light,* and *Another World.* As more women have taken to jobs outside the home, P&G has turned to sponsoring prime-time shows as well.

P&G's advertising is of such magnitude that they employ 10 ad agencies that compete with each other in promoting P&G products of the same type. For instance, in laundry detergents Compton has the Tide account, Young & Rubicam has Dash, Dancer Fitzgerald Sample has Oxydol, Grey has Duz and Bold, Doyle Dane Bernbach has Gain, and Leo Burnett has Cheer and Era.

P&G is also the largest purveyor of free samples and cents-off coupons: they really believe you'll like their products if you try them. They put a lot of money into research and development ($173 million in 1978). In the 1950s they sponsored the research that identified fluoride as an anticavity agent, and they reaped the rewards with Crest. More recently they synthesized sucrose polyester, which someday may find its way into your body as a cooking oil. Scientists at the University of Cincinnati's medical school found it effective in reducing cholesterol levels.

Before marketing a product P&G tries to be sure it will be a success. First they test it on hundreds of their own employees, then on panels of consumers—hundreds of thousands of them each year. P&G will stick with the product only if it wins a majority of consumer votes against all major competitors. For toothpaste or mouthwash, where individual tastes may vary quite a bit, P&G is satisfied with 55% approval; for a new toilet paper it has to be 80%. Once they've decided on a new product, they ease into the market gradually, starting in just a few cities. Their salespeople are notoriously aggressive in trying to grab the best shelf space in supermarkets.

But selling consumer products is not an exact science, and even P&G takes it on the chin sometimes. Ever hear of Teel toothpaste, Extend mouthwash, or Hidden Magic hair spray? Those are some items that went before the public and failed.

Sometimes when a new product doesn't rise to the top, P&G stays and fights—as in the case of Pringle's "new-fangled" potato chips, introduced in 1968. P&G mushed up dehydrated potatoes, loaded them with preservatives, molded them all into the same size and shape, fried them, and packaged them in containers that looked like tennis ball cans. They figured they had solved two of the potato chip's biggest problems: short shelf-life and crushability. Pringle's took off at first, perhaps from sheer novelty, but sales soon dropped. It seems people like their chips in different sizes and shapes. Besides, Pringle's cost more, and their preservative load may have turned off many people who were starting to notice ingredients. Having invested some $70 million in Pringle's, P&G decided to change them instead of abandoning them. They took out the preservatives, added two new varieties (a "Rippled Style" and a thick "Country Style"), and lowered the price.

P&G both starts products from scratch—Pringle's and Pampers disposable diapers, for examples—and buys other companies (Duncan Hines and Folger's). No matter how they do it, they like to be in first place. And they usually are. They bought the Folger's coffee business in 1963, and it took them 15 years to bring the brand into national distribution and first place in ground coffee sales. But they still trail General Foods in the instant coffee market and in overall coffee sales.

About 40% of P&G's sales comes from detergents, fabric softeners, and cleansers and about a third from "personal-care products" like soap, toothpaste, deodorant, shampoo, toilet paper, and diapers. Just under one-fourth comes from foods, and about 6% from a few minor fields including cellulose pulp and animal feed ingredients. Foreign business accounts for a little over a fourth of sales.

But if you had to guess which among all these products brings in more money to P&G than any other, which would you pick? The answer is Pampers disposable diapers, which in 1978 accounted for about 11% of the company's total sales, or about $900 million.

History. A story is told that when P&G decided in 1956 to reduce the price of their stock by exchanging two shares for each one outstanding, a stockbroker told an elderly client that Procter & Gamble was going to split. "What a shame," she said, "they've been together so long!"

William Procter, a British candlemaker, and James Gamble, an Irish soapmaker, joined their businesses in Cincinnati in 1837. The two men were married to two sisters, and company lore has it that their father-in-law suggested the partnership. The chief raw material for both candles and soap was animal fat, and Cincinnati, known as "Porkopolis," was a great hog-butchering center. Procter ran the office, and Gamble ran the factory. As the business expanded into several river-front factories and a downtown office, the two met in Procter's parlor on Saturday nights to discuss business. When the Civil War started, they were the largest company in Cincinnati. They had also developed their trademark, a circle containing the man in the moon and 13 stars, a version of which appears to this day on all their products.

P&G supplied soap and candles to the Union army during the Civil War and got even more business from the public when it was over in 1865. That same year young Thomas Edison landed a job as a P&G mechanic and set up an electrical device to speed messages from the office to the factory, two miles away.

Each cofounder had three sons who entered the business, and by the 1880s the second generation was running the company. It was Procter's son Harley who first displayed the marketing savvy for which the company became famous. When P&G introduced a new kind of white soap in 1878, Harley Procter came up with the gimmick of carving a groove in the middle of each laundry-size bar so that the buyer could break it into two toilet-size cakes. The right brand name came to him in church on a Sunday in 1879, during a reading of the 45th Psalm: "All thy garments smell of myrrh, and aloes, and cassia, out of the ivory palaces whereby they have made thee glad." Ivory Soap was born.

Later a customer surprised them by ordering "more of that floating soap." P&G guessed that a workman had accidentally left a stirring machine on too long and that an irregular batch of soap, laced with air bubbles, had slipped through. They changed the formula to make every bar float. Harley Procter had the soap chemically analyzed to find out the percentages of useless impurities: uncombined alkali, 0.-11%; carbonates, 0.28%; mineral matter, 0.-17%—total, 0.56%. That information spawned one of the most famous advertising lines of all time: "99 44/100% Pure."

Their next major brand name, Crisco shortening, appeared in 1911 during the tenure of William Cooper Procter, the cofounder's grandson. Crisco was made from the same cottonseed oil that went into some of their soaps. In the 1920s P&G popularized a new art form—soap sculpture—blanketing public schools with instructions for carving bars of Ivory and putting up prize money for an annual national contest that attracted thousands of entries.

In 1930 William Cooper Procter handed the presidency to Richard R. Deupree, who had risen through the sales department. For the first time neither a Procter nor a Gamble headed the company. Deupree was president until 1948, then chairman until 1959. During this period P&G became the nation's leading seller of consumer products. In 1932 P&G treated America to its first soap opera, a daytime radio drama called "The Puddle Family."

The company's biggest breakthrough came just after World War II, when they introduced Tide detergent ("gets clothes cleaner than any soap!"). The detergent culminated 20 years of research. Laundry soap didn't work in hard water, where high mineral levels were present, and it left "soap curd," like bathtub ring, in the washtub. P&G concocted a complex chemical compound that actually pulled oil and grease out of clothes and dissolved the dirt into the wash water, and revolutionized America's laundry habits before their main competitors, Lever Brothers and Colgate-Palmolive, realized what was happening. The astounding rise of Tide and other heavy-duty laundry detergents went hand in hand with the rise of automatic washing machines: in 1946, 3% of American homes had one; by 1955 it was 33%.

Having abolished much of the drudgery of the laundry room, P&G marched into the kitchen. The Duncan Hines label had come into being after a group of struggling farm cooperatives, trying to compete against much larger food companies, approached Roy H. Park, the proprietor of a small advertising agency in upstate New York. Park struck a deal with Duncan Hines, who was known for his guides to restaurants, to use his name on various food labels. Park licensed the name to many small food companies. The brand became well known on all sorts of products, the most successful being a line of pancake mixes made by Nebraska

Consolidated Mills (now ConAgra). Then P&G decided they wanted it. They bought Park's company in 1956, put the Duncan Hines name on their new line of cake mixes, and disbanded the licensing operation. So a line of products created to help small companies fight big ones was snapped up by a giant, leaving many of the small firms brandless again.

Neil H. McElroy, who rose through P&G's advertising department to take over the presidency in 1948, was named secretary of defense by President Eisenhower in 1957. He was the first official to proclaim the "missile gap," a national preoccupation for years to come. In 1959 he returned to P&G as chairman, retiring in 1971. During the next Republican administration P&G lent another executive to Washington. Bryce N. Harlow, who joined the company in 1961, became Richard Nixon's chief lobbyist on Capitol Hill in 1969. He returned to P&G at the end of 1970, then went back to the White House in June 1973, after Nixon's staff had been severely depleted by the Watergate scandal. In April 1974 he returned again to P&G, where he served as vice-president for national government relations until 1978.

Progress, P&G style, marched on. They entered the paper products field in 1957 when they bought little Charmin Paper Mills, and they proceeded to roll over the longtime industry leader, Scott Paper. They launched Pampers in 1961, they became the owners of Folger's in 1963, they challenged Listerine in 1965 with Scope. In the 1970s they introduced Sure deodorant, Era liquid detergent, Bounce fabric softener, Dawn liquid detergent, Coast deodorant soap, Folger's flaked coffee, and Rely tampons.

P&G was slow moving into overseas markets, but they have been making up for lost time with their customary aggressive marketing. They're now a powerful factor in the soap and detergent markets of Western Europe, going head-to-head with Unilever, Colgate and Henkel. In Japan they have entered into a joint venture with a local company, Nippon Sunhome of Osaka.

Addressing stockholders in 1978, Chairman Edward G. Harness said: "I see no reason why this company can't double its business every 10 years."

Reputation. Procter & Gamble is known as a company that does their homework.

They're highly regarded for their efficiency, and they're feared as competitors. Secrecy is another of their trademarks. Harness once said: "We've long believed there's nothing to be gained by telling our competitors how we do things."

YOU MAY HAVE HEARD OF THEM: THE NATION'S 50 BIGGEST ADVERTISING SPENDERS IN ALL MEDIA

Total Ad Expenditures, 1978

1. PROCTER & GAMBLE $554 million
2. SEARS ROEBUCK $418 million
3. GENERAL FOODS $340 million
4. GENERAL MOTORS $266 million
5. K MART $250 million
6. PHILIP MORRIS $237 million
7. WARNER-LAMBERT $211 million
8. FORD MOTOR $210 million
9. BRISTOL-MYERS $193 million
10. CHRYSLER $189 million
11. AMERICAN HOME PRODUCTS $183 million
12. R. J. REYNOLDS $183 million
13. AMERICAN TELEPHONE & TELEGRAPH $173 million
14. GENERAL MILLS $170 million
15. MOBIL $163 million
16. PEPSICO $156 million
17. BEATRICE FOODS $150 million
18. UNILEVER $145 million
19. NORTON SIMON $145 million
20. ESMARK $141 million
21. RCA $140 million
22. COCA-COLA $139 million
23. McDONALD'S $137 million
24. JOHNSON & JOHNSON $134 million
25. U.S. GOVERNMENT $129 million
26. GULF + WESTERN $127 million
27. J. C. PENNEY $125 million
28. INTERNATIONAL TELEPHONE & TELEGRAPH $123 million
29. COLGATE-PALMOLIVE $123 million
30. CBS $122 million
31. GENERAL ELECTRIC $121 million
32. SEAGRAM $120 million
33. HEUBLEIN $118 million
34. ANHEUSER-BUSCH $117 million
35. AMERICAN CYANAMID $115 million
36. KRAFT $114 million
37. RICHARDSON-MERRELL $105 million
38. PILLSBURY $104 million
39. GILLETTE $99 million
40. REVLON $92 million
41. CONSOLIDATED FOODS $92 million
42. SMITHKLINE $91 million
43. RALSTON PURINA $91 million
44. NABISCO $91 million
45. EASTMAN KODAK $86 million
46. CHESEBROUGH-POND'S $85 million
47. B.A.T. INDUSTRIES $82 million
48. KELLOGG $80 million
49. LOEWS CORP. $79 million
50. STERLING DRUG $78 million

Source: *Advertising Age,* September 6, 1979.

What they own. Forty-two plants in the United States, from Massachusetts to California, but mostly in the Midwest and the South. Twenty-seven plants in 13 foreign countries, the majority in Canada and Europe, with others in Peru, the Philippines, and Lebanon. They also hold long-term leases on extensive timberlands to supply their pulp mills in Florida and Alberta, Canada.

Who owns and runs the company. The Procters and the Gambles are long gone from active duty, but it is likely that many of their descendants own sizeable blocks of the stock. One of them, Olivia Procter Maynard, ran for lieutenant governor of Michigan in 1978 and released a financial disclosure statement that put her net worth at nearly $900,000. P&G operates the oldest profit-sharing plan in the nation—it began in 1887—and this plan holds the largest block of stock (about 8% of all the shares). P&G is famous in the business world for their training programs. Many of their graduates hold top jobs at other companies: General Foods, Pepsico, Scott Paper, Monsanto. But most hirees stay at the company, attracted by the combination of a good salary, a strong benefits program, and a long-time winning streak. P&G is known for throwing young recruits into the firing line. It has been said that there is probably no other company in America that has so many people under 30 managing important pieces of business. "We're not anxious to dispatch people to ivy-covered buildings where they sit in classrooms, hear lectures and sing songs," said Harness. "Instead we give them something to do." In 1978 P&G announced the election of eight new top executive officers. Their average age was 44 and they had an average of 20 years experience with P&G.

There's an almost evangelistic quality about life within Procter & Gamble. *Fortune* put it this way: "People who work for P&G believe the products they make and market *are* better. As they see it, they're engaged in something fundamentally worthwhile." At Christmas time P&G gives all their employees a gift package of "selected delicacies of the holiday season." Twice a year, usually in February and September, they hold "Dividend Day" programs for the Cincinnati employees. "This is a time for enjoyment and getting acquainted. It is also a day intended to personally remind you that, whatever your job, you are a partner who actively contributes toward and shares in the profits of Procter & Gamble."

In the public eye. You name it and P&G has been accused of it, from polluting sewage systems with their detergents to portraying women in an unfavorable light in their commercials. They have generally tried to be responsive. In 1957 they got into the bleach business by buying Clorox. Ten years later the Supreme Court made them sell off Clorox, ruling that P&G was a big enough boy to get into bleach on their own without buying up the biggest company in that business. Since then P&G has been chary about buying others. In 1977 they stopped buying coffee beans from the African country of Uganda after church groups objected that such purchases helped to prop up dictator Idi Amin. The minority share of P&G's U.S. workforce is about 15%—and they hold 7.7% of positions classified as "officials and managers." Women make up 24.3% of P&G's work force, but they hold only 10% of the top jobs. In the all-important P&G sales ranks, women have only 8.4% of the jobs (but that proportion has nearly doubled since 1976). Addressing managers in 1977, Chairman Harness advised them that P&G operates in "a framework of enlightened self-interest," adding: "There are those who criticize us for making what they regard as large profits. We make no apologies for the profits we have earned. Earnings are precisely what we are in business for."

Where they're going. P&G likes to point out that every new product they have developed has derived from their original soap-making business. From soap came detergents, then shampoo and toothpaste. They started mixing cottonseed oil in with animal fats in their soap recipes around the turn of the century, and from that came shortening, oil, and eventually peanut butter. The pulp from the cottonseeds led to paper towels, toilet paper, and disposable diapers. Now they're working on a birth-control device that uses a spermicidal agent similar to the element in detergents that loosens the dirt from clothes. In the late 1970s they entered the prescription drug field with medicines for acne and Paget's disease, a bone abnormality. They are test-

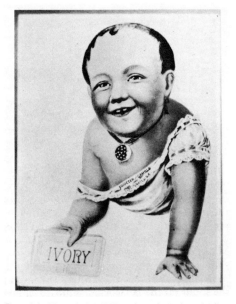

The original Ivory baby, 1887, and a rather ethereal advertisement for the floating soap at the turn of the century. Ivory is one of the oldest brands in America. It was 100 years old in 1979.

ing disposable diapers for incontinent adults in nursing homes, a market that has been virtually ignored in the past. They already make disposable surgical gowns, and they predict that the material used in them will someday replace cloth towels and sheets in hospitals and hotels. The cost is too high now, they say, but the price of detergents has been climbing in recent years. If Tide gets too expensive, P&G will be right there with the answer in the form of a product that needs no laundering. In the last few years they've been test-marketing a tampon (Rely) and a new disposable diaper (Luvs). They have developed an artificial cocoa butter from palm oil, which may show up as "artificial chocolate." They're also working on a dry carbonated soft drink and have registered a patent for a drinking glass with the powder lodged at the bottom: just add water and presto!—instant soda pop.

P&G apparently put their powdered soft drink on the back burner in mid-1980 when they bought Crush International after spirited bidding over the sale price with Dr Pepper. The final price tag: $53 million. Crush makes soft drinks under the brand names of Crush, Hires, and Sun Drop. Industry observers also expect P&G to experi-

ment with a cola drink to compete with Coca-Cola and Pepsi-Cola.

Stock performance. Procter & Gamble stock bought for $1,000 in 1970 sold for $1,356 on January 2, 1980.

Access. 301 East Sixth Street, Cincinnati, Ohio 45202; (513) 562-1100.

Consumer brands.

Dish detergents: Ivory Liquid; Joy; Dawn.
Dishwasher detergent: Cascade.
Laundry detergent: Bold; Cheer; Dash; Duz; Era; Gain; Oxydol; Tide; Dreft; Ivory Snow.
Bar soap: Ivory; Camay; Coast; Lava; Safeguard; Zest.
Household cleaning products: Comet; Mr. Clean; Spic and Span; Top Job; Bounce; Downy; Biz.
Food products: Crisco shortening and oil; Duncan Hines; Fluffo; Jif; Pringle's; Puritan Oil.
Toilet paper: Charmin; White Cloud.
Paper towels: Bounty.
Disposable diapers: Luvs; Pampers; Puffs.
Toothpaste: Crest; Gleem.
Hair Products: Prell; Head & Shoulders; Lilt.
Deodorants: Secret; Sure.
Tampons: Rely.
Moisture cream: Wondra.
Mouthwash: Scope.
Coffee: Folger's.
Soft Drinks: Crush; Hires; Sun Drop.

Broadcasters

Sales: $2.0 billion
Profits: $159 million
Forbes 500 rank: 258
Rank in television networks: 2
Founded: 1941
Employees: 9,400
Headquarters: New York, New York

What they do. For 20 years the best things about ABC were the jokes they inspired. How do you end the Vietnam War? "Put it on ABC and it will be cancelled in 13 weeks." Where is Patty Hearst? "Alive and hiding on ABC's Friday night schedule." But there are no ABC jokes anymore. From 1976 through 1979 ABC beat out CBS and NBC as the top-rated network, and in 1980 they finished only a shade behind CBS. And as their Nielsen ratings have gone up, so have the prices they can charge the companies who want to peddle beer, deodorants, and cars to the viewing audience during the three minutes of commercials aired in each half-hour of evening prime time. From 1975 to 1978 ABC almost quadrupled their broadcasting profits from $82 million to $311 million.

How has ABC risen from being the "number 3 network in a two-and-a-half network market," as they used to be known? As always, the key to their success has been putting on programs that will attract the largest audience. In their drive to the top, ABC's strategy has been to appeal to children (who are said to control the TV dial in most homes) and affluent youth (the free spenders advertisers want to reach) with a combination of silliness ("Happy Days," "Laverne and Shirley," "Mork and Mindy") and titillation ("Charlie's Angels," "Three's Company," "Soap"). As an ABC executive explained in 1976, "We're giving them the same old garbage done a little better." ABC buys these shows from television production companies like Norman Lear or MTM. ABC's programmers schedule the shows against the competition to get the most favorable mix of ratings, then send them out on the network, composed of 200 affiliates and ABC's five owned-and-operated stations in New York, Los Angeles, San Francisco, Detroit, and Chicago. (Stations along the network receive fees for the use of their airtime.) Then ABC waits nervously for the all-important ratings.

Like the other television networks, ABC started out in radio. Their radio network today includes 14 AM and FM stations owned by the company and about 1,600 affiliated stations. Unlike rival CBS, ABC is mainly engaged in broadcasting, which accounts for 87% of their revenues. A major part of the remainder comes from recently acquired publishing properties. They now own a number of trade and specialty magazines, including *Modern Photography*, *High Fidelity*, and *Wallaces Farmer*, one of the oldest and most famous farm journals. Their *Los Angeles* magazine had more pages of advertising than any other American monthly in 1978, and their Word Division—religious books—came out with *The Gift of Inner Healing* by Ruth Carter Stapleton (Jimmy Carter's sister) and Billy Graham's *How to be Born Again*.

ABC also owns and operates three recreational parks in Florida: Weeki Wachee Spring, Silver Springs, and Wild Waters. The ABC Entertainment Center at Century City in Los Angeles includes three theaters, restaurants, and shops.

History. ABC is one of the few major corporations started by government order. In 1941 the Federal Communications Commission forced NBC to sell one of their two radio networks—called the Red Network and the Blue Network. NBC kept the more profitable Red Network. Edward Noble, heir to the Life Savers fortune, bought the Blue Network and christened it the American Broadcasting Company. ABC's first home in the former New York Riding Club Arena always had a vague smell of horse manure, symbolic of the performance of the fledgling network. ABC had a difficult time in the late 1940s and early 1950s making the transition to television. During the 1950s, the Golden Age of Television, ABC broadcast live 186 hours of the Army–McCarthy hearings since they were the only network without daytime programming.

But in 1953 they got a boost when they merged with United Paramount, the movie–theater business of Paramount Pictures, which had been separated from its parent by antitrust action. (ABC finally sold the last of their movie theaters in 1978.) The merger gave ABC money to work with, and they promptly lent Walt Disney $4.5 million to complete Disneyland, in return for a Disney show. This was the first time a movie company had produced a show for television, but by 1955 ABC convinced Warner Brothers to follow Disney's example, and ABC soon had series like "Maverick," "Lawman," and "Colt .45."

But in ABC's first two decades they rarely challenged the supremacy of the other two networks. The network's best moments came from their sports department, which took over the number 1 spot on the strength of their "Wide World of Sports" show (which introduced the instant replay during the Texas-Texas A&M football game on Thanksgiving Day, 1961), Monday Night Football, and coverage of the Olympics. Nevertheless, they just barely survived takeover attempts by ITT, Norton Simon, and Howard Hughes.

ABC finally reached the top in 1976 through the efforts of the man "with the golden gut," mass-media programmer extraordinaire Fred Silverman. For $300,000 a year, a paid-up $1 million life insurance policy, stock options, and homes on both coasts, ABC induced Silverman to leave CBS in 1975. He was worth it. The day he was hired ABC's stock shot up two points on the stock exchange—a total increase of $34 million.

Under Silverman's leadership ABC introduced the shows intellectuals love to hate: "Laverne and Shirley," "Bionic Woman," and "Love Boat." ABC also snapped up most of the daytime ratings by expanding their soap operas to one hour and featuring controversial topics like feminism and abortion. Although Silverman was lured to greener pastures by NBC in 1978, the lineup he instituted is still the backbone of ABC's schedule.

Reputation. In New York CBS's elegant skyscraper is known as "Black Rock," and NBC's headquarters, at 30 Rockefeller Plaza, is known as "30 Rock." Inevitably, ABC's Manhattan building was called "Little Rock." And to some people it's "Schlock Rock."

Who owns and runs the company. Leonard H. Goldenson, who organized the Paramount merger in 1953, was still running the company in 1979, at the age of 74. Chairman Goldenson is the largest individual stockholder, with 1.4% of the shares, and is paid $750,000 a year. President Elton Rule makes $650,000. Still, the stars make more than the executives. Henry Winkler, who plays the Fonz, earns $80,000 per episode of "Happy Days." At 24 episodes per year, that adds up to $2 million. ABC has one woman and one black director in the person of Mamie Phipps Clark, the director of the Northside Center for Child Development in New York; and one woman officer, treasurer Ann Maynard Gray.

In the public eye. ABC has always been weak on news, but under the direction of Roone Arledge, the man who built their sports department, that is changing. In a highly publicized move in 1976, ABC offered Barbara Walters of NBC's "Today" show a $5 million contract to coanchor the news with Harry Reasoner. As *Forbes* pointed out, if Walters had increased the ratings by even 0.6 of a Nielsen point, her contract would have been paid off. But the Reasoner/Walters team flopped. Arledge stepped in with a new format. "World News Tonight" features a team of three anchors located in London, Washington, and Chicago, all tied together by satellite transmissions. The network's late-night coverage of the Iran hostage crisis in 1979 proved so popular that they immediately instituted the first network late night news show, which follows the late local news. According to *Newsweek*, Arledge has given his producers on the network's news specials greater freedom to do "multipart, in-depth looks at insurance frauds against the elderly and sexual harrassment of women on the job." Barbara Walters's interviews run the gamut from Richard Nixon and the Shah of Iran to popular stars like Farrah Fawcett, Cheryl Ladd, and Bo Derek.

Blurring the line between news and entertainment is not new at ABC. KGO-TV, ABC's owned station in San Francisco, pioneered with the "happy talk" news format that features a chatty, jocular delivery by news anchors, often accompanied by an emphasis on sex, violence, and sensationalism. This format made KGO the top-rated local news show for many years and inspired imitators all over the country.

In 1980 ABC ran a full-page newspaper ad that announced, "We are honored to be chosen" to cover the 1984 Olympics in Los Angeles. They neglected to mention that they outbid the other networks by $60 million for the "honor."

By their own report ABC's work force includes 38% women and 18% minorities; the figures for management positions are 28% and 11%.

Where they're going. ABC's success has brought in lots of cash, and since they are forbidden by law from expanding their broadcasting holdings, in the last three years they've been moving into publishing.

How "Little House" Gets to Your House:

You're sitting at home on a Monday night watching *Little House on the Prairie*. The screen is alight with the doings of the Ingalls family there in Walnut Grove, Minn. You're absorbed in the story and totally unconcerned about how in heaven's name that picture actually arrived in your living room.

In truth, it traveled a path more tortuous than the one Odysseus took on his celebrated voyage home from the Trojan War. Only quicker. The hero of Homer's *Odyssey* needed ten years to get where he was going but Michael Landon's image hits your screen in less than a second, once the whole intricate broadcast process is set in motion.

Let's follow one segment of *Little House on the Prairie*, starting from when its producers have finished filming it at Simi Valley, 50 miles northwest of Los Angeles, and have edited it into satisfactory final form.

The first thing the producers do is make four copies of the film—two 35 mm and two 16 mm—and hand them in to NBC's Burbank offices. The Burbank folks keep two

copies (one of each size) and put the other two on a plane to New York's Kennedy Airport, where they're picked up by a courier. He delivers the prints to an NBC facility called the Film Exchange in Englewood, N.J., just across the Hudson River from New York.

At Englewood, a film editor doctors the prints, inserting blank spots (called "black slugs") of precise duration into the film where commercials and promotional announcements will eventually go. Then he sends the 16 mm print to NBC's headquarters in the RCA Building at Rockefeller Center in Manhattan. Meanwhile, in NBC's master control room those commercials and "promos" are put into a computer, ready to be melded gracefully with the *Little House* episode.

At precisely 8 P.M. Eastern Time on Monday night, that computer in New York sends a command via cable to Englewood. A film projector there hums into action, beaming its picture straight into the innards of (what is in effect) a TV camera, transmogrifying the image into a TV signal, and sending *Little*

House on the Prairie on the first leg of its journey to your home. (Simultaneously, the 16 mm print in New York starts up on a separate camera chain, in case trouble with the Englewood transmission develops in the ensuing hour.)

Instantly, the airborne picture jumps from Englewood, by microwave, to an antenna atop the Empire State Building. From there it's funneled by cable into NBC's master control room, where—in an hour-long stint of scrupulously timed computer switching—the program and the commercials are dovetailed expertly into one seamless whole.

Next, the signal departs Rockefeller Center for a three-mile trip south on coaxial cable under the streets of Manhattan, to AT&T's Television Operating Center at the foot of the Avenue of the Americas. (All three networks send their pictures there.) Actually, it's *two* three-mile trips south because the program routes travel on parallel routes: one down the west side of Manhattan, one down the east side—just in case an underground steam-pipe rupture or flood should abort the signal.

In the future you might expect two things from ABC: (1) they'll acquire other non-broadcasting properties, or (2) they will be bought up by someone else looking for a good cash machine.

Stock performance. American Broadcasting Companies stock bought for $1,000 in 1970 sold for $3,226 on January 2, 1980.

Major employment centers. New York City and Los Angeles.

Access. 1330 Avenue of the Americas, New York, New York 10019; (212) 887-7777. Address inquiries and complaints to Audience Information Department.

A TV Signal Has a Drama All Its Own

Having thus arrived at A T & T, the signal is then sent to the building's roof, where a microwave transmitter beams it outward over the airways to the nation at large. Since microwaves don't follow the earth's curvature, microwave relay stations are perched on high ground every 40 or 50 miles all over the U.S. Each of them receives the *Little House on the Prairie* picture, then amplifies it and sends it on its way to the next station.

When the picture signals reach the microwave relay closest to the NBC affiliate in your area, they're captured and channeled right into that TV station's master control room. There, an engineer pushes buttons at precise intervals to insert local commercials over the few remaining "black slugs" in the program. The picture then leaves the control room (via cable or microwave) to the station's own transmitter, from which it's broadcast to the rooftop antenna on your home.

The final leg of *Little House on the Prairie* 's incredible journey is the few dozen feet from your roof to your television set. In your set the elec-

tronic signals that started back in Englewood, N.J., are reconstituted into a picture. And there you are, installed comfortably in front of your television set, observing the Ingalls family's latest adventures. (If you're on a cable-TV system, the NBC affiliate's signal is intercepted by the cable company's antenna and transmitted to your home by wire.)

If you live in the Eastern or Central time zones, the *Little House on the Prairie* picture has made its way from Englewood, N.J., to your home in milliseconds. Viewers in Eastern Time Zone cities like Boston and Cincinnati are seeing the program at 8 P.M., while folks in Central Zone towns like Minneapolis and Dallas are seeing it simultaneously at 7 P.M. their time.

In the thinly populated Mountain Zone, however, the NBC affiliates in places like Helena, Mont., Salt Lake City, Utah, and Flagstaff, Ariz., tape the program as it reaches them at 6 P.M., and then play it for their audiences on a delayed basis. Meanwhile, back in Burbank, NBC technicians are preparing the two film copies of *Little House on*

the Prairie that were left behind in California. (Remember them?) At 8 P.M. Pacific Time (11 P.M. in New York), they broadcast the program to states in that time zone: California, Nevada, Oregon, and Washington. Thus, viewers in the East and West get their prime-time programs from 8 to 11 P.M., and the two zones in the middle have a 7–10 P.M. prime time.

Hawaii's needs are met quite simply: NBC merely ships a video-tape copy of the program by plane to station KHON-TV in Honolulu, and the people there broadcast it to the islanders in routine fashion. Alaska's situation is more complicated. Entertainment programming such as *Little House* come by video-tape and is broadcast up to several weeks later. (More timely programs are fed to Alaska by satellite.)

So stop complaining. Considering what they must go through to get to your home, it's a miracle we have any television programs at all.

By Neil Hickey. Reprinted from *TV Guide*, July 28, 1979.

Consumer brands.

Television stations: WABC-TV (New York City); WLS-TV (Chicago); KGO-TV (San Francisco); KABC-TV (Los Angeles); WXYZ-TV (Detroit).

Radio stations: WABC-AM (New York City); WXYZ-AM (Detroit); WLS-AM (Chicago); KGO-AM (San Francisco); KABC-AM (Los Angeles); WMAL-AM (Washington, D.C.); WPLJ-FM (New York City); WRIF-FM (Detroit); WDAI-FM (Chicago); KSFX-FM (San Francisco); KLOS-FM (Los Angeles); KAUM-FM (Houston); WRQX-FM (Washington, D.C.).

Magazines: Los Angeles; Modern Photography; High Fidelity; Homes.

Specialized publications: National Insurance Law Service; Environmental Protection Law Service; Hotel and Motel Law Service; Schwann record and tape catalogs; *Word Incorporated* religious books; *Industrial Finishing; Office Products; Infosystems; Assembly Engineering; Machine & Tool Blue Book; Woodworking & Furniture Digest; Quality; Chilton* industrial, automotive, and business magazines.

Farm publications: Prairie Farmer; Indiana Prairie Farmer; Wallaces Farmer; Wisconsin Agriculturist; Hog Farm Management; Feedlot Management; Dairy Herd Management; Farm Store Merchandising; Feedstuffs; Tack 'n Togs; Home and Garden Supply Merchandiser.

Leisure attractions: Weeki Wachee Spring, Silver Springs, and Wild Waters, outdoor recreational facilities in Florida; ABC Entertainment Center, Century City (Los Angeles).

CBS

Sales: $3.7 billion
Profits: $201 million
Forbes 500 rank: 127
Rank in advertising revenues: 1
Rank in television broadcasting: 1
Founded: 1926
Employees: 38,700
Headquarters: New York, New York

What they do. CBS is chairman William Paley's candy store. For more than 50 years Paley has dominated CBS, and in the process he has done more than any other person to shape television and radio broadcasting in the United States. Through CBS, the world's most powerful advertising medium, he has helped sell more products than any man in history. And as the final arbiter of taste at the dominant television network, he has determined what programs Americans will see in their homes and what events will be brought to their attention as news.

The business of CBS is selling air time to advertisers. To the celebrity magazines and the gossip columnists, CBS is the galaxy of stars who have stood before the network's radio microphones or paraded on the screen behind the CBS eye logo: Jack Benny,

The Look of Indigestion

Some inner experiences cannot be shown photographically—the feeling of an attack of indigestion, for instance. So the [TV ad] producer may turn to a computer-animation studio like Dolphin Productions in New York for help. With Pepto-Bismol, for example, we see a woman sitting on a white sofa with her terrier. "Indi . . ."—she turns purple, and her swollen belly wiggles toward the dog—"gestion." The dog gets up; he backs off, fearful. Now a construction worker gets hit: His belly fills out in orange.

Then the logo's words get coated with pink liquid. It pours down inside the white letters that spell out COATS, SOOTHES, RELIEVES. How's it done? First the Dolphin crew records the image of a real environment for the background. Then they place the actor who is about to suffer in front of a blue curtain. His image is fed into an analogue computer that allows Dolphin to manipulate his shape to express a particular form of digestive distress—rubbery bones, billowing belly. Appropriate colors, such as purple,

green, and orange, are washed over the actor at the same time. Then, showing the background throughout, the Dolphin team assembles the pieces so that we can watch the real picture dissolve into the "unreal" one while the surroundings remain unchanged. The entire scene is then wiped away by a huge bottle of Pepto-Bismol while the announcer reverently repeats the product's name.

Reprinted from Jonathan Price, *The Best Thing on TV* (Viking, 1978).

Amos 'n' Andy, Burns and Allen, Lucille Ball, Ed Sullivan, Jackie Gleason, Mary Tyler Moore, Archie Bunker, Edward R. Murrow, Eric Sevareid, and Walter Cronkite. But to the managers at "Black Rock," the network's black granite headquarters in mid-town Manhattan, the programs are something they give away. CBS's reward comes from the advertisers of soap and cars and fast-food chains who are willing to pay $100,000 for a 30-second spot on a top-rated prime-time show like "Dallas." How much CBS can charge for a minute of air time depends on how many millions of people are tuned to the network at that hour. A drop of one percentage point in CBS's Nielsen rating over an entire television season can cost them $27 million in profits before taxes. Is it any surprise to learn, then, that a CBS executive can't tell whether a program is "good" until he sees the ratings the next morning?

Until ABC stole away CBS's number 1 spot in the late 1970s, CBS had dominated the Nielsen ratings for 20 years. More than any other broadcaster, William Paley had been able to anticipate what shows would attract the largest audiences. Even in his 70s, at a time when most corporate executives were strolling golf courses, Paley was deciding which of the pilot shows would be purchased for broadcast on CBS's network, which comprises 200-odd affiliates and their 5 owned stations in the top media markets of New York, Chicago, Los Angeles, Philadelphia, and St. Louis. He was right often enough to make CBS extraordinarily profitable: their broadcast operations—which include the TV and radio networks, the news and sports divisions, the 5 owned television stations, and the 14 owned radio stations—account for nearly 60% of their profits on only 40% of their sales.

Because federal regulations prohibit CBS from using the cash generated by their money machine to buy more TV stations, CBS has expanded heavily into other entertainment and media businesses. The CBS Records Group is the nation's largest record company, marketing records by the likes of Bob Dylan, Barbara Streisand, Billy Joel, and Zubin Mehta on labels such as Columbia, Epic, and Odyssey. The CBS Columbia group runs the Columbia Record and Tape Club, the world's largest record club (more than 4 million members); sells hobby kits and handicrafts by direct mail; makes and sells Fender electric guitars and pianos, Gemeinhardt flutes, Rodgers organs, Lyon & Healy harps, and the famous Steinway pianos used in concert halls around the world; manufactures educational toys and games such as Tinkertoys and Erector Sets; and sells stereo components through Pacific Stereo, the nation's largest chain of retail stereo stores. CBS has become a major publisher too. They own Holt, Rinehart and Winston, one of the nation's largest textbook companies. They also publish paperback books under the imprints of Popular Library, Fawcett, and Crest, and such magazines as *Woman's Day*, *Field and Stream*, and *Road & Track*, to name just a few. CBS's nonbroadcasting operations haven't always been healthy—for a while on Wall Street CBS was known derisively as a "purchaser of the last resort"—but the steady flow of profits from the television network has made it easy to buy other businesses.

History. William Paley, son of a Russian Jewish immigrant who made a fortune in the cigar-making business in Philadelphia, invested in the struggling 22-station Columbia Broadcasting System in 1928, just two years after it was founded. He had begun to see the enormous possibilities in radio in 1925 when, while his father and uncle were away, he took $50 a week from the cigar company's advertising budget to sponsor the "Miss La Palina Hour" on WCAU, a Philadelphia radio station. (La Palina was the name of the company's cigar.) Paley's uncle was furious at the waste of money, but his father soon noticed that radio advertising gave a far greater boost to company sales than thousands spent on print. When an opportunity arose to buy into CBS, Paley's father was behind him with the checkbook.

Paley didn't know much about the technical side of radio—that was the special genius of David Sarnoff, the founder of RCA and rival NBC—but Paley knew how to sell. He understood before anyone else in the industry that the key to radio's success was large audiences. So while Sarnoff was charging his NBC affiliates a fee to broadcast the network's shows, Paley decided to give his programming free to CBS's affiliates. All he asked in return was the right to take over any part of an affiliate's schedule for sponsored network shows. The affiliates were delighted to have the free programming, and Paley could march into advertis-

William S. Paley meeting with Eleanor Roosevelt in 1949 at a broadcasting industry luncheon.

ers' offices with an offer to sell time on network shows that would be heard, at a regular hour, by millions of people coast to coast. Within a decade CBS expanded to 114 stations, and the company's sales went up twentyfold.

The young network's ratings grew throughout the 1930s. Comedians like Phil Harris and Fred Allen and singers like Bing Crosby and Kate Smith took over the evening CBS time slots, and daytime audiences were held spellbound by a series of family dramas sponsored by soap companies (the first "soap operas"). But it was not until after World War II that CBS began to win the majority of the prime-time audience away from NBC. That CBS finally began to establish ratings supremacy was due to Paley's overwhelming concern with programming. He made a study of what America liked and didn't like on its radios, and he realized that only the best stars of radio would be able to make the transition to television, then on the horizon. So in 1947 and 1948, his checkbook in hand, he staged his famous "Paley raids" against NBC, luring away stars like Amos 'n' Andy, George Burns and Gracie Allen, Jack Benny, Red Skelton, and Edgar Bergen and Charlie McCarthy with offers of high salaries and tax breaks. NBC's Sarnoff refused to match

Paley's offers. After the raids Sarnoff angrily demanded of Paley how he could have violated the unwritten agreement between the networks not to raid one another's stars. Said Paley: "Because I needed them." Within a year CBS was number 1.

The lead carried over into the television era because the stars Paley stole from NBC were hits in television as they had been in radio. Other popular programs were quiz shows like "The $64,000 Question," but television's image was badly damaged when it was discovered some of the shows were rigged.

Paley moved into the 1960s by hiring James Aubrey, Jr., as president of CBS. Aubrey was a huckster's huckster, convinced that television programmers were putting on shows that were too sophisticated for the American audience. What television needed, he wrote in a famous memo, was more "broads, boobs and busts." Aubrey filled the CBS lineup with "The Beverly Hillbillies," "Mr. Ed," "Petticoat Junction," "The Munsters," and "Hogan's Heroes," a comedy about a Nazi POW camp. According to David Halberstam in his book, *The Powers That Be,* Paley disliked Aubrey's shows. A man of impeccable taste, a member of the board of the Museum of Modern Art, an insider in New York high society, Paley would return to work after a weekend with his rich and cultured friends and tell his executives that they needed to find higher-quality shows for CBS. But by the end of the week his obsession with the ratings always returned. Told once that CBS had beat out NBC in 9 out of 10 daytime shows, Paley replied, "That damn NBC always hangs in there for one."

Reputation. America's tastemaker. For 30 years CBS has set the standards that television has lived by, both in their entertainment and in their news coverage, which has always surpassed that of the other networks.

What they own. CBS has bought a lot of companies with histories of their own. In 1980 their Epic Records was 25 years old; Holt, Rinehart & Winston, 110; Creative Playthings, 40; *Field & Stream,* 84; and Steinway (born in Hamburg, Germany), 100.

Who owns and runs the company. Chairman Paley, who owns 7% of the stock, is by far the largest shareholder at CBS, and his holdings rewarded him in 1979 with an income of $6 million. Paley also continues to run the show at CBS. When he reached the mandatory retirement age of 65 in 1966, Paley promised he would step aside in favor of CBS president Frank Stanton, who for years had served as the company's public spokesman and had run the corporate side while Paley took care of the programming. But five minutes before the news release would have gone out to make the changeover official, Paley changed his mind about retiring. And when Stanton reached 65 in 1973, Paley cast him aside. The same fate befell Stanton's successor, Arthur Taylor, who was fired in 1976, just after the Nielsen ratings put CBS in second place for the first time in 21 seasons. Following Taylor was John Backe, from CBS's publishing division, who was even given the title of chief executive officer. But in May 1980 Paley forced Backe out too, hinting that Backe, who had presided over CBS's return to the top of the ratings, was too much concerned with profits and not enough of a statesman. Some insiders believed that Backe's success was too threatening to Paley.

The man who replaced Backe on the hot seat was Thomas Wyman, who came from Polaroid by way of Green Giant and Pillsbury. But not everyone expects him to be at CBS long. "He's got a nice contract," a market analyst told the *Wall Street Journal* shortly after Wyman's appointment, "and since he doesn't know beans about broadcasting he's got several years to learn about it before he gets pushed out."

In the public eye. In many ways CBS *is* the public eye. Since more people get their news from the CBS "Evening News" than from any other single source, their decisions about what is newsworthy are a powerful force in shaping how we see the world around us. News people generally regard

The Grandmother Shortage

In the spring of 1979 ten advertising people met in the New York offices of Steve Horn, Inc., to discuss locations for a series of five TV commercials that Horn was to film for the N. W. Ayer advertising agency and its client, American Telephone and Telegraph. Besides Horn, who directs filmed TV commercials, those present were Horn employees Ray, Joan, Cheryl, Michael, and Alayne; and Gaston and Jerry, who work for N. W. Ayer. Thanks to writer Michael Arlen, who was also on the scene, future generations will be able to ponder the conversation which took place:

Alayne: "Look, the Long Island Game Farm is fantastic, but the problem is we can't use the camel."

Gaston says: "O.K., we cancel the camel."

Linda says: "How about llamas?"

Steve says: "Llamas are terrific. I like llamas, except they spit."

Jerry says: "How badly do we need llamas?"

Alayne says: "Actually, research says kids only remember the little things they can pick up—the cuddly bunnies. Research says if you show a little kid a llama or a camel he usually doesn't remember he's seen one."

Jerry says: "What does he think he's seen?"

Gaston says: "I think a mix might do something for us. How about if we had a kangaroo in the background?"

Steven says: "I don't see that we need a kangaroo."

Alayne says: "Anyway, they don't have a kangaroo."

Gaston says: "O.K., cancel the kangaroo."

Steve says: "Let's see, where do we stand on the zoo?"

Linda says: "Vincent is Polaroiding it this afternoon."

Steve says: "O.K. I think now we ought to talk grandmothers. I think we've got some problem with grandmothers."

Gaston says: "I don't see that we have any big problem."

Steve says: "Well, we've got film on every available grandmother in the country right here in the office."

Linda says: "The trouble is each grandmother has been used so many times."

Steve says: "So it seems to me we have three or four grandmothers that are interchangeable—except, of course, for the black grandmother. I think the grandmother-and-grandfather situation needs to be worked out carefully."

Dialogue from Michael Arlen, "Thirty Seconds," *The New Yorker,* October 15, 1979.

THE 18 LARGEST CORPORATE SUPPORTERS OF PUBLIC TELEVISION

1977–1978 Contributions

EXXON	$8,912,000
MOBIL	$7,386,000
ATLANTIC RICHFIELD	$4,147,000
SUN COMPANY	$1,817,000
ALLIED CHEMICAL	$1,760,000
McDONALD'S	$1,500,000
GULF OIL	$1,430,000
MARTIN MARRIETTA	$1,258,000
XEROX	$1,050,000
MRS. PAUL'S KITCHEN	$ 953,000
RAYTHEON	$ 856,000
TEXACO	$ 820,000
HOFFMAN LaROCHE	$ 737,000
PRUDENTIAL INSURANCE	$ 625,000
CHUBB & SON	$ 600,000
INTERNATIONAL BUSINESS MACHINES	$ 454,000
AMERICAN TELEPHONE & TELEGRAPH	$ 407,000
POLAROID	$ 400,000

Source: *Mainliner*, July 1979.

Business Week (before Wyman's appointment): "This is more than a commercial company today. We have a balance sheet . . . but we also have a high degree of responsibility to the public. Maybe I was lucky—I invented fairness and balance when I was 32—but today I personally represent that responsibility, and the man who succeeds me should represent it too." It's Tom Wyman's turn at the bat.

Stock performance. CBS stock bought for $1,000 in 1970 sold for $1,116 on January 2, 1980.

Major employment centers. New York, New York; Stamford, Connecticut; Los Angeles, California.

Access. 51 West 52nd Street, New York, New York 10019; (212) 975-4321.

Consumer brands.

Television stations: WCBS-New York; KNXT-Los Angeles; WBBM-Chicago; WCAU-Philadelphia. KMOX-St. Louis.
Radio stations: WCBS-New York; KNX-Los Angeles; WEEI-Boston; WBBM-Chicago; WCAU-Philadelphia; KCBS-San Francisco; KMOX-St. Louis.
Records: Columbia; Jet Records; Barry White's Unlimited Gold Records; ARC/Columbia; Epic; Odyssey.
Record club: Columbia Record and Tape Club.
Musical instruments: Steinway pianos; Lyon & Healy harps; Gemeinhardt flutes and piccolos; Fender electric guiters and amplifiers; Fender-Rhodes electric pianos; Rogers drums; Gulbransen organs; Leslie speakers.
Stereo specialty stores: Pacific Stereo; SoundWorks.
Toys: Gabriel; Child Guidance; Gym-Dandy; Creative Playthings; Wonder; Tinkertoy; Erector sets; Potterycraft; Othello; Pop-Up Pinball; Bucky; The Wonder Horse.
Magazines: Woman's Day; Field & Stream; Mechanix Illustrated; Road & Track; World Tennis; Sea; Cycle World; Pickup Van & 4WD.
Books: Holt, Rinehart & Winston; Popular Library; Fawcett; Crest.

CBS as the best of the networks. In 1968, during the Tet offensive in Vietnam, Walter Cronkite decided to go to Siagon to see for himself what was happening. After learning the worst, Cronkite went to the roof of the Caravelle Hotel in Saigon, with the rumble of bombs and artillery in the background, and reported to the American people that the war could not be won. To some people, that was not news. But the fact that Cronkite would say it gave skepticism and pessimism about the war the kind of respectibility they had never had before. According to David Halberstam, even Lyndon Johnson, who had struggled continually to keep CBS on his team, recognized as much. Watching the Cronkite broadcast, Johnson turned to an aide and told him that if he had lost Walter Cronkite, he had lost the average American.

Where they're going. In 1980 CBS set up a new unit to provide programs to cable TV stations, but in the opinion of most observers, the company is not in the forefront of the new technology. The *Wall Street Journal* even reported that although Backe had been experimenting with computerized information systems, which he felt was the wave of the future, Paley looked askance because he "never fully understood the concepts and they didn't appeal to his sense of glamour." As for a successor, Paley would seem to be searching for a mirror image. He told

Newspaper and
Magazine Publishers

DOW JONES & COMPANY, INC.

Sales: $441 million
Profits: $51 million
Rank in daily newspaper circulation: 1
Founded: 1882
Employees: 4,400
Headquarters: New York, New York

What they do. Dow Jones runs the news machine that keeps Wall Street ticking. If you ever listen to radio or television news, then you're familiar with the Dow Jones Industrial Average. This stock market barometer, adjusted every half hour throughout the day, signals the rise and fall of the stock prices of 30 major industrial companies on the New York Stock Exchange. Dow Jones, the company that picks the stocks that go into "the Dow," also maintains two other stock price averages: one based on 20 transportation companies, one based on 15 utilities.

However, figuring the Dow Jones averages is only a small part of what they do. Dow Jones publishes the *Wall Street Journal*, the nation's largest-selling daily newspaper (it eclipsed the *New York Daily News* in early 1980 and now sells close to 2 million copies a day). They also publish *Barron's*, a business and financial weekly; *Book Digest*, a monthly collection of excerpts from new best-sellers that busy executives don't have time to read in full; a string of 19 daily and 6 weekly newspapers in small towns from Cape Cod, Massachusetts, to Medford, Oregon; and the *Asian Wall Street Journal*, a Hong Kong–based daily that focuses on business in the Far East. They run the Dow Jones News Service, known familiarly as the "broadtape" or the "news ticker" (not

to be confused with the New York Stock Exchange's stock ticker, which prints out stock prices on a narrow tape). The news ticker sends out business news in a constant stream over a teletype system to banks, stockbrokers, corporations, and newspapers. Dow Jones owns the publishing house of Richard D. Irwin, which produces college-level textbooks on business, economics, and social sciences. They run a computerized "news retrieval" service that makes instantly available anything published by the *Journal, Barron's,* or the ticker in the previous 90 days.

The *Wall Street Journal* is one of the most unusual daily newspapers in the United States. It is published only on Monday through Friday, and skips some holidays. Firm in the belief that "one word is worth a thousand pictures," they don't publish any photographs, except in the ads, and only occasionally illustrate a story with a half-column-wide drawing. They dispense with the major news events of the day in a column of one-paragraph entries and fill their pages with news of profits, mergers, and interest rates. Each day they publish several major, in-depth articles on a wide variety of subjects, from education to world affairs to the state of the economy. The *Journal* has won eight Pulitzer Prizes.

The paper is not for everybody, as they would be the first to admit. The *Journal's* audience consists largely of business and government executives, lawyers, doctors, and professors (people who are most likely to have stockholdings). Readers have an average household income of $52,000 and net worth of $400,000. Nine-tenths of the paper's subscribers around the country receive their copies on the day of publication, thanks to the *Journal's* elaborate printing

THE WHO PLUGGED WHAT QUIZ

The following pairs are incorrectly matched. Can you identify the product each celebrity actually plugged? (Answers on the next page.)

Celebrity	Product Plugged
GARY COOPER	Lux dishwashing soap
ELEANOR ROOSEVELT	Wheaties
MARILYN MONROE	Great Books
SONNY LISTON WITH ANDY WORHOL	Volkswagen cars
ERNEST HEMINGWAY	Parkay margarine
KING EDWARD VII OF ENGLAND	Lustre-Creme Shampoo
DOUGLAS FAIRBANKS	Whitman's chocolates
ADLAI E. STEVENSON	Pabst Blue Ribbon Beer
CHARLIE CHAPLIN	Bulova watches
JOHN WAYNE	Braniff Airlines
PRESIDENT WILLIAM McKINLEY	Old Gold cigarettes
RONALD REAGAN	Ballantine Ale
MARY PICKFORD	Lucky Strike cigarettes
BUZZ ALDRIN (astronaut)	Van Heusen shirts
JACKIE ROBINSON	Angelus player pianos
CHARLES LINDBERGH	Waterman fountain pens

setup. The pages are put together in Chicopee, Massachusetts. Photographic images of each page are then transmitted via a satellite 22,000 miles above the equator to most of the paper's 12 printing plants in 10 states, where the presses roll in the middle of the night. The papers are delivered in the morning, either through the mail or by private delivery systems. The reason the *Journal* rarely misses delivery is that they do the work of the Postal Service, sorting their copies not only by zip codes but by blocks or by companies or other destinations.

History. Charles H. Dow and Edward D. Jones were young newspapermen from Providence, Rhode Island, who came to New York independently around 1880. They both landed jobs as financial reporters in the Wall Street area. In 1882 they started their own financial news service, called Dow, Jones & Company, and set up shop in a basement on Wall Street, behind a soda fountain. Dow would go out and cover the news, taking shorthand notes on his shirt cuffs, while Jones stayed in the office as the "desk man." A third partner, Charles M. Bergstresser, also worked as a reporter. Jones would edit and dictate the stories to four or five clerks, who would write them out by hand in books of tissue paper with carbon paper between the leaves, making up to 24 copies at a time. Messenger boys would deliver bulletins to the news service's clients throughout the day.

The business prospered, and in 1883 they started publishing a recapitulation of the day's bulletins, called the *Customer's Afternoon Letter.* Soon they abandoned the system of handwritten bulletins in favor of a small press. By 1889 the company had 50 employees, and the partners decided to convert the *Letter* into a newspaper. The first edition of the *Wall Street Journal* came off the press on July 8, 1889. In 1897 they installed their first "ticker," a mechanical grandfather clock-like device that required winding every half hour.

Jones retired to Providence in 1899. Dow and Bergstresser sold their shares in the company in 1902 to Clarence Barron, their Boston correspondent; Dow died later that year. The indefatigable Barron, who stood 5'6" tall and weighed more than 300 pounds, wore out several male secretaries in succession as he ceaselessly dictated memos to his editors wherever he was—in the bathtub, barber chair, or men's room, or while dummy at bridge. He started *Barron's* weekly in 1921, with himself as editor, and he expanded the Dow Jones ticker service to cities across the country. Barron died in 1928. The next year, just eight days before the stock market crash, the *Wall Street Journal* started a West Coast edition in San Francisco.

The Depression dealt the *Journal* a heavy setback, as some of their readers were busy jumping out of windows high above Wall Street. Circulation sank from 50,000 to 28,000. Dow Jones executives decided to try to broaden the paper's appeal by including more news of general interest. The man who shaped the *Journal* of today was Bernard Kilgore, who became managing editor in 1941. Under Kilgore reporters often worked days or weeks on a story to provide a complete, in-depth article. Several features were introduced that have remained ever since, including "Review and Outlook" (now "The Outlook"), "Tax Report," and "Washington Wire." Kilgore became president of Dow Jones in 1945 and chairman in 1966, a year before his death. Under his direction the Journal's circulation grew from 33,000 in 1941 to 100,000 in 1947; 500,-000 in 1957; and 1 million in 1966.

Dow Jones's only spectacular flop was a Kilgore brainchild: the *National Observer*, a weekly newspaper that summarized and analyzed the news and carried feature stories on general-interest topics. Dow Jones started the *Observer* in 1962, and it lost $16 million before they finally folded it in 1977.

In 1978 they bought *Book Digest*, a monthly with a circulation of about 1 million that carries excerpts from about seven best-sellers each issue. In 1980 they sold a 20% interest in it to *Readers Digest* in exchange for circulation and distribution expertise and services.

Reputation. Although its editorial page is fiercely conservative, the *Wall Street Journal* has admirers across the political spectrum. *Newsweek* solicited opinions from the following readers in 1980: Claude O. Goldsmith, vice-president for tax and finance at Atlantic Richfield: "It's indispensable. You're afraid to go through the day without reading the *Wall Street Journal.*" Theodore R. Eck, economist for Standard Oil of Indiana: "The reporters are thorough. They check their sources very carefully and very rarely get a story wrong." Stanley K. Sheinbaum, a Los Angeles economic consultant

---

ANSWERS TO WHO PLUGGED WHAT QUIZ

1. GARY COOPER: Pabst Blue Ribbon beer (1948).

2. ELEANOR ROOSEVELT: Parkay margarine (early 1950s). The former First Lady appeared in a Parkay TV commercial in exchange for air time to promote a charitable cause.

3. MARILYN MONROE: Lustre-Creme Shampoo (1953).

4. SONNY LISTON: Braniff (1969).

5. ERNEST HEMINGWAY: Ballantine Ale (1952).

6. KING EDWARD VII: Angelus player pianos (1910). "His Majesty King Edward VII chooses an Angelus player-piano," proclaimed the ad, which showed the corpulent monarch regally garbed in ermine, clutching his scepter, and looking as if only the best could possibly be good enough for him. "Can any intending purchaser . . . afford to overlook this most remarkable endorsement . . . to the superior merits of the Angelus?" inquired the ad.

   Whether they could resist the pitch or not, readers might have been amused to think of the king sitting down of an evening to impress his royal visitors by rendering a few selections on the player piano—a contraption that cranked out the sounds of a virtuoso performance automatically, while the person at the keyboard simply pretended to play the appropriate keys.

7. DOUGLAS FAIRBANKS: Lucky Strike cigarettes (1928).

8. ADLAI E. STEVENSON: Great Books (1962). In the ad Stevenson was quoted as saying: "In the pages of these beautiful volumes truth stands out—ready to guide anyone concerned with where our world is going."

9. CHARLIE CHAPLIN: Old Gold cigarettes (1928). "It seems that Strongheart and Rin-tin-tin are the only motion picture actors who don't smoke them," said the Little Tramp.

10. JOHN WAYNE: Whitman's chocolates (1954). The Duke did three decades of testimonials. For his 1970s endorsement of the drug Datril 500, he got $400,000.

11. PRESIDENT WILLIAM McKINLEY: Waterman fountain pens (1900). McKinley was up for reelection at the time. In those days, before TV with its paid political announcements allowed candidates to sell themselves to audiences of millions, McKinley probably figured the pen ad would give him useful publicity.

12. RONALD REAGAN: Van Heusen shirts (1954). As a B-movie star in the 1940s and early 1950s, before getting elected as California governor in 1966, Reagan did many endorsements, including the one that went: "At General Electric, progress is our most important product."

13. MARY PICKFORD: Lux dishwashing soap (1928).

14. BUZZ ALDRIN: Volkswagen cars (1972). "The car, truly, is wired along the same principle as a space craft," declared the Apollo moon landing hero, somewhat ungrammatically.

15. JACKIE ROBINSON: Wheaties (1950).

16. CHARLES LINDBERGH: Bulova "Lone Eagle" watches (1927).

Source: Robert Atwan, Donald McQuaid, and John W. Wright, *Edsels, Luckies, and Frigidaires: Advertising the American Way*, 1979.

and a longtime backer of left-liberal causes: "I consider it the most important newspaper in the United States. I learn more about the workings of the American economy from the *Journal* than I do from the radical critics or the more professional business journals."

What they own. Twelve *Wall Street Journal* and *Barron's* printing plants across the country, from Federal Way, Washington, to Orlando, Florida, and 21 plants for the little local newspapers. A 49% interest in the *Far Eastern Economic Review*, an English-language weekly magazine published in Hong Kong (the rest is owned by the *South China Morning Post*, a Hong Kong daily on whose presses the *Asian Wall Street Journal* is printed—and Dow Jones owns 10% of the *Post*). A 30% interest in a newsprint mill in Virginia (the *Washington Post* is an equal partner) and a 40% interest in one in Quebec.

Who owns and runs the company. Clarence Barron, the *Journal's* owner in the early twentieth century, married a widow with two daughters in 1901, when he was 46. He left a controlling interest in Dow Jones to one of his stepdaughters, Jane Barron Bancroft, whose heirs now own 60% of the stock. Two of Jane Bancroft's daughters, Jessie B. Cox and Jane B. Cook, each own 16%; combined, their shares were worth about $180 million in 1980. Jessie Cox's son, William C. Cox, Jr., is a Dow Jones advertising executive and a director. Also on the board are William M. Agee, chairman of Bendix; J. Paul Austin, chairman of Coca-Cola; Richard D. Wood, chairman of Eli Lilly; and directors of Mobil and Sears, Roebuck.

Warren H. Phillips, who became president of Dow Jones in 1972 and chairman in 1978, joined the *Journal* as a proofreader in 1947 after being rejected by Columbia University's Graduate School of Journalism. He is generally regarded as the architect of the company's diversification program in the 1970s. At the beginning of the decade more than 90% of Dow Jones's sales came from the *Wall Street Journal;* ten years later the figure was closer to 60%—even though the paper had grown considerably in the meantime.

In the public eye. Laissez-faire capitalism, a much abused and abandoned philosophy, still has a staunch champion in the *Wall*

> **Newsrooms were 99% white in 1968. In 1979 they were 95.5% white while minorities make up 17% of the audiences they write for. Two-thirds of the nation's 1,762 dailies employ no minorities at all.**
> —*Gannetteer*, February 1980.

Street Journal's editorial page. "We're pro free enterprise—but often the business community isn't," *Journal* editor Robert L. Bartley told *Newsweek*. The *Journal* has blasted Chrysler for seeking a federal bailout and General Motors for pressuring suppliers to conform to wage and price guidelines. Ralph Nader is a favorite villain. Although many *Journal* staff members may have more liberal ideas, they often find the paper's stance helpful. "The fact that so many businessmen agree with our editorials is very useful," reporter Frederick C. Klein explained. "It gives us an entree we wouldn't normally have."

Where they're going. The *Wall Street Journal* has been the nation's fastest-growing daily newspaper. In 1980, as circulation hit 1.9 million, they announced plans to "significantly expand" their news coverage and divide the paper into two sections for the first time. They said they would start to cover five areas they hadn't paid much attention to in the past: small business, real estate, marketing and advertising, technology and new products, and regional business news. At the same time they said they were going to try to cut back their circulation a bit because of limited newsprint supplies. They reduced their radio and TV promotion and raised the newsstand price from 30 to 35¢. They were just selling too many newspapers; circulation rose 16% in 1979.

Stock performance. Dow Jones stock bought for $1,000 in 1970 sold for $639 on January 2, 1980.

Access. 22 Cortland Street, New York, New York 10007; (212) 285-5000.

Consumer brands.

Newspapers: The Wall Street Journal; The Asian Wall Street Journal; Ottaway newspapers.
Magazines: Barron's; Book Digest; Far Eastern Economic Review.
Books: Richard D. Irwin; Dow Jones Books.

GANNETT

Sales: $1.1 billion
Profits: $134 million
Rank in number of newspapers: 1
Rank in newspaper chains: 2
Rank in broadcast chains: 9
Founded: 1906
Employees: 24,000
Headquarters: Rochester, New York.

What they do. *Chillicothe Gazette. Muskogee Daily Phoenix. Sioux Falls Argus-Leader.* Now you know why Gannett has been described by the *Berkeley Monthly* as the chain that buys "small Mom and Pop dailies in one-newspaper towns." A less folksy description has been "a chain of small monopolies." However, in 1979 Gannett took over the *Oakland Tribune* (California) and the *Cincinnati Enquirer*, both big-city newspapers with sharp competition, which may mean they intend to step up from the bush leagues to the big leagues of journalism. Even now there is nothing bush league about Gannett's overall size and circulation. They seem to add new papers every few months; in early 1980 the total was 82, spreading from the Virgin Islands across 35 states and a stretch of Pacific Ocean to Guam. Although the average circulation of their individual papers was only about 40,-000, it added up to nearly 3.6 million—more than the combined circulation of the *New York Times, Los Angeles Times, Washington Post,* and *Chicago Tribune.* Gannett has started only one newspaper from scratch: *Cocoa TODAY,* in the Florida town where company chairman Allen Neuharth lives.

Often referred to as a monster or mammoth among newspaper chains, Gannett has also been called "the chain that isn't" because of a laissez-faire policy that makes their combined voice, according to an article in the *New York Times Magazine,* "like a choir where everyone sings something different." Although the *Times* says this means nobody pays any attention to them, Gannett proudly displays their slogan: "A world of different voices where freedom speaks."

The quality of Gannett papers is also uneven. They take as much as 60% of their copy from wire services (the *New York Times* and *Los Angeles Times,* in contrast, are 90% staff written). They tend to be thin on national and international news and have been called editorially flabby. Gannett has the dubious distinction of being the only big chain without a single prestigious newspaper. On the other hand, when Gannett takes over a paper, staffers often say it is improved. If a monster, remarked an *Oakland Tribune* columnist, they are "a very benevolent monster." In 1980 Gannett News Service won the Pulitzer Prize for public service. Gannett has won a total of 12 Pulitzers.

One word everyone agrees on for Gannett: *prosperous.* Those one-newspaper towns are an easy bet for lucrative advertising and expandable circulation. (The *New York Post's* owner, Rupert Murdoch, said running a monopoly newspaper was a "license to steal money forever." And in 97% of the U.S. towns that have daily papers, the paper is a monopoly.) Gannett's revenues crossed the $1 billion mark in 1979; they have a 12-year streak of rising profits. Professor Melvin Mencher of the Columbia University School of Journalism said in 1974 that Gannett talks "as if the business of journalism is business and not journalism." More recently a former employee observed that at Gannett, "the idea is to make money, not change the world."

History. Gannett's expertise at buying and running newspapers, rather than originating them, started with their founder, Frank E. Gannett. Soon after he bought his first newspaper, the *Elmira Gazette* (New York), he merged it with three other upstate New York papers to form the Gannett Company in 1906. By the time he died in 1957 Frank Gannett had accumulated 30 newspapers and a string of radio and television stations. He took over more newspapers than any other publisher without the help of an inheritance. Frank also set the vaguely Republican tone than many Gannett papers have today. In fact, he made an unsuccessful bid for the Republican presidential nomination back in 1940. He financed his campaign by selling stock to his employees, although the firm didn't actually go public until 1967.

In 1978 Gannett pulled off a colossal annexation to what was already the country's biggest collection of newspapers. With the acquisition of Arizona-based Combined Communications (CCC), they instantly became a power in the broadcast and billboard worlds as well. Like Gannett, CCC had been gobbling up media at a rapid rate,

and had 7 TV stations, 13 radio stations, and the second-largest outdoor advertising business in the country, together with the *Oakland Tribune*, the *Cincinnati Enquirer*, and the influential Louis Harris polling organization before being gobbled up themselves. Congressman Morris Udall, a critic of massive corporate control of the media, found the merger alarming, "a case of a whale swallowing a whale."

Gannett's financial picture changed radically when the FCC approved the merger in June 1979, after more than a year of deliberation. In 1978 newspaper advertising and circulation brought in 97% of their revenues; in 1979 that figure sank to 78%. The difference was just about evenly divided between broadcasting and outdoor advertising. Revenues themselves leaped from $690 million in 1978 to over $1 billion in 1979.

Until the recent Oakland and Cincinnati acquisitions, Gannett's largest newspapers were their two flagships in Rochester, New York, the *Democrat and Chronicle* and *The Times-Union*, with a combined circulation of 140,000; their smallest is the *Pacific Dateline*, a Guam evening paper with a circulation of 2,000. In an apparent effort to brighten up their journalistic reputation, Gannett is pumping money and experienced staff into the *Oakland Tribune*. They have added a jazzed-up morning edition of the *Trib*, with a new name (*East Bay TODAY*) and a new price of one thin dime. And they have brought in a distinguished black journalist, Bob Maynard, as editor—responding to the fact that Oakland's population is predominantly black. Maynard is the first black editor of a U.S. metropolitan daily.

Reputation. "Sumptuous growth" is what *Barron's* called Gannett's nonstop accumulation of newspapers and the endless swelling of totals in the dollar columns. "The bland leading the bland" is what *Newsweek* predicted would be the quality of U.S. journalism as the last independent newspapers were picked off by giant corporate chains like Gannett.

What they own. Besides 82 dailies and 20 weeklies in 35 states (their largest concentration is in their home state of New York) and 13 radio and 7 television stations in the Midwest and West, Gannett owns the Gannett News Service in Washington, D.C.; Louis Harris Associates in New York; and outdoor advertising facilities in Canada, New Jersey, Connecticut, and the West. They also own the Empire Newspaper Supply Company, which provides their papers with cheap newsprint, typewriters, pencils, and ink. In early 1980 Gannett bought Gateway Productions, a New York maker of television documentaries and business films, and Filmpower, which does postproduction film and videotape work.

Who owns and runs the company. Allen Neuharth, Gannett's chairman and president since 1970, wears two watches: one set for Rochester time (where he has an apartment adjoining his office), the other set for whatever city he is in that day. He works a 12–15 hour day in the New York City, Rochester, or Washington office, and takes a lot of trips in the Gannett jet. He sees his wife, Florida state senator Lori Wilson, only on weekends in Cocoa, Florida. The *Los Angeles Times* describes him as "one of the most fascinating, enigmatic, and powerful—albeit least-known—figures in the publishing world today." A friend says, "When Al wears a sharkskin suit, it's hard to tell where the shark stops and he begins." Gannett recently got their first black and only woman director, Dolores Wharton, a member of the National Council on the Arts.

The Gannett Foundation owns 15% of the company's stock.

In the public eye. The 1978–79 merger of Gannett and Combined Communications stirred a wave of controversy on the short- and long-term effects of huge corporations controlling all the sources of information in the United States. Although everyone says there is absolutely no editorial interference from the top at Gannett papers, Congressman Udall thinks it's bad enough that the power is there: he's not comforted that it isn't being abused *yet*. According to Udall and other critics (like University of California, Berkeley, journalism professor Ben Bagdikian), the potential abuses are far reaching and may enter the mainstream of our lives without our even noticing. They point out that corporate decisions about how to run the media are very likely to be influenced by the drive for financial and political power.

Gannett has been making a concerted effort to hire and promote women and minorities; Neuharth has appointed 5 women publishers and 14 women editors during his tenure.

The company has fought against unionization, so far managing to keep more than half their employees out of unions. Gannett has a policy of retraining employees displaced by technological advances (like printers).

And the nation's largest newspaper chain is being sued by the world's smallest republic. President Hammer De Roburt of Nauru, a tiny atoll about halfway between Guam and Australia, asserts that he was libeled by Gannett's *Pacific Daily News,* which has a circulation of 18,000. President De Roburt is seeking $37.5 million.

Where they're going. Almost three-quarters of the country's dailies are owned by chains, including Gannett; Gannett's got their eye on the other one-quarter. Their short-term goal: an even 100 newspapers. But they are clearly out for more than newspapers now. They changed their logo in 1979. The motto beneath it used to be "A world of different newspapers." Now it is "A world of different voices." Those different voices include radio, TV, film, and billboards—for starters.

Stock performance. Gannett stock bought for $1,000 in 1970 sold for $3,246 on January 2, 1980.

Access. Lincoln Tower, Rochester, New York 14604; (716) 546-8600.

Consumer brands.

Newspapers: See "Who Owns Your Local Paper" chart in this chapter.
Television: KPNX-Phoenix, Arizona; KARK-Little Rock, Arkansas; KBTV-Denver, Colorado; WXIA-Atlanta, Georgia; WPTA-Fort Wayne, Indiana; WLKY-Louisville, Kentucky; KOCO-Oklahoma City, Oklahoma.
Radio: MUZAK-Arizona; KIIS and KIIS-FM-Los Angeles; KSDO and KEZL-San Diego, California; WVON and WGCI-FM-Chicago, Illinois; WCZY-Detroit, Michigan; KSD and KCFM-St. Louis, Missouri; WWWE and WDOK-Cleveland, Ohio.

KNIGHT RIDDER

Sales: $980 million
Profits: $88 million
Forbes 500 rank: 465
Rank in newspaper chains: 1
Founded: 1892
Employees: 14,500
Headquarters: Miami, Florida

What they do. Knight-Ridder delivers more newspapers to the doorsteps of American homes than any other publisher. At the end of 1978 they were publishing 34 daily papers, whose combined circulation topped 3.7 million on weekdays and 4.3 million on Sundays. In 19 cities they publish the only newspapers in town, and they publish three of the biggest newspapers in America: *Detroit Free Press, Miami Herald,* and *Philadelphia Inquirer.* Gannett may have more papers, but Knight-Ridder has more readers. Gannett shies away from situations where they have to compete, but Knight-Ridder slugs it out with tough competitors in Philadelphia and Detroit.

Knight-Ridder papers (mostly the Knight side) have won more Pulitzer Prizes—23—than any other paper or chain except the *New York Times.* The hallmark of Knight papers has been a clean, modern look: short sentences, short paragraphs, sharp photography. They spend heavily to modernize their facilities, and as a result they operate the most up-to-date printing plants in the industry. Unions represent 60% of their work force.

Although they follow a policy of local autonomy for papers, Knight-Ridder sees to it that the links in the chain perform profitably by sharing technology and ideas among all the member papers. Staff people move from one paper to another. There's a steady flow of information among the papers. And training seminars are conducted for managers to improve their skills.

Knight-Ridder publishes some of the fattest newspapers in America. In California their *San Jose Mercury-News* (the *Mercury* is published on weekday mornings, the *News* in the evenings, and the *Mercury-News* on Saturdays and Sundays) carries more advertising columns than any other newspaper in the country after the *Los Angeles Times.* Not too far behind is the *Miami Herald,* an-

other blockbuster paper and the dominant daily in Florida's Dade County. The *Miami Herald* accounts for 18% of all the Knight-Ridder revenues. The second-biggest contributor is the *Philadelphia Inquirer* and its sister evening paper, the *Philadelphia Daily News,* which bring in 17% of the money; after that it's the *Detroit Free Press,* 12%, and then the *San Jose Mercury-News,* 10%. In short, four publishing properties account for nearly 60% of Knight-Ridder's revenues.

The local character of their newspapers becomes clear when you look at where Knight-Ridder's money comes from. Advertising from local merchants accounts for 40% of their total income; the classified advertising sections (autos for sale, help wanted, and the like) contribute 25%; and circulation income—what readers pay for the paper—brings in 20%. Other advertising, principally from national companies, contributes only 10%. If Knight-Ridder had to depend solely on income from readers, their sales would be $196 million instead of $980 million.

Since the Knight-Ridder papers used over 600,000 tons of newsprint in 1978, at a cost of $345 per ton, they wisely bought a one-third interest in a newsprint mill in Dublin, Georgia. The mill began operating in 1979.

History. Two wealthy newspaper families, the Knights and the Ridders, joined forces in 1974 to establish the huge chain that Knight-Ridder is today. John Knight and his younger brother, James, built up the larger and more prestigious half of the merger from a paper they inherited from their father, Charles Landon Knight. The paper, the *Akron Beacon Journal* in Ohio, had been bought by the elder Knight in 1903. John became editor and publisher on his father's death in 1933. John had used a pseudonym when he first started on the paper as a sportswriter because, as he says, "I was ashamed of the stuff"; however, his "Editor's Notebook" column later won a Pulitzer Prize.

James Knight got his own paper to run in 1937, when the brothers bought the *Miami Herald,* now the pride of the chain. The brothers bought more papers in Detroit, Chicago, North Carolina, Georgia, Kentucky, and, in 1969, Philadelphia. John Knight gave each paper's editor complete autonomy, but he stressed balanced reporting, civic responsibility, and good appearance.

While C. L. Knight was buying his first paper in Akron, Herman Ridder was running the *Staats-Zeitung,* the leading German language newspaper in the United States, which he had purchased in 1892. His three sons, Bernard, Victor, and Joseph, took over the paper on their father's death in 1915, and soon afterward they bought other papers, including the *Journal of Commerce,* a New York shipping daily (which Knight-Ridder still operates). At the time of the merger with Knight, the Ridders owned 18 dailies in Minnesota, South Dakota, Seattle, California, Indiana, Michigan, and Colorado.

Reputation. Knight-Ridder is proud of not imposing an editorial viewpoint on their papers. In the 1976 presidential election some papers supported Carter, others Ford. It's a custom that goes back to John Knight, who, although a lifelong Republican, supported more than 1,000 Democrats for public office. *Business Week* said in 1970 that some "critics call him simply an opportunist who bends with every prevailing public wind." In any case, there's no particular slant to a Knight-Ridder paper. The common denominator is that they make money. If they don't, as the *Chicago Daily News* didn't, they are sold.

What they own. Thirty-four daily papers; 12 suburban weeklies in California and Florida; 22 printing plants in 16 states; and 4 television stations, all ABC affiliates, in Flint, Michigan, Providence, Rhode Island, and Albany, New York.

Who owns and runs the company. In 1979 the two Knight brothers—James and John —still owned 30% of the stock, while three Ridder cousins—Bernard H. Jr., Bernard J., and Walter T.—held 7%. They all hold board seats. The company has been headed since 1976 by Alvah H. Chapman, Jr., a financial man and graduate of the Citadel (a military academy in Charleston, South Carolina), who began his career with the *Columbus Ledger-Enquirer* in Georgia. He succeeded former Pulitzer Prize-winning editor Lee Hills, who became president in 1967, when John Knight stepped aside. Knight now holds the position of editor emeritus.

John Knight was 85 years old in early 1980, and his life has been flecked with trag-

TOP DAILY NEWSPAPERS

Daily Circulation (1979)

1. NEW YORK DAILY NEWS 1,607,040
2. WALL STREET JOURNAL 1,599,559
3. LOS ANGELES TIMES 1,013,565
4. NEW YORK TIMES 841,890
5. CHICAGO TRIBUNE 780,626
6. CHICAGO SUN-TIMES 675,995
7. NEW YORK POST 631,104
8. DETROIT NEWS 628,574
9. DETROIT FREE PRESS 607,647
10. WASHINGTON POST 578,831
11. SAN FRANCISCO CHRONICLE 504,644
12. NEWSDAY 497,759
13. BOSTON GLOBE 482,578
14. PHILADELPHIA BULLETIN 462,137
15. PHILADELPHIA INQUIRER 418,148
16. NEWARK STAR LEDGER 408,038
17. MIAMI HERALD 398,239
18. CLEVELAND PLAIN DEALER 386,194
19. WASHINGTON STAR 342,760
20. HOUSTON CHRONICLE 339,573
21. HOUSTON POST 325,085
22. MILWAUKEE JOURNAL 324,167
23. KANSAS CITY TIMES 317,370
24. CLEVELAND PRESS 300,708
25. LOS ANGELES HERALD EXAMINER 300,595
26. KANSAS CITY STAR 280,635

Source: *Editor & Publisher,* December 29, 1979. Since then the *Wall Street Journal* has moved into first place.

edy. His first wife died eight years after they were married in 1921. Their eldest son, John, Jr., was killed in action in Germany in 1945. Their youngest son, Frank, died in 1948. In 1970 grandson John Knight, III, who was then at Oxford University in England, wrote a "Dear Granddad" letter about the Vietnam war, which his grandfather reprinted in the column he wrote in the Knight papers. Young John Knight told his grandfather that the violence on American campuses resulted "because, after more than six years of peaceful protests, kids are still being sent to their deaths in this sense-

Who Owns Your Newspaper?

1. **KNIGHT-RIDDER** (*Average weekday circulation: 3.7 million*).
   FLORIDA—*The Miami Herald; Tallahassee Democrat; The Bradenton Herald; Boca Raton News*; PENNSYLVANIA—*The Philadelphia Inquirer* and *Philadelphia Daily News*; MICHIGAN—*Detroit Free Press*; CALIFORNIA—*San Jose Mercury* and *News*; (Long Beach) *Independent* and *Press-Telegram*; (Pasadena) *Star-News*; MINNESOTA—*St. Paul Pioneer Press* and *Dispatch; Duluth News-Tribune* and *Herald*; NORTH CAROLINA—*The Charlotte Observer* and *News*; OHIO—*Akron Beacon Journal*; KANSAS—*The Wichita Eagle* and *Beacon*; KENTUCKY—*The Lexington Herald* and *Leader*; INDIANA—*The* (Fort Wayne) *News-Sentinel*; (Gary) *Post-Tribune*; GEORGIA—*The Macon Telegraph* and *News; The Columbus Enquirer* and *Ledger*; COLORADO—(Boulder) *Daily Camera*; NORTH DAKOTA—*Grand Forks Herald*; SOUTH DAKOTA—*Aberdeen American News*.

2. **GANNETT** (*Average weekday circulation: 3.4 million*).
   ARIZONA—*Tucson Citizen*; CALIFORNIA—*The Oakland Tribune; Salinas Californian; The* (San Bernardino) *Sun*; (San Rafael) *Independent-Journal; Stockton Record; Visalia Times-Delta*; COLORADO—*Fort Collins Coloradoan*; DELAWARE—*The* (Wilmington) *Morning News* and *Evening Journal*; FLORIDA—(Cocoa) *Today; Fort Myers News-Press; Pensacola Journal* and *Pensacola News*; GUAM—(Agana) *Pacific Daily News*; HAWAII—*The Honolulu Star-Bulletin*; IDAHO—*The* (Boise) *Idaho Statesman*; ILLINOIS—(Danville) *Commercial-News*; *Rockford Register Star*; INDIANA—(Lafayette) *Journal and Courier*; (Marion) *Chronicle-Tribune; The* (Richmond) *Palladium-Item*; IOWA—*Iowa City Press-Citizen*; KANSAS—*The Coffeyville Journal*; LOUISIANA—(Monroe) *World* and *News-Star; The Shreveport Times*; MICHIGAN—(Battle Creek) *Enquirer and News*; (Lansing) *State Journal*; (Port Huron) *Times Herald; Sturgis Journal*; MINNESOTA—*Little Falls Daily Transcript; St. Cloud Daily Times*; MISSOURI—*The Springfield Daily News; The Springfield Leader & Press*; NEBRASKA—*Fremont Tribune*; NEVADA—*Nevada State Journal; Reno Evening Gazette*; NEW JERSEY—*The* (Bridgewater) *Courier-News*; (Camden) *Courier-Post*; NEW MEXICO—*The New Mexican*; NEW YORK—*The* (Binghamton) *Evening Press* and *The Sun-Bulletin*; (Elmira) *Star-Gazette; The Ithaca Journal; Niagara Gazette; Poughkeepsie Journal*; (Rochester) *Democrat & Chronicle* and *Times-Union; Saratogian Tri-County News*; (Utica) *Observer-Dispatch* and *Daily Press; Westchester Rockland Newspapers*; (Westchester County) *Today; The* (Mamaroneck) *Daily Times; The* (Mount Vernon) *Daily Argus; New Rochelle Standard-Star; The* (Nyack-Rockland) *Journal-News*; (Ossining) *Citizen Register*; (Port Chester) *Item*; (Tarrytown) *News; White Plains Reporter Dispatch; Yonkers Herald Statesman*; OHIO—*Chillicothe Gazette; The Cincinnati Enquirer; The* (Fremont) *News-Messenger; The Marietta Times*; (Port Clinton) *News-Herald*; OKLAHOMA—(Muskogee) *Daily Phoenix & Times Democrat*; OREGON—(Salem) *Oregon Statesman* and *Capital Journal*; PENNSYLVANIA—(Chambersburg) *Public Opinion*; (New Kensington-Tarentum) *Valley News Dispatch*; SOUTH DAKOTA—(Sioux Falls) *Argus-Leader*; TENNESSEE—*The* (Nashville) *Tennessean*; TEXAS—*The El Paso Times*; VERMONT—*The Burlington Free Press*; VIRGIN ISLANDS—*The* (St. Thomas) *Daily News*; WASHINGTON—*The Bellingham Herald; The Daily Olympian*; WEST VIRGINIA—(Huntington) *Herald-Dispatch*; WISCONSIN—*Green Bay Press-Gazette; The* (Wausau) *Daily Herald*.

3. **NEWHOUSE** (*Average weekday circulation: 3.2 million*).
   ALABAMA—*The Birmingham News; The Huntsville Times* and *News*; (Mobile) *Press* and *Register*; LOUISIANA—*The* (New Orleans) *Times-Picayune* and *The States-Item*; MASSACHUSETTS—(Springfield) *News* and *Union*; MICHIGAN—*The Ann Arbor News; The Bay City Times; The Flint Journal; The Grand Rapids Press; Jackson Citizen Patriot; Kalamazoo Gazette; The Muskegon Chronicle; The Saginaw News*; MISSISSIPPI—*The* (Pascagoula) *Mississippi Press-Register*; MISSOURI—*St. Louis Globe-Democrat*; NEW JERSEY—*The* (Jersey City) *Jersey Journal; The* (Newark) *Star-Ledger*; NEW YORK—*Staten Island Advance; Syracuse Herald-Journal* and *The Post Standard*; OHIO—*The* (Cleveland) *Plain Dealer*; OREGON—(Portland) *Oregon Journal* and *The Oregonian*; PENNSYLVANIA—*The* (Harrisburg) *Evening News* and *The Patriot*.

4. **TRIBUNE** (*Average weekday circulation: 3.2 million*).
   Chicago Tribune; New York Daily News; CALIFORNIA—(Escondido) *Times-Advocate; The* (Palo Alto, Redwood City) *Peninsula Times-Tribune*; (Van Nuys) *Valley News*; FLORIDA—*Fort Lauderdale News*; (Orlando) *Sentinel Star; Pompano Beach Sun-Sentinel*.

5. **TIMES MIRROR** (*Average weekday circulation: 2.1 million*).
   Los Angeles Times; Dallas Times Herald; CONNECTICUT—*The Greenwich Time; The Hartford Courant*; (Long Island) NEW YORK— *Newsday; The* (Stamford) *Advocate*; CALIFORNIA—*Orange Coast Daily Pilot*.

6. **DOW JONES** (*Average weekday circulation: 1.9 million*).
   The Wall Street Journal; Ottaway newspapers: MASSACHUSETTS—*Beverly Times; Cape Cod Times;* (Gloucester) *Daily Times; The* (New Bedford) *Standard-Times; The* (Newburyport) *Daily News; The Daily Peabody Times;* CONNECTICUT—*The* (Danbury) *News-Times;* MISSOURI—*The Joplin Globe;* MINNESOTA—(Mankato) *Free Press;* (Owatonna) *People's Press;* OREGON—*Medford Mail Tribune;* NEW YORK—(Middletown) *Times; The* (Oneonta) *Daily Star; The* (Port Jervis) *Union-Gazette;* (Plattsburgh) *Press-Republican;* PENNSYLVANIA—*The* (Sharon) *Herald; The* (Stroudsburg) *Pocono Record; The* (Sunbury) *Daily Item;* MICHIGAN—*Traverse City Record-Eagle;* KENTUCKY—*The* (Ashland) *Daily Independent.*

7. **SCRIPPS-HOWARD** (*Average weekday circulation: 1.9 million*).
   ALABAMA—(Birmingham) *Post-Herald;* CALIFORNIA—(Fullerton) *Daily News Tribune;* COLORADO—(Denver) *Rocky Mountain News;* NEW MEXICO—*Albuquerque Tribune;* OHIO—*The Cincinnati Post; Cleveland Press; Columbus Citizen-Journal;* PENNSYLVANIA—*The Pittsburgh Press;* TENNESSEE—*The Knoxville News-Sentinel; Memphis Press Scimitar* and *Commercial Appeal;* TEXAS—*El Paso Herald-Post;* FLORIDA—*Hollywood Sun-Tattler; The Stuart News;* KENTUCKY—*The* (Covington) *Kentucky Post;* PUERTO RICO—*San Juan Star.*

8. **HEARST** (*Average weekday circulation: 1.4 million*).
   NEW YORK—(Albany) *Times-Union* and *Knickerbocker News;* CALIFORNIA—(San Francisco) *Examiner; Los Angeles Herald Examiner;* MARYLAND—(Baltimore) *News-American;* MASSACHUSETTS—*Boston Herald American;* TEXAS—*Midland Reporter-Telegram; Plainview Daily Herald; San Antonio Light;* WASHINGTON—*Seattle Post-Intelligencer.*

9. **COX** (*Average weekday circulation: 1.3 million*).
   GEORGIA—(Atlanta) *Journal* and *Constitution;* TEXAS—*Austin American-Statesman; Longview News* and *Journal; Lufkin News; The* (Port Arthur) *News; Waco Tribune-Herald;* OHIO—*Dayton Daily News* and *The Journal-Herald; The* (Springfield) *Sun* and *Daily News;* FLORIDA—(Daytona Beach) *Journal* and *News; The Miami News;* (Palm Beach) *News;* (West Palm Beach) *Post* and *Evening Times;* ARIZONA—(Mesa) *Tribune.*

10. **THOMSON** (*Average weekday circulation: 1.1 million*).
    64 small-town dailies.

11. **COWLES** (*Average weekday circulation: 1.0 million*).
    The Des Moines Register and *Tribune* publishes *The Jackson* (Tennessee) *Sun* and *Waukesha* (Wisconsin) *Freeman; The Minneapolis Star* and *Tribune* publishes *The Rapid City* (South Dakota) *Journal, Great Falls* (Montana) *Tribune* and *South Idaho Press.*

12. **CAPITAL CITIES** (*Average weekday circulation: 1.0 million*).
    ILLINOIS—(Belleville) *News-Democrat;* TEXAS—*Fort Worth Star-Telegram;* MISSOURI—*Kansas City Star* and *Times;* MICHIGAN—(Pontiac) *Press;* PENNSYLVANIA—*Wilkes-Barre Times Leader.*

13. **NEW YORK TIMES** (*Average weekday circulation: 1.0 million*).
    The New York Times; FLORIDA—*Gainesville Sun; Lake City Reporter; The* (Lakeland) *Ledger; Leesburg Commercial; Ocala Star-Banner; Palatka Daily News;* NORTH CAROLINA—*The* (Hendersonville) *Times-News; The* (Lexington) *Dispatch; Wilmington Star-News.*

14. **PARK NEWSPAPERS** (*Total average daily or weekly circulation: 425,000*).
    Daily newspapers: NEW YORK—(Lockport) *Union-Sun & Journal; The* (Norwich) *Evening Sun; The* (Ogdensburg) *Journal;* GEORGIA—*The* (Warner Robins) *Daily Sun* and *Houston County News;* VIRGINIA—(Manassas) *Journal Messenger;* INDIANA—*The* (Plymouth) *Pilot News;* NEBRASKA—*Nebraska City News-Press;* FLORIDA—*The* (Brooksville) *Daily Sun Journal;* OKLAHOMA—*McAlester News-Capital & Democrat;* NORTH CAROLINA—*The* (Kannapolis) *Daily Independent; The* (Morganton) *News Herald; The* (Newton) *Observer-News-Enterprise;* (Statesville) *Record & Landmark.*

    Weekly newspapers: NEW YORK—*Canton St. Lawrence Plaindealer; Massena Observer; Potsdam Courier & Freeman;* INDIANA—*Bremen Enquirer; Nappanee Advance-News;* OKLAHOMA—*Hartshorne Sun;* (Quinton) *Times; Bixby Bulletin; The* (Tulsa) *Southside Times; Jenks Journal;* NORTH CAROLINA—*The Valdese News.*

    Shoppers' giveways: GEORGIA—*South Macon Sun* and *Houston County News* (Warner Robins); NEW YORK—(Ogdensburg) *Rural News;* (Lockport) *Tri-County News;* (Norwich) *Chenango Shopper;* NEBRASKA—(Nebraska City) *Tri-State Weekly;* VIRGINIA—(Manassas) *Suburban Virginia Times;* FLORIDA—(Brooksville) *Smart Shopper;* INDIANA—(Plymouth) *Farm & Home;* OKLAHOMA—(McAlester) *Southeast Oklahoma News;* (Sapulpa) *Green Sheet;* ILLINOIS—(Macomb) *Business News;* NORTH CAROLINA—(Newton) *County News Interprise.*

less, unnecessary war." Five years later John Knight, III, then working in Philadelphia on the *Daily News*, was stabbed to death. A year later John Knight married for the third time (his second wife had also died).

In the public eye. At Knight-Ridder's annual meeting in 1977 Clare Plevinsky, a shareholder, rose to ask why there were no women on the board of directors. At the same meeting Ann Wrenn, an employee, rose to ask about the company's policies on hiring women. Chairman Lee Hills said then that one out of every five supervisors at Knight-Ridder was female. A year later they named Ann Wrenn treasurer. In 1979 they named their first woman director: Barbara Barnes Hauptfuhrer, active in Philadelphia community work.

Knight-Ridder publishes a Spanish section of the *Miami Herald* to serve the needs of the 500,000 Cubans in the area.

The *Philadelphia Inquirer* story of 1975 that won the Pulitzer Prize for public service exposed the habit of Philadelphia cops of beating confessions out of murder suspects. The Justice Department later filed suit against the city and police force for institutionalized brutality. In 1980 the *Inquirer* won its fifth consecutive Pulitzer for its coverage of Three Mile Island. Knight-Ridder reporters also broke the 1972 story about Democratic vice-presidential candidate Thomas Eagleton's electroshock therapy for depression.

Where they're going. Knight-Ridder is introducing zoned editions for different parts of metropolitan areas to give the papers a more local character. Although they would like to keep buying newspapers, they also intend to buy more TV stations.

Stock performance. Knight-Ridder stock bought for $1,000 in 1970 sold for $2,261 on January 2, 1980.

Access. One Herald Plaza, Miami, Florida 33101; (305) 350-2650.

Consumer brands.

Newspapers: See "Who Owns Your Local Paper" chart in this chapter.
Television: WJRT (Flint, Michigan); WPRI (Providence, Rhode Island); WTEN (Albany, New York).

The New York Times

Sales: $653 million
Profits: $36 million
Rank in daily newspaper circulation: 4
Rank in Sunday newspapers: 2
Founded: 1851
Employees: 6,800
Headquarters: New York City

What they do. In 1975 a *New York* magazine writer called the eight-column front page of the *New York Times*, with its narrow, layered headlines and its crowded, old-fashioned look, "the Stradivarius of journalism, a beautiful instrument that nobody has improved on." Like the classic violin, the *Times* is venerable, authoritative, inimitable. New Yorkers have strong feelings about their paper, reflected in sayings like "Times change, but the *Times* doesn't," or "If it isn't in the *New York Times*, it hasn't happened."

The first paper many U.S. presidents and foreign heads of state reach for in the morning, the *New York Times* is America's unofficial national newspaper. A quarter of its 865,000 daily copies go to readers outside the New York metropolitan area, in 50 states and 87 foreign countries, making the *Times* the nation's most widely distributed local newspaper. And the 500-page, four- to seven-pound Sunday *Times* is an institution in itself, with an average circulation of nearly a million and a half.

But those popular sayings don't always tell the truth. The *Times* has certainly had to change with the times. Even that old Stradivarius, the front page, was remodeled in 1976, its eight columns reduced to six. The reason was not aesthetic but economic: by trimming three-quarters of an inch from their newsprint reels, the Times was able to save $4 million a year. And they needed it.

In the last two decades the *Times* has had to come of age as a business. It looks, with hindsight, like the inauguration of a new era.

Prestige they had: 46 Pulitzer Prizes by 1979 (compared, for instance, with the *Washington Post's* 16) and a reputation as the intellectual's newspaper, with review sections that powerfully influenced book publishing and the New York performing arts.

News they had: by far the largest volume, both foreign and domestic, of any paper, and the largest news-gathering force. By 1978 there were 30 full-time foreign correspondents in 22 bureaus around the world; 375 reporters, editors, and photographers in the block-long Manhattan newsroom; 35 in Washington; 65 more reporting from Albany, Trenton, Miami, Denver, Houston, San Francisco, and many other cities; plus 500 part-time "stringers." In addition, the New York Times News Service had nearly 500 subscribing newspapers, magazines, and broadcasters; and, just for insurance, the *Times* themselves subscribed to nine news services.

But a business organization they didn't have: "We were organized like a forest of bamboo trees," publisher Arthur Ochs Sulzberger told *Business Week*, looking back on the 1960s. "Everything went straight up the organization to one person and nothing ever came together anywhere."

Muscle and grit to fight the unions they didn't have: their 1970 capitulation to the typographers, in which they gave an unheard-of 43% wage increase over three years without getting a single concession on the vital issue of automation, was described by Sulzberger a few years later as "humiliating."

And a grip on marketing—the skill, and the will, to sell both newspapers and advertising in rapidly changing urban circumstances—they didn't have. That turned out to be the most important. In the 1960s, while the core of their readership went rushing to the suburbs, the *Times* just went on turning out all the news fit to print. Meanwhile their old readers were switching to suburban papers, and advertisers were switching with them. City people were getting disproportionately poor, black, Hispanic, and old: less likely to read newspapers, less likely to buy advertisers' products. Downtown stores, a crucial source of ad revenue, were declining. Television competed for advertising and gave alternate news sources. By 1976 *Newsday*, a New York metropolitan area daily, had captured 62% of the Long Island market, leaving the *Times* only 11%. And since the suburbanites who still bought the *Times* often read it during their commute to the city, big-spending supermarkets withdrew their business, preferring to advertise in a paper that stays home, where the grocery list gets drawn up.

A giant newspaper strike in 1962–63 forced four New York papers to fold. Although the *Times* survived, they lost about $7 million and went into the red for the first time since 1898. Several attempts to broaden the company's interests in the 1960s fizzled. But in the 1970s they successfully transformed themselves from a one-paper company to a communications conglomerate. They got a slew of magazines, including *Family Circle, Golf Digest,* and *Tennis,* which in 1978 brought in over a quarter of their revenues. They acquired 11 newspapers in Florida and 3 in North Carolina, accounting for another 8% of income. To the classical music station they already owned in New York City they added television stations in Memphis, Tennessee, and Fort Smith, Arkansas, and two New Jersey cable TV systems. They went into book publishing: scholarly books at Arno Press, textbooks at Cambridge Book Company, and general books at Quadrangle/Times Books. They started their news service—now twice as big as its nearest competitor—and began producing a variety of educational and research materials. With the Washington Post Company and the IHT Corporation they publish the *International Herald-Tribune,* the Paris-based English-language newspaper. And they have 35% to 49% interests in three Canadian newsprint companies that supply 90% of the paper for the *Times.* The *New York Times* now accounts for just over half of the company's revenues. The benefits of expansion showed up dramatically in 1978: after a three-month strike in which the *Times* lost about $13 million, the company still returned a modest profit.

Since 1978 the *Times* has been changing its format to meet the needs of different audiences. The have developed "magazine-style" sections for each day: sports on Monday, science and education on Tuesday, food on Wednesday, home decoration on Thursday, arts and entertainment on Friday. The news of Connecticut, New Jersey, and New York are combined in a single section, and a beefed-up business section has been added. Although their West Coast edition failed in 1964, they are trying again with a Chicago edition, and are offering home delivery in Boston at no extra cost.

The old dowager empress of intellectual newspapers may be getting a bit trendy to compete with the suburban chains, but she still sees herself as primarily responsible, in the words of *Times* columnist James Reston, "to the historian of 50 years from now."

History. The *Times* was a penny paper when it was started in 1851 by Henry J. Raymond and George Jones. Its coverage of the Civil War and the Tammany Hall–Boss Tweed scandals made it a strong popular paper, but by the 1890s the *New York Times* couldn't compete with the sensationalism of Joseph Pulitzer's *World* and William Randolph Hearst's *Journal.* Hard hit by the panic of 1893, the *Times* fell to a daily circulation of 9,000 copies and was losing money every week.

In 1896 Adolph Ochs came to the paper's rescue. The son of German Jews who had come to America to escape persecution, Ochs began working around newspapers in Knoxville, Tennessee, at the age of 11; he bought his first newspaper, the Chattanooga *Times,* when he was 20. (The Chattanooga paper is still in the Ochs family, although not part of the Times Company. Adolph's granddaughter, Ruth Holmberg, is the publisher.) When Ochs bought the *New York Times,* he cut the price from 3¢ to a penny, to compete with Pulitzer and Hearst. He also cleaned up the typeface and added a Sunday magazine, book reviews, and a snappy slogan: "All the news that's fit to print." The balanced, if sometimes dull, reporting style favored by Ochs is still honored at the *Times,* as is the tradition of referring to men in the news as "Mister," with the exception of criminals and athletes.

Adolph's son-in-law Arthur Hays Sulzberger, the husband of his only daughter, Iphigene, ran the paper from 1935 to 1961, when the job passed to Arthur's son-in-law, Orvil Dryfoos. But when Dryfoos died only two years later, Adolph's grandson Arthur Ochs Sulzberger (known as "Punch") was forced to step up to the publisher's seat.

At 37 Punch wasn't quite ready to assume such responsibility. A *Times* executive commented on the young heir: "When Punch chooses people, the main thing is whether he likes them personally or not. And so all the top people are very intelligent, enjoyable, extremely likable. The only problem is that they don't know or care that much about business." Philip Graham, who himself married into his job as publisher of the *Washington Post,* called the *New York Times* of that period "not so much a business as a charitable institution."

Punch has learned quite a few lessons with time. Between 1970 and 1974 he brought the company into the modern business world, with tightly disciplined budgets, sophisticated planning, reorganization, younger managers, and successful acquisitions. In 1970 he buckled under the demands of tough union leader Bert Powers. But in 1974, with another strike shaping up, he treated Powers to a tour of the company's well-organized strike-busting capability. Not least among the weapons in his arsenal was the fact that the newspaper, which at that point accounted for about 60% of revenues, could be shut down for the major part of the year and the company could still break even. As *New York* magazine put it, the *Times,* "once a fat pussycat, was . . . looking very much like a tiger."

Reputation. A seat of power. In his 1969 book *The Kingdom and the Power,* former *Times* man Gay Talese unfolded a drama of New York and Washington editors battling like feudal barons. Besides sustaining epic struggles within, the *Times* wields awesome power outside. The paper was accused of communizing Cuba after publishing Herbert Matthews's coverage of the Castro guerrilla campaign in the Sierra Madre. Some historians believe that if the *Times* had not suppressed what they knew about the planned Bay of Pigs invasion in 1961, it might not have occurred. *Times* stories about the 1966–67 bombing of civilian targets in North Vietnam drastically altered public opinion, and the publication of the Pentagon Papers made and changed history. In Talese's words, the *Times* is an "institution that influences the world."

What they own. Two *Times* publishing plants in New York City and Carlstadt, New Jersey. Facilities for 6 of their Florida and North Carolina newspapers as well as for their television and radio stations in Memphis and New York. Interests in three Canadian pulp plants, and 40% of a new plant in Maine that will soon be the world's largest producer of magazine-quality paper.

In 1977 people laughed when the staid *Times* aped Time's *People* magazine by launching *Us.* In April 1980 *Us* was sold to Macfadden.

Who owns and runs the company. The New York Times Company is dominated by the Ochs-Sulzberger family. The Ochs Trust, which is administered by Iphigene Ochs Sulzberger (daughter, wife, mother, and mother-in-law of *Times* publishers, and a director of the company since 1917), and her son Arthur Ochs Sulzberger, the current publisher, together own over 70% of the stock. Iphigene's three daughters—Marian S. Heiskell (married to Andrew Heiskell, recently retired chairman of Time), Ruth S. Holmberg, and Judith S. Levinson—all sit on the board. Aside from female family members, there are no women or blacks on the board, which includes *Times* columnist James Reston and former Pennsylvania governor William W. Scranton.

In the public eye. After backing Republicans in the 1940s and 1950s, the *Times* supported Kennedy, Johnson, Humphrey, McGovern, and Carter for president.

In 1974 a class action suit against the company for discrimination against minorities was initiated and is still pending. In the same year the *Times* was cited in another class action suit for discrimination against women employees. The company agreed to change their affirmative action plan to promote women to top management jobs and pay $233,500 to employees plus $100,000 to cover their legal fees.

Over two-thirds of the *Times* employees are members of one of the 13 unions at the paper. The Pressmen's Union struck the *Times* (and two other New York papers) in 1978 to protest reduced staffing and increased mechanization. The strike lasted 88 days. But the company was willing to take an operating loss that year to effect automation and the "demanning" of the newsroom.

Where they're going. The big dream for a long time has been a national edition—and satellite delivery may soon bring that about.

Ninety-four percent of all households in Cleveland receive daily newspapers—the highest percentage of any city in the nation, according to *Retailing Today*. Kansas City is the runnerup with 90%, followed by Philadelphia (83%), Milwaukee (81%), and Buffalo (81%).

Stock performance. New York Times Company stock bought for $1,000 in 1970 sold for $547 on January 2, 1980.

Access. 229 West 43rd Street, New York, New York 10036; (212) 556-1234.

Consumer brands.

Newspapers: The New York Times; see also "Who Owns Your Local Paper" chart in this chapter.
Magazines: Family Circle; Golf Digest; Tennis.
Book publishing: Arno Press; Quadrangle/New York Times Books; Cambridge Books.
Information systems: The New York Times Index, a reference source; *The Large Type Weekly; The School Weekly;* The Information Bank, computerized storage; Teaching Resources Corporation; Microfilming Corporation of America.
Television and radio broadcasting: WREG-TV (Memphis, Tennessee); KFSM-TV (Fort Smith, Arkansas); WQXR-AM and -FM (New York City).

Newhouse

Sales: $1 billion (estimate)
Profits: $100 million (estimate)
Rank in newspaper chains by circulation: 3
Founded: 1922
Employees: 15,000
Headquarters: New York City

What they do. S. I. Newhouse, working out of a battered brown briefcase, built his newspaper group into a $1 billion business, the third-largest newspaper chain in the country at the time of his death in 1979. He insisted he wasn't out to get rich, just to provide for his family. His family operation was once described by *Forbes* as "half early Rothschild, half corner grocery store." At one point it had 64 Newhouse cousins, brothers, in-laws, and other relatives on the payroll. The business encompasses:

Twenty-nine major newspapers across the country, with a total circulation of 3.2 million (the heart of the Newhouse fortune).

Seven Condé Nast magazines, including *Vogue, House & Garden, Mademoiselle, Glam-*

our, *Bride's,* and *Gentlemen's Quarterly,* with a total circulation of 6.1 million.

The Sunday newspaper supplement *Parade,* with a 21 million circulation nationwide.

Five radio stations and cable television interests in a score of communities, with more than 250,000 subscribers.

Random House, one of the nation's largest and most prestigious book publishers.

Even before Newhouse bought Random House in 1980, *Forbes* said, "By the most conservative standards, the Newhouse properties are worth well over $1 billion. They are unencumbered by a penny of debt and except for a 49% interest in a paper mill, are 100% owned by the Newhouse family or by trusts they control."

At one time there were 31 Newhouse newspapers—only two ever failed. They also once owned six television stations. In 1979 they sold five TV stations to the Times Mirror Company for $82 million because the stations were located in cities where the Newhouse family also owned newspapers, and they assumed the government would eventually order them to be sold on antitrust grounds; the sixth station, in Portland, Oregon, had been sold earlier.

History. Samuel I. Newhouse bought the *Staten Island Advance* in 1922 for $98,000 and Random House publishing in 1980 (posthumously) for upward of $65 million; in between he built one of the country's largest communications empires.

"S. I.," as he always was known, became a press lord of sorts, but not with the usual trappings of the corporate executive. He had no permanent office, plush or nonplush, and no secretary. His briefcase was his office. His deals were made in hotel or motel rooms in the cities where he touched down in characteristic peripatetic style to buy newspapers. He kept such a low profile that he was often unrecognized on the few occasions he ventured to walk through the offices of the papers he bought.

Newhouse was born in 1895 in a tenement on Manhattan's Lower East Side, the eldest of eight children. He skipped high school because of poverty. Some reports say he left school at 12, others say 13 or 14. Some say he then took a job as an office boy with magistrate Hyman Lazarus in Bayonne, New Jersey, starting for nothing; others say it was a $2-a-week beginning wage. One report says he enrolled in a three-month business course in lieu of high school and was turned down at the first place he applied for a job because of his size —a mere 5'2". But all, including Newhouse, seem to agree that the job he landed, with Lazarus, determined his future career.

Lazarus had taken over the faltering *Bayonne Times* as payment for a bad debt. He told his clerk, who was then 17, to "take care of it until we get rid of it." Instead, Newhouse revived the paper by cutting costs and stimulating local advertising.

By 1916 Newhouse was making $30,000 a year, mostly in profits from the *Bayonne Times,* and had begun putting his relatives on the payroll. By 1922 he was able to buy the *Staten Island Advance* for $98,000. This small paper in the smallest of New York City's five boroughs became the cornerstone of the Newhouse empire. Profits from that begat the *Long Island Press* in 1932, the *Newark Star-Ledger* in 1933, the *Long Island Star-Journal* in 1938, the *Syracuse Journal* in 1939 and two years later the *Syracuse Herald-Standard,* the *Jersey Journal* in 1945, and the *Harrisburg Patriot* in 1948. Newhouse became a collector of newspapers, but he was never quite able to explain his urge to own them. "They might as well have been shoe factories," his brother Theodore once said.

In most cases he preferred to pay cash. Until 1955, when he borrowed money to pay for the *Birmingham News* and *Huntsville Times,* he concentrated on picking up low-cost properties. But that changed. His $42 million purchase of the *New Orleans Times-Picayune* and *New Orleans States-Item* in 1962 was the highest price ever paid for newspaper properties in one city, a record broken by himself five years later when he paid $54 million for the *Cleveland Plain Dealer.* His lifetime shopping spree produced other records, the last of which was the $305 million purchase of the eight Booth newspapers in Michigan three years before he died, reportedly the highest price ever paid in an American newspaper transaction.

Newhouse jokingly claimed to have bought the Condé Nast magazines as a 35th wedding anniversary present for his wife, the former Mitzi Epstein, a one-time student at New York's Parsons School of Design, whose abiding interest was fashion.

Reputation. The Newhouse papers aren't known as crusaders and prizewinners. They are, by and large, solid business properties which have become that way through cost cutting and keeping up with the times technologically. Unions have been resisted, and their reporters are not known for having high salaries. Newhouse papers do not have to toe to an editorial line. "My papers have different philosophies, and they're about as wide apart as they can get. Some are Democratic, some are Republican. I am not going to try to shape their thought," Newhouse said in 1968. The policy was copied by other chain publishers.

What they own. Their 29 daily newspapers are located in 11 states. The seven Condé Nast magazines are *Vogue, Glamour, House & Garden, Mademoiselle, Self, Gentlemen's Quarterly,* and *Bride's* (and British, French, Italian, and Australian editions). They own three radio stations in New York, Alabama, and Pennsylvania, as well as 15 cable TV systems in Texas, Wyoming, and Nebraska, under the name of Daniels Cable TV of Denver, Colorado. Newhouse owns almost half of a paper mill.

Who owns and runs the company. The Newhouse family. There never was a so-called chief executive officer in this operation—although it was generally understood that S. I. ruled the roost and called the shots, with top management divided among family members. Since S. I.'s death his two sons, S. I., Jr. ("Si") and Donald, have assumed roles as chiefs, along with brothers Norman and Theodore, who also continue to run their designated areas of the Newhouse empire. Si heads the Condé Nast operation; Donald, newspapers in the East; Norman, the Midwest and South from New Orleans, where he lives; and Ted travels to properties in the West as well as to Springfield, Massachusetts. A nephew, Richard E. Diamond, has the helm at the *Staten Island Advance;* another nephew, Robert Miron, works at broadcasting headquarters in Syracuse. A platoon of others is expected to come along and remain in the business—no one can sell out except to a relative.

In the public eye. A $15 million gift from the Newhouse Foundation established the S. I. Newhouse School of Public Communications at Syracuse University, the college both S. I.'s sons attended for three years. The S. I. Newhouse Foundation dispenses funds to charities. Other beneficiaries include Rutgers University's S. I. Newhouse

Center for Law and Justice and The Mitzi E. Newhouse Theater at Lincoln Center.

Where they're going. It's up to S. I.'s heirs, but the Random House acquisition shows that Newhouse is sticking to publishing—books and periodicals.

Access. Newhouse has no corporate headquarters. Samuel I., Jr., has offices at Condé Nast, 350 Madison Avenue, New York, New York 10017; (212) 880-8800. Donald is at the *Newark Star-Ledger,* Star Ledger Plaza, Newark, New Jersey 07101; (201) 877-4141. And Norman works out of the *New Orleans Times-Picayune,* 3800 Howard Avenue, New Orleans, Louisiana 70140; (504) 586-3785.

Consumer brands.

Magazines: Vogue; Glamour; House & Garden; Mademoiselle; Self; Gentlemen's Quarterly; Bride's; (Sunday supplement) *Parade.*
Radio: WSYR-Syracuse, N.Y.; WAPI-Birmingham, Ala.; WTTA-Harrisburg, Pa.
Newspapers: See "Who Owns Your Local Paper" chart in this chapter.

Park

Sales: $60 million (estimate)
Rank in newspaper chains: 50
Founded: 1942
Employees: 1,200
Headquarters: Ithaca, New York

What they do. In 1977, when he bought WONO-FM in Syracuse, New York, Roy H. Park accomplished something that broadcasting giants like CBS, NBC, and ABC have not been able to do yet: put together the biggest collection of broadcasting properties allowed under the regulations of the Federal Communications Commission. The FCC rules say that a single owner may hold no more than seven AM radio stations, seven FM radio stations, and seven TV stations—for a total of 21. Park's purchase of the Syracuse station put him right at the mark. He has stations in a dozen cities stretching from Birmingham, Alabama, to Seattle, Washington. The biggest of his TV stations is Birmingham's WBMG, a CBS affiliate.

Although he can't buy any more stations, there's nothing to stop Park from gathering newspapers. And he keeps picking them up, one after another. In mid-1980 he had 42 under his belt, all small-town papers: 17 are dailies; 12 are weeklies; and 13 are shoppers' weeklies that are given away. The largest of the papers is the *Union-Sun & Journal* in Lockport, New York, with a paid circulation of 18,000. The total circulation of all the Park newspapers is a little over 425,000, less than the circulation of the *San Francisco Chronicle*.

But Roy Park, who was born in Dobson, North Carolina, is quite happy with this mix. "We know how to operate in small towns," he says. "We wouldn't know how to operate in New York City, Buffalo, or Oakland. I'm really a country boy—I've still got a little hayseed in my hair."

Park operates through a maze of companies—about 50 of them—and they are not consolidated under any one corporation, nor is any of them "public" in the sense that shares of stock are available to the public. The two principal corporate entities are Park Broadcasting and Park Newspapers. But Park's interests extend to other areas, too: he's in the outdoor advertising business (renting billboard space), and he's active in real estate. How much of his estimated $60 million annual sales comes from publishing and broadcasting is not known, nor is Park required to tell anyone. His companies are private.

History. Roy Park, who was 70 years old in 1980, is now on his third career. After working his way through North Carolina State University, where he edited the campus paper, Park went into public relations and advertising work for farm cooperatives, first in North Carolina and then, beginning in 1942, in Ithaca, New York, where he ran an advertising agency primarily to serve the state's big farm co-op, GLF. The farmers who made up this co-op had a problem that they brought to Park: they felt they had good products but were no match for the big food processors because they lacked a well-known brand name. Park set out to find one for them. His search led him to Duncan Hines, who, in the 1940s, was widely recognized as an authority for travelers on where to stay and eat, publishing guides where hotels and restaurants were reviewed. The "Recommended by Duncan Hines" sign was displayed by establishments passing his inspection, which was far less rigorous than the standards now employed by the Mobil Travel Guides. (Hines, who liked to eat ice cream over corn flakes for breakfast, once said: "Usually the difference between the low-priced meal and the one that costs more is the amount you pay the doctor or the undertaker.")

Park persuaded Hines to lend his name, but his clients then had second thoughts about entering the brand-name marketplace. So Roy Park embarked on his second career, setting up a new company, Hines-Park Foods, to license the Duncan Hines name to other companies around the country. "We shipped the labels to the products, not the product to the labels," explained Park. The idea caught hold immediately. A lot of companies were hungry for a recognized name to put on their products, and for a royalty on sales, Park gave them one. By 1952 he had licensed 124 companies to use the Duncan Hines label—83 were ice cream makers; 12 were bread bakers; and others made orange juice, frozen peas, salad dressing, coffee, chili con carne, and pickles.

By 1955 more than 200 products were carrying the Duncan Hines name, and these products were doing annual sales of $50 million. The licensing had been ex-

AMERICA'S TOP MAGAZINES

Magazine (Publisher)	Total Sales (1979)*	Circulation	Ad Cost per Page
1. TV GUIDE (*Triangle*)	$552 *million*	20,044,375	$ 55,000
2. TIME	$349 *million*	4,293,387	$ 40,960
3. READER'S DIGEST	$240 *million*	18,036,216	$ 64,500
4. NEWSWEEK (*Washington Post*)	$236 *million*	2,929,888	$ 29,275
5. PLAYBOY	$176 *million*	5,995,605	$ 31,310
6. PEOPLE (*Time*)	$170 *million*	2,394,660	$ 19,000
7. SPORTS ILLUSTRATED (*Time*)	$169 *million*	2,280,047	$ 25,900
8. FAMILY CIRCLE (*New York Times*)	$155 *million*	7,948,017	$ 44,900
9. BETTER HOMES & GARDENS (*Meredith*)	$144 *million*	8,023,592	$ 44,395
10. WOMAN'S DAY (*CBS*)	$143 *million*	7,809,827	$ 44,960
11. PENTHOUSE	$138 *million*	4,632,141	$ 20,700
12. GOOD HOUSEKEEPING (*Hearst*)	$136 *million*	5,270,124	$ 33,130
13. PARADE (*Newhouse*)	$130 *million*	21,035,928	$111,945
14. BUSINESS WEEK (*McGraw-Hill*)	$129 *million*	793,524	$ 15,560
15. McCALL'S MAGAZINE	$123 *million*	6,519,804	$ 38,675
16. NATIONAL ENQUIRER	$116 *million*	5,186,800	$ 16,600
17. NATIONAL GEOGRAPHIC MAGAZINE	$116 *million*	10,037,676	$ 54,280
18. LADIES' HOME JOURNAL (*Charter*)	$106 *million*	5,832,279	$ 30,240
19. COSMOPOLITAN (*Hearst*)	$ 95 *million*	2,733,496	$ 14,855
20. U.S. NEWS & WORLD REPORT	$ 95 *million*	2,052,250	$ 19,800
21. REDBOOK MAGAZINE (*Charter*)	$ 88 *million*	4,457,061	$ 25,145
22. FAMILY WEEKLY (*CBS*)	$ 76 *million*	12,218,539	$ 63,630
23. THE STAR (*Murdoch*)	$ 70 *million*	3,199,044	$ 12,300
24. FORTUNE (*Time*)	$ 57 *million*	699,040	$ 14,650
25. GLAMOUR (*Newhouse*)	$ 56 *million*	1,889,711	$ 11,650
26. THE NEW YORKER	$ 50 *million*	498,382	$ 7,600
27. HUSTLER	$ 50 *million*	1,546,118	$ 7,500
28. FORBES	$ 47 *million*	671,855	$ 10,990
29. SOUTHERN LIVING	$ 44 *million*	1,685,964	$ 14,115
30. VOGUE (*Newhouse*)	$ 40 *million*	988,799	$ 9,300
31. MIDNIGHT GLOBE	$ 39 *million*	1,690,442	$ 6,700
32. SUNSET	$ 37 *million*	1,378,132	$ 11,590
33. POPULAR MECHANICS (*Hearst*)	$ 34 *million*	1,630,719	$ 12,690
34. POPULAR SCIENCE (*Times Mirror*)	$ 34 *million*	1,812,183	$ 14,205
35. SEVENTEEN (*Triangle*)	$ 34 *million*	1,411,539	$ 9,525
36. HOUSE & GARDEN (*Newhouse*)	$ 34 *million*	1,054,236	$ 11,900
37. SMITHSONIAN	$ 31 *million*	1,761,267	$ 15,000
38. FIELD & STREAM (*CBS*)	$ 31 *million*	2,047,288	$ 15,400
39. OUTDOOR LIFE (*Times Mirror*)	$ 30 *million*	1,741,976	$ 13,900
40. N.Y. TIMES SUNDAY MAGAZINE	$ 30 *million*	1,412,481	$ 8,450
41. POPULAR PHOTOGRAPHY (*Ziff-Davis*)	$ 29 *million*	825,834	$ 17,920
42. PREVENTION (*Rodale*)	$ 28 *million*	2,268,097	$ 10,745
43. CONSUMER REPORTS	$ 28 *million*	2,229,000	NA
44. LIFE (*Time*)	$ 28 *million*	1,328,598	$ 15,000
45. EBONY (*Johnson*)	$ 28 *million*	1,256,411	$ 10,638
46. NATION'S BUSINESS (*U.S. Chamber of Commerce*)	$ 26 *million*	1,212,360	$ 12,600
47. MADEMOISELLE (*Newhouse*)	$ 26 *million*	974,046	$ 7,375
48. NEW YORK MAGAZINE (*Murdoch*)	$ 26 *million*	402,685	$ 6,500
49. PSYCHOLOGY TODAY (*Ziff Davis*)	$ 25 *million*	1,176,920	$ 14,540
50. HOUSE BEAUTIFUL (*Hearst*)	$ 24 *million*	849,070	$ 9,715

*Includes advertising, subscriptions, and newsstand sales.

Source: *Folio*, January, 1980.

tended to makers of electric coffeemakers, toasters, pepper mills, and outdoor barbecue grills. The Duncan Hines program was called "the last chance for the independents." By far the most successful of the licensees was Omaha's Nebraska Consolidated Mills (now ConAgra), a flour miller that had no previous experience with consumer products. They marketed a line of Duncan Hines cake mixes that soon had the leaders—Betty Crocker, Pillsbury, and Swansdown—worried. The Duncan Hines brand rose to the number 2 position in the marketplace.

There then followed an ironic turn of events. Procter & Gamble, the king of the soap and detergent business and longtime marketer of Crisco shortening, decided they wanted to enter the cake mix field— and they ended up, in 1956, buying out Hines-Park and the Duncan Hines cake mix business of Nebraska Consolidated Mills. But P&G was interested only in cake mixes; they were not about to run a food-licensing operation. So all the other licensing arrangements went by the boards—and a scheme that had started out as a boon to small companies wanting to fight the big companies ended up in the hands of the largest advertiser in the country.

As part of the deal with P&G, Roy Park signed on as a consultant for three years. He was impressed at the way the Cincinnati marketing powerhouse bought up gobs of radio and television time to promote their many brands, and that impression led him to this third career, this time on the media side of the advertising equation.

In 1962 he went to his home state to buy a television station: WNCT in Greenville, North Carolina. That was followed by purchases of other stations—in Chattanooga and Johnson City, Tennessee, and Roanoke and Richmond, Virginia. In 1972, as he began approaching the maximum number of stations he could have, Park turned his attention to print, his first love (while he was running his advertising agency in Ithaca, he also published two magazines, *Co-Op Power* and *Cooperative Digest*). The first paper he bought was the *Daily Sun* in Warner Robins, Georgia. It was followed by 40 others in the next eight years. His latest purchase, in early 1980, was an 80-year-old daily, the *Concord Tribune* of Cabarrus County, North Carolina, with a circulation of 12,000. Along the way Park also bought outdoor advertising companies in New York and Pennsylvania. Headquarters for all his operations remains in Ithaca, home of Cornell University.

Park's strategy is to buy newspapers and stations with cash (usually borrowed from a bank) and then let the local managements run them; no editorial line comes out of Ithaca. Park is mainly interested in seeing that the properties turn a profit. Only 30 people are employed at Park headquarters in Ithaca.

Reputation. Roy Park is known as an entrepreneur who knows how to read a financial statement. He's a patient builder. He's not a reformer, and he doesn't use his papers or stations to advance any political or ideological cause.

What they own. In addition to his media empire, Roy Park owns citrus groves in Florida, a real estate enterprise in South Carolina, farm and timberlands in North Carolina, and a lot of real estate in Ithaca, including 88,000 square feet of office space at the Terrace Hill complex where his companies are based. This complex once housed his first advertising client, GLF, which became Agway and moved to Syracuse, New York.

Who owns and runs the company. Roy Park.

In the public eye. Roy Park has bought seven papers in his native North Carolina. In 1979, after he bought the *Record & Landmark* in Statesville, North Carolina, and the *News-Herald* in Morganton, North Carolina, another Tarheel paper, the *Daily Record* of Hickory, North Carolina, went out of its way to praise Park for persuading the local people to remain in charge. The paper editorialized: "At the rate Roy Park is going he may one day have a significant impact on the North Carolina press. Given some of the barracudas in our industry, he is going about it in a reassuring way."

Where they're going. There are some 1,750 daily newspapers in America; Park has 42 . . .

Access. Park Newspapers or Park Broadcasting, Terrace Hill, Ithaca, New York 14850; (607) 272-9020.

Consumer brands.

Daily newspapers: See "Who Owns Your Local Paper" chart in this chapter.
Television: WTVR-Richmond, Virginia; WBMG-Birmingham, Alabama; WSLS-Roanoke, Virginia; WNCT-Greenville, North Carolina; WJHL-Johnson City, Tennessee; WDEF-Chattanooga, Tennessee; WUTR-Utica, New York.
Radio: WTVR-AM and -FM, Richmond, Virginia; KEZX-FM, Seattle, Washington; WHEN-AM and WONO-FM, Syracuse, New York; WNCT-AM and -FM, Greenville, North Carolina; WNAX-AM, Yankton, South Dakota; KRSI-AM and KFMX-FM, St. Louis Park, Minnesota; WDEF-AM and -FM, Chattanooga, Tennessee; KWJJ-AM and KJIB-FM, Portland, Oregon.

Reader's Digest

Sales: $1 billion (estimate)
Profits: $100 million (estimate)
Rank in monthly magazines: 1
Founded: 1922
Employees: 10,000
Headquarters: Pleasantville, New York

Opening the mail at the *Reader's Digest* office in 1936. Even in those days there were 10,000 pieces of circulation mail received daily.

What they do. It looks so deceptively simple. You just digest articles that appear in other magazines. You stick to home, family, and uplifting stories. It sounds trite. But it works. DeWitt Wallace and his wife, Lila Acheson Wallace, started it in 1922 on $1,300 of borrowed funds. What they started became the most successful magazine in the history of publishing.

The Wallaces knew precisely what they wanted the *Reader's Digest* to be. They had an incredibly sure touch in knowing what Americans want to read. They didn't ape fashion. When everybody was smoking cigarettes, they denounced the habit. When everyone was selling stock to the public, they remained private. They depended on their readers so much that they didn't accept advertising in their U.S. edition until 1955. And when they did, they refused to take any ads for cigarettes, liquor, drugs, and other products they found distasteful.

Today, more people read the *Reader's Digest* than any other magazine in the world. Only *TV Guide* sells more copies in the United States—20 million versus the *Digest*'s 18 million. But the *Digest* is easily the world's largest-circulation magazine when you consider the 39 editions in 15 languages sold in 164 countries—making their worldwide sales about 30 million copies a month. Total readership is estimated at around 100 million. According to a *Digest* estimate several years ago, the amount of paper used to print the United States edition for one year could produce a 5½-foot-wide ribbon that would girdle the earth 15 times. The *Digest* comes into one out of four American homes each month, almost always through the mail; nine-tenths of their sales are through subscriptions rather than newsstands and supermarkets. It's a tiny format—only about 5" × 7"—but it costs $65,000 to buy a page of advertising in it.

But the magazine itself produces only about one-third of the company's sales.

Reader's Digest is also one of the world's largest hardcover book publishers, and another third of their sales comes from books—chiefly *Reader's Digest Condensed Books* but also a yearly almanac, a popular home-repair guide, and lavishly illustrated coffee-table books that the *Digest* publishes on a made-to-order basis only after polling their readers as to whether they would be interested in buying such a thing.

Another third of their money comes from the sale of records, tapes, and assorted items such as globes and first-day commemorative stamp covers, all of which they offer through the mail to the people on their huge subscription list—the envy of every direct-mail marketer in the country. Four times a year they conduct a giant sweepstakes, sending out 40 million pieces of mail to promote the magazine and their various other products.

The magazine that has made it all possible is a unique American institution which has been imitated countless times, never very successfully. Samuel A. Schreiner, Jr., a *Digest* editor for 15 years who recounted his experiences in *The Condensed World of the Reader's Digest*, noted that the magazine's central message "can almost be summed up in a word: optimism. Through wars and rumors of war, through depression and inflation, through fire and pestilence, it keeps telling people that the world is not only a pretty good place but can be made better, that life is what you make of it, that laughter is the best medicine, that there's no sting in death."

Another classic characteristic of the *Digest* is their legendary conservative, superpatriotic political stance. The *Digest,* as Schreiner put it, has long been convinced "that the world would be better off without Washington bureaucrats, Communists of every kind but particularly Russians and Chinese, economists who think inflation might be more tolerable than unemployment, most union leaders who have been depicted as Communists and/or gangsters depending on the times, federal revenue agents, environmentalists who even in the interests of saving animals might inhibit the growth of industry, young people who don't take the *Digest* to heart or even read it, and Democrats." *Digest* readers, however, seem to ignore the political lectures for the most part. The magazine's own readership polls, according to Schreiner, give the highest popularity marks to "departments, jokes, corking good dramatic tales, nostalgic tear jerkers, how-to-do-it pieces on health, wealth, marriage, local civic affairs."

The *Digest* is famous for articles "condensed" from other magazines. Actually, they originate many of these pieces. Some of them are simply published in the *Digest* as original material. But others are first "planted" in other magazines, then condensed and reprinted in the *Digest.* The magazine goes through this rigamarole to maintain the appearance of what it was originally—a "digest" encompassing the best of other publications. To come up with the rest of their articles, *Digest* editors comb every issue of more than 500 publications, looking for that elusive something that makes a *Reader's Digest* story. At the same time they keep their eyes open for short, humorous items for the various departments such as "Laughter Is the Best Medicine" and "Life in These United States."

When they find a worthy article, it goes through a rigorous editing process to reach an almost mystical level of simplicity, economy, and directness. Numerous editors successively chop and whittle what might start out as 8 or 10 large magazine pages into two or three pocket-size *Digest* pages. The *Digest* is "the best-edited magazine in America," according to Norman Cousins, former editor of the *Saturday Review.* "The words lift right off the page into your mind." Henry Kissinger was once quoted as saying, "Don't ever write anything more

complicated than a *Reader's Digest* article for Nixon." Nixon himself has been a *Digest* contributor, as have Billy Graham, Norman Vincent Peale, and Dwight D. Eisenhower.

History. The founder and guiding genius behind *Reader's Digest* is DeWitt Wallace, a Presbyterian minister's son. Wallace conceived the idea of the magazine in late 1918 while laid up in an Army hospital at Aix-les-Bain, France, recovering from shrapnel wounds he received in the closing days of World War I. Passing the time by going through American magazines, he decided that most of the articles were about four times too long. Wallace conceived the idea of a "service for readers" that would select the most worthwhile articles from current magazines and assembled a sample copy of what he already called the *Reader's Digest.*

In 1921 Wallace married Lila Acheson, another preacher's kid. The couple rented an office under a speakeasy in New York City's Greenwich Village, borrowed $1,300, and printed 5,000 copies of the first issue of the *Reader's Digest,* which appeared in February 1922 and promised "thirty-one articles each month from leading magazines —each article of enduring value and interest, in condensed and compact form." There was one article for every day of the month. Among the titles in the first issue: "How to Keep Young Mentally," "Henry Ford, Dreamer and Worker," "What Kind of Husband Are You?", and "Advice from a President's Physician."

Wallace spent much of the magazine's first year in the New York Public Library, scouring the magazines and writing out in longhand condensed versions of the articles he liked. The magazine was well received from the start, and circulation reached 7,000 within the first year. Late in 1922 the Wallaces moved the operation to the suburban town of Pleasantville, in Westchester County, north of New York City.

The *Digest* kept a low profile through its early years. Until 1929 it was sold only by subscription—partly because Wallace viewed his magazine as a kind of "association" to which his subscribers belonged, partly because he was afraid that if the *Digest* became too visible, editors of other magazines might see it as competition and stop letting him reprint their material, and imitators might rise up to squeeze him out of business once they saw how good the idea was. In fact they tried, but only Wallace, who has been described as "the average American par excellence," had a flawless sense of what a mass audience wanted in a magazine. By 1936 circulation had reached 1.4 million. The first foreign edition appeared in Britain in 1938. In 1939, with circulation at 3 million, the Wallaces moved the magazine a few miles away to Chappaqua, but their mailing address remained in Pleasantville—they knew they couldn't invent a better name themselves. Pleasantville now has an enormous post office to handle the tons of *Digest* mail.

In the 1930s and 1940s the magazine paid contributors more than almost any other magazine, and many of the most famous writers of the day started showing up in its pages, including Alexander Woollcott, Fulton Oursler, John Gunther, James Michener, and Max Eastman. For a long time several small magazines such as the *American Mercury* survived solely because of the *Digest*'s contracts for reprint rights.

Not until 1955 did the U.S. edition of the *Digest* accept any advertising (the overseas editions had run ads all along). When they finally did, they announced grandly, "The same unprejudiced and uninfluenced reports of the world we live in will be found in these pages each month." But they didn't accept their first beer and wine ads until 1978, and not until 1979 did they open their pages to hard liquor advertisers. They have never printed cigarette ads, though; the *Digest* was one of the first magazines to warn of the dangers of smoking, long before the 1964 surgeon general's report.

Condensed Books, the *Digest*'s first—and most successful—sideline, began in 1950. Five hardcover volumes are published each year, each volume containing condensed versions of five new books, mostly novels. Americans buy an estimated 11 million volumes of Condensed Books each year, and another 6 million are sold overseas. Most authors whose books are condensed don't mind seeing their precious prose pruned back since they usually receive more money in *Digest* royalties than they do from the original publication of their books.

In 1959 the *Digest* strayed from the printed word into phonograph records, issuing albums of music with broad appeal and a dash of self-improvement, such as "Music of the World's Great Composers." In 1965 they bought the publishing house of Funk and Wagnalls, but they got rid of it six years later.

When the magazine turned 50 in 1972, they published a booklet with glowing testimonials from such world leaders as President Nixon, West German Chancellor Willy Brandt, Israeli Prime Minister Golda Meir, Jordan's King Hussein, and Philippine President Ferdinand Marcos.

Reputation. The *Reader's Digest* has always been an object of scorn and derision from literati and publishers of less-lucrative magazines. *Christian Century* once called it a "delightful mishmash of family corn, cultural mediocrity and political reaction." To millions of Americans, however, it is a source of hope and inspiration. The magazine's files are stuffed with testimonials from readers who credit the *Digest* with saving their lives, or at least improving them dramatically. They also demonstrate their loyalty by renewing their subscription 70% of the time—a remarkably high rate for a magazine. To charges that they are "old-fashioned" and "square," the *Digest* cheerfully pleads guilty. "We answer by saying we address ourselves to the widest possible audience," former editor Hobart Lewis once told the White Plains (New York) *Reporter Dispatch*. "The 'intellectuals' who criticize us fail to recognize that we can be read—and are read—by highly educated persons as well as lesser educated persons. Just because we're clear doesn't mean we're superficial."

What they own. Unlike most huge publishers, the *Digest* owns no forests, paper mills, TV stations, or the like. Their headquarters in Westchester County sits on 155 beautifully landscaped acres overlooking the Saw Mill River Parkway. The central building is a three-story red brick affair built in 1939 at a cost of $1.5 million and styled after the recreated Colonial village of Williamsburg, Virginia. The *Digest* also owns the high-speed presses on which the magazine is printed in Dayton and Buffalo, but they let other companies run them.

In 1980 Reader's Digest got a 20% interest in *Book Digest*, owned by Dow Jones, in exchange for providing *Book Digest* direct mail and other subscription and distribution services. *Book Digest* prints excerpts of about seven best-selling books a month and has a circulation of about 1 million.

At the end of 1978 the *Digest* had assets totaling $325 million.

Who owns and runs the company. DeWitt and Lila Wallace, who both turned 90 in

1980, own all the voting stock. (They have given a few shares of nonvoting stock to favored employees.) They don't publish financial statements, so figures of sales and profits are only guesses. The company has a 12-member board of directors that includes Laurance Rockefeller and a former chairman of New York's Chemical Bank, but the board has no real power since, in the end, only the Wallaces have a vote. DeWitt Wallace is still active editorially and is reportedly on the phone daily with his editors, and Lila Wallace still selects the folksy paintings that decorate the magazine's back covers.

Although many people in the magazine business change jobs frequently, most *Digest* staffers stay for years. For half a century, all employees have received year-end bonuses of about 15% of their salaries. The company subsidizes meals in the company cafeteria, where a full lunch runs around $1 and beverages are free. Everybody gets four weeks of vacation each year, and the whole operation shuts down every Friday in May, providing a month of three-day weekends. Working hours are a leisurely 8:30 to 4, with time off for lunch and coffee breaks. The company pays half the cost of any self-improvement course an employee takes, from Dale Carnegie to transcendental meditation; if the course is job-related, the company pays for it all.

In the public eye. The Wallaces and the Reader's Digest Foundation, which they own, have given an estimated $100 million to assorted charities and civic causes over the years. Upon their 50th anniversary in 1972, the *Digest* published a summary of their philanthropies over the previous 10 years, in which the foundation and company together had given $19.6 million to various causes, including nearly $9 million for education and youth. In 1977 the *Digest* agreed to pay more than $1.5 million to settle a class action suit on behalf of 2,600 current and former women employees, who charged sex discrimination. In 1969, at the height of the Vietnam War, the *Digest* inserted detachable flag decals into all 18 million copies of the U.S. edition.

Where they're going. The biggest question in Digestland is what will happen when the Wallaces are gone. They have no heirs, and their plans for disposing of the enterprise are a secret. Speculation abounds. One theory holds that control will pass to the magazine's top officers. Another school of thought predicts the triumph of the "bottom-line boys," business managers concerned only with profit who might kill the golden goose by disrupting the delicate editorial formula. Schreiner cites one wild, unattributed theory more intriguing than the rest: that when Wallace goes, the *Digest* goes with him. In this scenario the magazine would simply cease publication upon Wallace's death. He started it, and he could end it, rather than let it pass into less-competent hands and possibly become a travesty of its earlier, nobler self. But Wallace has said publicly he hopes the *Digest* is around 500 years from now. Meanwhile, the Digest is working on a condensed version of the Bible.

In 1980 the Digest introduced a new magazine, called *Families*, aimed at helping parents and children "cope with the '80s." To figure out how much they should charge for it, they test marketed it in different cities at three separate prices: $1.25, $1.95, and $2.49.

Access. Pleasantville, New York 19750; (914) 769-7000. The headquarters is open for tours every working day, and visitors can see the impressive array of Impressionist and post-Impressionist paintings that Lila Wallace has assembled, including works by Degas, Matisse, Cezanne, Monet, and Picasso. It's said to be the second most valuable art collection in Westchester County—after the Rockefeller family's at Pocantico Hills.

Consumer brands.

Reader's Digest magazine, records, tapes, books and Condensed Books; *Families* magazine.

TIME INC.

Sales: $2.5 billion
Profits: $143.9 million
Forbes 500 rank: 264
Rank in publishing: 1
Rank in newsweeklies: 1
Rank in cable television: 2
Founded: 1923
Employees: 23,400
Headquarters: New York City

What they do. Henry Robinson Luce, who was born in China and went to Hotchkiss prep school and Yale University, invented modern, slick, American-style magazine journalism—and this company is his monument. It's the largest publishing company in the world. The Time-Life offices in New York—for more than 40 years they have been housed in Rockefeller Center—have long served as a mecca for the bright young wordsmith out of an Ivy League college. At Time Inc. he would find a cordon of Mount Holyoke graduates who did his research and typing. Their magazines, *Time* and *Life*, mirrored the world for a lot of Americans—and they were read overseas as the American version of the gospel. Intellectuals often vented their ire against the publications, but when they went overseas themselves they devoured *Time* magazine (or read it guiltily on airplanes). *Life* pioneered photojournalism and was in its heyday the most important mass-circulation magazine in the world—and indeed it was copied around the world.

Over the years Time Inc. has added *Fortune, Sports Illustrated, Money,* and *People. Time* sells 5 million copies of its weekly summary of significant developments in politics, business, world affairs, sports, science, and culture. All in all, the company that Luce built sells close to 28 million magazines each month.

Still, magazines provide only about one-fourth of Time's sales these days. They take in more money from forest products. Time is the largest private landholder in Texas. Their Temple-Eastex subsidiary owns timberland there that's larger than the state of Rhode Island. Since Time bought Temple Industries in 1973, the Temple family of Texas has owned the largest block of Time's stock. Temple-Eastex makes lumber and other building materials as well as paperboard for file folders and paper plates.

They even do some heavy construction work. Time's Inland Container company makes corrugated cardboard boxes for everything from eggs to refrigerators.

Time does a brisk business in book publishing too. Their Time-Life Books division issues handsome hardbound sets on everything from wilderness areas to gourmet cooking. The company estimates that one of every seven homes in the United States has a Time-Life book on the shelf. They own the Boston-based publishing house of Little, Brown. The Book-of-the-Month Club, also owned by Time, allows 1 million members to buy the latest popular titles without having to visit a bookstore. Time also sells record albums and facsimiles of great art works through the mail. They've published the daily *Washington Star* since 1978 (the much larger *Washington Post* owns Time's arch-rival, *Newsweek*), and they own a string of suburban weekly newspapers around Chicago.

Time is a major force in video, or nonbroadcast, television. They own Home Box Office, a pay TV network that beams movies and special programs via satellite to local cable TV systems across the country. Their American Television and Communications, based in Denver, is the nation's second-largest owner of cable systems, after Teleprompter. Time-Life Films makes TV specials like "Eleanor and Franklin" as well as video cassette tapes. In another realm of electronics, Time runs SAMI (Selling Areas-Marketing, Inc.), a Chicago-based computer service that monitors the movement of 80% of the nation's food products from wholesalers to supermarkets.

History. Henry Luce was born in Tengchow, China, in 1898, the son of a missionary, and he stayed in that country until he left for prep school in Connecticut at age 15. His growing up in China had a profound and permanent effect on his view of the world. As Robert T. Elson reports in his company history, *Time Inc.*, Luce once said, "I was never disillusioned with or by America, but I was, from my earliest manhood, dissatisfied with America. America was not being as great and as good as I knew she could be, as I believed with every nerve and fiber God Himself had intended her to be."

Luce devoted his publications to the cause of shaping America along the lines of the divine plan. To Luce, this meant glorifying the Republicans, discrediting the

Democrats, and rallying support for right-wing dictators around the globe (as an old China hand, Luce was especially fond of Chiang Kai-shek)—all in the guise of rounding up the news each week. "Henry Luce was a Calvinist and a conservative," says David Shaw of the *Los Angeles Times*, "and his view of the world was *Time's* view of the world—morally, socially, intellectually and, most important of all, politically." David Halberstam, in his book *The Powers That Be*, called Luce "a national propagandist . . . the most important and influential conservative-centrist force in the country." The German weekly *Der Spiegel* once said, "No other American without a political office—with the possible exception of Henry Ford—has had a greater influence on American society." Luce's second wife, Clare Boothe Luce, served two terms as a Republican congresswoman from Connecticut and was appointed ambassador to Italy by President Dwight Eisenhower.

Time magazine started in 1923 as a collaboration of Luce and a classmate of his from Hotchkiss and Yale, Briton Hadden. They began with $86,000, which they raised through friends and fellow classmates. Circulation had risen to about 220,000 in 1929, when Hadden died of a streptococcus infection at age 31. Luce continued to rule until his death in 1967.

Time's punchy prose style changed the voice of American journalism. Writers of "Timestyle" strung out adjectives (Huey Long was "button-nosed, pugnacious, curly-headed, loose-jawed, incredible"); coined new words (G. K. Chesterton was a *paradoxhund*, the U.S. drugstore *omnivendorous*); and helped themselves to other languages (*kudos* from Greek, *tycoon* from Japanese). Word order was jumbled to catch the reader's eye: "Into family chapels went he, robbery of the dead intent upon." (In 1936 the *New Yorker* magazine published a profile of Luce written in Timestyle by Wolcott Gibbs, including sentences like "Backward ran sentences until reeled the mind," and "Where it all will end, knows God!")

Luce started *Fortune*, a lavishly designed business magazine, in 1930. The next year *Time* initiated a radio drama, "The March of Time," to dramatize the news in that week's issue. In 1935 the program was adapted to film for movie theaters, featuring newsreel footage and dramatic reenactments of events. In 1936 Luce bought *Life*, a venerable but failing humor magazine, and invented mass-circulation photojournalism.

Time entered the forest products business in 1939, when they helped Champion Paper build a paper mill in Houston. In the early 1950s Time and the Houston Oil Co. started the East Texas Pulp and Paper Company, later called Eastex. In 1954 they launched *Sports Illustrated*. Time-Life Books began in the early 1960s, at first repackaging material from *Life* magazine. They expanded their computerized Chicago subscription center to create Selling Areas-Marketing in 1966, and in 1968 they bought Little, Brown. Activity reached a fever pitch in the early 1970s, as they moved into cable TV; started *Money*, a magazine of personal finance; folded the weekly *Life*; bought Temple Industries; started *People* in 1974; and bought the Book-of-the-Month Club in 1977. They picked up the *Washington Star* and Inland Container in 1978, and the same year they transformed *Fortune* from a monthly to a biweekly and revived *Life* as a monthly.

Reputation. They are much more than a magazine company today, but that's still the image which lingers. *Time* reaches five times as many people as the *New York Times*. And Time has always been a good place to work; they pay well, and benefits are super.

What they own. Their New York headquarters building (jointly owned with Rockefeller Center, Inc.) and several other offices scattered around the country and overseas. 1.1 million acres of timberland and three forest products plants in southeast Texas; 24 corrugated box plants in the United States and Puerto Rico.

Who owns and runs the company. Arthur Temple, grandson of Temple Industries' founder, became vice-chairman of Time in 1978. His cousin, Robert T. Keeler, also sits on the board. Henry R. Luce's son, Henry Luce, III, is a director. The all-white board includes such corporate titans as the chairmen of Borg-Warner and IBM and the president of Xerox. There are also two women directors, Matina S. Horner, president of Radcliffe College, and Joan D. Manley, who started in publishing as a secretary at Doubleday and became head of Time-Life Books. The Henry Luce Foundation owns 6.7% of the stock. Time chairman Andrew Heiskell and president James R. Shepley, who joined the company in 1937 and 1942, respectively, retired in 1980. They were replaced by a three-man team headed by president and chief executive J. Richard Munro, who served as publisher of *Sports Illustrated* and later turned Time's video operations from a $2.8 million loser in 1975 to a $68 million profit-maker in 1979.

The 1980 management change was significant in that the new leaders—Munro, Ralph P. Davidson, and Clifford J. Green—all came up from the business side. Heiskell started out as science editor of *Life*. Shepley was Washington bureau chief for *Time*.

In the public eye. *Time* has long been criticized for having a conservative bias. John Meyers, publisher of *Time*, admitted in 1980 that "we're pro-business, very pro-business." And David Shaw of the *Los Angeles Times* noted that Marshall Loeb, former economics editor of *Time* before moving over to become managing editor of *Money*, used to profile business leaders in such a flattering way that in-house critics used to dub his column "The Lives of Our Saints." That in-house critique is also part of the tradition of Time Inc. Many have left "to tell all."

Where they're going. Heavily into video. Time is "the leading force in the growing new fields of video," the *New York Times*

reported in 1980. All their video operations are growing rapidly. At the end of 1979 Wall Street financial analysts were predicting that Time would rake in more profits in 1980 from video than from either magazines or books. Time is now perfectly situated to capitalize on the emerging field of "electronic publishing."

Major employment centers. New York City; Chicago; Diboll, Texas.

Access. Time & Life Building, Rockefeller Center, New York, New York 10020; (212) 586-1212.

Consumer brands.

Magazines: Time; Life; Fortune; Sports Illustrated; Money; People.
Books: Time-Life; Little, Brown; Book-of-the-Month Club.
Records, films, video cassettes, filmstrips: Time-Life.
Art reproductions: New York Graphic Society; Alva Replicas.
Video: Home Box Office; American Television and Communications.
Newspapers: Washington Star; Pioneer Press (18 suburban Chicago weeklies).
Lumber: Temple.

TIMES MIRROR

Sales: $1.6 billion
Profits: $146.5 million
Rank in daily newspaper circulation: 3
Rank in cable television: 6
Founded: 1881
Employees: 24,256
Headquarters: Los Angeles, California

What they do. "The Chandlers invented Los Angeles," wrote David Halberstam in his 1979 study of the media, *The Powers That Be.* Since the 1880s the Chandler name has been synonymous with the *Los Angeles Times* —one of the worst newspapers in the country, as Halberstam notes, until Otis Chandler took over in 1960 and in a single generation turned it into one of the best.

Otis not only transformed the *Times* but built Times Mirror into the nation's biggest, most sophisticated newspaper-based publishing empire. Starting at the top, there's the *Los Angeles Times*, the third-biggest U.S. daily, with a circulation of more than 1 million, an editorial staff of 600 (including 200 reporters), and foreign correspondents in 20 countries. Then they own six other newspapers, including Long Island's *Newsday* (with over 500,000 circulation), the *Hartford Courant*, and the *Dallas Times-Herald*. Newspapers bring in just under half of Times Mirror's money. They've got a gaggle of book publishers, ranging from mass-market paperbacks (New American Library) to lavish art books (Abrams). Books bring in 15% of revenues. Then magazines: *Popular Science, Outdoor Life, Golf, Ski,* and the weekly bible of the baseball addict, *Sporting News*.

That's a lot of paper, right? So it helps that Times Mirror owns a quarter of a million acres of trees in Oregon and Washington and mills producing all kinds of forest products—above all, newsprint. Paper and wood products provide about 20% of their revenues.

The electronic media haven't been left out: two Texas television stations and cable TV systems in 13 states.

Times Mirror's list of miscellaneous enterprises makes interesting reading too: medical books, law books, syndicated features, telephone directories, road maps, flight manuals, graph paper, filmstrips, slide rules.

Now back to the *Los Angeles Times* for a few footnotes. It has the largest volume of advertising of any daily in the country, and it was the first major paper to eliminate linotype machines in favor of computerized typesetting—a change initiated in the late 1960s. (Meanwhile the *New York Times* management was being smashed in negotiations with the typographers union, which successfully resisted automation until the mid-1970s. The LA paper, on the other hand, has not been unionized.) Thanks to their early conversion to automation, they make more money than any other paper.

This supermodern operation, with its coast-to-coast network of subsidiaries, belongs to a company that 20 years ago owned virtually nothing but the *Los Angeles Times*, a newspaper reputed to be so reactionary and parochial that its editors were loath to concede the world was round.

History. General Harrison Gray Otis was a Civil War hero from Ohio who joined the fledgling *Los Angeles Times* in 1881, bought a piece of it the next year, and picked up the rest in 1886. Meanwhile Harry Chandler, a sickly young man from New Hampshire who had come to Southern California for his health, had gotten hold of the city's newspaper circulation routes. Chandler helped Otis wipe out the rival *Tribune* by getting his newsboys to "forget" to deliver it, then cemented the partnership by marrying the General's daughter.

From the start, the *Times* knew its enemies. In one of the General's purple passages, they were "the apostles of disorder, the missionaries of unrest, the jawsmiths of closed-shop unionism, the haters of honest industry, the acquisitionists of other people's property, the brawlers, the larcenists, the dynamiters, the I.W.W.'s, and the friends of raising the devil. . . ." When, during a strike in 1910, the *Times* building was bombed and 20 people were killed, the General became more virulently antiunion than ever. The paper attacked the 40-hour week, saying workers would use their spare time in "the only diversions they know—pool, poker, drinking and petty agitation."

Between 1881 and 1886 LA's population grew from 5,000 to 100,000, and the Otis-Chandler family amassed a fortune in real estate as the city swelled. They weren't just spokesmen for the big money community; they were leaders of it. Otis was an officer or director of 35 California corporations. And the *Times*, says Halberstam, was "the instrument and weapon of a vast and expanding economic order. Its job was to tame, intimidate and silence political enemies of that order and to allow the order to grow as quickly, with as little interference and debate as possible. Its job was not so much printing information as withholding it."

General Otis's son-in-law, Harry, a man after his own heart, took over the paper in 1917. By the 1930s he owned 2 million acres of land in Southern California and had big interests in shipping, road construction, oil, Goodyear Tire, and much more. The *Times* virtually owned the Republican Party (and thus City Hall) and the police chief, and Harry used his power to push programs that advanced his economic interests (harbors, freeways, the squelching of mass transit). In the 1930s *Time* magazine—hardly a left-leaning journal—branded the *LA Times* as "the most rabid labor-baiting, Red-hating paper in the United States."

Typical of the paper's tactics was their coverage of the election in 1934, when muckraking writer Upton Sinclair ran for governor of California on a radical platform. The news pages ran photos of hobos coming in boxcar loads to support Sinclair —but the photos were fakes, made with extras in a Hollywood studio. When a young *New York Times* reporter covering the election asked the *LA Times*'s chief political writer where Sinclair was speaking, he was told: "Forget it. We don't go in for that kind of crap that you have back in New York of being obliged to print both sides. We're going to beat this son-of-a-bitch Sinclair any way we can. We're going to kill him." And Sinclair was beaten in one of the dirtiest election campaigns in California's history.

Over the years a number of promising young conservative politicians were the paper's proteges. Halberstam says the *Times* "created Richard Nixon" and imbued him with "a sense that he could get away with things, that the press was crooked and could be bought off."

Harry's son, Norman Chandler, became chairman in 1941. Norman's wife Buffie upgraded the family image by devoting her prodigious energies to support of the arts. She was the main force behind the $34 million Los Angeles Music Center and was an influential member of the board of directors at Times Mirror.

Norman and Buffie's son Otis, who became publisher in 1960 at age 32, is (as *New West* puts it) "a Chandler of a different stripe." He occasionally votes Democratic. He hired some of the best journalists in the country, including liberal easterners, and gave them freedom to write as they wished. Asked where his more liberal views came from, he says that his Andover roommate was the black son of a janitor and that he rubbed shoulders with many black athletes as a champion shotputter at Stanford and a captain of the air force track team. An avid surfer and big-game hunter, Chandler's latest avocation is race car driving. In his first professional race in 1978 he and his partner drove a Porsche and got a $5,000 prize.

The *Times* has won 7 of its 10 Pulitzer Prizes under Otis Chandler's stewardship, and the company has generally improved other papers they've bought. *Time* magazine, which had dismissed the *Dallas Times-Herald* as "just another tired evening paper," said it had become one of the best

newspapers in the South since its 1970 takeover by Times Mirror. But there have been some flops too. In 1963 they bought World Publishing, the nation's biggest publisher of bibles and second largest publisher of dictionaries. Ten years later World was washed up, run out of business by Times Mirror's interference. The *Mirror* part of the company name recalls another failure: an afternoon paper they started in 1948 and gave up 14 years later.

Reputation. In Halberstam's words, "a modern, civilized, highly sophisticated, computerized empire." The *Times* has been called "the world's most financially successful newspaper."

Who owns and runs the company. Otis Chandler took up big-game hunting about the same time he took over the *LA Times*. His trophy room has over 100 heads, plus a few complete animals (they wash and blow-dry the lion on the front lawn once a year).

Chandler's and *Times* bosses of an earlier era were more interested in shooting down political opponents. A former colleague said of Otis in 1968: "His chief characteristic is . . . like a killer instinct. He means to become the best, by God, newspaper publisher in the world, and he is well on the way." Big game of journalism, watch out!

In 1977 boy wonder Tom Johnson—reporter at 14, White House fellow at 23, assistant presidential press secretary at 24, confidant to President Lyndon Johnson at 27, editor at 31, publisher at 33—took over the newly created post of president of the *Los Angeles Times*. He was 35. Three years later he became publisher, the first non-family member to get the job, which had been held by Otis Chandler for nearly 20 years. Chandler will replace the retiring chairman of Times Mirror in January 1981. His son Norman is in training to inherit the kingdom. He became editor-in-chief in 1980.

In the public eye. *Thinking Big*, a 600-page history of the *LA Times* by Robert Gottlieb and Irene Wolt, suggested that the Watts riots in the 1960s came as a shock to the people of Los Angeles because the *Times* hadn't reported on the existence of Watts. In the last census blacks, Chicanos, and Asian-Americans made up nearly 23% of Los Angeles County's population, and they were expected to be in the majority by 1980.

But *Times* coverage of minority communities is spotty, and their efforts to deliver papers in poorer sections of LA are faint-hearted. Marketing specialists, speaking of demographic profiles, point out that most poor people don't buy newspapers, and those who do don't buy advertisers' products. Otis Chandler has said it doesn't make financial sense to direct the paper to low-income readers.

Where they're going. Into broadcasting. In 1979 they completed a deal with Newhouse Broadcasting to buy five television stations in Syracuse and Elmira, New York; Harrisburg, Pennsylvania; Birmingham, Alabama; and St. Louis, Missouri.

Stock performance. Times Mirror stock bought for $1,000 in 1970 sold for $1,814 on January 2, 1980.

Access. Los Angeles, California 90053; (213) 972-3700.

Consumer brands.

Newspapers: Los Angeles Times; Dallas Times Herald; Greenwich Time; The Hartford Courant (Connecticut); *Newsday* (Long Island, New York); *The Advocate* (Stamford, Connecticut); *Orange Coast Daily Pilot.*
Television stations: KDFW (Dallas); KTBC (Austin, Texas); WSYR (Syracuse, New York); WSYE (Elmira, New York); WTPA (Harrisburg, Pennsylvania); WAPI (Birmingham, Alabama); KTVI (St. Louis, Missouri).
General books: The New American Library; New English Library; Abrams; Southwestern; Signet; Mentor; Meridian.
Professional books: Matthew Bender; Mosby; Year Book Medical Publishers.
Magazines: Sporting News; Outdoor Life; Popular Science; Golf; Ski; Homeowners How To; Ski Business; Sporting Goods Dealer.
Telephone directories: Times Mirror Press.

 Triangle Publications

Sales: $650 million (estimated)
Rank in magazine circulation: 1
Founded: 1933
Employees: 2,300
Headquarters: Radnor, Pennsylvania

What they do. It may strike some people as entirely fitting that the most popular reading matter in America is a television program magazine. It may strike others as fitting that this magazine comes from a company whose first publication was the *Daily Racing Form.* In any case, it's a fact that one out of every five magazines sold in the United States is an issue of *TV Guide.* People spend more on that pocket-size schedule than on any other magazine in the world. Each week 20 million copies are sold —two-thirds of them to individuals who

50 Million Pennies From Heaven

It began [in 1956–57] with the need to put more bite into an aging Digest promotion letter which began, 'An ancient Persian poet once said, "If thou hast two pennies, spend one for bread and the other to buy hyacinths for the soul. . . ."' Somebody got the idea of sending out two pennies with each letter, inviting the reader to return one against his subscription to the soul-satisfying Reader's Digest. This involved sucking out of the market 100 million pennies in return for 1 million Digest dollars. The Mint got into the act when it appeared that the Digest was stripping the whole New York area of pennies, and magazine executives had to make hasty arrangements to have 60 million pennies shipped into New York from other spots around the country. Meanwhile, the floor in the warehouse where the Digest pennies were stored collapsed under the weight. Nevertheless, the letter went out, pennies and all, and brought a return worth the effort and money.

Reprinted from Samuel A. Schreiner, Jr., *The Condensed World of the Reader's Digest* (Stein & Day, 1977).

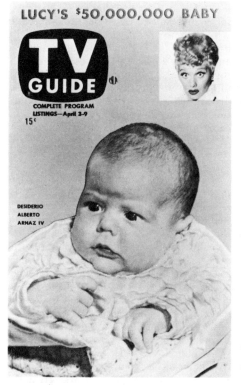

The first issue of *TV Guide:* April 3, 1953.

Walter H. Annenberg, founder of *TV Guide,* former Ambassador to the Court of St. James, friend of Richard M. Nixon.

plunk down 40¢ each to get the same listings that are available in every daily paper in the land as well as in scads of handouts from supermarkets and pharmacies. Subscriptions, at $20 a year, account for the other third of *TV Guide*'s circulation. In a year they sell more than 1 billion copies—three times the worldwide circulation of the runner-up magazine, the monthly *Reader's Digest.* Around the company headquarters on Philadelphia's Main Line there's a joke: "Each week we lose more copies of *TV Guide* off the backs of our trucks than most other magazines sell."

The owner of this gold mine is Walter H. Annenberg, who came up with the idea for *TV Guide.* His corporate vehicle is Triangle Publications, owned by him and his family. Triangle also publishes *Seventeen,* a monthly magazine that sells 1.4 million copies full of advice on fashion, beauty and love, aimed at teenage girls (it's sometimes called "The Acne and the Ecstasy"). Still in the house is the *Daily Racing Form,* bible of the serious horse bettor. In 1980 Triangle launched a more high-brow television magazine, *Panorama.*

But *TV Guide* is Triangle's pride. It's actually two publications in one. There's the slick-paper national edition, a "wraparound" with color pictures and articles about national TV; and there are the local listings, inserted in the middle. More than 300 workers at offices in 28 cities assemble the information for 101 different local editions, feeding it all to a computer complex at the Radnor, Pennsylvania, headquarters. The computer combines the local listings with national network shows and lays out the listings and ads for 9,000 different pages that make up the various local editions. They also have a computerized file of summaries of some 21,000 movies and 150,000 syndicated TV shows. For a station showing reruns of "I Love Lucy," the computer will issue something like, "Lucy tries out some ill-acquired Spanish when Ricky's mother comes to visit." *TV Guide* prints the local sections at 18 plants around the country and then binds them into the national edition, which is printed at three plants in Tennessee, Texas, and California. The magazine brings the company $550 million a year—$200 million of it from advertising.

A full color page in *TV Guide* costs an advertiser $60,000.

History. Moses Annenberg, a Jewish immigrant from Germany, got a job when he was 15, around the turn of the century, with William Randolph Hearst's *Chicago Examiner*. He worked his way up to circulation manager and held a command post during the bloody newspaper circulation wars that marked the beginning of the Al Capone era in Chicago. In the 1920s Annenberg and two other Hearst employees bought the *Daily Racing Form;* in 1933 he bought out his partners and started investing in other publications, including newspapers in Philadelphia and Miami. But his fortune came from a wire service that connected racetracks with bookies—a nationwide operation so vast that he was AT&T's fifth-largest customer. His annual income, one of the highest in the nation, was estimated at $1 million. In 1939 Annenberg was sent to prison for income tax evasion. His only son, Walter, was indicted in the same case, but those charges were later dropped. Walter gained control of Triangle after his father's death in 1942.

Walter Annenberg was running the family's *Philadelphia Inquirer* when he got the idea for *TV Guide* in 1952. He bought up several little television magazines that had sprung up locally—including *TV Digest* in Philadelphia, *TV Forecast* in Chicago, and *TV Guide* in New York—and started the unique format of local listings inside a national edition. Merrill Panitt, who had been the television columnist for the *Philadelphia Inquirer,* was installed as the first managing editor when *TV Guide* made its debut on April 3, 1953. The initial circulation was 1.5 million, but it soon began to go down. By August it had dropped to 1.3 million. They couldn't figure out why until someone looked out and saw people enjoying the summer sunshine. When fall came, sales climbed—and then kept on climbing until *TV Guide* took over the entire field. In 1974 it became the first magazine ever to sell more than 1 billion copies in a year.

Annenberg was a major fundraiser for Richard Nixon, and in 1969 he was rewarded with appointment as U.S. Ambassador to Great Britain. It was a selection greeted with much hooting on both sides of the Atlantic. *Time* said: "In London, where verbal agility is an almost indispensable social grace, Annenberg's bloopers stand out like Mao badges in Moscow." A British magazine called his style "folk-baroque, with the native *bonhomie* and verbal felicity of W. C. Fields." But Annenberg held the ambassador's post for five years, refurbishing the embassy at a personal cost of $1 million. It was during this time that he also dismantled a large part of his communications empire. He sold the *Philadelphia Inquirer* and *Daily News* (an afternoon tabloid in Philadelphia), plus 19 radio and TV stations. In 1972 he shut down the *Morning Telegraph*, another racing sheet.

But the name on top of the *TV Guide* masthead is still Walter H. Annenberg.

Reputation. To some it may seem ironic that the nation's best-selling weekly magazine is devoted to the most antiliterate force in society. But *TV Guide* has gained respect for its journalistic competence, and it's not adverse to biting the hand that feeds it. The *Wall Street Journal* reported in 1978 that the magazine's profile of actor Jack Lord was so unflattering that *TV Guide* reporters were banned from the set where "Hawaii Five-O" is filmed. Neil Hickey, *TV Guide*'s bureau chief in New York, said in a 1978 article that the television networks treat the public "as an immense herd of dimwitted sheep to be delivered to the highest bidder."

What they own. A new five-story *TV Guide* headquarters in Radnor, plus the regional offices; a *Seventeen* office in New York; a *Racing Form* office in Hightstown, New Jersey.

Who owns and runs the company. Walter Annenberg probably owns about half of Triangle, and his seven sisters share the other half. Exact figures are hard to come by since Triangle doesn't sell stock to the public and publishes no financial information.

In the public eye. As a newspaper publisher, Walter Annenberg was known for conducting smear campaigns against public figures and holding grudges against people. For a while the name of Dinah Shore was even blacklisted from the pages of *TV Guide*. The *Philadelphia Inquirer* waged a fierce campaign for the merger of the New York Central and Pennsylvania Railroads, attacking gubernatorial candidate Milton Shapp, who opposed the merger, at a time when Annenberg was the largest single stockholder in Pennsylvania.

Annenberg also contributed huge sums to charities. He was one of the founders of the Albert Einstein College of Medicine in New York, and his bequests made possible the Annenberg School of Communications at the University of Pennsylvania. But in 1970, reflecting on Annenberg's career as a publisher, Edward W. Barrett, former dean of the graduate school of journalism at Columbia University, said the sale of the *Philadelphia Inquirer* to the Knight newspaper chain "may well prove to be Walter Annenberg's greatest service to Philadelphia and to journalism."

Where they're going. Annenberg spends much of his time these days on his 1,000-acre estate, Sunnylands, at Palm Springs, California, where Richard Nixon is always a welcome guest. Annenberg's only son committed suicide in 1962—and he now has no immediate heir. The betting is that he will eventually sell *TV Guide.* Annenberg was 71 years old at the start of 1980.

Access. Radnor, Pennsylvania 19088; (215) 293-8942.

Consumer brands.

Publications: TV Guide; Seventeen; Panorama; Daily Racing Form.

The Washington Post

Sales: $593 million
Profits: $29 million
Rank in daily newspaper circulation: 10
Rank in newsweeklies: 2
Founded: 1877
Employees: 5,200
Headquarters: Washington, D.C.

What they do. Eugene Meyer was already a rich man who had built enough nationally influential careers for several lifetimes when he rescued the moribund *Washington Post* from the auction block in 1933. He bought it anonymously for $825,000. His purpose was not to make a financial killing.

Meyer bought *The Washington Post* because he saw an opportunity to build something good with it, a characteristic attitude that was always linked with Meyer's Midas touch. Meyer believed that "the newspaper's duty is to its readers and public at large, not to the private interests of its owner." He wasn't interested in merely subsidizing the *Post.* Its transformation was his crowning achievement.

In the two decades under his leadership the *Post* not only quadrupled its circulation but attracted the editorial talent that made it one of the country's great newspapers. The *Post,* now the nation's fifth-largest daily by circulation (602,000 daily; 828,000 Sunday), is the paper that broke the Watergate story—a scoop that may have added more to its prestige than the 16 Pulitzer Prizes it has won.

Now in the hands of Meyer's daughter, Katharine Meyer Graham, *The Washington Post* dominion includes the nation's second-largest weekly news magazine, *Newsweek,* which has its own book division, and sports magazine, *Inside Sports.* The Post Company also owns two other newspapers, four television stations, a syndicated writers' group, and a news service jointly operated with the *Los Angeles Times* that has 350 client newspapers here and abroad on six continents.

Getting the three editions of the *Post* out each morning involves 400 reporters, editors, artists, and researchers; 1,300 press operators; and 600 circulation, advertising, and business employees. At least 25 tons of metal are used in the printing plates for the average daily press run of more than 600,-000 copies. The *Post* goes through 3,000 tons of newsprint a week, enough each year to reach around the world 27 times, at a cost of over $300 a ton. Half of the *Post*'s paper is supplied by affiliate paper mills in Nova Scotia, Canada, and Richmond, Virginia, that they hold interests in. Five million pounds of black ink, at a cost of 15¢ a pound, are used to print the *Post* each year. The average cost of paper and ink in one daily *Post* is 18¢, and the newspaper sells for 20¢, which is why over three-quarters of the *Post*'s revenue comes from advertising. The *Post* controls almost three-quarters of all Washington print ads.

The *Post* is distributed mainly by direct home delivery, within the city and to large parts of Virginia and Maryland, landing on the doorsteps of government worker, ghetto dweller, and Congress member alike. It is frequently thought of in tandem with the *New York Times;* the fact that it has four pages of funnies, while the *Times* has none, points to a big difference in the readership of the two prestigious family-owned daily newspapers. In circulation the Post ranks after the *New York Daily News,* the *New York Times,* and the *Los Angeles Times,* although the Washington area is only one-eighth the size of New York City and Los Angeles.

Like the New York Times Company and Times Mirror of Los Angeles, the Washington Post Company sold stocks to the public and grew into a communications corporation to secure the survival of the flagship newspaper. The company's other well-known publication, *Newsweek* magazine, has a circulation of close to 3 million and ad revenues of $170 million. *Newsweek's* book division publishes subscription series books, *Great Museums of the World* and *Wonder of Man,* as well as condensed books.

The Washington Post Writer's Group syndicates columnists David Broder and Ellen Goodman, cartoonist Herbert Block (Herblock), and others. The *Trenton* (New Jersey) *Times* and the *Everett* (Washington) *Herald* are Post Company papers. The company publishes the International *Herald Tribune* in partnership with the *New York Times* and IHT Corporation.

Broadcasting represents 12% of the company's income, magazines and books 42%, and *The Washington Post* 41%. Almost half the company's employees work at the *Post.*

History. When Stillson Hutchins, a staunch Democrat and former politician, started the penny paper called *The Washington Post* in 1877, Pennsylvania Avenue had a wooden sidewalk and the downtown Federal Triangle was a redlight district known as "Hooker's Division" (in honor of General Hooker, who had herded some 4,000 prostitutes into one area of town).

By 1888 the *Post* was famous enough to inspire John Philip Sousa to compose the "Washington Post March." A year later Hutchins retired, selling the paper to Frank Hatton and Beriah Wilkins, who gave the paper a conservative bent. They sold the *Post* to John Roll McLean, publisher of the *Cincinnati Enquirer,* who used the *Post* as a "pedestal of power." McLean was influenced by the yellow journalism of his friend William Randolph Hearst, and the *Post* became a sensationalist paper.

Edward McLean, who inherited the paper from his father in 1916, was known as the "playboy publisher." Perhaps he bore the curse of the Hope Diamond, which his wife Evalyn owned; in any case, he became a drunken wastrel who roamed the world with Rose Davies (sister of actress Marion Davies, Hearst's mistress) and died in a hospital for alcoholics. The *Post* lost all credibility because of Edward's involvement in the Teapot Dome scandal of Warren G. Harding's administration. The newspaper was auctioned off in 1933.

The *Post's* new owner, Eugene Meyer, was the son of an intellectual Jewish family. His French-born father came to the United States in 1859 at 17 with a letter of introduction from the famous French merchant bankers, Lazard Frères. His mother was a rabbi's daughter; his uncle was the Grand Rabbi of France. Eugene bought a seat on the New York Stock Exchange in 1901 at the age of 26, when he was not too long out of Yale. In 1915 he was worth more than $50 million. By the time he bought *The Washington Post* in 1933, he had won and lost and again won fortunes in the copper industry, worked closely with Bernard Baruch in wartime policymaking, organized Allied Chemical, played a role in the early development of General Motors, and served as governor of the Federal Reserve Board and ex-officio board member of the Reconstruction Finance Corporation. He was later to become the first president of the World Bank.

To say he had a way with money would be an understatement. "Watch out for this fellow Meyer," warned J. P. Morgan, "because if you don't he'll end up having all the money on Wall Street."

One story has it that on an emergency trip to San Francisco, where he was going to see if his sisters had survived the 1906 earthquake, Meyer had to wait in Chicago for the afternoon train. With $30,000 in his money belt and a little time to kill, he strolled into a broker's office, where a stock quotation caught his fancy. By the time he boarded the westbound train, he had bought the stock and sold it for a profit of $2,500, which he took in cash.

Although the Meyers lived amid the luxuries that people of education, taste, and wealth can enjoy, Eugene had a sincere interest in public service as well as private pleasures. Meyer was reputed to have learned to play craps with the boys in the newsroom of *The Washington Post.* Most importantly, he cleaned up the *Post's* style and politics and stressed balanced reporting. His biographer and longtime associate at *The Post*, Merlo J. Pusey, wrote that the credo by which Meyer lived his life was, "Know everything about your task, work harder than anyone else and be absolutely honest."

In 1946, when he became president of the World Bank, Meyer handed the *Post* over to his daughter, Katharine, and her husband, Philip Graham, a lawyer who became publisher of the paper. Graham made the *Post* a huge newspaper during his 15 years in charge. He bought the rival *Times Herald* from *Chicago Tribune* owner Col. Robert McCormick in 1954 and merged it with the *Post.* He bought two radio stations, opened bureaus in Paris and London, and set up a news service with the *Los Angeles Times.* His greatest coup was the 1961 acquisition of *Newsweek*, which he snatched from under the noses of the magazine's longtime editor, the Doubleday Publishing Company, and newspaper czar S. I. Newhouse, all of whom wanted it. The Vincent Astor Foundation, which owned the magazine, gave the Post Company the nod after *Newsweek's* managing editor and president confided to the Astor representative, a Mr. Betts, that they had fallen in love with Phil Graham. Betts, using more dignified language, indicated that he felt the same way.

Phil Graham championed integration, attacked Senator Joseph McCarthy, and was a great friend of John Kennedy. In 1963 he shot himself in the head after recurrent manic-depressive episodes and hospitalizations.

The services at the National Cathedral were attended by President Kennedy, members of the Cabinet, Supreme Court, and Congress, friends from the city government and the press. The next day Senator George Smathers, who had roomed with Phil Graham in college, said: "If Phil Graham had any fault or weakness, I think it would be that of being too greatly concerned about the problems of other people, and of all humanity, and he resented and brooded over the fact that he could do nothing about many of them."

Graham's wife Katharine became publisher of the *Post*, a job for which she may have been better prepared than her father or husband (since they had started out at the top): Katharine had been a $21-a-week reporter for the *San Francisco News* before joining the *Post* as a reporter in 1939. Katharine was no mover or shaker herself, but she knew who was. She hired Benjamin Bradlee, the former Washington bureau chief of *Newsweek*, as editor, and Bradlee turned the *Post* into the lively, down-to-earth paper it is today. He introduced a weekend section, as well as three weekly zoned editions specifically for Virginia, Maryland, and the District.

As publisher, Katharine Graham "accepts her responsibility rather than asserts her authority," as writer Martin Mayer says. At meetings she sits in the back, only occasionally asking a question. She keeps her opinions to herself. Ben Bradlee revealed in 1968 that he didn't know Katharine's views on Vietnam. She claims that the "first tenet of this business is that you stick up for your editors."

Reputation. When 2,500 journalists apply for 18 positions, as happened at the *Post* in 1976, you know you have a newspaper that is both popular and respected. The Watergate stories helped put the *Post* on the world map, although it was already a prestigious, prize-winning paper.

What they own. Two buildings (of seven and nine stories) in Washington, 13 acres in Virginia (being developed as a printing plant), 10 acres in Maryland, plants and offices for the *Trenton Times* in New Jersey, and the *Everett Herald* in Washington state. The Post owns interests in warehouses in Virginia, plus Bowater Mersey Paper of Nova Scotia and Bear Island Paper of Virginia. Their four television stations are WDIV Detroit; WJXT Jacksonville, Florida; WPLG Miami (named for Philip Graham); and WFSB Hartford, Connecticut.

Who owns and runs the company. "You know, publishers' sons are famous dopes," joked Katharine Meyer Graham when she made her own son Donald publisher of the *Post* in 1979. Donald is the fourth member of the Meyer-Graham family to run the *Post* since his grandfather bought it. Katharine Graham is chairman and controls half of the stock. She has been a director since 1957. Donald, a 33-year-old Harvard graduate, Vietnam veteran, and former D.C. policeman, owns 13.3% of the voting interests of the company; his siblings, William, Stephen, and Elizabeth Weymouth, own another 20%. The directors, including Katharine's brother, Dr. Eugene Meyer, III, own half of the class B stock. Class A stockholders, primarily the Grahams, elect eight directors, whereas Class B stockholders elect only four.

Donald Graham says he has no plans to change the *Post*, but as editor Ben Bradlee points out, "Donnie can do anything he wants. He's got the A stock."

In the public eye. The strike by *Washington Post* press operators in 1975 received lots of publicity because the strikers began on October 1 by trashing the pressroom—an act that symbolized resistance to mechanization—and by beating up a foreman. Newspaper Guild members (editors and reporters) crossed picket lines and kept the paper going, so the *Post* missed only one day of publication during the four-month strike. The previous year Newspaper Guild members had staged an abortive strike, not over wages (*Post* editorial wages are the highest of any Guild paper in the country, averaging $29,000 a year), but over humiliating treatment.

Washington's population is 85% black. Although the *Post* donated their D.C. radio station, WTOP-FM, to predominantly black Howard University in 1971, and although the paper had more black employees and more coverage of black community events than other big-city papers, the Equal Employment Opportunity Commission backed up a charge of racial discrimination made by black reporters in 1972.

Also in 1974 the commission charged the *Post* with discrimination against women. Two years later 20% of the newsroom was female.

Where they're going. The company is concentrating on the *Post* now that the paper has a new publisher and Bradlee is nearing retirement age. The *Post* is worried about the acquisition of the *Washington Star* by *Time* in 1978, which is promising to sink $60 million in the *Star* to compete with the *Post*. Bradlee calls the new *Star* the "biggest challenge since Nixon."

Access. 1150 15th Street, N.W., Washington, D.C. 20071; (202) 334-6000.

Consumer brands.

Newspapers: The Washington Post; Times (Trenton, New Jersey); *Herald* (Everett, Washington).
Magazines: Newsweek; Inside Sports.
Book publishing: Newsweek Books.
Television broadcasting: WDIV (Detroit); WJXT (Jacksonville, Florida); WPLG (Miami, Florida); WFSB (Hartford, Connecticut).

> **Lurid murder stories, colorful headlines, and plenty of comics characterize yellow journalism. The term itself originated with a popular yellow-inked comic strip, "The Yellow Kid," which appeared first in Joseph Pulitzer's *World* newspaper, and then in William Randolph Hearst's *Journal*, both leading New York practitioners of sensationalist reporting.**

7

.GHT CATCHERS

Sales: $8 billion
Profits: $1 billion
Forbes 500 rank: 40
Rank in cameras: 1
Rank in film: 1
Rank in film processing: 1
Founded: 1880
Employees: 124,800
Headquarters: Rochester, New York

What they do. Kodak makes cameras that everyone can afford. Their strategy is to get those cameras into the hands of everybody who can hold one; they then make their money off the film and processing. Their share of the film market is so overwhelming that no one else even comes close.

Kodak has dominated the photographic market for so long that their name has become almost synonymous with amateur cameras. Hardly a tourist attraction on earth has gone unphotographed by an Instamatic, and it's a rare family reunion in America that doesn't get recorded on Kodak film. The advertising slogan coined by founder George Eastman nearly a century ago is more apt now than ever: "You press the button, we do the rest." Kodak provides everything the average shutterbug needs: simple cameras, easy-to-load cartridge film, and labs to develop and print the pictures (for those who haven't yet switched to "instant" cameras, which Kodak also makes). For the professional photographer they make darkroom chemicals, photographic paper, camera filters, and a wide range of 35-millimeter films. They also make home-movie cameras, film, and projectors. The Kodak name and their distinctive yellow film boxes are known around the world. Nearly 40% of Kodak's sales and one-third of their employees are outside the United States. In 1979 they started selling film in China.

Eastman Kodak also dominates their hometown of Rochester, New York, where 50,000 Kodak employees (in a city of 300,-000) make cameras, film, chemicals, and papers for everything from vacation snapshots to probes of Mars. Kodak is one of the world's largest users of silver, which goes into both film and photo paper: 75-pound bars of silver bullion are dissolved in acid to form crystals, which are then mixed with gelatin made from the bones and hides of cattle and pigs. This concoction goes into the film's emulsion, or light-sensitive layer. The emulsion is coated onto a base of paper or plastic made by Kodak in Texas and Tennessee.

But the consumer photographic market is only part of the picture for Kodak. They make lithographic plates for offset printing of magazines, newspapers, and books. They make a blood-testing machine that photographically analyzes blood samples. They make X-ray film. They compete with Xerox in office copiers, and they make microfilm systems—the equipment to put images on microfilm as well as retrieve them.

These photo-related activities account for about four-fifths of Kodak's sales. The rest comes from Eastman Chemicals, which manufactures the plastic the large Pepsi and 7-Up bottles are made of. They also make "natural" vitamin E and a bread softener for the baking industry. They spin out fibers for acetate dresses and cigarette filters. They make dozens of industrial chemicals and plastics that go into such things as garden hoses, steering wheels, candles, printing ink, and synthetic marble.

History. As a young bank clerk in Rochester, George Eastman decided in the late 1870s to take a Caribbean vacation. A coworker suggested he take pictures of his trip, so Eastman bought a photographic outfit—only to discover he would need a packhorse to carry it all: enormous camera, heavy tripod, light-tight tent, glass plates and tanks, chemicals, and a water jug. Eastman decided to skip the trip and concentrate on photography. He plunged into photographic literature and experimented constantly in his mother's kitchen with techniques to make dry plates, which would eliminate much of the cumbersome equipment needed in wet-plate photography. In 1880, satisfied with his formula, Eastman rented a loft in Rochester and started making dry plates commercially. In 1884 he astounded the photographic world with a new product: film in rolls, with a roll holder adaptable to almost every camera on the market. The company became the Eastman Dry Plate and Film Company.

In 1888 Eastman introduced the Kodak camera, a light, portable device that sold for $25 and came with enough film for 100 pictures. When you finished the roll you sent it, camera and all, to Rochester, with $10. There the film was developed and printed and new film inserted. The name Kodak was Eastman's invention, which he arrived at by trying many combinations of letters starting and ending with "K." He explained: "The letter 'K' had been a favorite with me—it seems a strong, incisive sort of letter."

Eastman Kodak continued to introduce products designed to interest more and more people in photography. In 1900 came the first Brownie camera, which sold for $1 and used 15¢ rolls of film. In 1923 Kodak introduced a home-movie camera, projector, and film.

Kodak's philosophy has always remained the same: get lots of people to take pictures and make it as easy for them as possible. They have never turned their attention to making professional-quality cameras—not because they couldn't, but because they

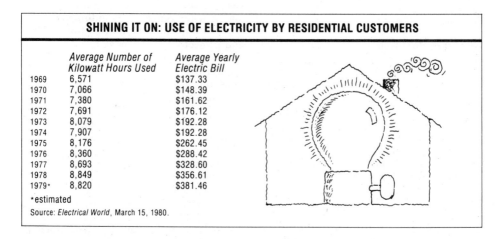

SHINING IT ON: USE OF ELECTRICITY BY RESIDENTIAL CUSTOMERS

	Average Number of Kilowatt Hours Used	Average Yearly Electric Bill
1969	6,571	$137.33
1970	7,066	$148.39
1971	7,380	$161.62
1972	7,691	$176.12
1973	8,079	$192.28
1974	7,907	$192.28
1975	8,176	$262.45
1976	8,360	$288.42
1977	8,693	$328.60
1978	8,849	$356.61
1979*	8,820	$381.46

*estimated

Source: *Electrical World*, March 15, 1980.

don't want to. They are well aware that the money is in the amateur end of the market, especially in film and processing. They're also considered masters at motivating people to take pictures. Theodore Levitt, Harvard Business School professor, put it this way: "Kodak sells film, but they don't advertise film. They advertise memories."

After his company's success was assured, Eastman became a major philanthropist, establishing children's dental clinics and giving millions of dollars to the University of Rochester, MIT, the Tuskegee Institute, and his own employees. In 1932, at the age of 77, after asking his doctor precisely where his heart was located, the ailing Eastman went home and calmly shot himself. His suicide note read: "To my friends. My work is done. Why wait? G. E."

The company continued to issue an endless stream of new products. Kodachrome, the first successful amateur color film, hit the market in 1935. In 1951 they came out with the Brownie hand-held movie camera. Tri-X black and white film, for shooting in dim light, appeared in 1954.

But Kodak's most revolutionary product in modern times appeared in 1963: the Instamatic camera, with film in a foolproof cartridge. Now there was no more agonizing over threading film on a spool or loading the camera in the dark. The camera was

A silver-thatched George Eastman, founder of Kodak, posed for this photograph in 1921 when he was 67 years old. Eleven years later, concluding his work was done, he shot and killed himself.

a huge success for Kodak, making all other amateur cameras obsolete and leading to a tremendous increase in picture taking. By 1976 Kodak had sold an estimated 60 million Instamatics; during the same period, all their worldwide competitors combined sold some 10 million cameras in the United States. In 1965 Kodak did the same thing for home movies, introducing an easy-to-load cartridge and a line of equally simple cameras and projectors. In 1972, when Kodak may have figured that everybody already had an Instamatic, they produced the Pocket Instamatic, a miniature version whose sales took off four times faster than the original Instamatic had done nine years earlier.

But not until 1976 did Kodak finally come out with an "instant" camera—almost 30 years behind Polaroid. When Edwin Land invented the instant camera in the 1940s, Kodak dismissed it as a toy and turned down a chance to market it. So Land's Polaroid Corporation sold it themselves. When Polaroid introduced instant color film in 1963, Kodak supplied the elaborately layered negative, but Polaroid held the patent. Kodak's problem in developing an instant camera of their own was that they had to come up with an original system that didn't breach any of Polaroid's patents. When they finally thought they had done so, Polaroid sued them for patent infringement anyway.

Kodak's biggest legal problem has come not from Polaroid but from several smaller film, camera, and processing companies. Since 1973 these firms—including Berkey Photo, GAF, Argus, and Fotomat—have filed separate antitrust suits, claiming that Kodak's share of the photographic market constitutes an illegal monopoly. One suit asked that Eastman Kodak be broken up into 10 separate companies. Others sought to declare *Kodak* a generic term, so that anybody could make cameras or film and label them Kodak.

An impressive array of lawyers have lined up on both sides of these actions. Cyrus Vance, who became Jimmy Carter's first secretary of state, represented GAF at one point. John Doar, who was special counsel for the House Judiciary Committee's impeachment investigation of President Nixon, was Kodak's chief lawyer in the Berkey case, which came to trial in 1978. (Kodak paid him $300,000 a year to handle the case.) Kodak lost that case and was ordered to pay $87 million in damages, but an appeals court threw out most of the judgment and ordered a new trial on most of the charges.

The Justice Department over the years has made a few rumblings about antitrust action against Kodak. But the last significant government move against them came in 1954, when the company signed a consent decree agreeing to stop selling film with the cost of Kodak processing included, a practice the government considered monopolistic. The agreement did not extend overseas, however, and American tourists in Europe still find that the Kodak film they buy there includes processing—redeemable anywhere in the world.

Reputation. George Eastman was a straitlaced Victorian bachelor who lived with his mother in his Rochester mansion. The company he founded has stayed almost as straitlaced. A lawyer for *Penthouse* magazine called them "the high priests of morality" in 1980 when Kodak refused to return some allegedly lewd photos of Cheryl Rixon, the magazine's Pet of the Year. As late as the 1970s all Kodak executives who wished to keep their secretaries past 5 P.M. were required to call a chaperone, and liquor was strictly banned from expense-account reimbursements. When the presidency devolved for a time in the early 1970s on Gerald Zornow, a colorful character who wore loud shirts and liked to hang out after work in a corner bar, the *Wall Street Journal* was moved to call him, "by Kodak standards, a veritable hippie."

What they own. Close to 200 buildings on 2,000 acres in Rochester. A photographic plant in Colorado; chemical factories in Tennessee, Texas, Arkansas, and South Carolina; a gelatin factory in Massachusetts. Ten processing labs, 8 equipment service centers, and 42 consumer-information centers around the country. Manufacturing plants in eight foreign countries, and numerous offices around the world, from Australia to Zambia.

Who owns and runs the company. Kodak employees, through a savings and investment plan, own slightly less than 2% of the company. On the all-male board 8 of the 14 directors are career Kodak executives, and the only one who started with Kodak later than 1950 is the company's general counsel. Directors from outside the company include the chancellor of the University of Rochester (which owns a sizable chunk of the stock, through donations), the president of Procter & Gamble, and one black lawyer.

Walter Fallon, who became chairman in 1977, started in 1941, worked his way up through the film emulsion operation, and directed the development of the Pocket Instamatic in the early 1970s. Colby Chandler, who replaced Fallon as president, started in 1950 and came to head up Kodak's assaults on Polaroid and Xerox: instant cameras and office copiers.

In the public eye. Kodak has been a focus of civil right actions since 1967, when a group called FIGHT (Freedom, Integration, God, Honor—Today) pressured Kodak to hire and train 600 hard-core unemployed blacks in Rochester. The late Saul Alinsky, a community organizer and professional radical, gained national attention for the FIGHT cause by urging Kodak stockholders to withhold their annual meeting proxies from the company's management. Kodak called in Daniel Patrick Moynihan, a Harvard professor and later senator from New York, as a mediator, and the two sides eventually reached an agreement whereby Kodak would send teams into Rochester's black neighborhoods to interview unemployed for jobs.

Kodak has pulled off the near-miraculous feat of avoiding unionization over their century of existence. They have done it by paying their employees well and showering them with fringe benefits, including hefty annual bonuses (called "wage dividends") averaging as much as $2,000 per employee, long vacations, and an abundance of social activities, like chess and football, movies, ski trips, and belly-dancing classes.

The University of Rochester has been a great beneficiary of Kodak's largesse over the years. Although he quit school at age 14, George Eastman was one of the first American industrialists to realize that the local university could be a training ground for future technicians, and he gave the school a big block of Kodak stock. Rochester is now one of the nation's 10 richest universities, with 490,000 shares of Kodak (worth $25 million in 1980) as well as sizable chunks of Xerox and IBM. In 1979, according to *Forbes*, Kodak employed 1,370 University of Rochester graduates.

Where they're going. Most amateur photographers get tired of their cameras after a few years and stop taking so many pictures, so Kodak has to keep devising new products to stir up fresh interest. The company has already outlined one novel product they may decide to make: a small, flat camera that would hold a film disc with a dozen or so frames.

Stock performance. Eastman Kodak stock bought for $1,000 in 1970 sold for $584 on January 2, 1980.

Major employment centers. Rochester, New York; Kingsport, Tennessee; Windsor, Colorado.

Access. 343 State Street, Rochester, New York 14650; (716) 724-4000. Complaints about Kodak products should be sent to Photo Information, Consumer Markets Division, at the Rochester headquarters. The Rochester plant is open for tours at 9:30 A.M. and 1:45 P.M. every weekday except holidays.

Consumer brands.

Cameras: Instamatic; Ektra 1; Tele-Ektra 1; Ektralite 10; Ektramax; Colorburst; Handle.
Film: Kodachrome; Kodacolor; Ektachrome; Tri-X; Vericolor.
Photographic paper: Ektacolor.
Office copiers: Ektaprint.
Fibers: Kodel.

> **About 94% of all American households have cameras, according to *Financial World*. The average household spends more than $60 a year for photographic equipment and supplies.**

▤ Polaroid

Sales: $1.4 billion
Profits: $36 million
Forbes 500 rank: 361
Rank in instant photography: 1
Rank in camera and film sales: 2
Founded: 1937
Employees: 18,416
Headquarters: Cambridge, Massachusetts

What they do. Polaroid stockholders await their annual meetings the way theatergoers anticipate a Broadway opening night. Reporters, photographers, stockholders, and Wall Street analysts all gather to watch the spectacular show of inventions that founder Edwin Land puts on each year.

The 1980 annual meeting was Land's farewell as chief executive officer (a post he held for 43 years), and it marked the first time any corporate meeting was held in Boston's Symphony Hall. During the session the world-renowned Empire Brass Quintet performed works by Bach, Handel, and Friederich. The *Wall Street Journal* described the meeting as "a setting of orchestrated adulation." A typical Polaroid annual meeting starts off with Land lit by spotlights on a darkened stage where he demonstrates the company's latest technological breakthroughs. The meeting is usually a mixture of show business with regular business. In 1979 the proceedings were interrupted to allow shareholders to wander around the cavernous Polaroid warehouse in Needham, outside Boston, and witness the instant filming of various staged tableaux (at one station a couple was enjoying a real lobster dinner). When one shareholder objected to these demonstrations, pointing out that other companies "don't do this," Land snapped: "That's because they have nothing to show."

Polaroid likes to perform technological miracles, and all but their most recent miracles have paid off handsomely. Ever since 1948, when Edwin Land introduced the public to his first instant camera, Polaroid has been popping up with inventions and then creating enormous demand for them in the marketplace—first for the Polaroid Land camera and more recently for the popular SX-70 instant camera and such esoterica as sonar-focusing devices.

Although Polaroid got their start in 1937 with Land's invention of a process for polarizing light, and they still use the process in sunglasses and a few other products, most of the company's business is done in the field of instant photography. Their SX-70 is the best-selling camera of all time. Polaroid has recently come up with a spin-off—the SX-70 Sonar OneStep, in which an inaudible sound wave emitted from the camera finds the subject and returns to the lens with automatic focusing instructions, all in a matter of a few microseconds. The One-Step self-focusing camera has forged to the lead in the cheap ($30 and under) camera market, outselling its nearest rival, the Kodak Handle, by better than 2 to 1. Other Polaroid cameras include the Pronto Land Camera, the Pronto Sonar OneStep, and the Polaroid Model 600 (for professional use); they range in price from $40 to $525 for the Model 600.

But like Gillette, which makes razors to sell its blades, Polaroid makes cameras to sell their film. Most of the profit (as much as 80% of it) is there, so Polaroid makes 28 different kinds of instant films, plus a wide variety of specialty films for medical diagnostic X rays, microscopes, and oscilloscopes.

History. While an 18-year-old undergraduate at Harvard in 1928, Edwin Land experimented with light waves and discovered a method for polarizing light—essentially, eliminating rays in a light beam unless they were traveling on a single plane, thus reducing glare. His process involves polarized light using polyvinyl alcohol sheets.

Thinking of obvious applications in the auto industry, Land dropped out of school to pursue his experiments.

It took Land nine years to perfect his process. In 1937 he founded Polaroid—but Detroit turned down the Land process for sun visors and headlights when they found that polarized sheets deteriorated in heat. Polaroid began making sunglasses instead, boomed during World War II with the manufacture of goggles, glasses, and filters, and then sagged after the war. The company lost $2 million in 1947 and desperately needed a new product to sell. Land was ready with the idea.

During a vacation in Santa Fe, New Mexico, in 1943, Land snapped a picture of his three-year-old daughter. When she asked how long it would take before she could see the finished product, Land wondered if it might be possible to develop and print a photograph inside the camera. Obsessed with the idea, he went to work, and by 1947 he startled a group of optical scientists with the first demonstration of instant photography. The Polaroid Model 95 was born. The camera weighed more than four pounds, produced sepia-toned pictures of varying quality in 60 seconds, and retailed for $90. It was an equally instant success.

Although it has been greatly refined, the basic process Land discovered for instant photography has remained essentially the same. *Time* magazine describes the process this way: "A negative inside the camera is exposed and then brought into contact with a positive print sheet. Both are then drawn between a pair of rollers, which break a tiny pod of jelly-like chemicals that spread

Just Tell Them What They Want

In the early 1970s the U.S. camera market seemed to fall into two leagues: the simple, mass-market Kodak and Polaroid products priced under $100, and the expensive ($500 and up), sophisticated, single-lens reflex Japanese models. But the Japanese companies, looking for a new and bigger share of the camera market, suddenly broke the rules and introduced a product halfway between: the automatic single-lens reflex camera, which looks like a fancy camera and uses 35 mm film but has the automatic light setting, focusing, and other mechanics of mass-market instants. The price was neatly pinpointed between the other two types of camera, at $200–$250.

Could such a half-breed attract buyers? A camera with plastic parts no professional would touch, and a professional appearance that could scare off the family photo-snapper?

The answer is a resounding yes (with a little bit of friendly persuasion). Canon introduced its AE-1 camera in 1975 with a blitz of television

across the sheet, producing a finished picture in seconds."

Sales of the Model 95 spurted ahead each time Land introduced another improvement. In 1950 he introduced black-and-white instead of the original sepia-toned instant photography; in 1960, 15-second pictures and automatic exposure; in 1963, color film and film cartridges; in 1965, the low-priced Swinger; and in 1971, the Square Shooter.

But Land's biggest achievement has undoubtedly been the SX-70. In 1963 Land realized that the world was ready for a compact instant camera that would combine negative and positive print in a single sheet, eliminating the "garbage" (Land's term) from previous models that littered the landscape at popular tourist sites. Unsure—and uncaring—whether the new idea would prove commercially feasible, Land went ahead anyway—tampering with a product that was already immensely popular and eventually throwing half a billion dollars into the project. Inventing or perfecting an idea mattered more to Land than resting on the profits of a past success. Mark Olshaker wrote in his biography of Land, *The Instant Image*, about a stockholder who asked Land about the bottom line (long-range profits) of a new invention. Land answered, "The only thing that matters is the bottom line? What a presumptuous thing to say! The bottom line is in heaven."

Land's inventing intuition was right in perfecting the SX-70. When it debuted in 1972, the camera was an inch-thick, seven-inch-long, fold-up instant miracle. The most miraculous thing about it was the film.

Thinner than the hyphen in SX-70, it contained eight separate chemical sheets protected by an "opacifier" layer that kept out the sun's rays while the picture developed *outside* the camera. Each of the eight dyed layers responded to a different light frequency when exposed, resulting in brilliant color. Because the dye used was metallic, the finished product didn't fade when exposed to extreme light for a long period. Kodak, Polaroid's chief competitor, was completely nonplussed, and to this day they have been unable to match Polaroid's achievement. Polaroid executives still take great delight in taping Kodak instant prints to their windows and watching them fade into nothingness in a matter of a few days.

After the SX-70, Land turned his efforts to instant movies. They proved to be the first Land-made miracle that didn't pan out. Problems that Polaroid thought minor when the system was introduced were the downfall of Polavision. The hand-held camera was equipped with a bright light that frequently annoyed subjects, especially small children. The show only lasted about 2½ minutes, and the resulting print was terribly grainy. But the worst problem with Polavision was its timing. In 1978, when the instant movies were finally introduced after 12 years of planning, the public was no longer interested in home movies. Demand for existing systems had been dying off for several years. Polaroid was caught unaware with a massive amount of unsold Polavision systems, and their earnings fell by a disastrous 70% in 1979. Land, who had seen Polavision as the crowning achievement of a brilliant career, stepped

ads featuring Australian tennis star John Newcombe and other athletes, claiming that anyone could use the camera (even an athelete!) because all that's required is to "aim and shoot."

The result: by the end of 1978 Canon's sales were up 500% from 1974, the year before the AE-1 was first marketed. Over 50% of the 35 mm, single-lens reflex buyers who walked into a camera store in America asked for the AE-1.

In effect, five Japanese camera makers—Canon, Minolta, Olympus, Pentax, and Nikon—created the product and then, through advertising, created a huge market for it.

The newfound desires of American camera buyers were so vehement, in fact, that Nikon—which stuck for a while to their exclusive, professional-quality line of cameras—took a profit drop from $3.9 million in 1974 to $1.8 million in 1978 before they brought out their own automatic, the Nikon EM.

down as chief executive officer at the age of 70 in April 1980, although he continued to serve as chairman.

Land's real crowning achievement may have been not any single invention but the creation of a billion-dollar company, this late in the twentieth century, from products for which there was little demand until Land thought of them. His creations have resulted in 524 U.S. patents under his name. (He was inducted into the patent office's National Inventors Hall of Fame in 1977.) Although he never did return to graduate from college, Land holds more than a dozen honorary degrees. He and his staff have therefore always referred to him as Doctor.

Reputation. Although Polaroid stock has fallen during the 1970s, Land's brainchild remains a glamorous company with a reputation for innovation that has remained unscathed in spite of the Polavision fiasco. Wall Street will not forgive Land for an erratic earnings record, but he never put much store in applause from that sector. Attending the 1980 annual meeting, Bill Clark, editor of *Camera 35*, commented: "Dr. Land said that making money is a by-product of research and development, which put him years ahead of most American management."

What they own. Polaroid holds Land's 524 patents, although some of the earliest have long since passed into the public domain. It will be years before anyone can duplicate the SX-70 film, even if they wanted to invest the half-billion dollars necessary to do it.

Who owns and runs the company. Land's 12½% of Polaroid gives him effective control of the company. The next biggest stockholder is J. P. Morgan, with 9%. The other directors and officers hold less than 1%, and William McCune, Land's successor as chief executive officer, has only 0.07%. Tall and bow-tied, McCune looks like the archetypal New Englander. An M.I.T. engineer, he joined Polaroid in 1939.

In the public eye. Polaroid as a corporation reflects Land's self-image as inventor-scientist-businessman-philosopher-humanitarian. They have donated money or some other form of assistance to some 143 different community projects in the Boston area, and Cambridge mayor Barbara Ackerman

> Polaroid's instant movie system, Polavision, has been a bust with consumers—its pictures are not the brightest, the film lacks sound, the film cartridges are difficult to edit, and an hour of film costs $240 (list). In a desperate Christmas (1978) promotional pitch, Polaroid offered to send a live Santa Claus to the home of any consumer buying the system during a three-week period. Customers living outside major urban centers were sent free Santa Claus suits instead. Polaroid delivered 3,000 Santas and 10,000 suits.

says, "Polaroid is the only industry in this city that you can go to for money, for land, or for some other contribution to the community. Polaroid considers itself a neighbor and actually does neighborly things."

A few years ago Polaroid achieved their long-stated goal of employing approximately 10% blacks, which corresponds roughly to the percentage of blacks in the U.S. population. But in 1970, according to *Time* magazine, "a dozen black militant employees tacked up posters on company billboards accusing Polaroid of supporting apartheid in South Africa by allowing their cameras and film to be used for internal passports and by paying their black South African employees lower wages than their white counterparts." When Land discovered that the charges were true, he appointed a group of black and white employees to visit South Africa and study the case, saying, "Your decision will be implemented, whatever it is." The group decided to stop selling to the apartheid government, and Land was as good as his word. In 1977, when Polaroid discovered that their South African distributor was violating the agreement not to sell to the government, Polaroid stopped shipping product to that country.

Director of Community Affairs Robert Palmer served as chairman for the Massachusetts State Advisory Committee on Corrections, and in 1972 he mediated a 10-day revolt at Massachusetts State Prison.

Where they're going. Polaroid may still realize some benefits from the Polavision drubbing. Two possibilities predicted in an April 1980 *Fortune* article are a cheaper method of manufacturing color film and the creation of an instant slide system. Whatever Land, who is still doing research in the lab, and his staff have cooking has not been revealed, but Wall Street is intrigued. Polaroid's research and development expenses climbed 27% to $109 million in 1979, so Land may have something up his sleeve for the next annual meeting.

Although the price of silver, one of the main ingredients in Polaroid film, rose dramatically in 1980, Polaroid hasn't suffered much—largely because of a long-standing practice of stockpiling the precious metal. After a great deal of hesitation, however, the company recently announced a film price hike of 13%.

Stock performance. Polaroid stock bought for $1,000 in 1970 sold for $224 on January 2, 1980.

Major employment centers. Cambridge, Waltham, and Norwood, Massachusetts. All are near Boston, where Land can draw on the talent of Harvard and the Massachusetts Institute of Technology.

Access. 549 Technology Square, Cambridge, Massachusetts 02139; (617) 577-2000. They do not offer plant tours, however, consumers may call (800) 225-1384 toll free.

Consumer brands.

Cameras: SX-70; SX-70 Sonar OneStep; Pronto Land Camera; Pronto Sonar OneStep; One-Step Land Camera; Polaroid Model 600; Polavision Land Camera.
Film: Polaroid film (various sizes and speeds); Land film; Polacolor; Polacolor 2; Polavision Phototape film.
Accessories: Q-Light; Polatronic Flash attachment; Polaroid TwiLight; Polavision Instant Replay; Polavision player; Polavision cassette.

The average amateur photographer uses a camera for three or four years before growing tired of it and setting it aside.

XEROX

Sales: $7 billion
Profits: $563 million
Forbes 500 rank: 52
Rank in copiers/duplicators: 1
Founded: 1947
Employees: 104,736
Headquarters: Stamford, Connecticut

What they do. "Please," the corporation's lawyers exhort the public, "don't say 'I'll Xerox a copy for you.'" The proper phrase, they contend, is "I'll make a duplicate for you on the Xerox copier." So entrenched have Xerox copying machines become in the lives of just about everyone that the company name is fast becoming a common verb. They fear that if their name becomes generic and ends up in the public domain, they'll lose their valuable trademark, just as Bayer lost *aspirin.*

This company, whose name has become such a common term, is the greatest business success story of the post–World War II era. No other firm the size of Xerox has ever been built in so short a time. Between 1959, when Xerox introduced the world's first convenient office copier, and 1974, their last year of steadily expanding profits, their sales exploded from $33 million a year to $3.6 billion; their profits mushroomed from $2 million to $331 million; and the price of their stock soared from $2 a share to $172, creating a number of surprised millionaires. Any way you measure it, the company had grown 100 times bigger in 15 years. The executives who presided over this astounding period of growth were not case-hardened corporate types but an unassuming family businessman and a liberal lawyer who went on to become a leading U.S. diplomat. In the same short period, their photocopying machines dramatically transformed the nature of office work. They made carbon paper and mimeograph machines obsolete, cut down drastically on typing time, and created unprecedented mountains of paper work.

The copiers that Xerox leases, and sometimes sells, to offices throughout the world account for more than three-fourths of their total revenues. Xerox also sells the paper and chemicals necessary for the machines' proper feeding, an appetite that generates between 10 and 15% of their revenues. In 1978, 450 billion photocopies were made in U.S. offices; Xerox accounted for more than a third.

The company also deals with words in another way—by publishing them. Xerox sends out *My Weekly Reader* to elementary school classrooms, issues *Publishers Weekly* for the book personnel of the country, and publishes *Library Journal.* Through other subsidiaries they make electronic word processors, digital printing systems, and computer disc drives. Half their sales come from outside the United States.

History. Xerography, from the Greek words for *dry* and *writing,* is basically a process that uses static electricity to make copies instantly on plain paper. Every office worker takes it for granted today, but it took Chester Carlson, a patent attorney and amateur physicist, several years of dabbling in his kitchen in New York City to discover the fundamental principles of what he called electrophotography. By 1937 he had enough of a process to patent it, and he set up a small lab behind a beauty parlor in nearby Astoria, Long Island, to pursue his experiments. His breakthrough came on October 22, 1938, when he duplicated a glass slide on which he had written: "10-22-38 Astoria."

Selling his process was more difficult and frustrating than inventing it. Over the next six years Carlson was turned down by more than 20 companies he thought might be able to develop his invention into a useful product, including RCA, IBM, Remington Rand, and General Electric. Even the National Inventors Council, known for its tolerance of what others might think are far-out notions, dismissed him.

Finally, in 1944, the Battelle Memorial Institute, a nonprofit research organization in Columbus, Ohio, became interested. They signed a royalty-sharing contract with Carlson and began to develop the process. In 1947 Battelle entered into an agreement with a small photographic paper company in Rochester, New York, called Haloid, giving the company the right to develop an "electrophotography" machine. Chester Carlson joined Haloid as a consultant.

Haloid's president, Joseph C. Wilson, had grown up with the business. His grandfather, Joseph R. Wilson, had been one of the company's founders in 1906, and his father, Joseph R. Wilson, Jr., had worked for the

This was Chester Carlson's first xerographic apparatus. It never worked very well—and it wasn't until 1959, 20 years after Carlson invented xerography, that the first convenient office copier was produced.

firm from the start. Young Joe succeeded his father as president in 1945 at age 36. Colleagues and stockholders regarded Wilson with fond admiration. John H. Dessauer, a longtime Xerox research chief, recalled in his memoirs, *My Years with Xerox,* that Wilson possessed "a quiet, unpretentious candor" that made strangers feel as though "he and they were old friends." Wilson died in 1971, but his memory is revered: at Xerox's annual shareholders' meeting in 1980, a member of the audience led the crowd in a round of applause for him.

As Haloid and Battelle continued to develop electrophotography, Wilson declared that the process needed a more distinctive name. Battelle consulted a Greek scholar at Ohio State University in Columbus, who suggested *xerography.* The machine itself, they decided, would be called XeroX (the second capital "X" was later dropped to lowercase).

Haloid introduced their first copier in 1949, but it was slow and complicated. They found the early models were better for making mimeograph masters than for copying documents. Still, they were sure they were on the right track, and they continued to tinker with the invention. In 1958 they optimistically changed the name of the company to Haloid Xerox, and in the following year came their big breakthrough: the first dependable, easy-to-use document copier. The 914 copier, so named because it could copy sheets as large as 9 by 14 inches, was a phenomenal success, and the company was off like a skyrocket. Within three years they were ranked among the *Fortune* 500 companies. In 1961 they changed their name again, this time to Xerox. By then, Chester Carlson, the inventor of the process, began to reap royalties of several million dollars a year. By the time he died in 1968, he had given away some $100 million to charities and foundations, including $5 million to the Center for the Study of Democratic Institutions in Santa Barbara, California.

Joe Wilson believed strongly that a corporation had a duty to support the institutions which made possible a free, healthy, and educated society. In the 1960s Xerox came to be associated publicly with liberal political ideas. This stance was largely inspired by Wilson and Sol Linowitz, a Rochester lawyer who started representing the company in 1950 and eventually rose to chairman of the board. Linowitz later headed the U.S. negotiating team that worked out the 1978 treaty for the return of the Panama Canal to Panama, and afterward he became a special U.S. ambassador to the Middle East. Xerox launched a new era in television advertising in 1964 when they spent $4 million to sponsor a six-part prime-time series on the United Nations commemorating the organization's 20th anniversary. The programs were devoid of commercials except for announcements at the beginning and end of each broadcast: "Xerox Corporation is privileged to bring you the following major television event," and "This program has been one of a series produced and telecast as a public service through funds provided by Xerox Corporation."

The UN series established Xerox in the public mind as a humanitarian and socially responsible company—and a master of the soft sell. (Xerox tried to extend this advertising approach to print journalism in 1975 when they "sponsored" a 23-page bicentennial profile of America by Harrison Salisbury in *Esquire* magazine. In exchange for full-page ads at the beginning and end of the article, Xerox paid Salisbury's $40,000 fee, kicked in $15,000 for expenses, and guaranteed *Esquire* another $115,000 in advertising over the next year. The arrangement provoked a firestorm of controversy among print journalists, many of whom saw it as a dangerous blurring of the distinction between editorial matter and advertising, and in the end *Esquire* agreed not to commission any more "sponsored" pieces.)

Wilson and Linowitz also moved Xerox into a new field: education. In 1962 they bought University Microfilms of Ann Arbor, Michigan, the nation's principal source of microfilmed copies of everything from doctoral dissertations to back issues of obscure publications. Then they added American Education Publications, publisher of *My Weekly Reader* and *Current Events*, read by millions of schoolchildren; R. R. Bowker, publisher of *Books in Print*, *Library Journal*, and *Publishers Weekly*; and Ginn, the Boston-based elementary textbook publisher.

Xerox Bags the Feds

In 1960, when Xerox started marketing their first easy-to-use office copier, the 914, they placed an elaborate six-page, four-color, die-cut advertisement in *Fortune* and *Business Week*. One feature the ad emphasized was that the new machine could make copies on any kind of paper. John H. Dessauer, Xerox's research chief at the time, tells of an unexpected response in his book, *My Years with Xerox*. The ad drew a letter from a skeptical "high government official" in Washington who demanded proof of what he suspected was an exaggerated claim. Sol Linowitz, the company's legal counsel, asked the coordinator of the 914 task force whether the machine could even make a copy on a paper bag. He was assured there was no reason why it couldn't. "Fine," said Linowitz. "Copy his letter on an ordinary bag and mail it back without comment to the man who wrote it." Xerox never heard any more about it.

Partly as a result of their phenomenal growth, and the accompanying problem of what to do with their money, Xerox has suffered some setbacks. In 1973 the Federal Trade Commission filed a complaint charging Xerox with illegally dominating the market for office copying machines. As a result, Xerox agreed to make their 1,700 patents available for a fee to any company wanting them, agreed to help companies develop products based on those patents, and agreed not to prevent employees from going to work for a competitor. But, shrugs Xerox, the patents that were so important during their early development are now of lesser significance. Besides, by offering licenses under Xerox patents, they may be able to obtain in exchange licenses for technology under patents held by others.

Perhaps Xerox's most disastrous mistake was their attempted entry into the computer manufacturing business in 1969. They bought Scientific Data Systems, a California maker of scientific computers, from its founder, Max Palevsky, for $900 million worth of stock. Xerox hoped to slug it out with IBM, but they lost $100 million in five years and finally pulled out in 1975.

Now the company is entering the telecommunications business. They've filed a petition asking the Federal Communications Commission for a lightly used portion of the upper radio spectrum to use in a high-speed, satellite-based communications network. Xerox wants to build and operate the network nationwide, thereby providing business users with high-speed transmission of digital computer data (256,000 bits of information per second) and business documents as well as offering video and long-distance conferences through a combined satellite and microwave radio link. In 1979 an exchange of stock brought them Western Union International (WUI) and their network of telecommunication facilities, including submarine cables and satellites.

In 1978, after growing up as a liberal company in the same town as notoriously stuffy Eastman Kodak, Xerox packed up and moved their corporate headquarters from Rochester to the New York City suburb of Stamford, Connecticut.

Reputation. Age may be hardening Xerox's arteries. In 1977 they placed on their board William E. Simon, the former secretary of the treasury who has gone on record as opposing corporate grants to educational institutions that harbor critics of the free-enterprise system. As corporations go, though, Xerox is firmly in the liberal camp. At an annual meeting in the 1970s, the *Wall Street Journal* reported, an angry stockholder who assailed the company's hefty contributions to charity received this reply from chairman C. Peter McColough: "You can sell your stock or try to throw us out, but we aren't going to change."

What they own. Xerox has research, manufacturing, and sales subsidiaries throughout the world, including South Africa. The latter operation, Xerox is quick to point out, complies with the code of conduct adopted by the European Economic Community for progressive personnel policies for nonwhite South African employees. Their largest interests outside the United States are Rank Xerox Ltd., of London, and Rank Xerox Holding B.V., of the Netherlands. Xerox owns 51% of both companies, and Rank Xerox Ltd. in turn owns 50% of Fuji Xerox, a big Japanese company.

Who owns and runs the company. C. Peter McColough, a Canadian-born lawyer who joined Haloid in 1954, rules the company as chairman, chief executive officer, and chairman of the executive committee from behind his custom-designed black stand-up desk. David T. Kearns, who became president in 1977, joined Xerox in 1971 after 17 years at IBM, where he headed the data processing division. The board of directors includes four Ph.D.'s; one woman, Joan Ganz Cooney, head of the Children's Television Workshop; and one black, Vernon Jordan, president of the National Urban League. The company's directors and officers together own about 1% of the stock.

In the public eye. Xerox was the first company in the nation to adopt a social service leave program, in which employees can take as much as a year off, with full pay and benefits, to devote to some worthy cause. Among other things, Xerox leave-takers have counseled Chicano youths in Los Angeles, created a model classroom for teaching mentally retarded preschoolers, helped former convicts return to their communities, established a medical clinic for troubled kids, and edited an equal-rights-for-women newspaper.

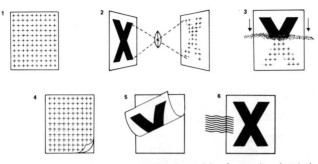

Xerography is based on two principles: materials of opposite electrical charges are attracted, and certain materials become better conductors of electricity when exposed to light. Here is how the process works.

Xerox has been embroiled in several lengthy multimillion-dollar suits in their young lifetime, most of them involving antitrust actions stemming from their de facto monopoly of the copier business for so many years. The biggest one came in 1973 when SCM Corporation sought damages of $1.5 billion from Xerox. After a 14-month-long trial, a jury awarded SCM $37.3 million in 1978, but the trial judge set aside the award and ruled that, under the law, Xerox wasn't liable for money damages. SCM appealed. Xerox hailed the judge's ruling as a victory for "the cause of inventiveness."

Twelve separate suits between IBM and Xerox were terminated in 1978 when the two behemoths entered an agreement for an exchange of all patent licenses covering both companies' information-handling products. In addition, IBM paid Xerox $25 million as part of the pact.

Where they're going. The copier business just isn't what it used to be for Xerox. For one thing, it's pretty well saturated—nearly every office has one by now. For another thing, a lot of other companies started getting into the act in the 1970s, starting with IBM and Kodak and followed by a flock of Japanese companies making smaller models. There are now more than 24 companies in the field. Although copiers still provide nine-tenths of Xerox's sales, Xerox has been looking hungrily at other fields. Lately they've been taking aim at the "office of the future": an electronic wonderland of "intelligent" copiers, word processors, high-speed printers, and other computer-linked gear that are supposed to revolutionize the way office work is done. If Xerox's forecasts are correct, the *Wall Street Journal* reported in 1978, "over the next several years the mountains of paper work that it helped to create gradually will melt into an uncluttered world where files are stored electronically and mail zips from desk to desk via computers and television screens."

To cash in on what they may see as a vast future market for the electronic devices creeping into all our lives, Xerox opened four experimental retail stores in the Dallas-Fort Worth area in 1980. If all goes well, they hope to dot the country with them. The stores sell Xerox copiers plus a lot of other products from different manufacturers: Hewlett-Packard calculators, Panasonic dictation machines, Apple computers, Remington Rand typewriters. If Xerox is guessing right—if every home will one day have a computer, or a terminal linked to computers at the bank, the store, or the office—then their retail stores may be the wave of the future.

Stock performance. Xerox stock bought for $1,000 in 1970 sold for $587 on January 2, 1980.

Access. Stamford, Connecticut 06904; (203) 329-8711.

Consumer brands.

Xerox copiers, paper.
Publications: My Weekly Reader; Current Events; Books in Print; Library Journal; Publishers Weekly; Ginn textbooks; University Microfilms.

8

MA BELL AND PA COMPUTER

Telephone Operators

Sales: $45.4 billion
Profits: $5.7 billion
Forbes 500 rank: 3
Rank in telephones: 1
Founded: 1877
Employees: 1,030,000
Headquarters: New York City

What they do. Hardly anyone could turn on a radio or television set or open a magazine in late 1979 and early 1980 without being urged to "Reach out and touch someone" through a long-distance telephone call. American Telephone and Telegraph urged you to make more long-distance calls, and their commercials pounded home the message with popular musicians who sang the "Reach out" theme song in rock, soul, country, and other arrangements. The making of one of the many TV commercials in the ad campaign even became the subject of a book, *Thirty Seconds*, by Michael J. Arlen, a writer for *The New Yorker* magazine.

Why was Ma Bell spending so much money to advertise? After all, AT&T has been the archetypal American monopoly for as long as anyone can remember. They own about four-fifths of the telephones in the United States. Every day more than half a billion conversations travel back and forth between the 138 million phones of AT&T's Bell System. With more than 1 million people on the payroll, AT&T is the nation's largest private employer. They also have the largest number of stockholders of any company in the world—almost 3 million—and they make more profit than any other company in the world. In 1979 only 65 American companies took in as much money in sales as AT&T rang up in after-tax profits. The company is so big that hardly anyone can figure out how it all works; just keeping it together is a feat of organization. For example: AT&T puts out so many newspapers and magazines for their own employees that they recently launched a new one just to give their in-house editors tips on putting out good publications.

Big as they are, however, AT&T's role in the communications industry is changing. A decade ago they advertised: "We may be the only phone company in town, but we try not to act like it." Since then Ma Bell has been dragged into a brand new arena: free enterprise. Competition in a limited form has come to AT&T as a result of several court decisions and Federal Communications Commission rulings. Now if you don't like the phone company's service or prices, in some cases you can take your business across the street. Instead of paying AT&T monthly "rent" on your telephone, you can buy a phone from another company and plug it into the Bell System. If you own a business that makes a lot of long-distance calls, you can save 15% to 30% by hooking up with one of several "specialized transmission services," which relay calls via independent microwave or satellite networks and hook into the Bell System at both ends. Big corporations can wire their offices with entire phone systems made by Ma Bell's rivals and link them up with the Bell System at the plant gate.

The competition cuts two ways. For several years AT&T has been edging into the vast computer field, already well populated with giants. The coming war between AT&T and IBM over electronic transmission of data promises to be the most exciting corporate collision of the 1980s. In the earlier, simpler days of computers, AT&T and IBM knew whose turf was whose, and they both stayed on their own. If computer companies needed to send information from one machine to another, across town or across the country, they sent it on AT&T's wires. As computers became more sophisticated, however, the line between the two functions began to blur. AT&T developed a new system of computerized switching centers to allow computers made by different manufacturers to "talk" to each other. AT&T even came up with a new phrase to explain what they were up to: *data communications*, which fell somewhere between processing and transmission.

Strictly speaking, AT&T is just the parent company that holds together about 24 subsidiaries that operate regional telephone systems in all states but Alaska and Hawaii,

plus two other subsidiaries that build the equipment and develop new technology. Together, the whole works is called the Bell System. AT&T owns 17 regional telephone companies outright; they have the lion's share of 4 others, ranging from 86% to 89.9% of the stock, and they hold minority interests in 2 more. Western Electric, a wholly owned subsidiary, makes the telephones and other equipment and is one of the nation's largest industrial corporations by itself, ranking 17th on the Fortune 500 list. Bell Laboratories, the subsidiary that does AT&T's research and development, is one of the most celebrated research facilities in the world. Seven Bell Labs scientists have won Nobel Prizes. AT&T's Long Lines Department handles interstate long-distance calls.

In every other major country in the world, the phone company is owned and run by the national government. Here Ma Bell is a "regulated monopoly." The FCC oversees AT&T's interstate activities, such as long-distance calls, while state regulatory commissions approve the rates of the regional telephone companies. In general, AT&T is allowed to set their rates so as to reap a profit return based on the amount of money they have invested in the system. To keep Ma Bell honest, the regulatory bodies are allowed to examine the company's books. As a practical matter, however, phone company finances are so complicated that the state agencies, which typically have small staffs and budgets to match, often despair of trying to understand all the talk of "rate bases" and "accelerated depreciation" and end up giving Ma Bell whatever she asks for.

For years AT&T considered themselves a "service" company with a "natural monopoly." Now, in their new competitive environment, they've decided they're a "marketing" company instead. That's why you can now get Mickey Mouse and Snoopy phones from the Bell System. (It wasn't so long ago that telephones came only in basic black.) That's also why they've decided to push their "Reach Out" theme vigorously. They now take in more money from long-distance than they do from local telephone service—$20 billion for long distance versus $18 billion for local service in 1978—and the percentage has been rising steadily over the last several years. Ma Bell is counting on long distance to make up for a lot of the money she's losing to the competition.

There are 165 million telephones in the homes of America.

> **Alexander Graham Bell never kept a telephone in his study because he resented interruptions.**

History. Every schoolchild has heard the story of Alexander Graham Bell, the Scottish-born inventor of the telephone. Hard at work in his laboratory in Boston, hot on the trail of an electrical dance that would transmit human speech, Bell called for his assistant: "Mr. Watson, come here, I want you." Watson came running from another room, where he had heard his master's voice come over the wires.

What is less well known is that the identity of the telephone's inventor had been a matter of great dispute. Bell's patent was the subject of 600 separate challenges. Bell's chief rival was Elisha Gray of Chicago, cofounder of the Western Electric Manufacturing Company. Gray had announced that he was working on a speaking telephone in a "caveat," or warning to other inventors, which he filed at the Patent Office in Washington on February 14, 1876, just hours after a similar patent application had been filed on behalf of Bell's rudimentary device, which didn't even work yet. The celebrated incident involving Bell and Watson took place the following month. In 1888 the U.S. Supreme Court ruled in Bell's favor by a vote of only 4 to 3.

Alexander Graham Bell's background was in the physiology of human speech, not electricity. His grandfather, Alexander Bell, was a Shakespearean actor who became the head of an elocution school in London that specialized in curing stammering, and he is widely believed to have been the inspiration for Professor Henry Higgins in George Bernard Shaw's play *Pygmalion*. The inventor's father, Melville Bell, was an elocution teacher in Edinburgh who devised a system to teach deaf people to speak intelligibly. Alexander Graham Bell himself was teaching his father's system at schools for the deaf in New England when he began his telephone experiments. Soon after he perfected his invention, Bell married one of his deaf students, disappeared from the telephone picture, and lived a quiet life as a tinkerer and an instructor of the deaf until his death in 1922.

The Bell Telephone Company, founded in 1877, expanded so rapidly that it needed large infusions of capital. The money came from the bankers of Boston, who got control of the company in return. In the precarious early years Bell managed to beat back a savage attack from Western Union, the telegraph company. Western Union bought the rights to Elisha Gray's devices, set up a subsidiary called the American Speaking Telephone Company, and hired a young inventor named Thomas Alva Edison to build a better telephone. Edison came through with a model much improved over Bell's, and the Bell company sued for patent infringement. At the time, Western Union was preoccupied with fighting off a takeover raid by Jay Gould, the dread financial predator. Bell and Western Union settled their fight out of court, with Western Union agreeing to get out of the telephone business and Bell agreeing to pay Western Union 20% of Bell's telephone rental receipts for 17 years. The company, which became known as American Bell Telephone in 1880, went through several reorganizations before settling on an arrangement in 1899 that has lasted ever since: American Telephone and Telegraph, which started as a subsidiary of American Bell to handle long-distance service, became the parent company of the Bell System, in charge of providing long-distance service and overseeing the regional telephone companies.

Shortly after the turn of the century control of AT&T passed to a group of bankers led by J. P. Morgan. The man they installed as president in 1907, Theodore Vail, spent the next 12 years consolidating AT&T's hammerlock on America's telephone system. Bell's original patents had expired in 1893 and 1894, and thousands of independent local telephone companies had sprung up from coast to coast. AT&T had a distinctly low opinion of competition, and they fought the independent companies with all the weapons at their disposal: gobbling them up, undercutting their prices, and refusing to connect their devices to the Bell System, which owned almost all the nation's long-distance lines.

Vail viewed the telephone business as a natural monopoly and saw no advantage to the public from "destructive competition." In 1909 AT&T saw fit to extend their natural monopoly into the telegraph business, and they bought 30% of Western Union's stock, giving Bell effective control of the telegraph company. In 1910 Vail became president of Western Union, and the boards were rearranged to have seven directors in common; in effect, the two companies were merged into one. Public indignation was rising over the growing power of AT&T. In 1913, under pressure from the Justice Department and the Interstate Commerce Commission in the new Democratic administration of President Woodrow Wilson, AT&T agreed to three things: (1) to sell their Western Union stock (the word *telegraph* in their name has been excess baggage ever since), (2) not to buy any more independent telephone companies without the approval of the ICC, and (3) to let other phone companies connect with the Bell System lines. Vail said he had "no serious objection" to public control of telephone rates, and AT&T accepted government regulation as a way to keep the government trustbusters off their back and to protect the Bell System from competition from upstart telephone companies. At the time of the "antitrust" agreement, AT&T controlled 50% of the telephones in the country. The figure is now closer to 80%.

Western Electric was founded in Cleveland in 1869 and moved soon thereafter to Chicago, where they made such devices as the world's first commercial typewriters and Thomas Edison's "electric pen," predecessor to the mimeograph machine. In 1881 Bell Telephone bought a large interest in the company, which began supplying AT&T's equipment a year later. Bell Labs and Western Electric have developed many of the technological milestones of the twentieth century, including sound motion pictures (1926), television transmission (1927), radio astronomy (1933), digital computers (1938), the transistor (1947), microwave relay (1948), the silicon solar cell (1954), lasers (1958), and satellite communications (1962).

AT&T has also been heavily involved in defense work. In World War II they built half the radar used by the U.S. armed forces. AT&T's Sandia Corporation, based in New Mexico, has played a central role in the development of nuclear weapons from the beginning of the atomic age. AT&T built the Nike missile systems, the DEW (Distant Early Warning) line of radar defense, the Sentinel and Safeguard antiballistic missile systems, and much of the equipment for the U.S. space program. They collaborated with the National Aeronautics and Space Administration on Telstar, the first international communications satellite, which was launched in 1962. AT&T also built the Defense Department's Autovon network, which connects all the U.S. military installations in the world.

Reputation. Almost everyone has had a gripe with the phone company at one time or another. Ma Bell is constantly under pressure from groups representing consumers, labor, women, and minorities, pro-

Lamb's Larynx and a Dead Man's Ear: The Evolution of the Telephone

Alexander Graham Bell's father and grandfather were British elocution instructors, and Bell set out in their footsteps at an early age. At 16 the inventor and his older brother built a speaking machine—an artificial skull that housed bits of tin, India rubber, and a lamb's larynx. By blowing through it they could make it cry "Ma-Ma!" Young Bell also figured out how to manipulate his Skye terrier's mouth and vocal cords to make the dog utter something that sounded like "How are you, Grandmama?" Things really began to fall into place with the "phonautograph" that Bell built in 1874 at age 27, two years before he developed the telephone. This macabre device employed the ear of a dead man connected to a lever. When words were spoken into the ear, causing the ear-drum to vibrate, the lever traced a sound-wave pattern on a piece of smoked glass. Bell began to speculate how a membrane might cause an electric current to vary in precise conformity with spoken sound waves. Thus the principle of the telephone was born.

Source: John Brooks, *Telephone: The First Hundred Years* (Harper & Row, 1976).

Hello, hello from the top: 3 early Bell leaders

Theodore N. Vail, who never went beyond high school, is credited with doing more than any other person to shape the Bell System as a regulated monopoly. He first served as president of Bell between 1885 and 1887, left the company, and then returned in 1907, at the age of 62, to steer the company for the next 12 years. He believed in telling stockholders what was happening. "If we don't tell the truth about ourselves, someone else will," he said in 1911.

Harry Bates Thayer, who was born in Vermont and graduated from Dartmouth, succeeded Vail as president in 1919 and held the post until 1925 when he became chairman for three years. He carried out Vail's policies faithfully. Vail once said: "Sometimes Thayer comes into my office and we just sit and look at each other."

Walter S. Gifford was born in Salem, Massachusetts, graduated from Harvard in 1904 and immediately joined the Chicago office of Western Electric at $10 a week. His Yankee father distrusted all corporations, and when his son was given a raise to $24 a week after two years, he said: "Any damn fool can make a success in a corporation." Gifford became president of AT&T in 1925 and held that post until 1948. He always wore a bow tie. He once tried wearing a monocle.

testing employment practices and spiraling rates. At the same time, the company likes to point out that the United States has the most reliable and efficient phone system in the world. Long-distance rates, they add, have actually declined over the long run, not just relative to the cost of living, but in hard dollar amounts. In 1915, according to the company, a three-minute coast-to-coast call during business hours cost $20.70; in 1930, $9; in 1950, $2.50; and in 1980, $1.30.

What they own. Poles, wires, and cables alongside or underneath almost every street and highway in the land. Office and equipment facilities everywhere. Western Electric has 24 manufacturing plants and 40 service centers across the country, and Bell Labs has 16 facilities in 8 states. The Bell System also owns some 133 million telephones, which they rent to the rest of us. What does it all add up to? $113 billion. That was the value of AT&T's assets at the

start of 1980. No company has more—not Exxon, not the Bank of America, not General Motors, no one.

Who owns and runs the company. Roughly 1 out of 75 Americans owns stock in AT&T. For years it was considered the blue chip of blue chips, a stock that could not possibly lose money, although this reputation is a bit tarnished today. It has also long been called a "widows' and orphans' stock," a favorite of small investors looking for a safe bet.

No single person or institution owns enough AT&T stock to exercise much influence, so the company is essentially management-run. The board of directors includes such corporate heavyweights as the board chairmen of Mobil, U.S. Steel, Union Pacific, Carter Hawley Hale Stores, the Deere farm machinery company, and the New York Stock Exchange; plus the presidents of Levi Strauss and Columbia University. Also on the board are one black (Jerome H. Holland, former U.S. ambassador to Sweden) and one woman (Catherine B. Cleary, a Wisconsin banker). Charles L. Brown, who took over as chairman from John deButts in 1979, grew up with the company: his father worked for AT&T for 37 years. In 1979 Virginia Dwyer was appointed vice-president and treasurer of AT&T, becoming the highest-ranking woman in the history of the company.

The routes to the top in AT&T provide a clue as to which regional telephone companies are well regarded at headquarters. Chairman Brown used to be president of Illinois Bell in Chicago. William M. Ellinghaus, who replaced Brown as AT&T's president, was president of New York Telephone. Two other directors are former presidents of Bell System companies: William S. Cashel, Jr., from Bell Telephone of Pennsylvania and Diamond State Telephone (Philadelphia), and James E. Olson, from Indiana Bell (Indianapolis) and Illinois Bell. But there's nobody on the board from the southern or western phone companies.

In the public eye. In 1974 the Justice Department launched a new assault on AT&T: an antitrust suit accusing them of having an illegal monopoly. According to the suit, AT&T had tried to obstruct potential competitors by refusing to let them hook their equipment to the Bell System. The suit seeks to break up AT&T into several smaller units in an effort to promote competition in the telephone industry. If the government wins, AT&T will have to sell off Western Electric as an independently owned and operated company, and Western Electric itself will have to be split into two or more competing companies. The government would also like to see "some or all" of the Long Lines Department separated from the regional phone companies and the research and development operations of Bell Labs set up as an independent company.

As soon as the suit was filed, then-chairman deButts vowed that AT&T would fight to the finish. By 1979, with the trial still several years off, Ma Bell had already spent more than $100 million on the case. The case was not expected to go to trial before 1982.

AT&T has drawn fire for their treatment of women and minority workers. In 1973,

after the Equal Employment Opportunity Commission filed charges of racism and sexism against the company, AT&T signed a consent decree to end employment discrimination. In 1979 the government said Ma Bell had done a good job. During that period, 1972 to 1979, minority employees in management doubled. Women now hold 36% of the jobs in management. Minorities now represent 17.4% of AT&T's work force; Ma Bell is thus the largest employer of blacks in the nation. The company also reported progress on moving men into jobs traditionally held by women. In 1972, for example, only 1.4% of telephone operators were men; by 1979 about 8% were men.

Business Week reported in 1979 that Ma Bell has frequently exerted "an unusual control over workers through technical and administrative systems," but that her current work force, "dominated by the independent-minded, better-educated 'baby boom' generation, is rebelling." But the magazine added that Ma Bell recognizes the problem and in fact has "created a new management unit to respond to it." To AT&T watchers, the news came as no great surprise. AT&T employees have been subject to many efforts at human engineering over the years—programs the company has designed to manage their enormous population. John Brooks recounts in his book *Telephone* how Western Electric became a pioneer in industrial relations in 1924 when they cooperated with the Harvard Business School, the National Academy of Sciences, and the National Research Council on a study of working conditions at a Western Electric plant at Hawthorne, Illinois. The decade-long studies, Brooks wrote, "introduced students of industry to the now-famous 'Hawthorne effect': that workers under study increase their production whether such factors as plant illumination are raised or lowered, suggesting that the increase is caused not by the nature of the change but by the change itself. The Hawthorne studies, if they did not exactly benefit the worker, at least showed him that the company was thinking about him."

Where they're going. AT&T hardly thinks of themselves as a "telephone" company anymore. That's old hat, and besides, the residential telephone market is saturated. They now want to be a "communications systems company," involved with computers and transmission of data. When the Justice Department had been after them, in 1956, AT&T signed a consent decree, agreeing to stay out of the new data processing field, which was left to the unregulated computer companies like IBM. The regulated Bell System agreed to stick to transmitting messages or moving information. As the clear line between *data processing* and *transmission* began to fade, the FCC decided to try to redraw it, laboring for four years to define *communications* and *data processing,* without much success. Finally in 1980 they voted to give AT&T virtual free rein in the "data communications" field. As part of the same decision they ruled that phone companies will have to stop renting phones to residential users—by 1982 we're all supposed to own our own phones. Furthermore, AT&T will have to run Western Electric in "arm's length" fashion—that is, the two operations will have to keep their money separate. The idea is to prevent AT&T from undercutting the competition by subsidizing Western Electric's telephone sales once we all have to start buying our phones.

Back in the humdrum world of telephones, AT&T says Bell Labs has perfected "lightwave communications"—transmitting information as pulses of light through hair-thin glass fibers, rather than as electrical impulses over wires. Ma Bell predicts that her lightwave technology is the wave of the future.

Stock performance. AT&T stock bought for $1,000 in 1970 sold for $1,072 on January 2, 1980.

Access. 195 Broadway, New York, New York 10007; (212) 393-9800. On the local front, dial "O" for Operator and go from there.

Consumer brands.

New England Telephone (Boston); Southern New England Telephone (New Haven); New York Telephone (New York City); New Jersey Bell Telephone (Newark); Bell Telephone of Pennsylvania (Philadelphia); Diamond State Telephone (Philadelphia); Chesapeake and Potomac Telephone (Washington, D.C.); Chesapeake and Potomac Telephone of Maryland (Baltimore); Chesapeake and Potomac Telephone of Virginia (Richmond); Chesapeake and Potomac Telephone of West Virginia (Charleston); Southern Bell (Atlanta); South Central Bell (Birmingham); Ohio Bell (Cleveland); Cincinnati Bell (Cincinnati); Michigan Bell (Detroit); Indiana Bell (Indianapolis); Wisconsin Telephone (Milwaukee); Illinois Bell (Chicago); Northwestern Bell (Omaha); Southwestern Bell (St. Louis); Mountain States Telephone (Denver); Pacific Northwest Bell (Seattle); Pacific Telephone (San Francisco).

Backfire in the Lobby

On August 10, 1962, Senator Russell Long of Louisiana burst through the Senate cloakroom and onto the floor, where the Senate was in the midst of a heated debate (and filibuster) over the Communications Satellite Act. He broke in on Senator Frank Moss of Utah, his ally against the bill that would have given AT&T complete control over all communications satellites. Long asked for the floor and got it, opening with these words:

"When this bill first started out I thought it was as crooked as a dog's hind leg. I am now convinced that that would be a compliment. . . ." He went on:

"I should like to ask the Senator from Utah whether the telephone company has offered him the kind of proposal that it has offered me?

"Has the Senator had proposals made to him that he could own a telephone building in his state and that the telephone company would make the loan and endorse the loan to build a building in a big city in his state just on the assurance that the Senator would give sympathetic consideration to the company's problem, if he would go along with them, and that the company would then build the building and endorse the mortgage loan and engage the bank to make the loan with the probability that he would wind up eventually being worth $5 million or $25 million?"

The telephone company did not get exclusive rights to the use of communications satellites.

Source: Joseph C. Goulden, *Monopoly* (G. P. Putnam's Sons, 1968).

General Telephone & Electronics

Sales: $10 billion
Profits: $645 million
Forbes 500 rank: 28
Rank in telephones: 2
Founded: 1926
Employees: 214,000
Headquarters: Stamford, Connecticut

What they do. General Telephone is the phone company for rural America. A distant second to Ma Bell, with only 8% of the phones in the United States, General services backwaters the Bell System left behind: rural areas in Texas, the Midwest, the Southeast, and the Pacific Northwest. The two major exceptions are in California and Florida: General controls 5 million phones in Long Beach, west Los Angeles, many of the sprawling suburbs of southern and northern California, and the growing Tampa, Florida, metropolitan area. But many of their customers pine for Ma Bell. The *Wall Street Journal* reported in 1971 that "some battle-wise residents of the Los Angeles area deliberately try to avoid living in General Tel service areas when they shop for new apartments." The situation didn't seem to have improved much eight years later, when the *Los Angeles Times* detailed the woes of a small business served by General Tel that was "looking for a new office . . . in Pacific Telephone [AT&T] territory" after five years of being "plagued by dead lines, a continuous dial tone, a delayed dial tone, static, interference from other conversations, the line going back to tone after a number was dialed, fast busy signals and calls that never rang through," while people who tried to call the company got "false

busy signals, a recording repeat that the number was not in service, disconnects and notice from information operators that there was no such listing."

GTE's 19 regional telephone companies provide about half their sales and four-fifths of their profits. The rest of their business is in electronics and electric consumer products. Sylvania, which GTE bought in 1958, makes TV sets and stereos and is a major force in TV picture tubes, flash bulbs for cameras, and light bulbs. GTE makes telephone switching machines for the Bell System as well as for their own companies. They also make TV sets under the Philco label.

History. At two crucial moments in their history General Telephone has had cause to say a heartfelt, "Thank you, Paine Webber." General was founded in 1926 by Sigurd Odegard, an owner of a small Wisconsin phone company who decided during a vacation to Southern California that he'd like to buy a small, independent telephone company in Long Beach. With the help of Chicago utilities magnate Marshall Sampsell and financing by a Paine Webber investment house partner named Morris LaCroix, Odegard set up Associated Telephone Utilities, a holding company that was soon gobbling up other independent phone companies. But the Great Depression brought disaster. Despite loans from a New York banking group, the company went broke; in 1934 they were reorganized under the bankruptcy laws as General Telephone, with LaCroix and the bankers in control.

General was content with modest growth and regular dividends until Donald C. Power, an Ohio utilities lawyer, was persuaded to take over as president in 1950. Power immediately launched an expansion program, buying the Automatic Electric Company, a telephone equipment manufacturer, and merging in 1958 with Sylvania, a large electronics company, in a deal quietly engineered because Paine Webber was the investment banker for both firms. The two deals gave General for the first time the factories and know-how to make the new electronic switching systems a modern phone company needs. In the 1970s, however, telephone use shot up dramatically in southern California, General's biggest service area, and the company found themselves without enough equipment or trained employees to service the new demand. Barraged with complaints, the company announced late in 1979 that they would spend $3.8 billion over five years on equipment to improve their service.

Reputation. They may be the number 2 phone company, but if they're trying harder, it doesn't show.

What they own. Besides their 19 phone companies, General has plants in Mountain View, California, and Needham, Massachusetts, that design and make sophisticated electronic warfare equipment for the U.S. military. Altogether their "products group" has over 150 plants, a third of them in foreign countries around the world.

Who owns and runs the company. Theodore F. Brophy, who became chairman in 1976 after 13 years as general counsel and 4 as president, continues General's tradition of having a lawyer at the helm. The firm's presidency then remained vacant for more than 3 years until Thomas A. Vanderslice, former head of General Electric's power-plant division, was lured to General Telephone. In 1979 the directors included one woman (37-year-old Sandra Moose, vice-president of a Boston consulting firm), the chairmen of two big oil companies (Maurice F. Granville of Texaco and Howard W. Blauvelt of Conoco), and a former secretary of labor (John T. Dunlop, who served in the Ford administration). No individual or institution controls much of GTE's stock; the company's directors and officers control only about one-tenth of 1%.

In the public eye. Between 1971 and 1975 General Telephone made $14 million in questionable payments to influence government decisions in 28 countries, according to a Securities and Exchange Commission complaint. Some $5 million of the total allegedly went to a group of investors in connection with GTE's sale of their partial interest in the Philippine Long Distance Telephone Company. A $6 million payment was aimed at influencing what the SEC described as "the highest levels of the Iranian government" during the reign of the shah to land a $600 million contract to expand Iran's telephone system. (Iran's revolutionary government stopped work on the project in 1979.) And the payments didn't just go overseas. GTE left New York City for Stamford, Connecticut, in 1973, but they kept the contract to supply Sylvania light bulbs to the New York subway system—and in 1979 they were fined $10,000 for paying an $11,500 bribe to a New York transit official to swing the contract their way. (The official was fined $10,000 and sentenced to two years in prison.)

Where they're going. By the beginning of the 1980s telephone companies and computer companies were starting to act so much like each other that it was almost getting hard to tell them apart. AT&T, IBM, and ITT all sallied into the field of data communications, a new area that represented a fusion of two previously distinct areas: data processing (by computers) and data transmission (over phone lines). GTE got into the act in 1979 when they bought Telenet, a Virginia-based company that runs a nationwide computer data switching network.

Stock performance. General Telephone stock bought for $1,000 in 1970 sold for $942 on January 2, 1980.

Access. One Stamford Forum, Stamford, Connecticut 06904; (203) 357-2000.

Consumer brands.

General telephones; Sylvania and Philco televisions; Sylvania light bulbs, flash bulbs, stereos.

A single glass fiber of the kind used by the telephone company to transmit communications can carry 800 voice messages, or information equivalent to 50 million bits (units of computer-stored information) per second. That is enough capacity to carry the contents of more than 40,000 typical library books from the Library of Congress in Washington, D.C., to Los Angeles in one hour.

Computer People

CONTROL DATA CORPORATION

Sales: $3.3 billion
Profits: $119 million
Forbes 500 rank: 150
Founded: 1957
Employees: 45,168
Headquarters: Minneapolis, Minnesota

What they do. Control Data believes doing well is compatible with doing good. Business exists to deliver the goods and services needed by society, says William C. Norris, chairman and founder of this Minneapolis-based computer and financial corporation, and what the United States needs are more and cheaper energy, rebuilt cities, better health care and education, and more skilled jobs. Norris thinks there are profits to be made in providing these services, and he wants Control Data to be the company to reap that bonanza.

Norris bases his social strategy on Control Data's computer operations, two-thirds of the company's business. A designer and manufacturer of large computers, they sell or rent their machines to government agencies, universities, and corporate research departments that need the huge "number crunchers" to solve complicated engineering and scientific problems. The information supplied by the computers is applied to aerospace engineering and design, weather forecasting, oil exploration, and control of refineries and electric power networks. In partnership with Honeywell and NCR, Control Data also makes and sells peripheral computer equipment: the terminals, printers, memories, and disc drives used to enter, store, and retrieve data from computers. Some of this equipment is sold to other computer makers for incorporation into their systems; the rest goes directly to users who attach the devices to their machines (usually IBM models).

Manufacturing operations bring in about 60% of the company's computer revenues, but a growing share of their business is in services. Control Data's 9 North American and 13 overseas centers sell computer time to customers who need access to a large computer but cannot afford one themselves. Major customers are banks, brokerage houses, government agencies, and about half the *Fortune* 500 companies (the 500 largest industrial corporations). The company also owns Ticketron, the computerized ticket service, and Arbitron, a television and radio audience rating service.

Norris is pinning his social strategy on supplying computer and educational services to the little guy too. The key to this goal is PLATO, a sophisticated computer-based education system that Control Data makes available through leased display terminals at colleges, high schools, prisons, and corporations, and at 69 Control Data learning centers around the country. These centers, hooked to a central computer, offer 500 hours of courses ranging from remedial math and basic English to financial management. The customers are job trainees funded by either their employers or government job programs. Control Data is also setting up 15 business and technology centers to sell management advice and computer access to small businesses, and they have plans to provide similar services to small farmers.

The noncomputer arm of Control Data is Commercial Credit, a finance and insurance company based in Baltimore. Their 800 offices in the United States and Britain make personal, auto, and installment-buying loans to more than 1 million customers. Commercial Credit also serves businesses that want to finance or lease cars, aircraft, machinery, and Control Data computers.

History. Control Data was founded in Minneapolis in 1957 when William Norris left his job as general manager of the Univac computer division of Sperry Rand to fulfill his dream of running a big computer company. As a computer man, he understood the futility of directly challenging IBM's dominance, so he decided to concentrate where IBM was weakest: huge computers needed for scientific uses. Twice in their first decade Control Data nearly sank under the expense of developing their initial systems, but by 1968 they had established a reputation as the technical leader in big computers. That same year Norris also made one of his most important management decisions: he filed an antitrust suit against IBM. Although the suit was expensive, it ended happily for Norris when, in 1973, IBM agreed to sell their data processing services subsidiary, Service Bureau Corp., to Control Data for an unbelievably low price of $16 million. Control Data came away with 40 data processing centers, 1,700 trained employees, a time-sharing network, and some well-developed computer programs. On top of that, cash-rich IBM threw in direct and indirect payments totaling about $100 million. *Business Week* valued the settlement at a quarter of a billion dollars.

Reputation. A company that does more than talk about social responsibility. While government and business were wringing

How Many Robots Does It Take to Screw in a Light Bulb?

PUMA, the most advanced industrial robot from Unimation, Inc.—the U.S. leader in robotics—still has a long way to go to catch up with its science fiction counterparts. Described by Fred Reed in *Next* magazine, PUMA, which resembles a fireplug equipped with five-joined arms powered by five electric motors, has gripper "hands" and computer brains that lie in a box separate from PUMA's body. Small and quiet enough to avoid intimidating human co-workers, PUMA is being tested in General Motors plants alongside human assemblers.

Like most of the new breed of robots, PUMA is a fast learner. To teach or program it, an engineer simply puts PUMA's gripper over an object and pushes a button on its "teach box." PUMA gets a message to "Remember this place." Then the engineer closes the little robot's grippers on the object

PUMA is to pick up, pushing a button that tells the robot "Remember to do this." Next, PUMA's human instructor moves the robot's gripper over the container, into which PUMA is supposed to deposit gadgets, pushing PUMA's Remember button. When the engineer finally pushes PUMA's Go button, the obedient robot will move gadgets to the receptacle until someone reprograms it—or pulls its plug.

PUMA's helpfulness, however, can go too far. For example, it will grab for a specified object in the spot where it expects to find it, but if the object happens to be even a few inches away, PUMA will happily grab handfuls of air and deposit them in the receptacle. Lacking either vision or tactile feedback, the hard-working PUMA makes mistakes no human assembler would make. Programmed to screw a light bulb into a stereo panel, PUMA does fine as

long as panel and bulb are where they're supposed to be. But if the panel is a fraction of an inch out of position on the conveyor belt, the robot pushes the bulb into blank metal spaces between sockets, never realizing why it won't screw in no matter how much it's twisted. Or, if a bulb arrives upside down in its tray, PUMA cheerfully tries to screw it into the panel upside down.

If PUMA's human co-workers have to spend a lot of their time positioning product parts for the robot, productivity inevitably drops. Mindful of this potential drawback of robot assemblers, PUMA's creators plan to give PUMA vision via a camera linked to image-processing gadgetry, and sensory "feel" may come next.

Source: Fred Reed, "The Robots Are Coming, The Robots Are Coming," *Next,* May/June 1980.

their hands over the plight of central cities, Control Data was building plants in ghetto areas of Minneapolis-St. Paul and Washington, D.C. *Business Week* reported in 1979 that some Wall Street analysts believe Control Data's "social orientation far exceeds its business orientation."

What they own. Control Data owns savings and loan companies in Ohio and Texas and three insurance companies: American Health and Life, Calvert Fire, and Gulf.

Who owns and runs the company. Since the beginning William Norris has been the undisputed boss. Though often criticized both inside and outside the company for holding the reins too tightly, Norris has insisted on doing things his own way—above all, on forging Control Data's unique social strategy.

In the public eye. William Norris has backed his rhetoric about corporate social responsibility with a wide range of programs that make Control Data a model of enlightened business. In 1979 they fielded a new unit, City Venture, to rehabilitate slum buildings in Toledo, Minneapolis, and other cities. They have made impressive gains in the number of minorities and women they employ and promote. Control Data also has a program to find and place orders with minority businesses.

In 1978, however, they pleaded guilty to charges of paying $200,000 in bribes between 1967 and 1973 to officials of an undisclosed foreign country. They were penalized $1.4 million for this indiscretion.

Stock performance. Control Data stock bought for $1,000 in 1970 sold for $468 on January 2, 1980.

Major employment centers. Minneapolis, Baltimore, and Oklahoma City.

Access. 8100 34th Avenue South, Minneapolis, Minnesota 55420; (612) 853-8100.

> The Connecticut-based Unimation is helping to develop a sheep-shearing robot for use in Australia where there are 130 million sheep but only 14 million people.

HEWLETT PACKARD

Sales: $2.4 billion
Profits: $203 million
Forbes 500 rank: 225
Rank in electronic testing and measurement instruments: 1
Rank in minicomputers: 2
Founded: 1938
Employees: 42,000
Headquarters: Palo Alto, California

What they do. Hewlett-Packard measures things. They are the nation's number 1 maker of highly sophisticated electronic measurement and testing instruments that can analyze radio waves coming out of a transmitter, measure herbicide levels in food, find the source of trouble in a computer which has broken down, detect pollution in water samples, or test Olympic athletes for drugs. The magazine they publish for their employees is called *Measure.* Many of the things they measure now were not accurately measurable before Hewlett-Packard invented the equipment.

They were one of the first electronics companies to set up shop near Stanford University, 40 miles south of San Francisco. Now so many high-technology companies have appeared nearby—more than 1,000 by 1980—that the area is known as Silicon Valley (after the basic material used in electronics parts). The trend got a big push in the early 1950s when Dr. Frederick Terman, a Stanford electrical engineering professor, encouraged his students and others to start companies in Stanford's 8,000-acre industrial park, rather than migrate to the East Coast, where electronics technology was focused then. Firms that have sprung up or opened branches there include IBM, Memorex, National Semiconductor, Intel, and Syntex. The 25-mile-long area has produced many of the major advances in computers, lasers, and electronics.

Hewlett-Packard doesn't make anything for the average consumer. Nearly all their products are sold to other companies, scientific laboratories, and hospitals. They do make a few hand-held calculators, but not the $10 mass-market kind that do simple arithmetic; they make advanced programmable models which they sell to scientists and engineers for $60 to $120.

They make computers too—small models

What may have been the world's first computer was this cumbersome machine called Eniac, built by J. Presper Eckert, Jr., and John W. Mauchly at the University of Pennsylvania. Forming the Eckert-Mauchly Computer Corp., they sold their first Eniac to U.S. Army Ordnance in 1946. Remington Rand (now part of Sperry Rand) later bought out Eckert-Mauchly and produced their first Univac in 1951.

such as "desktop computers," not much larger than a typewriter, for general business use. Their medical electronic equipment division makes electrocardiographs, bedside patient monitors, and a "fetal telemetry" system that can monitor the heartbeat of an unborn baby and broadcast the information to a terminal across the room.

Electronic testing and measurement devices, their original business, now account for less than half their sales. They take in almost as much money from electronic data products, including calculators and minicomputers.

"We're not geared to compete strictly on a price basis," a company executive once told *Business Week*. "We feel we have to add something that is not already available." Rather than try to sell more products than their competitors, they concentrate on developing more advanced ones for which people will be willing to pay premium prices. Hewlett-Packard made a big push in the 1970s to sell more products in foreign countries, and now nearly half their sales are overseas, chiefly in Europe. The U.S. government buys one-seventh of their output. To build all their gadgetry, Hewlett-Packard uses scarce materials like gold, gallium, and sapphire as well as more common substances like aluminum, steel, plastic, and, naturally, silicon.

History. William Hewlett and David Packard started their business in Packard's garage in Palo Alto, California, in 1938. (In another Palo Alto garage, 26 years earlier, Lee DeForest perfected the vacuum tube, leading the way to radio, television, and computers; the site is now known as the "birthplace of electronics.") Hewlett and Packard were recent engineering graduates of Stanford, where they had studied under Professor Terman.

Their first product was a new type of audio oscillator—a device for measuring sound waves. Hewlett had designed the circuitry for an electrical engineering thesis. They baked the paint onto the instrument panels in Packard's kitchen oven. Their first big order came from Walt Disney Studios, which bought eight of the oscillators to help create the elaborate sound system for the movie *Fantasia*.

During World War II Professor Terman was in charge of the government's antiradar project at Harvard, and he arranged for Hewlett-Packard to build microwave signal generators for his project. After the war, when the new electronics business started to boom, Hewlett and Packard were ready for it. With Hewlett as the technological innovator and Packard handling the business side, the company was soon turning out as many as 24 new products a year. They bought a few other companies in the late 1950s and early 1960s, including a pioneer in electrocardiograph equipment and a maker of gas chromatographs, devices that measure the chemical content of gases. In 1972 they introduced the world's first hand-held scientific calculator, which they called an "electronic slide rule." The calculator, partly designed by Hewlett, sold for $395. An outside firm they hired to do a market research study advised them not to make the device, calling it a toy, and some Hewlett-Packard executives tried to stop the project, but Hewlett was determined. The calculator proved to be enormously popular, and they had the field to themselves for two years until Texas Instruments produced something similar.

Reputation. They've always been known as one of the best-managed companies in the electronics industry, and it's a reputation that clings to them even as they grow larger and larger. Just how highly they're regarded on Wall Street is clear from the Forbes 500 rankings: they place 388th in asset size, 225th in sales, and 120th in profits. In market value—the total value of what all their stock would sell for—they place 41st among all 500 companies.

What they own. Their Palo Alto headquarters sits on 80 acres leased from Stanford University. They have 8 other plants in California; 10 more across the country from Oregon to Massachusetts; 2 in Germany; and 1 each in France, Scotland, Brazil, Japan, Malaysia, and Singapore.

Who owns and runs the company. Both founders, now past 65, are still on the board, although they no longer actively run the company. John A. Young, an engineer who came up through the ranks, became president in 1977 at age 45. David Packard, who was still board chairman in 1980, took a three-year leave of absence at the beginning of Richard Nixon's first administration to become deputy secretary of defense. (Packard's career at the Pentagon was not particularly distinguished. According to *Business Week*, asked later what his biggest accomplishment there had been, Packard thought for a moment and replied, "I gave up smoking.") Packard owns 21% of the stock, worth about $350 million in early 1980. He is also a director of Boeing and Standard Oil of California. In 1954 he became the youngest member of the Stanford Board of Trustees. William Hewlett, who was president until 1977, owns 17% of the stock, worth about $285 million. He is also on the boards of Chrysler and the Chase Manhattan Bank. Both founders have set up foundations: the Hewlett Foundation and the David and Lucile Packard Foundation.

Of the all-male board, 9 of the 18 members are Hewlett-Packard executives. One director from outside the company is Luis Alvarez, a University of California physicist who won the Nobel Prize in 1968 for his studies of subatomic particles. Also on the board are James Hodgson, U.S. ambassador to Japan during the Nixon and Ford administrations, and two medical doctors.

Hewlett-Packard goes to great lengths to promote a feeling of esprit de corps among their employees. The company calls it "the HP way" or "the 'people' philosophy." They devote a lot of energy to trying "to

There's 1 1/16 Born Every Minute

Computer scientists are sometimes criticized for their lack of sensitivity to worldly things that can't be interpreted literally. This tendency may be traced back as early as the nineteenth century, to Charles Babbage, an eccentric mathematical genius who spent much of his life designing a steam-powered "analytical engine" the size of a football field. (He died before ever coming near to building it.)

Babbage was offended by the inaccuracy contained in Alfred Lord Tennyson's line of poetry, "Every moment dies a man/ Every moment one is born." Upon reading the line, Babbage penned a note to the poet admonishing him that "if this were true, the population of the world would be at a standstill," and recommended that Tennyson change the line to read, "Every moment dies a man/ Every moment 1 1/16 is born."

Source: *Time,* February 20, 1978.

keep that small-company feeling" in a big organization. "Motivation is the difference between a championship ball team and an ordinary ball team," Packard has said. Employees are allowed to set their own work hours as long as they arrive and leave within specified two-hour periods in the morning and afternoon and put in eight hours a day. The company maintains 12 vacation spots near their plants where employees can camp and fish. They have a generous profit-sharing plan and stock-purchase program. They don't bid on short-term government contracts that would involve hiring lots of people and then laying them off at the end of the project. As one executive explained, "When you come to work at HP we hope we are offering you a permanent job." In an industry known for high turnover of skilled workers, their work force is unusually stable.

In the public eye. Of their employees in the United States, 18% are minorities and 41% are women. They have a program of "loaning" professionals to teach at predominantly minority colleges.

Where they're going. Into fiber optics. This new technology for transmitting electronic data through tiny strands of glass promises to revolutionize the electronics field, according to people in the business.

Stock performance. Hewlett-Packard stock bought for $1,000 in 1970 sold for $2,296 on January 2, 1980.

Major employment centers. Palo Alto, California; Loveland, Fort Collins, and Colorado Springs, Colorado; Boise, Idaho.

Access. 1501 Page Mill Road, Palo Alto, California 94304; (415) 856-1501. Questions or complaints should be addressed to the Public Relations Department at the Palo Alto headquarters. For plant tours contact the local public relations officer or the Palo Alto PR department.

Consumer brands.

Hewlett-Packard calculators.

Honeywell

Sales: $4.2 billion
Profits: $240 million
Forbes 500 rank: 106
Rank in control systems: 1
Rank in computers: 5
Founded: 1885
Employees: 86,328
Headquarters: Minneapolis, Minnesota

What they do. If the steel companies provide the sinews of the body industrial, and the energy companies supply the life blood, Honeywell makes the nervous system. Honeywell's products are the technological eyes, ears, noses, and brains that have enabled manufacturers to automate everything from oil refining to beer bottling. Consumers are probably most familiar with Honeywell's thermostats, which regulate home furnaces and air conditioners, but the company sells most of their thousands of products to other manufacturers.

Honeywell is known as the company that controls the control industry. Their environmental control division, in addition to producing home thermostats, makes and sells devices that regulate heating and electricity flow in commercial buildings. For large buildings, Honeywell sells computerized systems that incorporate small electronic brains, which they make at their Synertek subsidiary in California's Silicon Valley. For smaller buildings, which cannot afford a computerized heating system, Honeywell offers an energy management system that lets customers hook up to a central computer by telephone. Honeywell both designs these systems and makes many of the components, including motors, switches, valves, and electronic chips.

The other part of Honeywell's control business is making instruments and systems for automated industries. Using Honeywell systems composed of sensors, valves, switches, computers, and control panels, a few workers can monitor and control complex processes at chemical plants, refineries, sewage plants, steel mills, or electric utilities. Honeywell also makes scientific test instruments and systems for keeping traffic flowing smoothly on freeways and city streets. In all, controls account for half their sales.

No customer has more complex control problems than the Pentagon, and Honeywell is a major military contractor, doing about 10% of their business with the government. They make navigation systems for combat aircraft, guidance systems for nuclear missiles, infrared reconnaissance equipment (enabling attackers to see targets at night or through dense foliage), and torpedos. In the early 1970s they gained notoriety as the chief supplier of fragmentation bombs, one of the most brutal antipersonnel weapons used in the Vietnam conflict.

The largest single division at Honeywell, accounting for a third of their sales, is computers. Honeywell got into computers in a big way in 1970 when they bought out General Electric's computer operation. Now the fifth largest computer company in the United States, Honeywell also owns about half of Cii Honeywell Bull, a European company second there only to IBM. (Honeywell does about a quarter of their business overseas.) Honeywell's computers range from $3,000 minicomputers to large business systems with price tags of $7 million.

History. In 1883, when Minneapolis inventor A. M. Butz produced an automatic temperature controller by connecting a thermostat to a motor, he sowed the seed that would develop into an incredibly complex multinational company. Two years later Butz set up his first plant in a Minneapolis shed and hired the first six employees of his Consolidated Temperature Controlling Company.

William R. Sweatt invested $1,500 in Consolidated and was made a director in 1891, but he took no part in management because he had a business of his own to take care of. He took a more active interest in 1893, when he was asked to serve without pay as secretary-treasurer of the new company, now known as Electric Heat Regulator Co. In 1896, after Sweatt had worked gratis for three years, the directors voted him a salary retroactive to 1895. Sweatt received all the company's stock in 1902 after paying off the original investors.

Expanding rapidly, the firm was soon a leading manufacturer of "damper flappers" —automatic controls for coal-fired furnaces and oil burners. W. R.'s son, Harold Sweatt, started working for the company in 1913, was effectively running it by 1927, and became president in 1934. His brother Charles worked with him as vice-president for 20 years.

Honeywell entered the military world just before World War II, when they started making precision optical equipment for submarine periscopes and artillery sights. Experimental work in electronics led to the development of the first successful autopilot in 1941. They set up an aeronautical division in 1949 and got serious about making

---

Play Me a Nuclear War, Sam

On November 9, 1979, the United States was on a nuclear-attack alert for six minutes because one of the Defense Department's war games malfunctioned. A computer tape simulating a Russian attack was somehow sent out as the real thing. Ten jet fighters were launched, other jet pilots were alerted to man their planes, ICBM bases were placed on "low-level alert," and air traffic controllers across the country were notified. The controllers radioed all commercial aircraft in their sectors, telling them to be ready to land at the nearest airport at a moment's notice.

The error was detected before any significant action was taken, and Defense Department spokesmen called the incident "minor." According to one former Air Force missile launch officer, computer errors trigger false nuclear alerts "every couple of years."

—*Nation*, January 29, 1979.

guidance systems for planes and missiles. Once when their electronic engineers needed ceramic transducers, they simply bought a one-man ceramics company that produced the necessary piece. Honeywell entered the lucrative field of fire detection and alarm systems in 1957.

Their attempts to become a power in the computer industry got off to an inauspicious start in the mid-1950s, when Raytheon backed out of a joint enterprise (Datamatic Corp.) after two years of preparation, leaving inexperienced Honeywell floundering with the development and marketing of a huge business computer. Although some of their models became quite successful in the 1960s, they always lagged in profits because of the tremendous investments required in the fiercely competitive computer business. But they never gave up. In 1970 they rocked the industry with the announcement that they were buying General Electric's computer division. It took most of the next decade before that subsidiary—Honeywell Information Systems—was turning a profit.

Reputation. At a time when energy conservation is a prime concern, Honeywell's sophisticated controls are a hot item, but the business community questions whether they'll ever make it in the computer industry against the likes of IBM.

What they own. Domestically, the company owns facilities in almost every state. Internationally, Honeywell and their affiliates have plants and offices in about 60 countries throughout the Americas, Europe, South Africa, the Mideast, the Far East, and Australia.

Who owns and runs the company. Perhaps the most controversial leader was former chairman James H. Binger, still a director, who proclaimed at the 1971 annual meeting, amid controversy and protest over the war in Southeast Asia: "We have military forces in the field to be supplied and so long as this action continues, Honeywell intends to furnish material support."

The reins now are in the hands of chairman Edson W. Spencer, a former Rhodes

Take a Letter, XL2403

The secretary of the future will never take coffee breaks, hang around the water cooler, get sick, or ask for a raise. In fact, the secretary won't ask for any salary at all and won't be very pretty, either, what with jointed metal arms and single camera eye, but, considering the secretary's superhuman efficiency, the boss may not care.

However loyal and diligent, today's secretary, like other clerical workers, is among the least productive workers in the world. The secretary's efficiency may be gauged by the fact that major corporations spend an average of $6.41 for each one-page letter they compose, type, and mail, according to a recent IBM study. Office workers' salaries now account for some 50% of the total overhead costs of the average

U.S. corporation, and in government and some industries—banks, insurance firms, communications—that figure swells to 70–85%. Each year white collar workers nationwide earn about $300 billion—a sum that grows by 6–8% every year. Yet the average secretary spends scarcely more than half the working hours at the desk, waiting for work or absent the rest of the time. All but 19% of the secretary's job consists of tasks some robotics experts believe could easily be mastered by robots of the future, including filing, billing, and mailing, according to Creative Strategies International, a San Jose computer consulting firm. The rest—taking dictation, typing, and proofreading—could be handled by part-time secretarial workers, rendering the

full-time secretary extinct, or at least an endangered species.

So if the vision of offices staffed mostly by shirring, blinking robots sounds bizarre, to businesses it looks increasingly practical. Office salary costs have doubled in the past 10 years, but the price of electronic office equipment has plummeted, thanks largely to the advent of the silicon microchip. The microchips cheap and no bigger than sticks of chewing gum, are laced with tiny memory circuits capable of remembering and using thousands of items of information. When these miniaturized "brains" are coupled with mechanical devices like jointed movable arms, gripper hands, and camera "eyes," the result is robots able to handle many routine jobs once done by

scholar. His vice-chairman is Stephen F. Keating, a former FBI agent, naval air intelligence officer, and attorney.

In the public eye. Because of the fragmentation bomb production and the company's interests in South Africa, several annual meetings in the early 1970s were disrupted by protesters. The 1970 meeting, in fact, was aborted only 14 minutes after it began when shouting demonstrators began throwing bottles and breaking windows. They were finally forced out when guards used mace and billy clubs against them.

One of the most vocal demonstrators, and a loudly dissident stockholder, was Charles Pillsbury, scion of the flour-milling family whose headquarters are also in Minnesota. It was because Pillsbury gave Honeywell a contract to manufacture replacement parts for water meters and flour sifters in 1932 that Honeywell was able to survive the bleakest days of the Depression. Pillsbury's memorable question to Honeywell's chairman at the 1970 annual meeting: "Mr. Binger, how does it feel to be the Krupp of Minneapolis?"

Where they're going. Toward more involvement in energy conversion, conservation, control, and storage. Honeywell's big new office building in Minneapolis is said to incorporate the country's largest solar heating and cooling system. At one time they studied the practicality of windmill-generated electricity.

Stock performance. Honeywell stock bought for $1,000 in 1970 sold for $588 on January 2, 1980.

Major employment centers. Minneapolis (they're the largest employer in Minnesota), Boston, and Phoenix.

Access. Honeywell Plaza, Minneapolis, Minnesota 55408; (612) 870-5200.

Consumer brands.

Honeywell burglar and fire alarms, thermostats, smoke detectors.

---

people.

Robots have been lurking around American industry since 1960 or so, but, like the premicrochip computers, they were big, hulking contraptions, designed to do jobs too boring or dangerous for humans: yanking red-hot ingots from furnaces or spot-welding cars. The new breed of robot, with its microprocessor brain, is both more compact and far more sophisticated than the "classic" robot. And, although the robot secretary is still a vision for the future, robots are already replacing people on assembly lines. With 5,000 robots on the job in U.S. factories and 7,000 in Japan, robotics specialists predict the robot industry will grow from $60 million in sales in 1979 to somewhere between $700 million and $2.2 billion by 1990. Within the next 10 to 15 years, automatic speech recognition should enable people to chat with computers, and by the year 2038, computers may well have sufficient intellect to handle the jobs of bank tellers and construction workers. By that time, according to Walter Anderson, associate director of the U.S. General Accounting Office, "computers will be alive"—assuming life is defined by behavior rather than inner workings. These refinements, some experts predict, could spell the end for the human secretary.

On the other hand, our bumbling and tradition-bound species may never learn to work with robot superworkers. In 1977, for example, the federal government spent $80 million to computerize its office work, and that figure will swell to $300 million by 1982. Yet productivity is stalled at its normal, sluggish bureaucratic level, according to the General Accounting Office, because the agencies' human staff can't seem to learn how to use their hyperefficient electronic aides.

Besides, say some researchers, the typical corporate executive will fight the challenge to his prestige implied by loss of his personal secretary, no matter how efficient the robot successor might be. Says Creative Strategies' Larry Wells: "When a guy spends 15 or 20 years working his way up the ladder so he can have his own secretary, there's no way he's going to give her up for a machine."

IBM

Sales: $22.9 billion
Profits: $3 billion
Forbes 500 rank: 10
Rank in computers: 1
Rank in electric typewriters: 1
Founded: 1911
Employees: 337,119
Headquarters: Armonk, New York

What they do. What U.S. Steel was to the early twentieth century, what General Motors and Ford were to the Auto Age, IBM is to the Information Age. Most Americans used to spend their days on the factory floor making objects that could be driven, flown, worn, or eaten. Today, the majority of Americans work in offices to produce numbers, words, or images, and much of that production is done on equipment made by IBM.

IBM dominates almost all lines of products essential to the paper-shuffling economy of the Information Age. Their most important product is the computer. IBM controls about 60% of the U.S. market for computers and an even greater share overseas. They also dominate the market for business typewriters. In addition, IBM makes dictating equipment, electronic cash registers, photocopying machines, and word processors (the new electronic systems for typing, editing, and storing all kinds of information). By selling so much of the hardware essential to the Information Age, IBM has become a monolith of the modern economy. Among manufacturers, only the five largest oil companies and two giant automakers had greater sales than IBM in 1979, and only Exxon and AT&T had higher profits. The money comes in so fast that IBM has a cash hoard which earns the company about $400 million a year in interest, a sum larger than the profits of any but the most successful companies.

IBM owes their success to scientific innovation, organization, and sheer market power. They spend $1.3 billion a year on research and development, money that produces new IBM products and improvements in old ones. But even when IBM is not in the forefront of technology, as has often been the case with computers, they have been able to imitate the technical advances of others, incorporate them into IBM products, and sell them like mad. Their sales force has an almost fanatical devotion to the company, and even competitors praise their service organization, which keeps the computers and typewriters running. The sales personnel have ample reason for loving the company: When IBM announces a new line of computers, the industry goes into a tizzy—competitors worry whether their products will all be outmoded in one fell swoop; customers race to the phone to book an order to be certain of delivery within two or three years; and IBM salespeople tote up the business. For example, in 1979, when IBM announced their new 4300 series of medium computers, which process eight times as much information per dollar as their previous model, they were swamped with 42,000 orders, twice as many as they expected. Meanwhile, smaller companies, which had beaten IBM to the punch with cheap, fast computers, watched their business dry up. That's the joy of being number 1.

History. This enormous worldwide operation, which makes and sells some of the world's most sophisticated equipment, was built by one of the world's least sophisticated denizens, an Ohio farmboy named Thomas Watson. In the 1890s, in his first forays out of Elmira, Ohio, where the family farm was located, Watson held jobs as a traveling organ salesman, a sewing machine salesman, and a peddler of phony building company stocks (although he was unaware of it at the time). In 1899, after the stock swindle debacle, he went to work for John Patterson's National Cash Register Company in Dayton, Ohio. Under Patterson's tutelage, Watson soon rose to the upper echelon of the company and became their top salesman. Patterson then assigned him a special (and grossly illegal) duty, which Watson carried out in perfect innocence. He was to set up a company of his own for the supposed purpose of competing with NCR. In reality, however, Watson's company was to undercut competitor's prices on second-hand cash registers and thus eliminate anyone who stood in NCR's monopolistic way. In 1912 Watson, Patterson, and 28 others were indicted and convicted for the scheme (an appeals court later ordered a new trial that was never held). And in 1913, having successfully duped Watson, Patterson calmly fired his young protégé.

Paranoid Program Parries Shrinks

The computer at Stanford is OK, really, except it thinks everybody is out to get it.

Researchers created PARRY, a computer program designed to think and respond like a paranoid psychiatric patient, to help psychiatrists learn to deal with people suffering from the disorder. PARRY, a product of Yale University's Artificial Intelligence Laboratory, uses the SUMEX biomedical computer at Stanford Medical School, which has terminals at the University of California campuses in Los Angeles and Irvine. Doctors at all three schools can ask PARRY questions and get responses.

So far, PARRY has revealed as much about psychiatrists as about paranoids. In one experiment the doctors could ask the computer any question except the identity of the "patient." Unknown to the psychiatrists, half the responses came from PARRY; half from real paranoid patients who had volunteered for the experiment. When the psychiatrists analyzed the "patient's" ailment from responses to their questions, even experienced therapists were unable to tell the real paranoids from the computer.

Source: *Smithsonian,* March 1980.

Watson quickly recovered from the shock and took over a company called Computer-Tabulating-Recording Company, located near his old hometown in Elmira. The company had begun selling an electrical punch-card computing system developed for the 1890 census and had branched out into scales, meat slicers, and various adding machines. But sales had been slow, and Charles Flint, the financier behind the company, recognized the need for a super sales-man. Watson was his man. At Watson's order, the now-famous IBM THINK signs went up all over the company's offices, closets, and washrooms, and company salesmen gathered each morning for pep talks from Watson. Churchlike behavior was required of all employees; dark suits and white shirts were prescribed office wear, and smoking was forbidden on company premises. Watson even commissioned a company song-book with titles like "Ever Onward" and "Hail to the IBM" (International Business Machines was adopted as the company name in 1924). Sample lyrics:

Our voices swell in admiration;
Of T. J. Watson proudly sing.
He'll ever be our inspiration,
To him our voices loudly ring.

But these tactics worked: from the time Watson took over the company in 1914 until his death in 1956 at the age of 82, IBM boomed, thanks particularly to their colos-sally motivated sales force. In the 1920s and 1930s IBM totally dominated the market for time clocks and punch-card tabulators. In the 1930s and 1940s they pioneered the electric typewriter market while the established manufacturers slept soundly, never dreaming their standard makes would one day be obsolete. When Watson's son, Tom, Jr., took over the company in the 1950s, IBM, with 72,000 employees and sales of nearly $600 million, had become one of the nation's largest corporations.

Then came the computer. In 1951 Remington Rand delivered UNIVAC, the first computer designed for commercial use, to the Bureau of the Census, replacing some IBM machines. IBM was stunned. IBM officials had known about the development of computers and had seen early machines, but as Tom, Jr., later admitted, none had seen its possibilities. But IBM immediately jumped into the contest. They were blessed with several advantages. First, they were already a huge company, with lots of cash to pour into the expensive tasks of research, development, and manufacturing start-up. Second, they knew the market. IBM—un-like other giant companies such as GE and RCA that later entered the field—had a sales and service organization blanketing the country. This sales force knew what businesses needed in the way of information processing and accounting. So IBM, using the intelligence from the market-place, designed machines to fit the needs of their customers. The strategy worked. Within a few years IBM completely dominated the computer market. Some of their competitors, like GE and RCA, eventually decided to get out of computers; others, like Sperry Rand and Control Data, carved out specialized segments of the market where they would not feel the full brunt of IBM's power. In the 1960s and 1970s, IBM, with about 80% of the market, was as close to a monopoly as there was in the American economy.

Recently, however, the swift pace of technical change has begun to weaken IBM's hold on the industry. Advances in the technology of silicon chips have made it possible to reduce drastically the cost of processing a given amount of information and have simplified the manufacturing process, making it easier for small companies to come into the fray. Tiny Cray Research now dominates the market for sophisticated scientific computers. Companies like Amdahl (started by ex-IBMer Gene Amdahl) offer computers that can be plugged into existing IBM systems. Minicomputer manufacturers like Digital and Data General have convinced many customers that they don't need expensive, big machines from IBM. IBM has not taken this assault lying down, of course; they have gone into these new markets in a big way. However, IBM's new products have not always been up to snuff; their minicomputers have been a disappointment, their word processors are the butt of industry jokes, and their photocopying equipment has been full of bugs. Still, it's not time to shed any tears for poor IBM, as the enormous success of their new 4300 series proves. Their market share may be slipping, but the demand for computers is growing so fast that IBM can't help but get richer.

Reputation. A great company to work for. Although IBM is a huge, highly structured, disciplined organization, they manage not to bend, fold, spindle, or mutilate their workers. The largest nonunion company in the world, IBM is committed to paying their people at rates above those prevailing at competing firms. All workers are salaried, and firings are rare. The company's long-established "open door" policy entitles workers who think they've been wronged by bosses to appeal over their heads to higher echelons, even up to the chairman of the board. IBM holds free family-night dinners for employees, covers full medical and dental expenses, helps with children's tuition, finds homes for employees, holds annual Christmas parties for "IBM children," and has three country clubs that employees use at $1 a year. This paternal, Japanese-style policy may not suit everyone, but IBMers seem like a happy lot. They are the "true believers."

What they own. IBM owns and operates manufacturing and development facilities across the United States and Europe. There are major clusters of IBM plants in upper

The Art of Etching

The tiny components that are the bulk of a computer's functioning capacity start out as twinkling crystals of pure silicon, the clear element that makes up sand. The silicon crystals are grown like huge industrial versions of rock candy and sliced into razor-thin wafers about three inches in diameter. Each wafer will, after it is turned into an elaborately etched piece of miniature circuitry, be cut into about 250 fingernail-sized *chips*, the fundamental electrical parts of modern computers.

The chip circuitry is created a layer at a time. By etching the silicon wafer with layers of different impurities, the manufacturer makes it electrically conducting in some places and nonconducting in others. (Hence silicon is called a *semiconductor*.) A nonconducting zone placed between two conducting zones will act as an "off switch" to a current running through the circuit. A large enough electrical voltage applied to that nonconducting zone—either from an outside source or from another place on the circuit—will activate the "nonconducting" material and make it conduct, turning the switch "on" and letting current flow.

A complex, microscopic network of these zones is etched into the silicon, and the impurities that will make it work are baked onto the wafers. The result is a miniature electrical circuit board, with different combinations of conducting and nonconducting materials (or, more precisely, sometimes-conducting

Westchester County (where IBM has 2 million square feet of office space on 807 acres) near the company's headquarters in Armonk, New York, and in the Silicon Valley between San Jose and San Francisco.

Who owns and runs the company. IBM's board of directors reads like a Who's Who of America's political elite. Nicholas de B. Katzenbach, IBM's general counsel and a member of the board, is a former attorney general. William T. Coleman, Jr., was secretary of transportation in the Ford administration. Carla Anderson Hills is a former secretary of housing and urban development. William W. Scranton is a former governor of Pennsylvania, ambassador to the United Nations, and presidential candidate.

The IBM connection in Washington grew strongest under Jimmy Carter, who put three IBM directors in his cabinet: Cyrus Vance as secretary of state, Harold Brown as secretary of defense, and Patricia Harris as secretary of health, education, and welfare. In addition, Carter's first attorney general, Griffin Bell, came from a law firm that represented IBM's interests in the South, and undersecretary of state Warren Christopher was IBM's lawyer in the West. So no one should have been surprised when Carter decided to make the IBM team complete by appointing Thomas Watson, Jr., as U.S. ambassador to the Soviet Union. (His brother, the late Arthur Watson, was named ambassador to France by Richard Nixon.)

The IBM board is also populated with several top officials of other big companies, including Stephen D. Bechtel, Jr., chairman of the huge San Francisco–based Bechtel engineering and construction company; Irving S. Shapiro, chairman of du Pont; J. Richard Munro, who was named president of Time, Inc., in 1980; Richard W. Lyman, president of the Rockefeller Foundation and former president of Stanford University; and G. Keith Funston, retired president of the New York Stock Exchange.

Frank T. Cary took over from Tom Watson, Jr., as head of IBM at the beginning of 1973. A former IBM executive commented on the difference in leadership to *Business Week:* "The Watsons were worshipped. They were the anointed, not the elected. With Cary, we've moved from the king to a prime minister, and we view him as such." In 1980, when he turned 60, Cary stepped down as chief executive, remaining as chairman. The top job went to IBM's president, John R. Opel, who started with the company in 1949 as a salesman in Jefferson City, Missouri.

IBM is a favorite stock of every bank trust department, pension fund, insurance company, and university portfolio manager. And for good reason. By 1962, 100 shares of IBM stock, bought for $2,750 in 1914, had risen in value to $5,455,000. Their recent performance has not been so gratify-

A silicon micro-circuit chip

materials) functioning as transistors, diodes, and resistors— all the parts of old-fashioned electronics, done in miniature. The circuits are tested, cut into chips by a diamond cutter, externally wired (this is done by hand, and much of the industry sends its chips off to Malaysia and other places where labor is cheap to have the little gold wires attached to the chips), sealed in plastic, and delivered to the user.

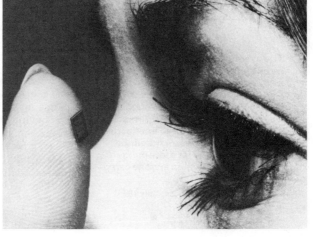

ing, but the total market value of outstanding IBM stock is greater than any company in the world. In 1979 IBM paid their 696,000 shareholders cash dividends totaling $2 billion.

In the public eye. In 1969 the Justice Department filed an antitrust suit against IBM, seeking to break the huge firm into several full-line computer companies. The suit has become a major industry in its own right. Tons of paper have passed hands, hundreds of witnesses have been interviewed, and millions of dollars have been expended by the company and the government. Evidence from past suits against IBM reveals that the company frequently has been a cutthroat competitor, but even so some of their rivals in the computer industry aren't eager to have IBM broken up; they would rather compete against one whale than three sharks. But the Justice Department, which has looked like a second-string team in the fight against an IBM crew led by former U.S. attorney general Nicholas de B. Katzenbach, is pressing ahead. Even if a decision is reached against IBM, the appeals will drag on for years.

Where they're going. Even with a slipping share in their major industry, computers, IBM has been pushing hard into new markets. In the late 1970s IBM made big inroads into NCR's dominance of the cash register market. Now IBM is going after Ma Bell. In partnership with Comsat and Aetna Life & Casualty Insurance, IBM has set up Satellite Business Systems, a company that will compete with AT&T in let-

ting computers talk to computers over a satellite network.

Stock performance. IBM stock bought for $1,000 in 1970 sold for $883 on January 2, 1980.

Major employment centers. Armonk, New York.

Access. Armonk, New York 10504; (914) 765-1900.

Consumer brands.

IBM typewriters, computers, dictating equipment, electronic cash registers, photocopying machines, word processors.

NCR

Sales: $3 billion
Profits: $235 million
Forbes 500 rank: 162
Rank in cash registers: 1
Founded: 1884
Employees: 62,000
Headquarters: Dayton, Ohio

What they do. Their electronic cash registers add up the bad news at the supermarket checkout counter. Their computers aren't as visible, but NCR is in there butting terminals with IBM, Burroughs, and Sperry Rand. This is the company that used to be known as National Cash Register, after their most famous product. They were the pride of Dayton, Ohio. But they almost didn't make it into the modern electronic era, having rested too long on past laurels. Then, out of the far East, came a savior: Warren S. Anderson. He turned the company around, making them a leading contender in the electronic office equipment market. According to *Value Line Investment Survey,* NCR now ranks second in the computer industry, accounting for 5 to 8% of shipments. They sell to stores. banks, and

> The average computer theft reported by corporations amounts to approximately $500,000. Charles F. Jacey, of Coopers and Lybrand, a New York City accounting firm told *Nation's Business:* "The computer criminal may be a mild-mannered intellectual carrying a floppy disk or magnetic tape reel, but he is far more dangerous to a company than anyone carrying a gun."
>
> —*Nation's Business,* July 1979

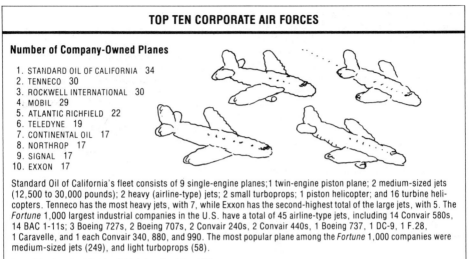

TOP TEN CORPORATE AIR FORCES

Number of Company-Owned Planes

1. STANDARD OIL OF CALIFORNIA 34
2. TENNECO 30
3. ROCKWELL INTERNATIONAL 30
4. MOBIL 29
5. ATLANTIC RICHFIELD 22
6. TELEDYNE 19
7. CONTINENTAL OIL 17
8. NORTHROP 17
9. SIGNAL 17
10. EXXON 17

Standard Oil of California's fleet consists of 9 single-engine planes; 1 twin-engine piston plane; 2 medium-sized jets (12,500 to 30,000 pounds); 2 heavy (airline-type) jets; 2 small turboprops; 1 piston helicopter; and 16 turbine helicopters. Tenneco has the most heavy jets, with 7, while Exxon has the second-highest total of the large jets, with 5. The *Fortune* 1,000 largest industrial companies in the U.S. have a total of 45 airline-type jets, including 14 Convair 580s, 14 BAC 1-11s; 3 Boeing 727s, 2 Boeing 707s, 2 Convair 240s, 2 Convair 440s, 1 Boeing 737, 1 DC-9, 1 F.28, 1 Caravelle, and 1 each Convair 340, 880, and 990. The most popular plane among the *Fortune* 1,000 companies were medium-sized jets (249), and light turboprops (58).

Source: *Business and Commercial Aviation*, December 1979.

---

governments, anyone who used to buy mechanical equipment. If your bank has one of those automated 24-hour tellers from which you can extract money by inserting a piece of plastic, you may have a steady relationship with an NCR product. NCR does more than half their business outside the United States. And Dayton is no longer the manufacturing base it once was for the company. Production is decentralized, with assembly operations scattered throughout the country.

History. Not so lovingly known as the "autocrat of the cash register," John Henry Patterson, a strong-willed man riddled with idiosyncrasies, didn't invent the cash register. But he practically invented American salesmanship, canned pitches, the hard sell, sales quotas, the first formal sales training manual, and one of the world's first company-sponsored sales training schools.

When the wiry, feisty, sandy-haired Patterson put up $6,500 in 1884 to buy a controlling interest in an obscure factory near Dayton that made those curious contraptions known then as "thief catchers," he may have had a product, but he certainly didn't have much of a market. The people of Dayton snickered, the seller gloated, and Patterson himself tried to back out. But he was stuck with the rights to a machine that enforced honesty among bartenders, cafe cashiers, and sales clerks—none of whom

wanted the new-fangled device on the premises.

Anybody else might have given up. Instead, Patterson built a model National Cash Register plant where he paternally plied employees with fringe benefits that were pioneer efforts at industrial welfare: showers, lockers, swimming pools, hot lunches, medical care, and inspirational lectures. Women employees were taught how to manage their homes, and children of employees were taught how to save their money, how to chew their food, and how to avoid scattering germs when they sneezed. In return, he demanded absolute obedience and high productivity.

At the same time, Patterson went about creating the most aggressive sales force ever assembled, introduced guaranteed territories, and provided energetic advertising support. The sales staff worked on straight commission and were sent out to cover the country with cash registers.

His "never take no for an answer" tactics succeeded, and by 1910 his company was doing 90% of the country's cash register business. This disturbed both Patterson and the Justice Department; Patterson wondered why he wasn't getting the other 10%.

When Patterson's opposition-crushing tactics got to be too much, the government slapped him with an antitrust suit. He drew a $5,000 fine and a year in jail, but in the nick of time the 1913 Dayton flood surged to his rescue, inundating the city with as much as 18 feet of water. As always, Patterson rose to the occasion. He moved food, tents, medicine, and hospital equipment onto company property; set his assembly line to turning out one rowboat every seven minutes; and saved the city. Evangeline Cary Booth, commander-in-chief of the Salvation Army, called him an instrument of the Lord. His sentence was reversed, 20,000 Daytonians celebrated with a victory parade, and Patterson went back to his unconventional business ways.

When he died in 1922, things calmed down at National Cash Register until William Anderson, a British national who spent the World War II years in a Japanese prison camp, became the man in charge. By all accounts (and there have been many), he rescued the company from almost certain extinction. He became president in 1972, and by his own description he had only one mandate: "For Pete's sake, straighten it out." He came from Japan, where he had transformed National Cash Register's subsidiary into what *Fortune* called a "showcase," the most profitable of the company's 45 foreign units. In Dayton he struck quickly at what he called "complacency and apathy," announcing: "Until we see a return to profitability, something akin to martial law will be in effect in Dayton." In 1974 he changed the company's name to NCR. He reorganized all the divisions: Five high executives retired early, and 17,000 people were lopped off the payroll. Dayton was hit the hardest: National Cash Register employed 20,000 persons there in 1969; Anderson cut that force to 5,000 by 1977. When 120 salespeople walked out after their earnings were reduced or they were relocated, Anderson said: "I want to provide careers for people, not make them rich quick. This is not a Las Vegas operation."

Reputation. National Cash Register was known as a producer of business leaders, among them Thomas Watson, founder of IBM, and Charles F. Kettering of General Motors. They're also known as a company that relied too long on past reputation.

Who owns and runs the company. NCR president Anderson strives to build from within, but he recruited Charles E. Exley, Jr., from Burroughs in 1976 to take the president's post (Anderson had previously been

> Business and government combined generate about 9,700 pages per second of memos, letters, reports, and other data. Though almost all of this data is currently sent by mail or by hand, *Financial World* predicted in 1979 that more than $20 billion would be spent by 1985 to send an increasing portion of this information via telecommunications by using satellite and computer technologies.

president as well as chairman). Among the board members brought in by Anderson are William G. Bowen, president of Princeton University, Cathleen S. Morawetz, professor of mathematics at New York University, and John Horan, chairman of Merck.

In the public eye. John Patterson left his mark in Dayton. There's Patterson Boulevard, Wright-Patterson Air Force Base (the Wright brothers were born in Dayton), and a statue of Patterson on park land he donated to the city. But the paternalism that used to be National Cash Register's hallmark is fading under Anderson's leadership. One vice-president described how it was in the pre-Anderson days: "We had a living retirement program going on here. At the old NCR, if it was raining, you could get a company umbrella." NCR's 1978 annual report was strictly business, with the company stating the goal as the recruitment and development of "the best minds available in the marketplace."

Where they're going. To the rest of the world with their computers, terminals, and software. NCR was one of the first companies to establish a business relationship with the People's Republic of China. William Anderson was himself born in China.

Stock performance. NCR stock bought for $1,000 in 1970 sold for $863 on January 2, 1980.

Access. 1700 South Patterson Boulevard, Dayton, Ohio 45479; (513) 449-2000.

Consumer brands

NCR computers, cash registers.

TEXAS INSTRUMENTS
INCORPORATED

Sales: $3.2 billion
Profits: $173 million
Forbes 500 rank: 151
Rank in digital watches: 1
Rank in electronic calculators: 1
Founded: 1930
Employees: 78,571
Headquarters: Dallas, Texas

What they do. Texas Instruments has brought a little bit of Japan deep into the heart of Texas. This Dallas-based company, the world's largest maker of calculators and digital watches, not only has bested the Japanese in the fiercely competitive consumer electronics business, but it has done so by borrowing Japanese-style management techniques. They call it "TI culture," and it means hard work, long hours, and an almost fanatical loyalty to the company. "There is a strong tendency in the Japanese culture to align personal goals with goals set by their companies," explains president J. Fred Bucy, who has created the same sort of environment at Texas Instruments. Others have less benign explanations of TI culture: "The company looks at its people as being completely interchangeable, kind of like auto parts," a former executive told *Business Week.*

But the machine seems to work. Since entering the semiconductor business in 1952, Texas Instruments has been a driving force in developing and applying the technologies that allow today's $300 hand-held calculators to perform functions that 25 years ago would have required a $200,000, three-ton computer. At the heart of their business are semiconductor integrated circuits—tiny silicon chips imprinted with many thousands of connected bits of information—that are the building blocks for the electronics industry. Texas Instruments makes these circuits in the United States in Dallas, Lubbock, Sherman, and Stafford, Texas, and Attleboro, Massachusetts, and sells them to manufacturers who use them as the little brains in computers, radios, televisions, cameras, games, autos, and home appliances. Sales of these components make up about half of their business. Another quarter of sales comes from digital equipment for consumers and businesses: calculators, watches, hand-held translators that will spell and pronounce foreign words, computers for office and home. Texas Instruments also designs and makes guidance systems for missiles and infrared sights that enable tanks to spot and destroy enemies in the dark.

History. Texas Instruments got their start in that most Texan of enterprises, oil exploration, which still accounts for one-tenth of their business. The original company, Geophysical Service, Inc. (GSI), was started in 1930 by Clarence Karcher, who invented the technique of using sound waves to map underground strata, and Eugene McDermott, a scientist with Geophysical Research Corporation in Houston. When the outbreak of World War II slowed oil exploration, GSI—which had been making electronic seismic equipment—got a contract to manufacture submarine-detecting devices for the Navy. After the war they decided to stay in the electronics business; helped along by Cold War military spending, the company, renamed Texas Instruments, grew rapidly.

The real breakthrough came in the 1950s. Texas Instruments was the first company to make transistors cheap enough to be commercially useful in radios. Four years ahead of their competitors, they produced silicon transistors for military applications. In 1958 Jack St. Clair Kilby, a scientist with Texas Instruments, invented the integrated circuit, which paved the way to miniaturized electronic systems by eliminating the need for masses of separate transistors joined by a maze of wiring. These inven-

---

THE BIG FIVE CHIPMAKERS

Sales*

TEXAS INSTRUMENTS $1 *billion*
NATIONAL SEMICONDUCTOR $600 *million*
MOTOROLA $575 *million*
INTEL $425 *million*
FAIRCHILD CAMERA AND INSTRUMENT
(*Schlumberger*) $350 *million*

*1979 sales for integrated circuits for various electronics and computer uses.

Source: *Business Week,* April 14, 1980.

tions were the stepping-stones to the electronic revolution, and they allowed Texas Instruments to grow rapidly, even in the face of competition from giants like GE and RCA.

By deciding to concentrate on the consumer market, Texas Instruments has lost out as the industry's technological leader to the small companies in California's Silicon Valley. Like many Japanese companies, they specialize in applying technologies and finding markets for them. One of hundreds of companies that decided to make electronic calculators and watches in the early 1970s, Texas Instruments swept to the top by constantly discovering ways of making their products cheaper. In 1974 their lowest-priced calculator, which retailed for $45, contained 119 parts; a comparable model in 1980, put together by robot arms on an automated assembly line, had 17 parts and sold for $10. As prices dropped, so did most of Texas Instruments' competitors.

Reputation. Texas Instruments doesn't have to build plants in Taiwan or Hong Kong because they keep salaries and wages low in Texas.

What they own. Texas Instruments makes their products in 48 plants worldwide, but the heart of their consumer operations is in Texas. The major plants are in Austin, Abilene, Dallas, Houston, Lubbock, Midland-Odessa, and Temple.

Who owns and runs the company. "Everybody in that organization is either from Texas or just out of school," a former manager told *Business Week*. J. Fred Bucy, who became president in 1976 at age 47, fits the model perfectly. Joining the firm in 1953 just after getting a master's degree from the University of Texas, Bucy worked his way up the ladder to become head of the semiconductor division, where he managed Texas Instrument's jump into calculators. He sets the tone for the whole company by taking home three briefcases and working until midnight. The largest block of TI stock—8% of the total—is owned by the employee profit-sharing trust, and the Republic Bank of Dallas votes these shares "in accordance with the employee's wishes." The next largest chunks are held by J. P. Morgan & Co. (6%), and Prudential Insurance (5%). The company's directors and officers own a total of 4%.

In the public eye. Texas Instruments is the

Moronic Micro-Mouse Beats Maze

Tension knifed through the crowd of engineers and computer scientists as the electronic mice toed the starting line. Competition was stiff: finalists gleaned from some 6,000 of the world's fastest and smartest computerized mice, created by an even greater number of human luminaries in the arcane science of computer design. The event was unprecedented in human or mouse history. It was the Amazing Micro-Mouse Maze Contest, sponsored by the Institute of Electrical and Electronics Engineers. The challenge: to create a computerized mouse able to find its way faster than all its rivals through an intricate maze, using

programmed-in memory and logic to traverse the unfamiliar pathways.

In trial runs leading up to the final race in June 1979 at the National Computer Conference in New York, engineers unveiled their top electronic rodents. Some of the computer mice looked like mice, and some looked like computers. One was programmed to exclaim in a squeaky voice, "Oh, rats!" whenever it took a wrong turn and bumped into a wall. Some mice could "see" via optical sensing devices, and some had spring-loaded whiskers to help them feel their way along.

There was a brilliant mouse named Moonlight Special,

after the 500 hours of moonlighting six engineers from the Battelle Northwest Research Laboratories of Richland, Washington, had invested in its design and assembly. Moonlight Special had optical sensors and a sophisticated microcomputer "brain" that enabled it to learn from its own mistakes as it negotiated the maze.

There was also a brainy contender named Cattywampus, but it suffered from a flaw common to mice and men: it moved faster than it could think. In a trial run Cattywampus shot forward at blazing speed, smashing into a wall and missing a turn it knew perfectly well it should make.

nation's third-largest nonunion company (after IBM and Eastman Kodak). Executives say there is no union because the workers don't want one, and because, as with Japanese companies, employees are happy with fringe benefits like recreation centers. But labor organizers who have spent 25 years and $3 million trying to make inroads say there is no union because Texas Instruments has one of the most effective antiunion operations in the country. To find out who was right, the *Wall Street Journal* in 1978 sent a reporter, Beth Nissen, to work on a computer assembly line at the Austin plant. She found that though Texas Instruments employees were paid 25% less than comparable IBM workers across town and had to work mandatory overtime and two Saturdays a month, they were afraid to talk about a union. Many veteran workers told her prounion employees were identified and fired by management. The reporter didn't last long. Within three weeks (during which time she tried consistently to talk with fellow workers about unions), she was fired for having failed to list a B.A. degree on her job application.

Where they're going. Texas Instruments,

which had sales of just over $3 billion in 1979, is aiming for $10 billion by 1990. The product they are counting on most is the personal home computer, which will be adaptable to such uses as family budgeting, video games, home learning, and control of appliances and security alarms. In 1979 they received a $14 million grant from the Department of Energy to develop a new method of converting sunlight into electricity, which the *Wall Street Journal* said "could significantly brighten the outlook for solar power."

Stock performance. Texas Instruments stock bought for $1,000 in 1970 sold for $1,411 on January 2, 1980.

Major employment centers. Dallas and Houston, Texas; Attleboro, Massachusetts.

Access. 13500 North Central Expressway, Dallas, Texas 75265; (214) 238-4855. They have a toll-free number for questions or complaints: (800) 527-4980; in Texas, (800) 492-4298. They do not encourage plant tours by the public.

Consumer brands:

Texas Instruments calculators, watches.

A critical moment came during a prefinals trial, when the high-IQ Moonlight Special faced off against a dumb but fast mouse named Harvey Wallbanger. Harvey was programmed to make only right turns, hugging the right-hand wall of the maze at all times, a tactic that required no intelligence but allowed the dimwitted mouse to make up in speed what it lacked in contemplative ability. Although Harvey's route through the maze was by no means the shortest, Harvey beat the far brighter Moonlight Special. The wall-hugging simpleton, created by three Hewlett-Packard engineers, looked like a shoo-in for the championship—unless the Battelle team

could come up with something better before the final race.

Back in their laboratory, the Battelle men hastily assembled a new model: Moonlight Flash, a high-speed mouse with hardly any brains but with Harvey's wall-hugging inclinations, enhanced by optical sensors. While Harvey groped blindly along, the engineers figured, Flash could gain an edge by seeing where it was going.

On final race day the Battelle engineers entered not only Flash but an improved, genius-caliber version of their original Moonlight Special. The low-brow Flash beat not only its fellow dullard, Harvey, but also the brainy Moonlight

Special and a host of other gifted rodents.

Exactly what this boded for the future of mice or men was unclear, but it seemed to be a setback for computer scientists who predict that artificial intelligence may someday make even the human brain obsolete. In the Amazing Micro-Mouse race, brute speed and a single-track mind triumphed over wit, and the champion of computer mice turned out to be just another dumb jock.

Source: *Smithsonian,* March 1980.

9

MONEY: THE BUSINESS OF IT

Bankers

Sales: $9.4 billion
Profits: $600 million
Forbes 500 rank: 31
Rank in banking: 1
Founded: 1904
Employees: 76,000
Headquarters: San Francisco, California

What they do. After the Bank of America branch in Isla Vista, California, near the campus of the University of California at Santa Barbara, was burned to the ground in 1970, *Ramparts* magazine quoted a 17-year-old's explanation of the torching: "Well, it was . . . the biggest capitalist establishment thing around."

That's about the size of it. B of A is the world's largest bank—and therefore an inevitable target no matter what they do or don't do. But the behemoth of banking hasn't forgotten that they were once the small-change Bank of Italy, known in San Francisco's Italian district as "the little fellow's bank," derided by fancy financiers as "the Dago bank in North Beach." Long after they had outstripped all their competitors in the banking world, B of A still showed an unusual willingness to listen to criticism. Louis Lundborg, who was chairman when the Isla Vista branch went up in smoke, might have responded by denouncing all protestors as lunatics. But in his book, *Future Without Shock,* he described the soul-searching the incident provoked and concluded: "The violence must be rejected, but the dissent and protest must not be."

In the high echelons of U.S. banking, B of A has always been a little different. The first and perhaps fundamental difference is that they aren't from New York, or even Chicago. B of A is a western bank, and their success has had much to do with the rough-and-tumble growth of California into the richest, most populous state in the union. Founder A. P. Giannini knew the eastern aristocrats looked down on him, and he was eager to show Wall Street that his bank was a force to be reckoned with. Once he was humbled by New York's House of Morgan, and once he had to fight for control of his own company, which was being taken apart by a Wall Street financier he had trusted. When World War II made California the greatest boom state for defense industries and military bases, B of A boomed with it. Shortly after VJ Day, Giannini announced with satisfaction: "The West has all the money to finance whatever it wants to. We no longer have to go to New York for financing, and we're not at its mercy."

Reduced to the basics, banking is an absurdly simple business. A bank collects money—and then lends out this money. Its profit (or loss) results from the difference between what it has to pay for deposits and what it gets for lending out the money it has. Let's say you put $1,000 into a savings account paying annual interest of 5%. If the bank is able to lend your $1,000 at 10% interest, the bank will make $100 on your money—and give you $50—and pocket the other $50. Blessed by being in a large, populous state that has allowed statewide banking, the Bank of America enjoys easy access to lendable funds. In California you are never far from a B of A branch. They have 1,120 branches, twice as many as their nearest competitor in the state (Security Pacific). Aside perhaps from the Chevron gas stations of California Standard, the B of A has the most visible presence of any company in California. These B of A branches hold about 40% of all the deposits in California banks. In mid-1980 the B of A system had 4 million regular savings accounts, 3.3 million personal checking accounts, and 500,000 business checking accounts. So vast is the Bank of America that even though most people in the country may have never heard of it, they rank first in many categories. They have more deposits than any other bank or savings and loan. They're the largest lender to consumers. They're the largest real estate lender. They're the largest lender to farmers. They're the largest lender to small businesses under the guarantee program of the Small Business Administration. In 1979 they accounted for 25% of all the SBA loans in California. They're also the largest lender to college students trying to pay their tuition.

In 1979 the B of A became the first bank to make more than $600 million in one year. How they did it is clear from their balance sheet figures. On deposits they held for their customers, they paid average interest of 8%; on their loans they collected average interest of 12%—that's a "spread" of 4%.

It was 1945 when Bank of America passed up New York's Chase Manhattan to become the biggest bank in the world. They haven't looked back since. On top of their California base they built a strong international network second only to New York's Citibank. Their overseas branches increased from 12 in 1960 to 114 in 1979. One of their subsidiaries, Bank of America/New York, controls Banca D'America e d'Italia, which has 89 branches in Italy; and their Bamerical International Financial Corporation owns Bankhaus Centrale Credit, with 27 branches in West Germany and West Berlin. Other B of A subsidiaries have 353 offices in over 100 foreign countries.

When all those branches are rolled into one, they result in assets of more than $108 billion, making them the largest nongovernmental financial institution in the world (surpassed only by the Federal Reserve Banks of New York and Chicago). At the end of 1979 the bank had deposits of $85 billion and had $57 billion in outstanding loans to businesses, governments, and consumers. Part of the loans to consumers was extended through credit cards, of which the B of A is probably the largest issuer. At the end of 1979 they had 8.3 million Visa and Master Charge cardholders who had charged $4.3 billion of purchases during the year. And at the end of the year the balances due—on which the bank collected 18% interest—totaled $1.9 billion. There was even a startling poster at the 1979 Canton Trade Fair in the People's Republic of China—a blowup of the familiar credit card, with the message in English and Chinese: "BankAmericard/Visa welcome here."

B of A ranges along the whole spectrum of financial services: computer leasing and financial data processing (through Decimus Corporation), investment research (BA Investment Management Corporation), travelers checks (BA Cheque Corporation), and real estate investment (BankAmerica Realty Services). In 1973 they bought GAC Finance, one of the nation's largest consumer loan companies with 382 offices in the United States and Canada, but now (as you might have guessed) the company is called FinanceAmerica Corporation.

History. Amadeo Peter Giannini was born in San Jose, California (just south of San Francisco) in 1870, the son of Italian immigrants who had come to California to run a hotel. His father died when he was seven, and his mother married Lorenzo Scatena, a wholesale fruit and vegetable dealer. At 15 A. P. was working the San Francisco water-

THE TOP 25 BANKS

Company and Headquarters	Total Deposits (1979)	Total Loans (1979)
1. BANK OF AMERICA (San Francisco)	$85.0 billion	$57.6 billion
2. CITICORP (New York)	$70.3 billion	$63.0 billion
3. CHASE MANHATTAN (New York)	$48.5 billion	$40.2 billion
4. MANUFACTURERS HANOVER (New York)	$38.2 billion	$25.5 billion
5. J. P. MORGAN (New York)	$30.3 billion	$22.4 billion
6. CHEMICAL NEW YORK (New York)	$29.0 billion	$20.5 billion
7. CONTINENTAL ILLNOIS (Chicago)	$24.0 billion	$23.1 billion
8. BANKERS TRUST (New York)	$22.4 billion	$16.1 billion
9. FIRST CHICAGO	$21.1 billion	$15.7 billion
10. WESTERN BANCORP• (Los Angeles)	$23.6 billion	$17.0 billion
11. SECURITY PACIFIC (Los Angeles)	$18.5 billion	$16.3 billion
12. WELLS FARGO (San Francisco)	$15.8 billion	$14.9 billion
13. IRVING BANK (New York)	$13.5 billion	$ 7.4 billion
14. CROCKER NATIONAL (San Francisco)	$12.5 billion	$10.5 billion
15. MARINE MIDLAND (New York)	$12.5 billion	$ 9.1 billion
16. FIRST NATIONAL BOSTON	$ 9.0 billion	$ 7.1 billion
17. MELLON NATIONAL (Pittsburgh)	$ 9.5 billion	$ 6.9 billion
18. NORTHWEST BANCORP (Minneapolis)	$ 9.6 billion	$ 7.5 billion
19. FIRST BANK SYSTEM (Minneapolis)	$ 9.0 billion	$ 6.9 billion
20. FIRST INTERNATIONAL BANCSHARES (Dallas)	$ 8.9 billion	$ 5.9 billion
21. REPUBLIC OF TEXAS (Dallas)	$ 7.6 billion	$ 5.4 billion
22. NATIONAL DETROIT	$ 6.9 billion	$ 4.6 billion
23. FIRST CITY BANCORP (Houston)	$ 7.6 billion	$ 4.6 billion
24. TEXAS COMMERCE BANCSHARES (Houston)	$ 7.2 billion	$ 4.9 billion
25. BANK OF NEW YORK (New York)	$ 6.9 billion	$ 4.3 billion

•Western Bancorp is the holding company for UCB, and banks in 10 other Western states.

front for his stepfather, bidding on shiploads of beans, peas, corn, potatoes, and other staples, then carting them back to be sold to small retailers in the city's burgeoning Italian community. Giannini proved to be a brilliant merchant and wound up marrying the daughter of a wealthy Italian businessman. When his father-in-law died a few years later, Giannini inherited a seat on the board of a little savings bank in North Beach, hub of San Francisco's Italian neighborhood.

At 31 Giannini was able to retire and build his dream home in San Mateo, a few miles outside town. But his frequent battles with the conservative directors of the savings bank led him in 1904 to set up his own lending institution, the Bank of Italy. Giannini believed the banks in San Francisco worked to exclude smaller consumers from loans, and he began to lend amounts as small as $25—often on no more collateral than his gut feeling about the debtor's intent to repay. His belief in the honesty of his clients paid off, and soon the Bank of Italy was known as "The Little Fellow's Bank."

The great San Francisco earthquake became a signal event in the bank's history. Giannini salvaged more than $1 million in gold, currency, and notes from the bank's vaults while the raging flames from the huge fire that followed the quake were only three blocks away. He took the cash and paper to his house in the suburbs and buried the gold in his garden. While the major banks downtown could not gain access to their vaults for days after the catastrophe, Giannini set up a tent and desk on a pier and proclaimed that his Bank of Italy was open for business. The bank was in a marvelous position to lend money for the reconstruction of the 25,000 buildings destroyed by the quake and fire. In 1909, when the state of California changed its banking law to permit banks to open branches, Giannini immediately set up his first branch outside San Francisco, in San Jose. By 1918 he had opened 24 Bank of Italy branches. But in 1921 the Federal Reserve Board ruled that no bank belonging to the federal reserve system could open new branches. Giannini's haughty competitors laughed to see his ambitions thwarted, but Giannini skirted the federal order by buying the Bank of America of Los Angeles, which had 21 branches, by using a loophole in the federal mandate. By 1926 Giannini was powerful enough to force the defeat of California's incumbent governor in favor of his own candidate, C. C. Young, who supported expansion of branch banking. The federal reserve soon relaxed its restrictions, and branches of both Bank of Italy and Bank of America began popping up throughout the state.

In 1931 an ailing Giannini stepped down from the chairmanship to travel abroad, having first created a holding company, Transamerica Corporation, to oversee the operations of his banks, which had spread beyond California. He appointed a Wall Street investment banker named Elisha Walker to head Transamerica, but as soon as Giannini was gone, Walker repudiated the founder's policies and began to dismantle his empire. Giannini had not counted on Wall Street's abiding hatred for his upstart bank and had underestimated the loyalty Walker owed to New York's financial elite. On returning to California A. P. led a populist crusade to recapture his empire, gathering up proxies from small investors all over the state through town meetings in which he denounced the "Wall Street racketeers" who were attempting to atomize his "Little Fellow's Bank." Giannini won the battle, but the Depression led many to question the validity of his populism—especially when his banks foreclosed on many Little Fellows' farms and businesses. During the Depression Giannini profited from having supported Franklin D. Roosevelt, who had earned the hatred of the eastern banking establishment by attacking Wall Street's "unscrupulous money-changers" in his first inaugural address. When the time came to finance the great western dam-building projects of the 1930s, Bank of America (Giannini had now consolidated operations under one name) got the bid.

Attending one of his last board meetings in 1945, Giannini snapped at a vice-chairman who was reading a boring list of figures, "For God's sake, Franny, give 'em the big news!" That was the news that B of A had overtaken Chase Manhattan in assets. *Ramparts* summarized Transamerica's holdings at the peak of their power and the eventual breakup by government fiat: "By 1948, Transamerica Corporation controlled 645 banking offices in California, Oregon, Nevada, Arizona and Washington. This was 41 percent of all bank deposits and 50 percent of all bank loans. The conglomerate also controlled insurance companies, finance companies, real estate operations and business services. But at the instigation of the Eastern banking aristocracy, a Federal Reserve Board order in 1952 (reinforced by a Special Act of Congress in 1956) thwarted Giannini's old dream of building his branch banking coast-to-coast. Transamerica Corporation and Bank of America were separated, leaving the giant bank to build its future on its California base."

When A. P. Giannini died in 1949, the reins were taken by his son Mario, who had been in training virtually all his life and had served as president for 13 years. Mario expanded the bank's operations overseas, as did his successors through the 1950s and 1960s. By 1970 B of A had become a prime international lender, following in the footsteps of their eastern rival, Citibank. They had offices everywhere, including Saigon in South Vietnam. But the 1970 Isla Vista razing really rocked them. Shortly afterward Chairman Louis Lundborg came out against the war in testimony before Congress. Newspaper headlines blared: "B of A Chairman—'War a Mistake.' " A year later, at the 1971 annual meeting of shareholders in San Francisco, President A. W. Clausen scarcely mentioned financial news, dwelling instead on the bank's "determination to aid minorities, preserve the environment . . . and be a catalyst for change in the 1970s." It was a performance that led the liberal weekly, the *New Republic*, to identify the Bank of America as the "antiwar bank."

Since that time, under the leadership of Tom Clausen, they have tried, on the one hand, to expand their business in many directions while at the same time putting in place a formal social responsibility apparatus that is probably the most extensive of any company in the nation.

Reputation. Solid, big, respectable, stuffy —and anxious to please. Hanky-panky is not something even their severest critics would accuse them of. In the mid-1970s Clausen hired a speechwriter and told her: "I'm tired of the biggest financial institution in the world being thought of as a regional bank." The B of A has been crying: "Pay attention to me!" In the 1970s they even forgave Wall Street for past indignities by agreeing to have their shares listed on the New York Stock Exchange.

The 1970 torching of the Bank of America branch near the University of California at Santa Barbara shook up the management of the bank, setting in motion a reappraisal of their social role.

What they own. Most of what the bank has is owned by others. That's the nature of banking. They concede that they own "no significant real property." They do have $100 million invested in their 52-story headquarters building in San Francisco.

Who owns and runs the company. Tom Clausen, who has been in charge since the first day of 1970, is a grouch in the morning, hates to say hello before 10 A.M. coffee, but affirms that he's "very mellow" by late afternoon. Colleagues say he's a perfectionist (he agrees), a nitpicker, and a workaholic. He has brought topnotch people into the bank, and he's not too proud to go outside to recruit them.

The B of A is a management-run institution. An employee benefit plan is the largest stockholder, owning 6.8% of the shares. Next is an old eastern rival, J. P. Morgan, with 2.4%. The board of directors reads like a *Who's Who* of California's top business leaders: Roy L. Ash (AM International); C. R. Dahl (Crown Zellerbach); John R. Grey (Standard Oil of California); Walter A. Haas, Jr. (Levi Strauss); Prentis C. Hale and Philip M. Hawley (Carter Hawley Hale Stores); Franklin D. Murphy (Times Mirror); Peter O'Malley (Los Angeles Dodgers); Donn B. Tatum (Walt Disney). The board also includes a black, former Federal Reserve Board member Andrew F. Brimmer; a Hispanic, Ignacio E. Lozano, Jr., publisher of *La Opinion;* and two

women, Barbara M. White, president of Mills College, and Lucia R. Myers, Los Angeles community leader.

Clausen insists that "equitable treatment of all employees is a source of pride for us," and the B of A went a long way during the 1970s to demonstrate that commitment, partially to make up for what they had not done previously. In 1972, 27% of their middle management and above were women, 8.5% were minorities. At the beginning of 1980 women held 49% of the management posts, minorities 18%.

In the public eye. The Bank of America is periodically raked over the public coals by human rights advocates, especially for their investments in South Africa. At the 1978 annual meeting, for example, Clausen and chairman C. J. Medberry spent much of their time fielding questions from stockholders on the bank's South Africa policy. Clausen explained: "Corporations have no business peddling politics, even high-minded politics, in foreign countries. We must defer to the government of the U.S. in matters involving other sovereign states." The Bank had about $200 million in outstanding loans to the South African government at the time.

B of A had a long-standing policy of forbidding top bank officials to join the boards of other companies. Crisscrossing directorships posed obvious risks of conflict of interest: what happens when the "cousin" corporation comes knocking at B of A's door for a loan? But in 1979 they changed the policy, and the following year president Clausen joined the board of Standard Oil of California, while chairman Medberry became a director of Georgia Pacific, the giant forest products company. A vice-president admitted there was some risk, but said he was sure the bank would be "extremely careful." Clausen said the main reason for the switch was that the bank's top people were becoming too "insular."

In 1980, after six years of legal wrangling, a California court ordered the B of A to turn over to the state some $20 million in withheld interest and service charges on dormant savings accounts. These were accounts that had apparently been abandoned by depositors. The B of A's policy in dealing with them was to stop paying interest on the accounts—and then, when the funds were turned over to the state after seven years of inactivity, the bank imposed a service charge. A Superior Court judge called it "simply inconceivable" that the B of A would not only not pay interest but also levy a service fee when they were using these funds "to earn money for themselves."

Where they're going. The B of A is looking forward to the loosening of regulations on commercial banks so that they can compete more effectively against savings and loans and other financial institutions for savings accounts. And if they ever allowed banks to go national, B of A would be there right away; they already have the appropriate name.

Stock performance. Bank of America stock bought for $1,000 in 1970 sold for $1,713 on January 2, 1980.

Access. BankAmerica Center, San Francisco, California 94104; (415) 622-3456. The B of A is a formidable publisher. They have an excellent series on how different small businesses work. They issue an annual report on their social responsibility programs. Their corporate conduct code and equal employment report are made available. Write Box 37000, San Francisco, California, 94137.

CHASE

Sales: $6 billion
Profits: $303 million
Forbes 500 rank: 64
Rank in banking: 3
Founded: 1799
Employees: 32,500
Headquarters: New York, New York

What they do. In 1973, when the Russians decided to let American banks open offices in Moscow, no one, least of all David Rockefeller, was surprised that the first bank they invited was his own Chase Manhattan. "To some extent the Soviets have believed their own propaganda to the effect that a small group of families, including our own, really run this country, while the government is just sort of a front," Rockefeller told the *New York Times.* "Therefore, if they're going to have a relationship with the U.S., they probably wanted to deal with the people who they thought really had the power." Rockefeller, of course, does nothing to dispel this impression, and for good reason. His reputation for power helps salve the pain of remembering that under his tenure as chief executive, Chase, once the largest bank on Wall Street, has fallen far behind rival Citibank.

The 1970s were a time of troubles at Chase Manhattan. Hundreds of millions of dollars of loans went bad, and the bank suffered the ignominy of being put on the Federal Reserve's list of "problem" banks, banks that need special watching by federal regulators. In the United States Chase lost business from regional banks whose burgeoning resources made it less essential for them to borrow money from big banks like Chase, which has long been an important "banker's banker." And overseas, Chase had a hard time making headway against Citibank's aggressive operation. So what did Rockefeller do? He called a press conference one afternoon in October 1972 and announced the firing of president Herbert P. Patterson. "Somebody had to take the rap," a Wall Street observer told *Business Week,* "and it wasn't going to be the guy who owns the bank."

For all Chase's difficulties, it's not time yet to think of them as underdogs. The nation's third-largest bank, with 226 branch offices in New York state and 105 branches and 37 subsidiaries around the globe, Chase remains one of the wealthiest and most powerful financial institutions in the world. To the average New Yorker, his local Chase branch probably looks like just another bank: it will deposit his paycheck, hold his savings, or make him a loan to buy a car. But the fact of the matter is that the average customer isn't a very important part of the Chase operation. Indeed, in the late 1970s Chase closed 43 of their New York branches, deciding to concentrate their individual banking on higher-income communities. It gave a new meaning to the bank's long-used slogan, "You have a friend at Chase Manhattan." In 1979 they adopted a new slogan, "You have the Chase behind you."

The people who really have a friend at Chase are the financial managers of big corporations, banks, and governments. To corporations Chase makes big loans for new factories and small loans to help through tight spots. Chase also specializes in helping big multinational corporations—particularly oil companies—move their money around the world, changing it from dollars to yen to francs to take advantage of the fluctuations in currency markets. As a banker's banker both at home and abroad, Chase holds the deposits of other banks and makes loans to them so they can make deals that would otherwise exceed their more limited resources. And for foreign governments, Chase helps in marketing the bonds they issue and serves as a major investor in government bond offerings. They are also active overseas in financing government-to-government trade and making loans to foreign countries, including many of the debt-ridden nations of the Third World.

The closing of some of Chase's New York offices is also a sign that they see their future overseas. From 1974 to 1978 Chase's foreign income went from one half to nearly two-thirds of their total. But the Chase retains enormous clout at home, not only through their loans to major corporations but through their control of huge trusts and even larger pension funds, enabling them to trade and vote big blocks of stock in companies like Exxon, CBS, United Airlines, and IBM.

History. From its beginning nearly two centuries ago, David Rockefeller's bank has been as much a political as a financial institution. The Manhattan half of Chase Manhattan began in New York City in 1799 as the local water company. That year a group of civic leaders, headed by political rivals Alexander Hamilton and Aaron Burr, convinced the city council and the state legislature to authorize the creation of a private company, the Manhattan Company, to supply the city with pure water to combat an epidemic of yellow fever. But Burr, the schemer, was interested in more than just water. Unbeknownst to Hamilton, he slipped a clause into the law, authorizing the Manhattan Company to engage in other business if it had any surplus funds. What Burr had in mind was a bank to challenge the dominance of the Bank of New York and the Bank of the United States, both operated by Hamilton's Federalist friends. (Burr's duplicity fanned the fires of the Burr-Hamilton antagonism, which ended in 1804, when Burr killed Hamilton in a pistol duel at Weehawken, New Jersey, the same spot where Hamilton's son had been killed years before by another anti-Federalist.) Not surprisingly, the Manhattan Company almost immediately discovered that the water system would not require their entire capital, and within six months the Bank of the Manhattan Company was opened on Wall Street. The bank prospered, but the water operation floundered, and in 1808 the state legislature agreed to let the Manhattan Company jettison the water operation by selling it to the city.

The Chase National Bank, the other half of Chase Manhattan, was founded in New York in 1877 by a 75-year-old former school teacher, John Thompson, who named the bank after Salmon P. Chase, secretary of the treasury under Abraham Lincoln. The bank didn't become a great force on Wall Street, however, until Albert H. Wiggin took over as president in 1911. One of the era's leading bankers, he masterminded a 20-year surge of growth and mergers that made Chase the nation's leading lender to industry. Wiggin capped his career in 1930 by merging Chase with Equitable Trust, the nation's eighth-largest bank, owned by John D. Rockefeller, Jr., and run by his brother-in-law Winthrop Aldrich. Wiggin was made chairman of the new bank, then the world's biggest, but in 1934 he and his associates were disgraced when congressional investigators discovered that they had used bank funds to speculate in Chase stock.

Aldrich ended up at the helm and the Rockefellers were in control.

Under Aldrich Chase National further developed their overseas business. They were the first to open branches in defeated Germany and Japan after World War II. But with consumer branches only in Manhattan, Chase was not in a good position to tap the prosperity that had come to middle-class America in the postwar era. So in 1955 Chase merged with the Bank of Manhattan, the nation's 15th-largest bank, whose 67 branches in other boroughs of New York City perfectly complemented their operation. The chairman of the new Chase Manhattan bank was John J. McCloy, an oil lawyer and former U.S. high commissioner for occupied Germany, known on Wall Street as "the head of the Establishment."

Reputation. Once the largest bank in the world, Chase has faltered recently, losing their lead to Citibank and Bank of America. The Rockefeller name has a cachet in international finance that no other bank can match but David Rockefeller is about to retire from the banking world.

What they own. Chase's most valuable property is their 60-story headquarters building in the Wall Street area, erected in 1961. In the building David Rockefeller has collected 1,600 modern art works by Cezanne, Wyeth, Rothko, and the like, valued in 1972 at more than $3 million.

Who owns and runs the company. Although penetrating the maze of the Rockefeller family empire is difficult, it is estimated that they own about 5% of Chase. David Rockefeller personally owns about 1.7%, worth more than $25 million in mid-1980. Rockefeller came to work at the bank shortly after World War II, at the invitation of his uncle Winthrop Aldrich. The youngest of the five sons of John D. Rockefeller, Jr., and the only one of them to go into a business career, David served a brief apprenticeship in various Chase vice-presidencies before becoming president and co-chief executive in 1960. He moved up to the chairman's post in 1969.

But Rockefeller has never been interested in the day-to-day operations of Chase. He is a power broker on an international scale, a man who travels the world ceaselessly, meeting with presidents, prime ministers, kings, sheikhs, dictators, and executives of the most powerful corporations. To keep track of his contacts, he has a card file of 35,000 persons he calls his foreign "friends." Sometimes Wall Street analysts have wondered what this globetrotting has to do with banking, but for an institution like Chase, banking and the exercise of power are one and the same thing.

Willard C. Butcher, who became president in 1972 and chief executive officer in 1980, will succeed Rockefeller as chairman in April 1981, when Rockefeller retires. Butcher has worked for Chase since he graduated from Brown University in 1947.

The 22-member Chase board includes a black, former transportation secretary William T. Coleman; a woman, Norma T. Pace of the American Paper Institute; the president of the University of Notre Dame, Father Theodore M. Hesburgh, as well as a bunch of corporate chairmen and presidents.

In the public eye. Chase Manhattan's close association with U.S. foreign policy, and David Rockefeller's prominence as a moving force in the Council of Foreign Relations and the Trilateral Commission, two pillars of the foreign policy establishment, have inevitably drawn the bank into controversy. In 1966 Rockefeller, a strong supporter of the Vietnam War, journeyed to Saigon to open a new Chase branch, a granite and sandstone fortress designed to withstand mine explosions and mortar attacks. The move triggered protests against the bank. So did Chase's 1965 decision to buy a major share in the second-largest bank in South Africa, which provoked picketing by civil rights groups and a campaign to convince individuals and institutions to pull their funds out of banks, like Chase, that supported the apartheid regime.

Chase's most controversial moment, however, came in 1979, when Rockefeller and Henry Kissinger, chairman of the bank's international advisory committee, put strong pressure on the Carter Administration to let the former shah of Iran into the United States. The shah had been Chase's best customer in the Middle East: according to one former Chase official, Iran's oil money deposits at Chase amounted in 1975 to $2.5 billion, or almost 8% of the bank's total deposits. When Rockefeller managed to persuade the government to admit the former shah, the Iranian government retaliated by announcing they would shift their deposits to other banks. However, Washington soon moved to protect Chase by freezing all Iranian assets in American banks. The shah had a friend at Chase Manhattan, and Rockefeller still has friends in Washington.

Chase, along with other big-city banks, has greatly increased their employment of minorities and upgraded their women into higher-level positions, but according to a 1976 study by the Council of Economic Priorities, Chase ranked 21st among 24 big banks in the country in their utilization of women. However, they were fourth in utilization of minorities, ranking only behind Crocker National, National Bank of Detroit, and Manufacturers Hanover.

Where they're going. Chase intends to speak out more on behalf of free enterprise (in case someone thought they were deserting to the other side). In 1980 both Rockefeller and Butcher endorsed this kind of approach, with Butcher saying: "It is unfortunate that in the last few decades, socialism has gained at the expense of private initiative and individual freedom in many parts of the world." Butcher also said Chase intends to work more on what he called "the quality of our relationship management," meaning, how we treat our customers. "Banking is a profession," asserted Butcher. "Is price the only reason you use a particular doctor or lawyer?"

Stock performance. Chase Manhattan stock bought for $1,000 in 1970 sold for $742 on January 2, 1980.

Access. 1 Chase Manhattan Plaza, New York, New York 10081; (212) 552-2222.

"As of January 23, 1980, there were $107.4 billion in U.S. currency and coins around the world. This equals about 2 percent of the amount of credit (approximately $5 trillion) outstanding in the United States alone, and is roughly equal to the reported assets of our largest bank (Bank of America or Citibank)."

—*Business and Society Review,* Spring 1980.

CITICORP✦

Sales: $10.9 billion
Profits: $541 million
Forbes 500 rank: 26
Rank in banking: 2
Founded: 1812
Employees: 51,600
Headquarters: New York, New York

What they do. Banks are stuffy, dignified, and oh so cautious—but at Citicorp they've broken the mold. Citicorp, owner of New York's First National City Bank, better known as Citibank, is all the things a bank is not supposed to be: adventurous, aggressive, daring. They don't have the Bank of America's stately airs or the high visibility that David Rockefeller brings to Chase Manhattan. What they have is a no-nonsense chief executive, Walter Wriston, and a team of young managers who have propelled Citicorp nearly to the top of the banking world: they now sit just behind Bank of America as the second-largest bank in the country. In 1978 Citibank held 4% of all the money on deposit with U.S. banks— $1 out of every $25. Only the Bank of America has more money in deposits, but Citibank lends out more money than the B of A: $63 billion versus $57 billion in 1979. They were able to do it because (1) they have the bulk of their deposits overseas, where loans tend to be big ones made to governments and multinational companies, (2) they have long had greater entree than the B of A to the big corporate borrowers, and (3) they have always been aggressive lenders (with the loan losses to show for it). The B of A may make more auto and home loans, but Citibank will make more loans for factories, mines, and other industrial developments. Walter Wriston would probably add another reason: "We're smarter."

Citibank is based in New York, but their turf is the world. With 840 banking offices in 92 foreign countries, they are by far the largest U.S. bank overseas. They have 75% of their deposits overseas, and for some time now they have been deriving more than two-thirds of their profits from international activities. In 1979, for example, Citibank had about $8 billion of loans outstanding to governments and their agencies. And they had another $9 billion out in loans to multinational corporations. Their

Visitors to the St. Francis Hotel in San Francisco get change in clean coins. That's because the hotel has a coin-washing machine in the basement. Here's coin washer Arnold Batliner putting a new load through. He says: "Pennies are the hardest to wash."

loans have financed such projects as a copper mine in the Philippines, a sugar refinery in Venezuela, a cattle ranch in Morocco, a steel mill in South Korea, a railroad in Gabon, and a geothermal energy project in Iceland. Their overseas activities range from consumer loans in Colombia to a computer service company in Hong Kong. They're the leading bank in the business of trading foreign currencies: for a fee they'll help you trade your dollars for any of 50 foreign currencies. The first U.S. national bank to go into the foreign market, Citicorp is today reaping an especially rich harvest in Saudi Arabia, where they were the first U.S. bank allowed. Asked by *Fortune* about the size of their Saudi deposits, Citicorp's chief international banker replied, "Just enough."

At home they're a tough competitor too. With 270 branch banks in the New York City area and 31 in upstate New York, Citibank aggressively goes after the savings and checking accounts of New Yorkers. Most offices have an automated teller that lets customers make deposits or cash checks 24 hours a day. Citibank is also experimenting with totally automated electronic banking kiosks for suburban shopping centers. Although federal law prohibits them from opening branches in other states, they have used their travelers check and credit card operations to reach across the nation. Some 80% of their Visa and Master Charge customers live outside New York state. And they go head-to-head with American Express in peddling their own Carte Blanche travel card and Citicorp travelers checks.

Citibank is currently in the midst of a major push to expand their consumer business, here and abroad. If there's money somewhere, Wriston wants it. He looks forward to the era of electronic banking, when Citibank will be able to do business anywhere in the country without having a physical presence outside New York.

History. Citibank's origins go back to founder Colonel Samuel Osgood—a close friend of George Washington and the nation's first postmaster general, a captain of the Minute Men, and the first commissioner of the U.S. Treasury. Formed as the City Bank of New York to replace the local branch of the defunct First Bank of the United States, the bank immediately pumped $1 million in subscriptions into government war loans to back the War of 1812, an unpopular cause among Federalist financiers in New England. In the early years the bank mainly served commercial interests: cotton, sugar, metal, and coal merchants. During the Civil War, when Congress established the first national banking system to create a uniform currency and a market for selling government bonds, the bank became the National City Bank of New York. The president at the time, Moses Taylor, also served as the treasurer of the company that laid the first transatlantic telegraph cable in 1866, which vastly aided international trade. The bank adopted the cable address of Citibank. As American businessmen came to believe that the key to prosperity was expansion into foreign markets, National City helped lead the way. In the early twentieth century bank president Frank A. Vanderlip lobbied strenuously to change regulations so that federally chartered banks could open branches overseas. Vanderlip won his fight in 1913, when Congress passed the Federal Reserve Act. The next year National City became the first U.S. national bank to open a foreign branch—in Buenos Aires—and in 1915 they became a worldwide banking empire when they bought the International Banking Corporation, with offices from London to Singapore.

At the same time, Citibank was pioneering in modern retail banking in the United States. Until the 1920s commercial banks did most of their business with corporations. Few people had checking accounts, and individual savers went to savings banks. But in 1921 Citibank began opening new branches to attract individuals, and in 1928 they became the first commercial bank to offer personal loans to consumers. In the 1950s and 1960s Citibank aggressively expanded their retail banking by following customers in their exodus to the suburbs. (The president during this period was James Stillman Rockefeller. Like their rival Chase Manhattan, Citibank was once part of the Rockefeller empire. William Rockefeller, younger brother of John D. Rockefeller and a cofounder of Standard Oil, became a major stockholder in the bank in the late nineteenth century and backed James Stillman, who was made president in 1891 and remained as chairman of the board until 1918. Stillman's daughter married Rockefeller's son, who begot James Stillman Rockefeller. Citibank overtook his cousin David Rockefeller's Chase Manhattan Bank in 1972.)

Citibank merged with the First National Bank of the City of New York in 1955 to become the First National City Bank. In 1961, under the guidance of vice-president (and later chairman) Walter Wriston, Citibank invented the certificate of deposit, with which depositors could get a higher interest rate on their deposits by agreeing to leave them for specified lengths of time. The bank's purpose was to lure back money that had gone off in search of higher returns from government bonds. In a coals-to-Newcastle move in 1963 they became the first U.S. bank to open a branch in Switzerland.

In 1968 Citibank started a major new trend among big banks when they created a "holding company," Citicorp, to take over ownership of the bank. The move allowed them to expand into several new areas, such as leasing, where federal law barred banks from operating—but said nothing about holding companies that happen to own a bank. Within six months several other banking giants formed holding companies of their own, including the Bank of America, Chase Manhattan, Manufacturers Hanover, Morgan Guaranty, and Chemical Bank.

Despite their huge size, Citibank has never been particularly well known in the United States outside New York City. The first time many Americans may have heard of them was in the late 1970s, when Citibank decided to go after the nation's credit card business in a big way. They blanketed the nation with 26 million offers of Visa and Master Charge cards—in the process angering many other banks who also issue the cards. A lot of people took them up on it: by 1980 nearly 6 million Americans held bank cards issued by Citibank. And Citibank had found a way to tap business outside their home state.

Reputation. Wall Street's nickname for Citibank is "Fat City," and they call Walter Wriston the banker's banker. But during New York's financial crisis in the 1970s, some people were bitter that the banks were profiting from the city's catastrophe. Matthew Troy, chairman of the New York City Council's finance committee, told the *Village Voice*'s Jack Newfield in 1975, "The bankers are bastards, and First National City Bank is the biggest bastard."

In his book *The Bankers*, published in 1974, Martin Mayer reported: "A First National City branch abroad has the same flavor as a First National City division in the United States—the same hard-driving, bright, vain people at the helm."

What they own. Citibank accounts for about 90% of Citicorp's business. Other businesses include Carte Blanche; Nationwide Financial Services, a consumer finance company; Citicorp Leasing, which leases aircraft (outside of airlines, they are the biggest owners of planes) and heavy equipment; and various consumer finance companies in Europe, Asia, and Latin America.

Citicorp's headquarters in New York City is a 39-story building on Park Avenue at 54th Street, but in 1978 they completed a 59-story tower, Citicorp Center, just across Lexington Avenue. The new building, shrouded in aluminum, pops out of the New York skyline in the early dawn when it glows with the first rays of sunlight. Viewed from the east or west, its roof has the shape of a right triangle—the building was supposed to have been heated and cooled by solar energy, but it didn't work out. At the ground level there's a three-story shopping bazaar with international restaurants, a bookshop, bakery, candy store, tobacconist, and other amenities. Hunkered under the tower is St. Peter's Lutheran Church, an ultramodern edifice that replaced the original structure, which had been on the block since 1907. Citicorp owns about 200 buildings around the world.

Who owns and runs the company. The man who has set the tone for Citibank's aggressiveness and derring do in recent years is Walter Bigelow Wriston, who became president in 1968 and chairman in 1970. Rated by fellow financiers as the most influential private banker in the country, he has earned the respect of colleagues by hiring the best Ivy League graduates and then pushing them to perform. His father, Henry M. Wriston, was president of Brown University for years. The younger Wriston got a master's degree from the Fletcher School of International Law and Diplomacy at Tufts University and served in the State Department during World War II. He started at Citibank in 1946. Tall, deepvoiced, bedecked with angular eyebrows, Wriston is known as a hard taskmaster with an acerbic tongue. In 1975 he expounded his philosophy at some length in an interview with *New York* magazine:

To understand the banking system in America, you have to understand the history of America. The country was settled with a wagon train. Every time the train stopped, four guys got off, built a city, and started a bank. That's why you've got 14,000 banks in this country, the only country in the world without nationwide banking.

The fundamental reason why banks built Taj Mahals was that the people figured their money was safe. The modern generation forgets that 1,000 banks failed in the city of Chicago in one week. But the Depression generation is still around and remembers, so banks traditionally build these enormous buildings —early Post Office modern—to look strong and forbidding. This didn't help the shareholders much, and the customers didn't particularly like it. So we began to market test mini-branches—storefronts is the political term for them —a room the size of this office, two girls, a counter, and a hotline to the computer. They perform the services that people want. They want to be able to cash a check, get a personal loan to buy a car, put a roof on their house, or pay the hospital bill, you name it. We don't pretend that this is the place where the treasurer of Esso goes to get a loan on oil reserves in Dubai—no way. These are community-oriented personal banking service branches. And instead of putting in a capital of a couple of million dollars, what you do is put in a very small capital, sort of a Robert Hall low-overhead operation, and hope that that supplies the services the community wants. That's brand new.

People who work in Citibank and Citicorp bleed when you stick 'em, their kids get sick, they've got financial problems, they're just as hot in the subway as you are, just as frustrated with the sales and income tax, pollution in the river, and the incinerator doesn't work. The fact that I go to work here and you go to work someplace else doesn't change our environ-

Vermonters vs. Banking

Long after it joined the Union, the state of Vermont refused to allow banks to operate within its borders. Bills to permit banks in Vermont were repeatedly introduced in the state legislature and as often defeated. In 1803, Vermont's governor offered the following rationale for keeping the banks out: Banks, by facilitating enterprises, both hazardous and unjustifiable, are natural sources of all that class of vices, which arise from the gambling system, and which cannot fail to act as sure and fatal, though slow, poisons to the republic in which they exist. . . . Banks tend strongly to draw off the dependence of debtors from their own exertions as means of payment, and to place it on the facility of increasing new debts to discharge the old. . . . Banks have a violent tendency, in their natural operation, to draw into the hands of the few a large proportion of the property at present fortunately diffused among the many. The tendency of banks seems to be to weaken the great pillars of a republican government, and at the same time to increase the forces employed for its overthrow. . . . As banks will credit none but persons of affluence, those who are in the greatest need of help cannot expect to be directly accommodated by them.

Source: Edward Hoagland, *Walking the Dead Diamond River* (Warner, 1974).

ment. As a citizen of the city and the country, my motives are the same as yours.

Citicorp's board of directors is about as powerful a group as you're ever likely to find gathered in one place at one time. In 1980 they included the chairmen of Exxon, Standard Oil of California, Du Pont, Xerox, Monsanto, Union Pacific, Kimberly-Clark, United Technologies, J. C. Penney, and Corning Glass Works; a former chairman of AT&T; a former secretary of the treasury, William E. Simon; a former member of the British House of Lords, Lord Aldington; a former minister of finance of Brazil (Citibank's biggest overseas profit center); one Harvard business professor; two women, Juanita M. Kreps, the former secretary of

commerce, and Eleanor H. B. Sheldon, former president of the Social Science Research Council; and one black, Franklin A. Thomas, president of the Ford Foundation. Citicorp's top executives sit on the boards of such giant companies as General Electric, J. C. Penney, United Technologies, Beatrice Foods, and Sears, Roebuck.

Bankers are a pretty anonymous group by and large, but not Citicorp's. Their 1979 annual report to stockholders included four pages of color photographs of their top management people, with a biographical paragraph on each one. There's a secret room at Citicorp where Wriston has tacked on the wall dozens of pictures of Citibank middle managers whom he calls "corporate property," meaning that they have been identified as the up-and-coming stars.

Unclaimed $25 Billion

Some $25 billion in "lost" money languishes in the coffers of banks, insurance companies, utilities, and other corporations because the rightful owners don't know it's there. These depositors, policyholders, and shareholders could get their money simply by showing up to demand it, but chances are that most of them will never learn it exists. The corporations that hold these forgotten funds are not exactly straining themselves trying to track down the owners.

In 1979 journalist Bonnie Goldstein checked into the fate of these lost funds. She found, among other things, that a California bank owed Bob Hope and Lucille Ball money they had left in old accounts. According to the bank, neither of these customers could be reached. "Obviously, it wasn't looking very hard," remarked Goldstein in an article for The Washington Monthly.

Naturally if private corporations got to keep all this loot indefinitely, they would have

no incentive to seek its owners. Aware of this snag, all the states have passed laws requiring companies to turn over unclaimed funds to the state treasury, usually after seven years. The money goes into the state's general revenues, where the government supposedly keeps it safe and sound until its owners appear.

How hard do states try to find the owners of forgotten money? Not very. Efforts to locate owners are mostly token gestures, such as putting small-print ads in the back pages of local newspapers. New York, which got $45 million in unclaimed cash in 1978 and earned another $9 million in interest on its booty, advertises for owners in an obscure publication called the New York State Register. Of course, if any of the people whose money the government is holding happened to turn up at the state treasury to ask for it, the state would hand it over. But someone who doesn't remember he has $500 coming from an insurance company

he paid premiums to for years isn't likely to drop by the treasurer's office to demand the cash. Meanwhile, states manage to return only about 11% of the funds in their care.

Why is the money forgotten in the first place? Banks wind up with a lot of unclaimed cash because of social mobility. People move, leaving small accounts behind. But banks don't simply let the money sit—the owners might show up to claim it, or the state will ultimately scoop it up. To hang onto this treasure trove, banks have cleverly devised ways of annexing the cash for themselves. The most common strategy is unadvertised "service charges" on dormant accounts, which drain them of their money. The Bank of America has helped themselves to $14–20 million this way. At the First National Bank of Boston they have a different system: money in all inactive accounts of less than $42 is automatically transferred into the general bank-

In the public eye. Ralph Nader catapulted Citibank into the news in 1971, when a study group of his charged the institution with siphoning off funds from poor neighborhoods, "taking money from those who can least afford it and giving it to those who need it the least." In a 547-page study Nader's group charged that Citibank snubbed people who needed home mortgages, disregarded New York's desperate fiscal plight while reaping benefit from municipal activities, paid their low-level people poorly, and generally ran "a slovenly but ever-expanding operation."

Citibank lashed back, claiming the Nader report contained many glaring inconsistencies and was built on basic misconceptions about the role of banking. Chairman Wriston charged that the report "largely ignored the vast store of information provided to the study group through interviews that lasted hundreds of hours and cost the bank many thousands of dollars." When the Nader group continued their probe with a study of Citibank's trust department, Wriston issued a memo to the bank's 37,000 employees, ordering them not to talk to Nader's people. In 1974 the Nader group issued an expanded report in book form, titled *Citibank*, written by David Leinsdorf and Donald Etra. The book concluded among other things that trust departments, which manage pension funds, should be split off from commercial banks. Wriston called the book "basically a retread."

The Securities and Exchange Commission began an investigation of Citibank in

---

ing fund where it can be used to make loans on which the banks make money.

Insurance companies have other ways of keeping people's forgotten funds. "Rather than count on people to forget about their money, insurers often simply don't tell them about it in the first place," Goldstein found. Kenneth Leon of Baltimore, for example, became a life insurance beneficiary when he was one week old. His parents, who bought the policy, evidently never told him about it. For 19 years they paid premiums, building up a cash value of $550.60. When they quit paying because of financial setbacks, Metropolitan Life sent notices that the policy had lapsed. But the company never bothered to nofity Leon that he was entitled to the $550.60.

Uncashed dividend checks are a third kind of lost money. When a shareholder fails to cash a dividend check, the funds are treated like unclaimed bank deposits. Corporations, like banks, are sup-posed to turn over money from uncashed dividends to the state after seven years, but the government suspects this doesn't always happen. Several firms, including J. C. Penney and Standard Oil of California, have refused to open their books to government auditors who want to check for unclaimed dividend money.

States, like banks, insurers, and other corporations, justify keeping unclaimed cash on the ground that it's impractical to track down all the people who have it coming. To test this, Goldstein looked up some of these people herself. Scanning names at the Maryland Department of Miscellaneous Revenues, which maintains lists of owners, she picked 15, after eliminating "the obvious toughies, like 'Cub Pack 14' or the 'Volunteer Fireman's Christmas Club.' "

With no more than two-and-a-half hours' work, Goldstein had reached almost half the people on her list and advised them how to collect a previously unclaimed $3,100. One of the people she telephoned was a 69-year-old retired hospital janitor who didn't know he had $1,000 coming from a life insurance policy.

Goldstein found 7 of the 15 simply by using the phone book. Her biggest effort, she reported, was walking to the Library of Congress to get an old Baltimore city directory, which led her to a pastor who had moved from a Baltimore church to one in Wilmington, Delaware. That case took only 20 minutes to solve; the others, even less.

"If, in my little experiment, I managed to return almost half the money owed in a few hours, what could a state—with its access to official records—do? One suspects a good faith search could easily be financed out of the interest the states earn on the unclaimed funds," contended Goldstein.

Source: *The Washington Monthly,* July/August 1979.

Dow Jones Averages:
What Are They Talking About?

"The Dow Jones Industrial Average fell 10 points to hit this week's low of 850." Thus TV and radio news commentators provide Americans with what is often their only piece of daily information about the business world.

Though the Dow Jones Industrial average relates to the behavior of the stock market, it does not describe what happened that day to all stocks sold on the market, nor does a change of one point in the Dow Jones average mean that stocks had risen or fallen an average of one point (one dollar) in value. In fact, the Dow Jones Industrial average is the most imprecise of three measurements of day-to-day stock market activity. But the Dow Jones is by far the most popular among news media, partly because of its age (created in 1897) and because the Dow Jones company publishes the most widely circulated business newspaper in the country, the *Wall Street Journal*.

There are actually four Dow Jones stock averages — one for 30 industrial corporations, and others for 20 transportations, 15 utilities, and a combined average of all 65 stocks. When created in 1897 the Industrials average used only 12 companies, and the average was computed by adding the prices of the 12 stocks and dividing by 12. Since that time other stocks have been added and subtracted from the list (the most recent change was the replacement of Anaconda by 3M in 1976). Through the years many of the companies have "split" their stocks to make it easier to purchase them. In other words, if a stock is reduced from $40 to $20 a share ("split 2-for-1"), the stock is then selling for only half of its original price though its actual value has not changed (there are twice as many shares so the stockholders are just as well off as before the split). Because there have been so many splits in the past 80 years, the prices of the 30 industrial stocks are no longer

divided by 30 but by a figure closer to 1.4. Mathematically that means that the Industrials average is far higher than the actual average price of the shares on the stock exchange (in 1979 the average stock cost $29.20).

Because of dissatisfaction with the Dow Jones averages, Standard & Poor's, a large stock research organization, developed their own stock average based on 500 stocks (that acounted for about 86% of the total value of the nearly 1,500 stocks traded on the New York Stock Exchange). Using high-speed computers, the Standard & Poor's 500-stock index is much more scientific because, besides representing a wider spectrum of stocks, it takes into account the total number of shares of stock that each company offers, thus giving more weight to companies with larger numbers of shares like AT&T.

The New York Stock Exchange got into the act themselves in 1966 when they began publishing their own index based on all of the stocks traded on the exchange. Part of the impetus for their action was their feeling that the public was being misled by headlines that proclaimed that the Dow Jones had dropped by 20 points when the average share of stock only lost about 50 cents. Though the Standard & Poor's and NYSE indices are more precise, it's a rare day that the three don't move in the same direction.

Here are the stocks used in the Dow Jones averages:

Dow Jones Industrial
Average stocks:

Allied Chemical
Alcoa
American Brands
American Can
AT & T
Bethlehem Steel
Chrysler
DuPont
Eastman Kodak
Esmark
Exxon

General Electric
General Foods
General Motors
Goodyear
Inco
International Harvester
International Paper
Johns-Manville
3M
Owens-Illinois
Procter & Gamble
Sears Roebuck
Standard Oil of California
Texaco
Union Carbide
United Technologies
U.S. Steel
Westinghouse Electric
Woolworth.

Dow Jones Transportation
Average stocks:

American Airlines
Burlington Northern
Canadian Pacific
Chessie System
Consolidated Freightways
Eastern Air Lines
McLean Trucking
Missouri Pacific
Norfolk & Western
Northwest Airlines
Pan Am
St. Louis San Francisco
Santa Fe
Seaboard Coast
Southern Pacific
Southern Railway
Transway International
TWA
United Airlines
Union Pacific.

Dow Jones Utilities
Average stocks:

American Electric Power
Cleveland Electric
Columbia Gas Systems
Commonwealth Edison
Consolidated Edison
Consolidated Natural Gas
Detroit Edison
Houston Industries
Niagara Mohawk Power
Pacific Gas & Electric
Panhandle Eastern Pipeline
Philadelphia Electric
Peoples Gas
Public Service E&G
Southern California Edison.

1980, the *Wall Street Journal* reported, based on "allegations that the bank evaded European taxes and violated foreign exchange laws in certain countries." The allegations stemmed from a $14 million suit filed by David Edwards, a former officer in Citibank's European money trading division, who charged that the bank on several occasions had illegally shifted profits arising from currency-exchange transactions out of branches in Paris, Milan, Frankfurt, and other European cities into a branch in Nassau that Citibank maintained as a tax haven. Edwards's suit charged that the bank had wrongfully fired him despite a company policy that calls on employees to report illegalities. Citibank denied any wrongdoing but acknowledged that they had undertaken a study of their own into the affair.

In March 1980 10 Protestant and Roman Catholic agencies with combined investment portfolios of $250 million said they would no longer do business with Citibank, "America's largest lender to South Africa."

Where they're going. To South Dakota. They planned to move their credit card operation (2,500 employees) out of New York in 1980 to escape their home state's "usury laws," which limit interest rates on unpaid balances. South Dakota allows a maximum rate of 24% on the first $500 outstanding and 18% on the rest, whereas New York limits the annual maximum charge to 18% on the first $500 and 12% on the balance.

Citibank announced a new service in 1979: an art investment program, in conjunction with the Sotheby Parke Bernet auction galleries, by which their more well-heeled clients can make wise decisions on purchasing valuable works of art. As Citibank explains, "It has long been a practice of some wealthy people to preserve their assets by putting about 10% of their net worth, exclusive of real estate, into works of art and other tangible articles. Inflation is causing more Americans to adopt this same investment strategy." Of course, they don't believe just anybody should start tying up large chunks of money for several years in art works. They said they would "suggest this strategy only to customers who are prepared to invest $1,000,000." For their troubles they charge an annual fee of 2% of the value of the portfolio. That's $20,000 on their $1 million minimum. And they intend to reappraise their customers' collections periodically.

Stock performance. Citicorp stock bought for $1,000 in 1970 sold for $1,450 on January 2, 1980.

Access. 399 Park Avenue, New York, New York 10043; (212) 559-0349.

CONTINENTAL BANK
CONTINENTAL ILLINOIS NATIONAL BANK AND TRUST COMPANY OF CHICAGO

Sales: $3.4 billion
Profits: $196 million
Forbes 500 rank: 140
Rank in banking: 7
Founded: 1857
Employees: 10,132
Headquarters: Chicago, Illinois

What they do. Continental Illinois is banker to the industrial heavyweights of the Midwest and, increasingly, of the world. They're the largest bank between New York and San Francisco. But if you want to open an account or take out a loan at Continental, you have to go to 231 La Salle Street in downtown Chicago. That's because, although federal law says a bank can open branches throughout one state, some states—Illinois is one—have limited banks to just one office. Colorado is another state where branch banking is not allowed, and in 1980 James P. Thomas, executive manager of the Independent Bankers of Colorado, explained why: "The populists that framed the state constitution in 1877 wanted to make sure you could look your banker straight in the eye."

Since Continental couldn't go after the deposits of millions of individuals all over Illinois, they looked around for other sources of growth, and in the 1960s and 1970s they made an all-out effort to get the business of large corporations—especially the multinationals. By 1979 they had more than 100 offices in 39 countries, serving some 420 multinational corporations. If their international department were split off, it would rank by itself as Chicago's third largest bank. Their New York subsidiary, Continental Bank International, is one of the leading forces in the foreign exchange market. Continental offers Chicago consumers all the usual banking services, from checking accounts to Visa and Master Charge cards, but their main attention goes to their big-business customers, both at home and abroad.

History. Continental Illinois, offspring of a series of bank mergers in the 1920s and early 1930s, traces their lineage back to the Merchants' Saving, Loan and Trust Company, which started in Chicago in 1857. Twice in their early years they narrowly escaped disaster. In October 1871 the great Chicago fire burned through the city, destroying the bank's offices and all their records, but it didn't reach their cash and securities. Then in the 1930s Continental was almost sunk by the Great Depression; only an infusion of $50 million from the federal government's Reconstruction Finance Corporation kept them afloat.

The man who guided Continental through the shoals of the Depression was Walter J. Cummings, sent in by Reconstruction Finance to look after the government's money. Cummings's conservative, low-risk policies were just what Continental needed during the Depression, but they didn't suit the prosperous postwar years, when Continental's growth lagged. In 1959, at age 80, Cummings stepped aside in favor of David M. Kennedy. Over the next 10 years Kennedy, in the words of the *New York Times*, "transformed a hidebound, hyperconservative bank into one of the most dynamic and progressive forces in American banking." He set out to encourage loans to corporations, telling his loan officers to stop worrying so much about risk and start thinking about growth. He also launched Continental into international banking, which now accounts for about a fifth of their business. These aggressive policies spurred new growth and helped Kennedy land a spot as Richard Nixon's secretary of the treasury.

No sooner had Kennedy gotten his government job in early 1969 than he was assailed by Wright Patman, head of the House Banking Committee, who attacked Kennedy's ownership of more than $1.2 million worth of Continental Illinois stock as a conflict of interest with his duties as treasury secretary. (The veteran Texas congressman had waged a similar battle against Treasury Secretary Andrew Mellon in 1932, starting impeachment proceedings that led to Mellon's resignation.) Kennedy

Credit cards are made out of polyvinyl chloride, a plastic with many industrial uses. It takes one gallon of crude oil to manufacture 20 credit cards. In 1979, 20 million gallons were used to supply credit cards to the United States.

sold the stock. Nixon later replaced him with nonbanker John Connally.

Reputation. An energetic newcomer to the international banking scene, Continental Illinois is making competitors forget what they thought they knew about stodgy midwestern bankers.

Who owns and runs the company. The board of directors of Continental Illinois reads like a roll call of the Midwest's industrial giants. There are representatives from Deere, Commonwealth Edison, Inland Steel, Esmark, Borg-Warner, FMC, International Harvester, Standard Oil of Indiana, Sears, Chicago Bridge & Iron, DE-KALB AgResearch, and IC Industries (owner of the Illinois Central Railroad). The board includes a black woman, Chicago attorney Jewel S. Lafontant, former U.S. deputy solicitor general, and a Jesuit priest, the Rev. Raymond C. Baumhart, president of Loyola University of Chicago.

Continental Illinois has had one of the worst records of any big commercial bank in the placement of minorities and women in upper-level positions. A 1971 study by the Council on Economic Priorities ranked Continental eleventh among 24 major commercial banks in minorities in higher-level jobs; when this study was updated in 1975, Continental slipped to 15th place. The 1971 study ranked Continental 15th in their proportion of women in managerial positions; by 1975 Continental had slipped to 22nd. It wasn't until the late 1960s that Continental allowed women in their executive dining room.

In the public eye. Continental is one of the few banks in the nation to release a regular report on their "social responsibility activities." In 1977 and 1978, they reported, they spent $10.5 million in "social investments." They have taken a leading role in urban redevelopment in Chicago, especially in the rundown areas bordering the downtown

Continental Illinois may have only one place of doing business on Chicago's
La Salle Street—but it's quite a place.

district. One of their pet projects is Little
Village, a neighborhood on the near southwest side; in March 1979 Neighborhood
Housing Services opened an office there.
NHS is a nonprofit corporation, with more
than 40 offices around the country, whose
goal is to revitalize and rebuild deteriorating inner-city neighborhoods. Continental
Bank has given the Little Village project
$375,000 to be used over a five-year period.
It is the first NHS site in the country to be
funded entirely by one institution.

Continental is one of the largest lenders
to South Africa. Five Protestant and Catholic religious organizations, which own over
10,000 shares in the corporation, have sponsored resolutions at annual meetings since
1977 asking for full disclosure of loans to
South Africa and "how each reported loan
category contributed to the well-being of
the black majority and their struggle for
full political, social and economic equality."
The bank's official view is that "the promotion of trade and investment and the support of economic development within
South Africa will prove to be a most important vehicle for correction of the problem of
apartheid." The church groups' requests
have been overwhelmingly rejected at
stockholder meetings.

The Air Line Pilots Association sued
Continental in 1973 on behalf of some 6,000
United Air Lines pilots whose pension
fund the bank had managed. The suit
charged that the bank had lost $7 million of
the pilots' money in the late 1960s and early
1970s by investing in stocks of companies to
which Continental had made substantial
loans, including Penn Central, the railroad
that went bankrupt. The pilots yanked
their fund out of Continental in 1971.

Stock performance. Continental Illinois
stock bought for $1,000 in 1970 sold for
$1,800 on January 2, 1980.

Access. 231 LaSalle Street, Chicago, Illinois 60693; (312) 828-2345. The main bank
building is available for tour; call (312) 828-
4506.

> Every day U.S. consumers report the
> loss of 30,000 credit cards. Approxi-
> mately 1 million of the 15.4 million
> cards lost yearly are stolen and used
> to ring up $400 million in unautho-
> rized charges.

J. P. Morgan & Co.

Sales: $3.6 billion
Profits: $288 million
Forbes 500 rank: 129
Rank in banking: 5
Rank in trust holdings: 1
Founded: 1839
Employees: 10,287
Headquarters: New York, New York

What they do. J. P. Morgan is America's largest stockholder. With more than $15 billion invested in the stock market, Morgan holds nearly 2% of all the stock owned by Americans. They're one of the top five investors in more than 50 major corporations, including ITT, Sears, American Express, Bank of America, and Citicorp.

The banking part of the operation, which accounts for 95% of the company's business, is called Morgan Guaranty Trust. In the words of the *Washington Post,* Morgan Guaranty occupies the "precise center, geographical as well as metaphorical, of financial America and even of the financial world." The Morgan bank has been implanted on the corner of Wall and Broad Streets, next door to the New York Stock Exchange, since 1873. The institution's seven-foot thick concrete foundation extends straight down to bedrock, and the Morgan bank is as steady as their foundation.

Morgan is a commercial bank, but they don't spend their time issuing automobile and home loans to the average person off the street. They do provide personal checking and other banking services to about 14,000 well-heeled customers, who must keep a minimum of $5,000 in their checking accounts—but Morgan doesn't solicit their business. Instead, Morgan serves corporations, governments, foundations, and institutions at home and abroad. More than $20 billion a day pass through the bank in the form of oil company payments to oil countries, foreign currency sales, loans to multinational corporations, or purchase of treasury bills. Morgan has lent money to build nuclear power plants in Spain, mine coal in the American Midwest, and, in one of the largest bank loans ever ($943 million in 1972), drill oil in the North Sea.

The center of Morgan's power is their trust department, which holds and manages the money of more than 7,500 individuals, estates, and large institutions, such as universities and corporations. Much of the money Morgan holds in trust consists of the pension and profit-sharing funds of companies like General Motors and Mobil. Unlike most other banks, Morgan accepts a trust account only on the condition that Morgan gets full authority to invest the money as they see fit. Morgan's customers are in the hands of the bank's portfolio managers (those who decide which stocks to buy and sell, and when). From behind their roll-top desks in Morgan's trust department offices on New York's Fifth Avenue, the 50 portfolio managers work closely with 45 research analysts in managing some $25 billion of other people's money.

Morgan's presence in the stock market can be overwhelming. During the course of 1974, Dan Rottenberg reported in the *New York Times,* Morgan's trust department bought nearly two-fifths of all the Goodyear Tire stock purchased on the New York Stock Exchange; nearly one-fifth of Sterling Drug, Gillette, and Marriott; and one-tenth of International Paper. At the same time, they sold about one-seventh of all the Baxter Laboratories and Schlumberger stock sold that year, as well as more than one-tenth of Upjohn and Howard Johnson.

What all this buying and selling presence means is *power.* Certain key Morgan managers have the authority to make what Morgan calls "global decisions" to buy or sell on behalf of all of Morgan's pension funds. "Because of the sheer size of Morgan's orders," Rottenberg related, "it often takes days, weeks or even months to buy or sell the shares it wants. In 1970, Morgan made a global decision to buy Du Pont, which was then selling at $110. When the price rose to $185, a global decision was made to sell it. The stock continued to climb to about $200, then began to fall. When it fell below $150, Morgan simply stopped selling it and waited for the price to rise again, whereupon Morgan resumed selling Du Pont. This cycle repeated itself several times, and it took two years for Morgan to complete its selling of Du Pont. But by its patience it was able to come away from the experience with an average sale price of $175."

Morgan also helps companies plan and negotiate mergers and acquisitions with other companies. They transfer stocks for 1,000 American corporations. In other words, if you buy a stock in one of these companies, you receive the stock certificate

J.P. Morgan Board of Directors

WALTER H. PAGE Chairman of J. P. Morgan and director of Merck.

LEWIS T. PRESTON President of J. P. Morgan and director of General Electric.

RAY C. ADAM Chairman of NL Industries, and director of American Broadcasting, Cities Service, Metropolitan Life Insurance.

J. PAUL AUSTIN Chairman of Coca-Cola, and director of Dow Jones, Federated Department Stores, General Electric, Southern Mills, Trust Company of Georgia.

JAMES O. BOISI Vice chairman of J. P. Morgan and director of Cities Service.

R. MANNING BROWN, JR. Chairman of New York Life Insurance, and director of Associated Dry Goods, Avon, Louisiana Land & Exploration, Union Camp, Union Carbide.

CARTER L. BURGESS Chairman of Foreign Policy Association, and director of Ford Motor, GAF, Kennecott Copper, Roanoke Electric Steel, SmithKline.

FRANK T. CARY Chairman of IBM, and director of American Broadcasting, Merck.

EMILIO G. COLLADO President of Adela Investment, former executive vice president of Exxon, and director of Discount Corporation of New York, Republic Management.

CHARLES D. DICKEY, JR. Chairman of Scott Paper, and director of British Columbia Forest Products, General Electric, INA.

JOHN T. DORRANCE, JR. Chairman of Campbell Soup, and director of Carter Hawley Hale, the Penn Mutual Life, Vlasic Foods.

WALTER A. FALLON Chairman of Eastman Kodak, and director of General Motors and Rochester Gas and Electric.

LEWIS W. FOY Chairman of Bethlehem Steel, and director of Brinco, Goodyear Tire & Rubber, Metropolitan Life.

HANNA H. GRAY President of the University of Chicago, and director of Cummins Engine.

ALAN GREENSPAN President of Townsend-Greenspan and Company, former chairman of the President's Council of Economic Advisers, and director of Alcoa, General Foods, and Mobil.

HOWARD W. JOHNSON Chairman of the Corporation of Massachusetts Institute of Technology, and director of Champion International, Du Pont, Federated Department Stores, John Hancock Mutual Life.

EDWARD R. KANE President of Du Pont.

JAMES L. KETELSEN Chairman of Tenneco.

ROBERT V. LINDSAY Chairman of the Executive Committee of Morgan and director of the Chubb Corp. and St. Joe Minerals.

HOWARD J. MORGENS Chairman emeritus of Procter & Gamble, and director of General Motors, Communications Satellite.

ELLMORE C. PATTERSON Former chairman of the Executive Committee of J. P. Morgan and director of Engelhard Hanovia, the Atchison, Topeka and Santa Fe Ry., Bethlehem Steel, Communications Satellite, Federal Reserve Bank of New York, General Motors, Santa Fe Industries, Standard Brands, and Schlumberger.

DONALD E. PROCKNOW President of Western Electric, and director of Bell Telephone, CPC International, Ingersoll-Rand, Prudential Insurance.

WARREN M. SHAPLEIGH Vice chairman of Ralston Purina, and director of Brown Group, First National Bank of St. Louis, Midland Container, Missouri Pacific, Tidewater, St. Louis Union Trust.

GEORGE P. SCHULTZ President of Bechtel, and director of Sears Roebuck.

DENNIS WEATHERSTONE Vice chairman of J. P. Morgan.

Source: J. P. Morgan proxy statement, March 12, 1979; Standard & Poor's Register of Corporate Directors, 1980.

and any dividend checks from Morgan. When you sell the stock, Morgan also records that information for the company. Morgan does more stock transfers than anyone else in the world. They allocate 10 floors of a building and 1,000 employees for just this purpose.

Morgan does a little over half their business abroad, mostly in the industrialized nations—but they've also made substantial loans to developing nations in the Middle East, Africa, southern Europe, and South America.

History. Morgan's preference for investing in huge corporations rather than financing home mortgages and auto loans comes directly from their founder. J. Pierpont Morgan, wrote E. L. Doctorow in *Ragtime:*

was that classic American hero, a man born to extreme wealth who by dint of hard work and ruthlessness multiplies the family fortune till it is out of sight. He controlled 741 directorships in 112 corporations. He had once arranged a loan to the United States Government that had saved it from bankruptcy. He had single-handedly stopped the panic of 1907 by arranging for the importation of one hundred million dollars in gold bullion. Moving about in private railroad cars or yachts he crossed all borders and was at home everywhere in the world. He was a monarch of the invisible, transnational kingdom of capital whose sovereignty was everywhere granted. Commanding resources that beggared royal fortunes, he was a revolutionist who left to presidents and kings their territory while he took control of their railroads

They Know Who Owns America

"Who Owns America?" is an interesting question that hardly anyone asks any more.

An exception is a New York–based nonprofit organization, Corporate Data Exchange (CDE), whose main mission in life is to ask and answer that question.

In 1980 CDE issued the third in a series of manuals detailing the ownership of major American companies. The first two covered the transportation and food industries. The third one tackles banking and finance, reporting on 240 companies —commercial banks, savings and loan associations, insurance companies, investment managers, small and large loan companies.

So who does own the Bank of America, the nation's largest bank? You turn to that page in the CDE manual and find that the largest holder, with 7% of the shares, is the bank itself as trustee for the employee benefit plan. The second-biggest holder, with 2.4% of the shares, is New York's J. P. Morgan. In third place, with 1.7%, is New York's Citibank, the nation's second-largest bank.

There's something curious right away. The Bank of America and Citibank are supposed to be bitter rivals for first place in banking, but the people who invest Citibank's money feel so highly about the Bank of America they own a big chunk of the stock.

Next you turn to the Citibank page—actually Citicorp, for the holding company where the bank is lodged— and you discover that the largest holder is J. P. Morgan: they have 4.1% of the shares.

So you turn next to the nation's third-largest bank,

THE TOP THREE INTERNATIONAL CREDIT CARD COMPANIES 1978		
	Number of Cards in Circulation	Volume of Charges
1. VISA	73.9 *million*	$29.0 *billion*
2. INTERBANK (*MasterCharge*)	68.8 *million*	$27.6 *billion*
3. AMERICAN EXPRESS	9.5 *million*	$12.4 *billion*

and shipping lines, banks and trust companies, industrial plants and public utilities.

Morgan was not a self-made man. His father, Junius Spencer Morgan, made a fortune as a banker in the London firm that was the predecessor of Morgan Grenfell (Morgan Guaranty still owns 31% of that bank). J. P. opened his own foreign exchange office in 1860, at age 24. According to Lewis Corey in *The House of Morgan*, his office grew successful not because he was a financial wizard and speculator like Andrew Carnegie and John D. Rockefeller, but because he knew how to organize and pick good partners. He believed that "men owning property should do as they like with it." What he liked to do was put together corporate monopolies. Among his creations were the U.S. Steel, International Nickel, General Electric, and Western Union combines. Morgan personally disliked Rockefeller and Carnegie, both of whom he considered had humiliated and swindled him. Morgan liked to employ handsome young men in his bank, and he liked to dally with pretty young women on his vacations. He was never at a loss for admirers despite an unfortunate physical characteristic: a bulbous red nose, the result of a chronic skin disease that had haunted him since early manhood.

In 1912, the year before his death, Morgan testified before the House Committee on Banking and Currency, which was attempting to prove that Morgan, with many interlocking directorates and financial ties, had a stranglehold on the American economy. Morgan professed bewilderment. The

Chase Manhattan, and at least here you get some flesh-and-blood people. Chase's employee plan holds the largest block of stock—2.8%—but the second-biggest owners are the Rockefellers, with 2.4% (this is David Rockefeller's bank, remember).

New York's Manufacturers Hanover—known in the business as "Manny Hanny"—ranks fourth in the nation in asset size, and here, too, the employee profit-sharing plan ranks first, with 7.4% of the shares; good old J. P. Morgan is second (2.7%) and Citibank fourth (2.6%).

J. P. Morgan, whose bank name is Morgan Guaranty Trust, turns up on nearly all these rosters. It is the fifth-largest bank in the country. So who owns it? The CDE breakdown shows the largest holder to be the Baltimore mutual fund manager T. Rowe Price, with 3% of the shares, followed by First National Bank of Boston (2.7%), Chase Manhattan (2.6%), and Citibank (2.6%).

If you think this is beginning to look a little like incest, you're right. Who owns the banks? Why, the other banks. They own each other. They buy each other's stock. The Morgan people own 4.2% of the largest bank in Arizona, Valley National; 2.5% of the largest bank in the Midwest, Continental Illinois; 1.9% of the largest bank in Texas, First International Bankshares; and 2.3% of Northwest Bancorp of Minneapolis, owner of 84 banks in seven midwestern states.

CDE finds all these interlocking patterns wicked, suggesting that they raise "serious antitrust implications." Another interpretation is that it's more mindlessness than conspiracy at work. Large pools of money collect at the same place, and they're traded back and forth.

CDE does perform a service, however, by laying it out for us. And they do point to some bizarre consequences. For example:

•The pension funds of U.S.

Steel and Bethlehem Steel have a total of $133 million invested in the stock of Citibank, Chemical Bank, Continental Illinois, the Mellon Bank, Western Bancorp, First Chicago, Wells Fargo, J. P. Morgan, Security Pacific, and Rainier Bancorp.

•These 10 banks have loaned $593 million to Japanese steel companies.

•American steel companies—and the United Steelworkers union—have complained about Japanese steel imports throwing Americans out of jobs.

•So the retirement funds of American steelworkers are being used to support banks whose lending helps Japanese companies drive the steelworkers out of jobs.

You see what happens when you ask "Who owns America?"

Copies of CDE manuals are for sale from CDE, Room 707, 198 Broadway, New York, New York 10038.

driving force in the world of finance, he maintained, was not money but character.

"Is not commercial credit based primarily upon money or property?" asked the committee's lawyer.

"No, sir," Morgan responded. "The first thing is character. . . . Because a man I do not trust could not get money from me on all the bonds in Christendom."

Pierpont's son, J. P. Morgan, Jr., took his father's place in 1913. The younger Morgan organized the merger of several public utilities into United Corporation and of food companies into Standard Brands in 1929. That same year, the National Bank of Commerce of New York, which had been founded in 1839 in a basement on Wall Street, merged into Guaranty Trust of New York. Guaranty Trust and J. P. Morgan later merged in 1959.

Today the J. P. Morgan company acts as a holding company for the Morgan Guaranty Trust and five subsidiaries that provide international loans, construction funds, government investments, and accounting services to the bank. The bank does not spend extra money on branches or employees. Outside of their five Manhattan offices, they have only two others in the country—in San Francisco and Houston. They have only one-fifth as many employees as Citicorp, but they make $1 in profit for every $2 that Walter Wriston's bank makes.

Reputation. The stuffiest of the stuffy. Writer Andrew Tobias once quoted a Wall Street financial analyst as saying, "Morgan is the only company left that moves from the office at 4:30 to tea at the Racquet Club at five. They have more preppies per employee than anyone else in town." As of 1973, according to Tobias, all but 3 of Morgan's top 14 officers had gone to Harvard, Yale, or Princeton. Morgan has a slogan to describe themselves: "First-class people doing first-class business in a first-class way." But Tobias notes that, their snobbish self-appraisal aside, "no one disputes that they are a first-class bank."

What they own. Their total assets were $43.5 billion at the end of 1979. But Morgan's huge blocks of stock belong to their clients, for the most part, not to the bank. They have 28 offices in Europe, Asia, and South America, and they hold a 50% interest in Bank Morgan Labouchere of Holland. They have lesser interests in banks

J. Pierpont Morgan, founder of the Morgan Bank, and his son, J. P. Morgan, Jr., who succeeded him as head of the bank in 1913.

and businesses in 34 foreign countries in Europe, South America, Asia, and the Middle East.

Who owns and runs the company. In 1929, when J. P. Morgan, Jr., headed the bank, his 18 partners held 99 directorships in 72 corporations. Today the 25 directors hold 86 directorships in about 70 corporations, which include Du Pont, General Motors, Mobil, General Electric, Ford Motor, Union Carbide, Goodyear, General Foods, ABC, Kennecott, Merck, and Sears, Roebuck.

Among the all-white Morgan directors in 1979 were the chairmen of Coca-Cola, New York Life Insurance, IBM, Scott Paper, Campbell Soup, Eastman Kodak, Bethlehem Steel, Tenneco, and the Massachusetts Institute of Technology; George P. Shultz, the president of Bechtel and former secretary of the treasury; Alan Greenspan, former chairman of the President's Council of Economic Advisers; Carter L. Burgess, chairman of the Foreign Policy Association; and one woman, Hanna H. Gray, president of the University of Chicago.

A Morgan family connection still exists through Walter H. Page, who became chairman in 1978 and is married to J. P. Morgan's granddaughter Jane. Most of the top shareholders in Morgan are banks and insurance companies. For instance, in 1977 First National Boston had 2.8%, Chase Manhattan 2.6%, and Citicorp 2.6% of the stock. But the top owner, with 3%, was the Baltimore mutual fund manager, T. Rowe Price.

Some of the advantages of working at Morgan include free lunches five days a week, five-week vacations, the services of three resident doctors, and a profit-sharing plan that can boost earnings by 15%.

In the public eye. Morgan has funded Shakespeare plays on public television as well as neighborhood rehabilitation in the Bedford-Stuyvesant area of Brooklyn and in the Bronx. They were the first bank to initiate an assistance program to a black business school (Atlantic University) in 1973. They provided a $300,000 grant and experts, and hired students for summer work-study at their New York headquarters. Morgan also assists minority contractors in obtaining loans and bonds.

Despite several shareholder resolutions sponsored in the last few years, Morgan refuses to curtail loans and investments in such countries as South Africa and Saudi Arabia. In fact, as chairman Page observed in the *Washington Post*, "Hardly a day goes by when there isn't somebody from Morgan Guaranty in Saudi Arabia."

Where they're going. Federal guidelines announced in 1980 that restrict the amount of money banks can lend could result in even more power for the banks. Small businesses may lose out as banks become more selective about granting loans. One Morgan executive told the *New York Times*, "We will become the arbiters of who gets money and who doesn't." One indication of who Morgan thinks should get the money came in May 1980, when 13 banks headed by Morgan and the First National Bank of Dallas approved a loan of $1.1 billion to Herbert and Nelson Hunt, the sons of billionaire oilman H. L. Hunt, whose plans to corner the world's silver market had backfired not long before.

Stock performance. J. P. Morgan stock bought for $1,000 in 1970 sold for $1,564 on January 2, 1980.

Access. 23 Wall Street, New York, New York 10015; (212) 483-2323.

THE TOP LIFE INSURERS

If you started a new life insurance company and took in $1 million a day from your policyholders, you still wouldn't rank among the top 25 life insurers in the nation. The following are the 15 life insurers who collected more than $1 billion in 1979 from their policyholders. The figures are what the insurers call their premium income.

1.	PRUDENTIAL	$8.0 *billion*
2.	METROPOLITAN LIFE	$5.9 *billion*
3.	AETNA	$4.7 *billion*
4.	EQUITABLE LIFE	$4.6 *billion*
5.	TRAVELERS	$3.6 *billion*
6.	NEW YORK LIFE	$2.6 *billion*
7.	CONNECTICUT GENERAL	$2.4 *billion*
8.	JOHN HANCOCK	$2.2 *billion*
9.	BANKERS LIFE	$1.4 *billion*
10.	LINCOLN NATIONAL	$1.3 *billion*
11.	NORTHWESTERN MUTUAL	$1.2 *billion*
12.	MASSACHUSETTS MUTUAL	$1.2 *billion*
13.	TEACHERS (*TIA*)	$1.1 *billion*
14.	OCCIDENTAL LIFE	$1.0 *billion*
15.	MUTUAL OF NEW YORK	$1.0 *billion*

Insurance Sellers

LIFE & CASUALTY

Sales: $11.4 billion
Profits: $560 million
Forbes 500 rank: 23
Rank in health insurance: 1
Rank in casualty-property insurance: 3
Rank in life insurance: 4
Founded: 1853
Employees: 37,540
Headquarters: Hartford, Connecticut

What they do. Aetna Life & Casualty will insure anything human, anything that moves (autos, boats, planes), or anything that stands in one place (homes, factories, offices, and so on). They are the world's number 1 "multiple-line" insurance company, peddling every kind of insurance under the sun, and in 1979 they took in more than $9 billion in premiums. They are the largest health insurance company, writing about 7% of all the health policies in the United States, many of them through group plans taken out by the employees of other companies. In 1979 their Aetna Life subsidiary sold more life insurance than all but two other companies: Prudential and Metropolitan Life. They're ahead of well-known names like Connecticut General, Travelers, and Mutual of New York.

How many Aetna insurance policies are there? About 35 million at the end of 1979. These policies are sold through independent agencies and brokers—there are about 24,000 of them in the United States. Aetna maintains 660 field offices across the country—and the majority of Aetna employees work in these offices. Nearly a third of Aetna employees work in the home office at Hartford.

Aetna differs from the big mutual life insurers (Prudential, the Met, Equitable), which are owned by their own policyholders. Aetna is a stock company, owned by people who buy Aetna stock on the New York Stock Exchange. Aetna is the nation's largest stock insurance company.

Aetna gets their revenues from two main sources. One is, of course, premiums—the money people pay to maintain their policy. But the other big flow comes from investment income. The money Aetna collects from policyholders gets invested, primarily in bonds, mortgages, and common stocks. During 1979 Aetna had around $25 billion to play around with—and their financial division has 725 employees who do the playing. In 1979 their income from investments totaled $2 billion, which exceeded the total sales of such companies as Polaroid, Revlon, McDonald's, and Quaker Oats.

Aetna's cash machine has also spilled into noninsurance businesses. They're real estate developers on their own (they own one of California's largest home builders, Ponderosa Homes), they're lenders to business through Aetna Business Credit, and they own chunks of other businesses, including 32% of Geosource, a company that helps others to find oil, and 30% of the New England Whalers, an ice hockey team. In 1979 Aetna made profits of $31 million from what they call "diversified business" (meaning noninsurance).

History. In 1850 a Hartford businessman and jurist named Eliphalet Bulkeley formed The Annuity Fund as a subsidiary to the Aetna Fire Insurance Company, which had been doing business in New England since 1819. The Annuity Fund sold life insurance to New Englanders until 1853, when Bulkeley and a few investors branched off and made the Fund into a separate company. One of the prime motivations for the split was a New York State law that said life insurance could not be carried out by a fire insurance company. So Aetna started out as a life insurer—and got back into property insurance business later.

Aetna survived in a period when a number of other companies were going broke, mostly because Bulkeley was committed to slow growth—determined not to sell more insurance than claims might force them to pay off. The company also established a reputation for prompt payment of claims. Their first claim, in 1851 (when Aetna was still called the Annuity Fund), took only two-and-a-half months to pay—in spite of the fact that it had taken nearly two months for the news to reach Hartford that the insured man had died of a fever contracted in the jungles of Panama. Another key factor in their early growth was a high-powered sales drive engineered by Dr. Thomas B. Lacey, who began as the company's medical examiner and then traveled across the country enlisting agents to sell the Aetna policies. He's regarded as the "father" of Aetna's agency system.

Bulkeley died in 1872 and was succeeded by Thomas Ostrom Enders, the company's chief administrator. It was Enders who introduced "participating" policies in which dividends were returned to policyholders based on investment earnings. When Enders died in 1879, the next Aetna president was Morgan Bulkeley, the son of the company's founder. Under his leadership, which lasted for 43 years, Aetna began offering many different kinds of insurance. They began writing accident insurance in 1891, health insurance in 1899, workmen's compensation in 1902, and automobile insurance in 1907.

Aetna and Morgan Bulkeley were also major factors in the history of Hartford and the state of Connecticut. While serving as president of Aetna, Bulkeley was also mayor of Hartford for three terms (1879–87), governor of Connecticut for four years (1887–91), and a U.S. Senator from Connecticut (1905–11). And Aetna also contributed to the Hartford skyline their home office building, near the state capitol. The headquarters, with a tower similar to that of Independence Hall in Philadelphia, is the largest building of colonial design in the world.

Aetna's fourth president was Morgan

Bulkeley Brainard, grandson of founder Eliphalet Bulkeley and nephew of Morgan Bulkeley. He succeeded his uncle in 1922 and proceeded to reign until 1955. His conservative policies paid off. When the 1929 stock market crash occurred, Aetna had only 12% of their assets in common stocks. And during the Depression farm foreclosures turned them into big property owners.

Brainard moved Aetna into the writing of group insurance for companies. By the time he retired Aetna was collecting more than $300 million a year in group premiums.

Much of the company's recent history was intertwined with the social and economic problems confronting the nation. Under Olcott Smith, chairman from 1963 to 1972, and John Filer, chairman since then, Aetna expanded mightily in many directions, and they also developed programs that identified Aetna as a company concerned with the social problems of the United States. The question is: could they do otherwise? When the cities were burning in the 1960s, one of the largest fire insurers was Aetna.

Reputation. One of the giants of the insurance industry, they're known as a company that makes a good try at merging profit motives with social responsibility considerations.

What they own. $13 billion worth of bonds, $7 billion of mortgage loans, $1 billion of preferred stocks, $650 million of common stocks. They have also joined with IBM and Comsat General to form Satellite Business Systems, designed to compete against AT&T in the telecommunications business.

Who owns and runs the company. When John H. Filer got the nod to head the company in 1972, there was a sigh of relief among people who were rooting for a social responsibility type as against a business type. A native of New Haven, Connecticut, and a Yale Law School graduate, Filer has been closely identified with "do good" efforts, both within Aetna and outside the company. From 1973 to 1975 he headed up the Rockefeller-funded Commission on Private Philanthropy and Public Needs, an inquiry into charity that became known as the "Filer Commission." One of its recommendations was for corporations to increase sharply their giving (a move that Aetna has made).

On Aetna's board are two women, Beryl Robichaud, a senior vice-president of McGraw-Hill, and Barbara Hackman Franklin, a senior fellow at the University of Pennsylvania's Wharton School and a former senior commissioner of the U.S. Consumer Product Safety Commission; and a black attorney, Hobart Taylor, Jr. David M. Roderick, chairman of U.S. Steel,

sits on Aetna's board, and Filer sits on his board.

As of mid-1980 the largest shareholder in Aetna was Los Angeles-based Teledyne, a conglomerate built by ex-Littonite Henry Singleton. Teledyne owns insurance companies, and these companies had accumulated 5% of all Aetna's shares.

In the public eye. Aetna stirred up some controversy in the late 1970s, when they began a campaign of print advertising criti-

The Brooklyn Carp's Revenge

Aetna Life & Casualty, like other insurance companies, is resigned to the reality that the unexpected and incredible will happen to at least some of its policyholders. Still, even the minds of seasoned claims adjusters can be boggled. The company pays tribute to their most bizarre claims by issuing a list of them each year as a press release. On April Fools' Day, 1980, Aetna sent out a decade's gleanings of these gems of improbability, of which the following are typical:

A butcher's helper tried to collect from his employers, claiming it was his boss's fault he broke his leg falling over a frozen rooster. The butcher, charged the helper, started a fracas by hitting him with a petrified duck after an argument. Acting in self-defense, the helper retaliated with a frozen turkey leg. As the fight escalated, dozens of fowl were brought into play as weapons, then discarded on the floor. Stumbling over the litter of frosted birds, the helper tripped on the gelid cockerel, falling fractured to the floor.

Attacks by food are not as uncommon as one might think. In Brooklyn a carp pulled from its tank in a delicatessen leapt from the weighing scale and sank its

teeth into the bare foot of the woman who had intended to take it home for dinner.

Aetna also offers the case of the pugnacious cat that launched an unprovoked assault on a woman and her dog when they strolled by. Dog and human were treated for their wounds, after which the dog owner visited the cat's house to complain to its owner. This time the unrepentant feline fell upon the dog owner with such fury that it knocked her to the floor, biting a chunk out of her ear before satisfying its lust for combat.

The foibles of pets are but a drop in the insurer's bucket of payable woe. One policyholder, tormented by mosquitoes at night, sprang from his bed and sprayed the pests generously. He awakened next morning to find his bedroom walls speckled and streaked with the bright-red enamel paint he had sprayed in the mistaken belief it was insecticide.

Aetna, in fact, would not mind at all if its policyholders refrained entirely from every form of do-it-yourself home improvement. One insured man tried to roof his office with the help of a friend. For safety's sake the men tied a

rope to the bumper of their parked truck, securing the other end to the one who was doing the roofing as he worked on the opposite side of the building. Eventually the assistant, tired of hauling heavy loads of shingles around the building, forgot about the rope and moved the truck. Launched like a missile into the treetops, the roofer suffered only a broken wrist.

Even this stellar bungle pales in the minds of insurance adjusters compared to the case of the New England town constables who helped burglarize a home. The officers spotted a group of men loading a van with valuables from a house. Guns at the ready, the constables demanded to know what was going on. One of the hoods convinced the police he was the owner of the house, taking possession of his rightful belongings after a bitterly fought divorce. Ever sympathetic to the sufferings of a wronged husband, the gullible cops holstered their pistols and helped load the van. The homeowners returned to find their house stripped.

cizing juries for awarding huge amounts to plaintiffs in malpractice and accident suits, which Aetna claimed was principally responsible for the high cost of health and liability insurance premiums. The advertising drew strong criticism and one lawsuit that likened the company to a professional gambler who tries "to change the odds."

They are well-known for their program to hire and promote minorities and women, and they're one of the few American companies with a vice-president for corporate social responsibility. Aetna was stung in 1979 by a Federal Trade Commission report that said people who bought life insurance policies got only a 1.3% return on their money. Filer called the FTC study a "reckless misrepresentation."

Where they're going. In 1980 Aetna announced a plan to provide $15 million in mortgage loans for inner-city residents across the country; Aetna president William Bailey told the *Washington Post* that the plan offered a "real possibility of reclaiming [these] neighborhoods."

Stock performance. Aetna stock bought for $1,000 in 1970 sold for $2,574 on January 2, 1980.

Major employment centers. Hartford, Bloomfield, and East Hartford, Connecticut.

Access. 151 Farmington Avenue, Hartford, Connecticut 06156; (203) 273-0123.

Consumer brand.

Aetna insurance.

When General Custer rode into battle at Little Big Horn, his life was insured under a $5,000 policy from New York Life.

Metropolitan
Life Insurance Company

Sales: $9.1 billion
Profits: $234 million
Rank in life insurance: 2
Founded: 1863
Employees: 52,300
Headquarters: New York, New York

What they do. Metropolitan is the dowager of the life insurance industry: old, stodgy, and very, very wealthy. For many years the largest life insurance company in America, New York–based Met has fallen behind rival Prudential in total assets and amount of insurance sold. But the Met's fall from the number 1 spot hasn't left them penniless. Twenty-three feet below ground at the Met's Manhattan headquarters there's a vault that contains certificates representing nearly $45 billion in assets. This horde remains one of the largest stashes of wealth in the country.

The Met accumulated their wealth by selling life insurance—lots of life insurance. More than 15 million Americans and Canadians are insured by the Met, and the total life insurance in force at the Met reached more than $324 billion in 1979. This means that if all Met's policyholders were to die tomorrow, the Met would owe the survivors $324 billion. Insurance is basically a bet by the company that you, the policyholder, won't die. You are, unfortunately, betting on the other side.

About 60% of the Met's coverage is in group insurance—policies sold to companies like General Motors or other organizations to provide death benefits to employees or members. Most of the rest is ordinary life insurance sold to individuals. And the Met's empire continues to grow: in 1979 the company's 20,000 salespeople sold $41 billion worth of new life insurance policies.

This is the kind of growth that usually makes stockholders smile. But not at the Met. Metropolitan is not a stock company, but a mutual company, owned and controlled—at least in theory—by the policyholders. Holders of Metropolitan Life policies participate in the company by receiving yearly "dividends," although a more appropriate term might be *rebates*. These dividends might be much larger if the Met didn't constantly beat the bushes looking for new customers. The Met has a

THE TOP PROPERTY INSURERS

In 1979 individuals, families and companies spent a total of $88 billion to insure their property (cars, homes, boats, buildings) against all manner of calamities (collisions, fires, earthquakes). The top 10 insurance companies collected 37.4% of all these payments (known in the industry as premiums). Here are the top 10 property insurers and their market shares:

1.	STATE FARM	8.05%
2.	ALLSTATE (*Sears*)	5.03%
3.	AETNA LIFE	4.32%
4.	TRAVELERS	3.03%
5.	INA	2.95%
6.	LIBERTY MUTUAL	2.95%
7.	HARTFORD (*ITT*)	2.93%
8.	FARMERS	2.77%
9.	FIREMAN'S FUND (*American Express*)	2.7%
10.	CONTINENTAL	2.67%

sales force of 20,000. They maintain 10 regional "head offices" in Tampa, Florida; Tulsa, Oklahoma; San Francisco, California; Ottawa and Ontario, Canada; Aurora, Illinois; Johnstown, Pennsylvania; Warwick, Rhode Island; Dayton, Ohio; and New York City. In 1977 *Business Week* reported that turnover among the Met's salesmen was running at 8,000 per year; 12 years ago the Met sales force numbered 32,000.

History. Metropolitan was started in 1863 by a wealthy promoter named Simeon Draper. With his extensive political and military contacts, Draper hoped that his National Union Life and Limb Company could capture the market for insuring Yankee soldiers fighting in the Civil War. Unfortunately, soon after the company was started the Union Army suffered stunning losses, and Draper began to lose interest in the business. Over the next few years the company floundered, going through a succession of managements and name changes, finally emerging as Metropolitan Life in 1868.

The Met didn't have major success, however, until they began to sell industrial insurance in 1879. Industrial insurance was a capitalist version of the burial societies workers had set up among themselves to pay benefits to the wives and children of dead comrades. Noting the success of industrial insurance in England, the Met im-

ported 500 English agents and sent them out to working-class neighborhoods to sell inexpensive policies for about a few pennies a week. In the boom-and-bust cycle of the American economy in the late nineteenth and early twentieth centuries a high proportion of workers failed to meet their payments, which meant they couldn't collect on their policies, and they forfeited their initial payments to Metropolitan. It was this heavy emphasis on the lucrative industrial insurance business that powered the Met to the top of the insurance world, a position it would not lose until the early 1970s.

Companies, like individuals, inherit characteristics. Much of the Met's conservatism is traced to the long reign of the Eckers—Frederick H. Ecker, Sr., who became president in 1929 and was chairman until 1951, and his son, Frederick, Jr., who was chief executive officer from 1953 to 1963. The Eckers were very very cautious (and suspicious) people. They thought common stocks were too risky. They used to check how long female employees spent in the washrooms. Both Eckers died in 1964 (the elder Ecker was 95).

Reputation. *Fortune* once described the Met as "laboring under a burden of financial conservatism that critics equate with antiquation." They are usually the last to try anything new.

What they own. The tally of Metropolitan's assets is staggering: $3 billion in government securities; $20 billion in corporate bonds; $1 billion of stock; and $12 billion worth of mortgages on homes, factories, skyscrapers, shopping centers, and farms.

Who owns and runs the company. In theory, policyholders control management. They are entitled to vote on nominees for the board of directors, who in turn set policy and pick the management. In practice, however, the Met's management is autonomous and self-perpetuating. For much of this century the Met was run by the Eckers, who held various positions in the company from 1901 to 1964. Since 1969 the president and chief executive officer has been Richard R. Shinn, who climbed the ladder within the company from mail boy to head of the Met's group insurance operations.

The Met's board is loaded with powerful corporate types who keep a careful eye on what the company does with their $45 billion in assets. (Only Prudential, AT&T, Exxon, and five banks have larger assets than Metropolitan.) The board includes the top officers of Union Carbide, Consolidated Edison, Bethlehem Steel, Republic Steel, NL Industries, Crocker National Bank, and The Royal Bank of Canada, as well as former defense secretary Melvin R. Laird.

In 1976 a policyholder requested a ballot to vote for the directors. He received one, along with a letter pointing out that he could vote only for those already nominated "because no other nominations were made within the time limited by law." It seems that nominations must be filed at least five months before the election by at least one-tenth of 1% of all policyholders. Since the Met probably has more than 40 million policyholders, that means 40,000 names on your nominating petition.

Where they're going. In the early 1970s the Met started selling auto and homeowners insurance partly after seeing that Prudential had done it successfully. The move was also taken to keep the company's sales force happy, since in an era of inflation the declining appeal of life insurance as an investment had cut down on their commissions. But the salespeople are still leaving, and the Met ranks far behind the Pru in these fields.

Clear Days on the Insurance Front

People have complained for years about how difficult it is to understand what insurance companies are talking about. But Old Republic Life Insurance Company of Chicago has found a way to answer inquiries in one sentence.

In 1978 they were queried by a policyholder whose disability payments had been reduced by Old Republic after he started to receive Social Security benefits. Old Republic had this one-sentence reply:

The contract stipulates if the total monthly amount of loss of time benefits promised for the same loss under all valid loss of time coverage upon the insured person, whether payable on a weekly or monthly basis shall exceed the monthly earnings of the insured person at the time disability commenced or his average monthly earnings for the period of two years immediately proceeding a disability for which claim is made, which ever is greater, the Company will be liable only for such portion and amount of such benefits under the certificate as the amount of such monthly earnings or such monthly earnings of the insured person bears to the total amount of monthly benefits with the same loss under all such coverage upon the insured person at the time of such disability commences and for the return of such part of the premiums paid during such two years as shall exceed the prorated amount of premiums for the benefits and repaid hereunder but this shall no [sic] operate the reduced total monthly amount of benefits payable under all such coverage upon the insured person below the sum of $200, or the sum of the monthly benefits specified in such coverage, which ever is the lesser nor shall it operate to reduce benefits other than those payable for loss of time.

Access. One Madison Avenue, New York, New York 10010; (212) 578-2211.

Consumer brand.

Metropolitan insurance.

Sales: $12 billion
Profits: $278 million
Rank in life insurance: 1
Founded: 1873
Employees: 61,800
Headquarters: Newark, New Jersey

What they do. Since 1896 Prudential has used the Rock of Gibraltar to signify the solid character of their insurance. Their famous slogan, "The Prudential has the strength of Gibraltar," is still used, but a new version, "Get a piece of the Rock," is more in character with the aggressive management that has made Prudential the world's largest life insurance company. They pulled ahead of their staid old rival Metropolitan Life in the 1970s, and Metropolitan is now far behind "the Pru."

Like any large life insurance company, the Pru is made up of two complementary operations. One is the business of selling life insurance. Prudential's 24,000 agents, operating under the direction of the company's nine decentralized home offices, sold more than $44 billion worth of new life insurance in 1978, bringing the Pru's total life insurance in force to $330 billion. In other words, that's the amount of money Prudential would have to pay out if all their policyholders suddenly died at once. About half of their new sales were of policies to individuals; the other half were group insurance policies sold to companies or organizations for the protection of their employees and members. Americans have more than 50 million policies with Prudential.

The other side of the company is Prudential the investor. The Pru has more than $50 billion in assets, more than either Exxon or General Motors. In fact, only four companies—AT&T, Bank of America, Citicorp, and Chase Manhattan—have more assets than Prudential. Here's what the Pru does with all their money: they've put more than $6 billion in stocks; $20 billion in corporate bonds; $13 billion in mortgages on homes, hotels, shopping centers, factories, and farms; and $2 billion in real estate. A less conservative investor than rivals like Metropolitan Life, Prudential has gone beyond the traditional practice of buying only the bonds of well-established, big corporations to provide direct financing to small- and medium-sized companies. The results have been impressive: the Pru has consistently earned higher profits from their investments than their competitors.

Prudential's cash flow is such that every working day they have something like $24 million to invest.

History. The Pru was founded in Newark in 1873 by John Fairfield Dryden, a young Yale drop-out who was elected to the United States Senate in 1902. Originally named the Widows and Orphans Friendly Society, the company was set up to sell industrial insurance to working-class families. (Industrial insurance was low-cost insurance for workers that paid off just enough money when they died to bury them, with maybe a little left over for their widows.) Dryden found few takers at first, even after he changed the name to Prudential in 1875 in imitation of the huge English industrial insurer of the same name. In 1876 the young company managed to sell 7,000 policies, but they were still $1,500 in the hole by the end of the year. At one point, cash was so tight that a physician-director of Prudential stayed up all night nursing a pneumonia patient who had recently insured herself for $500. The doctor is quoted in *The Prudential,* a company history by Earl Chapin May and Will Oursler: "A claim of $500 would very likely wreck the company. The way to save it was to save the patient." The patient lived.

John Dryden went to England in 1876 to study how his successful English counterpart operated. Returning to the United States, he applied his lessons, dropping sickness benefits and recruiting his agents from the neighborhoods where he intended to sell insurance. Dryden sent his crew of agents door to door to peddle policies. They were known as debit men, because they came around each week collecting 3¢ or a nickel, which they marked off in a debit book. The agents had to work frantically for their $10-a-week commissions, but business boomed. Between 1876 and 1905 the value of industrial insurance policies in America grew from $500,000 to $2.5 billion. Although the entire life insurance business was lucrative, industrial insurance was particularly so. Two-thirds of the workers who took out Prudential policies were unable to keep up payments on their policies for the three years that Prudential demanded. If you missed your payments, Prudential pocketed the money you had already paid out and was not obliged to pay your family a cent if you died.

When the Pru had their twentieth anniversary, John Dryden commissioned the J. Walter Thompson advertising agency to come up with a trademark. Account executive Mortimer Remington rejected such solid symbols as the Matterhorn, Mount Everest, and the Rockies before hitting on Gibraltar. A sketch of the rock (minus the land mass at the base of Gibraltar because of a whim of the artist) first appeared in 1896—and it's been running in every ad since.

The Pru's early success was the result of riding the boom that carried along the entire industry. Their drive to the top, however, was accomplished by bucking the traditions of the industry. In 1946 president Carroll M. Shanks began a program of decentralizing the Pru's operations by setting up "home offices" in Chicago, Minneapolis, Boston, Houston, Los Angeles, Jacksonville, and Toronto. Shanks, in effect, created a number of different insurance companies, competing with each other for prestige within the company. Although rivals scoffed, they soon followed suit when Shanks's plan proved a success. Shanks saw the role of insurance in American life this way: "The insurance industry must play a big part. We have the experience, we have the equipment, we have the organization. We are providing protection and security in many ways to millions of people. I am an ardent advocate of welfare plans. But loss of freedom is too high a price to pay." In other words, there's no need for the government to give the citizen health and welfare protection, when the citizen can already get it by buying it from an insurance company.

Recently, as inflation has dampened the appeal of life insurance, the Pru has expanded into other fields. They now sell auto, health, and homeowners insurance, and they operate PruLease Inc., which leases nuclear-fuel cores to the owners of nuclear power plants. In fact, since 1967 Prudential has established 22 subsidiary companies; 4 of these operate outside the United States. Most of these operations brought Prudential nothing but red ink in their early years. For example, their property and casualty business, selling policies to insure homes and cars, lost $73 million in the first five years after it was started in 1971. But in 1978 it came through with its first profit: $2.4 million. The Prudential clout is such that seven years after launching this new business, they ranked 13th in homeowners insurance and 18th in auto coverage. More than 1 million cars and more than 850,000 homes are now insured by Prudential policies.

Prudential was quite candid about why they went into other fields: to shore up the income of their 24,000 agents, who were finding it hard to make ends meet selling only life insurance.

Reputation. In a conservative industry, Prudential has stuck out as a company ready to break with old practices.

TOP FIVE INSURERS OF HOMES

Total market: $7.9 billion (1978)

Market Share

1.	STATE FARM	14.2%
2.	ALLSTATE	8.9%
3.	AETNA LIFE	4.0%
4.	FARMERS	3.4%
5.	CONTINENTAL	2.8%

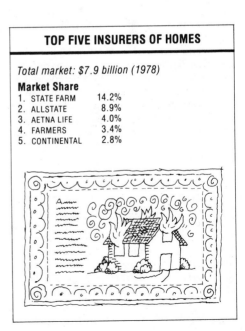

THE TOP FIVE AUTO INSURERS

Total market: $26 billion (1978)

Market Share

1.	STATE FARM	16.5%
2.	ALLSTATE	9.1%
3.	FARMERS	5.2%
4.	NATIONWIDE	3.5%
5.	AETNA LIFE	3.1%

What they own. Trademarks of the Pru are the skyscraper headquarters they have built for their nine home offices. Insurance companies like tall buildings (Metropolitan Life's Manhattan headquarters was the tallest building in America when it was built in 1909). The Pru owns the Empire State Building, at the top of the skyscraper list for many years. But the edifice complex of life insurance companies reached its ludicrous heights in the early 1960s in Boston. That was when Prudential decided to build a 52-story tower, then the tallest building outside of Manhattan, for their Boston regional office. It was probably no accident that the building was only three blocks away from the rival John Hancock Company's 26-story headquarters, until then Boston's tallest. And it was probably less of an accident that John Hancock soon announced plans for a new 60-story building. But the Pru had the last laugh. When the Hancock building was completed, it had the disconcerting habit of dropping its windows on the street below whenever the wind blew, leaving Hancock with a repair bill for $111 million and the dubious distinction of owning the world's tallest building with plywood windows.

Who owns and runs the company. Prudential is a mutual company, which means that it sells no stock and has no stockholders —control is supposed to rest with the policyholders through their policies. Policyholders are entitled to vote for directors, but the nominations are controlled by the management. Under New Jersey law 6 members of the 22-member board, usually prominent politicians, are appointed by the chief justice of the New Jersey Supreme Court. In practice the real control of the company rests with the management, which is headed by Robert A. Beck, chairman and chief executive officer, who was a financial analyst at Ford Motor before joining Prudential in 1951. He rose through the sales ranks, succeeding Donald S. Mac-Naughton, a lawyer who got to the top spot in 1969 after heading up a study of the Pru's home office. By the time he was through he knew more about the company than anyone except his predecessor, Orville E. Beal.

In the public eye. Newark, New Jersey, Prudential's headquarters city, was once a thriving industrial hub and the financial center of New Jersey. Today much of it looks like a war zone. In the aftermath of the 1967 riots in the city, Prudential pledged loans for the ravaged central city and helped back social programs in black neighborhoods. The company still makes social action investments in renewal projects in ghetto neighborhoods and has an affirmative action program in hiring: 26% of new home-office employees in 1978 were from minority groups. But the company has recently moved their Eastern home office out of the Newark headquarters into a suburban location. As Newark's largest employer, Prudential has it in their power to help decide if Newark will be, as Mayor Kenneth Gibson has warned, the first American city to die.

Access. 745 Broad Street, Newark, New Jersey 07101; (201) 877-6000.

Consumer brand.

Prudential insurance.

Money Handlers

Sales: $4.7 billion
Profits: $345 million
Forbes 500 rank: 86
Rank in travelers checks: 1
Founded: 1850
Employees: 41,000
Headquarters: New York, New York

What they do. American Express has perfected to a fine art the making of money by handling other people's money, although they like to describe their travelers checks as one of providing "security, convenience and a sense of confidence to our customers." In the process of delivering such intangibles they devised one of the tastiest money-making schemes ever conceived. For a fixed fee (1%) they generously give you the opportunity to lend them money (interest free).

Another cash generator is the American Express credit card. This wasn't American Express's idea—Diners Club was first—but with their experience in making money off money Amex quickly captured first place in the business until the banks realized that their thunder was being stolen. The bank cards—Visa and MasterCharge—turned this business into a lending operation, enabling cardholders to pay only a small amount of what they owed. American Express doesn't permit this—they require their cardholders to clear their charges promptly (no credit extended). But American Express makes money from their card in two ways:

1. They charge an annual fee. In mid-1980 this fee went up from $25 to $35. With more than 10 million members (2.1 million are outside the United States), Amex thereby boosted their annual dues collection by $70 million (cardholders over age 65 were exempt from this increase).

2. They discount the bills that are forwarded to them by stores, hotels, restaurants, airlines, and other businesses that accept the American Express card (there were 389,000 of these establishments at the start of 1980). The discount is the cut American Express takes for handling these transactions for establishments. They send back money—but not as much as the bill was. The discount varies, depending on the type of establishment and how quickly Amex has to fork over the money, but the upper range is believed to be 5%. The quicker an establishment wants to be paid, the bigger cut Amex takes.

The Fair Credit Billing Act of 1974 makes it unlawful for American Express or any other card issuer to prohibit businesses from offering customers a cash discount. In other words, if you run up a $100 bill in a restaurant and then try to use your American Express card, there's nothing to stop the owner from coming to you and saying: "Look, American Express is only going to pay me $96 for this check. You can save $4 if you pay in cash now." (When's the last time you heard this offer made?)

American Express operates one of the world's biggest travel agencies—they have 1,000 company-owned and representative offices in 120 countries—but it's a business that has not been producing much profit. In fact, in 1979 the company's travel service operations ran at a loss.

San Francisco–based Fireman's Fund, the nation's eighth largest property and ca-

Henry Wells of Vermont and William C. Fargo of New York, whose names now grace the third largest bank in California, were founders of the company now known as American Express.

sualty insurer (they'll insure you against all manners of disaster), became part of American Express in 1968, and they fit in nicely, being another money handler. In 1979 they collected premiums of $2.5 billion. They have been accounting for about 50% of the total profits made by American Express. They insure 70% of the movies made in America.

History. In 1845 Henry Wells went into competition with the U.S. government. The operator of an express delivery company in Buffalo, New York, Wells decided that, at 25¢ a letter, the post office was charging too much to deliver mail between New York City and Buffalo. So Wells started delivering letters between the two cities for 6¢. Its monopoly challenged, the government responded with indictments and arrests, but it didn't recapture the postal business until it lowered its rate below that at which Wells could make a profit. The taxpayers of course picked up the tab.

Wells stayed in the express delivery business though, and in 1850 he joined forces with his two main competitors to form American Express. The new company grew rapidly, acquiring other competitors serving the rapidly growing Midwest. But the board of directors balked when Wells and his vice-president, William Fargo, proposed that American Express extend their business to California, where the Gold Rush was in full swing. So the two men set up their own company: the famous Wells Fargo & Co. And shortly thereafter another of their partners, John Butterfield, set up the Overland Mail and Pony Express.

During the Civil War American Express transported supplies to army depots, brought election ballots to troops in the field, and delivered parcels to parts of the Confederacy newly overrun by Union forces. But after the war business slumped, and American Express was forced to merge with a strong competitor, Merchant Unions. A big part of the express business had been in carrying valuables, precious metals, and cash, but when the post office introduced the postal money order in 1864, business began to slip. In 1882 American Express fought back by introducing their own money order, their first step into the financial field. Travelers Cheques made their appearance in 1891, and Amex sold $10,000 worth that year. By 1901 annual sales had passed $6 million. By the outbreak of World War I, Europe was dotted with American Express offices handling shipments and finances for travelers.

The war changed Amex's character forever. In 1917 the government nationalized the railroads and ordered the express companies to combine their operations into one big outfit, American Railway Express. Shorn of their original business, American Express fell back on their travelers check operation, but after the war American tourists flooded Europe and the company prospered. So sound was their operation that they continued to cash their travelers checks during the 1933 "Bank Holiday" when banks were closed and the nation's assets virtually frozen.

Episodes like that gave American Express a reputation for solidity and probity. So they were totally unprepared for the late 1970s, when the press and other companies began to treat them like just another corporation. One by one they tried and failed to acquire Book-of-the-Month Club, Philadelphia Life Insurance, and Walt Disney Productions. When they tried to grab McGraw-Hill's publishing company in early 1979, they were denounced for sleazy tactics and undermining the First Amendment. That same year Citcorp took out full-page newspaper ads, blazoned with inch-high lettering, that accused American Express of false and deceptive advertising for implying that their competitors' travelers checks were not as easily refundable. And to add injury to insult, Visa and Mastercharge decided to go head-to-head with Amex in the travelers check business, hoping to steal away some of Amex's 60% market share. Amex sold 40 million travelers checks in 1979 alone.

The *Washington Post* suggested in 1975 that American Express leads a charmed life by operating relatively free of government regulation, unlike the banks and other financial institutions. The *Post* quoted a Capitol Hill source as saying: "They fall through the cracks. Everybody thinks somebody else is regulating them. Actually nobody is."

Reputation. American Express was regarded for so long as an uptight, conservative Wall Street company, a world unto itself, that they were shocked to be accused of lying on TV and attempted subversion of freedom of the press. But they must still have some of that old respectability. When they went 50-50 with Warner in the cable TV business, analysts said the association gave Warner new credibility.

What they own. In addition to Fireman's Fund, Amex owns half of Warner Amex Cable Communications, which in late 1979 operated 140 cable TV systems with about 650,000 subscribers in 29 states; a pay-cable channel with 150,000 subscribers; a national pay-cable network of children's programming with over 1 million subscribers; and the country's only major "audience-participation" cable system, called Qube, in Columbus, Ohio.

Who owns and runs the company. Anticipating the eventual retirement of Howard Clark, the powerful chairman and chief executive who led the company through 17 years of spectacular growth, Amex started putting together a two-man team to replace him: James D. Robinson, III (called "Jimmy Three Sticks" because of the III after his name) and Roger H. Morley. The two seemed to work compatibly, with Robinson in charge of travel, insurance, public affairs, personnel, and administration, and Morley overseeing financial matters, including acquisitions.

When Clark took an early retirement in 1977, 41-year-old Robinson moved up from president to become chairman and chief executive officer; Morley, then 45, was named president. At the end of 1979 Morley resigned. Wall Street pundits said he was miffed because he didn't get the top job, and, furthermore, he lost to a younger man. Morley had also been under heavy fire for his role in the McGraw-Hill takeover attempt.

The board of directors includes Edwin D. Etherington, former American Stock Exchange president; Vernon Jordan, head of the National Urban League, (who became the first black director in 1977 and got them to discontinue all loans to the South African government or any of its agencies); and Martha Wallace, in charge of the Henry Luce Foundation, the only woman on the board.

In the public eye. It didn't help at all that American Express president Roger Morley was on the McGraw-Hill board of directors when Amex suddenly tried to walk off with the publishing firm in their pocket in 1979. Chairman Harold McGraw, Jr., likened Morley to a Trojan Horse—the enemy concealed within the city walls, smiling like a friend but actually plotting with leaders of his own company to take the publishing giant captive. Morley was on McGraw's financial and audit committees, so presumably Amex knew just what they would be getting when they offered the tremendous sum of $830 million in early January. By late February they had raised the bid to $976 million—and they were on the brink of a mortifying defeat.

In the interim, McGraw-Hill had filed a $500 million lawsuit, shouting "breach of trust" and "corporate immorality" in two-page major newspaper ads. American Express was shaken to see their supremely respectable name thus dragged through the mud. They countersued. Harold McGraw surprised many with the fury and effectiveness of his opposition. He was worried about McGraw-Hill's editorial independence (they publish Standard & Poor's financial information and 60 magazines, including *Business Week*, in addition to books) as well as about Morley's treachery. At last the bid expired, and Amex was left with empty hands—except for a bill of $2.4 million in legal expenses.

Where they're going. Despite failures and embarrassments in the acquisition arena, they'll still try to add major businesses, especially in communications and related fields. Chairman James Robinson's 1980 statement to stockholders urged the United States to be more aggressive in attracting tourists here (and thereby helping American Express as well as our balance of payments).

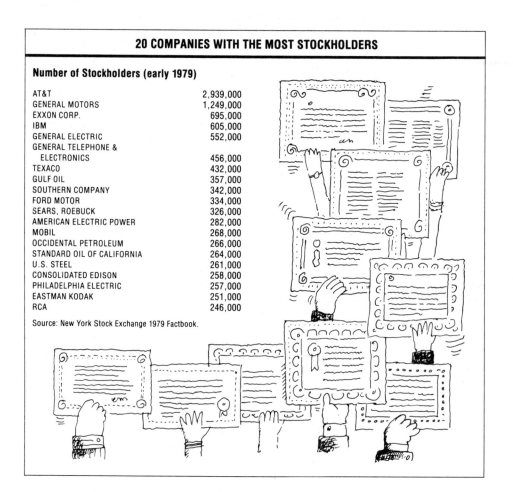

20 COMPANIES WITH THE MOST STOCKHOLDERS

Number of Stockholders (early 1979)

AT&T	2,939,000
GENERAL MOTORS	1,249,000
EXXON CORP.	695,000
IBM	605,000
GENERAL ELECTRIC	552,000
GENERAL TELEPHONE & ELECTRONICS	456,000
TEXACO	432,000
GULF OIL	357,000
SOUTHERN COMPANY	342,000
FORD MOTOR	334,000
SEARS, ROEBUCK	326,000
AMERICAN ELECTRIC POWER	282,000
MOBIL	268,000
OCCIDENTAL PETROLEUM	266,000
STANDARD OIL OF CALIFORNIA	264,000
U.S. STEEL	261,000
CONSOLIDATED EDISON	258,000
PHILADELPHIA ELECTRIC	257,000
EASTMAN KODAK	251,000
RCA	246,000

Source: New York Stock Exchange 1979 Factbook.

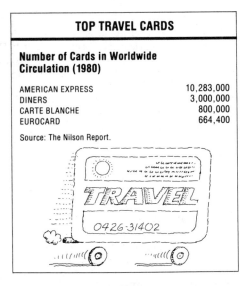
Stock performance. American Express stock bought for $1,000 in 1970 sold for $1,411 on January 2, 1980.

Major employment centers. New York City; Fort Lauderdale, Florida; Phoenix, Arizona.

Access. American Express Plaza, New York, New York 10004; (212) 480-2000.

Consumer brands.

Travel services: American Express.

Merrill Lynch Pierce Fenner & Smith Inc.

Sales: $2.1 billion
Profits: $118.7 million
Forbes 500 rank: 254
Rank as stock broker: 1
Founded: 1914
Employees: 26,000
Headquarters: New York, New York

What they do. "Well, the broker made money and the firm made money—and two out of three ain't bad."—Old Wall Street joke.

Stockbrokers make money by buying or selling stock with other people's money. They are middlemen. Whether they buy or sell, their commission is the same. Whether the stock they buy turns out to be a splendid or a rotten investment, their commission is the same. Author Andrew Tobias tells of a swanky New York brokerage firm that was entrusted with $175,000 to invest. The market was very good at the time; a lot of money could have been made. But in two months the firm, with much aid from a computer, turned the $175,000 into $10,000 —and collected $87,000 in commissions.

Merrill Lynch, Pierce, Fenner & Smith is the world's largest stock brokerage house. Their famous ad shows a thundering herd of bulls with the motto "Merrill Lynch is bullish on America," which means they're optimistic about the prospects of our capitalistic system. They ought to be: they *are* the system. And they are doing quite well. From nearly 400 offices across the country Merrill Lynch controls about 12% of the brokerage market, almost three times the share of their nearest competitor. Not satisfied with being the largest broker, they now call themselves a "complete financial services company"—which means they're casting an envious eye on the territory controlled by realtors, insurers, and bankers.

It's hard to talk about what Merrill Lynch does without getting enmeshed in the gobbledygook of high finance (commodities, securities, options, futures, municipals, over-the-counter, convertible debentures, liquid aftermarkets, and so on). But let's say you're an individual wanting to invest $1,000. If you want to put it in stock, you have to deal with a stockbroker. That's where Merrill Lynch comes in. They represent nearly 2 million Americans who buy and sell stocks. You just call up your local Merrill Lynch salesperson and place your order for $1,000 worth of XYZ Corporation at today's price on the New York Stock Exchange. Merrill Lynch relays your order to New York, where they have employees doing their customers' bidding on the floor of the stock exchange every day. If you don't have a particular stock in mind, their research division, staffed with analysts who keep track of entire industries, can make recommendations on which companies' stock to buy. Not that the experts necessarily know any better than anyone else. Andrew Tobias, in *The Only Investment Guide You'll Ever Need,* tells of an experiment in which three *Forbes* magazine executives threw 10 darts each at the *New York Times* stock page and then hypothetically invested $1,000 in each stock hit by a dart. After 10 years their stocks had risen in price by 50%—far better than most Wall Street investment "experts" had done.

Merrill Lynch has done more than any other brokerage firm to get the general public to play the stock market. They call it "People's Capitalism" and describe themselves as "the firm that brought Wall Street to Main Street." They did it through a high-powered mass advertising campaign that began just after World War II. Before then, as Peter Z. Grossman noted in *Financial World* magazine, "brokers wouldn't take on a new account unless the person showed his silver spoon at the door. To Merrill Lynch, if a person had a bank account, he could have a brokerage account. No order was too small; no portfolio was too small either. People were encouraged to drop into a Merrill Lynch office just to watch the ticker. Or ask a question. Or pick up some literature. Or get their portfolios evaluated without obligation." Merrill Lynch became "the broker of the little guy" and helped quadruple the number of stock market investors. One Merrill Lynch partner, Louis Engel, wrote an elementary guidebook in 1953 called *How to Buy Stocks* that proved enormously popular, going through dozens of printings and revised editions. In 1979 Merrill Lynch conducted 1,800 investment seminars and forums. One of them, staged in New York's Madison Square Garden, was transmitted via satellite to 20 cities.

Maybe you don't want to limit your investments to the New York Stock Exchange. Merrill Lynch also deals in over-the-counter stocks, which are simply bought and sold between dealers in free-wheeling fashion over the phone. If you really want to take a flier, Merrill Lynch will do your buying and selling in the highly speculative commodities market, where you gamble rashly on the future price of anything from plywood to pork bellies, (although you have to have $50,000 in ready cash before Merrill Lynch will help you dabble in commodities).

Or say you're not an individual at all but a corporation that wants to raise $100 million for a new glass-blowing plant. Merrill Lynch can help since they're also investment bankers, or underwriters. This means they will buy your new stocks or bonds at a price they negotiate with you and then turn around and sell them to the public for whatever the market will bear. To notify the public, they take out "tombstone ads" on the financial pages of newspapers, so named because they look like tombstones, with lots of white space and not much information—just the name of the company, the amount of money they're trying to raise, and the brokers who are handling the deal.

Or say you're a city that wants to raise $500 million for a new sewer system. Merrill Lynch will underwrite your municipal bonds and sell them to people looking for a low-risk, tax-free investment.

All these examples are just the traditional types of brokerage services offered by Merrill Lynch. They've spent the past 15 years branching out into a complete line of "womb-to-tomb" financial services, including home mortgages and life insurance. In recent years many bankers have complained that the Merrill Lynch bull is nosing into their china shops. Ever since the earliest days of the Franklin Roosevelt administration, stockbrokers and commercial banks have been fenced into two distinctly separate corrals. Banks accept deposits and lend money; brokers buy and sell stocks and bonds. But since 1977 Merrill Lynch has offered what they call Cash Management Accounts. Clients with extra money in their stock investment accounts with Merrill Lynch can have it invested automatically in interest-bearing money-market accounts, where they can draw it out through checks as easily as if the money were deposited in the corner bank. David Rockefeller, the head of Chase Manhattan Bank, has complained that Merrill Lynch should be subject to the same restrictions as banks if they want to get into banking business. But Merrill Lynch chairman Donald Regan sees it simply as "a blurring of lines as banks get more into our business."

History. Charles Edward Merrill, according to a Merrill Lynch publication, "had the physique of a Plymouth Rock rooster, the savvy and courage of a horse trader, and the soul of a poet." His knack for business surfaced early. As a youth in Jacksonville, Florida, he made pots of money selling newspapers at the edge of the red-light district to gentlemen who wanted to cover their faces on the way out. He went north to law school but dropped out to become a

The Ruin of the Franklin National Bank

How does a bank fail? Consider the Franklin National Bank, a Long Island financial institution which no longer exists. In 1974 it was the 20th largest bank in the country, with $5 billion in assets and over 100 branches. But the facade was deceptive.

A bank makes money by taking what its depositors deposit, and investing it for a profit. Banks can't play the stock market with depositors' money, but they can lend large sums to corporations, they can buy municipal or U.S. government bonds, they can lend to builders and small businessmen, and they can engage in foreign currency deals which, sometimes, net them profits from favorable exchange rates. Franklin National's founder, Arthur Roth, built up his bank in the 1950s and early '60s by using a variety of unorthodox techniques, including relying on verbal commitments and making real estate loans to people who didn't have other property to use as collateral. But because Long Island was experiencing a housing construction boom Franklin grew rapidly.

Part of the Franklin's early success (checkered as it was) came from New York state banking laws that forbade Manhattan banks from opening branches on Long Island. The Franklin's turf was assured—until the laws changed in the late '60s, and the big guys moved into Roth's territory. He countered by extending his own operations to Manhattan. This ill-fated move became the opportunity for Roth's own ex-public relations man, Harold Gleason, to stage a managerial coup that ousted the founder.

But the new management, which kept the downtown branches, couldn't make a Manhattan contender out of a suburban interloper. The Franklin found itself making risky loans to bring in the business which the other banks had shunned. In 1971 the Franklin lost $7 million. All this was merely the insecure foundation on which the bank's eventual downfall was

laid. In the summer of 1972 Italian financier Michele Sindona stepped onstage with the purchase of 21.6% of the Franklin (a controlling interest). Sindona had already skirmished with Italian banking authorities when he put some huge hunks of Italian business into foreign hands. *Fortune* magazine later reported that though Sindona's advisors warned him about buying into the Franklin, he answered, "Don't worry, I'm going to make most of my money in foreign exchange. That's the way I do it in my Italian banks."

Sindona brought in Paul Luftig from Bankers Trust as president. Luftig increased the bank's new loans, but he could do nothing about a large number of previously made loans, which yielded low interest and were becoming more and more expensive to maintain. Meanwhile, Sindona's men hired a new foreign exchange specialist: Donald Emerich, who had been fired from Continental Illinois Bank for unauthorized foreign exchange deals. Emerich's subsequent money deals cost the Franklin over $40 million.

By the end of 1973, the Franklin's troubles were no secret in banking circles. The bank was borrowing up to $1 billion on certain days in federal funds (pooled cash reserves the banks keep to lend each other) just to meet the need for cash. Rather than omit that year's third quarter stockholder dividend (which would have let the cat out of the bag to a lot of people with money tied up in the bank), the foreign exchange department put through a sneak transaction with one of Sindona's European banks, Amincor. The Franklin bought a huge amount of foreign currency from Amincor and then turned around and sold it back (the rates were, of course, rigged) at a $2 million profit. With that down on paper the Franklin could give out its dividend and keep the dirty linen in the closet awhile longer.

Desperate for a profit, the bank directors took a gamble. They bought $200 million worth

of U.S. government bonds. These bonds paid 7-8% interest, but to buy them, Franklin borrowed money from other banks on short term loans, at about 10% interest. On its face, that sounds like a deal that wouldn't tempt a Las Vegas rube. But it was the wisdom of the day that interest rates were about to fall. Since the loans were short term, Franklin hoped that when they were renewed, the interest would be low enough to make a profit on the government bonds. (Precisely the same unlucky bond gamble brought the near-downfall of the First Pennsylvania Bank in 1980).

But interest rates did not go down. They went up. By April 1974 the bank was losing $3 million a month on bad loans, bad debts, and bad foreign exchanges. The silent run was on. Both Morgan Guaranty and the Bank of America clamped down on the Franklin's access to their federal funds. The rumor of failure even reached the public: during the summer of 1974, customers withdrew over $1.7 billion—53% of the bank's deposits.

When the end came, it was quick. On an October Tuesday, the FDIC secretly took bids for a takeover. At 3 P.M. that day, when the bank closed, it was declared insolvent. Two hours later the winning bidder was announced. And the next morning, all branches opened as usual—but a sign was stuck in the window of each, reading, "European-American Bank & Trust Co.," the name of the winning bidder. The Franklin was no more. It was the biggest bank failure in U.S. history.

The victims in the Franklin fall were the bank's stockholders, who lost their investments clean. (The depositors just found themselves at a new bank). And, as for Michele Sindona, he did not escape unscathed. He lost his investment, and in 1980 a federal court gave him 25 years in jail and a fine of $207,000 for his part in the Franklin's demise.

bond salesman in Wall Street. In 1914 he opened his own underwriting firm, and within six months he took on a partner, Edmund C. Lynch. Merrill helped found Safeway Stores, and his company made millions of dollars in the 1920s selling stock for other new grocery chains. Merrill retired in 1930 and transferred his business to E. A. Pierce, the largest stock brokerage on Wall Street. Ten years later Merrill was persuaded to return to the firm, and the company joined with Fenner & Beane, a New Orleans–based brokerage. In 1958 the firm added the name of Winthrop H. Smith, who started as Charles Merrill's office boy and rose to head the company after Merrill's death in 1956.

It was under Merrill's direction in the postwar years that Merrill Lynch made their mark in the business. They introduced the idea of the salaried broker to assure customers that their broker was not simply interested in making a lot of trades to rack up commissions for himself. Their biggest innovation was reaching the small investor through mass advertising and demystifying the stock market for ordinary people. To the exclusive club of upper-class Wall Streeters this was abhorrent, like a crowd of rowdy touch footballers invading a gentlemanly game of golf at the country club. But Merrill Lynch's strategy worked. As the nation's population centers shifted south and west, Merrill Lynch followed, expanding their business to all sections of the country.

When the stock market collapsed at the end of the 1960s, more than 100 brokerage firms went out of business, but Merrill Lynch continued to turn a profit. Still, they sought a way to escape the ups and downs of the market, so they decided to branch out into other lines of business: insurance, real estate, and the like. To finance their expansion they took advantage of a 1970 rule that allowed brokerages for the first time to sell stock in their own company to the public.

Reputation. The toughest kid on Wall Street, Merrill Lynch is known at other brokerage houses as "those bastards." "They're all over the country, they're aggressive, and they've got the smarts," a banker at Citicorp once told the *New York Times;* "I admire them." But the flip side is that Merrill Lynch is reputed to be an autocratic operation with little room for decision making at the lower levels. Merrill

Lynch brokers commonly leave the company for firms where there is easier access to top officials and more local autonomy. In effect, Merrill Lynch is a training house for stockbrokers, and their salespeople are constantly being lured by other firms.

What they own. Merrill Lynch's major holding is the brokerage business of Merrill Lynch, Pierce, Fenner & Smith. The other 10% of the company is in real estate and insurance: American Mortgage Insurance provides home mortgages, and Family Life Insurance sells life insurance to mortgage holders. Merrill Lynch Relocation Services sells real estate services to employees who are transferring to jobs in new cities.

Merrill Lynch also has several international operations under the banner of Merrill Lynch International. Besides brokerage operations, the international segment has gone into banking. In 1979 Merrill Lynch's foreign activities accounted for about 15% of their sales.

Their headquarters, which they lease in New York City, occupies 45 floors of a 54-story building just off Wall Street.

Who owns and runs the company. The man who engineered Merrill Lynch's big move into other fields in the 1970s is Donald T. Regan, who became chairman in 1971. A Harvard Law School dropout, Regan joined a Merrill Lynch training class after serving as a marine colonel in World War II. Among competitors Merrill Lynch is respected, feared, and, in some quarters, hated. Says Regan, "I'd rather have our customers' needs and wants satisfied than have Wall Street satisfied that I'm a nice guy."

Managers of Merrill Lynch branch offices are expected to devote two or three hours a day to civic affairs, such as the United Fund and the YMCA. But one thing they don't do is rub elbows with their fellow brokers from other companies. As one critic declared to the *New York Times,* "They're No. 1 because they never tried to become part of the Wall Street family."

March 16, 1830, was the dullest day in the history of the Exchange—only 31 shares traded.

Their top men are mostly ex-office managers from Spokane or Buffalo or God knows where. They're brought here and they don't even try to develop relations outside the firm. . . . To most of the other firms Wall Street is a great club or cozy partnership—the good old way-of-life crap. To Merrill Lynch executives that's useless sentiment."

The board of directors in 1979 included William P. Rogers, the former secretary of state and attorney general; Hedley Donovan, the recently retired editor-in-chief of Time, Inc.; and one woman, Jill Ker Conway, president of Smith College. Merrill Lynch's directors and officers control a little over 3% of the stock.

In the public eye. In 1976 Merrill Lynch paid $1.9 million to settle two federal suits brought by the Equal Employment Opportunity Commission charging racial and sex discrimination. They also agreed to implement a $1.3 million, five-year affirmative action plan to employ more women and minorities.

In 1977 the Securities and Exchange Commission fined them $1.6 million for supplying some 4,000 customers with "false and misleading" research reports about Scientific Control, a Texas computer company that went bankrupt in 1969. As part of the settlement, seven Merrill Lynch salesmen were temporarily suspended from trading stocks.

Where they're going. Merrill Lynch intends to become a major power in real estate: by 1983 they plan to have 50 residential real estate brokerages nationwide, with 15,000 to 20,000 agents.

Access. One Liberty Plaza, 165 Broadway, New York, New York 10080; (212) 766-1212. Their headquarters houses an Investment Information Center that's open for tours.

Top 50 Black Businesses

1979 Sales

1. MOTOWN INDUSTRIES (*records, movies*)	Los Angeles	$65 *million*
2. JOHNSON PUBLISHING	Chicago	$61 *million*
3. FEDCO FOODS	Bronx, NY	$45 *million*
4. H. J. RUSSELL CONSTRUCTION	Atlanta	$41 *million*
5. JOHNSON PRODUCTS (*cosmetics*)	Chicago	$35 *million*
6. VANGUARD OIL & SERVICES	Brooklyn, NY	$35 *million*
7. AFRO-INTERNATIONAL (*exports*)	New York, NY	$32 *million*
8. SMITH PIPE & SUPPLY	Houston	$32 *million*
9. GRIMES OIL	Dorchester, Mass.	$30 *million*
10. WALLACE & WALLACE ENTERPRISES (*fuel oil*)	St. Albans, NY	$26 *million*
11. CHIOKE INTERNATIONAL (*defense equipment, crude oil*)	New York, NY	$25 *million*
12. COMMONWEALTH HOLDING (*mfg., real estate, building materials*)	New York, NY	$17 *million*
13. DRUMMOND DISTRIBUTING (*liquor wholesaler*)	Compton, Calif.	$16 *million*
14. L. H. SMITH OIL	Indianapolis	$16 *million*
15. MISSO SERVICES (*computer dealers*)	Washington, D. C.	$16 *million*
16. PORTERFIELD WILSON PONTIAC, GMC TRUCK	Detroit	$16 *million*
17. DICK GIDRON CADILLAC	Bronx, NY	$16 *million*
18. HOUSING INNOVATIONS	Boston	$15 *million*
19. COMMUNITY FOODS	Baltimore	$15 *million*
20. AMERICAN DEVELOPMENT	Charleston, S.C.	$15 *million*
21. WOODRUFF OLDSMOBILE	Detroit	$14 *million*
22. DICK HARRIS CADILLAC	Detroit	$14 *million*
23. COCOLINE CHOCOLATE	Brooklyn, NY	$14 *million*
24. AL JOHNSON CADILLAC	Tinley Park, Ill.	$13 *million*
25. MEL FARR FORD	Oak Park, Mich.	$13 *million*
26. S.T.R. CORPORATION (*retail food*)	Cleveland	$13 *million*
27. GOURMET SERVICES	Atlanta	$13 *million*
28. BROADCAST ENTERPRISES NATIONAL	Philadelphia	$12 *million*
29. PORTERFIELD WILSON MAZDA-HONDA	Detroit	$12 *million*
30. TRUE TRANSPORT	Newark, NJ	$12 *million*
31. THACKER CONSTRUCTION	Atlanta	$12 *million*
32. ESSENCE COMMUNICATIONS (*magazine publishing*)	New York, NY	$12 *million*
33. PREPAC (*vinyl and fabric packaging*)	Bronx, NY	$12 *million*
34. JACKSON OIL	Baltimore	$11 *million*
35. P. F. INDUSTRIES (*athletic footwear mfg.*)	Bristol, R.I.	$11 *million*
36. RALEIGH GUIDE OLDSMOBILE-CADILLAC	Fairfield, Ohio	$10 *million*
37. CAPITOL CITY LIQUOR	Washington, D. C.	$10 *million*
38. CENTURY CHEVROLET	Upper Darby, Penna.	$10 *million*
39. R. L. DUKES OLDSMOBILE	Chicago	$10 *million*
40. DELTA ENTERPRISES (*mfg.*)	Greenville, Miss.	$10 *million*
41. INNER CITY BROADCASTING	New York, NY	$10 *million*
42. TECHNOLOGY DEVELOPMENT (*electronic systems*)	Santa Clara, Calif.	$10 *million*
43. M & M PRODUCTS (*hair care products mfg.*)	Forest Park, Ga.	$10 *million*
44. PRO-LINE (*cosmetics mfg.*)	Carson, Calif.	$ 9 *million*
45. TRANS-BAY ENGINEERS & BUILDERS	Oakland, Calif.	$ 9 *million*
46. PAYTON WELLS FORD	Indianapolis	$ 9 *million*
47. TYNES CHEVROLET-CADILLAC	Dalaware, Ohio	$ 9 *million*
48. LANDMARK FORD	Fairfield, Ohio	$ 9 *million*
49. CONYERS FORD	Detroit	$ 9 *million*
50. SAM JOHNSON LINCOLN & MERCURY	Charlotte, N.C.	$ 9 *million*

Source: *Black Enterprise*, June 1980.

10

FROM THE EARTH

Petroleum Pumpers

AtlanticRichfieldCompany ◆

Sales: $16.2 billion
Profits: $1.2 billion
Forbes 500 rank: 15
Rank in petroleum: 8
Rank in copper: 3
Rank in aluminum: 5
Rank in silver: 1
Founded: 1866
Employees: 50,700
Headquarters: Los Angeles, California

What they do. Atlantic Richfield brings up the left wing of the petroleum industry. Not that they have a "share-our-wealth" philosophy or anything like that. In terms of wrenching a dollar of profit from sales and assets, they rank close to the top of their industry. But they often break ranks with the rest of the industry. Arco's two leaders —chairman Robert O. Anderson and president Thornton F. Bradshaw— are not conventional oil company executives. Neither is an engineer; both have broad intellectual interests. In their 1978 annual report Arco stated as a company goal the management

of operations "to achieve a maximum return on invested capital"—a phrase that could be found in the literature of any major corporation—but they quickly added the qualifier, "within a framework of responsible corporate behavior," a phrase not found all that often.

Arco was the only oil producer ever to take a stand against the now-discarded oil depletion allowance, a measure that saved petroleum companies millions of dollars in taxes. They were the first major oil company to support diversion of highway tax funds for mass transit uses. In 1978 they contributed $25,000 in a futile attempt to defeat the California tax reduction measure known as Proposition 13.

Through an artful series of mergers and acquisitions beginning in 1966, Arco became one of the major natural resource companies of America. They operate or have an interest in more than 36,000 producing oil and gas wells, which provide 80% of their requirements. (They buy the rest on the open market.) They have a petrochemical operation whose sales alone would make Arco a billion-dollar company (5% of every barrel of crude goes into petro-

Gasoline delivery, 1915.

chemicals). They own Anaconda, the nation's third-largest copper and fifth-largest aluminum producer. They're strip-mining in the Powder River Basin of Wyoming, on their way to becoming one of the nation's largest coal producers.

Arco is in the position the United States wants the country as a whole to be in: their energy sources are largely domestic, and they have only a minor involvement in the Middle East. It was an Arco drilling team that in 1968 discovered oil in Prudhoe Bay off Alaska—the largest oil field yet discovered in North America. The find boosted Atlantic Richfield into the top tier of the petroleum industry. The Alaskan fields now account for more than a third of Arco's daily production of 567,900 barrels of crude oil. Oil, once it's pumped up, is transported to refineries where it's turned into gasoline, other fuels, and feedstocks for chemical plants. Arco has four refineries, all in the United States—at Houston; Philadelphia; Carson, California; and Cherry Point, Washington. Their gasoline is marketed under the Arco name through some 8,500 retail outlets, primarily in the Far West, the Great Lakes area, and the Northeast. Among domestic petroleum companies (Exxon, Texaco, California Standard, and Gulf are considered international companies) Arco ranks second only to Standard Oil of Indiana.

History. As big as Atlantic Richfield is, it bears the stamp of one man: Robert Orville Anderson, a complex, restless figure on the American business scene who is said to be most comfortable when he's riding horseback on his 100,000-acre spread in New Mexico. An associate recalls Anderson sitting in a meeting on Wall Street, looking at his watch, seeing that it's 4:00 P.M. and muttering, almost automatically, "Well, it's time to saddle up."

Anderson grew up amidst the concrete of Chicago, where his father, Hugo Anderson, was a lending officer at the First Chicago National Bank. The Anderson family lived on the city's south side in the shadow of the University of Chicago, a Rockefeller-endowed institution that was transformed, beginning in the late 1920s, by the late Robert Maynard Hutchins, the boy wonder and *enfant terrible* of U.S. education. Hutchins established a two-year college where students had little choice in course selection: they would read Aristotle, Marx, Freud and other great thinkers before settling on a narrow specialty. Attached to the university was a laboratory school—a grammar school and high school where professors sent their children. It was also the place where Hugo Anderson sent his son. Bob Anderson went to the University of Chicago from kindergarten through college.

Hugo Anderson was well acquainted

with the oil industry. He was known as the banker who first extended loans based on oil in the ground. And when his son went off to New Mexico, Hugo Anderson helped to finance his purchase of a small refinery in the southeastern part of the state.

Bob Anderson was, to put it mildly, a great success as an independent oil operator, first in the refinery business and then as a wildcatter. He bought a West Coast refinery and retail operation, selling it off in 1957 to Gulf Oil at an enormous profit. His New Mexico production company struck oil, and in 1962 he sold it to Atlantic Refining of Philadelphia, receiving in return 500,000 shares of stock. At that point, when he was 44, Bob Anderson was ready to retire from the oil business. He had bought huge ranches in New Mexico and Texas, and he enjoyed that life. In addition, he was ready to succeed Walter Paepcke as director of the Aspen Institute for Humanistic Studies at Aspen, Colorado. Paepcke was another "great ideas" man from Chicago. He was chairman of Container Corporation of America (later to become part of Mobil), and he had started the Aspen retreat as a place where businessmen could be exposed to humanistic values. It was a place made to order for Bob Anderson—and he has remained close to it.

What brought Bob Anderson back into the petroleum business? This: his Atlantic Refining shares made him the largest stockholder in the company and gave him a seat on the board. It didn't take him long, sitting on that board, to realize that Atlantic Refining, a remnant of the Rockefeller Standard Oil Trust, was a poorly managed affair, with no great chances of surviving unless it had better direction. So in 1965 Bob Anderson came down off the mountain and went to Philadelphia to give that direction. "I figured," he said once in an interview, "that I would get in there when I was 47—and get the hell out on my 50th birthday." However, that wasn't the scenario that unfolded in Philadelphia.

Atlantic Petroleum Storage Company, later known as Atlantic Refining Company, had been founded in 1866 by Charles Lockhart, James S. Wright, and other early pioneers of the Pennsylvania oil industry. Atlantic became part of Standard Oil in 1874 and was set loose by the 1911 Supreme Court decree breaking up the Rockefeller-owned Trust.

Joining Atlantic Refining in 1956 was Thornton Bradshaw, a former teacher at the Harvard Business School. He became president of Atlantic in 1964, shortly before Bob Anderson arrived in Philadelphia to assume the chairmanship. They have worked together in those positions for 15 years, a team record matched by few other leaders in business. Here's what they did during those years:

1966: Atlantic Refining, primarily an eastern company traditionally short of crude, merges with Richfield Oil, a West Coast company with an uneven career (it nearly went under in the Depression before being rescued by Cities Service and Sinclair Oil).

1968: Arco strikes oil in Alaska.

1968: Arco's headquarters are moved to New York to be closer to the financial wellheads.

1970: Arco acquires the bulk of the assets of Sinclair Oil, a 54-year-old petroleum company built by Harry F. Sinclair, a buccaneer who served a jail term for his part in the Teapot Dome scandal of the 1920s.

1972: Bob Anderson, never fond of New York City, moves the company's headquarters across the country to Los Angeles (where he also can commute more easily to his New Mexico ranch).

1977: Arco acquires Anaconda for cash and stock worth about $700 million in one of the biggest acquisitions in business history.

Result: Coming into the decade of the 1960s there were three separate oil companies—Atlantic, Richfield, and Sinclair—producing gasoline and selling it at more than 30,000 service stations under three different brand names. By the end of the 1970s there was one company selling gasoline at 8,500 stations under one brand name: Arco.

When Bob Anderson arrived in Philadelphia in 1965, Atlantic Refining had total revenues of $825 million and profits of $66 million. The company ranked 68th on the *Fortune* 500 list. Today revenues of $16 billion rank the company 13th on the *Fortune* 500 list. Profits, at $1 billion, are more than revenues were in 1966. Yet there are fewer employees in the petroleum part of the business today than in 1970.

Reputation. They're known in the oil industry as "Bob Anderson's company." Wall Streeters love Arco because of the company's heavy dependence on U.S. energy

Arco chairman Robert O. Anderson.

sources. Despite their huge growth, they are still known as a company that can move quickly. If there's anything Anderson dislikes, it's deliberation by committees.

What they own. Petroleum is a capital-intensive industry. Arco's assets exceed $12 billion, and capital expenditures run to more than $1 billion a year. One of the minor assets is the British Sunday newspaper *The Observer,* which Anderson had Arco buy in 1976 to save it from extinction. Anderson called the purchase "a modest bet on the survival of England." The British press hailed the move at the time as follows: "A Stetson-Hatted Liberal to the Rescue."

Who owns and runs the company. Bob Anderson. Although institutions—banks, insurance companies, mutual funds, and other investment companies—own substantial blocks of Arco stock, there's no doubt who's in charge. With 500,000 shares worth approximately $50 million at the start of 1980, Anderson is the largest single stockholder. He has never shown much sympathy toward critics who say that boards of directors should be expanded to include members of different groups in the population as a whole. Arco's board is all-white and all-male. Bradshaw, the chief

lieutenant, has been a more visible leader than Anderson, having represented Arco to public groups. In a speech he made in 1976 Bradshaw complained that corporate boards have been populated by "too many lawyers, too many investment bankers, too many men, too few women, too few minorities." Thornton Bradshaw, meet Bob Anderson. In 1979 the board of directors awarded Anderson an extra retirement benefit. They decided, in effect, to back-date his employment to 1942 instead of 1964, when he first joined the company. As a result, when he retires, Anderson will get $374,685 a year instead of $111,821.

In the public eye. Bradshaw says: "No decision is made in the boardroom of Atlantic Richfield without first considering its social and political implications." In 1976 the Council on Economic Priorities published a study of oil refinery pollution, ranking 61 refineries in 22 states. The combined ratings showed Arco to have the best overall record in controlling emissions.

While other oil companies rail regularly against the "ogres" in Washington, Arco has not joined this anvil chorus. Indeed, in 1977 Bradshaw wrote an article for *Fortune* in which he stated: "The myth of American free enterprise persists. . . . I think it is time to look at our economic system realistically. My own premise is that business does not now operate in a free-enterprise system, but rather as part of a unique mix of private and government forces. In that mix the government role cannot and should not be denigrated."

Such is the litigious nature of the oil and mining industries that Arco is currently a defendant in more than 40 legal actions, ranging from antitrust suits brought by various states to a complaint by Alaskan Eskimos that Arco and others have abridged their aboriginal rights.

Where they're going. Arco is now producing 2 million tons of coal a year; they expect to be mining 30 million tons by 1990. They have one of the largest stakes in solar energy of any oil company, having invested $25 million to accelerate the work of Energy Conversion Devices, a Troy, Michigan, company in the forefront of research into substances that convert sunlight into electricity. Meanwhile, Arco has also pushed ahead with convenience store outlets at their self-service gasoline stations. If the oil ever gives out, they can give 7 Eleven a run for their money.

Stock performance. Arco stock bought for $1,000 in 1970 sold for $1,857 on January 2, 1980.

Access. 515 South Flower Street, Los Angeles, California 90071; (213) 486-3511.

Consumer brands.

Arco gasoline and motor oil.

Sales: $4.3 billion
Profits: $367.7 million
Forbes 500 rank: 217
Founded: 1963
Employees: 8,000
Headquarters: Jacksonville, Florida

What they do. Charter is a shipful of nervous operations managers who have to keep one eye on the company and another on their unpredictable, swashbuckling boss, Raymond Mason. With his saber clenched between his teeth, Mason swings from one new acquisition to another, seeming to pay little attention to how these companies are run. It has been said that Mason doesn't even recognize many of his own top-flight operations men. The *Wall Street Journal* has likened Mason to "a teenager who lays out all his savings for a car that barely works."

Still, it was Mason's Captain Blood–like antics that built his father's near-bankrupt lumber yard into a $4 billion corporation in 15 years; today they have fingers in publishing, broadcasting, insurance, and real estate. But Mason's shining achievement— and the company gold mine—is Charter Oil, now one of the nation's top twenty oil companies. Mason bought a few Dixie Vim gas stations, located mostly in the South, in the late 1960s and picked up 900 Billup and Super-Test stations and a rusty refinery in Houston in 1970. Today Charter has another refinery in the Bahamas and is a major refined oil supplier—160,000 barrels per day, a number which will certainly be

going up, thanks to the Bahamian deal. Oil operations account for nearly 90% of Charter's sales.

History. The Mason Lumber Company was founded in Jacksonville in 1919 by Raymond's father. In 1959 the nearly bankrupt lumber business was bought by the Pierce-Uible Company, a local land-development firm eventually taken over by Raymond Mason. He changed the name to Charter Company in 1963 and designated himself president. In 1968 the lumber yard was torn down, and a motel went up in its place.

Mason quickly began building his wheeler-dealer reputation. In 1965 he bought the Jacksonville National Bank. When home building in Florida suffered a decline the following year, he took on a Florida title insurance company and a mortgage company in Puerto Rico. But Mason's first truly great leap of faith came in 1970, when California's Signal Oil announced they were interested in dumping some of their petroleum assets—all big losers—at bargain-basement prices. With a shrug and a hearty "What the hell?" Mason stepped in and picked them up. When the Arab oil embargo hit in the early 1970s, Charter, with their domestic assets, was in position to clean up.

All this profitability seemed to make Mason nervous, so he bought *Redbook* magazine and a large magazine printing plant from Norton Simon in 1975, later adding other publications and radio stations. Mason, a voracious reader who often buys books by the bagful, loved the idea of dabbling in the publishing game.

Then, in 1979, Mason took his biggest gamble yet. He bought a refinery on Grand Bahama Island from Edward Carey, older brother of New York Governor Hugh Carey. The refinery was in receivership and $485 million in debt to the Libyan and Iranian national oil companies, which supplied the refinery with its crude. Mason arranged a deal with the creditors (the terms of which have not been disclosed) and now seems to be making a go of it. Meanwhile Mason is busying himself looking for something else to buy and is already swinging, saber in teeth, to the next ship.

Reputation. A "comer," as they say on Broadway. Mason's hell-for-leather management and acquisition style reminds Wall Street of Dr. Armand Hammer, the Occidental Petroleum chairman who built his company from nothing into a $9 billion firm in 20 years.

What they own. The world's fifth-largest oil refinery, in the Bahamas. Four magazines: *Redbook, Ladies' Home Journal, Sport, The Discount Merchandiser.* The Dayton Press, one of the nation's largest magazine printing plants, in Dayton, Ohio. Five radio stations: WOKY-AM, Milwaukee; KCBQ-AM, San Diego; KSLQ-FM, St. Louis; WMJX-FM, Miami; and WDRQ-FM, Detroit. An insurance company. Real estate and related assets valued at $44.7 million.

Who owns and runs the company. Raymond Mason's 3 million shares, which represent about 17.5% of the company's stock, make him the largest single shareholder. But his good friend Edward Ball controls 23% through the St. Joseph Paper Company, one of the Alfred I. du Pont family holdings. Ball is trustee of these holdings—and a counselor to Mason. Mason is known as a "hayseed tycoon," an image helped along by his thick southern drawl and predilection for wearing garishly patterned neckties and needlepoint belts made by his wife, Minerva.

In the public eye. Mason got some unwanted attention when, in the mid-1970s, he decided to use the power of his presses to cement relations with the Saudis, with whom he was negotiating for crude oil supplies. Dubbed "Project Faisal," the $8 million public relations campaign proposed by Mason involved planting favorable articles on the Saudi royal family in *Redbook* and other Mason publications. The king said no when Jack Anderson, Washington columnist, blew the whistle.

Mason has a penchant for personal diplomacy. According to the *Wall Street Journal,* in 1973, during the Arab oil embargo, he flew to Saudi Arabia with the idea of having King Faisal buy Gulf Oil. The king apparently liked the idea, but Gulf didn't. Then in 1975 he flew William Seawell, chairman of Pan American World Airways, to Teheran to try and save a deal in which Iran would have become a major shareholder in the airline.

Where they're going. Look for Mason to make beautiful music with another one of his good friends, Armand Hammer of Occidental Petroleum. The two almost merged their respective operations in 1970. In early 1980 Occidental said they would sell Permian, the nation's largest crude oil marketer, to Charter. But that deal fell through, too.

Not stopping to catch his breath, Mason went on to make a deal in early 1980 with Karl Eller, media wunderkind who built Combined Communications into a $300 million company before selling out to Gannett in 1979. Charter and Eller were to go 50-50 in a new company to be called Charter Media, the agenda calling for them to be active in newspapers, outdoor advertising, cable television, radio-TV stations, and other magazines. Their first move was to buy the *Philadelphia Bulletin.*

Stock performance. Charter stock bought for $1,000 in 1970 sold for $11,250 on January 2, 1980. In 1979 they were the biggest gainer on the New York Stock Exchange, with their stock 580% higher at the end of the year than at the beginning.

Access. 208 Laura Street, Jacksonville, Florida 32202; (904) 358-4111.

Consumer brands.

Service stations (some with convenience food-stores): Billup; Super Test; Dixie Vim; Charter.
Publications: Ladies' Home Journal; Redbook; Sport; Discount Merchandising; Philadelphia Bulletin.
Radio stations: WMIL-FM, Milwaukee; WOKY-AM, Milwaukee; KCBQ-AM, San Diego; KLSQ-FM, St. Louis; WDRQ-FM, Detroit; WMJX-FM, Miami.
Insurance: Charter Security Life.
Mail order sales: Joy's Ltd.; the Hamilton Mint.

Big oil firms control 72% of U.S. high-quality retrievable uranium ores, and they mine 60% of the nation's uranium. Gulf Oil owns 18% of domestic uranium reserves and a substantial amount of Canada's uranium.

Sales: $12.6 billion
Profits: $815.4 million
Forbes 500 rank: 20
Rank in oil: 10
Rank in coal: 2
Founded: 1911
Employees: 42,780
Headquarters: Stamford, Connecticut

What they do. It's a long way from Ponca City, Oklahoma, to Stamford, Connecticut; and if you look at profits, sales, and assets, Conoco has indeed come a long way. But even now a bit of the Ponca City dust seems to blow occasionally through the Conoco home office in Stamford—sometimes in the form of the wildcat fever that got the company going in the first place.

This once-tiny oil company struck it big in Libya in 1958, and now almost half their profits flow from African and Middle Eastern oil. The rest comes from the United States (34%), Canada (14%), and the North Sea (2%); with another 4% from wells in the rest of the world, principally Indonesia and Micronesia. Most of this oil is sold in the form of gasoline through Conoco service stations in Europe and the United States (mainly in the Midwest, Southwest, and Rocky Mountain areas). But Conoco also sells gas through stations that look like independents battling the majors: FasGas in Texas and the upper Midwest, Fast Gas and Econo in the West, Kayo in the East, and Jet on the West Coast and in the Midwest and Southwest. They sell in 42 states.

Conoco also has vast coal reserves in the western United States, mined by their Consolidated Coal subsidiary. And their chemical division is the world's fourth-largest producer of polyvinyl chloride, used to make records for the music industry.

History. E. W. Marland was one of Oklahoma's first wildcatters when he struck oil —a lot of it—on land belonging to a Cherokee named Willie Cries-for-War in 1911. It was his strike near Ponca City that touched off the Oklahoma "black gold" rush and made Marland's company one of the area's biggest producers. Needing a marketing outlet for his oil, in 1929 Marland merged with a Denver company, Continental Oil & Transportation, whose history can be traced back to 1875. Marland took the name of the Denver company, maintaining headquarters in Ponca City. In 1929 revenues were $90 million. Continental began selling gasoline and other petroleum products in the American Southwest in the 1930s.

Growth was slow until after World War II, when Conoco hired Leonard F. McCollum away from Standard Oil of New Jersey in 1947. McCollum decided to play with the majors and, after the 1958 Libyan strike, began selling in Europe. By 1964 Conoco had bought 1,000 gas stations in the United Kingdom, West Germany, Austria, Belgium, and Luxembourg. The 1966 addition of Consolidated Coal, with 14.3 billion tons of reserves, made Conoco the largest coal company in the United States (they are first in reserves, but Peabody outproduces them).

McCollum moved the company's base from Ponca City to Houston in 1950. In 1964 he moved the headquarters to New York to be closer to his bankers. In 1970 Continental decided to move to the suburbs (where the bankers live), and so they relocated to Connecticut. In 1979 the company's name was changed to their major brand name, Conoco.

Reputation. Conoco is widely known—in the industry and in labor circles and among public interest groups—as a hard-nosed company that spends an inordinate amount of time railing against government regulations. Their coal subsidiary has one of the worst safety records in coal mining.

What they own. Besides their oil and coal, more than 324,000 acres of mineral rights in the uranium-rich portions of the western United States.

Who owns and runs the company. Employee savings plans own 5% of the stock. Ralph E. Bailey, chairman since 1979, is a coal man.

In the public eye. Conoco has been the target of sex discrimination suits. In 1978 they agreed to pay $370,000 to 78 women who had been illegally denied jobs under the EEO guidelines.

In that same year a grand jury in Houston indicted the company for falsifying records and selling oil in excess of federal regulations. Conoco pleaded no contest to one felony and one misdemeanor count and paid a total of $3 million in refunds, fines, and penalties.

They have been under fire for their safety record in coal mining. In 1973 a public interest group organized a "Campaign Continental," issuing a counter-report to the company's annual report. The counter-report said:

Consolidation . . . maintained its record as the foremost killer among American coal mines in 1972. Thirty-two men died in Consol mines last year. Consolidation's record for deaths is phenomenal when compared to other companies. Peabody Coal, the company closest to Consol in production, had seven deaths. Over a four-year period from 1968 to 1972, Consol maintained the highest death rate per million man hours of any coal company, with 165 men dead.

A 1972 report by the National Council of Churches also took Consolidation to task for their mine safety record. The report stated that "safety training for new miners consists of a one-day session, a lecture welcoming them to Consol, giving each man a copy of the union contract, and briefly describing a few basic safety principles. Then the men tour a mine and a preparation plant and are assigned to work with an experienced miner."

Stock performance. Conoco stock bought for $1,000 in 1970 sold for $3,566 on January 2, 1980.

Major employment centers. Stamford, Connecticut; Houston; Ponca City, Oklahoma.

Access. High Ridge Park, Stamford, Connecticut 06904; (203) 359-3500.

Consumer brands.

Gasoline: Conoco; FasGas; Jet; Kayo; Econo.

FROM MOPED TO SATURN V: HOW FAR THEY GO ON A GALLON OF FUEL

MOPED (*motorized bicycle*)   120 *miles*
HARLEY-DAVIDSON 1200 (*motorcycle*)   50 *miles*
VOLKSWAGEN RABBIT DIESEL (*automobile*)   42 *miles*
MODEL A FORD (*automobile*)   25 *miles*
PIPER CHEROKEE (*light plane*)   13-1/2 *miles*[1]
MASERATI QUATTROPORTE (*automobile*)   7 *miles*
GMC ASTRO (*semitruck*)   4 *miles*[2]
GM (*diesel locomotive*)   632 *yards*[3]
BOEING 747 (*jumbo jet*)   280 *yards*[4]
ULTRA-LARGE CRUDE OIL CARRIER (*supertanker*)   31 *feet*[5]
SATURN V (*rocket*)   4 *inches to infinity*[6]

[1]At 144 miles per hour.
[2]Fully loaded.
[3]At 70 miles per hour, pulling 40–50 fully loaded freight cars.
[4]Carrying 385 passengers at 39,000 feet.
[5]At 17 miles per hour and fully loaded, this ship needs 40 gallons of fuel to travel its own length.
[6]In the course of launching a manned exploration vehicle toward the moon, Saturn V's first stage burned 15 tons of fuel per second for 2-1/2 minutes while gaining 36 miles of altitude and 6,000 miles per hour of speed (for an average of 4 inches per gallon); stage 2 consumed one ton per second for 6-1/2 minutes while climbing to 108 miles and gaining a speed of 17,400 mph; stage 3 burned twice, for a total time of 8 minutes, gulping 182 gallons of fuel per second before reaching 24,900 mph, and escaping the earth's gravitational field. The total fuel consumed was just over 1 million gallons (by weight, 21% kerosene; 33% liquid hydrogen; and 45% liquid oxygen). In fairness to Saturn V, which comes out something of a fuel-guzzler, it should be pointed out that the other figures in the table are based on crusing speeds and would all be drastically reduced for climbing while accelerating. Furthermore, once free of earth's gravity, you need not have stopped at the moon; after 200 days Saturn V's million-gallon boost would have carried you 120 million miles—with the average fuel economy of a Moped!

EXXON

Sales: $79.1 billion
Profits: $4.3 billion
Forbes 500 rank: 1
Rank in oil: 1
Rank in natural gas: 1
Rank in retail gasoline sales: 1
Rank in shipping fleet: 1
Founded: 1870
Employees: 130,000
Headquarters: New York, New York

What they do. Only about a dozen nations on earth have larger gross national products than Exxon's annual sales, which roughly match the GNPs of countries like Mexico, Sweden, and Iran.

Every hour, around the clock, Exxon rings up nearly $10 million in sales; with each passing second they reap another $150 in profits. Their international headquarters at Rockefeller Center in New York City is often called the "United Nations of Oil." A wall of television screens and computers records the movements of 500 Exxon ships as they set out from 115 ports to 270 destinations, with cargoes of 160 kinds of oil to be delivered to 65 countries. On the top floor, John D. Rockefeller's own desk is displayed.

Two thousand miles away, in Houston, Texas, the Exxon USA headquarters reflect another aspect of the world's largest moneymaking machine. The engineer-executives look out of their skyscraper on a young city built by the tough characters who drilled the first Texas oil wells at the turn of the century. Many of the managers are graduates of the "Exxon Academy," as they call their huge refinery at Baton Rouge, Louisiana.

Exxon is so enormous that even if you took away all their foreign operations, they would still rank among America's biggest 10 companies—even though only one-third of their sales and less than one-fifth of their oil production come from the United States. Their chemical operations, which make ingredients for everything from fertilizers to truck tires, would be one of the nation's five largest chemical companies. They also own the third-largest coal reserves in the United States.

Exxon is one of the original multinational corporations. Rigs working for Exxon or companies they partly own pump oil in the Arabian deserts, the North Sea off Britain, the Gulf of Mexico, Alaska's North Slope, and the wilds of Indonesia. The crude oil is distilled into gasoline, heating oil, or jet fuel at refineries in California, Texas, New Jersey, Montana, Louisiana, Wales, Rotterdam, and Saudi Arabia. (Exxon refines more than twice as much oil outside the United States than inside.) Each day 6 million motorists pull into Exxon's 65,600 gas stations around the world. The company sells gasoline in 45 of America's 50 states, but two-thirds of their filling stations are in foreign countries, from Guatemala to Thailand.

Like the other big oil companies, Exxon has the problem of making so much money they don't know what to do with it all. Exxon's profits in 1979 were up 55% from 1978. In the first quarter of 1980 they surpassed AT&T to become the world's biggest profit maker. In an effort to get rid of some of their spare change in 1979, they agreed to spend $1.2 billion to buy Cleveland-based Reliance Electric, supposedly because the company has developed an energy-efficient electric motor. They have ventured into copper mining, uranium mining, and nuclear fuel production, and they are a rapidly growing force in advanced office machines such as word-processing equipment. Still, less than 1% of their sales comes from non-petroleum-related activities.

History. John D. Rockefeller, born in 1839, seems to have inherited his character in equal portions from his con artist father and his stern, Calvinist mother. Peter Collier and David Horowitz present a telling portrait of his early years in their book *The Rockefellers*. The father, William Avery Rockefeller, was a tall, effusive, barrel-chested man who amassed great sums of money first by flimflamming the Iroquois Indians near his home in upstate New York and later by selling patent medicines, including an elixir he claimed could cure cancer. He gave medical consultations to the gullible country folk for $25—a good two months' wages. In 1849 he was indicted for the rape of a young woman who had worked in the Rockefeller household, and he left the county soon afterward. He moved his family to Cleveland in 1853 so that he could take advantage of the settlers streaming west in covered wagons with their life savings. He often went away for long periods, and finally he disappeared altogether. Years later, a reporter working for Joseph Pulitzer discovered that the elder Rockefeller survived to the age of 96 and spent his last 40 years living under an assumed name in South Dakota in a bigamous marriage with a woman 20 years his junior.

The task of setting the children on the path of righteousness fell to the mother, Eliza Davison Rockefeller, described as a "thin, hatchet-faced woman with flaming red hair and equally stark blue eyes." She studied the Bible and filled young John with maxims he carried through life, such as "Willful waste makes woeful want."

Upon graduating from high school in 1855, John D. Rockefeller chose to go into business rather than to college. He got a job as a bookkeeper with a Cleveland commodity merchant for $3.50 a week—10% of which he faithfully donated to the Baptist church. After three years he had saved $800, and he decided to start his own commodity business with a partner, Maurice Clark. Needing another $1,000, he turned to his father, who had promised each of his children that amount when they turned 21. John was only 19½, but his father agreed to lend him the money at 10% interest until he came of age. "I cheat my boys every chance I get," the father liked to say. "I want to make 'em sharp."

Commodity prices rose sharply during the Civil War, and the new firm of Clark & Rockefeller made impressive profits. But a development even more far reaching than the war was emerging around Titusville, Pennsylvania, where Edwin Drake had drilled the world's first successful oil well in 1859. Oil had been established as the cheapest, most efficient of illuminants, and

Remember Esso?

The most expensive name change in business history took place in 1972 when the Standard Oil Company (New Jersey) adopted the new designation Exxon Corporation. Also changed at that time was the company's major brand name, Esso, which also became Exxon. The basic reason for the switch was rooted in the historic 1911 Supreme Court decision breaking up the Standard Oil Trust into 34 companies. Today, 14 of the original 34 companies survive as Atlantic Richfield, Borne Chemical, Buckeye Pipeline, Chesebrough-Pond's, Conoco, Exxon, Marathon Oil, Mobil, Pennzoil, Standard Oil Company of California, Standard Oil Company (Indiana), Standard Oil Company (Ohio), Trans Union, and Washington Oil.

When the trust was dissolved, seven of the companies retained the name "Standard Oil." The largest was Standard Oil Company (New Jersey), which introduced the brand name Esso on the eastern seaboard in 1926. Esso was derived from the initials S. O. (standing for Standard Oil), and when Jersey Standard tried to introduce this brand name into other territories, they were challenged by the other Standard Oil companies. In 1935 Indiana Standard secured a court order locking up most of the Midwest for their Standard stations, keeping Esso out. When Indiana Standard goes outside the Midwest, they use the brand name Amoco (American Oil Company). Ohio Standard stations fly the banner Sohio. California Standard uses the Chevron brand name.

After finding that it could use the Esso name in only 19 eastern and southern states, Jersey Standard began selling under two other names in the rest of the country: Humble in Ohio and Enco elsewhere. Meanwhile, they continued to press in the courts for the right to use the Esso name everywhere. That effort ended in 1969 when the Supreme Court refused to entertain the idea. So Jersey Standard set up a task force to come up with a new corporate name and a new brand name to end the confusion about "Standard Oil."

Exxon emerged as the winner from 10,000 names dredged up by the computer. It was first tested on stations in September 1971. The corporate name was changed on November 1, 1972. The last Esso sign on a service station came down in the spring of 1973. (The brand name change was domestic only; Esso still survives overseas.) *New Yorker* writer John Brooks, whose story of the name change appears in his book *The Games Players,* said the cost of the switch had been estimated at $100 million, that cost including signs and insignia for 25,000 service stations, plaques for 22,000 oil wells and 18,000 buildings and storage tanks, 55,000 signs warning about underground pipelines, 300 million sales slips, and 11 million credit cards.

But the change was accomplished with a minimum of protest from employees, shareholders, and customers. John Brooks had the last word: "The company's rash act of 1972 overthrew one of the oldest axioms of business theory—that a successful trademark is sacrosanct, and that to change it is suicide."

it quickly started to replace candles and whale oil. The "oil regions" sprouted derricks overnight, and dozens of refineries sprang up, first in Pittsburgh and New York and then in Cleveland. In 1863 an acquaintance of Clark came to the partners with a proposition to start a refinery. Rockefeller dipped into his savings and invested $4,000 as a silent partner. At first he saw it as an unimportant sideline, but as the oil boom continued he began to devote more of his attention to it. In 1865, at the age of 26, he bought out the others and took control of the business. His refinery was already the largest in Cleveland, and he was determined to expand. Around this time a startled bystander happened to see Rockefeller in his office, jumping into the air, clicking his heels, and rejoicing to himself, "I'm bound to be rich! Bound to be rich! *Bound to be rich!*"

With this goal in mind, Rockefeller set out to control the industry. He realized that the big money in oil would not be made at the well since prices collapsed every time someone struck a new find. The key to success, he saw, was to control the refining and transportation of oil. Borrowing heavily from Cleveland banks, he expanded his refining capacity and leased all the available tank cars from the railroads, leaving his competitors with no way to ship their oil out of Cleveland. Next he negotiated an agreement with the Lake Shore Railroad to give him secret rebates on the crude oil he shipped from the oil regions to Cleveland and the refined oil he sent from Cleveland to the East Coast. In return, he guaranteed to ship 60 carloads of oil a day. With his freight advantage secure, Rockefeller formed a new company in 1870, called Standard Oil.

In the same year several railroads came up with a new plan: they would secretly combine with the largest refiners in each major refining center, to the benefit of both parties. Freight rates would go up, but the refiners in the scheme would get their money back through rebates on their shipments and additional "drawbacks" on the shipments of other refiners who were not in on the arrangement. Rockefeller saw it as a way to get rid of his bothersome competitors in Cleveland: they could either collapse their businesses into his, in exchange for stock, or they would be bankrupted by the rebate scheme. His younger brother, Frank Rockefeller, who was a partner in a firm competing with Standard Oil, was told by John D.: "We have a combination with the railroads. We are going to buy out all the refiners in Cleveland. We will give everyone a chance to come in. . . . Those who refuse will be crushed. If you don't sell your property to us, it will be valueless." Frank did not sell, and he went bankrupt. He remained bitter for the rest of his life and eventually moved his two children's bodies from the family burial plot in Cleveland so they would not have to spend eternity in the company of John D. Rockefeller.

Rockefeller looked back on this period with great piety. "The Standard was an angel of mercy," he told a biographer late in life. It was a situation, he explained, of "the strongest and most prosperous concern in the business . . . turning to its less fortunate competitors . . . and saying to them, 'We will stand in for the risks and hazards of the refining business. . . . Come with us, and we will do you good.'" Within three months Rockefeller bought up all but 3 of his 25 competitors in Cleveland. Standard Oil controlled one-quarter of the nation's refining capacity, but Rockefeller was not satisfied. He raised his sights and convinced more independent refiners in New York, Philadelphia, Pittsburgh, and the oil regions to come into the Standard combine, and he did it with such secrecy that almost no one knew about his oil monopoly until it was a fait accompli. By 1880 Rockefeller was refining 95% of the nation's oil.

At the time, American companies were prohibited from owning shares in other companies in other states. To get around this restriction, Rockefeller devised an oil trust, which owned shares in each of the component companies—pretending all the while that the companies were independent. He lavished bribes and "deals" on state legislators. He drove his competitors out of business by undercutting their prices until they gave up, and he expanded his power by buying oilfields across the country. At the same time he moved quickly into foreign markets. By 1885, 70% of Standard Oil's sales were overseas.

As the extent of Rockefeller's power gradually became known, public opinion forced the passage of antitrust laws in several states. But by 1888 Rockefeller was able to take advantage of a New Jersey law that allowed corporations to hold shares in companies outside the state. He reorganized the trust as a holding company, called Standard

Oil (New Jersey), which owned shares of all the other companies. President Theodore Roosevelt's Justice Department brought suit in 1906, under the Sherman Anti-Trust Act of 1890. The case worked its way to the Supreme Court, which in a historic decision in 1911 declared Standard Oil an illegal monopoly that had sought to "drive others from the field and exclude them from their right to trade."

Out of the dissolution came 34 separate companies, including Standard Oil of New York (later Mobil) and Standard Oil of California. The companies were still owned by the same stockholders, and Rockefeller himself held a quarter of the shares. The money has held together well over the years: the Rockefeller family and Rockefeller Foundation now own about 1.75% of Exxon, 2% of Standard Oil of California, and 1.75% of Mobil. New details of the Rockefeller money came to light in 1974 during the Senate confirmation hearings of Vice-President designate Nelson Rockefeller, the founder's grandson. According to Anthony Sampson in his book, *The Seven Sisters*, "The total value of the assets of all living descendants of John D. Rockefeller was estimated at that time at two billion dollars."

By the time of the split, John D. Rockefeller had retired from actively running the company (although he lived to be 97 years old). In his place was John D. Archbold, who first met Rockefeller when the two were bitter rivals in oil refining. Archbold, like many others, had eventually sold out to Rockefeller in a secret deal. He was a jovial, popular Irishman who was known to be a hearty drinker until Rockefeller forced him to "sign the pledge." Under Archbold, Standard Oil of New Jersey (or Jersey Standard, as it was often called) had to become newly aggressive in search of oil supplies since they were now cut off from the other companies that had supplied their crude oil for years.

Archbold's successor, Walter Teagle, was the son of an early Pennsylvania oilman who had also sold out secretly to Rockefeller. Teagle ruled Jersey Standard for 20 years, with a three-month hunting-and-fishing vacation each year. The modest size of Jersey's oil holdings pushed Teagle to buy 50% of Humble Oil Company of Texas in 1919 (secretly of course) and then look abroad for more oil as the flowering automobile age called for fantastic amounts of

> John D. Rockefeller's obsession with economy continued to rule his business operations even after his refinery had long since burgeoned into Standard Oil. According to *Great Stories of American Businessmen*, Rockefeller was watching cans of oil being soldered shut in one of his plants one day when he asked how many drops of solder were used on each can. When he heard that each can got 40 drops of solder, he asked if 38 would do. No one knew, so Rockefeller had workers try sealing some cans with only 38. A few cans leaked, but with exactly 39 drops of solder they stayed sealed. Thereafter, 39 drops of solder sealed each can, saving some $2,000 a year.

petroleum. Jersey expanded to South America and naively hoped to get into the Soviet Union after the Russian Revolution of 1917. Prior to the revolution, the Nobel brothers of Sweden had controlled about a third of the Russian oil production. In 1920, even though the Red armies had seized the Nobel properties, Teagle made a secret deal in which he bought out the Nobels for $11.5 million. He was obviously banking on the Bolsheviks being toppled. A company historian conceded that the deal with the Nobels "appears to have been one of the most ill-considered ever made" by Jersey.

But Jersey Standard had the right political muscle working for them when the first international oil cartel was formed in the Middle East after World War I. The Turkish Petroleum Company (later known as the Iraq Petroleum Company) was organized to exploit the oil resources believed to lie in the old Turkish Empire (Turkey and what is now Syria, Iraq, Jordan, Saudi Arabia). It was originally the idea of the extraordinary entrepreneur, Calouste Gulbenkian, who was to get 5% of the action. Backing him after the war were the British and the French, who felt they had a right to the spoils because they had defeated the Turks. The United States had never declared war against Turkey, but they objected vigorously to the cozy arrangements being worked out by the French and British. The State Department insisted on an "open door" policy—code words for "American participation." Under orchestration of the State Department, seven American oil companies were yoked together in the Near East Development Corporation to advance

American oil interests in the Middle East. Many were not all that eager to play this imperialistic role, and in the end only two remained: Jersey Standard and Mobil. They were to share a 23.7% interest in Iraq Petroleum. They joined with Anglo-Iranian Oil (later to become British Petroleum), Shell, the French national oil company, and Gulbenkian in the famous Red Line Agreement of 1928, the one that reserved to themselves as a group the oil resources of the Middle East (minus Kuwait and Iran). Each promised not to act independently in that area. This marked the start of American involvement in Middle East oil. Also in 1928, Teagle traveled to Achnacarry Castle in Scotland for a summit meeting with the boss of Shell (Sir Henri Deterding), the boss of Anglo-Iranian (Sir John Cadman), and other oil lords (including William L. Mellon of Gulf). In that secret conclave they hammered out the "As Is" agreement, a bold and on the whole successful attempt to make sure the world's oil resources would remain in their hands.

Teagle's reign ended when some of the company's dealings with Hitler's Germany came to light. Jersey Standard and the I. G. Farben chemical company of Germany had made a secret research agreement as early as 1926. After Hitler came to power in 1933, Jersey gave Germany the patents for a lead vital to the production of aviation fuel. The Germans in return were supposed to develop a formula for synthetic rubber, the secrets of which they would reveal to Jersey, but World War II intervened. Thurmond Arnold, the Justice Department's crusading antitrust chief, charged Jersey with obstructing American research on synthetic rubber. Senator Harry Truman, heading a committee investigating national defense, suggested that the agreement might be treasonable. Teagle resigned in 1942, a nervous, broken man. Jersey Standard insisted that the research agreement with the Germans was crucial to the U.S. development of 100-octane aviation fuel, synthetic rubber, and TNT derived from petroleum. Ironically, Hitler was upset with I. G. Farben for the agreement with Jersey. But Farben asserted that in fact their agreement with Jersey helped the Germans develop essential war material.

Jersey Standard's supply of oil and wealth grew sharply after World War II when they were cut into the Arabian American Oil Company (Aramco), by their two American sisters, Standard Oil of California and Texaco. Then, in 1954, the State Department once again came to the aid of Jersey Standard. After the CIA-aided overthrow of the socialist government of Dr. Mohammed Mossadegh in Iran and the return to power of the Shah, Jersey Standard and the other giants of the world petroleum industry organized a new consortium to operate the Iranian oil properties previously exploited by one company: British Petroleum. As the official history of Jersey Standard puts it, the company was invited by "the Iranian and U.S. governments" to revive the oil industry that was considered "essential to Iran."

In Saudi Arabia, Jersey Standard was given a 30% cut of the operation. In Iran they got 7%. These participations cemented Jersey Standard's position atop the world oil industry. They went on to discover oil in many other places—Libya, the Netherlands, Alaska, the North Sea (it seems that wherever there's oil, there's Exxon)—but none of these finds matched their flow from the Middle East. Even today, after the oil-producing countries have acted to take direct control of their resources, Exxon continues to derive a major part of their crude oil from those fields—under different arrangements to be sure. Now they are more like agents of the governments in power. In 1980 Exxon told their shareholders that 56% of the company's crude oil was coming from "governments or government oil companies under various agreements." Standard Oil of New Jersey became Exxon in 1972 to enable the company to sell their gasoline under one name in the U.S. market. They had wanted to go national with their Esso name, but the other Standard Oil companies objected, and the courts upheld these objections. At the time of the name change this was the company that advertised their gasoline by telling you to "put a tiger in your tank." They no longer do that. In fact, because of the energy crisis, Exxon has not advertised their gasoline since 1974. (Instead they only promote their motor oil, service, or various ideological messages about the energy crises. All oil companies have done the same, so that they are no longer among the top media advertisers. Only Mobil is in the top 100 advertisers because of their Montgomery Ward subsidiary.) Once again the world has changed on the company, and once again they are adapting. In 1974 *Time* pointed out that Exxon has "survived wars, expropriations, brutalizing competition, muckraking attacks and even dismemberment by the U.S. Supreme Court."

Reputation. If everybody hates the oil companies, then Exxon, as the biggest company in the industry, may be the most hated of them all. Exxon is aware of their unpopularity. "Public attitudes toward the company and the industry are quite negative," chairman Clifton C. Garvin, Jr., told shareholders at the 1978 annual meeting. To help reverse these attitudes, Exxon is building an energy pavilion in the "Future World" section of Walt Disney World in Florida. "We're impressed with the fact that they attract over 20 million people there," Garvin said. In 1979 Garvin, a quiet, reserved engineer, argued the industry's position on TV, appearing on the Phil Donahue show, where he faced housewives angered by the escalating gasoline prices. "The audience appreciated his guts, if not his logic," said *Fortune*.

What they own. Sixty-two refineries in 33 countries. Thirteen thousand wells in the United States, Canada (Exxon's 70%-owned Imperial Oil subsidiary is Canada's largest oil company), Europe, the Middle East, Africa, Australia, and the Far East.

At the end of 1978 Exxon's reserves—how much oil they still had left to pump up—were valued at $45 billion. At the end of 1979, thanks to price increases, those reserves were valued at $88 billion.

Who owns and runs the company. Management succession at Exxon has worked like clockwork, with engineers making their way up a long ladder. It has been suggested that to reach the top you need the stamina of a mountain climber. Engineer Monroe Rathbone retired in 1965, succeeded by another engineer, Michael Haider, who retired in 1970, passing the baton to another engineer, J. Kenneth Jamieson, who retired in 1975 when he was succeeded by Garvin, who at 53 was the youngest chief executive since 49-year-old Eugene Holman was picked in 1944. Exxon's second in command is Howard C. Kauffman, a year younger than Garvin, and also an engineer. But they come from different ends of the business. Garvin came up through refining and chemicals, Kauffman

from production and exploration.

The "big boss" era is over; now everything is run by committee. The standard "Exxonism" for a command, *Time* has reported, is: "You may want to consider this." The 17-member board of directors includes eight present or former Exxon executives; two foreign corporation heads, one British and one German; the board chairman of Procter & Gamble and United Technologies; one woman (Martha Peterson, president of Beloit College), and one black (Randolph W. Bromery, chancellor of the University of Massachusetts at Amherst). Exxon has made a determined effort to boost their minority and female employment. As a percentage of their U.S. work force, both have doubled in the past 10 years. Minorities now represent 16% of total employees, women 23%. Exxon said they hired 11,153 persons in 1979—19% were minorities, 41% were women.

In the public eye. Exxon is the nation's most generous dispenser of charitable contributions. In 1978 they gave away $28 million to education and the arts, sponsoring everything from minority engineering programs to the "MacNeil/Lehrer Report" news show on public television. In 1979, while their profits were jumping 44%, they increased their giving by 16% to $38 million ($7 million of which was contributed abroad). Exxon's charitable contributions budget is five times what it was at the start of 1970.

Exxon doesn't make the noise that Mobil does in defending themselves, and they have not been involved in a lot of scandals. In 1972, when Nixon's chief fundraiser, Maurice Stans, came around, he was supposedly ushered out of chairman Jamieson's office abruptly. In 1974 *Time* magazine reported that although Italian newspapers had been filled with stories about oil companies bribing government officials, "no such charges have been hurled against Exxon's Esso Italiana." Shortly after that Exxon signed a consent decree with the Securities and Exchange Commission in which they disclosed some $55 million of questionable payments in Italy between 1963 and 1972.

Where they're going. "Exxon," in the words of chairman Garvin, "is and will remain primarily an energy company." At the same time they've decided to go head to head with the twin giants of the office equipment business, IBM and Xerox. They are clearly aiming at the "office of the future" market with their Qyx "intelligent typewriters," Vydec text editors with display screens, and Qwip telephone facsimile devices, which send photographs over phone wires. It's admittedly a tough business to break into, but if anybody has the resources to do so, it's Exxon.

Stock performance. Exxon stock bought for $1,000 in 1970 sold for $1,785 on January 2, 1980.

Access. 1251 Avenue of the Americas, New York, New York 10020; (212) 398-3000.

Consumer brands.

Gasoline: Exxon; Esso (outside the United States); Imperial (Canada).
Motor oil: Uniflo.
Office equipment: Vydec text-editing system; Zilog microcomputers; Qyx typewriters; Qwip telephone facsimile devices.

PRINCES OF PETROLEUM:
THE 10 HIGHEST PAID OIL COMPANY EXECUTIVES IN 1979

	Cash and Cash-Equivalent Forms of Remuneration*	Other Forms of Remuneration**	Total all 1979 Remuneration
1. RAWLEIGH WARNER, JR. *Mobil:* Chairman	$3,593,440	$ 46,750	$3,640,190
2. WILLIAM P. TAVOULAREAS *Mobil:* President	$1,973,148	$1,026,077	$2,999,225
3. ZOLTAN MERSZEI *Occidental:* President and C.E.O. of Hooker Chemical	$1,120,610	$ 351,272	$1,471,882
4. ALEX H. MASSAD *Mobil:* Executive Vice President	$ 996,044	$ 293,929	$1,289,973
5. MAURICE F. GRANVILLE *Texaco:* Chairman	$ 969,619	$ 152,020	$1,121,639
6. RICHARD F. TUCKER *Mobil:* Executive Vice President and C.E.O. of Container Corp. of America	$ 870,032	$ 638,438	$1,508,470
7. ROBERT O. ANDERSON *Atlantic Richfield:* Chairman of the Board and Chief Executive Officer	$ 797,110	$ 449,687	$1,246,797
8. HAROLD J. HAYNES *Standard Oil, California:* Chairman	$ 794,099		$ 794,099
9. PAUL J. WOLFE *Mobil:* Executive Vice President	$ 745,779	$ 675,218	$1,420,997
10. JOHN F. BOOKOUT *Shell:* President and C.E.O.	$ 703,072	$1,037,200	$1,740,272

*Includes: salaries, director's fees, and bonuses; securities and property; insurance benefits or reimbursement for insurance by the company; personal benefits; and company contributions to employee's savings program.

**Contingent forms of remuneration, including: stock options, accrued stock appreciation rights, deferred payments, unexercised stock options, and incentive plans contingent upon performance.

C.E.O. = Chief Executive Officer.

Source: Proxy statements issued first quarter 1980.

Gulf

Sales: $23.9 billion
Profits: $1.3 billion
Forbes 500 rank: 8
Rank in oil: 5
Rank in retail gasoline sales: 5
Rank in coal: 16
Founded: 1901
Employees: 58,300
Headquarters: Pittsburgh, Pennsylvania

What they do. Gulf entered the 1970s like a lion—and left like a lamb. None of the other big oil companies took the beating that this Mellon-controlled petroleum pumper did during the past decade. They were rocked by payoff scandals that ended when their chairman and three other top executives were forced to leave the company. They had to close hundreds of their U.S. gasoline stations. They were accused by a Pittsburgh corporate neighbor of conspiring to drive up the price of uranium. And finally, as the decade drew to a close, Gulf was well on their way toward losing a main source of their crude oil.

It's incredible that Gulf was not only still standing but standing so tall. Their 1979 results ranked them 8th in sales, 10th in profits, 14th in market value, and 27th in assets among all U.S. corporations. In the American oil industry, only four companies—Exxon, Mobil, Texaco, and Standard of California—had greater sales. Gulf has been traditionally considered one of the "Seven Sisters," the term used to describe the seven reigning international oil companies (the other six are Exxon, Shell, Mobil, Texaco, British Petroleum, and Standard of California). But their inclusion in this select group is now being questioned. Indeed, *Business Week* found a London oil economist who said flatly that Gulf no longer belonged in this top tier.

If anything disqualifies Gulf from this top-tier ranking, it's their ever-decreasing access to the rich oil deposits below the desert sands of Kuwait, a Persian Gulf country the size of Hawaii. Gulf has been taking oil out of there since 1946, reaping enormous profits. In the early 1970s, when Middle East oil sold for $2.50 a barrel, Gulf's profits—after production costs, taxes, and royalty payments—was $1 a barrel. Gulf used to lift anywhere from 1 million to 3½ million barrels of oil a day from Kuwait. So their daily profit was more than $1 million—from Kuwait alone. But those were the days when Gulf and their partner, British Petroleum, owned and controlled the Kuwaiti oil operations. Gulf had so much oil coming from Kuwait that they brought in Shell as their major customer for this crude. An adept marketer, with filling stations girdling the globe, Shell always had need for crude oil. By contrast, Gulf was never any great shakes at selling gasoline—they would just as soon sell the crude to others, taking their profit early in the game. Gulf loaded the Kuwaiti oil on their tankers and sold it around the world. They became Japan's number 1 oil supplier. They built South Korea's first oil refinery, and that was to be a source of one of their major gaffes during the 1970s.

The Kuwaiti oil fields were taken over by the government of Kuwait in the wake of the formation of OPEC (Organization of Petroleum Exporting Countries). Gulf is still there, but more as a supplicant now. And Kuwait has sharply reduced the amount of crude oil it's willing to give Gulf. From more than 1 million barrels of Kuwaiti oil a day in 1974, Gulf was cut back to 520,000 barrels in 1976. In early 1980 the Kuwait government was preparing to reduce the Gulf share to 150,000 barrels a day.

In short, Gulf went from a crude-rich to a crude-short company. In 1974 they reported their crude oil and natural gas production at 2.7 million barrels a day. By 1978 that output had dropped to 1.6 million barrels—and that was prior to the most recent Kuwait cutback. Gulf's net loss in the 1970s: more than 1 million barrels of oil a day.

It's not as if Gulf has been reduced to a pygmy or anything like that. They're still the seventh largest crude oil producer in the United States, and they rank as the nation's fifth largest producer of natural gas. They operate eight refineries in the United States and sell through 17,000 Gulf service stations in 29 states in the East, South, and Southwest. One out of every 10 stations in the country flies the orange Gulf disc. Gulf is also one of the largest oil producers in Canada. They have six refineries there, and they produce much of the oil that comes out of Nigeria, Angola, Gabon, and Zaire. They're still taking oil out of Venezuela through long-term purchase agreements.

In addition, Gulf has expanded their non-petroleum operations. They mine coal and uranium, and they have an extensive chemicals and plastics business. Their nonoil activities generate sales of more than $2 billion a year.

But the key change for Gulf was in the Middle East. Access to Kuwaiti oil had made Gulf one of the international petroleum giants, separating them from companies such as Standard Oil of Indiana and Atlantic Richfield, whose crude sources were largely domestic. It had also turned Gulf into a company deriving two-thirds of their profits overseas. But that game seems to be over—for Gulf anyway. They're now getting more than half their profits from U.S. operations. The "Seven Sisters" have become "Six Sisters."

History. Engineer Anthony Lucas, in partnership with Pittsburgh investors James Guffey and John Galey, hit the biggest oil gusher then known on January 10, 1901, at Spindletop Hill near Beaumont, Texas. Their worst mistake may have been borrowing most of the necessary start-up capital from the Mellon family. In May of the same year Andrew and Richard Mellon, sons of Pittsburgh banker Thomas Mellon, organized the J. M. Guffey Petroleum Company and set Guffey up as president. The Mellon family was already a major force in the aluminum business (Alcoa), and the brothers saw Guffey's gusher as the first step toward challenging John D. Rockefeller's Standard Oil Trust. Six months after setting up Guffey, the Mellons started to build a refinery at Port Arthur, Texas, and they organized another company called Gulf Refining, named after the nearby Gulf of Mexico.

In 1902 the brothers sent their nephew, William Mellon, to Texas. He had had previous experience in Pennsylvania's oil fields before being forced to sell out to Rockefeller. Mellon and Guffey were two different persons. Guffey was a self-dramatizing promoter who wore big black hats, stovepipe trousers, and loud waistcoats. Mellon was a meticulous businessman who resented

> The United States consumes about 10,000 gallons of petroleum a second.

Guffey's showboating and disorganization. So in 1907 the Mellons bought out Guffey and formed Gulf Oil. Pioneer Guffey was understandably bitter. He later complained, "I was throwed out."

The Mellons needed their financial resources to make Gulf viable. The Spindletop field went dry after 20 months. But they soon found oil in what was then Indian territory, now Oklahoma. They then developed other fields in Louisiana and West Texas. In 1912 crude oil refined for gasoline used mostly for cars passed oil refined into kerosene used for lamps in sales for the first time. And in 1913, sensing which way the wind was blowing, Gulf opened the world's first drive-in filling station in Pittsburgh. By 1923 the Port Arthur refinery was using a new catalytic cracking process called "Alchlor" to refine the crude oil piped into it—and the refinery was then the world's largest. Gulf had also by then moved into oil production in Mexico and Venezuela, and they built new refineries in Bayonne, New Jersey, and Philadelphia, Pennsylvania, to process their crude. In the mid-1920s they had more than 1,000 Gulf service stations in the country.

Oil and politics have nearly always been intertwined—and Gulf's history is no exception. They were the beneficiaries, after World War I, of the struggle for power in the Middle East. It wasn't their idea to explore for oil in that part of the world. They were propelled there by federal officials who wanted an American presence in the Middle East, where the British and the French were in the process of dismembering the old Ottoman Empire. In 1921 Herbert Hoover, then secretary of commerce, persuaded seven U.S. oil companies to act together to raise the American flag in the Middle East. In that group were Jersey Standard (now Exxon), Standard Oil of New York (now Mobil), Texas Oil (now Texaco), Sinclair Oil, Atlantic Oil, Mexican Oil—and Gulf. After considerable diplomatic pressure, the American consortium was permitted to take a 23.75% stake in the Iraq Petroleum Company, which was set up not merely to exploit the oil resources of Iraq but any oil that might be found in a huge area stretching from Turkey down to the tip of Saudi Arabia. British Petroleum, Royal Dutch Shell, and the French national oil company each also got a 23.75% stake in the company. This was the famous "Red Line Agreement," so called because it was marked in red on a map by Calouste Gulbenkian, the legendary Armenian entrepreneur who was known as "Mr. Five Percent" because he received a 5% interest in Iraq Petroleum as the original promoter of the company. It was said that he drew the red line because he was the only one in the meeting that set up IPC who knew the boundaries of the former Ottoman Empire. Iraq Petroleum was born as a cartel. The deal was: all together—or nothing. Within the Red Line, which encompassed Turkey, Syria, Iraq, Saudi Arabia, and what is now Jordan, all exploration and production were to be conducted by the group. None of the members could act independently within that area. Iran was outside the Red Line, but British Petroleum already had the concession there. Also just outside the Red Line was the little sheikdom of Kuwait, lodged between Saudi Arabia and Iraq at the upper end of the Persian Gulf and recognized as an independent state by the Turks since 1756.

Negotiations to form IPC went on for three years, between 1925 and 1928. Gulf and four other American companies eventually dropped out of the consortium, leaving Exxon and Mobil as the U.S. contingent. But while they were still part of the team, Gulf was approached by a Major Frank Holmes, a New Zealander who had obtained the oil concessions for Bahrain, a group of islands in the Persian Gulf, and Kuwait. Gulf was all for exploring for oil in Bahrain but had to get permission from the other Red Line partners, who said nothing doing. Kuwait, however, was another matter—it was outside the Red Line and Gulf was free to proceed on their own there. The hitch was that British Petroleum, which often acted as if they owned the entire Middle East, didn't like American companies encroaching on their domain, so they tried to block Gulf's entry into Kuwait. But it turned out that Gulf had some strong diplomatic cards to play. In March 1932 President Herbert Hoover appointed his former treasury secretary as the U.S. ambassador to Britain. He was none other than Andrew Mellon, one-time president of Gulf Oil. From his strategic position in London Mellon argued vociferously the case for Gulf, in which his family happened to own a 25% interest. In fact, at one point he sent a stiff note supporting Gulf's claim to the British Foreign Office, an action which earned him a reprimand from the State Department.

In the end the Gulf-BP conflict ended in a typical international oil settlement. On December 23, 1934, Gulf and BP signed an agreement with Kuwait for joint exploration. Oil was first found in Kuwait in 1938, but World War II postponed development. The first shipment of oil did not leave Kuwait until 1946. It turned out to be another fabulous Middle East discovery, producing 3 million barrels a day. Gulf's share was more than all the crude they pumped in the United States and other parts of the world. Kuwaiti oil gained Gulf admission to the Seven Sisters. They were, by all accounts, the least sophisticated of the seven. In his book, *The Seven Sisters*, Anthony Sampson observed that the "Pittsburgh executives could never quite come to terms with this strange alliance with a tiny territory at the other end of the world. They took most of their political advice from their partners BP, who gave them patronizing lectures on how to deal with the Arabs."

In 1960 Gulf, awash with money, began their own political maneuvering. Through a largely dormant subsidiary they had in the Bahamas, Gulf began funneling money to politicians at home and abroad. The record of Gulf's payments later became a matter of public record. There were bizarre stories. A Gulf accountant, William C. Viglia, went back and forth between the Bahamas and different points in the United States, usually carrying bundles of $25,000 in cash. He became so friendly with the customs officials that they never examined his baggage. Between 1960 and 1966 he carried some $2 million into the United States. He would fly back to the Bahamas as soon as he made his delivery. The Gulf people he delivered the money to—like Claud Wild, Gulf's Washington representative—then disbursed the funds to Democrat and Republican politicians. Wild later testified that for 10 years he gave $10,000 a year to Senator Hugh Scott, who was Republican leader in the Senate. Frederick A. Myers, a Gulf employee for 47 years, testified that he gave money to politicians in various places —once, he said, he handed a sealed envelope to Indiana Congressman Richard L. Roudebush in the men's washroom of a Holiday Inn in Indianapolis. The Good Government Fund, a legitimate Gulf government action committee, did record that a $2,000 payment was made to Roudebush on that date. In 1971 Wild, solicited by Nixon fund raiser Maurice Stans, gave $100,000 in cash to the Nixon reelection committee.

Gulf's payments to overseas politicians were also lavish. In Kuwait they joined with BP in spending $2 million to build a beach club—at the request of the Kuwaiti government. They also spent $2.8 million on a large plane for the ruling sheik of Kuwait. In 1963 Gulf began building a huge refinery at Ulsan, South Korea. Called the "Pittsburgh of Korea," it represented a Gulf investment of $200 million. When a high official of President Park Chung Hee's government asked for a $1 million contribution in 1966, Gulf's president, Bob R. Dorsey, authorized the payment, which reached Korea via the Bahamas and two Swiss bank accounts. In 1970, during a trip to South Korea, Dorsey was confronted by S. K. Kim, a Korean political leader who demanded $10 million. Dorsey testified later that Kim was brutal in his request, telling the Gulf leader: "I'm not here to debate matters. You are either going to put up the goddamn money or suffer the consequences." Dorsey bargained him down to $4 million.

The $12 million in illegal and questionable payments that Gulf made over this period were never disclosed to the Gulf board, the State Department, or the Mellons. The slush fund disclosures, made in the wake of the Watergate investigation, triggered a 364-page report prepared by Gulf's attorneys at the insistence of the Securities and Exchange Commission.

One month after the publication of this report in December 1975, the board of directors forced Dorsey and three other top executives to resign. The *Wall Street Journal* called the board room drama a "morality play," with the five directors representing the Mellon interest acting the part of jury, appropriately assisted by director and Roman Catholic nun, Sister Jane Scully, president of Carlow College. The *Journal* described the marathon board meeting (one session lasted from 9 A.M. to 1:15 A.M.) this way: "The Mellon representatives and their lawyers flatly advised the 63-year-old Mr. Dorsey at one point that they 'weren't bargaining for a resignation,' one source recalls. Moreover, they ruled out any 'Ford-type pardon' settlement that might have released Mr. Dorsey from future liability in litigation arising from Gulf's slush-fund scandal. And the Mellon forces warned the Gulf chairman that they had the votes to oust him if he refused to resign, the sources

say."

Dorsey, who had been employed by Gulf all his working life, had no choice but to resign. The new chairman, Jerry McAfee, took the opportunity of a 75th-anniversary publication to apologize to stockholders. "We very much regret the mistakes of the past and the unhappy results of those mistakes," he wrote, "and have taken every reasonable step possible to minimize their recurrence. For all practical purposes, this chapter is now closed, and our greatest challenge is to restore our confidence in ourselves and our credibility with others."

Reputation. Gulf is seen today as a company in transition. They emerged from their scandal-ridden 1970s not merely with a sullied reputation but considerably poorer in access to crude oil because of developments in the Middle East. They are still getting their house in order.

What they own. Gulf has 50,000 wells capable of producing oil, the vast majority of them in the United States. They estimate their worldwide oil reserves at 2 billion barrels. Gulf owns the largest tanker fleet operated under the U.S. flag: 17 vessels of 90,000 deadweight tons. They have chemical operations at numerous locations, but their main petrochemical plants in the United States are at Cedar Bayou and Port Arthur, Texas; Philadelphia, Pennsylvania; and Welcome and Alliance, Louisiana. Their big plastics plants are at Cedar Bayou and Orange, Texas, and Marietta, Ohio. Gulf's Pittsburgh & Midway division operates nine coal mines in five states. They produce about 9 million tons of coal a year, supplied mainly to electric utilities. Gulf mines uranium in the United States and Canada— and the Canadian operation has landed the company as a defendant in a number of antitrust suits alleging that Gulf participated in a worldwide cartel to drive up the prices of uranium. Gulf's Pittsburgh neighbor, Westinghouse, was one of those filing suit. They had to renege on 28 uranium-delivery contracts because of the price escalation. Gulf pleaded that they were forced to participate in the cartel at the behest of the Canadian government.

Who owns and runs the company. Even the Mellons may be getting nervous about their investment in Gulf. In their February 1979 filing with the Securities and Exchange Commission, Gulf disclosed that the various Mellon heirs and foundations had reduced their holdings from over 20% to 16%. In February 1980 the Mellon holdings were down to 11%. The Mellons are well represented on the Gulf board through Nathan W. Pearson, the family financial adviser; James H. Higgins, chairman of the Mellon National Bank; and James M. Walton, president of the Carnegie Institute and a grandson of William L. Mellon. After the Mellons forced Dorsey to resign in 1976, they brought Jerry McAfee down from Gulf-Canada to head the company. McAfee's job is to restore confidence. *Business Week* described McAfee's style as opposite to Dorsey's. "McAfee is affable, Dorsey was aloof," said the magazine. "Dorsey refused to ride in elevators with other employees, but McAfee rubs elbows with the rank and file in the lobby coffee shop of the Gulf Building."

In the public eye. They would like to get out of it.

Where they're going. Looking for oil—in the Gulf of Mexico, the North Sea, the Baltimore Canyon off the New Jersey coast, places where they're not likely to be expropriated. McAfee has called a halt to possible mergers with companies outside the energy field. His predecessors explored mergers with Rockwell International (aerospace), CNA (insurance) and Ringling Bros.–Barnum & Bailey (entertainment).

Stock performance. Gulf stock bought for $1,000 in 1970 sold for $1,116 on January 2, 1980.

Major employment centers. Houston and Port Arthur, Texas; Philadelphia, Pennsylvania.

Access. Gulf Building, Pittsburgh, Pennsylvania 15230; (412) 263-5000. Customer inquiries or complaints may be addressed to Customer Service, Gulf Oil Company—U.S., 2 Houston Center, 909 Fannin Street, Houston, Texas 77002.

Consumer brands.

Gulf gasoline and motor oil.

The world's first drive-in gas station, at Baum Boulevard and St. Clair Street, Pittsburgh, Pennsylvania, December 1913.

Harbor Heights Fuel Co.

Sales: $505,000
Profits: $38,000
Founded: 1899
Employees: 2 full-time, 2 part-time, 1 summer helper
Location: Sag Harbor, New York

What they do. In partnership with his parents, Jane and Van, Jack Van Kovics runs the Harbor Heights Fuel Co., a Mobil gas station on Long Island, New York. Besides selling gas and TBA (trade shorthand for tires, batteries, and accessories), they fix cars and sell and deliver home fuel oil.

Jack Van Kovics does simple repair work that can stand frequent interruptions or shows people how to do their own repairs, often lending customers tools and letting them work in back of the garage. This policy allows many people in the area to creep around for years in old cars that other mechanics shun.

Harbor Heights serves about 300 customers a day, mostly local regulars and a few of what Jack calls "self-reliant types" from other towns.

Because their accounting method throws together revenues from gas, TBA, fuel oil, and repairs, the Van Kovics don't know exactly how much comes from each. But they are sure that the sale of gas brings no profit at all. Since 1973 federal regulations have put a mark-up ceiling of 16.2¢ on a gallon of gas sold—just enough to cover Harbor Heights' current overhead costs. They sell gas purely to bring customers to the station.

The Van Kovics are currently surviving on profits from the sale of motor oil, TBA, and home fuel oil delivered by Jack's father, Van. Repairs are the least profitable aspect of the business—partly because most are charged, and there is often a delay of a month or two before payment. Interest on money the Van Kovics borrow to cover costs until customers pay their bills costs Harbor Heights $11,000 a year.

Harbor Heights buys its gas from Mobil under a contract that is renewable every two years. The Van Kovics believe that if it were not for federal regulations, Mobil would not bother to supply independent stations like theirs. They find their relationship with Mobil "not much different from our relationship with LILCO (the electric utility) or the telephone company. The larger the organization, the more mistakes they make. . . . We're always having to check the bills and accounts."

History. Harbor Heights began one night in the 1890s when Jack Van Kovics' great-grandfather, Jim "Big Six" McMahon, raced a locomotive along the now-defunct Bridgehampton-Sag Harbor line, took the final corner too fast, and drove the train off the end of the tracks onto Main Street. This mishap cost Big Six his job as an engineer with the Long Island Railroad. He settled in Sag Harbor and, on a low hill not far from the scene of the accident, started the coal and hauling business that was to become the Harbor Heights Fuel Co.

The ancient Dutch dray, an unusual sloped wagon now parked next to the pay phone at Harbor Heights, was used by Jack's grandfather, Jim MacMahon, Jr., who drove it around town picking up dead horses for Big Six's hauling business. But father and son did not see eye to eye. Big Six continued with coal and hauling, and Jim got into house moving, demolition, and property speculation during the Depression. In 1931 Jim bought Harbor Heights gas station, which had been a Mobil station since 1927, operating out of the shingle shed that still serves as the front office. In 1943, when Big Six died, Jim started running the coal business from the property behind the gas station, moving in a two-car garage to serve as an office.

The gas station became a family business in 1954 when Jane Van Kovics, Jim's daughter, began to operate it with her husband, Van, and 13-year-old Jack. The first summer Jane, Van, and Jack also ran a Dairy Queen franchise on the Southampton

---

At least 7 trillion cubic feet of natural gas are deliberately burned off in oil fields around the world every year. If a way of safely transporting the gas could be found, just two-thirds of this would be enough to supply the year-round needs of the 41 million natural gas-fueled homes in the United States.

Jack Kovics.

bypass. With the $3,000 they earned on ice cream, they started a fuel oil business. Jack worked mostly for his grandfather in the next 10 years, shoveling coal and cutting firewood.

In 1967 they discontinued the coal business—"not," Jack pointed out, "because coal was impractical, but because people got lazy and didn't want to go digging around in the cellar." Since 1967 they have emphasized the gas station.

Reputation. "You have to argue with Jack to get him to do anything that isn't absolutely essential," says a regular customer. Gas costs a little more at Harbor Heights than at nearby stations, but many people still buy gas there, apparently trusting Harbor Heights to serve them in other ways, such as keeping their cars on the road at minimum expense.

What they own. "If someone offered us $325,000, I'd take it and run like a thief," says Jack. If you were to call his hand, here's what you'd get:

A 200-foot square lot which, with the building, is valued at $75,000.

The building, consisting of the original 1927 shed, now the front office, heated by a large coal stove; the two-car wood garage

that Jim MacMahon moved to the property in the 1930s; and two surviving wings of a building otherwise destroyed by fire (also moved in by MacMahon). These segments, loosely joined, are attractively faced with cedar shingles.

There is one island with three pumps, which the Van Kovics bought from Mobil for $1 when the oil company would no longer service them.

And vehicles—two fuel-oil trucks, a Bronco jeep, and a pickup—worth $25,000.

Who owns and runs the company. Jane, Van, and Jack Van Kovics are equal partners. Van runs the fuel business, Jack runs the gas station, and Jane (who used to run the gas station) does the accounts for both.

In the public eye. Jim MacMahon, Jr., had the longest run as mayor (13 years) in Sag Harbor history. Some attribute his popularity to his having kept many poor families supplied with coal during the Depression. Jane Van Kovics is a three-term village trustee. Jack shows similar inclinations, although at the moment his main public activity is coaching the high school soccer team.

Harbor Heights is routinely "hit up by every possible charity: Girl Guides, B'nai Brith, you name it. . . ." And they pay up.

They also spend about $1,200 a year to advertise in such publications as school yearbooks, the volunteer firemen's magazine, and the local horse show program. They feel they have to support the people who produce these publications, although it's unlikely the advertising brings in any new customers.

Where they're going. Costs have increased by 48% over the past three years. This fact, combined with the fluctuating gas supply, creates pressures never felt before by the Van Kovics. To stay in business Harbor Heights must either raise prices—the alternative favored by Jane and Van—or increase volume, which Jack prefers. "My parents are probably right, but it's very hard for me emotionally to tell a guy, 'I'm going to tune up your car and it's going to cost you two days' salary.'" Jack has hired a full-time mechanic and begun to take on some of the major repairs he used to turn away when he worked alone. Because of the same money pressures Harbor Heights is experiencing, many former "self-reliant types" can't afford the time off their jobs to work on their cars and are handing them over to Jack—a development that saddens him.

A further threat lies in gas-supply regulations. "The gas stations take the brunt of the government's policies. The governor didn't have to put his head into people's cars to check that they didn't have more than half a tank of gas. We did." Such procedures and coping with angry gas lines are at odds with Harbor Heights's way of doing things.

The present gas-allotment system can easily finish off an independent gas station that may be forced to close down for days at a time unless its owners know how to petition the government for more gas. Fortunately Jane Van Kovics has proved adept at wading through red tape and making the right phone calls, and thus far Harbor Heights has been adequately supplied.

"Right now," Jack says, "I don't think the business could survive if any one of us left." The Van Kovics have begun a feasibility study to see if Jack could run the business alone if Van or Jane should want to retire.

Access. Hampton Road, Route 114, Sag Harbor, New York.

Mobil

Sales: $44.7 billion
Profits: $2.0 billion
Forbes 500 rank: 4
Rank in oil: 4
Rank in natural gas: 4
Rank in retailing: 9
Rank in paperboard packaging: 1
Founded: 1866
Employees: 216,000
Headquarters: New York, New York

What they do. A 1977 Mobil ad featured a cartoon of seven women, all but one flat chested. The accompanying copy read, "Can't tell the sisters apart? Mobil's the one with the extra dimension."

It's not only Mobil's sexist advertising that sets them apart from the other major international oil companies that make up the Seven Sisters. Where other oil giants seem happy to collect enormous profits and keep their mouths shut, Mobil seems intent on picking fights with anybody who thinks the oil companies are getting more than their share from the ongoing energy crisis. They spend millions of dollars a year to defend Big Oil. Since 1972, for instance, they have run an ad every Thursday morning in the lower right-hand corner of the *New York Times'* Op-Ed (opposite editorial) page. This same ad also appears weekly in the editorial sections of other major newspapers: the *Wall Street Journal, Washington Post, Boston Globe, Chicago Tribune,* and *Los Angeles Times,* and often in more than 100 other newspapers across the country when oil becomes a hot political issue. Because of their aggressive stance, Mobil has become a lightning rod for criticism of the oil industry. The *New York Times* reported that President Jimmy Carter singled out Mobil as "perhaps the most irresponsible company in America."

Government officials are not alone in their annoyance with Mobil. Other oil companies were upset when Mobil announced in 1974—when gas lines were extending around the block at service stations across the country—that Mobil was going to put some of their profits into buying Montgomery Ward, the nation's ninth-largest retailer. Today Mobil gets about 20% of their sales from products totally unrelated to the energy business. Mobil's Container Corpo-

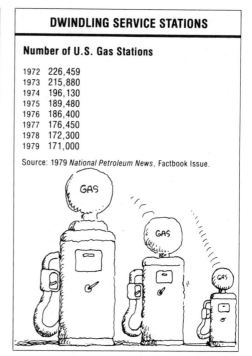

ration (part of the Montgomery Ward purchase) is the world's largest maker of paperboard containers. Mobil Chemical makes more disposable plastic products than anyone—items like polystyrene egg cartons and food trays. They also make the Hefty trash bags advertised on TV by comedian Jonathan Winters. Mobil even owns the company (W. F. Hall Printing of Chicago) that prints *Playboy, National Geographic,* and *Ebony* magazines as well as paperbacks for Avon, Bantam, Random House, and other publishers. In fact, if all Mobil's nonoil businesses were separated out, together they would rank as one of the 35 largest corporations in America.

Mobil isn't about to leave the oil business, however. Their sales rank them as the second-largest oil-based company—behind Exxon. But unlike Exxon, Mobil does not have a large surplus of oil; in industry terms the company is "crude-short." Mobil's own oil wells pump just barely enough to keep the company's refineries busy. (Mobil's refineries in 21 countries produce about 2 million barrels a day.) What makes Mobil particularly precarious is that so many of the company's oil wells are located in the politically volatile Middle East (80% of their crude oil comes from the OPEC) countries.

What they may lack in production, however, they make up in one of the most extensive marketing networks in the industry. Mobil sells gasoline in more than 100 countries through approximately 37,800 retail dealers, about half of which are located in the United States. They're especially strong in New York and New England, where gas stations with Mobil's flying red horse capture between 14% and 17% of the total market, but they're in every state of the union except Alabama, Mississippi, Alaska, and Hawaii.

Mobil has bought up a lot of coal fields in the western United States and Illinois, but the company has not yet begun to mine them. They are already in the uranium business, however. With two U.S. extraction plants in operation, Mobil produced 332,000 pounds of uranium in 1979.

Mobil also puts out America's best-selling travel guide. Since 1958 more than 20 million copies of the *Mobil Travel Guide* have been sold. They rate more than 400,000 restaurants, motels, hotels, and resorts; only about 250 get the four-star rating, only 30 get five stars ("one of the best in the country").

History. Mobil's first oils were meant for horses, not cars. In 1866 a Rochester, New York, carpenter, Matthew Ewing, devised a method for making kerosene by distilling crude oil in a vacuum, and his Vacuum Oil Company was soon manufacturing various lubricants, especially Vacuum Harness Oils used for tanning leather. Thirteen years after Vacuum was formed, John D. Rockefeller bought the lubricant company, and in 1882 he made Vacuum part of his newly organized Standard Oil Trust. That same year he also set up the Standard Oil Company of New York (Socony) as the administrative arm of the trust. Socony refined and sold gasoline in New York and New England, which soon became known in the industry as "Soconyland" because the new company was supplying 92% of that area's oil needs by 1911.

It was in 1911 that the Supreme Court broke up Rockefeller's oil trust into 34 companies, including Vacuum and Socony. Because Socony (which became Mobil) never owned any oil wells of their own under the Rockefeller trust, much of Mobil's subsequent history has been a mad scramble to get their own supplies. In 1918 they bought Magnolia Petroleum Company of Texas, whose oil wells, pipelines, and refinery (in Beaumont) became Socony's primary source in the United States. But Magnolia couldn't meet the needs of Socony's customers in the Far East.

Socony had developed a huge market in China in the early 1900s by introducing kerosene lamps (called *mei foo*, from the Chinese symbols for Socony, meaning "beautiful confidence"). In 1926 Socony found a supplier for all the kerosene lamps of China by buying General Petroleum, which had oil wells in California's Central Valley and a 200-mile pipeline (the world's first) to their refinery on the coast near Los Angeles. Socony became truly nationwide in 1930, when they purchased White Eagle Oil & Refining, with refineries in Kansas and Wyoming and service stations in 11 midwestern states. In 1931 Socony joined forces with Vacuum, their former sibling in the Standard Oil Trust. In the meantime, Vacuum had become a major seller of motor oils throughout the world and operated 1,500 filling stations of their own in Michigan, Indiana, and Ohio.

Socony-Vacuum began selling their oil and gasoline under the Mobil brand name and used a flying red horse as their symbol at the pumps. (They changed their company name to Socony-Mobil in 1955 and to Mobil in 1966.) But the new company was still crude-short. To serve their growing markets in the Far East, they joined in 1933 with Jersey Standard (now Exxon) in a venture called Stanvac (paralleling the Caltex organization formed by Texaco and California Standard). Using Jersey Standard's oil wells and refinery in Indonesia and Socony-Vacuum's huge marketing apparatus in the Far East, Stanvac built an oil-selling operation in 50 countries that spread from the east coast of Africa to New Zealand. Federal trustbusters broke up Stanvac in 1962, leaving each company with half the assets of the operation.

Socony-Vacuum's most productive effort to secure a steady supply of oil came in 1948, when they were allowed to buy a 10% interest in the Arabian American Oil Company (Aramco), the Saudi Arabian company then owned jointly by Standard Oil of California and Texaco. Actually they were offered more. They could have shared a 40% chunk with Jersey Standard (now Exxon), but, in one of the classic blunders of petroleum history, they opted for less. Jersey Standard took all it could get, and it came away with 30%, making them equal partners in Aramco with Socal and Texaco. In 1974 Mobil negotiated an additional 5% of Aramco's oil supplies. As *Business Week* described the deal, "With merely the stroke of a pen (plus some big dollars, no doubt), Mobil 'found' more oil in 1974 than most oil explorers come across in a lifetime."

Traditionally crude-short Mobil has not pinned all their hopes on Middle East fields. Although *Business Week* once characterized their exploratory efforts as "not only less than the others' but also less venturesome," they seem to have stepped up their efforts sharply in recent years. They discovered the Stratfjord oil field, the largest in the North Sea, and in 1979 oil was discovered for the first time beneath the Atlantic Ocean off Newfoundland. Called the Hibernia discovery, the Newfoundland field is believed to be a major find—and Mobil has the largest interest: 28%. Through another stroke of the pen—and a big cash payout—Mobil also expanded their U.S. oil production by 22,000 barrels a day by purchasing the oil and gas operations of General Crude. The price: $792 million.

If Mobil hasn't been sinking as much money into the ground as some competitors, they have certainly been sinking profits into other businesses. The most significant, of course, was their 1974 purchase of Montgomery Ward. The country's first mail-order business was founded by Aaron Montgomery Ward in Chicago in 1872. Ward's catalog, called "The Great Wish Book," went from a 24-page pocket-sized booklet in 1874 to a two-pound, 544-page catalog in 1893. Although Ward's started in the mail-order business 15 years before

Sears, they lost their lead early in this century. They ensured the gap between themselves and Sears would grow larger when Ward's directors turned down General Robert E. Wood's suggestion in 1924 that they open retail outlets. Wood, then a Ward's vice-president, quit, joined Sears, and led that company's expansion into retail sales, becoming the dominant force in U.S. retailing. Ward's survived the Depression, thanks to the strong guiding hand of Sewell Avery, but after World War II they began to slide downhill as Avery, convinced a depression was coming again, refused to invest in new facilities. The company was on the upswing when Mobil took it over. Today Montgomery Ward has 419 department stores in 42 states and 516 catalog stores. About one-fourth of Ward's sales are mail-order purchases. (Ward's made one other lasting contribution to Americana in 1939: they introduced a Christmas campaign featuring Rudolph the Red-Nosed Reindeer.)

Along with Montgomery Ward, Mobil got Container Corporation of America, which in 1968 had merged with Ward's to form a company called Marcor. CCA ended the age of the cracker barrel. In 1926, when the company was started by Walter Paepcke, much of what consumers bought was kept and shipped in wooden barrels and crates, or burlap sacks. CCA developed a vast array of practical and artfully designed paperboard containers that are now part of American culture. Breakfast cereal, bath soap, motor oil, frozen orange juice, furniture, appliances—whether you eat it, drink it, sit in it, clean with it, smoke it, or put it in your car, CCA probably packaged it.

Walter Paepcke, who died in 1960 at the age of 63, was a prominent patron of the arts and the main force behind the conversion of Aspen, Colorado, from a ghost town to a major resort and cultural center. He helped to found the Aspen Institute for Humanistic Studies, where corporate executives and intellectuals gather to be reminded of the eternal verities of life. But the main force behind the Aspen Institute today is another oil company: Atlantic Richfield.

Reputation. Mobil has been run by accountants, lawyers, and smooth-talking Ivy League businessmen rather than the typical refinery-educated oilmen who run other oil companies. Yet for all their charm and managerial expertise, Mobil has a pugnacious image that extends beyond their carefully cultivated public relations campaign. One former Mobil executive described his former colleagues to the *Wall Street Journal* as "smart people who are alley fighters." Their stance may have something to do with their crude-short position: like the short kid on the block, they have to make up for size with bravado.

What they own. They own 45,019 oil wells; 6,922 natural gas wells; 110 million acres of undeveloped oil and gas reserves; 37 refineries with a capacity of 2.7 million barrels a day; 96 oceangoing tankers; 40,955 miles of pipeline; 3.9 billion tons of coal reserves; 44 domestic and 16 foreign chemical plants; 860,000 acres of timberland; 22 paperboard plants; 47 shipping container plants; 8 plastic container plants; and an 80% interest in Mobil Tyco Solar Energy Corporation, formed to make solar cells that convert sunlight directly into electricity.

Who owns and runs the company. The Rockefellers still have a chunk of the company, more than 2 million shares (worth some $160 million in early 1980).

Rawleigh Warner, Jr., has been chairman since 1969. He's a Princeton-educated lifelong Mobil executive who's constantly trying to upgrade Mobil's public appearance. A retired Mobil executive told the *Wall Street Journal* that, because of Warner, "there are to be no plastic plants and a limited number of signs at Mobil gas stations. Office buildings and even our tankers are supposed to look nice."

Warner's right-hand man is William Tavoulareas, Mobil's president since 1969. The Brooklyn-born son of a Greek immigrant, Tavoulareas joined Mobil as an accountant (he later got a law degree) and has become the company's tough negotiator. A veteran oilman told the *Journal*, "Tav isn't one of the boys. He isn't an oilman, he's a numbers man. The executives at other companies have a rapport with each other. Tav doesn't. He's looked on as a sharp operator who's all too willing to exploit an advantage. And he doesn't give a damn." Tavoulareas came under some fire in 1979 for setting up his 24-year-old son, Peter, as a partner in Atlas Maritime Company, which operates Mobil's ships. He contended there was nothing improper, adding, "I come from a Greek background where relatives help relatives."

Mobil is one of the few oil companies (Exxon is another) to have placed a black on their board: William Kennedy, head of North Carolina Mutual Life Insurance.

In the public eye. Some people call the public TV network, PBS, the "Petroleum Broadcasting Service," in large part because of Mobil. Since 1971 Mobil has sponsored such award-winning TV productions as *Masterpiece Theater, Upstairs, Downstairs, The First Churchills,* and *Ten Who Dared.*

The man behind Mobil's sponsorship of these public TV shows, as well as the weekly Mobil ads on editorial pages across the country, is Herbert Schmertz, vice-president for public affairs and a Mobil director. Schmertz, who worked in the presidential campaigns of John, Robert, and Ted Kennedy, runs a $20 million-a-year public relations operation that is itself highly controversial. In a lengthy article about Schmertz in *Esquire* magazine in 1977, Michael Gerrard pointed out that Schmertz "controls nearly three hours of television time and choice space in leading newspapers." He compared Schmertz's influence to that of TV producer Norman Lear, but said that "his primary audience numbers only 535"—the U.S. Congress, "which largely determines how unfettered and prosperous Mobil can become."

Mobil's massive public relations campaign has not prevented an ongoing battle between the company and President Jimmy Carter. The conflict has been over Mobil's rejection of Carter's plan for a windfall profits tax and the voluntary price guidelines. At one point, Mobil ran an ad titled, "Sorry, Mr. President, you've been misled."

Mobil has also been attacked for their activities in South Africa. The United Church of Christ singled out the company for discriminating against their nonwhite employees in that country. A resolution asking Mobil to change their policies was rejected by 98% of Mobil's stockholders at the 1972 annual meeting.

In 1976 Mobil was accused of having fashioned an elaborate and secret chain of bogus companies to disguise the flow of $20 million worth of oil from Mobil's South African subsidiary to companies located in Rhodesia. At the time the United States was observing a United Nations embargo of Rhodesia. An investigation by the U.S. Treasury and the United Nations was launched but did not result in any charges against the corporation.

Where they're going. Into real estate, where they've spent more than $100 million since 1973. Their biggest project to date has been the Mei Foo condominium complex in Hong Kong that houses 65,000 people. It is the world's largest residential condominium, with 110 20-story buildings. They've also bought undeveloped land near San Francisco, Atlanta, Dallas, Ft. Lauderdale, and Washington, D.C. They're also still looking for oil. They found it recently in Tunisia, Cameroon, and in waters offshore Canada. Their Hibernia tract 200 miles off the east coast of Canada may be a sensational find.

Stock performance. Mobil stock bought for $1,000 in 1970 sold for $2,391 on January 2, 1980.

Access. 150 East 42nd Street, New York, New York 10017; (212) 883-4242.

Consumer brands.

Mobil gasoline and motor oils.
Plastic products: Hefty trash bags; Guestware dishes.
Stores: Montgomery Ward.

Occidental Petroleum Corporation

Sales: $9.6 billion
Profits: $562 million
Forbes 500 rank: 29
Rank in coal: 4
Rank in sulphur: 4
Founded: 1920
Employees: 34,200
Headquarters: Los Angeles, California

What they do. Occidental Petroleum—or "Oxy," as they're known on Wall Street—is a $9 billion one-man band. The man is Dr. Armand Hammer, the retired physician who took over the exhausted, $3 million wildcat operation in 1957 and built it into one of the nation's top 10 oil companies in less than 20 years.

Hammer is an octogenarian wonder, the Metternich of the bargaining table. His Gulfstream jet, with its cork-lined bedroom, sweeps him from capital to capital and keeps him in nearly constant motion. Hammer will spend one day in Moscow, where he began his business career in the 1920s, trading American wheat for Russian caviar and furs with V. I. Lenin, and where he maintains chummy relations with Brezhnev & Co. Those relations helped Hammer to work out the details of Oxy's $20 billion deal to build Russian fertilizer plants, in exchange for Russian ammonia and natural gas—a deal estimated to be the largest international trade agreement in history until the Russian invasion of Afghanistan created a hostile Soviet-American atmosphere and, at least temporarily, scotched the deal. In the meantime Hammer has worked out an Oxy-coal-for-Romanian-phosphates swap in Bucharest, involving at least 14 million tons of coal. Hammer doesn't think small.

The next day Hammer may turn up in Tripoli to oversee Oxy's vast oil interests there or to confer with Muammar al Qaddafi, the Libyan head of state. After quick side trips to Saudi Arabia and Egypt, Hammer may then instruct his pilot to head for Edinburgh, where the Oxy chairman can keep an eye on his North Sea oil fields. During a meeting with Scottish advisers Hammer will jot notes on sheets of white typing paper. At the end of the meeting he will jam the crumpled sheets into his pockets and head back to his Gulfstream. In spite of Oxy's size, Hammer still insists on running it out of his head—helped along by an occasional peek at the mangled white sheets in his pockets.

Following a jaunt back to Miami, Hammer will sit down with Albert Gore, the former Tennessee senator who now heads Oxy's Island Creek Coal Company—the nation's third largest, which also produces most of Oxy's sulfur. After lunch Hammer may fly north to Niagara Falls to see what Oxy's Hooker Chemical subsidiary is up to in the Love Canal area, the area where in 1978 hundreds of families were evacuated when noxious materials started bubbling up in basements. Some claim the problem was caused by chemical dumping by Hooker Chemical in the 40's and 50's. When the resulting birth defects and lawsuits aren't keeping them in the harsh glare of

Occidental's Dr. Armand Hammer.

publicity, Hooker tries to concentrate on fertilizer, industrial chemicals, and agricultural soil additives.

Sunday might find Hammer on *Meet the Press*, where in late 1979 he assured a national television audience that we should not worry about Russian arms buildups: "I still think the Soviets want peace, and I believe they want peace badly enough that they will not do anything to involve us in a war." Or it might find him in his Los Angeles home, running Oxy from his den. His employees say that Hammer thinks nothing of calling any part of the world at any time of day or night, and they estimate his personal phone bill at more than $1 million a year. This is understandable—Oxy derives more than 90% of their profits from non-U.S. operations.

Those operations are primarily exploring for and producing oil. Seventy percent of Oxy's revenues are from oil and gas, all of which is sold in crude form to others for refining and sale to consumers. Chemicals represent about one-fifth of their business and coal 7%.

History. It might be said that Armand Hammer did not strike oil: oil struck him. He came to Los Angeles in 1956 to retire gracefully with his third wife and the enormous amounts of money he had made through shrewd business investments. He looked around for a tax shelter—something that would give him a nice loss for his income tax return—and settled on Oxy. The company had a few tired-out wells in California and total assets of $120,000. They had also failed to pay their stockholders a dividend since 1934. Hammer bought most of the stock and loaned Oxy even more, but instead of gobbling up his dollars, Oxy struck oil south of Los Angeles. Confounded in his search for a loser, Hammer decided to come out of retirement and go into the oil business.

It was a strange end for Hammer. His father had been a radical leftist physician in New York City—he had named his son in honor of the "arm and hammer" insignia of the Socialist Labor Party in 1898—and his leftist contacts in America had given young Armand a toehold in Russia after the Bolshevik triumph there. Hammer went to Russia with a medical degree and $60,000 worth of much-needed medical supplies shortly after World War I and met Lenin. The Soviet leader thanked him and suggested the wheat-for-furs trade—even offering Hammer the concession on an asbestos mine in southern Russia. Hammer jumped at the chance and, by 1930, had made several million dollars in Russian-American trade—both on his own and as the agent for other American businesses.

When Stalin came to power and cracked down on foreigners, Hammer fled to the United States with an enormous cache of Russian Czarist and Soviet art. Selling it in special shows at American department stores, he made more millions. Soon he was dabbling in a wide variety of businesses, everything from art (the Hammer Galleries) to J. W. Dant bourbon, from manufacturing beer barrels to selling Angus bull semen to breeders.

After Occidental's bonanza in southern California, Hammer brought his wheeler-dealer techniques to the oil business—to the chagrin of the big league oilmen. They thought of him and his new company as pushy parvenus, especially after Libya. Hammer had been using Oxy's new-found wealth to buy up smaller American companies in oil-related fields, but the 1961 Libyan oil strike changed all that. As soon as he heard of the strike, Hammer flew to Libya and convinced King Idris that the "Big Boys" would try to come in and exploit Libya just as they had exploited the rest of the Middle East. Idris granted the oil concession to Oxy, and Oxy became one of the Big Boys.

In the early 1960s, at the request of the Kennedy administration, Hammer returned to Russia to talk trade with the Soviets. He took with him a few personal letters from Lenin and soon discovered that the epistles were tantamount to having the keys to the country. Everywhere he went the letters brought tears to the eyes of Soviet officials, from Khrushchev down to local party functionaries. Hammer forged a relationship with the Soviets that continues today. Even now, some companies find it difficult to swing a contract with the Russians unless Armand Hammer is in on the deal. His relationship with and his gifts to the Soviets—everything from expensive art to American diet books (for fatter functionaries)—made it possible for Hammer to strike his $20 billion, 20-year fertilizer deal in the mid-1970s.

Will "The Doctor" Ever Be Soda King?

The folks at Church & Dwight, makers of Arm & Hammer Baking Soda, wish Occidental Petroleum chairman Dr. Armand Hammer would change his name. A lot of people think the doctor *owns* the baking soda manufacturer, according to an article about Oxy's chief by Daniel Yergin in the June 1975 *Atlantic Monthly*. In fact, Hammer says he once thought about buying it, and he still thinks about it occasionally.

Hammer relates: "I used to have a boat and my boat had the arm and hammer on it. Every place I went people would say that he must be the Soda King and finally I said to my brother— we were in the distilling business —let us buy it so we do not have to apologize." That was nearly 30 years ago; Hammer still says, "I have got my eye on it."

HOW THE BIG OIL COMPANIES RANK

	Sales	U. S. Oil Production (Barrels per Day)	Rank	World Oil Production[1] (Barrels per Day)	Rank	Reserves[2] (Barrels)	Rank
1. EXXON	$79.1 *billion*	791,000	(1)	4.4 *million*	(1)	6.2 *billion*	(1)
2. MOBIL	$44.7 *billion*	369,000	(9)	2.1 *million*	(4)	2.1 *billion*	(7)
3. TEXACO	$38.3 *billion*	526,000	(4)	3.6 *million*	(2)	2.7 *billion*	(3)
4. STANDARD OIL (*California*)	$29.9 *billion*	386,000	(7)	3.2 *million*	(3)	1.7 *billion*	(10)
5. GULF	$23.9 *billion*	382,000	(8)	1.7 *million*	(5)	1.9 *billion*	(9)
6. STANDARD OIL (*Indiana*)	$18.6 *billion*	494,000	(5)	849,000	(6)	2.6 *billion*	(4)
7. ATLANTIC RICHFIELD	$16.2 *billion*	537,000	(3)	568,000	(8)	2.6 *billion*	(5)
8. SHELL OIL	$14.4 *billion*	481,000	(6)	508,000	(9)	2.3 *billion*	(6)
9. CONOCO	$12.6 *billion*	142,000	(11)	482,000	(10)	2.1 *billion*	(8)
10. PHILLIPS PETROLEUM	$ 9.5 *billion*	263,000	(10)	436,000	(11)	1.2 *billion*	(11)
11. STANDARD OIL (*Ohio*)	$ 7.9 *billion*	610,000	(2)	610,000	(7)	3.8 *billion*	(2)

[1] Crude oil production figures include condensates and natural gas liquids.

[2] Reserves are what the companies own underground. Geological and engineering data indicate with "reasonable certainty" that this amount of oil is recoverable in future years. However, the reserve figures here understate the access of the big international oil companies. In the cases of Exxon, Texaco, Standard Oil of California, and Mobil, these reserve figures do not include any of their interests in the Arabian American Oil Company (Aramco) because "release of this information has not been approved by the government of Saudi Arabia." In the cases of Texaco and Standard Oil of California, the figures also exclude, for similar reasons, their stake in the oil fields of Indonesia. And in the case of Gulf, the reserves do not include their stake in Kuwait and Nigeria (places now accounting for about half their oil production).

Much criticism has been directed at Hammer over the years. He has been called a show-boater. Occidental was charged by the SEC with failing to mention the prospect of major losses on their tanker leases when they tried to sell stock in 1971, and by the press of announcing the same oil strike two or three times over as if they were separate strikes, sending Oxy stock skyrocketing. Some have even claimed that Hammer inadvertently sparked OPEC (the Organization of Petroleum Exporting Countries).

When the coup led by Muammar al Qaddafi deposed King Idris in 1970, Occidental was in a vulnerable position. Because they were then almost completely dependent on Libyan oil, Qaddafi's threatened nationalization of oil reserves could have finished Oxy. Qaddafi ordered Oxy's production slashed in half. Hammer tried to find another company that would rescue him by selling him oil at cost, but no one would. Perhaps they enjoyed watching the uppity Hammer squirm. Hammer had no choice but to agree to sell 51% of Oxy's Libyan operation to Libya (for only $136 million). The deal sent shock waves throughout the oil world. Other nations, emboldened by Qaddafi's success in reclaiming his nation's oil reserves, followed suit. Today, control of the world's oil supply lies mostly with OPEC—not, as before 1970, with the giant American oil companies.

Reputation. According to a 1975 story in *Atlantic*, Hammer "repeats like a prayer that every man has his price." Hammer's promotion of the company went a bit farther than the Securities and Exchange Commission was willing to allow on one occasion. In 1964 Hammer publicly announced "a gold deposit" on Oxy land in Montana and the price of Oxy's stock jumped $4. In 1966 he said, "We may have one of the largest iron ore deposits in the Western part of the United States." But nothing further was ever heard about the supposed "finds." The SEC has forced Hammer to sign a "consent decree" indicating that he will refrain from such enthusiasm in the future.

What they own. Oxy's share of the Libyan oil operation is about 141,000 barrels a day, but their percentage of the take is falling as Libya continues to nationalize. To replace this operation, Oxy has moved into the British North Sea, where they now produce about 117,000 barrels a day. In addition, Oxy has extensive oil and gas interests in Peru, Bolivia, Colombia, Trinidad, and Pakistan—although the last three are not currently producing. They have also become involved in off-shore drilling in the Gulf of Mexico and the coast of California.

Who owns and runs the company. Although Hammer owns less than 1½% of Oxy stock, it is evident that "The Doctor," as his employees call him, runs Oxy with an iron fist. He is alleged to have boasted that he had the entire board of directors "in his pocket". That's one reason literally dozens of directors and officers of the company have come and gone since Hammer took over. Another is Hammer's "favorite son" routine. At least half a dozen presidents have been through Oxy's revolving door in the last decade. Each claimed that Hammer had told him he would inherit the chairmanship but had brought in someone new a year or so later. Today the heir apparent is Hungarian-born Zoltan Merszei, a 30-year veteran of Dow Chemical. A security analyst said in a 1979 *Fortune* story: "Oxy stock will go up ten points once the Doctor kicks the bucket."

In the public eye. The event that has given Oxy the biggest black eye has been the infamous Love Canal. Ironically, Oxy had nothing to do with it.

The Love Canal was a half-mile trench off the Niagara River in upstate New York when Hooker Chemical bought it in the 1940s. Until 1953 they used it as a dump for toxic chemicals. Then they filled it in and sold it to a local school district for $1 for use as a school site. The deed included a clause absolving Hooker of any liability for damages caused by the disposed chemicals.

The chemicals that leached into nearby basements have been associated with a number of diseases, including cancer, and several birth defects. In 1978 the state evacuated 239 families and reimbursed them for their homes. Although dumping at the canal stopped in 1953, and Oxy did not buy Hooker until 1968, it is Oxy that has taken the brunt of the public blame for "Love Canal."

Where they're going. According to Merszei, the current heir apparent, "Dr. Hammer was remarkable in getting the pillars of industry into place. All I have to do is put on the roof, the walls, and build an edifice." Which Merszei may do—if he lasts.

Stock performance. Occidental stock bought for $1,000 in 1970 sold for $1,124 on January 2, 1980.

Access. 10889 Wilshire Boulevard, Los Angeles, California 90024; (213) 879-1700.

Since the mid-nineteenth century some 2.5 million holes have been sunk in the search for oil.

The world's first energy crisis was precipitated in 1920 by newspaper reports that the United States would run out of oil by 1925. American oil companies then began negotiating with the British and French for shares in their Middle East petroleum resources. The world oil cartel eventually formed by the Seven Sisters—British Petroleum, Exxon, Gulf, Royal Dutch-Shell Group, Mobil, Standard Oil of California, and Texaco—controlled all Middle East oil and two-thirds of the international oil supply until the rise of OPEC in the early 1970s.

King Edward IV of fifteenth-century England decreed that a barrel of eels or herrings should be exactly 42 gallons. According to an April 1980 *New Yorker* article, the standard barrel established by this royal act became a measure of crude oil 400 years later, when it was adopted by the Council of Producers, a group of early U.S. oil drillers, in 1872.

The cylindrical steel containers you sometimes see stacked outside refineries should not be confused with barrels of oil. They are *drums* of oil and contain fifty gallons each. Oil never actually travels in barrels; it's just measured that way.

Sales: $9.5 billion
Profits: $891 million
Forbes 500 rank: 30
Rank in oil: 12
Founded: 1917
Employees: 30,000
Headquarters: Bartlesville, Oklahoma

What they do. When people talk about the big oil companies, they usually don't mention—or even think of—Phillips. But Phillips is no pygmy. They're the 11th largest oil company in the United States, ranked by sales, and in 1979 they made more money than Sears, Roebuck—the nation's largest retailer. One reason they don't usually get lumped with the likes of Exxon, Mobil, and Shell is that their offices are still in the tiny Oklahoma town where they were born. However, appearances can be deceiving. Phillips now produces oil in 7 countries and is looking for more in 21 others.

The geography of Phillips' oil production changed dramatically during the 1970s. As the decade opened they were producing 138,000 barrels of oil a day in the United States (40% of it from Texas) and 53,000 barrels outside the country. In 1979 Phillips pumped 121,000 barrels of oil a day in the United States (a third of it from Texas) and 166,000 barrels outside the country. The big difference is the North Sea. Phillips drilled the first successful fields there, in the Norwegian section, and now they get one-third of their total energy production from seven fields in the Greater Ekofisk Development in the Norwegian North Sea. More importantly, that's oil with fewer political complications than Middle Eastern oil.

The 1970s were fateful for Phillips in another important respect. A class action suit provoked by illegal political payoffs forced the company to broaden their board of directors to the point where outsiders (people not working for the company) now hold the majority of seats. Phillips is more open to public scrutiny these days. Before the suit, according to *Business Week*, management ran the company "as if it were its own private preserve."

Phillips is probably best known to American consumers in the Midwest and Southwest through their Phillips 66 gas sta-

tions. They have 13,600 of these stations, but that's far fewer than they had in the 1960s, when they thought of themselves as an up-and-coming national gasoline marketer. Through expansion in the Northeast and Far West, they had built their marketing network to a whopping 27,000 stations, but Phillips has since pulled out of both regions. Phillips' share of the national gasoline market is less than 4%.

Phillips is also an important chemical producer, with annual sales of $2 billion a year. They are a leader in the production of cyclohexane, the principal component of nylon, and they make various plastics such as Marlex and nitrogen fertilizers. Phillips also used to be known for an amateur basketball team, the Phillips 66ers, which they sponsored, but they folded the team in 1968.

History. Frank Phillips was born in Scotia, Nebraska in 1873 and grew up primarily in Iowa, where he became a ranch hand and, later, a barber. His business acumen came to the fore in his tonsorial enterprise—in the 1890s Phillips had a chain of three barber shops and had invented his own rainwater-based cure for baldness, "Phillips' Mountain Sage."

After marrying the local banker's daughter in 1897, Phillips sold his barber shops and became a traveling bond salesman. In just a few years he earned commissions of $75,000 and began investing the money in speculative oil leases in Oklahoma. In 1903 he set up Anchor Oil in Bartlesville and began drilling. His first two wells were dry holes, but they were followed by 80 gushers. To help with the business, Frank brought his two brothers, L. E. and Waite Phillips, down from Iowa. Meanwhile, he set up Citizens Bank and Trust, which prospered and eventually became the First National Bank of Bartlesville.

In 1917 Frank and L. E. incorporated Phillips Petroleum Company to replace Anchor. Under the leadership of "Uncle Frank" (as his employees called him), Phillips Petroleum underwent phenomenal growth—due largely to Frank's nearly evangelical faith in research and development. An observer once said, "Nothing sounds crazy to Frank Phillips if it comes from an intelligent mind." Because of Phillips's R & D department, they rapidly took the lead in airplane fuel development and also discovered a new process—called thermal polymerization—for the conversion of waste gas into gasoline.

The first Phillips gas station opened in Wichita, Kansas, in 1927. At a meeting of directors and officers, called to decide on a name for the new gasoline, someone suggested that U.S. Highway 66, which ran from Amarillo, Texas, to Chicago, was the center of the proposed marketing area and should lend its name to the station. This was rejected as being too narrow a definition for an ambitious company like Phillips. Then an official who had just returned from a test drive recalled that he had told the driver that the car "goes like 60 with our new gas." The driver checked the speedometer and noted that they were actually going 66 miles an hour. One of the directors asked where they had tested the gas. "On Highway 66," was the reply. Concluding that the gods of gas had spoken, the board unanimously voted to name their product "Phillips 66."

Frank Phillips was chairman until his retirement in 1949. During that time he earned a reputation for rugged individualism sometimes verging on eccentric egoism. Among other things, he constructed a 4,000-acre retreat near Bartlesville named "Woolaroc," complete with a lodge modeled after his Nebraska birthplace and stocks of exotic birds and animals. He was also a generous patron of the Boy Scouts and acquired a sizeable collection of southwestern art and Indian artifacts, which later became a museum. He died in Atlantic City, New Jersey, in 1950.

Uncle Frank's successor as chairman was one William Keeler, a one-sixteenth Cherokee Indian whom President Harry Truman named chief of the Cherokee tribe. During his tenure the tribe built in northeast Oklahoma a reconstruction of an eighteenth century Cherokee village called Tsa-La-Gi, which charges tourists $1 for a tour and monologue on Cherokee history. This was Keeler's homage to the 4,000 Cherokees who died along the "Trail of Tears," when President Andrew Jackson sent soldiers to herd the Indians westward from their native Georgia.

Under Keeler, Phillips went into partnership with the Egyptian government on a drilling concession "the size of the state of Oklahoma," as Keeler put it, and they began exploring in the North Sea and on the Alaskan North Slope. Thanks to these decisions, and to the lock the other majors had on Saudi Arabia and the rest of the Arab nations, most of their oil is non-OPEC. Planned or not, this has turned out to be Phillips' greatest blessing.

Reputation. "More a persistent plodder than a pioneer when it came to developing new energy sources," observed *Business Week* in 1978. "Phillips was among the last of the majors to search for foreign oil." So everyone was flabbergasted when they weighed in with their North Sea strike in the early 1970s—it was the most significant new find in many years. Phillips likes to describe themselves as "an international company that stayed home."

What they own. At the end of 1979 Phillips valued their investments in properties, plants, and equipment at $4.8 billion. Included were some 8,400 miles of pipelines, 9 crude oil tankers, 5 U.S. refineries (at Borger and Sweeny, Texas; Kansas City, Kansas; Woods Cross, Utah; and Great Falls, Montana), and 34 chemical plants in 13 states. They own 6,300 patents, more than any other oil company.

Who owns and runs the company. William F. Martin, who came up through the ranks of the accounting and finance departments, became president in 1971 and took over from Keeler as chairman at the beginning of 1974. At that time William C. Douce, from chemicals and sales, became president and chief operating officer. Thanks to a successful public-interest class action suit brought against the company in 1975, the board is now heavily weighted with nonmanagement directors. In 1979 only 5 of the 15 directors were full-time company officers. The Phillips board is probably the only one in the petroleum industry to include two women: Dolores D. Wharton, a black whose husband is also a leading educator, and Carol C. Laise, former U.S. ambassador to Nepal.

The largest block of stock, 6.7%, is held by Phillips' employees through their Thrift Plan. Employees may invest up to 5% of their salaries in stock during their first five years in the company and as much as 10% later. The company will then match half their investment in the employees' names. Since Phillips stock value has nearly quadrupled in the last 10 years, some employees are doing pretty well these days.

In the public eye. Phillips maintained a multimillion dollar political slush fund

The 10 Toughest Corporate Bosses

When *Fortune* magazine tried to write a story about the corporate world's ten toughest bosses, they immediately ran into a problem: fear. Trembling subordinates of the awesome leaders refused to be quoted by name in print, and even ex-colleagues insisted on anonymity lest the bosses' vindictive power smite them from afar.

The subordinates' responses made it easy to define one key quality of the Tough Ten: the ability to inspire respect tinged with terror. As Robert Malott, chairman of FMC Corporation, once explained to a group of his managers: "Leadership is demonstrated when the ability to inflict pain is confirmed."

One other common trait that emerged from the scores of interviews *Fortune* conducted was single-minded dedication to the job and the insistence that subordinates be equally devoted. Running a corporation is a 20-hour-a-day, seven-day-a-week job, Beatrice Foods' former chairman, Wallace Rasmussen, once told a meeting of company presidents.

"What about your wife and family?" asked one executive.

"Get rid of them if they get in the way," snarled Rasmussen.

Here is *Fortune's* Tough Ten, listed alphabetically, not in order of ferocity:

Robert Abboud, former chairman and chief executive officer, First Chicago Bank
Thomas Mellon Evans, chairman and chief executive officer, Crane
Maurice Greenberg, president and chief executive officer, American International
Richard Jacob, chairman and chief executive officer, Dayco
David Mahoney, chairman and chief executive officer, Norton Simon
Alex Massad, executive vice-president, Mobil
Andrall Pearson, president,

PepsiCo
Donald Rumsfeld, president and chief executive officer, G. D. Searle
Robert Stone, executive vice-president, Columbia Pictures
William Ylvisaker, chairman and chief executive officer, Gould

And here are some of the things their co-workers told *Fortune* about the Tough Ten:

Richard Jacob: "Do something wrong and he lands on you, all 300 pounds of him." Known as Old Rough-Tough, the bulking Jacob is a former World War II warrant officer who still acts like one. At a meeting of security analysts, when one of the analysts repeatedly interrupted Jacob while he was talking, Jacob threatened to kick the man in a sensitive part of his anatomy if he interrupted again.

Maurice "Hank" Greenberg: "Extremely blunt . . . accomplished at belittling people in front of others. . . . You haven't achieved any standing if you haven't experienced his wrath." "He pays little attention to time zones, so he is always calling people at home or dragging them off the golf course. The people who report to Hank are put under pressure that could be considered unreal."

Robert Stone: "Known as Captain Queeg when he ran Hertz. . . . A galley master who, hearing that the rowers would die if the beat were raised to 40, would say, 'Make it 45.'"

William Ylvisaker: "Uses Marine Corps boot-camp approach . . . creates aura of power and wealth and reminds people it all flows from him. . . . They won't go to the bathroom without his permission."

The article elaborated at length on Crane's Thomas Mellon Evans, about whom a subordinate said his "most glaring trait is his lack of feeling for people." A manager

considering accepting a job with an Evans-controlled company once phoned a former Evans co-worker for advice. "How old are you?" asked the survivor. "50." "Well, if you want to see 55, I'd think twice about it."

Some people rate Evans as the toughest of the Tough. "Next to Tom Evans, they are pussycats," said one man who has worked with a number of demanding bosses. "He's the toughest man I have ever known."

Some companies with bosses who rated in the Tough Ten have flourished; others haven't. With abrasive Robert Stone at the helm, Hertz's profits in the 1970s multiplied fourfold, to $60 million. But at First Chicago, during Robert "Idi" Abboud's reign as chairman, the bank's profits dropped 14% in 1979. What's more, since Abboud took over in 1975, First Chicago has lost 200 managers, and insiders say the high turnover makes it difficult to attract first-rate replacements. "There has been a history of the messenger being shot for bringing bad news," a former vice-president told the *Wall Street Journal*.

The boardroom table turned on Abboud shortly after *Fortune* ran their Tough Ten story. In May 1980 the executive committee at First Chicago decided to get rid of "Idi" and his second-in-command, Harvey Kapnick. The committee said the two men had been quarrelling enough to cause "unrest in senior management."

So when tough bosses fail, they, too, can be fired. Subordinates seldom pause to mourn the loss of the tyrant when he is toppled from his throne in the executive suite. In fact, at First Chicago employees were heard singing, "Ding-dong, the witch is gone."

Source: *Fortune*, April 21, 1980.

from 1964 to 1972, $50,000 of which was personally handed to Richard Nixon by William Keeler in Nixon's New York apartment in 1968. Nixon has denied receipt of any such payment. In 1975 Keeler pleaded guilty to violations of federal election laws and received a fine. Another $100,000 contribution that Phillips had made to Nixon's 1972 campaign was returned to the company in August 1973. Phillips also made about $125,000 in illegal contributions to Texas politicians from 1974 through 1979; they pleaded guilty and paid a $50,000 fine. In 1977 the company pleaded guilty to what the *New York Times* described as "federal tax charges alleging a global conspiracy to conceal $3 million in Swiss bank accounts and a secret cache at company headquarters."

Phillips's political and financial hanky-panky resulted in a class action stockholder suit by a Los Angeles public-interest law firm. As a result, in 1976 Phillips was ordered to include six members from outside the company on their board of directors—three named by the plaintiff lawyers, and the other three approved by them. One of the new directors was a U.C.L.A. Business School Dean Harold Williams, whom President Carter later made chairman of the Securities Exchange and Commission.

Where they're going. Phillips has a money machine in the North Sea, principally in fields located within Norway's territorial waters. Their platform complex near Ekofisk alone provides enough oil to power the city of Chicago for a year—and production from Ekofisk is increasing in the 1980s.

Stock performance. Phillips stock bought for $1,000 in 1970 sold for $3,979 on January 2, 1980.

Major employment centers. Bartlesville, Oklahoma; Borger, Texas; and Houston, Texas.

Access. Phillips Building, Bartlesville, Oklahoma 74004; (918) 661-6600. An exhibit hall on the second floor of the Phillips Building is open for tours Monday through Friday from 8 A.M. to 5 P.M. Tours of most Phillips plants and refineries are available for students and other groups on a request basis.

Consumer brands.

Phillips 66 gasoline and Trop-Artic motor oil.

Shell Oil

Sales: $14.5 billion
Profits: $1.1 billion
Forbes 500 rank: 16
Rank in oil: 7
Rank in natural gas: 2
Rank in U.S. refinery runs: 3
Rank in retail gasoline sales: 4
Founded: 1912
Employees: 35,000
Headquarters: Houston, Texas

What they do. The bright yellow scallop shell on a red field means gasoline to motorists around the globe. It's the most ubiquitous gasoline brand in the world. Shell is part of an international oil company that manages to appear American or British or Dutch, as the case or country may be. Here in the United States the Shell banner flies over 16,500 service stations in 43 states— and these stations are the most productive dispensers of gasoline in the nation. Texaco, for example, has 10,000 more stations than Shell, but they pump about the same amount of gasoline: 9 billion gallons a year. Up to 1980 less than half the gasoline pumped at Shell stations came from crude oil produced by Shell. Shell is a company that has been traditionally short of crude, which is the stuff that comes out of the ground and becomes gasoline when run through refineries. But Shell people, as anyone in the industry will tell you, have been superb marketers—ready, willing, and able to sell more gasoline than they produce. That characteristic has set them apart from crude-rich companies making their money on the production side and caring little about the final marketing of the product.

According to one oil business saying, Shell can sell the stuff but never find it. They're rectifying that by buying it. In the tail end of 1979 Shell made a dramatic move to shore up their U.S. resource base when they bought a little known, privately owned California crude oil producer, Belridge Oil. The price—$3.6 billion—made it the biggest acquisition in American business history. The resulting 44% increase in domestic oil reserves will not make Shell completely self-sufficient, but it takes them a long way in that direction. Shell called the acquisition "the capstone of our 1979 achievements." Those achievements included Shell's first $1 billion profit year. In 1979 only 13 American companies made more money than Shell Oil of Houston.

Because of their short supply, Shell has concentrated on doing more with what they have. At one point during 1978 they roared into first place in retail sales of gasoline in the United States, and they remain one of the leaders, with about 8% of the total market in 1979. They are number 1 in sales of jet fuel, with about 18% of that market. And they are a giant in the chemical industry. Their chemical operations, largely based on petroleum by-products, soared to sales of $2.5 billion in 1979. In their 14 major chemical product lines—which include synthetic rubber, detergent alcohols, and polystyrene—they rank first in 10, second in 2, and third in the other 2. They place among the 10 largest U.S. chemical producers.

The American company is clearly the most important asset of that Anglo-Dutch hybrid, the Royal Dutch/Shell Group.

History. Royal Dutch/Shell was put together by as unlikely a combination as you can imagine. The inspiration was self-defense against the rampaging American oil trust assembled by John D. Rockefeller. In 1906 Shell Transport—an oil company founded by Marcus Samuel, a Jewish merchant in London—merged with Royal Dutch, an East Indies oil company headed by a xenophobic Dutchman, Henri Deterding. Samuel had named his company Shell after the cargo of seashells he used to bring back from the Far East in the mid 1800s. After the merger, which created the initial Anglo-Dutch financial complex, Samuel was out. Deterding took over, intent on fighting Rockefeller's Standard Oil all over the world, and by the beginning of World War I he had established satellites in almost every part of the globe, including Russia, Rumania, Venezuela, Egypt, and Mexico.

In 1912, a year after the Supreme Court had broken up the Standard Oil Trust, Deterding moved into the United States to battle John D. on his home turf. His first base was a depot at Tacoma, Washington, which received Shell oil shipped from Sumatra. A terminal and refinery were then built at Martinez, California, on the northern end of San Francisco Bay. Before long Shell was producing oil in the United

States—they made important discoveries in California and acquired oil-producing companies in other parts of the country. By 1929 Shell gasoline was being sold in all 48 states. A year earlier Deterding had arranged his famous "As Is" cartel, getting Jersey Standard and other major producers to carve up world markets among themselves, setting prices and allocating oil. It was an arrangement that was to stand until 1942.

By the 1930s Deterding's erratic behavior had become rather embarrassing to fellow directors. He wrote in his memoirs, "If I were dictator of the world—and please, Mr. Printer, set this in larger type—I would shoot all idlers at sight." The anticommunism he had picked up from his second wife, a White Russian, turned into a pro-Nazi fervor when he married his German secretary. He retired to Germany, where he died six months before World War II broke out. Hitler and Göring sent wreaths to his funeral.

These histrionics had little effect on the development of Shell Oil in the United States, which was expected to—and did—succeed independently in the American market. They find their own crude oil, marketing it domestically, do their own research, and establish their own petrochemical operations. There's an interchange of ideas—and of some top managers—in the Royal Dutch/Shell Group, but the national entities operate with a high degree of autonomy. In that sense Shell is more of an international organization than the big U.S. multinationals. No matter where Coca-Cola, General Motors, or Exxon operate, they are likely to be regarded as American; that's not automatically the case with Shell.

The national Shell units in the world have a fair degree of independence, but it's not blanket autonomy. For example, Shell of the United States was precluded from exploring for oil in the Middle East—that was considered Royal Dutch/Shell turf. As a result, Shell really had to scramble for oil in the United States. On the other hand, right now Shell of the United States is dickering with the Saudi Arabian government for the construction of a $2 billion petrochemical facility.

Until 1939 Shell had three independent bases in San Francisco, St. Louis, and New York. The two eastern offices were then merged, with San Francisco continuing to function separately until 1949, when everything was consolidated in New York. In 1970 Shell moved their headquarters to the new oil capital: Houston.

Reputation. In a time when many oil companies seem indifferent to motorists at best, Shell still wants you to pull up to their pumps. They pay a lot of attention to the way their stations look, and they generally try to make it pleasant for you. They have to, since retail gasoline sales are such an important part of their business.

What they own. At the close of 1979 Shell had proved U.S. crude oil reserves of 2.2 billion barrels that, at their present rate of production (175 million barrels a year), would last only about 10 years. The big kicker in 1979 was Belridge Oil, which has more than half a million barrels of crude oil reserves. When they had to come up with $3.6 billion in cash to buy Belridge, Shell borrowed $3 billion from two banking syndicates. It was easy as pie.

Who owns and runs the company. It's complicated, but here's how it works: 69.4% of Shell Oil stock is owned by the Royal Dutch/Shell Group, which in turn is 60% owned by Royal Dutch Petroleum of the Netherlands and 40% by Shell Transport and Trading of London. Shell Oil stock not owned by the Group is traded on the New York Stock Exchange like any other stock. Shares of Royal Dutch and Shell Transport are also traded on the New York Stock Exchange, so you can buy shares of the two-thirds-owned American child or shares of either of the parents. Take your pick. In the opinion of many Wall Streeters, American investors are major owners of all three stocks. So it's difficult to say what, if any, nationality this company has. Management is an international mix too. John Bookout, a Louisiana geologist, became head of Shell Oil in 1976, succeeding a Briton, Harry Bridges. In 1965 Monroe E. Spaght, who was president of Shell Oil, became the first American to serve as a managing director of Royal Dutch/Shell. Asked how it was to work there, he said: "In Shell Oil Company you come to work on Monday morning and start saying, 'What'll we do now? What's our next step? How do we make more money?' Here your first chore on Monday morning is to see how much you've got left of what you had on Friday evening."

In the public eye. Shell's major advertising effort of recent years has been a "Come to Shell for Answers" program, featuring a series of booklets offering motorists various kinds of help—mainly on how to take care of their cars.

The Oil, Chemical & Atomic Workers (OCAW) struck Shell in 1973, calling for a boycott in a dispute over whether the union could have some say in monitoring health and safety conditions at refineries. Shell rejected the demand as a dilution of their control over plant operations.

In 1975 Shell put up $1.5 million to settle a class action suit brought on behalf of residents of Martinez, the California town where Shell first refined oil in America. The refinery had installed a new system that, according to the suit, spewed a yellow sticky substance over the town, ate the paint off cars, caused vibrations that cracked walls, and triggered cough spasms. Letters were sent to 10,000 present or former Martinez residents asking them to present claims.

Early in 1980 Shell came through with one of the largest single grants ever made to cancer research: $2 million for the testing of a promising new anticancer agent, interferon, a natural substance made by the body to ward off virus infections.

Where they're going. Under the name Pecten, Shell is exploring for oil in 10 countries, but they're bullish about finding it here too. They believe that 40% of the oil the country will need in 1990 "will come from fields not yet discovered." Shell believes that two-thirds of the oil and gas yet to be discovered in the United States lie under public lands, and so they are saying to Washington: "The ball's in your court. We're ready."

Stock performance. Shell Oil stock bought for $1,000 in 1970 sold for $2,451 on January 2, 1980.

Access. One Shell Plaza, P.O. Box 2463, Houston, Texas 77001; (713) 241-4083. Consumer complaints should be addressed to Shell Oil Company, P.O. Box 80, Tulsa, Oklahoma 75012. Toll-free number for complaints is (800) 333-3703.

Consumer brands.

Shell gasoline; Fire & Ice motor oil.

Chevron Standard Oil Company of California

Sales: $29.9 billion
Profits: $1.8 billion
Forbes 500 rank: 7
Rank in oil: 3
Rank in retail gas sales: 7
Founded: 1879
Employees: 39,700
Headquarters: San Francisco, California

What they do. Standard Oil of California (Socal) brings up the "right wing" of the American oil industry. They have a long history of aloofness and indifference to public opinion. As late as the 1970s male black receptionists in two-toned brown livery outfits padded through the executive suites of the company's headquarters in downtown San Francisco. Not until 1965 were women allowed to work even as secretaries on the building's 18th floor, the domain of Socal's top managers. "This is a *very* stuffy company," a Socal official boasted to Anthony Sampson, author of *The Seven Sisters.* Many people were enraged when Otto Miller, Socal's chairman at the time, sent a letter in 1973 to all the company's stockholders and employees, calling for support for "the aspirations of the Arab people" in the Middle East, without mentioning Israel's aspirations.

For Standard Oil of California it was all in a day's work. They were the first oil company to penetrate Saudi Arabia, and they still get more than four-fifths of their crude oil from the eastern hemisphere—mostly the Middle East, and particularly Saudi Arabia. It's understandable that they would want to stay on the good side of the sheiks because without Middle Eastern oil they would be hard put to keep their position as the largest company in the American West and the seventh largest company in the United States.

The company is so big and complex that even they can't always figure out what they're doing. In 1979, for example, the *Wall Street Journal* reported that Socal was profiting as much as $4 million a day from their participation in the Arabian American Oil Co. (Aramco), the consortium that produces Saudi Arabia's oil. Socal and the other member companies, according to the report, were paying $2 to $5 a barrel less for Saudi oil than what the other members of the Organization of Petroleum Exporting Countries (OPEC) were charging. The *San Francisco Chronicle* questioned Socal's deputy controller, who acknowledged that the company was benefitting from the "two-tier" price system. "But because of the complexities of the international oil business," he added, "it's a benefit we cannot calculate." They made out all right, though, since their 1979 profits were up 64% over 1978.

They have a lot to keep track of. They have a fleet of 77 ocean-going tankers that ship oil to and from 38 refineries, owned wholly or partly by Socal, in 19 countries. They have the second largest refining capacity in the country, with 12 refineries in the United States. They sell gasoline at 14,000 filling stations in 40 states, plus a few more in Canada, Central America, Puerto Rico, and Tahiti. Most of their stations operate under the Chevron name, but they're still called Standard in the Southeast, where they bought Standard Oil of Kentucky in 1961, in a rare move to expand their retail network. Their oil wells in the United States stretch from the Gulf of Mexico to the California coast.

Socal's real strength has always been in producing oil, not going out of their way to sell it to motorists. They've generally been content to sit on their vast Middle Eastern concessions and their huge California market, where they're the state's largest supplier of gasoline. They pump much more oil out of the ground than they could hope to sell through their stations, so they unload the rest on other companies. Much of their business is transacted overseas. In 1979 they sold a little over 1 million barrels of oil a day in the United States, compared to nearly 2 million barrels in foreign countries.

They find other uses for petroleum too. Socal is one of the world's largest asphalt producers, and they are among the nation's top three producers of garden fertilizers and pesticides, which they market under the name Ortho.

History. Socal began when Demetrius Scofield, a nomadic oilman from Pennsylvania, and some partners founded the Pacific Coast Oil Company in California in 1879. At that time John D. Rockefeller's Standard Oil Company was shipping oil around the Horn to California. After oil was discovered under Los Angeles, Rockefeller waged a ruthless price war and forced Scofield to sell his company to Standard in 1900. When the Supreme Court broke up the Standard Oil Trust in 1911, Scofield came back as head of the Standard Oil Company of California, 1 of 34 companies that emerged from the Rockefeller empire.

By 1919 Socal was providing more than one-fourth of the total U.S. oil production, more than any other company. But it was the Arabs who really made Socal's fortune.

Shortly before World War I, an Armenian entrepreneur named Calouste Gulbenkian had put together a syndicate called the Turkish Petroleum Company to explore for oil in Iraq. By the early 1920s ownership was divided among British Petroleum, Shell, the French government, and seven American oil companies, including Standard Oil of New Jersey and Mobil. Gulbenkian retained a 5% interest for himself. He also got the participating companies to agree that none would seek oil concessions in the former Ottoman Empire except through the syndicate, which was now called the Iraq Petroleum Company. Since no one was quite sure what constituted the former Ottoman Empire, Gulbenkian drew a red line on the map encircling the area he meant: Turkey and the entire Middle East except for Iran and Kuwait. It was called the Red Line Agreement, and it lasted until 1948.

Around the same time word began to circulate that there might be oil in Arabia. Standard of California, which was not a member of Gulbenkian's syndicate, paid $50,000 for the right to explore for oil on the Persian Gulf island of Bahrain, and in 1932 they struck oil. Enter King Ibn Saud, a desert warrior who had only recently subdued his enemies on the Arabian peninsula and named the whole territory after his clan—Saudi Arabia. The king was in desperate need of money, and he put the Arabian oil concession up for grabs. He wanted to be paid 50,000 British pounds in gold. The Iraq Petroleum Company cautiously tried to bargain with him, but Socal saw that this was no time for haggling. They quickly put up the gold. Soon their Arabian oil fields were producing so much oil that they couldn't handle it. They had to cut in Texaco just to be able to do something with all that oil. In 1936 Texaco's marketing and refining network in the eastern hemisphere merged with Socal's production operations in Bahrain to form Caltex, a 50-50 partnership. Socal's concessions in Sumatra, Java, and New Guinea were later added to the partnership.

After World War II Standard of New Jersey and Mobil bought into the lucrative Saudi Arabian operations, now known as Aramco. American engineers and their families moved in to run the oil show, giving rise to this peculiar scene in one settlement described by Sampson: "Bungalow houses spring up in neat rows, with creepers up the walls and green lawns alongside the desert, and a complete suburb formed itself with a baseball park, a cinema, swimming pools and tennis courts. It was an astonishing optical illusion, looking like a small town from Texas or California,

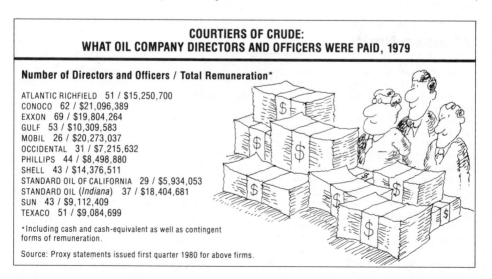

COURTIERS OF CRUDE:
WHAT OIL COMPANY DIRECTORS AND OFFICERS WERE PAID, 1979

Number of Directors and Officers / Total Remuneration*

ATLANTIC RICHFIELD 51 / $15,250,700
CONOCO 62 / $21,096,389
EXXON 69 / $19,804,264
GULF 53 / $10,309,583
MOBIL 26 / $20,273,037
OCCIDENTAL 31 / $7,215,632
PHILLIPS 44 / $8,498,880
SHELL 43 / $14,376,511
STANDARD OIL OF CALIFORNIA 29 / $5,934,053
STANDARD OIL (*Indiana*) 37 / $18,404,681
SUN 43 / $9,112,409
TEXACO 51 / $9,084,699

*Including cash and cash-equivalent as well as contingent forms of remuneration.

Source: Proxy statements issued first quarter 1980 for above firms.

whence many of the inhabitants came; except that it was ringed around with a high barbed-wire fence, with beyond it an expanse of limitless desert, with only a few oil wells and pipelines to break the monotony."

The arrangement worked fine, from Socal's point of view, until the 1970s, when the OPEC nations banded together to boost the price of oil dramatically and the Saudis announced their intention to take over Aramco.

Reputation. Socal has been known for years as a predominantly white, male, Christian company that wanted to stay that way. Anthony Sampson, in *The Seven Sisters*, characterized them as making "a positive cult of conservatism." *Forbes*, in 1971, characterized the management as following "the old Cal Standard tradition of saying as little as possible to anyone from the outside." In a national survey of graduating business students in the early 1970s, Socal ranked 49th out of 50 corporations rated on their social responsibility. For a while dissident employees at the company put out an underground newspaper, *The Stranded Oiler*.

What they own. They own 27,000 oil wells and and 2,000 gas wells around the world, with proved reserves of 1.7 billion barrels of oil, but they're not counting the crude they're getting from Saudi Arabia and Indonesia "because release of such information has not been approved" by the governments of those nations. In 1975 Socal bought 20% of AMAX, a huge mining company; in 1979 they tried to buy more but were rebuffed by AMAX's board.

Who owns and runs the company. Otto Miller, who stepped down as chairman in 1974, ran the company as an autocrat. In the late 1960s George Ball, former undersecretary of state, held a board seat. Ball then argued that it would be good politics to let British companies own a part of Aramco; shortly after that Ball was not renominated for a director's position.

Most Socal executives who make it to the top are engineers who have come up through the oilfields and refineries. Harold J. Haynes, who became chairman in 1974, is a civil engineer from Texas. Haynes is aware of the company's fabled public-be-damned posture and would like to improve their image. In an interview with Robert Scheer of the *Los Angeles Times* in 1979, he admitted, "I know that we have a miserable public image and I know that a lot of this is our own fault. And I say that because there were many, many, many years, in fact up until about 1973, where the oil business took the position or the attitude that our business was our business and nobody's but ours. And we wouldn't any more have sat down and talked to you for two hours about our business than we would have gone to the moon."

The various descendants of John D. Rockefeller own more than 2% of Socal, and David Rockefeller's Chase Manhattan Bank controls nearly 1.5%. Eight of the 14

"Poison Ivy"

Ivy Lee was one of the first practitioners of the craft of corporate public relations. The son of a Georgia preacher, Lee spent childhood evenings listening to family friend Joel Chandler Harris spin his nostalgic Uncle Remus stories about vanished plantations, faithful slaves, and kind masters of a South that had never existed. Thus born into revisionism, Lee was in later life to raise it to the level of an art form.

Ivy Lee eventually num-bered among his clients the likes of Walter Chrysler, Charles Schwab, George Westinghouse, Henry Guggenheim, American Tobacco, General Mills. He created the Wheaties slogan "Breakfast of Champions." But it is through his work for Standard Oil of New Jersey and the Rockefeller family that he is best remembered. John D. Rockefeller, the founder of the Standard Oil Trust, had long suffered from bad press: so bad, in fact, that when he tried to donate $100,000 to the Congregational Church for missionary work, the gift was denounced by many church leaders as "tainted money" ill-gotten by the foremost robber baron of the age. Rockefeller had been verbally indicted by none other than Teddy Roosevelt as one of America's "malefactors of great wealth"; and if any literate American still had generous feelings toward John D., there was always Ida Tarbell's muckraking *History of the Standard Oil Company* to dissuade him.

directors on the all-white board are Socal executives. Other directors include Carla Anderson Hills, former secretary of housing and urban development and the only woman on the board; Alden W. Clausen, president of the Bank of America; David Packard, chairman of Hewlett-Packard and former deputy secretary of defense; and George H. Weyerhaeuser, president of Weyerhaeuser.

In the public eye. Socal has a knack for making headlines. Here are just a few of their appearances in the past decade:

1970: A fire on a Socal drilling platform off Louisiana caused a massive oil slick in the Gulf of Mexico. The secretary of the interior charged the company with 147 violations of federal drilling regulations.

1971: Two Socal tankers collided in San Francisco Bay, causing an enormous oil spill.

1972: Backers of a "clean environment" initiative on the California ballot charged Socal with setting up a phony "front group" called Californians Against the Pollution Initiative to defeat the proposal.

1976: The California Air Resources Board found "the worst air pollution violation ever detected" at the Socal refinery in El Segundo.

1977: The California Franchise Tax Board charged that Socal owed the state $156 million in back taxes on profits from the Saudi Arabian oil holdings.

1978: Chevron USA, the company's domestic arm, doubled the rent on many of their service stations leased by independent dealers in California, shortly after California voters approved Proposition 13, which slashed property taxes.

1979: Chevron Chemical agreed to recall its weed killers containing Silves, a chemical believed responsible for causing cancer and birth defects.

For Haynes, it's just part of the job. As he told Scheer of the *Los Angeles Times*, "Look, we are accused, we are charged, we are maligned and everything else. We are a big company, and that is just going to happen . . . . Sure, we get fined, I mean, hell, I am sure you haven't gone through life without a traffic fine or something . . . . I am sure that during the course of time that we have been sitting here that we have probably had two or three more charges filed against us."

Where they're going. Socal hopes to keep taking oil out of Saudi Arabia as long as there's oil to lift—and as long as the Saudi Arabians will let them. But they are also hedging their bets by exploring alternative energy sources. In June 1980 they announced ambitious plans to extract oil from their vast shale deposits in Colorado. Between now and 1990 Socal could spend as much as $5 billion on this project. The plan is for the shale project to yield 50,000 barrels of oil a day by 1988 and 100,000 barrels a day by the early 1990s. Right now Socal is taking 2 million barrels a day out of Saudi Arabia.

Stock performance. Standard Oil of Cali-

But the darkest day for the Rockefeller name was April 20, 1914, when a seven-month-old strike by 9,000 miners at Colorado Fuel and Iron, a Rockefeller-controlled company, came to a bloody climax. The miners and their families had moved out of the company's Colorado mining camps and settled in tent cities that the United Mine Workers had set up nearby. A company of militia, paid by C F & I, had positioned themselves on a hill above Ludlow, one of the tent cities, to watch over the town. Just after daybreak on April 20, a shot rang out and the nervous militia opened fire on the town, their bullets setting the tents on fire. By nightfall, 40 miners were dead. The next morning workers discovered the bodies of two women and 11 children who had suffocated beneath the floorboards of the burning tents. Criticism of Rockefeller (who had been in New York at the time) was both instant and vicious. One Denver paper wrote that "every prayer Rockefeller utters is an insult to the Christ that died for suffering humanity"; and the opening lines of a story in the *Cleveland Leader,* in Rockefeller's home town, read, "The charred bodies of two dozen women [sic] and children show that ROCKEFELLER KNOWS HOW TO WIN!"

Enter Ivy Lee.

John D. Rockefeller, Jr.—universally known as "Junior"—sought Lee out in May, a month after the slaughter, to ask him to improve the family's public image. Lee had

fornia stock bought for $1,000 in 1970 sold for $2,205 on January 2, 1980.

Major employment centers. San Francisco Bay area and Los Angeles, California.

Access. 225 Bush Street, San Francisco, California 94104; (415) 894-7700. A free public exhibit, "The World of Oil," at 555 Market Street, San Francisco, California, is open weekdays from 9 A.M. to 4 P.M. Send complaints about dealers to Chevron USA, P.O. Box H, Concord, California 94524; about credit cards to P.O. Box 5010, same address. Toll-free numbers: (800) 642-2462 in California, (800) 227-1677 in other states. Call (415) 233-3737 for information about oil spills or exposure to poisonous Chevron and Ortho products.

Consumer brands.

Gasoline: Chevron; Standard (in the Southeast).
Fertilizers and pesticides: Ortho.

> Since World War II, the industrialized world has used more petroleum and nonfuel minerals than had been utilized in all previous human history. During that period the United States has consumed about 40% of the total.

Standard Oil (Indiana)

Sales: $18.6 billion
Profits: $1.5 billion
Forbes 500 rank: 13
Rank in oil: 6
Rank in U.S. oil production: 4
Rank in natural gas: 5
Rank in retail gasoline sales: 2
Rank in unleaded gasoline sales: 1
Founded: 1889
Employees: 52,300
Headquarters: Chicago, Illinois

What they do. Indiana Standard is the oil company of middle America, established by John D. Rockefeller in Indiana to refine Ohio oil for midwestern farmers. While the other majors were scrambling furiously for oil in the Middle East, Indiana Standard was content to remain in the Midwest. Their headquarters are still there (in a Chicago skyscraper overlooking Lake Michigan), and their Standard brand is still the Midwest's dominant brand of gasoline—although they sell in other regions under the Amoco trademark. They supply some 22,400 gas stations, mostly in the Midwest, East, and Southeast.

Indiana Standard's radio and television commercials talk up independence from OPEC (Organization of Petroleum Exporting Countries), which isn't surprising since

---

gone to work for the *New York Journal* after graduating from Princeton in 1898. There he had written about corporations, becoming fascinated by both their power and their defects. But Lee was not a muckraker. He believed that he could use the same aggressive journalistic techniques to improve the image of big business. In 1903 he left the *Journal* to become a corporate publicist. He was working for the Pennsylvania Railroad when Junior came to him and said, with

characteristic understatement, "I feel that my father and I are much misunderstood by the press and the people of this country. I should like to know what your advice would be on how to make our position clear."

Lee began by issuing bulletins on events in Colorado to a network of "opinion makers" he had built up in his 11 years in the business. Some of corporate America's first press releases, the bulletins consisted of selected newspaper reprints, statements by

leading citizens, and assorted other material, fashioned in such a way as to justify the actions of the Colorado Fuel and Iron company. One of them contained a misstatement by the vice-president of Colorado's Law and Order League to the effect that the gunshots from the militia had not been responsible for the death of the women and children; rather, the victims had carelessly overturned a stove in their tent.

These bulletins, later collected in a booklet called *The*

they're chiefly known as a domestic oil company. But the company that claims "America runs better on American oil" got 42% of their oil in 1978 from overseas—principally from Iran, Egypt, and South America. Although they lost their Iranian operation after the recent revolution there, Indiana Standard still gets a sizeable portion of their oil from foreign sources: and the Value Line Investment Survey reported in January 1980 that the company is "making a bundle outside the U.S." from their refining, marketing, and transportation businesses.

Traditionally, Indiana Standard has been known as a super sales organization that was short on crude, meaning that they had to buy oil from others to fill their marketing needs. They have been closing that gap in recent years with an aggressive exploration program, and in 1978 they drilled nearly 1,000 wells—300 more than any other oil company. The result has been that Indiana Standard, which used to buy half of the oil they sold to consumers, now only buys 20% and pumps the rest themselves. They have the capacity to produce about 1 million barrels of crude oil a day and refine almost 1.5 million barrels at their 13 refineries worldwide, the largest of which, at Texas City, Texas, has a capacity of 415,000 barrels a day.

Indiana Standard has been on a very hot streak. In 1970 they were making profits of $300 million. In 1980 they were heading toward profits of $2 billion. They now rank 4th among all U.S. oil companies in size of reserves (a measure of how much oil they have left).

History. Indiana Standard is probably the only oil company that had 10 million barrels of oil before they even existed. In 1886, ignoring the objections of his associates, John D. Rockefeller bought up all the oil he could get from Lima, Ohio—which was plenty since nobody else wanted the smelly "skunk oil." A high sulfur content rendered the Lima crude worthless. But Rockefeller stored it and built the largest oil refinery in the country on 300 acres of swampland in Whiting, Indiana, near Chicago. Then he waited for someone to figure out how to process sulfur oil. A man named Frasch successfully treated it with copper oxide in 1899, and soon Indiana Standard was supplying 10% of all U.S. oil.

Indiana Standard used horse-drawn tank wagons to deliver their kerosene oil, harness oil, stove gas, and axle grease to farmers in 1892—the first door-to-door rural free delivery in the country. They were one of the first companies to hire petroleum chemists, and a pair of their scientists discovered how to crack a petromolecule under pressure to double the amount of gasoline obtained from a barrel of crude oil.

After the dissolution of the Standard Oil Trust in 1911, Indiana Standard found themselves an oil company without oil. They merged with American Oil Company (Amoco) in 1925, gaining access to oil in

---

Struggle in Colorado for Industrial Freedom, made Lee infamous in literary circles. Upton Sinclair called him "Poison Ivy." Carl Sandburg wrote that Ivy "is below the level of the hired gunman and slugger. His sense of right and wrong is a worse force in organized society than that of the murderers who shot women and burned babies at Ludlow." But, in a letter to Junior, Lee revealed that he was aware of the need to do more than propagandize: "It is of the greatest importance that as early as possible some comprehensive plan be devised to provide machinery to redress [the miners'] grievances." Junior took his advice, and a grievance procedure was set up that same year.

Gradually, Standard's policy toward publicity ("Uncover no surface unnecessarily," as Starr Murphy, Rockefeller's personal attorney, had once stated it) began to change. Lee undertook to alter the image of John D. Senior from bloodless robber baron to sweet, harmless, generous old man. Lee suggested that Rockefeller begin to give out money to people on the street; so John D. began carrying a bag of dimes and nickels to hand out to adults and children, respectively—usually accompanying the gift with some fatherly Scottish maxim, such as "A dime for the bank; a penny to spend." Lee planted newspaper stories about Rockefeller the human being: his trips to church, his relations with his neighbors, his golf games,

Mexico and Venezuela, which they sold to Standard of New Jersey in 1932. Indiana Standard worried about expropriation (Mexico did nationalize foreign-owned oil in 1938), so they stuck close to home in the oil fields of the Rockies, Gulf Coast, and Canada for the next 24 years.

It took a South Carolinian to jolt Indiana Standard out of their midwestern complacency. John Swearingen joined the company in 1939 as a 20-year-old engineer. By 1960 he was chairman, and he's been shaking up the company ever since. He threw out 10 directors of a two-thirds-owned subsidiary because they objected to being absorbed by Indiana Standard. Once he threatened to throw a nun out of an annual meeting for speaking out of turn. And he actually has tossed hostile shareholders out of meetings. Swearingen is less an oilman than a businessman: "We're not in the energy business. We're trying to give our shareholders the best return on their money."

Swearingen's blunt style has earned some enemies, particularly Dr. Armand Hammer, chairman of Occidental Petroleum, which Swearingen attempted to take over in 1975. The oil industry named him chairman of the American Petroleum Institute, the industry's trade association, in 1978. Under Swearingen's guidance, Indiana Standard now has oil, mineral, and chemical operations in 40 countries.

Reputation. In the Midwest, Standard stations are as plentiful as cornfields. You might think their midwestern image would bring snorts of elitist derision from Wall Street; but, on the contrary, one New York oil analyst told the *Wall Street Journal* in 1979 that Standard has "the best management in the oil business." And Swearingen added "I'll stack our management team up against any company. It's the best I've ever seen."

What they own. Ten of Indiana Standard's 13 refineries are in the United States. Their transportation system includes 19 tankers, 15,000 miles of pipeline, 1,800 trucks, and 2,500 railroad cars.

Who owns and runs the company. In 1974, when Nelson Rockefeller was undergoing his Senate confirmation hearings for the vice-presidency, he had to disclose all his family's holdings. At that time he revealed that the Rockefellers still own two-tenths of 1% of Indiana Standard. That may not sound like much, but at the time that two-tenths of 1% amounted to about $12 million. The all-white, all-male board of directors includes members from such midwestern companies as Zenith, First National Bank of Chicago, and Eli Lilly. None of the directors lives east of Pittsburgh or west of Chicago. The largest single holding is the 8.5% chunk owned by employee savings plans.

In the public eye. The Amoco tanker *Cadiz*

etc.; all the while arranging for the recipients of Rockefeller charity to make public speeches of gratitude while Rockefeller himself remained modestly silent. As Lee began to successfully publicize more than $500 million in charitable contributions from John D., the old man's image began to soften.

Lee bolstered Junior's image as well. When World War I came, he planted stories on Junior's supposed spare-time habit of knitting scarves for the doughboys

overseas.

When the war ended, Lee convinced the Rockefellers and other oilmen to band together to form the American Petroleum Institute, with an eye to continuing cooperation between oil companies in peacetime—especially in the area of public relations, which, of course, was handled by Ivy Lee.

Lee continued to handle the Rockefellers' publicity for the next 15 years, on an annual retainer of $10,000. He publicized their endow-

ment of Colonial Williamsburg, Virginia, and he convinced the Associated Press to rewrite the obituary they had on file for John D., which had been compiled from muckraking sources like Ida Tarbell's book, in favor of more flattering material collected by Rockefeller's authorized biographer, W. O. Inglis.

But Lee ended his life in disgrace. In 1934 Standard Oil of New Jersey had sent him to Germany to consult with I. G. Farben, the German

TOP CORPORATE GIVERS

The following table, showing 22 of the top 25 business contributors to charity in 1978, was constructed by *Everybody's Business* from data prepared by the Conference Board, an industry research organization. The board supplies a table showing the dollar amounts given by the top givers minus the names of the companies. *Everybody's Business* has filled in the blanks by consulting with people knowledgeable about corporate philanthropy.

Contributions (1978)

1. EXXON $27.6 *million*
2. AT&T $24.3 *million*
3. GENERAL MOTORS $21.0 *million*
4. IBM $20.3 *million*
5. SEARS ROEBUCK $16.6 *million*
6. ? $12.6 *million*
7. FORD $11.5 *million*
8. GENERAL ELECTRIC $10.1 *million*
9. MOBIL $9.7 *million*
10. KODAK $9.1 *million*
11. ARCO $8.4 *million*
12. XEROX $7.8 *million*
13. DAYTON HUDSON $7.1 *million*
14. U.S. STEEL $6.7 *million*
15. DU PONT $6.7 *million*
16. ? $6.1 *million*
17. SHELL $6.0 *million*
18. ? $5.6 *million*
19. MONSANTO $5.6 *million*
20. PROCTER & GAMBLE $5.6 *million*
21. STANDARD OIL OF INDIANA $5.6 *million*
22. GULF OIL $5.3 *million*
23. GENERAL MILLS $5.3 *million*
24. STANDARD OIL OF CALIFORNIA $5.3 *million*
25. ITT $5.0 *million*

Other companies in the top 50 are: number 31. AETNA, $3.8 *million*; 34. BANK OF AMERICA, $3.7 *million*; 41. CITICORP, $3.3 *million*; 44. TEXACO, $3.2 *million*; 47. LEVI-STRAUSS, $2.9 million; 48. UNION CARBIDE, $2.9 *million*; 50. JOHN DEERE, $2.7 *million*.

---

petrochemical monopoly, on ways to improve Farben's image, and that of the Third Reich, to which the German company was closely tied. Standard had entered into a cartel with Farben in the 1920s, and the business relationship continued even after Hitler's rise to power. When Lee returned from Germany, he underwent a severe inquisition before a Special House Committee on Un-American Activities. When the testimony was released, the storm of adverse publicity was dev-astating. Headlines like "Lee Exposed as Hitler Press Agent" broke his spirit and what was left of his health. He was already dying of brain cancer when he testified before the Committee, but the brutal public criticism may have hastened his end. When Lee died John D. deserted him, refusing to answer reporters' questions about the man who had rebuilt his image. Even Junior delayed his letter of condolence to Lee's widow by nine months. Only Nelson Rockefeller, Jun-ior's son, sent her a telegram reading, "The country has lost a great leader." But Lee's best epitaph may have been written by America's ambassador to Berlin, who noted in his diary, "It is only another of the thousands of cases where love of money ruins men's lives. . . . I cannot say a commendatory word about him to the State Department."

Source: Peter Collier and David Horowitz, *The Rockefellers: An American Dynasty* (Holt, Rinehart, and Winston, 1976).

broke in two on the rocks off Portsall, France, in 1978. The 120,000 tons of oil in the ship's cargo formed a slick 70 miles long and fouled the Brittany coast. Amoco has refused blame for the largest oil spill in history, and they're now in the middle of a court battle over $2 billion in damages claimed against them.

Indiana Standard has a good record for minority employment and purchasing from minority-owned businesses. In 1979 they ranked third among companies that bought supplies from minorities, behind only General Motors and Ford Motor, with $75 million in purchases. Indiana Standard also helped restructure the building trades in Chicago—for years an all-white institution —by insisting on heavy minority employment during the building of their Chicago skyscraper. However, the Federal Trade Commission found that Amoco denied credit cards to applicants who live in certain "high-risk" zip code areas; most of Amoco's blacklisted zip code areas have mostly nonwhite populations.

Where they're going. Indiana Standard made their first move into solar energy with the acquisition of the Solarex Solar Cell Company of Maryland in 1979. Two attempts to buy into the coal industry have failed, but that doesn't mean Swearingen and his team are giving up—they're still on the lookout for an available mining company.

Stock performance. Indiana Standard stock bought for $1,000 in 1970 sold for $3,286 on January 2, 1980.

Access. 200 East Randolph Drive, Chicago, Illinois 60601; (312) 856-3800.

Consumer brands.

Petroleum products: American; Amoco; Standard. *Tires, batteries, and auto accessories:* Atlas.

Of the 25 top-ranked industrial corporations on the Fortune 500 list for 1979, 13 were oil companies, including numbers 1 (Exxon), 3 (Mobil), and 5 (Texaco).

Sales: $7.9 billion
Profits: $1.18 billion
Forbes 500 rank: 42
Rank in oil: 9
Rank in domestic crude oil: 3
Founded: 1870
Employees: 24,145
Headquarters: Cleveland, Ohio

What they do. Standard Oil of Ohio— usually known as Sohio—was small potatoes in the oil industry just 10 years ago. In 1968, the year before Sohio entered an agreement with British Petroleum to pump oil out of Alaska's North Slope, the company had assets of only $770 million and net profits of only $70 million. They didn't even qualify as a major oil company in those days. But by the end of 1979 they ranked as the ninth largest corporation in America (measured by the market value of their stock). In that year Sohio had assets of more than $9 billion—quite a success story for a company that had plodded along for a century just selling gasoline in their home state. With virtually no oil reserves of their own, Sohio was forced to buy crude oil from others and run it through their refineries in Lima and Toledo, Ohio, and Marcus Hook, Pennsylvania. Sohio still operates those same three refineries, but now the oil they process there is all their own. The North Slope has given them more American crude than any other oil company.

Sohio wanted a piece of the Alaskan action so badly that they sold 53% of themselves to British Petroleum, owners of the biggest share of the North Slope find. (The marriage was also convenient for BP, which badly needed outlets for all that oil, and which until then had little access to the gigantic American gasoline market.) That deal turned Sohio from a little regional company into an oil industry heavyweight almost overnight. Three quarters of their assets and almost all their production is now tied up in Alaska. The statistics are startling. Sohio's 10,000 wells in the lower 48 states produce only about 22,000 barrels a day, while their 156 Alaskan wells spew out half a million barrels. It all happened so quickly that Sohio can't process more than about 70% of what they pump out of the ground, and they still don't own any of the tankers that carry their Alaskan oil through the Panama Canal to the Gulf Coast.

Despite the British and Alaska connections, Sohio remains a midwestern company. They sell gasoline mainly in the Midwest and East, supplying some 2,600 service stations that in turn sell more than 650,000 gallons a year. In their marketing area (stretching along the East Coast from Maine to Virginia and westward to Michigan), Sohio sells about 9% of the gasoline, 5% of the heating oil, and 14% of the jet fuel. But in their home state Sohio gasoline commands a full quarter of the market. Outside Ohio their gasoline sells under the names of BP, Boron, Scot, and Wm. Penn. Their Vistron subsidiary makes and sells chemicals and plastic products out of Lima, Ohio. Sohio's seven coal mines are in Illinois and Indiana. Before Alaska, the farthest they ventured from the Midwest was Colorado and Utah for oil shale and New Mexico for uranium.

History. Sohio was the first link in John D. Rockefeller's chain of Standard Oil companies. John D. started out in Cleveland in 1870, but by 1899 his base was the Standard Oil Company of New Jersey (now Exxon). When the Supreme Court ordered Jersey Standard to divest themselves of the other 36 companies in 1911, Sohio was left with one refinery in Cleveland, a few stations and tankwagons, and no oil. They scrambled to buy crude right up to the 1970 merger with BP.

Life since the deluge of oil has not been without its problems. Because 46% of British Petroleum is owned by the British government, Sohio is often accused of acting in the British interest. A letter to a Cleveland newspaper suggested that Sohio's chairman register as a foreign agent.

To finance the Alaskan project, Sohio had to borrow $936 million from 76 lending institutions. They've had tankers stuck in Alaskan ice and pipelines thwarted in California. But all in all they have indeed struck it rich.

Reputation. Sohio demonstrates how intricate the international oil business can get. It's an American-owned company 53%-owned by a London-based company that is in turn 46%-owned by the British government. It's also the original member of the oil empire out of which Exxon, Mobil, and Standard of California were carved. Most Americans know nothing, and care less, about all that. They're just filling up with Sohio, BP, and Boron fuels.

What they own. Sohio's greatest asset is their 53% share in the Prudhoe Bay oil field in the North Slope of Alaska. They own a third interest in the four-foot-wide, 800-mile-long Trans-Alaska Pipeline (TAPS). Sohio also owns wells in Texas, Louisiana, and Oklahoma; the Visitron Corporation; and the Old Ben Coal Company.

Who owns and runs the company. Alton W. Whitehouse, who replaced Charles Spahr as chairman and chief executive officer of Sohio on Spahr's retirement in 1977, is a popular fellow with Sohio stockholders because he's the one who negotiated the deal with BP, causing Sohio stock to shoot up. But members of Sohio's management team are a trifle nervous. Because BP owns 53% of Sohio, they could conceivably move in and take over day-to-day management any time they wanted. Whitehouse discounts this—pointing to the fact that BP only has 3 members on the 16-member Sohio board of directors—but BP's majority ownership could, of course, easily change that situation. Other directors include former secretary of state William P. Rogers and one black man, Hobart Taylor, Jr., a lawyer and former vice chairman of the Equal Employment Opportunity Commission.

In the public eye. Sohio hit the headlines most recently in 1979, with their on-again, off-again plan to run a pipeline from Long Beach, California, to refineries in the central and eastern United States. The project had once been economically viable and was considered, by the U.S. Department of Energy, to be vital to the U.S. policy of energy independence. But Chairman Whitehouse blamed years of delay brought about by California state bureaucracy and a tangle of red tape for the company's eventual decision to withdraw from the project and ship their Alaskan oil by tanker through the Panama Canal instead. Governor Edmund G. Brown, Jr., challenged that assessment, arguing that only eight days remained in the permit process before Sohio could have

This is the world's first commercially productive offshore oil well, sunk by Kerr-McGee in the Gulf of Mexico in 1947. A barge tied to the platform served as a warehouse and the crew's headquarters.

begun construction of the docking facilities. But Michael Peevey, president of a pro-energy coalition of business and labor groups, said "the regulatory maze we've created in this state makes it almost impossible to site a major energy plant of any kind."

Sohio does a fair amount of public affairs publishing and broadcasting. They published and distributed 100,000 copies of economist Milton Friedman's articles on free enterprise and another pamphlet on Sohio's ideas on future energy supplies. Much of their PR is currently aimed at Alaska, where they have run into strong opposition from environmentalists. They sponsor two television shows, a radio broadcast, and a scholarship program to help train young Alaskans in petroleum technology.

Where they're going. "The sky's the limit as to what we can do," according to Glenn Brown, a Sohio vice-president. Maybe so, but they had better act fast. The Prudhoe Bay oilfield is scheduled to go dry by the late 1980s, and Sohio isn't likely to find another oilfield to replace it. They're hedging their bets by investing in other energy projects like coal gasification, shale oil, nuclear fusion by laser beam, and synthetic fuels.

Stock performance. Sohio stock bought for $1,000 in 1970 sold for $4,227 on January 2, 1980.

Major employment centers. Cleveland, Lima, and Toledo, Ohio; Anchorage, Alaska.

Access. Midland Building, Cleveland, Ohio 44115; (216) 575-4141.

Consumer brands.

Gasoline: Sohio (Ohio); Boron (Pennsylvania, Michigan, Kentucky, West Virginia, Indiana); BP; Scot; Wm Penn (New England and Mid-Atlantic states).
Fertilizer and agricultural chemicals: Sohigro.

Sales: $38.3 billion
Profits: $1.8 billion
Forbes 500 rank: 6
Rank in oil: 2
Founded: 1902
Employees: 67,841
Headquarters: White Plains, New York

What they do. It's hard to feel sorry for an oil company, especially one that makes well over $1 billion a year in profits, but once-mighty Texaco has fallen on hard times. For many years they were more profitable than any other oil company. They were the only company ever to put filling stations in all 50 states. They sold more gasoline than anyone else. They had vast oil reserves in the United States as well as the Middle East, and they had built up a worldwide marketing system as if they thought the oil would never run out.

In the late 1960s and 1970s everything started to change—that is, everything but Texaco. While other oil companies worried about their Middle Eastern supplies and hedged their bets by searching for oil in places like the Alaskan North Slope and in the North Sea, Texaco stayed put. Their attitude seemed to be: "Why change a winning act?" As a result, their slogan from the 1950s, "Number One—Second to None," was sadly out of date by the 1970s. Their fabulously rich oil reserves in the United States began to dry up. Their gasoline sales fell to an inglorious fourth place, behind Shell, Amoco, and Exxon. While their competitors sharply reduced their total number of filling stations, Texaco kept their network of 40,000 stations intact. When they finally joined the movement, they attacked with a meat ax, closing down more than 10,000 stations over a 10-year period. They abandoned the idea of being everywhere, and they pulled out of several states in the northern Midwest.

Don't get out your handkerchief yet, though. In 1979, the year the Carter administration decontrolled the price of domestic crude oil, Texaco's profits rose a whopping 106% over 1978. They're still the nation's sixth largest company of any kind. They have more than 20,000 oil wells in the United States, which produce more than half a million barrels of oil a day. They get

four times as much crude oil from the Middle East. To ship it around they have a fleet of 130 ocean-going vessels, including 43 mammoth tankers. They own 7,000 miles of pipelines, and they have part interests in nearly 30,000 more miles. They own 72 refineries, wholly or partly, in 35 countries. They sell petroleum products in nearly every country in the world, either by themselves or through their Caltex affiliate, a 50-50 marketing venture with Standard Oil of California. Their reach extends into every country except the Soviet Union, Vietnam, Cambodia, Cuba, and the Warsaw Pact nations of Eastern Europe. They also make a broad range of petrochemicals that go into such products as plastics, detergents, and cosmetics.

History. When Spindletop Hill—at 10 feet high, about the closest thing Texas has to a mountain—brought in a tremendous gusher in 1901, a former Standard Oil employee named Joseph Cullinan decided to get his share. With a New York investment banker, Arnold Schlaet, as his partner, Cullinan formed the Texas Fuel Company in 1902 and began drilling near Spindletop, just outside Beaumont, Texas. Within a year he had 36 storage tanks full of Spindletop oil and a 20-mile pipeline to the deepwater port at Port Arthur, Texas.

Everywhere Cullinan drilled he hit oil. By 1904 Texaco produced 5% of all American oil out of fields in Sour Lake, Texas, and parts of Louisiana and Oklahoma. The next year they opened a sales office in Europe. By 1908 they had sales operations in all but five western states. Most of Texaco's oil was sold for home lamps, to run the boilers of Southern sugar planters, or to power locomotives. When the automobile era came in, Texaco's far-flung sales and marketing network formed the basis for an extensive chain of service stations.

Meanwhile Cullinan was establishing a ruthless management style that was to last through his successors into the 1970s. He once accepted leadership of an oil field firefighting crew on Spindletop only on the condition that he could shoot disobedient firefighters. Later, when Schlaet and a group of eastern backers forced him out of the company, Cullinan demonstrated his ability to hold a grudge: he moved to a new company in Houston's Petroleum Building and took to flying a skull and crossbones from the flagpole as his personal protest against privilege and oppression.

Texaco became an international company in one bold leap in 1936, when they joined with Standard Oil of California (Socal) in a share-the-pie venture that endures to this day. Socal was the first oil company to drill in Saudi Arabia, where they discovered so much oil they didn't know what to do with it. Socal needed more capital to develop the enormous Arabian reserves, and they were woefully short of places to sell the oil. They cut Texaco in, and the two companies formed Caltex, a joint marketing company to transport and sell the Middle Eastern oil throughout the world. Thus Saudi Arabia became one of Texaco's prime crude sources. Today, nearly all the oil that Texaco and Socal sell in the eastern hemisphere is sold through Caltex (except in Europe, where the joint company was broken up in 1967).

Soon after the establishment of Caltex came one of the more extraordinary phases of Texaco's history. *The Texaco Story*, a company biography written by Marquis James, tells how Texaco bravely contributed to the American World War II effort and supplied the Royal Air Force with the fuel to defeat Hitler in the Battle of Britain. The book fails to mention, however, that Texaco was also supplying the Nazis prior to the U.S. entry into the war. Texaco's autocratic president, Torkild Rieber, a Norwegian protege of Cullinan, had outraged President Roosevelt in 1937, when Texaco ships taking oil to Belgium kept winding up in Franco's ports in Spain at the height of the Spanish Civil War. In all, Texaco sold Franco $6 million worth of oil (on credit, to be repaid after the war)—a blatant violation of the neutrality act. He continued to ship oil to Germany after the outbreak of World War II in Europe, sending his tankers out of neutral ports, and grew so close to Hitler's regime that he served as courier in January 1940, for Göering's peace plan, which required the surrender of Britain. Roosevelt rejected the plan.

In June 1940, as France was falling, Rieber celebrated at a party at the Waldorf-Astoria, and a German lawyer named Dr. Gerhardt Westrick arrived in New York, supposedly on a commercial mission to companies like Texaco with extensive German interests. While he was in New York, Texaco paid Westrick's salary, kept him entertained at company expense, gave him an office in their Chrysler Building headquar-

ters, and provided him with a large house in Scarsdale, New York, where he entertained influential American businessmen and presented the Nazi case in its best possible light.

Shortly thereafter, William Stephenson, the British Intelligence chief in New York, revealed Westrick's true purpose in the pages of the *New York Herald Tribune*. Westrick, it seems, was actually working out of Texaco's New York office on a Nazi intelligence mission (in fact, a very accurate review of the American aircraft industry prepared by Texaco's economists had been sent to Berlin from Nazi agents in the Chrysler Building headquarters). The ensuing publicity so enraged Texaco shareholders that they compelled Rieber to resign in an angry meeting. Texaco then began sponsoring the Metropolitan Opera broadcasts, which they have continued ever since.

After the war and for the next two decades, Texaco was satisfied to sit on their vast reserves and market their gasoline on the new federal interstate highway system and on virtually every other highway and dirt road in America. Under the leadership of Augustus C. (Gus) Long, Texaco expanded their operations into every state. Their stations provided a full range of services to motorists: gasoline, lubricants, repairs. Texaco advertised on national radio and TV, "You can trust your car to the man who wears the star," and they set up a huge credit card network. It was expensive, and they often lost money on the system, but they didn't care—it sold a lot of oil, and they had plenty to sell.

Texaco has always liked to use good front men. In the 1930s they sponsored Ed Wynn on radio. Now they're paying Bob Hope to deliver serious messages to the public about Texaco's commitment.

Gus Long continued in the buccaneering tradition of Cullinan, without the firearms. He demanded loyalty and once reportedly fired a Texaco employee he saw filling up at an Esso station. He was a strict penny pincher, carefully husbanding the number of keys to the executive washroom and driving hard bargains with everyone from suppliers to the lowliest Texaco gas station operator. He insisted on personally okaying every expenditure over $10,000, and he kept salaries as low as possible. Even today, Texaco's three senior vice-presidents earn less than two-thirds as much as Exxon's. When Texaco moved their home office from New

York City to suburban White Plains, they neglected to inform their employees that they would be working an extra 45 minutes per day for the same salaries as before.

Reputation. The big oil companies have traditionally been a rough and tumble lot, but Texaco is even too rough for the rest. "We all hate Texaco," says an Exxon man in Anthony Sampson's book *The Seven Sisters.* "If I were dying in a Texaco filling station," a Shell man added, "I'd ask to be dragged across the road." Sampson observed, "Texaco has always taken pride in being the meanest of the big companies, the loner in the western." At the same time, he points out, maybe they're just "the most honest and least self-deceiving" of the big oil companies. They've never pretended to be anything other than what they are: "a concern for making money, as quickly as possible, not a benevolent institution for world peace."

What they own. Besides all their wells, tankers, refineries, and filling stations, Texaco has crude oil reserves of nearly 3.3 billion barrels worldwide. At the rate they're pumping it out, they have about 12 years' worth.

Who owns and runs the company. Much of Texaco's stock is held by "institutional investors": banks, insurance companies, mutual funds. The biggest block of stock, a little over 5%, belongs to the company's employees' investment plan and is held by Manufacturers Hanover Trust and Morgan Guaranty Trust.

Texaco's management is extremely inbred. Their top 36 executives, all white males with an average age of 55, have worked for the company for an average of 30 years. In 1980 John K. McKinley, Texaco's president since 1971, was named chairman of the board to succeed Maurice F. Granville. Also on the board of directors are Admiral Thomas H. Moorer (retired), former chairman of the Joint Chiefs of Staff; William Wrigley, head of Wrigley

chewing gum and owner of the Chicago Cubs; Sir Arthur Patrick H. Forbes, the Earl of Granard; Dr. William J. McGill, president of Columbia University; and one woman, Dr. Lorene L. Rogers, president of the University of Texas at Austin.

In the public eye. Finding a complimentary—or even neutral—news clipping about Texaco is a rare event. Government agencies seem to be after them all the time: the Department of Energy for overcharging customers, the Occupational Safety and Health Administration for safety violations (a Texaco refinery fire at Port Arthur, Texas, killed eight workers in 1977), the Justice Department for anticompetitive activities, Congressional investigators for holding back natural gas from production until prices went up. One exception to the flood of bad publicity came in the fall of 1979, when President Carter praised Texaco for announcing a "freeze" on heating oil prices through the winter, and he urged other oil companies to follow their lead. Texaco was quick to correct the president —they hadn't promised any such thing, they said.

Where they're going. Texaco has recently made major oil strikes in the North Sea and off the coast of New Jersey, and the finds just might be large enough for Texaco to reestablish themselves as an industry leader. Meanwhile, like the other big oil companies, they're extending their stake in the energy field by moving into uranium, oil shale, coal, and tar sands.

Stock performance. Texaco stock bought for $1,000 in 1970 sold for $942 on January 2, 1980.

Access. 2000 Westchester Avenue, White Plains, New York 10650; (914) 253-4000.

Consumer brands.

Gasoline: Fire Chief; Sky Chief.
Motor oil: Havoline.

Miners

Alcan Aluminium Limited

Sales: $3.7 billion
Profits: $289 million
Rank in aluminum production: 2
Founded: 1928
Employees: 63,200
Headquarters: Montreal, Canada
U.S. headquarters: Cleveland, Ohio

What they do. For years Alcan Aluminium (they use the British spelling and pronunciation) was just the Canadian subsidiary of Alcoa, the American aluminum giant. Today Alcan is not only an independent company but Alcoa's major competitor. They account for 16% of the noncommunist world's aluminum supply.

Alcan produces more than 1.5 million metric tons of aluminum, about a third of which goes to American manufacturers—their biggest customers—who turn it into parts for the auto, construction, and electrical industries. Only about 14% of Alcan's aluminum remains in Canada. The rest goes to Europe (23%), Latin America (7½%), or Africa and Asia (26%). Most of the ore Alcan uses to make this aluminum comes from Alcan-owned mines in Jamaica, Australia, and Guinea.

The process for making aluminum requires enormous amounts of electricity, and Alcan generates most of their own from hydroelectric dams. They are now the world's largest nonutility producer of electricity. In Canada they produce so much that they even sell some of it to public utilities for consumer use.

History. Alcoa set up their first Canadian subsidiary in 1899 and had added several

more by 1928, when they decided to put all their Canadian operations and several other foreign holdings under one corporate flag. The new company was dubbed Aluminium Limited and operated as a separate subsidiary until 1945, when a U.S. Circuit Court antitrust decision forced Alcoa to sell most of their holdings in Alcan. Alcan immediately became the second-largest aluminum concern in the world.

Alcan's leaders retained strong familial ties to Alcoa. Former Alcoa chairman Arthur Vining Davis appointed his brother, Edward K. Davis, as Alcan's first president in 1928. Nathanael Davis followed his father Edward as president in 1947. Alcan got their first non–Davis family president in 1972, when Davis stepped up to the newly created post of chairman and made way for Paul H. Leman, a French Canadian, to become president.

Because Alcan produces so much electricity, their energy costs have always been much lower than those of any other aluminum producer. But they have had trouble converting that advantage into profits. They followed a postwar strategy of producing primary aluminum for fabrication by companies in the United States; by 1958, however, most of Alcan's potential customers had begun their own smelting operations. Alcan only recently recovered from this goof. Now they turn raw aluminum into their own finished products.

Reputation. How can you do $4 billion of business a year—and still be an unknown? Easily, if you sell nothing directly to consumers. Alcan is a behind-the-scenes giant.

What they own. Principal plants are located in Canada, Jamaica, and seven other countries. But their most valuable possession is a 30-mile stretch of the Saguemay

River in Quebec, which they own outright and use to run the generators that produce much of their electricity.

Who owns and runs the company. Nathanael Davis still serves as chairman of the board, although president David M. Culver is the chief executive officer who runs the firm. Culver, an employee of Alcan for over 30 years, describes himself as a "go-and-see manager rather than a sit-and-study one." The *New York Times* agrees that "he spends little time sitting. He walks the two miles to work from Montreal's exclusive Westmount district (where his house is clad in aluminum siding)."

The Kingdom of Norway (which gave half of their state-owned aluminum company to Alcan in exchange for a chunk of Alcan stock in the early 1960s) is the largest stockholder, with 3%. Holland's Sonnenberg family, which sold Alcan the Hunter-Douglas aluminum company for stock in 1975, follows closely with 2%.

In the public eye. Alcan has two major political headaches: one at home in the political uncertainty fostered by the French separatist movement; and the other in cash-starved Jamaica, where the government has been demanding advance payments for Jamaican bauxite shipments. The company has also had significant labor difficulties in the last decade. In the mid-1970s strikes idled Alcan plants for weeks at a stretch.

Where they're going. As the cost of electricity continues to rise—doubling and tripling in parts of the United States— Alcan's self-generated electrical costs remain essentially the same. Alcan's competitors in the United States pay an average of 18¢ for the electricity used to smelt one pound of aluminum, while Alcan's cost in Canada averages about 3¢, according to analyst John Ing. Most other companies will be forced to pass along increased energy costs to consumers. Alcan won't, and should finally begin to make inroads on Alcoa's markets. They could become the world's largest aluminum company in the next decade.

Stock performance. Alcan stock bought for $1,000 in 1970 sold for $1,838 on January 2, 1980.

Access. 1 Place Ville Marie, Montreal,

Quebec, Canada H3C 3H2; (514) 877-2340; and 100 Erieview Plaza, Cleveland, Ohio 44114; (216) 323-6918.

Sales: $4.8 billion
Profits: $504.6 million
Forbes 500 rank: 83
Rank in aluminum production: 1
Rank in bauxite mining: 1
Founded: 1888
Employees: 46,000
Headquarters: Pittsburgh, Pennsylvania

What they do. Had there been no Alcoa, there might never have been an aluminum industry. Beverage cans would be made out of steel (without pop-tops); a host of household appliances and utensils would be made of heavier, more expensive materials; and the governments of Jamaica, the Dominican Republic, and Surinam would be vastly different.

Alcoa, together with U.S. Steel, Gulf Oil, and the Mellon Bank, virtually owns and operates Pittsburgh, Pennsylvania, and has a lot to say about what happens in American heavy industry. After jettisoning Alcoa Wrap in the 1950s, they apparently decided ordinary consumers were beneath them. They now sell their aluminum products almost exclusively to other major companies: principally to the auto, canning, aerospace, electrical, and construction industries. Why they bother to advertise on television ("Alcoa Can't Wait . . . For Tomorrow") remains a mystery.

Alcoa began in 1889 by manufacturing a single aluminum teakettle and a few hundred pots and pans. Today they are the largest producer of aluminum in the world, accounting for 25% of U.S. and 16% of world production. They are also the world's largest miner and shipper of bauxite, the reddish ore that produces aluminum oxide (or *alumina*). Most of this bauxite comes from huge, open-pit mines in Arkansas, Brazil, the Caribbean, Guinea, Western Australia, and Surinam; it is then shipped to U.S. smelters with an annual capacity of 1.7 million tons (although Alcoa also has another 485,000 tons of overseas smelting capacity).

All this smelting requires enormous amounts of electricity. The process for separating aluminum from its oxide, which Alcoa's founders devised and which is now used by all aluminum companies, basically consists of sending a strong electrical charge through a chemical bath in a huge vat. Alcoa generates about half of the energy required to run these smelters from their own hydroelectric and fossil fuel plants; the rest comes from private and state-owned utilities. They estimated that the 11 billion kilowatt hours they used in 1967 could have run about 4 million homes for one year.

Since 1960 Alcoa has also invested in real estate. They created the $1 billion Century City complex in Los Angeles, and since 1972 they have been developing residential properties in Malibu, California, San Francisco, California, and Jupiter, Florida.

History. Although aluminum is the most plentiful metal in the world, comprising one-twelfth of the earth's crust, it was virtually unknown 100 years ago. A Danish physicist named H. C. Oersted first used a chemical process to make tiny globs of aluminum in 1825. A bar of aluminum, now valued at a little over 70¢, would have gone for $545 as recently as 1854 because of the exorbitant cost of refining the ores and clays which contained it. The metal was so rare during that period that the French emperor Napoleon III had his artisans design an aluminum table service for guests who deserved something better than mere gold.

It remained for a 22-year-old Oberlin College graduate named Charles Martin Hall to find an inexpensive way to separate aluminum from its oxide. In October 1885, after experimenting with several different catalysts, Hall found that he could produce a cheap aluminum by dissolving alumina in a bath of molten cryolite, a salt compound, and passing an electrical current through the solution. Hall immediately applied for a patent on his process, and in 1888 he convinced a Pittsburgh metallurgist and soldier named Captain Alfred Hunt, along with some other local businessmen, to help him set up the Pittsburgh Reduction Company.

Arthur V. Davis, a 21-year-old Amherst College graduate, helped pour the company's first aluminum ingot and became their first salesman. Because there were no existing markets, Davis borrowed a mold for a teakettle and tried to sell the idea to a local merchant. The merchant didn't go for the kettle, but he did order 2,000 pots. Davis snatched up the order for pots and then spent several days searching for equipment to make them. This was the first practical application of aluminum.

But few other merchants were willing to take a chance on the new metal, and in 1889 the company was in dire need of $4,000 to meet an overdue note. They went to Pittsburgh's Mellon Bank, where Andrew W. Mellon agreed to give them the money they needed to stay in business in exchange for stock in the company. In 1891 Pittsburgh Reduction was reorganized with Mellon, his brother Richard, and the bank holding about 1,200 of the 10,000 shares. By the 1920s the Mellons had increased their ownership to about 33% (a percentage the family held until 1973), giving them effective control of the company.

With the prestigious Mellons on board, Pittsburgh Reduction began to grow by leaps and bounds. In 1891 they outgrew their tiny Pittsburgh plant and shifted to New Kensington, Pennsylvania. In 1893 they became the first industrial user of Niagara Falls's hydroelectric power for a new smelter located nearby. During the next two decades, with a patent-insured monopoly on the aluminum refining process (and therefore the entire industry), they staged an aggressive campaign to convince makers of metal products to switch to aluminum. By 1907, when the company adopted its present name, aluminum had been used in buildings (even the cupola atop St. Gioacchino Church in Rome), boats, automobiles, kitchen utensils, surgical instruments, electrical transmission wires, and the Wright Brothers' airplane. Aluminum foil followed in 1910.

Alcoa's early monopoly made it difficult for competitors to gain a foothold. The company had begun mining their own bauxite in 1903 and effectively controlled the major known sources of the ore in the United States by 1910. In 1912, shortly after their patent expired, the U.S. Justice Department charged Alcoa with antitrust violations and forced the company to seek government approval before acquiring new plants or mines. This was the first blow in what was to be a long battle. An eight-year Federal Trade Commission investigation gave Alcoa a clean bill of health in 1930; in 1942 a U.S. District Court dismissed what was then the longest court case in history— another Justice Department antitrust suit against Alcoa. It wasn't until 1946 that Alcoa was finally broken up, forced to yield many of their aluminum processing patents and plants to competitors. At that time, Alcoa controlled 90% of the primary aluminum business in the United States; Reynolds Metals, their closest competitor, had only 7%. In addition, Alcoa was forced to sell off Aluminium Limited (later Alcan), their Canadian subsidiary. Today Alcan has annual sales of $3.7 billion and is almost as large as its progenitor. Together the two companies control about 30% of the world's aluminum business and nearly 50% of North American production.

Reputation. Even though their monopoly has been broken up, Alcoa still seems to determine the world's aluminum price. Whatever level Alcoa sets, the other companies are sure to follow. They are also the most technologically advanced aluminum company and lead the way in the search for improved reduction processes and new applications.

What they own. Alcoa estimates that their bauxite reserves in Arkansas, Australia, Jamaica, Brazil, Guinea, and the Dominican Republic will last for at least 40 years (although contracts in some countries run out before that). Alcoa owns more than 50 plants worldwide, as well as a shipping company, equipment manufacturer, and an electric utility. Alcoa owns real estate developments and hotels in Pittsburgh, Los Angeles, San Francisco, and Seattle.

Who owns and runs the company. W. H. Krome George joined Alcoa in 1942 as a chemical engineer. Although he soon got into the financial end of Alcoa, the *New York Times* claims that he "is still enough of an engineer to pull a slide rule out of his desk drawer as soon as the conversation gets around to figures." George became president of the company in 1970, and chief executive officer and chairman of the board in 1975. The Mellon family and foundations held about one-third of Alcoa's stock until 1973, when they sold 8.6%—leaving them approximately 25% of the total. Although there are no Mellons currently on the board of directors, they are represented by Na-

than Pearson, their financial adviser, and by John Mayer, a former chairman of the Mellon Bank. The Hunt and Davis families also hold significant portions of Alcoa stock. Alfred Hunt, grandson of Captain Hunt, is a director and officer; his brother Torrence is a vice-president. The board has one black— Franklin Thomas, president of the Ford Foundation.

In the public eye. Like other aluminum companies, Alcoa has had political problems in Jamaica since the election of the Michael Manley government in 1972. The Jamaicans have acquired 51% of the bauxite mining operations, but they have only a tiny share in the refineries where bauxite is turned into alumina. Alcoa is less affected than other companies because since 1972 they have cut their dependence on Caribbean bauxite from 84% to 38% of their needs.

In 1976 Alcoa disclosed in a filing with the Securities and Exchange Commission questionable payments totaling $348,300— $25,000 of which was reportedly solicited by Vincent W. de Roulet, U.S. ambassador to Jamaica during the Nixon administration. The ambassador suggested to Alcoa that the money be put up to finance a program to promote U.S. investments in Jamaica. De Roulet resigned his post in 1973 after being declared persona non grata by the Jamaican government.

Alcoa is influential and active in three small Third World nations. In Jamaica and the Dominican Republic the company mines bauxite. In Surinam bauxite, alumina, and aluminum production provide 90% of the country's foreign exchange, almost all of it split between Alcoa and Royal Dutch Shell.

Public pressures forced Alcoa's 51%-owned Australian subsidiary to embark on a massive reforestation project in western Australia in 1963. Over the last 16 years the company has strip-mined about 2,000 hectares (1 hectare = 2.471 acres) of land and replanted about 1,200 of that; today they are restoring about 270 hectares per year. Company spokespeople are so proud of their tree-planting project that Aussie journalists joke that Alcoa really stands for American Lumber Company of Australia.

Where they're going. In 1973 Alcoa announced the first major change in the alu-

THE BIGGEST IN METALS

Sales (1979)

1. ALCOA	$4.8 *billion*
2. REYNOLDS METALS	$3.3 *billion*
3. KAISER ALUMINUM	$2.9 *billion*
4. AMAX	$2.9 *billion*
5. KENNECOTT	$2.4 *billion*
6. ASARCO	$1.7 *billion*
7. PHELPS DODGE	$1.3 *billion*
8. ST. JOE MINERALS	$1.1 *billion*
9. COMMERCIAL METALS	$1.1 *billion*
10. CABOT	$1.1 *billion*

Sales: $2.9 billion
Profits: $365 million
Forbes 500 rank: 169
Rank in molybdenum: 1
Rank in coal: 3
Founded: 1887
Employees: 17,360
Headquarters: Greenwich, Connecticut

What they do. You need to know three things about AMAX right away: they're very big; they're very old; and they're very complicated. No other outfit takes so many different kinds of metals, minerals, and other substances from the earth as AMAX does—at least not in such huge quantities. If it's in the ground, AMAX will mine it. And when it comes out of the ground, AMAX will refine it. And when it's refined, AMAX will sell it. They carry on these activities anywhere in the world, either singly or in combination with others. Incest has long been a way of life in the mining world.

The most important of their products, accounting for about a quarter of their sales, is molybdenum, a gray metal used as an alloy to toughen steel and iron. AMAX is by far the largest producer of this metal. In 1979, when world consumption of "moly" was 178 million pounds, AMAX produced 92 million pounds. They mine molybdenum at the Climax Mine near Leadville, Colorado, and the Henderson Mine near Empire, Colorado. The moly concentrates are shipped from the mine to AMAX conversion plants at Langeloth, Pennsylvania; Fort Madison, Iowa; Rotterdam, Holland; Spigno Monferrato, Italy; and Stowmarket, England.

AMAX shipped 34 million tons of coal in 1979 from 11 mines in Illinois, Indiana, Kentucky, and Wyoming—all but one surface mines. They achieved a record of some kind on December 4, 1979, when their two strip mines near Gillette, Wyoming, loaded eleven 110-car trains in one day.

AMAX ranks as the second-largest tungsten producer in the United States; they operate the major nickel refinery in the country at Braithwaite, Louisiana; they're the leading producer of copper powders; they have their hands on 3,000 barrels of oil a day; their smelter at Carteret, New Jersey, can turn out 190,000 tons of copper a year

minum smelting process since Hall invented his electrolytic method in 1885. The new process combines alumina with chlorine in a chemical reactor where the resulting oxide is converted into aluminum oxide. It requires about 30% less electricity and is thus much less vulnerable to power reductions or cut-offs—and it will reduce the number of employees needed. Under the old method 100 workers produced about 50,000 tons of aluminum per year. Alcoa estimates that a dozen workers could do the job with the new process. It also eliminates the need for fluoride which causes the industry's most serious air pollution problem.

Alcoa is also searching for other sources of aluminum. Nearly all common clays contain aluminum, but Alcoa believes that kaolin clay will yield as much as 40% alumina —compared with about 38% for bauxite. Kaolin can also be strip-mined cheaply.

Early in 1980 Alcoa announced that they planned to increase their U.S. production by 25% in the next five years.

Stock performance. Alcoa stock bought for $1,000 in 1970 sold for $1,155 on January 2, 1980.

Major employment center. Pittsburgh, Pennsylvania.

Access. 1501 Alcoa Building, Pittsburgh, Pennsylvania 15219; (412) 553-4545.

Consumer brands.

Wear–Ever utensils and Cutco cutlery.

from recycled materials; and they're producing silver at Twin Buttes, Arizona; Boss, Missouri; and Sauget, Illinois.

Their great growth has been in the past decade but their history can be traced back to the eighteenth century.

History. The early Christians had the odd idea that there was something sinful about lending money and collecting interest from the borrower. That's why so many Jews went into banking. Later on, as credit began to grease the wheels of industry, the Christians changed their minds and formed their own banks, keeping the Jews out. In 1700, before the Christians were fully converted to banking, there was a Jewish banking house—Liebmann Cohen—in the German feudal kingdom of Hannover. And that's the real start of today's AMAX. Cohen became the fiscal agent of the Hannover court and later financed mining ventures in the Harz Mountains. The business flourished and led in the nineteenth century to a branch in Frankfurt, where Philipp Abraham Cohen acted as sales representative for the minerals extracted in the Hannover-Braunschweig district of Germany. Philipp Cohen's daughter, Sara Amalie, married Rafael Moses of London, who anglicized his name to Ralph Merton. Merton's son established the London metal-trading company known as Henry R. Merton & Company. The English and German branches of this company grew in tandem during the latter part of the nineteenth century and added other associates: the Ellingers, the Hochschilds, and the Ladenburgs.

The Ladenburgs, a Frankfurt family also related by marriage to the Mertons, opened a private banking firm—Ladenburg, Thalmann & Company—in New York City in 1880. In 1884 Berthold Hochschild came from Germany to join the New York company, which was active already in the international trading of metals. In 1887 the London and Frankfurt companies joined with the New York company to establish a new entity, the American Metal Company, to be active in the treatment and trading of metals—but not the mining, because that was considered too risky for the London and Frankfurt merchants.

This German-English-American combine prospered during the early years of this century. There were no more than 40 stockholders, and most were related to one another. It was a "family" company that operated on an international scale.

World War I brought profound changes. The English branch, Merton, deemed to be a satellite of the German company, went out of business. And in 1920 the U.S. government sold the German interest in American Metal to a group of investors. From then on the American company had to stand on its own.

The other main tributary of today's AMAX, the Climax Molybdenum Company, was formed in 1918 to develop mining claims in Colorado. American Metal, which had an office in Denver, was one of the early investors in the company, whose main mine was at Climax, Colorado. There, on the western slope of the Rocky Mountains, they mined molybdenum. It was much in demand during World War I but afterwards the market evaporated. The mine was closed in 1919, not to open again until 1924. When it did reopen, it was under the leadership of a brilliant chemical engineer, Brainerd F. Phillipson, who became an evangelist for moly, convincing the steel and auto industries of its value as a toughening and anticorrosive agent. In 1925 Climax sold 718,000 pounds of moly. By 1929 they were selling 2.8 million pounds. During all this time Climax maintained a close relationship with American Metal, which ran the mill that extracted the molybdenum from the ore. During the 1930s American Metal expanded on their own, moving into mining ventures in Africa, Canada, and the United States.

The two tributaries were joined on the last business day of 1957, forming American Metal Climax. They shortened their name to AMAX in 1974.

The company remained primarily a copper and molybdenum producer until a hard-driving mining engineer, Ian MacGregor, assumed the helm in 1969. Sales were then $550 million a year. MacGregor transformed AMAX, pushing them into oil and gas, nickel, aluminum, tungsten, and iron ore. In 10 years he more than quadrupled AMAX's size. Some analysts criticized him for overborrowing. His reply, according to one source, was: "I don't care what

> Coal was first mined commercially in the United States about 12 miles from Richmond, Virginia, in 1745.

Ore being hauled under the Continental Divide through a 14-mile tunnel (the world's fifth longest railroad tunnel). The tunnel connects AMAX's Henderson underground molybdenum mine with the mill, both in Colorado.

the balance sheet looks like, I'm going to acquire natural resources and someday they'll be valuable."

MacGregor stepped down in 1977 and was succeeded by a French mining engineer, Pierre Grousseland.

Reputation. AMAX has had labor and environmental problems, but they have scored some points for their sympathetic responses to these challenges. On one point there's no argument: no mining company makes the kind of money AMAX does. And from their profits they have fashioned a public relations program that has made them the mining industry's leader in artful dissemination of information. Write for their annual report, and see for yourself.

What they own. It has been said that every mining company is related to every other mining company through a web of interlocking financial arrangements. AMAX is certainly no exception. They own 50% of Alumax, the nation's fourth largest aluminum producer, in partnership with Japan's Mitsui (45%) and Japan's Nip-

pon Steel (5%). They own 50% of the primary aluminum reproduction plants at Ferndale, Washington, and Frederick, Maryland, in partnership with Howmet Aluminum, a French company. They have a 29.8% interest in Botswana RST Limited, a company mining nickel and copper in the southern African country of Botswana. AMAX's partners here are Anglo-American Corp., the big South African gold company, Charter Consolidated, and the Botswana government. They own 16.4% of Roan Consolidated Mines, a Zambian copper mining company controlled by the Zambian government. They own 29.6% of Tseumb Corporation, which produces and sells copper, lead, silver, cadmium and zinc concentrates from ores mined in Namibia in Southwest Africa. They own 17.3% of O'okiep Copper, a miner and smelter of copper in South Africa. They own 65% of Canada Tungsten Mining, and they are equal partners with Anaconda in the operation of the Twin Buttes copper mine near Tucson, Arizona. They are also 50-50 partners with Homestake Mining in the development of lead deposits in southeastern

Missouri. They have a 75% interest—Inco has the other 25%—in Heath Steele, operator of a lead, zinc, and copper mine and mill in New Brunswick, Canada. In Australia AMAX has a 25% participation in the mining of the Mt. Newman iron ore properties. Their partners there are two big Australian companies, CSR Limited (30%) and the Broken Hill Proprietary Company (30%), Japan's Mitsui (7%) and C. Itoh (3%), and England's Selection Trust (5%). Back in Arizona they have a partnership with Asarco: the Eisenhower Mining Company, formed in 1976 to develop copper deposits 20 miles south of Tucson. They own 11% of the French Rothschild holding company, Imetal, which in turn has stakes in a bunch of other mining and metal companies, including a big nickel producer in New Caledonia and Copperweld, an American specialty steel producer. In 1979 they acquired a 22% stake—since increased to 30%—in Adobe Oil & Gas, a U.S. producer of oil and natural gas, and in 1980 they moved to acquire Rosario Resources, a silver miner with oil and gas properties in Canada. And they do all this with only 17,360 employees.

Who owns and runs the company. The largest shareholder is Standard Oil of California, which acquired 21.7% of AMAX's stock for $333 million in 1975. Socal would like to increase their holdings but AMAX has discouraged their overtures. It's tough even for a big shareholder to dictate policy or take over the company because AMAX has a staggered election for the board of directors: there are 18 seats on the board and six different directors are elected each year for a term of three years. One of the directors, Walter Hochschild, is a descendant of the founder. He owns 3.2% of the shares. Another large holder, with 8% of the shares, is the London-based mining finance company, Selection Trust (they have fingers in mining pies all over the world). Former transportation secretary William T. Coleman, Jr., a black attorney, is a director. Offspring of AMAX founders have enlisted in various liberal causes. Adam Hochschild was one of the founders of the San Francisco-based progressive monthly *Mother Jones*. And in 1973 various descendants of Max Schott, founder of Climax Molybdenum, sued AMAX charging the management and the company with operating "illegally and immorally" in southern Africa.

> **Alumax's Intalco aluminum plant in Ferndale, Washington uses as much electricity as the entire city of Tacoma, which has a population of more than 150,000.**

In the public eye. AMAX is still remembered in Colorado for the huge deep-pit scar their Climax mine left on the western slope of the Rockies. In 1967, though, AMAX began a unique project in the Denver area. The company had discovered a deep molybdenum deposit on the east side of the Rockies, within the Arapaho National Forest, just 40 miles from Denver. Rather than charging ahead on their own, AMAX consulted for three years with environmental groups to plan a mining operation that would be as clean as possible. A task force, called "Experiment in Ecology," consisting of both AMAX people and environmentalists, was established. This task force went into every phase of the mining and processing operations. The group decided that the best site for a processing facility was an area on the west slope of the mountains. But this was 14 miles from the mine shaft on the east slope, separated from the mine by a 12,000-foot Continental Divide. The solution provided by AMAX engineers: tunnel 9.5 miles under the Continental Divide for a railroad to deliver the ore to the mill. It was a costly but environmentally sound decision. There were other decisions of that kind—but the mine, which cost AMAX $500 million, was opened on schedule in 1976 with no flack from environmental groups. The Henderson mine has been hailed as a model of corporate social responsibility. And it led AMAX to establish an Environmental Services Group as a permanent function in the company.

Where they're going. Probably to look for more oil and gas. They're also going to keep Standard Oil of California out of their hair.

Stock performance. AMAX stock bought for $1,000 in 1970 sold for $1,889 on January 2, 1980.

Access. Greenwich, Connecticut 06830; (203) 622-3000.

The ANACONDA Company ▲

Sales: $1.6 billion
Rank in copper: 3
Rank in aluminum: 5
Rank in silver: 1
Employees: 24,574
Founded: 1882
Headquarters: Denver, Colorado

What they do. Anaconda is an international ostrich. When the government of Chile under Salvador Allende nationalized the copper mines in 1971, Anaconda was evidently taken by complete surprise. They were scooping two-thirds of their copper production and three-fourths of their profits out of Chile. By comparison, their fellow copper miner Kennecott was apparently more aware of the political realities, and had reduced their Chilean operations to the point that only about one-tenth of their profits came from there.

Anaconda is still the nation's third-largest producer of copper and fifth-largest in aluminum. Their Wire and Cable Division turns out everything from high-voltage transmission lines to household wiring. They also make small parts for everyday objects—pens, lamp sockets, household appliances, office machines.

History. Marcus Daly, who was said to be able to "see farther into the ground than any mining man," came to San Francisco from County Cavan, Ireland, in 1858. He worked in mines in the West for several years, eventually becoming involved with George Hearst, the mining tycoon and father of William Randolph Hearst. Daly persuaded Hearst that he should buy the Anaconda vein of silver ore in Montana and set Daly up with one-fourth of the business for getting the ore out of the ground. As it turned out, the mine was rich in copper ore rather than silver. Daly built a smelter on the site of what is now the town of Anaconda, Montana, to refine the metal.

By 1895 Anaconda had become the world's number 1 producer of copper, which was then coming into great use in electrical wiring. In 1899 the Standard Oil Trust bought Anaconda in a deal that provoked angry public outcry. According to *The Rockefellers* by Peter Collier and David Horowitz, three executives of the trust—

William Rockefeller (John D.'s brother), James Stillman, and H. H. Rogers—bought Anaconda with a $39 million check from Stillman's National City Bank. Anaconda's former owners agreed not to cash the check for a while. The threesome immediately formed a new company out of Anaconda and sold stock to the public. The $75 million worth of shares they sold not only paid off the $39 million uncashed check, but also returned a tidy profit of $36 million. Although John D. Rockefeller was not involved in the scheme and withdrew his personal funds from National City Bank in protest, he was blamed by the public for the "Rockefeller plot" of selling the same company twice.

In 1923 Anaconda bought the Chile Copper Company from the Guggenheim family. The Guggenheims framed the $70 million check in their office in New York City. For the next half-century Anaconda extracted vast amounts of copper (more than 300,000 tons a year during most of the 1960s), principally from their huge mine at Chuquicamata in the northern Chilean desert. It's the most productive copper mine ever found in the world. In 1969 alone Anaconda sold nearly half a billion dollars' worth of Chilean copper. During that period the company was led by Charles M. Brinckerhoff, who had worked as an engineer and supervisor in the northern Chilean mines for nearly 25 years.

After the Chileans finally kicked them out, Anaconda received only token compensation from the U.S. government. To meet the company's huge losses from the Chilean takeover, Anaconda axed losing operations and sold 670,500 acres of timberland in Montana for $117 million. But it was too little, too late. In January 1977 Atlantic Richfield (Arco) bought Anaconda for about $700 million and moved the company's headquarters from New York City to Denver, closer to the mines. (Arco's coal mining operations are run out of Denver.) Anaconda left behind their plush Wall Street offices with richly paneled walls and uniformed attendants—relics of the nineteenth-century opulence that characterized the golden years of the mining business. They also said goodbye to a staff mechanic who tended the antique car collection of an Anaconda executive.

Reputation. Arco hopes that Anaconda's ostrichlike past has been buried in some of their closed mines now that Arco's profit-first managers are running the company.

What they own. A huge open-pit copper mine near Butte, Montana and a smaller one in Utah. A smelter in Anaconda, Montana, two copper refineries, nine copper-and brass-fabricating plants, and eighteen wire- and cable-manufacturing plants throughout the United States. They lease two aluminum plants and uranium mines in New Mexico from the Laguna Indians.

Who owns and runs the company. When Arco took over, they placed several oil executives at the top. Jim Morrison, a gasoline marketing man, became president of Anaconda Copper.

In the public eye. Anaconda was in the spotlight of world attention during the much-publicized Chilean takeover of the copper mines in the early 1970s. In 1980 Anaconda again hit the newspapers when irate Arco stockholders demanded that the company not pursue a new venture in Chile so long as the military government in that country continues to deny elementary human rights. The stockholders' resolution, sponsored by a coalition of seven church groups and soundly defeated at the Arco 1980 annual meeting, referred to Anaconda's exploration of a new copper mining site 180 miles north of Santiago. (Chile's government also granted Arco the right to drill for oil off the coast.)

In the United States Anaconda has been involved in a series of scrapes with federal and local officials over environmental and health hazards posed by their huge mining operations. For instance, the Berkeley open-pit mine began eating away portions of Butte, Montana and now covers about 20% of the city's area. The company was in open conflict with local officials in 1973 after more than 1,000 houses had been razed for the pit's expansion, which town leaders claimed had also contributed to the decline of the uptown business district. Anaconda suggested that the entire business center be relocated to an area that includes the town's only remaining park—a suggestion that met with open hostility from many Butte residents. An Anaconda spokesman, P. Largey MacDonald, responded to the outcry by saying, "If the weather is bad, it's blamed on the Anaconda company."

Anaconda has a long history of bitter and

> In copper mining an average of 6,000 pounds of earth must be moved to get an ultimate yield of 15 pounds of copper. At a mine near Tucson, Arizona, Anaconda hauled out 153 million tons of waste—half the amount necessary to dig a Panama Canal—to reach its first touch of ore.

often bloody labor disputes. A strike at a Montana mine in 1968 continued for eight and a half months until the White House intervened.

Where they're going. Arco plans to expand Anaconda's uranium and aluminum mining to make them less dependent on copper. In 1980 Anaconda joined with Sweden's LM Ericsson Telephone Company in a joint venture to market telecommunications equipment in the United States and several other countries. Ericsson is one of the world's largest telephone equipment manufacturers. They will now go head to head here with Western Electric.

Access. 555 17th Street, Denver, Colorado 80202; (303) 575-4000.

ASARCO

Sales: $1.7 billion
Profits: $259 million
Forbes 500 rank: 302
Rank in smelting and refining: 1
Rank in refining silver: 1
Rank in refining copper and lead: 2
Rank in refining zinc: 4
Founded: 1814
Employees: 12,500
Headquarters: New York, New York

What they do. In 1975 American Smelting and Refining Company changed their name to the acronym Asarco. But a truly descriptive name for Asarco's global operations would be a mouthful: International Miners and Refiners of Antimony, Asbestos, Bismuth, Cadmium, Coal, Copper, Gold,

Limestone, Silver, & Zinc.

For a large part of their history Asarco made most of their money from smelting (the process of melting down and separating ore) and refining (purifying the molten metal) minerals unearthed by other companies. But today three-quarters of their sales comes from metals from Asarco's own mines. Asarco has open-pit copper mines in Arizona and Peru, coal mines in Illinois, silver mines in Idaho and Mexico, zinc mines in Tennessee, asbestos mines in Canada. Their Australian subsidiary is one of the world's largest producers of copper, silver, lead, and zinc.

Still, Asarco smelts and refines more metal ore than anyone else. They buy raw material from other companies and then sell the refined products either on the open market, or back to the original miner. The refined metals eventually reach consumers in a multitude of forms: flashlight batteries and galvanized coatings on nails (zinc); electrical equipment and car radiators (copper); car batteries, stained glass, paint, and gasoline (lead); light-sensitive coating on photographic film (silver).

According to Asarco, since 1899 their refineries have "produced more than 26 million tons of copper, enough to make a household size wire that could be strung 26,000 times around the world; 26 million tons of lead, enough to make 2.5 billion automobile batteries; approximately seven million tons of zinc, which would coat and protect from corrosion a highway guard rail long enough to cross the U.S. 1,400 times; and over six billion troy ounces of silver, enough to mint eight billion silver dollars."

History. The company began as a consolidation of mines, smelters, and refineries. In 1814 the Gunpowder Copper Works, the ancestor of Asarco's Baltimore refinery, was supplying copper to the company started by Paul Revere in colonial days. Ac-

cording to John H. Davis in his book *The Guggenheims: An American Epic*, Asarco was organized into a labyrinthine network of mining and metal-processing concerns by William Rockefeller (the brother of John D.) and H. H. Rogers (the same two who made a killing out of buying and selling Anaconda in 1899) and Adolph Lewisohn. They asked the Guggenheims (the family that founded Kennecott) to join the American Smelting and Refining trust, but the Guggenheims refused. Instead, the Guggenheims increased production at their own mines. When workers struck Asarco in 1900, Asarco's stock began to fall, and the Guggenheims were able to buy into Asarco. A year later the Guggenheims owned 51% of the company, Daniel Guggenheim was chairman of the board and president, his brother Solomon was treasurer, and brothers Isaac, Murry, and Simon became directors. A member of the Guggenheim family continued as head of the company until the retirement of Daniel's son-in-law, Roger Straus, in 1957.

The Guggenheim control did not continue unchecked, however. In 1922 non-Guggenheim members of the Asarco board accused the Guggenheims of milking Asarco's mine exploration funds for other Guggenheim businesses. (Daniel had a secret staircase that connected his office at Asarco with his Guggenheim family office downstairs.) At any rate, Daniel and three of his brothers gave up their seats on the board, although Simon became president of Asarco.

Early in this century Asarco took over five mines in Mexico and another in Peru, and in 1928 bought control of Michigan Copper & Brass, which later changed its name to Revere Copper & Brass, makers of Revere cooking- and tableware. In the 1930s they took over a gold mining company in Nicaragua and the Mount Isa silver-lead-zinc mine in Australia. Under the direction of Roger Straus, Asarco continued to pick up mines all over the globe to ensure a source of metal for their smelters.

Their latest business venture is in solar power. They jumped into the burgeoning solar industry in 1975 when one of their subsidiaries purchased a solar collector firm called Sunworks.

Reputation. The "melting pot" of the metals industry.

What they own. Asarco has substantial investments in three of the world's great mining companies: Southern Peru Copper Corporation, M. I. M. Holdings Limited of Australia, and Mexico Desarrollo Industrial Minero. They also own asbestos mines in Canada, lead and zinc mines in Bolivia and Newfoundland, Midland Coal Company in Illinois, and American Limestone Company in Tennessee.

Asarco owns a third of Revere Copper and Brass, a major fabricator of copper, brass, and aluminum and a producer of primary aluminum. Add to that the Federated Metals Corporation, Lone Star Lead Construction Corporation, Enthone, Asarcon Federal Products Division, Federated Genco, and Cement Asbestos Products Company, and the picture of their grip on the nonferrous metals industry becomes fully etched.

Who owns and runs the company. Bendix Corporation became the largest shareholder with stock purchases in 1978 and 1979. They own 20% of Asarco. William M. Agee, chairman of Bendix, and Malcolm Baldrige, a Bendix director, both sit on Asarco's board.

Between October 1977 and April 1978, Asarco made agreements with nine banks for loans totaling $230 million, of which Chase Manhattan loaned $35 million and Manufacturers Hanover Trust loaned $25 million. Willard C. Butcher, president of Chase, and James R. Greene, former vice-president of Manufacturers, both sit on Asarco's board. Charles F. Barber, chairman of Asarco since 1971, is himself a Chase director.

In the public eye. Asarco has run afoul of many an antipollution law, and they seem to make strenuous efforts to avoid restrictions whenever possible. They have received delays and variances from air pollution regulations in Texas and the state of Washington and are contesting proposed air quality standards in Arizona. The U.S. government has sued them on behalf of the Papago Indians over water rights in Arizona, at the Mission and San Xavier mines. Their Canadian asbestos operation has been the target of another series of lawsuits.

El Paso, Texas, was once described as having the worst pollution in the United

For U.S. aluminum production 90% of the bauxite needed is imported, and half of the bauxite imports come from Jamaica, Surinam, Haiti, Guyana, and the Dominican Republic. Three companies—Alcoa, Reynolds, and Kaiser—refine 65% of the aluminum produced in the United States.

States because of the lead-filled dust coming from Asarco's smelters there. The company was sued for $1 million by the city of El Paso and the state of Texas before signing a consent agreement that pledges them to a massive environmental control program. When the Amarillo, Texas, zinc facility was closed, city leaders objected so strongly that Asarco "rewarded" the city with a new copper smelter. Then-president Charles Barber told the town: "When changes were made you did not panic. You did not seek to be instant heroes of the new environmental religion."

Where they're going. Because of market fluctuations, strikes, and labor shortages, the company experienced very little growth between 1974 and 1978. Their future depends on the world need for the metals they produce and the degree to which succeeding political administrations hold the line on environmental issues. Their tremendous silver production is a reliable asset, and they are increasing their silver mining capacity.

Stock performance. Asarco stock bought for $1,000 in 1970 sold for $1,154 on January 2, 1980.

Major employment centers. Tucson, Arizona; El Paso, Texas; Wallace, Indiana.

Access. 120 Broadway, New York, New York 10005; (212) 732-9500.

Consumer brands.

Revere cooking- and tableware.

ENGELHARD
MINERALS & CHEMICALS CORPORATION

Sales: $18.1 billion
Profits: $349.7 million
Forbes 500 rank: 14
Rank in precious metals fabrication: 1
Rank in mineral & metal commodity trading: 1
Rank in oil trading: 1
Founded: 1903
Employees: 11,600
Headquarters: New York, New York

What they do. Engelhard is virtually unknown, even in business circles, though their annual sales surpass those of such industrial giants as U.S. Steel, Du Pont, and Shell Oil. But many people would recognize the fictional character inspired by the man who shaped the company: Auric Goldfinger, the infamous James Bond antagonist. Charles Engelhard was a close friend of Ian Fleming, author of the Bond novels. The fabulously wealthy Engelhard, known as the world's platinum king, had homes in five countries, a fleet of private planes, and a stable of 250 racehorses. As an influential "checkbook Democrat," he hobnobbed with presidents Kennedy and Johnson. To cap the image, he smoked Old Gold cigarettes.

Engelhard today is actually two companies: a precious metals company and a trading company. The metals company, Engelhard Industries, buys gold, silver, and platinum from mines in South Africa, Canada, and elsewhere, and refines them at factories in New Jersey, Massachusetts, and overseas for use in industrial products such as X-ray film and catalytic converters for auto exhaust systems. They also mine some nonmetallic minerals, such as kaolin, in Virginia.

Nearly half of Engelhard's overall sales comes from trading crude oil and petroleum products. Philipp Brothers also does a brisk business buying and selling industrial commodities, such as steel, plastics, fertilizers, copper, molybdenum, sugar, grain, and cement. Usually they buy the goods from a producer, take ownership for a few hours or weeks, and sell them to an industrial customer. The key to success in the trading business is market intelligence: knowing where to buy a product in one place and sell it for more somewhere else. Their corporate nervous system in New York City is laced with telephones, telex machines, and computers, keeping their traders in constant touch with hundreds of shifting markets around the world. Their communications network is rivaled only by those of the Pentagon and the CIA. (In fact it may even be more advanced: Philipp Brothers had the good sense in 1978 to close their Iran office three months before the outbreak of street fighting that toppled the Shah, and rumor has it that CIA agents are continually trying to pump Philipp Brothers traders for information.)

Philipp Brothers even has their own Swiss bank, Phibrobank, which acts as an investment banker for raw materials producers, especially those in poor countries that have trouble getting bank loans. In return for helping to finance a new mine or other facility, Philipp Brothers often obtains a long-term contract to act as the selling agent for whatever is produced.

History. Engelhard Minerals & Chemicals is the offspring of an uneasy marriage between freewheeling American entrepreneurship and the German-Jewish urban merchant tradition. Charles Engelhard inherited his company from his father, built it into a global precious metals empire, and filled it with his Princeton chums, Democratic Party cronies, and, in the overseas operations, a few dukes and counts. In 1967 the company merged with Minerals & Chemicals Philipp, about 20% of which he already owned.

Oscar and Julius Philipp had started their metals trading business around the turn of the century, with offices in London and Hamburg, and in 1916 they moved their operations to New York. Philipp's current chairman, Ludwig Jesselson, came to the United States from Berlin in 1937. The Philipp traders lead quiet lives, often working 12- to 14-hour days, and they keep their mouths shut about the particulars of what they're doing, such as the names of customers and suppliers, or their volume of trade in any given line. When Charles Engelhard died in 1971 at age 54, a collision between the two worlds was inevitable. The Philipp contingent won, and soon afterward most of the top Engelhard men cleared out.

Engelhard surfaced briefly in the news in early 1980 when the price of silver plunged dramatically. Nelson Bunker Hunt and W. Herbert Hunt, sons of the late Texas oil tycoon H. L. Hunt, had contracted with

Philipp Brothers to buy enormous quantities of silver in what the *New York Times* described as "a speculative bender." The Hunts agreed to buy 19 million ounces of silver at $35 an ounce—a purchase of nearly $700 million. Political turmoil in the Middle East had driven the price of silver past $50 early in the year, but as tensions relaxed, the price plunged to around $15. The Hunts, unable or unwilling to pay for the silver, negotiated a way out: they turned over to Engelhard the exploration rights to 3.5 million acres of oil and gas properties in Canada's Beaufort Sea, worth an estimated $500 million to $750 million, along with 8.5 million ounces of silver. One Wall Street financial analyst told the *New York Times*, "It looks like they had the Hunts over a barrel and made the most of it."

Reputation. Engelhard's tight-lipped approach comes from a trading tradition that goes back at least to the fifteenth-century Venetian merchants. Their stock is bought and sold on the open market, but one Wall Street analyst has called them "perhaps the most reluctantly public company in the world." They are undoubtedly the nation's largest company without a public relations department.

What they own. Fifty trading offices worldwide. Precious metals plants in five countries and three states. Two pig iron mills in Brazil, a fertilizer plant in Florida, and assorted mines and mills in Georgia, Virginia, Vermont, and Oklahoma.

Who owns and runs the company. The biggest block of stock (close to 30%) is controlled by Harry Oppenheimer, who dominates the world's diamond and gold markets through his De Beers Consolidated Mines and his Anglo American Corp. of South Africa. Engelhard's South African connection may prove to be a liability: some Arab countries are boycotting Anglo American because of their sale of diamonds to Israel. An extension of the boycott to Engelhard "could put a serious crimp in Philipp Bros.' trading business," according to *Business Week* in March 1980.

Ludwig Jesselson, the driving force behind the Philipp Brothers trading operation, owns 3.3% of Engelhard's stock, worth about $37 million. Both Jesselson and Engelhard chairman Milton F. Rosenthal were past 65 and going strong in early 1980.

Where they're going. Some U.S. government officials, angered by the prospect of global merchants growing rich in times of shortages, have called for restrictions on the operations of the international traders, particularly in oil and grain. Engelhard doesn't seem very worried. "The world needs traders," Jesselson told *Business Week* in 1979. "We serve as an apolitical, international clearinghouse for essential goods."

Stock performance. Engelhard Minerals & Chemicals stock bought for $1,000 in 1970 sold for $2,841 on January 2, 1980.

Access. 1221 Avenue of the Americas, New York, New York 10020; (212) 764-3700.

Goldfinger vs. the Hippopotamus Factor

Charles W. Engelhard, the gold tycoon whose shrewdness and opulent lifestyle made him the model for Ian Fleming's cunning character Goldfinger, suffered only one business failure while building the global precious metals empire that earned him a $300 million fortune before his death in 1971.

In his obituary the *Wall Street Journal* told how Engelhard met his lone defeat when he followed Fleming's advice. The ensuing debacle would have made even James Bond cringe.

Fleming, a longtime friend of Engelhard's, suggested that they invest together in an African timber estate on the banks of the Zambesi River in Mozambique. Not until too late did they learn that in the dry season the Zambesi reverses direction and

flows inland, making it impossible to float timber to port.

When the two luckless investors tried to recoup their loss by planting crops on the estate, the Zambesi's hippopotami lumbered greedily out of the river and ate all the tycoon's vegetables.

Source: *Wall Street Journal*, March 3, 1971.

Inco

Sales: $2.5 billion
Profits: $142 million
Rank in nickel: 1
Employees: 52,581
Founded: 1877
Headquarters: Toronto, Ontario
U.S. headquarters: New York, New York

What they do. For nearly 60 years International Nickel Company (now called Inco) and the nickel industry were one and the same. Inco controlled 90% of the non-communist world's nickel market as late as the 1950s. They still produce and sell more nickel than any other company in the world.

Nickel is not in itself an end product. It's a metal that adds strength, durability, and heat resistance to the metal it's coupled with, usually steel, to make turbines, batteries, water desalination equipment, and especially armaments and stainless steel products.

The barren "moonscape" around Sudbury, Ontario, in the north of Canada, bears stark evidence of the mining and refining of the world's largest sulfide nickel deposits, and Canada's biggest mining operation. Inco also mines copper, platinum, iron, and titanium there—all metals found in the nickel ore.

Inco's only nonmetal industry is ESB Ray-O-Vac, which produces batteries, electrical products and motors, plastics, and chemicals. They bought it in 1974.

History. Nickel's early history could be characterized as a substance in search of a use. The Chinese used *packtong* (nickel) for minor decorative purposes. Europeans began producing "German Silver" in 1824, using the nickel for money and, later, as a base for silver plating. Nickel contributed the name and material for the U.S. 5¢ coin.

Nickel mining operations got under way in North America with the founding of Orford Copper in New Jersey in 1877, and Canadian Copper in Sudbury, in 1886. Almost all the nickel produced went directly to the steel industry, which J. Pierpont Morgan successfully monopolized in 1901. The next year Morgan and U.S. Steel interests bought Canadian Copper, Orford, and a few other smaller companies. They also acquired mining rights in Sudbury and the South Seas island of New Caledonia, the two major sources of nickel. With all of these holdings they formed a new trust, International Nickel Company, based in New Jersey.

The rise of the automobile industry pushed steel, and with it nickel, to new heights of prosperity, but as a former Inco president once told *Forbes*, "The introduction of nickel-steel into armaments was the most important single factor in the development of the nickel industry." Inco sold Canadian nickel to both sides during World War I but stopped aiding the Germans because of public opposition, according to *The Big Nickel: Inco at Home and Abroad* by Jamie Swift.

By the end of the 1920s Inco was supplying almost all the world's nickel. The company's Wall Street law firm, Sullivan and Cromwell, thought Inco would face antitrust suits in the United States, so John Foster Dulles, a senior partner in the law firm, long-time Inco director, and future secretary of state under Eisenhower, advised a stock transfer to the Canadian subsidiary from the American parent in New Jersey, thereby making Inco a Canadian corporation. According to *Forbes*, "Inco's new northern home was a sanctuary from high taxes and the threat of antitrust. Had it remained an American company, Inco would almost certainly have shared the fate of the great aluminum monopoly, Alcoa." Until recently Inco remained predominantly owned and managed by Americans. Inco still has offices in both Toronto and New York, although chairmen now rule from Toronto and Canadians now own about half of the company.

With virtually no competition (the Rothschild's Société Le Nickel, the world's oldest nickel company, and the Canadian-based Falconbridge had the other 10% of the market), Inco reaped huge profits with the help of high nickel demand from the Korean and Vietnam wars. Inco never bothered to move with the times, or learn new marketing techniques, because they didn't have to. But then the bubble burst in the 1970s as more aggressive companies took over Inco's markets. Inco's share of the world nickel market is now down to about 30%. Inco had no long-term debt in 1968; they now owe $1.2 billion.

Reputation. Inco, last of the Morgan-organized monopolies, retains an autocratic air. Even the *Wall Street Journal* concedes that one of Inco's main problems is "employee bitterness."

What they own. Besides mining operations in Ontario and Manitoba, Canada, Inco owns an 80% interest in nickel mines in Guatemala and a 55% interest of mines in New Caledonia, as well as full ownership of mines in Indonesia. Inco operates refineries in Canada, England, and Wales. Their subsidiary, ESB, has 92 plants in 22 countries.

Who owns and runs the company. Institutions—banks, insurance companies, mutual funds and the like—are the big holders of Inco stock. The investors are Canadians and Americans. Directors and officers own together two-tenths of 1% of the stock. Running the company today is an American, Charles F. Baird, who was under secretary of the Navy under Lyndon B. Johnson. During World War II he served in the Marines, and he reenlisted when the Korean War broke out. Baird moved from New York to Toronto in 1980, shortly before being promoted to chairman. He once described the Sudbury mining complex as a "paramilitary organization," explaining: "Mining and smelting are industrial activities that require a lot of discipline. You can't have people coming in there and doing what they like. It's a tough business and there are a lot of tough people in it."

In the public eye. Inco has had labor problems for many years. In 1966 there was a series of wildcat strikes punctuated by violence. In 1969, 17,000 Canadian workers walked off the job for four months. In 1978–79 they struck Inco for nine months.

In the early 1970's, Inco's refinery towers spewed out so much sulfur dioxide and soot that nothing but low brush grew for 10 miles around the Sudbury refinery, and the drinking water was brown and foul. The union claimed that conditions at Sudbury caused miners to suffer chronic bronchitis, silicosis (inhalation of silica dust), and a variety of cancers. Workers had to endure temperatures that sometimes reached 150° F in the areas near the furnaces.

Sudbury workers lived in a company camp five miles out of town. Room and board was deducted from their wages. One worker told *Last Post*, a socialist paper in Canada, "It's not the camp so much that's bad, it's the boredom—shit, you'll see 20 miners watching some women's cooking program." Women are not allowed in the camp.

Although Inco's Levack mine had the highest number of accidents for Ontario mines in 1970–74, the Levack superintendent was quoted in *The Big Nickel* as saying, "A lot of reported accidents are not accidents at all. The men fake them because they don't want to work." Inco's hard line on labor escalated under former chairman Edward Grubb, a man known for making English refinery workers save time by drinking tea from a thermos, rather than brewing the tea fresh each morning at a break.

The 1979 Inco report to the Securities and Exchange Commission states that the company is in "substantial compliance" with environmental, health and safety regulations in all of their operations.

Inco is spreading to the Third World now, with new mines in Lake Izabal, Guatemala, and Soroak, Indonesia.

Where they're going. Inco would like to do something about improving employee morale. Even Baird admitted to the *Wall Street Journal* that "people were ashamed to be working for Inco." He promised to spend more time communicating with employees but said that his first priority is "to see our existing assets produce a higher return."

Access. One First Canadian Place, Toronto, Ontario M5X1C4 Canada; (416) 361-7511. U.S. office: 1 New York Plaza, New York, New York 10004; (212) 742-4000.

Consumer brands.

Exide, Willard, Wisco, Ray-O-Vac batteries.

About half of all U.S. coal is dug from surface (strip) mines, which outnumber underground mines two to one.

KAISER ALUMINUM & CHEMICAL CORPORATION

Sales: $2.9 billion
Profits: $232 million
Forbes 500 rank: 166
Rank in aluminum: 3
Founded: 1931
Employees: 26,865
Headquarters: Oakland, California

What they do. Kaiser Aluminum began as an afterthought to Henry J. Kaiser's postwar industrial empire and emerged in the mid-1950s as the empire's dominant member. But Kaiser's empire ceased to exist when the parent company—Kaiser Industries—sold off their three children in 1977. (The other two are Kaiser Steel and Kaiser Cement and Gypsum.)

Kaiser Aluminum mines their own bauxite ore (outside the United States), refines it into aluminum oxide, smelts this into raw aluminum, and sells primary aluminum products to smaller manufacturers around the world. While aluminum production accounts for 75% of Kaiser's business, they also make chemicals used in the aluminum reduction process and have branched out into agricultural and industrial chemicals as well. Their Kacor Realty subsidiary handles residential and industrial real estate in southern California and Hawaii.

History. Henry J. Kaiser was the last of the great self-made American industrialists. He differed from his predecessors (such as Rockefeller and Carnegie) principally in that he became a liberal Democrat with a strong sense of the social responsibility of corporations.

Kaiser was a bald, hulking human dynamo who stood six feet tall, weighed 240 pounds, rose daily at 5:30 A.M., and had a knack for getting his own way. "Henry Kaiser is like a happy elephant," said one associate. "He smiles and leans against you. After a while, you know there's nothing left to do but move in the direction he's pushing." He was fond of spouting homilies like "Problems are only opportunities in work clothes"; "There's only one time to do anything and that's today"; and "Find a need and fill it."

Born to German immigrants in upstate New York in 1882, Kaiser quit school at age 13 and got a job in a dry goods store in Utica to help support his family. To earn extra money he took photographs after hours, and he later became a traveling photographic salesman. At 23 he had his own photographic studio and supply store, and he later opened stores in Florida and the Bahamas. Around this time he courted Bessie Hannah Fosburgh of Norfolk, Virginia, whose guardian, a wealthy lumberman, deemed Kaiser an unfit suitor. Kaiser headed west to prove himself worthy and found a job in a hardware store in Spokane, Washington. Rising quickly to city sales manager, he returned east, married Bessie in 1907, and returned with her to Spokane.

As a hardware salesman Kaiser called on contractors; soon he went to work for one of them, a gravel and cement dealer. In 1913, when he was 31, a British Columbia road-building company he was dealing with went out of business in the middle of a project. Kaiser convinced a Vancouver bank president to lend him $25,000 and finished the job himself. With $19,000 profit from the deal, Kaiser was off and running in the construction business.

A population boom in the American West during the next two decades created a need for water supplies and hydroelectric power—which in turn gave rise to a dam-building boom. Together with five other large firms Kaiser helped build the Hoover, Bonneville, and Grand Coulee dams. When World War II broke out, the same six companies moved into shipbuilding, despite the fact that none of them knew anything about it. By the war's end they had turned shipbuilding into an assembly-line industry.

After the war Kaiser was able to augment his construction business by picking up several aluminum processing plants in Washington state and Louisiana for a song from the federal government. Alcoa, almost the entire aluminum industry at the time, had built the plants for wartime production and was being forced to sell them in the wake of an antitrust case. At first, no one seemed to want them; popular wisdom had it that the market would be glutted with aluminum once the war was over. But Henry Kaiser figured he might need aluminum for the cars he was planning to build. A Korean War–era slump in car buying forced him to scuttle his Kaiser-Frazer auto manufacturing business in the early 1950s, but by then Kaiser Aluminum was going strong—thanks to an unexpected sevenfold increase in aluminum demand brought on by aggressive marketing by Alcoa and Reynolds

Metals. Kaiser Aluminum could thank the competition for their success.

Today Kaiser's almost accidental aluminum company is their biggest asset, with annual production capacities in excess of a million tons and operations in 23 foreign countries.

Reputation. Under the Kaisers this company built a strong national reputation for social responsibility. The new chairman, Cornell Maier, seems intent on continuing this tradition, albeit in his own fashion. Maier has been active on many fronts. He has run full-page ads in newspapers to attack the television networks for not giving companies such as Kaiser the time to express their views on energy, government red tape, and free enterprise. (One ad began, "Is the free enterprise system an endangered species?") He has worked to keep the Oakland Raiders football team in Oakland and has supported efforts to open up jobs for unemployed youths.

What they own. Most of Kaiser's bauxite comes from Jamaica. They were the first American aluminum company to reach an accommodation with the Jamaican government over "Jamaicannization" of bauxite resources. Other principal sources and processing plants are located in Australia and Ghana. Two of Kaiser's four American primary aluminum plants are in Washington state; the others are in Louisiana and West Virginia.

Who owns and runs the company. At the start of 1979 the Kaiser family still controlled 13% of the shares, with 10% held by an employee savings and profit-sharing plan. Edgar F. Kaiser, who dismantled the empire assembled by his father, stepped down as chairman in 1978. He was then 70 years old and had worked in the company since 1930. (His father died in 1967 at age 85.) There are no longer any Kaisers on the board, but Edgar has been named chairman emeritus and an honorary director for life. It's clear, though, that the reins of the company have been grasped firmly by Cornell Maier, who was born poor in South Dakota, grew up in Los Angeles, and has never worked for another company. In his midfifties, Maier has already taken the titles of chairman, president, and chief executive officer. He is not bashful about speaking his mind and he mounts many a podium. *San*

Francisco Examiner columnist Dwight Chapin called him "one of the most visible top corporate executives anywhere," a visibility earned in part by the utilization of Carl Byoir & Associates, one of the nation's largest public relations outfits.

In the public eye. Kaiser has a long history of community involvement. They have erected 19 Kaiser Hospitals through the company's health foundation and have one of the best employee health plans in the country. It was the first of the Health Maintenance Organizations (HMOs) and served as a model for later programs of the U.S. Department of Health, Education and Welfare. Kaiser has been a principal backer of the Oakland Renaissance program to restore the city's downtown area.

In 1978 Kaiser sponsored a "work-learn" summer program, in which high school students took morning classes and worked jobs in the afternoon. Kaiser picked up both the teachers' and students' salaries. Kaiser also "adopted" Oakland High School, donating facilities and employees' time to rehabilitate the dilapidated structure. In response to city budget cutbacks caused by California's Proposition 13, Kaiser established an "Adopt A Park" program among local businesses and led the way by taking responsibility for keeping Oakland's 88-acre Roberts Regional Park open to the public.

In 1979 Kaiser was honored at a special dinner by the National Association for the Advancement of Colored People for the company's actions in a reverse discrimination case. A white employee had sued the company, claiming that Kaiser discriminated against him in choosing two black workers with less seniority for a training program. Despite the recent Bakke case (which ended with a Supreme Court decision in favor of the white plaintiff), Kaiser defended their position in court—and won.

Where they're going. Since 1976 Kaiser has been dumping many of the unprofitable companies picked up during the previous two decades. Today there isn't a loser in the corporation. With aluminum demand and prices up, Kaiser has all it can do to fill the orders.

Stock performance. Kaiser stock bought for $1,000 in 1970 sold for $1,023 on January 2, 1980.

Major employment centers. Spokane, Washington; New Orleans-Baton Rouge, Louisiana; Ravenswood, West Virginia.

Access. 300 Lakeside Drive, Oakland, California 94643; (415) 271-3300.

ⓚ Kennecott
♀ Corporation

Sales: $2.4 billion
Profits: $130.4 million
Forbes 500 rank: 213
Rank in copper: 1
Rank in gold: 2
Founded: 1915
Employees: 24,000
Headquarters: New York, New York

What they do. Kennecott has always been synonymous with copper. They mine more of the shiny metal than any other company. But in 1980 they took "Copper" out of their name; they're now Kennecott Corporation, reflecting the big change the company has been going through since the early 1970s when Chile's president, Salvador Allende, threw them out of that country. Kennecott had been running the world's largest underground copper mine for more than a half century in Chile.

Today less than half of Kennecott's sales come from copper. They mine gold, silver, and molybdenum (an ingredient in alloys such as stainless steel). Their Carborundum Company makes electric "pilot lights" for gas appliances as well as a long line of industrial products for use in steel making, oil drilling, and the like. Their Chase Brass & Copper turns out copper and brass in strips and sheets for cars and electrical power generators.

History. Kennecott was born in the early part of this century in the wilds of Alaska, where the Morgan and Guggenheim interests built a $25 million railroad to reach a new copper find.

At the beginning of this century virtually all of the copper reserves in the American West, as well as almost all the smelters used to refine the metal, were in the hands of the Guggenheims. Meyer Guggenheim, the family patriarch, had emigrated from Swit-

zerland to Pennsylvania in 1848, where he peddled stove polish and a distilled version of coffee to housewives in Amish country. He got his big break during the Civil War, speculating in clothes and foodstuffs. After the war he made even more of a fortune by importing lace and embroidery from Europe. In 1881 Meyer bought a one-third interest for $5,000 in two lead and silver mines near Leadville, Colorado. Months after he bought out one discouraged partner, the mines became a bonanza. They returned $15 million to the Guggenheims before the ore was depleted.

Meyer saw mining as the way to make each of his seven sons a multimillionaire. According to John H. Davis in his book *The Guggenheims: An American Epic,* "Meyer gathered his seven sons around a long mahogany table in his office, and gave each a stick. He then told them to break the sticks and they did as he told them. Then he produced a bundle of sticks held together by a band, and asked each son to break the bundle. The bundle was passed around. None of the sons was able to break it."

"You see, my boys," Meyer said, "singly the sticks are easily broken, together they cannot be broken. So it is with you. Together you are invincible. Singly, each of you may be easily broken. Stay together, my sons, and the world will be yours. Break up and you will lose everything."

The sons stuck together and soon controlled 80% of the silver, copper, and lead market. According to Davis, by the early part of the twentieth century, the Guggenheims became one of the five richest families in America, along with the Rockefellers, Vanderbilts, Mellons, and Fords; and they were the second wealthiest Jewish family in the world, after the Rothschilds.

After the Leadville bonanza, the Guggenheims closed down their lace/embroidery business and moved to New York in 1888. They opened mines in Mexico in 1890, and bought a controlling interest in American Smelting and Refining in 1901. But their prize holding became a fabulous copper find in remote Alaska. In 1907 the Guggenheims and J. P. Morgan formed the Alaska Syndicate, which bought a steamship line, a fishing fleet (the largest in western United States, Canada, and Alaska), forests, and 200 miles of right-of-way for the $25 million railroad to the copper mine.

But the railroad proved to be a problem. It cost so much to build that the Guggen-

The largest open-pit copper mine in the United States, Bingham Canyon, near Salt Lake City, Utah, operated by Kennecott.

heims had to join all their copper holdings together into one corporation and sell millions of dollars' worth of stocks and bonds to finance the Copper River and Northwestern Railroad. The result, in 1915, was Kennecott Copper, named for a glacier near the Alaskan mine.

Kennecott copper flooded the market. Their copper was the cheapest to produce in the world. Kennecott workers in Alaska were paid $3 a day; $1 of that was spent on a bed, and $1.50 for three meals. The American public railed against the "Guggenmorganization of Alaska," and the "Morganheim" interests. One of the Guggenheim sons, Simon, became a U.S. senator, and supported measures favorable to the Guggenheim interests in Alaska.

Soon afterward Kennecott bought El Teniente, the world's largest underground mine, in Chile. Over the next 50 years Kennecott reaped enormous profits, taking more than 7 million tons of copper from Chile, until the government of Salvador Allende nationalized the mines.

Sensing the wave of nationalism that was rising in Chile in the 1960s, Kennecott re-

duced dependence on Chilean copper, which at that time accounted for about 25% of their profits. They greatly expanded domestic copper production and moved into other metals. When Allende nationalized the mines in 1971, Kennecott's rival Anaconda was devastated, but less than 11% of Kennecott's income depended on Chile by that time.

Kennecott no longer depended on Guggenheims, either. By the early 1970s, the Guggenheim office existed mainly to take care of investments. The seven sons had died, and their descendants had little interest in mining. The name Guggenheim now adorns a modern art museum in New York City, a hospital, a palace in Venice, a pavilion at the Mayo Clinic, a band concert shell in New York City's Central Park, and a series of grants to the arts.

In 1968 Kennecott bought Peabody, the nation's largest steam coal producer, but the Federal Trade Commission forced them to get rid of it in 1976 through an antitrust action. With about half of the $1.2 billion from the sale of Peabody, they bought the Carborundum Company, prompting a vicious fight for control led by a group of stockholders who thought the money should have been distributed to them in dividends instead. The stockholder faction was led by T. Roland Berner, chairman of Curtiss-Wright, a sagging aircraft engine business. Berner lost, but he did end up with seats on the Kennecott board of directors for himself and two associates.

Reputation. One year after Kennecott got kicked out of Chile, *Forbes* called the company a "sleeping giant living off its past." Complaints about management incompetence fueled the unsuccessful Curtiss-Wright takeover attempt. By 1979 the company had recovered so nicely that *Forbes* proclaimed them a "model of purpose compared to the disarray of barely a year ago."

What they own. The largest copper reserves in the United States. Four open-pit mines, including the biggest one in the world—the massive Utah Pit near Salt Lake City. An underground mine in Missouri that produces lead, zinc, and silver. More than 80 plants to process their metals, of which half are in the United States. Remaining plants are in Latin America, Europe, Canada, Australia, and New Zealand.

Who owns and runs the company. Curtiss-Wright owns 11% of the stock. Chairman Thomas D. Barrow, who came over from Exxon after the takeover fight, is the largest individual stockholder, with a little more than 1% of the stock.

In the public eye. Mining companies in the West have a tradition of creating towns near their mines, retaining ownership, and snuffing them out when they're no longer needed. Lark, Utah, was such a town, with 476 citizens, many of them retired. Lark was originally owned by another mining company, U. V. Industries, which sold it to Kennecott in 1977. Kennecott wanted to ex-

pand their waste dumps from a nearby mine and gain a water supply for their copper recovery process.

Eleven days before Christmas Kennecott called a town meeting to inform the citizenry that none of the land or home-rental leases would be renewed. Homeowners had 60 to 90 days beyond their expiration dates to move their houses or leave them to Kennecott bulldozers. Kennecott would not buy any of the houses, nor would they pay moving expenses.

The national media then pounced on the story. Newspapers across the country carried photographs of elderly people preparing to leave their little houses. An embarrassed Kennecott, insisting "we're not Scrooge," finally offered homeowners $11,000 each and renters $1,500 to relocate, plus extra money for improvements they had made.

Stock performance. Kennecott stock bought for $1,000 in 1970 sold for $673 on January 2, 1980.

Access. 161 East 42nd Street, New York, New York 10017; (212) 687-5800.

Kerr-McGee Corporation

Sales: $2.7 billion
Profits: $160 million
Forbes 500 rank: 186
Rank in uranium: 1
Founded: 1929
Employees: 11,100
Headquarters: Oklahoma City, Oklahoma

What they do. Kerr-McGee is a splendid example of how successful an oil company can become when their chairman is one of the most powerful members of the United States Senate. The company is a trail blazer. In 1947 they drilled the world's first offshore oil well. In 1952 they were the first oil company to expand into the uranium business. And in 1979 they became the first nuclear firm to go on trial for their safety record, in the famous Karen Silkwood case.

Though they may be best known now for

their nuclear operations, Kerr-McGee is primarily an oil company. Three-fourths of their sales come from petroleum. They operate oil and natural gas wells, along with refineries, in Texas, Louisiana, and Oklahoma. They also control offshore wells in the Gulf of Mexico, the North Sea, and the Persian Gulf off Abu Dhabi. They sell gasoline at some 1,600 Deep Rock and Kerr-McGee filling stations in the Midwest and the South.

In the late 1970s Kerr-McGee started strip-mining coal in Wyoming, tapping reserves they had bought 20 years earlier. They still sit on vast coal deposits in six other states. About one-fifth of their sales come from chemicals, such as soda ash from California, potash from New Mexico, and phosphates from Florida. The chemicals are used in fertilizers, window glass, laundry detergents, dry-cell batteries, and other products. Kerr-McGee also happens to be the nation's second-largest producer of railroad crossties.

The troubled nuclear power industry accounts for only about 5% of Kerr-McGee's sales. They mine uranium underground in New Mexico and at a strip-mine in Wyoming, and they process it into fuel for nuclear power plants at a factory in Oklahoma.

History. Robert Kerr was born in a log cabin in Indian Territory (later part of Oklahoma). In 1929, after he had become an attorney by studying law on his own, Kerr and his brother-in-law, James Anderson, bought an Oklahoma oil-drilling company for $5,000 in cash and $25,000 in I.O.U.'s. Anderson supervised the drilling while Kerr scouted for people who would allow oil wells sunk on their property. In 1936 Kerr bought out his brother-in-law, and the next year he hired Dean McGee, a prominent oil geologist from Phillips Petroleum, another Oklahoma firm. McGee's name was added to the company's in 1946.

Kerr handed the reins to McGee in 1942 and plunged into politics, becoming the first Oklahoma-born governor of that state. Six years later he was elected to the U.S. Senate, where he became a leading advocate of the oil industry. When Kerr entered politics, his company was just one of many small regional oil firms; by the time of his death in 1963, it was a giant. In the early 1950s, when the government decided to promote "atoms for peace," Kerr-McGee started buying uranium mines and landing contracts from the Atomic Energy Commission worth hundreds of millions of dollars. They moved into coal in 1957, buying huge deposits in Oklahoma, Wyoming, and elsewhere. At the same time, Senator Kerr pushed through Congress a $1.2 billion project to make the Arkansas River navigable from the Mississippi up to Tulsa—right next to Kerr-McGee's coal deposits.

Kerr died on New Year's Day in 1963.

Reputation. Kerr-McGee is a "colorful name in the history of the energy business," the *New York Times* once pointed out, one that has long been associated with "power politics and rawboned wildcatters." But *Forbes* suggested in 1973 that the company "has been getting cautious and unimaginative." When the oil drilling rights in the North Sea went up for grabs in 1971, chairman Dean McGee recalled, "We bid $1 million on what we thought was one of the few tracts worth bidding on. Well, that one sold for $52 million. . . . So we wound up with nothing."

Who owns and runs the company. Chairman and chief executive Dean McGee, who turned 75 in 1979, owns 3.2% of the stock. Two of the senator's kin, Breene and Robert, Jr., are on the all-male board of directors.

In the public eye. Many people know Kerr-McGee through the Karen Silkwood case, which first came to national attention through the reporting of Howard Kohn in *Rolling Stone* in 1978. Silkwood was a worker in the company's Cimarron, Oklahoma, plutonium plant. Safety conditions there were so poor, she charged, that the plant posed a danger to workers and the public. Silkwood died in a mysterious car crash in 1974 while she was on her way to meet with a *New York Times* reporter and a representative of the Oil, Chemical and Atomic Workers Union. Documents that she reportedly had with her to support her claims that the plant was unsafe were never found. Silkwood's relatives sued Kerr-McGee for negligence, and in 1979 a jury awarded her family $10.5 million in damages. Silkwood became a symbol and a martyr for the opponents of nuclear power. Kerr-McGee closed the plutonium plant in 1975 after the government chose not to renew their contract

Where they're going. The nuclear star dimmed in the late 1970s. Besides the unsolved problems of plant safety, disposal of nuclear wastes, and protection from would-be terrorists, the industry is torn from within. Westinghouse, one of the nation's largest builders of nuclear reactors, sued Kerr-McGee and several other companies for allegedly conspiring to drive up the price of uranium ore by 500%. Publicly Kerr-McGee still maintains that "nuclear power is one of the most viable long-term energy options available to the United States." If public policy eventually forecloses that option, they still have coal reserves to fall back on.

Stock performance. Kerr-McGee stock bought for $1,000 in 1970 sold for $2,274 on January 2, 1980.

Access. Oklahoma City, Oklahoma 73125; (405) 270-1313.

Consumer brands.

Deep Rock and Kerr-McGee gasoline.

PEABODY COAL COMPANY

Sales: $816 million
Profits: $54 million
Rank in coal: 1
Founded: 1883
Employees: 15,000
Headquarters: St. Louis, Missouri

What they do. Everybody keeps dropping Peabody Coal like a hot potato. The nation's largest coal producer, operating 48 mines in 12 states, Peabody hasn't been independent since 1966, when they sold out to Kennecott Copper. Kennecott was forced to unload them—and Peabody is now owned by a consortium consisting of five industrial giants and one financial powerhouse. Despite rising production and increasing reliance on coal as an energy source, Peabody has often been a drain on the pocketbooks of their owners (whoever they happen to be). And on top of that they are not generally beloved by the people

---

BIG COAL MINERS

Production (1977)

1. PEABODY	65 *million tons*
2. CONSOLIDATION (*Conoco*)	48 *million tons*
3. AMAX (*Standard Oil of California*)	28 *million tons*
4. ISLAND CREEK (*Occidental Petroleum*)	17 *million tons*
5. PITTSTON	14 *million tons*
6. U.S. STEEL	14 *million tons*
7. ARCH MINERAL (*Ashland Oil*)	13 *million tons*
8. NERCO (*Pacific Power & Light*)	12 *million tons*
9. BETHLEHEM MINES (*Bethlehem Steel*)	11 *million tons*
10. PETER KIEWIT	10 *million tons*
11. AMERICAN ELECTRIC POWER	10 *million tons*
12. WESTERN ENERGY (*Montana Power*)	10 *million tons*
13. OLD BEN (*Sohio*)	10 *million tons*
14. NORTH AMERICAN COAL	9 *million tons*
15. PITTSBURGH & MIDWAY (*Gulf Oil*)	8 *million tons*

*These 15 companies mined 40.6% of the U.S. bituminous coal production in 1977.

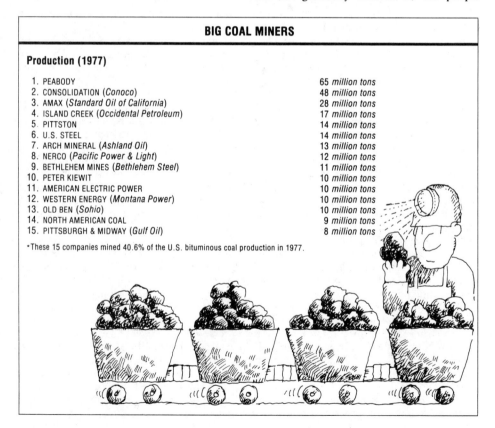

who work for them.

Peabody's surface (strip) and underground mines yield more than 60 million tons of coal per year. They have long ranked as the number 1 coal miner, producing between 10% and 12% of the U.S. total. Most of their coal is sold to utilities; their largest single customer is the Tennessee Valley Authority. Peabody claims that in a ranking of all suppliers of energy (oil, coal, gas, and uranium) they would place sixth, measured in terms of BTUs (British thermal units) produced in this country.

History.

"And Daddy won't you take me back
to Muhlenberg County
Down by the clear water where
Paradise lay
I'm sorry my son but you're too late
in asking
Mr. Peabody's coal train has hauled
it away."

—"Paradise," a folk song by John
Prine

Francis S. Peabody opened a coal yard in Chicago in 1883. The company sold coal at both the wholesale and retail levels, but it was not until 1896 that Peabody went into mining in downstate Illinois. By the end of the century they had four mines in Williamson County. Early in this century Peabody acquired 46,000 acres of coal reserves in the Midwest, some of which are still being mined. Utilities controlled by Samuel Insull, Jr.—notably Commonwealth Edison and People's Gas of Chicago—took control of Peabody, their largest supplier, in 1928, but this combination was broken up at the request of dissatisfied shareholders in 1934.

During the 1920s and 1930s the Peabody mines became bloody battleplaces for warring labor factions. John L. Lewis, president of the United Mine Workers (UMW), beat back a challenge to his leadership in 1926 when he disclosed that his longtime opponent, Illinois miner Frank Farrington, was secretly on the Peabody payroll as a $25,000-a-year consultant. The board promptly suspended him. Later on Illinois miners affiliated with the Progressive Union charged that Lewis was working in collusion with Peabody. On January 4, 1933, the Illinois National Guard was called out to enforce peace at the Peabody mine in

Taylorville, Illinois, after a violent struggle between striking miners and working miners left 2 dead, 14 wounded, and 18 jailed on murder charges.

From 1895 to 1955 Peabody was strictly an underground miner. During that period their mines produced a total of 440 million tons of coal from nine states and Canada. But in the 1950s the impact of strip-mining, which produced low-cost coal, as well as fuel conversion to oil and gas, was beginning to be felt. In February 1955 Stuyvesant Peabody, Jr., grandson of the founder, resigned. Four months later Peabody merged with Kansas City–based Sinclair Coal, an experienced strip-miner headed by the Kelce family: father David, the pit boss; brother Merl, the timekeeper; brother Ted, a shovel operator; and brother Russell, the president.

Between 1957 and 1963 Peabody built or acquired 24 additional mines, thereby becoming the largest strip-miner in the nation. Their output doubled to more than 54 million tons of coal a year. But the Kelces decided that running the nation's largest coal company wasn't nearly as much fun as building it. So in 1966 they sold out to Kennecott Copper for more than $500 million. That started a long, ridiculous battle with the Federal Trade Commission, which claimed Kennecott had violated the antitrust laws and should be forced to sell Peabody. The FTC argued that Kennecott, because of their copper mining expertise, was a "potential entrant" into coal mining and should not be allowed to buy their way in at the top. The FTC said Kennecott had signaled their interest in coal mining by acquiring Peabody. Kennecott responded to this Catch-22 logic by saying that if that was the case, the only people they could logically sell Peabody to would be people who didn't want the company (in other words, didn't want to go into coal mining). Nevertheless, the FTC prevailed, and Kennecott put Peabody on the block in 1974. After more than four years of trying to find a buyer to pick up the money-sieve Peabody had become as the result of incessant work stoppages and high capital costs (much of it health and safety-related), Kennecott finally found their buyer in the form of a group of six companies headed by Newmont Mining. In 1978 Kennecott sold Peabody Coal for $1.2 billion. Many observers were amazed they got so much for it.

Reputation. *Fortune* called it a "black jewel that bedevils its owners."

What they own. Peabody operates mines in Colorado (2), Montana (1), Arizona (2), Indiana (8), Kentucky (18), Ohio (3), Arkansas (1), Missouri (4), Oklahoma (1), and Illinois (4). They also own coal reserves, but no mines, in Alabama, New Mexico, North Dakota, Utah, and Wyoming. In the western states, where most of the mines are on federal lands, Peabody is the second-largest leaseholder. Mining is capital intensive, meaning it depends largely on machinery and equipment rather than people—and this is especially true of strip-mining, where giant shovels do all the work. This characteristic is reflected in Peabody's assets, stated by *Fortune* to be $1.3 billion. At Peabody's River King mine near Marissa, Illinois, a giant shovel mines 9,000 tons of coal every 24-hour working day.

Who owns and runs the company. The shareholders are Newmont, a mining company (with a 27.5% interest); the Williams Companies, an Oklahoma pipeline company and fertilizer producer (27.5%); Bechtel, world's largest engineering and construction company (15%); Boeing, world's largest plane builder (15%); Fluor, another big California-based construction firm (10%); and the nation's third-largest life insurer, Equitable Life (5%). In 1977 they installed Roderick Hills, former chairman of the Securities and Exchange Commission, as head of Peabody—and he lasted a year. A top Peabody executive, asked whether Hills had been forced to resign, told the *New York Times:* "I wouldn't say he wasn't, and I wouldn't say that he was." Named to succeed Hills in 1978 was Robert H. Quenon, who came to Peabody from Carter, Exxon's coal-producing unit.

In the public eye. Environmentalists, labor unions, and occupational safety regulators have all had their run-ins with Peabody. Nearly all Peabody's mines were shut down for nearly four months in 1977–78 as a result of an industry-wide strike. In the first 10 months of 1975 Peabody had 14 miners killed at its mines, and the United Mine Workers went to court to get union safety inspectors on Peabody property. In a 1977 report to employees the company said that one of its "major policies . . . is that every effort is made to comply

fully with all applicable laws and regulations."

Where they're going. No place.

Access. 301 North Memorial Drive, St. Louis, Missouri 63102; (314) 342-3593.

**REYNOLDS
ALUMINUM**

Sales: $3.3 billion
Profits: $177.1 million
Forbes 500 rank: 145
Rank in aluminum: 3
Founded: 1919
Employees: 36,200
Headquarters: Richmond, Virginia

What they do. Reynolds Metals is a semifeudal state, largely owned and operated by the aristocratic Reynolds family of rural, fox-hunting Virginia. In the 60 years since Richard S. Reynolds began manufacturing tinfoil for his uncle R. J.'s cigarette packs, the Reynolds Metals Company has become one of the so-called Big Four aluminum producers of the world. Anyone who drinks Miller beer in cans, or eats Brown-In-Bag foods, or wraps leftovers in Diamond Foil or Reynolds Wrap uses their products. They make nearly one-fifth of the nation's aluminum.

Reynolds Metals controls virtually every aspect of their business, relying on no outside suppliers for their basic materials. The bauxite ore they refine into aluminum comes from Reynolds-owned mines in Arkansas, Jamaica, and Haiti. Reynolds turns this primary aluminum into airplane and auto parts, housing materials like siding and storm doors, parts for major appliances like refrigerators and air conditioners, aluminum cans, kitchen utensils, aluminum foil, stadium seating, parts for farm and garden sheds, and the cigarette foil that R. S. started out with. In addition, Reynolds makes such esoteric items as aluminum pharmaceutical packaging, aluminum paste for metallic paints, and aluminum powder for use in biodegradable detergents and mining explosives. Of their total aluminum output, about one-fourth goes into construction products, one-fifth into packaging, one-fifth into transportation goods (airplane and auto parts), and one-tenth into electrical products.

History. In the summer of 1902 R. J. Reynolds convinced his nephew, R. S. Reynolds, to leave law school and enter the family tobacco business, which R. J.'s father had founded at Winston-Salem, North Carolina, after the Civil War. R. J.'s success helped to establish the Reynolds clan as part of the new southern aristocracy that emerged from the rubble of the war. He prophesied that R. S. was too shrewd a businessman to be happy in the stultifying legal profession; and true to his uncle's prediction, R. S. soon became the tobacco company's master merchandiser. R. S. was largely responsible for turning Prince Albert loose tobacco and Camel cigarettes into industry leaders.

But by 1913 R. S. had tired of the tobacco business and set off on his own. He first tried manufacturing household cleaners, but failed when industries supplying materials for World War I were given railroad shipping priorities. Unable to obtain his raw materials, R. S. spent the war years making gunpowder drums for the war effort.

Then in 1919, realizing that the sudden increase in cigarette consumption during the war had outstripped the supply of tinfoil used in cigarette packaging, R. S. borrowed $100,000 from his uncle's tobacco company and founded the U.S. Foil Company in a small one-story building in Louisville, Kentucky.

The company's overnight success was due to R. S.'s choice of factory sites. His competitors milled their foil in eight- to twelve-story buildings, which meant that a great deal of money and labor were wasted lifting the lead and tin to upper floors. But Reynolds, forced to make do with a one-story building, had his milling machines installed in long rows—thus eliminating the need for costly hand lifting. When his competitors instigated a price war, Reynolds was able to undersell them by several cents per pound on the finished foil.

R. S. was also the first cigarette foil manufacturer to recognize the advantages of the lighter, cheaper aluminum over the traditional lead/tin alloy. In 1928 he built the first aluminum foil plant in Louisville and,

after buying out the shares the tobacco company held in his business, formed Reynolds Metals. By 1930 the company had annual sales of $13 million and had moved the headquarters to New York. They continued to grow during the Great Depression, helped along by their 1935 discovery of a method of rotogravure printing on aluminum, which enabled them to enter the field of aluminum packaging. In 1938 the office moved south again, to Richmond, Virginia. (Richard S. Reynolds, Jr., son of the founder, had struck out on his own and founded Reynolds & Co., a stock brokerage firm that became Reynolds Securities and was later merged into Dean Witter. But when the company left New York for Richmond he went with them, becoming an assistant to the president. R. S., Jr., became president in 1948 and chairman in 1963.)

In 1937, faced with aluminum shortages, R. S. went to Europe in search of a new source of raw materials. He was startled to find aluminum production capacities in Germany at 800 million pounds—more than twice the combined capacity of England, France, and the United States. Reynolds guessed (correctly) that Hitler meant to use the aluminum for military airplane construction, and he decided to increase his own capacity, borrowing $15 million to build the company's first smelting plant near Sheffield, Alabama, and buying raw bauxite ore wherever he could find it. When Pearl Harbor plunged the nation into World War II, Reynolds Metals was already geared up for wartime production. By 1945 the company had a capacity of 450 million pounds, which exceeded the entire U.S. production in 1940.

After the war Reynolds turned this capacity over to construction and consumer uses. In 1947 they introduced Reynolds Wrap, which quickly passed Alcoa Wrap as the leader in the foil field, as well as a host of other products ranging from kitchen utensils to fabricated freight car parts. In 1948 R. S. began to yield some control of the company to his four sons—R. S., Jr., David, William, and J. Louis. The brothers were chiefly responsible for the company's rapid overseas expansion and the marketing of several new products in the 1950s and 1960s. Some of those products, like the all-aluminum beverage can, were immediate successes; others, like the Tapper aluminum home beer keg and the Aluminaut, an all-aluminum submarine, were not.

By the beginning of the 1970s Reynolds was losing money. A program in the mid-1960s to increase production capacity by 20% ended up costing the company almost twice the projected cost of $325 million; and when it was finished, the demand for aluminum suddenly leveled off. At least that was the company's explanation. But Wall Street stockbrokers and other critics attacked the nepotism in the company's management, claiming that the brothers held the reins too tightly when they should have been hiring professional managers from outside. R. S., Jr., had brought in a financial consulting firm to streamline the operation; but after the reorganizational dust had cleared, the reins of command were still firmly in the hands of the Reynolds family.

Reputation. More than any other company in the industry, they have been evangelists in finding new uses for aluminum. *Forbes* said in 1974, "The Reynolds boys changed aluminum from an exotic industrial raw material into a fabricated end product."

What they own. Reynolds has a bauxite mine in Arkansas; fluorspar mines in Colorado and Kentucky; an estimated 2 billion tons of coal in Wyoming; and foreign subsidiaries in 19 nations. Two plants, in Texas and Arkansas, convert raw bauxite ore into alumina (the oxide that yields primary aluminum). This primary aluminum then goes to one of 43 plants in 18 states that manufacture ingots, sheet, and wire and turn them into Reynolds products.

Reynolds also has mines and plants in Jamaica, Haiti, and Brazil. They even have a hand in distributing their finished products, with 90 sales agencies and 34 distributors located in most major cities of the world.

Who owns and runs the company. Photographs of the Reynolds Metals hierarchy are a study in family resemblance. The board includes three sons of R. S. Reynolds —David P. (who became chairman in 1976), J. Louis, and William G. A cousin of theirs, A. D. Reynolds, is a vice-president, and William G. Reynolds, Jr., is the company's treasurer.

The family, which owns about 18% of Reynolds's stock, also contributes to the company's sense of feudalism through its prominent position in Virginia society and politics. They are longtime supporters of the Democratic Party and are often named to business committees by Democratic administrations. J. Louis Reynolds's son, Sargent, was Virginia's lieutenant governor until his death in 1971.

In the public eye. In 1973 Reynolds International pleaded guilty to charges of violating government sanctions against importing Rhodesian ores and was fined $5,000. More recently, in 1979 the Federal Aviation Administration began a search for what it termed "substrength aluminum"—several million pounds' worth—which Reynolds had shipped to airplane manufacturers in the United States and abroad.

A major miner of Jamaican bauxite, they sold 51% of their mines and land to the Jamaican government in 1975.

Reynolds has received kudos for their aluminum recycling program, which since its inception in 1969 has recycled more than 13.7 billion aluminum cans and paid out $100 million to participating consumers. By the end of 1979 aluminum accounted for 60% of the beverage cans—and nearly 75% of the beer cans—made in America. Reynolds recycles more than half as many cans as they make.

Where they're going. Reynolds recently introduced a new product which they hope will eventually replace the tin can. This is the Flex-Can: a flexible aluminum food pouch, already in use by the military for some food rations. Reynolds also has spent, and continues to spend, millions in the attempt to convince the auto industry to move into all-aluminum engine blocks and other parts. Until recently they've had little success. But gasoline shortages have persuaded some automakers to try the lighter, more energy-efficient engine blocks in test models, and Reynolds hopes to make Detroit into an increasingly large aluminum market in the coming years.

Stock performance. Reynolds stock bought for $1,000 in 1970 sold for $1,102 on January 2, 1980.

Access. 6603 West Broad Street, Richmond, Virginia 23261; (804) 281-2000.

Consumer brands.

Reynolds Wrap and Diamond Foil household foil; Brown-in-Bag oven cooking bags; Redi-Pans semirigid containers; Flex-Can food pouch.

Tree Cutters

Boise Cascade Corporation

Sales: $2.9 billion
Profits: $174.9 million
Forbes 500 rank: 167
Rank in forest products: 5
Founded: 1931
Employees: 35,704
Headquarters: Boise, Idaho

What they do. It took Boise Cascade only 15 years to change from a 98-pound weakling into a Paul Bunyan. As recently as 1956 Boise was an acorn-sized, three-sawmill lumber company; but by 1970 the Boise family tree included branches in paper products and office supplies, lumber, prefabricated housing, land development, and even mobile homes. They were one of Wall Street's wonder companies—what an investment broker once called "a prototype acquisitor"—and president Robert V. Hansberger was so busy buying up companies that his swift-moving hands seemed an eternal blur.

Lightning struck in 1973. Setbacks in real estate development and housing, coupled with the growing ecology movement, brought Boise to the brink of ruin. Hansberger was forced out. A new management started selling the companies he had snatched up during the 1960s, and today Boise Cascade is strictly a forest products business. Everything they do starts with trees and ends as lumber, plywood, newsprint paper products, and "composite" (cardboard) packaging.

History. The Boise Payette Lumber Company had been one of Idaho's largest producers during the 1930s and 1940s; but a postwar building boom rapidly depleted their timber stands. When a 36-year-old Robert Hansberger came aboard in 1956, Boise was a tired, marginal lumber company.

Hansberger, who had held several management jobs in the lumber industry, turned things around overnight. Realizing that new products like plywood and wallboards had created burgeoning markets for the forest products industry, he set out to make his company large enough to build a pulp mill. Within months he had set up a merger with Cascade Lumber of Yakima, Washington, and with the additional borrowing power Boise Cascade was able to begin construction of their first mill near Wallula, Washington. The following year Boise added a corrugated container plant at Burley, Idaho, and began manufacturing containers for products like motor oil and frozen foods.

Hansberger was a product of Harvard Business School's famous Class of '47, a group of young men who had enrolled immediately after World War II and then charged out to take the reins of a booming economy with their fresh, academically inspired ideas. Hansberger's idea was "free-form management," and to implement it he installed graduates of the nation's top business schools in Boise's upper levels. They were treated as autonomous equals and given the authority to operate and expand Boise's various divisions. In the affluent 1960s these intellectual "young tigers" (Hansberger's phrase) built Boise into the third-largest forest products business in the nation—behind only Georgia-Pacific and Weyerhaeuser. By 1969, only 13 years after Hansberger had taken the helm, the tigers had flanked their president through some 33 mergers and acquisitions that brought the company annual revenues to more than $1 billion.

This pell-mell expansion left Boise with very little cash and an enormous debt. Since Hansberger and his tigers wanted cash to get into the high-risk recreational land development game, they set up a 1969 merger with Ebasco Industries. Formerly Electric Bond and Share Company, Ebasco had begun as a General Electric subsidiary in 1905 and later became one of the world's largest utility holding companies, with power plants throughout Latin America. At the time of the deal with Boise, Ebasco had $66 million in blue chip stocks, $300 million in Latin American government bonds payable in American dollars, and more than $100 million in cash. That gave Hansberger all he needed for his real estate deals, and Boise rapidly began setting up resort home developments near artificial lakes and golf courses. Boise threw so much money into the real estate game that by 1971, 44% of their revenues came from real estate speculation and development.

Then the bottom began to fall out.

Boise had bought several smaller development companies in California. These companies had salesmen who exaggerated, overpromoted, and made misleading statements to prospective buyers. One Boise ad said: "You can't buy a bad piece of real estate in California." Some of the buyers complained to California's attorney general, who filed suit, and in the next two years Boise shelled out nearly $60 million in settlements. (Some observers said that if the prosecutors had pushed as hard as possible, they might have sunk the company.)

In addition to legal troubles the early 1970s brought an unexpected slump in the homebuilding industry, which affected Boise's prefab business. At the same time the heightened ecological concern made it more difficult for Boise to get approval from many planning agencies for the company's recreational developments. When problems with the waste-disposal system at the company's Lake Tahoe condominium development fouled the lake water, a group of conservationists at the University of California in Berkeley dubbed Boise Cascade "Polluter of the Year." As if all this weren't enough, President Nixon's wage-and-price freeze crippled Boise's new mobile home business. Boise posted a $37 million loss in 1971. From a 1969 high of $81.87, Boise's stock fell to $11.10 a share in 1972. At this point, Hansberger resigned and John Fery, one of the young tigers (a Stanford Business

School graduate), moved into the president's office.

Fery replaced Hansberger's free-form management with a rigid hierarchical structure and began selling off subsidiaries, using the proceeds to cover real estate losses until Boise was out of the development game. Slowly but surely he returned Boise to businesses they knew—in the less profitable but less risky forest products field. Fery's policies paid off: 1978 was the best earnings year in Boise's history in spite of prolonged strikes at company paper mills.

Reputation. The days of the "wonder company" and the "young tiger" philosophy are gone forever. They may not be as exciting as they once were, but they've reduced their debt, sold off their consumer businesses—and they're making money.

What they own. 2.7 million acres of timberland, mostly in the Pacific Northwest. They lease about 3.8 million acres from the provincial governments of Ontario and New Brunswick, Canada.

Who owns and runs the company. Before he sold out in the mid-1970s Hansberger's Boise holdings amounted to about $20 million, making him the largest stockholder. Now that honor goes to Fery, who in 1979 owned 55,000 shares worth about $2 million. Boise has one female director, Anne L. Armstrong, former U.S. ambassador to Britain. Every full-time salaried employee may contribute up to 10% of his or her pay to the company's investment savings plan, and Boise matches one-half of the employee's contribution (up to 3% of total annual compensation). Translation: if you're making $20,000 and contribute $1,000 to the plan, the company will put in $500. After five years you can take your money and run.

In the public eye. The ambitious Hansberger was a member of presidential committees on urban housing and environmental quality, sat on the boards of cultural and educational institutions, and got the company involved in business ventures that reflected social consciousness (in New York's Harlem, for example, Boise helped stake the nation's largest black-owned construction company). But since Hansberger's departure—and since being battered by their collisions with ecology groups and the courts in the early 1970s—Boise has kept a low profile, except for a soft-sell campaign on TV to associate them with "Mother Nature" and all the good things in life.

Where they're going. Fery announced a $2.3 billion improvement plan in 1979 to revamp and expand plants and equipment, rather than to move into new fields. He said Boise has "weathered the bad times" and will stick close to the forest.

Stock performance. Boise Cascade stock bought for $1,000 in 1970 sold for $453 on January 2, 1980.

Access. One Jefferson Square, Boise, Idaho 83728; (208) 384-6161.

 **Champion International**

Sales: $3.8 billion
Profits: $247.1 million
Forbes 500 rank: 122
Rank in forest products: 4
Rank in printing and writing papers: 2
Rank in milk cartons: 2
Rank in plywood: 2
Founded: 1891
Employees: 43,000
Headquarters: Stamford, Connecticut

What they do. Champion is known for their fine papers; but they also make a lot of plain brown paper bags. That's not all. So insatiable are the plywood plants, sawmills, lumber mills, pulp and paper mills, and package factories of Champion International that their 3.4 million acres of timberland supply only half the wood they need. With more than 100 manufacturing facilities in 18 states, Champion makes and sells a long line of wood-derived products, from envelopes to hardwood flooring.

Champion Office Products is the nation's largest office products wholesaler, selling furniture, accessories, and supplies to retail outlets. Another unit, Nationwide Papers, distributes writing and printing papers. These two distribution units do three-quarters of their business in products supplied

by hundreds of manufacturers besides Champion.

History. Champion International was created by the 1967 merger of U.S. Plywood with Champion Paper & Fibre. Champion Paper & Fibre's predecessors had been two turn-of-the-century paper companies. Reuben Robertson, the founder of Champion Fibre, married the daughter of the founder of Champion Coated Paper. U.S. Plywood was founded in 1919 by Lawrence Ottinger, who borrowed $500 to start a company that sold casein glue and World War I–surplus plywood (then a new building material). They didn't get into manufacturing until 1932. (A descendant, Richard Ottinger, is a liberal New York congressman who was narrowly defeated in a 1970 race for the U.S. Senate. His voting record as a congressman made him an enemy in some business circles.)

What may have looked like an ideal marriage in 1967 led to bitter fighting over everything from who gets to use the trees (the plywood or the paper people) to the name of the company. The company first went under the name U.S. Plywood–Champion Paper. The Champion International name was adopted in 1972, which was also the year strongman Karl R. Bendetsen (he commanded the U.S. internment camps for Japanese Americans during World War II) retired at 65, leaving the company in the hands of a former Occidental Petroleum executive, Thomas Willers. Bendetsen had already moved Champion into furniture (Drexel Heritage) and carpets (Trend). Willers, who had worked at Occidental's Hooker Chemicals Corporation, also wanted to expand Champion into chemicals. But Bendetsen, still on the board, didn't like what was happening, and he used his influence to have Willers fired in 1974. The top position was then given to Andrew C. Sigler, who had started with Champion as a sales trainee in 1957.

In the next three years Sigler sold off more than a dozen businesses and emphasized that Champion was going to stick to what they knew best: the forests. That strategy did not preclude the 1977 acquisition of Hoerner Waldorf, the nation's fourth-largest producer of paper packages (grocery bags, folding cartons, cardboard boxes). Hoerner Waldorf itself was formed from the 1966 merger of Hoerner Boxes and Waldorf Paper. The original Hoerner's history goes back to 1920 in Keokuk, Iowa, when the Purity Oats Company needed boxes to ship rolled oats. And Waldorf started in 1886 in St. Paul, Minnesota, when the Baker-Collins Company began printing labels and stationery. Hoerner-Waldorf had acquired the Albemarle Paper Company in 1968.

"The fact is," said *Forbes*, "Hoerner Waldorf and Champion fit beautifully." Champion wanted to get into the packaging business, and Hoerner Waldorf needed trees.

Reputation. Graphic arts people have a high regard for what Champion calls their "fine papers." The company's printed materials, including their annual report to stockholders, look sensational. Their "Imagination" series, a spare-no-expense publication that uses as many kinds of Champion paper in as many ways as a graphic designer can think of, has become a kind of creative catalog in the design field.

What they own. They own 19 softwood plywood plants, 17 sawmills, 34 other wood-processing plants, 6 paper mills, 23 box plants, 24 sheet plants, and 42 other paper and packaging facilities.

Who owns and runs the company. Sigler was named chief executive officer in 1974 but Bendetsen retained his board seat, drawing monthly retirement benefits of $10,450. In 1980 they added their first female director: Elizabeth J. McCormack of the Rockefeller Family Associates.

In the public eye. In their 1978 report to the Securities and Exchange Commission, Champion disclosed eight antitrust actions pending against them in various courts across the country. The most serious were the folding carton conspiracy case, which they agreed to settle for $20 million, and the corrugated container conspiracy case, which they agreed to settle for $24 million. Both involved the Hoerner Waldorf operations.

Where they're going. Sigler says: "We'll go to that part of the world where there's wood." Champion already has a stake in the Brazilian rain forest.

Stock performance. Champion International stock bought for $1,000 in 1970 sold for $760 on January 2, 1980.

Major employment centers. Hamilton-Cincinnati, Ohio area; Pasadena–East Texas area; Canton-Asheville, North Carolina area.

Access. 1 Champion Plaza, Stamford, Connecticut 06921; (203) 358-7000.

Sales: $2.8 billion
Profits: $133.5 million
Forbes 500 rank: 173
Rank in forest products: 6
Founded: 1870
Employees: 32,000
Headquarters: San Francisco, California

What they do. A child of the California Gold Rush, Crown Zellerbach got started when a young entrepreneur realized that San Franciscans were rolling in gold but had no paper to write their accounts on. From a pushcart operation in 1870 Crown Zellerbach developed into one of the giants of the forest products industry, controlling millions of acres of timberland and towering over competitors in the western United States and Canada. Crown Zellerbach newsprint rolls through the presses of 250 Western newspapers, including those in the Hearst chain; their slick paper becomes the pages of *Time*, *Newsweek*, *TV Guide*, and *Sunset*. Their household towel and tissue brands—Chiffon, Zee, and Nice 'n Soft—are market leaders in the West. They also produce bags, boxes, stationery, lumber, plywood, printing ink, and industrial chemicals.

History. In 1848, when gold was discovered at Sutter's Mill, San Francisco was a shanty town of 1,000 people. Two years later the population was 25,000. The goods needed to stabilize the prosperous young city were scarce and expensive: a bucket of water cost $1; a quart of whisky, $40. Anthony Zellerbach, a middle-aged immigrant from Bavaria, arrived in San Francisco in 1868 penniless after failing to make his fortune in the gold fields of the Sierra Nevada mountains. With a wife and two children to support, he decided to sell the least expensive commodity—paper. Soon "Job Lot" Zellerbach was pedaling paper out of a 15-square foot room and pushing his heavily laden cart to printers about town. By 1887 his clever son Isadore (I. Z. for short) had joined the family business. When the 1906 earthquake and fire destroyed all their San Francisco stores and warehouses, they moved across the Bay to Oakland, where, just the day before, I. Z. had purchased another paper company and its entire stock. As one of the few paper suppliers, Zellerbach's supply was in great demand. But I. Z. rationed paper to his regular customers at normal prices, and his refusal to profit from the earthquake established his reputation in the city's business community. A year later I. Z. built the first new business structure in San Francisco after the great earthquake and fire—a seven-story company headquarters. Soon sales offices were opened in Portland, Seattle, Salt Lake City, and San Diego.

In the late 1800s, while "Job Lot" was selling what paper he could get his hands on, other West Coast entrepreneurs were trying to develop reliable local sources of paper. At the time paper was either imported from the East (by way of wagon trains or ships that went around Cape Horn) or made in small local paper mills that used straw or rags for pulp. But there were never enough rags, and occasionally shiploads of rags were brought over from China. When, in the late nineteenth century, East Coast manufacturers figured out an economical way to make paper from wood pulp, a few of their western counterparts realized they could solve their paper shortage problem once and for all. Loggers had begun to chop down the Pacific Coast's forests in the 1840s, but they had scarcely made a dent in the vast timberlands. In the Pacific Northwest the forests were so thick that one acre contained more timber than five acres of heavily wooded areas of Maine or Michigan.

In 1889 the Willamette Pulp & Paper Company began producing the West Coast's first wood pulp paper from a site on the Willamette River, just south of Portland, Oregon. Soon afterward a group of New York financiers followed suit by opening their own mill, called the Crown Paper Company, downstream. Over the next two decades Crown Paper became a major supplier of paper products in the West, including a special kind of tissue paper used to package citrus fruits from California's lush Central Valley. The man responsible for Crown's domination of this fruit paper wrapping market was Louis Bloch. A dropout from the University of California medical school, Bloch began his career in the paper industry as a baler in a small bag plant in San Francisco, where he was paid 75¢ for a 19-hour day. Bloch rose quickly in Crown and helped to negotiate several mergers, including the 1914 merger between Crown and their upstream competitor, Willamette. The Crown Willamette Paper Company, as the new company was called, became the nation's second largest manufacturer of paper.

Fortune smiled on I. Z. Zellerbach once again when in 1927, while touring the battlefields of France, I. Z. ran into Louis Bloch, who was also on vacation. I. Z. suggested a merger, "so you and I can take things easy and let the young fellows do the work," and persisted until Bloch agreed. The resulting Crown Zellerbach Corporation had assets of $92 million in 1928—impressive even by eastern standards.

Crown Zellerbach managed to show a profit for all but one year of the Depression, and during this period the third generation of family management began with the entry of I. Z.'s two sons, James David and Harold. In 1933 J. D. took a then-radical position for a corporation when he supported unionizing efforts by millworkers and loggers. Hints of progressive thinking were also present in the company's early reforestation practices.

After World War II, during which they supplied materials needed for the war effort at cost, Crown Zellerbach started to grow again. Their first big move was to purchase a large pulp and paper mill in British Columbia. They made their first foray outside the West Coast in 1956, when they bought a box company that brought along with it 400,000 acres of southern timberland, a Louisiana paper mill, as well as 17 container plants. Throughout the sixties Crown Zellerbach continued to expand in the United States and several foreign countries, including Holland and Chile. Their growth in eastern U.S. markets led to plant purchases in New York and Virginia in 1978.

Reputation. Although they are one of the largest players in the paper industry,

Crown Zellerbach is not much known outside the West. They have a big presence in the San Francisco Bay Area, which is dotted with their philanthropic contributions to the arts. The Wall Street gang is suspicious because Crown's profit performance is like a yo-yo. And it took them to 1979 to top the profits they made in 1974.

What they own. They own 3.4 million acres of North American timberland; 13 pulp and paper mills; St. Francis Insurance Company of Bermuda.

Who owns and runs the company. Until recently the company has been in tight Zellerbach and Bloch control. William Zellerbach, Anthony's great-grandson, serves as a director and as president of the distribution subsidiary, Zellerbach Paper Company. He holds nearly 200,000 shares of stock—worth about $8 million in early 1980. Former President Reed Hunt initiated the era of non-family management when he took office in 1959. Charles R. Dahl, who joined the company in 1950, was elected chief executive officer in 1970. *Forbes* said it was hard for him to change anything because "the company was dominated by torpor at the operating levels."

In the public eye. The Zellerbachs have long been culturally and politically active. J. D. was a Marshall Plan administrator and an ambassador to Italy under Eisenhower. Harold was a civic leader and patron of the arts—president of the San Francisco Art Commission for 28 years and a director of museum, ballet, and opera organizations. Through foundations he donated millions of dollars to universities and the arts. He died in 1978, but his name is still a fixture in the cultural life of the Bay Area, from the Neighborhood Arts Program truck christened "Harold" in his honor to the University of California's plush Zellerbach Auditorium, which he helped finance with a $1 million gift. Construction of San Francisco's controversial Performing Arts Center, which opened in September 1980, was assured by a $1 million family donation.

Crown Zellerbach conserves by drawing 50% of their energy from wood and pulp wastes and company-generated hydroelectric power. However, Crown Zellerbach mills have been cited for water pollution violations, and the company has been accused of foot dragging in complying with clean air and water standards. They are no stranger to antitrust suits, either, with several cases pending against them for alleged price fixing and other violations.

Where they're going. In 1979 there were rumors that Phillips Petroleum was considering a takeover of Crown. Chairman Dahl reared back and said that would be dastardly of Phillips at a time when the president was beseeching oil companies to put their profits into energy. In early 1980 Crown drilled and found gas on their Louisiana properties.

Stock performance. Crown Zellerbach stock bought for $1,000 in 1970 sold for $1,251 on January 2, 1980.

Access. One Bush Street, San Francisco, California 94104; (415) 823-5000.

Consumer brands.

Toilet paper, facial tissue: Chiffon; Marina; Nice'n Soft; Comfort; Silk.
Paper towels: Spill-Mate; Tuf'n Ready; Zee.
Paper napkins: Linensoft.

Sales: $1.3 billion
Profits: $61.7 million
Forbes 500 rank: 381
Rank in playing cards: 1
Founded: 1881
Employees: 19,300
Headquarters: New York, New York

Diamond International has a problem: inexpensive disposable lighters have become very popular with smokers. It's a problem because Diamond is a big match maker. In fact, they got started in 1881, when the owners of America's largest match makers banded together to form Diamond Match. They were the first to make safe wooden kitchen matches. But if the match business is on the decline, Diamond is consoled by the booming casino business —first in Nevada and then in Atlantic City. That's good news because Diamond owns the Cincinnati-based United States Playing Card Company, the country's largest manufacturer of playing cards under such labels as Bicycle, Bee, and Congress.

Diamond International harvests wood on 1.4 million acres in nine states. In some 45 plants across the country they convert that wood into lumber, packages, labels, checks, business forms, tissues, egg cartons, clothespins, toothpicks, and ice cream sticks. But their fastest-growing business is a retail network of Diamond Building Supply Home Centers, where they sell hardware, tools, lumber, and other homebuilding materials. There are more than 116 of these stores operating in 17 states (the biggest concentrations being in California and New England). Diamond International seems to be most proud of having paid dividends to stockholders every year since 1882; only seven other companies listed on the New York Stock Exchange have paid dividends longer. In 1978 Diamond paid a cash dividend of $2.20 per share. The biggest recipient: France's Generale Occidentale, which bought 600,000 shares (about 5.5% of the stock) in 1979 and was seeking control.

Access. 733 Third Avenue, New York, New York 10017; (212) 697-1700.

Consumer brands.

Matches, clothespins, toothpicks: Diamond.
Paper towels, tissues, napkins: Vanity Fair.
Playing cards and games: Bee; Bicycle; Congress; Tally Ho; Po-Ke-No; Gypsy Witch.
Retail stores: Diamond Building Supply Home Centers.

Georgia·Pacific

Sales: $5.2 billion
Profits: $327 million
Forbes 500 rank: 74
Rank in forest products: 1
Rank in plywood: 1
Rank in lumber: 3
Rank in gypsum: 3
Founded: 1927
Employees: 40,000
Headquarters: Portland, Oregon

What they do. Georgia-Pacific knows exactly what they want to do: cut down trees and turn them into plywood, lumber, and paper. They just can't decide where to run their show. Since opening their doors in 1927, Georgia-Pacific has shifted headquarters from Atlanta, Georgia, to the West Coast—first to Olympia, Washington, and then to Portland, Oregon. Now they plan to return to Atlanta. Georgia-Pacific has extensive tracts of timber in both regions—about four million acres all together. They moved to the West to acquire stands of Douglas fir. Now they see that their southern pine forests (most of them acquired after the move to the West) mature much more quickly—25 to 50 years against 65 to 70 years for a Douglas fir. They can therefore be cut twice as often. There's one other important reason for the move back to the South: three-fourths of Georgia-Pacific products are sold in the eastern states. So Georgia-Pacific (accent on the first syllable) is whistling Dixie once again.

While they may be confused about where to place their headquarters, Georgia-Pacific has never been confused about forests: they view them as money-making resources. Few companies are as good as Georgia-Pacific at squeezing profits out of a tree. Just compare their record with International Paper, whose wood resources dwarf Georgia-Pacific's.

They perfected the technique for manufacturing plywood—and they're number 1 in softwood plywood. They account for 3% of the nation's lumber production. They make wood flooring, siding, and paneling. They produce 13% of the nation's gypsum products, used primarily in drywall construction. Building products account for 70% of their sales. They have also become a large paper producer, accounting for 3% of national output. They make household tissues, paper plates, printing paper, bags, and cardboard boxes. Their tissues are sold under the brand names Coronet and M-D—and also under store labels.

Georgia-Pacific is in the chemical business, too. They went into that business in 1959 to supply the chemicals needed in their plywood plants—resins, for example, to make the glue that holds the plywood layers together. They now make a bunch of basic chemicals for their lumber and pulp and paper plants as well. They're now producing a billion pounds of formaldehyde a year—plus polyvinyl chloride, ammonia, and chlorine, among others. They use 28% of the chemicals they produce and sell the rest to other manufacturers. Their chemical sales are $400 million a year.

History. Many of the big players in the forest products industry started with a strong base: they owned a lot of tree-filled lands. That wasn't the case with Georgia-Pacific. Owen Cheatham, who claimed to be a descendant of Benjamin Franklin, founded the Georgia Hardwood Lumber Company in Augusta, Georgia, in 1927 on an investment of $12,000. He didn't own any land. He simply bought lumber from southern mills and resold it. He was a good salesman. During World War II his company was the largest supplier of lumber to the armed forces. By that time he was also operating five sawmills, but he still didn't own any timberland.

In 1947, when the company was 20 years old, they bought a plywood mill in Bellingham, Washington. Sales were still only $24 million a year. It was in plywood that the company was to make their mark. While veneers (thin layers of wood) had been used by furniture manufacturers for nearly a century, it took two discoveries of the 1930s to make plywood possible. These were synthetic resin adhesive and the so-called "hot press process," which compressed thin layers of glued wood together under heat. These developments made water-resistant plywood a reality. The new product was composed of alternating sheets of veneer tightly glued together, with the grain of each adjacent ply running in a different direction. The result was a wood product that resisted both warping and splitting and was relatively easy to shape. It also had greater structural strength than steel of the same weight. After World War II plywood became a big hit in the construction trade—and Cheatham's company was the first to recognize its potential.

They bought additional plywood mills in Washington and Oregon in 1948, and in that same year changed their name to the Georgia-Pacific Plywood Lumber Company. Headquarters were still in Georgia. And the company was still landless. It was not until 1951 that Cheatham embarked on the timber-buying program that was to stand the industry on its ear. Cheatham and his sidekick, Robert B. Pamplin, were not only plywood innovators, they were financial innovators. They charged into banks and insurance companies and persuaded them to finance the company's purchase of forestlands, pointing out that with an aggressive program of harvesting they would get their money back quickly. Between 1951 and 1957 they borrowed $160 million and bought timberland in the West and in the South. They increased their assets ninefold during that period. In 1953 they moved headquarters nearly 3,000 miles to Olympia, Washington, near one of their plywood mills. A year later they set up headquarters in Portland, Oregon, a state in which they had acquired significant amounts of timberland.

Cheatham and Pamplin continued to follow this strategy: they borrowed heavily to expand their operations in the West and the South. They bought timberlands and manufacturing facilities. Overnight they became a giant of the industry. Between 1955 and 1965 they increased their size by seven times. Once they were a nothing in the forest products business. Suddenly, as the 1970s dawned, only two companies were bigger: Weyerhaeuser and International Paper.

In fact, Georgia-Pacific became so big that they were forced by the Federal Trade Commission in 1972 to sell 20% of their assets. Thus was born Louisiana-Pacific. At birth Louisiana-Pacific ranked as the nation's sixth-largest lumber manufacturer. One competitor griped: "It's bad enough having one Georgia-Pacific for competition, let alone having two." These fears have been borne out. Louisiana-Pacific started off with sales of $270 million; by 1979 sales had climbed to $1.3 billion.

Georgia-Pacific is still buying up others. In 1979 they bought Hudson Pulp & Paper, adding more than 500,000 acres of timberland in Florida and Maine to their resource base.

Georgia-Pacific built a 30-story headquarters building in Portland in 1970. It's the second-tallest building in the city. But in 1978 they decided they would move back to the South in 1982. The decision angered many people in Portland. One resident told the *Los Angeles Times:* "There's a feeling that they came up from the South, liked our trees, cut them down and now they're going back."

Reputation. Georgia-Pacific is regarded as the tough guy of the forest products industry. They blame conservationists and government agencies for timber shortages. But they're beloved on Wall Street for their moneymaking ability.

What they own. They own 4.8 million

acres of timberlands in the United States, Canada, and Brazil, with exclusive cutting rights on another 1.3 million acres in the United States and Indonesia; over 200 plants and mills in the United States, Canada, the Philippines, Brazil, and Indonesia; a 66-year supply of gypsum quarried and mined in seven states and Canada; 92 billion cubic feet of natural gas and 3.3 million barrels of oil in the Gulf of Mexico.

Who owns and runs the company. For their first 49 years of life Georgia-Pacific had only two leaders. The first was their founder, Owen Cheatham, who built up the company in the South and then moved the headquarters across the country. Cheatham retired as chairman in 1967 and died in 1970. His successor, Robert Pamplin, joined Georgia-Pacific as an accountant in 1934. Both were known as autocratic managers who were also risk-takers. "We don't move by committees," Pamplin once told a reporter for *Finance* magazine. "If you don't know enough about something without going to a committee, you haven't got any business being in it. . . . If you need a decision here, you can get it, and if you can't get it from anyone else, come to me and I'll make it." Pamplin stepped down as chairman in 1976 and was succeeded by Robert Floweree, who joined the company in 1952 after his family sold their interest in an Oregon sawmill to Georgia-Pacific. In 1978 Pamplin resigned from the Georgia-Pacific board in a huff because of a new pension plan adopted for salaried employees. Pamplin thought the pension provisions were too costly. The *Wall Street Journal* reported that Pamplin had "ruled with an iron hand." Adoption of the pension plan was probably the first time the board had gone against him. And the last.

In the public eye. In 1968 34 Congressmen asked Georgia-Pacific not to cut a 3,000-acre stand of virgin redwood that was about to be included in a national park. Three other lumber companies who had received similar requests obliged, but not Georgia-Pacific. The redwoods they couldn't wait to cut amounted to about 1/1,000th of their holdings. In 1972 they ranked eighth in a field of 21 pulp and paper companies measured by the Council on Economic Priorities on the adequacy of their pollution control. In 1978 the CEP reported that the company had rectified most of their problems with water pollution at their seven pulp mills.

Georgia-Pacific has an all-white, all-male board of directors. The only female officer is Mary A. McCravey, who is the company's secretary, a post she has held for some 20 years. About a quarter of Georgia-Pacific's U.S. employees are minority group members but they are heavily concentrated in lower-level positions.

Where they're going. Back to Georgia, where they will complete by 1982 a 52-story skyscraper at 123 Peachtree Street (on the site of the theater where *Gone with the Wind* premiered in 1939). They will then replace Coca-Cola as Georgia's biggest corporation. They will keep 500 employees in Portland and have offered to move 400 to Atlanta. Julian Cheatham, brother of the founder of Georgia-Pacific and a director of the company, explained the company's move by saying that people in the South welcome industries with "open arms. . . . They're glad to get you." Cheatham heads his own investment company in Portland. It wasn't known whether he's planning to make the move to Atlanta.

Stock performance. Georgia-Pacific stock bought for $1,000 in 1970 sold for $999 on January 2, 1980.

Access. 900 S.W. Fifth Avenue, Portland, Oregon 97204; (503) 222-5561. There's bass fishing in Lake Georgia-Pacific at Crossett, Arkansas; a Forest Historical Museum at Fort Bragg, California; a Forest Historic Museum at Portland headquarters; and a forest research center at Mosby Creek, Oregon.

Consumer brands.

Toilet paper: Coronet; Coronet Prints; M-D.

Until oil was discoverd in the Middle East in 1908, the Standard Oil Company, owned by John D. Rockefeller, controlled two-thirds of the oil supply known to the world.

INTERNATIONAL PAPER COMPANY

Sales: $4.5 billion
Profits: $525.3 million
Forbes 500 rank: 90
Rank in forest products: 2
Rank in paper: 1
Rank in corrugated shipping containers: 1
Rank in specialty newsprint: 1
Founded: 1898
Employees: 51,000
Headquarters: New York, New York

What they do. International Paper is living proof that when you own enough acres of timberland, you can make a lot of mistakes and not suffer too badly. The trees keep growing, the mills keep running, and the managers continue convivial lunches in New York with their bankers. International Paper owns or controls close to 20 million acres of North American forestland, which they believe makes them the largest private holder of timberland in the world. Still, Wall Street analysts and financial reporters seem irked that the company doesn't do more with these resources—in other words, pile up bigger profits. If all the speculations about management at International Paper were collected, they would fill a fair-sized scrapbook.

International is the world's leading supplier of printing and writing papers. About 40% of their business is in packaging materials, which they make into cartons and boxes or sell to other container manufacturers.

Out of their forests and mills every year come millions of board feet of lumber and plywood, sold mostly to the construction industry, though they themselves own some building materials stores.

International Paper's sales from manufacturing operations outside the United States were close to $1 billion in 1978; one-quarter of that was newsprint made in Canada and sold to U.S. customers.

They also own Davol, a maker of innovative medical and health products, such as a closed-wound suction set and electro-surgical equipment.

History. International Paper began in 1898 with a merger of 20 New England and New York paper mills. For many years their self-image was "massive," and their sole purpose to cut trees and keep the mills running. While other companies innovated and experimented, International just bought more mills and more land. Despite a management that was stolid and unimaginative, International Paper grew into a behemoth that, though it had no real problems of survival, had no bright prospects either.

From 1943 until the 1960s International Paper was lethargically run by the Hinman family; when Edward Hinman took over in 1966. One former executive told *Forbes*, "I never once heard him make a decision. He'd say, 'That's very interesting,' and leave the room." Hinman stayed in the board room long enough to embark on a program that turned out to be disastrous. Between 1968 and 1970 International Paper acquired Davol, two housing development companies, and built a $50 million plant to make tissues and disposable diapers. Davol turned out to be a solid investment, but the housing companies fell right into a real estate recession. And the tissue factory? Banging heads with Procter & Gamble and Kimberly-Clark brought $14 million losses the first two years.

In 1969 the board brought in Frederick R. Kappel as chairman to stem the mounting losses. Kappel was retired chairman of American Telephone & Telegraph, and he worked only part-time, trying to bring some order to the place. In 1971, when Hinman left the company, Kappel brought in as the new chief another AT&T veteran, Paul Gorman (he had been head of Western Electric). Kappel then left. Gorman, who said in advance he wanted to stay only two years, brought in a bunch of managers from Mobil, and the reorganization of IP continued. When Gorman stepped down as planned in 1973, the board went outside again and lured J. Stanford Smith, a 37-year veteran of General Electric, to become chairman. Smith began saying that the company was in the "land resources management business" rather than simply a forest products company and steered International Paper through a merger in 1975 with General Crude Oil of Houston, an oil exploration and production firm that operates in Canada and on the Gulf Coast. Smith also initiated the company's first rudimentary management-training program. But the program had not been in place long enough to groom a new president for the company. The board again picked an outsider, Edwin A. Gee of Du Pont, who became president in April 1978 and replaced Smith as chairman in January 1980.

Gee said his top priority as chairman was to strengthen top management so his replacement could come from within the corporation. Gee had a maverick image with Du Pont—he zipped around the Wilmington, Delaware, headquarters in his Jaguars and Porsches—and he seemed to change the atmosphere at International Paper's New York offices by appearing in a cardigan sweater and golf socks. Gee was behind several major deals in the summer of 1979, when International Paper sold off General Crude Oil for about $800 million and bought Bodcaw, which owns 320,000 acres of soft pine forests. Gee also plans to spend $4 billion by 1983 to update facilities and build the world's largest linerboard mill in Mansfield, Louisiana.

Reputation. International Paper's reputation as the stumbling giant of the industry is attributed to poor management. They have had to go to outside corporations for their last three leaders, and in recent years have recruited other executives from NATO and Citibank. One officer imported from an oil company kept referring to paper mills as refineries.

What they own. International Paper owns 7.1 million acres of U.S. timberland (69% in the South, 24% in the Northeast, 7% in the West). In addition, they own 1.3 million acres in Canada, and they lease 11 million more in Quebec. They own 16 paper mills in the United States, 7 in Canada, and 1 in Italy; 86 packaging plants in 27 states, 7 foreign countries, and Puerto Rico; and numerous lumber mills, plywood facilities, and other plants.

Who owns and runs the company. No one really owns International Paper—it's like a headless monster. All the directors and officers together own little more than one-tenth of 1% of the stock. When Edwin Gee came from Du Pont to be president in 1978, some Wall Street analysts criticized the selection because he had no experience in the forest products industry; International Paper responded that while at Du Pont Gee had sold pigments to the paper industry. Another IP executive said: "See who got us into these problems in the first place—experts in the paper business." To get Gee,

International Paper forked over a onetime payment of $700,000 (to cover his DuPont benefits), bought his house in Wilmington for resale, and moved him to New York, for a grand total of $529,200. In addition, his starting salary was $250,000 a year, plus a guaranteed $150,000 incentive bonus for 1978.

One of Gee's first recruits was John A. Georges, a 49-year-old chemical engineer from Du Pont. He's now vice-chairman and a possible successor to Gee. In 1980 a disgruntled, ex-IP executive described to *Business Week* the turmoil of the past decade: "Kappel and Gorman spoke AT&T management language. Then Gorman brought in a lot of senior people from Mobil Corp., and they had their own language. We had some more of that with Smith's GE language. And now we've got Du Pont. You have to keep learning a new vocabulary."

In the public eye. Mill closings are a fact of life for a forest products executive, but not for the families of employees. When International Paper decided to unload their plant in Panama City, Florida, in 1978, a worker remarked bitterly: "I'm going to send the president of the board word that I hope he had the same kind of Christmas that 950 families in Panama City have had. . . ." (From their sale of the Panama City plant and 420,000 acres of associated woodlands, International Paper realized $90 million in profits.)

In 1973 the controversial closing of the International Paper mill in Temiscaming, Quebec, was the subject of a Canadian Film Board documentary called *The Town That Wouldn't Die.*

In 1970 International Paper was deluged with protests after running a two-page magazine ad featuring the story of "the disposable environment—the kind of fresh thinking we bring to every problem."

Where they're going. As long as we're in this disposable age, International Paper has a bright future, no matter who's running the company.

Stock performance. International Paper stock bought for $1,000 in 1970 sold for $996 on January 2, 1980.

Access. 220 East 42nd Street, New York, New York 10017; (212) 490-6000.

✳ Kimberly-Clark Corporation

Sales: $2.2 billion
Profits: $314.4 million
Forbes 500 rank: 241
Rank in forest products: 9
Rank in sanitary napkins: 1
Rank in tampons: 3
Rank in facial tissues: 1
Founded: 1872
Employees: 29,867
Headquarters: Neenah, Wisconsin

What they do. It may seem ludicrous to think of a stand of trees turning into Kleenex, but that's mainly what Kimberly-Clark does. Most of the big forest products companies convert the trees they cut down into lumber, plywood, boxes, and papers that are sold, for the most part, to other companies. Kimberly-Clark does sell some lumber and newsprint, but about 60% of their sales are in disposable consumer products sold under well-known brand names. In addition to pop-up tissues, they make menstrual-care products (napkins and tampons); paper towels; toilet paper; napkins; and the disposable linens, gowns, and wrappers used widely in hospitals. Kimberly-Clark thus has more of a feel for the consumer marketplace than other forest products companies, which makes them more outgoing than their competitors, and perhaps more responsive to public concerns. There's frequently a high moral tone to their business pronouncements.

The main ingredient in Kimberly-Clark's products is pulp, the result of mashing wood or other plant life with water or chemicals. Wood pulp is used predominantly, but the company also uses pulp from sugarcane stalks (called bagasse) to make the wadding for Kotex napkins; flax straw pulp from the northern Midwest and Canada for the thin papers of cigarettes, tea bags, and Bibles; and cotton pulp for fine writing paper. The company even mashes used paper and recycles it into pulp to make new paper.

The average American uses 8.3 boxes of facial tissues a year, which amounts to $500 million in sales; Kleenex holds 35% of that market. The average American household uses 7.5 rolls of disposable household towels a year, for sales of $930 million; Kimberly-Clark brands (Kleenex and Hi-Dri) hold about 15% of that market. The average American woman uses 100 sanitary napkins a year, bringing in sales of $350 million; Kimberly-Clark brands (Kotex and New Freedom) hold about 45% of that market. That same "average American woman" uses 91 tampons annually—a $250 million market, of which Kotex tampons' share is 10%.

Though nearly 40% of Kimberly-Clark's sales are in foreign countries, the United States provides almost 80% of their profits.

History. Kimberly-Clark has always been based in Neenah, a town in east-central Wisconsin seven miles south of Appleton, on Lake Winnebago. In 1872 four young men of Neenah invested $7,500 apiece to establish a business making newsprint from linen and cotton rags; before that the nearest source of newsprint had been a mill 300 miles east of Wisconsin. The company was named for two of the principals, John A. Kimberly and Charles B. Clark. (Later a mill town on the Fox River north of Appleton was named for Kimberly.) Of the four founders only John Kimberly survived beyond the first decade of this century. Elected president when the company was incorporated in 1880, Kimberly held that position until 1928, when he died at age 90. Clark, who became a congressman from Wisconsin, died in 1891.

In their early days Kimberly-Clark made newsprint, writing paper, and wrapping paper. They were the first to manufacture paper for printing photographs on a rotary press, a process called rotogravure. For many years after 1915 virtually all the rotogravure printing done in America was on paper from Kimberly-Clark mills. During World War I, when surgical cotton was in short supply, Kimberly-Clark scientists came up with a substitute—a creped cellulose wadding made from bagasse and called "cellucotton." This discovery was to change Kimberly-Clark in an unexpected way. Army nurses found a new use for the wadding: as a sanitary napkin that could be thrown away rather than laundered and reused. In 1920 Kimberly-Clark warily introduced the napkin to consumers as Kotex. Embarrassed to be associated with such a personal product, they set up a separate sales company, International Cellucotton Products, and marketed Kotex in a plain brown wrapper.

In 1924 another consumer product arrived: Kleenex. Also assigned to International Cellucotton, they promoted it first as a substitute for the "cold cream towel" that used to be found in bathrooms to remove cosmetics. Once again consumers showed the company which way to go, writing to say what a great disposable handkerchief it made. The hankie appeal was tested in Peoria, Illinois, in 1930—and it far outdrew the "cold cream towel" pitch. When they began national advertising to promote Kleenex as a disposable handkerchief, sales doubled. Kotex and Kleenex developed into Kimberly-Clark's one-two punch. They became such familiar household words that many people still use them as generic terms for facial tissues and sanitary napkins.

During World War II International Cellucotton signed up the cartoon character Little Lulu to promote Kleenex. At the time Margaret Buell, Little Lulu's creator, drew the cartoon for the old *Saturday Evening Post*. Curtis Publishing, publisher of the *Post*, gave permission for the character to be used in ads, if the ads ran only in newspapers. A few years later Curtis changed their mind and gave Mrs. Buell an ultimatum: choose between the *Saturday Evening Post* and Kleenex. She chose Kleenex, and Little Lulu and Kleenex were a team for 16 years. International Cellucotton was finally admitted into the Kimberly-Clark corporate embrace in 1955. It was in the 1960s that Tampax's tampon began to make serious inroads in the menstrual-care market, as the product of choice for young people. Kimberly-Clark stayed with their older customers—and saw their market share drop each year.

Kimberly-Clark established their first base outside the United States in the 1920s, when they built a paper mill at Kapuskasing, Ontario. In 1926 they became partners with the *New York Times* in building a newsprint mill at Kapuskasing. They began selling Kleenex and Kotex abroad in 1925; today they operate in 21 countries and sell their products in about 160 countries.

Reputation. On Wall Street some observers regard Kimberly-Clark as a "paper tiger" because they have lost ground to competitors in recent years. In 1976 *Forbes* said the company's "once-mighty roar now sounds more than a little squeaky." On the other hand, employees and communities know Kimberly-Clark as a company that cares about them. You just can't make those people on Wall Street happy.

What they own. Kimberly-Clark made their first timberland purchases in 1902. Today they own nearly 1 million acres in the United States, primarily in Alabama, Georgia, and South Carolina. And they have access to one of the largest forest resources of any wood products company through their leasing of 11.8 million acres of government land in Ontario, Canada. They sold their 320,000 acres of California forestland in 1979.

Who owns and runs the company. William E. Kimberly, great-grandson of the founder, was named senior vice-president in charge of consumer products in 1979, but he is not on the board of directors. Darwin E. Smith, who rose from the legal and financial sides, became chief executive officer in 1971. Kimberly-Clark seems to have a more interesting board than most companies. The members include two women—Pastora San Juan Cafferty, a social service administration professor at the University of Chicago, and Dr. Evalyn Stolaroff Gendel, a clinical professor at the University of California medical school; Claudio X. Gonzalez, head of Kimberly-Clark's Mexican subsidiary; and Father John P. Raynor, president of Marquette University.

Kimberly-Clark offers employees some unusual benefits. In addition to the traditional health insurance programs, they have at Neenah a $2.5 million physical fitness complex, staffed by 15 full-time health-care professionals, who work with employees on an illness prevention program. All costs are paid by the company. Kimberly-Clark also has a widely heralded "dollars-for-culture" plan, in which the company pays tuition for employees who want to pursue courses in any field (they don't have to be job-related). Each employee receives an annual allotment of about $480 for such educational purposes. If the money is not used, it reverts to the company at the end of the year.

In the public eye. Kimberly-Clark is one of the few companies in the forest products industry that was not a party to an antitrust suit during the closing years of the 1970s. In 1977 the company instructed all their advertising agencies to refrain from buying commercials on any programs marked by "excessive violence or antisocial behavior." In 1978 they issued to directors a series of background papers on their South African operations, indicating that they were considering a proposal to sell their 39% interest in a South African company, Carlton Paper. The board of directors went to South Africa for nine days, visiting the Carlton facilities and meeting with religious, political, business, and academic leaders. Finally they decided that the investment in South Africa should be retained because "it is one of the many positive forces for change" in that country. The board also stated that future investment in South Africa would be viewed in light of the "progress of the South African government towards eliminating laws and practices which deprive employees of their human rights."

Stock performance. Kimberly-Clark stock bought for $1,000 in 1970 sold for $1,028 on January 2, 1980.

Access. Neenah, Wisconsin 54956; (414) 729-1212. Consumer complaints or inquiries should be addressed to: Consumer Communications Department, West Office Building, Neenah, Wisconsin 54956.

Consumer brands.

Menstrual-care products: Kotex; New Freedom; Fems.
Facial and bathroom tissue: Kleenex; Boutique; Casuals; Little Travelers; Man-Size; Delsey; Popee; Dawn; Wondersoft.
Paper towels: Kleenex; Boutique; Teri; Hi-Dri; Thick & Thirsty.
Disposable diapers: Kleenex; Huggies; Super Dry.

∩ead

Sales: $2.6 billion
Profits: $141 million
Forbes 500 rank: 197
Rank in forest products: 7
Rank in paper: 5
Founded: 1846
Employees: 28,500
Headquarters: Dayton, Ohio

What they do. Mead used to be thought of as a sleepy little family-owned paper company, but no more. After fending off a 1978 takeover attempt by Occidental Petroleum, and waging one of the most vicious inter-company battles in history, Mead gained a new respect from the business community.

Mead made possible America's love affair with the throwaway container. They are the world's largest supplier of cardboard beverage carriers (like the six-pack) and a pioneer of packaging for the food and beverage industries. Besides making things easier to carry home from the grocery store, Mead has 1.4 million acres of U.S. timberland from which they produce lumber, furniture, and paper products. These account for about 75% of their profits. The rest comes either from industrial parts like rubber fittings for the oil-equipment industry and precision castings for autos, or from coal mining. They sold about 800,000 tons of coal to the steel industry in 1978.

History. In 1846 Colonel Daniel Mead bought a part interest in the small Ellis, Chafflin & Co. paper mill in Dayton, Ohio. By 1882 he had succeeded in buying out his partners and renamed the firm Mead Paper. But after his death in 1891, his heirs allowed the company to sag. In 1905 Mead fell into receivership.

Salvation came in the person of one of the colonel's grandsons—a polo-playing 28-year-old named George Mead—who made a public stock offering and managed to turn the company around by 1915, in spite of a serious paper slump in 1908–1909. By the 1920s, Mead's researchers had discovered a way to convert wood chips into cardboard; and by 1930, the company had several plants making cardboard for the container industry.

George Mead retired in 1942 and a new generation of managers took over, helped along by the post–World War II economic boom. By 1970 Mead had picked up more than 40 smaller companies in such fields as steel, coal, rubber, cement, fabrics, and school and office supplies. By 1978 they became a primary target for acquisition-hungry Occidental Petroleum. Mead's new president, Warren Batts, decided to fight the merger, and the battle was on.

Mead executives devoted their entire time for months fighting the deal. Their strategy was to shock Occidental into withdrawing by airing the oil company's extensive line of dirty laundry. They publicized the fact that Oxy chairman Armand Hammer had been convicted of illegal campaign contributions in 1972; they accused Oxy of fraud and extortion; and, perhaps more damaging, they played on the public's animosity toward Hooker Chemical, an Oxy subsidiary which had poisoned the Love Canal area in upstate New York with chemical discharges. In December 1978, after five months of bloody combat, Occidental gave up, but not before the David-and-Goliath warfare had captured Wall Street's imagination and sent Mead stock skyrocketing. (Once the fight was over, the stock price went down sharply.)

Reputation. As the result of the takeover battle, Mead is now seen as a tough, independent company with a solid management group. It will be a while before a big company with Oxy-like skeletons in its closet attempts a forced merger with them. In 1979 the *New York Times* called them "born-again."

What they own. Mead has three main paper manufacturing plants in the United States: at Chillicothe, Ohio; Kingsport, Tennessee; and Escanaba, Michigan. They are supplied primarily by 665,000 acres of company-owned U.S. timberland; (another 750,000 acres are leased).

Who owns and runs the company. The Meads are still prominent. Two Meads and a Mead brother-in-law sit on the board. So does Barbara Jordan, the former Texas Congresswoman, the only black and the only woman on the board. The fight against Occidental was led by Warren L. Batts, who joined the company in 1971 and became chief executive officer in 1978. Batts was credited with reorganizing the management during the 1970s and putting Mead on a more competitive basis. He set the tone for the defense against Oxy, coming to the office one day wearing a blue sweatshirt that bore the words "ferocious management" and a picture of a lion. Early in 1980 Batts, 47, suddenly announced his resignation for "personal reasons." James W. McSwiney, who held the top post for 10 years prior to the election of Batts, moved back into the chief executive's chair.

In the public eye. Mead is one of the few corporations with employee membership on a committee of the board of directors. This is their Corporate Responsibility Committee, which meets four times a year to decide what civic activities Mead will participate in and what charities they'll contribute to, and it also monitors such programs as equal employment opportunity. The committee is composed of six directors and six employees.

Where they're going. Like many other paper companies—most notably, Boise-Cascade—Mead got their fingers burned in the late 1960s by dabbling in real estate. Made more cautious by the experience, Mead has now chosen to look into more stable areas. At the moment they're looking into data processing. They've developed LEXIS, an electronic law library for lawyers and law schools. In 1979 they introduced a small terminal model that will give lawyers access to LEXIS from their desks. And now they have followed up with NEXIS, an electronic library of newspapers and magazines.

Stock performance. Mead stock bought for $1,000 in 1970 sold for $1,800 on January 2, 1980.

Access. Courthouse Plaza Northwest, Dayton, Ohio 45463; (512) 222-6323.

SCOTT

Sales: $1.9 billion
Profits: $137.1 million
Forbes 500 rank: 277
Rank in forest products: 10
Rank in toilet paper: 1
Rank in paper towels: 1
Rank in wax paper: 1
Founded: 1879
Employees: 20,400
Headquarters: Philadelphia, Pennsylvania

What they do. Scott is the defending champion of what's known as the Great Toilet Paper War. They originated soft toilet paper and used to advertise it quite frankly as a product that wouldn't give you hemorrhoids. Scott recently lost a couple of battles to Procter & Gamble (P & G's Charmin and Bounty brands have captured number 1 positions in toilet paper and paper towels, respectively), but Scott still produces more toilet paper, paper towels, paper napkins, and wax paper than anyone else.

Scott sat back in their Philadelphia headquarters, as *Forbes* says, "apparently cocksure of predominance" before they realized they were under siege from Procter & Gamble. They have retaliated by greatly increasing their advertising and by introducing seven types of toilet paper, three kinds of paper towels, three styles of paper napkins, and premoistened tissues for babies—but they now have to fight a lot harder for each dollar of profit.

Scott supplies almost half the wood pulp necessary for their paper products from their own timberland. Some of this pulp is also used to make paper for printing and book publishing.

Scott has branched into areas where P & G is not represented. They now make polyurethane foam for carpet cushions and soundproofing. They also produce lighting fixtures and aluminum and rattan furniture. But household papers account for 63% of their sales.

History. During the Victorian era most Americans used outdoor privies and rough sheets of yellow paper clamped together with staples as their toilet paper. E. Irvin and Clarence Scott, two brothers who sold scratch paper and bags from a pushcart trundled through the streets of Philadelphia in 1879, changed all that. The brothers bought tissue in large rolls from manufacturers and converted it to toilet rolls for home use, especially for the new indoor bathrooms then coming into vogue.

After a brief, and disastrous, foray into the bicycle business (one of their Great Scott bikes fell apart during an important race), they stuck to the toilet paper business, which had as many as 2,800 brand names (such as Foldum, Twilldu, Krect, and Kowntit). In 1905 Irvin's son, Arthur Hoyt Scott, convinced his father to push only a few quality tissues. He also thought up the company's slogan, "soft as old linen," to describe Scott's soft tissue.

By 1907 Scott had also introduced the paper towel, after they received a shipment of paper too rough to use for toilet tissue. The company broke into national magazine advertising in 1919, but their masterpieces of crassness did not appear until the 1930s, when they pictured a suffering man alongside the headline, "I've got to have a minor operation" (hemorrhoids). Other ads read, "They have a pretty house, Mother, but their bathroom paper hurts."

After Arthur's death in 1927, his former Swarthmore College fraternity brother, Thomas McCabe, took over as president and served as chief executive officer for 40 years (he is still a director). Scott maintained their big lead in paper under his management but they were stunned at first by the Procter & Gamble challenge. P & G, in effect, beat Scott at their own game. After buying the small Charmin paper mills, they had special machinery built to produce a super-soft tissue. And on that product edge they built the long-running, highly successful "Don't Squeeze the Charmin" campaign. P & G did to Scott what Scott had done to their competitors 50 years ago. Scott's comeback is being directed now by their new president, Morgan Hunter. He was trained by Procter & Gamble.

Reputation. Philadelphia gentlemen who seem ill cast for front line duty in the toilet paper war.

What they own. They own 3.2 million acres of timberland in Washington, Ala-

THE BIG TEN PAPER COMPANIES

Sales (1979)

1. GEORGIA–PACIFIC	$5.2 *billion*
2. INTERNATIONAL PAPER	$4.5 *billion*
3. WEYERHAEUSER	$4.4 *billion*
4. CHAMPION INTERNATIONAL	$3.8 *billion*
5. BOISE CASCADE	$2.9 *billion*
6. CROWN ZELLERBACH	$2.8 *billion*
7. MEAD	$2.6 *billion*
8. ST. REGIS PAPER	$2.5 *billion*
9. KIMBERLY–CLARK	$2.2 *billion*
10. SCOTT PAPER	$1.9 *billion*

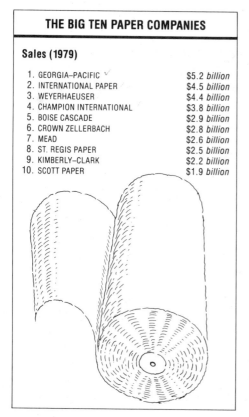

bama, Mississippi, Georgia, Florida, and South Carolina. They also own timberland in British Columbia and Nova Scotia. Their 26 plants are in 15 states, mostly in the Midwest and the East. Scott owns interests in subsidiaries in 17 countries throughout South America, Europe, the Far East, Canada, and Australia.

Who owns and runs the company. The 1979 proxy statement showed that Thomas B. McCabe, then 86, was still the largest single shareholder, with 2% of the stock. Charles D. Dickey, Jr., who joined the company in 1946 as a salesman, became chief executive officer in 1973. He was described by *Forbes* as "a shy, numbers-oriented man who isn't given to communicating." Seeing no one below him as a possible successor, Dickey brought in Morgan Hunter in 1979. Hunter resigned from the presidency of R. J. Reynolds Tobacco to take the Scott challenge. Since 1977 Claudine B. Malone, a black woman who teaches at the Harvard business school, has been on the board.

In the public eye. Scott paid $1 million in fines and penalties to the state of Wisconsin and the federal government for water pollution violations at their Oconto Mills, Wisconsin, pulp mill, which they closed in 1978. However, their mill in Everett, Washington, now has one of the most effective pollution-control systems in the paper industry, thanks to an investment of $55 million during the 1970s. The company told stockholders in 1979 that the Everett plant now emits only "an occasional puff of steam."

Where they're going. Scott has such valuable properties that they can always sell some of them to make money while they battle the likes of P & G. As 1980 got underway Scott was moving to sell 100,000 acres of timberland on Vancouver Island in British Columbia. The sale was expected to balloon Scott's profits by some $50 million.

Stock performance. Scott stock bought for $1,000 in 1970 sold for $536 on January 2, 1980.

Access. Scott Plaza, Philadelphia, Pennsylvania 19113; (215) 521-5000.

Consumer brands.

Toilet paper: ScotTissue; Waldorf; Soft-Weve; Lady Scott; Family Scott; Cottonelle; Soft'n Pretty.
Paper towels: ScotTowels; Viva; Job Squad.
Table products: Scotkins; Viva; Scott Family napkins.
Facial tissues: Scotties; Lady Scott.
Food wraps: Cut-Rite waxed paper.
Sanitary napkins: Confidets.
Baby wipes: Baby Fresh.
Furniture and lighting products: Brown Jordan.

Sales: $1.4 billion
Profits: $151 million
Forbes 500 rank: 359
Rank in forest products industry: 11
Founded: 1852
Employees: 15,175
Headquarters: Wayne, New Jersey

Union Camp's profits are in the bag—the paper bag, that is. They got their start in 1852 when a Pennsylvania schoolteacher named Francis Wolle invented the first machine to manufacture paper bags, and to this day the company still makes more of them than anyone else. They're also one of the biggest lumber producers east of the Mississippi River, and they enjoy the dubious distinction of operating the largest chemical business of any forest products company, turning out such wood-based items as tall oil rosin, fatty acids, and turpentine derivatives.

Although Union Camp's executives work out of an office right across the Hudson River from New York City, this is very much a Southern company. Their 1.7 million tree-filled acres are located in six south-

> **62,860 trees must be cut down to provide pulp for a single Sunday edition of the *New York Times*.**

ern states: Alabama, Florida, Georgia, North and South Carolina, and Virginia. Most of these trees are cut and fed into pulp and paper mills or lumber and plywood plants. About 60% of the pulp and paperboard that emerges from the mills is then run through a network of 32 plants for conversion to paper bags and corrugated boxes. The rest is sold to other converters.

Union Camp also owns Moore Handley, which operates a chain of 48 Homecrafters stores in six southeastern states. These sell building materials to professional builders and do-it-yourself homeowners alike. A Moore Handley wholesale division runs a franchise hardware business under the Hardware House trade name.

Large donations to the federal Nature Conservancy (including 50,000 acres of Virginia's Great Dismal Swamp and another 15,000 acres of Georgia's Okefenokee Swamp) have not erased Union Camp's past performance on environmental issues. In 1935, when they built their massive paper mill—the world's largest—in Savannah, Georgia, during the Depression, the city agreed in writing to excuse Union Camp from all responsibility for air or water pollution. The city even promised to pay Union Camp's legal expenses to the tune of $5,000 per lawsuit. By the early 1970s, the Savannah mill was responsible for an estimated 80% of the pollution flowing into the Savannah River. A Union Camp manager at the time responded to questions about the possibility of industrial pumping drying up the underground water supplies: "I don't know. I won't be here." The company's environmental protection plan of the early 1970s can be summed up in the remarks of Union Camp's director of Air and Water Pollution: "It probably won't hurt mankind a whole hell of a lot in the long run if the whooping crane doesn't quite make it."

Stock performance. Union Camp stock bought for $1,000 in 1970 sold for $2,040 on January 2, 1980.

Access. 1600 Valley Road, Wayne, New Jersey 07470; (201) 628-9000. The company's paper mill in Franklin, Virginia, has a tour for the general public on the second Wednesday of every month at 7:30 P.M. The mills in Savannah and in Montgomery, Alabama, also provide tours.

Weyerhaeuser

Sales: $4.4 billion
Profits: $512.2 million
Forbes 500 rank: 93
Rank in forest products: 3
Rank in lumber: 1
Rank in plywood: 3
Rank in treeplanting: 1
Rank in home building (single-family): 5
Founded: 1900
Employees: 48,000
Headquarters: Tacoma, Washington

What they do. Timbermen used to be like hunters, chopping down virgin stands of forest and dragging away the spoils. Today they're more like corporate farmers—thanks to Weyerhaeuser, by their own description "the tree-growing company." Each year Weyerhaeuser (pronounced *wire-houser*) plants close to 200 million trees in their vast forests, which cover more ground than the state of Massachusetts. They own nearly 6 million acres of timberland, about half of it in the Pacific Northwest, where the main tree is Douglas fir, and the rest in the South, where the lofty southern pine holds sway. They also cut trees on government land in Canada and the Far East.

Just as Chinese chefs are said to use every part of the duck but the quack, Weyerhaeuser has a customer for just about every part of the tree but the bark (and they have found a few uses for that too). When a felled tree arrives at a Weyerhaeuser lumber mill, it is scanned by lasers and aligned by a computer for the best possible cuts into boards. Much of the wood that can't be used for lumber goes into plywood, which is laminated in sheets from several pieces of wood. Leftover parts are chopped into chips and ground into pulp, which provides the basic material for paper, corrugated cardboard, grocery bags, milk cartons, and a host of other products from photographic film to the disposable diapers sold by J. C. Penney. Remaining scraps, shavings, and sawdust go into particleboard (reconstituted "boards" made of little wood pieces pressed and glued together) or artificial fireplace "logs"; or they are burned to produce heat and power for Weyerhaeuser's mills, which ge..erate two-thirds of the energy they use. Many of Weyerhaeuser's trees by-pass this treatment by being shipped as logs to Japan —a controversial practice in the Northwest. Nearly one-third of Weyerhaeuser's sales come from outside the United States.

Chopping down trees is only half of Weyerhaeuser's business. Joyce Kilmer may have been right when he said that only God can make a tree, but Weyerhaeuser believes in giving the deity a helping hand. They have pioneered what they call high-yield forestry, combining genetics, soil analysis, and computer science to determine how to get the most cubic feet of wood out of the forest in the shortest amount of time. A Weyerhaeuser tree, chosen from parents who grew straight, tall, and fast, starts as a seedling in an outdoor nursery, where it is irrigated, fertilized, and sprayed with animal repellent to keep deer and other creatures from having it for lunch. Around age 3, when it is a foot or so high, it is transplanted to the forest. There it is periodically bombarded with fertilizers from helicopters, while its neighboring alders, unwanted by Weyerhaeuser, are wiped out by herbicides. (They used 2,4,5-T, the Vietnam defoliant, until the Environmental Protection Agency temporarily suspended its use.) Every five years the forest is thinned out from below, with weaker trees removed to give more light and growing space to the others. The harvest comes when the trees are about 50 years old, and a crew clear-cuts an area of 250 acres or so, cutting down every tree. Weyerhaeuser figures they get twice as much lumber from an acre as Mother Nature could produce left to her own devices. Within a year they plant the next crop.

In recent years Weyerhaeuser has become a user of lumber as well. They bought up a string of local developers and builders, from Pardee in Los Angeles to Babcock in Coral Gables, Florida, and they are now a major homebuilder.

History. Frederick Weyerhaeuser came to the United States from Germany in 1852, at age 18. After a stint as a brewer's apprentice in Pennsylvania, he noticed that "brewers became confirmed drunkards" and moved to Illinois, where he worked in a sawmill and lumber yard. His boss went broke in the panic of 1858, and Weyerhaeuser bought the yard at a sheriff's auction. Over

---

PRICE-FIXING COSTS PAPER COMPANIES $535 MILLION

The major paper companies paid out over $535 million in fines and damages between 1972 and 1978 for illegally fixing prices on paper bags, plywood, and folding cartons. The cases, brought by the Justice Department or the Federal Trade Commission, saw the following actions taken against the offenders:

Amount of fines or damages*

1. CONTAINER CORPORATION OF AMERICA (*subsidiary of Mobil*) $58 million
2. WEYERHAEUSER $54 million
3. CHAMPION INTERNATIONAL (*Hoerner Waldorf division*) $47 million
4. INTERNATIONAL PAPER $42 million
5. OWENS-ILLINOIS $33 million
6. CONTINENTAL GROUP $32 million
7. BOISE CASCADE $26 million
8. FEDERAL PAPER BOARD $16 million
9. STONE CONTAINER $15 million
10. MEAD $14 million
11. WILLAMETTE INDUSTRIES $11 million
12. DIAMOND INTERNATIONAL $11 million
13. ST. REGIS PAPER (*Michigan Lithographic*) $11 million
14. POTLATCH $10 million

*Some cases are still under appeal.

Source: *Forbes*, June 15, 1979.

---

the next 40 years he built a prosperous lumber business, heading a syndicate that bought up sawmills and timberlands in Wisconsin and Minnesota. In 1891 he moved his family to St. Paul, where his next-door neighbor was James J. Hill, the Northern Pacific Railroad tycoon. Hill sold Weyerhaeuser 900,000 acres in Washington for $6 an acre, and the Weyerhaeuser Timber Company was born. Soon Weyerhaeuser picked up another 200,000 acres in Oregon for $5 an acre. By the time he died in 1914, he had bought nearly 2 million acres of timberland in the Northwest at an average price of $8.80 an acre. Most of that land is still on the company books at the original cost, for tax purposes. The real value of Weyerhaeuser's timber holdings is estimated at around $7 billion.

The company grew fast, boosted by cheaper shipping provided by the 1914 opening of the Panama Canal and the surge in demand for forest products during World War I. In the 1930s Weyerhaeuser adopted the slogan "Timber is a crop" and pioneered the concept of maintaining a perpetual harvest on the land, in contrast to the prevailing practice of "cut and run." In 1941 they dedicated the nation's first tree farm, in Washington State.

Weyerhaeuser acquired southern lands

after World War II, buying logged-out areas of Mississippi and Louisiana and replanting them. In 1957 they added 400,000 acres in North Carolina when they bought Kieckhefer Container and Eddy Paper. In 1969 they picked up more land in Oklahoma and Arkansas by buying Dierks Forests.

Weyerhaeuser operates out of one of the most spectacular corporate headquarters in America. The five-story building between Seattle and Tacoma overlooks a 10-acre lake and, beyond an expanse of forests, commands a view of majestic Mt. Rainier. Its rooftop terraces are covered with ivy. Inside are tapestries of forest scenes and a jungle of potted plants. It houses a library, barber shop, and gym. The company's president and his chief lieutenants occupy top-floor offices separated only by shoulder-high partitions. There are very few doors in the complex, which was designed by Skidmore, Owings & Merrill.

Reputation. To many environmentalists the timber industry seems one of the worst corporate offenders against the health and dignity of the earth. Paper mills and sawmills foul the air and pollute the water. Clear-cutting of timber is seen as the sylvan equivalent of strip-mining. High-yield forestry, with its scientifically grown trees, is another triumph of galloping monoculture. Weyerhaeuser works hard to minimize the objectionable effects of their activities, and they usually manage to stay several strides ahead of their competitors. At times they have even won grudging admiration from the ecology movement. *Audubon* magazine once published an article on Weyerhaeuser titled "Best of the S.O.B.'s."

In 1976 *Money* magazine selected them as one of the best companies in America to work for.

What they own. Besides their sprawling forest, Weyerhaeuser has nearly 200 manufacturing plants worldwide, where they turn out a broad range of forest products from plywood in Arkansas to turpentine in North Carolina to doors in Wisconsin. They make veneer in the Philippines, milk cartons in Venezuela, and cardboard boxes

A Forest of Clones

The supertree is born in a laboratory, miles from any forest. Brought to life in a cloudy solution of chemical nutrients, it begins as a sliver of wood no bigger than a fingernail paring, carved from a parent tree that yields thousands of other, identical, slices. Floating in their jars of nutrient fluid, the sliver and its army of siblings are destined to become the forest of the future—the lumberman's dream —a forest of perfect clones.

Nurtured in the laboratory, the slivers sprout roots and green needles, becoming "plantlets." Transplanted to a greenhouse, the clones grow in an artificial climate where nothing can mar their perfection. In the guarded silence of the greenhouse, untouched by nibbling deer or drenching rains or wayward gusts of wind, the future forest

of supertrees grow sturdy, straight—and as identical as pingpong balls.

Grown from the cells of a parent tree selected for its superior traits, the infant supertree and its siblings were, literally, chips off the old block. They do not merely resemble the parent: they duplicate it down to the last knothole. Like the parent, they grow faster and straighter than ordinary Douglas firs. No random mating of forest firs, no accidental mingling of unpredictable genes, no seeds falling to the forest floor to sprout in sun and rain, can create the supertrees of the new factory forest. Creations of science from birth to harvest, the clones are programmed to produce twice as much lumber per acre as any forest nature ever grew.

At three years of age the

supertree and its fellow clones, all exactly one foot tall, are planted on a 250-acre plot of naked ground in the Pacific Northwest, at the heart of a vast Douglas fir forest. Once the site of a natural stand of towering firs and hemlock, the plot, clear-cut by loggers, is as bare as the face of the moon. Where the ancient forest stood, the high-yield clones are planted in rows as straight as freeway lanes.

Bombarded from helicopters with herbicides to kill off competing trees, with pesticides to ward off insects, and with nitrogen fertilizer to speed growth and replace nitrogen once fixed in the soil by older trees, the supertrees shoot upward. All the same kind, same age, same height, they look less like a forest than like a Christmas tree lot.

Despite their accelerated

in South Africa.

Who owns and runs the company. The Weyerhaeusers. George H. Weyerhaeuser, great-grandson of the founder, has been president and chief executive officer since 1966. He holds less than 2% of the stock, but other members of the family—and other families closely associated with the Weyerhaeusers—probably own much more. The only full-time company employee to hold a seat on the board, as of early 1980, was George H. Weyerhaeuser. The board is thus dominated by big stockholders and outside people like Robert O. Anderson, chairman of Atlantic Richfield, and Robert S. Ingersoll, former U.S. ambassador to Japan. George H. Weyerhaeuser became the second-most-famous kidnap victim of the 1930s (after the Lindbergh baby) when, at age nine, he was snatched on his way home from school in 1935. He was freed when his family paid $200,000 in ransom, which was later recovered.

The Weyerhaeuser people have long been reputed to hold important interests in other timber giants of the West. In a paper done at the University of Oregon in 1974, sociologist Marvin Dunn found that the Weyerhaeusers had strong stock interests in Boise Cascade, Potlatch Industries, and Arcata.

William Ruckelshaus, the first head of the Environmental Protection Agency (and acting attorney general who lost his job for refusing President Nixon's order to fire special prosecutor Archibald Cox in 1973), became a Weyerhaeuser senior vice-president for law and corporate affairs in 1976.

In the public eye. Weyerhaeuser has become the number 1 U.S. lumber supplier to Japan, chiefly because U.S. law forbids the export of unprocessed logs cut on public lands and most Weyerhaeuser timber comes from their own private forests. Exports of logs to Japan now accounts for nearly one-fifth of Weyerhaeuser's sales. Homebuilders have screamed that they are draining the market of wood that ought to stay in the United States, and labor unions have joined the protest, complaining that the lumber should at least be processed here. Weyerhaeuser counters that it is

---

growth rate, the clones will never become sky-reaching giants like their predecessors—trees that were tall before white men set eyes on the Pacific Northwest 200 years ago. Inefficient as lumber producers, old Douglas firs grow slowly after the age of 125, sometimes decaying inside as much as they grow. In the lifetime of one 250-year-old fir, lumbermen say, they could produce five trees on the same spot with high-yield forestry, clear-cutting and replanting every 50 years.

So, at 50, the supertree and its siblings will be cut down for lumber, leaving a 250-acre bald patch where a fresh set of tiny tree clones will be planted. By clear-cutting and replanting, high-yield forestry produces two or even three times as many cubic feet of wood, or "cunits,"

as the natural forests. Long before the clone forest reaches "financial maturity," thinning will have cut its tree population to about 150 per acre, compared with hundreds more in a natural fir forest. But nature's average tree would be only 11.8 inches in diameter, whereas every high-yield supertree will be 18.8 inches in diameter—producing 16,000 cunits of wood per acre compared to half that amount for nature's forest.

Before the end of this century Weyerhaeuser, the lumber company that pioneered high-yield forestry, will have cut down all but 6% of its old Douglas fir forests on millions of acres in the Pacific Northwest. High-yield forests will replace them. Environmentalists protest that the lumbermen are turning stately forests into squatty tree

farms, forever altering the scenery of the Northwest and endangering wildlife and the forest itself. Animals and birds, environmentalists contend, need the natural variety of tree and plants in a virgin forest to feed and breed, even if they could survive aerial bombardment with pesticides and herbicides. Even when the lumbermen plant several strains of cloned trees, they are drastically reducing the genetic variability that has helped forest plants survive attacks of pests and disease.

Weyerhaeuser says their factory forests will thrive and support wildlife. But how will they look, compared to a natural forest? "Not that much different," avows company chief George Weyerhaeuser, "as long as you're not looking for a cathedral."

cheaper to ship a log from the West Coast across the Pacific to Japan than overland to Montana, that their exports do not affect the domestic price of lumber, that the Japanese don't use standardized lumber sizes and would rather cut up the logs themselves, and that West Coast lumbermills don't have the capacity to handle that many more logs anyway. What's more, they say, Weyerhaeuser's log exports help the nation's balance-of-payments situation by offsetting some of those Toyotas and Panasonics.

Other critics have charged that Weyerhaeuser is destroying the balance of nature through use of pesticides, herbicides, and fertilizers. They suggest that by breeding trees for certain desirable qualities, the company's geneticists are exposing the forest to possible disaster. Intent on producing efficient trees, the company may be planting entire forests with varieties unable to withstand the ravages of some attacking blight, which a naturally diversified forest could resist. The company dismisses such fears: they would be the last to want their forests destroyed, and they spend a lot of money on research to avoid any such catastrophe. The real issue, they argue, is whether the country wants its lumber companies to produce enough timber to meet the demand for wood and paper at prices people can afford.

In 1978 Weyerhaeuser and two other companies were convicted of a plywood price-fixing conspiracy. If the verdict stands on appeal, Weyerhaeuser estimates, the three companies might have to pay as much as $2 billion in damages.

Where they're going. They plan to keep growing them and, much later, mowing them down. The company has often been known to sacrifice a short-term profit for long-term growth. Their philosophy comes from founder Frederick Weyerhaeuser, who said, "This is not for us, nor for our children, but for our grandchildren." A Douglas fir planted in 1980 should be ready to harvest around 2030.

Stock performance. Weyerhaeuser stock bought for $1,000 in 1970 sold for $1,567 on January 2, 1980.

Major employment centers. Longview, Washington; Springfield, Cottage Grove, Oregon; Plymouth, North Carolina.

Access. Tacoma, Washington 98477; (206) 924-2345.

Consumer brands.

Prestologs (fireplace logs).

11

INDUSTRIAL HEAVYWEIGHTS

Steelmakers

United States Steel Corporation

Sales: $12.9 billion
Losses: $383 million
Forbes 500 rank: 18
Rank in steel: 1
Founded: 1901
Employees: 166,848
Headquarters: Pittsburgh, Pennsylvania

What they do. On display at Pittsburgh's Carnegie Institute is *diplodocus carnegiei,* the skeleton of a huge dinosaur dug up in 1898 by an archeological expedition funded by the famous steelmaker Andrew Carnegie. When it roamed the earth, *diplodocus carnegiei* was a fearsome creature, dwarfing other animals. But it was also ponderous, slow, and unable to adapt to new conditions, and, alas, it soon perished. Mulling over the fate of *diplodocus carnegiei* cannot be any comfort to the citizens of Pittsburgh, one of America's last old-fashioned industrial cities, but nowhere should it give greater pause than at the headquarters of the other dinosaur Carnegie bequeathed to Pittsburgh: the U.S. Steel Corporation.

Since 1901, when it was founded as America's first billion-dollar company, U.S. Steel has been the biggest steelmaker in the United States. Today, Big Steel, as the company is known, turns out about 23% of the steel used in the country each year. U.S. Steel handles all aspects of steel making. They mine their own raw materials (iron ore in Minnesota; coal in Alabama, Kentucky, West Virginia, Pennsylvania, Illinois, Indiana, and Colorado; limestone in Alabama, Michigan, and Pennsylvania); ship them on their own rail lines, barges, and Great Lakes cargo vessels; and make steel at plants in Pennsylvania, Ohio, Alabama, Texas, Utah, California, and the Chicago area. The steel products they fabricate at their mills around the country include plain steel sheets and strips for automobiles and refrigerators, or coated sheets (with enamel, zinc, or tin) for washing machines, roofing, or cans. Steel plates (flat-rolled products thicker than sheets)—sometimes as wide as 200 inches and as thick as 15 inches —form hulls of ships and walls of nuclear reactors. Steel bars come in an array of shapes for construction uses. Structural steel made by U.S. Steel's American Bridge division holds up the Sears Tower and the John Hancock building in Chicago, the Pan Am building in New York, and the San Francisco–Oakland Bay Bridge. About a quarter of their production is sold to the transportation industry (cars and railroads), 15% goes to construction, and 10% each goes to machinery and containers. In all, steel accounts for about three-quarters of Big Steel's business.

But the steel business is not what it used to be. Although the American economy has doubled in size since 1955, steel production has gone up only 17%. Aluminum, plastic, and cement are increasingly used as a replacement for the heavy metal. Since the Arab oil embargo of 1973–74, automakers, the largest steel customers, have worked overtime cutting the weight of their cars to get better gas mileage, and most of the pounds they have shed have come from their steel orders. So U.S. Steel has looked to branch out into other areas. About 7% of their sales now come from their chemical divisions, which produce industrial and

coal chemicals, polystyrene resins, and fertilizers. They also manufacture gas- and oil-field drilling and pumping equipment, cement, and shipping containers. But the profits from their other operations haven't been large enough to stanch the hemorrhage of red ink from their steel business; in 1979 U.S. Steel closed 16 plants, putting 13,-000 employees out of work, and had losses of $383 million.

History. Many companies are born brash and aggressive and then grow cautious and timid as old age sets in. U.S. Steel was born old. Founded in 1901, the crowning achievement of the great wave of business consolidations that swept the United States at the turn of the century, U.S. Steel symbolized a whole era in American economic history: the Steel Age. From the Civil War

The Paradoxical Tycoon

"How much did you say I had given away, Poynton?" Andrew Carnegie asked his secretary shortly before his death.

"$324,657,399."

"Good heaven!" cried the magnate. "Where did I ever get all that money?"

Andrew Carnegie spent his life until age 65 buying and building business. He ruined competitors and advanced his own select troop of "young geniuses." Wall Street nicknamed the 5'1" steelman "the little Scotch pirate." He created havoc in industry and amassed one of the most astounding fortunes in the history of the world. He was the richest man in the world when he retired, but not when he died. True to a promise he made early in life, Carnegie gave away over 90% of his wealth in his own lifetime.

He proposed a method of "scientific philanthropy," of doing things for the masses "better than they would or could do for themselves." His actual giving sometimes looked more like sentimentalism with a dash of good taste. His list of preferred fields for philanthropy were, in

descending order: universities, free libraries (he founded over 2,500), hospitals, parks, public meeting and concert halls, swimming baths, and — right behind those baths — churches. (Carnegie was an avowed nonsectarian who disapproved of anyone imposing one faith upon another. Requests for Carnegie money to fund missionaries fell on deaf ears.)

Carnegie's first public philanthropy was an 1873 gift of $25,000 to his native town of Dunfermline, Scotland, for building a swimming bath. By the time he retired in 1901 he had also founded the Carnegie Institute in Pittsburgh ($36 million) including a museum, library, art collection and music hall. (In 1892 an expedition from the museum went to Wyoming and dug up the fossil remains of a great dinosaur which they named *Diplodocus carnegiei*). Carnegie gave a grant to the university at Pittsburgh and a pipe organ to the Swedenborgian church in Allegheny, Pennsylvania, which his father had attended. (The organ soon plagued him; when word of the gift got

around he was besieged by requests from other churches. The noted agnostic gave away 7,689 organs before he was through, costing $6,248,312).

He established the Carnegie Foundation for the Advancement of Teaching. Originally a pension fund for college professors, the foundation's board of directors set such high standards for admission to the fund that a general reassessment and raising of standards in higher education throughout the country resulted. Schools changed their curricula and rewrote their charters to qualify for the fund. (Carnegie's board were the cream of the academic elite: Charles Eliot of Harvard, Woodrow Wilson, then president of Princeton, and a dozen other heads of top U.S. universities). By 1909 the foundation was the *de facto* accrediting agency for colleges in the United States. In 1917 it created a Teachers Insurance & Annuity Association to take care of pension insurance while the foundation turned all of its $16.25 million toward the study and advancement of teaching. TIA is now the 13th

to World War I, the iron and steel industry was the backbone of the American economy, forging the rails that spanned the continent, the wire that fenced the prairies, and the beams and girders of the new cities, bridges, and factories. But like the economy itself in those days, the steel industry was a boom-and-bust affair, unstable, unpredictable, and fiercely competitive. U.S. Steel was Wall Street's attempt to end that instability.

The company was put together in 1901 by J. Pierpont Morgan, the famous financier. Several smaller steel companies had already joined together, with some of their mergers sponsored by Morgan, to head off ruinous price-cutting that plagued steelmakers in the 1890s. Like many other businessmen of the era, Morgan had no liking for the rough and tumble of competition and was appalled by the waste and duplication of free enterprise. He wanted an orderly industry. But no merger of steel companies was likely to bring peace to the industry unless it included Andrew Carnegie's Carnegie Steel, the most efficient producer in the industry.

Andrew Carnegie was born to a weaver in Dunfermline, Scotland, in 1835. Mechanization put his father out of business, and the family moved to the United States in 1848. They settled with relatives in Allegheny, Pennsylvania, near Pittsburgh. Young Carnegie's first job, at age 13, was as a "bobbin boy" in a textile factory, at $1.20 a week. He jumped at an offer to become a telegraph messenger boy in Pittsburgh a few years later. He learned the name and face of every important person in the city and became one of only three people in the largest life insurance company in the United States.

Woodrow Wilson got Carnegie down to Princeton for a visit, and plied him with arguments on why the school should have a law faculty and a science school and a great deal more. After the visit, as Carnegie was boarding his train, he said to Wilson, "I know exactly what Princeton needs and I intend to give it to her." "What?" asked the delighted Wilson. "It's a lake. Princeton should have a rowing crew to compete with Harvard, Yale, and Columbia. That will take young men's minds off football." Carnegie abhorred football. Princeton got an artificial lake.

For ten years, Carnegie revelled in giving away money. He was criticized by many, sometimes for doing too much, sometimes for doing too little. William Jennings Bryan charged him with sullying the arts with his ill-gotten gains, and the American theologian William Tucker Jewett said Carnegie was "trying to make charity do the work of justice." But he was praised by his beneficiaries. British cities frequently gave him the "Freedom of the City," a medieval honor, when he donated a library to a town. He collected them with glee. ("I have 52 and British Prime Minister William Gladstone has only 17!" he exulted.) The New York Herald kept a running box score on who spent his money quicker, Carnegie or John D. Rockefeller.

But Carnegie couldn't spend it fast enough. By 1911 he had given away $180 million; that was only half of his fortune. And the remainder grew at 5% a year from interest. In November of that year, tired of the game and interested in going into politics, Carnegie created the Carnegie Corporation of New York, gave it $125 million, and told the directors to "promote the advancement and diffusion of knowledge among the people of the United States." For the board he had chosen the heads of his other trusts, and in addition his three faithful secretaries — who had, miraculously, kept track of all the money until that time. The Herald's box scores went off the scale and ended with a final tally, "Carnegie: $332 million; Rockefeller: $175 million."

At one time or another, everyone from William Gladstone to unpublished authors to the anonymous masses beseeched Carnegie for part of his money. He received 400 to 500 letters a day asking for funds, all screened by secretary James Bertram. Mark Twain, who always addressed Carnegie as Saint Andrew, wrote the most charming of the begging letters:

"You seem to be in prosperity. Could you lend an admirer a dollar and a half to buy a hymn book with? God will bless you. I feel it. I know it. N.B. If there should be another application this one not to count. P.S. Don't send the hymn-book, send the money. I want to make the selection myself."

Twain reportedly took Carnegie's refusal with good grace.

country who could transcribe Morse code by ear. The Pennsylvania Railroad stole him from his telegraph employers in 1853, and he quickly advanced from secretary to division superintendent.

Carnegie bought his first stock—in the Adams Express Company—at age 20, raising the cash for it by mortgaging his mother's house. According to Leon Wolff's book, *Lockout*, when he received his first dividend check (for $10), Carnegie remarked prophetically, "Here's the goose that lays the golden eggs."

Most things the young entrepreneur touched turned to gold. He speculated on some oil land in Pennsylvania, which was fertile. He bought into and reorganized the Keystone Bridge Company. When in 1864 his friend, Tom Miller, was betrayed by a partner in the Kloman iron works venture, Carnegie and Miller set up a competitor to Kloman, the Cyclops Iron Company. (Its one eye stared straight at Kloman.) The mills went up in the winter of 1865–66, and by March Kloman was negotiating to become a Cyclops subsidiary. The two were united before Cyclops ever rolled a beam, under the name of the Union Iron Mills. Carnegie had entered the iron business.

Carnegie bought control of the Edgar Thomson Steel Company at Braddock, Pennsylvania, in 1873 and the Frick coke works in 1883. He bought ore land in Pennsylvania and leased rights to the Mesabi range on Lake Superior from John D. Rockefeller.

The stodgy reputation of USS today has roots in Carnegie. "Pioneering don't pay," he said. He hesitated about converting to the Bessemer process until he met the "crazy Frenchman" in London and saw a demonstration of the steel-making technique. Carnegie grabbed the next steamer home and proclaimed "The day of iron has passed—steel is king!" The conversion of his plants from iron to steel was completed in a frenzy.

Carnegie set about building an industrial empire that soon outstripped all rivals, making him the "Steel King" of the world. By the turn of the century Carnegie Steel alone made more steel than the entire British steel industry. Considering that in 1885 Great Britain had been the world's leading steel producer, it was a startling achievement. How did Carnegie do it?

Like most successful enterprises of the time, Carnegie's steel empire grew with the help of powerful inside connections in critical industries; mergers and acquisitions; sharp dealing; and of course plain fraud, as when Carnegie Steel sold the U.S. government a batch of inferior, overpriced steel armor plate. Carnegie's old railroad connections gave him an inside track when the railroads began replacing their iron rails with steel, especially since the Pennsylvania was first to make the switch. But if secret finagling played a role in the company's spectacular growth, so did Carnegie himself. A gifted manager, salesman, and high-level business diplomat, he built a streamlined operation that turned out steel faster, cheaper, and more efficiently than any rival firm. His superintendents rushed materials from process to process, speeding the transfer of steel ingots from blast furnace to rolling mill by pouring the molten steel into molds on rolling flatcars.

Carnegie kept an iron grip on every phase of his company's operations, refusing even to sell stock in Carnegie Steel lest it weaken his control. He took in partners but always retained the majority interest, forcing partners to sign an agreement that gave him the right to expel them—but denied them the power to oust him. When Carnegie used his profits to finance expansion instead of paying dividends, his frustrated partners were powerless.

Along the way Carnegie broke all efforts by financiers and manufacturing trusts to defeat him. In the 1890s the U.S. steel industry's capacity finally outgrew its markets. When this had happened in other industries, financiers like J. P. Morgan had set up holding companies, called trusts, to keep prices artificially high by controlling production and eliminating competitors. In the late 1890s the leaders of several trusts pressured Carnegie to join—among them the Morgan-backed colossus known as Federal Steel. Carnegie stood fast against "Trusts and other swindles. The Carnegie Steel Company should never in my opinion enter any Trust," declared Carnegie.

J. P. Morgan became even more actively interested in making an amalgamated steel company after a December 1900 dinner speech by Carnegie's president, Charles W. Schwab, who spoke glowingly about steel prospects. In his biography, *Andrew Carnegie,* Joseph Frazier Wall recounts that after a long meeting with Schwab at Morgan's New York home, the financier finally said, "Well, if Andy wants to sell, I'll buy. Go and find his price." Schwab went to Carnegie, who after a day's deliberation agreed. He asked $480 million. Carnegie picked up a piece of paper, scribbled a few of his company's vital statistics on it, and handed it to Schwab. Schwab took the paper to Morgan, who looked at it and said simply, "I accept this price." That was it—the biggest deal to date in American industry. Carnegie explained his exit from business by saying that he wanted to retire and devote his life to education and philanthropy. He eventually gave away 90% of his wealth, or $324 million.

To Carnegie Steel Morgan added his own combines, Federal Steel and National Tube, and five other amalgamated steel companies. The result was a monolith that controlled 65% of the U.S. steel industry. But U.S. Steel was not designed to be a sleek, efficient producer. Morgan was a banker, not a steelmaker, and he made his profit on the deal from his fees for arranging the consolidation. So Big Steel started life with watered stock, a lot of obsolete mills, and an almost unmanageable mixture of divisions and subdivisions.

From the beginning U.S. Steel was slow, conservative, and vulnerable to more efficient rivals. Judge Elbert Gary, the Morgan man who served as the first chairman of Big Steel until his death in 1927, used to call together the leaders of the industry and lecture them on the need for stable prices. These informal price-fixing sessions, known as "Gary dinners," helped provoke a federal antitrust suit against U.S. Steel in 1911 (the Supreme Court ruled in favor of the company in 1920). A conservative company dominated by New York financiers, they were reluctant to abandon obsolete and poorly located Pittsburgh mills. Instead of moving mills closer to Detroit, they instituted a "Pittsburgh Plus" price system under which all steel was priced as if it had been made in Pittsburgh, and won a "gentlemen's agreement" from the industry not to locate in Detroit. But not all companies could be persuaded to stop competing, and by 1930 U.S. Steel's share of the market had fallen to 40%.

The onset of the Depression didn't improve matters. In 1929 company president James Farrell, like Gary before him, was reminding steel industry executives that "we must get into our minds that all customers do not belong to the man who wants to cut the price to get the business." While

Bethlehem Steel, the nation's second largest steel maker, was organized in 1904 by Charles M. Schwab. Above is a shot of Bethlehem's Grey mill, which began in 1908 to roll the structural steel that made skyscrapers possible.

Big Steel's operations were hit heavily by the economic slump, other smaller steel companies weathered the storm without major damage. In his memoirs, writer Dwight MacDonald describes his conclusion after doing a four-part series on U.S. Steel for *Fortune* in the mid-1930s: "The more research I gathered, the more it became evident that the biggest steel company in the world benefited neither its workers (wages were low . . .), its customers (prices were kept high . . .), nor its owners (who got slim dividends)."

Not much has changed since then. U.S. Steel does have better relations with their workers—at $10.60 an hour steel workers are the highest paid in any industry, and in 1973 they signed a no-strike agreement with the companies—but Big Steel is still old-fashioned and inefficient. U.S. Steel's plants are the oldest in the industry: their "newest" integrated steel mill was built in 1953, and their major mills at Gary, Indiana, and Fairfield, Alabama, were constructed at the turn of the century. As a result, U.S. Steel's share of the market has fallen to 23%, and their return on the stockholder's investment has fallen to 4.6%, less than investors would make in a savings account.

Reputation. A museum piece. In early

1980 the *Wall Street Journal* said: "The root of U.S. Steel's problems does indeed seem to be a longstanding resistance to change. As the economic and political circumstances facing the industry have altered over the past 20 years, U.S. Steel has failed to accommodate to them as well as other steelmakers have."

Eye Sinister

Pinkerton's detective agency is well known as the largest company in the $1 billion armed-guard industry. Less well known is the agency's sensational, violent history—in particular, its role in labor battles against early industrial unions.

Alan Pinkerton, a Scottish barrelmaker, was born in Glasgow in 1819 and fled to America in 1842. He settled in Illinois, where he ran down a counterfeiting ring and was made sheriff, first in Kane County and later in Cook County, centered in Chicago. He was an abolitionist, a leader in the Underground Railway, and a close friend of John Brown. He organized a detective force for the sheriff's department in Chicago, and in the 1850s went into business for himself as the Pinkerton National Detective Agency, specializing in train robberies. His slogan was "We never Sleep"; his trademark an open left eye ("eye sinister"), origin of the term *private eye.*

Pinkerton uncovered the "Baltimore Plot" to assassinate president-elect Lincoln. He headed the first U.S. Secret Service during the Civil War. His agents infiltrated and broke the Molly Maguire coalminers' gangs in the 1870s, the Scott-Dunlap bank robbers, and the Dr. Meyer "murder-for-profit" ring. With his sons, William and Robert, he chased innumerable Wild West bandits, among them the McCoys, the border bandits, and the James and Younger brothers. The agency established one of the

first "rogues' galleries," where criminals' pictures were posted.

Pinkerton died in 1884, but his sons continued and expanded the agency. In 1880 they had convinced the nation's jewelers to band together as the Jewelers Protective Union and hired Pinkerton's. The American Bankers Association followed suit. The record was impressive: from the association's inception until 1909, banks without Pinkerton detectives suffered 1,097 robberies (and a loss of almost $1.5 million), while protected banks were robbed only 202 times (for $154,000). Thieves were known to return bank loot anonymously when they found out Pinkerton detectives were assigned to the case.

When workers first organized and struck the steel, railroad, and coal industries, threatening damage to property and death to "scabs," owners and management turned to the Pinkertons for paid protection. Agency detectives became undercover agents who infiltrated unions and gathered evidence of their plans, legal and illegal. In the rail uprisings of 1877 agents infiltrated the Trailman's Union as soon as it began to gather members. The Baltimore & Ohio issued an order to discharge all union members, and Pinkerton supplied their names. With Pinkerton assistance the Pan Handle line was able to fire union members just four days after the union was created. Strikes by the union

were utterly foiled. That same year 20 members of the Pennsylvania coalminers' Molly Maguire organization were hanged after their group was infiltrated by Pinkerton man James McParland.

Between 1869 and 1892 Pinkerton operatives worked exclusively for management in 77 strikes. The 2,000 active agents and 30,000 reserves outnumbered the nation's standing army. The agency gave preference in hiring to ex-soldiers and ex-policemen, and union encounters with them were often violent. Pinkertons and police frequently broke up crowds of striking workers with billy clubs. Agency operatives were active at the Haymarket massacre in Chicago on May 4, 1876, after which even the governor of Illinois conceded that in previous years "a number of laboring people, guilty of no offense, had been shot down in cold blood by Pinkerton men."

"The mere sight of a Pinkerton watchman's blue uniform in a strikebound area was enough to enrage the union men," records James D. Horan in *The Pinkertons: The Detective Dynasty That Made History.* In the 1888 Burlington railroad strike an operative who shot and killed a striker "vanished just in time from being lynched." Historian Leon Wolff remarked in *Lockout* that, among Pinkerton's agents, "an unpleasant number of them were trigger-happy."

One of the few defeats for Pinkerton forces, and an enduring blot on the company

What they own. Steel plants in Ohio, Pennsylvania, Chicago, Indiana, Alabama, Texas, Utah, and California, plus 28 marketing centers across the United States. The corporation owns or leases land with about 3.7 billion tons of coal reserves. They own 30 bulk cargo vessels and seven self-unloading vessels, plus over 20 chemical plants.

---

record, was a battle during the violent strike at Andrew Carnegie's Homestead steelworks near Pittsburgh. On July 1, 1892, after workers closed down the plant, the town instituted martial law (the mayor was one of the strikers) and sealed off Carnegie's property. Intent on repossessing the works, Carnegie chairman Henry Clay Frick ordered the Pinkertons to get in and take over.

"A total of 316 men were collected in New York and Chicago. Mostly unemployed, or drifters, a few college lads trying to earn a little money between semesters, a hard core of Pinkerton regulars, some hoodlums and out-and-out criminals on the run, they comprised a typical group of agency guards," recounted Wolff.

Strikers had blocked the roads and ringed Homestead with armed lookouts, so the men left Pittsburgh, at 2:00 A.M. on July 6, in two barges. A tugboat towed them quietly up the Monongahela River, the nonregulars unaware of the nature of their assignment. They arrived in Homestead two hours later, amid a fusillade of rifle shots from shore.

An enraged crowd of 10,000 strikers and their families greeted the Pinkertons by the dim early light. The people of Homestead were armed with sticks, bricks, pistols, revolvers, and Civil War–vintage carbines. They held the two barges under seige all day in a sweltering sun. (The Pinkertons' tug abandoned them early, taking out some dead and wounded men.) Deaths and injuries mounted throughout the day from gunfire, homemade bombs, a small cannon on shore, and burning oil (Carnegie's) dumped on the water by strikers in an attempt to incinerate the barges. Strikers shot down a white handkerchief some Pinkertons waved through a porthole several times during the seige. At dusk the town finally accepted the Pinkertons' surrender. But those who made the long "escorted" walk to captivity in the local theater were beaten, maimed (one had his eye put out by a woman with an umbrella), and pelted by mobs of strikers, women, and children. One man reportedly stabbed himself to death with his penknife after being repeatedly beaten, unable to stand any more of the bloody day's events.

After heated arguments union leaders persuaded the mob not to lynch the guards outright. Bloody and battered, they were put on a special train to Pittsburgh. An estimated 9 strikers and 7 Pinkertons were dead, 40 strikers and 20 guards shot. And some 300 Pinkertons had been wounded on their forced march through the town.

Nevertheless, Pinkerton's did not give up strike work. The same James McParland who broke the Molly Maguires eventually became head of the agency's Denver office and worked for the Mineowners Association as it tried to scuttle the Western Federation of Miners. At least one Pinkerton played his undercover role so well he went to a 1903 UMW convention as a delegate. The agency also tried to undermine the reputation of labor organizer Mother Jones by circulating stories about her alleged work in red-light districts of Denver, Chicago, Omaha, and San Francisco.

In 1937, after congressional hearings the previous year on industrial espionage, Pinkerton's finally got out of strike work.

"That is a phase of our business that we are not particularly proud of and we're delighted we're out of it," Robert Pinkerton, II, later told the *New York Times*.

Today the agency is much more sedate. Over 90% of its business is in rented guards. Still a huge enterprise (with 21,000 guards, 100 offices, and 1979 revenues of $260 million), the company got its first nonfamily president in 1967, the year they went public. A major stockholder is Warren E. Buffett, an Omaha investor with interests in the *Washington Post* and the Ogilvy & Mather advertising agency. Most of the company's staff is college trained, and many are ex-FBI agents. Although electronic security systems have cut into their business lately ("When was the last time you saw a guard in a bank?" asks Chase Manhattan protection director Gerald J. Van Dorn), Pinkerton's still never sleeps.

The company also has interests in Canada, South Africa, Guyana, Indonesia, Gabon, Italy, Venezuela, India, and Spain.

Who owns and runs the company. The employee pension plan holds the largest single block of stock: 11 million shares or 13% of the total, according to a 1980 report by Corporate Data Exchange. Next in line is the founding father, J. P. Morgan & Co., with 2.5% of the shares, although there has been no direct Morgan control since J. P. Morgan, Jr., served as chairman of USS from 1927–32. The board of directors, composed of white males, owns about 0.2% of the stock. Chairman and chief executive David M. Roderick is a 20-year veteran of the company who came up through the ranks of the nonsteel operations. President William R. Roesch, formerly of Jones and Laughlin Steel and Kaiser Steel, is one of the few outsiders ever to hold a top job at Big Steel, and Wall Streeters have their fingers crossed that he can overcome the company's hidebound traditions. Already he has reversed U.S. Steel's fierce resistance to pollution controls, and, to the amazement of everyone, in 1979 he hired experts from Japan's Nippon Steel to advise the company on improving the output of a blast furnace at their Gary plant.

U.S. Steel touched off a management revolt when they decided to withhold wage increases for managers in 1980, although they had just signed a three-year contract for wage increases with the United Steelworkers union. "It's really insulting that the board isn't paying us what it's paying the union members," a plant foreman told the *Wall Street Journal.* "Some of the people I supervise already make more than I do. The union guys are laughing at us."

As of early 1978, Du Pont owned 1.3% of U.S. Steel.

In the public eye. Steelmaking is a dirty business, but in the 1970s U.S. Steel was in no hurry to clean up their operations. According to EPA officials, U.S. Steel had a "record of recalcitrance second to none." "None of the major steelmakers have moved quickly to comply with environmental regulations over the past 10 years," the *Wall Street Journal* reported in 1980, "but U.S. Steel's opposition was particularly bitter. The company fought environmental regulations in state and federal courts all over the country, and it made liberal use of threats to close plants if regulations were enforced." But the company signaled a new policy in 1979 when they agreed to spend $400 million to clean up pollution at nine plants in Pennsylvania.

Having given up the battle against pollution controls, U.S. Steel has turned their artillery on imported steel. U.S. Steel says that Japanese and European steel producers, who captured 16% of the U.S. market in 1979, are dumping steel here at prices below the cost of production. They say that foreign steelmakers have an unfair advantage because they receive government subsidies and do not have to meet tough antipollution laws. Although the Carter administration in 1977 instituted a system of tariffs to keep out cheap foreign steel, in 1980 U.S. Steel broke with other steel companies and filed formal charges of "dumping" against seven European countries.

But the administration and industry critics denied that the steel imports represented a danger to the industry. They pointed to a study by Merrill Lynch which shows that since 1959 most of the gains made by foreign producers have come at the expense of U.S. Steel, the industry's least efficient producer. They also argued that banning imports would reward U.S. Steel's poor management and penalize steel consumers with higher prices. It didn't help U.S. Steel's case when the Japanese press reported in May 1980 that Big Steel had contracted to buy Japanese steel to sell at their West Coast service centers. Asked about the purchase by the *Wall Street Journal,* a company spokesman said, "We aren't going to have any comment."

Where they're going. U.S. Steel has instituted a new plan to shut down unprofitable plants, hoping that somewhere inside the dinosaur there lurks a snarling tiger. They also want to crack down on labor and invest more money in the company's nonsteel operations.

In 1980 United States Steel decided to temporarily close down The Edgar Thomson Works, the first plant ever built by Andrew Carnegie, and one of the oldest in the Pittsburgh area; 2,000 of the plant's 2,300 workers were laid off. When U.S. Steel closed down two plants in Youngstown, Ohio, in 1979, laid-off plant workers tried to buy the plant and continue to run it themselves. U.S. Steel claims they can't sell the plants to a group that would become a tax-subsidized competitor. Just before Christmas 1979, 83 plaintiffs charged U.S. Steel with breach of contract over the closing of the plants. They are represented by lawyer Staughton Lynd, a former anti-Vietnam war activist. The case was still in court in mid-1980.

Stock performance. U.S. Steel stock bought for $1,000 in 1970 sold for $778 on January 2, 1980.

Access. 600 Grant Street, Pittsburgh, Pennsylvania 15230; (412) 433-1121.

Chemists

Sales: $3.2 billion
Profits: $168 million
Forbes 500 rank: 154
Rank in chemicals: 7
Founded: 1907
Employees: 43,750
Headquarters: Wayne, New Jersey

What they do. American Cyanamid is a sprawling chemical company that lately has been raging out of control. When they're not fending off lawsuits, strikes, or attacks from federal regulatory agencies, Cyanamid manufactures a long line of drugs, medicines, chemicals, toiletries (Old Spice men's cologne, Breck shampoos), and plastics, like Formica. They still make fertilizers—their original product—as well as a number of agricultural pesticides that they sell under such aggressive brand names as

Avenge, Counter, and Prowl (known as "Stomp" in the European market).

For years one of Cyanamid's biggest assets has been their Lederle Laboratories subsidiary, which pioneered in antibiotics (aureomycin, achromycin) and a number of sulfa drugs. Today Lederle contributes about $600 million to Cyanamid's sales, primarily through sales of Stresstabs Vitamins, antibiotics, and assorted anticancer agents.

History. Cyanamid was founded in 1907 because a civil engineer named Frank Washburn wanted to build a dam. Washburn had already built three hydroelectric dams in the South and had ambitious plans for an even larger one. But first he had to find a use for it. He had heard of a new German process for extracting nitrogen from the air and combining it with lime and carbide to form cyanamid, a basic element in fertilizer; he was delighted to learn that the process required an enormous amount of electricity. Washburn went to Germany and bought the American rights to the process. Then he built his dam in Ontario, Canada, set up American Cyanamid to use the electricity it produced, and went on building dams.

When Washburn died in 1922, a staid Quaker lawyer named William Brown Bell, who had been Washburn's assistant, became Cyanamid's president. Bell was *so* staid that he reportedly referred to others as "thees," common to the Society of Friends, but in the mid-1920s, faced with an agricultural depression, Bell broke out of his conservative mode and began buying up small chemical companies. In 1930 he bought Lederle, which had been founded in 1906 by a New York City physician and health officer to produce diphtheria antitoxin. By 1930 the company had expanded into antitoxins and sulfa drugs. They remained Cyanamid's biggest money-maker until the 1970s.

When Bell finally stepped down after 28 years as president, his successors continued buying other companies. Notable among these were the Formica Company in 1956, the John Breck Company in 1963, and the Shulton Company, makers of Old Spice and Pierre Cardin fragrances, in 1971.

Reputation. In late 1977 *Forbes* described American Cyanamid as "ingrown and a bit inept." The magazine noted that Dr. James Affleck, the Princetonian chemist who is Cyanamid's chairman and president, presides over a nine-member executive committee composed primarily of Princetonians and chemists. The article went on to point out a few blunders in Cyanamid's corporate history—such as the 1974 decision to build a $4.8 million plant to compete with a company they could have bought outright for $5 million.

What they own. In addition to Breck, Shulton, Formica, and their 38 chemical and medical subsidiaries around the world, Cyanamid owns an insurance company in Bermuda and an optical company in New York. When Cyanamid paid $100 million of its stock for Shulton in 1971, Clifford D. Siverd, who was then president, explained: "We've always wanted a men's line."

Who owns and runs the company. In 1972 the descendants of William Brown Bell were reported to hold 29% of the stock, but that holding is not visible anymore. There are no Bells on the board, and in 1979 the

company identified their largest stockholders as the National Bank of Detroit (with nearly 6% of the shares). A large individual holder (nearly 2%) is director George L. Schultz, who sold his Shulton company to Cyanamid.

The rest of the stock is held by more than 90,000 stockholders. Normally, American Cyanamid holds their annual meeting in Portland, Maine, where the company was originally chartered, but in 1974 they decided to hold an informational meeting in Wayne, New Jersey, in an attempt to gauge their stockholders' interest in the company. Only 250 people showed up.

In the public eye. Six separate incidents in the last decade have caused Cyanamid's public image to slip from bad to worse. In 1969 they lost a price fixing suit over their antibiotic drug tetracycline. Four years later the Georgia State Water Quality Control Board ordered Cyanamid to clean up the sulfuric acid waste-disposal systems from their Savannah plant, which had apparently been killing fish in the Savannah and Wilmington rivers. In 1976 Cyanamid disclosed that their subsidiaries, principally Lederle Laboratories, had made $1.2 million in illegal or irregular payments abroad. In 1978 the company agreed to pay workers at their Westwego, Louisiana, chemical plant 36 months of back wages for having locked out 441 members of the Oil, Chemical, and Atomic Workers Union. Also in 1978, 1,300 workers struck Cyanamid's Bound Brook, New Jersey, plant, claiming that the company understated health hazards and concealed illnesses caused by carcinogenic chemicals in the plant. Cyanamid was unmoved. Said plant manager Eldon Knape, "We don't run a health spa."

Finally, they made headlines because of an incident at their Willow Island, West Virginia, chemical plant in 1979. Fearing that the presence of certain lead compounds in parts of the plant might lead to birth defects among their employees' offspring, Cyanamid offered their women workers a choice: quit, be demoted, or be sterilized. Five Cyanamid employees took the latter course, and four told the *New York Times* in January 1979 that they deeply regretted their decision. The Occupational Safety and Health Administration and the labor unions at the plant condemned the company for coercion, job discrimination, and the violation of basic women's rights;

OSHA later fined Cyanamid $10,000.

Where they're going. They're considered a prime takeover candidate.

Stock performance. American Cyanamid stock bought for $1,000 in 1970 sold for $1,289 on January 2, 1980.

Access. Verdan Avenue, Wayne, New Jersey 07470; (201) 831-1234.

Consumer brands.

Cleaning products: Pine-Sol; Lemon-Sol.
Surface covering: Formica.
Fragrances: Nina Ricci; Pierre Cardin, Tabac Original.
Grooming: Old Spice; Breck.
Vitamins: Stresstabs; Centrum.

Sales: $9.3 billion
Profits: $784 million
Forbes 500 rank: 33
Rank in chemicals: 2
Founded: 1897
Employees: 55,900
Headquarters: Midland, Michigan

What they do. Dow is everything they say a big corporation is supposed to be (but often isn't): aggressive, bold, independent, efficient, tough minded, and very successful. In the last decade this "chemical company's chemical company" has leapfrogged rivals Monsanto and Union Carbide to become Du Pont's closest competitor in the industry. Even more impressive, for several years in the middle 1970s Dow reaped higher profits than all rivals—including Du Pont—despite smaller sales. And Dow will not be content with anything less. When president Zoltan Merszei, one of the company's most successful executives, let profits fall slightly from their previously spectacular levels, he was moved up to chairman in 1978 after only two years on the job because "a younger manager can more easily cope with the challenges of a changeable and demanding world."

Dow's main business is supplying chemicals to other industrial and chemical companies. Using oil, coal, natural gas, salt, and ocean water, they make inorganic chemicals like soda, solvents, and chlorine, which are used in dry cleaning, paper making, and water treatment; and organic chemicals like acetone, ethylene glycol, glycerine, and phenol, which are used to make plastics, polyester fiber, and antifreeze. Sales to other industrial companies account for 60% of Dow's business. Another third of Dow's business is in plastics and packaging material. Dow is most familiar to consumers as the maker of Saran Wrap, the plastic film that has driven waxed paper from the American kitchen. Dow also makes Handi-Wrap, a cheaper plastic film; Ziploc food-storage bags; Styrofoam polystyrene foam; and a wide range of plastic moldings, coatings, and plastic intermediates used by the construction, electrical, food, and plastics industries. Other Dow divisions make herbicides, insecticides, and antibiotics.

A voracious consumer of hydrocarbons—oil, natural gas, and coal—Dow gets about three-fifths of their U.S. needs from plants along the energy-rich Gulf Coast. At Freeport and Oyster Creek, Texas, amid a company-owned network of 500 miles of pipelines for gathering natural gas and oil, Dow has set up a complex of four major plants employing nearly 8,000 workers. As part of the company's strategy for energy independence, one of the plants in the complex is a crude-oil processing plant, which will supply fuel oil to meet all their Gulf Coast needs for steam, electricity, and petroleum feedstocks, the raw material for many chemicals. Dow not only produces three-quarters of their own electricity and steam, but in 1978 their energy conservation program saved the equivalent of 23 million barrels of oil, an amount equal to one day's

> The three largest chemical firms in the world are West German (BASF, Hoechst, and Bayer). Only three American firms are among the 10 largest (Du Pont, ranked 4th, Dow, 6th, and Union Carbide, 7th). The other four top chemical companies are European: Imperial Chemical (British), Montedison (Italian), Rhone-Poulenc (French), and Royal Dutch Shell (Dutch/British).

consumption by the entire United States. Other major Dow chemical plants are in their headquarters city, Midland, Michigan, where the local utility is building a nuclear power plant to provide Dow with electricity and steam, and in Pittsburgh, California, next to the San Francisco Bay Area's large refinery complex.

History. Dow Chemical was founded in 1897 by Herbert Henry Dow to extract bromine and chlorine from the large deposits of underground brine around Midland, Michigan. To chlorine bleach, the company's first product, they slowly added a variety of other chemicals: chloroform in 1903, ethylene in 1915, phenol in 1922. One of Dow's less popular early products was mustard gas, which they made during World War I.

The company's major growth began after World War II, when research resulted in the discovery of whole new families of plastics. Dow introduced Styrofoam in 1944 and Saran Wrap in 1952. In 1960 they began their aggressive program of expansion. Dow's strategy rested on two major assumptions: the first was that overseas markets would be hot areas of growth. A latecomer to overseas expansion, Dow plotted their course carefully. They first established a beachhead by marketing products imported from the United States, then followed up by building chemical plants overseas. Dow now sells about 45% of their products abroad and has major chemical plants in the Netherlands, West Germany, Brazil, Japan, South Korea, and Yugoslavia. Their second assumption was that the best way to finance this growth was to borrow money. Convinced that the governments of the world were committed to inflation as a permanent way of life, Dow gambled by borrowing heavily in the hope that they could pay back their debts in cheapened dollars. The gamble has paid off. Not only has inflation accelerated, but the explosion of oil prices during the 1970s has pushed up chemical prices even faster than the prices of most goods, which means that Dow has more dollars to pay off their debts than they had anticipated.

Reputation. One of the best-managed companies in the world. Dow has made phenomenal gains in one of the most competitive industries.

What they own. Dow has interests in various other companies around the globe. They own 50% of Dow Corning, Dowell Schlumberger, and Asahi-Dow. In 1979 their participation in other companies returned them profits of $123 million or 15% of their total profits. One of Dow's holdings is a Swiss bank (Dow Banking).

Who owns and runs the company. Although two members of the Dow family still sit on the board of directors, the company is run by management people, who hold 14 of 16 board seats. (The directors and their families hold 2% of Dow stock.) The man who took over as president in 1978 when Zoltan Merszei moved upstairs was Paul F. Oreffice, formerly head of Dow's domestic operations. An outspoken critic of government overregulation, Oreffice, in 1977, cut off all Dow's donations to neighboring Central Michigan University after Jane Fonda gave a speech on campus criticizing big corporations in general and Dow in particular. In a letter to the university's president, Oreffice announced that Dow would give no gifts to the school "until we are convinced our dollars are not expended in supporting those who would destroy us" and until Oreffice had been invited to campus to "balance the scales." Oreffice got his invitation.

In the public eye. Dow is no stranger to controversy. During the Vietnam War they were attacked for making napalm, the jellied incendiary that sticks to its victims, burning deep holes into their bodies. Although Dow employment recruiters were mobbed on many campuses, Dow made no apology for their actions. However, they quietly allowed themselves to be outbid on the contract when it came up for renewal.

In 1975 Dow announced plans to build a new petrochemical plant in northern California across the Sacramento River from their existing Pittsburgh chemical complex. Dow filed for the 65 local, state, and federal permits needed to approve the project, pledging that they would abide by all laws protecting the quality of the water and air. Environmentalists objected, lawsuits were filed, hearings dragged on interminably. When an air-pollution-control officer ruled that the law would permit no new emissions in the area, Dow offered to reduce emissions at their existing complex by an amount more than the new plant would produce. The pollution board nixed the plan. After two years of delays, Dow decided to teach California a lesson. Declaring that the state's permit processes were too involved and too expensive, Dow canceled the project.

Where they're going. Dow is giving Alaska a shot at having the petrochemical complex nixed in California.

Stock performance. Dow Chemical stock bought for $1,000 in 1970 sold for $2,807 on January 2, 1980.

Access. 2030 Dow Center, Midland, Michigan 48640; (517) 636-1000.

Consumer brands.

Food-storage products: Saran Wrap; Handi-Wrap, Ziploc bags.
Cleaning products: Dow Bathroom Cleaner.
Drugs: Novahistine cold preparations; Rifadin and Rifocin antibiotics.

Sales: $12.6 billion
Profits: $939 million
Forbes 500 rank: 21
Rank in synthetic fibers: 1
Rank in gell explosives: 1
Rank in chemicals: 1
Founded: 1802
Employees: 134,200
Headquarters: Wilmington, Delaware

What they do. Du Pont, the nation's largest chemical company, Delaware's largest employer, and the company that was, for more than a century, America's national armorer, is generally credited with having "invented" the modern corporation. They introduced the "family-tree" style of organizational chart in the early 1900s, delegating authority to various levels of managers and committees within the company, and then used it to reorganize General Motors after they demonstrated its usefulness at Du Pont.

For generations—from 1802 until 1971—the company was run by one du Pont or another. (In 1961, after 159 years of confusion, company lawyers finally decided that the company is spelled "Du Pont"—uppercase "D"—and the family "du Pont"—lowercase "d"). They tended to keep to themselves in a little cluster of estates along Delaware's Brandywine river, where they built their first black powder plant and where they produced three-fourths of the nation's explosives until the end of World War I. The family seemed to defy the trends of twentieth century business because as the company grew into a vast, multibillion dollar empire, there were always young du Ponts coming up to take the helm, continuing the family dynasty in seeming contravention of the move to professional management. And their control over the private and public sectors of life in Delaware increased to the point where the du Pont family now wields power in the state's largest banks, newspapers, charities, and the University of Delaware as well as in much of the state's political life. In the last few years alone, du Ponts have served as Delaware state legislator and attorney general (W. Laird Stabler), state senate majority leader (Reynolds du Pont), and Delaware congressman and governor (Pierre S. du Pont IV).

Although they finally sold their last dynamite plant a few years ago, Du Pont is still the largest manufacturer of gell explosives (made from soft plastic materials). But the company's mainstays for the last 50 years have been their chemical, plastic, and synthetic fiber businesses. They invented nylon, for example, and developed rayon—as well as a host of other synthetic dyes and chemicals. They pioneered research in fluorocarbon chemistry, eventually creating Teflon resin, later used in nonstick cookware; "SilverStone" scratch-resistant cookware finishes; and Freon, the chemical that made electrical refrigeration possible. They synthesized Lucite, a clear plastic used in everything from auto glass to house paint. And, just to keep their hand in the original family business, they built and operated the world's first plutonium plant in the state of Washington to fuel the atomic bombs dropped over Japan in 1945.

Today Du Pont has four major lines of business. Their fiber business, which turns out carpet and apparel threads like Orlon and Dacron, accounted for $4.1 billion—or

33%—of Du Pont's sales in 1979. This was followed by the specialty products division, which produces everything from "Rain Dance" car wax (one of Du Pont's few consumer brands) to film, cookware coatings, explosives, and a line of firearms and ammunition, and which had sales of $3.5 billion, or 28% of the total. Making plastics, artificial resins, and synthetic rubbers for the auto and other industries contributed $2.8 billion (22%) of the total; the rest ($2.1 billion, 17%) came from petrochemicals and additives for agricultural feeds. The company has 87 plants in 27 states, turning

Did Du Pont Suppress a Family Biography?

When Gerard C. Zilg's book about the du Pont family was published in 1974, it looked like a sure-fire winner. The New York Times gave it a rave review, and the Book-of-the-Month Club picked it as a Fortune Book Club selection. Du Pont: Behind the Nylon Curtain seemed certain to win fame and money for its 29-year-old author.

But Zilg's book flopped. In fact, it virtually disappeared. Today it is nearly impossible to find a copy in any library or bookstore. Prentice-Hall printed only 13,000 copies, and Zilg made no profit for the five years he spent researching and writing the book. New York Times critic Robert Sherrill called "something of a miracle...masterful...a comprehensive, cohesive, balanced, vibrant, gossipy biography of a family."

In 1978 Zilg sued both the Du Pont company and Prentice-Hall, charging that the two had joined in a corporate conspiracy to suppress his book and destroy its chances of commercial success. In his $5 million suit, filed in U.S. District Court in New York, Zilg claimed that Du Pont bigwigs, after reading a leaked prepublication manuscript of his book, became so alarmed at its

potential for damaging the Du Pont image that they launched a corporate plot to scuttle the book. Since Du Pont could not prevent publication, Zilg charged, the company launched a campaign to stop Prentice-Hall and Book-of-the-Month from advertising or distributing it widely.

Du Pont and Prentice Hall vehemently denied any back-stage effort to scuttle Zilg's book, and Book-of-the-Month officials said the club cancelled Du Pont because a club official felt sections of the book might leave the club open to a libel lawsuit. Whether there was actually a corporate plot to suppress Zilg's book is to be aired when the case comes to trial (scheduled for late 1980).

During the pretrial legal proceedings, Zilg's lawyers have obtained a number of internal Du Pont documents, backed up by sworn statements from company officials, that shed an interesting light on the inner workings of Du Pont's public relations apparatus.

According to the documents, Du Pont suspicions were first aroused in June 1973, when the current family patriarch, Irénée du Pont, Jr., then senior vice-president of the company, got

a letter from Zilg asking for an interview. "Suspicious. Five years ago. Warning by someone," wrote du Pont on Zilg's envelope, alerting the firm's public affairs department. For the next year, internal Du Pont memos show, Bettina F. Sargeant and other PR employees checked into Zilg's background, even contacting Richard Williams, head of the Eleutherian Mills-Hagley Foundation Library where Zilg did research for the book. A Sargeant memo quotes Williams as calling Zilg "a professional radical" and suggesting that "General Motors can supply additional information on Zilg as he has been an allegedly militant activist in attempting to organize GM labor forces."

A subsequent Du Pont check with GM turned up nothing, and a memo to Harlan L.P. Wendell— who reported to the company's executive committee—confessed that public affairs employees had exhausted their sources on Zilg and "I regret to report that we have come up with very little that is helpful."

While this cloak-and-dagger project was underway, other Du Pont documents show, the company was sparing no effort to get a copy of the impending

out more than 1,700 products, almost all of which are sold in turn to other manufacturers and fabricators. Du Pont also has plants in Germany, the Netherlands, the United Kingdom, and Argentina. International business now accounts for one-third of their sales and 40% of their profits. They rank as one of the largest U.S. exporters: their 1979 exports were $1.7 billion.

Du Pont is so big that they've even set up their own phone system, enabling them to avoid AT&T and save 75% of the cost of commercial toll rates. The system gives 170 locations in the United States direct-dial ac-

---

book before it hit the stands. "Let's arrange to obtain and review a copy ASAP," urged a note from then-public relations chief Thomas W. Stephenson, dated June 11, 1974. Two days later, Du Pont memos show, a partially edited copy of Zilg's manuscript was in company hands. According to pretrial testimony, a Prentice-Hall salesman delivered the manuscript to Greenwood Bookstore in Wilmington, Delaware, where a former Du Pont employee who worked in the store gave it to J. Bruce Bredin, brother-in-law of Irénée du Pont. Bredin claimed it was merely a coincidence that he arrived in the store just after the copy of the manuscript appeared.

Soon after the company obtained Zilg's manuscript, Du Pont public affairs officials learned of the Book-of-the-Month Club contract to distribute *Du Pont*. In July 1974, according to his own memo, Harold G. Brown, Du Pont's assistant vice president of public affairs, telephoned Vilma Bergane, a book club editor. "I told Ms. Bergane that the manuscript had been read in Wilmington by several persons, including attorneys, and that they

described it as 'scurrilous' and 'actionable,'" wrote Brown.

After more Du Pont phone contacts and a meeting at the book club's offices, Book-of-the-Month on July 26, 1974, notified Prentice-Hall that they would defer issuing a Book-of-the-Month Club edition of Zilg's book. A few days later, the club backed out of their contract with Prentice-Hall entirely.

Prentice-Hall recognized that their profits from Zilg's book would be hurt by the book club's decision, as internal letters from Prentice-Hall's own attorneys show. One such note argued that Zilg could "bring action against us for our failure to take action against BOMC." Yet the publishers made no legal moves against either Du Pont or the book club. And when Zilg urged that Prentice-Hall call a press conference to air the controversy, the publishers refused, despite what then-editor Bram Cavin later testified was "the greatest opportunity in the world to sell the book."

Zilg bought the unsold 700 copies of his book from Prentice-Hall and is now selling them himself (for $12.95 from Probe Publishers, P.O. Box 326, New York, NY 10014). He is also trying to get another publisher to issue

the book in paperback.

You don't have to read very far into Zilg's 623-page opus to discover why Du Pont's public relations department was so exercised.

As Zilg depicts them, the du Ponts of today "employ more servants than Britain's royal family, own more yachts, cars, swimming pools, planes, and estates than any other family in recorded history." According to Zilg, they are the world's richest family—far wealthier than the Rockefellers.

—Du Pont patriarch Irénée du Pont spent much of his time during the 1950s at his walled Cuban estate, Xanadu, where, according to Zilg, his pride and joy was his herd of attack-trained iguanas. At a command from Irénée, the three-foot-long lizards would come to his side standing at attention; at a second command, they would attack a target to kill.

—Of the 1,600 or so living du Ponts, 250 constitute what Zilg calls the "inner circle," of which only 50 "make up the all-powerful inner core of the family." Zilg says that these du Ponts "own controlling interests in over 120 multimillion dollar corporations and banks," including: Du Pont, General Motors, Uniroyal, Boeing, Penn Central, Hercules Chemical, Atlas Chemical, Chemical Bank of New York, United Fruit (now United Brands), Continental Can (now Continental Group), North American Rockwell (now Rockwell International), and the Philadelphia Phillies baseball team.

cess to each other as well as to telephones in 40 metropolitan areas. The network handles 100,000 Du Pont-related calls a day.

History. Eleuthère Irénée du Pont de Nemours was born near Paris in 1771, the second son of Pierre Samuel du Pont, who had been elevated to the French nobility in 1784 for his efforts during the negotiations to end the American Revolutionary War. At the age of 16 Irénée enrolled in the prestigious Essonne laboratory to study under Antoine Lavoisier, the famed chemist in charge of manufacturing the French government's gunpowder. But when his education was interrupted by the French Revolution in 1789, Irénée went to fight beside his father in defense of the monarchy. After King Louis XVI was beheaded in 1793, Pierre was imprisoned. Although he was eventually released, the continuing turmoil in France and fears for his own safety persuaded Pierre to emigrate to the United States in 1797.

Irénée went with him and, with his experience in Lavoisier's lab a decade before, planned to go into the gunpowder business. Thomas Jefferson, who had known of his father from the treaty negotiations, encouraged him and recommended a site on Delaware's Brandywine river, which was central to all the states at that time and provided sufficient water power to run the

The time: 1900. The scene: powdermen working at Du Pont's mills on the Brandywine River near Wilmington, Delaware. Du Pont operated the gunpowder mills from 1802 to 1921. There's now a museum there devoted to America's early industrial history.

mills. Irénée and his older brother, Victor, then returned to France to raise the necessary capital and, in April 1801 E. I. du Pont de Nemours was founded. When the first Du Pont black powder went on sale in 1804, the federal government was the buyer.

Du Pont rapidly established a reputation for superior gunpowder, but because most of their profit came from nonmilitary sales, the American military demands during the War of 1812 forced Irénée and his company into debt. An explosion in 1815 at one of the mills killed nine workmen and destroyed a large section of the plant. Three years after Irénée's death, in 1834, his two sons, Alfred and Henry, were able to buy out the French backers. They continued to head the company until 1889, during which time Du Pont expanded into the manufacture of smokeless powder, dynamite, and nitroglycerine.

Du Pont was run by Eugene du Pont until his death in 1902. After the funeral there appeared to be no du Ponts qualified to take the helm. A five-member board of the eldest du Ponts prepared to sell the company, but the idea proved to be anathema to three cousins: Alfred, Pierre, and Coleman. They considered the company their birthright and managed to convince the elders to sell the company to them for no money down. They quickly discovered that their conservative elders had vastly undervalued the du Pont holdings, and Pierre uncovered an old ledger that revealed Du Pont to be the secret owner of one of the other two largest gunpowder firms, Hazard & Company. The shrewd Coleman then went to the third gunpowder firm, Laflin & Rand, and made what seemed to be a very generous offer to buy them out for stock in a dummy company Coleman had set up. When the offer was accepted, the three cousins found themselves in control of 56% of the U.S. explosives business, with assets conservatively estimated at $60 million, for a cash investment of a few thousand dollars in incorporation fees. Profits from the business quickly paid off the elders for the purchase of Du Pont, now one of the nation's largest corporations.

Previously Du Pont had functioned as a sort of gigantic one-man show, with various arms and branches making different products—over all of which Du Pont's president was expected to keep a close eye. But with the addition of Hazard and Laflin & Rand and their operations across the country, the cousins recognized a need for another method of operation. As a model they used the experience of two of their underlings, Amory Haskell and Hamilton Barksdale, who had reorganized the company's dynamite business by building an elaborate but efficient sales organization in 1892. In 1903 the cousins kicked Haskell and Barksdale upstairs and, with their help, began the reorganization of the unwieldy empire they had created. The result of the shuffle was a streamlined Du Pont, with Coleman as president, overseeing three major divisions (one for each of the company's main products—black powder, dynamite and explosives, and smokeless powder). Manufacturing was concentrated in a few large plants strategically located around the country, and a nationwide marketing department formed around the skeletal sales force established by Haskell and Barksdale. They also added a department to do explosives research, and put up a headquarters building in downtown Wilmington to house the administrative staff. Another reorganization in 1911 added another level of management between president Coleman and the divisions, with Barksdale, as general manager, now in charge of the various divisions.

The reorganizations, with their elaborate family-tree charts and levels of managers, revolutionized American big business, especially after 1917, when Pierre bailed out the struggling General Motors by buying 23% of the stock and applying the organizational skills perfected at Du Pont. Du Pont held control of GM until the early 1950s, when a federal antitrust action forced them to sell.

Meanwhile Du Pont chemists had been experimenting with a product known as guncotton—an early form of nitroglycerine —and those experiments had led to the company's involvement in the textile business. By the end of World War I it was obvious that peacetime uses for artificial fibers and plastics would produce far more profit than explosives, and in the 1920s the company began acquiring the rights to French technology for producing cellophane. Their own experiments improved on it by making it moistureproof, thus transforming cellophane from a decorative wrap into a packaging material for food and other products. Also in the 1920s Du Pont began to produce another French invention, rayon, as a clothing fiber, and they invented a process for using a stronger version of the fiber in auto tire cord.

Gradually Du Pont began to move away from explosives and into synthetics. The most important Du Pont discovery—the one that changed their public image to that of a dignified chemicals and plastics company—was the 1930 creation of nylon. Made from coal, water, and air, the new fiber rapidly gained acceptance as a material in undergarments, chiefly women's stockings, as well as tire cord, auto parts, and brushes. Lucite, a clear and tough plastic resin, soon followed, as did the company's discovery in 1938 of Teflon, another resin used primarily in nonstick cookware. Soon it seemed that Du Pont was introducing a new wonder plastic or fiber every year as the likes of neoprene (synthetic rubber), Orlon, Dacron polyester, and Mylar rolled out of Du Pont's research labs. The company quickly became the world's master synthesizer.

The last du Pont to head the company was Lammot du Pont Copeland, who during the 1960s decided to throw millions of dollars into promoting Corfam, a synthetic leather developed by Du Pont researchers. The decision proved a costly one, eventually costing Du Pont more than $150 million. The dynasty may have ended with him, at least as far as having a du Pont run the Du Pont company. Copeland's son, Lammot Copeland, Jr., was no heir apparent. "Motsey," as he was called, went to Harvard, worried about "creeping socialism," and dabbled in various ventures ranging from newspapers to a carwash. In 1970 he had to seek protection from his creditors, filing for bankruptcy in a petition that listed his assets at $26 million and his debts at $62 million, making it, as the *Wall Street Journal* said, "one of the biggest personal busts of recent times."

By then Motsey's father, the great-great-grandson of the company's founder, had already relinquished the chief executive's post. He had stepped down in 1967 and was succeeded by Charles B. McCoy. McCoy was not a du Pont, but he was the son of a Du Pont executive and had virtually grown up in the company. The big change, and the one that rocked the business world even though it had been clearly signaled, was the selection of Irving Shapiro in 1974 as the new chairman and chief executive officer of the company. Shapiro's father, an immigrant from Lithuania, had been a pants presser in Minneapolis (one of Irving's brothers eventually took over the business), and Irving had grown up poor, wearing shoes with cardboard soles. He went to the University of Minnesota and became a lawyer, and he was then part of the Justice Department team that prosecuted the 11 leaders of the U.S. Communist Party after World War II. In 1951, despite opposition at Du Pont to a Jewish lawyer, Shapiro was hired to work in the Du Pont legal department at Wilmington for $12,000 a year.

At Wilmington, Shapiro confronted his old employer, the Justice Department, playing a major role, on Du Pont's behalf, in the federal antitrust suit that ended with the company being forced to sell their 23% interest in General Motors. Shapiro was the principal architect of the final settlement, which called for Du Pont to distribute their GM shares to Du Pont stockholders. The Internal Revenue Service wanted to treat that distribution as a dividend, taxable as ordinary income. What Shapiro did then was described as follows by *Fortune:*

> In one of the most successful corporate lobbying efforts in history, Du Pont got a bill through Congress in 1962 that saved the individual stockholders an estimated $1 billion by permitting them to account for the GM stock they received as a return on capital, taxable at capital-gains rates. Shapiro directed the company's campaign in Congress and designed the divestiture plan.

By that time Shapiro probably knew more about Du Pont than any du Pont, and he rose swiftly in the company, becoming assistant general counsel in 1965 and vice-president and a member of the executive committee in 1970, the year Motsey filed for bankruptcy. He was named vice-chairman in 1973, making him clearly in line for the top job, but when his selection was announced, *Fortune* still called it "wildly improbable," because he was a nontechnical person at the head of a science-oriented

company. "What is most astonishing of all," added *Fortune*, "is that the son of a poor Jewish shopkeeper should move to the top of the most family-dominated of the nation's major corporations."

As 1980 dawned, Shapiro was still there, although the du Ponts have not exactly disappeared. Five family members and one in-law sit on the board of directors.

Reputation. Most people still think of Du Pont as a sort of national sorcerer, creating miracle fibers and plastics out of nothing through the alchemy of their research and development labs, but the fact is that Du Pont hasn't introduced a genuine miracle for some time, and has even had some notable failures. Lammot du Pont Copeland's Corfam experience was one of these, and the company periodically announces the discovery of "another nylon," which then simply becomes just another fiber. But many industry observers are still waiting to see what becomes of Du Pont, a family company that for so long avoided the trend toward professional managers and that now seems to be going the depersonalized way of all corporations.

What they own. Delaware, according to Ralph Nader. In 1973, *The Company State*, by James Phelan and Robert Pozen, reported the findings of a Ralph Nader study group on the relationship of the Du Pont corporation and family to the state of Delaware. Among other things, the book noted that Christiana Securities, the du Pont family company that held the largest block of Du Pont shares, owned 100% of Wilmington's only newspaper, *The News-Journal* and controlled the Wilmington Trust Company and the Delaware Trust Company, two of the state's largest lending institutions. Du Pont directors also served on the boards of the state's two utilities: Diamond State Telephone and Delmarva Power and Light. Many people, besides Du Pont, disputed the significance of the Nader findings. *Fortune* said the study was "so naive and riddled with errors and misrepresentations that it sank with hardly a ripple."

What Du Pont does own are manufacturing facilities at 87 locations in 28 states, plus manufacturing outposts at 44 locations in 18 foreign countries. The company's physical properties are valued at $10.8 billion—the bulk of them in Texas, Delaware,

The squeeze bottle was introduced in 1947 by Dr. Jules Montenier. He made a white, opaque polyethylene bottle of Stopette deodorant that rocked the cosmetics industry. Within 6 years over 14 million squeeze bottles were produced for more than 2,000 different products.

Tennessee, New Jersey, Virginia, North and South Carolina.

Who owns and runs the company. Du Pont family members still own about 35% of the stock, worth about $2.3 billion. (The family also owns an estimated $1.2 billion in General Motors stock, plus another $1.5 billion in other properties.) Pierre Samuel du Pont fathered a brood that now numbers more than 1,700 people whose interest in chemicals has diluted with their numbers. All these du Ponts are rich, although some more than others, and most still live in Delaware. Some sense of how much money the du Ponts still have in the company is

Help Wanted: Prefer Healthy Male Cockroach

"1984 is already here," says Anthony Mazzochi, leader of the Oil, Chemical and Atomic Workers International Union.

Mazzochi was interviewed in a *New York Times* investigation of "genetic screening," a process chemical companies have quietly begun using on their employees. Company doctors analyze the genetic makeup of an employee—or a job applicant—to determine whether he or she is predisposed to be vulnerable to hazardous chemicals used in the workplace. Or, as industry doctors put it, to determine whether the person's genes are "defective."

With a small sample of blood, the same amount taken for a routine blood test, a technician runs a battery of tests that reveal genetic character. If a company geneticist declares an employee to be "hypersusceptible," that worker can become ineligible to work in areas where certain toxic chemicals are in the environment.

The major proponents of screening are Dow and DuPont, who say they've screened thousands of workers over the past decade. Now the practice has spread from chemicals into the steel and battery industries.

The programs in use or under consideration by companies have been developed over the past 15 years. Meanwhile, both the scientific assumption made by proponents of screening and the idea of the tests themselves have polarized researchers in industry and science and caused outrage among union leaders.

From the start, genetic screening involved genetic variations associated with sex and race. (The Equal Employment Opportunity Commission has about 40 cases on file of people who charge they've been barred from jobs because of alleged hypersusceptibility. Nearly all are women.) Persons with genetic blood disorders like sickle-cell anemia, thalessimia, or deficiency of an enzyme known as G-6-PD are thought, by some doctors, to be at "special risk" from benzene, nitrosamines, nitrites, and lead. What groups have these problems? American and African blacks, certain Italians, Greeks, Yugoslavians, Arabs, Jews of Mediterranean or Middle Eastern descent, Chinese, Filipinos, and East Indians, for starters. An alleged predisposition to harm from industrial agents that trigger bronchitis and emphysema also might give an employer pause about hiring Swedes, Danes, and Norwegians (or people of that ancestry) to work near those chemicals.

The assertion that these groups do in fact have predisposed vulnerabilities is not universally accepted by scientists. (Neither is the assertion that pregnant women must not work around lead because it may cause birth defects. Nonetheless, General Motors says it will not hire fertile women of child-bearing age to work around the element.) Even more hotly debated is the question of whether an industry has the right to screen in the first place.

Opponents of screening feel that susceptible people should be regarded as the canary-in-the-coal-mine, a harbinger of sickness that will eventually harm even the most resistant. They're afraid the chemical companies will kick out workers rather than clean up toxins in the workplace. "The allowable level of benzene in the environment should be such that the most sensitive human being does not get sick. I have as much right to be healthy as anyone else. But some in industry are saying that because you have less G-6-PD, you do not have the same rights as other Americans to be employed and to be healthy," comments MIT biology professor Dr. Jonathan King.

The backers of screening insist that it isn't economically possible to make the workplaces safe for all. They say screening gives workers "a chance to alter their employment goals and enjoy better health."

"I think that in the '80s, we are going to see a lot of victim-blaming," warns union-leader Mazzochi. "The emphasis will be not so much what you work with, it will have to do with who your mother and father were."

Source: *New York Times*, February 3, 1980.

apparent from the stock held by the five family members on the board of directors. In mid-1980 their combined holdings amounted to over $85 million; Irénée du Pont, Jr., has over $40 million; Edward B. du Pont, over $20 million; Wm. Winder Laird, over $11 million; Hugh R. Sharp, Jr., over $9 million; and Lammot du Pont Copeland, over $5 million. Many du Ponts have moved out of Delaware and into other businesses, such as Robert R. M. Carpenter, a cousin, who owns the Philadelphia Phillies baseball team. The family still maintains their eighteenth-century French custom of staging a "calling" on New Year's Day: male members of the du Pont clan gave candies and flowers to female members. But these days every member has to wear a name tag.

Of the 24 Du Pont board members, 17 are company executives, and 2 work for the du Pont-controlled Wilmington Trust Company. Also on the board are the chairman of AT&T and the head of the Massachusetts Institute of Technology. Du Pont's board, broadened since Shapiro took the reins, includes a black, former Federal Reserve Board member Andrew F. Brimmer, and two women, Ruth Patrick, 71-year-old scientist, and Margaret P. MacKimm, public relations director of Kraft. Du Pont reported in 1980 that one-third of the graduating college students they hired in 1979 were minorities or women.

In the public eye. Much of Du Pont's newsworthiness over the years has stemmed from their constant antitrust battles. Since the three cousins established their explosive monopoly in the early 1900s, Du Pont has come under repeated investigation for allegedly monopolizing segments of the auto, chemical, plastic, and synthetic fiber industries—most recently in 1979, when a Federal Trade Commission judge dismissed a suit charging Du Pont with monopolizing the titanium dioxide pigment market. Du Pont is still being sued by the feds, however, this time for alleged violations of the Federal Water Pollution Control Act centering on the dumping of pollutants into the Delaware river. If the feds win, the maximum penalty would be $15,000. Du Pont makes that much profit in 30 seconds. In 1979 Du Pont contributed $8.5 million to education, health care, and other social services. Among corporate givers they rank 15th.

Where they're going. It has been a long time since Du Pont came up with a startling new invention, but this may be changing. In 1980 the company increased their already huge research and development budget by 15% to a total of $475 million. Much of that increase went to life sciences, a discipline Du Pont has never been known for (although their Endo Laboratories makes pharmaceuticals). Du Pont has 4,000 scientists and engineers working in research. Surely they'll come up with something.

Stock performance. Du Pont stock bought for $1,000 in 1970 sold for $1,154 on January 2, 1980.

Access. 1007 Market Street, Wilmington, Delaware 19898; (302) 774-1000.

Consumer brands.

Du Pont paints.
Plastics and fibers: Orlon; Dacron; Quiana; Lucite; Lycra; Teflon; Mylar; SilverStone; Kevlar.
Rain Dance paste wax; Remington guns and ammunition.

Monsanto

Sales: $6.2 billion
Profits: $331 million
Forbes 500 rank: 60
Rank in chemicals: 5
Rank in nylon: 2
Rank in acrylic fibers: 2
Rank in phosphates: 1
Rank in aspirin: 1
Founded: 1901
Employees: 63,000
Headquarters: St. Louis, Missouri

What they do. "Without chemicals," say the Monsanto ads, "life itself would be impossible." And of course so would Monsanto. They're an industry giant, making a long line of chemicals, plastics, and fibers derived mainly from petroleum, natural gas, and phosphate ore. Many of these are "building-block" chemicals that end up in products made by other companies, although Monsanto does carry through some raw materials to a finished stage.

THE TOP 10 U.S. CHEMICAL PRODUCERS

1979 Sales

1. DU PONT $12.6 *billion*
2. DOW CHEMICAL $9.3 *billion*
3. UNION CARBIDE $9.2 *billion*
4. EXXON $6.7 *billion*
5. MONSANTO $6.2 *billion*
6. W.R. GRACE $5.3 *billion*
7. ALLIED CHEMICAL $4.3 *billion*
8. SHELL OIL $3.6 *billion*
9. AMERICAN CYANAMID $3.19 *billion*
10. CELANESE $3.15 *billion*

Source: *Chemical Week*, April 23, 1980.

They make and market Lasso, the largest selling herbicide in the United States. They're responsible for the AstroTurf that has replaced grass in many ball parks. They are the world's largest manufacturer of aspirin: they produce and sell it in bulk to other manufacturers. They are also the leading producer of the chemicals used to make detergents, which they supply to the soap and detergent companies. Their two leading textile fibers are Acrilan and Ultron. Their largest-selling plastic is Lustran, used to make appliance housings and automotive parts (dashboard panels, for example). Basic to Monsanto is their position as the world's largest producer of acrylontrile, a versatile petrochemical used in the production of nylon fibers, acrylic fibers, and thermoplastics.

It's tempting for a Monsanto manager to think that the company could develop their own consumer products and sell them under their own brand names. But there are two problems with this temptation. One is that such a move would bring Monsanto into competition with their own customers. The second is that whenever Monsanto has taken this route, the results have been disastrous. Monsanto was the company that developed the low-sudsing detergent All. However, when they learned how much money it would take to promote a detergent brand in the consumer marketplace, Monsanto people blanched. In 1957 they sold the All name to Lever Brothers, agreeing to continue manufacturing the product.

Agricultural chemicals represent only 15% of Monsanto's sales but half their profits. Among their herbicides, in addition to Lasso, are Roundup, Machete, and Avadex. They also make the Polaris plant-growth regulators.

History. In 1901 John Francis Queeny, a purchasing agent for a St. Louis wholesale drug house, failed to convince his employer to manufacture saccharin instead of importing it from Germany. So with an investment of $5,000 Queeny established his own saccharin production company, naming it Monsanto, after his wife's maiden name. The Monsanto Chemical Works made their first profit—$10,600—in 1905. By then they were also making caffeine and vanillin. Sales passed the $1 million mark in 1915.

World War I was a turning point for Monsanto and other members of the U.S. chemical industry. Previously they had been almost totally dependent on materials imported from Europe, mainly from Germany; now they had to produce their own from scratch. Monsanto realized that they were really on their own when their researchers went to libraries to look up German chemical processes and discovered that the Germans had preceded them: the pages describing these processes had been torn out of the books. Monsanto began making aspirin in 1917 when the German patent expired. By 1918 they had ceased to be a one-factory company and were well on their way to becoming the diversified chemical producer they are today.

By World War II Monsanto was an integral part of the American industrial scene. The 1942 annual report to shareholders was prefaced with this explanation: "It is with regret that we abandon our past practice of transmitting to our shareholders an inform-

In 1953 Monsanto vice-president John L. Gillis stepped into the first Corvette delivered in St. Louis. He got the honor because the sports car's plastic body contained Monsanto's resins.

ative and interpretive annual report . . . the necessity of secrecy imposed by our national interest surrounds much of the activities upon which the company has been engaged." They were referring to the crucial role of the chemical industry in the war effort. Or as one Monsanto executive put it: "America rolled on rubber, the war would roll on rubber, and Monsanto styrene would become a crucial necessity of the wartime synthetic rubber program."

Monsanto met the challenge and pushed full steam ahead on the production of styrene. A newly acquired plant in Texas City, Texas became the focus of this activity. But on April 16, 1947, the plant burned to the ground in the aftermath of a tremendous explosion of ammonium nitrate aboard a French freighter tied up near the Monsanto plant. It was the worst disaster in Monsanto's history. The death toll was 512—145 of whom were Monsanto employees. Monsanto was completely blameless—they had nothing to do with the ammonium nitrate or the French freighter—and they collected insurance claims of $17.3 million. Two years later a new plant stood on the ashes of the old.

Through acquisitions and internal development the Monsanto product line grew longer and longer. It grew so long, in fact, that in 1964 they took the *chemical* out of the corporate name. Sales crossed the $1 billion mark in 1962.

A major turning point in Monsanto's history came in 1960, which was the year Edgar Monsanto Queeny stepped down as head of the company. He had taken the reins in 1928, when he was 30 years old, after his father, John Francisco Queeny, discovered he was incurably ill with cancer. It was Edgar Queeny who built the company into an industrial power. A taciturn leader whose nickname was "Stoneface," Edgar Queeny looked askance at modern political and social developments. He opposed the New Deal. He once pulled Monsanto out of the National Association of Manufacturers because the group didn't come out for high tariffs on chemical imports. Queeny was an only son, and he and his wife had one son who died shortly after birth. Edgar Queeny died in 1968, his wife, Ethel, in 1975. According to Dan Forrestal, who wrote a history of the Monsanto company, *Faith, Hope & $5,000*, there are no known members of the Queeny family left. What survives is the Monsanto name.

Reputation. Edgar Queeny once said Monsanto should be identified with policies and practices "which in an individual would be good morals and good manners." Monsanto's image today is blurred. In the business community they are regarded as a company that has failed to achieve a consistently adequate return on assets. To the outside world they became known as the producers of various chemicals—PCB, vinyl chloride, acrylontrile, methapyrilene, the herbicide Agent Orange—which caused, or were suspecting of causing, ills ranging from birth defects to cancer.

What they own. Monsanto has 64 plants in the United States and another 34 in 20 foreign countries. International operations account for a third of sales. Monsanto is two-thirds owner of Fisher Controls, a Marshalltown, Iowa, maker of process controls, including valves, regulators, and pneumatic controllers. (Britain's General Electric Company owns the other third.)

Who owns and runs the company. In 1972, after a series of mistakes and dismal earnings, Queenyless Monsanto went outside their ranks to find a new chief executive. They found him at their biggest customer, Procter & Gamble. John W. Hanley, who had spent 25 years at P & G, was hired away to bring new life to Monsanto. It was a raid that angered Procter & Gamble. Howard Morgens, chairman of P&G, vented his anger in a *Fortune* interview: "We had worked closely with Monsanto for years. They could walk into our offices and talk to anybody. When a company does that, there is an unwritten code not to offer a job to one of your customer's people. It's an unfortunate thing for a good supplier to do to one of its best customers." Charles H. Sommer, who was then chairman of Monsanto, pursued Jack Hanley after investigating and finding that P&G had no alternative sources for the phosphates they were buying from Monsanto.

The gamble was worth it for Monsanto. Hanley pulled them out of markets where they were weak (this entailed selling or closing 50 businesses) and got the company back on the profit trail. He knew what he had to do. Before taking the job, he asked people what Monsanto was like. The reply was: "They're a great bunch of guys, but they're all going in different directions." Hanley brought to Monsanto the professional management that is the hallmark of P&G. After a few weeks on the job he eliminated weekday golf games and the noontime cocktail. His model is "an organization where responsibility is pushed down to the lowest level." Hanley's children call him "Fossy," a cross between fussy and bossy.

On the Monsanto board are two unusual directors: Jean Mayer, a nutritionist who is president of Tufts University, and Margaret Bush Wilson, a St. Louis attorney who has been chairman of the National Association for the Advancement of Colored People since 1975. Monsanto's record in equal employment opportunity is not outstanding. The company reported in 1979 that minorities and women now make up 6.3% of all employees in managerial positions, "a sixfold increase in the past five years."

In the public eye. Monsanto made charitable contributions of $5.7 million in 1978, slightly more than the average level of corporate contributions (based on a percentage of pretax profits). Monsanto says they rank second in the chemical industry in terms of the dollar value of business placed with minority- and female-owned businesses—$12 million in 1978, double the 1977 allocation.

Monsanto now has in place what it calls "one of the most far-reaching industrial health monitoring systems in existence." This system will medically track each Monsanto employee "through his or her entire career, helping to assure an early alert to any hazard."

According to the Securities and Exchange Commission, Monsanto has made $461,000 in "questionable payments" to officials of foreign governments. However, the company has refused to reveal where some of the under-the-table payments occurred.

Where they're going. Health care, including production of pharmaceuticals, seems to have caught Monsanto's eye. In the middle of 1979, after closing their European nylon operations, they hired Howard A. Schneiderman as senior vice-president for research and development. He was formerly dean of the School of Biological

Without Advertising, Monsanto Itself Would Be Impossible...

"We don't have to apologize for making chemicals," says Robert A. Roland, president of the Chemical Manufacturers Association of America. The CMA hired J. Walter Thompson, one of the most prestigious advertising agencies in the country, to prove the legitimacy of their profession. A $3 million pilot program of positive publicity for the chemical industry should blossom into a media blitz costing $5 million-plus per year in the 1980s. And that's just the CMA; the 1979 advertising tab for image-building in the industry overall was estimated at $10 million. For one year.

Why the effort? Chemical companies have been held in low public esteem in recent years. The Love Canal scandal at Niagara Falls, "midnight dumping" of toxic wastes, as well as numerous spills, explo-

sions, ruined rivers, and injured workers, put chemical companies lowest on the list of 13 industries surveyed for public trust in 1979 by New York polling group Yankelovich, Skelly & White. In fact, the distance between the chemical makers and the industry next above them in credibility is "quite large," the pollsters say.

Individual companies have been wise to image cleanup for some time. Monsanto started the movement in 1977 with a $4.5 million ad campaign ("Without chemicals, life itself would be impossible"). They've spent as much or more every year since. DuPont followed the lead with a $4 million campaign, and its image budget for the 1979–80 television season was estimated at $8 million. Hooker Chemical (the Love Canal defendant) spent

a total of $250,000 to $300,000 for advertisements refuting unfavorable editorials in the *New York Times* and in *Business Week*. Dow Chemical took the theme "Common Sense—Uncommon Chemistry" for print and TV ads that featured employees discussing the company's active desire to save the environment, as well as worker health and safety. Estimated budget: $1 million.

"They're putting their money into ads and not the cleanup," complains Thomas C. Jorling, former assistant administrator at the Environmental Protection Agency. "Why don't they shape up?"

That would be uncommon chemistry indeed.

Source: *Business Week,* October 8, 1979.

Sciences at the University of California at Irvine. One Monsanto product already in test is a polymer that seems effective in helping the body reject tumor cells. Monsanto has also committed $23 million to a joint cancer research venture with Harvard University.

Stock performance. Monsanto stock bought for $1,000 in 1970 sold for $1,639 on January 2, 1980.

Major employment centers. St. Louis, Missouri; Houston, Texas.

Access. 800 North Lindbergh Boulevard, St. Louis, Missouri 63166; (314) 694-1000. Send inquiries or complaints to Les Fries, manager of the consumer inquiry center, at St. Louis headquarters. The toll-free telephone number is (800) 325-4330, extension 3404.

Sales: $9.2 billion
Profits: $556 million
Forbes 500 rank: 34
Rank in chemical industry: 3
Rank in dry-cell batteries: 1
Rank in antifreeze: 1
Rank in plastic bags: 1
Founded: 1886
Employees: 113,300
Headquarters: New York City

What they do. A decade ago Union Carbide refused to attend government conferences discussing how to clean up air pollution. Today their chief executive spends a quarter of his time talking to politicians and opinion leaders, and the company plasters their public service ads across the pages of newspapers and magazines. Union Carbide has learned that if you can't beat them, you can at least bend their ears.

Union Carbide is an industrial behemoth that takes elements from the earth and air and fashions them into chemicals. They rank third among U.S. chemical companies, behind Du Pont and Dow; 1979 was the first year Dow edged them out of second place. They're seventh largest in the world market.

They make a few consumer products, such as Prestone antifreeze, Eveready batteries, Glad plastic wrap, and Simoniz car wax. Generally, though, Union Carbide is twice removed from the marketplace. They sell their basic products to other industrial producers who also don't sell to consumers. For example: their largest customer, the steel industry. Carbide sells oxygen, chromium, manganese, and other materials to steel companies, who use the products to run the furnaces at their steel mills.

Union Carbide is tops in the production of polyethylene (the world's most widely used plastic), glycol (used to manufacture polyester fiber and antifreeze), urethane foam, nitrogen, tungsten, vanadium, uranium, welding equipment, and sausage casings. They also make herbicides, insecticides, waste-water-treatment systems, blood analyzers, and radioisotopes. Carbide operates the government-owned nuclear facilities at Oak Ridge, Tennessee, and Paducah, Kentucky.

History. Union Carbide grew from a carbon company started in 1886 that produced the first dry cell battery and originated the Eveready trade mark. In 1917 a group of New York financiers patched it together with four other companies to form the Union Carbide and Carbon Corporation. When the United States entered World War I, the company moved from metallurgy and carbon products to gases and chemicals. World War II pushed Carbide into the atomic energy program.

In later years Carbide tried their hand at consumer goods, which have higher profit margins than commodity chemicals. In the 1970s they introduced a long line of flops: Chaste, a feminine deodorant; Tight Spot, a foot deodorant; Stud, an oil additive; and Drydees, a disposable diaper. (Drydees alone set them back $15 million.)

Bulk chemicals are where Union Carbide excels, but even there they've had problems, thanks to headlong, thoughtless expansion. They've sold at least a dozen businesses in the last few years, including their $300 million petrochemical operation in Europe.

Sluggish is a term frequently used to describe them, but lately they've been trying

The Million Dollar Paycheck

		Salary and Bonus	Total 1979 Compensation*
1. FRANK E. ROSENFELT** *president and chief executive officer*	MGM	$ 194,000	$5,063,000
2. RAWLEIGH WARNER, JR. *chairman*	MOBIL	$ 902,000	$4,313,000
3. RICHARD W. VIESER *executive vice-president*	McGRAW-EDISON	$ 76,000	$2,635,000
4. BARRIE K. BRUNET *executive vice-president*	MGM	$ 121,000	$2,451,000
5. PAUL P. WOOLARD *senior executive vice-president*	REVLON	$ 630,000	$2,368,000
6. MICHEL C. BERGERAC *chairman, president and chief executive officer*	REVLON	$ 900,000	$2,339,000
7. WILLIAM P. TAVOULAREAS *president*	MOBIL	$ 770,000	$2,313,000
8. R. M. HOLLIDAY *chairman*	HUGHES TOOL	$ 286,000	$2,124,000
9. SIDNEY J. SHEINBERG *president and chief operating officer*	MCA	$ 330,000	$1,984,000
10. JAMES M. BEGGS *executive vice-president*	GENERAL DYNAMICS	$ 320,000	$1,975,000
11. JAMES D. ALJIAN *consultant*	MGM	$ 60,000	$1,840,000
12. J. ROBERT FLUOR *chairman, president and chief executive officer*	FLUOR	$ 638,000	$1,784,000
13. E. CARDON WALKER *president and chief executive officer*	WALT DISNEY	$ 245,000	$1,521,000
14. T. F. BRADSHAW *president*	ATLANTIC RICHFIELD	$ 524,000	$1,516,000
15. EDWARD B. WALKER III *executive vice-president*	GULF OIL	$ 425,000	$1,492,000
16. O. C. BOILEAU *vice-president*	BOEING	$ 167,000	$1,338,000
17. THOMAS D. BARROW *chairman and chief executive officer*	KENNECOTT COPPER	$ 834,000	$1,309,000
18. JESSIE I. AWEIDA *chairman and chief executive officer*	STORAGE TECHNOLOGY	$ 500,000	$1,296,000
19. WILLARD F. ROCKWELL, JR. *chairman*	ROCKWELL INTERNATIONAL	$ 578,000	$1,270,000
20. LEE A. IACOCCA *president*	CHRYSLER	$1,266,000	$1,266,000
21. HENRY WENDT *president and chief operating officer*	SMITHKLINE	$ 301,000	$1,256,000
22. M. T. STAMPER *president*	BOEING	$ 339,000	$1,159,000
23. ROBERT F. DEE *chairman and chief executive officer*	SMITHKLINE	$ 406,000	$1,142,000
24. H. S. GENEEN *chairman*	ITT	$ 636,000	$1,116,000
25. C. C. GARVIN, JR. *chairman*	EXXON	$ 830,000	$1,078,000

*Includes stock options and stock appreciation rights. Companies often give their top executives the right to buy a specified number of shares of company stock at the market price (a "stock option"). If the price of the stock increases at a later date, the executive may exercise his option to buy the stock at the original price. The difference between the price he was allowed to purchase the stock and the actual market value when he bought it is shown in this chart. Stock appreciation rights work similarly except that the executive does not actually have to buy the stock—he simply receives a payment that reflects the increased value of the company's stock.

**Rosenfelt's income package equalled $2,531.50 per hour (assuming 50, 40-hour work weeks).

Source: Sibson & Co., *Business Week*, May 12, 1980.

to rouse themselves from their torpor. They weeded out their older managers by inducing 1,000 of them to retire early. In 1980 the company began to move their headquarters from their New York skyscraper on Park Avenue to the greener pastures of Danbury, Connecticut, to attract talented young managers with families.

The exit from New York was not without controversy. Top officials of New York state, headed by Governor Hugh Carey, tried to dissuade Carbide. In a 1976 meeting Carbide explained to these officials that a $20,000-a-year employee would save $922 a year in taxes by moving to Connecticut, a $80,000 executive would save $5,837, and a $200,000-a-year man would save $11,600. According to *New York Times* reporter Fred Ferretti, writing in *Barron's*, Warren Anderson, majority leader of the New York State Senate, replied to this argument by saying: "Do you mean to say you're going to tell your stockholders you're moving just to save yourself some personal income taxes?" The embarrassed Carbide people then said the real reason was that they couldn't attract bright professional and technical people to the New York scene. They told of one Carbide manager who refused a transfer to New York, saying, "I don't want to move my family to the jungle."

Reputation. Early in 1979 the *Wall Street Journal* was still able to describe Carbide as "an unwieldy giant run amok, plunging into often mindless new ventures." The company is working hard to turn that image around. Executive vice-president Douglas H. Freeman says, "Larger is not where our aim is. We want to be more profitable. We'd drop $1 billion in sales off tomorrow if that would help."

What they own. Some 500 plants, mines, and mills in 37 countries. The value of their properties is higher than all but 18 other U.S. companies.

Who owns and runs the company. The architect of Carbide's turnaround has been William S. Sneath, who became chairman and chief executive in 1977 and whose father also worked for Carbide. A Harvard Business School graduate, he's the first nonengineer in recent times to head the company. Moving up with him at the same time—into the president's post—was Warren M. Anderson. Both Sneath and Anderson have spent their entire working careers with Carbide. The Brooklyn-born Anderson took a chemistry degree at Colgate but came up through the Carbide sales ranks.

At the end of 1979 Carbide employed more than 10,000 minorities and over 19,000 women, representing 13% and 24%, respectively, of their U.S. work force. The comparable figures for 1962 were 3% and 16%. The evidence that the company is aware of their previous insularity shows in these recent additions to the board of directors: Jerome H. Holland, a black and former U.S. ambassador to Sweden; Kathryn D. Wriston, an attorney (and wife of Citicorp chairman Walter Wriston); Russell E. Train, former administrator of the Environmental Protection Agency and president of the World Wildlife Fund; and Roberto de Jesus Toro, president of the Banco de Ponce in Puerto Rico, home of a major Carbide petrochemical facility.

A recent count showed that the largest single holder of Carbide stock (2.4%) is the trust department of Morgan Guaranty, on whose board sits R. Manning Brown, Jr., chairman of the New York Life Insurance Co. and a director of Union Carbide.

In the public eye. In the late 1960s and early 1970s Union Carbide was virtually Environmental Enemy number 1. Environmentalists called their Alloy, West Virginia, iron-alloy plant "the smokiest factory in the world"; an outdoor statue of St. Anthony there had to be cased in plastic because pollution from the Union Carbide plant was turning it black. When Carbide threatened to lay off 625 workers in Ohio to offset the cost of pollution control, Ralph Nader called it "environmental blackmail." The company stonewalled efforts to clean up several of their plants, and by the time they finally yielded to public and government pressure, they were widely seen, as *Fortune* said, as "a reactionary ogre obsessed with profits."

> **Women account for 98% of all secretaries, 94% of all typists, 78% of all clerical workers, 95% of all private household workers, less than 10% of skilled workers, and less than 5% of top management employees.**

Since then the company has taken long strides toward correcting their problems and improving their image. They spent $35 million to clean up the Alloy plant, which is now considered a model of pollution control. They are sponsoring a study of 40,000 Carbide workers to determine the health effects of working with chemicals. Carbide has also developed a new type of "molecular sieve" to strain pollutants out of water.

Where they're going. They're trying to act like a responsible corporate citizen— and they are still shedding girth. In June 1980 they announced the sale of half their metals business—silicone, manganese, specialty chromium, and calcium carbide—to a Norwegian-Canadian combine for $285 million.

Stock performance. Union Carbide stock bought for $1,000 in 1970 sold for $1,135 on January 2, 1980.

Access. 270 Park Avenue, New York, New York 10017; (212) 551-2345.

Consumer brands.

Prestone antifreeze; Eveready dry-cell batteries; Glad plastic wrap and bags; Simoniz car wax.

Earthmovers

☐ CATERPILLAR

Sales: $7.6 billion
Profits: $492 million
Forbes 500 rank: 45
Rank in earth-moving equipment: 1
Founded: 1928
Employees: 89,400
Headquarters: Peoria, Illinois

What they do. Pass a building site, an oil field, a logging operation, or a place where a new road is being graded, and you're almost certain to see a piece of Caterpillar equipment. They are the world's largest earth mover, clearer of jungles, and reshaper of mountains—the makers of road graders and scrapers, bulldozers, backhoes, forklifts, and dump trucks, all painted Caterpillar's trademark bright yellow for easy identification. They control about half the western world's market for heavy construction equipment, and account through their exports, for almost $2 billion of the foreign currencies flowing into the United States. Cat makes hugh bulldozers costing up to $500,000 each. In 1979 they converted their traditional bright yellow color to a butterscotch yellow after the Occupational Safety and Health Administration issued new regulations that caused Cat to change to a lead-free paint.

Caterpillar—or "Cat" to their friends and foes alike—manufactures this equipment in one of their 26 plants: 15 in the United States, 3 in the United Kingdom, 2 each in France and Brazil, and 1 each in Australia, Belgium, Canada, and Mexico. The equipment then goes out to Cat's network of 253 dealers worldwide, who sell it to the heavy construction industry. Cat also manufactures a line of diesel engines for their heavy equipment as well as for on-highway trucks, marine use, and electric power–generating systems.

Cat is very attractive to Wall Street investors. They rank 45th in sales, 43rd in profits in the country, and 28th in market value (the price of one share of stock multiplied by the total number of shares).

History. Caterpillar's roots are in California's Sacramento Valley, where two companies—the Holt Manufacturing Company and the C. L. Best Tractor Company—started simultaneously in the mid-1880s. The Holt company was the more notable of the two, especially after Benjamin Holt, the company's founder, hit on the idea of running a tractor on crawler tracks rather than the iron wheels which sank into the mud of California's farmland. The crawler track, which allowed big, clumsy equipment to move over the dirt easily, was dubbed the "Caterpillar" by the company. It inspired the 1915 British invention of the armored tank. When the war ended, the U.S. Army gave their tanks to states and counties to use in road construction work. Their rugged efficiency at this task surprised construction contractors and the Holt Company alike.

But after the war the Holt company began to drift, heavily burdened with debt and under strong competition from Best Tractor. In 1925 a San Francisco stockbroker proposed a merger between the two, and in 1928 the Caterpillar Tractor Company was born. Headquarters were moved to Peoria, in order to be closer to the bulk of their farmer customers; but soon the company's new president, Raymond Force, decided there was more growth potential in the earth-moving and construction businesses, and the company began to concentrate their efforts there. By 1929 they were a major force in the field. Force's decision to expand into foreign markets helped Cat to weather the Depression. Between 1929 and 1933—the time of the first Soviet five-year plan—Caterpillar sold the Soviet Union $18 million worth of equipment.

Caterpillar also began to establish a reputation for homespun management under Force, a reputation that was cemented under his successor, Louis Neumiller. Neumiller's "industrial version of the Boy Scout law," as *Fortune* called it in 1963, consisted of homey axioms on duty and honesty. A sample: "There is but one Caterpillar and wherever it is, you will find it reaching for high levels of integrity, achievement and quality—standing first and foremost for the rights and dignity of the individual and wishing to make associa-

Red Faces in Peoria

There were lots of red faces in Peoria in the summer of 1979. It seems Caterpillar had sent a 95-ton bulldozer, which they called the world's biggest and most powerful earth mover, to a major international exhibition in Moscow in the hopes of selling the machine to the Russians after the show for a reported $500,000. Though Cat had no firm contract when they shipped it (at a cost of $30,000), they had good rea-

son to believe it would be picked up, especially after Premier Alexei Kosygin showed up at the exhibition and spent time talking with Cat executives about the marvelous vehicle. Cat officials gave the premier a $25 model of the bulldozer, which he played with for 10 minutes and asked for another to take back to the "boss"—party chairman Leonid Brezhnev. But when the exhibition closed, no order was forth-

coming, and the Soviets demanded that Cat pay $45 a day rent to keep the bulldozer at the exhibit site and $60 a day to provide a 24-hour guard. Eventually the Soviets bailed Cat out of the dilemma and bought the machine—reportedly at a substantial discount.

tion with the Company a life-satisfying experience." Neumiller also established another Caterpillar tradition: coming up through the ranks. Of the top three Cat executives today, only one has been to college.

Reputation. Caterpillar has a well-deserved image as a tight-lipped, conservative company—so conservative that they almost never innovate, preferring to let their competitors make the mistakes and then coming out with a superior product. As Neumiller once said, "We do it the second or third ime, and we do it better."

What they own. Cat's biggest asset is their reputation for quality. Cat equipment has a lower down-time (when equipment is out for repairs) than any of their competitors. Their parts department is known for its efficiency: if a Cat part needs replacing, it's there the next day.

Their buildings, machinery, and equipment were valued in 1979 at $3.6 billion—at original cost. They owe more than $1 billion.

Who owns and runs the company. Cat is a place where traditional American values matter. Fancy degrees and prestigious schools don't count for much at Cat. On-the-job training does. Neither president Robert Gilmore nor former (until 1977) board chairman William Naumann graduated from college; they both started as apprentice machinists. Two of Caterpillar's three top officials, Gilmore and executive vice-president E. J. Schlegel, were born in Peoria, and the third, chairman Lee Morgan, comes from Aledo, a smaller Illinois town. They're a tight bunch; Gilmore and Morgan live two blocks away on the same Peoria street. All of Cat's directors are white, middle-class men. The board includes such captains of industry as David Packard, chairman of Hewlett-Packard, and Rawleigh Warner, chairman of Mobil Oil.

The strong following Cat has on Wall Street is indicated by 82% of their shares being held by institutions such as banks, insurance companies, mutual and pension funds. Employee investment-funds in 9 countries own more than 6% of the shares, and the employees are allowed to vote the shares allocated to them.

Employees represented by the United Auto Workers struck Caterpillar for 78 days at the end of 1979, eventually signing a contract that will give them more than $10 an hour. About 10% of Cat's U.S. work force are minorities.

In the public eye. Although Caterpillar's reputation for corporate secrecy is legend, they came into the glare of the spotlight recently when the Soviets arrested F. Jay Crawford, of International Harvester. Marshall Goldman, an associate director of Harvard's Russian Research center, complained that Caterpillar, "Harvester's chief competitor, not only publicly refused to protest (like all the other companies with Moscow offices), but reeled in the contracts the Soviets suddenly started to divert its way in an effort to prevent a united front." In fact, Cat did not receive any Harvester contracts from the Soviets—those went to a Japanese company—and they claim they made their protest through the proper channels.

Caterpillar is envied in the business world for their Code of Worldwide Business Conduct, a felicitous expression of ethical values that in the hands of other corporate wordsmiths comes out reading mealymouthed. Many companies have used it as a model. One example from the code: "The law is a floor. Ethical business conduct should normally exist at a level well above the minimum required by the law." Caterpillar was conspicuous by their absence from the long roster of companies disclosing questionable payments overseas—and Cat does about half their business abroad.

Where they're going. Cat intends to take over more and more of the lucrative diesel engine market. They recently contracted with Ford Motor to share in the marketing and servicing of the diesel engines Cat makes. This is important since it gives Cat a much more global reach than they had before: they now have what *Forbes* calls a "big chunk" of the medium-sized truck diesel engine market as a result.

Stock performance. Caterpillar stock bought for $1,000 in 1970 sold for $1,906 on January 2, 1980.

Major employment centers. Peoria, Aurora, and Joliet, Illinois.

Access. 100 Northeast Adams Street, Peoria, Illinois 61629; (309) 675-1000.

Coddled Criminals

In 1975 the Fruehauf Corporation, its Chairman, and its President were found guilty of conspiring to evade more than $12 million in federal taxes. Three years later after long and expensive legal maneuverings paid for by the corporation, President Robert D. Rowan and Chairman William E. Grace finally had to resign their jobs in the expectation that they would soon be in jail.

Soon thereafter the judge in the case had a change of heart about the sentence, and the two men escaped jail. Although Fruehauf had been bankrolling Rowan and Grace all along, the Board now wanted to rehire them and reinstate them in all their former glory. To support this action Fruehauf published, in its 1979 Notice of Annual Meeting of Shareholders, a list of twenty-eight American executives who between 1971 and 1978 had

been indicted for or implicated in crimes. The company argued that, since half of these executives had been retained or rehired, Fruehauf had ample precedent for doing the same.

Rowan and Grace have now been reinstated at Fruehauf, but the company has done the rest of us a service by providing the following list of coddled corporate criminals.

AMERICAN AIRLINES. George Spater, chairman and chief executive officer, was implicated in illegal corporate political contributions in 1973. No criminal charges were brought. He resigned as chairman and did not seek reelection as a director.

AMERICAN SHIP BUILDING. George Steinbrenner III, chairman and CEO, was indicted in 1973 for illegal corporate political contributions and fined $1,000. He resigned as chief executive officer but remained chairman.

ASHLAND OIL. Orin E. Atkins, chairman and CEO, was indicted in 1973 for illegal corporate political contributions and fined $1,000. He retained his jobs with Ashland.

AMREP. Howard Friedman, president and director, was indicted for fraudulent land sales and mail fraud in 1976. He was sentenced to six months in prison but the sentence was later reduced. He resigned as director and suspended himself as president upon conviction, and resigned as president when appeal lost. AMREP rehired him as an employee after prison term was completed.

BORMAN'S. Arnold Faudman, director and executive vice president, was indicted for obstruction of justice in 1977 and served 2½ years in prison. He resigned from Borman.

BRANIFF AIRWAYS. Harding L. Lawrence, chairman and CEO, was indicted for illegal corporate political contributions in 1973. He was fined $1,000 but kept his job.

BROWNING. John Val Browning, president and director, was indicted in 1976 for obstruction of justice and customs infringements. He resigned upon indictment.

CARNATION. H. Everett Olson, chairman and CEO, was indicted for illegal corporate political contributions in 1973 and fined $1,000. He retained his job.

CIRCLE F INDUSTRIES. Edward A. Ring, chairman and CEO, was indicted for antitrust price-fixing in 1977. He was fined $20,000 and sentenced to 30 days in prison with 17-month suspended sentence. He kept his job with Circle F, but later retired and was retained as consultant to company.

Michael St. John, president and director, was indicted for the same violation. He was fined $5,000 with 18-month suspended sentence, and kept his job.

CONTAINER CORPORATION OF AMERICA. R. Harper Brown, president and director, was indicted for antitrust price-fixing in 1976. He was fined $35,000 and sentenced to 2 months in prison, but the fine and sentence were later reduced. He resigned as president, but retained directorship and elected vice chairman in 1977.

CONTINENTAL OIL. Wayne E. Glenn and Williard H. Burnap, vice-chairmen, were implicated in questionable foreign and domestic political payments in 1976. No criminal charges were brought, but both resigned.

DIAMOND INTERNATIONAL. William J. Koslo, executive vice president and director, was indicted in 1976 for antitrust price-fixing. He was fined $15,000 and was ordered to do 7 days of community work. He retained his job at Diamond International and subsequently became chairman and CEO.

FLORIDA STEEL. E.L. Flom, president and director, was

indicted in 1974 for antitrust price-fixing. He was fined (amount unknown) but kept his job.

GOODYEAR TIRE & RUBBER. Russell D. Young, chairman and CEO, was indicted for illegal corporate political contributions in 1973, and fined $1,000. He retired as CEO after conviction, retired as chairman three months later, but kept his directorship.

GULF OIL. Bob R. Dorsey, chairman and CEO, was implicated in illegal corporate political contributions and questionable foreign payments in 1975. No criminal charges were brought, but he resigned.

LOCKHEED. A. Carl Kotchian, president and vice-chairman, and Daniel J. Haughton, chairman and CEO, were implicated in questionable foreign payments in 1975. No criminal charges were brought but they resigned.

J. RAY McDERMOTT. C.L. Graves, chairman and CEO, was indicted for antitrust price-fixing and mail and wire fraud in 1978. He pleaded no contest and fined (amount unknown). Civil charges are still pending. He resigned as chairman and CEO two months after indictment for reasons of health, but retained directorship.

3M. Harry Heltzer, chairman and CEO, was indicted for illegal corporate political contributions in 1973 and fined $500. He resigned as CEO and did not seek re-election as director.

NATIONAL GYPSUM. Colon Brown, chairman and CEO, was indicted for antitrust price-fixing in 1973. He was fined $50,000 and received 6-month

suspended sentence, but it was reversed on appeal, and a new trial was ordered. He resigned as director after conviction but stayed as unpaid consultant.

NORTHROP. Thomas V. Jones, chairman, president and CEO, was indicted in 1974 for illegal corporate political contributions, and fined $5,000. He resigned as chairman in July, 1975; resigned as president and reinstated as chairman in February, 1976.

OCCIDENTAL PETROLEUM. Armand Hammer, chairman and CEO, was indicted for illegal personal political contributions in 1975. He was fined $3,000 and ordered to 1 year probation. He kept his job.

PHILLIPS PETROLEUM. W.W. Keeler, chairman of the board and CEO, was indicted in 1973 for illegal corporate political contributions, and fined $1,000. He retired as president and did not seek reelection as director.

TECHNICAL TAPE. Gerald Sprayregen, chairman and CEO, was indicted for securities fraud in 1977. He was sentenced to 1 year in prison. During his imprisonment his duties were assigned to another person, but he retained the job and resumed duties upon release.

TELEPROMPTER. Irving Kahn, chairman and CEO, was indicted in 1971 for bribery and perjury. He was sentenced to 5 years in prison and resigned from his post.

U.S. GYPSUM. Graham J. Morgan, chairman and CEO, was indicted in 1973 for antitrust price-fixing. He was fined $40,000 and given 6-month suspended sentence. He kept his job.

Reprinted from *Business and Society Review,* Spring 1980, "Corporate Criminals Who Kept their jobs," by Robert Stuart Nathan. Nathan's original article and chart appeared in *Harper's,* January 1980.

JOHN DEERE

Sales: $4.9 billion
Profits: $310 million
Forbes 500 rank: 80
Rank in farm equipment: 1
Founded: 1837
Employees: 65,400
Headquarters: Moline, Illinois

What they do. Deere is about as complicated as an Illinois cornfield. They're
America's number 1 farm equipment
manufacturer, selling more than $3.5 bil-
lion worth of tractors, plows, combines,
and the like each year to farmers all over the
world, all the while relying on the time-
honored Midwestern values of hard work
and what *Fortune,* in 1976, called playing
"fair and square." They're also one of the
nation's fastest-growing corporations. In
the decade just ended, Deere's sales quintu-
pled—a growth rate faster than Xerox and
more than twice as fast as either IBM or
Texas Instruments.

Deere did it by knowing what the world's
farmers wanted. After World War II they
were the first to spot a trend in farming
away from labor and toward heavy machinery. They capitalized on the trend by pouring twice as much money into research and
development as their competitors—as
much as 4¢ for every dollar in sales—and by
asking farmers what they needed. By the
mid-1960s their research and aggressive
overseas expansion programs had coupled
to move Deere past International Harvester
as the country's top farm-equipment manufacturer.

A replica of the steel plow invented by John Deere—it
marked the start of a company that's now the leading
maker of farm equipment.

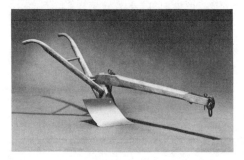

Deere also sells industrial equipment like
bulldozers, backhoes, and forklifts, and
they sell consumer products like garden
tractors and lawnmowers as well, but farm
equipment still accounts for three-fourths
of Deere's sales. Understandably they like
to stay in touch with the farmers they serve.
Their award-winning rusted steel and
smoked glass headquarters, which *Mainliner*
magazine has called "a corporate Versailles," sits on 1,000 acres of landscaped
grounds in the middle of the cornfields near
Moline, Illinois. And you can bet those
cornfields are all tilled by green and yellow
plows and tractors with leaping deer logos
on the sides.

History. John Deere was an enterprising
Vermont blacksmith who in 1837 moved to
Grand Detour, Illinois, and invented the
first self-cleaning steel plow. The plow was
curved to one side, which enabled it to cut
a clean furrow slice without frequent stops
having to be made to scrape off the dirt; it
represented a major improvement over the
cast-iron plows then in use in the Midwest,
which bogged down periodically in the
sticky prairie soil.

Over the years John Deere's successors
continued to innovate. They invented the
first automatic wire-tie hay baler, which
packages and ties hay bales, and the first
bale ejector, which tosses the bales into a
following wagon. But their most valuable
asset was their relationship with Midwestern farmers. During the tough times of the
Depression, Deere continued to extend
credit to their customers on their most expensive equipment, even though it often
took years to collect on debts they had written off in the mid-1930s. The policy resulted
in repeat business and business from the
sons of old customers. Deere thought so
much of their customers that they hired Dr.
Janet Travell, who treated President John
Kennedy's back, to design a tractor seat for
them. Today, throughout the Midwest toy
Deere tractors are fixed to rural mailboxes
like little coats of arms—and some farmers
say that if their local John Deere dealer sold
underwear, they'd buy it.

Since 1837 Deere has had only five chief
executives—all related by blood or marriage to the Deere family. The current chief
executive officer, William Hewitt, married
the boss's daughter and took over in 1955
after his father-in-law, Colonel Charles
Deere Wiman, the founder's great-grand-

son, died of cancer. Under Hewitt, Deere made what U.S. Department of Agriculture specialists called the most significant innovation in farm machinery since World War II. The innovation was a combine that harvested and shelled ears of corn right in the field through the use of a "corn head," an attachment that looks something like a giant hair clipper and scrapes individual kernels off the ears, cutting harvesting time by hours. The corn head now comes in sizes wide enough to harvest six rows at a time. Deere also introduced the first "hay cuber," which cuts and compresses up to five tons of hay every hour into one- by two-inch blocks—perfect for cows. In this form hay is also easier to handle, ship, and store.

Hewitt also encouraged the company to go after the "Cadillac market"—the top 20% of farmers who earn most of the farm cash income. To help produce and sell to that market, Deere cataloged on computer tape by crops grown and other data 1 million farmers. Hewitt also decentralized Deere to the point where each factory is now responsible for all aspects of one category of machines, from design and testing right through manufacturing.

Finally, under Hewitt's prodding, Deere expanded overseas, where they now sell $1 billion in farm equipment a year, although they still trail International Harvester, which had a big jump on Deere in foreign markets. *Fortune* writer Charles Burck described how Hewitt made this move in 1956 not too long after he arrived in Moline from his native San Francisco. Hewitt called in one of Deere's top factory men, Harry Pence, and asked him to investigate possible acquisitions overseas. Pence had never been outside the United States in his life, and according to Burck, he replied, "Hell, Bill, I don't even know where those places are." Hewitt snapped back: "Harry, go and buy you and your wife plane tickets, fly around the world and find out where they are." Pence went off on a two-month trip, leading to the acquisition of a German tractor company, Lanz, and the building or acquiring of plants in five other countries.

Reputation. *Fortune's* 1976 article summed up the Deere reputation succinctly. "Deere is a culture as well as a corporation. . . . They still think of themselves as the corporate descendants of John Deere—an innovative artisan who made an honest product and dealt honestly with his customers."

Deere people pride themselves on being square shooters, and that's one reason they're known as such a good company to work for: a company survey a few years ago turned up the astonishing fact that 90 of the company's top 100 executives began their careers there.

What they own. Deere's most valuable "possession" is their network of 5,100 dealerships worldwide (2,300 in the United States). Many of them carry up to 15,000 parts in their warehouses—some for tractors that are 40 years old. Deere's service and parts distribution depot near Moline, Illinois, is open 24 hours a day, seven days a week, shipping parts anywhere in the United States the same day orders arrive.

Who owns and runs the company. Hewitt, a former San Franciscan, was an odd choice to head up the corniest of the cornbelt companies. Old friends told *Fortune* that he had an extraordinary "love of style and flair, and an unswerving commitment to having everything that surrounded him to be the best." Many Deere watchers doubted he'd last a year as company president when he succeeded Wiman; but Hewitt not only lasted, he remade Deere. One of his first acts on taking over was moving Deere out of their musty, 90-year-old headquarters in Moline and onto their landscaped grounds, in a building designed by Eero Saarinen. But his commitment to art and culture hasn't deprived Hewitt of a sense of showmanship. In 1960 he introduced a new tractor by airlifting all 5,000 dealers to Dallas for a Texas barbeque and fireworks in the Cotton Bowl. Then, in the

The Eero Saarinen-designed headquarters of John Deere sits in the middle of the Illinois cornfields. It symbolizes the sophistication of the company, called by *Forbes* "the country slicker."

jewelry department of Neiman-Marcus, a ribbon wrapping a huge gift was clipped and the sides of the box fell down to reveal a shining new tractor with a diamond tiara hanging from the hood.

In the public eye. Deere has a long-standing reputation for community involvement. The John Deere Foundation regularly donates money to health, educational, and cultural organizations, and their artist-in-residence program, which features a series of well-known artists such as pianist Barbara Nissman, brings culture to the culture-starved midwestern town where Deere has facilities. Deere also supports youth groups like Future Farmers of America, 4-H, and the Outstanding Young Farmer program.

Where they're going. Overseas. Deere was slow to get into the foreign market—10 years behind International Harvester, their main competitor in the international farm-equipment field. When they finally made their move in the 1960s, Deere rapidly took over 10 to 12% of the market, compared with about 15% for IH. They now have plants in Europe, South Africa, Venezuela, Australia, Mexico, and Japan.

Stock performance. Deere stock bought for $1,000 in 1970 sold for $3,629 on January 2, 1980.

Major employment centers. Moline, Illinois; Waterloo and Davenport, Iowa.

Access. John Deere Road, Moline, Illinois 61265; (309) 792-8000.

INTERNATIONAL HARVESTER

Sales: $8.4 billion
Profits: $370 million
Forbes 500 rank: 37
Rank in heavy-duty trucks: 1
Rank in farm machinery: 2
Rank in earth-moving equipment: 2
Founded: 1902
Employees: 97,660
Headquarters: Chicago, Illinois

What they do. Archie McCardell is a man with problems. The chief executive officer of International Harvester, the nation's largest producer of heavy-duty trucks, was brought in from Xerox in 1977 and given a fancy contract to turn slumping Harvester around. Then the company was hit by the longest strike in their history—172 days in 1979 and 1980—and suffered a six-month loss of almost half a billion dollars. Some industry analysts now predict that International Harvester could become the Chrysler of the industrial equipment world.

That would be a hard pill for Harvester to swallow. They are the oldest of the industrial equipment companies, the successor of the McCormick Harvesting Machine Company, which in turn traced their origins back to Cyrus McCormick's 1831 invention of the reaper. Today Harvester makes more than harvesting machines for farmers. They also make heavy gasoline- and diesel-powered trucks and tractors; International Scout four-wheel drive vehicles; lawn and garden tractors for home use; earth-moving equipment for construction;

THE TOP 10 IN RESEARCH AND DEVELOPMENT SPENDING

R & D Spending (1979)

1. GENERAL MOTORS $1.9 *billion*
2. FORD $1.7 *billion*
3. IBM $1.4 *billion*
4. GENERAL ELECTRIC $640 *million*
5. UNITED TECHNOLOGIES $545 *million*
6. BOEING $525 *million*
7. KODAK $459 *million*
8. ITT $436 *million*
9. DU PONT $415 *million*
10. EXXON $381 *million*

Source: *Business Week*, July 7, 1980.

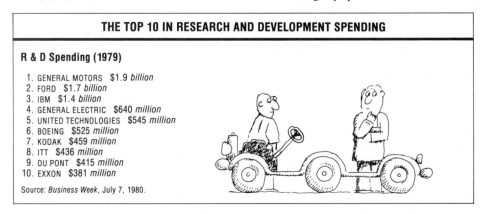

and turbine-driven compressors, generators, and pumps for the oil and natural gas industries. The biggest part of their business is trucks: one of every four heavy-duty trucks in America was made by Harvester.

While more than a third of their employees are outside the United States, and nearly 30% of their sales are overseas, Harvester has been cutting back their foreign operations. In the last few years they've sold seven foreign subsidiaries in places like Kenya and Peru, although they still have a significant presence in Europe and Africa, with 16 plants on the two continents, in addition to 26 at home.

History. Although Cyrus McCormick invented the reaper in 1831, it took him 10 years to sell his first one. By 1848 his patent had expired, and McCormick was forced to maintain his lead in farm equipment through salesmanship techniques. He advertised, offered a warranty, and even extended credit to his customers—all of which were innovations at the time.

The first reapers were bulky, ungainly vehicles, so noisy that slaves or farmhands had to walk alongside the machine to calm the horses that pulled it. At the Great Exhibition in London in 1851 the *Times* of London derided the reaper as "a cross between . . . a chariot, a wheelbarrow, and a flying machine." But the machine still won first prize.

Photographic reproduction of an N.C. Wyeth painting shows Cyrus Hall McCormick in his hour of triumph: the demonstration of the world's first successful mechanical reaper in 1831. That's supposed to be 22-year-old McCormick striding behind his invention.

In 1902, after Cyrus's death, the McCormick company merged with Deering Harvester Company and three smaller machinery makers to form International Harvester. Their development in the early 1900s of high-wheeled vehicles known as "auto-wagons" for farmers made Harvester a pioneer in motorized trucks. (They also made a short-lived foray into auto production.) By the 1930s, after buying up a few more companies, Harvester was also involved in construction equipment, making a few crawler-type tractors for farm and industrial use. Harvester even tried to get into the consumer market with refrigerators, freezers, and air conditioners after World War II, but the move didn't pan out. Today the only general consumer items they make are lawn and garden tractors and the International Scout, a jaunty passenger vehicle popular among hunters and other off-road drivers.

Since 1831 a McCormick descendant always either ran the company or stood in the wings waiting to take over; but when Brooks McCormick decided to step down in 1977, the line ended. McCormick brought in Archie McCardell, the number 2 man at Xerox with a reputation as a tough cost-cutter, and when McCardell took over as chief executive officer, he proved that his reputation was well-deserved. He began by cutting out deadwood, forcing the retirement of several Harvester executives, and demanding tight budgets. But he ran into trouble when he sent a group of outside consultants through the plants to increase efficiency. Increasing efficiency meant, in many cases, toughening work rules that the United Auto Workers, which represents most of Harvester's employees, had spent 30 years winning. The confrontation led to a 172-day strike, in which the company appears to have won most of the bargaining issues. But the economic impact of the strike was devastating and the company was only beginning to recover by late 1980.

Reputation. McCardell was thought to be pulling Harvester out of the doldrums until the strike hit. The company's competitors filled the gaps left by the strike, and Harvester's stock prices began to slip. They posted a loss of $222 million for the quarter ending January 31, 1980—the first quarter of the strike, which began in November—and $257 million for the next quarter. While McCardell remains optimistic about the rest of the year and the immediate future, one stock market analyst told the *Wall Street Journal* on May 8, 1980, that Harvester "lost more than they'll ever gain back" as the result of the strike.

Who owns and runs the company. Someone else who lost a great deal from the strike is McCardell himself. He came on as one of the biggest bonus babies in corporate history, with a contract that called for a $1.5 million bonus for leaving Xerox and coming over to Harvester, a salary of $460,000 (since raised to $525,000) a year, and other incentives that amounted to $300,000 in 1979. But it was all tied to a deal that enabled him to buy $1.8 million of Harvester stock with $1.8 million loaned to him by the company at 6% interest. The deal was that if McCardell achieved certain profit goals over a seven-year period, the entire loan would be forgiven—he would not have to pay back any of it. But the strike obviously put a crimp in those plans. Far from reaching his profit goals, McCardell was losing money in 1980, and Harvester's stock was going nowhere.

McCardell's management style was described by *Fortune* as "amiably dead-serious." He smokes cigars, works in his shirtsleeves, and frequently kicks his shoes off in the executive suite. But he's also very demanding and does not hesitate to tell suppliers that their service is lousy, or his managers that their budgets are too big.

In the public eye. Harvester may face an even more serious problem because of their farm tractors. In late 1979 a jury awarded Merlin Stambaugh, an Illinois farmer, a total of $15.6 million as a result of an accident he suffered while working on a Harvester tractor. Stambaugh claimed a flaming geyser of gasoline shot out of the tractor's gas tank, causing serious burns on his body. He contended that the company had made an error by designing the gas tank to sit on top of the engine. Harvester claimed the accident took place because of a mistake on Stambaugh's part rather than a design flaw. But at least a dozen other farmers have filed similar suits against Harvester stemming from injuries they suffered from accidents while working with Harvester tractors built between the early 1950s and the mid-1970s that had gas tanks on top of the engines.

Where they're going. McCardell is optimistic about the future at Harvester, but he seems to be alone in that assessment, especially if the opinion of a Harvester crane operator can be believed. The *Wall Street Journal* reported in May 1980 that Harvester's labor relations had been dealt a severe blow by the strike and quoted the crane operator as saying that "quality will drop—you'll see." McCardell, he said, had "cut the vein that carries the blood to the system, and that's the workers." If productivity does indeed drop, Harvester will be hard-pressed to compete against John Deere and Caterpillar, their two principal opponents.

Harvester also announced in 1980 that they would soon jettison their International Scout division. A Texas entrepreneur named Edward Russell plans to buy the Scout division for an undisclosed sum and thinks the four-wheel drive sport-utility vehicle has a bright future. But the Scout was too small for McCardell, who told the *New York Times,* "It has too low a market share in volume," which is McCardell-ese for "It's a loser." McCardell is cutting the division loose as part of a cost-cutting effort. There will certainly be more cuts to come. McCardell has to make Harvester as efficient as their competitors by 1984 in order to get his $1.8 million loan forgiven.

Stock performance. International Harvester stock bought for $1,000 in 1970 sold for $1,581 on January 2, 1980.

Major employment centers. Chicago and Moline, Illinois; and Fort Wayne, Indiana.

Access. 401 North Michigan Avenue, Chicago, Illinois 60611; (312) 836-2000.

Consumer brands.

International Scout four-wheel drive vehicle, International Harvester trucks and tractors.

> **As of March 1978, 43% of all women in the labor force were single, widowed, separated, or divorced, and worked to support themselves and their dependents.**

A Plant Builder, an Oil Field Logger, and a Nuclear Reactor Supplier

FLUOR CORPORATION

Sales: $3.5 billion
Profits: $98.7 million
Forbes 500 rank: 139
Rank in construction/engineering: 5
Founded: 1912
Employees: 21,500
Headquarters: Irvine, California

What they do. Fluor is a world-class engineering and construction firm, building plants, refineries, offshore drilling platforms, and other structures of enormous scale. Their current projects include a $5 billion Aramco plant in Saudi Arabia to process waste gases, a $4 billion South African complex to produce gasoline from coal, and—in China—the world's largest copper mine. Fluor's major customers are foreign governments, oil companies, chemical producers, and utilities. Half their work is overseas. They compete against the likes of Bechtel, Brown & Root, Pullman Kellogg, Foster Wheeler, and Combustion Engineering.

History. The company was founded in California by John Simon Fluor, a Swiss-born carpenter. One of his first customers was Southern California Edison; another was Richfield Oil. They grew largely as a builder for the petroleum industry, acquiring numerous other companies along the way.

Reputation. Fluor is one of the sources automatically considered by any government or company interested in putting up a large-scale industrial complex. They have an elite corps of engineers ready to go anywhere in the world to build.

Who owns and runs the company. The Fluor family owns a big chunk of stock, and another big block is held by an employees' trust fund. The company is headed by the founder's grandson, J. Robert Fluor, a former Air Force pilot who races thoroughbred horses.

Toledo-based Owens-Illinois is the world's largest producer of glass packaging, operating 61 plants in 14 countries. In 1976 William F. Niehous, their general manager in Venezuela, was kidnapped by a terrorist group from his Caracas home. Rescued three years later, he is shown here arriving at Toledo Airport on July 2, 1979, greeted by his family. By the following day his hair was neatly trimmed above his ears. Niehous is now vice-president and director of administration for corporate technology at Owens-Illinois.

America's Biggest Corporate Employers

Number of Employees

1. AT&T	1,030,000	26. UNION CARBIDE	113,300
2. GENERAL MOTORS	839,000	27. HALLIBURTON	112,100
3. FORD MOTOR	506,500	28. FIRESTONE	107,000
4. SEARS ROEBUCK	472,000	29. TENNECO	107,000
5. GENERAL ELECTRIC	401,000	30. XEROX	104,736
6. ITT	379,000	31. ARA SERVICES	100,000
7. IBM	337,119	32. TRW	97,900
8. MOBIL	216,000	33. BOEING	97,800
9. GENERAL TELEPHONE	214,000	34. BETHLEHEM STEEL	97,700
10. J. C. PENNEY	211,000	35. INTERNATIONAL HARVESTER	97,660
11. K MART	208,000	36. McDONALD'S	96,000
12. WOOLWORTH	202,600	37. PEPSICO	95,500
13. UNITED TECHNOLOGIES	198,000	38. CATERPILLAR TRACTOR	89,400
14. U. S. STEEL	166,848	39. BEATRICE FOODS	88,000
15. CHRYSLER	157,958	40. 3M	88,000
16. GOODYEAR	154,000	41. TWA	87,500
17. SAFEWAY STORES	144,000	42. SPERRY	87,300
18. WESTINGHOUSE ELECTRIC	141,776	43. HONEYWELL	86,328
19. DU PONT	134,200	44. SCHLUMBERGER	85,000
20. EXXON	130,000	45. McDONNELL DOUGLAS	82,700
21. EASTMAN KODAK	124,800	46. SINGER	81,000
22. RCA	118,000	47. CONSOLIDATED FOODS	80,900
23. FEDERATED DEPARTMENT STORES	117,151	48. BENDIX	80,600
24. ROCKWELL INTERNATIONAL	115,162	49. R. J. REYNOLDS	80,000
25. GULF + WESTERN	113,700	50. TEXAS INSTRUMENTS	78,571

In the public eye. Fluor will work for any government that pays it. For example, they're helping the South African government reduce its dependence on imported oil by building a coal gasification plant. They've also tried to help burnish the image of Saudi Arabia, a big Fluor client. In 1978, after the Saudi minister of industry complained to Fluor about his country's poor image in the United States, Bob Fluor set out to do something about it. He called together the executives of 40 companies doing business in Saudi Arabia and asked them to fund a $22 million Middle East Studies Center at the University of Southern California, to be run by a former Arabian-American Oil company employee and controlled by the donors. "Although this is not the way an academic body connected to a university is usually governed," noted *Harper's*, "it suggests the way a certain kind of businessman thinks when he donates money. . . . Every university has to deal with such donors, usually by either politely showing them the light or politely showing them the door, but Bob Fluor was the chairman of the board of trustees." When protests by the USC faculty and the Los Angeles Jewish community blocked the center, Fluor's vice-president of public relations said the affair had been distorted by "the Jewish press."

Stock performance. Fluor stock bought for $1,000 in 1970 sold for $5,604 on January 2, 1980.

Major employment centers. Irvine; Houston; Greenville, South Carolina.

Access. 3333 Michelson Drive, Irvine, California; (714) 975-2000.

Schlumberger

Sales: $3.5 billion
Profits: $658 million
Forbes 500 rank: 131
Rank in oil-well testing: 1
Founded: 1919
Employees: 85,000
Headquarters: New York, New York

What they do. Their name is Schlumberger—pronounced "Schloombear-zshay" —but to oilmen, they're "Slumber-jay," the world's foremost oil-well testers. They're a French company, but they're incorporated in Curaçao (an island in the Netherlands Antilles) and have their headquarters on Park Avenue in New York City. Schlumberger's real home, though, is any place in the world where crews of roughnecks are drilling for oil.

When an oilman is drilling a well and wants to know what's at the bottom, he calls Schlumberger. One of their field crews (usually composed of a young engineering graduate and a few technicians) comes out to the well site in a van crammed with computerized sensing equipment. They drop a "sonde" (a long, slender electronic probe) down the well, and as it descends it sends back to the truck readings on the character of the rock formations in the well. With these readings the computer makes a log of the well, from which the engineer can divine whether the well will be a producer or a dry hole. This probing is vital to the oil industry—without it, estimated *Forbes* in 1978, oil exploration costs would double or triple—and no company does more of it than Schlumberger: they control an estimated 75–80% of the world market for wireline services, as the probing is known. Schlumberger's reputation in the field is such that, no matter what company is performing the probe, oilmen refer to the process as "running a Slumber-jay."

Testing oil wells requires sophisticated electronic equipment, which Schlumberger manufactures for their own use at plants in Houston and France. They have also moved into electronics, which now accounts for 40% of their business. They make meters, instruments, and control systems for electric utilities in Europe and the United States, and in 1979 they bought Fairchild Camera and Instruments, a big producer of semiconductors, tiny integrated circuits used in computers, calculators, and televisions.

History. Conrad Schlumberger and his brother, Marcel, were born in the late 1800s in the Alsace region of France, an area that had been hotly disputed with the Germans for centuries. Because the region was then under German control, the brothers moved to Paris in order to avoid becoming German citizens. There Conrad became a phys-

New York-based Continental Group is the nation's largest manufacturer of packages — packages of all kinds (cans, boxes, plastic containers). Here's John Roskos, a line maintainer at the Continental plastics plant in Milltown, New Jersey, holding two large PVC bottles. Across the country — at Continental's Forest Industries plant at Pittsburg, California — a "gorilla" greeted incoming employees to distribute a free banana and drive home a message about the importance of safety. Continental claims to have one of the best safety records in industry.

ics professor and experimented with minerals, trying to determine whether they could be identified by their degree of resistance to electricity.

By the end of World War I Conrad had a resistance-measuring device accurate enough to sell, and with Marcel, a mechanical engineer, he began to measure the shapes of subsurface mineral deposits for mining companies. By 1927 the brothers had added a service measuring the amount of electricity generated by water and oil. Two years later Shell Oil hired them to use their technique probing wells in Venezuela and California. Soon they were using the process to probe wells in the Soviet Union, and by 1938 the company was running probes on a thousand wells a month around the world.

Conrad died in 1936, leaving Marcel in charge until the early 1950s, when his son,

Pierre, took over, moving the headquarters to Houston. Pierre decided to forbid any further involvement of Schlumberger relatives in the company in order to encourage ambition in his employees, and when Pierre stepped down in 1965, he was succeeded by a professional manager, Jean Riboud. Under Riboud, Schlumberger has aggressively applied new technologies in the booming oil-drilling market and has expanded into the glamorous electronics industry. Known as "the IBM of the energy crisis," Schlumberger has become one of the favorite companies of Wall Street investors. Though their sales of $3.5 billion put them 131st on the 1979 *Forbes* 500 list in terms of sales, their profits of $658 million topped all but 2.1 companies. Even more impressive is that the total market value of their stock (the price of the company's stock times the total number of shares) ranked them 5th—only IBM, AT&T, Exxon, and General Motors ranked ahead of Schlumberger.

Reputation. In addition to being known for accuracy, Schlumberger is known for hiring very young field engineers—frequently just out of graduate school. These graduates have a tough life: on call 24 hours a day, working and living out in the desolate country where the rigs are, operating a probe and interpreting the data sent back for as long as 30 consecutive hours, and forced to troubleshoot any equipment problems on the spot. On the line is a half-million dollars worth of sensitive electronic equipment and millions of dollars worth of the client's investment in an oil well. It's no wonder that 30% of new Schlumberger engineers quit or are fired in the first 18 months.

Who owns and runs the company. Jean Riboud himself has an interesting history. Born in France, he joined the French Resistance during World War II, was captured by the Germans, and spent two years in Buchenwald. After recovering from the tuberculosis he had contracted at the concentration camp, Riboud moved to New York and met Marcel Schlumberger, who invited

him to join his firm. When Riboud asked what his job would entail, Schlumberger told him he "hadn't the foggiest idea." Riboud took the job anyway and rapidly rose to the top of the ladder. After taking over in 1965, Riboud moved the headquarters to New York and decorated the walls with Magritte oil paintings. He is hardly the model of the modern corporate executive, preferring to work out of his Paris apartment much of the year and numbering among his friends Italian film director Roberto Rosselini and writer Jean-Jacques Servan-Schreiber, author of *The American Challenge.*

Although American investors now own more than half of the company's stock, the largest single block of shares is still controlled by the Schlumberger family.

Where they're going. Schlumberger is hedging their bets by expanding into the electronics field. Their Sangamo Weston subsidiary is making residential electric meters with small electronic microprocessors that will allow utilities to vary rates according to the time of day.

But Riboud expects Schlumberger to be in the oil business for a long time to come. "We've explored less than two percent offshore on the continental shelf," he told *For-*

Why Are There So Many Delaware Corporations?

It takes about an hour to charter a corporation in Delaware, a state that works overtime to keep itself attractive as a corporate haven.

It all started in the nineteenth century, when states began to make laws allowing companies to incorporate without a lot of legislative red tape. The landmark law was the 1896 New Jersey code, which gave companies such leeway that they rushed to New Jersey from all parts of the nation, just to incorporate there.

Delaware tried to elbow out its neighbor, first by imitating its law and then by undercutting its franchise tax. But the big break came in 1913.

Woodrow Wilson, then governor of New Jersey, decided his state was harboring too many trusts, and he got his legislature to pass a stricter law. Business flowed to little Delaware.

Over half the states in the nation now have laws to attract incorporating business, but Delaware maintains its lead. The nearly $60 million a year paid in business franchise taxes and fees provides over 10% of the state's total tax revenues.

The laws that keep Delaware ahead are constantly refined and amended. ("There are automobile companies that disappeared because no one paid attention to what

the public wanted," warns Delaware attorney S. Samuel Arsht.) The legislature gets advice on the modifications from the 30 lawyers that make up the General Corporation Law Committee of the Delaware State Bar Association. The committee has been accused of going beyond mere advice to tell the legislature exactly what to do. "That's true," admits one committee member, "but the law has to be written by people who know what's going on, and the Delaware legislature is not really sophisticated enough to do the job alone."

Source: *Fortune,* February 13, 1978.

tune in 1973; "there is still an extraordinary amount of oil yet to be discovered. The oil business will last."

Stock performance. Schlumberger stock bought for $1,000 in 1970 sold for $11,317 on January 2, 1980.

Major employment centers. Houston, Texas; Atlanta, Georgia; and Benton Harbor, Michigan.

Access. 277 Park Avenue, New York, New York 10017; (212) 350-9400.

 **Westinghouse**

Sales: $7.3 billion
Profits: $331 million
Forbes 500 rank: 49
Rank in nuclear power plants: 1
Rank in elevators: 2
Rank in light bulbs: 2
Founded: 1886
Employees: 141,776
Headquarters: Pittsburgh, Pennsylvania

What they do. The nuclear reactor at Three Mile Island was *not* built by Westinghouse. That's the good news about this big Pittsburgh company. They run a distant second to General Electric in the electric equipment field, and their story in the last decade is a continuing tale of disasters, including an unsafe train-control system, defective turbine generators, broken contracts, and a nuclear power plant being built on the slope of an active volcano. It is a story that gives new meaning to the company's old slogan: "You can be sure if it's Westinghouse."

Most of Westinghouse's business is in electricity. A pioneer in the field, they make everything needed to get electricity from the power plant to the consumer. They are the leading manufacturer of nuclear power reactors, with 40% of the market, and the second-largest maker of turbine generators for conventional power plants. At major factories in Pittsburgh; Buffalo, New York; and Bloomfield, New Jersey, they make transformers, circuit breakers, electric mo-

tors, complex control systems for industry, truck refrigeration, and elevators. These industrial products bring in almost half of their profits. Westinghouse sells about half of this equipment to electric utilities.

Once a major manufacturer of home appliances, Westinghouse now confines their consumer electric business to light bulbs, a market in which they run a strong second to GE. Westinghouse's single most important customer is the U.S. government, which accounts for about 10% of their business. Among the items Westinghouse makes for the Pentagon are radar for combat aircraft and launching systems for the Trident and MX nuclear missiles.

The parts of Westinghouse that aren't related to electricity or defense include several big 7-Up bottling plants; the Linguaphone Institute (world's largest supplier of home-study language courses); and land-development companies in Pelican Bay on Florida's Gulf coast, Half Moon Bay near San Francisco, and Coral Spring, Florida, a Westinghouse-owned community of over 30,000 "featuring a constantly upgraded life-style." Westinghouse also operates five television and nine radio stations, sells the Longines-Wittnauer brand of watches and develops educational aids and programs sold to schools.

History. Westinghouse Electric Company was founded in 1886 by George Westinghouse, one of the great inventors of the nineteenth century. At 40, having already invented the air brake for trains, electric signals for railroads, and a series of devices for the first practical transmission of natural gas, Westinghouse turned his attention to the problem of transmitting electrical current over long distances. He settled on alternating current (AC) to accomplish this feat. Alternating current had actually been the brainchild of Nikola Tesla, a former Edison associate, who realized that sending power over long distances would require high voltages, which would then need to be sent through transformers to reduce the voltage for home use. Direct current, then in use and favored by Edison himself, was generated from batteries and couldn't provide sufficient power to outlying communities. Westinghouse paid Tesla $1 million for his AC patents and began to sell AC systems, installing them in 130 towns in his first two years in business.

In the twentieth century Westinghouse

began to manufacture electrical products—everything from lightbulbs to major appliances—and they pioneered in atomic power and nuclear reactors for ship propulsion. But the company never managed to make significant inroads on General Electric, their larger competitor. One problem was that Westinghouse was what *Business Week* in 1963 called "abnormally dependent" on utility customers. Utilities were almost all regulated and were relatively few in number, giving them an enormous advantage when discussing prices with their suppliers—of which Westinghouse was second only to GE. Because they concentrated on this market for their huge turbines and generators, Westinghouse got a late start in the post-World War II home appliance market, where GE was cleaning up. By the time Westinghouse realized what was happening and jumped in with both feet, other competitors had risen to challenge for a piece of the market. By the late 1950s competitors were cutting each other's throats with costly "white sales," which cut prices of appliances by as much as 40%. At the same time Westinghouse was beginning to have other problems as well. The company was caught in a scheme with GE and 27 other companies to fix prices on all kinds of electrical products. Westinghouse was fined $372,000 by the court, and two company executives were given prison terms.

After this fiasco in the late 1950s, Westinghouse began to suffer a seemingly endless epidemic of glitches in their engineering systems. An automatic train-control system designed for San Francisco's Bay Area Rapid Transit District (BART) proved defective. It was supposed to guide the district's ultramodern trains along the tracks at high speeds and close intervals—as little as two minutes apart. But Westinghouse's system could not detect trains that were supposed to be sitting still on the tracks, and "mystery trains" made ghostly appearances from time to time on the master control board and then, just as mysteriously, disappeared. BART sued and won.

Then Westinghouse's main business—utility generators—began to come apart. In the mid-1970s Westinghouse lost a large chunk of business to GE when their turbine generators proved defective, prompting 10 utilities to sue them for $225 million. But then in 1975 came the biggest disaster of all. To win customers for their nuclear reactors, Westinghouse had promised utilities millions of pounds of uranium fuel at the mid-1960s price of $9.50 a pound. But by 1975 the price had soared to $40 a pound, and Westinghouse was forced to admit that they would be unable to honor their contracts. Seventeen angry utilities sued, and by early 1980, 16 had been settled at an estimated cost to Westinghouse of $1.5 billion. In turn, Westinghouse has sued 12 domestic and 17 foreign companies, claiming that the firms illegally formed a cartel to push up the price of uranium. Ironically, one of the companies Westinghouse is blaming is their Pittsburgh neighbor, Gulf Oil, and social occasions at Pittsburgh's elite Duquesne Club are understandably tense these days.

Some industry analysts have pointed to organizational problems as the cause for Westinghouse's various faux pas, noting that former president Mark Cresap died suddenly in 1963, at a crucial period in Westinghouse's reorganization. One financial columnist accused them of simple "managerial incompetence," and a brief tour through the headlines of the nation's more prestigious financial journals shows that every few years someone new arrives at Westinghouse to pick up the pieces of the most recent mess. "The Changes At Westinghouse" (*Fortune*, August 1958), "Breaking a Pattern of Woes" (*Business Week*, August 31, 1963), "Westinghouse Invents a New Westinghouse" (*Fortune*, October 1967), and "What Bob Kirby (current chairman) Has Wrought in Adversity." These are hardly the headlines used to describe companies that are going places; Westinghouse was finally forced to sell off to White Consolidated their once profitable major appliance business in 1975.

Reputation. For 20 years Westinghouse executives have been proclaiming that they see the light at the end of the tunnel of Westinghouse's woes, but there is suspicion in many quarters that what they have been seeing are GE's tail-lights disappearing into the distance.

What they own. The gem of their operations is Westinghouse Broadcasting Company, which owns five television and nine radio stations in large media markets and has been an outspoken critic of sex and violence on TV. Westinghouse also owns the world's largest 7-Up bottling operation, in Southern California, and the Longines-

Wittnauer Watch Company.

Who owns and runs the company. Robert E. Kirby, an engineer and Harvard Business School graduate, who has been with Westinghouse since 1946, became chairman in 1975. The board of directors includes a black lawyer, Hobart Taylor, Jr., and a female economics professor, Marina Whitman, who has served on the U.S. Council of Economic Advisors. Directors and officers, as a group, own less than 1% of stock.

In the public eye. In 1978 Westinghouse pleaded guilty to charges of having falsified government documents to hide $323,000 of bribes to an Egyptian official; they were fined $300,000. But their biggest scandal may involve a $1.1 billion nuclear power plant they are trying to build in the Philippines. Westinghouse has acknowledged paying a fee, as much as $35 million, to the firm of Herminio T. Disini, a close friend of Philippine President Ferdinand Marcos, for his help in obtaining the contract. According to Philippine officials, Westinghouse got the contract without submitting detailed specifications and despite the fact that officials calculated the plant was overpriced by as much as several hundred million dollars. Worst of all, the plant is being built on the slope of an active volcano, in an area subject to both earthquakes and tidal waves. Westinghouse denies that the plant will be unsafe, but in June 1979, following the accident at Three Mile Island, Marcos suspended construction, and the U.S. Nuclear Regulatory Commission held up an export license for the reactor.

Where they're going. Until recently Westinghouse's hopes were pinned on the power-generating business, but the U.S. market for nuclear plants has disappeared, and conservation efforts have caused the demand for electricity to level off, slowing the pace of new power-plant construction. Now the huge, sprawling company is looking more to their defense business and a miscellany of other enterprises, including construction, real estate, industrial products, and old standbys like light bulbs.

Stock performance. Westinghouse stock bought for $1,000 in 1970 sold for $692 on January 2, 1980.

Access. Gateway Center, Pittsburgh, Pennsylvania 15222; (412) 255-3800.

Consumer brands.

Light bulbs: Westinghouse.
Radio stations: WINS New York; KFWB Los Angeles; KYW Philadelphia; WBZ Boston; WIND Chicago; WOWO Fort Wayne; KDKA (WPMT-FM) Pittsburgh; KODA-FM Houston; KDAX-FM Dallas.
Television stations: WBZ Boston; KPIX San Francisco; WJZ Baltimore; KYW Philadelphia; KDKA Pittsburgh.
Watches: Longines-Wittnauer.

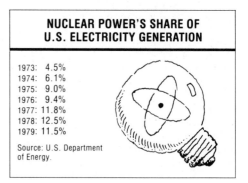

NUCLEAR POWER'S SHARE OF U.S. ELECTRICITY GENERATION

1973: 4.5%
1974: 6.1%
1975: 9.0%
1976: 9.4%
1977: 11.8%
1978: 12.5%
1979: 11.5%

Source: U.S. Department of Energy.

12

IN TRANSIT: RAILS TO ROCKETS

Railroaders

Amtrak

Sales: $381 million
Losses: $620 million
Rank in passenger trains: 1
Founded: 1971
Employees: 19,928
Headquarters: Washington, D.C.

What they do.   Everything wrong.

History.   Set up by Congress in 1971 to take over the nation's entire passenger railway service from private industry, Amtrak has become the little engine that says "I think I can't, I think I can't." Amtrak passengers *know* they can't; but in the face of Amtrak's suicidal instincts and Congress's seeming determination to goad them into jumping off the bridge, there's not much passengers can do but complain.

Within the first 40 days of Amtrak's existence, they suffered a massive strike, horribly mangled schedules, and a derailment in southern Illinois that left two dead and several injured. Since then Amtrak has racked up no less than 13 passenger deaths. There were 39 derailments in 1976; 36 in 1977. Passenger safety had always been relatively certain under the private sector, but today veteran porters on what used to be the Burlington Northern's run tell nervous passengers, "You're in the good Lord's hands now." Another disenchanted crewman once told a reporter, "This is no job; it's a disease."

What happened?

Almost all of Amtrak's problems are politically inspired. They took over lines private railroads were threatening to cut because of unprofitability; and Amtrak was placed under a congressional mandate to make them profitable again. Roger Lewis, the Nixon appointee who served as Amtrak's first president, was an aerospace executive with no railroad experience. He was saddled with the task of eliminating vast chunks of Amtrak's unprofitable railroads, but he soon discovered that the only lines he could cut were the ones in the districts of the least powerful congressmen. Several little-used lines in West Virginia, for example, which is represented by Senate Majority Leader Robert Byrd, are still with us today.

Washington has also kept Amtrak from modernizing their trains and repairing their rails—which contributes to the system's lousy safety record. "It boggles the mind that we're supposed to get people out of their 1979 autos with 1947 equipment," says current president Alan Boyd. His immediate predecessor, Paul Reistrup, left because, he said, Amtrak was his "own little Vietnam."

One problem is that Congress seems to think passenger service can be run profitably. No other passenger train service in the world does. Great Britain spent $728 million to subsidize its rail passenger system in 1978; Amtrak, a much more enormous system, received only $500 million. France spent $930 million in the same year, and tiny Japan spent $4.1 *billion* to help its rail system. The United States is currently contributing $2.4 billion every year to the World Bank to help railroad development in other countries, and $10 billion on highway construction and maintenance.

Reputation. The wino of the rails. Amtrak critics claim that "uncountable numbers" of prospective Amtrak passengers "have been lost by ineptitude and sloth, if not by outright refusal to accommodate demand." In June 1979 an estimated 1.4 million passengers were turned away by Amtrak as a result of overbooking and inefficiency. (The figures come from Amtrak's own computers.)

What they own. Virtually all of the nation's passenger lines. A few, such as Southern Pacific's San Francisco commuter train, are still held by private industry. These also operate at a loss, but nothing like Amtrak's.

Who owns and runs the company. Every taxpayer in the United States owns a chunk of Amtrak, but that doesn't mean they have any control over it. Congress runs Amtrak, which means, in essence, that no one really runs Amtrak.

In the public eye. Amtrak's public relations expertise is demonstrated by the fact that 6 million of the people who called Amtrak in June 1979 got a busy signal.

Where they're going. Nowhere.

Access. 400 North Capitol Street, NW, Washington, D.C. 20001; (202) 383-3000.

BURLINGTON NORTHERN

Sales: $3.3 billion
Profits: $175.6 million
Forbes 500 rank: 149
Rank in railroad mileage: 1
Rank in rail freight sales: 2
Rank in air freight sales: 3
Founded: 1849
Employees: 52,485
Headquarters: St. Paul, Minnesota

What they do. Burlington Northern, with 26,000 miles of track, is easily the longest of the nation's private railways—but that doesn't mean they're the best run. The result of literally hundreds of mergers over the years, BN tracks run out of Chicago, virtually encircle the Midwest, and then meander out to Seattle and Vancouver, as well as from Denver to Galveston, Texas. Because some of their component companies were formed during the great railroad land grab of the 1800s, Burlington Northern also has vast land holdings (2.4 million acres) in 11 western states, plus mineral rights on 6 million acres of land they no longer own. Freight hauling accounts for 83% of Burlington Northern's money, and transporting coal makes up nearly a quarter of that.

Burlington Northern Air Freight, founded in 1972, has grown rapidly and now operates out of 86 airports in the United States. They are ranked third among air freight handlers.

WHERE OUR ELECTRICITY COMES FROM	
Top Fuels Used to Make Electricity	
Fuel or Power Source	*Percentage of Electricity Produced (1978)*
1. COAL	44.3%
2. OIL	16.5%
3. GAS	13.8%
4. WATER (*hydroelectric*)	12.7%
5. NUCLEAR	12.5%
Source: U.S. Department of Energy and U.S. Department of Commerce.	

History. The Burlington Northern story is one of the most convoluted in American railroad history. The first of the railroads that eventually became Burlington was the Aurora Branch Railroad, founded in 1849 and consisting of 12 miles of second-hand scrap iron spiked to wooden rails. In 1864, after several mergers and acquisitions, the railroad had 400 miles of track, mostly in Illinois, and began calling itself the Chicago, Burlington & Quincy Railroad Company. (Burlington, Iowa, was the western terminus of the line.) By 1901 the C B & Q was an amalgamation of not fewer than 204 railroads; and in that year the Northern Pacific and the Great Northern railroads bought the company.

The Great Northern was the brainchild and labor-of-love of Jim Hill, a burly, one-eyed empire-builder who was largely responsible for the development and population of a stretch of America between Minnesota and the state of Washington: he constructed a vast network of railroads over unfriendly terrain in the 1880s without benefit of the land grants that had made Union Pacific and Central Pacific possible. Once he completed his road in 1893, he advertised widely for farmers, lumberjacks, and businessmen to move out into Montana and the states of the Pacific Northwest and turn the barren, desolate terrain into something resembling a civilization.

Hill built his railroad along a 1,500-mile route roughly paralleling that of the Northern Pacific, completed a few years earlier. Both roads began in the northern Midwest and ran through Minnesota, North Dakota, Montana, and Idaho, out to Seattle, Washington. After their joint purchase of the C B & Q it seemed natural for them to merge; but a Supreme Court antitrust decision that same year (1901) blocked the move. Nevertheless, the two roads continued to function almost as though the merger had gone through—even occupying the same headquarters building in St. Paul, Minnesota, in 1915, with a wall down the center of the building to keep them in technical compliance with the Court's ruling. The wall finally came down in 1970, when Chief Justice Earl Warren approved the merger, although traces of it can still be seen in what is now the main office of Burlington Northern—as the resulting company came to be called.

In April 1980 the Interstate Commerce Commission approved the merger of Burl-

The legendary James J. Hill (left), builder of the Great Northern Railroad, who opened up the entire Northewest, is shown here with his son, Louis W. Hill, at the Omaha Land Show in 1911.

ington Northern with the St. Louis–San Francisco Railway (Frisco), creating the longest railroad in U.S. history. Burlington Northern wanted Frisco largely because their combined tracks plot a direct rail route between the coalfields of Montana and the industrial plants in the Deep South, such as those around Birmingham, Alabama.

Reputation. Quick to merge, slow to move. Although Norton Simon, the Los Angeles investor who was Burlington Northern's biggest stockholder until 1974, spent 23 years urging management to develop the resources under their land, Burlington Northern is still only scratching the surface. Estimates are that Burlington Northern has the rights to one-fifth of the coal reserves in Wyoming, North Dakota, and Montana—which have 44% of the na-

> Railroads carried about 75% of all intercity freight traffic in the United States in 1929. Today that figure has dropped to about 35%.

tion's total coal reserves—but Burlington Northern still removes only a paltry percentage.

What they own. All that coal, easily the company's biggest potential money-maker. At Simon's insistence (he scolded management for 15 minutes at the 1973 annual meeting), Burlington Northern hired Robert Binger, a professional forester by training, to develop their timber and mineral resources. Company wits call him "Ranger Bob."

Who owns and runs the company. Norton Simon sold his stock in disgust in January 1974. At that time he held about 5% of Burlington Northern stock; today, nobody owns more than one-fourth of 1% of it. All 49 of the directors and officers as a group hold a grand total of 2%.

In the public eye. In April 1977 the Securities and Exchange Commission determined that Burlington Northern wasn't taking very good care of their tracks and hadn't bothered to inform their stockholders of that fact. In the railroad business that's important news: repair and maintenance of track is a major expense, and the Interstate Commerce Commission, which regulates the railroads, can shut down lines if tracks aren't in decent shape. The SEC was investigating whether by avoiding costly track repairs, Burlington Northern might be keeping their profits artificially high. If the ICC one day ordered them to repair the tracks, profits could fall.

Where they're going. In 1945 there were 130 major railroads in the United States. Today there are fewer than 50. If rate deregulation of the industry comes, as expected, within the next few years, Burlington Northern may be one of the dozen or fewer to survive the inevitable shopping spree for smaller railroads—at least, that's what *Forbes* suggests.

Access. 176 East Fifth Street, St. Paul, Minnesota 55101; (612) 298-2121.

> "Railroads move about four times as much freight traffic per gallon of fuel as big trucks and 125 times as much as cargo aircraft.... One double-track railroad can accommodate the traffic of a 20-lane superhighway."
>
> —American Association of Railroads

MISSOURI PACIFIC

Sales: $2.0 billion
Profits: $180 million
Forbes 500 rank: 267
Rank in railroad revenues: 8
Founded: 1849
Employees: 21,095
Headquarters: St. Louis, Missouri

What they do. You might think that the first railroad to carry passengers west of the Mississippi would have had a big advantage during the transcontinental fever of the 1800s. And you might also think that a St. Louis railroad with the chutzpah to call itself "The Pacific" a full 20 years before the 1869 Golden Spike ceremonies would have had the tenacity to make it to that ocean eventually. But you'd be wrong. Even today, after scores of mergers and acquisitions, the westernmost point on the Missouri Pacific line is still El Paso, Texas—hardly a surfer's paradise.

MoPac—as they're known by their competitors—is about as far from sea air as a company can get. Their 11,500 miles of main line track crisscrosses the Midwest from Chicago to El Paso and from New Orleans to Omaha. And although recent mergers have left them with a cement company and a valuable natural gas pipeline (from Louisiana to St. Louis), three-fourths of MoPac's business still comes from their railroad. They carry chemicals, grain, automobiles and auto parts, coal, and a variety of other commodities throughout the grain belt and the dust bowl.

History. When the Union Pacific and Central Pacific (which later became the Southern Pacific) railroads finally met in Utah in 1869, a few hundred people were present for the celebration. But when Tom Allen staged the groundbreaking for the Missouri Pacific Railroad in 1851, more than 25,000 people showed up. It was undoubtedly the biggest party St. Louis ever had (40 gallons of brandy and 10 gallons of rum were consumed by dignitaries alone), and everyone present was convinced that Allen would be at the coast in a few years. Allen threw another party the following year, when his railroad reached Cheltenham, five miles outside the St. Louis city limits. Thirteen years later, well after Union Pacific and Southern Pacific had begun laying the first transcontinental track, Missouri Pacific had made it all the way to Kansas City. Allen may have been slow, but he knew his public relations.

Financial difficulties made it possible for New York financier robber baron Jay Gould to pick up the MoPac at bargain prices in 1879 and add it to his collection. MoPac underwent a series of boom-and-bust cycles, receiverships, and bankruptcies until 1960, when a new ownership and management began to turn things around.

Reputation. One industrial customer says the MoPac is now "offering better service than any railroad I've ever seen." The new management's belt-tightening and efficiency measures have made Mopac quite possibly the fastest-growing railroad in the United States.

What they own. Just in case hard times hit the rail industry again, MoPac has gone into trucking. Their midwestern truck routes cover more than 20,000 miles of highway.

Who owns and runs the company. Downing Jenks is the man responsible for turning MoPac around. At the time he was hired to run MoPac in 1960, he was in charge of the Rock Island railroad. But his railroad roots are much deeper. *Forbes* described his background:

> Jenks is one of that small breed who begin learning about railroading almost as soon as they learn to read and write and do arithmetic. His grandfather had helped James J. Hill build the Great Northern. His father, Charles O. Jenks, was a vice-president. While still in his teens, Jenks worked summers as a chainman on the Spokane, Portland & Seattle. After Yale, where he majored in industrial engineering, he worked briefly for the Pennsylvania Railroad before joining his father on the Great Northern. For six tedious years, his father refused to promote his son above the rank of trainmaster; if young Downing wanted to run a railroad, he would have to get there the hard way. He did. In 1948, when he was 33, young for railroading, he was made general manager of the Chicago & Eastern Illinois Railroad.

Where they're going. Federal policy now seems to favor deregulation of the rail industry, which would open the way to a series of mergers. The 13 major western roads would crunch down to 4 or 5. MoPac plans to merge with the biggest one of them all, Union Pacific.

Stock performance. Missouri Pacific stock bought for $1,000 in 1970 sold for $3,397 on January 2, 1980.

Access. 9900 Clayton Road, St. Louis, Missouri 63124; (314) 991-9900.

Norfolk and Western

Sales: $1.4 billion
Profits: $199 million
Forbes 500 rank: 347
Founded: 1838
Employees: 21,930
Headquarters: Roanoke, Virginia

What they do. They used to say that all Norfolk & Western had to do was run coal-laden freight cars down a hill, bring the empties back up, and count money. That's no longer true. Although coal still accounts for close to 40% of Norfolk's business, they now haul a wide variety of other commodities—from chemicals and food products to automobiles and auto parts—over a system that stretches from Omaha and Kansas City to Buffalo, New York, and Norfolk, Virginia. A subsidiary line, the Delaware & Hudson, picks up the Norfolk freight in Buffalo and moves it as far as Vermont and Montreal.

History. Founded in 1838, Norfolk & Western is the oldest of the nation's major railways. Their original eight-mile track connected Petersburg and City Point in Virginia. By 1858 the company had a single track from Norfolk to Bristol, in the western part of the state. At the same time, the basic route of the Wabash Railroad was taking shape in the Midwest. In 1870 Wabash connected Keokuk, Iowa, with Toledo, Ohio.

Norfolk's relationship with coal began in

1892, when they opened their first lines into the coal fields of West Virginia. Northward expansion during the next decades enabled the Norfolk to begin hauling coal for the steel industries of Ohio and Pennsylvania, their biggest customers until well after World War II. In 1964 Norfolk merged with Wabash and four other railroads to form the present system. They bought Delaware & Hudson in 1968.

Reputation. A well-run, no-nonsense railroad. The more compact eastern railroads have traditionally had an easier time maintaining schedules than their far-flung western counterparts, but Norfolk's on-time rate of 85% is seen as phenomenal in the industry.

What they own. A total of 116,000 freight cars and 1,660 locomotives moving over more than 7,000 miles of track.

Who owns and runs the company. Lawyer John Fishwick has been running the Norfolk since 1970. Soon after he took over, he got annoyed with how cluttered the railroad's yards looked. So he ordered the whole company into the yards for a massive one-day cleanup operation. "Thousands and thousands of people, union and management, turned to and picked up the refuse," one Norfolk official told *Business Week.* Norfolk's board of directors also includes top-flight financiers like the Mellon Bank's John Mayer and such captains of industry as Alcoa's W. H. Krome George and Kennecott Copper's William Wendel. Because of the numerous mergers over the years the 10-member board controls only one-tenth of 1% of the stock; two members have none at all.

In the public eye. In 1978 the Brotherhood of Railway and Airline Clerks struck Norfolk & Western for 82 days, with the main issues centering on job protection. The railroad refused to settle the strike, letting it go on until it was ended by the appointment of a Presidential Emergency Board. In their 1978 annual report to stockholders, Fishwick boasted that Norfolk was able to continue running, although at reduced capacity, through the help of supervisors and union members who crossed the picket lines in ever-increasing numbers as the strike wore on. In the end, Norfolk was moving 50% of their traffic with only 15% of their normal work force. As a result, said

Fishwick, "We did discover opportunities . . . to get work done with fewer people than we have used in the past, and we are putting that information to good use wherever we can."

Where they're going. Norfolk & Western is nervous about a proposed merger between their competitors Seaboard Coast line and Chessie (for Chesapeake & Ohio) Systems, which would create the nation's second-largest railroad. With that in mind Norfolk and Southern Railway are trying to merge to create the nation's third largest road.

Stock performance. Norfolk & Western stock bought for $1,000 in 1970 sold for $1,057 on January 2, 1980.

Major employment centers. Roanoke, Cleveland, and St. Louis.

Access. 8 North Jefferson Street, Roanoke, Virginia 24042; (703) 981-4530.

Sales: $2.6 billion
Profits: $227.7 million
Forbes 500 rank: 199
Rank in railroads: 6
Founded: 1863
Employees: 39,468
Headquarters: Chicago, Illinois

What they do. Although many people may still think of the Atchison, Topeka and Santa Fe Railway as the setting for the 1946 Judy Garland movie *The Harvey Girls,* or as the title of that movie's hit song, today's Santa Fe is more than that. In fact their thrust has changed so much that in 1980 the Value Line Investment Survey called them "an oil company which happens to own a railroad and some other transportation and natural resources businesses."

Santa Fe now operates four main businesses:

1. The railroad, which has 12,200 miles of track stretching from Chicago to Califor-

One of the early Santa Fe railway stations in Ponca City, Oklahoma, birthplace of the Marland Oil Company, one of the predecessors of today's Conoco.

nia's Central Valley and San Diego and from central Texas up to Nebraska. In 1979 they carried 109 million tons of freight, coal accounting for 16% of these shipments.

2. A natural resources group that develops Santa Fe's extensive oil, gas, coal, and uranium reserves.

3. A forest products division that converts the company's trees into plywood and particle board.

4. A real estate and construction arm that sells and develops Santa Fe–owned land.

Oil is by far the big gusher. Santa Fe ranks as one of the nation's largest producers of heavy crude oil. In 1979 the federal government decontrolled the price of heavy oil. As a result the price went from $5.50 per barrel on August 16, 1979, to $24.40 by the end of the year—and Santa Fe's profits shot through the roof, rising 38% in one year. Oil accounted for nearly a third of the company's 1979 profits but less than 9% of their sales.

History. Santa Fe's early history is interwoven with that of the state of Kansas. Founded in 1860 by men from Topeka and Atchison, Kansas, the railroad didn't lay one inch of track until 1868, largely because of disruptions caused by the Civil War. It took four more years before the railroad reached Dodge City, about 300 miles west of Topeka. Soon Dodge City came to be the end of the trail for the cowboys from Texas who drove their cattle north to be shipped by the Atchison, Topeka and Santa Fe line to packing houses to the east. In 1884 800,-000 head of cattle were put on Santa Fe trains out of Dodge City. Though the company warmly greeted the revenues from the enormous cattle trade, Santa Fe passenger train conductors carried guns when collecting fares out of Dodge City, and the rambunctious cowboys there shot out locomotive headlights. The town's sheriff, Bat Masterson, could offer little protection to the young railroad's property or employees from the cowboys.

It was not until 1882 that Atchison, Topeka and Santa Fe track actually reached Santa Fe, New Mexico. A few years later, the line stretched to San Diego and San Francisco to the west, and to Chicago to the east.

One of Santa Fe's principal contributions to rail travel may well have been the introduction of decent food for travelers to the Wild West. Until Fred Harvey began operating Santa Fe's whistle-stop food concessions in the 1870s, the trip by rail entailed greasy, expensive meals in a seemingly endless chain of hash-houses. Harvey, an Englishman with a penchant for fine linen and silverware, brought *haute cuisine* to the American prairie. He eventually took over operation of the Santa Fe dining cars, and "Meals by Fred Harvey" became Santa Fe's slogan.

His waitresses—known as "Harvey Girls"—were recruited from New England and the Midwest and lived in dormitories where they were closely watched by matrons. Keith L. Bryant, Jr., in his *History of the Atchison, Topeka and Santa Fe*, described their attire: "Dressed in black shoes and stockings, plain black dresses with an 'Elsie collar' and a black bow, and a heavily starched white apron, their hair plainly done with a white ribbon, the 'Harvey Girls' stood in sharp contrast to the 'painted ladies' of the nearby saloons." Nearly 5,000 lonely Westerners married "Harvey Girls," and one former Harvey employee estimated that at least 4,000 babies were named after Fred Harvey.

The Harvey food and lodging business is now part of the Honolulu-based Amfac. Santa Fe has no interest anymore in feeding people. They became Santa Fe Industries in 1967.

Reputation. Santa Fe used to be known on Wall Street as a potential giant that had unaccountably fallen asleep—sort of the Rip Van Winkle of railroads. But Santa Fe seems to be waking up as they hear oil gurgling under their bed.

What they own. In addition to their rail holdings, Santa Fe owns a 2,750-mile pipeline network, a small trucking subsidiary, 650,000 acres of timberland, and oil wells now producing 46,500 barrels of crude a day. Their biggest petroleum source is the sprawling Midway-Sunset field in California: 20,000 barrels a day.

Who owns and runs the company. Institutional investors are the major owners. The 31 largest holders, including many banks, insurance companies, mutual funds, and such entities as Yale University and the

Ford Foundation, held a total of 12% of the stock in 1975. The architect of Santa Fe's growth in the 1970s was John Shedd Reed. He was elected chief executive officer in 1974. The board of directors has a strong Chicago contingent, including John T. Rettaliata, chairman of the Chicago branch of the Banco de Roma.

Where they're going. Santa Fe is now bound hell-for-leather into the oil business. But they're not neglecting their coal-carrying railroad business. They planned to spend $390 million in 1980 to improve their rail facilities, including the following: 140 new and 85 rebuilt locomotives; 2,075 new, 638 rebuilt, and 217 modified freight cars; 1,290 piggyback trailers; 466 miles of new and reconditioned welded rail; and 1.8 million new ties. And as long as everyone else in the railroad business is merging, they will too. Their intended marriage partner: Southern Pacific.

Stock performance. Santa Fe Industries stock bought for $1,000 in 1970 sold for $2,167 on January 2, 1980.

Access. 224 South Michigan Avenue, Chicago, Illinois 60604; (312) 427-4900.

Southern Pacific

Sales: $2.6 billion
Profits: $180 million
Forbes 500 rank: 190
Rank in railroad mileage: 3
Rank in rail freight revenues: 2
Rank in title insurance: 1
Founded: 1861
Employees: 46,500
Headquarters: San Francisco, California

What they do. It's hard to believe that today's Southern Pacific Company, with their conservative, stale-cigar-smoke image, could have grown out of one of the nineteenth century's most avaricious monopolies—but that's exactly what happened. Robber barons Leland Stanford, Mark Hopkins, Charles Crocker, and C. P. Huntington turned their railroad into the prototypical American monopoly through the time-honored techniques of graft, bribery, fraud, and outright mendacity. In the process they built the state of California and inspired Frank Norris's muckraking 1901 novel, *The Octopus.*

The partners put together a railroad that now stretches from Portland, Oregon, down to Los Angeles, then east to Houston, and finally north again to St. Louis. Complete with their other branches, Southern Pacific now has more than 13,000 miles of main line—enough to stretch four times across the United States.

But the story of Southern Pacific is still basically the story of the Far West, and the fates of the two are inextricably linked. A beneficiary of massive federal land grants during the railroad's construction in the 1860s, Southern Pacific still owns and leases some of California's most valuable farm land, which is situated conveniently near the railroad's various rights-of-way. Next to the federal government Southern Pacific is the largest landlord in California, Nevada, and Utah. They own 3.8 million acres in those three states and hold the mineral rights to an additional 1.3 million.

In addition, Southern Pacific has 2,480 miles of pipeline, owns 450,000 acres of prime western timberland, owns part of the 1,200-room New Orleans Hilton Hotel, and invests in geothermal energy development. They have even gone into competition with Bell Telephone: their microwave communications system called "Sprint," which they lease to other companies, may handle about 3% of A T & T's long-distance phone traffic by 1984. Southern Pacific's three trucking companies (Pacific Motor Trucking, Southwestern Transportation, and Southern Pacific Transport of Texas and Louisiana) handle some 4 million freight movements a year.

History. It all started with a visionary engineer named Theodore "Crazy Ted" Judah, who found the first feasible rail route through the forbidding Sierra Nevada mountains in 1860 and spent the next year trying to pry money out of San Francisco financiers to build his railroad. Despite a reputation as a pushy lunatic, four Sacramento merchants finally agreed to back him. Huntington and Hopkins ran a small hardware store, Stanford was a wholesale grocer, and Crocker was in the dry goods business. The four formed the Central Pacific Railroad Company and gave Judah $35,000 to begin laying tracks from Sacramento to the mining country of Nevada. What they originally wanted was a monopoly on the silver mining trade; but when President Lincoln signed the Pacific Railroad Act in 1862, the partners realized they had a shot at building the western link of the first transcontinental railroad—and reaping immense profits once it was done.

The four men functioned like a well-trained team of stage horses. The burly, profane, 265-pound Crocker took command of the army of white men and Chinese to build the road. To the Chinese he assigned the task of nitroglycerin demolition. While working with the strange new explosive, many of them were blown to bits; Crocker simply shrugged and sent in a new crew. When it came to carving a ledge in the side of a sheer cliff, Crocker had a group of Chinese lowered down from the top in baskets —with orders to pick away at the rocks until they had made enough holes for the nitro.

Hopkins, meanwhile, was in charge of the money end. A scholarly, religious man, he was not above an occasional oversight when the interests of the railroad called for it. When a congressional investigation inquired after some $23 million in federal

Demolishing Racism in Its Tracks

The competition to lay the most track in the first transcontinental railroad was so fierce that the two roads intentionally missed each other. The Central Pacific's Chinese and the Union Pacific's Irish road graders had gone more than a hundred miles past each other while the roads' owners haggled over a meeting point. One Saturday night, after a serious liquor session, some of the Irish laborers shot and killed several of the Chinese. Within a few days the Chinese, who had become expert at demolition during the Sierra crossing, blew up more than 20 of the Irish. Thereafter acts of overt racism toward the Chinese were few and far between—at least on the railroad crews.

grants to the railroad, Hopkins explained that the books had mysteriously disappeared. That ended the investigation.

Stanford, who had been involved in California politics since 1857, managed to get himself elected governor of the new state in 1861. He signed no fewer than seven pro-railroad bills into law during his tenure—one of them granting his railroad $10,000 for every mile of track the partners laid inside the state. Meanwhile, Huntington was in Washington convincing Congress to give them $16,000 for every mile of track laid in the flatlands and $48,000 per track-mile laid over mountainous terrain. When he wired Stanford about the federal deal, the governor had the state geologist determine that the Sierra Nevada range actually began only seven miles east of Sacramento: the partners had moved an entire mountain range more than 24 miles.

When Crazy Ted complained about his four backers and their questionable dealings, he was quietly squeezed out. By 1864, before the road was even out of California, the four partners had taken over his Central Pacific shares. He died a few years later.

By 1868, the year before the Golden Spike marked the joining of the Central Pacific with the Union Pacific, the four partners had quietly bought a controlling interest in the Southern Pacific Railroad, which ran a line from San Francisco down to San Jose, a distance of 47 miles. The four had worried that Southern Pacific might compete with them in setting up the vital, final link to San Francisco—which, as a city, had owned the SP. Helped by Stanford's political connections, the partners took over the tiny railroad and set up Huntington as its president. Stanford continued as president of the Central Pacific and became vice-president of the SP.

The 1854 Gadsden Purchase, by which the United States acquired the southernmost portions of Arizona and New Mexico, had made possible a southern route across the mountains. The partners were anxious to build there. Several years later they completed a link between San Francisco and Houston as part of the Southern Pacific system, which then absorbed Central Pacific.

By 1900 a map of California showing reclaimed desert land, telegraph lines, rail lines, ferry systems, farming areas, and vital resources was largely a map of the SP empire. Where Southern Pacific went, so went civilization—and the same is largely true today. The railroad created Reno, Nevada, as well as Fresno, Modesto, Truckee, and Coalinga, California—all of which were set up to encourage growth along the Southern Pacific lines. From nothing Southern Pacific created California tourism: building the Del Monte, Shasta Springs, and Coronado hotels and advertising them across the country. They started *Sunset Magazine* in 1898, hoping to use it to attract newcomers and settlers to California. People came to the Golden State in droves, and those who tilled the land soon made the state into the country's biggest agricultural producer—with Southern Pacific trains and tracks strategically placed to haul California's fruits and vegetables to a hungry nation. Today food products are the principal cargo carried on Southern Pacific, the second-largest rail freight carrier in the United States.

Despite Southern Pacific's rich landholdings, some financial analysts criticize the company for not doing more to convert those properties into profit-making ventures (as are some other big railroad landholders, notably the Union Pacific). Nevertheless, Southern Pacific remains a formidable power in California. In March 1979 *New West* magazine concluded that "the hidden empire of Southern Pacific is so vast that it controls virtually every important area of policy and growth in California: energy, land, transportation, urban development, and environment."

Reputation. Although Southern Pacific as a whole is generally considered a bit stodgy, some subsidiaries are downright feisty. Gus Grant, head of Southern Pacific's microwave communications company, keeps a cartoon on his office wall showing him at-

A typical locomotive lasts 15 years; a freight car, 30 years; and track, 60 years.

The first "piggybacking" by railroads took place in the 1800s when circus wagons were occasionally transported by rail.

Railroad Revenues (1979)/Number of Employees

1. CONRAIL $3.9 *billion*/87,500
2. BURLINGTON NORTHERN $2.6 *billion*/52,485
3. SOUTHERN PACIFIC $2.2 *billion*/46,500
4. SEABOARD COAST $2.1 *billion*/37,000
5. CHESSIE SYSTEMS $1.9 *billion*/38,500
6. SANTA FE INDUSTRIES $1.9 *billion*/39,468
7. UNION PACIFIC $1.8 *billion*/30,637
8. MISSOURI PACIFIC $1.4 *billion*/21,095
9. SOUTHERN RAILWAY $1.4 *billion*/21,431
10. NORFOLK & WESTERN $1.4 *billion*/21,930

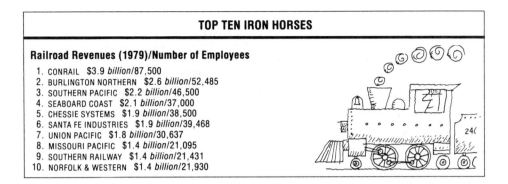

tempting to slay the giant Ma Bell. Between 1978 and 1979 he increased the number of Southern Pacific Communications customers from 1,000 to more than 24,000.

Even the other divisions of Southern Pacific seem to be slowly rousing themselves to activity. Although Southern Pacific had not completed a merger or acquisition since 1964, they recently picked up Ticor, Inc., the nation's largest writer of title insurance. The acquisition was greeted by general applause on Wall Street, apparently because Southern Pacific had finally *done* something.

What they own. Southern Pacific is one of the nation's largest developers of industrial parks. They currently have 73 industrial developments, strategically located along Southern Pacific rail lines near highway interchanges. They own 2% of California's land surface.

Who owns and runs the company. Benjamin F. Biaggini, SP's chairman, has been with the railroad 44 years. He was paid $328,000 in 1978. Biaggini owns about 15,-000 shares of SP stock worth $500,000 in early 1980. Surrounding him on the all-male, all-white board of directors are heavy industry people including Stephen Bechtel, Jr., chairman of the Bechtel engineering firm, Thomas M. Evans, the wheeler-dealer chairman of Crane, and a bunch of top mining executives.

In the public eye. Southern Pacific works hard at keeping a low public profile, but a group of 7,500 noisy commuters has forced them into the open in recent years. Like most American railroads, Southern Pacific has found passenger service unprofitable. They have repeatedly tried to discontinue their only passenger run, the San Jose–San Francisco commuter service. "I'm the biggest philanthropist in the Bay Area," bemoans Southern Pacific's colorful chairman, B. F. Biaggini, who is a member of the exclusive Bohemian Club. "I give away $9 million a year to wealthy commuters." But each time Southern Pacific has tried to dump the commuter line, the commuters successfully plead with California's Public Utilities Commission for continuation of the service.

Where they're going. Southern Pacific is one of a group of companies that have combined to form what they like to call a "landbridge" across the continent. The combine is able to pick up freight from Japan unloaded at San Francisco, move it to eastern American ports, and then send it off to Europe faster and more cheaply than it would go via the Panama Canal route. They see the landbridge as a growing business.

Although their every effort to date has failed, Southern Pacific still dreams of becoming the first truly transcontinental railroad. They almost did it in 1978; but Seaboard, the southeastern railroad with links from New Orleans to Florida and Virginia, backed out of a merger at the last minute. In May 1980 they announced a merger with an old rival: the Santa Fe.

Stock performance. Southern Pacific stock bought for $1,000 in 1970 sold for $1,-034 on January 2, 1980.

Major employment centers. The San Francisco Bay Area, Los Angeles, and Houston.

Access. One Market Plaza, San Francisco, California 94105; (415) 362-1212.

Sales: $1.5 billion
Profits: $161 million
Forbes 500 rank: 343
Founded: 1894
Employees: 21,431
Headquarters: Washington, D.C.

What they do. The Southern Railway's management could get down on their knees and give thanks for the Civil War. Because of the destruction of most of the South's railroads during the war, and the tight economy that followed, the companies which were eventually combined to form the Southern laid track only where it was absolutely necessary. As a result, Southern has just 10,000 miles of track to maintain—and almost all of it is in nearly constant use. That keeps profits high and contributes to Southern's reputation as perhaps the nation's best-run railroad.

Southern's lines are all still south of the Mason-Dixon Line, with freight trains running from Washington, D.C., down to New Orleans, and from Florida up to Cincinnati and East St. Louis. More than half their business comes from hauling lumber, chemicals, coal, and aluminum-bearing kaolin clay. Southern has had to make it as a railroad because that's just about all they do.

History. The ubiquitous J. Pierpont Morgan formed the Southern out of more than 30 bankrupt southern railways in 1894. The company operated unspectacularly until after World War II, when an industrial boom swept the South. The man who made sure that Southern shared in the region's new prosperity was D. William Brosnan, who headed the line from 1962 to 1967. Brosnan tried to slash the payroll by intro-

A railroad classification yard is a vast place where freight trains are moved around from a computerized control room. It's like a toy train set—only for real. This is an aerial view of Southern Railway's four-mile-long yard at Linwood, North Carolina. It routes thousands of cars each week.

ducing track-maintenance machinery and automating aspects of the repair shops. To demonstrate that railroad firemen didn't do anything, Brosnan hired some untrained men as "firemen" and told them to do nothing but sit in the locomotive cab.

The unions took a dim view of Brosnan's antics, but they were up-in-arms when Brosnan simply laid off 1,562 workers of the Central of Georgia Railway after Southern bought the smaller railroad in 1963. After four years of bitter legal fighting, the Interstate Commerce Commission concluded that Southern had acted with "callous disregard" of employee rights, and the road was forced to pay about $20 million in severance pay to the laid-off workers. Southern's board didn't like the outcome, and Brosnan was removed as chairman shortly after the ICC ruling, though he still sits on Southern's board. "We're still tough, but we try to avoid picking fights with the unions just to put them in their place like we used to [under Brosnan]," George Scott Paul, Southern's executive vice-president, told the *Wall Street Journal* in 1976.

In recent years Southern has urged new industries locating in the South to build their plants close to Southern's tracks. In 1978 alone more than 100 new or expanded manufacturing plants, warehouses, and electricity generating plants made firm pledges to invest $5.9 billion in new facilities (representing 8,400 new jobs) near Southern's routes. Included in this latest influx are new plants of corporate giants like Miller Brewing, Philip Morris, Procter & Gamble and PepsiCo's Frito-Lay, as well as a Duke Power nuclear reactor.

Reputation. Southern is every bit as down-home as corn grits—only heavier on the corn. Their managers wear little green lapel buttons, with nothing printed on them, which are supposed to symbolize "Go!" to less-motivated employees.

What they own. Southern has more than 47,000 of their own freight cars and 812 locomotives. They also still have 142 passenger cars—a legacy from the pre-Amtrak period. Southern won the hearts of many southerners in 1971 when they decided to continue operating their famous Southern Crescent passenger train themselves, refusing to turn it over to Amtrak. They doubted that Amtrak would provide the kind of service Crescent passengers were used to and

which they felt an obligation to provide. Finally in early 1979, after years of steady losses, Southern capitulated and the line is now part of the Amtrak system. A company spokesman said that Southern felt they had "gone the extra mile" in trying to make private passenger service feasible on their route that went from Washington, D.C., to New Orleans via Atlanta.

Who owns and runs the company. L. Stanley Crane, who became chief executive officer in 1977, started with the Southern in 1937 as a laboratory assistant. He succeeded W. Graham Claytor, Jr., who resigned to become Secretary of the Navy. Morgan Guaranty Trust holds the largest block of shares (4.3% of the total), and they have been represented on the board by Ralph F. Leach. Also on the board is R. L. Ireland III, partner in another Wall Street outfit active in railroad financing: Brown Brothers Harriman.

In the public eye. There were lots of crimson faces at Southern's home offices in early 1976 when the press carried accounts of how Southern had paid for a two-day hunting trip by then–Secretary of Agriculture Earl Butz at "Brosnan Forest," a 15,000-acre Southern-owned retreat near Charleston, South Carolina. Butz, who reportedly bagged a wild turkey on the outing, later paid the company back for his expenses. The Butz affair was apparently only the tip of the iceberg, however. In November 1979 Southern admitted that it had illegally entertained customers at Brosnan Forest, which has two man-made lakes and facilities for fishing, hunting, and golf. Southern paid a fine of $1.9 million in federal court for 95 separate instances when Southern had hosted trips by shippers' representatives at Brosnan Forest between 1974 and 1978.

Where they're going. Southern plans to merge with the Norfolk & Western.

Stock performance. Southern stock bought for $1,000 in 1970 sold for $2,329 on January 2, 1980.

Major employment centers. Atlanta, Chattanooga, and Birmingham.

Access: 920 15th Street, NW, Washington, D.C. 20005; (202) 628-4460.

Sales: $4 billion
Profits: $382 million
Forbes 500 rank: 112
Founded: 1862
Employees: 30,637
Headquarters: New York, New York

What they do. Today, after almost 120 years, Union Pacific continues to profit from an incredible land grab scheme dreamed up by its founders and shrewdly nursed by their heirs.

Although Union Pacific is still known primarily as a railroad, almost half their profits come from the mineral resources that lie beneath the land the founders cajoled, bribed, and swindled from the U.S. Congress in the 1860s. As of 1979 they had crude oil reserves of 111 million barrels and natural gas reserves of 964 billion cubic feet —almost all within the continental United States. Their Champlain Oil subsidiary has 5,008 oil and 989 gas wells in the United States and Canada, plus refineries which produce a daily total of 43,684 barrels of oil and 251 million cubic feet of gas.

The railroad itself is a basically wishbone-shaped piece of track extending from Council Bluffs, Iowa, to a point in western Wyoming, where a northern fork runs to Seattle and a southern branch meanders down to Los Angeles. Altogether, the system contains 9,700 miles of track—5,100 miles of main line and 4,600 miles of branches and side-tracks on which about 332 million tons of freight are moved annually.

Union Pacific trains haul more than 17 million tons of coal a year, much of which comes from their vast Wyoming coal reserves. They also mine and process more than 1,000 tons of uranium every day at plants near Casper, Wyoming.

History. After the first federal survey was completed in 1820, the region now occupied by Kansas, Nebraska, Wyoming, and Colorado appeared on maps as "The Great American Desert"—an area thought to be populated only by prairie dogs and Indians. Because of this reputation very few settlers moved there. Had it not been for the Cali-

fornia gold strike of 1849, and for the ensuing population explosion on the West Coast, there would have been no need to cross the great desert.

If the need to move people from coast to coast made a transcontinental railroad desirable, it was the legend of the desolate "Desert" that enabled a New York medical man named Thomas Durant to initiate the land grab. Together with a few cronies, Durant convinced Congress to sweeten the pot for the railroad's eventual builders with sizable land grants, loans, and a federal bond issue. In 1862, helped along by bribes from the Durant group and convinced that the land was worthless, Congress passed the bill creating the Union Pacific railroad and offering 10 square miles of land for every mile of track completed.

Even with this kind of compensation Durant and his buddies had a tough time attracting investors—especially since the Civil War munitions industry offered more rapid returns. But the unflappable Durant simply returned to Congress and "convinced" them to double the size of the land grants and allow Union Pacific to offer their own bond issue. This second law was duly passed in 1864.

Construction began in Omaha, Nebraska, in 1865 and rapidly captured the public's imagination. The Central Pacific Railroad was starting simultaneously from California, and the two were to link up at some as yet unspecified point. Because the federal loans and land grants depended on track mileage, the two companies staged a hell-for-leather race to lay the most track. Each offered enormous wages for the times and cut corners wherever possible to save time—building trestles out of wood where masonry was required, chopping down whatever timber stands they could find along the route for use as ties and telegraph poles (sometimes while holding the timber owners at gunpoint), even working all night when the full moon made that possible.

Town-building fever followed—sometimes even preceded—construction. Dozens of shanty cities sprang up in the path of the oncoming railroad. One Union Pacific investor, Grenville Dodge, used his inside connections to learn the railroad's path through Wyoming. As a result, he was able to plot and build Cheyenne, Wyoming, before the Irish immigrant laborers even had the first cross-ties in sight. North Platte,

Nebraska, Julesburg, Colorado, and Laramie, Wyoming, all resulted from the same fever—all built in advance, just waiting for the vital transportation link to reach their new villages.

By 1869, when the two railroads were finally linked in the Golden Spike ceremony at Promontory Point, Utah, Union Pacific had been granted more than 18,000 square miles of territory—an amount of land equal to the combined areas of Vermont and New Hampshire. Some of this was sold to settlers along the way in the hope that cheap land would increase railroad business; but most of it was kept by the railroad. Settlers who bought Union Pacific land usually discovered too late that they owned only the surface rights to their properties: Union Pacific had kept the subsurface mineral rights for themselves.

Three years later scandal hit Union Pacific. Durant and an eccentric crony named George Francis Train had correctly guessed that the real profits would come from the building of the railroad, not from its eventual operation. With that in mind in 1864 they created the Credit Mobilier of America, a construction company that supplied Union Pacific with building materials. Durant and Train would buy the materials, charge an exorbitant markup, and sell the goods to the railroad. By early 1872 they had defrauded Union Pacific's investors of $23 million.

When the scandal broke later that year, both Durant and Train were long gone. Durant had been forced out of the Credit Mobilier by a Boston investor named Oakes Ames, who ironically ended up taking most of the blame for the fraud while Durant retired to the Catskills. Train, who had run unsuccessfully three times for the Democratic nomination for President, quit Credit Mobilier to run for dictator of the United States in 1873. He would later turn up fighting for the French Communards, defending free-love advocate Virginia Woodhull, and beating the record of Jules Verne's Phineas Fogg by circumnavigating the globe in only 67 days. He died a pauper in a New York hotel in 1904. An epitaph printed in the Louisville *Courier-Journal* described him as having "the brains of 20 men, all pulling in different ways."

By the 1890s, thanks to the Credit Mobilier scandal and other mismanagement, the Union Pacific Railroad was bankrupt. Wall Street financier E. H. Harriman, one of the last of the robber barons, bought the company at auction just prior to the turn of the century. Known as "the little bookkeeper," Harriman had made his first killing in a stock deal at the age of 26. Bernard Baruch later described his stock dealings as "the epitome of all that was dashing." But others despised his voracious appetite for profit; Teddy Roosevelt even went so far as to call him a "wealthy corruptionist" and an "enemy of the Republic."

Harriman began his Union Pacific career by simply biding his time. During the early years of the twentieth century he was content to keep a very low profile, repair the now-rusted Union Pacific rails, and dig for the coal that lay beneath his Wyoming right-of-way. His strategy soon became apparent. When times were good and the rail industry prospered, Harriman squirreled away the Union Pacific profits and looked on as his competition spent all their cash on expansion. But he knew that bad times were inevitable; and when they hit, Harriman was able to pick up smaller railroads at bargain prices and build the teetering Union Pacific into the nation's premier railroad. The strategy continued under his son Averell, later governor of New York and U.S. diplomat, who also built the nation's first winter resort in Sun Valley, Idaho, during the 1930s.

After the Second World War, however, even Union Pacific fell on hard times. Airlines and the trucking industry combined to deal the rail industry a critical blow, and passenger service declined rapidly. Today Union Pacific has no passenger service, and their freight transportation accounts for only half their total revenues. The rest comes from the mineral rights in Wyoming and elsewhere, for which they have Thomas Durant to thank.

In 1969 Union Pacific formed a partnership with Standard Oil of Indiana to drill for oil on Union Pacific right-of-way. But Union Pacific kept for themselves the mineral rights to the northeast corner of every one of the 640-acre squares of land. When Standard hit oil or gas, Union Pacific drilled another well in their own corner for an added bonanza.

Reputation. Union Pacific is almost universally regarded in investment and banking circles as the railroad that knows how to squeeze the most money out of the "iron horse."

What they own. More than 7 million acres of coal-rich western land, as well as their more than 70,000 freight cars and 1,500 locomotives.

Who owns and runs the company. Although Union Pacific is a western railroad, their headquarters remain in New York, close to their financial wellsprings. As late as 1974 the Harriman family interest held control through their holdings of 3% of the stock, but by 1976 they no longer showed up among the 50 largest shareholders. Elbridge T. Gerry, 70-year-old grandson of Edward H. Harriman, was still on the board in 1979. The UP has always been important to the Mormon community of Salt Lake City.Brigham Young once served on the board, and Salt Lake is now represented on the board by George S. Eccles, chairman of First Security Bank of Salt Lake City, and his nephew, Spencer F. Eccles, president of the bank. With 17,400 shares (a fraction of 1%), George Eccles is the director with the largest stockholdings.

James Evans was named president in 1969 and chairman in 1977. He's a soft-spoken lawyer and former banker whom the *New York Times* once described as having "a voracious appetite for figures and detail." He's the first nonrailroad man to head the railroad since E. H. Harriman.

> 23,373,000 railroad cars carried 1.4 billion tons of commodities all over the United States in 1978. Coal filled 19% of the freight cars and weighed in 28% of the total tonnage.

In the public eye. Union Pacific's robber baron background finally may be catching up with them. Five lawsuits have been filed by Wyoming ranchers since 1977, charging that Union Pacific (known as "Uncle Pete" by the ranchers) has no right to the mineral deposits beneath their land. They claim that the deeds issued to their ancestors or the previous owners originally included mineral rights and were fraudulently changed by Union Pacific after the buyers mailed the signed deeds back. Though UP board chairman James Evans dismisses the suits as "frivolous," the company's main source of profit is at stake.

Where they're going. Back to the rails. Chairman Evans told the *New York Times* in late 1978, "We could always drill more oil wells or open more mines. But our investment in the oil business is very unsatisfactory at the present time. We see enormous room for growth on our railroad." As soon as that appeared in print, Evans wrote a letter to the *Times* pointing out that in 1978 the road was investing $300 million in energy resources and $240 million in the railroad. Just over a year later Evans and officials of the Missouri Pacific announced that they had opened discussions about a possible merger between the two railroads.

Stock performance. Union Pacific stock bought for $1,000 in 1970 sold for $3,185 on January 2, 1980.

Major employment centers. Omaha, Nebraska; Fort Worth, Texas; and Los Angeles, California.

Access. 345 Park Avenue, New York, New York 10022; (212) 826-8200.

The End of the Liners

Once the world's great ocean liners—the Queen Mary, the France, the Michelangelo, the United States—ferried passengers across the North Atlantic. As recently as 1957 more than 1 million passengers crossed the Atlantic on 70 steamers.

Today only Cunard's QE2 is left on the North Atlantic run, every year carrying 50,000 passengers, who pay from $850 to $6,000 each for a crossing. Cost constraints make it unlikely that there will ever be another ship like the QE2, which is longer than three football fields and higher than an eight-story building, and carries up to 1,700 passengers and 960 crew.

Motor Carriers

BEKINS

Sales: $244.3 million
Profits: $95 million
Rank in intra-city moving and storage: 1
Rank in interstate van lines: 5
Founded: 1891
Employees: 6,700
Headquarters: Los Angeles, California

Martin and John Bekins made a smart move when they relocated their moving company from Sioux City, Iowa to Los Angeles in 1895. As California grew Bekins did too, becoming the state's largest mover and storer of household goods. They are also an interstate mover, ranking fifth in that field. Operating a fleet of 4,900 vehicles that average 1,000 moves a day, Bekins has also expanded into related businesses: termite control, self-storage warehouses, building

The scene is 1906 in San Francisco, just after the great earthquake and fire. Martin Bekins is pointing to the upper floors of the Bekins Mission Street warehouse, which was completed after the quake. Note the three-horse teams, needed to navigate the San Francisco hills.

maintenance, guard services.

The Bekins family still owns 43% of the company. Four Bekins cousins, grandchildren of the two founders, sit on the board, but only one, Milo Bekins, Jr., is active in day-to-day management. Peter De Wetter, onetime mayor of El Paso, Texas (where he had a moving company that he sold to Bekins), took over the top job at Bekins in 1971. In 1975 he spent a week as a crewman on a Bekins moving van to learn about the business from a different perspective. But in 1979, after two consecutive years of declining profits, the Bekins family members forced De Wetter to resign as president and Albert L. Labinger succeeded him as president.

Access. 1335 South Figueroa Street, Los Angeles, California 90015; (213) 749-9111. You can write to Bekins for "City Survival Guides," which give information about the 20 most-moved-to destinations in the United States; and "Books for Kids About Moving," a bibliography of children's story books dealing with moving.

Sales: $4.7 billion
Profits: $123 million
Forbes 500 rank: 85
Rank in bus carriers: 1
Rank in bus manufacturing: 1
Rank in bacon: 1
Rank in hot dogs: 2
Rank in canned meats: 1
Rank in needlecrafts and yarns: 1
Founded: 1914
Employees: 50,912
Headquarters: Phoenix, Arizona

What they do. Everyone associates Greyhound with the bus marked by the symbol of the running dog. But hot dogs? Yes. And computers, jet aircraft, fire insurance, museum installations, pizza mix—to name a few of their various enterprises.

No longer "just the bus company," Greyhound has recently been touting itself as "the *omni* bus company." In little more than a decade they have changed from a Chicago-based bus transportation and bus manufacturing business to the epitome of the modern conglomerate, headquartered in a skyscraper in Phoenix, Arizona.

The transformation began in 1962 when the bus company got into the business of leasing ocean vessels and jet planes. But the really dramatic step was taken in 1969, when Greyhound absorbed Armour, the venerable meat packers and makers of Dial soap as well as other consumer products from ammonia to yarn. At that time Armour, also based in Chicago, was three times Greyhound's size.

If you take a cross-country trip on a Greyhound bus, you can eat at Greyhound fast-food restaurants along the way, use Greyhound money orders, cover your luggage with Greyhound insurance, or view a show on the arts of ancient Nubia that is touring the world in displays designed by a branch of Greyhound. You may not be able to escape Greyhound by flying, either: they own and lease more jets than some airlines. Workers on the Alaska Pipeline eat food supplied by Greyhound.

History. Greyhound rose out of the combination of a number of small bus lines around the country. The earliest was in the Mesabi iron-ore region of Minnesota: Eric Wickman charged miners 25¢ for a round trip from Hibbing to Alice in 1914. The next year he carried school children and others in his seven-seat Hupmobiles, and even attempted the 90-mile trek to Duluth. Other tiny buslines in California, Wisconsin, Georgia, and Florida eventually came together in 1925.

"Greyhound" was the nickname of the first vehicles manufactured as buses by Frank Fageol (later the Peterbilt company). By 1930 the company had adopted the running dog as their trademark, and Chicago as their headquarters. Greyhound offered better and cheaper service than the railroads (buses are still more fuel efficient than trains, or any other form of transportation, for that matter). During the Second World War Greyhound's patriotic pitch was: "Serve America now, so you can see America later."

Greyhound had little to worry about in the 1960s. They were twice the size of their nearest bus competitor, Continental Trailways, and they controlled almost half of the country's bus routes under Interstate Com-

The Greyhound bus—1929.

merce Commission license. So they began to buy other businesses, including Armour. Dating back to 1867, Armour was a giant of the meat-packing industry, a pioneer in meat canning, and the developer of the first, and perennially best-selling, deodorant soap, Dial. When Armour was in financial trouble in the 1960s and likely to be snapped up by an eastern conglomerate, local powers influenced Greyhound's Gerald Trautman to buy Armour and keep it in Chicago. Trautman complied—then surprised and dismayed Chicagoans by moving both Greyhound and Armour to the Southwest in 1971. Why he picked Phoenix is not exactly clear—though he did happen to own a house there. Greyhound is now the biggest business in the state.

Reputation. The Greyhound dog no longer runs on diesel fuel, or even on Armour hot dogs, but on the power of computers, equipment leasing, and other profit-raising parts of their business.

What they own. Greyhound owns over 5,-000 buses, costing about $100,000 apiece, which are manufactured at Greyhound plants in Canada, North Dakota, and New Mexico. The bus service runs to all states but Hawaii, so Greyhound support systems like terminals, food services, and maintenance centers can be found around the country, too.

Who owns and runs the company. First and foremost, Gerald Trautman, chairman since 1966 and overseer of the expansion that has catapulted Greyhound to a place among the nation's top 100 corporations. Trautman, who had represented Greyhound as an attorney for 20 years, took firm hold of the reins when he became chairman, quickly firing all executives whose visions of the future conflicted with his. Eventually he even axed his own protégé, James L. Kerrigan, who headed the transportation division. A 1978 Greyhound Lines press release presented a glowing image of Kerrigan's

The Greyhound bus—1980.

leadership; two years later Trautman commented dryly on his former heir apparent: "He let the business go downhill." Kerrigan is now chairman of Greyhound's chief bus competitor, Trailways.

Directors and officers own less than 1% of the company's stock. The board of directors includes a woman (Martha W. Griffiths, a lawyer) and a black (John Johnson, publisher of *Ebony* magazine).

In the public eye. Potential and current women drivers won a class action suit against Greyhound in 1976. The women charged that the 5'7" height requirement for drivers amounted to a discriminatory policy. In another legal action the Mount Hood Stages, an Oregon bus line was awarded $18 million in damages in 1979. The court found Greyhound guilty of antitrust violations for having diverted passengers from Mt. Hood to Greyhound buses.

Greyhound paid a $5,000 fine for illegal contributions to the presidential campaigns of President Nixon and Senator McGovern of about $16,000 in 1972. Gerald Trautman had solicited the donations from his executives. The company now has a "Good Government Project," which solicits contributions from executives for political candidates. In 1978 Greyhound supported 222 candidates for office (54% Republican, 46% Democrat).

Greyhound employs Joe Black, a former relief pitcher for the Brooklyn Dodgers, as their representative for minorities, and Black has helped Greyhound's reputation in minority communities.

Where they're going. Greyhound is still committed to the motto, "Take the bus, and leave the driving to us." They're making buses for urban mass-transit systems, and they're supplying 197 buses to Saudi Arabia, where Greyhound will run a private bus service for Aramco personnel.

Stock performance. Greyhound stock bought for $1,000 in 1970 sold for $865 on January 2, 1980.

Access. Greyhound Tower, Phoenix, Arizona 85077; (602) 248-4000.

Consumer brands.

Food products: Armour Star; Golden Star; Decker Quality; Veribest; Miss Wisconsin; Tes-Tender; Cloverbloom; Appian Way Pizza; Treet.

Other household products: Dial and Tone soaps; Parson's ammonia; Bruce floor-care products; Magic sizing; Manpower toiletries; Malina and Bucilla knitting yarns.

Insurance: Verex; Travelers Express and money orders.

Food services: Post House; Faber Enterprises; Prophet.

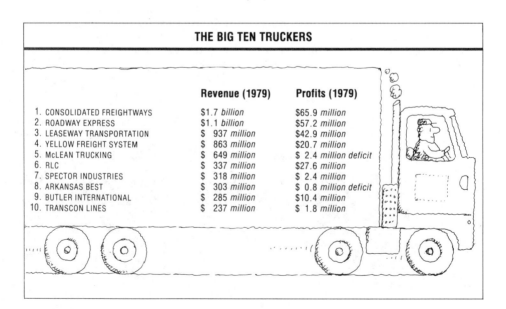

THE BIG TEN TRUCKERS

	Revenue (1979)	Profits (1979)
1. CONSOLIDATED FREIGHTWAYS	$1.7 *billion*	$65.9 *million*
2. ROADWAY EXPRESS	$1.1 *billion*	$57.2 *million*
3. LEASEWAY TRANSPORTATION	$ 937 *million*	$42.9 *million*
4. YELLOW FREIGHT SYSTEM	$ 863 *million*	$20.7 *million*
5. McLEAN TRUCKING	$ 649 *million*	$ 2.4 *million deficit*
6. RLC	$ 337 *million*	$27.6 *million*
7. SPECTOR INDUSTRIES	$ 318 *million*	$ 2.4 *million*
8. ARKANSAS BEST	$ 303 *million*	$ 0.8 *million deficit*
9. BUTLER INTERNATIONAL	$ 285 *million*	$10.4 *million*
10. TRANSCON LINES	$ 237 *million*	$ 1.8 *million*

Sales: $1.1 billion
Profits: $57 million
Forbes 500 rank: 425
Rank in trucking: 1
Founded: 1930
Employees: 23,000
Headquarters: Akron, Ohio

Roadway considers excessive government regulation one of the nation's "more serious problems," but the company is quite happy with the Interstate Commerce Commission's regulation of the trucking industry, and opposes deregulation. Under the eyes of the ICC Roadway has emerged as the nation's number 1 trucker. Their routes blanket the East, and they are fanning out to the West. They've expanded by buying smaller truckers, more than 20 in the past decade. At the start of 1979 they operated a fleet of 22,359 tractors, trailers, and trucks, serving 40 states, with terminals in more than 400 cities. They carried 11,910,000 shipments in 1978. Roadway's average shipment is 1,174 pounds hauled 988 miles.

Galen Roush, a lawyer, and his brother Carroll founded Roadway in Akron in 1930. Carroll sold his shares in 1956, and Galen died in 1976. Roush family members still control 42% of the stock but are no longer active in day-to-day management. W. F. Spitznagel, who was elected chairman and president in 1978, has 26,000 shares (13%) worth about $650,000; his salary was $432,000 in 1978. Roadway has long rewarded efficient, profit-producing managers with cash and stock bonuses that have made some of them millionaires. In 1978 they set

aside $15 million for bonus payments to salaried employees.

Stock performance Roadway stock bought for $1,000 in 1970 sold for $4,160 on January 2, 1980.

Access. 1077 Gorge Boulevard, P.O. Box 471, Akron, Ohio 44309; (216) 384-1717.

Sales: $3.4 billion
Profits: $83 million
Rank in motor carriers: 1
Rank in package delivery: 1
Founded: 1907
Employees: 105,000
Headquarters: Greenwich, Connecticut

What they do. United Parcel Service—UPS as they are known across the land—delivers small packages in direct competition with the U.S. Postal Service. However, there are differences. Whereas the Postal Service generally loses money, UPS always makes money. Whereas the Postal Service is government owned, UPS is privately owned—by the managers and supervisors who work for the company. Whereas the Postal Service has a monopoly on delivery to mailboxes, UPS picks up and delivers door-to-door. And whereas the Postal Service is obliged to accept virtually all packages weighing 50 pounds or less and shorter than 120 inches. Dealing with small packages has enabled UPS to automate their sorting and loading. Sophisticated conveyor belts speed shipments on their way. The weight limit also means that a UPS shipment can be handled by one man. (While more women are popping up in those brown uniforms, UPS drivers are still predominantly male.) UPS is proud of the efficiency of their delivery systems. Defenders of the Postal Service say UPS is "skimming the cream off" of the small shipment business, which accounts for their ability to turn a profit.

UPS now delivers more than 1.4 billion packages a year (five million packages a day

---

WHO CARRIES THE MOST PASSENGERS?

People Carried Between Cities (1979)

BUSES	378 *million*
PLANES	308 *million*
TRAINS (*not including commuters*)	21 *million*

during the Christmas season), twice as many as the Post Office. They operate in all 50 states under the authority of the Interstate Commerce Commission and state regulatory agencies, which puts them in the class of a "common carrier," whose services must be available to all comers. But UPS does little or nothing to solicit customers. They employ very few salespeople and they don't advertise, so many people are probably unaware that they could be using UPS to send packages. (All it takes is a phone call, and the cost is usually comparable to U.S. postage.) Most UPS deliveries are still for businesses.

History. Serving businesses is how this company grew up. They were born in Seattle in 1907 when Jim Casey founded the American Messenger Company. He had six messengers, two bicycles, and a telephone. He soon began delivering parcels for merchants in a Model T Ford refitted for carrying packages and a year later added seven motorcycles. From the start, the drivers had to look neat: they wore suits, ties, and caps. By 1918 Casey's company was handling all the deliveries for three of Seattle's largest department stores. In 1913 American Messenger became Merchants Parcel Company. After World War I, renamed United Parcel Service, the company expanded to other cities, offering local stores a contract delivery service. The first UPS cars hit the streets of New York in 1930, and by the end of their first year there UPS was delivering for 123 New York stores. By the early 1950s they were serving stores in 16 metropolitan areas; the ubiquitous brown trucks gave people the impression that UPS was an extension of the downtown department stores.

This department store image still clings to UPS even though the company radically changed their course in 1953 when they began to offer a door-to-door parcel pickup-and-delivery service for wholesalers, manufacturers, and others (translation: everybody). Today this is the biggest part of their business. The delivery system even includes a cross-country air parcel service, which delivers more packages than Federal Express, Emery, Purolator, or any other dispatcher. Called their "Blue Label" air service, it accounts for 2% of UPS volume and 10% of their profits. In 1980 a 10 pound package traveling from New York to Los Angeles cost $37 via Federal Express; the price was $10.31 via UPS's chartered 747, which makes the rounds between Los Angeles, San Francisco, Dallas, Atlanta, and New York. UPS guarantees delivery within two days.

Reputation. UPS is known for requiring rigid adherence to dress codes and standardized procedures. Employees are expected to be neat—which means, in UPS terms, no pins on the uniform, no hair below the collar, and no "excessively

Light a Fire in That Christmas Tree

Trucker talk works on a straightforward principle: you can't call things by their right name; it's gotta be something different. The more colorful the words, the more likely they'll keep a *bedsteader* (sleepy driver) awake while he rolls down his *religious road* (highway full of potholes) on *baloney skins* (bald tires) in *Georgia overdrive* (coasting in neutral, an East Coast term; in the West it's *Mexican overdrive*), searching for *hundred-mile coffee* (strong enough to keep you alert for 100 miles) along *Radar Alley* (Interstate

90 between Cleveland and the New York State line).

Trucking songs have made words like *smokey* (a state trooper) common knowledge, but there are still terms unknown outside the truck-stop parking lots, where the *gear jammers* (truckers) *light a fire* (turn on the ignition) in their rigs. For instance, the names they give to the trucks they drive:

Bedbug hauler: moving van
Cat engine: one made by the Caterpillar company; driving one is *dangling the cat*

Christmas tree: truck with many clearance lights; also *rolling lighthouse*
Corn binder: International Harvester Corp. truck; also known as *In Hock Constantly* truck
Dirge: Dodge tractor
Dog catcher: any truck fast enough to catch and pass a Greyhound bus
Fix or Repair Daily: Ford tractor
Gandy dancer: weaving truck
Garbage hauler: truck carrying vegetables or fruit
Jimmy: General Motors truck; also *General Mess of*

bushy" sideburns. In *The Corporate Personality*, British designer Wally Olins caught the UPS spirit, noting that the company "practices elitism through a private language and complex symbolism. . . . Delivery trucks . . . are called package cars. . . . The name of the manufacturer is removed and certain modifications are made to most of the bodies to disguise the vehicles' origins. No UPS vehicle has Mack, GMC, Chevrolet, Dodge or Ford badges on it. All UPS package cars are washed daily. . . . Everything is standardized and coded: a flat tire is a 471, a road service call is a 388. . . . UPS . . . is in many ways a private world, carefully developed with the intention of making people behave predictably."

What they own. 40,000 brown vehicles.

Who owns and runs the company. UPS is completely private, with no stock in the hands of the public. What little is known about them results from their having to file reports with the Interstate Commerce Commission. Only managers and supervisors—about 9,000 of them now—hold UPS stock, some of it bought, but much of it awarded to them for their performance as profit producers. When UPS managers leave the company (and not many do) or retire, the stock has to be resold to the company. As of 1975 the UPS Managers Stock Trust held nearly half the stock. James Casey, the founder, held 2.46%, and other longtime employees—Harold and Paul Oberkotter, James P. McLaughlin, Preston David, and Charles Forman—held chunks ranging from one-quarter of 1% up to 1.9%.

George C. Lamb, who joined UPS in 1952, succeeded Harold Oberkotter as chairman in 1980. Founder Jim Casey holds the title of honorary chairman; he was 92 in 1980.

In the public eye. The UPS passion for efficiency has provoked a number of labor disputes. Employees represented by Teamsters unions in 15 eastern states struck the

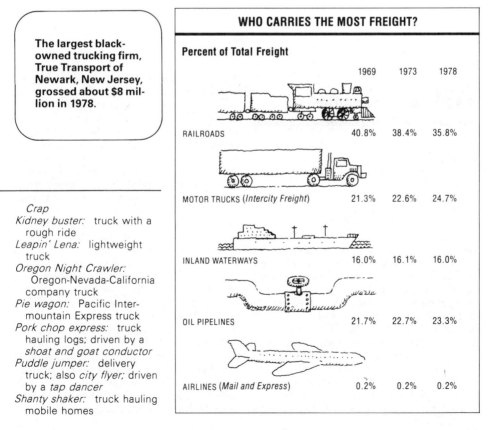

The largest black-owned trucking firm, True Transport of Newark, New Jersey, grossed about $8 million in 1978.

Crap
Kidney buster: truck with a rough ride
Leapin' Lena: lightweight truck
Oregon Night Crawler: Oregon-Nevada-California company truck
Pie wagon: Pacific Intermountain Express truck
Pork chop express: truck hauling logs; driven by a *shoat and goat conductor*
Puddle jumper: delivery truck; also *city flyer;* driven by a *tap dancer*
Shanty shaker: truck hauling mobile homes

WHO CARRIES THE MOST FREIGHT?

Percent of Total Freight

	1969	1973	1978
RAILROADS	40.8%	38.4%	35.8%
MOTOR TRUCKS (*Intercity Freight*)	21.3%	22.6%	24.7%
INLAND WATERWAYS	16.0%	16.1%	16.0%
OIL PIPELINES	21.7%	22.7%	23.3%
AIRLINES (*Mail and Express*)	0.2%	0.2%	0.2%

company for 12 weeks in 1976, and in 1974 a Teamsters union pulled New York employees off their UPS jobs for 87 days. A Teamsters official, Ron Carey, said: "UPS is hardnosed. If they catch a guy with an infraction, he's discharged. They don't give the union guy a chance to sit down and try to work something out."

Access. 51 Weaver Street, Greenwich, Connecticut 06830; (203) 622-6000.

Airline Operators

 **AmericanAirlines**

Sales: $3.3 billion
Profits: $87.4 million
Forbes 500 rank: 148
Rank in airlines: 2
Founded: 1930
Employees: 38,000
Headquarters: Dallas–Fort Worth, Texas

What they do. By a macabre quirk of accounting, American's worst disaster helped produce their highest ever profits. American collected nearly $24.3 million in insurance payments after the May 25, 1979, crash of their DC-10 at Chicago's O'Hare airport that killed 273 people. The insurance money contributed to American's record of $95 million in profits for the spring of 1979. A government investigation later determined that faulty maintenance procedures by American contributed to the crash.

Built by a far-sighted Texan, Cyrus Rowlett Smith, American Airlines reigned the skies as the leading U.S. airline until they were upended 20 years ago by United Airlines. United forged to the top by a simple end-around play: they bought a floundering carrier, Capital Airlines. American never regained the top spot and experienced such management traumas that in 1973 they recalled "C. R." Smith from retirement to take the helm again at the age of 74. C. R. held the fort for seven months until American was able to lure smiling Albert V. Casey (publisher of the *Los Angeles Times*) from the Times-Mirror Company in Los Angeles to New York as their new chief executive. Casey led American from a deficit of $20 million in 1975 to record profits of $134 million in 1978, and he then shocked New York City officials by moving the airline's headquarters to Texas, specifically to the Dallas–Fort Worth airport where his brother, John Casey, is based as vice-chairman of Braniff International. *Business Week* suggested that Casey was miffed because he had failed to gain acceptance in New York's ruling circles. Casey replied that since American is a domestic airline, it "belongs in Mid-America."

American does fly over a good part of the country. At the start of 1979 they had flights out of 56 cities in 28 states, plus service to several Caribbean islands and a few spots in Canada and Mexico. They added 10 new destinations, including Miami, Las Vegas, Minneapolis–St. Paul, and Nassau, Bahamas, in 1979. Passenger tickets account for 84% of their revenues.

History. American likes to trace company origins back to Charles Lindbergh. In 1926 Lindbergh, then a little-known barnstormer, flew a load of mail from Chicago to St. Louis in a World War I surplus biplane, a model nicknamed "The Flaming Coffin." Airmail was the chief commercial use of airplanes at the time, and the service was heavily subsidized by the federal government. Lindbergh worked for Robertson Aircraft, one of a hodgepodge of 85 aircraft-related companies consolidated into American Airways in 1930.

American Airways flew a weird assortment of Fords, Lockheeds, Condors, and half a dozen other types of planes. In 1931 they became the first airline to have a plane built to their own specifications: a nine–passenger, single-engine Pilgrim 100-A.

C. R. Smith, a tall, gruff, dynamic Texan, got into the airline business almost by accident. A. P. Barrett, owner of the Texas-Louisiana Power Company, hired Smith as an assistant treasurer in 1926. Two years later Barrett bought Texas Air Transport and asked Smith to run it.

When American Airways became American Airlines in 1934, Smith became president. Believing that the future of aviation lay in carrying passengers, not mail, Smith introduced a Curtiss Condor plane with sleeping berths—sort of a flying Pullman car. At the same time, American flights started carrying stewardesses.

Smith viewed air transportation as a product that could be marketed "like a box of Post Toasties." Selling it, in his opinion, was "fully as important as producing it." Up until then most airline advertising had consisted of a schedule and a picture of an airplane. Smith confronted the big taboo of airline advertising head-on: "Afraid to fly?" read the headline on a 1937 ad. American's routes to California flew over the deserts of the Southwest—"The Sunshine Route," they called it, implying safer flying weather

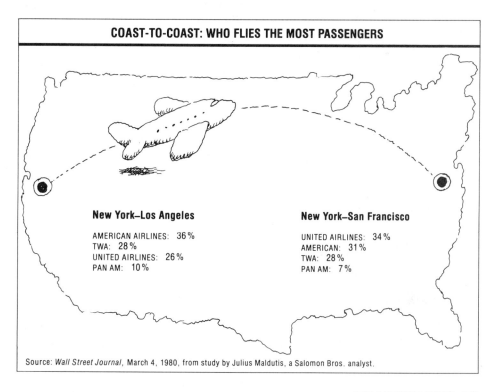

COAST-TO-COAST: WHO FLIES THE MOST PASSENGERS

New York–Los Angeles

AMERICAN AIRLINES: 36%
TWA: 28%
UNITED AIRLINES: 26%
PAN AM: 10%

New York–San Francisco

UNITED AIRLINES: 34%
AMERICAN: 31%
TWA: 28%
PAN AM: 7%

Source: *Wall Street Journal*, March 4, 1980, from study by Julius Maldutis, a Salomon Bros. analyst.

than on United's flights across the Rockies. When a United plane crashed in the mountains near Denver, American's ads boasted of "The Low-Level Routes to the West."

Nevertheless, the early years were unprofitable for American, as well as other airlines, because of high costs and low passenger volume. The dominant transport plane in the mid-1930s was the 14-seat Douglas DC-2. C. R. Smith thought a bigger plane would stand a better chance of making money, so he had Douglas Aircraft design the 21-passenger DC-3, destined to become one of the most famous commercial planes in history. American had DC-3s in the air by 1936; they also turned their first profit that year: a tidy $4,600. By the end of the decade they were the country's number 1 airline.

Smith married Elizabeth Manget, a Dallas Junior Leaguer, in 1938, but the marriage had to compete with his love for American Airlines. After a four-day honeymoon Smith dropped his bride off at their apartment and disappeared to his office for the next day and a half. Ultimately the airline won: they were divorced, and from then on Smith lived in a bachelor apartment in New York decorated with paintings of Western scenes by Frederic Remington and Charles Russell.

During World War II Smith served as deputy commander of the Air Transport Command, the center of the war effort's air operations. By the end of the war he had become a major general. After the war he returned to American Airlines and outfitted the airline with all new planes, which represented the biggest outlay of money any airline had ever made. In 1949, while United was still flying DC-3s, Smith had a good laugh on his chief competitor by donating American's last DC-3 to a museum.

In 1953 American offered the first nonstop coast-to-coast flights aboard their 80-seat DC-7s. That same year they surpassed the Pennsylvania Railroad as the world's largest passenger carrier in terms of sales. In 1959 they ushered in the American jet age with their Boeing 707s.

Smith left the airline in 1968 to become secretary of commerce during fellow Texan Lyndon Johnson's last year in the White House. He was succeeded at American by George A. Spater, a quiet, professorial lawyer who collected first editions of Virginia Woolf, lunched with the New York literati, and shunned the company limousine to commute by train. Spater became one of Watergate's earliest casualties when he announced in 1973 he had made an illegal $55,000 corporate contribution to President Nixon's reelection campaign. American had been turned down repeatedly in their requests for new routes, and Spater may have thought his donation would lead to more favorable treatment from the Civil Aeronautics Board. The directors sacked Spater in 1973 and brought back C. R. Smith.

In 1977 American introduced the Super Saver coast-to-coast fare to fill their big jets. United and TWA fought to stop the scheme before the CAB, but they lost—and also started offering Super Savers. It was the

AIRLINE INDUSTRY FUEL BILL

1978: $4 *billion*
1979: $6.5 *billion*
1980: $10 *billion* (*anticipated*)

FUEL BILL: $10,000,000,000.

kind of promotion true to the C. R. Smith tradition.

Reputation. Under the C. R. Smith regime, American was known for years to traveling businessmen as one of the most professional and efficient airlines in the country. After Smith left, things got so bad in the early seventies that one American vice-president sent a note to 140,000 regular passengers apologizing for the poor service. They have been trying to recover their old reputation ever since, telling their employees that "American's leadership image has been built on a tradition of service excellence."

What they own. American owns 167 airplanes and leases another 84. Their Sky Chefs division serves in-flight meals for American and 36 other airlines, prepared in their "in-flight" kitchens at 26 airports. In 1976 they went into the oil business by buying Howard Corp., a Dallas-based company with 3,600 oil and gas wells. They used to run the Americana hotel chain but the hotels lost money for 14 years in a row and were finally unloaded in 1979.

Who owns and runs the company. The largest individual stockholder is Richard Gruner, a West German millionaire who once published the German weekly *Stern*. Gruner, who owns 5.6% of American (worth $14 million in 1980), also owns smaller chunks of Continental Airlines and Pan Am. Casey, chairman and president, held only 16,000 shares in 1979 but had options to buy 21,000 more. The directors include Carla Hills, secretary of housing and urban development under President Ford; Antonio Luis Ferré, president of the Puerto Rican Cement Company; and Christopher Edley, executive director of the United Negro College Fund.

In the public eye. American Airlines boasted "the best safety record in the history of commercial aviation" until their 1979 crash in Chicago. It was the worst disaster in U.S. aviation history. American had to pay a record $500,000 fine imposed by the Federal Aviation Administration for improper maintenance of their DC-10s

In 1973 two company officials were indicted for accepting bribes and kickbacks in return for the contract to print the airline's in-flight magazine, *American Way*. Walter Rauscher, an executive vice-president and one of the company's top four executives, was sentenced to six months in jail; the other defendant, who worked under Rauscher, skipped the country.

In 1977 American rehired 300 flight attendants fired between 1965 and 1970 because they had become pregnant. The airline also gave the attendants $2.7 million in back pay in one of the largest civil rights settlements ever.

Where they're going. From their new base in Middle America, American will be plotting once again how to regain the lead they lost to United two decades ago.

Stock performance. American stock bought for $1,000 in 1970 sold for $329 on January 2, 1980.

Major employment centers. New York, Tulsa, Dallas–Fort Worth, Los Angeles, and Chicago.

Access. P.O. Box 61616, Dallas–Fort Worth, Texas 75261; (214) 355-1234. American has no regular tour program, but visitors can go through the Flight Academy and Learning Center at Fort Worth by appointment. Complaints should be directed to E. M. Dieringer, Director, Consumer Relations, at the Dallas–Fort Worth headquarters.

> La Motte Cohu, president of American Airways (now American Airlines) in the early 1930s, was plagued for a time with complaints over lost luggage. Cohu summoned his station managers from around the country and arranged to have their baggage lost in transit. "We had a lot more efficiency after that," said Cohu to the *New York Times*.

> Fuel represented over 25% of average total costs for international air carriers in 1979.

WHY DODGE THIS QUESTION:

Afraid to Fly?

WE know that fear keeps many people from enjoying the advantages of air transportation. *So why should we be silent on this subject?* Regrettable as it is, the records show there *have been* accidents and fatalities in *every* form of transportation. What we do not understand, is why some people associate danger with a transport plane more than they do with a train, a boat, a motor car, an interurban, or a bus. Is it because airline accidents have received more publicity?

The fact is, there *are* risks involved in *all* kinds of travel.

It is also a fact that the *air transportation industry has shown greater progress and achieved a much higher standard of efficiency in a shorter span of years than any other form of transportation the world has ever known.*

Why quote statistics? They are not always conclusive. They are often only controversial. I could show you figures to prove that you would have to fly around the world 425 times — or make approximately 14,165 flights back and forth between New York and Chicago — before you would be liable to meet with an accident. Do these statistics overcome your fear of flying? I think not. There is only one way to overcome that fear — and that is, to fly.

Many of our regular passengers, who now prefer air travel to any other form of transportation, admit they were very timid about their *first* flight. Perhaps you say: "It is my business if I want to go on being afraid and confine myself to

By *C. R. Smith*

PRESIDENT
AMERICAN AIRLINES, INC.

slower forms of transportation." No one questions that. The question is: "Is it good business?" Maybe your competitor is flying. Many people lived and died who never rode on a train because *they* were afraid. Today we smile at those old-fashioned fears. And today, to the more than a million airline passengers of last year, the fear of air travel is just as old-fashioned.

American Airlines, Inc. has carried more than a million passengers. These people travel by air for the same reason they use the telephone, send telegrams, and ride in elevators. It is a quicker, more modern, more efficient way to accomplish what they want to do.

Are airlines safer than railroads? You can find intelligent people to take both sides of the argument.

Whether you fly or not, does not alter the fact that *every* form of transportation has *one* thing in common — risk! No form of transportation — on the ground, on the water, or in the air — can guarantee its passengers absolute immunity from danger.

This whole subject of fear about flying can be summed up as follows: PEOPLE ARE AFRAID OF THE THINGS THEY DO NOT KNOW ABOUT. You would be equally afraid of trains if you had never ridden on one.

As soon as you become acquainted with air transportation your fear will be replaced by your *enjoyment of the many advantages of air travel.*

AMERICAN
AIRLINES INC.

In this historic 1937 advertisement American Airlines dared to ask the question everyone else in the industry was afraid to ask. President C.R. Smith's answer said, in part: "I could show you figures to prove that you would have to fly around the world 425 times — or make approximately 14,165 flights back and forth between New York and Chicago — before you would be liable to meet with an accident. Do these statistic overcome your fear of flying? I think not. There is only one way to overcome that fear — and that is, to fly."

Braniff paid artist Alexander Calder $100,000 to paint this DC-8 jetliner which was in service on Latin American routes. At the unveiling in 1973 Braniff's leader, Harding Lawrence, said: "More people will see this painting by a famous artist in a shorter time than perhaps any other in history."

BRANIFF INTERNATIONAL

Sales: $1.3 billion
Loss: $44.3 million
Forbes 500 rank: 365
Rank in airlines: 7
Founded: 1928
Employees: 12,000
Headquarters: Dallas–Fort Worth, Texas

What they do. On one day in 1978 Braniff added service to 16 new cities. The federal government had just lifted most restrictions on which routes airlines could fly and Braniff saw it as a chance to leap to prominence. Their routes lace the Midwest from Minneapolis to Houston, and they also fly to the Northeast, Florida, and California. They are a major carrier to Central and South America, and they have a few flights to Europe, too.

History. Braniff is the only major airline named after its founder: Thomas Braniff, whose younger brother Paul started flying a five-passenger Stinson Detroiter between Tulsa and Oklahoma City in 1928. Tom Braniff steadily expanded the airline throughout the Midwest and Texas and into South America before he died in a private plane crash in 1954. Braniff now flies a fleet of 108 planes—more than 80% of them Boeing 727s.

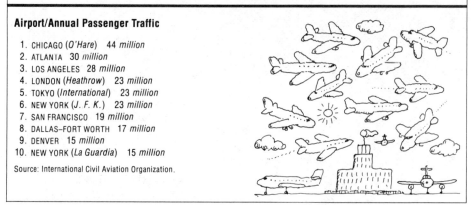
In 1965 Harding Lawrence, a Texan who (as the *New York Times* put it) looks "as though the Ashley Famous Agency had sent him over to play the part of a dynamic airline president," became president of Braniff. Two years later he married Mary Wells, chairperson of the successful Wells, Rich, Greene advertising agency. Mary Wells had created Braniff's dazzling ad campaign of the mid-1960s that celebrated "the end of the plain plane." Braniff painted their jets in bright shades of the rainbow and became the airline that "gets you there with Flying Colors." They outfitted their flight attendants in Pucci-designed uniforms. In 1969 Braniff added a new phrase to American speech: "When you've got it, flaunt it." A series of Braniff television commercials made seatmates of pairs of celebrities such as Andy Warhol and Sonny Liston, Mickey Spillane and Marianne Moore, and Whitey Ford and Salvador Dali. In the mid-1970s they commissioned Alexander Calder to design new paint jobs for two planes, which featured wavy blocks of bright colors and were prominently signed "Calder." Despite Braniff's flashy jet-set image, however, 70% of their passengers are business travelers—the highest percentage of any airline.

Mary Wells didn't have a hand in Braniff's commercials in the early '70s because the Wells, Rich, Greene agency dropped the Braniff account and took on TWA shortly after the Lawrence-Wells marriage. But in 1979 Wells, Rich, Greene resigned TWA and became the Braniff ad agency once again. The *New York Times* once called Harding Lawrence and Mary Wells "America's corporate lovebirds."

Unfortunately for Braniff, their big expansion of 1978 came at a time when the price of jet fuel was skyrocketing. Although they had made money in earlier recessions when other airlines were losing heavily, they found themselves operating in the red by mid-1979.

In the public eye. In 1972 Braniff made an illegal $40,000 corporate contribution to the Nixon campaign. After the donation was revealed, the Aviation Consumer Action Project, a group affiliated with Ralph Nader, persuaded the Civil Aeronautics Board to investigate Braniff's procedures for handling cash. The investigation of the political contribution also revealed that Braniff was giving rebates and excessive commissions to travel agents. Braniff paid a $300,000 civil penalty for this activity. At the time it was the largest penalty in CAB history.

Who owns and runs the company. Lawrence became chairman of the board in 1968. Braniff's vice-chairman John Casey is the brother of American Airlines chief executive Albert Casey. Three women sit on the board of directors, including Anne Armstrong, former U.S. ambassador to Great Britain.

Stock performance. Braniff stock bought for $1,000 in 1970 sold for $917 on January 2, 1980.

Access. P.O. Box 61747, Dallas–Fort Worth Airport, Texas 75261; (214) 358-6011.

CONTINENTAL AIRLINES

Sales: $927.6 million
Loss: $13.2 million
Forbes 500 rank: 487
Rank in airlines: 10
Founded: 1934
Employees: 12,200
Headquarters: Los Angeles, California

What they do. The story of Continental Airlines is the story of Robert Six, the last of the old scarf-and-goggles aviators in the airline business. As president he ran Continental with an iron grip from 1938 to 1975, and he was still chairman as 1980 opened. Most of Continental's flights stay west of the Mississippi. Their only international flights (besides one to Calgary, Alberta) cross the Pacific via Hawaii to Micronesia, Japan, Australia, and New Zealand.

History. Bob Six's aviation career began around the time Charles Lindbergh made his transatlantic solo flight. After dropping out of St. Mary's High School in Oakland, California, Six got a job as a bill collector for the Pacific Gas and Electric Company—but he was fired for taking flying lessons on company time. In 1929, at age 22, he got his pilot's license. Six years later he married Henriette Erhart Ruggles, daughter of the board chairman of the Charles Pfizer chemical firm. In 1937 he borrowed $90,000 from his father-in-law and bought a 40% interest in the Southwest Division of Varney Speed Lines, a three-year-old company that flew three planes on a mail route between El Paso, Texas, and Pueblo, Colorado. Within a year Six became president, moved the company from El Paso to Denver, and changed the name to Continental Airlines.

In Denver, to publicize the line, the flamboyant Six organized a group of top Continental executives as "The Six Guns," decked them out in western regalia, including frock coats and 10-gallon hats, and took them around to fast-draw contests (they won several). Six stands 6′ 4″, weighs 210 pounds, dominates any room he walks into, and has a penchant for marrying rich or famous women. He was twice divorced and twice remarried—first to Broadway star Ethel Merman in 1953, then to television performer Audrey Meadows in 1961. In 1963 he moved Continental's headquarters to Los Angeles. He and his wife live in the Hollywood Hills, and they also keep a 1,200-acre ranch in Colorado.

Unlike many airline executives, who constantly push for higher fares, Six always thought the way to make more money in the airline business was to increase passenger volume. In 1963, over the strenuous objections of United, American, and TWA, he got the Civil Aeronautics Board to approve an economy fare between Chicago and Los Angeles that was 20% below what the others charged. The others reluctantly followed suit.

Six, a staunch Democrat, maintained close connections with the Democratic administrations of John Kennedy and Lyndon Johnson. In 1965 he hired Pierre Salinger, who had been Kennedy's press secretary, as a Continental vice-president. (Salinger left in 1967.) During the 1960s Continental managed to win several new route approvals. Just before President Johnson left office, he approved a new Continental route from the United States to Australia and New Zealand, and Continental ordered four Boeing 747s to make the flights. But when Richard Nixon became president in January 1969, he canceled Johnson's approval and awarded the route to American Airlines instead. Continental ended up mothballing their 747s in New Mexico, at a cost of about $13 million a year, until they managed to unload three of them on the government of Iran in 1975. In recent years Continental has continued to have close relations with political figures: they made John Connally a director in 1978. Also on the Continental board is Irma Baker Lyons, widow of George T. Baker, the founder of National Airlines. Six's right-hand man for years was Harding Lawrence, who left to become president of Braniff in 1965.

Stock performance. Continental stock bought for $1,000 in 1970 sold for $863 on January 2, 1980.

Access. Los Angeles International Airport, Los Angeles, California 90009; (213) 646-2810.

DELTA AIR LINES

Sales: $2.4 billion
Profits: $137 million
Forbes 500 rank: 215
Rank in airlines: 5
Founded: 1929
Employees: 33,000
Headquarters: Atlanta, Georgia

What they do. All routes lead to Atlanta on Delta, a hard-nosed, no-nonsense company that started with two World War I surplus "Flying Jennies" and now fields 200 mid-sized jets—half of them Boeing 727s. Delta flies to 85 cities in 31 states. Most of their destinations are in the South and the Midwest, but they also make some long hops to California, Venezuela, and London. Since they bought Northeast Airlines in 1972 they have been flying to several cities in New England as well.

History. Delta began as a crop-dusting experiment in Louisiana in the 1920s, when the boll weevil was terrorizing the southern cotton fields. One of their pilots was an agricultural agent named C. E. Woolman. By 1929 the crop-dusting operation had expanded into a mail and passenger airline called Delta Air Service. Woolman became president in 1945 and continued to run the company until his death in 1966.

Delta got through the early years without much competition in the South. Although airlines make most of their money on long flights, Delta learned to turn a profit on short routes, through careful scheduling so that their short runs feed into their longer ones.

Reputation. Delta's image is one of "determinedly grim efficiency," *Newsweek* magazine has observed. "We don't squander our money on things like goofy advertising," chairman W. T. Beebe remarked.

In the public eye. Like many southern companies, Delta has managed to avoid unions almost entirely: only their pilots and dispatchers are organized. The airline goes to great lengths to avoid layoffs, keeping pay and benefits ahead of those of their competitors.

Delta's ability to make money is legend-

ary in the airline industry. In 1975 and 1976 they made more profits than any other air carrier. In 1977 they ranked third behind United and Northwest. In 1978 they were second to United, and in 1979 they again made more money than any other airline.

Stock performance. Delta stock bought for $1,000 in 1970 sold for $1,283 on January 2, 1980.

Access. Hartsfield Atlanta International Airport, Atlanta, Georgia 30320; (404) 346-

EASTERN

Sales: $2.9 billion
Profits: $57.7 million
Forbes 500 rank: 168
Rank in airlines: 4
Founded: 1928
Employees: 37,100
Headquarters: Miami, Florida

What they do. Eastern Airlines rose to glory under a World War I flying ace and was later saved from bankruptcy by an astronaut. Eastern's first routes went up and down the Eastern Seaboard, and most of their flights still take off and land east of the Mississippi. They fly to 13 cities in Florida alone. They also make a few runs to the West Coast, Texas, Mexico, and the Caribbean.

History. Eastern's roots go back to Harold Pitcairn, a young pilot and airplane builder who flew the county-fair circuit in the 1920s, operating out of a barnyard near Philadelphia. One year after Congress authorized the post office to contract for airmail transportation, he was low bidder on the contract to carry U.S. mail between New York and Atlanta (he offered to do it for $3 a pound). Before Pitcairn had even flown his first bag of mail, the post office extended his route to Miami. By the time he started carrying the mail, he had built a fleet of eight single-engine, open-cockpit biplanes, a model he called the Pitcairn Mailwing, and rounded up a crew of barnstormers and World War I veterans to fly the planes.

Pitcairn was more interested in designing planes than running a business, though. In July 1929, while aviation stocks were still booming on Wall Street, he sold his company for $2.5 million to North American Aviation. The new owners changed the company's name to Eastern Air Transport.

Eastern was the first airline to fly passengers between New York and Florida. By 1932 it was possible to fly from New York to Miami in one day. Eastern advertised this breakthrough with a radio jingle: "From frost to flowers in 14 hours." Th plane left New York at 8:00 A.M., stopping at Philadelphia, Baltimore, Washington, and Richmond, where the passengers got off for lunch. Then it stopped again in Raleigh, Florence, Charleston, Savannah, and Jacksonville, where dinner was served. After one more stop at Daytona Beach, the plane arrived in Miami at 9:50 P.M.

Nevertheless, the airline floundered during the early Depression years when the postmaster general withdrew all mail contracts in 1934. The man who turned things around was Eddie Rickenbacker, the nation's top flying ace in World War I, who had shot down 26 German planes and won the Congressional Medal of Honor. Before the war he had been a race car driver. Afterward he and a partner started Florida Airways, but Rickenbacker got out and went to work for General Motors as a sales executive in the Cadillac LaSalle division. General Motors bought a controlling interest in North American Aviation in the early 1930s, and in 1935 they installed Eddie Rickenbacker as general manager of Eastern Air Transport.

Rickenbacker slashed costs, drove his people hard, and started turning modest profits for Eastern, according to Patrick Kelly's *The Sky's the Limit.* But GM wasn't satisfied, and in 1938 they found a group of investors who offered $3.25 million for Eastern. GM was ready to take it when Rickenbacker quickly lined up a group of his own, including Laurance Rockefeller, and made a better offer. GM sold the division to Rickenbacker's group.

Rickenbacker, who was called "the captain" at Eastern, ran a one-man show. His goal, after safety, was to fly the most planes at the least cost. To get maximum use of their planes, Eastern often would schedule flights that left in the middle of the night. But since they had a monopoly on most of their routes in the early years, they could

Eastern's Frank Borman in training for his 1968 NASA moon mission.

pretty much run the airline at their own convenience. Profits had risen to $14.7 million by 1956.

At the same time, however, customers were complaining loudly about lost luggage, poor treatment, late flights, and reservations that weren't honored. Rickenbacker's obsession with economy was driving customers away, and by 1956 the Civil Aeronautics Board had allowed competitors to fly on all of Eastern's routes.

In 1961 Eastern introduced the Air-Shuttle, linking Washington, New York, and Boston. The flights leave every hour and require no reservations; if the plane is full, they bring out another one. The Air-Shuttle had become so popular by the gas-short summer of 1979 that Eastern was unable to accommodate the thousands of people who lined up for the planes each day—which of course provoked more complaints about Eastern's service.

Eastern ran into severe financial turbulence in the late 1960s and early 1970s, when heavy debts and mounting losses

threatened to send the company down in flames. They lost $57 million in 1973 and $96 million in 1975. With the airline near collapse in 1975, Eastern installed as president Frank Borman, the former Apollo 8 astronaut who became famous by reading to the nation from the book of Genesis while orbiting the moon on Christmas Eve of 1968.

Eastern employees call Borman "the colonel." He requires the men at headquarters —now in Miami, not New York—to wear white shirts and dark suits, and drinking at lunch is tacitly forbidden. He frequently turns up in television commercials for his airline. He personally called on Elizabeth Bailey, a member of the Civil Aeronautics Board, to apologize. An Eastern flight attendant had called board member Bailey a "witch" for insisting on a no-smoking seat. When he took over, he cut the ranks of top executives nearly in half and sold off several of Eastern's aging fuel-guzzling airplanes. He also got Eastern's employees to accept some unusual cost-cutting measures, including a one-year wage freeze and a scheme by which the company would withhold 3.5% of employees' salaries as a hedge against corporate losses. At the end of 1979 Eastern workers got only one-third of their withheld wages back, but Borman passed out ten shares of Eastern stock (worth $8.50 a share) to each full-time employee.

Borman's energetic efforts may be paying off. Under his leadership the company made $39 million in 1976, $28 million in 1977, and $67 million in 1978. Still, they haven't paid their stockholders a dividend since 1969, and the company is more than $1 billion in debt.

Reputation. For many years Eastern was known to travelers as the airline with the worst food, the poorest service, and the sur-

Eastern Airlines Flies a Hard Bargain

Hammering out deals is one of the most crucial jobs at an airline. Somebody has to work out the arrangements to buy hundreds of millions of dollars' worth of airplanes and then go to the banks and insurance companies to try to borrow the money. Vast fortunes can ride on the smallest of details.

For years the chief wheeler-dealer at Eastern Airlines was Charles Simons, executive vice-president. In the late 1970s Simons negotiated one of the biggest deals Eastern had ever made—the $778 million purchase of 23 jets built by Airbus Industrie, a German-French-Spanish consortium. Eastern liked the planes, but Simons thought they might be slightly too big for the airline's routes. He worked a provision into the contract that Airbus would forgo certain payments from Eastern for a period of time unless the airline filled at least 58% of the Airbus seats with paying customers. In 1979, the first full year of service for the planes, Eastern filled 57% of the seats—and the airline didn't have to pay a penny.

How did the ingenious Simons arrive at the 58% figure? As he later explained to a *Wall Street Journal* reporter, he picked it "out of thin air."

liest employees. In recent times they have been trying hard to improve their image.

What they own. Eastern has been trying to switch to more economical aircraft and may be the most energy-efficient in the industry. They now have 9 Airbus A-300s, a wide-body made by Airbus Industries, a French-German-Spanish consortium, and they have 14 more on order. This was the first major crack in the U.S. domination of the world airliner market. No U.S. airline had bought a European-made jet since the early 1960s.

Who owns and runs the company. Laurance Rockefeller is still the dominant stockholder, with 2.6% of the stock. He as well as Harper Woodward, a consultant to the Rockefeller family interests, and Felix Rohatyn of the Lazard Frères investment banking firm sit on the board. Frank Borman is chairman, president, and chief executive officer.

In the public eye. Eastern was an early leader in the hiring of black pilots, and still outdistances the other carriers in this area.

Where they're going. In 1980 Eastern retaliated against carriers who had invaded the Florida market by beginning transcontinental service from New York to Los Angeles and San Francisco.

Stock performance. Eastern stock bought for $1,000 in 1970 sold for $534 on January 2, 1980.

Major employment centers. Miami, Atlanta, New York.

Access. Miami International Airport, Miami, Florida 33148; (305) 873-2211.

The U.S. merchant marine carries only 4% of our foreign commerce and ranks 10th in size among the fleets of the world. Not since the 1850s has the U.S. merchant fleet been a challenger for primacy on the high seas. Then almost as numerous as the reigning British fleet, Yankee clippers transported 76% of American foreign trade.

National Airlines

Sales: $589.4 million
Profits: $14.4 million
Founded: 1934
Employees: 7,900
Headquarters: Miami, Florida

What they do. National Airlines was widely known for the "Fly Me" advertising campaign that angered feminists in the early 1970s. A more apt slogan later in that decade might have been "Buy Me," since National was the object of a year-long fight that saw Pan Am, Eastern, and two smaller airlines, Air Florida and Texas International—all try to take the company over. Pan Am prevailed in 1979.

National specializes in getting people in and out of Florida. Their flights to and from the Sunshine State go in three general directions: north to New York, west to Los Angeles, and east to Paris and London. At the height of the winter travel season National sends 10 DC-10 flights to Florida every day from New York's La Guardia airport.

History. National began as a 142-mile mail route between St. Petersburg and Daytona Beach, Florida, in 1934. The pilot, ticket agent, mechanic, and sole proprietor was George T. Baker, a former airplane salesman in Chicago who picked up odd flying jobs under the name of National Airlines Taxi Service. As the company grew, Baker moved his headquarters to Jacksonville in 1939 and to Miami in 1946. His big break came in 1944, when the Civil Aeronautics Board decided to give Eddie Rickenbacker's Eastern Airlines some competition by letting National fly the New York–Miami route. Baker was quick to conjure up sales gimmicks to lure customers away from Eastern. While Eastern flights carried male stewards, National loaded their planes with attractive female "hostesses." Baker introduced cut-rate excursion fares and beat Eastern with the first nonstop flights between New York and Miami. In December 1958 National became the first domestic carrier to use jets—renting two brand-new Boeing 707s from Pan Am for the winter months. National inaugurated flights to California in 1961 and to Europe in 1970.

Total Number of Passengers

1. EASTERN 42,748,000	11. NORTHWEST 11,708,000
2. DELTA 40,495,000	12. AIR FRANCE 10,789,000
3. UNITED 36,082,000	13. PAN AM 10,043,000
4. AMERICAN 31,263,000	14. CONTINENTAL 9,878,000
5. TWA 22,653,000	15. SAS 8,662,000
6. BRITISH AIRWAYS 16,904,000	16. SAUDI ARABIAN 7,964,000
7. AIR CANADA 14,587,000	17. NATIONAL 6,598,000
8. BRANIFF 14,511,000	18. MEXICANA 6,208,000
9. LUFTHANSA 12,887,000	19. AIR INTER 5,921,000
10. WESTERN 12,069,000	20. OLYMPIC 5,023,000

Source: *Air Transport World*, March 1980.

Lewis "Bud" Maytag, Jr., a 35-year-old heir to the Maytag washing machine fortune and an aviation enthusiast who had been president of Frontier Airlines, bought Baker's National stock in 1962 and took over as president, chairman, and chief executive. Maytag turned over the chairman's seat to Dudley Swin of Carmel, California, later that year, but upon Swin's death in 1972, Maytag took the job back. He relinquished the presidency in 1976 but stayed on as chairman and chief executive.

National was shut down for a total of nearly a year between 1970 and early 1976 during three long strikes: a 116-day clerks' walkout in 1970, a 108-day mechanics' strike in 1974, and a 127-day flight attendants' strike that lasted five days into 1976. Maytag was never known for his liberal attitudes toward labor or minorities. The *Wall Street Journal* said, "Much of what National employees had to say about Mr. Maytag, particularly the pilots, was unprintable."

The takeover fight of 1978–79 was a politically charged battle royal. Leon Jaworski, the former Watergate special prosecutor, entered the fray as a lawyer on behalf of Texas International. Pan Am's case was pushed by Sol Linowitz, the Pan-ama Canal treaty negotiator who sat on the Pan Am board, and the fight also attracted Senators Jacob Javits and Daniel Patrick Moynihan of New York, the state where Pan Am's corporate headquarters are located. Frank Borman, the astronaut turned Eastern Airlines chairman, plugged away from a third direction. When Pan Am finally won, the victory was sweet: they had been trying to get domestic routes for years and for most of the 1970s they were losing money while National was coining it.

Who owns and runs the company. Pan Am. Bud Maytag had been National's biggest stockholder, owning 317,000 shares or 4% of the total. The Pan Am $50-a-share purchase thus enriched him by $15.9 million. He could have stayed on, but quickly left, surprising no one who knows him.

Stock performance. National stock bought for $1,000 in 1970 sold for $2,089 on January 2, 1980.

Access. P.O. Box 592055, Airport Mail Facility, Miami, Florida 33159; (305) 874-4111.

Total Number of Planes

336 **UNITED** (18 B747, 153 B727, 59 B737, 37 DC-10, 69 DC-8)
255 **EASTERN** (125 B727, 5 DC-8, 84 DC-9, 34 L-1011, 7 A300)
251 **AMERICAN** (136 B727, 72 B707, 10 B747, 28 DC-10, 5 Convair)
232 **TWA** (11 B747, 95 B707, 74 B727, 14 DC-9, 30 L-1011, 8 Convair 880)
200 **DELTA** (100 B727, 51 DC-9, 23 DC-8, 26 L-1011)
142 **PAN AM/NATIONAL** (43 B747, 53 B727, 31 B707, 15 DC-10)
106 **NORTHWEST** (21 B747, 63 B727, 22 DC-10)
103 **BRANIFF** (85 B727, 3 B747, 15 DC-8)
 68 **CONTINENTAL** (52 B727, 15 DC-10, 1 Sabreliner)

(Note: The initials in parentheses represent the following aircraft manufacturers: A, Airbus Industries; B, Boeing; DC, McDonnell Douglas; Convair, General Dynamics; L, Lockheed.)

NORTHWEST ORIENT

Sales: $1.3 million
Profits: $72.5 million
Forbes 500 rank: 376
Rank in airlines: 8
Founded: 1926
Employees: 10,680
Headquarters: St. Paul, Minnesota

What they do. Northwest calls their airline Northwest Orient to draw attention to their flights to Japan, Hong Kong, and the Philippines. They were the first airline to fly the Great Circle route from New York over the Aleutians to Hong Kong—a route nearly 20% shorter than the conventional one via Honolulu. Their domestic routes radiate from Minneapolis to the big cities of the Northeast and south to Atlanta and Florida. They also make several short hops around the sparsely populated territory of North Dakota, Montana, Wyoming, and Idaho. In 1979 they started flying to Europe for the first time, with flights to Scotland and Scandinavia.

History. In their obsessive and successful drive to keep costs down and profits up, Northwest gained a reputation for slow service, long delays, and frequent strikes. The person who set the company's austere tone was Donald Nyrop, a former chairman of the Civil Aeronautics Board who was brought in to rescue the foundering company in 1955 and stayed at the helm for the next 24 years. The *Wall Street Journal* called him "the Vince Lombardi of airline executives." His devotion to the bottom line was unlimited. If he found a paying customer unable to get a seat on a crowded Northwest flight, he would get off himself and wait for the next plane. During his reign Nyrop boasted that Northwest's headquarters at the Minneapolis–St. Paul airport—a drab, windowless building with no pictures on the walls and no doors on the men's toilet stalls—cost the company only $1.75 a square foot while competitors were paying $10 or more.

Northwest owns their entire fleet of 106 planes—22 DC-10s, 21 Boeing 747s, and 63 Boeing 727s; while many of their competitors are stuck having leased planes at high rates.

In 1929 there were 117 licensed women pilots. By 1977 over 21,000 women were licensed. The first female commercial pilot in the country was hired in 1973; there still is no woman 747 captain.

U.S. passenger airlines employed approximately 38,000 commercial pilots in 1979. About 100 (0.3%) were black, and 200 (0.5%) were female. Only one pilot was a black woman.

When Nyrop retired in 1978 he was succeeded by M. Joseph Lapensky, an accountant who rose through the ranks at Northwest. Most observers expected him to continue Nyrop's policies but the employees were pleasantly shocked in the summer of 1979 when he handed out $100 bonuses for their handling of heavy passenger loads during a strike that grounded United. As the *Wall Street Journal* said, "It was the first time Northwest employees could recall getting anything without a prolonged battle."

Melvin Laird, President Nixon's secretary of defense, sits on the all-male board of directors.

Stock performance. Northwest stock bought for $1,000 in 1970 sold for $987 on January 2, 1980.

Access. Minneapolis–St. Paul International Airport, St. Paul, Minneapolis 55111; (612) 726-2111.

Sales: $2.5 billion
Profits: $76.1 million
Forbes 500 rank: 206
Rank in airlines: 6
Founded: 1927
Employees: 41,668
Headquarters: New York, New York

What they do. Pan Am: the very name suggests the intended glory. In the years before World War II, Juan Trippe built an airline that appropriated for itself first place in world aviation as if that were its natural birthright. When World War II ended Trippe picked up where he left off. Pan Am was number 1 in the world skies. What he failed to realize was that the world had changed. That failure brought Pan Am to the brink of total collapse.

Pan Am remains the nation's first international carrier, the only one with a truly global reach. As their TV commercials boast, Pan Am flies to "68 places in 47 lands on six continents." Their fleet of jetliners flies 143,000 miles a year, carrying more than nine million passengers, with an average of 183 passengers per flight. They estimate that their 747 jumbo jets are in the air an average of 13 hours every day. Three-fourths of their sales come from passenger tickets, 15% from freight transport, the balance from charter flights and mail runs (the original business).

In the old days Pan Am functioned practically as a branch of the State Department —and there are still vestiges of that role. When trouble breaks out anywhere, Pan Am gets the call from the U.S. government. In recent years they brought American citizens home from flare-ups in Iran and Lebanon, and they helped to evacuate Americans from Saigon at the end of the Vietnam War.

Their days as a colonizer are reflected in their worldwide hotel chain, the Intercontinental: 92 hotels in 49 countries. Trippe was so enamored of the international airline business that he never sought routes in the United States. And when Pan Am tried in the 1970s to get a piece of the U.S. action, they were turned back repeatedly by the Civil Aeronautics Board. They finally got their foothold on the first day of 1980, when they took possession of National Airlines, the nation's 11th largest domestic carrier. It was a purchase regarded by many industry analysts as a salvation for our largest international airline. Pan Am, at long last, had come home.

History. Until 1969 Pan Am was a one-man show. The man who ran it was Juan Trippe, who put together the backers to finance a small mail-carrying operation in the 1920s and built it into the world's largest air transport company by 1930.

Trippe, born in 1899, was the son of a wealthy New York stockbroker. His mother named him after a favorite aunt named Juanita. His name opened many doors when his company moved into Latin America. He attended Yale until 1917, when he quit to enlist as a bombing pilot in the Naval Reserve Flying Corps. In love with aviation from the age of 10, Trippe returned to Yale after the war and formed the Yale Flying Club with a group of bankers' sons and two sons of Cornelius Vanderbilt. As early as 1919 Trippe believed that "a flight across the Atlantic Ocean is a perfectly safe and sane commercial proposition and not a gigantic gamble."

When Trippe's father died suddenly in 1920, Trippe used his inheritance to buy nine sea-going Navy biplanes at the junk price of $500 each and formed Long Island Airways. The object was to perform a kind of "air taxi" service, ferrying businessmen around New York and nearby Long Island towns. It failed, Trippe later recalled in Matthew Josephson's excellent history of Pan Am, *Empire of the Air*, because in those days pilots "were show-offs who would work at some county fair for $500, then get drunk and take the next day off."

But in 1925 the Kelly Air Mail Act was passed by Congress, authorizing the Post Office Department to make long-term contracts for the transport of airmail over designated routes at a maximum rate of $3 a pound. Trippe, financed by his rich buddies from Yale, jumped at the chance: they each threw in $25,000 and formed Colonial Air Transport to carry airmail from Boston to New York and back. They won the first airmail contract ever issued. In 1927 they bought two three-engine Fokker planes for $37,000. The Fokkers were big enough to carry both passengers and mail—and for the first time Colonial was in the passenger business. That same year a schism emerged among the stockholders, and Colonial was sold to what is now American Airlines.

Trippe and his friends then bought another company, Aviation Corporation of the Americas, to bid for the rights to a Key West–Havana mail route. However, they soon discovered two other companies in the bidding as well: Florida Airways, founded by World War I flyer Eddie Rickenbacker, and a tiny operation called Pan American Airways. Both were shoestring airlines and readily accepted the merger proposal the wealthy Trippe group offered. The group joined forces in 1927, keeping the Pan American name.

Business was slow at first. There was plenty of mail between the two areas, but most prospective passengers were still terrified at the prospect of flying over water. Pan Am pilots in Havana even resorted to walking into bars and challenging American tourists to come with them into the wild blue. Eventually the speed of air travel won over enough customers for Pan Am to make a go of it. One of those customers was Chicago gangster Al Capone, who, with his four bodyguards, was in a hurry to check up on his interests in the Havana casinos. He told the ticket agent, "Better see it's a

safe plane. If anything happens to us, it won't be so healthy for you fellas."

Trippe secured exclusive rights to fly between the U.S. and Cuba. They expanded operations to other Caribbean islands and then into South America where competition was such that extraordinary measures were apparently taken—such as stealing competitors' gasoline, which frequently left planes and passengers stranded in the middle of jungles. When airmail traffic fell off, and thus threatened to deprive Pan Am of their $2-a-mile federal payment for each 800 pounds of mail carried in the Caribbean, Pan Am agents began sending each other well-wrapped bricks, according to *Business Week*.

These tactics may have helped Pan Am establish their supremacy in the international air lanes, but it was Trippe, with his astonishing bargaining ability, who clinched it. *Business Week* called him a "Metternich when dealing with foreign governments," and an Air France executive said "he doesn't run an airline; he's a politician." United's chairman, William Patterson, believed Trippe "should have been our ambassador to Moscow."

Pan Am's hegemony over international air routes was never stronger than at the end of World War II. The war had effectively destroyed all international commercial aviation activity except Pan Am's. Trippe argued that it was in the best interests of the nation to have a single airline, and he proposed that Pan Am become a regulated monopoly—like the telephone company. He even went so far as to offer to sell 49% of Pan Am to the federal government, but Congress would have none of it. It was the first diplomatic battle Trippe ever lost.

Before long he was to lose many others. The golden age of the airline industry was beginning, and Pan Am had to contend with an unheard of phenomenon: competition—at home and abroad. Trans World Airlines started to fly the Atlantic, United Airlines extended their routes to Hawaii. Worse yet for Pan Am, every nation in the world wanted to have an airline of its own, and the rules of the game specified that if a country allowed a foreign airline to land, they could then demand that their airline be allowed reciprocal landing rights. Pan Am—and Trippe—were unsuited for this kind of melee. The many years of unchallenged supremacy had lent Pan Am an air of arrogance that earned them a reputation for being one of the most unfriendly airlines in the world.

But as their share of the market eroded on the various oceans of the world, Pan Am continued to try and do business the way it always had done. Trippe, a tiger for new equipment, was one of the first to give Boeing a jumbo order for the 747 jumbo jet. After the founder left in 1969, his hand-picked successor, Najeeb Halaby, former head of the Federal Aviation Administration, presided over absolute disaster. Pan Am's declining portion of the overseas passenger trade, plus the expense of adding the new 747s to their fleet, kept the airline from making a profit until 1977. The board of directors got so fed up they pulled out a resignation letter Halaby signed when he was hired and accepted it in 1972 after 27 months of Halaby rule. They then brought in William Seawell and gave him stock and a lucrative contract to turn things around. It took him five years to do it. Things were so bad that when Congress turned down Pan Am's request for federal subsidies in 1975, the airline tried to talk the Shah of Iran into supporting them. When the Shah also refused to help, Pan Am appeared to be finished.

They had lost money for six straight years (the 1974 deficit was $81 million), they were deeply in hock to the bankers (a billion dollars or so), and they seemed to have no friends left in the world. A couple of things saved them. They shrank their system, giving up Trippe's missionary plan to touch down on every landing field in the world. And they found friends in their employees, many of whom had worked many years for Pan Am. The employees offered to take an 11% pay cut until the company was in the black again—and Seawell accepted. They also lobbied vigorously for Pan Am in the corridors of Congress and the Civil Aeronautics Board. In 1977, helped by tax-loss credits, Pan Am made a profit for the first time since 1968. The bankers breathed a little easier, and in 1979 they lined up behind Pan Am in their successful fight with Eastern and Texas International for control of National Airlines. Twenty-one banks gave Pan Am $300 million of credit to buy National stock.

Reputation. Pan Am is perceived abroad as *the* American flag carrier. The airline's manners under Trippe contributed to the "ugly American" image, but the present management has made strides in changing people's minds. They're more humble today.

What they own. Pan Am's fleet is surprisingly small, considering their reputation and worldwide range. Of the 87 planes in the fleet Pan Am owns only 59; they lease the rest. Consequently, they have an unusually high daily flight time per plane of 13 hours for 747s and nearly 7 hours for other jets. At the close of 1979, they were still close to $1 billion in debt.

Who owns and runs the company. Of the 19 directors, Seawell is the largest stockholder, thanks to his "Quick—save us!" contract. He held one-tenth of 1% of the shares in 1979. Because Pan Am pays no dividends, he gets no income from these holdings. And because Pan Am's stock has been depressed, his shares have never been worth much more than $500,000. Other board members in 1979 included city planner Marietta Tree, James S. Rockefeller, former chairman of Citibank, William T. Coleman, Secretary of Transportation in the Ford administration, and Sol Linowitz, a lawyer who was one of Jimmy Carter's chief negotiators in the Panama Canal treaty talks.

In the public eye. The chief issue before the public in the past decade has been, will Pan Am survive? One of their amazing feats was getting strong backing from employees during a period when they reduced their airline work force from 39,000 to 26,000.

Where they're going. They hope to get back into China (where they inaugurated Clipper service before World War II) as both a carrier and hotel operator. And as National Airlines gets folded into the system, look for "National" to disappear.

Stock performance. Pan Am stock bought for $1,000 in 1970 sold for $516 on January 2, 1980.

Major employment centers. New York and Miami.

Access. Pan Am Building, New York, New York 10017; (212) 880-1234.

Sales: $335.8 million
Profits: $23.1 million
Founded: 1949
Employees: 3,400
Headquarters: San Diego, California

What they do. PSA couldn't let well enough alone. In the 1950s and '60s they served as a model of how marvelously an airline could perform if it wasn't oppressed by federal regulations. By the end of the 1970s PSA had become an outstanding example of what can happen to a successful company that gets cocky, expands too far, and ventures into fields it knows nothing about.

PSA's bread and butter comes from the hour-long, 350-mile jaunt between San Francisco and Los Angeles, one of the most heavily traveled air corridors in the world. PSA flights leave hourly in each direction. They also fly to nine other cities in California between San Diego and Sacramento. For nearly 30 years PSA planes never strayed outside the state—which is how the company was able to stay out from under the regulatory wing of the Civil Aeronautics Board. Unlike interstate airlines, PSA could fly wherever and whenever they pleased, and could slash prices below those of their competitors—primarily United. When the federal government lifted most airline regulations in 1978, PSA started flying to Reno, Las Vegas, and Phoenix, and they plan flights to Seattle, Salt Lake City, Denver, Houston, and several cities in Mexico.

History. A group of World War II flying buddies started Pacific Southwest Airlines in 1949 with one plane, a rented war-surplus DC-3, which they flew on Fridays and Sundays between San Diego and Oakland via Hollywood/Burbank. Most of their early customers were Navy men on weekend passes, who thought of the company's initials as standing for "Poor Sailors' Airline." As PSA grew into a major California carrier, the company gained a reputation for tacky flamboyance: cofounder J. Floyd "Andy" Andrews, a mustachioed former Royal Air Force pilot, painted silly-looking happy-face grins on the noses of PSA planes

As a fringe benefit airline employees—and frequently other family members—can fly virtually for free, or at most for half-fare. For instance, an employee of American Airlines can take advantage of AA's agreements with 185 other lines and fly anywhere in the world for at least a 50% discount. Fifty of these airlines will give the AA worker a 90% discount, and 11 will honor AA's trip pass, exacting minimal charges only. In addition, 23 airlines will offer a 90% discount to AA employees or retirees, and their spouses, parents, and other eligible family members.

and decked out the stewardesses in beehive hairdos and go-go dancer costumes featuring red, orange, and pink hot pants. PSA replaced the Barbie Doll outfits with below-the-knee uniforms in 1976, but the "grinning birds" linger on.

Not content with merely running a profitable airline, Andrews got the urge in the late 1960s to expand into rental cars, radio stations, and lodgings. PSA bought four big California hotels, including the Queen Mary Hyatt in Long Beach and the San Franciscan on a then run-down and remote stretch of San Francisco's Market Street. PSA figured they could route their passengers into the hotels, but instead the hotels gobbled up about $2 million a year from the airline. PSA eventually sold off the nonairline operations (except for the Queen Mary, which they haven't been able to unload).

The biggest fiasco, however, involved airplanes. In the early 1970s, when they saw nothing but clear skies and dollar signs for their Los Angeles–San Francisco run, they ordered five Lockheed L-1011 TriStar jumbo jets, at $22 million each. An astonished executive at a competitor said, "It was like buying a Cadillac to drive over to visit your next-door neighbor." As soon as they put the first two into service in 1974, air travel dropped off and the price of jet fuel skyrocketed. PSA couldn't fill the huge planes with enough passengers to make a profit. Within a few months they mothballed the two they had and told Lockheed they couldn't use the other three. Lockheed held on to the $18 million PSA had deposited toward the three planes and in December 1978 sued the airline for another $15 million. PSA responded with an antitrust

THE TEN WORST AIR DISASTERS

1. MARCH 27, 1977
   Tenerife, Canary Islands
   Pan Am 747 and KLM 747 collided on a runway: 579 dead

2. MARCH 3, 1974
   Paris, France
   Turkish DC-10 crashed on take-off from Orly airport: 346 dead

3. MAY 25, 1979
   Chicago, Illinois
   American Airlines DC-10 crashed on take-off after losing engine:
   275 dead

4. JANUARY 1, 1978
   Bombay, India
   Air India 747 exploded: 213 dead

5. AUGUST 3, 1975
   Agadir, Morocco
   Charter Boeing 707 hit mountain: 188 dead

6. NOVEMBER 25, 1978
   Colombo, Sri Lanka
   Charter Icelandic DC-8 crashed in thunderstorm: 183 dead

7. OCTOBER 14, 1972
   Krasnaya Polyana, U.S.S.R.
   Aeroflot Ilyushin-62 crashed: 176 dead

8. JANUARY 22, 1973
   Kano, Nigeria
   Boeing 707 jet carrying Moslems from a pilgrimage to Mecca crashed
   in fog: 176 dead

9. SEPTEMBER 10, 1976
   Zagreb, Yugoslavia
   Yugoslav charter DC-10 and British Airlines Trident collided in
   midair: 176 dead

10. AUGUST 17, 1979
    Ukraine, U.S.S.R.
    Two Aeroflot jet liners collided: 173 dead

suit against Lockheed. Meanwhile, they were stuck with the two flying white elephants until 1978, when they managed to lease them to Aero Peru.

In the public eye. PSA had never had a crash until September 1978, when one of their 727s collided with a small Cessna over San Diego, killing 144 people. It was the worst plane crash in U.S. history until the following May an American Airlines DC-10 crashed in Chicago, killing nearly twice as many people. After the DC-10 disaster the Federal Aviation Administration took a hard look at airline maintenance, and in August 1979 they fined PSA $385,000—one of the largest penalties the FAA had ever handed down—for flying planes in

"unairworthy" condition. PSA countered that their planes were perfectly safe, that the FAA inspectors had misread PSA's maintenance logs, and that PSA had been unfairly singled out as part of the "new get-tough policy."

Stock performance. PSA stock bought for $1,000 in 1970 sold for $845 on January 2, 1980.

Access. 3225 North Harbor Drive, San Diego, California 92101; (714) 574-2100.

Black Executive Letter, a newsletter for black corporation executives, reports that 90 companies had blacks on their boards of directors in 1979, but the actual number of black directors is only 55 because some sit on more than one board.

TOP 10 FLIERS

Airline Revenues, 1979

1. UNITED $3.3 *billion*
2. AMERICAN $3.25 *billion*
3. TWA $3.0 *billion*
4. EASTERN $2.9 *billion*
5. DELTA $2.7 *billion*
6. PAN AM $2.5 *billion*
7. BRANIFF $1.35 *billion*
8. NORTHWEST $1.31 *billion*
9. WESTERN $932 *million*
10. CONTINENTAL $928 *million*

TWA

Sales: $4.3 billion
Profits: $8.6 million
Forbes 500 rank: 96
Rank in airlines: 3
Founded: 1928
Employees: 87,500 (airline portion: 35,700)
Headquarters: New York, New York

What they do. TWA is the only carrier with a strong presence at home, 241 cities, and abroad, 12 cities, and these airline operations generated revenues of $3 billion in 1979. Their hops are mostly long ones. They fly from the East Coast to the West Coast—and they have key midwestern hubs in St. Louis and Kansas City. TWA ranks third in the United States—after United and American. Most of their international flights end in European destinations, and they fly more passengers over the Atlantic Ocean than any other carrier (22% of this traffic, as opposed to Pan Am's 17%). It would seem, on the face of it, that this is an impressive airline operation. So why did they change their corporate name in 1979 from Trans World Airlines to Trans World Corporation?

They did it because the airline business, while big, has not been making as much money as the other things that TWA does —and the airline often loses money. Airline operations still bring in two-thirds of the revenues—but two-thirds of the profits have been coming from running hotels and serving food. TWA owns Hilton International, which operates 76 Hilton Hotels outside the United States, and Canteen Corporation, which feeds people through 197,-000 vending machines and 700 cafeterias in factories and offices. You're eating in a Canteen Corporation facility when you dine at the Metropolitan Opera House in New York, at Yankee Stadium, or at the Kennedy Center for the Performing Arts in Washington, D.C.

In 1979 they diversified further out of the airline business by adding two more subsidiaries: Century 21, a California-based real estate company, and Spartan Food Systems, operator of Hardee's fast-food restaurants in the South.

How TWA got to the point where they make more money on the ground than in the air results from a corporate history more tangled than most.

History. Transcontinental Air Transport was organized in 1928 by a group of investors who envisioned a coast-to-coast passenger service: air by day, rail by night. They hired Charles Lindbergh to survey the route, and in 1929 they inaugurated "The Lindbergh Line." Passengers boarded a Pennsylvania Railroad Pullman in New York in the evening, arriving the next morning in Port Columbus, Ohio, where they climbed aboard a Ford trimotor airplane and flew all day to Waynoka, Oklahoma. From there a Santa Fe Pullman took them overnight to Clovis, New Mexico. There they caught another plane for Los Angeles. The whole trip took 48 hours and cost $351.94 one way.

Transcontinental merged with Western Air Express, a Los Angeles operation, in 1930, to form Transcontinental and Western Air—TWA. One of the company's more promising young employees was Jack Frye, a former Hollywood stunt pilot who had specialized in flying movie stars to desert hideaways in Arizona. By 1934 Frye had become TWA's president, but he kept his pilot's license up-to-date by flying some routes himself. General Motors controlled TWA for a time during the early 1930s, but the government forced them to get rid of it. Control passed to the Lehman Brothers investment house and to John Hertz, owner of Yellow Cab. Henry B. duPont became chairman of the board in 1934.

In the late 1930s TWA's affairs became entwined with those of one of the most powerful and mysterious individuals in the annals of American industry: Howard Hughes. The eccentric Hughes had become wealthy at an early age when his father died and left him the Hughes Tool Company, the chief manufacturer of drilling bits for the entire oil industry. Hughes proceeded to make fortunes of his own in movies, electronics, and aviation.

At the urging of Jack Frye, who shared his passion for setting airplane speed records, Hughes bought control of TWA in 1939; over the years he increased his holdings to 78% of the company. Under Hughes and Frye TWA became the most technically advanced airline in the world. They pioneered pressurized planes that could fly passengers over bad weather rather than through it, and they were the first with

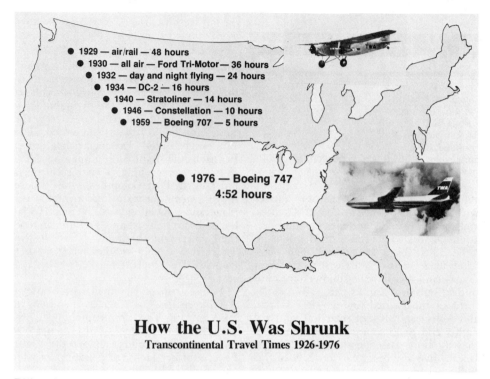

- 1929 — air/rail — 48 hours
- 1930 — all air — Ford Tri-Motor — 36 hours
- 1932 — day and night flying — 24 hours
- 1934 — DC-2 — 16 hours
- 1940 — Stratoliner — 14 hours
- 1946 — Constellation — 10 hours
- 1959 — Boeing 707 — 5 hours

- 1976 — Boeing 747
  4:52 hours

How the U.S. Was Shrunk
Transcontinental Travel Times 1926-1976

TWA tracks shrinking of the continental United States from the time of its first air-rail service in 1929 (with Ford Tri-Motor) to Boeing 747 service in 1976.

four-engine planes that could cross the Atlantic. After World War II they added 21,000 miles of international routes and changed the company's name to Trans World Airlines.

Around this time, it seems, Hughes eccentricities surfaced. He would hold up major business decisions for weeks while fretting over minute details of airplane design. He once disappeared with a new Lockheed Constellation from the TWA fleet and took it to the Bahamas, where he practiced landings for days on end, according to Patrick Kelly's *The Sky's the Limit.* Meanwhile, back at the office, Frye was trying to expand the company enough to accommodate the ambitious new routes TWA had taken on after the war. But Frye ran afoul of Noah Dietrich, the fiscal overseer of the Hughes empire, who persuaded Hughes that TWA was overextended and in financial trouble.

Hughes, through Dietrich, asked Frye to resign in 1947; he made it a condition for pumping any more money from Hughes Tool Company into the airline. He also moved the corporate headquarters from Kansas City to New York. But things just got worse. Ralph Damon, who became TWA's president, came over from American Airlines only to find that Hughes, for reasons of his own, had decided to cut back on advertising and promotion. The frustrated Damon died of a heart attack in 1955; he was succeeded by Carter Burgess, an assistant secretary of defense. Burgess lasted only 11 months, during which he never met Hughes in person.

In the mid-1950s airlines were competing to be the first to fly jet planes. While all the other airlines made plans and placed orders, Hughes pondered endlessly over whether to go with the Boeing 707 or the Douglas DC-8. When he finally made his decision, TWA was last in line to buy jets. To make matters worse, Hughes ordered 76 planes from Boeing and Convair—many more than TWA could hope to pay for. His plan was to use the hefty profits of the Hughes Tool Company to buy airplanes and then lease them to TWA—at a considerable tax saving to himself. Unfortunately, some officers of TWA saw it as a scheme to milk TWA for the benefit of Howard Hughes. Ultimately, a recession in the oil industry caused the Hughes Tool Company's profits to sag, and Hughes had to turn to a group of Wall Street investment bankers to help him pay for his airplanes.

While the bankers respected Hughes as an industrial tycoon, they considered him an erratic and unreliable individual. As a condition of any financial help, they insisted that he put his TWA stock in a trust under their guidance. After a series of bizarre negotiations that dragged on to the last minute of the last business day of 1960 —the bankers' deadline—Hughes agreed to their terms.

The bankers installed as president of TWA a Wall Street lawyer named Charles Tillinghast, who promptly slapped Hughes with an antitrust suit charging that he had monopolized aircraft purchases to the detriment of TWA. Hughes in turn sued the bankers for $300 million, charging that they had conspired to swindle him out of his airline. In 1973 the U.S. Supreme Court ruled in Hughes's favor in the antitrust suit, overturning a lower court's award of $145 million to TWA. Another suit by TWA against Summa Corporation, the holding company for Howard Hughes's business interests, charging Hughes with financial irresponsibility, is still pending in Delaware.

Although Hughes lost control of his airline, he had the last laugh. In 1966 he sold his TWA stock for $546.5 million. He got $86 a share. TWA has never again sold at that price. It entered 1980 selling at $16.

Reputation. TWA has the fuzziest image of all the major airlines. After being run for many years by an eccentric, they fell into the hands of bankers and lawyers. No one is quite sure where they're coming from— and they have made things increasingly difficult by getting into more nonairline businesses than any other carrier.

What they own. TWA has "one of the oldest, most fuel-inefficient fleets of any major United States carrier," according to Winston Williams of the *New York Times*. They have over 100 aging Boeing 707s and McDonnell Douglas DC-9s, which they will have to replace over the next few years for somewhere close to $4 billion.

Who owns and runs the company. The two biggest chunks of Trans World stock are controlled by the United Missouri Bank of Kansas City (11.2%) and J. P. Morgan & Co. (7.2%). The Kansas City bank holdings represent shares held in trust for TWA employees. The people in charge of the company are not seasoned airline operators, which may or may not be an advantage. Trans World chairman Edwin Smart is a former Wall Street lawyer. TWA president C. E. Meyer is an accountant. The directors include Arjay Miller, former dean of Stanford University's graduate business school and a former director and president of Ford Motor; Charles "Tex" Thornton, chairman of Litton Industries and leader of the World War II Air Force "Whiz Kids" (a group that included former defense secretary Robert McNamara, whose accounting systems revolutionized American business); and Jack Valenti, president of the Motion Picture Association of America. There are two

The Shah to the Rescue?

When Trans World Airlines was strapped for cash and woefully overextended on jumbo jets in the early 1970s, they turned to the Shah of Iran for help. The airline announced a deal in 1975 by which the Iranian Air Force would buy six of TWA's Boeing 747s for $99 million—a bargain basement price, considering that they cost $22 million to $25 million apiece new. As part of the deal Iran got an option to buy six more 747s from the airline. TWA hoped Iran wouldn't exercise the option —they didn't have all that many superfluous jets, it seemed—but as it turned out, the Iranians decided they wanted them all. TWA scratched around and came up with three 747s from Continental Airlines, but they had to provide the others themselves. "They were our best planes," one TWA man told the *Wall Street Journal*, "and to sell another three would only serve to further decimate our fleet." But a deal is a deal, and the Iranians insisted. Moaned TWA president C. E. Meyer: "It was agony."

women and one black on the board. The stockholders have not received a dividend since 1969.

Where they're going. "We have no plan to liquidate the airline," chairman Smart told the *New York Times* in 1978. "It's just a question of how large it should be." The answer seems to be: smaller. TWA has cut back flights on unprofitable routes, and between 1976 and 1978 reduced their fleet from 259 planes to 232.

Stock performance. Trans World stock bought for $1,000 in 1970 sold for $695 on January 2, 1980.

Major employment center. Kansas City, Missouri, where TWA has their operations and maintenance base and is that city's second largest private employer (after General Motors).

Access. 605 Third Avenue, New York, New York 10016; (212) 557-6162.

UNITED AIRLINES

Sales: $3.8 billion
Losses: $72.8 million
Forbes 500 rank: 117
Rank in domestic airlines: 1
Founded: 1926
Employees: 71,000
Headquarters: Chicago, Illinois

What they do. There is a basic similarity between the airline and hotel businesses, says Eddie Carlson, who was head of the Seattle-based Western International Hotels chain before becoming president of United Airlines. "At Western I was selling empty hotel rooms, here it's empty airplane seats."

As the nation's largest airline, United has a lot of seats to fill. They fly to and from most of the big cities of the Eastern Seaboard, across the Great Lakes states and the Midwest to California and Hawaii, up and down the West Coast, and from the Northeast down to Florida—in all, covering 112 cities in 32 states, Washington, D.C., and Canada. At the same time, they have quite a few hotel rooms to fill—about 26,000. Their Western International subsidiary operates New York's Plaza and San Francisco's St. Francis, as well as hotels in Hawaii and foreign countries from South Africa to Singapore. They run the revolving restaurant at the top of Seattle's Space Needle, a World's Fair relic that was reportedly a brainstorm of the civic-minded Eddie Carlson. The hotel business accounts for about one-twelfth of UAL's sales. The company also owns GAB Business Services, formerly General Adjustment Bureau, the nation's largest independent insurance claims adjuster (the people who come to see you when you have an insurance claim and who try to keep the amount of settlement down). All of the subsidiaries, including the airline, are part of UAL, the corporate name they created in 1968.

History. United Airlines began as just that —an amalgamation of several companies, all started by aviation pioneers, that joined together in the late 1920s and early 1930s. In his comprehensive history of U.S. air carriers, *The Sky's the Limit*, Patrick Kelly traces United's origins to 1926, when Varney Air Lines started flying a 460-mile route between Pasco, Washington and Elko, Nevada—a stretch of unlikely territory to be where American commercial air transport began. Several other air carriers were getting busy around the same time: Bill Boeing of Seattle was building planes and flying sacks of mail between Chicago and San Francisco with his Boeing Air Transport Company; Frederick Rentschler was making airplane engines at his Hartford,

The original stewardesses pose in 1930 for a publicity shot. The eight pioneers, all registered nurses, were: Ellen Church (upper left), who was the first: Alva Johnson (upper right); and (from left to right) Margaret Arnott, Inez Keller, Cornelia Peterman, Harriet Fry, Jessie Carter and Ellis Crawford. The idea for flight attendants came from Steve Stimson, a public relations man for Boeing Air Transport (a precursor of United Airlines). He first thought of using men but changed his mind after Ellen Church said to him: "Don't you think it would be better psychology to have women up in the air? How is a man going to say that he's afraid to fly when a woman is working on the plane?"

Connecticut, Pratt & Whitney Aircraft Co.; and Vernon Gorst's Pacific Air Transport was flying mail between Seattle and Los Angeles. Clement Keys, a Wall Street promoter, organized National Air Transport and won the airmail contract between Chicago and Dallas; and Bill Stout, backed by Henry and Edsel Ford, built the Ford trimotor airplane and flew passengers between Detroit, Chicago, and Cleveland on Stout Air Services.

By 1931 all these companies had fused into one: United Air Lines. (It wasn't until the 1970s that they decided to make *Airlines* one word.) The company flew the first coast-to-coast passenger flights along a route they called the "Main Line"—from New York to San Francisco via Chicago. In 1934 Congress decided that airlines had to be separate from airplane manufacturers, so Boeing and Pratt & Whitney were split off, and the presidency of United Air Lines devolved upon 34-year-old William Patterson, who had been in the aviation business for six years. At the same time, the company moved its headquarters from New York to Chicago.

Patterson was born in Honolulu, ran away from military school to sign on as a cabin boy with a sailing ship headed for San Francisco, and, when he arrived got a job as an office boy in the Wells Fargo Bank. He was a loan officer when Vernon Gorst, president of the fledgling Pacific Air Transport, came in to borrow some money so he could dredge up an airplane engine that was lying at the bottom of San Francisco Bay—the wreck of a plane that had crashed on take-off. Gorst didn't get that loan, but Wells Fargo did advance him $5,000 to overhaul his equipment, and Patterson developed a close interest in the affairs of Pacific Air Transport. In 1927 he helped negotiate the sale of the company to Boeing Air Transport, and the next year Boeing lured him to Seattle as an assistant to the president.

When Patterson took over in 1934, United Air Lines had revenues three times those of their nearest competitor, American Airlines. Over the next 32 years Patterson ran United with a banker's go-slow approach. They started with a virtual monopoly on the Chicago–New York route with a fleet of Boeing 247s, but TWA and American soon fielded their faster Douglas DC-2s and took away much of the business. By 1938 American was taking in twice as much money as United. United's competitors gained a further edge in the late 1950s when the airlines were placing their orders for jet planes. American ordered Boeing 707s, which became available two years earlier than Douglas's DC-8s, but Patterson doggedly held out for Douglas because of a supposed advantage in the seating layout.

United regained their long-lost position as the nation's top airline in 1961 not by attracting more passengers or changing policies, but simply by taking over financially weak Capital Airlines. Through the merger United gained a vast network of north–south routes in the East.

After Patterson's 1966 retirement the new chief executive was George Keck, an engineer who had worked his way up through United's maintenance department. Abrupt, aloof, unresponsive to suggestions from the board of directors and uncommunicative with them, Keck suffered a series of reverses in dealing with the unions and the CAB that damaged his credibility with the directors. In 1970, when United lost $41 million, the directors, led by Gardner Cowles (chairman of Cowles Communications) and Thomas Gleed (a Seattle financier), staged a palace revolt and gave Keck the ax.

To replace Keck, the board picked Eddie Carlson, president of the Western Hotels chain which United had recently bought. Carlson, a 5'7" dynamo, had entered the hotel business as a bellboy. Warm and outgoing, he had a gift for motivating his subordinates, from vice-presidents to cleaners, and to the people at United it seemed as if he had dropped out of the friendly skies to turn the company around. He held the company's losses to $5 million in 1971, and by 1974 he had boosted profits to nearly $100 million. A mechanic's strike in 1975 knocked United back to a $5 million loss that year, but by 1978 they had recovered spectacularly, chalking up a record profit of $302 million, though they lost $72 million in 1979—a year United experienced a month-long strike.

When he moved from the hotel business to the airline, Carlson brought along a bright young protégé named Dick Ferris as head of United's Food Services Division and his own heir apparent. Ferris became president of United in 1975 when Carlson moved up to chairman of both United and UAL. In 1978 Ferris became chairman of United and president of UAL.

Reputation. For years stuffy United had a strict policy of no more than two drinks per customer per flight. Carlson eased the rule a bit: now a passenger who really *insists* can have a third drink. But drunks aren't the only people United can't tolerate; they once petitioned the Civil Aeronautics Board to abolish the youth fares, claiming the kids were stinking up their airplanes.

What they own. More DC-10s than any other airline—37 of them. The rest of their 336-plane fleet (273 owned outright, 63 leased) consists of Boeing 727s, 737s, and 747s, and McDonnell Douglas DC-8s. Western International Hotels manages 49 hotels, 23 of them in the United States.

Sales: $729 million
Profits: $32.3 million
Founded: 1939
Employees: 9,000
Headquarters: Washington, D.C.

Who owns and runs the company. J. P. Morgan & Co. controls the biggest block of United's stock—6.8%. The all-male board of directors includes former astronaut Neil Armstrong, one black, and one Japanese-American.

In the public eye. In 1976 United agreed to give more than $1 million in back pay to minorities and women who had had a hard time being hired or promoted. At the time, it was the largest settlement ever made in a discrimination case that went to trial.

Where they're going. After the low-risk Patterson reign and the disastrous Keck interregnum, United seems to have gotten their competitive juices flowing again. While almost all other airlines cringed at the specter of deregulation (no more control of routes and fares by the Civil Aeronautics Board), Dick Ferris was the industry's loudest voice in favor, predicting it would be "the greatest thing to happen to the airlines since the jet engine." An executive at a competing airline remarked to the *Wall Street Journal,* "What Ferris wants is to have us for lunch, and I don't mean at McDonald's."

So far only a domestic airline, United now aims to become a major international carrier: next on the agenda are flights to Japan, Hong Kong, China, Mexico, and South America.

Stock performance. UAL stock bought for $1,000 in 1970 sold for $829 on January 2, 1980.

Major employment centers. Chicago, San Francisco.

Access. 1200 Algonquin Road, Elk Grove Township, Illinois (P.O. Box 66919, Chicago, Illinois 60666); (312) 952-4000.

What they do. U S Air claims they fly more passengers than Pan Am to more cities than American Airlines on more flights than TWA. If you live west of the Mississippi, though, chances are you've never heard of them, even under their earlier name of Allegheny Airlines. Most of their flights radiate out of Pittsburgh, their operating headquarters, and service the industrial Northeast.

When the nation's airlines were more or less deregulated in the fall of 1978, Allegheny snapped up a few routes to sunbelt spots like Tampa, Houston, and Phoenix. They decided that the name Allegheny sounded too much like "a small, regional carrier," so they changed in 1979 to U S Air, which they think suggests "a large and modern airline with nationwide service."

History. Richard C. du Pont, a glider buff and scion of the Delaware du Ponts, started the company in 1939 as All American Aviation, to deliver mail around the mountains of Pennsylvania and West Virginia. The company pioneered a method by which a plane, through a system of hooks and ropes, could swoop down to treetop level, drop off a container of mail, and snatch up the outgoing mail without having to land. During World War II the U.S. Army Air Corps adapted this method to rescue stranded fliers. Richard du Pont, while supervising the army's glider program, was killed in a glider crash in California in 1943.

The company became Allegheny Airlines in 1953 and grew as a regional carrier, subsidized by the federal government to shuttle passengers from the small cities of the East and "feed" them into the routes of the major airlines. In the mid-1960s Allegheny switched their fleet to jet planes and started concentrating on their longer, more profitable flights. Under Civil Aeronautics Board regulations, however, they had to continue to provide service to the smaller towns on their routes—towns like Hagerstown, Maryland, and Philipsburg, Pennsylvania. To satisfy the federal requirements, they spun off many of their "puddle-jumper" flights to independent pilots with smaller planes.

One of the directors is George Goodman, the author of many popular articles and books on financial matters under the pen name Adam Smith.

Stock performance. U S Air stock bought for $1,000 in 1970 sold for $655 on January 2, 1980.

Access. Washington National Airport, Washington, D.C. 20001; (703) 892-7000.

Plane and Missile Builders

THE ***BOEING*** COMPANY

Sales: $8.1 billion
Profits: $505.4 million
Forbes 500 rank: 39
Rank in commercial aircraft: 1
Rank in defense contracts: 7
Founded: 1916
Employees: 104,000
Headquarters: Seattle, Washington

What they do. When Boeing has the sniffles, Seattle sneezes. In 1980 Boeing was so healthy that Seattle was glowing. The city's largest employer had 104,000 persons on the payroll—and the "help wanted" sign was still out. Boeing was riding high on top of the aerospace industry.

To most people jets mean Boeing. And with good reason. Their 707 jetliner inaugurated the jet age in 1959. They have built 60% of the jets now in airline service. Every one of the jets designed by Boeing is still in production. The 727 trijet, a medi-

um-haul plane (it has a range of 1,900 miles), is the most popular plane in aviation history. Boeing has sold 1,780 of them.

In March 1980, as frosting on this cake, Boeing pulled a major coup by winning the biggest single Air Force contract since the Vietnam War: the $4 billion air-launched cruise missile system. This is a system whereby missiles armed with nuclear warheads are released from a bomber 1,500 miles away from the target; the missiles skim along at 500 miles per hour as low as 50 feet above the ground so that they avoid radar detection. They then smash the intended target with the force of 100,000 to 200,000 tons of TNT.

It was a sweet victory for Boeing. They had already bested McDonnell Douglas and Lockheed in the commercial airline market. Now they had bested the Pentagon's largest supplier, General Dynamics, in a series of flyoffs conducted over eight months. Air Force Secretary Hans Mark said: "Boeing's system is better."

The victory was significant enough to

land Boeing's chairman, Thornton Wilson, on the cover of *Time*'s April 7, 1980, issue. Boeing, said *Time*, now "dominates world aviation."

History. Boeing started out as a rich timberman's hobby. William Edward Boeing, a Yale graduate, originally came to Washington early in this century from Wisconsin to acquire timber properties. He learned to fly and bought the second pontoon plane built by aviation pioneer Glenn L. Martin. Boeing wanted the seaplane because he liked to fish, and it gave him quick access to lakes and rivers in British Columbia. After finding that it took six months to get replacement parts, the impatient Boeing decided to make his own plane. In 1916 he set up his "factory" in a boathouse on the shores of Lake Union near downtown Seattle. His stick-and-wire seaplane was built in six months—the first of thousands of Boeings. In 1919 Boeing and a World War I pilot, Edward Hubbard, organized an airmail service between Seattle and Victoria, British Columbia. Later they won the U.S. Post Office contract to carry the mail between San Francisco and Chicago. In other words, Boeing was both building planes and operating them—and by the end of the decade he and his associates, mainly Frederick B. Rentschler, had brought into being what would be recognized today as a conglomerate. Lumped into a New York–based holding company called United Aircraft were Boeing, the Seattle plane builder; Pratt & Whitney, the aircraft engine builder; Northrop, a maker of military planes; the Sikorsky airplane works (they built amphibians); and a bunch of regional airlines merged into a system called United Air Lines. It all came unglued in 1934 after a government investigation into collusion in the awarding of airmail contracts. Plane builders were then separated from plane operators. United Airlines emerged as an independent company based in Chicago. United Aircraft remained in the East with Pratt & Whitney as its main holding. And Boeing remained in Seattle to build planes. William Boeing retired, but the company bearing his name continued to function as one of the nation's leading plane builders. They made the P-12 fighters, the Stratoliner (the first four-engine plane to operate on transcontinental runs), and the famous Clipper flying boats used by Pan Am on international routes.

Boeing made their mark during World War II as a source of durable, reliable, and destructive bombers. Their B-17, the "Flying Fortress," dropped 640,000 tons of bombs on German targets, more than all the bombs dropped by all other Allied planes. The B-17 was used in the first mass missile attack in history when it released 106 glide missiles over Cologne, Germany. The B-17 was followed by the B-29, the "Super Fortress," the biggest airplane ever built up to that time. Martin Caidin, in *Boeing 707*, reported that the B-29 "seared Japanese industry and Japanese cities to an unbelievable wasteland of choked ash." During one raid on Tokyo the B-29s "burned to ash more than 19 square miles of the city." It was a B-29 that dropped the atomic bomb on Hiroshima in 1945.

After the war Boeing continued to make bombers—the B-47, the B-50, and the famous B-52. Their one entry in the passenger plane market was the Boeing 377 Stratocruiser, a huge double-decker transport used by Northwest Orient Airlines. In 1952, when the commercial plane market was dominated by Douglas and its DC series, Boeing decided to invest $16 million to develop a jet-powered prototype. It was a decision that put them ahead of the competition. The Boeing jet lifted into the air for the first time in 1954. American Airlines, which had always been first with the latest Douglas equipment, was impressed enough

A 95-ton Boeing 727 held in service for 20 years is expected to fly 25 million miles, make 45,000 take-offs and landings, and carry 3.5 million passengers.

Updating your fleet? Boeing 767s ready for delivery in the mid-1980s ran about $40 million each. By comparison, in the early 1970s a Boeing 747 cost around $24 million.

to place orders for the Boeing jets. The first scheduled flight of a jetliner took place on January 25, 1959: American Airlines Flight #2 left Los Angeles and swept across the country to New York in four hours and three minutes. The plane, which cost $5.5 million, was a Boeing 707. It put Boeing into a leadership position it has yet to give up.

Not that there wasn't some turbulence along the way. In the late 1960s and early 1970s Boeing was in a slump. They had opted to make the 747 jumbo jet, and when the planes were ready, the airline industry had no great need for them. From 1969 to 1972 Boeing didn't get a single order for a 747. Congress then halted Boeing's work on the controversial SST (Supersonic Transport), despite the frantic lobbying of Washington's Senator Henry Jackson, called "the Senator from Boeing" by the Pacific Northwest Research Center. Wilson was elected president in 1968, and he proceeded to slash Boeing's work force from 105,000 to 38,000. Seattle's unemployment rate soared to 13%. A billboard appeared in the city: "Will the last one to leave Seattle please turn off the lights."

Today Boeing's employment is back to what it was—and Seattle is a boom town. Boeing has sold more than 500 of the big 747s to airlines all over the world. Moreover, the company's productivity has been sharply improved. "In 1969," according to *Time*, "it took 25,000 Boeing workers to turn out seven 747s per month; today it takes 11,000."

Boeing's comeback has made the company the nation's largest exporter. In 1979 their sales of planes and spare parts outside the United States totalled $4 billion. That represented 4% of all U.S. manufactured exports.

Reputation. Boeing's planes stay in the air. They have an outstanding safety record, reflecting the engineering prowess of the company.

What they own. Most of Boeing's facilities are in the Seattle area. Their assembly plant at Everett is one of the largest plane factories in the world. Their Vertol plant in Philadelphia makes the Chinook helicopters.

Who owns and runs the company. The all-male, all-white board of directors includes David Packard, deputy defense secretary under Richard Nixon. Packard helped to arrange Lockheed's government-guaranteed loan.

In the public eye. With their product lineup, why was it necessary to bribe? In a report to the Securities and Exchange Commission, Boeing described details about questionable payments and outright kickbacks linked to foreign aircraft sales. This report was part of a settlement with the SEC. Some $3 million went to Japanese politicians, although the *Wall Street Journal* quoted officials "close to the airline industry" as saying that these rebates "weren't really needed to get the JAL [Japan Air Lines] orders."

Where they're going. Into the wild blue yonder, carrying people and missiles. Boeing engineers can get you to the moon, but not to Fenway Park. Their $100 million mass-transit system in Morgantown, West Virginia, has had troubles galore, and the light rail vehicles they built for the mass-transit system in Boston and San Francisco had operational problems. In 1978 Boston returned 35 of the cars to Boeing for repair. In 1979 Boeing checked out of the streetcar business.

Stock performance. Boeing stock bought for $1,000 in 1970 sold for $5,400 on January 2, 1980.

Major employment centers. Seattle, Wichita, Philadelphia.

Access. 7755 East Marginal Way South, Seattle, Washington 98108; (206) 655-2121.

GENERAL DYNAMICS

Sales: $4.1 billion
Profits: $185 million
Forbes 500 rank: 109
Rank in defense contracts: 1
Rank in liquid natural gas tankers: 1
Rank in tactical weapons systems: 1
Rank in lime production: 1
Founded: 1952
Employees: 77,100
Headquarters: St. Louis, Missouri

General Dynamics, more than any other aerospace company, is dependent on the Pentagon: government defense contracts account for two-thirds of their sales. John Jay Hopkins started the company in 1952, hoping to create the General Motors of the weapons industry. And that's just about what he did. The Electric Boat division (founded in 1899) makes submarines in Groton, Connecticut. The Quincy, Massachusetts shipyard (largest in the country and the site where a World War II inspector named Kilroy wrote "Kilroy was here" all over ship hulls) makes tankers. The F-16 fighter jet comes out of Fort Worth, Texas, while the Tomahawk cruise missile is made in San Diego, California. Tactical weapons in California, coal in the Midwest, lime in Chicago, and telecommunications in Florida and Missouri round out General's inventory.

David Lewis, a former president of McDonnell Douglas, was elected chairman in 1970, but the power behind the scenes is Henry Crown, a Chicago financier and one of the richest, but least known, men in the country. A group headed by Crown, who was 83 in 1980, owns about 20% of the company. His associates, who sit on the General Dynamics board with him, are his son, Lester Crown, and Chicago industrialist Nathan Cummings, founder of Consolidated Foods. In January 1980 General Dynamics raided their Seattle competitor,

Boeing, to recruit 52-year-old Oliver C. Boileau as president under Lewis. At the time Boeing and General Dynamics were competing for the biggest single Air Force contract since the Vietnam War: the air-launched cruise missile program. Three months later the decision came down from the Pentagon: Boeing. One of the first congratulatory calls to Boeing headquarters came from Boileau, who had spent 26 years with the Seattle plane builder.

Major employment centers. San Diego, Groton, and Fort Worth.

Stock performance. General Dynamics stock bought for $1,000 in 1970 sold for $5,450 on January 2, 1980.

Access. Pierre Laclede Center, St. Louis, Missouri 63105; (314) 862-2440. The company notes: "Since our customers are, for the most part, government and industry, some of our facilities are not open to touring groups."

GRUMMAN

Sales: $1.5 billion
Profits: $19.6 million
Forbes 500 rank: 341
Rank in defense contracts: 10
Founded: 1930
Employees: 26,000
Headquarters: Bethpage, Long Island, New York

Leroy Randle Grumman did not want to move to Pennsylvania with his employer, Loening Aircraft, so he started his own company in 1930. Today Grumman makes jets and weapons in the former potato fields of Bethpage, Long Island. The company is the largest employer on the Island, and probably the most paternal. Production employees are not unionized, they have never held a strike, they own one-third of the company's stock, and they each receive a Christmas turkey every year. But they are beginning to wonder if Grumman is the real turkey around Bethpage.

The company known for their World War II Navy fighters (Wildcat, Hellcat,

John P. Holland emerging from his Holland submarine, the U.S. Navy's first sub, purchased in 1900 from Electric Boat Co., a predecessor of General Dynamics.

Avenger) can't seem to get Navy contracts for their F-14 Tomcat. Perhaps the Navy couldn't afford the world's most expensive fighter. Or maybe the F-14's record of 25 crashes scared them off. Grumman has tried to reduce their dependence on the government by manufacturing yachts, aluminum canoes, firetrucks, buses, solar heating equipment, and computer systems, but defense contracts still account for 80% of their sales.

Iran temporarily bailed the company out with an order for the F-14, but the disclosure of Grumman's payments to agents in Iran cost them millions in restitutions to the Iranian government. In Japan, Mitsuhiro Shimada, a top executive of a major trading company, committed suicide in 1979 in the midst of an investigation of charges that some of the commissions paid by Grumman on the sale of their Hawkeye reconnaissance planes may have found their way into the pockets of Japanese government officials. In 1980 the Navy canceled a contract Grumman had to build a training system that simulates electronic warfare, charging that the company wasn't even close to meeting the delivery date. The Navy not only terminated the contract and awarded it to another company but demanded that Grumman return the $11 million they had received on the project. The crucial question for Grumman chairman John C. Bierwith: will Grumman be able to pull up and regain altitude, or will its 10-year downward spiral end in a crash?

Stock performance. Grumman stock bought for $1,000 in 1970 sold for $968 on January 2, 1980.

Access. Bethpage, Long Island, New York 11714; (516) 575-3344.

Lockheed

Sales: $4.1 billion
Profits: $36.5 million
Forbes 500 rank: 110.
Rank in commercial aircraft: 3
Rank in defense contracts: 4
Rank in NASA contracts: 5
Founded: 1913
Employees: 55,100
Headquarters: Burbank, California

What they do. The Lockheed payoff scandals toppled a Japanese prime minister, nearly brought down the Dutch monarchy, led to the resignation of an Italian minister, and caused acute embarrassment to government officials from Turkey to the Philippines. The 1975 disclosure of massive bribery to win overseas contracts, coming on top of a financial debacle six years earlier, threatened Lockheed's very existence. But the aerospace giant pulled out of the tailspin and by the end of the 1970s the headlines told the story. "Lockheed Comes in from the Cold," said the *New York Times.* "How Lockheed Got Back Its Wings," cried *Fortune.*

Lockheed has long been one of the world's prime suppliers of weaponry. They are, for example, the sole U.S. makers of submarine-launched missiles. They produce huge military cargo planes that have been sold to the Pentagon and defense establishments in 43 other countries. They have built more than half the space satellites launched by the United States. They are the acknowledged leader in what's called "spook" hardware, reconnaissance planes and satellites. The U-2 Gary Powers flew when he was shot down in 1960 over Russia was a Lockheed product.

Lockheed also competes in the commercial airline market with their L-1011 Tri-Star jet, a jumbo jet smaller than the Boeing 747 but larger than the DC-10. It was the mid-1960s decision to make this plane that precipitated Lockheed's financial troubles.

Headquartered in Burbank, California, Lockheed has plane-building plants sprawled across the suburbs of Los Angeles, where aerospace is the largest industry. Lockheed's Missiles & Space division is headquartered in Northern California, at Sunnyvale. And they build the big C-130 cargo carriers in a largely government-owned facility—said to be the largest aircraft plant in the world—at Marietta, Georgia.

History. "Oh what tangled webs we weave when first we practice to deceive." If only former chairman Dan Haughton and former president Carl Kotchian had heeded Shakespeare's verse, they might not have been forced out of Lockheed in 1975. Lockheed started out innocently enough in 1913, when brothers Allan and Malcolm Loughhead (who later changed the spelling of their name) flew their seaplane over San Francisco Bay. Three years later they estab-

To sell this airplane to Japanese airlines Lockheed paid out something like $12 million, most of it in bribes, including a $1.7 million secret payment to the Japanese Prime Minister, Kakuei Tanaka.

lished an aircraft company in Santa Barbara, working with designer Jack Northrop.

Malcolm left the company in 1919 to market hydraulic automobile brakes, and Northrop left soon after to form his own aircraft company, but Allan scored a hit in 1926 with the Vega plane, which Amelia Earhart later used in her solo flight across the Atlantic. Allan moved the company to the Los Angeles suburb of Burbank, and when Northrop and North American Aviation settled in Los Angeles, aircraft companies overshadowed even the movie industry.

But then the age of innocence ended. Lockheed went bankrupt in 1931, and Allan turned to selling real estate. Boston bankers Robert and Courtlandt Gross resurrected Lockheed for $50,000 in 1932, without Allan Lockheed (but with his name). Six years later the company entered the weapons industry, producing the Hudson bomber for the British. Lockheed has depended on the military contracts ever since.

After the Second World War, Robert Gross's dream of a "hanger in every home" never materialized, but another war did. "Korea was a Lockheed war," wrote Anthony Sampson in *The Arms Bazaar*. The conflict generated plenty of demand for Shooting Star fighters and Constellation transports. Lockheed became the biggest defense company in the country. They tried to attack the commercial airline business with their Electra plane, but the Electra couldn't manage to stay in the air, so

they concentrated on the NATO market for fighters.

The Starfighters that Germany bought in 1959 may have been promoted as the "missile with a man in it" by Lockheed, but Germans soon called them flying coffins and widow-makers, as 175 delicate Starfighters crashed, killing 85 pilots. (Lockheed paid damages of $1.2 million to widows of the German pilots in 1975.) Kai-Uwe von Hassel, Germany's minister of defense, proclaimed, "Those Lockheed rogues will never get into my office again." Von Hassel's son, a pilot, later died in a Starfighter crash.

With money flowing in from the Pentagon, Lockheed moved in the 1960s to reenter the passenger plane business that Boeing was dominating with its early jetliners. Boeing had announced that it was building the 747 jumbo jet. Lockheed—and McDonnell Douglas—both thought they saw an opening in the market for an airbus that would stand between the small jet and the jumbo. McDonnell Douglas began building the DC-10; Lockheed began building the L-1011 TriStar. Both raced to get to the market first.

In 1969 Lockheed ran into heavy squalls. They overran their budget on the C-5A cargo jet by $2 billion. Some critics charged it was because the company bid "unreasonably low" to get the contract. Senator William Proxmire said: "Lockheed has been milking the Pentagon for years." Lockheed posted a loss of $32 million for 1969 and advised the Pentagon that unless they received a money transfusion of $600 million they would have to stop work on four military projects. That was just the beginning. Lockheed had ordered the engines for the TriStar from Britain's Rolls-Royce. When that company had its own financial crisis (leading to bankruptcy and government takeover), the timetable for introduction of the L-1011 went out the window.

What it came down to in the end was this: the banks would not lend money to Lockheed unless the U.S. government guaranteed these loans. By a one-vote margin in the U.S. Senate in August, 1971, the government was authorized to guarantee up to $250 million in loans to keep Lockheed alive, much to the disgust of Senator Proxmire, McDonnell Douglas (which resented government aid to a competitor), and General Electric (which felt the financial difficulties served Lockheed right for bypassing the GE jet engines in favor of Rolls-Royce's).

Saved at the bell from a knockout, Lockheed then went on their way, dispensing money lavishly to overseas agents and government officials. It was the way the wheels of commerce had always been greased in foreign military sales. During this period Lockheed was run by two former accountants, Haughton and Kotchian, who had risen to the top in 1967. Both believed the payoffs were necessary to outmaneuver the competition; at least it appeared that way—neither argued about delivering fat payments to people of influence. It was alleged that Prince Bernhard of the Netherlands was one of the recipients of some payments, although this was not proved. Lockheed's agents included Middle East wheeler-dealer Adnan Khashoggi and Yoshio Kodama, a right-wing Japanese militarist who served three years in prison as a war criminal after World War II.

Congressional investigations in 1975 turned up questionable foreign payments by Lockheed of $25.5 million. In Japan, where former prime minister Kakuei Tanaka was eventually arrested and brought to trial, Lockheed became a household name, standing for corruption of public officials. On February 13, 1976, Haughton resigned his post. Kotchian had to be convinced in a four-hour meeting that he, too, had to go.

To save the company, the directors chose from among themselves a new leader: Robert Haack, an investment banker, former president of the New York Stock Exchange, a man described as one who "oozes integrity." Haack performed the miracle that was needed to rescue Lockheed. He went around the world "disabusing people," as he put it, "of the notion that we are 55,000 people all carrying black bags."

In 1977 he turned over the reins to a 20-year Lockheed veteran, Roy Anderson. And Anderson is smiling these days. In 1979 he led a contingent of Lockheed executives in a presentation to the New York Society of Security Analysts, who analyze stock for Wall Street investment houses. It was the first appearance of Lockheed before this group since 1967. After it was over an analyst said: "For the first time in 10 years there were no revelations of payoffs, no problems with cost overruns, no more crippling debts and no fears of bankruptcy."

Anderson himself said: "We've come a long way toward restoring our credibility."

Reputation. Lockheed was once called the "wounded giant of the aerospace industry." Robert Haack, in explaining how he tried to regain credibility for Lockheed, said he would pose the following question: "How many corporations in America could take these assaults and still be around to tell the story?"

Who owns and runs the company. The banks. The 1979 proxy statement showed J. P. Morgan & Co. owning a 9.4% stake in the company, nearly three times the combined holdings of 51 officers and directors. In addition, nine of the largest banks in the country, from Bank of America down to the Mellon Bank, were listed as holders of a

The major manufacturers of corporate aircraft are (in order): Cessna, Piper, Beech, Gates Learjet, Gulfstream American, and Rockwell.

The biggest concentration of the nation's aerospace workers—more than 40%—is in the Pacific states of California, Washington, Oregon, Hawaii, and Alaska.

Lockheed builds huge planes for the military at their gigantic manufacturing plant at Marietta, Georgia, which is mostly owned by the U.S. government. Here are 15 military transports—the C-141B StarLifters—in production at Marietta. The building covers 74 acres from door to door.

special class of preferred stock. That was part of their payoff for going along with Lockheed until the company could fly straight again.

In the public eye. They've had enough publicity to last a lifetime.

Where they're going. Now that rival McDonnell Douglas is struggling with the aftermath of the DC-10 crash, Lockheed hopes to be able to sell more of their Tri-Stars. By early 1980 they had sold 234 of them, compared to the 362 DC-10s sold by McDonnell Douglas.

Stock performance. Lockheed stock bought for $1,000 in 1970 sold for $2,000 on January 2, 1980.

Access. 2555 North Hollywood Way, Burbank, California 91520; (213) 847-6121.

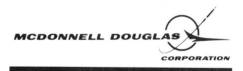

Sales: $5.3 billion
Profits: $199.1 million
Forbes 500 rank: 72
Rank in commercial aircraft: 2
Rank in defense contracts: 2
Rank in jet fighters: 1
Founded: 1920
Employees: 70,547
Headquarters: St. Louis, Missouri

What they do. McDonnell Douglas is a proud family aircraft builder trying to weather the storm surrounding their DC-10 passenger plane, the wide-bodied jet whose 1979 crash after takeoff from O'Hare International Airport in Chicago killed 273

Top 50 Pentagon Suppliers

Sales/Percent of U.S. Total

1. GENERAL DYNAMICS $3.5 *billion* / 5.52%
2. McDONNELL DOUGLAS $3.2 *billion* / 5.11%
3. UNITED TECHNOLOGIES $2.6 *billion* / 4.04%
4. GENERAL ELECTRIC $2.0 *billion* / 3.23%
5. LOCKHEED $1.8 *billion* / 2.84%
6. HUGHES AIRCRAFT $1.6 *billion* / 2.46%
7. BOEING $1.5 *billion* / 2.39%
8. GRUMMAN $1.4 *billion* / 2.16%
9. RAYTHEON $1.2 *billion* / 1.98%
10. TENNECO $1.1 *billion* / 1.73%
11. LITTON $832 *million* / 1.32%
12. CHRYSLER $809 *million* / 1.28%
13. NORTHROP $800 *million* / 1.27%
14. SPERRY $778 *million* / 1.23%
15. ROCKWELL INTERNATIONAL $684 *million* / 1.08%
16. WESTINGHOUSE $660 *million* / 1.04%
17. HONEYWELL $658 *million* / 1.04%
18. AT&T $570 *million* / 0.90%
19. IBM $553 *million* / 0.87%
20. MARTIN MARIETTA $519 *million* / 0.82%
21. FAIRCHILD INDUSTRIES $505 *million* / 0.80%
22. RCA $487 *million* / 0.77%
23. TEXTRON $477 *million* / 0.75%
24. TODD SHIPYARDS $449 *million* / 0.71%
25. GENERAL MOTORS $449 *million* / 0.71%
26. LTV $448 *million* / 0.71%
27. TRW $437 *million* / 0.69%
28. TELEDYNE $400 *million* / 0.63%
29. TEXAS INSTRUMENTS $374 *million* / 0.59%
30. FMC $352 *million* / 0.56%
31. SINGER $346 *million* / 0.55%
32. EXXON $341 *million* / 0.54%
33. FORD MOTOR $338 *million* / 0.53%
34. CONGOLEUM $336 *million* / 0.53%
35. BENDIX $297 *million* / 0.47%
36. HYUN DAI CONSTRUCTION $290 *million* / 0.46%
37. ITT $263 *million* / 0.42%
38. AMERICAN MOTORS $244 *million* / 0.39%
39. STANDARD OIL OF CALIFORNIA $241 *million* / 0.38%
40. AMERADA HESS $237 *million* / 0.37%
41. GENERAL TELEPHONE & ELECTRONICS $227 *million* / 0.36%
42. GENERAL TIRE & RUBBER $220 *million* / 0.35%
43. HARSCO $219 *million* / 0.35%
44. GOODYEAR TIRE & RUBBER $218 *million* / 0.34%
45. AL HUSEINI $206 *million* / 0.33%
46. NORTH AMERICAN PHILIPS $205 *million* / 0.32%
47. HERCULES $191 *million* / 0.30%
48. KAISER INDUSTRIES $186 *million* / 0.29%
49. MOTOROLA $186 *million* / 0.29%
50. MOTOR OIL HELLAS $184 *million* / 0.29%

Source: Department of Defense, for year ending September 30, 1979.

persons in the nation's worst air disaster. A subsequent investigation by the National Transportation Safety Board implicated the manufacturer by finding that the plane's design contributed to the accident. After the crash the Federal Aviation Administration grounded all the DC-10s for 37 days. In 1974 a DC-10 operated by Turkish Airlines crashed outside Paris, killing 346 persons. It's no wonder that *New York Times* aviation writer Richard Witkin called the DC-10 "one of the most controversial planes ever to fly the airways."

McDonnell Douglas makes one other commercial plane, the DC-9, a smaller jet. They have sold more than 1,000 DC-9s. But the main output of McDonnell Douglas "teammates" (as management likes to call employees) is military aircraft. Fighter planes account for more than half their sales. Throw in space systems and missiles and you've got three-quarters of their total business. Their F-4 Phantom is the most popular jet fighter in the world; they've made more than 5,000 of them since 1958. Between 1955 and 1979 they turned out 2,960 A-4 Skyhawks. Also in production at McDonnell Douglas are the F-15 Eagle, a jet fighter used by the air forces of the United States, Israel, Saudi Arabia, and Japan, and the F-18A Hornet, ordered by the U.S. Marine Corps and the U.S. Navy.

Making war planes has always been the forte of the McDonnell wing of this aircraft company. They may rue the day they decided to enter the commercial end of the business. They made that move in 1967 by annexing California's Douglas Aircraft Company.

History. The merger of McDonnell and Douglas in 1967 joined two of the oldest family-owned aviation businesses in the country. Donald Wills Douglas, son of a Brooklyn bank cashier, came to Los Angeles in 1915 with an engineering degree from the Massachusetts Institute of Technology. He started his own company in 1920 and produced his first plane, the Cloudster, two years later in an abandoned movie studio in Santa Monica. Two of Douglas's World Cruiser planes flew around the world in 1924, making the trip in six months and six days. The company's most famous series of planes, the Douglas Commercial (DC), got off the ground in 1933, with a Trans World Airlines order for 40 DC-2s. The DC-3, known as the "immor-

tal," was so perfect aerodynamically that engineers claimed it could glide if the engines failed. Airlines eventually bought 448 DC-3s—and they were steady sellers on the used plane market for many years. A DC-4 was the first presidential aircraft, ordered for Franklin Delano Roosevelt, and dubbed the "Sacred Cow" by journalists. The DC-6 became Harry Truman's "Independence."

After World War II Douglas continued to set the pace in commercial airlines. They never had another winner like the DC-3, but the DC-6 could fly 350 miles per hour and had a range of 2,600 miles, and the DC-7, introduced in 1953, became the first commercial plane to fly nonstop across the United States. Donald Douglas, Jr., took over as head of the company, but his father still called the shots. One shot he didn't call correctly was the jetliner. Seattle's Boeing beat Douglas to the punch. Boeing's 707 jet was making test flights while the first Douglas jet, the DC-8, was still undergoing wind tunnel trials on the ground. American Airlines, a major customer of Douglas, ordered Boeing 707s after being persuaded that the plane was faster and less expensive than the Douglas version. In 1959 American inaugurated coast-to-coast jet service with the 707. It was a lead Boeing was never to give up. Douglas went into a tailspin. It couldn't even produce DC-8s fast enough to meet demand. By 1966 it was losing money. And it was ripe for an overture from St. Louis, headquarters of McDonnell Aircraft.

James S. McDonnell, another strong-willed engineer, took a degree at Princeton (as did his sons and nephew, who all work for the company) and founded his company in 1939 with capital from friends (the only stranger to invest was Laurence Rockefeller). By wartime 1942 the McDonnell Company was a major industry in St. Louis. They were the first to make jet-propelled planes to operate from the decks of aircraft carriers. McDonnell's Banshee F2H-2 fighters, used in the Korean War, became famous through James Michener's *The Bridges of Toko-Ri*. Other well-known fighters followed: F3H Demon (the first swept-wing jet), Voodoo, and Phantom— the names all reflecting James McDonnell's interest in the occult.

Chairman James McDonnell (whom employees call "Mr. Mac") describes himself as a "practicing Scotsman" who is a stickler for details. He once calculated on his slide rule just how much to spike the eggnog to insure conviviality without rowdiness. On that same slide rule he figured how many calories and how much cholesterol were in the executive dining room menus ("one slice of corned beef $3 \times 2 \times \frac{1}{4}$"). His thriftiness is reflected in the company's balance sheet, which shows little debt compared to the enormous debts of most aerospace companies.

When McDonnell took over Douglas in 1967, it was hailed as a savior of a company threatened with collapse. By 1969 *Business Week* was reporting that the "consolidated company had come through stronger than either of the companies could ever have hoped to be individually." And in 1970 *Forbes* told its readers: "Once the sick man of its industry, McDonnell Douglas has become perhaps its healthiest major company. And Boeing, which came close a few years back to squeezing Douglas out of the commercial aircraft business, is today a danger-ously ailing firm." The reasoning here was that Boeing had thought "too big" when it decided to build the 747 jumbo jet, while McDonnell Douglas had gauged the market prospects perfectly by deciding to go full blast and build a flexible airbus: the DC-10.

Today, Boeing is on the cover of *Time* and McDonnell Douglas is wondering whether it will ever sell enough DC-10s to recover their costs.

Reputation. McDonnell Douglas is regarded as a premier builder of fighter planes for military forces here and abroad. But many people now go out of their way to avoid flying a DC-10.

What they own. McDonnell Douglas has not moved much from their original plants in St. Louis, Missouri, and Long Beach, California, but they now have a plant in Ontario, Canada.

Up From Nothin'

"Do you remember Jim Driscoll, that used to sell papers on Nassau Street?"

"Yes, I knew him; where is he?"

"He went out West about two years ago. He's doin' well. Got fifty dollars in the savings bank, and a good home besides."

"Who told you?"

"Mr. O'Connor. He had a letter from him."

"Jim can't write, nor read either. When he was sellin' papers in Nassau Street, he used to ask what was the news. Sometimes I told him wrong. Once I told him the President was dead, and he didn't know no better than to believe it. He sold his papers fast, but the last chap got mad and booted him."

"Well, Jim can write now. He's been to school since he was out there."

"He can do more'n I can. I can read easy readin', but I can't write no more'n a lamppost."

"Nor I," said Julius, "but I mean to learn."

Is this some odd snatch by an unknown author? Yes and no. The book it is taken from (called *Julius, or The Street Boy Out West*) is virtually unknown now. Its author went by a name most people think of as myth: Horatio Alger. But the real Alger was the most widely read writer in the history of the United States. His melodramatic stories of rags-to-riches success via hard work and honesty were serialized in such popular magazines of the late nineteenth century as *Munsey's* and *Argosy*. Published as books, they sold over 250 million copies. And although the real Alger has been forgotten—along with his heroes Ragged Dick, Ben Barclay, and Phil the Fiddler—his own name now symbolizes up-from-nothing success.

Horatio Alger, Jr., was the son of a Unitarian minister.

Born in 1834, he went to Harvard and was ordained a minister himself, but he gave up the pulpit for the pen. He was a financial success but gave most of his money away. Shy around women, he never married; he died in 1899.

Alger worked as private tutor for the sons of the Lehman, Harriman, and Cardozo families, and among his students was Benjamin Cardozo, later a justice of the U.S. Supreme Court. But his direct influence extended to a larger company. A list of avowed Alger fans includes many who went the path of Alger heroes: Henry Ford, George Eastman, Thomas Edison, John D. Rockefeller—to say nothing of Ernest Hemingway, F. Scott Fitzgerald, Carl Sandburg, and Joyce Kilmer.

Who owns and runs the company. "But Mr. Mac, you and the board made me president last year and you've just made me chief executive officer," complained Sanford McDonnell to his uncle, James McDonnell, in 1972.

"That's right," Mr. Mac replied, according to *Business Week*. "You're the CEO and I'm the boss."

Although the McDonnell Douglas mandatory retirement age is 65, octogenarian McDonnell is exempt as founder.

James McDonnell and his two sons, John and James III, own 20% of the firm. Sanford McDonnell, whose son is now in the company, too, owns less than 1%. Donald Douglas, Jr., still sits on the board of directors, but after the merger he played a smaller and smaller role, taking early retirement in 1974. A remarkable 90% of the employees own stock in the company, through employee savings plans, which hold 22% of the stock.

In the public eye. In 1970, just after McDonnell Douglas was awarded a $1 billion Air Force contract for the F-15 fighter plane, the U.S. Civil Rights Commission charged the company with lodging black workers in low-level jobs. The commission said that McDonnell Douglas had only 41 blacks among 4,898 officials and managers, and only 67 blacks among 6,709 professional employees. The Air Force then warned the company that unless they put into effect adequate affirmative action programs, the F-15 contract would be terminated. It never was—and McDonnell Douglas reported in 1979 that all their plants were "in compliance with government regulations."

Most companies accused of making illegal or dubious payments abroad settle the complaints out of court. Not McDonnell Douglas. In 1979 James McDonnell III, three other company executives, and the company itself were indicted by a grand jury on charges of bribery connected with sales of the DC-10 in Pakistan, Venezuela, Zaire, and the Philippines. Former Defense Secretary Clark Clifford was retained to defend the company. Chairman McDonnell said his son, the other executives, and the company were innocent. He said these payments were made in "difficult sales environments in many parts of the world" and were well known to the U.S. government at the time.

"THIS IS THE PRESIDENT OF McDONNELL DOUGLAS SPEAKING... WELCOME ABOARD THE TITANIC...."

This cartoon by *Los Angeles Times* cartoonist Paul Conrad struck a raw nerve. The people at McDonnell Douglas, found it "cruel and crude," reported A. Kent MacDougall, *Los Angeles Times* business writer. And the *Times*, after the cartoon appeared in 1979, shortly after the DC-10 crash in Chicago, received 53 letters criticizing the cartoon, none supporting it.

McDonnell Douglas is one of 30 companies to celebrate United Nations Day with a paid holiday for all employees.

Where they're going. They say they're going to stick with the DC-10. But they've decided not to compete with Boeing in the development of the next-generation commercial jet. They made that decision even before the DC-10 fatal crash in Chicago. So they're falling back on the Pentagon dependence they thought they were escaping with the Douglas marriage.

Stock performance. McDonnell Douglas stock bought for $1,000 in 1970 sold for $1,844 on January 2, 1980.

Major employment centers. St. Louis, Missouri, and Long Beach, California (Douglas Division).

Access. P.O. Box 516, St. Louis, Missouri 63166; (314) 232-0232.

NORTHROP

Sales: $1.6 billion
Profits: $90.3 million
Forbes 500 rank: 320
Rank in defense contracts: 15
Rank in unmanned target aircraft: 1
Founded: 1939
Employees: 31,200
Headquarters: Los Angeles, California

Northrop's specialty is called "tin-bending": making aircraft parts for other companies. Northrop makes the fuselage, doors, and floor beams of the Boeing 747 jumbo jet, and various components of the McDonnell Douglas F-18 Hornet fighter. They also make their own aircraft: their F-5 Freedom Fighter jet, which *Forbes* called the "Pinto of the fighter market," is the most widely used supersonic fighter aircraft in the world. Northrop delivers a new F-5 every three days.

Founder John K. Northrop, the designer responsible for the Lockheed Vega, the plane used by Amelia Earhart in her solo flight across the Atlantic in 1932, and the Black Widow night fighter of World War II, set up shop in Hawthorne in 1939; by the

time he left, the company was a mess. His successor, Thomas Jones, who became president in 1959, moved into subcontracting, unmanned target aircraft, defense systems electronics, and even a construction company in New York City. Although Northrop's holdings are mainly in California, they operate plants in Illinois, Virginia, Missouri, Massachusetts, and New Hampshire.

Jones also moved Northrop into bribery and scandal: he took $50,000 in cash out of his desk drawer in 1972 and handed it to Herbert Kalmbach as a contribution to the Nixon reelection campaign. For that indiscretion—it's illegal for a corporation to make such a political contribution—Jones was fined $200,000. Northrop was then forced to disclose that they had spent $30 million soliciting business overseas, "at least a half a million" of which, *Fortune* reported, "went to bribe officials in Indonesia, Saudi Arabia, and Iran." Here at home, according to Jack Anderson, Northrop entertained more than 30 admirals and generals, plus a bunch of Congressmen, at their private hunting preserve on Maryland's eastern shore. As Anderson says, "A little booze and banter will go farther than a discourse on the company's

The Harrowing History of Airplane Seating

"Please unbutton my coat" were A. C. Pheil's first words upon alighting from the Benoist seaplane flown by Tony Jannus from St. Petersburg to Tampa, Florida, on January 1, 1914. The ex-mayor of St. Petersburg was the first passenger aboard the world's first fixed-wing commercial air service. He needed assistance because he had spent the entire 23-minute flight perched on a wooden seat beside Jannus, exposed to the chill air of an unusually harsh Florida winter. Pheil had also been obliged to help the pilot tinker with the plane's balky machinery in flight, so his hands were frozen and coated with grease.

The former mayor paid $400 for his flight, which

was a model of comfort compared to earlier passenger conditions. The Wright Brothers had believed that air passengers would be content to lie on their stomachs, but by 1908 aerial pioneers had decided that sitting was the best flying posture. Crude passenger seats were installed aboard biplanes and triplanes, but the need for seat belts was overlooked until some passengers disappeared abruptly during storms.

The problem of passenger seating still bedeviled commercial aviation in 1932, when one of Donald Douglas's engineers made a cross-country flight in a Ford trimotor to test the rival firm's design for passenger comfort. The engineer reported that

his ride in Ford's unpressurized "tin goose" had been "like flying in an iron lawn chair with cotton in his ears."

The Douglas engineer's recommendations were built into the Douglas DC-2, a 14-passenger transport billed as "comfort with wings." Not only did the DC-2 have upholstered contour seats, thick carpeting, footrests, and plenty of leg room; an in-flight movie was shown aboard TWA's DC-2 in 1934. The film was called *Flying Hostesses.* Amid such luxury air passengers quickly forgot what their forebears had endured.

Source: Benjamin Lawson, "A Curmudgeonly View of Air Comfort," *Smithsonian,* September 1979.

WHO FLIES F-5s?

Country/Number of Planes Owned

TAIWAN 363	SWITZERLAND 72	MALAYSIA 20
IRAN 309	JORDAN 71	VENEZUELA 20
SOUTH KOREA 276	SPAIN 70	CHILE 18
UNITED STATES 145	THAILAND 57	LIBYA 18
CANADA 115	VIETNAM 47	INDONESIA 16
SAUDI ARABIA 114	BRAZIL 42	KENYA 12
NORWAY 108	MOROCCO 24	YEMEN 12
TURKEY 108	ETHIOPIA 23	TOTAL 2,285
NETHERLANDS 105	PHILIPPINES 22	
GREECE 77	SINGAPORE 21	

Northrop's F-5 fighter, the Volkswagen of short-range fighter aircraft, sells for $4 million plus options and has become the favorite of countries all over the world.

Source: *New York Times*, February 4, 1980.

---

methods."

As a result of these activities, Northrop was sued by an outraged stockholder. In the subsequent court-directed settlement Jones had to give up his position (though he continued as chairman) and the company had to add four independent directors to their nine-man board, giving the outsiders the controlling votes. And this arrangement was made permanent; people outside the company must now have 60% of the board seats. *Business Week* said it was the first time ever that minority shareholders had been able to impose "permanent, structural changes on a company."

Major employment centers. Hawthorne, California (aircraft division), Palos Verdes, California (electronics division), and Anaheim, California (electro-mechanical division).

Stock Performance. Northrop stock bought for $1,000 in 1970 sold for $3,475 on January 2, 1980.

Access. 1800 Century Park East, Los Angeles, California 90067; (213) 553-6262.

 **Rockwell International**

Sales: $6.3 billion
Profits: $263 million
Forbes 500 rank: 62
Rank in commercial aircraft electronics: 1
Rank in components for trucks: 1
Rank in defense contracts: 11
Rank in electronic computer systems: 1
Founded: 1919
Employees: 115,162
Headquarters: Pittsburgh, Pennsylvania

On January 27, 1967, three astronauts—Virgil Grissom, 40, Edward White II, 36, and Roger Chaffee, 31—burned to death in a fire that broke out inside an Apollo space capsule at Cape Kennedy, Florida. The ghastly accident touched off a barrage of criticism of the Apollo builder, North American Aviation. Nine months later North American, an aerospace company founded in 1928 in El Segundo, California, merged with a Pittsburgh outfit, Rockwell-Standard, whose origins go back to 1919, when they began to make truck axles in Oshkosh, Wisconsin. Of the two companies, North American was much the larger —it had sales of $2 billion to Rockwell-Standard's $635 million. But it was clear from the outset of this merger that the shots were to be called by the Rockwells: Colonel Willard F. Rockwell and his son, Willard, Jr. They had collected 50 companies before North American. Colonel Rockwell was once described by *Fortune* as someone who picks up and discards companies "like a gin-rummy player." The colonel himself once prophesied: "By 1980, 200 companies will control 60 to 75% of the world's gross national product, and we intend to be one of them."

Rockwell International ranks today as one of the 100 largest manufacturing companies in the world, with a product roster that spans many industries. They make all kinds of components for cars, trucks, and other vehicles: axles, drivelines, brakes, gear boxes, bumpers, wheels, door latches, universal joints, sun roofs, window regulators. "If it moves, we probably make something on it" is an old Rockwell boast. In the electronics area they make navigation, flight control, and communications equipment, including auto-pilot systems and the guidance and control systems for the Minuteman III intercontinental ballistic missile.

Still in place, and still having problems, is the California-based aerospace business. They suffered a setback in 1977 when President Jimmy Carter ruled against development of the B-1 supersonic bomber, a program that had made Rockwell a target of antiwar groups.

Rockwell has been the National Aeronautics & Space Administration's largest contractor since 1973. They function as the prime contractor on the Space Shuttle Program. But that's not all Rockwell does. They make gas meters, industrial valves, web offset newspaper printing presses (they're the largest maker), power tools, and industrial sewing machines and looms for the textile industry.

Shortly after they engineered the North American merger, the Rockwells lured Robert Anderson away from Chrysler to

Miss Hot Kiss Sells the Bomb

It looks like any other big time sales convention at Washington's Sheraton-Park Hotel. Women in skin-tight jump suits and magicians twisting disappearing coins try to cajole the buyers into their displays. Freebees are handed out like loose change. Food, drink, toys . . . no one in the crowd will leave empty-handed.

But this crowd is not the average cluster of well-heeled conventioneers; these are five thousand military officers and government officials, guests of more than 50 of the United States' biggest and most powerful armament manufacturers. And the displays are not simply new household hardware or automobiles. Together, they represent an arsenal of America's top-flight missiles, aircraft components, and strategic fighters.

Before finishing each year's defense budget, the Pentagon is invited to something called "The Aerospace Briefings and Equipment Displays." It is the military industry's version of a Tupperware party. . . .

For fifteen years, the industry has gathered in Washington to hold this military aerospace trade exhibition. It's a chance for the buyers and sellers to look each other over while appreciating the newest, most eye-catching products on the market. Unlike other exhibitions, the products often have the capability of leveling an entire city. But at a glance you wouldn't know it.

Our hostess leads us to the shine of aluminum walls and a small open stage about the size of a puppet theater. It is the Delco Electronics booth, and a sign reads, "Next briefing, three minutes." Music begins to chatter from the ceiling, and two attractive models dressed in abbreviated aviator costumes bounce up to the stage. The music gets louder, and the women, with practiced smiles, wave us closer. Over the loudspeaker we hear an announcer.

Voice: "Ladies and gentlemen, Delco Electronics, the makers of Delco's series of magic computers, welcomes you to view 'The Big Picture.' "

The Blonde: "Hello, I'm Janine."

The Brunette: "And I'm Cynthia."

The Empty Stage: "And I'm Delco's Big Picture!" . . .

The stage comes alive with floating mirrors, hands without bodies, and suspended pictures of sophisticated weapons components dancing playfully to the music. Janine tells of F-16 fighter controls while releasing small, flame-colored kites explaining inertial upper stage guidance computers. Little drawings of airplanes soar back and forth across the back scrim of the stage like poor animation for a Saturday morning children's education special.

Cynthia: "OK, I think we get the Big Picture."

Big Picture: "Then stick around, and get yourself a copy of my Big Picture puzzle, too."

When the lights at the stage dim, Cynthia and Janine hand out free puzzles of a soaring Delco-guided missile. Many of us take the opportunity to fill our free United Technology bags with extra Delco puzzles, a handful of Delco buttons, and assorted freeway maps of Washington.

. . .

If you want to sell a product, manufacturers believe, you need an entertaining twist. Facts and figures can be boring—even if the merchandise is a nuclear weapon. It's like selling cigarettes: Long lasting? Fine. But what about seeing some legs?

bring order to their industrial mélange. Anderson had been general manager of the Chrysler-Plymouth division and became unhappy when his subordinate at Chrysler, John Riccardo, was promoted over him. "It's not that I have to be on top," Anderson told the *Wall Street Journal.* "I just hate to be shafted." At Rockwell, Anderson advanced quickly, becoming president in 1970 and chief executive officer in 1974. Willard F. Rockwell, Jr., remained chairman. Then in 1978, according to *Business Week,* Rockwell tried to get the board to move Anderson up to vice-chairman "without clear authority." The board instead changed the bylaws to give Anderson complete control, having him report to the board rather than the chairman. "In short," said the *Wall Street Journal,* "Mr. Rockwell became an outside director of his own company." In 1979 Rockwell, then 65, retired from the company. He's still on the board, as is his son, S. Kent Rockwell, president of the company's utility-products group.

Stock performance. Rockwell stock bought for $1,000 in 1970 sold for $2,250 on January 2, 1980.

Access. 600 Grant Street, Pittsburgh, Pennsylvania 15219; (412) 565-2000.

More than one company has taken the cue. At the General Electric display, a hologram of a tightly-bikini'd model rubs a turning engine against her breasts whenever a buyer passes her vicinity. At Pratt and Whitney, the bite is more subtle:

The Pratt and Whitney representative is a short man standing before an audience of military officers and a new sophisticated turbo-engine, the JT15-D; his attention is disturbed by an extremely attractive woman rubbing her fingertips along the side of the display case.

P & W Representative: "Excuse me, Miss Hopkins, but we must get started."

Blonde model (fingertips off the display case): "Hotchkins, sir."

P & W Rep.: "All right, Miss Hot Kiss, but we really must get started."

Hotchkins: "Oh. Sorry."

P & W Rep. (to audience): "Good morning, ladies and gentlemen. My name is G. Evert Thornbeck—"

Hotchkins (jumping and waving wildly): "Hi, Mr. Hornbeck!"

P & W Rep.: "Thornbeck, not Hornbeck."

Hotchkins: "Oh. Sorry."

P & W Rep. (to audience):

"The JT15-D's design is less complex, and less cost-burdensome, and produces increased reliability factors."

Hotchkins (lips pursed to a captain in the audience): "I think I like the JT15-D."

P & W Rep. (stuttering): "F-furthermore, it passed severe F.A.A. tests on birds and ice . . . without a difficulty factor."

Hotchkins (rubbing thighs): "Well, you really do know your factors."

P & W Rep. (rubbing his own thighs): "In the JT15-D, hundreds of delicate and expensive compressor blades are replaced by one rugged, easily manufactured part."

Hotchkins: "That's wonderful." (Her fingers drop to her crotch and separate to about six inches.) "How can anyone put so many good qualities into just one package?"

P & W Rep. (blushing): "Um, um . . . we'll get into that later, Miss . . . um . . . Hot Kiss. Further, the fan turbine has two stages to achieve the small diameter to reduce engine size."

Hotchkins: "Heaven knows, I never could go for one of those big, bulky engines. I bet it's just about your size."

At the end of the show, a

more somber Pratt and Whitney representative walks forward clapping his hands, nodding to an assistant to hand out some rubber footballs. On the sides of the footballs is printed, "PRATT AND WHITNEY—WE'RE ON YOUR TEAM."

"I'm here representing Pratt and Whitney's aircraft division," says the new representative. He leafs through some notes and hides a hand in his jacket. "I've been with Pratt and Whitney for four years, and I've come to the point now where I've begun to feel like part of the team. And that's our subject for today—teamwork. I thought to get this started, I'd find out if we were really all together as far as teamwork is concerned. Now, colonel, I want you to think . . . of a card." His hand pulls out of his jacket, and he waves a fanned deck of cards. "A card that you would find in a normal playing deck, jokers not allowed, and I will name that card. Because here at Pratt and Whitney, you call the shots and we got the answers!"

This article by James E. Cohen appeared in the *The Washington Monthly* in November 1979 and is reprinted by permission.

Show and Tell

"After all, the best part of a holiday is perhaps not so much to be resting yourself, as to see all the other fellows busy working," wrote Kenneth Grahame in *The Wind in the Willows*. Every summer, Americans take to the mills, plants, and breweries of the nation and do just that: watch others work. The Guest Relations Association (representing 61 of 3,500 businesses and institutions that give in-house tours) estimates that in 1976 its business members alone entertained over 4.6 million visitors.

Who gives company tours? Just about everybody. Perhaps best known is the Corning Glass Museum in Corning, New York, followed closely by the Hershey Chocolate factory in Hershey, Pennsylvania. Hershey's tour became so successful in the early 1970s that it interfered with operations, and in 1973 the company built a separate, simulated chocolate factory for tourists. The site logged 1.6 million visitors in 1976.

But there are countless lesser attractions. If you're driving through Barre, Vermont, three makers of granite monuments (Rock of Ages, Associated Memorial Products, and Bilodeau-Barre Company) want to show you their stone. While waiting for the Alaska railroad in Fairbanks, you can drop in on the University of Alaska Musk Ox Experimental Farm. And if you're forced to lay over in Campbellsville, Kentucky, Campbellsville Industries will introduce you to the art of design and manufacture of church steeples and cupolas.

From among myriad potato chipperies and toymakers, kayak and cosmetics manufacturers, rose gardens and lily growers, cheesemakers and jam-producers and mitten-knitters, we've culled a list of out-of-the-way tours

you might take. But as we haven't ducked our heads in through the windows at the Dakota Sash & Door Company in Aberdeen, or any of the other places we mention, you'll have to make arrangements at your own risk:

Hydroculture, Inc., Glendale, Arizona. Dirtless gardeners! They have a 100-acre complex devoted to hydroponic (soilless) growing of vegetables and plants under controlled conditions.

Shields Date Gardens, Indio, California. These growers produce dates, tangerines, and grapefruit, and their tour includes a 30-minute presentation entitled "Romance and Sex Life of the Date."

Fred A. Stewart, Inc., San Gabriel, California. An orchid nursery where you can visit the laboratory (orchids are cloned!), bottle houses, and planting, shipping, and processing departments.

F.I.P. Corporation, Farmington, Connecticut. These people design and build the landscaped building complexes called "industrial parks." Their tour includes an explanation and a walk through their model industrial park prototype.

W. T. Armstrong Co., Elkhart, Indiana. Makers of flutes, piccolos, and saxophones.

AMAX Coal Company, Indianapolis, Indiana. Into the earth you go, to see coal being mined, washed, and processed prior to loading.

Westinghouse Learning Corporation, Iowa City, Iowa. Remember those standardized educational-testing questions you sat through in school? These guys do the test scoring, as well as providing other educational data services, consulting, opinion surveys, and computer-managed instruction (answers not included in tour).

Consolidated Popcorn, Schaller, Iowa. Popcorn producers.

A. Hoen & Company, Baltimore, Maryland. The oldest continuously operating lithographer in the country. Books, maps, advertisements, packing, and printing, since 1865.

Trojan Yachts, Inc., Elkton, Maryland. See a pleasure yacht built.

Charles River Breeding Laboratories, Wilmington, Massachusetts. You may dream of rodents for nights on end after a visit to the droves of laboratory rats and mice bred here.

American Fire Pump & Apparatus, Battle Creek, Michigan. A maker of fire pumps and fire trucks. They'll show you pumpers, aerials, elevating platforms, water towers, and custom-built fire-fighting equipment.

Gooch Foods, Lincoln, Nebraska. A pasta plant.

Kulis Freeze Dry Taxidermy, Bedford, North Dakota. No place for animal-lovers. You can investigate methods and equipment manufacture for freeze dry taxidermy.

Noba, Inc., Tiffin, Ohio. On the scene are facilities and bulls participating in artificial insemination of dairy and beef cattle.

Pensilco Corporation, One Silicon Way, Bradford, Pennsylvania. Makers of electronic silicon crystal slices for the computer industry. See crystal growing and slicing, centerless grinding, and polishing operations.

Spitz Space Systems, Chadds Ford, Pennsylvania. See the simulator equipment behind domed space theaters. The tour includes a visit to a small planetarium classroom, the manufacturing plant, and a demonstration of the Space Simulator.

Garden Spot Badge Company, Lititz, Pennsylvania. A maker of award ribbons.

Dentsply International, York, Pennsylvania. See porcelain and plastic teeth produced, along with dental equipment.

Colonial Mill Farm, South Kingstown, Rhode Island. A friendly watercress farm.

Black Sun Herb Farm, San Antonio, Texas. A tour of historical buildings and gardens where they grow culinary and medicinal herbs.

Vitri-Forms, Brattleboro, Vermont. Makers of lasers and scientific apparatus—and also hand-blown glass flowers, jewelry, and animals.

The Orvis Company, Manchester, Vermont. Bamboo and glass fishing rod makers.

Aerocar, Longview, Washington. Did these far-sighted fellows choose the town of Longview for its name? They make experimental light aircraft and flying automobiles.

Companies provide a variety of accommodations for their visitors, from taped tours to free samples to guides speaking a handful of languages—the Mayflower Glass Factory in Latrobe, Pennsylvania, for example, will translate their tours into Croatian, Polish, Spanish, and Yugoslavian.

The United States is not your only tour territory.

Schedule that Puerto Rican vacation just right and you can view the cutting and sewing rooms of the Carol Foundation brassiere manufactory, pass through the funeral supplies at Buxeda Caskets, pop into Ford Gum & Machine's chewing gum plant and Marmoles El Rey's marble quarry, and end the day with a visit to Bacardi's distillery for a tour and free drinks—and then perhaps reel into one of the products of the Hamacas De Puerto Rico hammock factory with that last Bacardi in hand.

THE MOST EXPENSIVE ELECTRIC UTILITIES

1. CONSOLIDATED EDISON (New York)	7.6¢ *per kilowatt-hour*
2. HAWAII ELECTRIC LIGHT (Hilo)	6.7¢ *per kilowatt-hour*
3. SAN DIEGO GAS & ELECTRIC (California)	5.4¢ *per kilowatt-hour*
4. LONG ISLAND LIGHTING (Mineola, New York)	5.4¢ *per kilowatt-hour*
5. ORANGE & ROCKLAND (Pearl River, New York)	5.3¢ *per kilowatt-hour*
6. PUBLIC SERVICE CO. OF NEW MEXICO (Albuquerque)	5.3¢ *per kilowatt-hour*
7. UNITED ILLUMINATING (New Haven, Connecticut)	5.2¢ *per kilowatt-hour*
8. IOWA ELECTRIC LIGHT & POWER	5.2¢ *per kilowatt-hour*
9. BOZRAH LIGHT & POWER (Connecticut)	5.1¢ *per kilowatt-hour*
10. NARRAGANSETT ELECTRIC (Providence, Rhode Island)	4.9¢ *per kilowatt-hour*

And the Least Expensive

1. WASHINGTON WATER POWER (Spokane)	1.2¢ *per kilowatt-hour*
2. CHEYENNE LIGHT, FUEL & POWER (Wyoming)	1.3¢ *per kilowatt-hour*
3. PACIFIC POWER & LIGHT (Portland, Oregon)	1.4¢ *per kilowatt-hour*
4. IDAHO POWER (Boise)	1.5¢ *per kilowatt-hour*
5. MONTANA POWER (Butte)	1.5¢ *per kilowatt-hour*
6. PUGET SOUND POWER & LIGHT (Bellevue, Washington)	1.7¢ *per kilowatt-hour*
7. CP NATIONAL (San Francisco)	1.7¢ *per kilowatt-hour*
8. LOUISIANA POWER & LIGHT (New Orleans)	2.1¢ *per kilowatt-hour*
9. SOUTHWESTERN ELECTRIC POWER (Shreveport, Louisiana)	2.1¢ *per kilowatt-hour*
10. PORTLAND GENERAL ELECTRIC (Oregon)	2.3¢ *per kilowatt-hour*

Source: *Forbes*, March 17, 1980. Data from the National Utility Service, Inc.

13

FUN AND GAMES

Star Makers

Columbia Pictures

Sales: $629 million
Profits: $33.1 million
Founded: 1924
Employees: 3,800
Headquarters: New York, New York

What they do. Rita Hayworth. Clark Gable. Marlon Brando. Jean Harlow. John Wayne. Edward G. Robinson. William Holden. Kim Novak. Frank Capra. Howard Hawks. Dore Schary. Dorothy Parker. Ben Hecht. Many of Hollywood's greatest actors, directors, and screenwriters came together at Columbia Pictures during the Golden Era of the movies. The studio's trademark, a draped maiden in a Statue of Liberty pose, has appeared at the start of many classics: *It Happened One Night, Platinum Blonde, His Girl Friday, From Here to Eternity, All the King's Men, The Caine Mutiny, On the Waterfront.*

In recent years Columbia's dramas on celluloid have taken a back seat to the melodrama enacted in their own boardroom. In 1979 *Fortune* set the scenario like this:

A movie company is rocked by scandal when it discovers that one of its key executives stole $84,208 by forging checks and padding his expense account. The executive is suspended, then reinstated, and finally forced to resign—but not before negotiating a $600,000-a-year independent production contract with the company. The handling of the incident creates such mistrust between the board and the chief executive that a bitter feud ensues and the c.e.o. is fired. New managers are installed, others resign. Despite all the turmoil, the company becomes a star performer on the Fortune 500.

A new battle for control broke out at Columbia in 1980 between major stockholders Kirk Kerkorian and the Allen & Company investment firm. But in spite of the ruckus, Columbia has turned out several major box-office hits in recent years, including *Kramer vs. Kramer, The China Syndrome, The Deep, California Suite,* and *Close Encounters of the*

Third Kind. They also produce such television shows as "Fantasy Island," "Charlie's Angels," and the soap opera "Days of Our Lives." They shoot made-for-TV movies and produce TV commercials for companies like General Motors and Procter & Gamble. Production of films of all types accounts for about three-quarters of their revenues. Columbia owns country and rock radio stations in West Virginia, Alabama, and Utah. D. Gottlieb of Chicago, which they bought in 1976, is a leading maker of pinball machines, with plants in Illinois and North Dakota.

The profitability of a Hollywood movie no longer depends solely on exhibiting the film in theaters. Columbia and the other studios have learned to spin their movies off in other directions: records, books, games, home video cassettes, television rights, airline screenings. If the movie is popular enough, they can license manufacturers to turn out anything from lunch boxes to sleeping bags based on it. Columbia's D. Gottlieb subsidiary makes a Close Encounters of the Third Kind pinball machine. There's also the foreign market: about one-third of Columbia's take in 1979 came from outside the United States.

History. Harry Cohn, born of immigrant parents and raised in New York City at the turn of the century, followed his older brother Jack into the movie business after a try at vaudeville singing. In 1913 Jack had collaborated on *Traffic in Souls,* a movie about white slavery purportedly based on the "Rockefeller White Slavery Report" and the New York district attorney's investigation of the vice trust. The film proved for the first time that sex sells at the cinema —a lesson that has guided producers ever since. (An ad for the movie read: "A $200,-000 spectacle in 700 scenes with 800 players showing the traps laid for young girls by vice agents.")

Around 1920 Harry Cohn went to work for a film company his brother had started with a friend named Joe Brandt. At first they called themselves CBC Film Sales, from the initials of the three principals. The low-budget company soon became known in the industry as Corned Beef and Cabbage; maybe that's why they changed the name to Columbia Pictures in 1924. Harry Cohn, vice-president in charge of production, was based in Hollywood, while the others stayed in New York. At a time

when the young company badly needed capital, Harry Cohn happened to be courting an old New York girlfriend, whose only drawback was that she was already married. It wasn't such a drawback, as things turned out. Her husband, a prominent lawyer, was generous enough to give her $250,000 in a divorce settlement. She then married Cohn, who sank the money into Columbia. As the company grew, the brothers hired so many of their relatives that Robert Benchley dubbed it the Pine Tree Studio "because it has so many Cohns."

Harry Cohn became the prototypical Hollywood producer. Vulgar, gruff, uneducated; he wielded absolute power, firing underlings who made the wrong chance remark and elevating others who made the right one. Hollywood lore is rich with tales of Cohn's lust for young actresses trying to break into movies. A special passageway ran from his office to a dressing room occupied by a succession of starlets.

In his biography *King Cohn,* Bob Thomas tells of how the boss angrily summoned a writer and producer to his office. "You college men!" Cohn bellowed. "I pay you bastards thousands of dollars a week to know something, and what do I get? Ignorance!" It seems that in reviewing the script of an Arabian Nights fantasy, Cohn had come across an expression that struck him as anachronistic. "I never went to college like you sons of bitches, but I can tell you one thing: they didn't say 'yes, sirree' in 1200. It's all through this script, goddammit. You've got 'em all saying, 'Yes, sirree.' " The producer asked to look at the script. "But, Harry," he protested, "that's 'Yes, sire'!"

In contrast to the studio's boss, Columbia's movies, populated with gorgeous women in long gowns and handsome men in dinner jackets, gained a reputation for ultrasophistication. Trying to carve out a corner in an industry already dominated by giants like Metro-Goldwyn-Mayer and Paramount, but lacking the money to keep big stars under contract, Columbia had to lure them with good scripts and crack directors. They also took great care with the quality of their prints, and their sound was said to be the best in the business.

Cohn was president of the company from 1932 till his death at 67 in 1958. His judgment of scripts and stars, though phenomenally successful, was not infallible. He dropped Marilyn Monroe after a six-month tryout in 1949.

Cohn was succeeded by Abe Schneider, who had delivered newspapers to Columbia's New York office in the 1920s and had come up through the company's bookkeeping department. For a time the studio went on producing box-office hits (such as *Oliver* and *A Man for All Seasons*) under the guidance of studio chief Michael J. Frankovich. But they began to falter in the early 1970s after Frankovich left. Sinking money into costly flops, among them *Lost Horizon* and *1776*, they lost more than $80 million in three years. Some observers thought it was curtains for Columbia.

Exit Abe Schneider and enter the New York investment-banking firm of Allen & Co., which bought a controlling interest in Columbia in 1973 and installed Alan Hirschfield, an Allen employee, as president, and David Begelman, a leading talent agent, as head of the company's Hollywood movie operations. Under Begelman the studio rebounded with a string of winners, including *Shampoo*, *The Deep*, and the spectacularly successful *Close Encounters of the Third Kind*.

Shortly before the premiere of *Close Encounters*, in September of 1977, Begelman was abruptly suspended. The company discovered that he had forged $61,008 worth of company checks and diverted another $23,200 in questionable expense account items. Begelman had been drawing a $234,000-a-year salary, with bonuses and perks that boosted his pay to almost $400,000. According to the *Wall Street Journal*, he "had been an avid gambler in the past and lived consistently 'close to the financial precipice,' as one friend put it." Begelman, who repaid the money, later pleaded no contest to a charge of grand theft and was fined $5,000.

The fallout from the Begelman affair landed in the boardroom. Accounts of what happened inside the company vary, but Begelman was reinstated in December. Amid public outcry over his reinstatement he resigned the following February, but he left with a three-year independent-production contract that left him better off financially than when he was head of the studio. After Begelman's suspension, according to some reports, the majority of the directors insisted that he be reinstated, but Hirschfield resisted—either on principle or because he wanted to run the movie operation himself. According to others, the initiative to bring Begelman back came from Hirschfield himself. At any rate, relations between Hirschfield and the board deteriorated rapidly,

and in July of 1978 they asked him to resign. When he refused, they fired him. In his place they installed Francis T. Vincent, Jr., a Washington lawyer with no prior film experience.

Reputation. Since the early days of the industry, movie companies have been pawns in a tug-of-war between New York money and California operations. That game is still being played out today at Columbia: Allen of New York versus Kerkorian of California. Many observers foresee a full-scale fight between Allen and Kerkorian over control of the company.

What they own. The days are gone when nearly all films were shot on giant studio lots. The upkeep is just too expensive. So in 1972 Columbia sold their 14-acre lot in Hollywood and their 36-acre ranch in Burbank and formed with Warner Bros. a company called The Burbank Studios: the two companies take turns using Warner's 100-acre Burbank property when studio shots are called for. One of Columbia's most valuable assets is their film library; it contains 1,800 movies just waiting for the home video disc market to take off.

Who owns and runs the company. Although Allen & Company owns 10% of the stock, compared to Kerkorian's 25%, the board of directors is likely to remain on Allen's side through the end of 1981. When Kerkorian bought most of his Columbia stock in 1979, he signed an agreement with Columbia's management that he would not try to buy any more Columbia stock until January 1, 1982. Kerkorian also owns 48% of MGM, and the Justice Department tried to block his purchase of Columbia stock on antitrust grounds, but Kerkorian won in court.

Leo Jaffe, a longtime Columbia employee, became chairman in 1973. He reportedly cast the only vote to keep Hirschfield as president in 1978.

In the public eye. David Begelman, who moved over to MGM as head of their movie division in 1979, wasn't Columbia's only controversial employee. The company hired Clive Davis in 1974 to run their new record division, Arista Records, even though CBS had fired Davis as head of their record division a year earlier, accusing him of having misappropriated funds for such purposes as a $17,000 bar mitzvah for his son. Arista quickly rose to prominence under Davis, signing Barry Manilow, Patti Smith, the Grateful Dead, and others before Columbia sold Arista to Bertelsmann AG, a German company, in 1979.

Where they're going. Not to Los Angeles, even though most of their business is conducted there. MGM and Twentieth Century-Fox moved their headquarters out of New York years ago. In 1973 Columbia announced plans to follow suit, but they canceled the move two months later. There's really not much to move. Columbia is not a large employer. Control is where the money is.

Stock performance. Columbia Pictures stock bought for $1,000 in 1970 sold for $1,304 on January 2, 1980.

Access. 711 Fifth Avenue, New York, New York 10022; (212) 751-4400. (Allen & Co. has the same address.)

Consumer brands.

Columbia Pictures.

Sales: $797 million
Profits: $114 million
Rank in amusement parks: 1
Founded: 1923
Employees: 21,000
Headquarters: Burbank, California

What they do. Although a lot of people, especially intellectuals, have sneered at Walt Disney for 40 or 50 years, he was a true genius at film-making and, more than many of the other people who have worked in Hollywood, he put his stamp on American culture. His animated creatures on the screen captured the imagination of not only Americans but of just about everyone else in the world who saw the cartoons.

When Japan's Emperor Hirohito visited the United States he met the president and conferred with senators and congressmembers on weighty matters of trade between the two nations. But in the living rooms of Tokyo the highlight of the trip was a picture of Hirohito meeting with Mickey Mouse at Disneyland. Nikita Khrushchev threw a temper tantrum when he couldn't get into Disneyland.

Disneyland in Anaheim, California, and Disney World in Orlando, Florida, symbolize America to non-Americans around the world. So popular are they that social critics never tire of analyzing them. Michael Harrington, author of *The Other America*, visited Disney World and called it "a corporate utopia, a pretentious and socially conscious fun house." The German commentator Dankwert Grube insists that "German builders, architects, and above all, city planners should be forced, in chains if need be, to find out from the Mickey Mouse people how one can create an environment in which laughter flourishes and well-being is produced."

Most people don't need to be forced to visit Disney's parks or watch a Disney film. Debt-free, with $315 million in ready cash, Disney Productions is not only a grand nurturer of fantasy, it is also one of the most fruitful money trees in Hollywood.

The secret? Disney's public relations department calls it "imagineering" (imagina-

> David Friedman, chairman of the board of the Adult Film Association of America, estimates that 1979 pornographic tape sales were $7 to $7.5 million, or roughly 60–70% of the videotape business. However, *Merchandising* ranks *The Godfather* as number 1 on the videotape charts, followed by *Saturday Night Fever*, *Godfather II*, *M*A*S*H*, and *The Sound of Music*.
>
> —*Merchandising*, January 1980.

tion plus engineering). Ideas churned out by WED Enterprises (the company's creative center) are materialized into entertainment parks, movies, comic strips, TV shows, books, and music. In addition, Disney does a big business selling their name to makers of such things as coonskin caps and school desks. The two "theme parks" (Disney World and Disneyland) are their hottest items, however, accounting for 70% of income. Fourteen million people a year visit Disney World, which is now booking space a full 11 months in advance. Although box-office receipts for new films are down domestically (they're still climbing overseas), Disney's old movies, rereleased every seven years to catch yet another wave of tots (not to mention their nostalgic elders) are still referred to as "Fort Knox" in the Disney boardroom.

History. Despite the belief of many that Walt Disney was a great cartoonist, Disney's genius was as an idea man, decision-maker, and story editor. In fact, Disney was unable to draw Donald Duck or any of his other famous characters, according to author Richard Schickel in *The Disney Version*. Even Mickey Mouse was done by someone else—an old friend of Disney's named Ub Iwerks, who received screen credit for his handiwork in *Steamboat Willie* and other early cartoons. Disney was known to ask his animators to show him how to turn out a quick sketch of Mickey to accompany autographs. More embarrassing was the fact that Disney's signature bore no resemblance to the famous logo that appeared on all his products. According to Schickel, a number of people threw away authentically signed books and records under the impression that the autographs were fake.

Walt Disney grew up on a small farm in Missouri; his father was a member of the Congregational Church and a proponent of socialism. Schickel writes that Disney knew what "Protestant, middle-class, midwestern America" was all about. "What he liked, it liked." He also picked up a bit of anti-Semitism, which he showed in a rather nasty caricature of a Jewish peddler in his first big cartoon success, *The Three Little Pigs.*

Following the bankruptcy of his first cartoon business in Kansas City, Disney went to Hollywood in 1923 to join his brother Roy, who was turning out silent comedies in a garage. With a small staff of animators, Disney made the first Mickey Mouse cartoon *(Steamboat Willie)* in 1928, and suddenly he was in the animation business. After a long string of cartoon shorts, including *The Three Little Pigs*, which contributed the first hit song from a cartoon ("Who's Afraid of the Big Bad Wolf"), Disney decided to make an animated feature film in 1937. The result was *Snow White*, the film that put Disney Productions squarely in the black.

One animator remembers that Disney acted out the entire story of *Snow White*, playing all the parts, in several hours. It's a testimony to Walt Disney's talents as a story editor that Disney writers today, almost 15 years after Walt's death, still ask, "How would Walt have done it?" when working on a script. From 1932–1942 Disney won an Oscar every year but two. His cartoons were the first to get marquee billing. Disney never rested on the success of one cartoon; nor did he issue sequel after sequel of popular cartoons. He took chances on features like *Pinocchio* and *Fantasia*. (Walt Disney's comment on *Fantasia*, scored to classical music, was "Gee, this'll make Beethoven.")

During the 1950s, when TV was sapping Hollywood's strength, Disney's was the only studio to prosper. Walt realized early that television was a perfect mate for the

Walt Disney's Train Wreck Hobby

Since he worked 12-hour days, Walt Disney didn't have much free time. What little he had he devoted to a scale model, half-mile-long railroad that wound around his estate. A good deal of the Disneys'

social life revolved around giving visitors rides on the train; a select few were given cards designating them "vice-presidents" of the railroad.

When he was planning the road, Disney had his lawyers

draft right-of-way contracts for his wife and daughters to sign. He presented the documents so solemnly that the family stood poised with their pens before the impish cartoon king declared that their

Disney imagination; two shows—"The Mickey Mouse Club" and "Disney's Wonderful World"—soon proved it. Disney hocked his life insurance and peddled TV programs to raise money to build Disneyland, a shocking gamble at a time when the words *amusement park* conjured up images of wind-blown, trash-piled acres in crumbling seaside resorts. By 1960 he was sole owner of the most successful amusement park in America.

In 1966, when Walt Disney died of lung cancer at 65, his fantasy empire was booming. Since then the studio's animated films have lost much of their sparkle, but other projects Disney had planned were carried off successfully—particularly Disney World, which opened in Orlando, Florida, in 1971; and the more recent EPCOT (Experimental Prototype Community of Tomorrow), Walt's dream city, which opens in 1982 just two miles (by monorail) from Disney World.

Reputation. Mister Clean. Accused by Schickel of having a "rage to order, control, and keep clean any environment," Disney tries to project the most wholesome image in American business. Their dress and hair code makes the U.S. Marines look liberal and sometimes upsets employees—they have not been immune to strikes. Environmentalists dread the prospect of still more "theme parks" across the country. The Third World is offended by the paternalistic attitude toward "primitives" expressed in Disney films and cartoons. Animators say they've lost the old magic. But families keep trooping to their wholesome movies and mobbing their entertainment parks. Reputation depends on who's looking.

What they own. Disney's Orlando holdings (Disney World and EPCOT) amount to a plot of land the size of San Francisco. Then there's Disneyland, in Anaheim; the Burbank studio and offices; and a 708-acre ranch in the San Fernando Valley used for shooting their own movies and rented out to other motion picture producers.

Who owns and runs the company. Contrary to popular belief, Walt Disney does not send Tinkerbell down from Heaven with directives to the board. The chairman and chief executive officer is an old Disney hand, E. Cardon Walker, who was 64 in 1980. Walker joined the company in 1938 as a messenger, working his way up through the advertising department. In the president's spot is Ronald W. Miller, 46, who is married to one of Walt Disney's daughters. The 1979 proxy statement sent to shareholders disclosed that Roy E. Disney (son of Walt's brother Roy) held 5.2% of the stock. Another 6% was held by an employee stock ownership plan.

In the public eye. Disney was stung a couple of years ago by the sudden mid-project walkout of Don Bluth and 11 other animators, who complained of the tight-fisted attitude toward animation since Walt's death. Fred Calvert, another animator who had left earlier, claimed that "if Walt was still alive, it would have been Disney that made *Star Wars.*"

Where they're going. Disney recently discovered that there was such a thing as life after puberty, and accordingly went after a more adult audience in 1979 with *The Black Hole*—a $17.5 million science fiction thriller. Walker insisted that "we're not deserting the children," but Miller said: "Our society's changing, and we have to change with it."

EPCOT, due to open in 1982 in Florida, is Walt's $600 million dream of a sort of permanent, futuristic World's Fair—a planned, controlled community and a showcase for American technology, includ-

verbal consent would be enough. Then he donned his engineer's cap and began building, grading, and even digging a tunnel under his wife's prize flowerbeds.

Disney especially enjoyed planning wrecks because he had so much fun repairing the damage. Once, after buying two new engines, he told George Murphy (then an actor and one of the road's "vice-presidents"; later a U.S. senator): "Boy, we're sure going to have some wrecks now!"

Source: Richard Schickel, *The Disney Version* (Simon & Schuster, 1968).

ing solutions to problems of ecology, transportation, energy, and the like.

Another Disneyland is going up, too, but Disney won't own this one, in Tokyo. Despite the ardent response of the Japanese people to Hirohito's meeting with Mickey Mouse, Walker says no profit is worth the headaches of running a company in Japan. So Disney will take a 10% cut for design and maintenance while the Japanese foot all the bills.

Stock performance. Disney stock bought for $1,000 in 1970 sold for $1,562 on January 2, 1980.

Major employment centers. Orlando, Florida; Anaheim, California; and Burbank, California.

Access. 500 Buena Vista, Burbank, California 91521; (213) 845-3141. There are no organized tours of the studio, but consumers can write to Mike Spencer, Walt Disney Productions, at the above address for information.

Consumer brands.

Walt Disney (Mickey Mouse, Donald Duck, and other Disney characters are licensed to others).

MCA

Sales: $1.4 billion
Profits: $139 million
Forbes 500 rank: 362
Founded: 1924
Employees: 19,000
Headquarters: Universal City, California

What they do. MCA is probably the only entertainment company where top executives are required to wear suits and ties. "We're a business," explains one of the 19 vice-presidents. In an industry where turtlenecks, beards, shaggy heads, and jeans (albeit designer) are the norm, MCA—the biggest name in television and movie production—stands out like a CPA at a rock concert. In fact, until recently MCA executives wore only *black* suits. One observer

remarked when a group of the company's top men arrived at a conference, "Here come the penguins."

MCA has been the strong arm in Hollywood for as long as anyone would care to remember. They run, to put it mildly, a tight ship. Their Universal Studios, described as "a busy place," schedules as many as 300 shooting days in a month. This kind of scheduling has made some producers compare Universal to a factory turning out films like sausages. One sound editor says, "We're into quantity, not quality." MCA's recent hits have included *Jaws, The Sting,* and *Airport '75.*

Though movies contribute nearly two-thirds of MCA's revenue, an executive insists, "MCA is not a movie company; we're an entertainment factory." One of the country's biggest tourist attractions (3 million visitors a year) is the Universal Studios Tour. MCA also runs the concessions at Yosemite National Park and at several national landmarks. For 1980 they scheduled production of 20 films, over 11 hours of TV shows, several made-for-TV movies, 90 record albums, and 675 books, including such bestsellers as Steve Martin's *Cruel Shoes* and Mario Puzo's *Fools Die* (their publishing concerns include G. P. Putnam's and *The Runner* magazine). And there's more on the MCA conveyor belt: plans to add 40 Spencer Gift stores to the nearly 400 they had in 1979, and to expand their line of video discs, cassettes, and players. Their miscellaneous enterprises include savings and loan associations, computer and financial services, and real estate development.

Often called the General Motors of the entertainment industry, MCA keeps close tabs on costs. "You have to fill out requisition forms for just about everything. It can drive you crazy," a movie production assistant complained to the *Los Angeles Times.* Stories abound about secretaries who are allotted only so many pencils a month.

But even MCA loses track of the purse strings on occasion, according to Larraine Gary, who is married to president Sid Sheinberg and who played an important role in the MCA blockbuster *Jaws.* Originally budgeted to cost around $4 million, *Jaws* eventually devoured $9 million. Sheinberg is often credited with not pulling the plug as the film ate up more and more money. Yet Gary says her husband didn't realize how much *Jaws* was costing. "There was a screw-up between the production office and the accounting department," Sheinberg conceded. "If we'd known all the facts, we might have cancelled it."

Such screw-ups are rare at MCA.

Thirty-seven unions represent employees at Universal Studios. Pay and benefits are reportedly good, but when Universal gave a cost-of-living increase as specified in the contracts, MCA raised the prices of food in the employees' commissary and the monthly fees in company parking lots.

MCA is a company that garners more respect than love—respect not just from stockholders, who have seen the price of their shares multiply *seven times* in the past decade, but also from union representatives, who see chairman Lew Wasserman as a fair and honest man. Though a hard negotiator, Wasserman is known to stick religiously to a deal. Bill Howard, president of the AFL-CIO Hollywood Film Council, said in 1973, "If we only had Lew to deal with, we'd have no problems. He's spread a little thin these days, but he's a man of his word."

Writers and producers agree. "He's ice, pure ice in negotiations," says one writer. "He'll take your hair, your arms, your legs and even your fingernails in a deal, but he won't lie—he'll tell you." Many producers contend that MCA's businesslike approach to production is what makes Universal a growing concern, allowing them to make more and more films and create more and more jobs in an industry not known for steady employment.

History. There was a time in MCA's history when they weren't known as "General Motors" or "the factory"; they were "the octopus." The epithet referred to their hold on the biz. By the end of World War II they were the largest talent agency in the country, controlling half of the top-name stars and scooping up big 10% commissions. "Octopus" also referred to the ominous way they tended to wrap themselves around people. "They make me so mad I could cut their throats," bandleader Tommy Dorsey once told *Variety*, "but I've got to play ball with them." Ronald Reagan, Jimmy Stewart, Bette Davis—MCA had them all.

MCA was started by Jules C. Stein in 1924. In those days Stein (now in his eighties) was putting himself through the University of Chicago medical school by play-

ing "schmaltzy" violin and saxophone. Though he once told the *Wall Street Journal* he "was never a good musician," the money wasn't bad, and Stein and his band began getting more gigs than they could do themselves. So he started booking other bands into clubs and summer resorts in the Chicago area, charging the band leaders a commission. Business boomed. Meanwhile, Stein graduated, but he found the music business more compelling than the career in ophthalmology he had prepared for.

In 1924, with $1,000 capital, he founded the Music Corporation of America. By the early 1930s Stein had a flourishing national talent agency. In 1936 he signed on Lew Wasserman as national director for advertising and public relations. Wasserman, 22 at the time, quickly became MCA's top agent, at the same time acquiring an extensive knowledge of show business taxes and law. MCA moved to California in 1937, where Wasserman was the first agent ever to get stars a percentage of a movie's earnings instead of a straight salary, thus spreading income over many years and making James Stewart, among others, a millionaire.

In 1946 Stein made Wasserman, at age 33, president of MCA. Wasserman soon convinced Stein that television held the pot of gold at the end of the rainbow. Though the first years were lean, by the mid-1950s MCA's Revue Productions was solidly in the black, turning out such early favorites as "Alfred Hitchcock Presents," "Bachelor Father," and the "General Electric Theater" (hosted by Ronald Reagan). They became the nation's biggest producer of TV shows. Some of their most popular shows: "Wagon Train," "The Virginian," "Rockford Files," "Rich Man, Poor Man," and "The Six Million Dollar Man."

MCA did not start producing films for theaters until the mid-1960s, although they had been on the edge of the film industry for years. In the 1950s they bought Paramount's pre-1948 film library of over 750 films to rent to television. They also bought the Universal Studios lot, which they have since turned into one of the all-time greats of publicity. They charge admission to see an exhibit that is an advertising promotion for their own products. The Studios are the third-largest tourist attraction in southern California, and bring in about $20 million worth of income a year.

MCA finally took the plunge into theater

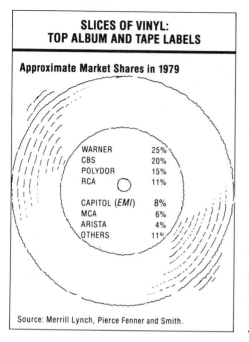

SLICES OF VINYL: TOP ALBUM AND TAPE LABELS

Approximate Market Shares in 1979

WARNER	25%
CBS	20%
POLYDOR	15%
RCA	11%
CAPITOL (*EMI*)	8%
MCA	6%
ARISTA	4%
OTHERS	11%

Source: Merrill Lynch, Pierce Fenner and Smith.

films in 1966 when they merged with Decca, the company that owned Universal. By this time they had completely given up their function as a talent agency and were ready to move over to the other side of the bargaining table as a film producer. They went on to become one of the leading motion picture makers. Their first big winner was *Airport* in 1970. *Jaws*, in 1975, broke all box-office records. *The Sting* was also a smash. *The Deer Hunter* won five Academy Awards in 1979. But MCA is still deriving more income from television films ("Quincy," "Rockford Files," and "The Incredible Hulk") than theatrical releases. In the 1979–80 season they were supplying eight hours of prime time (evening) network programming every week.

Reputation. Here's a vignette from the *Los Angeles Times* of the efficiency at debt-free MCA:

A writer went to start work on a film, parking in the space where his name had been stenciled on a sign. He found that the office he had just been assigned had been stripped bare—not even a trashcan. A call to his agent revealed that MCA had decided to cancel the film, though they would pay him. When he went back to his car, his name had already been removed from the sign, and there was a ticket on the windshield.

The 10-K is a detailed report companies are required to file with the Securities and Exchange Commission. Most companies will send it to those who request it free of charge. MCA will do that for shareholders; nonshareholders must pay $10.

What they own. Called the "tower of fear," "the black tower," and "the monolith," MCA's 15-story building dominates the San Fernando Valley landscape. It sits in the middle of a 420-acre complex of offices, restaurants, a hotel, an amphitheater, sound stages, and back-lot sets, called Universal City Studios. During the 1950s this was the site of the run-down Universal Studio lot. MCA bought it when most movie companies were trying to get rid of their properties to reduce overhead. According to *New West* writer Andrew Tobias, MCA wanted space to make their TV shows and they "realized that the San Fernando Valley was as populous as Baltimore—without a *single* good hotel." On the 420 acres MCA constructed the base of their filming operations, but also a hot tourist and leisure spot. Universal City's current value is estimated at $500 million.

Who owns and runs the company. Jules Stein is the biggest owner of MCA stock, with 16%. Stein, said to have made a separate fortune in the stock market, is one of the richest men in the world. *New West*'s Tobias wrote: "Call him the Four-Hundred-and-Six-Million-Dollar Man, give or take a couple of hundred million." The second biggest stockholder is Chairman Lew Wasserman, with 8%, about $10 million worth.

In the public eye. In 1974 MCA and environmental groups like the Sierra Club and Friends of the Earth started a long and loud fight over the development of Yosemite National Park. Having received the concession rights in the park, MCA proposed hotels, trams, tennis courts, and more, circulating a pamphlet which described Yosemite as "Nature's eloquent answer to a convention city. The perfect site for sales meetings, seminars, and conventions." The Sierra Club was outraged. The pamphlet was withdrawn. By 1978 the National Park Service had taken steps to severely limit the development, while MCA protested that "by federal law, the concessionaire is guaranteed a reasonable opportunity to make a fair profit."

This is the photograph Twentieth Century-Fox sends out when you ask for a picture of Sherry Lansing, head of production. Lansing's official title is president of Twentieth Century-Fox Productions.

In 1976 MCA put $3 million into a subsidiary called MCA New Ventures to finance blacks, other minorities, and women who have their own entertainment companies.

Where they're going. Lew Wasserman believes the market for home videodiscs (record discs that project images on a television screen) is "mind-boggling," and MCA plans to be the videodisc company that boggles the most minds. They have a powerful partner in IBM, with whom they have joined to form a company that will develop and market videodiscs.

Stock performance. MCA stock bought for $1,000 in 1970 sold for $7,365 on January 2, 1980.

Access. 100 Universal City Plaza, Universal City, California 91608; (213) 985-4321.

Consumer brands.

Movies: Universal.
Records: MCA Coral.
Book publishing: G. P. Putnam's; Jove; Berkley; Coward, McCann & Geoghegan.
Magazines: The Runner.
Retail and mail order stores: Spencer Gifts.
Financial services: Columbia Savings and Loan Association.
Recreation services: Universal Studios Tour and Amphitheatre; Yosemite Park and Curry Company; Landmark Services.

Sales: $658 million
Profits: $57.3 million
Founded: 1933
Employees: 6,300
Headquarters: Los Angeles, California

What they do. Saved by Darth Vader. And Obi Wan Kenobi, Luke Skywalker, a portly perambulating cylinder called R2D2, a platinum butler named Threepio, a laser-beam sword, and all the rest of the mythofantastic stuff that made *Star Wars* the biggest box-office attraction in movie history. Twentieth Century-Fox had been in financial quicksand for most of the last two decades. But in 1977 the Force was with them. Putting a modest $10 million behind a script that other big studios had turned down, Fox found themselves with a $200 million take at the end of the first year —a figure that has more than doubled since.

It wasn't the first time Twentieth Century-Fox had been snatched from the brink of ruin by a blockbuster. Cleopatra, who was the downfall of some prominent Romans 2,000 years ago, came back to haunt Fox in the early 1960s when they made a movie of the story. During the filming in Rome, Richard Burton and Elizabeth Taylor became lovers, leaving their spouses. The production went far over budget, soaking up money faster than Fox could pour it in, and it was never a great box-office hit. The company lost nearly $40 million in 1962. Just to keep going, they sold off 260 of the 334 acres on their back lot in Century City to the Aluminum Company of America for $43 million. Then along came *The Sound of Music*, the most successful film Hollywood had ever seen, to put Fox back on their feet.

After *Star Wars*, Fox found themselves in the unfamiliar position of having more money than they knew what to do with. They decided to do what anyone else would do—go on a shopping spree. They bought a Coca-Cola bottling company in Minnesota ($27 million); Aspen Skiing, the nation's biggest ski resort operator, with four big areas in Colorado ($48 million); Magnetic Video, which sells prerecorded video cassettes ($7 million); and Pebble Beach Corporation, which operates a luxury hotel, golf course, and related amenities on 3,750 acres of California's Monterey Peninsula ($72 million).

Back at the studio, Fox continues to issue 12 to 15 films a year. Offerings in recent years have included *Norma Rae, Breaking Away, Alien, The Rose, An Unmarried Woman, The Turning Point,* and *Julia.* In 1980 they released *The Empire Strikes Back,* a sequel to *Star Wars.*

Fox also has a finger in television, producing series like "M*A*S*H," "Paper Chase," and "Dinah!" They own and run TV stations in Minneapolis, Salt Lake City, and San Antonio. They process film for themselves and other movie makers and TV producers at a lab in Hollywood. In Australia and New Zealand they do what they're forbidden to do in the United States: they own movie theaters—more than 100 of them. They also have a money-losing record division that puts out albums by a few musicians of distinctly subsuperstar level, such as Barry White and Genya Raven.

History. Twentieth Century-Fox was founded and ruled for more than a quarter-century by the archetypal cigar-chomping movie mogul, Darryl F. Zanuck, who broke into the business in 1924 as a writer for Rin-Tin-Tin, the dog star, at Warner Brothers. Zanuck became Warner's production chief in 1927, at age 24. He quit Warner in 1933 and formed the Twentieth Century Company with Joseph M. Schenck, then head of United Artists. Two years later they merged with Fox Film, and Zanuck became vice-president of the combined company, in charge of production.

The studio's output included such award-winning films as *The Grapes of Wrath* (1940), *How Green Was My Valley* (1941), and *Gentleman's Agreement* (1947). The company's emblem of searchlights scanning a Hollywood sky symbolized the glamor that was Hollywood in its heyday. By the 1950s, however, Hollywood's Golden Age had lost its shine; the new mass medium, television, conquered the eyes of America. Movie audiences shrank by two-thirds, and film production declined by three-fourths. Studios could no longer afford exclusive contracts for private stables of stars and directors. Darryl Zanuck's son Richard explained the difference to John Gregory Dunne, author

of *The Studio:* "In the old days, my father could staff and cast a picture in minutes from the card file listing everyone under contract. Nowadays, planning a picture takes longer than making one. Jesus, you spend hours fighting with agents over billing, salary, fringe benefits, start dates, stop dates, the works."

Darryl Zanuck quit in 1956 and went to Paris to become an independent producer, filming such works as *The Sun Also Rises* and *The Longest Day.* Fox's new president, Spyros Skouras, a Greek theater owner, introduced the wide-screen CinemaScope system as an answer to the TV threat, but the movies Fox produced during his reign were generally duds. Zanuck, whose family held the largest block of the company's stock, returned to run the studio in 1962, just in time for the release of the disastrous *Cleopatra.* This time he stayed until 1969, producing such successes as *Patton* and *M*A*S*H.* Then he appointed his son Richard president, retaining for himself the role of chief executive. But *The Sound of Music* had given them the idea that lavish, big-budget productions were the ticket to box-office success. Unchastened by *Cleopatra,* they followed with expensive spectaculars: *Hello, Dolly!, Dr. Dolittle,* and *Tora! Tora! Tora!,* all of which were huge losers. Richard Zanuck resigned under fire in 1970, and his father was ousted four months later when financial vice-president Dennis Stanfill took over. (Ironically, Richard Zanuck went on to become an independent producer with David Brown, husband of *Cosmopolitan* editor Helen Gurley Brown, and made two smashes—*Jaws* and *The Sting* —for Universal, owned by MCA.)

Fox continued to flounder through 1973, when Alan Ladd, Jr., came in to run the film division and pulled out a string of hits culminating in *Star Wars.* In the next five years profits quadrupled, and Twentieth Century-Fox garnered 33 Academy Award nominations. But Ladd quit in 1979 over differences with Stanfill. In January 1980, in a move that rivaled the plot turns of any Hollywood fantasy, Fox announced that Ladd's successor as president of the film division would be 35-year-old Sherry Lansing, Hollywood's first woman production boss. Lansing had gone from being a script reader for an independent producer to a vice-president at MGM to a project director at Columbia Pictures, where she oversaw production of *The China Syndrome* and

Source: *Variety*, January 9, 1980, which uses actual dollars paid by movie theaters to distributors. These figures have *not* been adjusted for inflation. *Gone with the Wind* is thus competing against *Star Wars* with 1939 dollars. More people have paid to see *Gone with the Wind* than *Star Wars*, but *Star Wars* has collected much more in inflated dollars.

The Wages of Wookies

After the phenomenally successful *Star Wars* appeared in 1977, sales of spinoff items became nearly as unreal as the movie's fantasy galaxies: $100,000 worth of *Star Wars* T shirts sold in a month, $260,000 worth of intergalactic bubble gum. Sales of *Star Wars* toys, games, and gimmicks have brought in more than $200 million.

The movie itself—the most successful box-office attraction in history—has returned more than $500 million worldwide to Twentieth Century-Fox, more than $180 million of it in the United States.

Director George Lucas's company, Lucasfilm, gets 40% of profits from the film itself. Fox and Lucasfilm split royalties—5 to 10%—on retail prices of *Star Wars* merchandise. Insiders say their earnings have been over $20 million.

But hundreds of thousands of dollars have been spent in lawsuits against copyright pirates who marketed *Star Wars* toys without licenses. To keep the image of *Star Wars* pure, the FBI and the U.S. Customs office cooperated in cracking down on those who would try to profit illegally from associating liquor, cigarettes, or sex with the pure-minded heroes and heroines of the space adventure.

Source: *Atlantic,* March 1979.

Kramer vs. Kramer. Darryl F. Zanuck, the last of the hardboiled studio bosses, died just two weeks before her appointment.

Reputation. Budd Schulberg, author of the classic Hollywood novel *What Makes Sammy Run?*, singled out Fox as representative of an "atmosphere of paranoia" in 1980 Hollywood. In an article for the *New York Times Magazine*, Schulberg wrote: "Both at Fox and Columbia, each studio viewed the other as 'the enemy camp.' There was wild talk about suits and countersuits. Panic had reached the point where the brass at Fox had begun to fear that if I were to see 'the Columbia people' . . . I might write something 'so destructive as to threaten the very future of the company.'"

What they own. Besides all the subsidiaries they bought with their *Star Wars* profits, Fox still owns some 63 choice acres of their original studio lot, right next to Beverly Hills. Since they don't need a lot of real estate to make movies these days, they've been considering various plans to develop the land into commercial and residential property.

Who owns and runs the company. Dennis Stanfill, a former naval officer and Rhodes scholar, is a strong—some would say tyrannical—studio boss. He has bagged for himself the three top offices of chairman, president, and chief executive officer. Vice-chairman Alan Hirschfield, recruited from Columbia Pictures after Ladd's resignation, oversees much of Fox's film production; he is the one who hired Sherry Lansing. Fox's directors constitute an exclusive club—they include Princess Grace of Monaco (the only woman on the board); Paul Nitze, chairman of Aspen Skiing, former deputy secretary of defense, and Strategic Arms Limitations Talks negotiator; and former secretary of state William Rogers. There is one black director, John Johnson, publisher of *Ebony*. Fox's largest stockholder (20%) is Chris-Craft Industries, which owns television stations and makes boats.

Stock performance. Twentieth Century-Fox stock bought for $1,000 in 1970 sold for $2,304 on January 2, 1980.

Access: 10201 West Pico Boulevard, Los Angeles, California 90035; (213) 277-2211.

Consumer brands.

Twentieth Century-Fox movies, TV shows, records, tapes, and sheet music; Aspen Mountain, Buttermilk, Snowmass, Breckenridge Colorado ski resorts; The Lodge (Pebble Beach, California) luxury hotel.

> There were an estimated 12,275 movie theaters in the United States in 1978, of which 9,048 were indoors and 3,227 were drive-ins; 20% of theaters have more than one screen. Between 1976 and 1978 there was a 1% decline in total number of theaters but an 8% increase in the number of screens.

WARNER COMMUNICATIONS

Sales: $1.6 billion
Profits: $201 million
Forbes 500 rank: 312
Founded: 1918
Employees: 7,500
Headquarters: New York, New York

What they do. Warner is like the kid who has more toys than he knows what to do with. Not only do they own one of the nation's biggest film companies (Warner Bros.) and three of the major record companies (Warner Bros., Atlantic, and Elektra/Asylum/Nonesuch), but they have stuffed into their pockets a professional soccer team, a cosmetics firm, a fancy new cable TV system (the first to include audience participation), a paperback book publisher, a magazine distribution system, a maker of electronic games, and a toy company. On top of that, Warner Communications has made such TV programs as "Kung Fu" and "Streets of San Francisco."

The biggest slice of the Warner pie is music, which accounts for about two-fifths of their sales. Among the stars who have recorded for Warner's various labels are Rod Stewart, Linda Ronstadt, Bob Dylan, Fleetwood Mac, Led Zeppelin, and Joni Mitchell. For aficionados of less popular music, Warner's Nonesuch records are a treasury of hard-to-find Baroque music and music of faraway cultures such as Peru and Tibet.

Warner's movie and TV operations (accounting for about one-third of sales) have produced such box-office hits as *Superman*, *Blazing Saddles*, *Deliverance*, and *Dirty Harry*. Their Panavision subsidiary makes professional motion picture cameras and lenses used by many other filmmakers.

Warner's publishing division (accounting for less than 5% of sales) includes Warner Books, which publishes mass-market paperbacks; Judith Krantz's *Scruples* and Elia Kazan's *Acts of Love* are among their recent successes. They own DC Comics (*Superman*, *Batman*, *Wonder Woman*) and *Mad* magazine. Their Independent News distributes *Playboy*, *National Lampoon*, and other magazines.

Their toys and electronic games division (accounting for one-seventh of sales) includes Atari, which makes coin-operated video games such as Pong and Asteroids as well as video cartridges that allow you to play games—Space Invaders and 3-D Tic-Tac-Toe, for example—on your TV set; Knickerbocker Toy, makers of Raggedy Ann dolls and Sesame Street furniture; and Malibu Grand Prix, which builds mini-race tracks for amusement parks.

Warner's soccer team, the Cosmos, boosted the sport's popularity in the United States tremendously when they signed Brazilian soccer superstar Pelé in 1975; they play their home games at the Meadowlands Sports Complex in East Rutherford, New Jersey. Warner/Lauren is a line of perfumes and cosmetics to which fashion designer Ralph Lauren has lent his name.

Warner Cable (accounting for 5% of sales until American Express bought half interest in 1979) operates 144 cable TV systems in 29 states and recently started experimenting with two-way communications between home viewers and the TV studios. The system, called Qube, allows viewers to push buttons on a device that resembles a pocket calculator and register their various responses with a computer. Warner's 1979 annual report illustrated one use of the system: immediately after a speech by Jimmy Carter, Qube viewers were presented with an instant opinion poll. "Does the President's speech leave you: 1. Optimistic; 2. Pessimistic; 3. Confused." The tabulated responses appeared on the screen instantly; in this case, 61% were optimistic, 18% pessimistic, and 21% confused.

History. Jack, Sam, Harry, and Albert Warner were sons of a Polish immigrant couple who came to the United States around 1890. Charles Higham gives an account of the family's entry into the movie business in his book *Warner Brothers*. Their father, who had been a cobbler in the old country, tried to pursue his trade in Baltimore, but because business was too slow he became an itinerant seller of pots and pans. The family wound up in Youngstown, Ohio, where young Sam got a job as operator of a motion picture projector at a nickelodeon. When the owner went broke, Sam persuaded his father to pawn his watch and chain to buy the projector. The family set up a traveling show, exhibiting a print of *The Great Train Robbery* in surrounding towns. Sam cranked the projector, Jack sang and performed in blackface, and their 13-year-old sister Rose played the piano.

Seeking a permanent home for their operation, the brothers arranged with the owner of a building in New Castle, Pennsylvania, to set up a theater. They had no money for chairs, so they borrowed some from an undertaker on the understanding that if someone died, they would return the chairs for the funeral. From the theater business the brothers moved into making and distributing movies. By 1917 Sam and Jack Warner were turning out slapstick comedies in Los Angeles.

Warner Brothers, more than any other Hollywood studio, gained a reputation for making movies that dealt with political and social themes, usually in simple, low-class settings. Typical of their early offerings were *Open Your Eyes*, a 1919 semidocumentary on syphilis, and *Why Girls Leave Home*, the story of a naive young person shocked by the decadence of high society. Later movies in a similar vein included *Little Caesar*, in which Edward G. Robinson caricatured Al Capone as a ruthless, arrogant gangster; *I Am a Fugitive from a Chain Gang*, the story of a man who escaped from a barbaric Georgia prison; *The Petrified Forest*, a gangster movie starring Bette Davis and Humphrey Bogart, set in a seedy roadside service station in Arizona; and *Rebel without a Cause*, a sympathetic portrait of rebellious youth, starring James Dean.

At the same time, Warner Brothers gave the world Bugs Bunny and Rin-Tin-Tin (said to be one of "the most disagreeable dogs who ever lived"); Busby Berkeley's extravagant displays of choreography, among them *The Gold Diggers of 1933;* the swashbuckling adventures of Errol Flynn; serious film biographies of distinguished people like Florence Nightingale and Louis Pasteur; and the immortal Bogart classics, including *The Maltese Falcon* and *Casablanca*. They also built an enormous chain of movie theaters. By 1930 they owned one-fourth of the theaters in the country, but they were forced to get rid of them in 1949 when the government succeeded in breaking up joint ownership of movie studios and theater chains.

Warner Brothers' film studio went into a financial and artistic decline in the 1950s, and by 1969 the movie operation was virtually defunct. The company, known by this time as Warner Bros.–Seven Arts, consisted primarily of two record companies, Warner/Reprise and Atlantic Records. Steven Ross decided to add the company to the conglomerate he was assembling.

Ross, a former professional football player, may not know the exact difference between disco and soul, or what it takes to make a box-office smash, but he does know how to put a deal together. His first deal, made during the late 1950s, combined his father-in-law's New York City funeral business with a car-rental company and a parking lot operation. Ross realized that a funeral parlor doesn't use its limousines all the time, so he decided to rent them. That was the start of Abbey Rent-a-Car. As a promotional gimmick he tried offering free parking for his rental cars; he made a deal with Kinney, the city's largest operator of parking lots and garages. In 1961 he put all the operations together—funerals, car rentals, and parking, plus a building maintenance company—and called it Kinney Services. Five years later he bought National Cleaning Contractors and named the new firm Kinney National Service.

Ross's company took a turn for the glamorous in 1967, when he bought Ashley Famous, a glittering talent agency. His appetite for entertainment businesses whetted, Ross soon picked up Warner Bros.–Seven Arts.

Ted Ashley of Ashley Famous took charge of the motion picture company and within two years rebuilt it into one of the heavies of the industry. His first big hit was *Woodstock*, followed shortly by a John Wayne picture, *Chisum*. Warner Brothers had two of the box-office smashes of the 1970s: *The Exorcist* and *All the President's Men*. In 1971 the company sold the funeral business and changed their name to Warner Communications.

In 1979 they had the two top motion picture sellers in *Superman* and *Every Which Way But Loose*. Also in 1979 they provided a home for Alan Ladd, Jr., and two of his associates, who fled Twentieth Century-Fox after producing a series of hits, including *Star Wars* and *Silver Streak*. Their first film for Warner's was slated to be *Divine Madness* with Bette Midler.

Reputation. Warner doesn't like to be reminded of their roots in funerals and parking lots, but the references seem inevitable —as when *Forbes* detected "a morbid kind of justice" in Warner's profiting from possession by the dead (in *The Exorcist*). In 1974 *Fortune* characterized Warner's top executives as "a bunch of weirdos with beards

and turtlenecks, mauve cowboy boots, and Gucci loafers." But their reputation in the business world improved suddenly in 1979 when the eminently respectable American Express agreed to give them $175 million for half of Warner Cable, the company's cable TV subsidiary.

What they own. One record-pressing plant in Pennsylvania; three others in West Germany, England, and Brazil. Warner Brothers and Columbia Pictures jointly own a movie studio in Burbank, California. Their agreement allows both companies to use the studio. Employees of the two companies remain separate.

They own a 1,000-acre site in West Milford, New Jersey, formerly the home of Warner's "Jungle Habitat" amusement park. They hope to sell it. They pay annual rent of $4 million for their Rockefeller Center offices. They also own the rights to thousands of popular songs by such composers as George Gershwin, Cole Porter, Bob Dylan, and Rodgers and Hammerstein.

Who owns and runs the company. Records, movies, and books are fields that require relatively few people. Hardly any companies that take in $1.7 billion get by with 7,500 employees.

Like their enterprises, Warner executives tend to be an odd assortment of strong and unusual personalities. Take Atlantic Records founder and president Ahmet Ertegun. As the first person to record Ray Charles, Mary Lou Williams, Leadbelly, and Mable Mercer, Ertegun has been a key figure in the history of black music in America. He came to this country from Turkey in 1934, when he was 11 years old; his father was the Turkish ambassador. In 1978 he was featured in an almost book-length two-part profile in the *New Yorker*. The writer, George W. S. Trow, Jr., recounted innumerable stories about Ertegun's distinctive career, from the jazz concerts he staged in Washington in the 1940s to his close friendships with luminaries like Mick Jagger in the 1970s. He and a partner named Jerry Wexler were responsible for the rise to popularity in the 1950s of rhythm and blues—the music of LaVern Baker, Clyde McPhatter, and many others —which laid the groundwork for rock and roll. He started Atlantic Records in 1947 and linked up with Warner in 1967 for $17 million worth of Warner stock.

Mo Ostin and Joe Smith, known to everyone at Warner Bros. Records as "Mo and Joe," had, like Ertegun, an uncanny sense of style. During the 1960s, while other major companies were still hustling Andy Williams and Tony Bennett, Ostin and Smith were looking to San Francisco psychedelia and London's Carnaby Street. With Warner artists Bill Cosby and Peter, Paul, and Mary paying the bills, Mo and Joe began signing countercultural musicians like the Grateful Dead, the Mothers of Invention, Jimi Hendrix, and the Fugs. Mo Ostin (now president of Warner Bros. Records) and Joe Smith (president of Elektra / Asylum / Nonesuch) transformed Warner Bros. from a Frank Sinatra–type record company to a giant in rock music.

Perhaps the zaniest of the Warner clan is William Gaines, founder and mastermind of Warner's satiric *Mad* magazine. Gaines, who in his late 50s has shoulder-length gray hair and a beard, doesn't much mind being owned by Warner. As he told *Fortune* in 1974, "I can knock their movies in the magazine and know they won't sue me." Gaines cranks out *Mad* from a cluttered three-room suite in midtown Manhattan. He refuses to work in the posh corporate headquarters at Rockefeller Center, saying, "Who wants to move in with your parents?"

Gaines is justified in adopting the attitude of *Mad*'s famous Alfred E. Newman: "What, me worry?" Warner gives the companies they own what chairman Steven J. Ross calls "creative autonomy"; or as the annual report stiffly explains: "The corporation has frequently succeeded in acquiring companies whose strong, entrepreneurially inclined managements knew they could not thrive in an environment of creative second-guessing by a parent com-

pany." A New York banker has another version: "Steve Ross tells me he doesn't know what to do. There's Ahmet [Ertegun] and all these other strange guys and there is no way to understand what they are doing. They make half the profits for him but he doesn't understand how they do it. He says it's a little scary."

The Capital Group, a Los Angeles investment company, owns 8% of Warner's stock. Directors and officers own a total of 6.2%. The board is a family grouping, including in its ranks Edward Rosenthal, identified as "a grandfather of Ross's two children and the three children of another executive officer"; Jacob S. Liebowitz, former head of Warner Publishing, and his nephew, Jay Emmet. Rosenthal and Liebowitz were 80 and 77, respectively, in 1980. Also a director is consumer activist and onetime Miss America Bess Myerson.

Stock performance. Warner Communications stock bought for $1,000 in 1970 sold for $2,194 on January 2, 1980.

Access. 75 Rockefeller Plaza, New York, New York 10019; (212) 484-8000.

Consumer brands.

Records and music publishing: Warner Bros.; Reprise; Elektra/Asylum; Nonesuch; Atlantic; Atco; Cotillion.
Movies: Warner Bros.; Orion; Ladd.
Publishing: Warner Books; *Mad; Superman, Batman, Wonder Woman* comics.
Toys, electronic games, and home computers: Atari; Knickerbocker; Malibu Grand Prix.
Soccer team: Cosmos.
Cosmetics: Lauren; Polo; Chaps.

Innkeepers

HILTON

Sales: $514 million
Profits: $99 million
Rank in hotels: 3
Founded: 1919
Employees: 27,000
Headquarters: Beverly Hills, California

What they do. Hilton Hotels are not quite what they seem. There are, of course, Hilton hotels all around the globe—nearly 250 of them, renting tens of thousands of rooms from Chicago to Hong Kong. But Hilton owns no hotels outside the United States, even though there are 75 overseas Hiltons. The overseas hotels belong to Hilton International, which Hilton sold to TWA in 1967. Nor do Hilton Hotels own the 136 Hilton Inns in 124 cities around the United States. These inns are merely franchise hotels, which pay to use the Hilton name and reservation service. Hilton does own up to half of some of the 30 Hilton hotels they manage, including the Beverly Hilton, which is their headquarters. But the real core of the business is the group of 18 hotels Hilton owns outright; these hotels accounted for more than 90% of sales in 1978.

Hilton Hotels are turning a good profit, but not all of it derives from their skill in spreading fresh linen or delivering silver trays of eggs Benedict and orange juice. Of their total revenues, 36% comes from just two of the hotels they own, both in the same

city: the Las Vegas Hilton and the Flamingo Hilton, where profits from the roulette wheels and blackjack tables put bed-and-board income to shame.

History. The history of Hilton Hotels is enmeshed with the life of Conrad Hilton, which in turn was a tangle of religion, women, and ego. Born on Christmas Day, 1887, in San Antonio, Territory of New Mexico, "Connie" got business training from his father, Gus, and religion from his mother, Mary. Educated at the New Mexico Military Institute and the New Mexico School of Mines, he gained his first experience as a hotelier renting out rooms in the family house. Later he served in the legislature of the new state of New Mexico, founded a bank, and went off to World War I. Home again, Hilton began to think about his future. As he related in his autobiography, *Be My Guest*, he asked: "Was I content to become a fatter frog in this puddle?" He soon took a friend's deathbed advice to leave New Mexico to go and make a fortune in Texas.

In 1919, intending to buy a Texas bank, he took $5,000 to buy a hotel in the oil-boom town of Cisco instead. It was the beginning of his love affair with hotels. This first one, the Mobley, he called an old "dowager." He gave her a facelift and was off and running with partners L. M. Drown and Jay C. Powers to start a chain. By the mid-1920s they had eight hotels in Texas—but Powers was dead, shot by another partner as he came out of an elevator in a Hilton Hotel.

During the Depression Hilton came close to losing everything on several occasions. But at the 11th hour he'd pull a rabbit out of the hat and get it all back, usually giving St. Joseph the credit. When boom times returned, Hilton once again found himself with five hotels in Texas but minus his first wife, Marry Barron. He consoled himself after their divorce by buying hotels in San Francisco (the Sir Francis Drake), and Long Beach, California, and Albuquerque, New Mexico. But Hilton wasn't satisfied with renovating his dowagers, or even with the inns he built from the ground up; he wanted the biggest and the best. He was so obsessed with getting New York's Waldorf-Astoria (his "socialite") that he carried a picture of "her" in his wallet for years. Eventually she was his.

In the early 1940s Hilton started expanding abroad (in Mexico) and going for the big time in New York, buying and selling hotels as if he were in a Monopoly game. He was also heading for big trouble with the Roman Catholic Church, via Zsa Zsa Gabor. "I theenk I am going to marry you," she told him at their first meeting. Hilton laughed, but four months later he joined her at the altar and lost his rights to the Sacraments. It didn't last. Connie was disgusted by Zsa Zsa's cosmetic rituals, which he complained in his autobiography "could have been the rite of an ancient Aztec temple." But Zsa Zsa boasted later that she'd won over God. She'd find him on his knees praying, saunter past in a black negligee, and say, "Take your choice, Him or me." She said she won every time, but Hilton divorced her and comforted himself by buying the Waldorf (1950) and eventually the whole chain of Statler hotels.

This was the big time. Believing that "man with God's help and personal dedication is capable of anything he can dream," he founded Hilton International in 1948. Although it flourished, Hilton's elder son and prime heir, Barron, convinced him to sell the international hotels for a chunk of TWA stock. Barron apparently thought TWA's stock would go much higher (it didn't), and *Fortune* says he also "didn't properly value the worth of Hilton International." The elder Hilton bemoaned the mistake but put Barron in charge of the company, although he kept coming to the Beverly Hills office every day to give advice and arrange philanthropic projects. In his entire career Hilton took only one vacation, and that only for one month. Nevertheless, he lived 91 years. When he died in 1979, his hotel empire was still thriving, and he was back in the good graces of the church (even after marrying a third time in 1977).

Barron Hilton is the architect of the chain's current strategy of concentrating their resources on only their most profitable properties. In 1970 they went into Las Vegas and bought the largest hotel there—the International Hotel, owned by Kirk Kerkorian—and renamed it the Las Vegas Hilton. In the same deal they also picked up Kerkorian's Flamingo. In 1975 Hilton sold a 50% interest in six of their hotels to Prudential Insurance and used the $66 million in cash to build additions onto their hot Las Vegas hotels.

Reputation. Some Hilton Hotels, like the Waldorf Astoria, have a reputation for un-

So that's how it started: the first Hilton—the Mobley Hotel in Cisco, Texas, 1920.

surpassed style and chic. Other hotels, in outlying areas, are said to be downright mediocre. Overseas, Hiltons are usually quite elegant, and Hilton International is said to be contemplating a name change to avoid being associated with their American cousins.

What they own. In 1978 they owned 18 hotels in the United States (2 with gambling casinos) and partly owned 11 more; 136 Hiltons were franchised, and 19 unowned hotels were under their management.

Who owns and runs the company. Chairman and president Barron Hilton has all the marbles. In 1979 he owned about 3.5% of the company's stock, and if he takes up the option in his father's will to buy Conrad's shares over the next 10 years, he will own 28% of the stock, worth $192 million. Barron's brother Nicholas was in the news in the 1950s because of his short marriage to film star Elizabeth Taylor.

In the public eye. Henri Lewin, a vice-president in Hilton's Western Division, has been charged for illegally giving complimentary lodging, entertainment, and refreshments to a Teamster official. Hilton says that the offering of free lodging and other benefits "occurred in the ordinary course of business on the basis of factors unrelated to [his] union status." But the organized crime section of the Justice Department still thinks Hilton's generosity to the Teamsters is worth investigating.

Where they're going. To Atlantic City where they plan to open a 1,500-room luxury hotel and casino in early 1983. Also in the works is a plan to expand the New York Hilton into the world's largest hotel. A Moscow hotel currently holds the room-count record. Conrad Hilton didn't like that, and Barron means to change it.

Stock performance. Hilton stock bought for $1,000 in 1970 sold for $2,095 on January 2, 1980.

Access. 9880 Wilshire Boulevard, Beverly Hills, California 90210; (213) 274-7777.

Consumer brands.

Hotels: Hilton Hotels and Inns; Palmer House (Chicago); Waldorf-Astoria (New York City).

Sales: $1.1 billion
Profits: $56 million
Forbes 500 rank: 421
Rank in hotels: 1
Founded: 1952
Employees: 27,000
Headquarters: Memphis, Tennessee

What they do. Thirty years ago Memphis real estate developer and devout Baptist Kemmons Wilson figured that American families wanted clean, reliable, and economical places to stay when they motored across the country. Today, Holiday Inns has 296,000 rooms that say Wilson was right. With 1,741 hotels in 54 countries around the globe, Holiday Inns, now the world's large innkeeper, has changed the concept of a motel from a sleazy roadside lovers' rendezvous to a family lodging place.

Holiday Inns has also taken the motel business out of the hands of mom-and-pop operators and turned it into a high-rolling growth industry. In 1979 the Holiday Inns rang up about $7 million a day just in room rentals. They rented 74% of their rooms at an average rate of $32.65 per room. But that's only part of the business; the Holiday Inns' restaurants are second only to McDonald's as the biggest feeders in America.

What the average traveler may not know is that 1,495 of the units in the chain are operated as franchises, with some of the franchisers owning highly successful mini-chains within the system. To get a franchise to operate a Holiday Inn in the United States, you must make a downpayment of $5,000 plus $150 per room (the total minimum downpayment is $20,000). On top of that you must pay a 4% royalty on room sales and kick in another 2% of gross room sales for marketing and reservation services. The reservation services—the Holidex communication lines—are important. From one Holiday Inn you can reserve a room in another Holiday Inn anywhere and get a confirmation in minutes. If one inn is fully booked, the computer automatically seeks out the nearest available Holiday

Inn and offers it. You can also reach Holidex through a toll-free number and through airline reservation systems, travel agents, and the travel departments of 200 big companies. Holidex is used by 30% of the travelers who stay in Holiday Inns. And incidentally, it's the largest private communications network in the world.

Ranging in size from 48 to 715 rooms, the lodgings traditionally have been oriented toward the family on a budget and toward business people who want to save money. However, that direction is changing. In 1979 Holiday Inns bought Harrah's, a major Nevada casino operator, and announced that they intend to build a 500-room hotel in Atlantic City, New Jersey, with 500,000 square feet of casino space. Now weary travelers can spice up their stay in those locations with a bit of gaming before turning in for the night.

History. The world's largest hotel chain started on a miserable vacation 30 years ago. In 1951 Kemmons Wilson took his family on a holiday to Washington, D.C. Along the way they stayed in a succession of roadside tourist courts, the kind of fleabag motels that catered to traveling salesmen and clandestine lovers. Convinced that American families would flock to a clean, moderately priced, family-oriented motor hotel, Wilson went back to Memphis and put his building experience to work.

He opened his first Holiday Inn on the outskirts of Memphis in 1952, naming it after the movie *Holiday Inn*, with Bing Crosby and Fred Astaire. (The film introduced the Irving Berlin songs "White Christmas" and "Easter Parade.") The hotel, like no other in the area, boasted a swimming pool, free ice, free parking, and a dog kennel. What's more, children under 12 could stay without charge in their parents' room. Within a week all the Inn's 120 rooms, each with a private bath, were filled nightly as motorists welcomed an alternative to poorly equipped and carelessly operated tourist courts.

Soon Wilson had opened three more Holiday Inns on highways leading into Memphis, and had begun spinning dreams of a national chain.

He called upon another go-getter, Wallace E. Johnson, dubbed "the Henry Ford of the home building industry" by the *Saturday Evening Post*. In 1953 the two invited 75 home builders from other parts of the country to hear their franchise pitch. They found plenty of takers, and Holiday Inns, all predictable but reliable, soon started blooming along roadsides. In many cities they became the best places to stay.

The first non-United States Holiday Inn opened in 1960 in Montreal, the forerunner of others in Canada; the first European Holiday Inn was built in Holland in 1963; and when a unit was launched in 1971 in Anchorage, Alaska, the burgeoning chain claimed the distinction of having flags in all 50 states. By this time a Holiday Inn was being completed somewhere in the world every 2½ days.

Each Holiday Inn in the United States has a restaurant, but no liquor was served during the early years. When that dictum was reversed in 1960, the chain's image of sleepy, wholesome hostelries began a transition. Holidomes, of which there are now 102, were introduced, advertising themselves as recreational centers suitable for short family vacations or extended business stays. Each Holidome provides year-round recreational facilities, including swimming pools, saunas, exercise rooms, miniature golf, and table tennis, plus resort-style res-

So that's how it started: the first Holiday Inn—in Memphis, 1952.

taurant and lounge facilities.

The Arab oil embargo of 1973–74 and its resulting shortage of gasoline brought a steep decline in car travel and motel use, forcing Holiday Inns into a new direction. Roy Winegardner, a franchise operator, was chosen to run the company, and he replaced the hometown management with Harvard Business School graduates. To reduce Holiday Inns' reliance on the automobile, the chain started building more highrise units in downtowns and near airports, and increased the number of Holidomes.

But the most drastic and controversial phase of Winegardner's program was to put Holiday Inns into the gambling business. In 1975 he and his top managers put together an elaborate presentation to convince the largely Southern Baptist board of directors of the virtues of going into the hotel/casino business. The board voted down the proposal. Two years later, however, after the retirement of several of the antigambling directors, the proposal was resurrected, and the board, this time reading the bottom line instead of the Bible, passed it.

Reputation. Seasoned Holiday Inn guests know exactly what they're getting: two double beds, a Bible, writing paper, color TV, phone book, laundry bag, eight clothes hangers including four with trouser holders, six towels, three washcloths, a pitcher and two wrapped plastic water glasses, Kleenex, two bars of soap, a spare roll of toilet paper, and a sanitized strip on the toilet seat.

Holiday Inns have, of course, been ridiculed as being plastic. But, writes Judson Gooding, former associate editor of *Fortune* and managing director of *Next:* "Criticizing Holiday Inns for their taste is really criticizing the taste of the country itself, because the inns are decorated and operated so as to match, with the most rigorous exactitude, the nation's standards. . . . The only problem is that some people wish the nation's standards were different."

What they own. As the chain grew to become the world's largest, so did their need for about 7,000 nonfood products and supplies necessary to operations and maintenance. To meet these demands, Holiday Inns formed Inn Keepers Supply, a group equipped to design, engineer, and furnish a hotel from scratch; Innkare, a one-stop master distribution system for expendable sup-

plies; and Dohrmann, a major distributor of restaurant equipment and supplies. They sold Dohrmann in 1979.

Who owns and runs the company. When founder Kemmons Wilson, now a multimillionaire, retired as chairman in 1979, he said his future plans could well include becoming a Holiday Inn franchise holder himself. Asked by the *Wall Street Journal* why he didn't follow the lead of so many other executives and have an unlisted home phone number, he replied: "Why, someone might want to reach me; God might want to reach me."

Things have not been placid among the company's top executives since Holiday Inns decided to go into the gambling industry. In 1978 L. M. Clymer quit as Holiday Inns' president and chief executive, a decision he said he reached after months of Bible study and prayer. Although Clymer contended he wasn't judging his colleagues who considered gambling a proper business, he claimed he chose to resign because of "my overriding regard and respect for my Lord Jesus Christ."

He was succeeded as president by Roy E. Winegardner, who later took over as chairman when Wilson stepped down. A former plumbing contractor, Winegardner was an early Holiday Inn franchise holder, building up a chain of more than 40 Holiday Inns, most of which were sold back to the company for stock in 1970. He's known as a no-nonsense hotel operator whose holdings now are worth about $13 million.

In the public eye. The company has several antitrust suits pending against them, most filed by disgruntled licensees who feel they've been done in by Daddy.

One suit seeks to stop Holiday Inns from entering into license agreements with third parties without first giving an option to franchisers already operating in the area. Another suit charges that Holiday Inns declines to grant licenses to persons who own hotel or motel interests other than Holiday Inns.

Where they're going. They got out of the bus business in 1979 by selling Trailways, and they were reported to be looking for a buyer for their Delta Steamship Lines, bought in 1969. In 1979 they bought Perkins' Cake & Steak, a Minneapolis-based chain with 94 company-owned and 270 licensed restaurants in 33 states.

Who Sleeps the Most

	Sales 1978	Number of Hotels/ Properties	Number of Rooms or Beds (†)
1. HOLIDAY INNS	$1,900 *million*	1,718	286,529
2. SHERATON (*ITT*)	$ 800 *million*	402	102,109
3. RAMADA INNS	$ 759 *million*	644	93,000
4. U.S. ARMY	$ 756.6 *million**	1,145	756,645†
5. BEST WESTERN	$ 734.7 *million*	2,145	152,725
6. U.S. NAVY	$ 524.8 *million**	—	524,824
7. FRIENDSHIP INNS INTERNATIONAL	$ 390 *million*	1,493	93,000
8. HOWARD JOHNSON (*Imperial Group*)	$ 380 *million*	524	59,040
9. HILTON INTERNATIONAL (*TWA*)	$ 364.2 *million*	76	—
10. HILTON HOTELS	$ 359.4 *million*	184	67,231
11. INTERCONTINENTAL HOTELS (*Pan Am*)	$ 323 *million*	83	30,057
12. WESTERN INTERNATIONAL (*United Airlines*)	$ 294.3 *million*	50	26,000
13. HYATT HOTELS	$ 285 *million*	52	26,000
14. U.S. AIR FORCE	$ 279.5 *million**	—	279,500†
15. MARRIOTT	$ 244.8 *million*	56	22,658
16. VETERAN'S ADMINISTRATION HOSPITALS	$ 211.5 *million**	279	105,763†
17. TRAVELODGE	$ 190 *million*	517	38,461
18. DAYS INNS OF AMERICA	$ 176.9 *million*	289	42,305
19. QUALITY INNS	$ 171.1 *million*	300	33,717
20. U.S MARINE CORPS	$ 125 *million**	120	125,000†
21. TOPEKA INN	$ 107.9 *million*	73	12,400
22. AMERICANA HOTELS	$ 100 *million*	20	10,000
23. RODEWAY INNS	$ 100 *million*	148	18,200
24. LOEWS HOTELS	$ 90 *million*	15	—
25. MOTEL 6 (*City Investing*)	$ 87.9 *million*	254	25,473
26. AIRCOA	$ 85 *million*	26	6,770
27. AMFAC (*Hotels in U.S. and Hawaii*)	$ 84.1 *million*	25	—
28. RED CARPET INNS	$ 80 *million*	131	16,776
29. NEW YORK STATE OFFICE OF MENTAL HEALTH	$ 70.2 *million*	63	46,800†
30. HYATT INTERNATIONAL	$ 68.1 *million*	24	9,061
31. DUNFEY HOTELS	$ 61 *million*	22	8,990
32. LA QUINTA MOTOR INNS	$ 60 *million*	76	8,754
33. MGM	$ 58.7 *million*	2	3,800
34. UNITED INNS	$ 57 *million*	34	8,159
35. RADISSON HOTELS	$ 51 *million*	18	6,690
36. STOUFFER (*Nestlé*)	$ 50.1 *million*	20	7,042
37. HOSPITAL CORP. OF AMERICA	$ 50 *million*	127	20,000†
38. WINEGARDNER & HAMMONS	$ 49.7 *million*	40	6,900
39. HOSPITALITY MANAGEMENT	$ 48.8 *million*	22	5,170
40. AMERICAN MOTOR INNS	$ 48.1 *million*	54	7,458
41. SERCICO	$ 47.5 *million*	36	7,265
42. MOTOR HOTEL MANAGEMENT	$ 46.5 *million*	43	—
43. HOSPITAL AFFILIATES	$ 46 *million*	—	18,400
44. PRINCESS HOTELS	$ 45.9 *million*	7	3,550
45. WALT DISNEY WORLD	$ 45 *million*	4	2,919
46. UNIVERSITY OF WISCONSIN	$ 44.5 *million*	—	35,277†
47. THUNDERBIRD/RED LION	$ 43.8 *million*	37	6,130
48. HUMANA, INC.	$ 40 *million*	91	16,000†
49. EVANGELICAL LUTHERAN GOOD SAMARITAN SOCIETY	$ 39.1 *million*	—	18,224
50. NATIONAL COUNCIL OF YMCA'S	$ 38 *million*	—	37,480

Source: *Institutions*, July 15, 1979.

*Institutions magazine gives what they call a "commercial equivalent" to represent "sales" in such institutional settings as the U.S. Army and the VA Hospitals.

†Represents number of beds.

Stock performance. Holiday Inns stock bought for $1,000 in 1970 sold for $435 on January 2, 1980.

Access. 3742 Lamar Avenue, Memphis, Tennessee 38118; (901) 362-4001.

Consumer brands.

Hotels: Holiday Inns; Harrah's.
Steamships: Delta.
Restaurants: Perkins' Cake & Steak.

Sales: $1.5 billion
Profits: $71 million
Forbes 500 rank: 346
Rank in airline catering: 1
Founded: 1927
Employees: 63,600
Headquarters: Washington, D.C.

What they do. The liquor flows freely at the bars in 65 hotels and inns operated or franchised by Marriott in the United States. In 1974, while watching the libations being poured for a noisy crowd at a Marriott Inn bar, J. Willard Marriott, Jr., commented: "Look at 'em. Just like a slot machine." Marriott, head of the company founded by his father, then went to bed; he never touches the stuff himself. Like his father, he's a devout, hard-working Mormon who neither drinks nor smokes and who donates more than 10% of his income to the church. His wife, Donna, once said: "We belong to a church that believes in work. This is what his dad grew up with—the principle of work."

It's a principle that has worked its way into a chain of comfortable lodging places that have made their mark on the American scene. The 1,212-room Chicago Marriott was the largest new hotel opened in the United States in 1978. In that same year 430 rooms were tacked on to the New Orleans Marriott, making it the largest hotel in the South, with 1,354 rooms. Both are in convention cities—and that's a key to the Marriott strategy: they cater to business people.

They run establishments that are classier (and more expensive) than Holiday Inns. The rooms are a little larger, the beds a little longer, the fixtures less plastic, the service a little more attentive. It translates into the highest occupancy rate in the industry. Marriott, on the average, rents out more than 80% of their rooms. And at the end of 1979 they had 21,000 rooms to rent, double what they had in 1974.

Although hotels are the most visible signs of Marriott's presence, their main business is feeding people. Half their 1979 hotel revenues of $535 million came from sales of food and beverages in restaurants and bars and from room service. Some airlines have their own kitchens, but Marriott is the largest independent supplier of the meals and snacks eaten on planes. They have kitchens at 30 U.S. and 23 overseas airports, and they operate restaurants and shops at 10 airports. Marriott also feeds the employees at Xerox's corporate headquarters in Connecticut, those at the Federal Reserve Bank of Atlanta, and students and faculty at West Texas State College, among other places. In addition, they're in the restaurant business under other names: Bob's Big Boy coffee shops, Roy Rogers fast-food places, Farrell's ice cream parlors, and the Hot Shoppes.

They'll also feed you at their two Great America theme parks, one in Santa Clara, south of San Francisco, the other between Chicago and Milwaukee at Gurnee, Illinois. The parks attracted 5 million customers in both 1978 and 1979. Finally, Marriott operates three Sun Line cruise ships, the smallest part of their business, bringing in $34 million in 1979. They feed you there, too.

All told, they feed about 1 million people every day at 1,400 establishments.

History. The first establishment was a nine-stool 5¢ root beer stand at 14th and Kenyon Streets in the northwest section of Washington, D.C. It was opened in 1927 by a newly married couple, John Willard Marriott and the former Alice Sheets, both recently arrived from Utah with a franchise for A & W Root Beer. The stand did well during the hot summer months, but when a cold eastern winter descended on the capital, the customers disappeared. So the Marriotts did a quick turnaround and converted their stand into a Hot Shoppe, serving chili con carne and hot tamales. The recipes were borrowed from a cook at the Mexican Embassy.

Washingtonians took kindly to the fiery food, and it wasn't long before the Marriotts were running a string of Hot Shoppes in the Washington metropolitan area—and raising a family at the same time. They went into the airline catering business in 1937 with a contract to service Eastern Air Lines flights at the old Hoover Airport in Washington. Marriott has retained a close tie with their first customer: Eastern accounts for 15% of Marriott's airline catering business, more than any other carrier. Marriott built their first hotel—the Twin Bridges Marriott at Arlington, Virginia—in 1957.

In a profile of the company in 1974, *Washington Post* reporter Richard Cohen said: "If it is impossible to distinguish between Marriott, the corporation, and Marriott, the family, it is similarly impossible to separate the Marriotts from their faith and their heritage. They are Mormons who came east from the tiny settlement of Marriott, Utah, stark cattle and sheep country north of Salt Lake City. What they brought with them was a vision of America that dances in red, white and blue colors and testifies to their faith that man was created in the image of Pat Boone."

J. W. "Bill" Marriott, Jr., was reared in that tradition. He began working in Hot Shoppes restaurants when he was in high school. When he went off to the University of Utah, he got up at 5 A.M. to work in the Hot Shoppes restaurant there. He joined the company in Washington in 1956, became president of Marriott Hot Shoppes, Inc. in 1964 when he was 32, and succeeded his father as chief executive officer in 1972.

Bill Marriott has presided over the company's spectacular growth. When he was elected president, sales were $85 million a year. They crossed the $1 billion mark in 1977. Asked once about his social life, he said: "I don't have a social life. Friendship is an investment and friendship takes a lot of time. My priorities are the church, the family, and the business. After that I have very little time left over."

The company that started out as a root beer stand is now the largest private employer in Washington, D.C., with some 14,-000 people working for them in the nation's capital. In late 1978 they opened a new headquarters building in suburban Washington. The Washington metropolitan area has more Marriott hotels than any other city: five.

So that's how it started: here's J. W. Marriott standing in the doorway of the root beer stand he opened in Washington, D.C., in 1927.

Reputation. Marriott is proud that their hotels have won more 4-star awards in the Mobil Travel Guides than any other hotel company. The Marriott ads rub it in: "Twice as many as Hilton. Twice as many as Hyatt. And more than Ramada Inn, Western International, Sheraton, and Holiday Inn combined." Financial analysts appreciate the way Marriott makes money. In 1979, for the first time, Marriott made more money than Holiday Inns.

What they own. Less and less. Their goal now is to manage hotels, not own them. In 1978 they sold five of their hotels to Equitable Life, and they planned to sell six more to Equitable in 1980—although all the hotels they've sold continue to carry the Marriott name and are managed by Marriott. Only about one-third of Marriott's room capacity is in hotels owned by Marriott.

Who owns and runs the company. The Marriotts are in firm control. They moved early in 1980 to increase their stake in the company from 20 to 30%. J. W. Marriott, Sr., who was born in 1900, is still chairman; his son, J. W. Marriott, Jr., is president, and another son, Richard E. Marriott, is group vice-president. Alice Marriott is a vice-president and member of the board. The Marriotts have a long and close connection with the Republican Party. J. W., Sr., was chairman of the Nixon inaugural balls in 1969 and 1973. The highest non-Marriott officer in the company is Frederic V. Malek, who joined the company in 1974 and is now executive vice-president. A West Point graduate and former Green Beret in Vietnam, Malek was deputy director of the Office of Management and Budget under President Nixon. He was the author of the "Malek Manual," which explained to department heads how they could shift Democrats into meaningless jobs.

In the public eye. In 1970 Marriott hired F. Donald Nixon, the then-president's brother, as a vice-president; Nixon previously had been with Ogden Foods. A month later American Airlines switched their $500,000 Dulles Airport catering contract from Ogden to Marriott.

Marriott fights against any increases in the minimum wage and is no friend of unions. "Only one of its 51 hotels—the Essex House in New York City—is organized," reports *Business Week*, "and that contract was in place when Marriott bought the hotel 10 years ago." In 1978 Marriott executives boasted publicly of opening their Chicago Marriott, the only nonunion hotel in downtown Chicago, "without capitulating to the unions," as they put it. That same year J. W. Marriott, Jr., spent $7,000 of the company's money to send letters to all shareholders urging them to join a new organization, Citizen's Choice, which lobbies against "bigger government, higher taxes and increased government regulation." Marriott says: "If we don't stand up and fight for what we believe in, for the free enterprise system, we'll just go down the road like England and Sweden, to economic disaster."

Where they're going. In early 1980 Marriott had 50 new hotels in various planning or development stages. They operate three in the Middle East: two in Saudi Arabia and one in Kuwait. Asked at the 1978 annual meeting whether they would go into the gambling business, Bill Marriott said no, explaining: "Our business policy today is to avoid entry into major new businesses where we have no experience."

Stock performance. Marriott stock bought for $1,000 in 1970 sold for $1,106 on January 2, 1980.

Access. Marriott Drive, Washington, D.C. 20058; (301) 897-9000. Toll-free numbers: for hotel reservations, (800) 228-9290; for Sun Line Cruises, (800) 223-5760.

Consumer brands.

Hotels: Marriott; Camelback Inn; Essex House; Santa Barbara Biltmore; Marco Beach Hotel; Rancho Las Palmas; Breckenridge Pavilion; Tan-Tan-A Resort; Pavilion; Paraiso; Sam Lord's Castle; Lincolnshire Resort.

Restaurants: Bob's Big Boy; Roy Rogers; Farrell's Ice Cream Parlours; The Joshua Tree; Hot Shoppes; Jr. Hot Shoppes; Hogate's; Port O'-Georgetown.

Amusement park: Great America.

Cruise ships: Sun Line; Stella Solaris, Stella Oceanis, Stella Maria.

Casino Operators

Bally

Sales: $376.8 million
Profits: $46.3 million
Rank in slot machines: 1
Rank in pinball machines: 1
Rank in amusement arcades: 1
Founded: 1931
Employees: 5,600
Headquarters: Chicago, Illinois

What they do. Tough old ladies, high-priced call girls, country bumpkins, and New York executives all gather in Las Vegas to sit for hours in front of garishly lit slot machines. The casinos have no windows or clocks to distract the players from feeding nickels, dimes, quarters, and silver dollars into the slots and pulling down the handles on the one-arm bandits. Few voices are heard, but the casino rings with the sounds of sirens and bells that herald another jackpot and the clatter of coins as they hit the metal payoff tray.

Slot machines make more money for the casinos than blackjack, craps, keno, or the high-stakes baccarat together. And Bally supplies 80% of the slot machines in Nevada, the only state where gambling is legal everywhere.

They also make and sell 70% of the slot machines and German gaming machines (a no-arm bandit, the slot machine preferred in Germany) for the overseas market. Their German subsidiary Gunter Wulff contributes one-fifth of Bally's sales. The flipper pinball machine played by the Pinball Wizard in the movie *Tommy* was a Bally. Bally's Midway subsidiary makes arcade games and sells them to more than 100 Aladdin's Castles gaming centers, also owned by Bally.

Now that New Jersey has opened its borders to gamblers, Bally has built on the Atlantic City Boardwalk a luxurious hotel/casino complex called Park Place, although Bally's chairman, William O'Donnell, had to resign temporarily for his company to get a gambling license—pending an investigation for possible underworld connections. O'Donnell claims that Bally's legal problems are a matter of "image," or guilt by association: "After all, we do make machines people gamble on, and we are a Chicago company."

Bally recently gambled on the possibility that baseball hero Willie Mays can convince the public they don't hobnob with the Mob. They're paying Mays $100,000 per annum for 10 years to be their goodwill ambassador. It is hard to avoid a shady image when much of your business is outlawed in 48 states.

History. The first slot machine was invented in 1895, but Bally didn't get into the business until 1931, when a company known as Lion Manufacturing made a wooden slot machine called the Ballyhoo. After the Ballyhoo's inventor died, William O'Donnell, a Lion sales manager, tried to buy up the company. That's where the alleged Mafia connection came in. O'Donnell's friend Sam Klein arranged a loan, part of which came from Gerardo Catena, who makes everybody's list of underworld leaders. In 1975, when Klein was a vice-president and largest stockholder, he was forced out of the company and fined $50,000 by the Nevada Gaming Commission after he was spotted playing golf with Catena in Florida.

Lion Manufacturing changed their name to Bally in honor of the Ballyhoo. In 1963 they came out with the first electrome-chanical slot machine. Bally now makes 67 models. The machines are set to pay back 85–95% of what's put in, but a dollar slot still makes $70,000 a year, and it costs only $4,000 to buy.

Those figures have convinced Bally to move into casino ownership themselves. As O'Donnell admits, "The operations are the real profitable end of the business." Their Park Place casino opened in Atlantic City in 1980.

Reputation. "Sinful, crime-connected one-arm bandits? Or just good clean fun?" That's the question *Forbes* has posed. That's also what the Atlantic City and Nevada Gaming Commissions have asked.

What they own. Three of Bally's plants are in the Chicago area. Others are in Dublin, Ireland, and West Berlin, Germany. Their research and development and distribution plants are logically located in Reno and Las Vegas. In 1979 their 129 amusement arcades were leased in 27 states, Canada, and Denmark.

Who owns and runs the company. William T. O'Donnell, chairman of Bally since 1963, may or may not be running the firm. He had to put his stock (7.3% of the total) in a trust and resign at least temporarily, before New Jersey would issue the coveted Atlantic City gaming license. Richard Mullane is now chairman and president. Bally first sold stock to the public in 1959; the directors own 12.7% of the stock. Billy Weinberger, former president of Caesar's Palace in Las Vegas, is now in charge of Bally's Atlantic City operations. Midway Manufacturing, maker of Bally's arcade amusements, has a woman president, Marcine Wolverton. Alan Bible, former U.S. senator from Nevada, was elected to the board in 1975.

In the public eye. Absolutely nothing has been proved against Bally regarding alleged underworld connections, but the investigations continue.

William O'Donnell believes that slot and pinball machines are a necessary part of American life, and he says that the Ballyhoo fed a lot of people during the Depression. Bally devoted a full page of their annual report to a discussion of the "slot machine versus the state lottery." Their conclusion: "Slot machines could become an important

source of revenue for state and local governments as an alternative to raising taxes."

Where they're going. Toward the jackpot. Gambling is spreading like wildfire, and Bally's supplying the fuel.

Major employment centers. Chicago, Atlantic City, and Nevada.

Access. 2640 West Belmont Avenue, Chicago, Illinois 60618; (312) 267-6060.

Consumer brands.

Slot machines: Bally.
Amusement arcades: Aladdin's Castles.
Hotel/Casino: Park Place.

MGM 🦁

Sales: $491.3 million
Profits: $61.6 million
Founded: 1919
Employees: 10,200
Headquarters: Culver City, California

What they do. The once mighty roar of the Metro-Goldwyn-Mayer lion is now scarcely a meow. What's audible from MGM today is the whir of slot machines, the rattling of dice and chips, and the jingle of silver dollars on their way to the company till from the pockets of gamblers at MGM's Grand Hotels in Las Vegas and Reno. Although MGM is best known as the most glittering studio of Hollywood's golden era, their business these days is more in hotel/casinos than in movies.

It's possible to spend an entire vacation at an MGM Grand without setting foot outside the hotel. The 2,076-room Las Vegas hotel and its 1,015-room Reno counterpart are stuffed with restaurants, tennis courts, boutiques, swimming pools, casinos the size of football fields, and theaters that present lavish Hollywood-style floor shows and headline entertainers like Engelbert Humperdinck and Burt Bacharach. The luxury suites are named for stars from the MGM firmament; for instance, you might want to stay in the "Rhett Butler," named for the hero of the 1939 epic *Gone With the Wind*, one of the all-time biggest box-office attractions.

MGM hasn't lost sight of the movie business entirely; they've done all right with recent films like *Coma, Network,* and *The Goodbye Girl* (a coproduction with Warner Bros.). But MGM now makes only 5 or 6 movies a year, compared to 30 or more at their peak. They produce a few television shows too, such as the regular program "CHiPs" and shorter-run series like the 11-part "How the West Was Won." Only 1,600 of their employees work in movies and television.

Movies are risky, but casinos are sure bets. "Every year we have a *Gone With the Wind,*" MGM's principal stockholder, Kirk Kerkorian, remarked in 1979. What he meant was this: *Gone With the Wind* had grossed about $150 million by the mid-1970s. In 1978, the year the Reno MGM Grand opened, MGM's hotel and gaming operations brought in $219 million and made a profit of $56 million before taxes.

History. Three separate companies merged to form Metro-Goldwyn-Mayer in 1924. Metro was the property of Marcus Loew, whose parents had come to America from Austria. Around the turn of the century in New York, Loew started buying vaudeville theaters and nickelodeons, converting them into 5¢ movie houses. To ensure a steady supply of films, Loew bought a Hollywood production company called Metro Pictures in 1920.

Samuel Goldwyn was born Samuel Goldfisch in Warsaw in 1882. Concluding at an early age that there wasn't much future in the Warsaw ghetto, he ran off to Hamburg and eventually reached America. In 1913 he formed a movie production company in New York City with his brother-in-law Jesse Lasky and Cecil B. DeMille, but he was squeezed out three years later. He started a new movie company in 1916 with two Broadway producers, Edgar and Arch Selwyn. By combining their last names, they came up with the name for the business: Goldwyn Pictures. Sam, who was tired of "goldfish" jokes by this time anyway, liked the name so much that he took it for his own. The Goldwyn company bought a studio in Culver City, California, and started making silent movies with stars like Will Rogers and Tallulah Bankhead. Pressed for cash, the company sold $7 million worth of stock to the du Pont family of Delaware in 1919. Three years later Goldwyn was again squeezed out of his company, this time by the du Pont interests.

"Include Me Out": The Sayings of Sam Goldwyn

Samuel Goldwyn, the Polish-born producer who founded one of the Hollywood movie studios that went into Metro-Goldwyn-Mayer, never quite mastered the English language, although he lived in the United States for 80 years. He was famous for his malapropisms, known as "Goldwynisms"—hilariously mangled expressions, mixed metaphors, and syntactical blunders. Here are some:

Include me out.

I can tell you in two words: im possible.

A verbal agreement isn't worth the paper it's written on.

I never put on a pair of shoes until I've worn them at least five years.

A man who goes to a psychiatrist should have his head examined.

They're always biting the hand that lays the golden egg.

I don't think anybody should write his autobiography until after he's dead.

She's colossal in a small way.

Our comedies are not to be laughed at.

The trouble with this business is the dearth of bad pictures.

I read part of it all the way through.

This atom bomb is dynamite.

Every Tom, Dick, and Harry is named Sam.

Goldwyn maintained that he never uttered half the Goldwynisms attributed to him, blaming them on overzealous press agents and idlers around his studio.

Vowing never again to get mixed up with partners, Goldwyn went on to produce more than 70 movies over the next 35 years under the solitary banner Samuel Goldwyn Presents. He himself was never a part of MGM.

The third source of the company was Louis B. Mayer, who came to America from Russia in the late nineteenth century. Mayer soon built a chain of theaters and movie houses from Canada to Pennsylvania, and in 1918 he started a production company, which he soon moved to Los Angeles. When Metro-Goldwyn-Mayer was formed, Louis B. Mayer became the studio's production chief, a role he filled until he was forced out of the company in 1951. Mayer served for a time as state chairman of the California Republican Party.

MGM believed the main reason people went to the movies was to see movie stars. Accordingly, the casts of the MGM productions of the 1920s and 1930s constitute a virtual Who's Who of Hollywood: Buster Keaton, Erich von Stroheim, Clark Gable, Jean Harlow, Myrna Loy, the Marx Brothers, Peter Lorre, Charles Laughton, Johnny Weissmuller, Nelson Eddy, Jeanette MacDonald, Greta Garbo, Judy Garland. MGM seemed to be in perfect harmony with the moviegoers of America.

With their Hollywood production facilities and their nationwide chain of Loew's theaters, MGM controlled their movies from the making to the showing. The other big studios had their own theater chains as well. But the whole movie business changed in 1949 when the government forced an end to this practice. If you made movies, you could no longer control the theaters. MGM was forced to sell their theaters—which became the basis of the present-day Loews conglomerate.

Something else changed after World War II. Audiences, it seemed, were not so easily satisfied with escapist entertainment cooked up on a Hollywood lot. Television made rapid inroads into America's viewing habits. MGM still produced movies, but they frequently depended on gimmicks: song-and-dance musicals like *Singin' in the Rain* (1952), cast-of-thousands spectacles like *Ben-Hur* (1959), or Cinerama curved-screen extravaganzas like *How the West Was Won* (1962). In 1963 Elvis Presley made the first of a long string of movies for MGM, each one more idiotic than the last. By the end of the 1960s MGM couldn't seem to make anything much better than *Zabriskie Point* and *Strawberry Statement*—with occasional exceptions like *2001: A Space Odyssey*.

The company seemed to be sliding straight down the tubes. In July 1969 they announced they had lost a staggering $31 million in the previous nine months. That same month, when MGM was at their lowest point financially, a self-made California millionaire named Kirk Kerkorian stepped in and bought a controlling interest in the company, over the futile objections of the two largest stockholders, Time, Inc., and Edgar Bronfman of the Seagrams distilling empire.

Kerkorian, the son of an Armenian immigrant, served as a cargo pilot during World War II, and after the war he started buying and selling war surplus planes. The planes were cheaper in Hawaii, and Kerkorian came close to crashing in the ocean several times as he flew the planes back to the mainland. Borrowing $15,000 from the Bank of America, Kerkorian started a three-plane flying service, called Los Angeles Air Service, which made frequent stops in Las Vegas. He also gained a reputation for paying his debts on time, which impressed the people at the Bank of America.

He built his flying business into Trans International Airlines, which he sold for $1 million in 1962 but bought back a year later after having second thoughts. In 1968 he sold it again, this time to Transamerica Corporation, for $90 million worth of stock, which he sold a year later for $104 million.

Next Kerkorian bought 30% of Western Airlines, financed by $73 million in unsecured loans from his friends at the Bank of America. Around the same time he bought the Flamingo Hotel-Casino in Las Vegas and borrowed $30 million from a Nevada bank to build the International Hotel and Casino, Las Vegas's largest. Now he took aim at MGM. Armed with a recommendation from the Bank of America that said they considered him worth $70 million on his signature alone, Kerkorian persuaded a consortium of European banks to lend him the money to finance his MGM takeover.

But even millionaire wheeler dealers get strapped for cash sometimes, and Kerkorian found himself struggling to cover his debts. In 1970 he reluctantly sold his beloved International Hotel at a bargain price to Hilton Hotels, who renamed it the Las Vegas Hilton.

Meanwhile, back at MGM, Kerkorian installed a new management that set about slashing costs and selling assets to raise money. Mike Curb, the 25-year-old head of MGM Records (who was elected California's lieutenant governor in 1978), got into the swing of things by firing 239 of his division's 240 employees. MGM held a series of auctions on their back lot and then sold the lot. Most of their historic props were knocked down to the highest bidder, including the ruby slippers worn by Judy Garland in the 1939 classic *The Wizard of Oz* (they went for $10,000). In 1972 they sold the record division.

Kerkorian was not particularly interested in MGM as a show business company; he saw it primarily as his vehicle to get back into the hotel/casino business. The MGM Grand Hotel in Las Vegas, which opened in 1973, was even bigger than the International he had built and lost.

In 1980 MGM became two separate companies: MGM Grand Hotels and Metro-Goldwyn-Mayer Film Company. Stockholders received one share of each company for every share of MGM stock they owned. Part of the reason for the split, MGM said, was to beef up their movie operations; they wanted to avoid the image of "a hotel company that makes some films." Some observers suspected it was simply a maneuver to get rid of the bothersome movie company, a view that MGM hotly denied. To back up their professed intention to rebuild movie operations, they hired David Begelman in 1979 to head their motion picture division. Begelman produced several huge successes for Columbia Pictures before resigning in the wake of a check-forging scandal in 1978. MGM president Frank E. Rosenfelt said Begelman's assignment was to "return MGM to the glory days." Begelman said MGM planned to produce 12 to 15 theater movies a year, starting in the summer of 1981.

Reputation. "Actors think with their hearts," Sam Goldwyn once said; "that's why many of them die broke." The businessmen who steered MGM into casinos don't let glamor or sentimentality blur the bottom line. When the MGM lion was king of Hollywood, the Latin inscription over his head read, "Ars Gratia Artis"—Art for Art's Sake. A better motto today might be one that *Newsweek* suggested in 1978: "The House Never Loses."

What they own. Besides their Las Vegas and Reno hotels, MGM still owns 44 acres in Culver City. Their film lab there processes all the footage shot by Columbia Pictures as well as MGM—a total of 7 million feet of film each week, or about 1,400 miles, roughly the distance from Hollywood to Kansas City. They also own what they believe to be "the most valuable motion picture library in the world, never having sold a single negative." Every time the MGM lion roars on late-night TV or in a revival movie house, the company makes more money.

Who owns and runs the company. Kirk Kerkorian, who owns 48% of MGM's stock, is one of America's maverick tycoons. He rarely attends annual meetings of the companies he buys, and he doesn't get involved with managing the businesses. Like Howard Hughes, Kerkorian is attracted to Las Vegas and shuns publicity, but he doesn't have the late billionaire's eccentricities.

In 1976 Kerkorian bought 5% of Columbia Pictures and resigned as an MGM director to avoid any possible antitrust action. He later bought another 20% of Columbia, at which point the Justice Department tried—and failed—to force him to give up his Columbia stock. (The government has appealed.)

MGM boasts of their "unique and liberal" dividend policy, and Kerkorian gets a nice cash payment every three months. In 1979 he received quarterly dividends of $2.1 million, or a tidy $8.4 million for the year. Kerkorian's dividend checks stirred up quite a bit of controversy in the mid-1970s when he allegedly engineered two special dividend payments that netted him $11.1 million. The dividends were the first that MGM had declared in four years. The first one came just after the company had posted a $585,000 loss for the year, prompting the Securities and Exchange Commission to file a complaint, which was later settled by consent decree.

Cary Grant and Art Linkletter sit on MGM's board of directors.

Where they're going. To Atlantic City, like other big hoteliers. Following New Jersey's 1976 legalization of casino gambling in Atlantic City, MGM planned a 1,300-room Grand Hotel there, which they hope to open in the summer of 1981.

Stock performance. Metro-Goldwyn-Mayer stock bought for $1,000 in 1970 sold for $5,374 on January 2, 1980.

Access. 10202 West Washington Boulevard, Culver City, California 90230; (213) 836-3000.

Consumer brands.

Metro-Goldwyn-Mayer movies and TV shows. *Hotels/casinos:* MGM Grand–Las Vegas; MGM Grand–Reno.

New York City Off-Track Betting

Sales: $803 million
Profits: $85 million
Rank in legal offtrack betting: 1
Rank in New York City retail sales: 1
Founded: 1970
Employees: 2,500
Headquarters: New York, New York

What they do. Governments, like people, will do almost anything when they're hard pressed. New York City, strapped for funds, went into the bookmaking business. Their entry was sanctioned by New York state, which gets a piece of the action. Off-Track Betting, familiarly known as OTB, operates the business through 155 seedy branch offices scattered throughout the five boroughs of New York City. At an office you can place a bet on a horse or cash in a winning ticket (warning: if you hit a really big daily double or triple, they'll ask to see your social security number to report your legally gotten gains to the Internal Revenue Service). The OTB offices are located in high-traffic spots. There are no chairs, to discourage loitering, but the punters, a garrulous lot, loiter anyway. The most picturesque OTB station is in the rotunda of Grand Central Station, where the old ticket windows of the New York Central Railroad have been converted to cages where you place your bets. (Instead of buying a ticket on the "iron horse," you buy one on a real one.)

Many department stores—Franklin Simon, DePinna, Bonwit Teller, Stern's—

gave up on New York City, but OTB has a "product" they didn't have. OTB is now the biggest retail business in the city, outselling Macy's handily.

History. A special act of the state legislature authorized offtrack betting in 1970. It was passed at the behest of New York City, then mired in a desperate fiscal crisis. New York City Off-Track Betting was set up as a "public benefit corporation." The public was supposed to benefit in two ways: (1) legalized bookmaking would produce badly needed revenues for the city, and (2) the legalizing of betting would put a crimp into the operations of the illegal bookmakers.

Nine years later there was no evidence that OTB had seriously impaired the business of the bookies. And the revenues they generated for the state and local governments have been less than expected: in 1979 OTB gave New York City $62 million and New York state $17 million.

The people who run OTB complain that they're forced to compete against the bookies with one hand tied behind their backs. At the track the "house," in the form of the New York Racing Association, takes 14% of the money bet. The OTB take is 23%. The bookies pay track odds, so you can make more money betting a horse with them than with OTB.

The result has been virtual stagnation. In 1977, New Yorkers bet $782 million at the OTB windows, in 1978, $768 million, and in 1979, $802 million.

Reputation. If you can't get to the track or reach your bookie by phone, OTB is the next best thing.

What they own. About $8 million worth of property and equipment. Virtually all their offices are leased. Their 1980 rental commitment was $5 million.

Who owns and runs the company. New York City, for all practical purposes. The first boss was Howard "the Horse" Samuels, plastics millionaire who failed twice in races for the New York state governor's office. Then came Paul Screvane, former head of the New York City Sanitation Department. Next was Bernard Rome, who was a chief fundraiser for Mayor Ed Koch. After he took over, Rome found himself at odds with City Hall. He opposed moves to introduce casino gambling in New York, arguing that this would cut into OTB's business. City Hall thought otherwise, and so Rome was out of the money. He was replaced by John F. Keenan.

In the public eye. OTB has the most visible retail presence in New York City; you're never far from a station where you can bet your $2.

Where they're going. They want to televise live racing from the tracks. The races would be televised into the OTB betting parlors so that bettors could stand there and root for their horses. "We continue to believe," says OTB, "that television is the key to the racing industry's future."

Access. 1501 Broadway, New York, New York 10036; (212) 221-5461.

. PLAYBOY

Sales: $323 million
Profits: $11 million
Rank in men's magazines: 1
Rank in magazines: 11
Founded: 1953
Employees: 4,600
Headquarters: Chicago, Illinois

What they do. *Playboy* was the first of what author Tom Wolfe has called "the one-hand magazines," dedicated to the proposition that the average American male desperately wanted to see the girl next door with no clothes on—still fresh, lively, beautiful, and approachable, but with a dash of suggestiveness thrown in for fantasy enhancement. And because the average American male imagined himself to be more sophisticated than the run-of-the-mill voyeur, *Playboy* surrounded their girls-next-door with plenty of literary articles and stories; features on such male accoutrements as clothes, pipes, and cars; cartoons; reader polls on music; profiles of sports figures; and an advice column that dealt alternately with stereos, wines, and oral sex techniques.

From such things are empires made. Today Playboy Enterprises has a string of Playboy Clubs in the United States, England, and Japan; hotels; casinos in London (with more to come in Atlantic City); music and book publishing businesses; a division that licenses and sells *Playboy*'s famous rabbit-head logo on ties, handkerchiefs, cufflinks, and the like; and *Oui*, another one-hander that *Playboy* spun off to compete with the slightly raunchier brand of men's magazines that have sprung up. In 1978 Playboy bought a specialty magazine called *Games*, a monthly composed entirely of puzzles, contests, and tests, which came to them complete with a 500,000 circulation. *Free Enterprise* magazine cited it as "perhaps the most successful new magazine in the specialty market"; and because the reader is expected to go through *Games* clutching his pencil, it too might be considered a one-hander.

Rounding off the Playboy empire is the entertainment division, which got its start a few years ago with Roman Polanski's production of *Macbeth* (in which founder Hugh Hefner's name appeared above Shakespeare's). More recently they produced Peter Bogdanovich's *Saint Jack* and a made-for-TV movie for ABC called *The Death of Ocean View Park*. They also stage periodic jazz festivals, the most recent in 1980 in the Hollywood Bowl.

History. Clay Felker, editor of *Esquire* magazine and later founder of *New York* and *New West* magazines, refused to give young Hugh M. Hefner a $5-a-week raise in 1953; the result was one of the great success stories of twentieth-century publishing. With his $500 savings and a couple of friends, Hefner bought the rights to the famed Marilyn Monroe calendar and put together the first issue of *Playboy* on the kitchen table of his Chicago apartment. Uncertain whether there would be a second issue, they didn't put a date on the first (they weren't even sure whether to call it *Playboy;* the name *Stag Party* at first sounded more appealing). But the first printing of 50,000 sold out in days. So it went, through the second, third, and fourth issues; *Playboy* was on its way.

From the millions that rolled in during the next few years, Hefner built a reputation as America's premier playboy and inspired a generation of young males in matters of taste, dress, and affectation. During the late 1950s and early 1960s the nation's swinging bachelors wore smoking jackets, puffed straight, small-bowl pipes, listened to jazz on their stereos, read *Playboy*, and competed with each other for dates with large-breasted secretaries and airline stewardesses. They also believed in the so-called Playboy Philosophy, a column written by Hefner which espoused the theory that sex was healthy and needn't be procreative in purpose. Sex was good, clean fun, and every swinging bachelor with smoking jacket and small-bowl pipe owed it to himself to get some as frequently as possible. The quest was supported during the early 1960s by Helen Gurley Brown's *Cosmopolitan* magazine, which espoused a similar philosophy for single women. Together the two magazines did much to alter the nation's thinking and bring on the so-called sexual revolution of the 1960s.

Playboy's colossal success spawned a swarm of imitators in the 1970s—principally Bob Guccione's *Penthouse* magazine, which introduced female pubic hair for the first time on the pages of a general circulation periodical and forced *Playboy* to reassess its approach. According to *Esquire*, *Penthouse*'s approach was also to display the girl next door—but in heat. *Playboy* stuck to its guns with kittenishly suggestive models and unblemished bodies. The strategy seems to have paid off, as *Playboy* is still out in front with a circulation of 5.5 million and $60.4 million in advertising revenues. *(Penthouse, however, sells more copies at the newsstand than does Playboy.)*

Reputation. *Playboy*, perhaps more than anything else, symbolizes the change in sexual attitudes in America. In some circles it is what passes for modernity. But there's still a big part of America that rejects it. It took *Playboy* a long time to attract big national advertisers—and they still have difficulties on this score. In 1980 they touched off a storm at Baylor University, a Baptist college in central Texas, when they announced plans to come there to photograph and interview students. Abner McCall, the president of Baylor, excoriated *Playboy* as "just a cheap, pornographic magazine. Among our constituents they've got as much influence as Mao's little red book."

What they own. Casinos! Although the magazine is a money-maker, Playboy clubs and hotels have always been losers—main-

tained more for image enhancement than for profitability. But the London casinos rake in money from the wealthy of Europe and the oil sheiks of the Middle East, helping to keep the losers afloat. The five casinos bring in three times the profits that the magazines generate.

Who owns and runs the company. Hefner owns almost 72% of Playboy's stock and completely controls the company. The other 28% is held in tiny bundles, and countless thousands of readers buy one share each, for the simple reason that each Playboy stock certificate features a Playmate on the certificate. While Hefner embellishes his lifestyle at his Los Angeles and Chicago mansions, day-to-day operations are left mostly in the hands of president Derick Daniels, scion of a famous southern publishing family and former chief of news operations at the Knight-Ridder newspaper chain. Daniels became something of an oddity in the corporate ranks at Playboy by getting married his second day on the job. The one woman on the board of directors, vice-president Christie Hefner, is also Hugh Hefner's 28-year-old daughter.

In 1978, at the insistence of the federal Securities and Exchange Commission, Playboy conducted an audit of directors' compensation to determine whether Hefner and other officers received more than their income taxes showed. The audit turned up $796,413 in rent, lavish entertaining, and other personal expenses like a valet paid by Playboy for Mr. Hefner. He agreed to repay the company. One-fourth of the "Big Bunny's" (Playboy's DC-9 plane) flights were personal, so the plane was sold in 1976.

The company's worst years were 1975–1976, when *Hustler*, *Penthouse*, and other imitators, like pesky insects, were having the most success in luring away *Playboy*'s readers. At the same time, a number of deadweight Playboy Clubs were being jettisoned. During these dark times Hefner earned his stockholders' gratitude by passing up more than $1 million in dividends he could have collected personally and maintaining the regular payout to other shareholders. But then, he could afford it.

In the public eye. In 1970 Hugh Hefner wrote his editors a memo ordering an attack on feminists: "These chicks are our natural enemy. It is time to do battle with them." Nevertheless, two years later, the Playboy Foundation, with Hefner's agreement, made its first grant to a feminist organization (although the foundation had given grants to abortion rights groups since 1966), and it now gives a third of its $250,000 grant money to women's groups like Women's Right Project, Center for Women's Policy Studies, Women's Action Alliance, and the film, *With Babies and Banners,* a documentary on women strikers. Rochelle Korman, associate director of the Ms. Foundation, says, "I wish the money came from elsewhere. But at least it's being spent on good programs."

The Playboy Foundation has backed a lot of unpopular causes besides feminism. For years they were the sole support of the National Organization for the Reform of Marijuana Laws. They have also supported the abolition of capital punishment, the rights of military personnel, mental patients, welfare recipients, minors, and prisoners. The foundation has even given money to Al Goldstein, publisher of *Screw* magazine, in his fight with the postal service over mailing obscene materials (his magazine).

Where they're going. Playboy expected to have a hotel-casino up on the Atlantic City Boardwalk by the end of 1980.

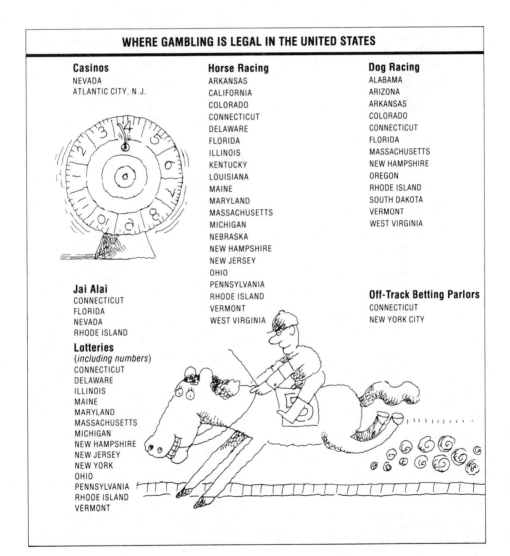

WHERE GAMBLING IS LEGAL IN THE UNITED STATES

Casinos
NEVADA
ATLANTIC CITY, N.J.

Jai Alai
CONNECTICUT
FLORIDA
NEVADA
RHODE ISLAND

Lotteries
(*including numbers*)
CONNECTICUT
DELAWARE
ILLINOIS
MAINE
MARYLAND
MASSACHUSETTS
MICHIGAN
NEW HAMPSHIRE
NEW JERSEY
NEW YORK
OHIO
PENNSYLVANIA
RHODE ISLAND
VERMONT

Horse Racing
ARKANSAS
CALIFORNIA
COLORADO
CONNECTICUT
DELAWARE
FLORIDA
ILLINOIS
KENTUCKY
LOUISIANA
MAINE
MARYLAND
MASSACHUSETTS
MICHIGAN
NEBRASKA
NEW HAMPSHIRE
NEW JERSEY
OHIO
PENNSYLVANIA
RHODE ISLAND
VERMONT
WEST VIRGINIA

Dog Racing
ALABAMA
ARIZONA
ARKANSAS
COLORADO
CONNECTICUT
FLORIDA
MASSACHUSETTS
NEW HAMPSHIRE
OREGON
RHODE ISLAND
SOUTH DAKOTA
VERMONT
WEST VIRGINIA

Off-Track Betting Parlors
CONNECTICUT
NEW YORK CITY

Stock performance. Playboy first sold stock to the public on November 3, 1971, at $23.50 a share. $1,000 bought then sold for $607 on January 2, 1980.

Major employment centers. Chicago, Los Angeles, and London.

Access. 919 North Michigan Avenue, Chicago, Illinois 60611; (312) 751-8000.

Consumer brands.

Magazines: Playboy, Oui, Games.
Books: Playboy.
Clubs/casinos: Playboy.

Sales: $407 million
Profits: $86.5 million
Founded: 1908
Employees: 5,500
Headquarters: North Miami, Florida

What they do. This is the company that introduced casino gambling in the rundown New Jersey resort of Atlantic City on May 26, 1978. Was it a winner? You better believe it. The casino at the Resorts International Hotel there is the world's biggest floating crap game. In the first full month of operation, June 1978, the casino had winnings of $16 million, or about $534,000 a day. A year later—in June 1979—the casino took in $22 million, or about $730,000 a day. In the next month—July 1979—they did even better: $24.8 million, or about $820,000 a day.

The gaming industry had never seen action quite like that. It's triple the winnings at the biggest casino in Las Vegas, the one at the MGM Grand. The casino at the Resorts hotel is enormous, measuring 60,000 square feet and housing 1,640 slot machines, 94 blackjack tables, 18 dice tables, 10 roulette tables, 2 big six wheels, and 3 baccarat tables.

Even after giving the state of New Jersey an 8% cut of these revenues, Resorts comes out way ahead. In 1977, before they became

the top croupier in Atlantic City, Resorts had total sales of $59 million, on which they made profits of $2.5 million. In 1979 their profits—$86 million—were greater than their 1977 sales.

Resorts is not new to gambling. They have been operating casinos and hotels in the Bahamas since 1967, when they decided to give up a paint company. Their other businesses include Chalk International Airline, which uses seaplanes to ferry people from downtown Miami to Bimini, Cat Cay, and Paradise Island in the Bahamas; Antilles Air, which uses seaplanes to move people about in the Virgin Islands and Puerto Rico, and Intertel, a detective agency that you can hire to investigate fraud, kickbacks, and kidnappings—and to make checks "on past associations and reputations extending beyond normal screenings and credit checks."

Intertel is an odd—or maybe logical (it depends on how you look at it)—business to be in for a company that has had to fend off repeated questions and accusations regarding involvements with shadowy figures and organized crime.

History. Once upon a time there was a company called Mary Carter Paint, a privately owned maker of latex and semigloss paint in Tampa, Florida. In 1958 a midwestern family named Crosby bought the company and installed gravel-voiced ex-stockbroker James M. Crosby, then 30 years old, as chairman. They bought some more paint companies. But James was not interested in paint. He was blueprinting a huge complex of hotel/nightclub/casinos over the United States, Central America, and Europe.

Meanwhile, down in the Bahamas, Huntington Hartford, art patron and heir apparent to the A & P fortune, was negotiating with a Swede named Axel Wenner-Gren for a piece of Nassau real estate known as Hog Island. Hartford saw "Hog" as the potential Riviera of the Caribbean, bought it, and renamed it Paradise Island.

Enter the Sir Stafford Sands, whom *Barron's* called "the brilliant, ruthless and corrupt Minister of Finance and Tourism" and the then "most powerful political force on the island." Unfortunately for Hartford, who had supported the opposing political party, Sands was in charge of doling out government licenses for Hartford's proposed operation. Paradise Island could have its licenses—if Hartford was not the sole owner.

In a long investigative piece in *Barron's* Gigi Mahon described how the Crosbys of Mary Carter Paint bought most of the interest in Huntington's island property, slowly squeezed him out entirely, and set about making the new Riviera a reality. The Crosbys got on the right side of Sands by hiring him as counsel. Sands secured the needed approvals, and in 1967 the Paradise Island Casino and Paradise Beach Hotel were opened. Richard Nixon was guest of honor at the gala celebration. The following year Mary Carter became Resorts International and the Crosbys, no longer interested in latex and semigloss, sold their paint companies. Over the next 10 years they put up the Paradise Island Hotel & Villas, the Britannia Beach Hotel, and the Ocean Club on the island. In 1978 they began operating the El Casino gambling complex in Freeport and bought 1,675 acres of land nearby.

But their biggest coup was betting on how the people of New Jersey would vote when confronted in 1976 with a referendum permitting gambling in Atlantic City. Betting on the outcome, Resorts bought the biggest hotel in the town—the stately Chalfonte-Haddon—before the vote on the referendum. When the voters said "yes" to gambling, Resorts was in on the ground floor. Their investments in and around Atlantic City include 56 acres of ocean-front land, a 576-acre tract on nearby Great Island, the Steel Pier (the longest amusement pier in the United States), and assorted other Boardwalk properties.

Their history is checkered with stories relating to their associations with people who have had scrapes with the law. Among the people they had dealings with in developing their business in the Bahamas were financial manipulators Bernard Cornfeld and Robert Vesco. Crosby, at one point, contemplated selling out to Vesco, who is now a fugitive in Costa Rica. Resorts was even linked to the Watergate escapade that was Richard Nixon's downfall. In 1977 *Barron's* reported:

"History and photographs tell us that Richard Nixon was no stranger to Paradise [Island]. A corporate yacht was put at his disposal. A shortsclad Crosby escorted a suited Nixon and [Bebe] Rebozo about this tropical lair. Nixon, in turn, escorted Crosby around the White House. And one report has it that after the '68 campaign,

President-elect Nixon wanted to repair to Paradise Island, but the Secret Service nixed the idea. Presidents of the United States did not hang out at gambling spots."

Resorts was also linked to underworld figure Meyer Lansky. Lansky's name was brought up repeatedly in 1976 and 1977 during a public hearing in Atlantic City on the fitness of Resorts to operate a casino. It was because of these past associations that the attorney general of New Jersey asked that Resorts be denied a license to operate a casino.

In 1966, when he was planning his entry into gambling, Crosby visited the Justice Department to get advice on people to hire to run casinos. He talked there with Robert Peloquin, who was then head of the department's organized crime strike force. Crosby was impressed by Peloquin, who later left to become counsel to the National Football League and then set up his own law firm with William Hundley, a former Justice Department colleague. Resorts was one of his first clients. In 1970 Peloquin set up a security services company, International Intelligence, or Intertel, with the financial backing of Resorts. Intertel, now a wholly owned subsidiary of Resorts, provides the security arrangements at all Resorts International casinos. When he was at the Justice Department, looking into the activities developing in the Bahamas, Peloquin wrote a memo in which he said Paradise Island seemed "ripe for a Lansky skim." After he began working for Resorts, Peloquin advised Crosby to purge people with underworld connections. Appearing at a news conference in Atlantic City in 1976, Peloquin said of Resorts:

"We've been investigated by the F.B.I., the Attorney General, the New Jersey State police. We came up as an extraordinarily clean company."

Reputation. Their reputation took a turn for the better in 1979 when the New Jersey Casino Control Commission granted them a permanent license, declaring: "There is absolutely no evidence of present organized criminal involvement in the applicant. . . ."

Who owns and runs the company. The Crosby family, headed by chairman James M. Crosby, and including brothers John and William and Henry Murphy (a brother-in-law), control 54% of Resorts' stock.

James Crosby and president I. G. Davis wield the power.

In the public eye. *Rolling Stone Magazine* (whom they're suing for libel for $100 million) accused Resorts International of being a CIA front that launders funds to support counterinsurgents in Central and South America, and charged further that they're mob-related and heavily into "casino-skims" of profits. A Watergate investigator told *Barron's* that "nothing was solved to my satisfaction" regarding Resorts' alleged involvement in Watergate. They were fined $144,000 for violations of New Jersey gambling regulations but got their permanent license anyway. They're being investigated by the Securities and Exchange Commission over their contributions to foreign and domestic political groups and public officeholders, over the sources of financing for their Atlantic City properties, and for a variety of other transactions. Again, according to *Barron's*, they have hired lawyers related to the New Jersey legislators who make decisions about the state's casino laws. On the positive side, they have been praised for helping to reduce unemployment in Atlantic City and for staffing their hotel/casino operations there with a work force that is more than 20% minority and 43% female.

Where they're going. Anywhere gambling's being legalized. If that's New York, they'll get into the action. If it's Miami, they'll be there. They're planning to open a second hotel/casino in Atlantic City.

Stock performance. Resorts International stock bought for $1,000 in 1970 sold for $8,200 on January 2, 1980.

Major employment centers. Atlantic City; and Paradise Island and Freeport, the Bahamas.

Access. 915 Northeast 125th Street, North Miami, Florida 33161; (305) 891-2500.

Childhood's Little Disappointments

The National Advertising Division (NAD) of the Council of Better Business Bureaus is supported by business to "assure the truth and accuracy of all national advertising." The following cases are excerpted from the first five-year report of the NAD's Children's Unit, published in 1980.

Money Maker, a magic trick (Five Star Gift Company)
Basis of Inquiry—A comic book advertisement for this toy device included the copy: "Insert blank piece of paper, turn knob, and PRESTO . . . out comes a real dollar bill." The advertising was questioned under the Children's Advertising Guidelines because of the implication that the product could transform an ordinary piece of paper into real currency. Actually, one must "secretly" insert a dollar bill in the device prior to performing the trick. When a blank piece of paper is later inserted, it appears that, by a turn of a knob, a transformation has taken place. The advertiser agreed to change its copy so as to correctly describe the product's operation.

Johnny Bench Batter Up, a toy (Fonas Corporation)
Basis of Inquiry—Print and television advertising for this batting-practice aid did not disclose that the bat shown was not included with the purchase. It also did not mention the fact that a cement base is necessary to stabilize the product. This base involves a separate purchase of an 80-lb. bag of cement plus the time to prepare a form (made from the packaging) and to mix and pour the cement. The Children's Advertising Review Unit questioned the advertising under its Guideline applicable to mentioning the need for additional purchases. The advertiser responded with the assurance that the copy would be changed to include the appropriate information.

Source: *An Eye on Children's Advertising Self-Regulation,* Council of Better Business Bureaus, 1980.

A Toy Maker

Mattel

Sales: $805 million
Profits: $30 million
Rank in toys: 1
Rank in circuses: 1
Rank in juvenile books: 1
Founded: 1945
Employees: 25,700
Headquarters: Hawthorne, California

What they do. The Barbie doll catapulted Mattel to fame and fortune, but a twist in fate, figures, and facts forced her creators out of the toy company they had built into the world's biggest. Elliott and Ruth Handler founded Mattel in 1945 and through an uncanny sense of potential fads and trends saw it grow to become the darling of Wall Street—only to plummet to near insolvency in a two-year period. In 1978 Ruth Handler and Seymour R. Rosenberg, executive vice-president and chief financial officer, were indicted for issuing false and misleading financial reports. The law of business is: grow. Not wanting to run afoul of that law, they tried to maintain the appearance of corporate growth in the face of sluggish sales. So they reported orders as sales when in fact shipments hadn't been made (and many of the orders were later canceled).

The Handlers resigned in 1975 after a

Cunning and Intrigue in the Toy Factory

In 1979, in a Brooklyn federal court, an artist named Christian Thee faced off against Parker Brothers, charging that the mammoth toy company had filched his ideas to create its Masterpiece board game—selling 3½ million sets without paying him a penny.

In his lawsuit Thee said he had submitted his idea to Parker for the art-auction game some years before Parker marketed Masterpiece. But when the toymakers came out with Masterpiece, charged Thee, they marketed it as an idea from Marvin Glass & Associates, the Chicago toy/game think tank renowned for windowless build-

ings, secrecy, and the fact that several employees were murdered on the premises when one of the toy engineers went berserk and started shooting his colleagues.

According to Thee, Parker had a long-standing secret relationship with Glass & Associates that enabled Parker to use outsiders' ideas without having to deal with those who submitted the concepts. Thee's lawyer, Carl Person, said that Parker forwarded the freelancers' ideas to Glass, which altered them enough to dodge copyright problems with the originators and then sold them back to Parker.

The Brooklyn jury awarded Thee 70% of the royalties Parker had paid to the Glass organization: $427,000. Masterpiece, however, is no longer on the market; Parker has discontinued it.

As of the end of 1979 two other cases were pending against Parker Brothers with charges similar to Thee's. Two similar suits have been filed against the Kenner Products Company, which, like Parker Brothers, is a toymaking subsidiary of General Mills.

Source: *The New Yorker*, December 10, 1979.

federal district court, at the behest of the Securities and Exchange Commission, ordered the company to restructure their board so that the majority of directors would be outsiders (people not employed by Mattel). Today there are new handlers at Mattel, which still holds the number 1 position in the toy industry.

Mattel makes a wide range of toys, including the new hand-held electronic games, but dolls, and accessories for the dolls, are their mainstays. Selling accessories for the dolls—not just clothes but even houses—has been an important marketing ploy for Mattel, what Elliot Handler called the old "razor and razor blade" tactic (you get hooked on one, you have to buy the other). Dolls account for nearly half their toy business. One of their recent entries was Baby Grows Up, "two dolls in one as she 'grows' from a baby to become a little girl with simulated feeding from her bottle." They have sold more than 112 million Barbie dolls.

Most of Mattel's toys are made outside the United States. For example, virtually all their fashion dolls, and the costumes for them, are made by Mattel in Hong Kong, Taiwan, and the Philippines or by independent suppliers in Hong Kong and Korea.

Mattel competes against 900 other U.S. toymakers. In 1978 Americans spent $3.4 billion on toys. Mattel captures an estimated 10% of that market, and they spend 11% of their toy sales (more than $40 million a year) on advertising to promote their wares. They do about a quarter of their business outside the United States, much of it in Europe, where they were delighted to find that toys remain popular longer than in America. Their Cheerful Tearful doll, for example, has been a best seller in Germany since 1966.

Toy profits enabled Mattel to buy other companies. They own Ringling Bros.–Barnum & Bailey Circus, Shipstads & Johnson Ice Follies, and Holiday on Ice. In 1979 they bought Wisconsin's Western Publishing, the nation's largest publisher of children's books (under the Golden imprint).

It's ironic that a company devoted to the innocence of children almost ruined their business by false and misleading statements and deception of its stockholders.

History. Ruth Handler, youngest of 10 children of Polish immigrants, was a secretary at Paramount Pictures in Los Angeles when she married Elliott Handler, an in-dustrial designer. Handler went into the picture-frame business and in 1945 found himself with a lot of extra frame slats. So he and Ruth started a business to make doll furniture. They sold $100,000 worth of doll toys in their first year and were in the toy business to stay. In 1955, by which time their sales had reached $6 million a year, they introduced toy burp guns. The Handlers then gambled by agreeing to sponsor Walt Disney's *Mickey Mouse Club* on TV for a year—and that was their big breakthrough. It was the first time a toy manufacturer had spent money on advertising throughout the year; previously advertising was done only for the Christmas season. The Handlers sold plenty of burp guns, and they also registered their brand name, Mattel, with the viewing audience (kids). (One slogan they used for years was: "You can tell it's Mattel, it's swell.")

The Barbie doll came along in 1959. Instead of the cherubic model the industry had long been making, Ruth Handler came up with a doll that looked like a buxom teenager. As she later explained it to the *New York Times:* "If a little girl was going to do role playing of what she would be like at 16 or 17, it was a little stupid to play with a doll that had a flat chest. So I gave it beautiful breasts." Barbie soon had a boy friend, Ken, and they both had extensive wardrobes (that were bought separately). Another Mattel winner was a talking doll, Chatty Cathy. Sales boomed, and by 1965 Mattel was doing more than $100 million a year, topping everybody in the toy industry, and their stock was listed on the New York Stock Exchange. In 1967 Ruth Handler was named Woman of the Year by the *Los Angeles Times.* In 1968 they introduced another spectacular seller, Hot Wheels, miniature model cars. Mattel could do no wrong in the toy business.

But in a few years they were doing everything wrong. In 1970 their plant in Mexico burned. The following year a shipping strike cut off their toy supplies from the Far East. Rather than report declining profits (a no-no on Wall Street), Handler and Rosenberg played with the books, logging sales they hadn't made and pushing expenses into the future, and setting off a chain of juggling that continued for two years. In early 1973 the company posted a $32 million loss just three weeks after assuring shareholders that everything was going along fine. Mattel's stock nosedived—and the investigation by the SEC followed.

Ruth Handler and Rosenberg eventually pleaded no contest to the charges brought against them. In 1978 Judge Robert Takasugi, sitting in federal district court in Los Angeles, fined them $57,000 apiece and gave them each 41-year sentences—which he suspended, ordering them both to do 500 hours of charitable work every year for the next five years. The judge told them: "The crimes each of you committed, in the opinion of this court, are exploitive, parasitic and I think disgraceful to anything decent in this society."

After the Handlers were deposed, Mattel was reorganized with a new board of directors and a management headed by Arthur S. Spear, who had been executive vice-president under the Handlers. By 1977 Spear had Mattel back on the road to profits.

Early in 1980 the Handlers sold almost all their Mattel stock, about 12% of the company, thus casting themselves out of the business they had founded. Their stock was then worth $18.5 million.

(Meanwhile, Ruth Handler has entered a new business, still giving fake breasts. She's co-owner of Ruthton, a company that makes prosthetic breasts for masectomy patients. And she still knows how to promote a product. During interviews with reporters she opens her blouse and encourages them to feel her breasts to see if they can tell which is real and which is prosthetic. "The left one is false," wrote Robert Lindsey of the *New York Times*.)

Reputation. They still seem to have a sure touch in the toy business, but there aren't many believers on Wall Street anymore. In early 1980 Mattel stock was selling at $6.50, a far cry from the $50 it sold for in 1971, even after they had introduced Kissing Barbie, who, the company said, "leaves her mark in many ways."

What they own. Mattel owns the best-known brand name in the toy market. By purchasing Western Publishing they became one of the largest commercial printers in the country. Western operates printing plants at Racine, Wisconsin; Poughkeepsie, New York; and Mt. Morris, Illinois. They print the Dell paperbacks, *Travel & Leisure* magazine, and the Foster and Gallagher mail-order catalogs.

Who owns and runs the company. In 1979, prior to the merger with Western, only two Mattel employees—chairman Arthur Spear and president Samuel B. Meason, who was recruited from Riviana Foods in 1976—sat on the 13-member board of directors. After the merger four Western directors joined the board. There's hardly a trace left of the old Mattel management.

In the public eye. Mattel ran ads across the country in 1979 to recall tiny plastic missiles that could be launched from their Battlestar Galactica toys, 2 million of which had been sold. The recall notice went out after a four-year-old boy died from swallowing one of the projectiles. Mattel offered to exchange the missiles for a Hot Wheels vehicle.

Where they're going. Into other businesses. They tried—and failed—to acquire the Macmillan publishing house in 1979. There may be other efforts. Seven banks have given Mattel a credit line of $125 million to finance purchases of other companies.

Stock performance. Mattel stock bought for $1,000 in 1970 sold for $240 on January 2, 1980.

What a Doll!

She may not walk and talk, but she kisses, suntans, bends, dyes her hair, drives a Corvette, and rides a 10-speed bike. She is the Barbie doll, the first doll with developed breasts. Over 112 million Barbies, Kens (her boyfriend), Skippers (her sister), Francies (her black friend), and other assorted friends and relatives have been sold since 1959. Clothing and accessories for the Barbie population currently sell at the rate of 20 million items a year.

About 2,000 people around the world collect Barbies, subscribe to "Barbie Bulletin" and "International Barbie Doll Collector's Gazette," or read *The Encyclopedia of Barbie Dolls and Collectibles,* whose coauthor, Sybil DeWein, owns 1,315 Barbies and friends and all the accessories.

An original, boxed 1959 Barbie, which sold for around $3 when it was new, brought $501.59 in 1978. New Barbie dolls cost about $6 to $9 in 1980.

Major employment centers. Hawthorne and East Los Angeles, California; South Plainfield, New Jersey.

Access. 5150 Rosecrans Avenue, Hawthorne, California 90250; (213) 644-0411. Their toll-free number is (800) 421-2887.

Consumer brands.

Mattel toys: Astro Blast rockets; Baby Grows Up doll; Barbie doll and dream house; Bee Gees Rhythm Machine; Brain Baffler computer game; Caterpillar trucks; Creepy Crawlers Thingmaker II; Dancerella doll; Drive Command cars; Godzilla; Horoscope Computer; Hug 'n Talk dolls; Las Vegas Pinball; Luv-a-Bubble and Baby Magic Tenderlove dolls; Magical Musical Thing; Mork and Mindy toys; The Power Shop toys; Scorches models; See 'n Say talking television; Softuf foam toys; Spinout 360 tricycle; Sir Galaxy robot; Superman Spinball Pinball; Tuff Stuff toys; Monogram's Snap-tite.
Entertainment: Holiday on Ice show; International Circus Festival of Monte Carlo; Rin-

gling Bros.–Barnum & Bailey Circus; Shipstads & Johnson Ice Follies.
Amusement park: Circus World.
Home computers: Intellivision.
Publishing: Western Publishing; Golden Books; Betty Crocker Recipe Cards; The Greenhouse.
Hobbies: Whitman checkers and chess games; Skil-Craft biology and chemistry sets; Handy Andy tool sets and dollhouse kits.

> **What happened to the Game called Happiness?**
>
> "We once had a Game Called Happiness, which stressed the need to help one another out and was not competitive. It bombed."
>
> —Dr. Dorothy Worcester, psychologist and vice-president of market research (and director of creative services) for Milton Bradley
>
> Source: *Saturday Review,* December 1979.

Book Publishers

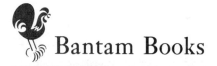

Bantam Books

Sales: $100 million (estimate)
Rank in paperback books: 1
Founded: 1945
Employees: 450
Headquarters: New York, New York

What they do. Things have changed in the paperback world since Bantam's fa-

mous rooster stepped into the ring to square off against Pocket Books' kangaroo: from the garish, laminated, easy-to-peel covers of the postwar years to the more sedate graphics of the 1970s; from the 200,000-copy press runs of 1946 to the 2.5 million run for Jacqueline Susann's *Love Machine* in 1970; and, most spectacularly, from the paltry paperback author fees of a few thousand dollars in the late 1940s to sums in the millions today.

Americans buy 400 to 500 million paperbacks a year, and Bantam has 15% of that market in their pocket. They have led the way in battles for big paperback titles, setting a record in 1975 when they paid $1.85 million for the paperback rights to *Ragtime* by E. L. Doctorow, then breaking it themselves by paying $3.2 million for the rights to Judith Krantz's *Princess Daisy*. You have to sell a lot of paperbacks to justify that kind of outlay, and Bantam does. Their Des Plaines, Illinois, distribution center moves more than 100 million books a year to over 120,000 bookstores, newsstands, supermarkets, schools, airports, and other outlets throughout the United States and Canada, and tens of thousands more to 110 foreign countries.

Bantam churns out 30 new paperbacks every month. To get the right to reprint hardcover books, they compete with other houses in auctions, usually conducted informally by phone or over lunch. But reprints of hardcover books aren't Bantam's only business. They also copublish with hardcover houses and do original paperbacks. They invented the "instant book"—a rocket-propelled job of writing and printing based on a current event that has overwhelmed public attention, like the Watergate hearings, the first lunar landing, Nixon's trip to China, or the 1967 Arab-Israeli war. The most instantaneous of the instant was *The Pope's Visit to the United States* in 1965, written and printed in less than three days.

Bantam's longtime editorial chief Marc Jaffe (who recently left to take over Random House's Ballantine Books) used to say that there is no mass market; there are many mass markets. Skilled in cashing in on them all, Bantam mixes distinguished literature (Doris Lessing, Philip Roth, Kafka, Homer) with an abundance of forgettable romances, adding whodunits; westerns; science fiction; topical nonfiction; diet, exercise, and cooking books; reference and educational works; volumes of crossword puzzles; books concocted from movies and TV series *(Star Trek Lives!)*; and practical tomes like *Winning Tactics for Weekend Singles* (advice not for swingers but for tennis players). Their all-time best-selling author is western writer Louis L'Amour, who has sold 100 million copies.

History. Ian Ballantine, an American graduate student at the London School of Economics, wrote a thesis on the economics of paperback publishing, then went home in 1939 and opened a United States branch of Penguin Books, which was having great success with paperbacks in England. At

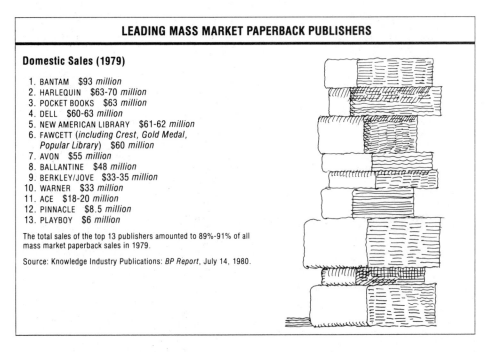

LEADING MASS MARKET PAPERBACK PUBLISHERS

Domestic Sales (1979)

1. BANTAM $93 *million*
2. HARLEQUIN $63-70 *million*
3. POCKET BOOKS $63 *million*
4. DELL $60-63 *million*
5. NEW AMERICAN LIBRARY $61-62 *million*
6. FAWCETT (*including Crest, Gold Medal, Popular Library*) $60 *million*
7. AVON $55 *million*
8. BALLANTINE $48 *million*
9. BERKLEY/JOVE $33-35 *million*
10. WARNER $33 *million*
11. ACE $18-20 *million*
12. PINNACLE $8.5 *million*
13. PLAYBOY $6 *million*

The total sales of the top 13 publishers amounted to 89%-91% of all mass market paperback sales in 1979.

Source: Knowledge Industry Publications: *BP Report*, July 14, 1980.

that time paperbacks (which had flared sporadically in the nineteenth century) were dead in America. But they were about to spring dramatically to life through Pocket Books, which also started in 1939. By the time Ballantine parted ways with Penguin in 1945 and was looking for backing to start his own company, Pocket Books had swept the country and had been bought by the rapidly expanding publishing empire of Marshall Field. Some big publishers were interested in stopping Field's expansion. Five of them hastily joined forces to snatch Grosset & Dunlap away from him, and Grosset in turn helped bankroll Ian Ballantine as a good bet to challenge Pocket Books. The other major backer was Curtis Publishing, publisher of the *Saturday Evening Post*. The new contender for the crown in lightweight publishing, which took the name Bantam, had an astoundingly heavyweight board of directors, including the

Conjuring Up The Exorcist

If not for a chance meeting between writer William Blatty and a Bantam Books executive, there would have been no *Exorcist* —no book, no movies, and, perhaps, no national obsession with demonic possession.

Blatty and Marc Jaffe met at a Hollywood party in December 1967. When Jaffe asked Blatty what he was working on, Blatty told him of an idea for a novel about demonic possession, but he said neither his own agent nor any publisher had found the story interesting. "It sounds pretty good to me," said Jaffe.

A few weeks later Jaffe got a letter from Blatty. It said: "I dreamed last night that I saw you standing at the confluence of Hollywood and Vine holding a massive cornucopia that spewed forth paperbacks and doubloons. In the dream you were smiling. I have since discussed the matter with my gardener, a certain Mr. Wisdom Tweed, who, it happens, is also a lay analyst, and together we concluded that my dream was a *bona fide* sign that the time had come to render unto Bantam a few jottings concerning the novel that has been simmering in my subconscious for some years."

Eight pages of electrifying background and outline followed. Then Blatty confided why he had not written the

book yet: "I am lazy and weak and insecure and can't resist those $100,000 screenplay assignments which aren't nearly the chore involved in writing a decent novel, and besides, I blew my cool and my cash in the stock market last year."

All of this, as it turned out, was Blatty's preamble to his pitch for a big advance. Without that, he said, he could not afford to take time to write the book, because it would be successful only with solid research. "The reader must feel that things like this have happened," Blatty contended in his letter. "He must sniff the unmistakable aroma of authenticity in the pages." Bantam, sniffing the unmistakable aroma of profit, bought all rights to *The Exorcist* for a relatively modest advance payment: $26,000. But Blatty did not immediately spin out his tale of possession. First he dashed off another $100,000 movie script, finally finishing *Exorcist* in 1970. Bantam arranged to have the book published first in hardcover by Harper & Row. Its success in hardcover prepared the way for its leap to the top of the best-seller list as a paperback in 1973, then again in 1974 after the movie was released. By the time *The Exorcist* slid off Bantam's best-seller list months later, it had sold 10 million paperback copies. No other book had ever returned

so much to Bantam on so small an initial outlay. Said Jaffe: "An editor is lucky if he has one like that in his career."

Blatty's novel was also indirectly responsible for a new look in paperback covers that helped sell other authors' novels of the supernatural. Bantam's art director and vice-president Leonard Leone calls it *"The Exorcist* look." The design formula calls for a deep purple or black background, title type exactly like *The Exorcist's*, and a symbol of some sort, small but bizarre and unearthly. "If you can get some blowing candles into it, that's always a real plus," says Leone.

"Blowing candles for some reason or other conjure up something in connection with death masks and skulls to suggest a bit of black mass, and if you get a white-faced woman with black hair, a sort of bloodless look, that's pretty good too."

One Bantam author, Frank Luria, had several novels about the supernatural on the book racks, but none sold well until Leone tried giving their covers *"The Exorcist* look." Sales of the Luria books "took off like a shot," reported Leone, with one book selling 350,000 copies.

Source: Clarence Petersen, *The Bantam Story: Thirty Years of Publishing* (Bantam, 1975).

heads of Random House; Harper & Brothers; Little, Brown; and Book-of-the-Month.

Ian Ballantine and his colleagues carefully chose the 20 titles on Bantam's first list in 1945: reprints of works by Mark Twain, John Steinbeck, F. Scott Fitzgerald, and Antoine de Saint-Exupery; a Zane Grey western; two books with *murder* in the title; some humor; some romance. It was a phenomenal success. They went from four to eight titles a month. Soon they had lots of competitors—Mentor, Signet, Fawcett, Dell, and Avon, to name a few. Newsstands and store racks were jammed with 25¢ books in the early 1950s. This was the era of the carnal cover and the purple blurb. "We had cleavage on *Little Women*," said one of Bantam's founders. In 1952 a congressional committee looking into pornography sharply criticized the paperback industry's "lurid" cover art and obsession with "the 3 S's": sex, sadism, the smoking gun. Meanwhile the market was glutted, new companies were spewing out paperbacks with about as much control as a volcano, and millions of unsold books were being returned to publishers.

In 1952 Ian Ballantine resigned from Bantam to start his own Ballantine Books, another paperback house. It took 18 months to replace him. In 1954—a year when 60 million unsold paperbacks from all publishers were dumped, some of them into an abandoned canal near Buffalo, New York— a skeptical Oscar Dystel was persuaded to take the Bantam presidency. Dystel had had a very successful career managing and editing such magazines as *Esquire, Coronet,* and *Collier's.* Comparing the paperback industry's tactics to "an army sending out 1,000 soldiers and getting 900 killed to capture an objective," he completely reorganized Bantam, had it running in the black by 1955, and stayed on to lead the company for the next 25 years.

Bantam history, according to *The Bantam Story,* by Clarence Petersen, is as colorful as Bantam book covers. It abounds with tales of breathtaking deals, blockbuster sales, anecdotes about famous writers, Hollywood collaborations, ingenious promotions, national (and sometimes international) phenomena touched off by massive paperback popularity. For example, there was "Jawsmania" that took over the country when the book (which preceded the movie) went through 18 printings and 6.2 million copies in six months. There was a flap in the French government over Leon Uris's *Topaz.* There was the time Garson Kanin tricked Dick Cavett into displaying his book, *Tracy and Hepburn,* on coast-to-coast TV for the third time by giving out complimentary copies while on the air.

The paperback industry is characterized by rapid turnover, and Bantam itself has had five owners in less than 35 years: Grosset & Dunlap, National General, American Financial, the Italian IFI International, and the German Bertelsmann Publishing Group.

THE BIGGEST BOOK PUBLISHERS

Book Sales (1979)*

1. TIME (Book-of-the-Month Club; Little, Brown; Time-Life Books)	$425 *million*
2. CBS (Holt, Rinehart & Winston; Praeger; Dryden; Fawcett Books; Gold Medal; Premier; Popular Library)	$340 *million*
3. McGRAW-HILL (Webster; Schaum/Paperback; Gregg; Standard & Poor's)	$335 *million*
4. READER'S DIGEST (Reader's Digest Condensed Books)	$333 *million*
5. DOUBLEDAY (Dell; Delacorte Press; Dial Press; Literary Guild)	$287 *million*
6. SCOTT & FETZER (Worldbook-Childcraft)	$279 *million*
7. GROLIER (Scarecrow Press; Franklin Watts)	$278 *million*
8. ENCYCLOPAEDIA BRITANNICA (G. & C. Merriam)	$275 *million*
9. SFN/SCOTT, FORESMAN (University Park Press; William Morrow)	$254 *million*
10. HARCOURT BRACE JOVANOVICH (Academic Press)	$237 *million*
11. TIMES MIRROR (New American Library; Harry N. Abrams; Matthew Bender; Year Book Medical Publishers)	$235 *million*
12. MacMILLAN (Berlitz Publications; Crowell Collier)	$228 *million*
13. PRENTICE-HALL	$208 *million*
Total**	$3.7 *billion*

*In 1979 the entire book industry sold books worth a total of $6.3 billion, roughly equal to the sales of Kraft that year. Fifty-eight corporations had sales larger than Kraft's.
**The total sales of these 13 companies represent 59% of all books sold in 1979. There are 1,250 companies in the United States that published at least three titles in 1979.

Source: Knowledge Industry Publications, *BP Report,* Vol. 5, No. 31, July 7, 1980.

Reputation. "Bantam is King of that skittish, pressure-cooker segment of the book world known as mass-market paperbacks," said the *New York Times Book Review* in 1980. The company is best known for expertise in defining and redefining the many mass markets and for aggressive, imaginative promotion.

What they own. The rights to Judith Krantz's *Princess Daisy*. At $3.2 million, the novel has to sell between 4 and 6 million copies to break even. But Bantam is betting that Krantz is the next Jacqueline Susann, the only other Bantam author to hit this range consistently.

Who owns and runs the company. The German Bertelsmann Group is headed by a former German Afrika Korps officer named Reinhard Mohn, who spent a large part of World War II interned in an American prisoner-of-war camp near Concordia, Kansas. Bertelsmann bought 51% of Bantam in 1977, and then bought the remaining 49% from the Italian IFI in 1980. Bertelsmann is Germany's largest publisher. In fact, Time Inc. is the only publisher in the world bigger than Bertelsmann. Despite their huge size, nearly 90% of Bertelsmann is still owned by the Mohn family, direct descendants of Carl Bertelsmann, who founded the company as a religious book publisher in 1835.

Reinhard Mohn admits that he is "no literary man," according to *Business Week*. He handles the business side of Bertelsmann by using the American management techniques he learned from Alfred Sloan's book, *My Years With General Motors*. Although Mohn dislikes politics, Bertelsmann owns three-quarters of Gruner & Jahr, publishers of the slick and influential magazines *Der Spiegel* and *Der Stern*. In 1979 Gruner & Jahr entered the U.S. market with a lavish $4-a-copy magazine, *Geo*.

Bertelsmann has announced that Bantam has complete autonomy, but they did help pick Bantam's new chairman, Louis Wolfe, formerly of Avon Books, who replaced Oscar Dystel on his retirement in 1979. Most of the final decisions on titles to be published by Bantam are made by a woman, editor Rollene Saal.

Where they're going. Bantam joined with publisher William Morrow in 1979 to form Perigord Press, enabling them to buy hard- and softcover rights to a book at the same time. They will remain separately owned and operated companies.

It is ironic, if coincidental, that since being taken over by companies from the two former Axis countries, Bantam has decided to reissue scores of World War II

Paperbacks for the People

A tragic-looking Indian mourns the death of his bride beside two lovers rapturously entwined and bathed in a peach-colored glow; nearby a monstrous shark shoots from the sea depths to seize a naked swimmer; below, a bikini-clad young woman strikes a pose designed to show that she has triumphed over the unsightly bulges of cellulite with the help of the book whose cover she adorns.

Whether the supermarket shopper who confronts this multicolored wall of decisions ultimately chooses *Bury My Heart at Wounded Knee, Once Is Not Enough, Jaws,* or

Cellulite, he or she is probably unaware that a scant 40 years ago the choice did not exist. Grocery shoppers had only to choose between radishes and romaine, and people who wanted books went to bookstores to buy them. When they did, they found mostly expensive hardcover editions. Seldom were books bought on impulse, as they often are now.

Today the paperback revolution has put books nearly everywhere, bringing them to a mass audience and transforming the reading habits of the nation. In markets, drugstores, newsstands, railroad stations—wherever magazines

are sold—mass-market paperbacks are present as a part of everyone's environment.

Paperbacks as such are nearly as old as the Republic; it is the way they are printed and marketed that has changed. As early as 1777 Americans could plunk down eight shillings for a paperback book: one or another of the 190 volumes of John Bell's "British Poets" series. Early publishers were quick to recognize the potential appeal of bargain-priced books, but, lacking either high-speed printing presses or mass-marketing channels, their first efforts to launch a paperback industry proved short-lived. In

DOUBLEDAY

Sales: $351 million
Profits: $17 million
Rank in hardcover book sales: 1
Rank in book clubs: 1
Founded: 1897
Employees: 5,700
Headquarters: New York, New York

> The cost of manufacturing (paper, printing, and binding) 4,000 copies of a typical 400-page hardcover book averaged $2.01 for each book in 1979, according to the *U.S. Book Publishing Yearbook*.

"glory novels" in a major War Books series that celebrates the heroism of the Luftwaffe as readily as that of the U.S. Marines. Bantam hit stores with a frontal assault of 15 war books in March 1979, to be followed by a new title each month until there are at least 60. An editor says that the series focuses on the positive aspects of war. Observing that the Vietnam-era disillusionment with war is past and there is a resurgence of enthusiasm for martial idealism, Bantam hopes to cash in with such titles as *I Flew for the Führer* and *A Helmet for My Pillow*.

Major employment centers. New York, New York; Des Plaines, Illinois.

Access. 666 Fifth Avenue, New York, New York 10019; (212) 765-6500.

Consumer brands.

Books: Bantam; Perigord; New Age.

What they do. Doubleday is probably the nation's largest publisher of hardbound "trade" books (those that are sold through general bookstores, as opposed to those aimed at special markets, like school and professional books). But only Nelson Doubleday, president, grandson of the founder, and owner of about 51% of the stock, knows for sure. And he isn't saying.

In fact, this private, family-owned company is so tight-lipped that nearly all the information in this profile came from a *New York Times* article of July 15, 1979, which called Doubleday "the Sphinx of Publishing." No information came from the company. Their treasurer responded tersely to our inquiries: "We do not publish financial information and, therefore, will not be able to send any to you."

The *Times* estimates Doubleday's yearly output of trade books at 700, quite a few more than any other firm publishes. The list usually includes a handful of best-sell-

---

1831 the Boston Society for the Diffusion of Knowledge took a crack at it, featuring hard-hitting titles like *Discourses Delivered before the Boston Mechanics Institute*; the venture sank without a trace.

Other paperback publishing enterprises followed, most of them only marginally successful at best. The one noteworthy exception was the dime novel. In its heyday, from 1860 to about 1910, the dime novel permeated American folkways as television does now. With bold, simple plots of mystery or sensational adventure, populated by pure-minded heroes

and blackhearted villains, these 10¢ paperbacks captured the imaginations of young Americans, becoming the nation's first mass-produced entertainment industry. They were the favorite reading of Civil War soldiers, as comic books later became for the G.I.'s of World War II. To meet the insatiable demand, authors like Horatio Alger, William Gilbert Patten, and Frederick van Rensselaer Dey churned out endless variations on their stock themes of the poor-but-virtuous-newsboy-turned-tycoon, the noble and fearless Frank Merriwell, and the invincible sleuth, Nick Carter.

Several billion copies of dime novels were printed, and their popularity gave book publishing a bigger share of the gross national product than it has ever enjoyed before or since.

The leading entrepreneur of the dime novel was Erastus F. Beadle, a marketing genius who abandoned the cloistered dignity of the bookshop to plaster every available surface with posters trumpeting the virtues of his product: *"Books for the Millions! A Dollar Book for a Dime!"* The runaway success of this promotion for his first book inspired Beadle to even flashier tactics. Edward S. Ellis, author of

ers, a handful of distinguished novelists and poets, and a raft of works aimed at the mass market—romantic fiction, mysteries, celebrity memoirs, how-to books, and the like.

But that's not where the money comes from. The biggest chunk of Doubleday's profits (about 35%) emanates from book clubs. Doubleday owns 15 of them, from the well-known Literary Guild (which they claim is larger than Book-of-the-Month Club and therefore the biggest in the nation), to the less well-known but still profitable Doubleday Book Club, Military Book Club, Doubleday Romance Library, and Graphic Guild—all of which Doubleday keeps well fueled through plenty of direct-mail advertising and spreads in Sunday newspaper supplements.

Doubleday's next biggest money-maker is probably their Laidlaw Brothers textbook subsidiary, which concentrates on the elementary and high school markets and accounts for about a quarter of the profits. Laidlaw is followed closely in the profits department by the company's manufacturing operation, which prints and binds virtually all the 60 million trade and book-club volumes Doubleday puts out and is reputed to be the most efficient printing operation in publishing. Most of Doubleday's competitors farm out their business to independent printers.

Bringing up the rear for Doubleday are

> The U.S. is the world's largest book exporter. About 40% of books exported go to Canada, 12% to the United Kingdom, 10% to Australia, 6% to Japan, and 3% each to Mexico and the Netherlands. The estimated 1980 total for U.S. books sold abroad exceeds $500 million.

their actual publishing concerns: primarily Dell (one of the nation's largest paperback houses), Dial Press, Delacorte Press, and, finally, Doubleday Publishing Company (the trade book outfit). Although hardcovers rarely make money by themselves, Doubleday keeps this part of their operation going strong by getting all they can out of film, paperback, foreign, and serial rights. The nationwide chain of Doubleday bookstores contributes only marginally to the company's coffers.

History. Frank Doubleday went to work for the publishing company of Charles Scribner's Sons in 1877, at the age of 15. Twenty years later he left to form his own publishing house in partnership with S. S. McClure, who had decided he wanted to publish books along with his prospering line of magazines, the most successful being *McClure's Magazine.* The partnership lasted

---

the second title Beadle ever published, a mass-market adventure called *Seth Jones, or the Captives of the Frontier,* later reminisced about Beadle's marketing strategies:

All of a sudden, all over the country, there broke out a rash of posters, dodgers and painted inscriptions demanding to know "Who is Seth Jones?" Everywhere you went this query met you. It glared at you in staring letters on the sidewalks. . . . In the country the trees and rocks and the sides and roofs of barns all clamored with stentorian demands to know who Seth Jones was . . . and just when it had

begun to be a weariness and one of the burdens of life . . . a new rush of decorations broke out all over the country . . . in the form of big and little posters bearing a lithographic portrait of a stalwart, heroic looking figure under. . . . And above or below this imposing figure in large type were words, "I am Seth Jones."

Beadle's success gave rise to imitators. Dime novels became big business, dominated by a few giants like Beadle and Adams, George Munro, Norman Munro, Street and Smith, and Frank Tousey. Beadle and Adams alone pub-

lished more than 7,500 novels, and their competitors were close behind. Horatio Alger's books alone—some 100 novels—sold about 250 million copies.

But competition and changing tastes ultimately killed off the dime novel. Rival hardcover and magazine publishers, joined by moralists who viewed dime novels as sensationalist trash, lobbied to deny dime-novel publishers the extremely low, subsidized second-class postal rate. Since dime novels were sold largely on newsstands and by mail order directly to readers, it was a stunning blow when the U.S. Postal Service

only three years: both men had dominating personalities and needed to be in charge. And Doubleday thoroughly dominated his company from 1900 until the late 1920s.

He had a number of extraordinary relationships with writers, the most famous being Rudyard Kipling, whom he had attracted to Scribner's and brought with him when he formed his own company. Once he nursed Kipling night and day through a critical bout with pneumonia. The friendship lasted to the end of their days. When Doubleday decided to accept a novel by Booth Tarkington—then poor and unknown—he climbed six flights of stairs to a dingy room to convey the good news personally. For over a year he contributed $50 a month to help support the obscure and poverty-stricken Joseph Conrad. Other writers in his stable in the early part of the century were Frank Norris, O. Henry, Arthur Conan Doyle, Willa Cather, Edna Ferber, and Booker T. Washington. But his most profitable author was a now-forgotten writer named Gene Stratton-Porter, a midwestern housewife whose works (with titles like *Moths of the Limberlost* and *Freckles*) stressed love of family, hearth, home, and nature.

Not all authors got such good treatment from Doubleday, according to an account in Charles A. Madison's *Book Publishing in America*. While he was abroad, his partner

Nelson Doubleday is a big man in publishing and baseball. He runs Doubleday & Co., which manufactures 50 million books a year. And following in the steps of his granduncle, Abner Doubleday, the reputed inventor of baseball, he bought the New York Mets, who rarely manufacture enough victories to climb out of the National League cellar.

accepted Theodore Dreiser's *Sister Carrie* after Frank Norris had declared it to be a masterpiece. But when Doubleday read the manuscript, he was offended by its realism, and his wife plainly pronounced the book immoral (it showed that a woman could sin and remain unpunished). Doubleday tried

revoked the publishers' second-class permits. Consignments of dime novels languished at depots, while the pulp magazines, now in lone, triumphant possession of the coveted second-class permits, flourished.

The rise of the pulps dealt the dime novel its final death blow, after a decade or so of declining popularity. Pulp magazines carried several stories in a single issue, their fiction was more varied and sophisticated, and they attracted more adult readers than dime novels, which appealed primarily to adolescents. Furthermore, by 1920 or so the dime novel was

suffering from a generation gap. The overblown heroics of a Deadwood Dick or Buffalo Bill adventure might have thrilled a boy of 1880, but his counterpart in 1920 had different tastes. Dime-novel publishers had always depended heavily on their own past stories as a source of free material, reprinting them year after year. Now they were stuck with titles that their readers found stale. By 1920 the dime novel was virtually dead.

Then, in 1939, came Gertrude the Kangaroo, bearing in her pouch the first Pocket Book. Her creator, Robert de Graff, "the father of the mod-

ern paperback," is credited with launching the present paperback revolution. As former president of a company that published low-priced clothbound reprints, he was convinced that cheap books could reach the same mass markets as cigarettes or shaving cream, provided they got the same widespread national distribution. Years later, describing his vision, de Graff made it sound deceptively simple: "My idea was to put out 25-cent books which could fit easily into a pocket or purse and to provide them with attractive picture covers."

At the time, though, pubto get out of the contract, but Dreiser insisted. So Doubleday saw to it that less than 650 copies of the book were distributed and less than 500 sold. Dreiser got so depressed he almost committed suicide and didn't try to write fiction again for 10 years.

George Doran, a publisher who merged his company with Doubleday in 1927, said Frank was "by extraction and practice ruthlessly Prussian." Once again the merger went on the rocks, and the leaders of Doran's company went their separate ways. Meanwhile Doubleday's health was failing. He made his son Nelson president in 1928, and Nelson was fully in charge when his father died in 1934.

Frank Doubleday had become known as the first of the business-oriented publishers, and Nelson was even more so. "I sell books," he once said, "I don't read them." When he died in 1949, a *New York Herald Tribune* writer characterized him as "one of the world's leading merchants of books," who "believed all books were written to be sold in quantity."

Nelson Doubleday, Jr., joined the firm after graduating from Princeton in 1954, then left in 1956 for a three-year stint in the Air Force. When he returned he quickly became a director and vice-president, but didn't take over as president until 1978.

Reputation. "We're chugging along. Nothing is happening and nothing looks like it's going to happen." That's all the satisfaction the *New York Times* reporter got from the vice-president, who communicated by phone that no one at Doubleday cared to be interviewed.

Until just a few years ago, their report to shareholders consisted of a few numbers scrawled on a blackboard at the annual meeting, which was held in a windowless boardroom. Nowadays Doubleday actually prints an annual report, but copies are about as rare as Gutenberg Bibles.

Doubleday's a conservative bidder in the auctions of hot book properties. They compete with the biggest, but an agent says that once a figure edges over $250,000, "they get pale in the face and begin to keel over."

Doubleday is famous for the number and breadth of their published titles, but the physical quality of the books on the list is less than breathtaking. A former employee said you can tell a Doubleday book with your eyes closed because "it feels so rotten." Doubleday is known for printing on crummy paper and binding their books with a glue that turns brittle so rapidly they often fail to survive a cover-to-cover reading.

What they own. The New York Mets. That's right—the baseball team. Nelson Doubleday is descended from Abner Doubleday, the man many say invented baseball. In January 1980 Nelson bought the team and, in an emotional press conference, announced that this perennial National

---

lishing insiders scoffed at de Graff's effort to revive the expired paperback business. But de Graff, fortified by his long stints with Doubleday and Garden City Publishing Company, and backed by three Simon & Schuster executives, launched Pocket Books with 10 titles, all reprints of hardcover classics and bestsellers: Emily Brontë's *Wuthering Heights*, Felix Salten's *Bambi*, Agatha Christie's *The Murder of Roger Ackroyd*, James Hilton's *Lost Horizon*, Thorne Smith's *Topper*, Dorothy Parker's *Enough Rope*, Thornton Wilder's *The Bridge of San Luis Rey*, Samuel Butler's *The Way of All Flesh*, Dorothy Brande's *Wake up and Live*, and *Five Great Tragedies* by William Shakespeare.

From the start, de Graff's distribution tactics were unorthodox. He wanted his Pocket Books in every subway, supermarket, drugstore, and backwoods trading post. No existing book marketing system reached these outlets, however. Early in 1941 de Graff's first sales manager, Wallis E. Howe, persuaded four wholesale magazine distributors to handle Pocket Books. Soon more than 600 newspaper and magazine distributors had signed up to display Pocket Books in the outlets they serviced. Pocket Books also supplied specially designed racks to their outlets —the first paperback racks ever to appear in American stores.

The success of Pocket Books soon silenced the skeptics. In their first 10 years of existence the firm sold more copies than all the bestsellers combined since 1880. Their success was sudden and phenomenal, and it set the pattern for the paperback avalanche that followed. *Pocket book* became synonymous with paperback, although other companies were soon trying to capitalize on de Graff's success. Penguin

League cellar-dweller would soon be transformed into the cream of baseball. A few months later, the *New York Times* carried a full-page ad appealing to the nostalgia of the great days of baseball, when New Yorkers screamed and wept over the Giants and Dodgers, and concluding with the motto, "The New Mets. The Magic is back."

Publishers have a way with words. How they intend to get the Magic back into the Mets' hitting and pitching remains as mysterious as the Sphinx's riddle.

Who owns and runs the company. The private company has less than 300 stockholders, and the great majority of shares belong to the family. Although Nelson Doubleday, Jr., with 51%, is clearly in control, other family members occasionally get uppity. Witness the case of Neltje Doubleday Kings, ex-wife of Doubleday's chairman John Sargent, and daughter of Nelson, Sr. Periodically Mrs. Kings decides to press her conviction that Doubleday ought to go public. She goes to the annual meeting, insists that the stock be listed on the New York Stock Exchange, and is voted down by Nelson. Things then return to normal.

Two men make the decisions at Doubleday. Chief executive Nelson, reported to have "a will of iron and a hellish temper," has the final say on everything. But the hour-to-hour decisions, according to the *Times*, are made by Nelson's most trusted

> The first black-owned publishing company, the National Baptist Publishing Board, was founded in 1896 by Richard Henry Boyd, a former slave who taught himself to read and write at age 30.

colleague, vice-president John O'Donnell—very private, sharp, tough, superbly efficient, "the sort of executive who causes people to quiver a bit in their boots."

In the public eye. That naked lady in the encounter group wasn't just there to heal her psychic wounds. She was there to write a novel. But she didn't tell anyone. She even signed a paper (as did all the participants) promising not to write anything about the 20-hour "nude encounter marathon" conducted by Los Angeles psychologist Paul Bindrim. A month later she signed a contract with Doubleday, giving her a $150,000 advance for *Touching*, which she churned out in about four months. When Bindrim saw how unmistakably he was portrayed in the leading character, and how scandalously the events of the marathon had been falsified and vulgarized, he sued. The resulting battle over whether a person can be libeled by a work of fiction brought swarms of writers, publishers, and literary agents out of the woodwork, sounding the alarm about First Amendment rights and the dan-

Books, a British paperback publisher, opened an American office in 1939, selling, like Pocket Books, through newsstands and magazine outlets. Ian Ballantine, head of Penguin, ultimately broke away to form Bantam Books, now a paperback giant, and later Ballantine Books. Still, Pocket Books has remained a force to be reckoned with: at the end of their first 25 years they had sold a spectacular 1 billion books, with 3,000 titles, making them, numerically, the biggest publisher in the history of the industry.

Yet without three interlocking developments there could have been no mass-market paperbacks. One was de Graff's pioneering use of distribution channels already established by the magazine and newspaper industries, which gave paperbacks national coverage equal to *McCall's* or *Reader's Digest*, along with distributors' confidence that they could get their money back from publishers if the books didn't sell. Another was the invention of the high-speed roll-fed printing press, which could mass-produce books economically. And third was the advent of short-term reprint agreements, whereby hardcover publishers grant paperback firms the right to reprint bestsellers for a specified length of time, usually five to seven years.

Today Americans buy more than 400 million paperbacks each year, choosing from 123,000 different titles sold in more than 100,000 retail outlets—figures that would astonish even Erastus F. Beadle himself.

gers of muzzling artists. But to no avail. The jury awarded $75,000 to Bindrim, agreeing that he had been libeled, and the California Appellate Court upheld the jury. Finally, the U.S. Supreme Court refused to review the case and let stand the lower court decision. Doubleday wouldn't have been in trouble, except that Bindrim's lawyer had told them the material was libelous when the hardback came out and they'd better not go issuing a paperback. The publisher asked author Gwen Davis if she'd libeled anyone, and she said of course not, so out came the paperback. The court called that insufficient investigation, and Doubleday had to share the blame with the author.

Then there was the case of *Alex Haley vs. Doubleday*. Haley's *Roots* was the nation's best-selling book within a month of its October 1976 publication by Doubleday, and it was still on top when Haley sued his publisher for $5 million in March 1977. He said they hadn't bothered to promote his book, they'd monkeyed around with paperback rights to his disadvantage, and they'd even inhibited hardcover sales. Altogether he counted five instances of breach of contract, and he thought $1 million apiece would be about right to soothe his outrage. Doubleday denied it all and flung back some accusations of their own (for instance, that it took Haley 10 years longer than he promised to deliver the manuscript).

The suit was dropped in 1977. When we phoned Doubleday in 1980 to ask if they could give any further information about the settlement, they said "No, and nobody else can either."

Access. 245 Park Avenue, New York, New York 10017; (212) 953-4750.

Consumer brands.

Books: Dell; Dial Press; Delacorte Press; Doubleday; Anchor; Laidlaw.
Book clubs: Doubleday Book Club; Literary Guild; Western Writers Club; Mystery Guild; Military Book Club; Doubleday Romance Library; Graphic Guild.
Bookstore: Doubleday Bookshop.
Professional baseball: New York Mets.

Close to 30,000 new book titles are added each year to the half-million U.S. books in print.

HBJ

Harcourt Brace Jovanovich

Sales: $413 million
Profits: $7.4 million
Rank in textbook publishing: 2
Founded: 1919
Employees: 7,800
Headquarters: New York, New York

What they do. For decades Harcourt Brace Jovanovich has been one of the nation's largest publishers of elementary and high school textbooks, as well as an eminent general book publisher. But recent developments indicate that HBJ would like to be something quite different. Why else would a publisher of grade-school math books suddenly buy into businesses as diverse as business magazines, seafood restaurants, TV stations, and amusement parks?

The first big headscratcher came in late 1976, when HBJ acquired Sea World—a San Diego–based trio of recreational parks (with the other two in Florida and Ohio) featuring trained whales and dolphins and other marine wonders. Sea World's operations also include an institute for the study of sharks, a chain of Captain Kidd Seafood Galley restaurants, and fish processing plants in California and Mexico. Then in 1977 HBJ bought the Petroleum Engineering Publishing Company, which made them the proprietor of 63 specialized business magazines from the *Pipeline and Gas Journal* to publications on cosmetics, toys, and tobacco. Adding these to the journals they already had for doctors, lawyers, farmers, teachers, and others, HBJ claimed to be tied with McGraw-Hill in the number of their business publications. In mid-1978 HBJ expanded further, acquiring television stations in Duluth, Minnesota.

What makes a book publisher go shopping like that? Well, greed may have something to do with it. Survival too. Book publishing is not the most lucrative business around, and it's not exactly a growth industry, at least not the way Wall Street means growth. So William Jovanovich, who has been HBJ's president for over 25 years, decided to go the conglomerate route and pick up a few nonpublishing businesses to bolster profits and make the stock a trifle more glamorous to investors.

HBJ's two top profit-makers in 1978 were

school publications (39%) and the Sea World group (31%). Next came university and professional publications (20%) and testing services (10%). The tests emanate primarily from another of the oddities in the HBJ stable: Psychological Corporation, a testing and consulting company founded and formerly owned by some 380 psychologists that works with business, government, and educational institutions. Finally, HBJ sells quite a lot of insurance to farmers in the Midwest. In fact, insurance provided slightly more profits (9%) than the tradebook department in 1978.

History. HBJ was originally Harcourt, Brace & Company—the result of two young men, Alfred Harcourt and Donald Brace, who were getting fed up with the conservative style of their employer, publisher Henry Holt, and were setting off on their own in the summer of 1919. Their first big success was economist John Maynard Keynes's now-famous *Economic Consequences of the Peace*, published in 1920. They soon branched out into fiction and poetry and in the 1920s published such distinguished authors as Sinclair Lewis, Carl Sandburg, T. S. Eliot, and E. M. Forster.

Harcourt, Brace had been a major textbook publisher from the start; William Jovanovich, who joined the firm in 1947, continued that tradition, first as head of the school department, then as president of the company from 1954. But he had other plans too. In 1960 the company went public, and soon afterward Jovanovich managed a merger with World Book Company, a major publisher of school and college textbooks. The greatly expanded company was renamed Harcourt, Brace & World. In the next 12 years they acquired over 20 more companies, but all had something to do with publishing. In the mid-1970s Jovanovich began to adopt more daring business strategies, such as the expansion into fish (both trained and frozen). He took the daring a step further in 1978 when he created a three-member Office of the President, adopting the corporate structure of companies like ITT, Kodak, Borden, and other conglomerates, but unheard of in the staid world of hardcover publishing.

To get Sea World, HBJ competed with—and beat—MCA, the giant entertainment conglomerate. Then Jovanovich tried to crack the mass-market paperback business with an imprint that linked his name with

that of the king of the Roman gods. But Jove Books fell flat despite an unprecedented ad campaign in *Publishers Weekly*, the industry trade journal. Ironically, MCA bought floundering Jove in 1979 and combined it with their own paperback enterprise, Berkley Books.

Human Nature, the slick magazine launched by HBJ in late 1977, was an idea whose time hadn't come. Jovanovich liked the magazine very much, but he didn't like the price tag—$4 million the first year, and dimming hopes that the venture would ever break even. With regrets, he folded his first attempt at a consumer magazine in March 1979.

HBJ is decidedly William Jovanovich's company—a fact reflected in the 1970 name change to Harcourt Brace Jovanovich. There are stories that Jovanovich, very proud of his Yugoslav heritage, was annoyed by frequent misspellings and mispronunciations of his name. He changed the name of the firm so that people would have to get it right.

Reputation. Restless. They not only want more companies, but they want them bigger. "We're actively looking at a lot of companies to buy," William Jovanovich told the *Wall Street Journal* in 1980. "We aren't looking at anything right now smaller than $40 million in annual sales."

What they own. A broad range of publishing enterprises, including general and educational books, tests, and magazines; Sea World's marine parks, research institutes, restaurants, and fisheries; two Duluth TV stations; several insurance companies, including Harvest, which serves mainly agricultural areas; and buildings in San Diego, San Francisco, Duluth, and elsewhere.

Who owns and runs the company. Chairman William Jovanovich is the author of two novels and a collection of essays in which he characterizes publishing as "one of the most civilized of worldly pursuits." His writings reveal a man of great erudition and charm. His business dealings reveal a man of relentless ambition with an increasing yen to engage in ventures that are more worldly and less civilized.

In 1978 the comparatively tiny ($32 million in annual sales) Marvin Josephson Associates, a talent agency that represents some of America's most eminent authors (and owns the Captain Kangaroo television series), managed to buy 8.6% of HBJ's stock. This took HBJ by surprise, and they filed suit, charging violations of the Securities Exchange Act. They later withdrew the suit and stated to *Publishers Weekly* that "both sides had agreed not to make any further comment about the litigation." Josephson kept their 8.6%.

Of the 15 directors, 4 are women, one being the author Anne Morrow Lindbergh. In 1980 former Minnesota Senator Eugene McCarthy joined the board.

In the public eye. William Jovanovich was a personal friend of the Yugoslav dissident Milovan Djilas and played a major role in the American publication of Djilas's works in the early 1960s. Two of the 11 pieces in *Now, Barabbas,* Jovanovich's essays on publishing, are devoted to Djilas's career and Jovanovich's relationship with him. They include the transcript of Jovanovich's 1962 testimony before a Senate committee investigating the Yugoslav government's attempts to interfere with publication of Djilas's works.

Where they're going. More expansion. Jovanovich speculated in a 1978 issue of *Publishers Weekly* that his next purchase might be an athletic team. But while Jovanovich was dabbling with dolphins, Nelson Doubleday, a rival publisher, hit a home run by buying the New York Mets in early 1980.

Stock performance. Harcourt Brace Jovanovich stock bought for $1,000 in 1970 sold for $531 on January 2, 1980.

Major employment centers. New York City; San Diego, California; Duluth, Minnesota.

Access. 757 Third Avenue, New York, New York 10017; (212) 888-2345.

Consumer brands.

Books: Academic Press; Dansville Press; Kurt and Helen Wolff Books; Harcourt Brace Jovanovich.
Book Club: The History Book Club.
Restaurant: Captain Kidd Seafood Galley.
Amusement parks: Sea World.
Insurance: Harvest.
Television stations: WDIO and WIRT.

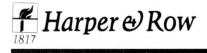

Harper & Row

1817

Sales: $167 million
Profits: $4.4 million
Rank in book publishing: 5
Founded: 1817
Employees: 1,900
Headquarters: New York, New York

What they do. When a chairman's annual letter to stockholders includes lines like "The year had a peculiarly intense, grueling, unsettling quality," you know the firm is in shaky times. Harper & Row, one of the nation's oldest publishing houses, may have bitten off more than they could chew when they bought the J. B. Lippincott Company in late 1978. After the last-minute battles were over and the dust had cleared, Harper's announced that they had somehow paid more than they'd meant to. The explanations were complicated and confusing, but the drift of it was that Harper's had bought about $21 million worth of a nebulous commodity called *good will*—a term that stands for the amount by which the purchase price exceeds the fair market value of the goods. In plain language, to get Lippincott, Harper's absorbed a loss of more than $21 million. They decided to spread the damage over 40 years, which means that $532,000 comes off the top of anything the company earns every year until 2020.

Still, Harper & Row is in no danger of going under. In 1979 they published over 1,200 new books, films, tapes, and records—including Gerald and Betty Ford's memoirs, Theodore White's *in Search of History,* the final volume of Alexander Solzhenitsyn's *Gulag Archipelago,* and memoirs by two more Nobel Prize winners: Anwar Sadat and Menachem Begin. Their sales of college and school textbooks reached $48 million. One bright spot, and the only obvious benefit from the Lippincott deal, was getting hold of a line of medical and nursing books that more than doubled Harper & Row's sales in the field of professional books. But even with that boost, the Lippincott purchase dragged Harper & Row's profits down to 60% of their 1978 level and caused some eyebrow-raising on Wall Street. While president Brooks Thomas huffily defended the deal as "the most important acquisition we have made in 162 years," one stock analyst said, "Let's put it this way. I'm glad it was done by someone I didn't have my money in."

In their fiscal 1980 year—the 12 months ended April 30, 1980—Harper's rebounded by posting record sales of $167 million and profits of $4.4 million, up 42% over the 1979 level (but still below the $4.9 million and $4.7 million earned in 1978 and 1977 when sales were far lower).

History. Fifteen-year-old James Harper was inspired to become a printer when he read Ben Franklin's *Autobiography* in 1810. After a couple of years' experience as printers' apprentices, he and his brother John set up their own shop in 1817. Two other brothers, Wesley and Fletcher, soon joined them. The quartet worked so well together, with the brothers playing different and complementary roles in the growing business, that the association lasted half a century and was broken only when James died in 1869. (The others died soon afterward, between 1870 and 1877.)

The Harpers' original idea had been to service New York's 33 booksellers, and their first book, a translation of Seneca's *Morals,* was printed for bookseller Evert Duyckinck. But they soon began publishing on their own. By 1830 they were the biggest publishers in the country, turning out a title a week.

In the 1830s they started launching series: Harper's Family Library, the Library of Select Novels, the Boys and Girls Library (which included the *Swiss Family Robinson,* the first American printing of that children's classic), the Classical Library. Their School District Library, geared to state school requirements, eventually brought out 295 volumes, which were distributed all over the country.

The Harper brothers developed a reputation for haggling with authors. In 1840 they sat down with William Cullen Bryant and the father of Richard Dana to bid for the rights to Dana's *Two Years Before the Mast.* The first offer was $200. Bryant and Dana wanted $500. After hours of negotiation the Harpers had barely budged, and a final price of $250 was agreed upon. In 1965 Harper & Row bought one copy of the first printing of *Two Years* for more than twice what was paid for the entire publishing rights in 1840.

In 1844 James Harper was elected mayor of New York. (He came back to the publishing business after one term.) By 1853 Harper & Brothers was the biggest publishing house in the world. That was the year the company's 16 buildings and virtually everything in them burned down. The night of the fire the brothers got together to plan the rebuilding of the company, which they accomplished in short order with warm support from business and community leaders.

Harper's New Monthly Magazine appeared in 1850 and soon became one of America's most important literary and intellectual journals. *Harper's Weekly,* started in 1857, carried the work of the famous political cartoonist Thomas Nast and political commentaries and features. *Harper's Bazaar,* aimed at women, began in 1867; it is still thriving (although now owned by the Hearst Corporation).

The most important figure at Harper & Row in the twentieth century has been Cass Canfield, who joined the company in 1924 and remained for more than 40 years, most of the time as president. In 1925 the legendary literary editor Eugene Saxton moved over from Doubleday, bringing with him a long list of popular writers like James Thurber, E. B. White, O. E. Rölvaag, Bernard De Voto, and Robert Benchley. The Harper & Row religious division, started in 1926, has published such distinguished authors as Teilhard de Chardin, Albert Schweitzer, Paul Tillich, and Bishop James Pike.

Harper & Brothers became Harper & Row in 1962, when the New York company merged with a big textbook house in Evanston, Illinois: Row, Peterson & Co. R. K. Row and Isaac Peterson had gone into business in Chicago in 1906 to publish *Essential Studies in English,* a book coauthored by Row. Their most successful series was the *Alice and Jerry* elementary school readers, which sold nearly 100 million copies.

In the 1960s, when publishing companies like Random House, Simon & Schuster, and Holt, Rinehart and Winston were being gobbled up by huge conglomerates, Cass Canfield took steps to safeguard Harper & Row's independence. First he sold a great slice of stock to the Minneapolis Star and Tribune Company, headed by John Cowles, Jr., who happened to be married to Canfield's stepdaughter. Then he raided Wall Street to get the business sophistication he reasoned was necessary for the book people to outmaneuver the money people.

He brought Winthrop Knowlton, a partner of a major investment banking firm and a former assistant secretary of the treasury, and Brooks Thomas, a corporate lawyer, into Harper's top management. Knowlton and Thomas subsequently became Harper & Row's chairman and president.

Reputation. Harper & Row published Herman Melville's *Moby Dick* (1851), among other giants of American literature, but to make it into the twentieth century they needed a loan from J.P. Morgan ($850,000). Now Wall Street people have come aboard to take the helm of what's considered a bastion of traditional publishing. Some people think they have hooked a white whale with Lippincott, but President Brooks Thomas explained: "We're just trying to steer the battleship in a slightly different direction."

What they own. Besides Lippincott, Harper & Row owns Basic Books, whose list of scholarly titles includes the collected works of Jean Piaget and Sigmund Freud. In 1977 they bought T. Y. Crowell, a big name in juvenile books and a publisher of reference works including *Roget's Thesaurus.* With Lippincott came the Ballinger Publishing Company, which produces specialized professional books.

Who owns and runs the company. The largest shareholder, with 32% of the stock, is the Minneapolis Star and Tribune, whose chairman, John Cowles, Jr., and president, Otto A. Silha, sit on the Harper & Row board. Cass Canfield, Jr., son of the former president and currently a senior editor at Harper's, owns about 4% of the stock and is on the board. Joseph and Barton Lippincott, who own a total of 4% of the stock, are also directors.

The Minneapolis Star and Tribune announced in mid-1980 that they were discontinuing *Harper's Magazine,* which they bought from Harper & Row in 1965. John Cowles, Jr., is the nephew of Gardner Cowles, Jr., who ran the Cowles Communications media empire, which in its heyday owned *Look* and *Family Circle* magazines as well as a TV station in Memphis (WREG), and a string of newspapers in Florida. Cowles killed *Look* in 1971, the same year they sold *Family Circle* and other properties to the *New York Times.*

In the public eye. In 1974, 320 Harper & Row employees in New York, members of

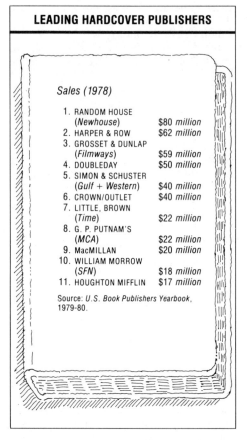

LEADING HARDCOVER PUBLISHERS

Sales (1978)

1.	RANDOM HOUSE (Newhouse)	$80 million
2.	HARPER & ROW	$62 million
3.	GROSSET & DUNLAP (Filmways)	$59 million
4.	DOUBLEDAY	$50 million
5.	SIMON & SCHUSTER (Gulf + Western)	$40 million
6.	CROWN/OUTLET	$40 million
7.	LITTLE, BROWN (Time)	$22 million
8.	G. P. PUTNAM'S (MCA)	$22 million
9.	MacMILLAN	$20 million
10.	WILLIAM MORROW (SFN)	$18 million
11.	HOUGHTON MIFFLIN	$17 million

Source: U.S. Book Publishers Yearbook, 1979-80.

an independent company union, staged the first and longest strike—17 days—in modern book publishing history. The average wage of the striking employees had been $190 a week; the new contract gave them raises totaling $46 a week over a three-year period. In 1977, 240 New York employees, now affiliated with the United Auto Workers, walked out again in a dispute over merit raises and cost-of-living increases; the strike lasted a week before a compromise was reached.

In 1978 chairman Winthrop Knowlton outlined a plan to combat unemployment: he proposed that corporations be given tax breaks if they taught reading to job applicants who are functional illiterates.

Stock performance. Harper & Row stock bought for $1,000 in 1970 sold for $636 on January 2, 1980.

Access. 10 East 53rd Street, New York, New York 10022; (212) 593-7000.

A Decade of Best Sellers

	Year First Published		Publisher	Number of Copies Sold
Fiction				
1. THE GODFATHER By Mario Puzo	1969	Hardcover Paperback	PUTNAM NEW AMERICAN LIBRARY	292,765 13,225,000
2. THE EXORCIST By William Blatty	1971	Hardcover Paperback	HARPER & ROW BANTAM	205,265 11,948,000
3. JONATHAN LIVINGSTON SEAGULL By Richard Bach	1970	Hardcover Paperback	MacMILLAN AVON	3,192,000 7,250,000
4. LOVE STORY By Erich Segal	1970	Hardcover Paperback	HARPER & ROW AVON	431,976 9,778,000
5. JAWS By Peter Benchley	1974	Hardcover Paperback	DOUBLEDAY BANTAM	204,281 9,210,000
6. THE THORN BIRDS By Colleen McCullough	1977	Hardcover Paperback	HARPER & ROW AVON	646,503 7,450,000
7. RICH MAN, POOR MAN By Irwin Shaw	1970	Hardcover Paperback	DELACORTE DELL	99,610 6,550,000
8. THE OTHER SIDE OF MIDNIGHT By Sidney Sheldon	1973	Hardcover Paperback	MORROW DELL	85,000 6,500,000
9. CENTENNIAL By James A. Michener	1974	Hardcover Paperback	RANDOM HOUSE FAWCETT	458,788 5,715,000
10. FEAR OF FLYING By Erica Jong	1973	Hardcover Paperback	HOLT, RINEHART, WINSTON SIGNET	100,000 5,700,000
Nonfiction				
1. THE LATE GREAT PLANET EARTH By Hal Lindsey and C. C. Carlson	1970	Hardcover Paperback	ZONDERVAN BANTAM	57,227 7,229,542
2. CHARIOTS OF THE GODS? By Erich Van Däniken	1970	Hardcover Paperback	PUTNAM BERKLEY PUBLISHERS	59,924 6,298,000
3. YOUR ERRONEOUS ZONES By Wayne W. Dyer	1976	Hardcover Paperback	CROWELL AVON	780,569 4,640,000
4. THE JOY OF SEX By Alex Comfort	1972	Hardcover Paperback	CROWN SIMON & SCHUSTER	1,000,000 4,236,000
5. FUTURE SHOCK By Alvin Toffler	1971	Hardcover Paperback	RANDOM HOUSE BANTAM	209,475 4,795,000
6. THE SENSUOUS MAN By "M"	1971	Hardcover Paperback	LYLE STUART DELL	410,000 4,500,000
7. ROOTS By Alex Haley	1976	Hardcover Paperback	DOUBLEDAY DELL	1,174,000 3,677,000
8. IF LIFE IS A BOWL OF CHERRIES—WHAT AM I DOING IN THE PITS? By Erma Bombeck	1978	Hardcover Paperback	McGRAW-HILL FAWCETT	702,926 3,440,000
9. THE TOTAL WOMAN By Marabel Morgan	1973	Hardcover Paperback	REVELL REVELL/POCKET BOOK	903,000 2,700,000
10. THE GRASS IS ALWAYS GREENER OVER THE SEPTIC TANK By Erma Bombeck	1976	Hardcover Paperback	McGRAW-HILL FAWCETT	463,915 3,116,000

Source: *The New York Times Book Review,* 12/30/79

Consumer brands.

Hardcover books: Harper & Row; Lippincott; T. Y. Crowell; Basic Books; Ballinger.
Paperback books: Torchbook; Colophon; Barnes & Noble; Perennial.

Sales: $880 million
Profits: $77 million
Rank in business magazine publishing: 1
Rank in educational publishing: 1
Founded: 1909
Employees: 13,240
Headquarters: New York, New York

What they do. McGraw-Hill started *Business Week* magazine two months before the stock market crash in 1929, expressing the view, contrary to popular opinion, in their first issue, that the economy wasn't really in great shape. A phenomenal success in spite of a slow start and a feuding family ownership, *Business Week* has become a prime information source for the business community. It carries more advertising pages than any other magazine in America, a championship for which it vies perennially with *The New Yorker;* the McGraw-Hill publication usually wins. Every year more than 750,000 people pay about $22 million to receive the magazine. Add $78 million in advertising revenues—and you have a $100 million magazine property.

McGraw-Hill is known primarily as a publisher of technical magazines and textbooks. They put out 60 magazines, such as *Chemical Engineering, Aviation Week & Space Technology, Electronics,* and *Medical World News,* thereby ranking as the largest publisher of trade magazines and newsletters. These publications account for 30% of their sales.

McGraw-Hill is a giant in the book field too; publishing a staggering 20,000 different books a year. They rank as the largest publishers of textbooks, and they have been striving to establish a presence in trade books, the industry term for novels and popular nonfiction. Kottmeyer's *Basic Goals in Spelling* is one of their big grade-school sellers, but they also published Erma Bombeck's *If Life Is a Bowl of Cherries, What Am I Doing in the Pits?* Books and educational services represent 40% of their business.

The reigning McGraw, Harold, Jr., rules the operation from new corporate headquarters in Rockefeller Center, a glassier, classier skyscraper box than the old green McGraw-Hill landmark on West 42nd

Street, in Manhattan's Hell's Kitchen, abandoned several years ago. It was there, just off New York's pornography row, that the family feuds festered. A former president, Jay McGraw, was ousted by other members of the family in 1950; it was said that he forced his brothers to make appointments to see him. Of the current leader a cousin told *Fortune* "He wanted me to be his damn briefcase carrier." It may have been this family dissidence that encouraged staid American Express to make a takeover bid for McGraw-Hill in 1979. Harold McGraw then rose to the occasion, beating back the invaders in a fierce battle in which he accused American Express of everything from lacking integrity to trying to destroy credibility of the press.

History. The two founders, James H. McGraw, Sr., and John Hill, started their publishing careers independently but almost simultaneously in the late 1880s by becoming involved in trade magazines that provide news and information about specific industries. McGraw, a schoolteacher in upstate New York, supplemented his salary by selling magazine subscriptions on the side. In 1886, when he tried to collect $1,500 owed to him from a nearly defunct magazine, *Street Railway Journal,* he was given a chance to buy the magazine instead. He immediately switched its emphasis from horsecars to electrification. At about the same time, Hill, a locomotive engineer, began contributing articles to *American Machinist* and *Locomotive Engineer.* Eventually he became owner of both.

The two were innovators, and each began to make a clear distinction between advertising copy and editorial matter, a previously fuzzy (and sometimes still fuzzy) area in trade journals. They also reported their circulations, a move that separated them from other business publishers who gave away their magazines and went to advertisers with tall tales of their readership. In 1909 the pair formed the McGraw-Hill Book Company to publish technical books. They kept their magazines apart, however. When Hill died unexpectedly in 1916, leaving five magazines and no heirs who cared to run them, his magazines were merged with McGraw's the next year.

McGraw-Hill continued to expand by buying other magazines and starting new ones to cover different trades and industries. The culmination of these efforts was

Business Week, a magazine to report on all aspects of business. In the late 1960s and early 1970s McGraw-Hill moved into other fields, most of them related to the original orientation of McGraw and Hill. In 1966 they paid $82 million to buy Standard & Poor's, one of Wall Street's major information sources. When the 1970–71 recession hit McGraw-Hill magazines, the Standard & Poor's bond rating service was put in the position of downgrading their own company's bonds (the lower rating a bond has, the higher interest the company has to pay on loans). Nevertheless, in 1972 McGraw-Hill went outside their normal territory to buy four television stations from Time, Inc., for $57.2 million. And in 1979 they signaled their interest in the new and fast-growing field of electronic information delivery by spending $103 million to buy Data Resources, a company run by noted economic forecaster Otto Eckstein. Data Resources supplies information, and makes predictions, from a computer-simulated model of the economy. Whether it will be as accurate as *Business Week* was in 1929 is another question.

Reputation. Have a manuscript you want to see in print? Take it to McGraw-Hill. They were suckered into contracting for Clifford Irving's monumental hoax, the "autobiography" of Howard Hughes. Then, adding humiliation to ignominy, the *New York Times* revealed—on the same day Clifford Irving and his collaborators were indicted—that large parts of another McGraw-Hill best-seller, *The Memoirs of Red Chief*, were plagiarized from a book published in the 1940s. Since those two frauds were uncovered in the early 1970s, cynics have been saying McGraw-Hill will publish anything. They have certainly put their name on enough tedious (self-financed) histories of corporations, including the modestly titled *Endless Frontiers, the Story of McGraw-Hill.*

On the other hand, they're regarded highly by professionals who use their publications and information services every day. If you're a contractor, architect, or security analyst, it's necessary to use *Dodge Reports, Sweet's Catalog,* or *Standard & Poor's Stock & Bond Guide* because they're all basic tools of their industries.

What they own. Licenses to operate four television stations: WRTV, Indianapolis;

KMGH, Denver; KGTV, San Diego; and KERO, Bakersfield, California. They're co-owners of thier headquarters building in Rockefeller Center. They have distribution centers in Highstown, New Jersey; Manchester, Missouri; and Novato, California.

Who owns and runs the company. Six grandchildren of founder James McGraw own 4.4 million shares, about 18% of the company. Chairman Harold W. McGraw, Jr., got the top job in 1975, shunting aside his two cousins, Donald McGraw and Donald's younger brother, John. Donald, who thought he should be chairman, was bitter and seemed eager to sell his 622,000 shares when American Express initiated their unsolicited takeover attempt in 1979. He is not on the board. John resigned as an officer in 1978 but remains on the board. "We haven't had Thanksgiving dinner at grandmother's house in a number of years," John remarks, describing the family rift.

Edward Booher, formerly head of McGraw-Hill's Book Division, was an early underestimater of Harold, who once worked under him. Booher says: "I did not respect him professionally." When Harold took charge of the company, he reorganized Booher out of a job. "It just never occurred to me," Booher later reflected, "that Harold would one day be my boss."

In 1979 the board of directors included eight white males over 60 and one woman, Kay Knight Clarke of Arthur D. Little, a research and consulting firm. William J. McGill, president of Columbia University, also sat on the board.

In the public eye. When American Express tried to gobble up McGraw-Hill for $1 billion in cash, Harold McGraw was surprised, shocked, furious, and adamant. His answer, and that of his board, was a loud and public No.

The fight itself became a media event—newspapers and magazines gave it extensive coverage—and some shareholders, most notably Donald, were unhappy with the board's inflexible negative attitude. But in the end Harold won—at a cost of $3.4 million in legal fees, $1 million more than American Express paid their lawyers.

Where they're going. "It's the wave of the future," said Harold McGraw in 1980. He meant computerized data banks containing precise information on an unlimited range of subjects, ready to be scanned and turned into dozens of publications tailor made for specialized audiences. Once a mere sideline, the business of providing detailed facts and figures to industries, governments, and individuals now brings in half of McGraw-Hill's money. It's called "data-based publishing," and you had to be as big as McGraw-Hill to become the leader in the field, compiling and collating masses of information, setting up the electronic hardware to process it, and mobilizing the sales force to market it.

The material retrieved from the data banks may turn into an international journal, a report for a particular person, or a regularly updated newsletter. The people to whom this information means dollars and cents are ready to shell out for it: the average McGraw-Hill newsletter costs $250 a year. But a subscription to *Platt's Oilgram News* (known, with its companion publication, *Platt's Oilgram Price Report*, as the Bible of the oil industry) costs $557 plus $100 for airmail. And the more exclusive *Platt's Oilgram Marketscan* carries an annual price tag of $2,300.

Stock performance. McGraw-Hill stock bought for $1,000 in 1970 sold for $996 on January 2, 1980.

Access. 1221 Avenue of the Americas, New York, New York 10020; (212) 997-1221. On the basement level there's a bookstore that probably has the largest collection of business books of any store in the country.

Consumer brands

Books: McGraw-Hill.
Magazines (business, trade, and professional): Architectural Record; Aviation Week & Space Technology; Business Week; Chemical Engineering; Chemical Week; Coal Age; Construction Methods & Equipment; Data Communications; Electrical Construction & Maintenance; Electrical World; Electronics; Engineering & Mining Journal; Engineering News Record; Fleet Owner; House & Home; International Management; Medical World News; Modern Plastics; National Petroleum News; Power; Textile Products and Processes; Textile World.
Information systems: Dodge Reports; Sweet's Catalog Files; Standard & Poor's.

RANDOM HOUSE

Sales: $150 million (estimate)
Profits: $5 to $10 million
Rank in general interest books: 1
Founded: 1925
Employees: 1,500
Headquarters: New York, New York

What they do. They provoked—and won—the most famous censorship case in the history of U.S. publishing (James Joyce's *Ulysses*, cleared of obscenity charges in 1933). For four decades they've published the nation's most famous children's writer, Dr. Seuss. And they had the most famous head of a publishing company, Bennett Cerf, who until his death in 1971 loved to publicize "the ham that I am" and whose smiling face was beamed into millions of American homes every week for 17 years on the popular TV show "What's My Line?"

Cerf's posthumously published memoirs, *At Random*, are crammed with intimate stories of his relationships with famous authors. How Eugene O'Neill spirited him down to the basement to listen to his beloved "Rosie"—a white player piano with naked ladies painted all over it. How James Joyce, potted, tried to sing him some Irish ballads, and was forcibly stopped by Mrs. Joyce. How Cerf rented a dress suit for William Faulkner to accept the Nobel Prize in. How young Truman Capote went to do a story on multiple murders in a small Kan-

Of the approximately 16,000 bookstores in the United States, between 4,000 and 5,000 are general bookstores, carrying both fiction and nonfiction. The rest of the nation's bookstores are more specialized, including about 3,000 religious bookstores and 2,500 to 3,000 college bookstores. An increasing share of the general books are being purchased in bookstore chains, two of which account for nearly one-third of all sales in general bookstores: the 524-store Walden Book chain, owned by Carter-Hawley-Hale, and the 364-store B. Dalton chain, owned by Dayton Hudson.

sas town dressed up in a pink velvet Dior jacket. How Gertrude Stein, when Cerf admitted on coast-to-coast radio that he didn't understand her work but was proud to be her publisher, replied, "I've always told you, Bennett, you're a very nice boy, but you're rather stupid." There are stories of James Michener, Sinclair Lewis, Robert Penn Warren; stories of haggling and howling with George Bernard Shaw, of setting up a luncheon between Cardinal Spellman and rough, tough Catholic novelist John O'-Hara (who called his publisher "Cerfie").

Besides their list of illustrious contemporary authors, Random House has over the years published the Modern Library classics, the *Random House Dictionary of the English Language,* and the *Random House Encyclopedia.* Since 1960 they have acquired several other important publishers; including Alfred A. Knopf (with their paperback line, Vintage Books), Pantheon Books, and the paperback house Ballantine Books. These companies are almost completely autonomous, each having its own editor-in-chief, editorial staff, and advertising and promotion people. Their offices are on separate floors of the Random House building (Random House occupies 13 of 60 floors). What they share is Random House's big sales staff and centralized accounting and shipping.

History. Twenty-seven-year-old Bennett Cerf regularly asked his boss, publisher Horace Liveright, to sell him the Modern Library. And Liveright (who was really quite fond of Cerf) regularly threw him out of the office. But one day in 1925 the flashy, fast-living Liveright, perennially in need of money, instead of saying "Get out of here!" to Cerf's request, said, "What will you give me for it?"

That was the start of Random House, which began as Modern Library, Inc. Liveright was publishing some of the greatest writers of the time, but Modern Library—inexpensive hardbound editions of classic and modern books—was his bread and butter. Cerf and his friend Donald Klopfer bought the line (112 book titles at the time) for $215,000 and made their investment back in two years. In 1927 they decided to start publishing luxury editions of books chosen "at random." When they told their artist friend Rockwell Kent about the new name, Random House, he immediately sketched a logo—a house that looked half-

cottage and half-mansion. The name and the logo have stayed unchanged for over half a century. Cerf and Klopfer ran the business with apparently uninterrupted good fellowship (for decades they had facing desks and shared the same secretary) until Cerf's death in 1971. Klopfer continued as chairman and became "chairman emeritus" on the firm's 50th birthday in 1975.

The history of Random House is pervaded by a kind of friendly good humor and lightly wielded (though nonetheless potent) intelligence that sprang largely from the personality of Bennett Cerf. One of his longest-serving editors, Jason Epstein, observed, "Bennett runs Random House as a conservative branch of show business." And Kopfer noted that Cerf was the only U.S. publisher who was ever a public figure —TV personality, subject of a 1966 *Time* cover story; compiler and editor of a string of best-selling joke books and a humor column carried by hundreds of newspapers; indefatigable lecturer, storyteller, and partygoer, vast enjoyer of fame and success, but always with a light touch, seemingly moved more by pleasure than by greed.

It was, nevertheless, Cerf's pleasure to build one of the biggest and richest publishing companies in the United States. And one of the most respected.

Random House grew slowly. Modern Library carried them through the Depression (although the luxury editions, which had sold out in the late 1920s, had to go). When Liveright died and his firm went under in 1933, Cerf flew first to Sea Island, Georgia, and then to California to sign Liveright's two premier authors: Eugene O'Neill and Robinson Jeffers. That same year Cerf and Klopfer made a deal with James Joyce: they'd get the American rights to *Ulysses* if they could clear it of obscenity charges. They engineered a seizure of the book by U.S. Customs, fought the charges up to the Supreme Court, and emerged with Judge John Woolsey's historic ruling in the book's favor.

Through the 1930s and 1940s they kept adding distinguished editors and authors. Modern Library grew and prospered. Juvenile books became an important department, with the Babar elephant stories, the Beginner Books series, and the phenomenal Dr. Seuss.

Going partly public (they sold 30% of the stock to outsiders) in 1959 was a watershed in company history. It led to a quick series of acquisitions that made Random House a richly diverse publisher with several distinctive and independent companies under their wing. The first, and most prestigious, was Alfred A. Knopf in 1960. Knopf is still regarded by many as the most distinguished literary publisher in the country, known for quality in physical production as well as in content ("I think that best-seller lists ought to be abolished by law," said 85-year-old Alfred Knopf in 1977). Knopf brought along a college division as well as a quality paperback line, Vintage Books. Also in 1960, Random House bought L. W. Singer, a big publisher of elementary and high school textbooks, and a year later Pantheon —founded in 1942 by Kurt and Helen Wolff, refugees from Nazi Germany who became the U.S. publishers of many European authors and of the scholarly Bollingen series. But Random House didn't get Pantheon's founders, who moved over to Harcourt Brace Jovanovich in 1960 to publish under the imprint Kurt and Helen Wolff Books.

The latest independent publisher to duck under Random House's umbrella was Ballantine Books, the mass-market paperback house, which Random House bought in 1973.

In the mid-1960s big conglomerates got interested in buying book publishers—

there was a whole mythology about electronic hardware and print software rounding each other out in the communications of the future. Random House, growing more profitable every year, was surveyed by several prospective buyers and was finally bought in 1966 by RCA, the electronics and communications giant that also owns NBC. RCA paid $38 million. Bennett Cerf was enthusiastic: "In the next 10 or 12 years, desks of school kids are going to look like miniature computer centers with all kinds of machines," he said in 1968. "They will take their examinations on something that looks like a typewriter, and the grades will come back from a central location in a matter of minutes. These machines we call the hardware. The publishers are going to supply the software, the material that is fed into these machines."

But when Random House's profits flattened out around 1977, RCA started looking for a buyer for the publisher. They finally found one in Newhouse Publications—owner of 29 newspapers, the Condé Nast magazines, *Parade* magazine, and a bunch of cable TV systems. The agreement to sell (for $65–70 million) was announced in early 1980. Random House operates as an independent subsidiary of Newhouse, a privately held company founded in 1922 by Samuel Newhouse and now headed by his two sons.

The Shreds of Failure

What happens to those mass-market paperbacks that sit unsold on supermarket and drugstore book racks? Like scrapped plans for secret military missions, they vanish into the cruel jaws of the paper shredder, carrying with them their authors' dreams of glory and their publishers' hopes of profit.

Shredding books that don't sell, ironically, is part of the system that makes it possible to mass market paperbacks, taking them outside the confines of bookstores and onto racks and newsstands wherever magazines are sold. The wholesale distributers who control these distribution channels for magazines grew enthusiastic about handling paperback books only after publishers agreed that books, like magazines, could be returned for refunds if they failed to sell. But the last thing any publisher needs is a warehouse full of rejected books—so, like unsold magazines, the returns are ripped to shreds.

When a wholesaler pulls books off racks, he first tears off their covers, then feeds the denuded pages into a shredder. The covers go back to the publisher, who marks them off in his debit columns and refunds the wholesaler's money. Baled in bundles, the shredded mix of book and magazine pages goes to scrap dealers.

Not every author's creation meets this violent end, no matter how badly it sells. Publishers try to recover "whole-copy returns" of higher-priced paperbacks, including classics and lavish, large-format books. Still, as the publishers are the first to admit, despite the most expert attempts to estimate each new book's potential public appeal and print only as many copies as readers will buy, roughly half of all mass-market paperbacks printed end up in the shredder.

Source: Clarence Petersen, *The Bantam Story: Thirty Years of Publishing* (Bantam, 1975).

Reputation. An editor's house. Bennett Cerf said that giving a trusted editor freedom was one of the lessons he learned from Horace Liveright. Many fine editors have been lured to Random House—and have stayed long years—because of the company's policy of giving editors their heads.

What they own. In addition to the Random House, Modern Library, Knopf, Pantheon, Vintage, and Ballantine imprints, the company has a large educational division producing textbooks and mixed-media materials.

Who owns and runs the company. Chairman Robert Bernstein, with Random House since 1957, was described by *Publishers Weekly* as a man "with a passion for freedom to publish." He has taken a strong interest in the fate of Soviet dissidents, many of whom have been published by Random and Knopf. The Soviet Union showed its appreciation by rescinding his visa to attend the Moscow International Book Fair in 1979. Bernstein also backed the Knopf suit on behalf of Victor Marchetti's *The CIA and the Cult of Intelligence,* which went all the way to the Supreme Court.

In the public eye. Twinkly eyed Oakland muckraker Jessica Mitford, who had attained fame with her exposé of the burial business, *The American Way of Death,* turned her sharp gaze on Bennett Cerf in 1970. Well, not exactly on Cerf, but on the Famous Writers School, for which Cerf and 14 other writers served as the figurehead "Guiding Faculty." The 15 appeared in innumerable ads, sometimes individually, sometimes together. "Here is Bennett Cerf," wrote Mitford in the *Atlantic Monthly,* "most famous of them all, his kindly, humorous face aglow with sincerity, speaking to us in the first person from a mini-billboard tucked into our Sunday newspaper: 'If you want to write, my colleagues and I would like to test your writing aptitude. We'll help you find out whether you can be trained to become a successful writer.' "

Mitford's investigations indicated that the ads were misleading if not fraudulent (implying that the "Guiding Faculty" actually had something to do with guiding students or judging the aptitude tests, which

they emphatically didn't); that Famous Writers, like its companion businesses, Famous Artists, and Famous Photographers, was a hard-sell of a shoddy product that often duped aspiring authors out of $900 for a course; and that the "Guiding Faculty" were lending their names in a very irresponsible way to a very questionable enterprise for, presumably, a very high fee which none of them was willing to discuss.

Her interview with Bennett Cerf had its amusing moments.

Cerf (cordial and charming): May I call you Jessica?

Mitford: I don't see why not, *Mortuary Management* always does.

Cerf: I think mail-order selling has several built-in deficiencies . . . a very hard sales pitch, an appeal to the gullible. . . . For God's sake, don't quote me on that 'gullible' business!

Mitford: Why do you lend your name to this hard-sell proposition?

Cerf: Frankly, if you must know, I'm an awful ham—I love to see my name in the papers.

The article provoked a torrent of letters, a few defending the school, most dumping on it. The "Famous" schools had become fabulously rich in the 1960s, expanding around the world. But their fortunes plunged in 1971. That was the year Cerf died, still appearing among the Famous Fifteen.

Where they're going. It's a divine marriage, proclaimed the bride and groom, and everything will be just as wonderful in the future as it's been in the past. When Random House was sold to Newhouse Publications in 1980, chairman Robert Bernstein said, "I'm very happy. We feel we will have financial stability and editorial integrity." And Samuel Newhouse, Jr., affirmed resoundingly that there would be "absolutely no changes" at Random House: "We have great faith in print, we have great faith in books, we have great faith in culture." Amen!

Access. 201 East 50th Street, New York, New York 10022; (212) 751-2600.

Consumer brands.

Books: Random House; Alfred A. Knopf; Vintage Books; Pantheon Books; Ballantine Books; Modern Library; Juvenile Books; Beginner Books; Del Rey Books.

AMERICA'S TOP 10 MANUFACTURERS THROUGH THE YEARS

Ranked by Sales Volume

1917
1. U.S. STEEL $2.4 *billion*
2. SWIFT· $875 *million*
3. ARMOUR· $577 *million*
4. AMERICAN SMELTING· $441 *million*
5. STANDARD OIL (*New Jersey*)· $412 *million*
6. BETHLEHEM STEEL $299 *million*
7. FORD MOTOR $275 *million*
8. DU PONT $270 *million*
9. AMERICAN SUGAR REFINING· $200 *million*
10. GENERAL ELECTRIC $197 *million*

1929
1. STANDARD OIL (*New Jersey*) $1.5 *billion*
2. GENERAL MOTORS $1.5 *billion*
3. FORD MOTOR $1.1 *billion*
4. U.S. STEEL $1.1 *billion*
5. SWIFT $1 *billion*
6. ARMOUR $900 *million*
7. STANDARD OIL (*Indiana*) $495 *million*
8. GENERAL ELECTRIC $415 *million*
9. WESTERN ELECTRIC $411 *million*
10. CHRYSLER $375 *million*

1945
1. GENERAL MOTORS $3.1 *billion*
2. U.S. STEEL $1.7 *billion*
3. STANDARD OIL (*New Jersey*) $1.6 *billion*
4. GENERAL ELECTRIC $1.4 *billion*
5. BETHLEHEM STEEL $1.3 *billion*
6. SWIFT $1.3 *billion*
7. ARMOUR $1.2 *billion*
8. CURTISS-WRIGHT $1.2 *billion*
9. CHRYSLER $995 *million*
10. FORD MOTOR $897 *million*

1955
1. GENERAL MOTORS $9.8 *billion*
2. STANDARD OIL (*New Jersey*) $5.6 *billion*
3. FORD MOTOR $5.5 *billion*
4. U.S. STEEL $3.2 *billion*
5. GENERAL ELECTRIC $3 *billion*
6. SWIFT $2.5 *billion*
7. CHRYSLER $2 *billion*
8. ARMOUR $2 *billion*
9. GULF OIL $1.7 *billion*
10. SOCONY-VACUUM OIL· $1.7 *billion*

1966
1. GENERAL MOTORS $20.2 *billion*
2. FORD MOTOR $12.2 *billion*
3. STANDARD OIL (*New Jersey*) $12.1 *billion*
4. GENERAL ELECTRIC $7.7 *billion*
5. CHRYSLER $5.6 *billion*
6. MOBIL $5.2 *billion*
7. TEXACO $4.4 *billion*
8. U.S. STEEL $4.3 *billion*
9. IBM $4.2 *billion*
10. GULF OIL $3.7 *billion*

1979
1. EXXON $79 *billion*
2. GENERAL MOTORS $66 *billion*
3. MOBIL $44 *billion*
4. FORD MOTOR $43 *billion*
5. TEXACO $38 *billion*
6. STANDARD OIL (*California*) $30 *billion*
7. GULF OIL $24 *billion*
8. IBM $23 *billion*
9. GENERAL ELECTRIC $22 *billion*
10. STANDARD OIL (*Indiana*) $18 *billion*

·Swift is now part of Esmark; Armour is now part of Greyhound; American Smelting is now Asarco; Standard Oil (New Jersey) is now Exxon; American Sugar Refining is now Amstar; Socony-Vacuum is now Mobil.

14

LIGHT UP AND DRINK UP

Cigarette Makers

American Brands, Inc.

Sales: $3.8 billion
Profits: $347 million
Forbes 500 rank: 120
Rank in cigarettes: 4
Rank in bourbon: 1
Founded: 1904
Employees: 54,500
Headquarters: New York, New York

What they do. The product of eccentric, willful leaders, American Brands continues today to puff away at what they know best: cigarettes. Despite the change in their name from American Tobacco, and despite bringing into their tent such products as Jim Beam bourbon, Swingline staplers, Sunshine Hydrox cookies, Jergens lotion, and Acushnet golf balls, the health of American Brands is sustained by cigarettes. Their four main brands are Pall Mall, Tareyton, Lucky Strike, and Carlton. Tobacco products—they're important cigar makers too—account for more than 60% of their sales.

Once they were the most powerful force in tobacco. Now they're only a shadow of their former leafy prominence. Not only are they no longer first in cigarettes, but they have slid to fourth place, with only brand, Pall Mall, ranked among the top 10 sellers. When reports linking cigarettes to a variety of deadly diseases began to appear regularly, smokers moved sharply toward filter cigarettes, and American was late in climbing on that bandwagon. They remained true to their original nonfilter products—and they suffered the sales consequences. Although filter cigarettes account for 90% of U.S. cigarette sales, only half of American Brands' cigarette volume is nonfilter.

American is the only U.S. tobacco producer with more cigarette sales outside the country than in it. That's because they own Britain's second-largest tobacco firm, Gallaher. In 1979 they bought Franklin Life Insurance, one of the 50 largest life insurers in the nation. Franklin does not offer a discount to nonsmokers.

History. It all started with James Buchanan "Buck" Duke, the man who controlled the industry more than anyone before or after him and who came within a hair's breadth of controlling all the tobacco in the world. Born in Durham, North Carolina, in 1857, he was the son of Washington "Wash" Duke, an independent dirt farmer who hated the plantation class, opposed slavery, and raised food and a little tobacco. Wash's opposition to secession didn't prevent the Confederate Army from drafting him, and after doing some time in a Union prison, he walked home to find his farm devastated by Sherman's fiery romp through the South. The war over, Union soldiers sacked most of the tobacco warehouses to stock up on Bright leaf (a mild and sweet tobacco) for a chew on the way north. Wash, with nothing else left, granulated Bright leaves, packed it into muslin bags, and peddled it as Pro Bono Publico ("for the public good") chew. The Dukes survived the winter on the proceeds and planted more the next spring. Things went better for Wash than he could have imagined. Some of the stolen Bright had made it north of the Mason-Dixon line, and now there was a sensational demand for it. In 1865 Wash sold 15,000 pounds of Pro Bono Publico chew.

But it was his son Buck who made it big. "I ain't going to be a preacher or lawyer," he told his Latin tutors at a Quaker Academy in New York state; "I'm going to be a businessman and make my pile." Returning home to enter the family business, he found he had serious competition in Bull Durham, a popular Liggett & Myers chew that deft advertising had made number 1 by the late 1870s. "My company is up against a stone wall," Buck wrote. He decided to go into the cigarette business, although he hated to. Cigarettes were effeminate by Southern standards; cigars were the gentlemen's smoke. But he went ahead anyway, moving 125 Russian Jewish immigrants to Durham in 1881 to roll his smokes. They rolled too few. In 1881 James Bonsack, a 21-year-old Virginia mechanic, invented a cigarette-rolling machine that actually worked (there had been previous, painfully complicated attempts), and by 1884 it could turn out 200 cigarettes a minute. Buck managed to tie Bonsack to a series of airtight contracts that gave him special privileges, such as a rebate if other companies used the machine. The contracts enabled Buck to undersell his competitors. Then, in a three-stage program, he moved to take over the entire American tobacco industry.

Move one: In 1887 he cut prices. Other cigarette manufacturers, unaware of the Bonsack deal, were puzzled by the price-cutting, but they also lowered their prices. Buck knew he could outlast them, and he did. Although they tried to buy him out, he refused, offered to buy them instead, and cut prices again. The other companies fell like dominoes. Kinney, the third largest, landed in Duke's hands first. Allen and Ginter sold out to him in 1889. Goodwin and a number of small operations followed. And in January 1890 Duke's lawyers created the American Tobacco Company out of what had been W. Duke, Sons and Company. Buck Duke controlled cigarettes.

Move two: The Plug War. Cigarette control secured, Buck began buying up plug (chewing tobacco) producers. Within half a year he drove plug prices down by 50%, forcing P. Lorillard, Liggett & Myers, Drummond, and Brown to the wall—at the same time "inviting" them to join his company. Again he outlasted his rivals, mainly by pouring cigarette profits into the "plug war" while opponents emptied their treasuries. In the end even Liggett & Myers, which had held out longer than the rest, fell, and Duke got the long-coveted Bull Durham brand in 1899.

Final move: He bought up independent cigarette, plug, and snuff makers, all of which could be "persuaded, bullied, or

TOP SELLING SMOKES

Brand (Company)	Billions of cigarettes (1979)
1. MARLBORO (*Philip Morris*)	103.6
2. WINSTON (*R.J. Reynolds*)	81.0
3. KOOL (*Brown & Williamson*)	56.7
4. SALEM (*R.J. Reynolds*)	53.2
5. PALL MALL (*American*)	33.9
6. BENSON & HEDGES (*Philip Morris*)	27.8
7. CAMEL (*R.J. Reynolds*)	26.3
8. MERIT (*Philip Morris*)	22.4
9. VANTAGE (*R.J. Reynolds*)	20.7
10. KENT (*Lorillard*)	19.3
11. CARLTON (*American*)	15.0
12. GOLDEN LIGHTS (*Lorillard*)	13.2
13. TAREYTON (*American*)	12.2
14. VICEROY (*Brown & Williamson*)	11.7
15. TRUE (*Lorillard*)	11.5
16. RALEIGH (*Brown & Williamson*)	11.3
17. VIRGINIA SLIMS (*Philip Morris*)	10.5
18. NEWPORT (*Lorillard*)	9.8
19. PARLIAMENT (*Philip Morris*)	7.7
20. L & M (*Liggett*)	7.5

Source: *Business Week*, December 17, 1979.

beaten into submission," as Robert Sobel put it in *They Satisfy*, a history of cigarettes in America.

Having control of the U.S. tobacco habit, Duke promptly attacked England, entering the British market in 1902. But the British weren't going to stand for it. Independent producers banded together, forming Imperial Tobacco Company, and withstood Duke's lowered prices. Not only that, they threatened to invade the U.S. market. At that point, a truce was called. The American and British companies agreed to keep out of each other's homelands and carve up the rest of the planet: Duke got America; Imperial got England; and British-American Tobacco, which they founded together, got the rest of the world. Duke was named chairman and got two-thirds of the stock.

In 1904 Duke reshaped his bundle of companies into American Tobacco Company. The only thing he didn't control was cigars, the one thing he wanted most for the prestige value. He had to settle for buying up the companies that manufactured pipes, tinfoil, and cigarette vending machines; and some stores.

But now Buck was in trouble. The U.S. government was after him on antitrust grounds (and because Teddy Roosevelt couldn't stand him), and the first anticigarette movement was underway. Cigarettes were damned as causing sterility, impotence, bad health, and the sickliness and death of users' children. "Tobacco that outlandish weed/ It spends the brain and spoils the seed," cried reformers, led by Lucy Page Gaston, a humorless midwestern woman who looked like Abraham Lincoln

and hounded the industry for 25 years. The main effect of her efforts was the destruction of Duke's little remaining competition —small producers who couldn't bear the loss of revenues that went with a drop in smoking. Duke was selling 9 out of 10 cigarettes in 1900. What finally brought Duke down was the 1911 antitrust suit in which the Supreme Court dissolved American Tobacco into Liggett & Myers, Reynolds, Lorillard, the original American Tobacco company, and a number of smaller companies. It also forced Duke to sell all his stock in British-American.

Depressed and morose, Duke left American Tobacco in 1912 and got into light, learning, and children (although he remained president of British-American). He started the Duke Power and Light Company in North Carolina. Looking for a suitable monument for himself, he gave enough money to Trinity College in Durham that they changed the name to Duke University. Otherwise, he spent his time doting on his daughter. He died in 1925, a relatively happy man of 69. He had outlived Lucy Gaston, who'd lost terribly. In 1900, 4.4 billion cigarettes were sold; at her death in 1924, 73 billion were sold. Ironically, she died of cancer of the throat.

Duke's successor at American, Percy Hill, wasn't the man for the job. Robert Sobel described him as "a gentle and effective staff man, he had been a perfect assistant . . . but Hill had few notions of his own." The company drifted and declined under his leadership from 1912 to 1925 and was unable to stand up to the Camel cigarettes R. J. Reynolds put out. Percy did

Smoking vs. Double Chins

In 1917 Lucky Strikes was a new brand of cigarettes, hopelessly outsold by established brands like R. J. Reynolds's Camels. Women were a potential new market, but in those days most Americans still looked askance at women who smoked. To overcome feminine inhibitions about smoking, American Tobacco's George Washington Hill

unleashed a barrage of ads aimed specifically at women, urging them, for example, to ward off double chins by smoking cigarettes instead of eating fattening candy. "Avoid that future shadow," advised one such Luckies ad, showing an elegant young woman with a taut jawline against a shadowed profile of a woman with sagging jowls.

So effective was the blitz that Luckies' annual sales climbed from $12 million to $40 million in only four years. The ad campaign, which cost $250 million between 1917 and 1938, ultimately enabled Luckies to overtake bestselling Camels.

leave American Tobacco one thing of great value, however: his son, George Washington Hill.

George Hill led the company into the era of mass advertising. If Camel and Chesterfield could make a Burley blend (a tobacco that could absorb liquid additives) that was capturing the market, he could, too. He blended Burley with Bright tobaccos in a smoke he called Lucky Strike, formerly a popular pipe tobacco. He liked the aroma—the blend smelled like morning toast. He introduced it in 1916 with the slogan, "It's toasted." Then he drifted off to World War I, returning in 1919 to go at it again. His devotion to Luckies was described by Sobel as "a missionary's devotion to Jesus."

Small, arrogant, and vulgar—famous for his cowboy hat and the Lucky between his fingers, and spitting on boardroom tables—Hill was a dream merchant who prided himself on manipulation. He teamed up with Albert Lasker, one of the pioneers of advertising, to make Luckies the number 1 smoke in 1931. They alternated with Camels for the top spot in all the years from 1930 to 1950. One of their famous campaigns was, "Reach for a Lucky instead of a sweet!" featuring opera singers and slim actresses. Testimonials from doctors said Lucky was a smoother smoke. Together Hill and Lasker are credited with starting more people on the smoking habit than anyone else in history. They also helped to break the taboo against women smoking in public. The company's directors tried several times to get rid of Hill, but he remained at American until he died of a heart attack in 1944. "I *am* the company," Hill howled, "and those bastards better not forget it!"

Hill didn't live long enough to experience the real disaster. In 1953 publicity linked cigarette smoking to lung cancer for the first time. "Hill would have known what to do about this health business," one Madison Avenue ad executive said. "He would have made cancer fashionable." But Hill wasn't around, and American completely missed the boat. People switched to filter cigarettes in astounding numbers, but American kept relying on Luckies and Pall Mall, another filterless cigarette that had been selling well since before World War II on the bizarre premise that its extra length (it was "king size") made it milder.

In 1963 Robert Barney "Brand-a-Month" Walker took the helm. Trying to catch up, he introduced one filter brand after another

in a buckshot approach to recapture the market. He put out a Bull Durham filter, a Sweet Caporal filter, a Roi-Tan cigarette-cigar hybrid. He mentholated and filtered Lucky Strike. But the only brands to stick were Carlton, the low-tar cigarette, and Silva Thins, aimed especially at women. In the process Walker invented the 100mm cigarette. American continued to lose ground. Lucky Strike disappeared from the top ten in 1969. Tareyton and Pall Mall fell from their lofty positions. American's share of the market sank from 35% in 1965 to 17.8% in 1971. By 1978 they were down to 12%.

American began buying nontobacco companies in 1966, with Sunshine Biscuits and James Beam Distilling. In 1968 they picked up Bell Brand foods and Duffy-Mott (apple and prune products), followed in 1970 by Swingline (staplers), Acme Visible Records (office filing equipment), Master Lock (padlocks), and Andrew Jergens (soap and lotion). They changed their name to American Brands in 1970.

Reputation. American Brands is known as the least flexible and most reclusive of the tobacco companies. They rarely talk about corporate citizenship. They give their back-of-the-hand to critics who raise the health issue. But stockholders love them. American was one of the original companies in the Dow Jones Industrial Average, and they believe in paying high dividends to their stockholders.

What they own. Tobacco plants in Virginia, North Carolina, Northern Ireland, and Wales. The Beam distillery owns 50 whiskey warehouses and four water reservoirs. Sunshine Biscuits has five bakeries, six snack food plants, one flour mill, and one dairy.

Who owns and runs the company. American Brands' chairman is Princeton graduate Robert Heimann, a one-time managing editor of the business magazine *Forbes*, who holds a Ph.D. in sociology from New York University. He built his career on the company's efforts to counter criticism of the tobacco industry, dragging out his typewriter to write *Sold American!* (1954) and *Tobacco and Americans* (1960), both tributes to tobacco's contribution to the nation. He joined the company in 1953 and ascended to the top when Barney Walker—the previous chairman, renowned for smoking 22 cigarettes at just one business meeting—dropped dead of a heart attack in a Manhattan hotel in January 1973. The president is John F. Walrath, who came along with the Andrew Jergens company in 1971. The board of directors has no women and no blacks. Asked why no women were on the board, Heimann said: "We do not select our directors on the basis of sex, race, color, or creed."

In the public eye. Donald Klock, a former president of the Duffy-Mott subsidiary, was convicted of income tax evasion in 1977 and sentenced to a year in prison and fined $20,-000. The James Beam distillery was found to have passed along some $165,000 worth of possibly illegal gifts of liquor between 1970 and 1977. They promised not to do it again.

In 1979 American was the defendant in at least six civil suits alleging racial and sex discrimination. And that wasn't the first time. In 1975 a federal judge ruled that they'd discriminated against blacks and women in job assignments and promotions at their Richmond, Virginia, pipe tobacco and cigarette plants. He ordered them not to hire another white male foreman until their percentage of blacks and women met the percentages of blacks and women in the Richmond area labor force.

American Brands is not noted for their record in philanthropy. Asked at the 1979 annual meeting how much money the company contributed to charity, Heimann declined to give a figure, saying that "comparisons can be odious." He then added: "Our policy on contributions is to limit them to deserving philanthropic, educational, and scientific activities which are not political, fraternal, sectarian, or social in purpose. They must be exclusively for public purposes, must receive wide public support, must be tax deductible, and must serve a wide segment of the community."

Where they're going. American is following the dictum of an advertising slogan they used for many years to promote their Tareyton brand: "We'd rather fight than switch." At the 1979 annual meeting Heimann said: "The company is favored with a corpus of people who have proved their ability to turn setbacks and disappointments into opportunities. Years ago we suffered a crushing blow when the cigarette

George Washington Hill, the man who made Lucky Strike the most popular smoke in the land during much of the 1930s and '40s, was the model for the role played by Sidney Greenstreet in Warner Brothers' 1946 movie, "The Hucksters."

scare—based though it was on questionable experiments in painting mice—made our nonfilter brands obsolescent almost overnight. Our people have met the challenge of that situation, to diversify, to move into new brands and new kinds of business, to keep earnings and dividends growing."

Stock performance. American Brands stock bought for $1,000 in 1970 sold for $1,899 on January 2, 1980.

Access. 245 Park Avenue, New York, New York 10017; (212) 557-7000.

Consumer brands.

Cigarettes: Carlton; Tareyton; Pall Mall; Lucky Strike; Silva Thins.
Cigars: Roi-Tan; La Corona; Antonio y Cleopatra.

About a third of the universally prized American tobacco crop is grown for export. In 1978 that meant the United States exported a total of 74 billion cigarettes.

Pipe tobacco: Half and Half; Paladin Blackcherry; Bourbon Blend.

Liquor: Jim Beam bourbon and Regal China trophy bottles and ceramic products; Spey Royal Scotch; Mr. and Mrs. "T" Bloody Mary Mix.

Food: Sunshine Cheez-its, HiHo crackers, Hydrox cookies, Wheat Wafers, Krispy saltines, Cinnamon Grahams, and other bakery products. Bell Brands and Blue Bell; Mott's applesauce, apple juice, and prune juice, Clamato, Beefamato; Grandma's Molasses.

Life insurance: Franklin Life Insurance.

Locks: Master.

Staplers: Swingline; Ace.

Tools: Spotnails.

Automotive products: Marson.

Golf balls and supplies. Titleist; Bulls Eye; Gold Club.

Soap, lotions, shampoo: Jergens; Gentle Touch; "Gee, Your Hair Smells Terrific."

Office supplies and equipment. Wilson Jones; Acme Visible; Swingline.

Knives and scissors: Case.

Sales: $15 billion
Profits: $500 million
Rank in cigarettes (world): 1
Rank in cigarettes (U.S.): 3
Founded: 1902
Employees: 250,000
Headquarters: London
U.S. Headquarters: Louisville, Kentucky

What they do. Only the Chinese state monopoly makes and sells more cigarettes than B.A.T Industries, a huge multinational whose name used to be British-American Tobacco. Literally born a multinational at the turn of the century, B.A.T has expanded into a sprawling operation that ranks as Britain's third-largest company. They operate 121 tobacco factories in 51 countries, sell 550 billion smokes a year (80% of the amount smoked in the United States), have the number 1 brand in 38 countries, and collect nearly twice the revenues of the two largest U.S. tobacco companies combined. They employ 100,000 people in their tobacco operations. And the last time they counted, they had about 700 brands of cigarettes, cigars, and pipe tobacco.

The U.S. market brings in about a third of their profits, thanks largely to their Louisville subsidiary, Brown & Williamson Tobacco, maker of Kool, Viceroy, Raleigh, and Belair. Kool is the big one. It's the third-best seller in the American cigarette market and the world's largest-selling mentholated cigarette.

Profits from cigarettes have enabled B.A.T to buy companies in nontobacco businesses in both Britain and the United States. They have become the largest British cosmetics company, with a roster of brands including Yardley, Lenthéric, and Germaine Monteil. They have bought paper companies in Britain (Wiggins Teape) and the United States (Appleton), and they have entered retailing on both sides of the Atlantic. In the United States they own Saks Fifth Avenue, Gimbel Brothers, and the Kohl supermarkets and department stores in Wisconsin.

But tobacco is still the main thing, accounting for three-quarters of their profits. It has made them the 25th-largest corporation in the world.

History. James Buchanan Duke, creator of the American Tobacco trust, controlled the U.S. tobacco market at the turn of the century. In 1901 he invaded England to make an all-out bid to control the British market as well. The Wills brothers, Player brothers, and other family-owned British tobacco producers banded together upon Duke's arrival, formed the Imperial Tobacco Company, and squared off to fight the flamboyant American. A bitter year-long price war came to an end only when Imperial took steps to invade the American market in retaliation. Exhausted and poorer on both sides for the battle, Duke and Imperial called a truce in 1902, sat down, and divided up the tobacco fortunes of the world. The terms: Duke would get America, Imperial would monopolize English tobacco, and together they would form the British-American Tobacco Company, which would get the rest of the world. Duke was British-American's first chairman. He also held two-thirds of the stock to Imperial's one-third.

That's the way things stayed until 1911, when the U.S. Supreme Court broke up Duke's American monopoly and ordered him to cancel the cartel he had with the British for dividing up the world tobacco market. He did, but Imperial held to their side of the bargain. They retained their stake in the company and they allowed British-American to develop the overseas markets while Imperial took care of the home market. One of the overseas markets British-American entered was the United States, where, in 1927, they bought a small company in North Carolina: Brown & Williamson.

It's fair to say that no company propagated cigarette smoking around the world as much as British-American. Their original strength was in British Commonwealth countries, but from there they expanded to the whole world. They distributed all the brands made by Imperial as well as popular American brands. To this day they still sell American Brands' Lucky Strike and Pall Mall outside the United States. One of their early conquests, between 1911 and 1923, a period when smokers switched from pipes to cigarettes, was China. They became the first foreign company to penetrate the vast Chinese hinterland beyond the coastal trading stations, and they did their work well—the Chinese are now among the heaviest cigarette smokers in the world. At one point the Chinese market was so big it accounted for 25% of British-American's business. British-American lost their companies in China during Japanese occupation of the Far East in World War II.

Brown & Williamson was an indifferent performer in the U.S. market until after World War II. Their main brand had been Raleigh, which was promoted by the inclusion in each package of coupons redeemable for products (when you saved up enough). They had one of the first major entries in the filter market: Viceroy. However, their major coup was Kool, which took off like a shot after the menthol content was reduced but maintained at a higher level than that of any other brand, enabling Brown & Williamson to stress repeatedly, "Come up to Kool." Kool's success was the major factor in moving Brown & Williamson from sixth to third place in the American market between 1961 and 1968. Kool became a particularly strong brand among blacks for reasons which have never been satisfactorily explained.

When Britain joined the European Common Market in 1972, Imperial and B.A.T decided to end their cartel agreement of 1902 (which had given Imperial the British market and B.A.T everything else but), before the Common Market tried to end it for them. This left B.A.T free of restrictive marketing agreements for the first time. They can sell everywhere now, and they do —in 140 countries around the world. In 1978 B.A.T introduced their State Express cigarettes in the British market; for the first time in 76 years this British company marketed a cigarette in their home country. In 1975 Imperial reduced their stake in B.A.T from 26 to 15%, and in 1979 they sold all their remaining shares for about $310 million. B.A.T, the company born of fighting parents, has far surpassed both of them in size, sales, and profits.

Reputation. B.A.T has an undisguised air of snobbery and self-importance, issuing pronouncements (printed on their own Wiggins Teape paper) about how benevolent they are in populating the world with cigarette factories and tobacco leaf farms. They're also tigers on getting the most output from each employee. They are currently phasing out their big cigarette fac-

Off with Their Noses

Present-day nonsmokers who seek to ban smoking in public places have some notable forerunners in early history. The Turkish Sultan Murad IV executed smokers, dispatching as many as 18 a day, and the first Romanov czar punished puffers by slitting their noses. King James I of En- gland despised smoking, denouncing it as "A custom loathsome to the eye, hateful to the nose, harmful to the brain, dangerous to the lungs, and in the black stinking fume thereof, nearest resembling the horrible Stygian smoke of the pit that is bottomless." Besides expressing his royal displeasure in print, King James increased tobacco import taxes by 4,000%. Smoking, however, continued to spread inexorably throughout Great Britain.

Source: *Time*, January 12, 1976.

tory at Louisville to concentrate production at a more efficient facility in Macon, Georgia. Brown & Williamson has long been an economic mainstay in Louisville.

What they own. The list of their subsidiaries covers two pages, in fine print, in their annual report. They're brewing beer in Brazil, operating hotels in India and discount stores in Britain.

Who owns and runs the company. Their chairman is Peter Macadam, who loves to make the point that he's multinational too. Born in 1921 in Buenos Aires, Argentina, he holds citizenship there and in England. He's fluent in five languages. Macadam joined B.A.T in 1946, after wartime service with the Queen's Bay Regiment. He worked for B.A.T in Argentina, Chile, and Hong Kong and was also responsible for B.A.T's operations in Kenya and Nigeria. He became chairman of the main board on April Fool's Day, 1976.

In the public eye. Anyone reading B.A.T's annual reports would have no idea that there's any controversy in the world about smoking and health.

Where they're going. They desperately need to come up with a low-tar cigarette in the big U.S. market—their share of the American market has fallen from 17.5% in 1974 to 14.5% in 1979. They are looking

> **Italy adopted a total ban on cigarette advertising in 1962. Since then cigarette sales in Italy have doubled.**

forward to getting back into the Chinese market, now that the Chinese are seeking foreign businesses.

Access. Windsor House, 50 Victoria Street, London SW1 HONL, England; Telex, 915795; telephone, (01)222 7979. General enquiries may be sent to Richard Haddon, head of corporate affairs. In the United States they have a new holding entity for their American properties, Batus, located at 2000 Citizen's Plaza, Louisville, Kentucky 40202; (502) 581-8000.

Consumer brands.

Cigarettes: Kool; Viceroy; Raleigh; Belair; Arctic Lights.
Chewing tobacco: Bloodhound; B&W Sun Cured; Red Duce.
Loose tobacco: Bugler; Target; Kite.
Snuff: Tube Rose.
Pipe tobacco: Sir Walter Raleigh.
Roll-your-own kit: Laredo.
Department stores: Gimbels; Saks Fifth Avenue; Kohl (supermarkets as well).
Cosmetics: Yardley; Lenthéric, Morny; Germaine Monteil; Cyclax; Juvena; Tuvaché.

British American Tobacco's chairman, Peter Macadam. He sells more cigarettes than anyone else in the world.

Sales: $946 million
Profits: $54 million
Forbes 500 rank: 478
Rank in tobacco: 6
Rank in Scotch whiskey: 1
Rank in canned dog food: 1
Rank in physical-fitness equipment: 1
Founded: 1822
Employees: 8,200
Headquarters: Montvale, New Jersey

What they do. Liggett makes the top-selling chewing tobacco: Red Man. They sell the top-selling Scotch whiskey, J&B. And they're also number 1 in canned dog food (Alpo) and barbells (Superstar, Challenger, and Champion). But those monumental triumphs failed to dispel the smoky cloud that hung over the company through the 1970s. The cloud was blown there by cigarettes.

Liggett's problem with cigarettes was not so much the health issue as their inability to sell them to people who continued to smoke. Their Chesterfield brand was once the third-largest seller. Their L&M filter was once one of the 10 top-selling brands, and in 1957 they held 14.5% of the cigarette market. They have done so poorly recently, however, that not one of their brands now ranks in the top 20. As a company they have dropped to sixth and last place in the cigarette business; their share of the total market has descended below 3%. Cigarettes still account for half their sales, but they brought in only 12% of the profits in 1978. Liggett was making more money from chewing and loose smoking tobacco than from cigarettes. Everything else the company does is highly profitable, so observers have been speculating that the cigarette business would be either sold off or disposed of in some other manner. Grand Metropolitan, a British hotel, liquor, and gambling company, made a bid for Liggett early in 1980, which Liggett resisted. To discourage Grand Metropolitan, Liggett sold one of their best properties, Austin Nichols. Standard Brands then made a bid for Liggett, but Grand Metropolitan topped that—and Liggett now belongs to Grand Metropolitan.

History. Liggett began as a snuff manufacturer in Belleville, Illinois. The snuff-making shop was opened in 1822 and moved to St. Louis in 1833. John Edmund Liggett, grandson of the founder, entered the business in 1844; he later joined with George S. Myers to form Liggett & Myers. From snuff, a pulverized tobacco snorted up the nostrils, the company moved logically into chewing tobacco. In 1876, when the nation was 100 years old, they brought out their Star plug chewing tobacco—and it swept the country. In the 1890s they went into the cigarette business with brands like Sledge, Music, Good Form, Tent, and Long Voyage. In 1899, two years after John Liggett died, they were swallowed by Buck Duke's American Tobacco trust. When the trust was dissolved in 1911, Liggett & Myers resurfaced with 625 brand names, including Piedmont and Fatima cigarettes, Star and Horse Shoe chewing tobaccos, and Duke's Mixture and Velvet pipe tobaccos. But the brand that became the company's big winner was Chesterfield. With R. J. Reynolds' Camel and American Brands' Lucky Strike it formed a triumvirate that did more than 90% of the cigarette business during the 1920s and 1930s. Chesterfield's famous advertising slogan was "They satisfy." In the 1920s they put a Chesterfield ad on billboards that became a classic: it showed a young man and woman in an outdoor setting, the man lighting a cigarette, the woman saying, "Blow some my way."

Liggett & Myers made nothing but tobacco products until 1964, when the U.S. Surgeon General's first report on smoking and health appeared. In that year they bought Allen Products, the maker of Alpo dog food. Then, as the company's cigarette business settled in for a long and unrelenting decline, they bagged these other businesses:

1966: Paddington, the J&B Scotch people.

1966: Carillon, importer of Grand Marnier liqueur.

1967: National Oats, maker of the 3-Minute brands of cereal, grits, and popcorn.

1968: Brite Industries, maker of watchbands (Brite, Kimtron, Roger Williams).

1969: Austin, Nichols, a major wine importer and the distiller of 101-proof Wild Turkey bourbon (sold to Pernod-Ricard of France, makers of Pernod liqueur, in 1980).

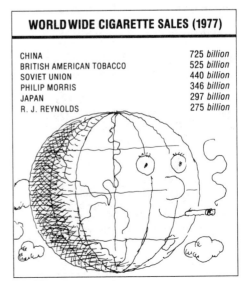

WORLD WIDE CIGARETTE SALES (1977)

CHINA	725 *billion*
BRITISH AMERICAN TOBACCO	525 *billion*
SOVIET UNION	440 *billion*
PHILIP MORRIS	346 *billion*
JAPAN	297 *billion*
R. J. REYNOLDS	275 *billion*

1970: Earl Grissmer, maker of Blue Lustre carpet shampoo.

1977: Diversified Products, maker of physical-fitness equipment, table tennis tables, and other sporting goods.

1977: Pepsi-Cola Bottling Co. of Fresno, California.

1978: Pepsi-Cola Bottling Co. of Stockton, California.

Reputation. Confused. In 1974 they relocated their corporate headquarters from New York City to Durham, North Carolina, near their main cigarette manufacturing facilities. In 1979 they moved back north, relocating their headquarters office in Montvale, New Jersey. In 1968 they changed their name from Liggett & Myers Tobacco to Liggett & Myers. In 1976 they changed it again to the Liggett Group. Now they're going British.

What they own. A slumping cigarette business and a prosperous bunch of alcoholic beverage brands.

Who owns and runs the company. Still in charge is Raymond J. Mulligan, who came up through the Alpo business. Grand Metropolitan, the British producer of J & B Scotch, is now the owner.

In the public eye. A lot of people in the country have it in for all the cigarette companies, but here's one that could probably be persuaded to flee the field.

Where they're going. It appears as if their problems are to be taken over by the British (as if they didn't have enough of their own).

Stock performance. Liggett stock bought for $1,000 in 1970 sold for $1,165 on January 2, 1980.

Major employment centers. Diversified Products, Opelike, Alabama; Allen Products, Allentown, Pennsylvania.

> **Americans smoked 615 billion cigarettes in 1978, an average of 9,667 cigarettes a year or 26½ cigarettes a day for the approximately 64 million smokers.**

Access. 100 Paragon Drive, Montvale, New Jersey 07645; (201) 573-4203. L&M in Durham has regularly scheduled tours.

Consumer brands.

Cigarettes: Chesterfield; Decade; Eve; Lark; L&M; Oasis; Picayune; Piedmont; St. Moritz.

Chewing and smoking tobaccos: Red Man; Red Horse; Union Standard; Pay Car; Tinsley's; W.N.T.; Spark Plug; Star; Horse Shoe; Velvet; Granger; Edgeworth; Rum and Maple; V.I.P.; Holiday; John Rolfe; Masterpiece; King Bee; Virginia Extra; Dinner Bell; Plow Boy; Summer-Time.

Spirits and wines: J&B; Royal Ages; Paddington of Canada; Catto's Gold Label; Izmira; Grand Marnier; Chateau de Sancerre and Lescours; Bombay; Langs; Punt e Mes; Achaia Clauss; Fazi-Battaglia; Bertani; Dopff; Vin Fou Blanc.

Pet foods: Alpo; Alamo; Liva-A Snaps; Char-O Snaps; Chik-N Snaps; Beef Snaps.

Sporting goods: Halex; Superstar; DP.

Food: 3-Minute brands, Super Pop popcorn; Butterflake; Lab-16; National.

Home-care products: Blue Lustre; Rinsenvac.

Watchbands: Brite; Medalist; Roger Williams; Ultra Twist; Carriage; Everything Chain; Charms for Chains.

Philip Morris

Sales: $6.1 billion
Profits: $507 million
Forbes 500 rank: 63
Rank in cigarettes: 2
Rank in beer: 2
Rank in soft drinks: 3
Founded: 1847
Employees: 65,000
Headquarters: New York, New York

What they do. Some people might think it would be hard to sell cigarettes these days, since the smoking habit has fallen from social grace. But you couldn't tell it from Philip Morris. This is the company that has stood the tobacco business on its ear in the past 25 years with high-visibility advertising attuned to the sounds of the city. If R. J. Reynolds is the company of the rural South, Philip Morris has the urban North under lock and key. That's where their Marlboro brand made it—first on TV and then, when cigarettes got kicked off the air, in print.

At the beginning of the 1960s Philip Morris was the smallest of the nation's six major tobacco companies, with about 9% of the market. Now they're the second largest, making close to one-third of the 700 billion cigarettes sold each year, and closing in on Reynolds. Their remarkable rise has resulted from some of the shrewdest marketing of consumer goods the country has ever seen. In times past, cigarette advertising usually depicted aristocrats or movie stars lighting up in stately settings. Then Philip Morris unleashed the Marlboro man, an earthy, ruggedly handsome cowpoke who rode into the sunset to the strains of the theme from the movie *The Magnificent Seven*. In 1968 they turned around and made a new cigarette for women—Virginia Slims—that capitalized on the growing feminist movement. They even succeeded with a cigarette whose only advantage was that it was longer than ordinary cigarettes—Benson & Hedges—and they did it with a thoroughly silly ad campaign that stressed the brand's disadvantages.

Philip Morris makes cigarettes for several other tastes too: Merit (low tar), Parliament (recessed filter), Saratoga (120 millimeters long), Alpine (menthol), and Philip Morris (unfiltered). Despite their aggressive marketing techniques, though, they have rarely been an innovator. They've preferred to let their competitors, chiefly Reynolds, establish new cigarette categories. Then they move in with a brand of their own. They followed filter-tipped Winston with Marlboro, low-tar Vantage with Merit, and extra-long More with Saratoga.

Marlboro knocked off Winston as the nation's best-selling brand in 1976. Philip Morris claims it's the best-selling cigarette brand in the world. Philip Morris captured 29% of the U.S. market in 1979. Outside the United States Philip Morris claims 6% of the market. They sell more than 160 brands of cigarettes in more than 170 countries. In at least 20 countries they have more than 15% of the market. Philip Morris is also America's leading cigarette exporter, with 42% of the export market. In 1978 their Swiss subsidiary bought the rights outside the United States to all the cigarette trademarks of the Liggett Group: L&M, Lark, Chesterfield, Decade, and Eve.

Cigarettes are only one bad habit (or, as they say, "simple pleasure") that Philip Morris promotes. Their other big one is beer. When they took over Miller Brewing in 1970, the company was languishing in seventh place among American brewers. Today Miller is number 2 and still climbing. They made their low-calorie "Lite" beer a staple in American refrigerators, and they even proved that a lot of American consumers would buy a high-priced "super-premium" beer that looked like a German import (Löwenbräu), even though it was brewed in Fort Worth, Texas, under license from the German brewer.

In 1978 they evidently decided to attempt another miracle when they shelled out more than $500 million for Seven-Up, the lemon-lime soft drink company that has 6% of the soft drink market. They revved up a new ad campaign designed to rival Coke (36% of the market) and Pepsi (22%). After their success with Miller, nobody is scoffing.

Philip Morris has fingers in a few other pies as well. They developed Mission Viejo in Southern California's Orange County. Located midway between Los Angeles and San Diego, Mission Viejo is a planned community of 44,000 souls, 13,000 homes, and various golf courses, tennis courts, shops, and swimming pools. They're now planning another community, Aliso Viejo, just across the freeway from Mission Viejo, overlooking Laguna Beach. In 1979 Mission Viejo accounted for 8% of all new homes sold in Orange County. Philip Morris also owns a group of companies that make paper products like fast-food wrappers, napkins, beer cartons, labels, and technical drawing paper. They even have a few chemical subsidiaries, Polymer Industries, Armstrong Products, that serve the textile industry. But industrial products, real estate, and soda pop add up to less than 10% of their sales. The rest is all cigarettes (64%) and beer (28%).

History. "Philip Morris, Esquire, Tobacconist and Importer of Fine Seegars," opened his shop on London's Bond Street in 1847. Seven years later he started making his own cigarettes, and in 1870 he introduced the Cambridge, Oxford Blue, and Oval brands. When he died in 1873, his brother and his widow took over the company, finally selling it to William Curtis Thomson in 1894.

Philip Morris prospered under Thomson. In 1901 a royal decree made them

How They've Sold the Cigs

Brand/Company/Slogan

In The Beginning (the turn of the century)

CAMEL / R.J. REYNOLDS / "Turkish and Domestic Blend" / "Don't look for premiums or coupons, as the cost of the tobaccos blended in Camel prohibits the use of them." / "I'd walk a mile for a Camel." (*slogan inspired by a golfer on the links who ran out of cigarettes*)

PIN HEAD / AMERICAN TOBACCO / "Famous Actresses" card series, notably those of Madame Rhea; "Rags to Riches" card series

CHESTERFIELD / LIGGETT & MEYERS / "A balanced blend of the finest aromatic Turkish tobacco and the choicest of several American varieties"

LUCKY STRIKE / AMERICAN / "It's toasted" / "A blend of Burley and Turkish Tobacco" / "Reach for a Lucky instead of a sweet." (*aimed at the weight-conscious woman*) / "L.S./M.F.T.—Lucky Strike means fine tobacco."

OLD GOLD / LORILLARD / "Eat a chocolate. Light an Old Gold. And enjoy both! Two fine and healthful treats!" (*a response to the Lucky Strike ads*)

The Depression

PAUL JONES / PHILIP MORRIS / "America . . . here's your cigarette." (*a slogan stressing Paul Jones's lower prices*)

WINGS / BROWN & WILLIAMSON / "Many smokers say, 'A friend recommends WINGS!' He's a real friend who enables you to save 33-1/3% on your cigarette bill!"

PHILIP MORRIS / PHILIP MORRIS / "Call for Philip Morris" (*featuring Johnny Roventini, a page from the Hotel New Yorker, appealing to the Depression desire to be rich*)

PALL MALL / AMERICAN / "Modern design makes the big difference" / "Something is happening to the cigarette business." (*to introduce Pall Mall's longer length*)

Second World War

CHESTERFIELD / L & M / "They satisfy." / "Keep 'em smoking!" / "You want steady nerves when you're flying Uncle Sam's bombers across the Ocean (names withheld for defense purposes and national security)."

CAMEL / REYNOLDS / "Our fighting men rate the best!" / Camels are the favorite! . . . in the Army . . . in the Navy . . . in the Marine Corps . . . in the Coast Guard!"

LUCKY STRIKE / AMERICAN / "Lucky Strike Green has gone to war!" / "So round, so firm, so fully packed, so free and easy on the draw" / "Sold American!" (*spoken by "Speed" Riggs, tobacco auctioneer, in competition with Philip Morris's Johnny Roventini*)

In Response to Health Concerns

OLD GOLD / LORILLARD / "An edge on mildness"

FLEETWOOD / AXTON-FISHER / "A cleaner, milder smoke"

CAMEL / REYNOLDS / "Not a single case of throat irritation due to smoking Camels" / "More Doctors smoke Camels than any other brand."

KOOL / B & W / "Guarded against colds"

PALL MALL / AMERICAN / "A longer finer and milder smoke" / "Outstanding, and they are mild."

L & M / L & M / "Just what the doctor ordered" (*a pitch for the filter tips*)

For the Real Man

WINSTON / REYNOLDS / "Winston tastes good like a cigarette should." (*They got a lot of mileage and free advertising off the ungrammatical English.*)

MARLBORO / PHILIP MORRIS / "Marlboro Country" / "You get a lot to like in a Marlboro."

CAMEL / REYNOLDS / "No other cigarette is so rich-tasting, yet so mild."

TAREYTON / AMERICAN / "Us Tareyton smokers would rather fight than switch!" (*complete with model with black eye*)

WINSTON / REYNOLDS / "If I'm going to smoke, I'm going to do it right."

For Women Only

VIRGINIA SLIMS / PHILIP MORRIS / "You've come a long way, baby."

The Bottom Line

CHESTERFIELD / L & M / "They *still* satisfy."

tobacconist for King Edward VII, and the following year, playing on the royal endorsement, they began selling their cigarette brands in the United States. By 1919 Philip Morris had been taken over by American stockholders, but it was not until 1929 that the American version of the company became a manufacturer. That's the year they bought a factory in Richmond, Virginia, and began rolling their own cigarettes.

Their big break came in 1930 when, in the midst of the Great Depression, the successors of the old Tobacco Trust, led by R. J. Reynolds, upped their prices. Philip Morris, Brown & Williamson (another firm of English origin), and several smaller cigarette makers countered by introducing economy brands. The company's major economy brand was Philip Morris itself, and in 1933 they began promoting it with one of the most popular and successful ad campaigns in cigarette history. They found a midget bellhop named Johnny Roventini working in the lobby of the Hotel New Yorker, gave him a page's uniform and a tiny pillbox hat set at a rakish tilt, and put him on the radio to "Call for Philip Morris." Soon Johnny's picture and famous line were on billboards and magazine ads across the country—and Philip Morris established a place for their economy cigarettes that they held even after the Depression had worn off.

After World War II Philip Morris picked up the Continental Tobacco Company and a few more plants in Louisville, Kentucky. But a deal they made in 1954 was to do more for the company than any other single event in their history. The deal was the purchase of Benson & Hedges, makers of Parliament cigarettes—but the popular Parliament brand wasn't nearly so valuable as Benson & Hedges's president, Joseph Cullman III.

Born and raised in New York, and a third-generation member of an American tobacco-growing family, Cullman brought to Philip Morris a senstitivity to the marketplace that became the company's hallmark. In three years he was president, making decisions that were to shape the industry for the next two decades. Cullman directed the marketing of Marlboro when it was introduced in the mid-1950s with its distinctive red-and-white fliptop box. When the brand was wheeled into New York City with the slogan "flavor, filter,

fliptop box," marketing history was made: it captured first place in 30 days. That phenomenal success gave Cullman and the group of hard-charging executives he collected around him a taste of blood they never forgot. As they moved up from the rear of the industry, they became intent on knocking off the guy on the next rung of the ladder. They did it first in cigarettes, moving from 6th to 2nd place, and then, after acquiring Miller Brewing in 1970, they did it in the beer business, moving from 7th to 2nd place.

Miller was a sleepy Milwaukee brewer when Philip Morris took it over. Their roots go back to 1855 when Frederic Miller, a 28-year-old German-born brewmaster, bought a small brewery just outside the city limits of Milwaukee. The Miller family ran it for nearly 100 years. When the last Miller to serve as president died in 1954, the brewery ranked 9th in the industry. Joe Cullman looked upon Miller as another Marlboro situation. Billed as "The Champagne of Bottled Beers," Miller was stuck with a genteel constitutency of occasional beer quaffers. They also let their beer stay on supermarket shelves too long. To effect the transformation of Miller, Cullman sent to Milwaukee a tough New York lawyer, John A. Murphy, who joked, "Every Irishman dreams of going to heaven and running a brewery." A Murphy-led Philip Morris team turned Miller around. They improved the beer quality, changed the packaging, introduced new beers (notably Miller Lite), and regaled TV watchers with a heavy barrage of clever advertising designed to reach "the blue-collar tonnage drinker." In 1970 Miller brewed 5 million barrels; in 1979 they brewed 36 million.

Cullman's other major contribution was the recognition that although Americans were smoking like chimneys, there were many more potential smokers outside the United States. It was his decision to make a major international push. Today Philip Morris International has annual sales of $2.5 billion.

The Cullman record was extraordinary. In 1957, when he became president, Philip Morris had profits of $17 million on sales of $400 million. When he stepped down as chairman in 1978, Philip Morris had profits of $335 million on sales of $5.2 billion. And that was during a time when their main product was under relentless attack as a cause of all kinds of deadly diseases.

Reputation. To anticigarette crusaders mobilized against the advertising of "cancer sticks," they're killers. To the consumers who spend billions every year for smoke and bubbly refreshment, they're providers of desired pleasures. To *Financial World* they're "magicians" whose "marketing miracles are famous on Wall Street," and whose profits have been leaping fabulously for over a quarter of a century. Only 37 companies in the United States made more money in 1979 than Philip Morris.

What they own. Seven cigarette plants around Richmond, Virginia (capable of rolling a total of 106 billion cigarettes a year), and two more in Louisville, Kentucky. Miller breweries in Wisconsin, New York, California, Texas, and North Carolina. The main Seven-Up plant in St. Louis.

Who owns and runs the company. George Weissman, former head of Philip Morris' overseas operations, succeeded Cullman as chairman in 1978. Weissman is one of the few businessmen who made the Nixon White House "enemies list"—he's a liberal Democrat. Cullman stayed on as a director, and his cousin Hugh Cullman is also on the board. There is one black woman director: Margaret Young, widow of Whitney Young, the late head of the National Urban League. When Young died in 1971, Joe Cullman was the prime mover in setting up the Whitney M. Young, Jr. Memorial Foundation, which gives fellowships to outstanding black students. Philip Morris gave the initial $100,000—and Mrs. Young went on the company board in 1972. Young serves on the board's committee on public affairs and social responsibility. Together, the directors and officers own a little over 2% of the stock.

In the public eye. Philip Morris claims that one reason for their success is their "patronage of the arts and humanities that led—even fostered—the nation's growing corporate interest in culture." The list of Philip Morris contributions to everything from "Art in the Factory" exhibits to bluegrass music festivals and symphony orchestras during a 15-year period fills 17 pages. Their interest in minority goals is also well known. John Murphy, Miller's president, once won the Roberto Clemente Award from the National Association for Puerto Rican Civil Rights. One out of every four employees is a minority group member.

Philip Morris contributes heavily to campaigns to defeat measures that would curtail smoking in public places. In 1979 113 measures were introduced in various state legislatures; only 8 were enacted.

Where they're going. Almost everyone in the soft drink business expects them to challenge Coke and Pepsi soon with a cola drink. Their Mission Viejo unit has bought the 22,000-acre Highlands Ranch just south of Denver, Colorado, where they plan to build a new community over the next 25 years.

Stock performance. Philip Morris stock bought for $1,000 in 1970 sold for $4,028 on January 2, 1980.

Access. 100 Park Avenue, New York, New York 10017; (212) 679-1800. To tour the Miller Brewing Company, write 4251 West State Street, Milwaukee, Wisconsin 53208, or phone (414) 931-2467. To tour the Philip Morris Manufacturing Center in Richmond, Virginia, call (804) 271-3342 or 271-3329.

Consumer brands.

Cigarettes: Marlboro; Marlboro Lights; Marlboro 100s; Marlboro Menthol; Benson & Hedges Regular and Menthol 100; Benson & Hedges Lights; Merit; Merit 100s; Virginia Slims; Parliament; Philip Morris; Alpine.

Beer: Miller High Life; Miller Lite; Miller Malt Liquor; Löwenbräu.

Soft drinks: 7-Up; Diet 7-Up.

RJR

Sales: $7.1 billion
Profits: $551 million
Forbes 500 rank: 51
Rank in cigarettes: 1
Rank in container shipping: 1
Rank in canned fruits and vegetables: 1
Founded: 1875
Employees: 80,000
Headquarters: Winston-Salem, North Carolina

What they do. Richard Joshua Reynolds, the founder of the R. J. Reynolds empire, used to foster the legend that he first rode into the twin hamlets of Winston and Salem, North Carolina, as a barefoot, illiterate farm boy atop a wagon load of his dad's tobacco—a myth of an innocent, simple southern underdog who made good. Although still headquartered in Winston-Salem, the business named for R. J. Reynolds has grown into an enormously wealthy international company run by a man with a reputation for never taking a back seat to anybody. They lead the nation in sales of cigarettes and pipe tobacco. They own the biggest vegetable and fruit packer in the United States (Del Monte). They sell more packaged Oriental food (Chun King) than anybody else. They operate the largest container shipping operation in the world (Sea-Land). And they happen to have an oil company—Aminoil—whose success in finding crude was triple the industry average in 1979 (they hit on 53% of their explorations).

When the 22-story Reynolds Building, shown at the left, went up in 1929 in Winston-Salem, North Carolina, it was the largest office building south of Baltimore. It was also the model for the Empire State Building, shown at the right. The same architects who designed the Reynolds structure designed the 102-story New York skyscraper, which went up in 1931. When the Reynolds Building celebrated its 50th birthday in 1979, officials of the Empire State Building sent a card saying, "Happy Anniversary, Dad." The building in Winston-Salem no longer serves as the headquarters for R.J. Reynolds Industries (they built a new glass structure in 1977) but it's still the headquarters of the tobacco division.

Profits from cigarettes made it all possible. One brand in particular—Camel—was central to their early fortunes. For 40 years Camel was at or near the top in U.S. cigarette sales, challenged only by American Tobacco's Lucky Strike. When filter-tip and mentholated cigarettes swept the industry after World War II, Reynolds named two brands for their headquarters city and continued to lead the industry. Their ungrammatical advertising slogan, "Winston tastes good, like a cigarette should," gave them the kind of notoriety they didn't mind at all. They now make one out of every three cigarettes smoked in the United States. Of the top 10 smokes, 4 (Winston, Salem, Camel, and Vantage) are Reynolds brands. They also make More, Now, and Doral.

R. J. Reynolds does nearly half their sales outside the tobacco area, but cigarettes remain the potent profit performers. Only about two dozen U.S. manufacturers make more profits than R. J. Reynolds—and tobacco accounts for 80% of those profits.

History. Contrary to the legend, R. J. Reynolds was no barefoot illiterate. After going to both college and business school, he borrowed money from his family to build a factory in Winston in 1874. By 1887 he was marketing 86 brands of chewing tobacco, some named for favorite girlfriends. Reynolds liked pretty women, liquor, horses, and business, but probably he liked business best. So when James B. (Buck) Duke of the American Tobacco trust used the financial panics of the 1890s to force R. J. to sell out, Reynolds was furious. Their confrontation, as told by grandnephew R. S. Reynolds, Jr., was recounted by *Forbes.* Said Duke: "I'll give $1 million for two-thirds of your company or I'll break you." Returned Reynolds: "Buck, my price is $3 million. Otherwise I'm going to walk out of here, and for every dollar you cost me, I'm going to cost American Tobacco a hundred." Duke paid the $3 million and Reynolds wired his brothers: "Prepare for good living."

But even though Buck Duke could buy practically anything, he couldn't run it all. Reynolds not only got his $3 million, but he continued to be active in the business, using Duke's money to build new, well-equipped factories. When the Supreme Court broke up Duke's monopoly in 1911, Reynolds regained his company, ready to lead tobacco

users from chewing to smoking.

Mulling over package designs for his new Kaiser Wilhelm cigarette shortly before the First World War, he had second thoughts: "I don't think we should name a product for a living man. You never can tell what the damn fool will do." So he named it Camel, to play up its Turkish tobacco content, and illustrated the pack with a portrait of Ol' Joe, a camel in the Barnum & Bailey circus that passed through Winston-Salem at the time. Soon after releasing Camel in 1913, Reynolds had the Kaiser to thank for its success: the company created a whole generation of loyal Camel smokers during World War I by giving away free cigarettes to American doughboys in France. Camel became the first national cigarette brand. Within 10 years of its introduction nearly half the nation's smokers were puffing on Camels. Their most famous advertising slogan was created on a golf course in 1921 when the golfing partner of an R. J. Reynolds ad executive ran out of cigarettes. "I'd walk a mile for a Camel," he said. Camel was an early radio and television advertiser, sponsoring the Camel Pleasure Hour on the radio in the 1930s and the Camel News Caravan, with John Cameron Swayze, on TV starting in 1948.

R. J. Reynolds's cigarettes may have gained the loyalty of millions of American smokers, but his business didn't hold the loyalty of his own family. After he died in 1918 his three sons went their separate ways, and his favorite nephew, Richard S. Reynolds, went off to start a foil factory, which started out making wrappings for R. J. Reynolds cigarettes and grew into Reynolds Metals.

Management of the tobacco passed into the hands of Bowman Gray, a salesman and protégé of the founder. The Gray family proceeded to run the company for the next 50 years, through Bowman, his brother James, and his son Bowman, Jr., who served as chairman until his death in 1969. Gordon Gray, brother of Bowman, Jr., became secretary of the army under Harry Truman, acted as an adviser to the next five presidents, and spent 19 years on the R. J. Reynolds board of directors. It was the Grays who fought American Tobacco's George Washington Hill and master adman Albert Lasker in the two-decade top-of-the-mountain fight between Lucky Strike and Camel, the alternating number 1 brands in the 1930s and 1940s. The Grays did very well indeed, but at the beginning of the Depression they made one mistake. Thinking people would rather smoke than eat, they raised prices. That opened the door for price-cutting smaller tobacco companies. Philip Morris was one that came through the door.

Reynolds ushered in the filter era with Winston in 1955, when many smokers were beginning to suspect that cigarette smoke just might be unhealthy, and maybe a filter would make it less so. When researchers started to establish clear links between cigarette smoking and lung cancer in the 1960s, R. J. Reynolds began to move into other businesses, as did other tobacco makers. They picked up Chun King in 1966 and Patio Foods in 1967. In 1969 they paid $115 million for McLean Industries, the owner of the huge Sea-Land shipping company, founded by a native Winston-Salem boy named Malcom P. McLean. In 1970 they spent $55 million for American Independent Oil (Aminoil), which had wells in Kuwait and Saudi Arabia. To herald their new businesses, they changed their name to R. J.

The 1970s saw the desegregation of many boards of directors of major U.S. corporations. Vernon E. Jordan, Jr., president of the National Urban League, was sitting on the boards of five major companies as the decade drew to a close: American Express, Bankers Trust, J.C. Penney, R.J. Reynolds Industries, and Xerox.

Reynolds Industries in 1970. Some Reynolds family members, who didn't run the company but still owned a lot of it, thought it was rubbish. "What do they know about ships or oil?" complained one grandson to *Forbes* in 1971. "They look like country boys with too much cash in their pockets." By 1979 they had an extra $618 million burning holes in their pockets, so they plunked it down for Del Monte, the San Francisco-based company that produces one out of every six cans of fruit and vegetables that pass through the nation's supermarket checkstands.

Reputation. The South is their bailiwick: they are the biggest company headquartered in the South, they are based in the biggest tobacco growing state, and their cigarette brands are strongest in southern rural areas. Juanita Kreps, formerly a vice-president at North Carolina's Duke University (founded on tobacco money), was a director of Reynolds from 1976 to 1977 before becoming secretary of commerce. After leaving the cabinet in 1979, she returned to the Reynolds board. In 1980 Atlanta-born Vernon E. Jordan, Jr., president of the National Urban League, was elected a director.

What they own. R. J. Reynolds Industries is the parent company of R. J. Reynolds Tobacco; R. J. Reynolds Tobacco International; Aminoil; Sea-Land Service (with a fleet of close to 50 containerized vessels); Del Monte; RJR Foods (including Hawaiian Punch; Patio, the nation's number 1 brand of frozen Mexican food; Chun King, the leader in canned Chinese food; Brer Rabbit molasses; and Vermont Maid syrup); and RJR Archer (plastic film packaging for supermarket meats and foil wrapping for grocery products such as margarine).

Who owns and runs the company. No descendants of the founder sit on the board, although as recently as 1971 *Forbes* reported that some 40 Reynolds family members owned a total of 7 or 8% of the stock. In 1979 the New York research outfit, Corporate Data Exchange, reported that the Z. Smith Reynolds Foundation owned 5% of the stock and the McClean family (Sea-Land) had another 1.5%.

Once known as a "feudal barony," Reynolds went through management upheavals during the 1970s. The key role was played by J. Paul Sticht, who engineered what *Business Week* called "a bloodless coup." Sticht was president of Federated Department Stores, the nation's largest department store chain, when he joined the Reynolds board in 1968. In 1972 a longtime Reynolds executive, David S. Peoples, was slated to become chairman, but Sticht opposed that appointment—and threatened to quit as a director if Peoples got the top position. Sticht then won over other directors who weren't company executives, and in a showdown vote in the board of directors he was named president and Colin H. Stokes, a veteran of 41 years at Reynolds, was elected chairman. The two ran the company as "partners," although Sticht said he made it clear at the start that "I was never going to work for somebody else." Sticht was elected chief executive officer in 1978. He has recruited many managers from outside the company. One, J. Tylee Wilson, came from Chesebrough-Pond to run the floundering foods division. He's now president.

In the public eye. David Peoples and two other top Reynolds managers—Charles B. Wade, Jr., and William S. Smith—were forced to resign as officers and board members in 1976 when it was disclosed they had been involved in funneling $65,000 to $90,000 of corporate funds into a secret account used to make illegal domestic political contributions. Three and one-half months later, still in 1976, Reynolds disclosed that their domestic political contributions were more like $190,000. They also reported then to the Securities and Exchange Commission that they had made some $25 million in questionable corporate payments in the U.S. and overseas since 1968—some $19 million of which were possibly illegal rebates made by their shipping company, Sea-Land. In 1978 Sea-Land was fined $5,000 for this violation of the Shipping Act.

R. J. Reynolds has long been an important financial resource in the southern communities where they operate. In 1956 they were instrumental in having Wake Forest University relocate from Wake County, North Carolina, to Winston-Salem. They continue to be one of the nation's largest contributors to independent colleges and universities. In the late 1960s, when riots struck many cities (and Winston-Salem had disturbances), they contributed $1 million

If all the cigarettes smoked worldwide in a year were placed end to end so as to form a single cigarette, the result would be more than 260 million miles in length. Its filter alone would reach half the distance from the earth to the sun.

to the establishment of a local citizens' coalition to improve housing and public transportation.

They were the first company to create a pastoral counseling program for employees, and they have sponsored one of the largest HMOs—Health Maintenance Organizations—in the nation. Called the Winston-Salem Health Care Plan, it delivers total health care for 35,000 employees of R. J. Reynolds and has been hailed as a model for other organizations seeking to combat the rising costs of Blue Cross-Blue Shield plans.

Minorities make up 22% of the Reynolds work force.

Where they're going. To China, the world's biggest cigarette market. Reynolds announced in 1979 that they would start selling Winston there, accompanied by ads on Chinese television. In 1980 they signed an agreement under which Camel cigarettes will be made and sold in China. Also in 1980 Sea-Land inaugurated the first regularly scheduled containerized shipping runs between the People's Republic and North America. Maybe the Chinese can teach the Chun King folks how to make a better chow mein.

Stock performance. R. J. Reynolds Industries stock bought for $1,000 in 1970 sold for $1,495 on January 2, 1980.

Access. Reynolds Boulevard, Winston-Salem, North Carolina 27102; (919) 777-2000. Their cigarette plant is open for tours daily. In 1979, 160,000 visitors went through it.

Consumer brands.

Cigarettes: Winston; Salem; Camel; Vantage; More; Now; Doral.
Little cigars: Winchester.
Smoking tobacco: Prince Albert; Carter Hall; George Washington; Madeira; Apple; Our Advertiser; Top.

Plug chewing tobacco: Days Work; Brown's Mule; Apple Sun Cured; Reynolds' Natural Leaf.
Pouch chewing tobacco: Work Horse.
Food and beverages: Del Monte canned foods, pineapples, bananas, raisins, catsup; Hawaiian Punch; Milk Mate chocolate-flavored syrup; Chun King Chinese food; Patio Mexican food; Vermont Maid syrup; Brer Rabbit molasses and syrup; My*T*Fine puddings; College Inn broth; Davis baking powder.

Brewers

ANHEUSER-BUSCH COMPANIES, INC.

Sales: $2.8 billion
Profits: $144 million
Forbes 500 rank: 175
Rank in beer: 1
Founded: 1860
Employees: 16,027
Headquarters: St. Louis, Missouri

What they do. Anheuser-Busch brews Budweiser, the world's best-selling beer. Bud has been the "King of Beers" almost from the moment the first kegs rolled out of their St. Louis brewery more than a century ago. Milwaukee brewers have occasionally challenged Budweiser's dominance —Pabst in the 1890s, Schlitz in the 1950s, and Miller in the 1970s—but none has ever toppled Bud from its throne for long.

The Busch family, which has run the company for four generations, would credit this success to their painstaking brewing process, chiefly to the beechwood-chip aging technique that keeps Budweiser in kegs for a month or more when other brewers market their beers after only 20 days.

But only the fiercest Budweiser partisans believe that their beer, of the hundreds of beers once brewed in America, rose to the top solely on its taste. Bud's real trump card has been aggressive marketing. From the days of cofounder Adolphus Busch—who promoted Budweiser by reproducing hundreds of thousands of copies of Cassily Adams's painting *Custer's Last Fight* for display in saloons—to the time of his grandson Gussie Busch—who paraded the Budweiser Clydesdale horses through parts of rural America where Prohibition sentiment lingered and who bought the St. Louis Cardinals baseball team—Anheuser-Busch has been a colorful, resourceful marketer. Their marketing strategy today, as *Business Week* put it, is to "bracket and pinion" other brewers with beers in all product categories: light (Natural Light and Michelob Light), premium (Busch and Budweiser), and superpremium (Michelob and Wurzburger, a German beer they plan to import in 1980). Although the rapid rise of Miller Brewing has captured much media attention in the last decade, Busch has raised its share of the market to 29%; during that time the number of brewers in the United States has gone from 92 to 41.

Budweiser has 11 strategically located breweries around the nation: two in California, two in Florida, and one each in Texas, Illinois, Ohio, Virginia, New Jersey, New Hampshire, and New York (they bought Schlitz' Syracuse brewery for $100 million in February 1980). Together these breweries have the capacity to produce and ship almost 47 million barrels of beer (in 1978 they became the first brewer to sell more than 40 million barrels in one year). Busch also makes corn syrup and starch at a plant in Indiana and produces baker's and brewer's yeasts at plants in New Jersey, California, Missouri, and Florida. Most of these products are sold to the food-processing industry. An entertainment division operates Busch Gardens entertainment theme parks in Tampa, Florida (The Dark Continent, styled on colonial Africa), and Williamsburg, Virginia (The Old Country, after seventeenth century Europe). But Busch's nonbeer businesses account for only 10% of their profits; the real money comes from those barrels of beer and their market position, which they zealously guard with the biggest advertising budget in the industry: $120 million.

History. Eberhard Anheuser, a St. Louis soap maker, took over a failing brewery in 1860, but his son-in-law, a German immigrant named Adolphus Busch, deserves the credit for making it a success. Together with Carl Conrad, a St. Louis restaurateur, Busch perfected the formula for Budweiser, which imitated the light beer brewed in the Bohemian town of Budweis. Busch guessed correctly that many drinkers would prefer the light brew to the heavy beers then on the market. (Ironically, Conrad had the trademark rights to Budweiser; Anheuser-Busch didn't buy the name until 1891.) Although Pabst became, in 1893, the first American brewery to sell 1 million barrels of beer, Budweiser overtook them in 1901. As the beer's popularity surged, the company even had two songs commissioned: "Budweiser's a Friend of Mine" in 1907, and the preposterous "Under the Anheuser Bush" a few years later. A second beer, Michelob, was introduced in 1896 but remained a draught-only beer until the 1960s, when it became the first of the "super-premium" brands.

Anheuser-Busch's biggest challenge came not from other competitors but from Prohibition. When the Volstead Act closed the breweries in 1920, president August Busch, the founder's son, struggled to keep the company alive. He turned from beer to yeast, refrigeration cabinets, bus and truck bodies, corn and malt syrup, and soft drinks —all the while lobbying to have Prohibition repealed. When Repeal finally came in 1933, Anheuser-Busch had trucks of beer ready to roll to the bars of St. Louis. But the struggle had taken its toll; in poor health, August Busch shot himself to death in 1934.

The biggest recent challenge to Budweiser's market dominance came in the 1970s from Miller Brewing, which had been bought in 1971 by Philip Morris, the cigarette manufacturer. Miller launched a low-calorie beer, Lite, and Philip Morris brought their marketing expertise to the launch. Miller put on a succession of award-winning TV commercials featuring former athletes, and the new beer surged in popularity. Anheuser-Busch quickly countered with Natural Light beer and their own award-winning commercial (starring language-mangling comedian Norm Crosby), and the battle was on. It was a bitter fight. Miller complained to the FTC that Natural Light contained unnatural ingredients. Busch retaliated by luring some of Miller's athletes away from Lite and over to Natural Light commercials. The smoke still hasn't cleared, but at the end of 1979 the standings read: Anheuser-Busch, 46 million barrels; Miller, 36 million barrels. And these two brewers are now doing more than 50% of the total business. In 1970 the two top brewers—Anheuser-Busch and Schlitz—had 30% of the market.

Reputation. Anheuser-Busch is not afraid of a beer brawl. They'll just wade right in and slug it out. In the mid-1970s, when Miller started to make their move and began talking about capturing first place, August A. Busch III said: "Tell Miller to come right along, but tell them to bring lots of money."

What they own. Eleven breweries from Newark to Los Angeles (the largest is in St. Louis). Two malt plants in Wisconsin and Minnesota. Four yeast plants in Missouri, New Jersey, California, and Florida. A corn-processing plant in Indiana. Two beer can factories in Florida and Ohio. St. Louis Refrigerator Car, a subsidiary that repairs and maintains 880 refrigerated railroad cars

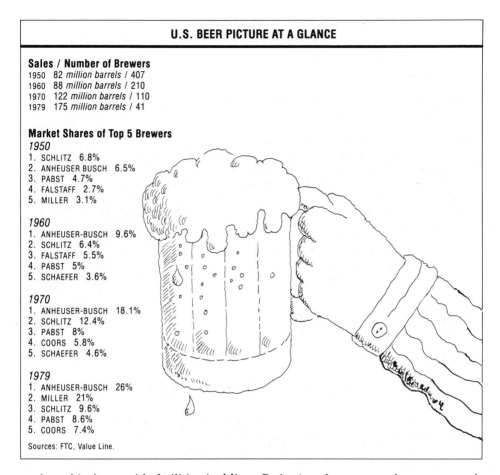

U.S. BEER PICTURE AT A GLANCE

Sales / Number of Brewers
1950   82 *million barrels* / 407
1960   88 *million barrels* / 210
1970   122 *million barrels* / 110
1979   175 *million barrels* / 41

Market Shares of Top 5 Brewers
1950
1. SCHLITZ 6.8%
2. ANHEUSER BUSCH 6.5%
3. PABST 4.7%
4. FALSTAFF 2.7%
5. MILLER 3.1%

1960
1. ANHEUSER-BUSCH 9.6%
2. SCHLITZ 6.4%
3. FALSTAFF 5.5%
4. PABST 5%
5. SCHAEFER 3.6%

1970
1. ANHEUSER-BUSCH 18.1%
2. SCHLITZ 12.4%
3. PABST 8%
4. COORS 5.8%
5. SCHAEFER 4.6%

1979
1. ANHEUSER-BUSCH 26%
2. MILLER 21%
3. SCHLITZ 9.6%
4. PABST 8.6%
5. COORS 7.4%

Sources: FTC, Value Line.

used to ship beer, with facilities in Missouri, Illinois, and Texas. Manufacturers Railway, a company that ships freight by train and truck. Amusement theme parks in Virginia and Florida (the Florida park, according to Anheuser, has "one of the world's largest privately owned wildlife collections"). A 3,000-acre residential and commercial real estate development near Williamsburg, Virginia. Two eight-horse teams of Clydesdale horses. The St. Louis Cardinals.

Who owns and runs the company. Busch family members own at least 15% of the stock. In 1979 the biggest chunk was still held by August A. Busch, Jr., honorary chairman, who stepped down as chief executive in 1975. The 79-year-old grandson of the founder had 6.4 million shares, which meant that in 1979 he collected cash dividends of $5.8 million. Busch's son, August A. Busch III, has been in training for his job since the day he was born. "Five drops of

Budweiser from an eyedropper were the first things in my mouth when I was a few hours old," he told *Fortune* when he took over the top spot in 1975. "Father had arranged it with the doctor, to Mother's dismay." "Augie," as he is known, brings with him a whole set of modern management skills, but he does not have the personal flair of his father, Gussie. A hard-driving salesman, Gussie used to whistlestop across the United States in an 86-foot stainless-steel private railroad car with a wood-paneled office, a sitting room, four conference rooms, kitchen, bar, and plenty of Budweiser. At home he would entertain wholesalers, retailers, and saloonkeepers at his 34-room French Renaissance chateau set on 220 acres of rolling land outside St. Louis. There his visitors could stroll quietly in the formal gardens; view the 350-yard fence made entirely of Civil War rifle barrels; or see the bison, North African mountain sheep, and rare deer in Busch's private wildlife park.

April 7, 1933: August A. Busch, Sr., inserts a letter to President Franklin Delano Roosevelt in the first case of Budweiser produced after the repeal of prohibition. He is flanked by his sons Adolphus Busch III (left) and Gussie Busch (right), who still serves as honorary chairman of the corporation and whose son is now president and chief executive officer. A year after this photo was taken August Busch, Sr., shot himself to death.

In the public eye. Budweiser will be the "official beer" of the 1984 Los Angeles Olympic Games—and it cost Anheuser-Busch only $10 million to get the nod. The Olympic Committee peddles the "official" designation in 164 product categories. Now Anheuser-Busch will be able to use the LA Olympics logo and mascot in their advertising, although they are not guaranteed a spot as a concessionaire at the actual event; that has to be negotiated separately.

The Securities and Exchange Commission in 1977 accused Anheuser-Busch of making $2.7 million in secret payoffs since 1971 to induce wholesalers and retailers to buy their beer. According to the SEC, Anheuser-Busch made false entries in their books to conceal the payments, which are illegal under federal law. The SEC bowed out of the case when Anheuser-Busch, while not admitting fault, agreed not to engage in illegal anti-competitive practices. The Treasury Department's Bureau of Alcohol, Tobacco and Firearms, working in cooperation with the SEC, extracted $750,000 from Anheuser-Busch to settle the payoff charges.

Where they're going. Anheuser-Busch intends to expand into snack foods and soft drinks, taking advantage of the network of distributors they already have in place. But their major target is domination of the beer market. Anheuser-Busch plans to spend $2 billion in the first half of the 1980s, most of it for additional brewing capacity of 18 million barrels. If all goes well, they hope to control 40% of the U.S. beer market by 1985.

Stock performance. Anheuser-Busch stock bought for $1,000 in 1970 sold for $616 on January 2, 1980. (Their stock began trading on the New York Stock Exchange for the first time in 1980.)

Major employment centers. St. Louis, Missouri; Tampa, Florida; Williamsburg, Virginia.

Access. 721 Pestalozzi Street, St. Louis, Missouri 63118; (314) 577-2000. You can tour the big brewery in St. Louis Monday through Friday from October to May, and Monday through Saturday from June to September. During the summer tours leave every half-hour. Children under 16 must be accompanied by an adult. For more information, call (314) 577-2153.

Consumer brands.

Beer: Budweiser; Natural Light; Michelob; Michelob Light; Busch; Anheuser-Busch Classic Dark (draught only).
Theme parks: The Old Country (Williamsburg, Virginia); The Dark Continent (Tampa, Florida).
Baseball team: St. Louis Cardinals.

Sales: $740.5 million
Profits: $68.4 million
Rank in beer: 5
Founded: 1873
Employees: 8,700
Headquarters: Golden, Colorado

What they do. Coors was once America's great cult beer. Between 1965 and 1975, when Coors was sold only in 11 western states, thousands of people—including former President Gerald Ford and ex-secretary of state Henry Kissinger—smuggled cases back East for their own consumption. Paul Newman and Clint Eastwood wanted it on their movie sets. When properly refrigerated, Coors had a light, clean taste unmatched by any other beer, so unmatched that, back in the days of the $1.25 six-pack, Coors was fetching $1 or more per can from bootleggers on Eastern Seaboard college campuses.

But times have changed in the brewing industry, and Adolph Coors, the victim of countless boycotts and strikes, has suffered more than most. The beer that shot from 12th to 4th place between 1965 and 1969, with virtually no advertising or promotion, fell back to 5th place in 1976 and experienced drastic drops in sales through 1978. What happened? At first the Coors family blamed the unions. But eventually they came around to admitting that a big part of the problem was that Coors had remained oblivious to the demands of marketing while their rivals carved up the territory and dazzled the drinking public.

"We thought we were doing the retailers a favor to bring beer to them," said Peter Coors after the company reluctantly opened a marketing department and put him in charge. "We got arrogant." They could afford to be arrogant when there never seemed to be enough Coors and they were doling it out selectively to clamoring dealers. In 1975 Coors was the top-selling beer in 10 of the 11 states where it was sold. It was quite a shock in 1976 when, for the first time since Prohibition was repealed, they couldn't sell all they made. The phalanx of new "light" and "superpremium" beers introduced by Anheuser-Busch and Miller, moved forward by enormous promotion campaigns, left Coors flat—like a can with a popped top.

Coors is not really in position to play ball with the big boys like Anheuser-Busch and Miller. All their beer is still produced in America's largest brewery in Golden, Colorado, where the company was founded. Because Coors is unpasteurized and uses no preservatives, it must be made, shipped, and stored in a refrigerated state. If left out, the beer will sour and become cloudy in seven days, and it goes bad in refrigerators in just a month, which is one reason Coors has always restricted sales to the western states. Another reason, according to a 1975 series of articles in *The Washington Post,* is an "obsession with control" that led to a fight with the Federal Trade Commission between 1973 and 1975. The FTC charged restraint of trade, including price-fixing, barring certain retail chains from carrying Coors, and intimidating distributors (for instance, some bars were told they couldn't get Coors unless they sold it exclusively). The company fought up to the Supreme Court but lost, and they had to remove restrictions on distribution. As a result, their marketing territory expanded from 11 to 16 states—all still west of the Mississippi—by the end of 1978.

Coors has several subsidiaries, including the nation's largest aluminum can manufacturing plant and a maker of porcelain products whose uses range from automotive seal rings to nose cones for missiles. But the miscellaneous companies provide only 10% of Coors's revenues. So if their beer business goes sour, they're in big trouble.

History. Adolph Herman Joseph Coors came to the United States in 1868 to avoid the German draft. After working at odd jobs in the East, he came to Colorado to start his brewery in 1873. The first articles of incorporation, in 1914, listed Adolph,

Sr., as president and treasurer, Adolph, Jr., as vice-president and secretary, and Grover Coors as general manager of the Golden plant. The company is still largely family-owned.

Coors got through Prohibition by using their plant to make near beer and malted milk. Adolph, Jr., took over when his father died in 1929. His first year's production of beer after the 1933 repeal of Prohibition was 123,000 31-gallon barrels; 30 years later production had reached 3.5 million barrels. That was when the mystique began. By 1974 Coors's production had trebled to more than 12 million barrels a year—one-third as much as Anheuser-Busch, the world's largest brewer.

This scenario of runaway growth was played out against a backdrop of boycotts and strikes brought on by proliferating charges of discrimination in employment and unfair labor practices. It started in 1966 with a strike organized by Mexican-Americans, who were practically unrepresented on Coors' work force even though they made up a large proportion of the local population. Other targets of strikers over the years were the infamous lie detector tests required of job applicants (who were reportedly asked about subversive or revolutionary leanings, drug use, crimes they had gotten away with, and even—although the company denied it—their sex lives) and a list of grounds for immediate dismissal that included making disparaging remarks about the Coors family or their beer or refusing to be frisked at work. The strikes and boycotts continued over 12 years, supported by an unlikely amalgamation of Teamsters, Chicanos, blacks, women, and gays.

Under the extreme pressure, not only from workers but from federal agencies like the National Labor Relations Board and the Equal Employment Opportunity Commission, Coors improved their minority hiring programs and liberalized some controversial policies. In mid-1979 a Mexican-American political group announced it was satisfied and withdrew from the boycott (although others still supported it). In December 1978 Coors won a battle with the Brewery Workers Union when nonunion employees voted that the local as their bargaining agent. Chairman Bill Coors (grandson of the founder) commented in 1979, "I see no resolution to our conflict with the unions. We're convinced we can sell beer without them."

Reputation. In 1978 *Forbes* said, "Coors ranks with J. P. Stevens on union hate lists." At the same time the employees dumped the union, Coors stepped up their public relations campaign with ads that featured smiling blacks, Chicanos, and women under the slogan, "At Coors, people make the difference." The new stance is an about-face from their old one. It includes aggressive marketing (as opposed to smug aloofness) and openness. For years, said a new "communications" expert, Coors hired public relations men to say, "No comment." By the end of 1978 they had a toll-free, round-the-clock number for journalists. Now, they say, "We're ready to answer any questions about the company at all."

What they own. Their brewery in Golden, Colorado, with 60 springs on the property that supply the "Pure Rocky Mountain Spring Water" they use to brew the beer. Coors Container Company, which makes aluminum cans in Golden and glass bottles in nearby Wheat Ridge. Coors Porcelain Company, which makes industrial ceramics in Colorado, Oregon, Oklahoma, California, and Arkansas. Coors Transportation Company, which runs a fleet of tractor-trailer rigs. Coors Food Products Company, which mills rice and makes a cocoa substitute from brewer's yeast in Arkansas. A natural gas field and a coal mine in Colorado that supply much of the energy for the brewery. Grain elevators to store barley in Colorado, Idaho, Montana, and Wyoming (the barley, an obscure strain called Moravian III, is grown under contract by 1,800 farmers).

THE 1979 BRAND LEADERS IN BEER

Sales

BUDWEISER 30.3 *million barrels*
MILLER 22.3 *million barrels*
PABST 12.8 *million barrels*
MILLER LITE 12.7 *million barrels*
COORS 11.3 *million barrels*
SCHLITZ 10.2 *million barrels*
MICHELOB 8.4 *million barrels*
STROH 5.8 *million barrels*
OLD MILWAUKEE 4.2 *million barrels*
OLD STYLE 3.8 *million barrels*

Source: *Beer Marketer's Insights.*

The world's largest brewery, owned by Adolph Coors in Golden, Colorado.

Who owns and runs the company. William Coors, chairman; Joseph Coors, president; Jeffrey Coors, senior vice-president; Peter Coors, senior vice-president . . . get the picture?

In 1975 Coors went semipublic, selling 14% of their stock (in a nonvoting category) to pay off a $50 million inheritance tax bill.

In the public eye. In 1960 Adolph Coors, III, grandson of the founder, was kidnapped and murdered. His brothers William and Joseph explain that that's one reason (along with their belief that a violent left-wing group is out to get them) for the employee lie detector tests.

Joe Coors spearheaded and bankrolled many ultraconservative projects and groups throughout the 1970s. These included the Committee for a Free Congress, dedicated to ousting "radical" congressmembers; the Heritage Foundation, a right-oriented research organization aimed at countering the influence of the Brookings Institution; and Television News, a TV news service designed to be an antidote to network news commentators like Walter Cronkite and Harry Reasoner, who are supposedly contaminated by liberalism.

As a regent of the University of Colorado from 1966 to 1972, Joe Coors took ardent stands against student radicalism and financed a newspaper to compete with the regular campus paper, which frequently caricatured him in the dress of an eighteenth-century Puritan.

President Nixon, the day before he resigned, nominated Joe Coors to the board of the Corporation for Public Broadcasting, and President Ford resubmitted the nomination. But the Senate Commerce Committee rejected him in 1975—the same year the Equal Employment Opportunity Commission sued the company for race and sex discrimination. In a 1977 settlement Coors admitted to no bias in the past but agreed to stick to nondiscriminatory practices in the future.

Coors's sales got a boost in 1979 when a Food and Drug Administration study detected nitrosamines, suspected as cancer-causing agents, in 40 brands of domestic and foreign beer—but not in Coors, because of their different method of heating barley malt. Coors was quick to capitalize on the study with ads in 400 newspapers proclaiming, "No nitrosamines in Coors beer." The implication, although Coors didn't say it, was that other beers might give you cancer, but not Coors.

Where they're going. All the way, in their competition with Miller and Anheuser-Busch. In 1978, after heated controversy within the company, they broke their century-long tradition of having only one beer. The introduction of Coors Light almost immediately boosted their flagging sales (nearly all the growth in the beer industry was coming from the new low-calorie products). In 1980, striking back against Miller's Löwenbräu and Anheuser's Michelob and

Wurzburger, they began selling a "super-premium" beer, Herman Joseph's 1868, in California. They called it that after the founder's two middle names and the year he came over from the old country as a penniless orphan.

Coors bought land in Virginia's Shenandoah Valley in 1979, with a view to brewing beer for the eastern market. But they've delayed construction because the eastern competition is so fierce; besides, the project has drawn the fire of ecological groups who think the brewery will foul the valley landscape. They do expect to be selling beer in Tennessee and Louisiana by early 1981, expanding their reach to 19 states.

Stock performance. Coors first sold stock to the public in 1975. That stock, bought for $1,000 in 1975, sold for $400 on January 2, 1980.

Access. Golden, Colorado 80401; (303) 279-6565. The brewery is open for tours without appointment from Monday through Saturday.

Consumer brands.

Beer: Coors Banquet; Coors Light; Herman Joseph's 1868.

Sales: $894.2 million
Losses: $50.6 million
Rank in beer: 3
Founded: 1849
Employees: 7,000
Headquarters: Milwaukee, Wisconsin

What they do. For a brief time during the 1950s Schlitz was the nation's number 1 brewer, but their gusto has evaporated over the past two decades. They're now in third place behind Budweiser and Miller. Schlitz brews five national brands of beer: Schlitz, Schlitz Light, Schlitz Malt Liquor, Old Milwaukee (a "popular-priced" brew), and Erlanger (a "superpremium" beer, introduced recently to compete with Anheuser-Busch's Michelob and Miller's Löwenbräu).

They have some of the most efficient breweries in the industry. In fact, they can brew more beer (25 million barrels a year) than they have been able to sell (about 17 million barrels). Part of their problem stemmed from a blunder they made in the mid-1970s when they tried to save money by fiddling with their beer recipe. They substituted cheap corn syrup for some of the costly barley malt and rushed batches through in half the time that most brewers spend. A lot of people apparently noticed the difference. Schlitz has since improved the formula, but they've had trouble luring back their old customers. To make matters worse, Schlitz introduced an inane television advertising campaign showing belligerent characters threatening harm to anyone who dared to "take away my gusto." They dropped the commercials after receiving hundreds of complaints, and they've since switched advertising agencies. Schlitz has also been rent by squabbles among the descendants of the founding family.

History. August Krug started a brewery in an abandoned restaurant in Milwaukee in 1849. A year later Krug brought from his native Germany his eight-year-old nephew, August Uihlein, who was followed in later years by three brothers. Krug died in 1856, and the brewery's young bookkeeper, Joseph Schlitz, assumed control. Schlitz later married Krug's widow, and in 1874 he renamed the brewery after himself. Schlitz died on his way to Germany to visit relatives when the steamer *Schiller* went down in the Irish Sea in 1875. The brewery then passed into the hands of the Uihlein brothers.

The line "The beer that made Milwaukee famous," which appears on every can and bottle of Schlitz, is one of the oldest advertising slogans in America. It came about as a result of the great Chicago fire of 1871. After the fire Chicago was desperately short of water, and its breweries were virtually destroyed. The Krug brewery in Milwaukee, hearing of those parched throats in Chicago, sent a shipload of beer down Lake Michigan. That "export" sale turned the company's beer into more than a local seller. They put the slogan on their label in 1894. Until 1949 Milwaukee was the only place where Schlitz brewed beer.

After World War II the number of breweries in the United States dropped dramatically. There were more than 350 in the early 1950s; 25 years later the number had sunk below 100. By the end of the 1970s the five biggest beer companies made 75% of the beer sold in the country. Between 1950 and 1977 Schlitz's share of the market doubled, from 7% to 14%, but they failed to match the surge of Budweiser and Miller. In 1957 Anheuser-Busch knocked them out of first place, and in 1977 Miller displaced them from second. In 1979, still on the downswing, Schlitz brewed about 10% of the nation's beer and lost $50 million doing it.

Reputation. Schlitz was slow to catch on to the trends that swept the beer industry in the 1970s. They were late realizing there were big markets for a low-calorie beer and a premium beer. They also found out too late that once people decide a brand of beer tastes bad, it's extremely difficult to win them back. As a Wall Street analyst explained to *Business Week*, "Brand loyalty among beer drinkers is extremely strong, but so is brand disloyalty."

What they own. Six breweries at Milwaukee; Memphis; Winston-Salem, North Carolina; Longview, Texas; Los Angeles; and Tampa, Florida. Five can manufacturing plants that not only fulfill all their requirements but produce enough cans to sell to other companies. (Value Line Investment Survey estimated that in 1978 Schlitz made more money selling cans than selling beer.) Schlitz also owns the Geyser Peak winery in California and holds a minority interest in three Spanish breweries: Cerveceras Asociados, Barcelona; La Cruz del Campo, Seville; and Henninger Espanola, Madrid.

Who owns and runs the company. The members of the Uihlein family—close to 500 of them—still control 75% of Schlitz's stock, and three Uihleins sit on the board of directors. However, the Uihleins have not been active in the day-to-day management of the brewery since 1976, when chairman Robert A. Uihlein, Jr., died. During the 15 years that he was in charge, the family presented a united front, but after his death family strife began to surface at the company's annual stockholders' meetings. At the 1977 gathering, David V. Uihlein, a former director, sharply criticized his relatives on the board for investing in breweries overseas and entering the wine business.

He blamed the board for Schlitz's falling share of the beer market and problems with the quality of the brew. Two other Uihleins on the board supported some of his criticisms, but a motion he made to delay voting on directors until he could assemble a slate of his own failed by a wide margin.

To replace Robert Uihlein as chairman, the board selected Daniel F. (Jack) McKeithan, Jr., who had married into the Uihlein family (but was divorced in 1974). McKeithan ushered in a whole new management team. He hired as president Frank Sellinger, former top aide at Anheuser-Busch. Sellinger moved up to vice-chairman in 1980, and to replace him as president, Schlitz brought in Jerome Vielehr, head of international trade at Coca-Cola. One of Schlitz's board members is Willie Davis, former all-pro defensive end for the Green Bay Packers and Schlitz's distributor in Los Angeles.

In the public eye. On top of their other woes, Schlitz found themselves in deep trouble with the federal government in 1978. The feds charged them with making illegal payments and kickbacks of $3 million to wholesalers and retailers to get them to feature Schlitz beer in such outlets as O'Hare International Airport and the Conrad Hilton hotel in Chicago. Schlitz was indicted on 747 different counts. To settle the complaints, the company paid a total of $761,000 in penalties and fines. As a result of the legal action, four of Schlitz's eight top marketing executives left the company.

Where they're going. Schlitz is trying to regroup so that they can at least get back to the point where they're producing as much beer as their plants are capable of. To save money, they closed their brewery in Hawaii (where they brewed Primo beer) and sold their big brewery in Syracuse, New York, to Anheuser-Busch. They introduced their "superpremium" beer, Erlanger, and they started to distribute Ramlosa Royal, a Swedish mineral water. The company also moved their advertising account to the J. Walter Thompson agency, which came up

Americans drink 11 times more beer than wine.

with a new slogan: "Beer makes it good, Schlitz makes it great." Speculation in the brewing industry is that if Schlitz cannot stop their sales slide, the company will be sold.

Stock performance. Schlitz stock bought for $1,000 in 1970 sold for $350 on January 2, 1980.

Major employment centers. Milwaukee; Longview, Texas; Van Nuys, California; Tampa, Florida; Winston-Salem, North Carolina.

Beer Wars

When John A. Murphy, president of Miller Brewing, gets to work in the morning, he wipes his feet on a rug imprinted with the Budweiser logo. On his desk is a four-inch voodoo doll named Augie Busch, after August Busch III, head of Anheuser-Busch, the makers of Budweiser. When Busch heard about the voodoo doll, he made one of his own with red hair (Murphy is an Irish redhead) and shipped it off to Murphy, complete with Busch's monogrammed stickpin protruding from its chest. Murphy responded by registering a new beer trademark, "Gussie," the well-known nickname of August Busch II, the Anheuser-Busch chairman's father.

All this may seem like harmless pranksterism, but to the captains of the brewing industry it symbolizes the

vicious fight for supremacy in the beer market between Anheuser-Busch, long the "King of Beers," and Miller Brewing, the upstart of the 1970s. "What we have now, according to *Saturday Review* writer Jonathan Evan Maslow, "is a knockdown, dragout Beer War, with companies intent on carving themselves a larger share of the beer-drinking market—through advertising blitzes if they can, but directly out of another brewer's flesh if need be."

The war really got its start in 1971 when Philip Morris, the tobacco company that had bought Miller the previous year, sent Murphy to Milwaukee to turn the ailing brewer around. At the time, Miller was seventh in the industry and losing ground at a slow but steady pace. Murphy began with what *Esquire* called "the greatest beer-

spilling since Eliot Ness." Beer goes bad if it's left on the shelves too long, and that had been a Miller problem for some time. Murphy pulled millions of bottles, cans, and barrels of beer out of stores and bars and emptied them. Since then every can or bottle of Miller's is dated for quality and shipped back to the brewer if it's unsold by the deadline.

Then Murphy began to move, ordering a new ad campaign from McCann-Erickson, the big New York-based ad agency. The new campaign focused on one of the most important, but little known, facts of brewing life: that about 30% of the nation's beer-drinkers drink 80% of the nation's beer. The brewer who controls that 30% controls the industry; so McCann-Erickson aimed their sights at the blue-collar beer drinker. The campaign featured ordinary working men knocking off after a hard day's work for "Miller Time" at a local bar. It worked. By 1975 Miller had moved into fourth place—ahead of Coors, but behind Anheuser-Busch, Schlitz, and Pabst.

Then came Murphy's master-stroke. Brewers had long known that raising their prices normally decreased their share of the market (the beer-buying public being notoriously fickle), but the increasing ad budgets the big brewers were forced to spend in order to keep pace with the competition were cutting

Anheuser-Busch hired former boxer Joe Frazier to tell TV viewers why he switched from Miller Light to Natural Light—one of the many episodes in the bitter beer wars.

Access. 235 West Galena Street, Milwaukee, Wisconsin 53201; (414) 224-5000. Send requests for information to John A. Rourke, vice president–public relations. Tours of the Milwaukee brewery are conducted daily every half-hour between 9:00 A.M. and 3:30 P.M.; call (414) 224-5252. Children must be accompanied by an adult.

Consumer brands.

Beer: Schlitz; Schlitz Light; Schlitz Malt Liquor; Old Milwaukee; Erlanger.
Wine: Geyser Peak.

---

sharply into profits. What was needed was a new product that would cost the same to produce but could be sold for a higher price. Murphy's solution was Miller Lite, the reduced-calorie beer that has been, by any measure, the biggest new product in beer history.

Low-calorie beer had been tried before but was normally dismissed by consumers as a novelty item. Murphy thought a major, national television campaign was in order. Once again McCann-Erickson got the call, turning the account over to a 38-year-old creative director named Bob Lenz, who had never worked on a beer account before. Lenz wanted a spokesman who had a "beery" quality about him (for "beery," read paunchy). His first choice was Eddie Egan, the real-life model for the detective in *The French Connection.* But Egan was under indictment at the time, so Lenz tried to talk Jimmy Breslin into it. Breslin said no, and Lenz finally settled on former New York Jets running back Matt Snell, whose poster he had seen while riding on a New York City bus. "We taped him," Lenz told *Esquire,* "and once we saw the result, we knew we were onto something." The campaign eventually included the likes of Bubba Smith, Mickey Spillane, Rodney Dangerfield, Billy Martin, Dick Butkus, and Joe Frazier. (They had to be ex-athletes. The advertising codes pro-

hibit current athletes from appearing in ads for alcoholic beverages.)

Shortly after the introduction of Miller Lite, Murphy launched Löwenbräu in an attempt to go after Anheuser-Busch's Michelob, the leading super-premium beer. Finally, Anheuser-Busch got nervous. In November 1977 they complained to the Federal Trade Commission that Miller wasn't playing fair. Löwenbräu, they said, was marketed as though it were the German beer of the same name brewed since 1383. Anheuser pointed out that Miller had merely bought the rights to use the name in America for a beer they were brewing by modern methods in Fort Worth, Texas. The Bureau of Alcohol, Tobacco, and Firearms directed Miller to change their advertising to make it apparent that Löwenbräu was not the German product. But Murphy, incensed at Anheuser-Busch's appeal to the feds for help, issued what was, in essence, a declaration of war. "We find it incredulous [sic] that the world's largest brewer would ask the FTC to protect them. It seems apparent that the crown on the King of Beers must be slipping."

In fact, Budweiser's share of the market was *growing,* but at a much slower rate than Miller's. The upstart was now the number 2 brewer in the nation. When Anheuser-Busch introduced their own "Natural Light" beer, Miller complained to the Federal

Trade Commission that there was nothing natural about Anheuser's product. The beer was replete with tannic acid and various other chemicals, they said in a 1979 press release, and using *natural* as the product's nickname was deceptive and "corrupt(s) the word's proper usage." The war was on, and Anheuser pointed out to the *Wall Street Journal* that same year that Miller was also "a chemical brewer." Miller admitted to the *Journal* that they use various chemical additives but quickly added that their processes met federal regulations.

The war has become downright nasty. Miller charged to the Bureau of Alcohol, Tobacco, and Firearms that Anheuser-Busch's Michelob Light was "simply watered-down Michelob," made by diluting regular Michelob with carbonated water. Anheuser-Busch's response was equally snitty. "[Michelob Light] is an all-natural beer, and unlike Miller Lite, doesn't contain any fungal enzyme or artificial foam enhancer." Miller then attacked Budweiser's famous "beechwood aging" process, a company symbol since the end of Prohibition. "We seriously doubt," said Miller, "that consumers understand that 'beechwood aging' consists of dumping chemically treated lumber into a glass-lined or stainless-steel beer storage tank."

Distillers

Heublein

Sales: $1.3 billion
Profits: $68 million
Forbes 500 rank: 378
Rank in vodka: 1
Rank in wine: 2
Rank in premixed cocktails: 1
Rank in fast foods: 2
Founded: 1875
Employees: 24,900
Headquarters: Farmington, Connecticut

What they do. During the last two decades Heublein has kept moving up breathlessly in the liquor business. Their three vodka brands—Smirnoff, Popov, and Relska—account for one-third of all the vodka downed in the United States. And Smirnoff has become one of the top-selling liquor brands in the world. Heublein likes to attribute their success to their ability to mesh their products with changing American lifestyles. As Chairman Stuart D. Watson puts it: "This new lifestyle provides consumers with more occasions for light and flavorful adult drinks such as our wines and spirits." Translation: Americans have more time to drink, they are drinking less hard whiskey (the "brown" stuff), and they have turned to light-looking drinks ("white" goods). Heublein masterminded the switch from whiskey to vodka, inventing and/or promoting a whole new bunch of mixed drinks that use vodka. The vodka boom started—where else?—in California and spread across the country, although it has yet to take deep roots in the Midwest. But Heublein is confident of the future.

The opportunities are to be sought through a long line of spirits and wines. Some Heublein distills themselves, some they import from other countries, and some they produce in the verdant grape-growing valleys of California. Alcohol is this company's business—and they do very well at it. They're particularly adept at insinuating their products into the modern, attractive, sporty settings that are the hallmarks of Smirnoff advertising. They spare no cost in photographing these settings; Smirnoff advertisements have featured the work of such world-famous photographers as Irving Penn, Gordon Parks, and Helmut Newton. They have been unswerving in their goal: to make Smirnoff part of the social fabric.

Heublein still makes the premixed cocktails they started out with in the 1890s, but vodka provides the big kick, aided by such helpful spirits as Black & White Scotch, Don Q rums, José Cuervo tequila, Lancers Wine, Harveys Bristol Cream sherry, Irish Mist liqueur, and Black Velvet Canadian whiskey. Figuring that wine is part of the new American lifestyle, Heublein bought the nation's second-largest wine seller, United Vintners (Italian Swiss Colony, Inglenook, Petri) in 1969. At the same time they bought one of California's great premium wineries, Beaulieu. The Federal Trade Commission challenged the United Vintners purchase in 1979, charging that it reduced competition in the wine business, and Heublein is still contesting this complaint. They were able to make a novel defense: the leading wine maker, Gallo, has forged further ahead since United Vintners was bought by Heublein.

Heublein would have been better off if they had stuck to vodka. Their venture with Hamm's Beer was a washout. And their 1971 purchase of Kentucky Fried Chicken has brought a lot of headaches even though this business was supposedly part of the

Best Selling Booze

Brand (type, marketer)	Sales (thousands of cases*) 1979
1. BACARDI (rum, Bacardi)	7,200
2. SMIRNOFF (vodka, Heublein)	6,300
3. SEAGRAM'S 7 CROWN (blend whisky, Seagram)	6,100
4. SEAGRAM'S VO (Canadian, Seagram)	3,825
5. CANADIAN CLUB (Canadian, Walker)	3,625
6. JIM BEAM (bourbon, Beam)	2,825
7. POPOV (vodka, Heublein)	2,800
8. J & B (Scotch, Paddington)	2,600
9. SEAGRAM'S GIN (gin, Seagram)	2,600
10. GORDON'S GIN (gin, Renfield)	2,525
11. CANADIAN MIST (Canadian, Brown-Forman)	2,425
12. WINDSOR SUPREME (Canadian, National)	2,400
13. DEWAR'S (Scotch, Schenley)	2,300
14. JACK DANIEL'S (Tennessee, Brown-Forman)	2,200
15. GILBEY'S GIN (gin, National)	2,000
16. CUTTY SARK (Scotch, Buckingham)	1,975
17. BLACK VELVET (Canadian, Heublein)	1,950
18. EARLY TIMES (bourbon, Brown-Forman)	1,700
19. JOHNNIE WALKER RED (Scotch, Somerset)	1,675
20. ANCIENT AGE (bourbon, Schenley)	1,650
21. GORDON'S VODKA (vodka, Renfield)	1,650
22. KESSLER (blend whiskey, Seagram)	1,625
23. BEEFEATER (gin, Kobrand)	1,600
24. CHRISTIAN BROS. (brandy, Fromm & Sichel)	1,600
25. TEN HIGH (bourbon, Walker)	1,500
26. KAMCHATKA (vodka, National)	1,400
27. CALVERT EXTRA (blend whiskey, Seagram)	1,375
28. FLEISCHMANN'S GIN (gin, Fleischmann)	1,350
29. GILBEY'S VODKA (vodka, National)	1,325
30. KAHLUA (liqueur, Walker)	1,300
31. SOUTHERN COMFORT (liqueur, Brown-Forman)	1,225
32. CHIVAS REGAL (Scotch, Seagram)	1,100
33. IMPERIAL (blend whiskey, Walker)	1,050
34. WOLFSCHMIDT (vodka, Seagram)	1,050
35. FLEISCHMANN'S PREFERRED (blend whiskey, Fleischman)	1,000
36. OLD GRAND-DAD (bourbon, National)	1,000
37. LORD CALVERT CANADIAN (Canadian, Seagram)	975
38. OLD CROW (bourbon, National)	975
39. CROWN RUSSE (vodka, Seagram)	800
40. SCHENLEY'S VODKA (vodka, Schenley)	800
41. McNAUGHTON'S (Canadian, Schenley)	775
42. OLD CHARTER (bourbon, Schenley)	775
43. TANQUERAY (gin, Somerset)	775
44. AMARETTO DI SARONNO (liqueur, Glenmore)	700
45. OLD FORESTER (bourbon, Brown-Forman)	700
46. RELSKA (vodka, Heublein)	700
47. RONRICO (rum, Seagram)	700
48. CASTILLO (rum, Bacardi)	650
49. CROWN ROYAL (Canadian, Seagram)	650
50. FLEISCHMANN'S VODKA (vodka, Fleischmann)	650
51. JOSE CUERVO (tequila, Heublein)	650
52. SKOL (vodka, Medley)	650
53. OLD TAYLOR (bourbon, National)	625
54. INVER HOUSE (Scotch, Wile)	600
55. JOHNNIE WALKER BLACK (Scotch, Somerset)	600
56. CANADIAN LTD (Canadian, Fleischmann)	550
57. HIRAM WALKER VODKA (vodka, Walker)	550
58. MR. BOSTON (vodka, Glenmore)	550
59. NIKOLAI (vodka, Seagram)	525
60. JACQUIN (vodka, Jacquin)	500
61. PASSPORT (Scotch, Seagram)	500
62. WILD TURKEY (bourbon, Austin-Nichols))	500

*There are 12 fifth-gallon bottles per case.

Source: Business Week, March 17, 1980.

new American lifestyle. They do have a $115 million-a-year food business headed by A-1, the top-selling steak sauce; Grey Poupon, the leading Dijon-type mustard; and the Ortega line of Mexican foods.

History. In 1875 Smirnoff vodka was the only brand Czar Alexander II would allow on his table. That's the year Gilbert and Louis Heublein set up a distilled spirits business in a Hartford, Connecticut, storefront. They couldn't guess that 65 years later Gilbert's grandson would decide to bring the Czar's favorite drink to the American people—or that the decision would revolutionize the company's fortunes and America's drinking habits. The Heublein brothers did pretty well establishing themselves in the liquor trade in the 1880s. By 1892 they were bottling the first prepared cocktails, selling them to hotels and restaurants and then directly to consumers. But Prohibition wiped out Heublein's main source of profits, so they turned to a seemingly unimportant company they'd acquired a few years earlier,

The Water of Life: A Capsule History

One forgotten but joyful day in prehistory, an early human discovered that fruit left to rot while damp transformed itself into an intoxicating brew with a strange power to lift the spirits of whoever drank it, temporarily softening the harsh realities of primitive life. For centuries afterward the phenomenon was regarded as a magical gift from the gods. In fact, the change was a simple chemical process called fermentation, which breaks down the starches in fruit, vegetables, or grain, turning them first into sugars, then into alcohol.

In time, experimentation revealed that the transformation could be hastened and the final product improved by adding yeast and/or sugar to the fermenting foodstuffs. Fermentation, controlled under modern winery or brewery conditions, is still the basic process that produces wine and beer.

Drinks created by fermentation typically contain no more than 16% alcohol. To make stronger alcoholic beverages like brandy, whiskey, gin, or vodka requires a second step: distillation. Exactly how people discovered that fermented fruit or grain could be heated to produce an alcoholic vapor which could then be cooled and condensed back into a highly potent liquid, no one knows. Various nations and individuals have claimed the honor, but the fortuitous discovery was probably made in the Far East before Christ was born. Primitive stills made of gourds and hollow bamboo tubes were used to make distilled liquors in China as long as 1,000 years ago. In India a potent drink called *arrack* was distilled as early as 800 B.C.

Knowledge of distilling probably reached Europe via the ancient Egyptians, who practiced the art starting in the eighth century B.C. Aristotle described the technique for distilling wine into brandy in the fourth century B.C.

Much later, in early Christian times, a Spanish alchemist named Albucasis rediscovered the process Aristotle described, claiming to have invented it himself. Albucasis, whose ninth-century experiments were aimed at finding the fabled elixir of eternal life, believed that the potent liquid he distilled was the miracle fluid he sought. For centuries afterward distilled liquors resembling modern brandy and whiskey were called *aqua vitae*, or water of life.

Wherever the credit belongs, European alchemists and monks kept distilling a closely guarded secret, reserving their potent liquors for the aristocracy and religious insiders.

How the secret reached the British Isles is a mystery, but in the sixth century a Welsh bard, Taliessin, composed songs in praise of mead and ale, demonstrating that the Welsh were familiar with distilling as well as malting and brewing, the first stages in making whiskey from grain.

When the Reformation broke up the monasteries in England and Scotland in the sixteenth century, monks were forced to work at trades. Many became brewers or distillers, spreading their secrets to a wider circle. Improved stills were devised, and the Scots learned to distill a distinctive kind of aqua vitae from their abundant barley crops, first "malting" the barley by steeping it in water and letting it germinate. This is still the key process in making true Scotch whiskey. The malted grain is dried over peat smoke in a kiln, cleaned, crushed, mixed with hot water to produce a "wort," to which yeast is added to help the fermentation. The fermented mash, or "wash," is distilled into whiskey.

Legend says that St. Patrick, a native of Scotland, brought the secrets of whis-

the British makers of A-1 Steak Sauce. Today they point to A-1 as the sole reason they survived the Prohibition decade.

When the revolution overwhelmed Russia in 1917, Vladimir Smirnoff fled to Paris, taking along the vodka formula that had won the imperial seal of approval. He had little luck trying to sell vodka in France, and an American who bought the U.S. rights to the vodka formula in 1933 was similarly unsuccessful. Scoffers called it "Martin's folly" when John Martin, grandson of Gilbert Heublein and then president of the company, decided to buy the Smirnoff rights in 1939 for $14,000. At the time Smirnoff sold only about 6,000 cases per year. But after World War II Heublein staged a massive campaign to change American drinking habits in favor of Smirnoff. They emphasized vodka's lightness and versatility, claiming that Smirnoff left the drinker "breathless"—which helped convince noontime drinkers and drinking drivers to give it a try. Heublein also introduced a number of new vodka-based drinks (bloody Mary, screwdriver, Moscow mule)

of the Distiller's Art

key making to Ireland along with Christianity. Galvanized either by faith or aqua vitae, the Irish reportedly emerged from the caves where they had been living half-naked to become the world's most cultured people.

Scots-Irish pioneers brought their whiskey-distilling skills with them to America, but they made little whiskey before the Revolution. Until then the favored drink of Colonial Americans was rum, distilled in the New England colonies from West Indies molasses, as part of the infamous three-way slave trade. Rum shipped to Africa's Guinea coast paid for slaves, who were shipped to the West Indies to work on sugar plantations. The plantation owners paid in molasses, which went to New England to be made into rum.

But the Revolution's British blockade, followed by a trade embargo and finally Congress's abolition of the slave trade, cut off most of the molasses supply. Scots-Irish settlers in the Shenendoah Valley were ready to fill America's thirst. From the 1700s the Pennsylvania settlers were raising bumper crops of rye—far more than they could eat or drink. A pack horse could carry only 4 bushels of grain to the markets of the Eastern seaboard. But if the grain were distilled into whiskey, the same horse could haul 24 bushels, condensed into two kegs of liquor. Whiskey became the frontier's money, to trade for manufactured goods like gunpowder, shot, iron, and nails.

Some of the Scots-Irish drifted still further, into Kentucky. There rye and wheat grew poorly, but corn flourished. The Kentuckians developed a new kind of corn whiskey, mellowed with a little rye. Before long, peddlars from the east were touring the rural bluegrass counties, bartering their wares for freshly distilled farm whiskey —colorless, sharp-tasting liquid sold in uncharred barrels as soon as it was made. By 1812 "Kentucky whiskey" and "western whiskey" were known and esteemed in eastern cities.

Eventually people noticed that the raw Kentucky whiskey mellowed on its journey east. Kentucky distillers started aging their product in kegs, to mellow it for sale. Ultimately, someone made the discovery that produced the first true bourbon: aromatic, mellow, and ruddy-colored. The transformation happened only when the corn whiskey was aged in new, charred kegs of white oak; then it lost its biting sharpness, gaining sweetness and a burnished hue.

Legend offers at least three explanations for the origin of the charred bourbon barrel, according to Gerald Carson's *The Social History of Bourbon.* One is that a distiller tried to reuse fish barrels to age his whiskey. To eliminate the fishy tang, he burnt the inside of the casks—and found that the whiskey aged in them was the best he had ever made. Another tale credits the breakthrough to a cooper who accidentally singed his barrel staves while heating them to make them pliable. Saying nothing, he sold an internally charred keg to a distiller, who subsequently insisted that all his barrels be charred. Yet another story claims that when Kentucky distillers started aging their product, a barrel shortage developed. Recycling used kegs, the distillers scorched them to drive off stale flavors.

Whatever the truth of the matter, aging in new, charred oak barrels is the feature that distinguishes bourbon from all other whiskies of the world.

that popularized vodka so quickly that by the 1960s vodka had moved from a footnote on the sales charts to a place in the top echelon. Heublein's success was spurred by the ease of vodka-making: unlike whiskeys, which may require years of aging, vodka can be produced in the morning and sold in the afternoon.

Vodka's strength today is awesome. In 1979 Heublein sold 10 million cases of vodka in the United States and another 5 million cases in the rest of the world. Vodka now outsells gin in the United States by a margin of better than 2:1. And Smirnoff now outsells every other alcoholic beverage brand with the exception of Bacardi rum.

Heublein's touch was not so sure in other places. They bought Hamm's beer in 1966, but that didn't work out at all. Unaware that canned beer has a very short shelf-life, Heublein failed to replace old cases with new ones. Hamm's went flat and musty in the coolers, and consumers began to leave it there. Unable to revive the brand, Heublein sold it in 1973 to Olympia Brewing.

Their initial experience in the wine business was not gratifying either. They began riding the pop-wine boom—and when that fad lost its kick, United Vintners lost their share of the market. They have now come back strongly by emphasizing table wines, where the big growth is. Their Inglenook label sold more than 5 million cases in 1979,

making it one of the industry's top sellers.

Kentucky Fried Chicken has been a disaster—they helped to knock Heublein's profits down from $73 million to $41 million in one year (1975–76)—but Heublein is determined to make this one work. Of the 17,500 persons employed by Heublein in the United States, 12,000 work for Kentucky Fried Chicken.

Reputation. Heublein is known as a smart marketing company, and their rebound from the KFC disaster was rapid enough that this image is mostly intact. They are a major advertiser in all media, promoting their wines and chicken on television and their harder stuff through billboards and print advertising. Here's their own description of how they do it: "Take a food or drink product, formulate it to satisfy most consumers' taste, name it memorably, package it smartly, price it wisely, distribute it widely, and promote it with feeling so that it etches into the consciousness of consumers ... The Smirnoff performance is a paragon."

What they own. Heublein makes vodka at plants in Allen Park, Michigan; Hartford, Connecticut; Menlo Park, California; and Paducah, Kentucky. They have wineries at eight California locations. They have the biggest liquor operation in South America through their 1973 purchases of Drury-Fasano and Dreher in Brazil. They also have a 49% interest in a Portuguese winery, Fonseca.

Who owns and runs the company. Stuart D. Watson, a former advertising man on Madison Avenue, came to Heublein as president in 1966 and became chairman in 1973. He was succeeded as chief executive officer in 1980 by Hicks B. Waldron, who came to Heublein in 1973 after 27 years with General Electric. John Martin, former chairman and descendant of the Heublein brothers, is the largest single shareholder, with 4.6% of the stock. Next is director Robert Trescher, who owns 3.3% The board has one black member, Lisle Carter, who is president of the University of the District of Columbia, and a former assistant secretary of Health, Education and Welfare. He was elected in 1979.

Where they're going. Heublein suffered a blow when the Shah of Iran was overthrown. They had built up a business of 300,000 cases of Smirnoff a year—but the Ayatollah Khomeini didn't believe in spirits (alcoholic, that is) and banished them from the country. But Heublein has high hopes elsewhere—in Brazil, where they have a new vodka distillery and where the population is expected to shoot from 112 million to 200 million by the end of the century, and of course in their home country, the United States, where Heublein feels that the era of "me-ism" is made to order for their products. Heublein feels they will do well even if gas shortages keep people at home because then they will do more home entertaining and that's where some 70% of distilled spirits are consumed. In Smirnoff's case it's even higher: 80% is consumed in homes.

Stock performance. Heublein stock bought for $1,000 in 1970 sold for $723 on January 2, 1980.

Major employment centers. Hartford and Farmington, Connecticut; and Louisville, Kentucky.

Access. Farmington, Connecticut 06032; (203) 677-4061. The following facilities are open for tours:

Heublein food processing plant at Oxnard, California (1500 East 3rd). Products made here include A-1 steak sauce, Ortega chiles and sauces, and Grey Poupon Dijon mustards. Tours by appointment only—call (805) 483-2377.

Beaulieu Vineyards, Rutherford, California. Open daily from 10 A.M. to 4 P.M. Free, no appointment needed.

Inglenook Vineyards, Rutherford, California. Open daily from 9 A.M. to 5 P.M. Free, no appointment needed.

Consumer brands.

Spirits: Smirnoff vodkas; Smirnoff Silver; Black

An early Colonial distiller named E. C. Booze sold a brand of whiskey called *Old Log Cabin*. Booze's name in time became a slang term for whiskey, although *Old Log Cabin* has long since vanished into the mists of history.

Velvet Canadian whiskey; Black & White scotch; Arrow cordials and brandies; Bahia Licor de Cafe; Heublein cocktails; The Club cocktails; José Cuervo tequila; Cuervo 1800; Don Q rum; Irish Mist liqueur; Milshir gin; Tullamore Dew Irish whiskey; Popov vodka; Relska vodka; Arrow Ostrova vodka; McMaster's Scotch and Canadian whiskies; Matador tequila; Malcolm Hereford's Cows; Yukon Jack Canadian Liqueur; Boggs Cranberry liqueur; Vaklova liqueur.

California wines, brandies, and champagnes: Beaulieu; Inglenook; Italian Swiss Colony; Petri; Annie Green Springs; T. J. Swann; Bali Hai; Sangrole; Mission Bell; Santa Fe; H. M. S. Frost; Esprit; Jacare; Gambarelli and Davito; Lejon; Jacques Bonet; Tipo; Hartley; Vin Kafe; Cappela; T. J. Socials; GMR; Zazie.

Imported wines: Lancers; Harveys Bristol Cream sherry; Bouchard Pere & Fils; Egri Bikaver Hungarian wine; Tokaji Aszu; Harveys other sherries and ports; Vinya Rose; Kiku Masamune sake; Taru sake.

Convenience foods: Kentucky Fried Chicken; H. Salt Seafood; Zantigo Mexican-American foods.

Sauces and specialty foods: A-1 Steak Sauce; Grey Poupon Dijon mustard; Ortega tacos, chiles, sauces, and Mexican-style foods; Snap-E-Tom tomato cocktail; Regina wine vinegars; Escoffier sauces; Steak Supreme sauce; Hart's dinner rolls, muffins, and buttermilk biscuits.

Seagram

Sales: $2.2 billion
Profits: $90 million
Rank in liquor: 1
Rank in blended whiskey: 1
Rank in wine: 3
Founded: 1924
Employees: 15,000
Headquarters: Montreal, Quebec
U.S. Headquarters: New York, New York

What they do. They're headquartered in Canada, but they do almost three-quarters of their business in the United States—and they sell their booze in 175 countries around the world. They own nine distilleries in Scotland, they have big vineyards in California, France, Italy, and Germany, and they're distilling whiskey at the foot of Mount Fuji in Japan.

That's Seagram, the company Samuel

"Mr. Sam" Bronfman started more than 60 years ago with a small distillery outside Montreal. Today they're the biggest liquor business in the world. Seagram produces spirits in 17 countries and makes wine in 10, and they market 150 brands of spirits and some 300 brands of wine and champagnes all over the world. Much of their production is for thirsty Americans. In the United States they sell Crown Royal, 7 Crown, V.O., Chivas Regal, The Glenlivet Scotch, John Jameson Irish Whiskey, Lord Calvert Canadian Whiskey, Four Roses, Wolfschmidt Vodka, Ron Rico Rums, Leroux brandies and liqueurs, and Christian Brothers brandy. They also make Paul Masson wines and sell the wines and champagnes produced by Christian Brothers, Barton & Guestier, Munn's, Kayser, and Schoonmaker.

But increasingly the booze business is taking on an international character, as spreading affluence is making it possible for drinkers in Europe, Japan, and Latin America to move up from local liquors to the more prestigious foreign products. While American sophisticates serve their dinner guests German wines imported by Seagram, Seagram is busy satisfying Germany's new-found taste for bourbon. In Great Britain, where the taste is turning to vodka, Seagram imports Stolichnaya, Russia's finest; meanwhile, their distilleries in Scotland turn out high-priced Chivas Regal for discerning drinkers around the world. When Japanese import duties made it difficult for imported whiskeys to make big inroads into the market there, Seagram, in partnership with Kirin, the big Japanese brewery, started to distill Robert Brown Scotch to sell to drinkers who wanted a premium Scotch with a foreign name.

With the exception of bottles and labels, which the company buys from various suppliers, Seagram controls their domestic manufacturing and distilling business from start to finish. They have their own grain elevators in Indiana and Illinois to hold the raw materials that are turned into whiskey, vodka, gin, and the like at their five distilleries and bottled in their six plants in the United States and Canada. What Seagram doesn't bottle immediately, they store in white oak barrels for aging periods between 4 and 12 years—and, yes, they make the barrels too. After the products hit the market, Seagram spends $120 million a year on magazine, newspaper, television, and bill-

board advertising. They are one of the largest advertisers in newspapers and magazines in North America.

Since 1963 Seagram has also dabbled in the oil and gas business, primarily in the American Southeast, where their Texas Pacific subsidiary pumps crude oil. In the last few years Texas Pacific has begun exploring in Europe and Asia, and in 1978 they went into production offshore in the Gulf of Mexico. In April 1980 Sun Oil offered a whopping $2.3 billion for most of Texas Pacific's reserves—an offer Seagram accepted.

History. The word *bronfan* means "brandy" in Yiddish, so it was perhaps fated that when Yechiel Bronfman fled Czarist anti-Semitism in Bessarabia and came to Manitoba in 1889, he would end up as a liquor distributor. He died a wealthy man in 1919. His sons, Sam and Allan, started selling booze by mail order during World War I. Although every Canadian province except Quebec was dry at the time, a quirk of the laws made it legal to sell liquor through the mails. When the provinces finally, one by one, regained their senses in the early 1920s and legalized liquor sales, Sam and Allan went into the distilling business. In 1924 they broke ground on their first distillery just outside Montreal, and in 1927 they bought out the much larger Joseph E. Seagram & Sons and adopted the name.

Sam and Allan chose the right time and place to go into the distilling business. Prohibition had been in effect in the United States since 1919, and Americans were thirsty for whiskey, paying exorbitant prices to anyone willing to flout the law and smuggle liquor from Canada. They could not be choosy about quality. In his 1979 biography of Sam Bronfman, *King of the Castle*, Peter Newman wrote that to make their Prohibition-era Scotch, the Bronfmans "reduced the sixty-five-overproof white alcohol to required bottling strength by mixing it with water, then added some real Scotch plus a dash of burnt sugar (caramel) for coloring." The Bronfmans then sold this whiskey to a little army of bootleggers who smuggled it south across the 49th Parallel.

An estimated 1.1 million gallons of Canadian whiskey were smuggled across the border in 1928, and again in 1929; estimates place the Seagram share of this trade at 50%

or more. But in 1930 the Canadian government banned liquor exports to any country that banned imports, which the United States had theoretically been doing since the passage of the Prohibition in 1919. Until the 1933 repeal the Bronfmans circumvented this law by shipping their whiskey to the French-owned island of St. Pierre, just off the Nova Scotia coast, and selling it to bootleggers who shipped it to the American Eastern Seaboard or back down the St. Lawrence River to upstate New York.

"We shipped a lot of goods," Mr. Sam told *Fortune.* "Of course, we knew where it went, but we had no legal proof. And I never went on the other side of the border to count the empty Seagrams bottles." The Treasury Department probably didn't count them either, but that didn't stop them in 1935 from levying $60 million in back excise taxes and import duties on Canadian distillers. Although the Treasury action was of dubious legality, it was backed by a threat to exclude Canadian imports, and Seagram agreed to pay $1.5 million.

After the repeal of Prohibition, Seagram was in a splendid position to cash in on the legal U.S. liquor market. Unlike their U.S. competitors, they had warehouses full of aging whiskey. Also, unlike American distillers who were most experienced at selling "straight" whiskeys (bourbon or rye) in bulk, Bronfman's old mail-order business had taught him the value of brand names. Until the mid-1930s Americans relied on local brands, distilled in one region and seldom distributed over more than a few states. Seagram introduced the first national brand in 1934: Seagram's 5 Crown, succeeded a few months later by 7 Crown. These were blended whiskeys, made from a combination of aged whiskey and neutral grain spirits. Lighter and smoother than the rye and bourbon Americans had been drinking before Prohibition, they were a big success, and by 1938 Seagram was on top of the liquor business.

Seagram's 7 Crown itself is legendary, both for its market rank and for its profitability. For more than two decades 7 Crown was the biggest-selling alcoholic beverage in the United States, at one point doing three times as well as its nearest competitor. One of the most popular, and most advertised, bar drinks in history has been "Seven and Seven"—7 Crown and 7-Up.

Seagram's Mr. Sam

Samuel ("Mr. Sam") Bronfman, owner-operator of the vast Seagram liquor empire, inspired abject terror among his employees. His colossal temper tantrums, in which he often hurled objects at his underlings, occurred almost daily.

One of those who could never get used to Mr. Sam's outbursts was Frank Marshall, director of export sales for Seagram during the early 1950s. Marshall was so upset by Mr. Sam's furies that he arranged his schedule so as to be out of town whenever Mr. Sam was in, and in when he was out. In case Mr. Sam returned without notice, Marshall would grab his suitcase, run out the back door, and fly off to whatever part of the Bronfman empire might

benefit from a surprise inspection. The system worked perfectly for several years while overseas sales were booming; but Bronfman eventually realized that he hadn't seen his export manager in some time and sent word out that he wanted to see him.

Marshall continued to dodge Mr. Sam for a few more months, but finally he had to return when Bronfman's 60th birthday party was scheduled. The main feature of the party was a film of Seagram's far-flung Egyptian officers toasting one another with Seagram's Crown Royal and of a Bedouin riding a camel across the desert with a bottle of V.O. under his belt. As the camel approached the camera,

Bronfman saw that the "Bedouin" was actually Marshall dressed up in a long nightshirt and a fez, staging the picture for the camera's benefit. He leaped out of his chair and screamed "There's the son-of-a-bitch! That's where he's been spending his time! Riding a goddamn camel!"

Once Bronfman had calmed down somewhat, Marshall meekly approached him from behind and whispered, "That film was taken on a Sunday, Mr. Sam." Bronfman's response has gone unrecorded.

Source: Peter Newman, *King of the Castle* (Atheneum, 1979).

But 7 Crown's profits were even more incredible. One of Seagram's 476 U.S. distributors said that its "margins are in a league with razor blades and Coca-Cola"; meaning that although Seagram's 7 Crown costs only pennies to make, it retails for upward of $75 a case. Distributors are making $9 or $10 a case, and most of them move between 50,000 and 100,000 cases a year. Seagram's per case profit has never been published, but even at a tiny fraction of their distributors' profit, multiplied by 476 distributors, Seagram makes tens of millions each year from 7 Crown alone.

Their leadership did not go unchallenged. Seagram was locked in a fierce competition with Lewis Rosenstiel's Schenley

No, it's not the University of Virginia, it's the entrance to the corporate headquarters of Brown-Forman in Louisville, Kentucky. The Brown family founded this distillery in 1870, and three generations of Browns have gone to the University of Virginia—hence the corinthian columns to remind them of their alma mater. And there are plenty in the company to remind. Brown-Forman, the distiller of Jack Daniel's, Early Times, Old Forester, and Canadian Mist whiskies, is a company that believes in nepotism. W. L. Lyons Brown, Jr., the president, is the great-grandson of the founder—and there are many other Browns in the company (six on the board alone). The company encourages all employees to have their relatives apply for jobs. The *Wall Street Journal* once estimated that one-seventh of the Brown-Forman work force was composed of relatives.

Industries for dominance in the industry. When distilling grain for liquor was banned as a wartime emergency measure in 1942, the two big companies were faced with the crucial decision of whether to restrict sales or to use inferior spirits distilled from potatoes or sugar cane. Bronfman chose to stick to grain spirits, thereby restricting his output, particularly of his cheaper brands. Rosenstiel, on the other hand, decided to use potato and cane spirits, which allowed him to keep production high and take over as the industry leader. But the guys at the bar rail were drinking Schenley's potato liquor only out of patriotic duty and sheer necessity, and when Seagram resumed full production after the war, they flocked to Bronfman's quality line, giving Seagram a lead they have never lost.

In the 1950s and 1960s Mr. Sam's uncanny knack for predicting and creating liquor tastes began to slip. Americans were turning away from blended whiskeys in favor of ever-lighter beverages—principally gin, vodka, and rum. Bronfman looked down his nose at vodka. He could never understand its appeal to drinkers: at an American Legion convention where a friend poured a case of vodka into a swimming pool, Mr. Sam stood up and cheered. As a result, Seagram never promoted their own vodka (Wolfschmidt) and lost ground to Heublein. But in the late 1940s Bronfman had begun to expand his empire overseas to Scotland, Jamaica, and France, and even as blended whiskey dropped in popularity, Seagram was ready with Scotch, rum, and wine. Now, no matter what drinkers order, Seagram has the liquor they want.

Reputation. When Bronfman died in 1971, Seagram changed for good. Mr. Sam was a brilliant pioneer in liquor marketing, but he overstayed his time, attempting to run the company until the age of 80. He stuck to his own ideas of what America should drink even while companies like Heublein, with younger leadership, were proving him wrong. "We were losing some of our customers to the obituary columns," a company executive admitted to *Forbes*. Still, there's no question who's the powerhouse of the liquor industry. Seagram has more than twice the sales of their nearest competitor. And Mr. Sam's sons run the show.

What they own. The jewel of Seagram's

worldwide empire is their 38-story U.S. headquarters on Park Avenue in Manhattan. Considered by many critics as New York's finest postwar skyscraper, the bronze and glass tower was designed by Mies Van der Rohe and Philip Johnson. Mr. Sam originally commissioned a more pedestrian design for the building, but his daughter Phyllis persuaded him to hire Van der Rohe and battled her way on to the company's building committee to see that the job got done right.

Who owns and runs the company. While he was alive, Mr. Sam ruled the company as a ruthless autocrat. Brother Allan had hoped that his sons, Edward and Peter, would be brought into the company after they finished college, but Sam intended to hand the company to *his* sons, Edgar and Charles. Because he controlled the family trust, Sam won the battle, creating a rift in the family that has never healed. Edgar Bronfman took over from his father as chief executive, and Sam's sons control 34% of the company's stock.

In the public eye. The U.S. liquor industry has always been viewed with suspicion by the federal government—a holdover from the days of Prohibition. In the past three decades there have been frequent accusations of bribery and political payoffs, particularly in the so-called control states where all alcoholic beverages must be sold through state-owned liquor stores. In the most recent case, in West Virginia in 1979, 18 companies including Seagram were charged with several counts of commercial bribery, and all pleaded guilty. A former state liquor commissioner was indicted on related corruption charges.

Also in 1979, Seagram was found guilty of 73 separate violations of the Federal Alcohol Administration Act, for political contributions between 1974 and 1976, and forced to pay a fine of $1.5 million—the largest penalty ever levied on a corporation.

Where they're going. At the moment in the liquor industry, wine is the up-and-coming commodity, and Seagram is one of the major producers. They own California's Paul Masson vineyards, one of the largest-selling brands, and they import Barton & Guestier wines from France and Brolio wines from Italy, and market Christian Brothers wines and brandies here in the United States.

Major employment centers. New York, New York; Lawrenceburg, Indiana; Louisville, Kentucky.

Access. 1430 Peel Street, Montreal, Quebec, Canada H3A 1S9; (514) 849-5271. U.S. office: 375 Park Avenue, New York, New York 10022; (212) 572-7000.

Consumer brands.

Whiskeys: Seagram's 7 Crown; Kessler; Calvert Extra; Four Roses; Seagram's V.O. Canadian; Seagram's Crown Royal; Canadian Lord Calvert; Harwood Canadian; Chivas Regal; Passport; Premium Bourbon; John Jameson Irish; White Horse; Benchmark; The Glenlivet; Famous Grouse; James Fox Canadian; Henry McKenna; Logan Deluxe; Jerome Irish; Canadian Masterpiece; Royal Salute.

Vodka: Wolfschmidt; Crown Russe; Burnett's; Nikolai.

Gin: Seagram's Extra Dry; Calvert; Sir Robert Burnett's.

Rum: Ronrico Puerto Rican; Myer's Jamaica; Palo Viejo; Grauado.

Others: Leroux brandies and liqueurs; Christian Brothers brandy; Olmeca tequila; Lochan Ora liqueur; Pasha liqueur; Vandermint.

Wines: Paul Masson; Christian Brothers; Gold Seal; Barton & Guestier (B&G); Mumm's; Kaiser; Frank Schoonmaker selections; Nectarose; Kijafa; Chateau de La Chaize; Chateau Larose Trintaudon; Les Charmes; Perrier-Jouet; Henri Marchant.

In 1978 Americans consumed about 430.7 million gallons of wine, of which 288.6 million were produced in California, 10 million in other states, and the balance in foreign nations. Italy was the largest exporter to the United States, shipping more than 39 million gallons. At an average price of $8 a gallon, Americans spent more than $3.2 billion on wine in 1978.

A Wine Maker

 Gallo

Sales: $475 million (estimated)
Rank in wine: 1
Founded: 1933
Employees: 2,000
Headquarters: Modesto, California

What they do. Gallo is a secret kingdom built on the profits made from cheap wine. Since their founding in 1933 the Gallo brothers—Ernest and Julio—have thumbed their noses at the press and anyone else who has asked what was going on behind their impenetrable walls in Modesto, California. Because the Gallo brothers and their families own the winery lock, stock, and barrels, they are not legally required to release much information about the activities of the world's largest wine-making company, and they are alone among major California wineries in refusing to allow public tours of their premises.

Still, analysts of the wine industry have come up with some pretty fair estimates of their clout. Gallo is certainly the largest winery in the world, controlling between one-fourth and one-third of the American wine market, leading *Time* magazine in 1980 to dub them "the General Motors of American wine." They produce and sell as much wine as their next three or four competitors *combined.* Of the 314 million gallons of California wine shipped in 1979, Gallo's share was 104 million. They buy so many California grapes to make it with that *Forbes,* in 1975, credited them with setting grape prices by themselves, keeping prices at an artificially high level to put the squeeze on their "less well-heeled competitors." They market more than 55 different varieties of wine: from the premium, corked varietals (French Colombard, Ruby Cabernet, and so

on) to popular, low-priced "jug" wines like Hearty Burgundy, to cheap "pop" wines (Boone's Farm) and wino favorites like Thunderbird. Gallo doesn't put their own name on their less sophisticated wines (Thunderbird and Ripple, for example), but if the label says it's from Modesto, you're drinking a Gallo product.

History. Ernest and Julio Gallo were born near Modesto and grew up working their father's small vineyard during Prohibition. Their father died in 1933, just before repeal, and the brothers decided to take their small inheritance (about $6,000) and produce their own commercial bulk wine—learning how to make it from two pamphlets Ernest found in the local library. While Julio pressed the grapes and made the wine, Ernest hopped a flight for Chicago and sold a distributor a contract for 6,000 gallons at 50¢ apiece. He continued east and eventually found enough distributors to buy the company's entire production, and the Gallos ended up with a $34,000 profit their first year. They plowed it back into equipment, as they did with their second- and third-year profits, until they were finally large enough in 1940 to buy bottling companies in Los Angeles and New Orleans.

In that year the Gallos marketed the first wine under their own name—mostly sherries and muscatels. Ernest recruited his own salesmen and instructed them to get the best possible shelf space from each store owner. Critics accused the salesmen of using intimidation techniques to achieve this goal, although others insist that the company simply offered dealers economic incentives, a month's free supply, for example, in exchange for good display. The wine sold well both because of its display space and its price—well below that of the larger wineries' products.

After the war Gallo was one of the first

wineries to automate, cutting production costs to the bone. They were the first winery to hire research chemists, the first to abandon traditional wooden storage barrels in favor of stainless steel ones, and the first to computerize their operations. But the most influential factor in establishing Gallo as the nation's premier wine maker has been Ernest's uncanny knack for predicting consumer tastes. For years Gallo researchers knew that ghetto blacks had been buying 40-proof white port and cutting the obnoxious aftertaste by adding lemon juice. At Ernest's instructions, they came up with Thunderbird (white port and citric acid) in the late 1950s; the product has been a staple of ghetto drinkers and winos ever since. Ernest also created the pop wine craze of the late 1960s and early 1970s. Julio, as an experiment, had carbonated the company's slow-selling Boone's Farm apple wine in 1969. When sales skyrocketed, Ernest ordered different varieties and flavors. By 1972, when the pop wine boom peaked, Gallo was selling six of the top entries, and 16 million cases to their competitors' mere 2 million. At that point Ernest shrewdly figured the market had topped off, and he plunged his pop wine profits into promoting dry table wines like Hearty Burgundy, which some wine connoisseurs rated one of the finest wines ever produced in its price range. In the mid-1970s Gallo introduced a line of fine varietals—a move that kept them one step ahead of their wine-drinking public, which has since proved itself ready for better and better wines. Gallo has always claimed that they make wines to suit the American palate. If this palate is now changing toward acceptance of dry table wines, as the sales figures suggest, Gallo will move into that area as well. They have, they point out, the greatest productive capacity in the industry—and they can adapt that to any taste preference.

Reputation. Known to generations of wine drinkers for their cheap wines, Gallo has begun to change their image by applying technological prowess to producing wines aimed for more discriminating palates. In the industry they're known for their secrecy, superb marketing skills, and occasional hardball tactics with distributors and labor unions.

What they own. Gallo owns facilities in and around Modesto that *Forbes*, in 1975,

said were "years ahead of the industry." But their biggest asset may be their bottling plant, built in 1958 and more than quadrupled in size over the years. James Walker, III, an analyst at Paine, Webber, told *Forbes* the plant "gave Gallo a 10% per bottle price edge over [their] competitors." This allowed Gallo to sell their wine at a loss and make a profit on the bottle! Until Heublein's United Vintners recently built a bottling plant for their wine business, Gallo's was the only such winery-operated plant. They also own 5,000 acres of vineyards and 2,000 acres of apple orchards, one of California's largest trucking companies, and several big wine distributors. Their own vineyards supply only about 10% of the grapes they need, the rest they buy from others—a total of 40% of California's wine grapes.

Who owns and runs the company. The Gallos continue to control 100% of their operation, although both brothers are now near 70. Ernest has always controlled the financial end of the business, leaving the actual production to Julio. The division of labor suits their personalities. Ernest is grim and unsmiling and is generally depicted as a tough businessman; Julio is a smiling, one-of-the-boys type who'd rather make a good wine than a good profit. Julio's son Robert appears to be the heir apparent.

Gallo is known as a great training ground, and former Gallo people are everywhere in the industry. Art Palumbo used to run Paul Masson for Seagram—he's out of Gallo; Dick Marr, president of Beringer—he's out of Gallo; Terence Clancy, president of Somerset Wine (a Norton Simon company)—he's out of Gallo; Richard Peterson, who's blending the Taylor Cellars line for Coca-Cola—he's out of Gallo. According to Paul Gillette, publisher-editor of the Wine Investor newsletter, probably three-fourths of the top people in the industry (outside the strong family-owned companies) spent some time at Gallo.

In the public eye. Gallo began to draw fire in 1973 for their labor policies—specifically, their policies toward Cesar Chavez's United Farm Workers Union. Ernest Gallo, a lifelong liberal, originally welcomed Chavez' union and signed with them in 1967 and again in 1970 as representatives of Gallo's grape harvesters. But in 1973 Gallo and the UFW split. Chavez accused Gallo of dirty dealings when many of Gallo's field hands signed instead with the Teamsters Union. A bitter strike and boycott of Gallo products followed and was not lifted until 1978, when the UFW returned as the representative of the field workers. In the interim Gallo's name became anathema to leftists, and frequent accusations of surveillance and thug tactics against the union members didn't help. Just how much the strike and boycott hurt Gallo may never be known because the only accurate records lie somewhere behind the palatial walls in Modesto.

Wine as Big Business

The U.S. wine industry was slow in getting started. At the turn of the twentieth century, annual production was not much more than a million and a half gallons—and the premier wine producing state was Ohio, with half a million gallons.

Prohibition devastated the industry, but, after Repeal, wine made a strong comeback—and California led the way. Many large companies—first in the distilling industry, later in a wide variety of industries—saw the opportunity and bought established wineries or created their own.

Schenley, now a subsidiary of Rapid-American Corporation, probably was the first to recognize the market potential of California premium wines. They bought the Cresta Blanca and Roma wineries in 1939. Schenley sold them in the early 1970s but still has small California wine holdings and also sells a large line of imports, including Portugal's popular Mateus line.

Seagram, the nation's largest distiller, purchased the Paul Masson winery at Saratoga, California, in 1946. In 1950 they bought a majority interest in Fromm & Sichel, exclusive marketing agent for Christian Brothers wines and brandies. Seagram also has an extensive import line, including B & G wines of France, Mumm Champagne, and Brolio, Ricasoli, and Bersano wines of Italy.

Coca Cola is a more recent entry in the U.S. wine sweepstakes. Since 1977 they have purchased Taylor, Hammondsport, New York (which earlier had purchased Great Western); Sterling, a small (100,000 gallons a year) but prestigious Napa Valley, California, winery; and The Monterey Vineyard, a medium-sized (1 million gallons a year) winery on California's Central Coast.

Coca Cola Bottling Company of New York, an independent corporation from the Atlanta-based soft drink giant, purchased California's Franzia Brothers winery, Chicago-based Mogen David (best known as a producer of kosher wines), and New Jersey–based Tribuno (best known for their vermouth, though they recently began importing Italian wines also).

Norton Simon, the New York-based conglomerate, owns California's San Martin winery and the large Somerset import line.

Beatrice Foods owns California's high-volume Brookside Vineyards.

Schlitz Brewing owns California's Sonoma-based Geyser Peak and neighboring Nervo wineries. Meanwhile, Philip Morris, the cigarette manufacturer and owner of Miller Brewing, also owns the Linde-

---

LARGEST U.S. WINE SUPPLIERS

1978 Total Shipments (estimate) / Market Share

1. E & J GALLO / 106 *to nearest million gallons* / 25%
2. UNITED VINTNERS (*Heublein*) / 56 *million gallons* / 13%
3. ALMADEN (*National Distillers*) / 26 *million gallons* / 6%
4. CANANDAIGUA / 16 *million gallons* / 4%
5. WINE SPECTRUM (*Coca-Cola*) / 14 *million gallons* / 3%
6. PAUL MASSON (*Seagram*) / 14 *million gallons* / 3%
7. GUILD / 14 *million gallons* / 3%
8. MONARCH / 12 *million gallons* / 3%
9. MOGEN DAVID (*Coca-Cola of NY*) / 11 *million gallons* / 3%
10. FRANZIA (*Coca-Cola of NY*) / 11 *million gallons* / 2%
OTHER U.S. WINERIES / 58 *million gallons* / 13%
IMPORTS / 94 *million gallons* / 22%

Total 1978 wine shipments (domestic and imported) in U.S.: 430.5 million gallons.

Source: *Beverage Industry,* 22 Feb 1980.

Accusations of Gallo's strong-arm tactics with distributors led to a Federal Trade Commission investigation which determined, in 1976, that Gallo had used their "dominant position, size, and power to lessen . . . competition in the sale and distribution of wines in the U.S. by engaging in various unfair acts . . . including . . . coercion of distributors." One of those complaining distributors charged that Gallo had driven him out of the business entirely for carrying a competing brand.

Access. Modesto, California 95363; (209) 521-3111.

Consumer brands.

Table and dessert wines: Gallo; Paisano; Thunderbird; Carlo Rossi; Eden Roc.
"Pop" wines: Boone's Farm; Spanada; Tyrolia; Pagan Pink; Madria Madria Sangria; Ripple.
Sparkling wines, champagnes, and cold duck: Gallo; Andre; Eden Roc.
Vermouth: Gallo.
Brandy: Eden Roc; E & J.

---

mann winery in Australia, a small but promising entry on the U.S. import market. And U.S. Tobacco owns Washington State's fast-growing Ste. Michelle Vineyards.

Standard Brands owns the large Julius Wile import business (Antinori Chianti and Williams & Humbert sherries, among other leading brands), sells California's Souverain wines, and also owns Fleishmann Distilling, which markets California's Weibel wines and brandies.

Brown-Forman, the Kentucky-based distiller (Jack Daniels and other leading brands), sells California's Korbel wines and brandy (half a million cases a year) and a number of imported wines, including Italy's Bolla wines.

Wine subsidiaries of Heublein, the Connecticut-based conglomerate (owner of Kentucky Fried Chicken), include California's Italian Swiss Colony (the nation's second largest producer), Inglenook, and Beaulieu Vineyard. The company also imports Lancers of Portugal, Bouchard of France, and Harvey's sherries.

National Distillers (Old-GranDad) owns Almaden, the nation's third largest producer, which subsidiary also markets a broad import line. American Distilling is another importer, as is Foremost-McKesson, parent of "21 Brands."

Switzerland-based Nestlé,

the chocolate company, has significant interests in the Beringer winery of St. Helena, California.

Los Angeles–based Young's Market Corporation, the big food and liquor wholesaler, owns burgeoning Buena Vista, a Sonoma, California, winery.

Liggett Group, a cigarette manufacturer, imports wines from Europe.

Then there is Getty Oil, which makes no wine but owns many acres of California vineyards under contract to Bronco Wine, a mass-market producer. And Los Angeles–based Tejon Land Co., which has extensive vineyard holdings. And Lazard Frères, the Wall Street investment banking firm, which owns vineyards and markets bulk wines.

Not all companies with wine interests have fared well. Pillsbury, the Minneapolis-based flour giant, bought Souverain of Rutherford, California, in 1972, and built two large, modern wineries. But in 1976, when they wanted to acquire the Steak and Ale fast-food chain, they sold their wine holdings to avoid federal and state liquor law problems. The loss, industry insiders estimate, amounted to $10 million.

Southdown, the Texas-based conglomerate, lost at least $1.5 million and possibly a good deal more when in

1977 they sold to Norton Simon the San Martin winery they bought just a few years earlier.

Risky though the wine industry is, it obviously has great appeal to big companies—and sometimes to former executives of big companies. Ely Callaway retired as president of Burlington Industries and founded Callaway Vineyards at Temecula, near Los Angeles. Brooks Firestone left the automobile tire manufacturer founded by his family to build and operate Firestone Vineyards in the Santa Ynez Valley, near Santa Barbara, California, in a joint venture with Japan's Suntory distillery interests.

Show-business celebrities also like the wine industry. Dick Smothers of the brother comedy team owns a small winery in Santa Cruz. Actor Wayne Rogers (of TV's "M*A*S*H" and "City of Angels") has vineyard holdings and recently was named to the board of directors of Almaden. Fred MacMurray owns vineyards, as did the late Alfred Hitchcock, and Frank Sinatra is part owner of a Los Angeles wine wholesaler.

— Paul Gillette

TOP 10 BLACK-OWNED BANKS

Assets

1. INDEPENDENCE BANK OF CHICAGO *Chicago, Illinois* $98 *million*
2. SEAWAY NATIONAL BANK OF CHICAGO *Chicago, Illinois* $81 *million*
3. INDUSTRIAL BANK OF WASHINGTON *Washington, D.C.* $60 *million*
4. FREEDOM NATIONAL BANK OF NEW YORK *New York, New York* $58 *million*
5. UNITED NATIONAL BANK OF WASHINGTON *Washington, D.C.* $56 *million*
6. FIRST INDEPENDENCE NATIONAL BANK OF DETROIT *Detroit, Michigan* $52 *million*
7. FIRST BANK NATIONAL ASSOCIATION *Cleveland, Ohio* $51 *million*
8. CITIZENS TRUST BANK *Atlanta, Georgia* $48 *million*
9. MECHANICS & FARMERS BANK *Durham, North Carolina* $45 *million*
10. LIBERTY BANK AND TRUST COMPANY *New Orleans, Louisiana* $38 *million*

Source: *Black Enterprise*, June 1980.

TOP 10 BLACK-OWNED SAVINGS & LOANS

Assets

1. FAMILY S&L (*Los Angeles*)	$89 *million*
2. CARVER FEDERAL S&L (*New York, NY*)	$83 *million*
3. ILLINOIS/SERVICE FEDERAL S&L (*Chicago*)	$81 *million*
4. BROADWAY FEDERAL S&L (*Los Angeles*)	$60 *million*
5. INDEPENDENCE FEDERAL S&L (*Washington, D.C.*)	$57 *million*
6. FOUNDERS S&L (*Los Angeles*)	$48 *million*
7. UNITED FEDERAL S&L (*New Orleans*)	$26 *million*
8. COMMUNITY FEDERAL S&L (*Washington, D.C.*)	$26 *million*
9. CITIZENS FEDERAL S&L (*Birmingham*)	$26 *million*
10. ADVANCE FEDERAL S&L (*Baltimore*)	$25 *million*

Source: *Black Enterprise*, June 1980.

TOP 10 BLACK-OWNED INSURANCE COMPANIES

Assets

1. NORTH CAROLINA MUTUAL LIFE	$185 *million*
2. ATLANTA LIFE	$107 *million*
3. GOLDEN STATE MUTUAL LIFE	$ 78 *million*
4. UNIVERSAL LIFE	$ 57 *million*
5. SUPREME LIFE OF AMERICA	$ 51 *million*
6. CHICAGO METROPOLITAN MUTUAL ASSURANCE	$ 40 *million*
7. MAMMOTH LIFE & ACCIDENT	$ 27 *million*
8. BOOKER T. WASHINGTON INSURANCE	$ 20 *million*
9. THE PILGRIM HEALTH & LIFE	$ 15 *million*
10. UNITED MUTUAL LIFE	$ 10 *million*

Source: *Black Enterprise*, June 1980.

LEADING CATEGORIES OF BLACK BUSINESS IN THE UNITED STATES

Type of Business/Number of Black-Owned Firms/Sales

AUTO DEALERS, SERVICE STATIONS 5,002 $1.1 *billion*
FOOD STORES 10,679 $786 *million*
MISCELLANEOUS RETAILERS 20,880 $590 *million*
EATING AND DRINKING ESTABLISHMENTS 13,008 $572 *million*
SPECIAL TRADE CONTRACTORS 17,126 $497 *million*
HEALTH SERVICES 14,560 $433 *million*
PERSONAL SERVICES 35,035 $399 *million*
BUSINESS SERVICES 15,461 $358 *million*
TRUCKING, WAREHOUSING 11,552 $353 *million*
INSURANCE CARRIERS 58 $249 *million*
GENERAL BUILDING CONTRACTORS 3,415 $215 *million*
AUTO REPAIR AND SERVICE, GARAGES 6,890 $185 *million*
BANKING 152 $140 *million*

(Miscellaneous retailers includes stores selling liquor, drugs, sporting goods, books, jewelry and cameras, etc.; special trade contractors includes plumbers, painters, etc.; personal services includes laundries, beauty salons, barber shops, etc.; business services includes advertising, building services, data processing, etc.)

Source: *Black Enterprise*, June 1980, based on Census Bureau data for 1977.

15

LEVIATHANS

Sales: $1.7 billion
Profits: $56 million
Forbes 500 rank: 307
Rank in Hawaiian sugar: 1
Rank in frozen french fries: 3
Founded: 1849
Employees: 23,700
Headquarters: Honolulu, Hawaii

What they do. Until just over a decade ago, Amfac was, in the words of chairman Henry A. Walker, "primarily a sugar company with a comfortable Hawaiian position in retailing, a small and not particularly profitable distribution operation in Hawaii and a lot of Hawaiian land." Today they're still a sugar company, and they still own a lot of Hawaiian land. But they're also a billion dollar conglomerate with hotels, department stores, drug wholesalers, and food-processing companies located all over the western United States. And they owe it all to the jet airplane.

The jet airliner made Hawaii a part of the United States in a way the 1959 Statehood Act never could. When the jet planes began flying across the Pacific to disgorge hundreds of sun-seeking tourists on the island shores, Hawaii boomed—and so did Amfac. Tourists needed hotels, hotels needed land, and so land prices soared. As a major landowner, Amfac was a big winner. But with all that valuable real estate, Amfac was a prime candidate to be swallowed by a bigger company. So in 1967, with Walker at the helm, they set out to make themselves too big to swallow.

"My starting instructions from the Amfac board were, number one, to enlarge the company," Walker told a reporter in 1979. "My second instruction was to find some way to decrease Amfac's overwhelming dependence on sugar. My third directive was to diversify the company geographically." Walker has carried out his orders well. Although Amfac is still Hawaii's biggest sugar producer, contributing 31% of the raw sugar to C&H Sugar, the cooperative that refines and markets sugar for Hawaii and California growers, Amfac's sugar and papaya operations account for only 8% of their total sales. The rest of their business comes from such areas as wholesale prescription drugs, electrical supplies, and construction materials; frozen french fries, mushrooms, and processed cheese; 25 hotels and resorts, including Maui's Royal Lahina, the King Kamehameha on Kona, the hotel at the Dallas-Fort Worth airport, and the Fred Harvey restaurants at the Grand Canyon; and their Liberty House chain of retail and department stores in Hawaii and northern California.

But the key to Walker's growth program has been the 65,000 acres of land Amfac owns in Hawaii. The steep rise in the value of their sugar fields has helped Amfac finance the smaller companies they bought on the mainland. And by developing and selling the most valuable parts of their island empire—in 1978 they sold 8 acres on Maui for $9 million—Amfac always has a steady flow of cash to buy new companies or expand old ones. And Walker intends to keep trading small pieces of Hawaii for big pieces of action on the mainland.

History. On November 28, 1848, the 156-ton brig *Wilhelmine* cast off from Bremen, Germany, and set sail for Hawaii. After 238 days at sea, the ship docked in Honolulu and its owner, a shrewd merchant named Heinrich Hackfeld, stepped off to become an agent for sugar growers and Hawaiian merchants. He also set up retail stores and sold imported building materials, laying the foundation for Amfac's later retailing and distribution operations. The company prospered, but the German ownership couldn't survive the anti-German hysteria of World War I. After the Alien Property Custodian seized the company in 1918 at the start of the war, their assets were picked up by their major competitors—principally Castle & Cooke, Alexander & Baldwin, and C. Brewer. The new owners changed the name from Hackfeld to American Factors (a factor is an agent) and concentrated their efforts on the sugar business. Later, the name was shortened to Amfac.

In 1967 the board of directors picked Henry A. Walker, Jr., as president and gave him his three instructions. Walker, a third-generation Hawaiian (his grandfather had been an advisor to the Hawaiian royal family), was an out-going, energetic executive. He threw himself into his assignment and, in the space of less than a decade, fulfilled the board's orders.

Reputation. They're known now as a steady—if not spectacular—performer. Walker's management has been a boon to the company, but there have been some failures, too. Amfac bought the Joseph Magnin chain of specialty clothing stores and found they didn't have the expertise to run it, eventually taking a loss of $21 million on the deal. They've also bought and sold several other outfits: five Liberty House stores in the northwest were sold to Marshall Field, and the Rhodes and Gano-Downs specialty stores in the Southwest also turned into lemons under Amfac leadership. But as long as Amfac can get a million an acre, they'll be able to afford a few mistakes.

What they own. Amfac values their assets at about $1 billion; but that figure grossly understates the real value of their Hawaiian land, which they report at its original cost. Some of that land was bought decades ago for agricultural use and has now become valuable resort real estate, like the million-an-acre land near the company's development at Kaanapali Beach on Maui. One of their goals is to develop and sell between $10 and $15 million worth of land each year while still increasing the value of their total land holdings. The way they increase that value is by developing the land into resort property.

Who owns and runs the company. Of the 15 board members of Amfac, 8 live in Hawaii, and 2 are women—Patricia Saiki, a Hawaii state senator, and Mary Anne Normandin, an assistant to the president of Lewis and Clark College in Portland, Oregon. About 22% of Amfac's stock is owned by Gulf + Western, Charles Bluhdorn's New York conglomerate.

In the public eye. Amfac has weathered some expensive antitrust battles lately—most notably, a 1974 fight with the Federal Trade Commission over alleged sugar price-fixing by Amfac and the other companies involved in C&H. The settlement they reached cost Amfac several million dollars.

Stock performance. Amfac stock bought for $1,000 in 1970 sold for $780 on January 2, 1980.

Access. 700 Bishop Street, Honolulu, Hawaii 96801; (808) 546-8111.

Consumer brands.

Food: C&H sugar; Fisher cheese; Monterey mushrooms; Lamb-Weston frozen potatoes; Pacific Pearl seafoods; Puna papayas.
Department stores: Liberty House; Kauai Stores.
Restaurants: Fred Harvey.
Hotels: Airport Marina; Amfac; Island Holidays; Metropolitan Motels.
Country clubs: Silverado Country Club (Napa, California).
Resorts: Grand Canyon National Park Lodges; Coco Palms Resort (Hawaii).
Financial services: Amfac Commercial Credit.
Nurseries: Amfac (Hawaii); Glenn Walters (Oregon); Selest (California).
Insurance: ARMS.
Tours: Hawaiian Discovery.

✪ City Investing

Sales: $5.0 billion
Profits: $133 million
Forbes 500 rank: 77
Rank in casualty insurance: 13
Rank in water heaters: 1
Rank in air conditioning: 3
Rank in magazine printing: 1
Rank in mobile homes: 3
Rank in home building: 4
Founded: 1904
Employees: 69,400
Headquarters: New York, New York

What they do. If there's a logic in City Investing's operations, it's known only to George T. Scharffenberger, who began buying companies in 1966, when he took over as president. He had learned his craft at Litton Industries, the mother company of conglomerates, where he rose to senior vice-president. Scharffenberger has parlayed a chunk of Manhattan real estate into a $5 billion empire that's now bigger than Litton. And he's still buying companies. In 1978 he bought Servomation, an operator of 110,000 vending machines, and the Red Barn fast food chain. He explained: "Housing and feeding people are people-oriented businesses. We house people, so why shouldn't we feed them?"

City Investing houses people through three companies: General Development, a Florida tract builder (80,000 people live in Port Charlotte, Port St. Lucie, and their five other communities); Wood Bros., a builder of single-family houses in Colorado, Texas, Arizona, New Mexico, Nevada, and Wyoming (average house price in 1979: $68,000); and Guerdon Industries, one of the nation's largest mobile home builders (15,000 in 1979, sold under such names as Great Lakes, Magnolia, and Statler).

But City's biggest business (37% of total sales) is property and casualty insurance, conducted through the 127-year-old Home Insurance Company. Home's specialty is insuring businesses against all kinds of disasters. In 1979 they collected premiums of more than $1.5 billion. They rank 13th among casualty insurers.

City's manufacturing operations include Rheem (water heaters, air-conditioning equipment, 55-gallon steel drums); and World Color Press, the nation's largest

magazine printer, with plants in three southern Illinois communities: Sparta, Effingham, and Salem. (They print *Forbes, Vogue, Money,* and *Cosmopolitan,* among other magazines.) In 1979 they added a company that's not people-oriented at all: Uarco, the country's second largest manufacturer of business forms (purchase orders, payroll checks, label markers).

History. City Investing was formed as a property investment company in 1904 by Robert E. Dowling, who had inherited a fortune from his father, an Irish immigrant who struck it rich in gold in California and then decided to go East to invest his loot in New York real estate. When Dowling died in 1943, control of City Investing passed to his son, Robert W. Through his dealings with several Broadway theaters and movie houses operated by City, the younger Dowling was led into a second career as a producer for the stage and screen and a cultural czar for New York City. Among the properties, City owned or operated the Astor, Victoria, Bijou, Helen Hayes, and Morosco theaters; the Hotel Carlyle; and the Parke-Bernet auction galleries. City remained mostly a real estate company until 1966 when Dowling handed over the reins to Scharffenberger, who immediately put his experience at Litton to work: in five years he boosted annual sales from $8 million to $1.5 billion. In one year, 1968, he bought Home Insurance, World Color Press, and the Motel 6 chain.

Reputation. City Investing is known in business circles as a highly leveraged company—meaning they owe a lot of money. At the end of 1979: $1.5 billion.

What they own. A California savings and loan association (Southern California Savings & Loan); a plastics manufacturer (Alma Plastics, Alma, Michigan); an aircraft maintenance firm (Hayes International, Birmingham, Alabama). They still own Sterling Forest, a 17,000-acre property 35 miles north of New York City. Acquired by Robert Dowling in 1954 for $850,000 and largely undeveloped, it was appraised at $76 million in 1966. City also owns 5.1% of Stokely-Van Camp, the canned- and frozen-food producer.

Who owns and runs the company. Scharffenberger and his wife held 1.7% of the stock at the start of 1980. The biggest stockholder (12.4%) was Sharon Steel, which in turn is owned by Miami investor Victor Posner's NVF Co., which has interests in numerous companies. Although City is headquartered in New York, Scharffenberger has continued to live in Los Angeles, where he has a 17-acre property on the Palos Verdes Peninsula and works at his hobby of beekeeping. The heir apparent is Peter Huang, a Shanghai-born executive who negotiated many of City's acquisitions and became president and chief operating officer in 1980. City has had only three chief executive officers: the two Dowlings and Scharffenberger.

City's 1980 annual meeting was held at Shea Stadium's Diamond Club after the company became part of the group that bought the New York Mets. City owns 6.5% of the Mets.

Where they're going. One thing always leads to another. One of City's best-performing units is Motel 6, the nation's largest chain of budget motels. They were called Motel 6 originally because they rented rooms for $6 a night. In 1979 their no-frills rooms rented from $10.95 up to $17.95 a night. Motel 6 had 29,000 rooms in 283 motels in 37 states at the end of 1979— and they plan to open 25 new ones every year for the next five years. Motel 6 is based in Santa Barbara, California. When another Santa Barbara company, Sambo's Restaurants, ran into heavy trouble in the late 1970s, their neighbors from Motel 6 came to the rescue—and City Investing now has a sizable minority investment in Sambo's.

Stock performance. City Investing stock bought for $1,000 in 1970 sold for $653 on January 2, 1980. Tamco Enterprises, a new company organized by Lyman Hamilton, ousted president of ITT, thought this price was so low that they offered nearly twice as much for the shares—and this offer was still pending in July 1980.

Major employment centers. New York; Chicago.

Access. 59 Maiden Lane, New York, New York 10038; (212) 759-5300.

Consumer brands.

Air conditioners: Rheem; Ruud.

Motels: Motel 6.
Mobile homes: Great Lakes; Magnolia; Leisurama; Statler; Wayco.
Insurance: Home Insurance.
Fast foods: Red Barn.

Dart Industries

Sales: $2.4 billion
Profits: $172 million
Forbes 500 rank: 219
Rank in door-to-door sales: 2
Rank in glass bottles: 3
Founded: 1902
Employees: 42,000
Headquarters: Los Angeles, California

What they do. Dart Industries is aptly named. You would know them better by some of their products—Tupperware, West Bend pots and pans, Duracell batteries— but the force that assembled and holds the company together is Justin Whitlock Dart, who has been working overtime since his prep school track-and-field days in the 1920s. Back then, according to *Current Biography*, Dart "carried a 56-pound weight and a 16-pound hammer wherever he went and hurled them at the unlikeliest moments, endangering the public safety but enabling himself to set several local records."

Dart entered Northwestern University (he was born in Evanston, Illinois, home of Northwestern) in 1925 and went on to play tackle on the football team, making the All-Big-Ten-Conference teams in his junior and senior years. He also had a campus romance with Ruth Walgreen, whose father founded the Chicago-based drugstore chain of that name. After graduation Dart and Ruth Walgreen were married, and Dart went to work in the basement of a Walgreen drugstore for $25 a week. He rose rapidly, becoming head of store operations (there were then 375 stores) by 1932. He is credited with a number of pioneering steps in drugstore merchandising. One was the placement of the prescription counter in the back of the store: this arrangement gave customers privacy and also led them past the displays of other products.

In 1939 Ruth Walgreen divorced Dart. Eight months later, on Christmas Day,

1939, Charles R. Walgreen, founder of the chain, died, leaving a large share of the business to his former son-in-law. A week later, on New Year's Eve, Dart remarried. His bride was an actress, Jane O'Brien, who played under the name Jane Bryan. Justin Dart stayed on at the Walgreen company for two more years, fighting regularly with two major stockholders—his ex-wife and her brother. In 1941 he left, enticed by a former fraternity brother, Edward J. Noble (the Life Savers millionaire), to join a chaotic Boston-based outfit founded in 1902 called United Drug, which made drugs and sold them (along with lots of other products) through drugstores named Rexall, Liggett, Owl, and Sontag (some they owned, some they didn't).

In 1943 Dart took complete charge of this hodgepodge and transformed it into a money-making enterprise, going with the Rexall banner and discarding most of the other names. In 1945 he moved the headquarters across the country to Los Angeles, saying the business could be managed from there "just as efficiently and certainly more comfortably" than from Boston. And he has managed the business from there ever since, although "it" has changed considerably. Not one operation is left from those early days. The last of the Rexall business was sold in 1978. In the fold today, in addition to Tupperware, are Thatcher Glass, third-largest maker of glass bottles, and a variety of plastics and chemical companies making garden hose, tubes for ballpoint pens, plastic cups, and Wilsonart decorative laminates (a Formica competitor).

Tupperware is the standout. They make durable plastic containers that are sold only through the home "party" system. (A Tupperware agent gets people to invite their friends to their homes for an evening of buying plastic containers.) Tupperware produces more than half of Dart's profits, and they rank second only to Avon in the sale of products direct to consumers in their homes.

Justin Dart, a stalwart of the Republican right wing, celebrated his 72nd birthday in 1979.

In 1980 Dart agreed to a merger with Kraft, the huge cheese and food-processing company based in suburban Chicago. The new company, to be called Dart & Kraft, was to be headed by Kraft's chairman, John Richman. Based on 1979 sales, the combined operation would have annual sales of nearly $9 billion and would be among the 30 largest U.S. industrial companies. Asked by the *Wall Street Journal* why his name was to precede the better-known name of Kraft, the crusty Justin Dart replied, "They wanted the innovative company's name out front."

Stock performance. Dart Industries stock bought for $1,000 in 1970 sold for $1,019 on January 2, 1980.

Access. 8480 Beverly Boulevard, Los Angeles, California 90048; (213) 658-2000.

Consumer brands.

Kitchenware: Tupperware.
Cookware: West Bend.
Batteries: Duracell.
Cosmetics: Vanda.
Plastic covering: Wilsonart.

FOREMOST McKESSON

Sales: $3.3 billion
Profits: $58 million
Forbes 500 rank: 143
Rank in dairy products: 4
Rank in wholesale drugs: 1
Rank in bottled water: 1
Rank in pasta: 1
Rank in liquor wholesaling: 1
Founded: 1833
Employees: 17,600
Headquarters: San Francisco, California

What they do. Foremost-McKesson is one of those companies that can't decide what they want to be when they grow up. On one hand they're Foremost, one of the nation's top five dairy firms, processing and selling milk, cheese, and ice cream products throughout the West. But then the company is also a middleman. McKesson, originally a pharmaceutical maker, is the nation's largest wholesale drug and chemical distributor, peddling other people's wares throughout the United States via more than 20,000 drugstores and nearly 6,000 hospitals.

The two companies had wandered aimlessly since the turn of the century until

1967, when Foremost's management decided that putting them together under one roof might help. It didn't. As recently as 1977 a San Francisco market analyst reported Foremost-McKesson's "record of limited accomplishment" and "limited growth potential," and the Gallagher Presidents' Report, a scorecard for corporate executives, cited Foremost-McKesson president William R. Morison for his "lack of achievement." Those are hardly terms financial types use to refer to a winner.

The reason for this dismal reputation? Well, sheer unwieldy size has something to do with it. Foremost-McKesson produces such diverse products as bottled water and Armor-All auto protectant, ORAfix denture adhesive and Mueller pasta, Yeast-Quick baking products and Gentec cotton swabs. Just to complicate this already Byzantine scenario, Foremost-McKesson also distributes other companies' products: Galliano and Amaretto liqueurs, Martin's V.V.O. and Ballantine's Scotch, St. Pauli Girl beer, and Mount Gay Rum, just to name a few. But that's not all. Foremost-McKesson also dabbles in homebuilding through their Ditz-Crane and Crocker Homes subsidiaries, which operate in California and Arizona. It takes remarkably astute management and careful organization to run an operation as diverse as all this. Unfortunately, Foremost-McKesson apparently may have neither.

History. John McKesson, scion of an old colonial family, opened a drugstore in Manhattan in 1833. In 1840 he took another New Yorker, Daniel Robbins, as a junior partner and changed the company name to McKesson-Robbins. They quickly became one of the most prestigious drug firms in the world, largely on the merits of their gelatin-capsule quinine pills. After the founder's death in 1891 McKesson's heirs continued to run the company, although constantly at odds with Herbert Robbins (Daniel's son) and chairman Saunders Norvell. In 1924 the McKessons (Irving, Donald, and George) split off to form the New York Quinine & Chemical Works, and in 1926 Robbins sold McKesson & Robbins pharmaceuticals to an ambitious young man named F. D. Coster. He began one of the most intriguing chapters in American business history.

Coster was as crooked as a dog's hind leg. His real name was Philip Musica, the son of a Neapolitan barber turned importer who brought Italian foodstuffs (cheese, olive oil, and so on) into New York. When shipments arrived, Philip went down to the docks and bribed the customs weigher to certify that Musica's imports weighed less than the scales showed. The family prospered from the import trade, moved to the more fashionable Bay Ridge section, and became leaders of the Italian community—until 1909, when father and son were arrested. Philip took the rap, paid a $5,000 fine, and served five months of a one-year sentence at Elmira Reformatory.

Upon his release, Philip convinced his father to go into the hair exporting business, shipping human hair overseas to wig makers, and the family prospered again. By 1913 they had $500,000 in bank loans, all supposedly secured by the company's stock of long, valuable hair. But when Philip went off in search of another loan, a bank investigator discovered that the hair in the Musica warehouses that was to have served as collateral consisted of worthless ends and short sizes. Detectives burst into the Musica home in Bay Ridge. They found no Musicas, but they did find the valuable hair under the floorboards. They nabbed Philip and his father in New Orleans just as their getaway ship was about to cast off. Philip once more took the blame and served three years in New York jails. He was released in 1916 and worked for the D.A.'s office as an undercover stoolpigeon named William Johnson, specializing in informing on German spies. Here his history gets foggy. He went into the poultry business during the war, and was indicted for suborning perjury in a murder case in 1920. But Musica was never convicted and never served another day in jail.

In the early 1920s he reemerged as Frank B. Costa, president of Adelphi Pharmaceutical Manufacturing Company in Brooklyn, ostensibly makers of hair tonic. Adelphi was actually a bootlegging front, and a profitable one; but Musica/Costa closed it down finally when his physical fear of his partner, Joseph Brandino, overcame his profit motive. He turned up again in 1926 at the head of Girard & Co., another hair tonic firm; and, relying on his favorite scam, built up a sizable clientele composed mostly of nonexistent companies. Using these phony accounts as collateral, he borrowed his way into a position where he could buy McKesson-Robbins. But now he was Frank Coster, businessman.

He headed McKesson for 13 years, and by 1938 was listed in *Who's Who*, although two-thirds of his biography was phony. McKesson's sales seemed to grow steadily until 1938, when the company treasurer began to notice that, although McKesson's raw-drug business showed huge profits, the profits were always plowed right back into the business. No cash ever seemed to emerge. The treasurer began an investigation that eventually revealed that Coster had stolen nearly $3 million from the company through phony buyers he had set up. Some of the money went to pay Brandino blackmail money; Brandino had rediscovered Coster and was threatening to expose him as Musica. In the end, in 1939, Coster/Musica shot himself, Brandino was convicted of blackmail, and McKesson-Robbins, humiliated by the ensuing publicity, withdrew into conservative, stodgy management practices that led to near-stagnation.

Foremost was the result of the marriage of Ferndale, California's Central Creamery, founded in 1905, and J. C. Penney's Foremost Dairy, founded in the 1920s in Jacksonville, Florida and named for Penney's prize bull. Foremost bought Golden Gate (formerly Central) in 1954 and went on to buy up other dairy companies for the next decade, although the new companies only made them bigger, not more profitable. In 1967 Foremost picked up McKesson—against McKesson's will. After the hostile takeover, Foremost was afraid to alienate the McKesson management further and left them in place to carry on business as usual; the result was that the two companies, unhappily linked, simply meandered through the world together with no apparent strategy for growth—or anything else, for that matter. It took Foremost three years to persuade McKesson to move their offices to San Francisco, where management could finally be centralized.

In 1974 the company's chief executive officer, Rudy Drews, resigned under pressure and opened his own corporate-merger consulting business. Drews went to Victor Posner, a Florida-based company takeover artist who owns Sharon Steel and several utility companies. Drews suggested that Foremost-McKesson was up for grabs and Posner grabbed, eventually piling up 10% of Foremost-McKesson's stock. But the company, led by Chairman William Morison, fought off the bid and managed to retain their independence. Posner still holds the stock and may try again. If he succeeds, Foremost-McKesson may one day have some direction.

Reputation. A lethargic corporation, ripe for a takeover by someone who knows what to do. Even new president Thomas Drohan, attempting to put the best possible face on the company's position, compared Foremost-McKesson with an elephant that was "finally off its knees and ambling noisily" in a *Business Week* story in 1977.

What they own. Foremost-McKesson dominates the market for bottled water in New York and California, with Eagle water in New York City, Alhambra in northern California, and Sparkletts in southern California. The company also owns the C. F. Mueller line of pasta, which has an interesting history of its own. Mueller was an old-line pasta maker in New York when New York University bought it as an investment to aid the administration's dreams of a na-

In-Flight Snack

Mergers don't make the overall economy grow at all: they just shuffle cash from one till to another. Since 1975, $100 billion has been passed back and forth in U.S. ownership shuffles. SEC chairman Harold M. Williams points out that the money "could have been devoted to new production and employment opportunities." As used in mergers, it doesn't "flow back as new capacity, improvements in productivity, innovation, new products or new jobs."

William E. Seawell, chairman of Pan Am, pleaded the case of the money-shufflers before the Civil Aeronautics Board. He was trying to convince the board to let Pan Am acquire National Airlines:

"I am tired of playing the role of the White Queen, who is told there is jam tomorrow, jam yesterday, but never any jam today. At Pan Am we believe we ought to get some today. . . ."

tional "law center" in 1947. They sold it to Foremost-McKesson 30 years later and are now building a new law school.

Who owns and runs the company. Morison remains as chairman, Drohan remains as president, and Posner remains as the largest shareholder, with 10% of the stock. In 1979 Posner made another small stock buy and announced that he was interested in buying still more, his stated purpose being to support a friendly buy-out bid by a group of private investors. But Posner's history of takeover bids makes this explanation laughable. It is entirely probable that Posner will be in the financial headlines again in the near future with yet another buy-out attempt at Foremost-McKesson.

In the public eye. Foremost-McKesson had a bad year in 1976. While Posner was pressing his first takeover try, Foremost lost a six-year dispute with the Crocker bank family over control of their Crocker Land Development Company subsidiary and was ordered to sell it off. They also were hit with a multimillion-dollar sex discrimination suit by female employees, a suit that is still pending. The Securities Exchange Commission charged them with making $6 million in payoffs to liquor dealers, and the company didn't deny it. They were also charged with making $231,000 in questionable foreign political contributions and signed a decree agreeing not to misbehave again in the future.

Stock performance. Foremost-McKesson stock bought for $1,000 in 1970 sold for $907 on January 2, 1980.

Access. One Post Street, San Francisco, California 94104; (415) 983-8316.

Consumer brands.

Food products: Foremost dairy products; Yami, and Fresh n' Fruity yogurt; Dolly Madison and San Francisco Mint ice cream; Mueller pasta products; Magic Shell dessert topping; Yeast Quick baking products; Milkman hot cocoa.
Bottled water: Sparkletts; Crystal; Alhambra; Aqua-Vend (from vending machine).
Wine and spirits: Liquore Galliano, Amaretto di Galliano, Sambuca di Galliano; Mohawk; Ballantine's Scotch whisky; Martin's V.V.O.; Canadian Rich n' Rare; Mt. Gay Barbados rum; Della Scala, Del Ventuno, and Sole di Roma wines; 8 Year Old Scotch; Muirhead's scotch;

Folonari Italian wine; St. Pauli Girl German beer; Rosegarden Liebfraumilch wines.
Household products: Armor-All Protectant, Cleaner, and Ultra-Plate.
Drug and health-care products: Sun Mark home health-care products; McKesson perscription drugs; Valu Rite over-the-counter products; Gentec hospital supplies; ORAfix denture adhesive.
Costume jewelry: Hi Lights.
Retail: Valu-Rite drug stores.

GRACE

Sales: $5.3 billion
Profits: $223 million
Forbes 500 rank: 73
Rank in chemicals: 5
Founded: 1854
Employees: 66,800
Headquarters: New York, New York

What they do. Peter Grace is a driven man, and his company, New York-based W. R. Grace, shows it. Since Grace became president in 1945, at the age of 32, he has routinely worked 80-hour weeks—except during the two-month annual budget reviews, when he works 112 hours a week. The result of this prodigious toil has been a complete transformation of the family business that was nearly a century old when he took over. At that time W. R. Grace was a transportation, trading, and agricultural mammoth that dominated the economy of South America's west coast. In 1950 Latin American operations brought in 66% of Grace's sales; in 1962 it was 19%; in 1977, zero. Shipping provided 28% of sales in 1950, 13% in 1962, zero in 1977. Chemicals moved in the other direction: from 6% in 1950 to 55% in 1977. The other wedges in the $5 billion corporate pie today have nothing to do with the company's original businesses.

W. R. Grace gets bigger, stronger, richer, and more diverse all the time, but outsiders may have a hard time seeing the rationale of a manic expansion combining chemicals and taco stands, coal mines and cowboy clothes, chocolates and automobile clutches. In a third of a century at the helm, Peter

Grace bought 130 companies and sold 60. It's no wonder he spends so many hours in the office; it's like straightening out a cluttered closet or storeroom.

The main business of W. R. Grace is now chemicals, accounting in 1978 for about half their sales. The nation's fifth-largest chemical producer, Grace produces ammonia, urea, phosphates, sulfuric acid, and nitric acid to make catalysts for oil refineries and auto emission systems, plastic food packaging, industrial cleaning compounds, germicides for hospitals, and compounds used in sewage treatment. Grace's most important chemical product is fertilizers, which they make at major plants in Tennessee, Florida, Oklahoma, and Trinidad. They dig anhydrous ammonia, the raw material for nitrogen fertilizers, out of the earth at their Florida phosphate mine. Grace is hoping to make fertilizer out of coal, which they mine in Colorado, in partnership with Hanna Mining Co., and to stop making it from the natural gas that flows from Grace's wells in California, the Southwest, the Rockies, and Libya.

The other big chunk of Grace's sales comes from a hodgepodge of consumer businesses. Grace owns 257 restaurants, ranging from "theme" dinner houses to fast-food stands and coffee shops. A lingering attachment to the company's south-of-the-border origins is perhaps reflected in their acquisition of the El Torito and Que Pasa restaurants and a string of Del Taco hamburger and taco stands. At the end of 1978 Grace also owned 69 Herman's sporting goods stores, 6 Sheplers western-wear outlets, and several chains of do-it-yourself home centers, in addition to one of the nation's largest book wholesalers, Baker & Taylor and four automotive parts companies in California, Nevada, and Ohio.

History. Grace was founded in Peru in 1854 by W. R. Grace, an emigrant Irishman who sailed to South America as a shipboard candlemaker and then began chartering ships to haul guano (bird droppings for fertilizer). He invested in Peruvian land, cotton mills, sugar, and resources like tin and nitrates. Forced to leave Peru in 1865 because of poor health, Grace reestablished his business in New York, buying ships to set up a triangular trade between Peru, the United States, and Europe. This was the beginning of the famous Grace Line. After

two terms as Mayor of New York, Grace died in 1904, leaving the business to first his younger brother, Michael, then his son, Joseph. When Joseph passed the reins to his son, Peter, in 1945, the company owned the Grace Lines; half of Pan American Grace Airways (Panagra, a major Latin American airline; Pan Am owned the other half); great plantation tracts in Peru, Chile, Colombia, and Central America; cotton mills and sugar refineries in Peru and Chile; and the Grace National Bank in New York.

The company was gigantic, but Peter Grace worried about depending too much on Latin America in an era when Latin Americans were chafing against Yankee domination of their economies—and he was right. So in the early 1950s Grace began getting into other businesses, starting with chemicals. In the late 1960s a military junta in Peru seized Grace's sugar plantations. By 1974 they were completely out of South America.

Reputation. It's inextricably bound up with the personality of the man who has run the company for over 35 years: powerful, unpredictable, unevenly mixed, intensely competitive, unbelievably energetic, detail-obsessed, never satisfied. *Fortune* characterized J. Peter Grace as a typical overachiever, whose aggressive style and torrent of achievements may mask an underlying insecurity that never goes away. Grace himself has said, "It's just like Babe Ruth. Every time he swung he was swinging for the center-field bleachers. He struck out a lot of times but he also hit a hell of a lot of home runs. I've never tried to play an errorless game. I play a very offensive, experimental game."

What they own. Besides chemical companies, restaurants, retailers, and coal and oil reserves, Grace owns American Breeders Service in DeForest, Wisconsin, the world's largest seller of bull semen for beef and dairy cattle breeding. *Cacaofabriek de Zaan,* a leading Dutch chocolate company, is one of the remnants of Peter Grace's abortive drive to become a General Foods of Europe.

Who owns and runs the company. Chief executive Peter Grace drives his employees as hard as he drives himself. Proclaiming that "numbers are reality," he makes his managers turn out reams of reports swarming with figures. One of Grace's favorite devices is the spreadsheet, a huge compilation of figures laid out on accordion-folded lengths of paper. Grace demands a spreadsheet on every major project; sometimes they have thousands of columns. It is not unusual for Grace to have the sheets tacked up in hotel corridors so he can study the numbers while walking down the hall. Besides his passion for numbers, Grace is known for wit, brashness, and sometimes bizarre behavior. He is fond of challenging fellow executives to arm-wrestling matches, seeing how far he can drive a golf ball while standing on one foot, and carrying a Cobra .38 Special revolver in a holster tucked under his belt.

The Grace family still owns about 5% of the company's stock, but the largest share, 28%, is held by a West German group headed by industrialist Friedrich Flick.

THE 50 LARGEST U.S. MULTINATIONALS

Foreign Sales / Foreign Sales As Percentage of Total Sales

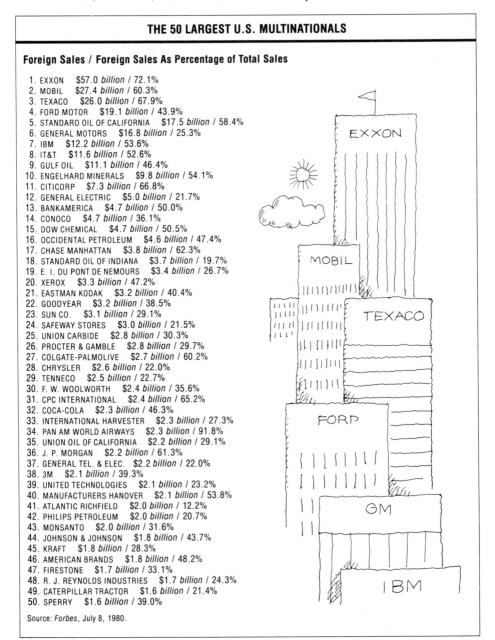

1. EXXON $57.0 *billion* / 72.1%
2. MOBIL $27.4 *billion* / 60.3%
3. TEXACO $26.0 *billion* / 67.9%
4. FORD MOTOR $19.1 *billion* / 43.9%
5. STANDARD OIL OF CALIFORNIA $17.5 *billion* / 58.4%
6. GENERAL MOTORS $16.8 *billion* / 25.3%
7. IBM $12.2 *billion* / 53.6%
8. IT&T $11.6 *billion* / 52.6%
9. GULF OIL $11.1 *billion* / 46.4%
10. ENGELHARD MINERALS $9.8 *billion* / 54.1%
11. CITICORP $7.3 *billion* / 66.8%
12. GENERAL ELECTRIC $5.0 *billion* / 21.7%
13. BANKAMERICA $4.7 *billion* / 50.0%
14. CONOCO $4.7 *billion* / 36.1%
15. DOW CHEMICAL $4.7 *billion* / 50.5%
16. OCCIDENTAL PETROLEUM $4.6 *billion* / 47.4%
17. CHASE MANHATTAN $3.8 *billion* / 62.3%
18. STANDARD OIL OF INDIANA $3.7 *billion* / 19.7%
19. E. I. DU PONT DE NEMOURS $3.4 *billion* / 26.7%
20. XEROX $3.3 *billion* / 47.2%
21. EASTMAN KODAK $3.2 *billion* / 40.4%
22. GOODYEAR $3.2 *billion* / 38.5%
23. SUN CO. $3.1 *billion* / 29.1%
24. SAFEWAY STORES $3.0 *billion* / 21.5%
25. UNION CARBIDE $2.8 *billion* / 30.3%
26. PROCTER & GAMBLE $2.8 *billion* / 29.7%
27. COLGATE-PALMOLIVE $2.7 *billion* / 60.2%
28. CHRYSLER $2.6 *billion* / 22.0%
29. TENNECO $2.5 *billion* / 22.7%
30. F. W. WOOLWORTH $2.4 *billion* / 35.6%
31. CPC INTERNATIONAL $2.4 *billion* / 65.2%
32. COCA-COLA $2.3 *billion* / 46.3%
33. INTERNATIONAL HARVESTER $2.3 *billion* / 27.3%
34. PAN AM WORLD AIRWAYS $2.3 *billion* / 91.8%
35. UNION OIL OF CALIFORNIA $2.2 *billion* / 29.1%
36. J. P. MORGAN $2.2 *billion* / 61.3%
37. GENERAL TEL. & ELEC. $2.2 *billion* / 22.0%
38. 3M $2.1 *billion* / 39.3%
39. UNITED TECHNOLOGIES $2.1 *billion* / 23.2%
40. MANUFACTURERS HANOVER $2.1 *billion* / 53.8%
41. ATLANTIC RICHFIELD $2.0 *billion* / 12.2%
42. PHILIPS PETROLEUM $2.0 *billion* / 20.7%
43. MONSANTO $2.0 *billion* / 31.6%
44. JOHNSON & JOHNSON $1.8 *billion* / 43.7%
45. KRAFT $1.8 *billion* / 28.3%
46. AMERICAN BRANDS $1.8 *billion* / 48.2%
47. FIRESTONE $1.7 *billion* / 33.1%
48. R. J. REYNOLDS INDUSTRIES $1.7 *billion* / 24.3%
49. CATERPILLAR TRACTOR $1.6 *billion* / 21.4%
50. SPERRY $1.6 *billion* / 39.0%

Source: *Forbes*, July 8, 1980.

The Flick family seems to have recovered nicely from the infamy it suffered in the Nuremburg trials, when Flick père was convicted and sentenced to seven years' imprisonment for his SS membership and his role in Nazi-instituted "slave labor, plunder, and spoliation."

Grace has one of the largest boards of directors in the corporate world: 34 men sit on the board. Two are black, Henry G. Parks, Jr., founder of a meat business in Baltimore, and Judge Harold A. Stevens.

In the public eye. According to W. R. Grace, when they were active in Peru, involved in chemicals, paper, mining, fishing, and sugar, to name just a few of their interests, they kept a very low profile, preferring to "stay out of the volatile politics so often characteristic of Latin American nations" (to quote from their company magazine, *Grace Digest*). And what good did that do them? Nothing. Their holdings were expropriated and the company said they didn't get credit for the good they did because of not blowing their own horn. So no more of that. In the United States W. R. Grace and their leader, Peter Grace, have become very active in putting forth their point of view. Grace's current prescription for U.S. ills:

1. Balance the budget.
2. Cut the top personal tax rate to 36%.
3. Adjust all profits for inflation before taxing.
4. Eliminate the capital gains tax.
5. Manage agricultural exports to strengthen the U.S. economy.
6. Let gasoline prices rise to "free market levels to encourage conservation."

Where they're going. After years of denying that W. R. Grace was unmanageable, Peter Grace announced in October 1979 that they are considering splitting up into as many as seven separate publicly held companies. Grace himself has opposed this plan in the past, but all the top contenders for his job are known to favor dividing up the company.

Stock performance. W. R. Grace stock bought for $1,000 in 1970 sold for $1,528 on January 2, 1980.

Access. 1114 Avenue of the Americas, New York, New York 10036; (212) 764-5555.

Requests should be sent to Product Information Service, (212) 764-5850 (collect calls are accepted).

Consumer brands.

Home improvement stores: Channel; Handy City; Handy Dan; Orchard Supply.
Sporting goods stores: Herman's World of Sporting Goods.
Leisure apparel: Sheplers; Bermans.
Coffee houses: Coco's; jojos.
Dinner houses: Moonraker; Plankhouse; Reuben's; El Torito; La Fiesta; Que Pasa.
Fast food: Del Taco; Naugles.
Restaurants: Annie's Santa Fe; Baxter's Street; Cano's; Chanteclair; Gorda Liz; Houlihan's Old Place; Reuben E. Lee; Sam Wilson's Meat Market.

Gulf + Western Industries, Inc.

Sales: $5.3 billion
Profits: $227 million
Forbes 500 rank: 70
Rank in cigars: 1
Founded: 1958
Employees: 113,700
Headquarters: New York, New York

What they do. When comedian Mel Brooks made the film *Silent Movie*, he depicted a company called Engulf & Devour, whose greedy, power-mad executives bought anything and everything just for the sheer pleasure of ownership. He was using Gulf + Western as his model; and, at times, the characterization seems accurate enough. Gulf + Western, under the direction of their acquisitive chairman Charles Bluhdorn, a post–World War II immigrant Wall Street sometimes calls "The Mad Austrian," has bought more than 100 companies since G + W's birth in 1958—80 in one six-year period (1965–1970) alone.

What makes this acquisitiveness even more remarkable is that those companies have practically nothing to do with one another. Today G + W is the nation's largest cigar maker (Consolidated Cigar) as well as being one of the largest apparel makers (Kayser-Roth) and auto parts supplier (A.P.S.). They make some of the nation's

Charles G. Bluhdorn, architect of Gulf + Western. "The man would have been happier in the era of Commodore Vanderbilt when businessmen were judged by the balance sheet rather than by what the press thought of them," said *Forbes* in 1979.

most popular movies and television shows through Paramount Pictures (*The Godfather, Love Story, Saturday Night Fever,* "Mork and Mindy," "Happy Days"), and they're one of the largest zinc miners in the United States. They own Madison Square Garden, which in turn owns the New York Knicks, the New York Rangers, the Washington Diplomats soccer team, Roosevelt Raceway in New York and Arlington Park Race Track near Chicago, and 80% of Holiday on Ice. They own Simon & Schuster publishing. They own Pocket Books. They own the Miss Universe and Miss USA pageants, Simmons mattresses, and Associates First Capital, a consumer loan and insurance chain. They even make the molds the U.S. Mint uses to press coins.

G + W's most controversial industry is their sugar business in the Dominican Republic. They own 264,000 acres there, 118,000 of which are used to grow sugar cane. G + W accounts for nearly one-third of the sugar grown in the Dominican Republic. Their holdings represent 8% of the arable land in the country. They are also active in many other fronts on the Dominican Republic, including livestock, growing of fruits, vegetables, and tobacco, and ex-

tensive tourist operations. During the peak season G + W employs 15,000 cane cutters in the Dominican Republic. Critics have charged that these workers are paid substandard wages; G + W counters that they pay 25% higher than the government and other sugar growers. An ongoing investigation by the U.S. Securities and Exchange Commission charges them with attempting to defraud the government and their own shareholders by concealing a $64 million profit in Dominican sugar.

G + W makes so many things in so many different places that Wall Street stock analysts frequently refuse to try to follow them, claiming the company is too complicated to recommend to prospective stockholders. One estimate has G + W selling 850 different products in all 50 states and in 50 countries overseas.

History. The word *conglomerate,* which became popular in the 1960s as a term for a hodge-podge of different companies operating under the same parent company, comes from the Latin verb *conglomerare,* to roll together into a ball. That's exactly what Charles Bluhdorn has done with his companies, and he's still rolling.

Bluhdorn fled Hitler's Austria in 1942 and came to the United States via England, working first as a $15-a-week clerk in a cotton brokerage firm. He then served as a private in the air force. Mustered out in 1946, he began working for a commodities broker just as the boss and his secretary went on vacation. He was supposed to sit and answer the phone for a couple of weeks, but instead Bluhdorn read a report on the malt business and called a few people in the malt industry in the Midwest. When the boss returned, he found Bluhdorn successfully playing the malt commodities market. At 23 he invested $3,000 in a coffee speculation venture and was a millionaire before his 30th birthday. His attitude on having outfoxed so many other, more experienced speculators was, "That'll show those goddamned bluebloods!"

In 1958 he decided to buy Michigan Plating, a small company with a practically worthless contract to manufacture the rear bumpers for the struggling Studebaker corporation. Believing he saw a market for auto replacement parts in the western United States, he put a Houston parts maker together with Michigan Bumper, and grandiosely titled his new possession

Gulf + Western—thinking he'd make the parts on the Gulf of Mexico, where labor was cheap, and ship them west. For a few years that's exactly what he did.

But Bluhdorn soon grew restless. In 1965 he made the first of his many moves into other fields, taking out an $83 million loan from Chase Manhattan Bank to buy New Jersey Zinc right in the midst of one of the worst worldwide zinc gluts in this century. Wall Street laughed at him; but Bluhdorn, a genius at analyzing financial statements, knew that the company was undervalued. He rapidly lopped off unprofitable divisions, streamlined the operation, and turned the company into a money-maker. Before Wall Street had the time to gasp, he was off and running, buying up companies at the rate of one every six weeks or so.

At first, he only bought companies that were willing to sell, cooing that he and they "would make a great team." But soon Bluhdorn had mastered the art of the "hostile takeover," buying unwilling companies by picking up sizable blocks of stock until he was the largest shareholder, and then forcing the rest to sell out to him. When asked about his intentions, Bluhdorn would usually say that G + W was only interested in these companies for "investment purposes." But more often than not, they would wake up to find themselves rolled up into Bluhdorn's ball. The few who got away were Armour meats, Allis-Chalmers equipment, Pan American Airways, and the A&P grocery chain.

Most of Bluhdorn's takeovers have been profitable for G + W, and his knack for turning unhealthy companies around has been astonishing. Generally, Bluhdorn provides his possessions with insurance, legal, tax, and financial aid but leaves them under their old management. One exception to this rule was Paramount, where he fired virtually the entire management and made himself president—even going so far as to help edit the film *Is Paris Burning?* himself, although he had no experience in filmmaking. When questioned about the mass firings, Bluhdorn simply snapped that "half the people here [were] an accumulation of 20 years of errors." Today, with recent winners like *Grease, Saturday Night Fever,* and *Heaven Can Wait,* Paramount is one of the industry's most profitable companies.

In spite of Bluhdorn's amazing track record in producing profits, he is not widely beloved. *Forbes* announced in a 1979 head-

line that he had "a $400 million credibility gap," the difference between what G + W stock was worth then and what it would have been worth if Wall Street trusted him. *Forbes* noted that few of Bluhdorn's investments were "made for the reasons given at the time"; they charged that the Houston parts business had been picked up because they owned some attractive real estate and that New Jersey Zinc was bought because they had assets Bluhdorn could use to buy Paramount. But another reason for the downgrading is Bluhdorn's abrasive personality. He continually responds to probing questions about his business by waving the American flag, talking about how only in the United States "could a guy like me build a Gulf + Western." He once told how he returned to the United States from a trip to the U.S.S.R. and kissed the airport concrete in front of an astonished customs official. He desperately wants the press to love him and his company, which explains the revolving door pattern in the company's public relations department. One former PR executive told *Fortune* in 1979 that Bluhdorn would never be satisfied with his PR men until he was "the fifth face on the Mount Rushmore of American business."

In 1979 *Fortune* said there was "a crisis atmosphere" around G + W, these days mostly because of the SEC investigation, involving a complaint of fraud against Bluhdorn and G + W for allegedly concealing profits from their Dominican sugar operation, a complaint fueled by testimony from Joel Dolkart, a former G + W lawyer and former friend of Bluhdorn who is also a convicted check forger. When Bluhdorn found out Dolkart had turned state's evidence, one source told *Business Week* in early 1980, "it was as if Kissinger had defected to Moscow."

Reputation. It's such that in 1979 Bluhdorn took out the most expensive print advertisement in history in order to improve the company's image. The ad was 64 pages in *Time,* consisting of the company's 1978 annual report. The cost: a staggering $3.3 million.

What they own. A better question might be "What don't they own?" In any case, their Paramount purchase brought them a 52-acre studio in Hollywood, complete with 32 sound stages. Their holdings in the Dominican Republic include the world's largest sugar mill, resorts, a dock and shipping facilities, and a railroad system. They also own a sugar mill, refinery, and an office building in Florida. They have 250 manufacturing plants in the United States and Canada, Puerto Rico, Jamaica, Australia, and other foreign countries, as well as 5 quarries and 16 concrete plants. Their zinc mines are located in Pennsylvania, Tennessee, Virginia, and New Jersey.

Gulf + Western also has sizable chunks of stock in, among others, Sherwin-Williams paint, Uniroyal tires, Amfac (the huge Hawaiian-based land and resort company), Cummins Engine, Jonathan Logan women's apparel, and the West Point–Pepperell bedding and linen company. In June 1980 G + W increased their stock ownership in General Tire to 15% and indicated they might just increase it again, this time to 25%. General Tire president M. G. O'-Neil told the *Wall Street Journal* at the time that he believed G + W was merely "making an investment," not going for another takeover.

Who owns and runs the company. Bluhdorn, who has been chairman since founding the company in 1958, owns over 6% of the stock, worth more than $50 million in 1980. But the most interesting shareholder at the moment is Carl Lindner, a controversial Cincinnati financier who bought 8.3% of the stock in late 1979 and who owns, among other things, large portions of the Gannett newspaper chain and United Brands. Lindner has an acquisitive streak every bit as wide as Bluhdorn's, but he denied to the *Washington Post* that he had any intention of acquiring control of Gulf + Western at present. The denial sounds a lot like Bluhdorn in his better days; and it could be that one of The Mad Austrian's favorite tactics is coming home to haunt him.

In the public eye. Church groups, stockholder resolutions, and an ABC news documentary have all focused on what ABC called the "state within a state" that G + W runs in the Dominican Republic. They own four resort hotels on the island, along with 90 other businesses, and Bluhdorn himself has a luxurious home, La Favorita, there. Under former dictator Joaquin Balaguer, a G + W ally, G + W got a free industrial zone which exempted them from taxes for 20 years. According to a report by the Corporate Information Center of the National Council of Churches in 1975, G + W was paying Dominican workers 35¢ an hour. Responding to these charges in 1978, G + W said that during the harvest season their field workers earned $100 a month—higher than three-fourths of all Dominican workers.

G + W also has extensive investments in South Africa, Thailand, Bolivia, and Paraguay. Their New York headquarters was bombed in 1977, allegedly by the FALN, a Puerto Rican terrorist group. G + W has holdings in Puerto Rico, too.

G + W bought the vacant cultural center building at Columbus Circle (across the way from their headquarters), had it refurbished, and then donated it to the City of New York with all operating expenses paid for two years.

Where they're going. Gulf + Western announced in June 1980 that they had come up with an electric battery for auto engines that would power a car at 55 miles per hour for 150 miles on a single charge. They have opened a production plant in Greensboro, North Carolina, to begin making the units and could be in limited production by 1983. At the moment, G + W estimates that the engines, which would weigh 1,200 pounds and cost about $3,000 apiece, would operate at a cost of only 2.3¢ a mile—one-third the cost of a conventional gas engine.

Stock performance. Gulf + Western stock bought for $1,000 in 1970 sold for $2,713 on January 2, 1980.

Access. 1 Gulf + Western Plaza, New York, New York 10023; (212) 333-7000.

Consumer brands.

Movies: Paramount.
Book publishing: Simon & Schuster; Summit; Sovereign; Pocket Books; Archway; Fireside; Touchstone; Wallaby; Monarch; Julian Messner; Wanderer.
Sports arenas: Madison Square Garden; Roosevelt Raceway; Arlington Park.
Sports teams: New York Knickerbockers; New York Rangers; Washington Diplomats.
Cigars: Don Diego; Don Marcos; Don Miguel; Flamenco; H. Upmann; Montecristo; Montecruz; Por Larranaga; Primo del Rey; Dutch Masters; El Producto; Muriel; Capitan de Tueros; Ben Franklin; Harvester; La Palina; Lovera; 1886; Tipalet; Dutch Treats.

Tobacco: Mixture No. 79, Old Grand Dad, Sutliff Private Stock, Heine's Blend pipe tobacco; Rogers Pouch tobacco.
Pipe lighter: Nimrod.
Candy: Schraffts; Lewis; King Kup; Wallace; Terry.
Auto parts: A.P.S.; Big A.
Swim and sportswear: Cole of California; Catalina; Sandcastle; Going Places; Bay Club; Malibu; Bob Mackie; John Newcombe.
Lingerie: Kayser.
Gloves: Kayser; Halston.
Sleepwear: Her Majesty; Nazareth.
Men's wear: Excello; John Weitz; Oscar de la Renta; Mavest; Tassel; Champion.
Belts: Paris.
Hosiery: No Nonsense; Easy to Be Me; Sheer Indulgence; Supp-hose; Mojud; Kayser; Interwoven; Esquire.
Slippers: Jiffies.
Shoes: Bostonian; Stetson; London Character; Pacer; After Six; Jack Nicklaus; Sandler of Boston.
Paper products: Nibroc, Pert, Purity towels and napkins; Paper Maid, Handi-Pac, Aristocrat food containers.
Matches: Monarch; Superior.
Loan offices: Associates.
Insurance: Capitol (life); Providence (property and casualty).

IC Industries

Sales: $3.7 billion
Profits: $106 million
Forbes 500 rank: 124
Rank in Mexican food: 1
Rank in boxed chocolates: 1
Founded: 1851
Employees: 65,200
Headquarters: Chicago, Illinois

What they do. What's a railroad doing making Midas Mufflers and Dad's Root Beer? This Chicago-based company, known for more than 100 years as the Illinois Central Railroad, has spent the past 15 years buying businesses that have little or nothing to do with trains. By 1978 their railroad contributed only one-quarter of their sales and 1% of their pretax profits. In fact, they don't even want the railroad. Its lines run mostly north and south along the Mississippi River, while most railroads go east and west. They've lost a lot of business to the cheaper barges that ply the Mississippi.

IC used to be a major force in automobile hauling, but they lost a big General Motors contract in 1975 to the Missouri Pacific Railroad, which operates along the same corridor. As a Missouri Pacific executive explained to *Forbes,* "If a fellow wants to lay down and take a snooze, I don't mind picking his pockets."

IC's stated policy for several years has been to sell the railroad—the only problem is that they haven't been able to find the right buyer. They thought they had found one in the Southern Railway, but talks with Southern broke down in 1979 and no other likely customer has appeared on the scene. "The railroad isn't like a used car," IC chairman William B. Johnson explained to the *Chicago Tribune.* "This isn't the kind of situation in which you . . . find a guy on South Wells Street and say: 'Psst. Do you want to buy a railroad?' "

In the meantime, IC is attending to their other businesses, which are concentrated in the railroad's home territory of the Midwest. Midas-International, an IC company since 1972, makes mufflers (4.5 million of them in 1978) in Illinois, Wisconsin, and Canada and sells them through more than 1,100 franchised Midas Muffler Shops across the United States, and in Canada, Mexico, England, Belgium, France, and Australia. Midas also makes recreational vehicles and trailers (18,000 in 1977) in Tennessee, Indiana, and California. In the mid-1970s Midas shops started offering other "under-the-car" products, such as shock absorbers, brakes, and springs.

Pet, which IC added in 1978, is the 95-year-old St. Louis–based company that started with evaporated milk and now makes a vast line of food products including Whitman Chocolates, Sego diet foods, and Old El Paso, the nation's best-selling brand of Mexican foods. IC's Pepsi-Cola General Bottlers bottles and distributes Pepsi to five major midwestern areas—Chicago, Des Moines, Kansas City, Louisville, and Cincinnati—with a combined population of more than 14 million. IC also owns two Chicago-based soft drink companies, Dad's Root Beer and Bubble-Up.

IC's first major nonrailroad company was Abex, formerly American Brake Shoe & Foundry, which IC bought in 1968. Abex makes brakes, wheels, and couplings for railroad cars; brake linings for cars and trucks; hydraulic systems for airplanes and ships; and specialized metal castings for industrial uses such as sugar mills and locomotives.

Like most railroads, IC owns a lot of valuable land, which they've picked up along their railroad lines. In the 1970s they decided they didn't need the land for the railroad, so they plunged into real estate development. IC is now a major partner in the Illinois Center, a complex of office buildings, hotels, and condominiums on 83 acres in downtown lakefront Chicago owned by the railroad. IC sold the land on which the New Orleans Superdome was built and held on to 11 adjoining acres, where such improvements as a Hyatt Regency hotel have been added. IC has also developed industrial parks in or near New Orleans, Memphis, and Fort Lauderdale. In 1978 real estate produced 14% of IC's pretax profits on just 2% of their sales.

History. The Illinois Central Railroad got its start in 1851, financed by European bankers who wanted to cash in on America's booming railroad business. For their first 16 years they operated only inside Illinois, but after the Civil War they started to expand vigorously, incorporating more than 200 separate railroads into their system. In 1867 they ventured across the Mississippi into Iowa, and in the following years their lines stretched southward through Kentucky, Tennessee, Arkansas, Alabama, and Mississippi, eventually reaching New Orleans. Other lines extended into South Dakota, Minnesota, Wisconsin, Indiana, Missouri, and Nebraska.

Until the 1960s the Illinois Central was content simply to haul passengers and freight up and down the Mississippi Valley and throughout the upper Midwest. Then William Johnson climbed aboard as president in 1966. Johnson had been a lawyer for the Pennsylvania Railroad and president of the financially troubled Railway Express Agency. At IC he engineered the purchases of Abex, Midas, Pepsi General, Dad's Root Beer, and Bubble-Up. In 1973 IC bought the Gulf, Mobile & Ohio Railroad, which was itself a combination of several venerable railroads, among them the Gulf, Mobile and Northern; the Mobile and Ohio; and the Chicago and Alton. The new railroad was called the Illinois Central Gulf. In 1975 the parent company changed their name to IC Industries.

Then Johnson started looking around for a healthy consumer-products company,

preferably in the food industry. After scouting several companies, he settled on Pet in 1978. But Pet, it turned out, didn't want to be bought. In an attempt to escape, Pet quickly tried to arrange a merger of their own with the Hardee's fast-food chain, which, according to *Business Week*, "would have made them too big for IC to swallow." But Johnson was not so easily rebuffed. "It takes Bill a long time to make up his mind," one of his advisers told *Business Week*, "but once he does, he's a very determined fellow." Pet tried to stop him in court, but a federal judge in St. Louis persuaded Johnson and Pet president Boyd F. Schenk to try to work out an agreement. As a result, Pet relented and Schenk became a member of IC's board of directors.

Reputation. IC Industries is well known by now—in business circles anyway—as a company that would rather sell root beer than run a railroad. And anyone riding their IC commuter line in and out of Chicago will testify to that.

What they own. 8,850 miles of railroad, plus some 45,000 freight cars and 1,000 locomotives; 46 Abex factories in the United States and 19 more in other countries; 65 Pet food plants in the United States, Canada, and Mexico; 311 Stuckey's stores along the nation's highways; 15 Midas factories in the United States and Canada; 10 Pepsi plants in the Midwest; big slices of Chicago and New Orleans.

Who owns and runs the company. The biggest piece of IC stock (13.8%) is owned by another railroad, the Union Pacific. Chairman William Johnson owns some 85,000 shares, worth about $2 million in 1980. The all-white-male board includes George T. Scharffenberger, chairman of City Investing; Graham J. Morgan, chairman of United States Gypsum; and Ralph E. Bailey, deputy chairman of Continental Oil.

Fortune's "Core Group"—262 companies which appear on both the 1955 and 1980 lists of the 500 largest U.S. industrial companies—have bought 4,500 other companies in the past 25 years.

Where they're going. Out of the railroad business, they hope.

Stock performance. IC Industries stock bought for $1,000 in 1970 sold for $846 on January 2, 1980.

Access. One Illinois Center, 111 East Wacker Drive, Chicago, Illinois 60601; (312) 565-3000.

Consumer brands.

Roadside restaurant/gift shops: Stuckey's.
Party supply stores: Vendome (California); 9-0-5 (Missouri).
Soft drinks: Dad's Root Beer; Bubble-Up.
Auto parts: Midas.
Candy: Whitman's; Stuckey's.
Mexican food: Old El Paso.
Canned milk: Pet.
Cereal: Heartland.
Snack food: Laura Scudder's.
Diet food: Sego.
Nuts: Funsten; Haig Berberian.
Fruit products: Musselman's.
Seafoods: Gulf Belle shrimp; Orleans oysters.
Bakery goods: Aunt Fanny; Pet; Pet Ritz pie crust; Downyflake waffles and frozen foods.

International Telephone and Telegraph Corporation

Sales: $22 billion
Profits: $382 million
Forbes 500 rank: 12
Rank in baking: 1
Rank in communications equipment: 2
Rank in property and casualty insurance: 7
Rank in hotels: 2
Founded: 1920
Employees: 379,000
Headquarters: New York City

What they do. ITT—known more formally as International Telephone and Telegraph—is the company that wrote the book on running a bunch of disparate companies. The problem is that the author of the book, Harold Geneen, is leaving, and no one else seems to know how to finish the story. After taking over as chief executive in 1959, Geneen, a brilliant and remorselessly hard-

driving manager, went on one of the most feverish buying sprees in corporate history. In 20 short years he grabbed 275 companies for ITT, turning the large but uninspiring telephone maker into the world's largest conglomerate. But at the same time Geneen was making his company very few friends. As the *New York Times* once wrote, "ITT to many Americans has become a three-letter symbol for corporate subterfuge and raw political power." That's not the kind of image most companies want, but ITT sees it as a plus. Even while the scandals surrounding their involvement in some of the more sordid episodes of the Nixon administration were at their height, Geneen's PR men assured British author Anthony Sampson that people would soon forget the scandals and remember only the company's name.

Ask someone about ITT and chances are the person won't reel off a list of businesses, being more likely to remember their involvement in Watergate or to recall that ITT tried to sabotage the election of Chilean president Salvador Allende. Part of the reason is that the "Geneen machine," as ITT is sometimes called, is almost too sprawling to keep track of. You're doing business with ITT when you stay at a Sheraton hotel, eat a Twinkie, have a sandwich on Wonder Bread, wash it down with a C&C Cola, read a book published by Bobbs-Merrill, buy insurance from The Harford Insurance Group, spread Turf Builder grass seed or fertilizer on your lawn, or dab a little Pavlova perfume behind your ears. If you pick up a telephone in Europe, odds are that it was made by ITT. They're second only to Western Electric in telephones and related phone equipment like cables and switching systems. Phone manufacturing is ITT's biggest business, accounting for a quarter of their sales, but it's primarily a foreign business. Although they sell switching equipment to Ma Bell, they make and market phones in Europe and Latin America, where they virtually own the market.

ITT isn't one of those companies that calls themselves a "multinational" just because they opened an office in Toronto. ITT has plants and does business in more than 80 countries around the world. Of their 379,000 employees, 215,000 are engaged in manufacturing overseas.

History. ITT was founded in 1920 by Sosthenes Behn, a sugar broker from the Virgin Islands, whose ambition was to build a phone company that would do for the world what AT&T did for the United States. He named the company International Telephone and Telegraph, deliberately inviting confusion with the names of his famous rival, and started out with phone operations in Cuba, Puerto Rico, and the Virgin Islands. In 1923 Behn got his first big break: a contract to operate the phones in Spain. But it took a decision of the U.S. government to turn ITT into a major multinational company. In a 1925 antitrust action AT&T's subsidiary Western Electric was ordered to sell off their overseas manufacturing operations. Backed by the Morgan bank, Behn bought AT&T's network of European plants and then sat down with AT&T and negotiated a secret cartel agreement not to invade one another's territory.

One of ITT's major operations was in Germany. Shortly after Hitler came to power, Behn met with the German dictator and soon, on the advice of Hitler's officials, installed some Nazis on the board of his German companies. One of them, Kurt von Schroeder, later an SS general and major source of financial support for the Gestapo, became a leading force in ITT German operations and Behn's liason with the Nazis. Under Schroeder's direction ITT companies in Germany expanded and got contracts to help in Germany's rearmament. Rather than repatriate ITT's German profits, Behn was happy in 1938 to let Schroeder buy a 28% share in Focke-Wulf, a manufacturer of bombers. Even after Pearl Harbor Behn's executives kept in contact with their German counterparts through meetings in Spain, and ITT's Swiss subsidiary manufactured equipment for Germany. But ITT played both sides of the street. While German bombers made by a partially owned ITT company were bombing American ships, ITT in the United States was making a directional finder that helped the U.S. Navy destroy German submarines.

ITT, in their devotion to profit, was above such considerations as nationalism, war, or morality. As Anthony Sampson writes in *The Sovereign State of ITT*, "If the Nazis had won, ITT in Germany would

If It's Monday, This Must Be Belgium

"On the last Monday of every month, a Boeing 707 takes off from New York to Brussels, with sixty ITT executives aboard, including Geneen or one of his deputies, with a special office rigged up for him to work in. They stay in Brussels for four days, enveloped in their own company capsule, spending most of their time in one of the marathon ITT meetings.

A meeting is a weird spectacle, with more than a hint of Dr. Strangelove. One hundred and twenty people are assembled in the big fourth-floor room, equipped with air-conditioning, soft lighting, and discreet microphones. The curtains are drawn against the daylight, and a big screen displays table after table of statistics. Most of the room is taken up with a huge horseshoe table, covered in green baize, with blue swivel armchairs and a name in front of each chair, with a bottle of mineral water and a volume of statistics. In the chairs sit the top men of ITT from all over Europe, like diplomats at a conference: in the middle are the senior vice-presidents. Among them, swiveling and rocking to and fro in his armchair, surveying the faces and gazing at the statistics, is an owlish figure behind a label saying Harold S. Geneen. . . .

The meetings, whether in Brussels or New York, are the central ordeal of the ITT discipline, the test that its men are attuned to the openness of the system. As Geneen explained to me, it is not enough for him to see the figures; he must see the expression of the man that presents them. . . ."

Harold S. Geneen, the man in the armchair, was then chairman of the board of ITT. The description above is from Anthony Sampson's observations during his visits to Brussels when he was writing *The Sovereign State of ITT.* Sampson added:

"For a newly joined manager—and especially from a company newly acquired by ITT—the ordeal can be terrifying; there are stories of one man fainting as he walked in and of another rushing out to get blind drunk for two days. For the hardened ITT man, it is no more than a routine test of sangfroid. 'You have to be prepared,' said one of them, 'to have your balls screwed off in public and then joke afterward as if nothing had happened.'"

Source: Anthony Sampson, *The Sovereign State of ITT.* (Stein & Day, 1973).

have appeared impeccably Nazi; as they lost, it reemerged as impeccably American." In fact, ITT actually had the audacity to file claims with the U.S. government for damage done to ITT plants by Allied bombers; in 1967 they received $27 million in compensation, including $5 million for damage to the Focke-Wulf plants.

But Behn merely laid the foundation for ITT. In 1959 he was succeeded by the man who transformed the company, Harold Geneen. A man without roots, Geneen was the perfect choice for a multinational company like ITT. Born in England, he came to America as a child, attended a series of boarding schools, and then quit school at 16 to devote himself to accountancy. Starting at an accounting firm in New York, he soon demonstrated his brilliance and his fanatic devotion to work and moved up the corporate ladder at Bell & Howell, Jones & Laughlin, and Raytheon. But he longed to be the boss of his own company, where he would not have the frustrations of dealing with the wishes of others. At ITT he got his chance.

Arriving at ITT, Geneen discovered that the company lacked management and discipline. Soon he set up what Sampson calls "the most intricate and rigorous system of financial control that the world has ever seen." All the lines of communication went to Geneen. He instituted regular meetings and flows of reports that allowed him to keep track of all the company's operations. "I want no surprises," he told his executives. Geneen (the "G" is soft as in Jesus, not hard as in God, as they say at ITT) even had a vice-president who provided him with secret dossiers on the performance and personal lives of his executives.

In the early 1960s Geneen started his merger spree. Convinced by Castro's nationalization of ITT's Cuban phone company that the telephone business was too much under the control of foreign governments, Geneen vowed to buy back into the United States to protect ITT's existence. Between 1960 and 1962 the company acquired 14 other firms. In 1963 they grabbed 13 more; in 1964, 19 more; in 1965, 16; in 1966, 11; in 1967, 13; and in 1968, 24. By the time Geneen finally stepped aside as chief executive officer in 1978, ITT had added 275 companies to their network and the company had come to be called the Geneen Machine—what Rand Araskog, ITT's chairman after Geneen, called "the most complex organization in American business."

The most important, and most fateful, of Geneen's acquisitions was one of the last—the Hartford Insurance Group. Until then ITT had made their acquisitions through offers of ITT stock. As the company grew, the price of the stock went up, making more acquisitions possible. But outside accountants were convinced that some of ITT's continuous profit growth was accomplished through Geneen's accounting wizardry and that ITT needed a company like the Hartford with a large flow of cash from premiums. Geneen was apparently convinced also. When the antitrust chief of the Nixon administration filed suit to stop the Hartford takeover, Geneen launched a furious lobbying campaign to turn the administration around. And in 1971 he succeeded. That June, just before the case was to have its final round in the Supreme Court, the chief of the antitrust division relented and signed a consent agreement with ITT. The agreement allowed the company to keep the Hartford Insurance Group (now responsible for about a fifth of their business), if they sold Avis Rent-A-Car, Levitt & Sons homebuilders, Canteen vending machines, and the fire business of Grinnell alarm.

The settlement raised a few eyebrows in Washington—but it set off a storm in February 1972 when columnist Jack Anderson revealed the existence of an internal memo by ITT lobbyist Dita Beard implying that Geneen had arranged favorable settlement by pledging to the White House a $400,000 contribution to finance the Republican National Convention in San Diego. At the bottom of the memo was Beard's notation: "Please destroy this, huh?" The day after Anderson's column appeared, ITT's Washington office was in a frenzy, as workers madly put their files through the paper shredder. Dita Beard disappeared to a Denver hospital, where she was visited secretly by E. Howard Hunt, of the infamous White House "plumbers." Wearing an ill-fitting red wig borrowed from the CIA and disguising his voice through a voice modifier, Hunt instructed her to denounce the memo as a fake (it wasn't). Eventually located by the FBI, Beard was questioned in her hospital room by a panel of senators sitting on the confirmation of attorney general Richard Kleindienst, who had supervised the settlement of the ITT-Hartford case. (Kleindienst pleaded guilty to a misdemeanor arising out of his testimony about the case.) It was a grand show, giving the nation a preview of Watergate and a glimpse of how Geneen used his power.

Reputation. The cloak-and-dagger corporation. One former ITT executive characterized the Geneen Machine this way: "ITT is like the British in India toward the end of the empire. The company is a compound; those inside are trusted; those outside are not."

What they own. In total, ITT owns $23 billion worth of factories, real estate, forests, coal, oil, and securities. About half their assets are in the United States.

Who owns and runs the company. The largest block of stock in ITT, 2%, is held by the investment plan for the company's salaried workers. Other large blocks are held by the Chase Manhattan and Morgan banks.

Geneen relinquished the chairman's position he held for 21 years at the end of 1979, but he continues as a member of the board, looking over the shoulder of the chief executive officer, Rand V. Araskog, who came to ITT from Honeywell in 1968. Geneen stepped down as chief executive officer in 1978 in favor of Lyman Hamilton, a cost-cutting specialist Geneen had brought aboard in 1962 from the World Bank. But Hamilton tried to cut some of Geneen's favorite companies, so Geneen cut him instead. One analyst told the *Wall Street Journal* in 1979, shortly after the ax fell, that "Hamilton showed his muscles too much. Geneen didn't want a really charismatic guy."

In his place, Geneen put Araskog, who wasted no time imitating the style of his boss. Geneen made a point of living in midtown Manhattan so he wouldn't waste time commuting, so Araskog is doing the same thing. In 1980 the board of directors "requested" him to buy a cooperative apartment near the office. And to make sure that the high price of Manhattan co-ops did not put too much financial strain on Araskog, who was paid only $700,000 in 1979, the board authorized the company to pay his interest on a $950,000 apartment loan. The board also made sure that Araskog would get the right kind of advice: they signed Geneen to a five-year, $1.5 million contract as a consultant, which will supplement his $243,097 annual pension.

THE TEN LARGEST CORPORATE LEGAL DEPARTMENTS

Legal Staff

AT&T 902
EXXON 384
GENERAL ELECTRIC 302
PRUDENTIAL 202
DU PONT 194
MOBIL 188
STANDARD OIL (*Indiana*) 179
GENERAL MOTORS 159
GULF OIL 152
BANKAMERICA 146

According to one company estimate, the cost of each in-house attorney is $110,000 a year.

Source: Law and Business Directory of Corporate Counsels, 1980-81.

In the public eye. Although part of the reason for Geneen's merger spree was to protect ITT from foreign government nationalization of their telephone operations, he had no intention of giving them up without a fight. In May 1970, through John McCone, a board member who was former director of the CIA, ITT approached CIA director Richard Helms about a joint CIA-ITT operation to ensure the election of a right-wing candidate in that year's Chilean presidential election. In a later meeting McCone pledged $1 million for a program to help Jorge Alessandri defeat Radomiro Tomic and Salvador Allende, both of whom had pledged to nationalize ITT's holdings. The Nixon administration rejected ITT's pro-Alessandri plan in favor of a block-Allende strategy, but the CIA helped ITT funnel funds to the right-wing candidate. When no candidate received a majority, the election was thrown into the Chilean Congress, where Allende was sure to win. The Nixon White House began plotting a coup to prevent Allende's taking power, but when the CIA approached ITT for help in throwing Chile's economy into a panic, ITT refused to cooperate. Nixon failed to keep Allende out of power in 1970, but in 1973 he helped the military overthrow the government, and the generals repaid ITT, which again runs subsidiaries in Chile.

Six years later, in 1979, ITT's muscle again came to the fore when the Justice Department dropped a criminal case against Edward Gerrity, a senior vice-president at ITT who had been charged with perjury for allegedly lying about ITT's role in Allende's overthrow. Federal lawyers were afraid that prosecuting Gerrity might bring out details of ITT's tangled relationship with the CIA and certain prominent Chileans, so the case was dropped in the interest of national security.

Where they're going. No one believes they'll go anywhere without Geneen navigating.

Stock performance. ITT stock bought for $1,000 in 1970 sold for $430 on January 2, 1980.

Access. 320 Park Avenue, New York, New York 10022; (212) PL2-6000.

Consumer brands.

Bakery products: Wonder Bread; Hostess Twinkies, cupcakes, and Sno-Balls.
Frozen food: Morton.
Lawn-care products: Scott's Turf Builder, Turf Builder Plus 2, and Grass Seed.
Meats: Gwaltney Ham; Great Dogs (chicken dogs); Genuine Smithfield.
Books: Bobbs-Merrill; Marquis Who's Who.
Soft drinks: C&C Cola.
Hotels: Sheraton.
Insurance: Hartford.

LITTON INDUSTRIES, INC.

Sales: $4.1 billion
Profits: $189 million
Forbes 500 rank: 108
Rank in microwave ovens: 1
Rank in aircraft guidance systems: 1
Rank in medical magazines: 1
Rank in defense contracting: 11
Founded: 1953
Employees: 77,700
Headquarters: Beverly Hills, California

What they do. The first modern conglomerate, a far-flung colossus of wildly disparate parts selected solely on the basis of whether they could make money for the parent company. Litton blasted off in the 1950s, had a spectacular rise and fall in the 1960s, crashed and nearly burned in the 1970s, but recovered in time to face the 1980s in relatively sober shape.

More than 100 different businesses operate under the Litton umbrella. As *Fortune* put it in 1979, "A customer may order a monkey suffering from leukemia or an artificial diamond; a log of geophysical soundings taken in the Bering Straits or a *McGuffey's Reader;* a microwave oven or a metal-grinding machine; a set of hand tools or a custom-made computer." Keeping all these divisions humming smoothly would be a remarkable feat if the whole thing had to be directed from the top, but Litton doesn't work that way. They have always bought going concerns and let them keep operating without a lot of interference. Charles "Tex" Thornton, founder and chairman of the Litton empire, once explained, "We had to grow fast. There wasn't time to learn a business, train people, develop markets. . . . We bought time, a market, a product line, plant, research team, sales force. It would have taken years to duplicate this from scratch."

To consumers Litton is probably best known for their microwave ovens. They make more of them than anyone else—1½ million a year. They make Monroe office calculators and Sweda electronic cash registers that use an optical scanner to read prices at supermarket checkstands. They make steel office furniture and machines that turn out automobile brake parts. Litton divisions make printed circuit boards for computers, oxygen monitors that regulate the atmosphere inside infant incubators, and robot warehouses that can store and retrieve small items at the push of a button.

Litton is heavily involved in "seismic prospecting," the frenzied search for oil and gas inspired by the soaring prices of the permanent energy crisis. Their Western Geophysical division, based in Houston, scours the globe for major oil companies, independents, and national oil monopolies such as Pemex in Mexico and Petrobras in Brazil. They have vast files of "speculative seismic explorations" conducted over the past 20 years, which they sell for a handsome price whenever an oil company wants data on a particular area.

They also happen to be the nation's leading publisher of medical magazines, such as *Medical Economics, Diagnosis,* and *Current Prescribing.* These magazines, loaded with ads from drug companies, are sent free to physicians across the country. Litton publishes the widely used *Physicians' Desk Reference,* an annual directory of prescription drugs. They also publish textbooks for all levels of students, from elementary school to college.

Through their ups and downs, Litton has gone in and out of many different businesses, but they've stayed in one crucial line all along: defense contracts. About one-fourth of their sales are to the government. In 1980 they were the Pentagon's 11th-largest supplier, making equipment for all branches of the armed forces. They make the ultimate in navigation and guidance systems for airplanes, helicopters, and missiles used by the air force. They make "mortar fire-control calculators" for the army and high-technology communications systems for the marine corps. They're a major supplier of destroyers to the navy, and they own the only shipyard built in the United States since World War II (the state of Mississippi financed its construction).

It's not just America's defenses that Litton is concerned with, either. In 1979 they landed a $1.6 billion contract to build a nationwide air-defense system for Saudi Arabia, where they were already working on an air traffic control system for the country's airports. The company was putting the finishing touches on four guided missile destroyers for the Iranian navy when the Shah's government was toppled, but the U.S. Navy obligingly took the weapons off Litton's hands.

History. Charles B. "Tex" Thornton, the genius behind the fabulous rise of Litton Industries, was born in a small town in north-central Texas just before World War I. His father deserted the family when Tex was young, leaving his mother to teach him the art of finance. She persuaded him to

invest money from odd jobs in real estate, and before long he had accumulated nearly 40 acres. By the time he was 14, every store in town would take his personal check. At 19 he started a combination gas station and Chrysler-Plymouth dealership.

In the mid-1930s Thornton went to Washington, earned a bachelor of commercial science degree, and got a job as a clerk in the Department of the Interior. He joined the Army shortly before Pearl Harbor and rose meteorically through the ranks, winning his first promotion within 48 hours and eventually becoming one of the youngest full colonels in the army. Thornton was charged with developing a system of statistical controls for the army air corps (later the U.S. Air Force). He later described it as "a fancy name for finding out what the hell we had by way of resources and when and where they were going to be required." It was an early form of data processing: for the first time the army could know exactly what equipment they had, from shoelaces to submachine guns, and what they were likely to need at various times and places.

After the war Thornton and a group of nine talented subordinates decided that, rather than go their separate ways, they would offer themselves as a package to American business. The group, known as the Whiz Kids (after a popular radio show), accepted an offer from Ford Motor Company. Out of the deal Ford got two future presidents—Robert McNamara (later U.S. secretary of defense) and Arjay Miller—as well as four division heads. But Tex Thornton ran afoul of his superiors and left Ford after only two years. He returned to Texas, paid a call on the state's biggest industry, Hughes Tool Company, and wound up taking a job as assistant general manager of another Howard Hughes company, Hughes Aircraft, in Los Angeles.

Thornton and Hughes parted company in 1953 under disputed circumstances. According to one account, Thornton quarreled with the reclusive Hughes over Thornton's lack of clear-cut operating authority. Another version has it that the government forced Hughes to get rid of Thornton and his assistant comptroller, Roy Ash, after the air force discovered the company had ripped them off to the tune of $43 million. Thornton and Ash were accompanied out the door by several other top Hughes executives and engineers, including the

> In 1979, 2,128 companies, worth a total of $43.5 billion, were bought by other corporations.

men who went on to found two other big companies, TRW and Teledyne.

Thornton and Ash started a company called Electro Dynamics, then went to Wall Street, borrowed $1.5 million, and bought a small vacuum-tube company owned by Charles V. Litton. They started piling on more companies as fast as they could. Within four years sales rose from $3 million a year to $100 million. Only $11 million of the increase came from Charles Litton's original business; the rest resulted from their acquisition of some 17 other firms.

Litton's appetite for companies was insatiable. They bought businesses that made calculating machines, cash registers, price tags, label adhesives, office furniture, trading stamps, and a vast range of electronics equipment, from medical devices to marine navigation systems. In 1961 they bought Ingalls Shipbuilding in Pascagoula, Mississippi, and suddenly became a major supplier of ships to the U.S. Navy.

Litton seemed to have the Midas touch. Their stock kept going up, up, up in the "go-go" economy of the early and mid-1960s, as more companies clamored to be bought and stock market speculators rushed to climb aboard the rocket-powered elevator. Litton pioneered the concept of transforming the traditionally staid annual report to stockholders into a high-class promotional brochure. Their report for 1967, produced at the peak of their prosperity, looked more like an art museum catalog than a business document, with full-color reproductions of stained-glass windows on nearly every page. It was the most expensive annual report a company had ever produced, costing Litton close to $500,000. Tex Thornton was riding high. At the behest of his fellow Texan Lyndon Johnson, he spent much of his time serving on presidential commissions, including the President's National Advisory Commission on Civil Disorders (the Kerner Commission) and the President's Commission on White House Fellows.

But Litton was starting to slip. In 1968, for the first time quarterly profits actually declined—a great shock to all those who had come to believe in Litton as an invincible money machine. Suddenly investors decided Litton wasn't such a blue chip after all, and between 1967 and 1974 the price of Litton's stock plummeted from $120 to $3. In 1971 the House Antitrust Subcommittee, in an investigation of corporate conglomerates, reported that Litton had created "an image of technological and organizational superiority" by developing "flamboyant sham into an art" through the use of "all the sophisticated accounting techniques and statistical gimmicks available."

In 1972 the company reported their first annual loss: $2.3 million. Shortly thereafter, Roy Ash, the Litton cofounder who had become the company's president, went to Washington to become director of the Office of Management and Budget in the Nixon administration. He was replaced by Fred O'Green, a former Lockheed engineer who came to Litton in 1962. O'Green sold off hopeless companies, closed several plants, and pumped money into a few divisions he thought could be revived. It has been a long haul, but he seems to have succeeded in turning the company around. The company lost $48 million in 1974, but in 1979 they reported record profits of $89 million.

Over the years so many Litton executives have left to head other companies or start their own that there's a term for them: Lidos, an acronym for Litton Industries dropouts (Litton prefers Ligrads, or Litton Industries graduates). Among them: Roy Ash, who went on from the White House to become chairman of Addressograph-Multigraph, now AM International; Harry Gray, who became head of United Aircraft, now United Technologies; Henry Singleton, who founded Teledyne, which is now the single largest Litton stockholder; Fred Sullivan, who became head of Walter Kidde & Co.; George Scharffenberger, who became head of City Investing and returned to Litton as a member of the board of directors in 1974; Russell McFall, who became head of Western Union Telegraph; and William McKenna, who became a one-man Who's Who, successively heading Hunt Foods, Norton Simon, Technicolor, and Sambo's Restaurants.

Reputation. A sadder but wiser conglomerate.

What they own. Plants in 75 cities in 29 states, from Massachusetts to California, and others in Canada and Western Europe.

Who owns and runs the company. Teledyne, a Los Angeles company founded in 1960 by Litton veteran Henry Singleton, is Litton's largest single stockholder, with

27% of the stock, which they bought at rock-bottom prices in the early 1970s. Chairman Tex Thornton, who turned 65 in 1978, owns a little under 3% of the shares, worth around $50 million in 1980. The board of directors includes Wallace W. Booth, former president of United Brands; William S. Banowsky, president of the University of Oklahoma; Norman H. Topping, chancellor of the University of Southern California; and one woman, Jayne B. Spain, a former vice-chairman of the U.S. Civil Service Commission.

In the public eye. Litton was a pioneer in the Cold War "systems" approach to supplying equipment to the Pentagon. The newly created air force, lacking the capabilities to design or produce the weapons they wanted, started "contracting out" the entire process of designing, building, and even maintaining weapons systems to private companies. Since no one, least of all the air force, had any idea how much a new bomber or missile system should cost, they issued contracts on a "cost-plus" basis: essentially, the companies could spend as much as they wanted, add on a percentage for profit, and send the Pentagon the bill. The other services, finding themselves lagging behind the upstart air force in technological prowess, soon adopted the same method.

The cost-plus practice has done much to boost peacetime defense budgets to record heights since World War II. Companies that find they can't finish a job for the amount they agreed on at the beginning can usually just go back for more. But from time to time certain government officials have objected to the massive cost overruns that seem to come with every new defense project. A large part of Litton's troubles in the 1970s stemmed from a protracted hassle with the navy over cost overruns on an order for 30 destroyers, in which Litton succeeded in raising the ire of crusty old Admiral Hyman Rickover. The company ended up paying the navy $173 million to settle the dispute, which caused a whopping $91 million net loss for Litton in 1978.

When Litton was still going great guns in the 1960s, they decided to move into the realm of social engineering. Three weeks after a military junta toppled the government of Greece, Litton signed a contract with the junta to concoct an "economic development" program for the entire geo-

graphical region of Crete and the western Peloponnessus—on a cost-plus basis, of course. Litton's plans consisted largely of promoting tourism, building a German brewery and a Litton electronics assembly plant, and growing brussels sprouts for export to Germany.

On the home front Litton got involved with the War on Poverty during the Johnson administration, landing a $12.8 million cost-plus contract to set up a Job Corps center at an unused navy base in Pleasanton, California. They scooped up youths from ghettos and poverty pockets across the country, put them through a "basic education" program, awarded them high school-equivalency diplomas, and placed about 40% of the "graduates" in the U.S. military (this during the height of the Vietnam War). In 1968 the General Accounting Office visited the center and found, among other things, that Litton had spent $337,000 on textbooks published by the company's Instructional Materials division—but since the Job Corpsmen could barely read, the books were lining closet shelves. Among the titles: *Forces and Vectors, The Dynamic Molecular Structure of All States of Matter, Newton's Law of Motion, The Theory of Relativity,* and *Understanding the Financial Page.*

Where they're going. Now that Litton seems to be back on the track, they may just start buying companies again (their last major purchase was New Britain Machine in 1968). They have a lot of extra money these days, and they have to do something with it. If they get stuck for ideas, they can always peer into the pages of the new magazine, called *Next,* which they launched in 1980. They describe it as the only magazine "specifically for the future"—where, after all, "we're going to spend the rest of our lives." Sample articles: "Arizona: The State of America to Come" and "Will There Ever Be a Jewish President?"

Stock performance. Litton stock bought for $1,000 in 1970 sold for $1,473 on January 2, 1980.

Access. 360 North Crescent Drive, Beverly Hills, California 90210; (213) 273-7860.

Consumer brands.

Microwave ovens: Litton.
Calculators: Monroe.
Book publishing: Van Nostrand-Reinhold.

Loews Corporation

Sales: $3.8 billion
Profits: $182 million
Forbes 500 rank: 118
Rank in cigarettes: 5
Rank in low-tar cigarettes: 3
Founded: 1919
Employees: 29,400
Headquarters: New York, New York

What they do. Loews chairman Laurence Tisch likes to say that his company is "really run like a delicatessen." By this he means that although Loews is a massive corporation with more than $3.8 billion in annual sales, it's still a family operation. Laurence Tisch and his brother, Preston, run the company and collectively own about 43% of Loews stock; their mother, Sadye, serves as the official hostess at their Miami Americana Hotel. Laurence's son, Andrew, is an officer at their recently acquired Bulova Watch subsidiary.

And, like a deli, Loews sells a little of this and a little of that. They don't just own a chain of hotels—they operate some of the more obscenely luxurious watering places in the world, like the Regency in New York (where investment bankers gather at breakfast to make deals) and resorts in Monte Carlo and Nassau. These hotels are a long way from Loews' first two hotels in New York City: the McAlpin and the Belmont-Plaza.

But hotels are only Loews' third-biggest money-maker. Most of their profits come from insurance and cigarettes, through Continental Casualty and Continental Assurance (both part of CNA Financial, which is almost four-fifths owned by Loews); and Lorillard, maker of Newport, Old Gold, and Kent cigarettes. Lorillard has moved into the number 3 position in low-tar cigarettes with the successful introduction of Kent III and Triumph. The Loews theaters, from which the conglomerate took the name, are now a small part of the company, although they have 128 movie screens in nine states.

Loews operates as a company that buys and controls other companies that make or sell services, but they also invest their spare cash in the stock market. That's why the company has been called a "mutual fund for widows" and "a mutual fund that sells cigarettes" by Wall Street analysts. Laurence Tisch, the mastermind of Loews's investments, told *Forbes,* "I think of stocks as businesses." He frequently buys stock in money-losing companies to give himself a base for buying the majority of the company in a future takeover bid. When the bid is successful, as in the case of CNA and Bulova, Tisch and his brother then throw out the old management, take tight control of operations, and turn their new possession into a money-maker. Tisch keeps a stock ticker next to his desk in New York and constantly amazes his lawyers by quoting the latest prices on stocks of obscure companies. But his expertise in playing the market has earned him quite a reputation on Wall Street. One analyst concedes that he gets nervous whenever Tisch is doing something he's not doing, and when investors learned that Loews had bought 10% of Gimbel's department store stock in 1972, the normally sluggish stock shot up four points. (Tisch was right, as usual: shortly afterward Gimbel's was bought by British-American Tobacco.)

History. Laurence and Preston Tisch founded their empire in 1946 on $125,000 from their father, a garment manufacturer who ran two children's summer camps. A few years before, Laurence had graduated from Pennsylvania University's Wharton School of Finance with a master's degree at the age of 18. The two brothers bought a New Jersey resort hotel they had seen advertised in the *New York Times* "business opportunities" section. Soon they began buying other hotels in Atlantic City, New Jersey, and the "borscht belt" of New York. They also began building their own in Florida.

An impending antitrust settlement pushed Laurence into Loews theaters. Marcus Loew, like many another Jewish immigrant in the early 1900s, had gotten a job in the fledgling motion picture industry. He started out in crank-up nickelodeons and began exhibiting films in 1919. Later he bought Metro Pictures and entered the production end of the new business. Then, in 1924, he merged Goldwyn Pictures and Louis B. Mayer Pictures to form Metro-Goldwyn-Mayer—MGM, one of the great studios in the history of Hollywood. The two businesses remained linked until after World War II when antitrust suits forced the company to separate film production from the theaters.

In 1959, aware that the antitrust settlement would force MGM to sell off their Loews theater chain, Laurence began buying all the Loews stock he could get his hands on. He thought the chain had vastly undervalued their land holdings—prime, downtown real estate sitting underneath the theaters—by at least $20 million, and when he took control in May 1960 he found out he was right. After selling off several unprofitable theaters, the Tisch brothers quickly doubled the chain's profits. This, together with Laurence's stock market aplomb and the success of their hotels, built the company's assets to $273 million by 1968.

In that year the Tisch brothers stunned the financial world by taking over Lorillard, a 200-year-old tobacco company that had been stagnating. (Lorillard's history goes back to 1760, when an 18-year-old French immigrant, Pierre Lorillard, started to make and sell snuff in New York City. The snuff mill his sons Peter and George built is still standing in the Bronx Botanical Gardens). What surprised Wall Street about the Tisch takeover was that Lorillard, with annual sales of $565 million, was three times the size of Loews.

Lorillard was then in horrible shape. All three of their major brands—Kent, True, and Newport—were in trouble. To turn things around, the Tisches bought in Curtis H. Judge, a Texan and a lawyer, who had just been fired by R. J. Reynolds over a policy dispute. It was Judge who spearheaded Lorillard's push during the 1970s into the low-tar-and-nicotine field with Golden Lights, Kent III, and Triumph. As a result, the Lorillard brands now have 10% of the total market and 17% of the fastest-growing segment of the market: the low-tar end. Also, they are advancing on fourth-place American Tobacco.

Reputation. Loews is known for their ability to take over losers and make winners out of them, even when they have to fire all the managers to do it, as they did with CNA. The Tisch brothers generally bring in their own managers and cut out such frills as fancy offices, excess secretaries, company planes, and private bathrooms. The Tisch style runs to sandwiches at the desk and no interoffice memos. At CNA they fired 1,400 employees and added only one person to the staff. When the Tisches sold the McAlpin Hotel to Sheraton and the Sheraton people came in, they found all the light bulbs had been taken away.

What they own. Lorillard, the hotels, and the theaters are wholly owned by Loews. They own 79% of CNA and 93% of Bulova Watch, once the premier watch company of America, which Loews bought in 1979. It's probably too early to tell whether Loews can bring Bulova back up to its former glory, but the Tisches have already put their distinctive stamp on the company— most of Bulova's management and several directors have been forced into early retirement. Whether the Tisches will be able to improve the Bulova product also remains to be seen. As one former Bulova manager recently admitted, "When Seiko ships out 30 watches, they all work—with Bulova, maybe 20 work."

Who owns and runs the company. With the Tisch brothers owning 43% of the stock, there's no question who runs the company, although Laurence is usually considered the "brains" of the family. He's the financial man and chairman; president Preston has a special personal interest in the hotel business. Stories about Preston's concern for the minutiae of his hotels are legend. The board of directors has no minority or female members.

In the public eye. Although Loews stays pretty much out of the spotlight, Laurence Tisch himself has donated $1 million to the United Jewish Appeal.

Where they're going. They haven't bought a company for a while, but no one expects that lull to continue for very long.

Stock performance. Loews stock bought for $1,000 in 1970 sold for $1,627 on January 2, 1980.

Access. 666 Fifth Avenue, New York, New York 10019; (212) 841-1000.

Consumer brands.

Cigarettes: Newport; Old Gold, Old Gold Lights; True; Kent, Kent Golden Lights, Kent III, Kent III 100s; Max 100s; Triumph.
Watches: Bulova.
Insurance: Continental Assurance; Continental Casualty.
Theaters: Loews.
Hotels: Loews.

The Tender Trap

The boss came in late, hung his jacket in the closet in his office, and sat down with the *Wall Street Journal* and coffee. He ran a medium-sized mining company, which had just branched into manufacturing. Six or seven things on his mind, the boss scanned the news pages and sipped his coffee. It was Friday.

Turning to the mail, he found a letter from Mr. Lance, head of another mining company. The boss mined coal, Lance mined zinc and other metals. The letter was peculiar: very friendly, Lance was suggesting a joint venture, or possibly a merger. In fact, Lance's company was prepared to make an offer. The boss was puzzled and vaguely suspicious. He set the letter aside.

In the language of corporate takeovers and mergers, Lance's letter seemed like a "teddy-bear pat," and after consulting a few of his executives, the boss pegged it as such. Lance's company clearly wanted to take over the boss's.

The boss knew that in the business world his company was a "sleeping beauty": a sort of sitting duck, attractive to other companies and ripe for a takeover. (One such, NN Corp., a Milwaukee insurance company, was approached at least 25 times between 1973 and 1980 by various conglomerates who wanted to buy.)

Lance was styling himself as a "friendly suitor" for the moment, but he would turn into a "black knight" if he got an unfavorable answer from the boss. He knew the boss's company was vulnerable—his investment bankers had told him so. (First Boston Co. has a "creative director" whose entire job is finding likely targets for acquisition. Morgan Stanley has a computer system called a "plum picker" for the same purpose.)

What made the boss's corporation so attractive? For one thing, the concern had a lot of cash reserves and no long-term debt. That meant any buyer would immediately have a lot of

money at his disposal once he took over the company. The cash could even be used to pay for the boss's business. (Eli M. Black, the financial juggler who headed United Brands, perfected the technique of buying cash-rich companies with money he borrowed from banks, then paying his debt to the banks with the cash from his new company. Black's method became popular in the merger heyday of the 1960s.)

The boss decided he didn't want to become a junior partner in Lance's operation, so he wrote and told Lance he wasn't interested. A week later came the "bear hug": another letter with an informal offer of $21 a share for the entire company, $4 a share more than the stock was selling for on Wall Street. Lance also told the boss that he was also informing the SEC, which requires 30 days' notice of large takeovers. The boss's heart sank when, after reading Lance's letter, he opened his *Wall Street Journal* and learned that Lance's company had quietly bought up 9% of the company's stock over the previous few months. The boss remembered how Morrison-Knudsen had had to buy back just such a chunk of stock from Crane Co. to keep out of Crane's clutches. "Paying ransom," it's called. Morrison-Knudsen kept their independence, but had to pay $14 million for stock that had cost Crane only $11 million.

The boss got on the horn. He called his lawyer in Washington, D.C., and told him to file SEC form 14-D, confirming his plan to fight the takeover. (Before 14-D is filed, a defending company can't say much of anything publicly about a takeover offer.) He called in his lawyers, his bankers, and his PR department. He cancelled his weekend golf game. Lance's offer was good for a week. If not accepted within that time, Lance would go directly to the boss's stockholders with an offer, "Saturday Night Special": a sudden, openly hostile grab for another

company's stock.

The boss's lawyers filed suits accusing Lance of antitrust violations, since Lance ran a mining company like the boss. The PR department sent out a barrage of press releases and letters to the stockholders, explaining that Lance's company just wanted to take over assets and fire employees, perhaps even folding up operations, whereas the boss could turn this company into a real winner. (The boss didn't go as far as Mead, which, when faced with a takeover bid by Occidental Petroleum in 1978, sent shareholders a letter citing Occidental chairman Armand Hammer's questionable past encounters with securities laws. In the letters, phrases like "criminal violations" and "fraudulent course of conduct" were underlined. Dictaphone made a similar counterattack against the Canadian corporation Northern Telecom in 1974. Dictaphone filed an antitrust suit, attacked Telecom's chairman and his management abilities, and got Senators Lowell Weicker and Abraham Ribicoff up in arms against the takeover of a Connecticut company by a hostile offer, and a foreign one at that. The startled Canadians withdrew at once. "They just weren't aware of what they were getting into," recalled one of Telecom's advisors.)

The boss's lawyers got a hearing under an antitrust statute. That threw Lance's one-week deadline out the window. The boss, when this news came through several days after his cancelled golf game, heaved a sigh of relief.

But what next? Once an offer has been made, it is difficult for a company to avoid being eaten up unless they take drastic action. Some takeover targets try quickly to make themselves unpalatable, like certain species of butterfly that look attractive to predators but taste so bad that in the end they're left alone. Carrier, under siege by United Technologies in 1978, agreed to buy Jenn-Air, another air conditioning manufacturer, the purchase of which added $90 million to the cost of gaining control of Carrier. Daylin shot down a takeover bid by W.R. Grace by threatening to buy a firm in the same lines of business as Grace (chemicals, natural resources), which would have made a Grace takeover violate antitrust laws. McGraw-Hill fended off a takeover by American Express in 1979 by creating such an uproar about freedom of the press (and Amex's unacceptably low offers) that the credit-card giant retired in defeat.

The boss wasn't happy. He didn't have many options, now that he had time to consider his position. He couldn't really impugn Lance's character. ("You really have to prove that he is guilty at least of rape, or you won't get the public's attention these days," notes one merger lawyer.) Lance, after all, was sending out letters and press releases, too, saying what a great company he had and what a great profit the stockholders would make if he took over.

His stock was going up because Wall Street expected the takeover to go through. The "arbitrageurs" (professional stock speculators) were moving in on the boss's stock wherever they could.

What the boss needed was stockholder support. Part of the company was in the hands of his people because he'd made sure there was a nice stock-option for executives. But the boss and his board of directors couldn't be sure of more than about 15%. Texas Gulf Co. once felt so potentially vulnerable to a takeover that they *gave* stock to all employees. But such moves require time and SEC approval. The boss began to feel that loss of independence was inevitable.

But that didn't mean he had to sell to Lance, the hostile "black knight." He figured he could do what Microdot did when that manufacturer of electrical connectors was under siege by General Cable. Microdot went out and found Northwest Industries, who played the role of a "white knight" (or "sweetheart"), a company that "rescues" the "target company" from the embrace of an "unfriendly suitor" with a much better offer. Pan Am played the white knight to National Airlines when little Texas International Airlines was trying to buy National (a company five times larger) for a low price.

The boss had a "black book" — a thick packet of emergency measures he had prepared in advance of just such a takeover emergency. Along with model press releases, suggested legal strategies and other antitakeover tactics, called "shark repellant," the black book contained a "sweetheart" list of 10 companies he judged to be friendly. He turned their names over to his investment bankers and took off for nine holes of golf and a brace of martinis.

The rest was bidding between Lance and the head of the white knight the boss's bankers chose, a Mr. Chevalier. Bid and counterbid, angling for position, sessions with stockholder-relations specialists, and a month later Chevalier's toothpaste-and-fast-foods conglomerate agreed to buy out Lance's stock and the rest of the boss's company at $28 a share, cash.

Since the boss agreed to the deal, he sent a letter to his stockholders announcing Chevalier's bid and requesting that the stockholders "tender" (hand over) their shares for the $28 price. Virtually all of the shareholders were expected to go along with the "tender offer" since they would receive a lot more for their stock at $28 a share than the $20 a share the stock was then selling for on Wall Street.

Happily, the offer was a truly friendly one. The marriage — a somewhat bigamous arrangement, as Chevalier had played this circuit before — was consummated. The boss became a division head of, say, the Bur-O-Dent Corporations.

Would he last? Some do, some don't. Bob Kinney let his little crab-canning operation merge with Gorton's Fisheries of Gloucester in 1953 and four years later was president of Gorton's. In 1968 he sold that company to General Mills and moved into their management. He was named president and chief executive officer in 1977.

Then again, there was Lester Rosskam, who headed the Quaker City Chocolate & Confectionery (maker of Good & Plenty candies). He merged with Warner-Lambert in 1974, confident that the bargain was good. Early in 1975 Rosskam quit. He told Don Gussow, author of *Divorce Corporate Style,* that he planned to write a sequel to Gussow's tome, titled *Corporate Rape.*

Sales: $5.4 billion
Profits: $655 million
Forbes 500 rank: 68
Rank in cellophane tape: 1
Founded: 1902
Employees: 88,000
Headquarters: St. Paul, Minnesota

What they do. Minnesota Mining & Manufacturing, known as 3M, likes to keep the competition shaking their heads and wondering, "Why didn't we think of that?" Why didn't Du Pont, who invented cellophane in the 1920s, think of putting a bit of stickum on the back of it, cutting it into strips, and selling it in a roll? If they had, they would have been the inventors of Scotch tape. For curious outsiders 3M has only a wry smile. They like to keep their cards close to the chest.

Though sometimes considered a chemical company, 3M defies classification. They make 84,000 products, many of them no more complex than the famous roll of Scotch tape. "We're a nickel-and-dime business," said former chairman Harry Heltzer. "Fortunately it all adds up." Unlike such other technological titans as IBM and Xerox, 3M has their bets spread over a lot of squares. Their literature doesn't even attempt to name all their products, but some of them are photocopiers, carbonless paper, microfilm, more than 500 kinds of pressure-sensitive tapes (including "peel-open" tabs used to seal cans of fruit and vegetable juice), Scotchlite and Reflecto-Lite reflective materials for highway signs, photographic paper, X-ray film, motion picture film, plastic lenses for eyeglasses, surgical masks, videocassettes, magnetic recording tape, tape recorders. and ceramic-coated granules used in shingles.

Although 3M won't get specific about how they manage to come up with 50 or more successful new products each year, former chairman Ray Herzog once explained that during any given year there are about 1,000 fresh ideas germinating in the 3M domain. The company hovers over their research and development department like a big mama bear with her cubs: proud, fiercely protective, and a bit indulgent. The company is known to go along with offbeat, even wild, ideas from inventors on the chance that this might be the big one. Said Herzog, "If a guy has a really good success pattern, I'll go along with him if he says he can go to the moon on Scotch tape."

3M goes along to the extent of plowing 5% of their annual sales into research (a quarter of a billion dollars in 1979). Some 3M inventors have advanced degrees, others didn't go beyond high school, still others stopped at grade school. Besides the main research labs, they have a special R & D department whose purpose is to find and build new businesses for 3M. Inventors often participate in developing and marketing their own creations. "We like . . . somebody personally involved with a particular product and let him carry the ball," says Herzog. Inventors who have climbed through the ranks can be found on 3M's board of directors. A. G. Bush, the father of Scotch tape, went on to become chairman.

3M's peculiar talent seems to be an ability to take a particular technology and find an abundance of commercial uses for it or develop a single product into dozens of marketable forms. They like to point out how one thing leads to another at 3M. For example, their Tartan all-weather, nonslip surfacing material was first used on horse racing tracks, later on the tracks at the Olympic Games in Mexico City in 1968, then on indoor playing fields, ship decks, and even on the farm (to line the floors of cow stalls). The original Scotch tape led to a vast array of tapes, including Scotchlite reflective material, used on billboards. Soon 3M was in the billboard business themselves. Then, since they were more or less involved with highway travelers, they started publishing a couple of magazines for them: *Travelaide*, a vacation guide, and *Where*, a local entertainment sheet for business travelers in 27 cities. Once they were in publishing, it was just a short hop to buying Media Networks, a magazine advertising-buying service, and Mall Advertising, an outfit that sells space on small billboards in shopping centers. Buying other companies is the exception for 3M: most of their growth has come from within.

History. 3M began in 1902 when a doctor, a lawyer, a butcher, and two railroad employees in Two Harbors, Minnesota, on Lake Superior's north shore, put down $1,000 each to start a mining business. They hoped to mine what they thought was corundum, a mineral nearly as hard as diamonds, and sell it to grinding-wheel manufacturers as a high-grade abrasive. Unfortunately, the ore in question turned out to be not corundum at all but a low-quality, relatively worthless mineral called anorthosite.

By 1905 the company was close to bankruptcy, but the partners managed to convince Lucius P. Ordway, a rich St. Paul plumbing supplier, that the "corundum" could be used to make sandpaper. Ordway put in $235,000—enough to cover the most urgent bills but not enough to meet their payroll. Many workers were paid in stock—the most worthless stuff in town, but nevertheless accepted by some local bartenders (one shot of cheap whiskey for two shares of stock). Ordway, who served as president from 1906 to 1909, insisted in 1910 that the company move to St. Paul, where he could keep an eye on it.

William Lester McKnight, a South Dakota farm boy, joined 3M in 1907 as an assistant bookkeeper. He quickly ascended to accountant, office manager, and sales manager. In 1916, at age 29, he became head of the company. Having experienced the full brunt of 3M's less than smooth start, McKnight resolved that 3M would never again have to go through such uncertainty.

As 3M began to eke out a business in sandpaper manufacturing, McKnight was establishing the guidelines that, to this day, are followed at the company: diversify, avoid price cutting, minimize the risk of information leakage by confining board membership to company officers, carefully patent products, license patents, increase sales at least 10% a year, expand production facilities, keep employee morale high, and maintain quality control.

Because of McKnight's insistence on quality control, 3M's sandpaper improved —and their reputation with it. They came out with waterproof sandpaper. During the 1920s they began to branch out, and in 1925 a lab assistant invented masking tape, which marked a major milestone in the life of 3M.

For their first 30 years 3M didn't advertise, except for a management-written series of hard-sell columns in the *Saturday Evening Post* in 1921. Still they managed to make money. Sales tripled in the 1930s, as 3M brought out more and more products.

From 1946 to 1969, 3M didn't grow so much as explode. Sales increased by 25 times and profits by nearly 50—although not without setbacks. 3M had come out with the first office copier, the ThermoFax, in the 1950s and had briefly dominated the market until Xerox introduced their superior office copier in 1960. 3M's machine sank off the sales charts. As former chairman Harry Heltzer explained, "We just didn't see Brand X coming."

William McKnight continued to run the company until he retired as chairman in 1966. By then he had accumulated 3M stock worth several hundred million dollars. A theater buff, he once owned the Martin Beck and St. James Theaters in New York, the Shubert in Philadelphia, and the Colonial in Boston. He backed several Broadway shows, including *Hello, Dolly!*, *The Music Man*, and *How to Succeed in Business Without Really Trying*. After his retirement he remained on the board until his death in 1978 at age 90.

Reputation. 3M has always cultivated a feeling of midwestern folksiness. Company publications quote 3M executives voicing such sentiments as "A great asset 3M has is the ability to laugh at itself and have a good time as it goes along" and "You have to have great faith in people. You have to outline the tasks and the challenges and encourage them to set their eyes on the heights."

Here's the 3M Symphony—the members of the orchestra are all Minnesota, Mining & Mfg. employees.

They're proud that *Money* magazine singled them out in 1976 as one of "Ten Terrific Companies to Work For." So it came as a great shock to 3M watchers when the company got Scotch-taped to the Watergate scandal in the 1970s.

What they own. They have 91 plants in the United States; 97 more in 38 foreign countries, where 3M gets 40% of their sales.

Who owns and runs the company. James H. Binger, William McKnight's son-in-law, is a director and controls about 1.9% of 3M's stock, about one-third of which belongs to the McKnight Foundation, of which Binger is a trustee. Binger was formerly chairman of Honeywell. John G. Ordway, the grandson of Lucius P. Ordway, is also a director and controls a little less than 1% of the stock. Lewis W. Lehr, who joined 3M as an engineer in the tape division in 1947, became chairman in 1980. The board includes two former Cabinet members, Joseph W. Barr (treasury, 1968) and Peter G. Peterson (commerce, 1972–73) and one woman, Norma T. Pace, an official of the American Paper Institute, a trade group.

In the public eye. In the mid 1970s government investigators discovered that 3M had maintained a $634,000 political slush fund used to funnel illegal corporate campaign contributions to various politicians over a 10-year period. The contributions included a $30,000 gift to Richard Nixon's 1972 reelection effort and other donations to such prominent figures as Minnesota Senator Hubert Humphrey and Arkansas Congressman Wilbur Mills. According to a federal indictment, 3M transferred money from a corporate bank account into a Swiss bank account and then channeled the cash back to a safe in the office of 3M's top financial officer. The company allegedly made false entries in their books to hide what happened to the money and lied about it on their income tax returns. As a result, 3M and several top officers were the subjects of a maze of criminal charges and civil lawsuits brought by the Watergate special prosecutor, the state of Minnesota, the Securities and Exchange Commission, and a stockholder. Chairman Harry Heltzer pleaded guilty to charges of making an illegal contribution and resigned from 3M under fire. Irwin R. Hansen, 3M's top financial officer, pleaded guilty to similar charges, resigned his post, and declined to run for reelection to the board of directors. Bert S. Cross, 3M chairman from 1966 to 1970, also declined to seek reelection to the board.

In 1979 3M was battling sex discrimination suits brought by the St. Paul Chapter of the National Organization for Women and the Equal Employment Opportunities Commission. At the same time, the company had no women executive officers.

Where they're going. One of 3M's latest products, announced in 1980, is a suntan lotion called "Mmm! What a Tan!" Borrowing some stickum from their adhesives division, they made a lotion that "adheres" to the skin even after a swim. It comes off with soap and water, they say.

Stock performance. 3M stock bought for $1,000 in 1970 sold for $916 on January 2, 1980.

Major employment centers. St. Paul, Minnesota, area; southern California; and Chicago area.

Access. St. Paul, Minnesota 55101; (612) 733-1110.

Consumer brands.

Household products: Scotch tapes; Scotch-Brite and Scrub 'n Sponge pads; Three-M-ite, Tri-M-ite, Wetordry, and Press 'n Sand abrasives; Scotchguard fabric protector; Post-it notes; Mmm! What a Tan! suntan lotion.

TOP BUYERS FROM MINORITY-OWNED COMPANIES

Total Purchases (1979)

GENERAL MOTORS $199 *million*
FORD MOTOR $108 *million*
STANDARD OIL (*Indiana*) $75 *million*
WESTERN ELECTRIC $67 *million*
J. C. PENNEY $65 *million*
IBM $54 *million*
CAMPBELL SOUP $36 *million*
R. J. REYNOLDS $34 *million*
SHELL OIL $34 *million*
BOEING $33 *million*
MOBIL $31 *million*
BORDEN $26 *million*

Office machines: Secretary and VQC copiers; 9600 facsimile transceivers.

Recording materials: Wollensak tape recorders; Scotch and Tartan recording tapes; Scotch videocassettes.

Prescription drugs: Theolair for asthma; Norgesic analgesics.

Paper: 3M carbonless paper.

Northwest Industries

Sales: $2.6 billion
Profits: $172 million
Forbes 500 rank: 195
Rank in Scotch whiskey: 3
Rank in western boots: 1
Rank in men's and boy's underwear: 1
Founded: 1968
Employees: 43,000
Headquarters: Chicago, Illinois

What they do. Northwest Industries was put together by a lawyer who used to have a reputation as a liberal Democrat. Starting with a railroad, which he then discarded, Ben Heineman assembled a holding company that buys other companies. By their own admission they are interested only in "industry leaders." In other words, they buy in at the top. Northwest's Lone Star Steel makes the piping that goes deep down into oil and gas wells. Their Microdot is the largest independent U.S. producer of ingot molds—large cast-iron forms in which molten steel solidifies to become ingots, mechanical tubing, construction pipe, and oil-transport pipe. Microdot is also the biggest name in connecting devices (seals, fasteners, couplings) for the automotive and aerospace industries.

Universal Manufacturing is the nation's leading producer of lamp ballasts—small transformers used in fluorescent and high-intensity lamps.

Velsicol Chemical, a maker of pesticides and industrial chemicals and resins, has been under attack recently for their production of Tris, a flame retardant purported to be carcinogenic.

Then there's the other side of this hulking hybrid: consumer products. Northwest's the largest manufacturer of western boots. They make car batteries. They own the Coca-Cola Bottling Company of Los Angeles as well as the Buckingham Corporation, importer of Cutty Sark Scotch whiskey and Mouton Cadet, a Bordeaux wine. Finally, Northwest owns Union Underwear, the world's largest manufacturer of men's and boy's underwear, mostly sold under the name Fruit of the Loom.

History. The story of Northwest Industries is largely the story of shrewd, sharp-tongued Ben Heineman, who has been described as "remote, autocratic, and supremely self-assured." Associates like to remember an annual meeting when a stockholder stood up and asked how much the company was going to make in the coming year. Having just pulled through a terrible year in which Northwest lost 23¢ a share, Heineman said, he wouldn't even hazard a guess. The stockholder then addressed the other officers: would *they* be willing to estimate earnings? Heineman cut in icily: "In this company, if the president doesn't care to hazard a guess, no one else does either."

The roots of Northwest Industries are in a railroad. Fresh out of Northwestern University Law School (where he graduated in the top 10 of his class), Ben Heineman won a suit for the preferred stockholders of Chicago and Great Western Railway. (At the time the railway was nearly moribund, and Heineman discovered that railroading was a business where a little intelligence could go a long way.) Not long afterward, in 1952, he was invited to take charge of another failing railway bought up by Chicago financier Frank Lyons. When Lyons acquired the large (but floundering) Chicago & Northwestern Railway in 1956, he made Heineman president. A secretary remembers when the new boss came to work, with his leg in a cast as a result of a fall. She breezily suggested that even though he was new at the job, he ought to take sick leave, since he wouldn't be able to work. Heineman snapped: "I don't think with my legs."

Ben Heineman soon gained a reputation as a railroad wizard. In 10 years he moved the Chicago & Northwestern from a $5 million deficit to a $26 million profit. He even got the Chicago commuter trains to run on time.

In the early 1960s Heineman added two

chemical companies to the railroad. He had hoped to merge an expanded C & NW line with other railroads, but the other railroads balked, and Heineman threw his energies into organizing Northwest Industries as a holding company. In 1968 Northwest became the parent not only to the railroad and the chemical companies, but also to Lone Star Steel, Acme Boot, and Fruit of the Loom.

In 1969 Heineman made a grab for B. F. Goodrich, the big Akron, Ohio, tire company. Goodrich did not want to be grabbed. An intense legal and financial battle ensued; *Forbes* invoked the names of Julius Caesar, Mao-tse Tung, and Napoleon to convey the sense of generalship, high-power strategy, and confrontation that characterized the fight. Northwest, the agressor, lost. Although they suffered some humiliation and loss of stockholder confidence, they managed to rebound in the 1970s and march on to new acquisitions. In 1970 they finally sold the C & NW railroad, which they had been trying to unload for several years. In 1976 they bought Microdot and a year later the huge Coca-Cola bottling company that serves half of California, four of the five main Hawaiian islands, and most of Nevada.

Reputation. Environmental problems at Velsicol have given Northwest a black eye, but they keep trying to position themselves as the "good guy" conglomerate. They run ads saying: "We're happy about our acquisitions, but we're not acquisition-happy," and "Sure, we've spent a lot buying companies ($575 million). But we've spent even more building companies ...."

Who owns and runs the company. "I am the antithesis of free-form management," said Ben Heineman in 1973. *Business Week* called his style one-man rule. But he gives a certain kind of autonomy to individual companies, believing in decentralization of day-to-day decisions and tight central control of goals and planning. He is the largest shareholder, with 2.2% of the stock.

In 1952 Heineman worked for Adlai Stevenson in his unsuccessful campaign for the presidency. The Northwest board is all-white, all-male.

In the public eye. Velsicol Chemical has been under fire not only for their carcinogenic Tris but for selling cattle feed con-

taminated with flame retardant PBB to Farm Bureau Services, a Michigan cooperative. One suit against them was dismissed, but they are still involved in litigation over the incident.

In Bayport, Texas, former Velsicol employees have filed a $12 million damage suit contending that the company did nothing to warn them about the dangers of the pesticide Phosvel. They say they suffered muscle paralysis, nervous-system disorders, vomiting, excessive sweating, blurred vision, difficulty in swallowing, and speech and memory blocks after working with the substance. A former supervisor said that workers in his plant were dubbed "the Phosvel zombies" because of obvious nervous afflictions: "It was a nightmare situation." The company, he said, "knew people were getting sick. They told me all those guys smoked marijuana. They said the guys were acid freaks."

Where they're going. The *Wall Street Journal* reported in early 1980 that they may be planning to get rid of Velsicol.

Stock performance. Northwest stock bought for $1,000 in 1970 sold for $5,636 on January 2, 1980.

Access. 6300 Sears Tower, Chicago, Illinois 60606; (312) 876-7000.

Consumer brands.

Underwear: Fruit of the Loom; Underoos; B.V.D.
Boots: Acme; Dingo; Polo; Ralph Lauren; Dan Post.
Liquor (imports): Cutty Sark, Cutty 12 Scotch whiskeys; Finlandia vodka; Mouton Cadet, Marquisat wines.
Bottled water: Arrowhead Puritas.

Fortune magazine first published their list of the 500 largest U.S. industrial corporations in 1955. Since then 185 of the companies on the original list have been bought by other companies.

RCA

Sales: $7.5 billion
Profits: $284 million
Forbes 500 rank: 48
Rank in color TV sets: 1
Rank in network TV broadcasting: 3
Rank in rental cars: 1
Founded: 1919
Employees: 118,000
Headquarters: New York, New York

What they do. "I have trouble knowing just what RCA is today," complained former RCA chairman Robert Sarnoff to business columnist Dan Dorfman in early 1980. "When I look at RCA, I see broadcasting, rent-a-cars, electronics, consumer products and finance. I'm confused."

You know that a company is one of the new breed of conglomerates, with lots of different kinds of products and services under their wings, when a former top executive of the company says he's confused about what the company is doing. What makes Robert Sarnoff's confusion even more remarkable is that it was he who started the transformation of the electronics and broadcasting empire created by his father, General David Sarnoff. Under Robert Sarnoff's reign (1966–75), RCA bought Hertz Rent-A-Car, Banquet Foods, a major producer of frozen fried chicken, Coronet rugs, and Random House, a leading book publisher. As with other modern-style conglomerates, RCA has been buying and selling companies at a rapid rate. In a period of several months in late 1979 through early 1980, RCA sold Random House to the Newhouse newspaper and magazine chain for about $70 million, bought C.I.T. Financial for more than $1 billion, and announced that they wanted to sell Banquet Foods. C.I.T. is a mini-conglomerate in their own right, operating consumer loan offices, North American Company for Life and Health Insurance, Gibson Greeting Cards, All-Steel office furniture, and Raco electrical outlet boxes.

Despite forays into other fields, RCA's main businesses are still related to electronics and their National Broadcasting Company. Much has been reported in recent years about NBC's woes as number 3 in a three-network race for top spot in the television ratings game. NBC even lured Fred Silverman, who had worked miracles in boosting the viewing audiences at ABC and CBS, to their helm. But NBC ranked last again in 1979, after Silverman had been running NBC for a year. No one should shed tears over poor NBC, which made more than $100 million in profits in 1979. NBC's "Tonight Show" is possibly the most lucrative TV show in existence, bringing in an estimated 10% of the network's profits—more profits than all of Random House. Johnny Carson, the star of the "Tonight Show" for 17 years, used his show's money-making clout to negotiate a new $5 million contract in 1980.

NBC serves 213 affiliated TV stations in the United States, reaching an estimated 99% of all homes with TV sets. NBC's radio network reaches 275 affiliated stations in the United States. The company also owns five local TV stations and four local radio stations.

RCA leads in the sales of color TV sets (selling one out of every five color TV sets bought in the country), but they face stiff competition from the Japanese imports. Most of RCA's TVs are made in the United States, though some are also manufactured in Canada, Taiwan, and Mexico. Another large chunk of RCA's business is in related electronics and communications fields. They have a global communications service and two communications satellites (a third was lost in space soon after lift-off in 1979), with three more due to be launched by 1983.

RCA spent $339 million on research and engineering in electronics in 1978, although $198 million of that sum came from the U.S. government for defense research. RCA scientists have been known to complain that the RCA labs are "mushroom factories —where they are kept in the dark, fed a lot of manure, and then are canned," but RCA used the services of 7,600 scientists, engineers, and technicians in 1978.

Though most of RCA's sales were from electronics and broadcasting, the single most profitable part of their business was in rental cars. Hertz is the undisputed leader of the car rental business, with 40% of the whole market. Avis claims they try harder, but they're still a poor number 2. Hertz is also the world's largest used car salesman, selling 60% of their rental cars after a year or two of service at their own used car lots in over 100 locations around the country.

History. RCA would perhaps never have been started if not for the paranoia of the U.S. government. In 1915 General Electric had been approached to sell the patent rights on their Alexanderson alternator for long-distance communications to the Marconi Wireless Telegraph Company, a British-owned firm. But after World War I acting secretary of the navy Franklin Delano Roosevelt strongly suggested that General Electric and their competitor, A T & T, buy out Marconi and set up a new company between them, thereby keeping this technology in American hands. The Radio Corporation of America (RCA) was incorporated in 1919, headed by General J. C. Harbord, but actually run by David Sarnoff, a 29-year-old who had never gotten past the eighth grade.

If the Navy was responsible for providing the impetus to set up RCA, David Sarnoff gets the credit for making it the huge communications network it became. Sarnoff and his family had emigrated from a dirt-poor Jewish *shtetl* in Minsk, Russia, in 1900. The family settled in the Jewish ghetto on the lower east side of Manhattan, and David hawked Yiddish newspapers at the age of nine to help his family out. Three years later, David bought a newsstand with $200 given him by a mysterious woman. (Years later Sarnoff met up with the woman again, and discovered that she had been the emissary of a rich man who gave out anonymous cash gifts to poor people.) At 15 David ran messages for a telegraph company, while he taught himself Morse code at night.

David Sarnoff, the founder and builder of RCA, and Guglielmo Marconi, inventor of wireless telegraph, got together in 1933 at the RCA transmitting center at Riverhead, Long Island. The Marconi company in America, where Sarnoff worked as a telegraph operator, was the predecessor of RCA.

He finally "hitched his wagon to the electron," as he later told his biographer, Eugene Lyons, who wrote *David Sarnoff*. He went to work as a wireless operator for Marconi. His big break came in 1912, when a very weak signal came over the experimental wireless station atop the Wanamaker building in New York: "S.S. Titanic ran into iceberg. Sinking fast." For 72 hours Sarnoff stayed at his post, laboriously copying down the names of 800 survivors of the "unsinkable" Titanic. He received a num-

His Master's Nipper

Nipper is the white fox terrier who's been listening quizzically to "His Master's Voice" coming out of the speaking horn of a victrola for almost 90 years, 28 of those years as the trademark of the Victor Talking Machine Company. When RCA bought Victor in 1929, they took little Nipper along with them.

Nipper was a real dog, the pet of British artist Francis Barraud, who painted the original oil of Nipper, "His Master's Voice," in the early 1890s. He sold a revised version to the Gramophone Corporation of Britain for 50 pounds sterling, with another 50 pounds for the copyright.

Victor acquired the North American rights to Nipper in 1901 and used him on all Victrolas and Victor records. In the 1930s and 1940s thousands of three-foot high papier mâché statues of the dog sat outside record stores. Nipper has been duplicated in plastic, china, sterling silver, bronze, cloth, paper, and cardboard; on belt buckles, beach towels, and the like.

The biggest Nipper, 25½ feet tall and weighing four tons, sits on top of the RTA Corporation (an RCA distributor) in Albany, New York. He cost $8,000 to build and erect in 1954.

Source: *Los Angeles Times*, October 30, 1978.

ber of promotions for his diligence.

When RCA took over Marconi, Sarnoff went along with the equipment. Some General Electric insiders tried to get rid of the uneducated Jewish immigrant, but Sarnoff held on. He was full of ideas about "radio music boxes" and broadcast stations, and he wrote memos about them to engineers. Westinghouse beat RCA to the first broadcast in 1920, but Sarnoff followed up with the first sports broadcast in 1921.

To broadcast the Dempsey-Carpentier boxing match from Hoboken, New Jersey, Sarnoff persuaded Roosevelt to loan him the navy's transmitter and ship it to New Jersey. He then got Marcus Loew to rig his theaters with loudspeakers to pick up the broadcast. Over 200,000 people heard the fight, which was a huge success for RCA.

Under Sarnoff's enthusiastic guidance, RCA soon began producing their own equipment (their catalog of 1922 exhibited radios costing $25.50 to $401), formed NBC in 1926, and started manufacturing records and victrolas when they bought Victor Talking Machine in 1930. General Electric and A T & T gave up their interest in RCA two years later.

By this time Sarnoff was head of RCA, and now he turned to a dream of sight and sound together. His engineers came up with the first television set, exhibited at the New York World's Fair in 1939. RCA came out with their first black and white sets for sale in 1946, for a cost of $375. Their electronic color TV followed four years later. Sarnoff was named "Father of television," although he did not invent it and rarely watched popular TV shows. His taste ran more to the Metropolitan Opera and Arturo Toscanini conducting the NBC orchestra. His six-story, 30-room townhouse had about 20 television sets, most hidden in the walls behind paintings.

General Sarnoff (he was promoted to one-star brigadier general during World War II while in communications—he never fired a gun) spent much of the 1950s speaking out against communism and wrote a pamphlet entitled "Political Offensive against World Communism." RCA built a ballistic missile early warning device for the government. By 1962 one-quarter of RCA's personnel worked on space/defense programs.

NBC, in the meantime, announced itself as the first all-color network and adopted a peacock symbol. The network was tops in advertisements and awards. The General.

(called the "Gen" by his three sons) saw an RCA radio make it to the moon with Neil Armstrong in 1968. In 1971 David Sarnoff died at the age of 80.

Under Robert's leadership, RCA took a $500 million loss when they dumped their computer business in 1971. He tried to cut costs by turning off the huge RCA neon sign above Rockefeller Center and by turning down the building heat. He moved beyond electronics into Hertz cars, Coronet rugs, and Banquet Foods. In 1975, after he accompanied his third wife, soprano Anna Moffo, on a concert tour, the RCA board asked for Robert's resignation. An RCA employee told the *Wall Street Journal*, "The General shouldn't have run RCA for so long, and his son shouldn't have run it at all." Ten months later, the man who took Robert's place, Anthony Conrad, also resigned over his failure to file income taxes for five years. (Conrad never explained this, and only after two years as a fugitive from New York did he turn himself in and pay the fine of $1,000.)

RCA's troubles continued with an embezzlement scandal by middle-level managers, the loss of a satellite, the decreased ratings of such NBC stalwarts as "Nightly News" and "Today," and the defection of four affiliate stations to ABC. But they hired Fred Silverman away from ABC, sold off Random House, and bought profitable C.I.T. Financial, the largest independent financial services firm in the country. They are waiting to see if Silverman delivers on his promise to make NBC number one by Christmas of 1980.

Reputation. RCA has been trying for a long time to get its act together. They have always been known as a "nice guy" company ill-equipped to handle itself in the tough business wars. Chairman Edgar H. Griffiths told *Business Week*, "RCA is a great technical company, it's a great innovator, but it stumbles."

What they own. RCA owns 15.8 million square feet of the 65 plants they operate in the United States and abroad. Their plants are located in Indiana, Ohio, Pennsylvania, New Jersey, Massachusetts, Illinois, California, Missouri, Arkansas, and Georgia—a total of 47 in the United States—as well as Malaysia, Taiwan, Ontario, United Kingdom, Brazil, and Mexico. They own nine TV and radio stations in New York, San

Francisco, Los Angeles, Chicago, Cleveland, and Washington, D.C. Antenna fields are located in Alaska, Florida, Louisiana, and other coastal areas. RCA owns 90 of the 1,500 Hertz offices around the country. The David Sarnoff research center occupies a 342-acre tract of land in Princeton, New Jersey.

Who owns and runs the company. Getting someone to run the store has been a big problem at RCA since the General left. Edgar H. Griffiths moved into the top slot in 1976 after Conrad resigned. Finding no one in the management ranks he wanted as his number 2, Griffiths recruited Maurice R. Valente from ITT. Valente became president of RCA in January 1980. Six months later he was fired, with Griffiths declaring bluntly and publicly that Valente's performance "didn't meet expectations." Two weeks later there was another public firing at RCA when Jane Cahill Pfeiffer was ousted as NBC chairman. She had also been a director of NBC, and her $400,000-plus pay ranked her as the highest-paid woman in U.S. business. Pfeiffer had previously spent 21 years with IBM, where her husband, Ralph A. Pfeiffer, Jr., is a senior vice-president. Griffiths, who commented freely on Valente's dismissal, had nothing to say about Pfeiffer's, but there was rampant speculation in the business press, some saying she couldn't get along with NBC program chief Silverman, others saying that Griffiths took an "intense dislike" to her.

A Broker in Companies

If you want to buy a company or sell one, call Eric Gleacher in New York at (212) 558-1964—he will put you together with a prospective seller or buyer. He may charge a stiff fee, but what's a commission, even a big one, when it gets you where you want to be—the seller of a company or the buyer of another one?

Gleacher has the contacts you need because he heads the mergers and acquisitions department of Lehman Brothers Kuhn Loeb, a major Wall Street investment banker. You can be sure he is waiting for your call, because Lehman Brothers ran a full-page advertisement in the *Wall Street Journal* listing his phone number and inviting readers to call if they were thinking of merging, acquiring, or selling out. The ad didn't even list the address of Lehman Brothers. These matters are better handled by telephone, don't you know? You wouldn't want to tip your hand to an unsuspecting company you're planning to knock off.

Now a full-page ad in the *Wall Street Journal* doesn't come cheap; it costs $36,000. But Gleacher—and his employers—obviously believe it's worth it to get their name before the restless troops out there. And that there are a lot of restless bodies is clear from the merger mania that has gripped the corporate world in the past few years.

When you run an ad, you naturally put your best foot forward. What Gleacher and Lehman Brothers did with their *Journal* space was to list the 51 transactions they helped to engineer over a 20-month period.

Lehman Brothers represented Bacardi, the rum people, when a $45 million stake in the company was acquired by Canada's Hiram Walker liquor enterprise (Canadian Club).

Lehman helped a Dutch bank, Algemene, gain control of the LaSalle National Bank of Chicago for $82 million, and then helped a Dutch insurance company, Nationale-Nederlanden, scoop up the Life Insurance Company of Georgia for $360 million.

Quite adept at helping foreign companies, Lehman assisted the Swiss company Nestlé in their $263 million acquisition of Alcon Laboratories.

Lehman did yeoman work for Hollywood's Twentieth Century-Fox, awash with all that *Star Wars* money: they brought into the studio Aspen Skiing Corporation for $49 million and Pebble Beach Corporation for $65 million.

Lehman fronted for Philip Morris in the tobacco company's $516 million purchase of 7-Up. They helped RCA dispose of their Alaska communications company for $200 million. And they helped put together one of the biggest mergers in retailing history: Skaggs Companies of Salt Lake City and American Stores of Wilmington, Delaware, a $311 million deal.

It's an impressive record. The 51 transactions completed by Lehman Brothers between January 1, 1978, and August 15, 1979, had an aggregate value of more than $6.7 billion. So if you want to be on Eric Gleacher's next buy-and-sell list, call him in New York.

Business Week said the biggest loser was Griffiths, who had previously been hailed as RCA's first efficient manager. Now he was depicted as a loner who surrounds himself with yes-men. Griffiths has been with RCA for 32 years. Born in Philadelphia, he now lives in a Philadelphia suburb and is driven 100 miles to his New York office every day.

In the public eye. In 1977 RCA threatened to close down recording studios unless unions relented on requirements that RCA considered "a financial burden"; the union granted RCA several concessions. That same year women employees won about $2 million from RCA in a sex-bias suit settlement.

RCA has supported urban renewal in Camden, New Jersey, and education programs to induce minorities to study engineering, and business. About 92 minority vendors sell $2.2 million worth of materials to RCA. About 12.5% of RCA employees are minorities, and 40% women, who occupy 17% of managerial, professional, and sales positions.

Where they're going. By 1981 RCA video-

Made in U.S.A. Foreign Owned

Many familiar names in the American marketplace are owned by foreign companies. Here's a country-by-country guide. The names preceding the U.S. products and services are those of their foreign owners.

Anglo-Dutch
ROYAL DUTCH SHELL: **Shell** oil. UNILEVER: **Wisk, All, Breeze, Rinso** and **Drive** detergents; **Lux, Dove, Caress, Phase III** and **Lifebuoy** soaps; **Signal** mouthwash; **Aim, Close-up** and **Pepsodent** toothpastes; **Imperial, Promise** and **Autumn** margarine; **Mrs. Butterworth's** syrup; **Lawry's** seasonings; **Spatini; Lipton** teas and soups; **Wish-Bone** salad dressings; **Knox** gelatin; **Pennsylvania Dutch** noodles; **Lucky Whip** and **Final Touch.**

Belgium
DELHAIZE–LE LION: **Food Town** stores and **Alterman's** supermarkets.

Brazil
COPERSUCAR: **Hills Brothers** coffee.

France
AGACHE-WILLOT: **Korvettes** discount stores. SOCIÉTÉ BIC: **Bic** pens and lighters. GÉNÉRAL OCCIDENTALE: **Grand Union** and **Weingarten's** supermarket chains. PERNOD RICARD: **Wild Turkey** bourbon.

Hong Kong
HONG KONG SHANGHAI BANKING: **Marine Midland** banks.

Japan
MATSUSHITA: **Quasar** TV sets. BANK OF TOKYO: **California First Bank.**

Netherlands
PHILLIPS: **Magnavox** TV sets and **Norelco** appliances. AHOLD: **Bi-Lo** food stores. BRENNINKMEYER: **Ohrbach's** apparel stores. NATIONALE NETHERLANDEN: **Life Insurance Co. of Georgia.**

Norway
OLSEN, LEHMKUL FAMILIES: **Timex** watches.

Sweden
ELECTROLUX: **Eureka** vacuum cleaners.

Switzerland
HOFFMANN-LA ROCHE: **Valium** and **Librium** tranquilizers; **Pantene** hair products. NESTLÉ: **Nescafé, Taster's Choice, Decaf** and **Sunrise** instant coffees; **Libby's** canned foods; **Stouffer's** restaurants and frozen foods; **Nestea; Nestlé** chocolate bars and **Quik; L'Oreal** cosmetics; **Crosse & Blackwell** food specialities; **Maggi** soups and **Souptime.** SANDOZ: **Ovaltine.**

discs will be available to consumers. These "records" can be hooked up to home television sets to show movies at any time—from classics like *Gone with the Wind* to more recent favorites like *The Godfather*. The research center is at work on solar cells to convert sunlight to electricity, also for the home.

Stock performance. RCA stock bought for $1,000 in 1970 sold for $651 on January 2, 1980.

Major employment centers. Indianapolis, Indiana; Camden, New Jersey; Lancaster, Pennsylvania.

Access. 30 Rockefeller Plaza, New York, New York 10020; (212) 621-6000.

Consumer brands.

Televisions and radios: RCA.
Rental cars: Hertz.
Frozen foods: Banquet.
Rugs: Coronet.
Records: RCA.
Greeting cards: Gibson, Buzza, Cleo Wrap, Pleasant Thoughts, Success.
Office furniture: All-Steel.
Video cassettes and discs: SelectaVision.

United Kingdom

B.A.T: **Kool, Viceroy, Belair, Arctic Lights, Raleigh** cigarettes; **Sir Walter Raleigh** pipe tobacco; **Tube Rose** snuff; **Bugler, Target** and **Kite** roll your own tobacco; **Bloodhound, B&W** and **Red Juice** plug chewing tobacco; **Saks Fifth Avenue** and **Gimbels** department stores; **Kohl** supermarkets. BEECHAM GROUP: **Macleans** and **Aqua-Fresh** toothpaste; **Sucrets** throat lozenges; **Cling Free** fabric conditioner; **Brylcreem** hair dressing; **Massengil** disposable douches; **Calgon** water conditioner; **Vitabath** bath products; **Hold** cough drops. BRITISH PETROLEUM: **BP, Sohio** and **Boron** gasoline. W. LYONS: **Baskin-Robbins** ice cream. NORTHERN FOODS: **Bluebird** meats. WELLCOME FOUNDATION: **Empirin** compound. RECKITT & COLMAN: **French's** mustard. IMPERIAL GROUP: **Howard Johnson** foods, restaurants and hotels. UNITED BISCUIT: **Keebler** baked goods. COATS PATONS: **Coats & Clark** textiles. TOOTAL: **American Thread.** GRAND METROPOLITAN: **Lark, Chesterfield, L&M** and **Decade** cigarettes; **Alpo** dog food; **Liv-A-Snap** pet treats; **3-Minute Oats; Super Pop** popcorn. TRUST HOUSE FORTE: **Pierre Hotel** (New York); **TraveLodge** motels; **Colony Kitchens** and **Hobo Joe's** restaurants. HANSON TRUST: **Ball Park** franks.

West Germany

TENGELMANN GROUP: **A & P** supermarkets. BAYER: **Alka-Seltzer; One-A-Day** vitamins; **S.O.S.** pads; **Chocks** and **Flintstones** children's vitamins. BERTELSMANN: **Bantam** books. HUGO MANN: **Fed-Mart** department stores.

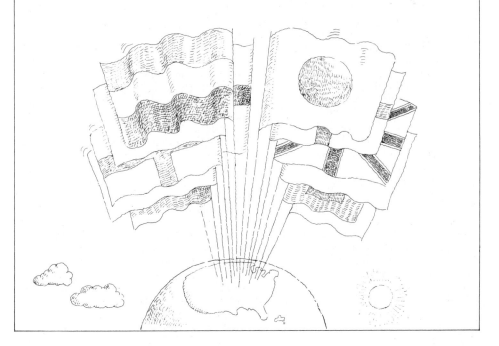

Consumer loan offices: C.I.T. Financial.
Insurance: North American.
Television stations: WNBC (New York City), KNBC (Los Angeles), WMAQ (Chicago), WKYC (Cleveland), WRC (Washington, D.C.).
Radio stations: WNBC-AM, WYNY-FM (New York City), KNBR-AM, KYUU-FM (San Francisco), WMAQ-AM, WXQX-FM (Chicago), WRC-AM, WXYS-FM (Washington, D.C.).

Sales: $11.2 billion
Profits: $570 million
Forbes 500 rank: 25
Rank in shipbuilding: 2
Rank in gas pipelines: 4
Rank in auto exhaust systems: 1
Rank in dried fruits and nuts: 1
Founded: 1943
Employees: 104,000
Headquarters: Houston, Texas

What they do. Tenneco has legal scrapes, labor troubles, and environmental problems in seven different industries. They're the youngest of the 25 biggest industrial companies in the country, but in less than 30 years they have bought more than 100 companies across the country and abroad (they do 19% of their business overseas) that provide everything from nuclear submarines and shower curtains to raisins and life insurance.

Tenneco started during World War II as the first company to build a natural gas pipeline from Texas, where they are based, to West Virginia. The company still reaps almost three-quarters of their profits from the energy business, but now they pump the gas and oil in addition to sending it through their pipelines. Most of Tenneco's oil and gas comes from the Gulf Coast, although they also drill oil in Arkansas, Oklahoma, Montana, the Dakotas, Arizona, New Mexico, Utah, Colorado, New Jersey, Georgia, California, Canada, Nigeria, and the North Sea. The 96,000 barrels of oil a day they produce are sold as Tenneco, Bay, Direct, U Fill 'em, and Red Diamond gasoline to southerners, and as home heating oil to northerners.

The Northeast is the major market for

the 1.5 billion cubic feet of natural gas that Tenneco pumps through 16,000 miles of pipelines. New York, Pennsylvania, and Massachusetts buy half their natural gas from Tenneco.

Founder Gardiner Symonds, disgusted with federal regulations on oil and gas, decided to "get into businesses where when you make a dollar you can keep it." A Tenneco ad details how Americans "spend the day" with Tenneco products. The juice you drink or the cereal you eat in the morning may come in a container made by their Packaging Corporation of America. Your car may be the one out of every three equipped with a Walker exhaust system or Monroe shock absorber. A snack of Sun Giant brand raisins or almonds is produced on the 900,000 acres of Tenneco West farmlands in California, Arizona, and Kansas. The garden tractor you use to mow the lawn could be from their J. I. Case company in Wisconsin, makers of farm and construction equipment. The plastic in your credit card could have been produced by the chemical division of Tenneco. Tenneco also operates one of the largest shipyards in the world at Newport News, Virginia, where workers overhaul cruise ships like the Queen Elizabeth II. Two-thirds of the shipyard's business is supplied by building and repairing nuclear vessels for the navy. Tenneco ranks as one of the 10 largest military contractors in the country.

History. The Tennessee Gas and Transmission Company was only two days old when the Federal Power Commission challenged them about their rates for natural gas. That's when founder Gardiner Symonds started looking for uncontrolled businesses to buy. Symonds had been put in charge of the Tennessee division of the Chicago Corporation for the purpose of constructing a 1,265-mile pipeline to connect the Gulf with the East in 1943. Just after the war Chicago sold Tennessee, and the new company became public with Symonds as president.

Symonds claimed that the biggest disappointment in his life was capable men who say "I have all I want. I want to slow down and quit." Nothing could be further from Symonds's character. He expanded the pipelines and got into chemicals in 1955. In 1961 he merged Tennessee Gas with Bay Petroleum to form Tenneco. And in 1964 he bought Packaging Corporation of America, which came with about 400,000 acres of timberlands in the South and Michigan.

Symonds's biggest coup, however, was the acquisition of the Kern County Land Company (now Tenneco West) in 1967. Some of the Kern land was first developed in the days of the Gold Rush, when two Kentucky lawyers, Lloyd Tevis and James Ben Ali Haggin, bought up California scrubland to sell to forty-niners. Irrigation later made the formerly arid land into a lush garden of alfalfa, barley, cotton, potatoes, asparagus, beans, and fruit.

Besides the 2.5 million acres of farmland with oil underneath some of the California acreage, Kern also contributed two manufacturers from Racine, Wisconsin: J. I. Case farm and construction equipment company, founded in 1842 by Jerome Increase Case, and Walker Manufacturing, makers of auto exhaust systems.

Obviously Tenneco had plenty at this point, but Symonds did not want to slow down and quit. One year after the Kern purchase he bought Newport News Shipbuilding of Virginia, a huge shipyard founded in 1886 by railroad magnate Collis Porter Huntington.

In 1971 Symonds died while he was still Tenneco's chairman, but his expansion policies have lived on after him. Tenneco includes more than 300 companies today, including Monroe shock absorbers of Michigan and Philadelphia Life Insurance.

Reputation. A company with an insatiable appetite for other companies and one that's in constant hot water with authorities. During the past five years they have been the targets of complaints by the U.S. Navy, the Justice Department, the Federal Power Commission, the Federal Trade Commission, the Federal Energy Regulatory Commission, OSHA, the Securities and Exchange Commission, and the Environmental Protection Agency.

What they own. Tenneco's plants, equipment, and property are worth $9 billion. They include 16,000 miles of natural gas pipeline, 700,000 acres of developed oil and gas land, and almost 4 million untapped acres. Tenneco owns 15,000 oil and gas wells, mostly in the United States, plus 419,000 acres of timberland in the South and in Michigan, as well as 860,000 acres of farmland in California, Arizona, and Kansas. The Newport News Shipyard sits on

475 acres in Virginia.

They own 150 factories in Britain, Canada, Italy, Australia, and about 11 other foreign countries, as well as the United States. They include 22 machinery plants, 37 auto parts factories, 49 chemical plants, and 50 packaging plants. Their 375 retail outlets for machinery are located in 141 countries.

Who owns and runs the company. About 6% of Tenneco's stock is owned by an employee savings plan managed by the Republic National Bank of Dallas. All the directors and officers together own less than four-tenths of 1% of the shares. The lone female director is Barbara Cox Anthony, also a director of Cox Broadcasting. In 1979 J. L. Ketelson, chairman, owned 21,900 shares worth about $800,000. He sits on the board of J. P. Morgan. In 1980 Peter T. Flawn, president of the University of Texas at Austin, was named to the Tenneco board.

In the public eye. An interviewer once asked Gardiner Symonds how he made decisions. He replied, "You just say, 'Get with it,' or 'Do it.'" Tenneco still "does it", often objecting to government regulation in the process. Consequently, the company has a history of run-ins with the law that extend back to their original clash over rates in 1943.

In 1977 a National Council of Churches group that owned $350,000 worth of Tenneco stock questioned the company's purchase of huge land tracts and policy of subleasing state lands to small farmers. The church group also brought up the California Labor Relations Board accusations against Tenneco for harassing United Farmworkers organizers during union elections.

Tenneco has also been accused of thwarting organizers at the Newport News shipyard. The United Steelworkers now represent the 16,500 workers at the yard after a three-year struggle with Tenneco that included a three-month strike in 1979 and a National Labor Relations Board election.

The Occupational Health and Safety Administration fined the Newport News yard $786,190 for 617 health and safety violations, including 54 willful violations, in the biggest case OSHA ever filed. Tenneco was cited for noise; deficiencies in medical programs; and exposing workers to high levels of lead, asbestos, silica, and other toxic substances. OSHA had previously cited and fined Tenneco for an explosion at their Chalmette, Louisiana, refinery that killed 13 workers in 1976.

Tenneco points out in their annual report that they support the cultural life of their hometown by sponsorship of the Houston Pops Orchestra summer concerts and the Houston Grand Opera. They also gave $1 million in 1978 to education, $100,-000 of which went to children of employees for college.

Stock performance. Tenneco stock bought for $1,000 in 1970 sold for $1,676 on January 2, 1980.

Major employment centers. Racine, Wisconsin; Newport News, Virginia; and Monroe, Michigan.

Access. Tenneco Building, Houston, Texas 77002; (713) 757-2131. Complaints may be sent to Ms. Virginia Vaughn, consumer affairs manager, (713) 757-4037.

Consumer brands.

Gasoline: Tenneco; Bay; Direct; U Fill 'em; Red Diamond.
Farm equipment: Case tractors.
Auto parts: Walker mufflers; Monroe shock absorbers; Mechanex; Speedy Muffler King.
Dried fruits and nuts: Sun Giant.
Insurance: Philadelphia Life.

⊤ Transamerica

Sales: $4.0 billion
Profits: $239 million
Forbes 500 rank: 111
Rank in rental cars: 3
Rank in charter airlines: 1
Founded: 1928
Employees: 27,100
Headquarters: San Francisco, California

What they do. After you've owned the world's largest bank, it's hard to get people to pay attention to an encore. Transamerica, a San Francisco holding company, started life as the parent of Bank of America, but government antitrust action forced them out of banking in the 1950s. Ever since they have lived—literally and figuratively—in the shadow of what was once their largest holding. But now after 20 years under the leadership of John R. Beckett, they have taken their place in the front ranks of conglomerates. The trouble is, no one knows who they are.

Transamerica comprises 10 major companies and many smaller ones. The largest, accounting for about 40% of their business, is Occidental Life Insurance, a Los Angeles company that ranks ninth in the life insurance industry in terms of the face value of

THE 10 LARGEST TAKEOVERS OF ALL TIME

	Bought By	Price	Year
1. BELRIDGE OIL	SHELL OIL	$3.65 *billion*	1979
2. TEXAS PACIFIC OIL	SUN COMPANY	$2.3 *billion*	1980
3. UTAH INTERNATIONAL	GENERAL ELECTRIC	$2.17 *billion*	1976
4. CIT FINANCIAL	RCA	$1.35 *billion*	1980
5. RELIANCE ELECTRIC	EXXON	$1.17 *billion*	1979
6. MARCOR	MOBIL	$900 *million*	1976
7. BODCAW	INTERNATIONAL PAPER	$805 *million*	1979
8. GENERAL CRUDE OIL	MOBIL	$763 *million*	1979
9. STUDEBAKER WORTHINGTON	McGRAW-EDISON	$723 *million*	1979
10. BABCOCK & WILCOX	McDERMOTT	$687 *million*	1977

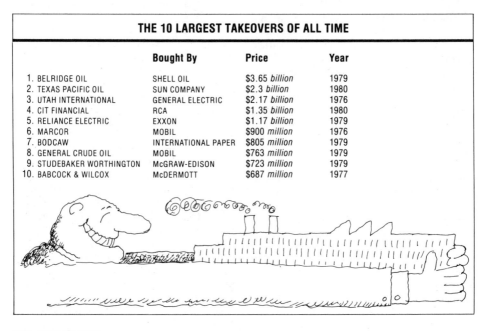

all their insurance policies. Occidental writes 34% of their insurance in California. They are heavy in term insurance (insurance that doesn't build up cash value).

The best known Transamerica company is United Artists, the film company founded in 1919 by Douglas Fairbanks, Sr., Mary Pickford, Charlie Chaplin, and D. W. Griffith. Unlike other movie companies, United Artists has no studios or stars under contract. However, as financial backer and distributor for films made by independent producers, United Artists has had such box office hits as *Annie Hall, Coming Home, Rocky,* and *Apocalypse Now.*

In transportation they own TransInternational Airlines, the world's largest charter carrier; Budget Rent a Car, the country's third-largest car rental firm; and a major moving company, Lyon Van & Storage. Pacific Finance Loans operates 504 loan offices in 23 states.

Transamerica's corporate staff, secretaries and all, numbers around 100. They have little to do with the day-to-day management of their many companies, acting mainly as bankers and management consultants to the subsidiaries, shuffling funds around to where they can be invested most profitably, giving advice, and watching the subsidiaries to see that they don't pull any surprises that would impair the overall financial performance.

History. Although they have long been a power in the financial world, Transamerica has never been popular on Wall Street. Founded in 1928 by A. P. Giannini as the holding company for his growing empire of western banks, including the Bank of America, Transamerica spent their first 25 years fighting a constant battle with jealous rivals on Wall Street and government regulators concerned about their near monopoly of western banking. In 1931 Giannini retired from Transamerica, leaving his banks in the hands of Elisha Walker, a Wall Street investment banker whom he had groomed as crown prince. No sooner had Walker taken over than he repudiated Giannini's policies and tried to break up the empire. Giannini fought back, finally ousting Walker in a furious proxy battle at the 1932 annual meeting.

Washington proved a more difficult opponent. In 1937, to appease their critics, Transamerica sold off 58% of Bank of America, but this was a cosmetic action at best since their people still controlled the board. Both the Securities and Exchange Commission and the Federal Reserve Board launched campaigns against Transamerica, which at the end of World War II controlled, through their holdings, 39% of the bank deposits and 50% of the bank loans in California, Oregon, Washington, Nevada, and Arizona. In the early 1950s they disposed of the last of their Bank of America holdings. But this still wasn't enough for Washington. In 1956 Congress passed the Bank Holding Company Act, forbidding bank holding companies from engaging in nonbank operations. (This act was passed specifically to foil Transamerica.) Faced with the choice of selling either their banks or their other operations, including Occidental Insurance, Transamerica decided to dispose of the banks, thus forming what is now Western Bancorporation, a holding company that owns 22 banks with 791 branches in 11 western states.

The task of re-creating Transamerica fell to John Beckett, a quiet San Francisco investment banker who was hired as president in 1960. In the 1960s, using Occidental as his base, he bought a clutch of companies, transforming Transamerica from an insurance holding company into a holding company for various kinds of businesses, most of them in the service field.

Reputation. Conglomerates tend to have a racy image—but not Transamerica. They're conservative operators, almost stuffy. Profiling the company in 1979, *Forbes* said: "Bland is beautiful."

What they own. Transamerica Delaval, their only manufacturing subsidiary, makes turbines, compressors, pumps, and condensers at 10 plants they own in New Jersey, California, Texas, Connecticut, Ohio, and West Virginia. Transamerica also owns the 17-story United Artists building in New York; the 32-story Occidental Center in Los Angeles; and their 48-story corporate headquarters in San Francisco, a spindly-legged, pointy-headed white pyramid that caused a furor before, during, and after its construction in 1970.

Who owns and runs the company. For 20 years, from 1960 to 1980, there has never been much doubt that Jack Beckett is the man in charge. For most of that time he held the titles of both chairman and president. At the end of 1979 he relinquished the president's position to James R. Harvey, one of his two executive vice-presidents, who has been with Transamerica since 1965. Beckett, who turned 62 in 1980, once said he believes in "running a business in a very orderly fashion, in which no one person dominates any part of it." He added: "The way we run things would carry us forward equally well in whatever business we are in." This orderliness was ruffled in 1978 when United Artists tried to leave the nest and aired their squabbles in the pages of *Fortune.*

The quarrel, as in most families, was about money. Arthur Krim and Robert Benjamin, the United Artist executives who originally sold the company to Transamerica in 1967, had been happy to have the strong backing of Transamerica in 1970 when they put big money into a series of films that went bust at the box office. But in the middle 1970s United Artists came up with a string of winners: *One Flew over the Cuckoo's Nest, Rocky,* and *Coming Home.* At a "pure" film company blockbuster movies send the company's stock soaring and line the pockets of the executives; at United Artists the loot ends up in the Transamerica

treasury. Krim and Benjamin were unhappy they weren't getting the payoff from their good movie judgment. They also resented the financial and management controls Transamerica had imposed after the 1970 debacle. For example, when United Artists' West Coast producer wanted a Mercedes, just like everybody else in Hollywood, corporate guidelines said he was only entitled to a Ford. Deciding that they didn't like life in the conglomerate, Krim and Benjamin decided to pull United Artists out of Transamerica.

But Transamerica, naturally, was not about to drop one of their best companies. "In successful times," Beckett told *Fortune* in 1978, "every company we've got wants to be off by themselves. That's life. And if the people at United Artists don't like it, they can quit and go off on their own." Within a week, Krim and Benjamin took up Beckett's invitation, leaving United Artists to set up a new film company, Orion.

In the public eye. The controversy over Transamerica's "Pyramid" building enlivened discussions in San Francisco during the late 1960s and early 1970s. It became, in fact, a cause célèbre, with critics maintain-

Many San Franciscans would have preferred it if Transamerica had kept its headquarters in this three-story ornate structure on the edge of the North Beach section where many Italian families live. Instead, amid much controversy, they built this pyramid across the street—and it's now the tallest structure in the city, topping the Bank of America building by about 75 feet.

ing that the building was another step in the "Manhattanization" of the city. Beckett and Transamerica defended the obelisklike structure as a contribution to the aesthetic appearance of San Francisco. Protests caused Transamerica to scale down the height of the building. It finally came in at 853 feet, but 212 feet of that consists of a spire that rises above the top floor of the building. Without the spire, the Pyramid is the third-largest building in the city; with it, the Pyramid is the largest, topping the Bank of America building, located a few blocks away, by about 75 feet.

Time seems to have justified Jack Beckett. When the building was going up in 1971, John Pastier, then the architecture critic of the *Los Angeles Times*, called the spire a "dunce cap" and charged that Transamerica and its architect, William Pereira, was "inflicting upon San Francisco an arrogant, exhibitionistic, yet strangely mediocre building." Another architecture critic, Alan Temko, labeled it "a large and pretentious folly." But the building has now won wide acceptance in the city, and in 1977, when *New York Times* architecture critic Paul Goldberger came to look at it, he wondered what all the fuss had been about. He said the building "may be flamboyant and a little silly, but it is also the most sensible new skyscraper in this city." Jack Beckett had the last word: "Anybody who comes to San Francisco, at least, will know who we are."

Where they're going. Interviewed by *Forbes* in May 1979, Beckett said Transamerica was no longer interested in buying other companies. "If we never made another acquisition in our life, we'd have a very fine company." A month later Transamerica paid out $210 million in cash to acquire a New York–based leasing company, Interway. It reminded some people of the ad Transamerica ran in 1967. Created by the Doyle Dane Bernbach agency, the ad showed Jack Beckett explaining his company:

I run a company called Transamerica.

> Companies which dread the expense of beating off hostile takeover bids can buy a new kind of policy from Lloyds of London called "tender offer defense expense insurance."

By almost any yardstick it's one of the biggest on the Big Board . . .

So what happens when I'm introduced to a new face?

"Transamerica? Oh yes. The airline."

If we'd wanted to be known as an airline, we'd have bought one.

In 1968 Transamerica did buy an airline, Kirk Kerkorian's TransInternational Airlines, now called Transamerica Airlines.

Stock performance. Transamerica stock bought for $1,000 in 1970 sold for $677 on January 2, 1980.

Major employment centers. Los Angeles; San Francisco Bay Area; and New York metropolitan area.

Access. 600 Montgomery Street, San Francisco, California 94111; (415) 983-4000. Inquiries to Jane W. Hall (vice-president, corporate relations). The 27th floor of the Pyramid is open to the public; it features a spectacular view of San Francisco Bay.

Consumer brands.

Rental cars: Budget.
Consumer loans: Pacific Finance.
Insurance: Occidental; American Life of New York; Transamerica; Wolverine; Riverside; Premier, Automotive.
Moving: Lyon Moving & Storage.
Films: United Artists.
Airlines: Transamerica Airlines.

Sales: $9.1 billion
Profits: $326 million
Forbes 500 rank: 35
Rank in commercial aircraft engines: 1
Rank in elevators: 1
Rank in air conditioning: 1
Rank in defense contracting: 3
Founded: 1925
Employees: 198,000
Headquarters: Hartford, Connecticut

What they do. "If you hear the sound of helicopter blades overhead, watch out! It may be Harry Gray." That's a joke told in some executive suites, but a lot of corporation presidents don't find it funny. Harry Gray is the chairman of United Technologies, and he's notorious for trying to take over companies that don't want to be taken over. He likes to travel about in Sikorsky helicopters, which his company makes. He is said to keep dossiers on some 50 companies that he may be interested in buying when the time is right.

When Harry Gray came over from Litton Industries in 1971, the company was called United Aircraft. Their chief divisions were Pratt & Whitney Aircraft (airplane engines), Sikorsky Aircraft (helicopters), Hamilton Standard (aircraft parts), and Norden (electronic gear for the military). Half their sales were to the U.S. government. Gray set out to reduce their dependence on the Pentagon and the volatile aerospace industry. He tacked on Otis (elevators and escalators), Carrier (air conditioning), Essex (wire and cables), Dynell Electronics (ship radar), Mostek (semiconductors), and Ambac (diesel power systems and fuel-injection equipment). Aerospace now accounts for less than half their sales, and the government buys only 23% of their wares.

The company has landed, more or less, but it's been rough. The managements of Otis and Carrier put up terrific fights to keep from being taken over, but Gray prevailed. Other companies have successfully staved him off. He tried and failed to get ESB Ray-O-Vac (batteries), Signal Co. (Mack trucks), and Babcock & Wilcox (power-generating equipment, including the nuclear reactor at Three Mile Island).

Actually, United Technologies' sales to the government have declined only in relation to everything else they do; in dollar volume, the figure has grown by two-thirds since 1972. As of 1980 the company was the nation's third-largest defense contractor (after General Dynamics and McDonnell Douglas), with orders from the Pentagon totaling $2.4 billion. In April 1980, when the U.S. military launched its ill-fated mission into Iran to rescue the American hostages, the raid was called off after three of the eight Sikorsky Sea Stallion helicopters broke down.

The company's Pratt & Whitney jet engines power F-16 fighters made by General Dynamics, and their Hamilton Standard division makes parts for other military and commercial planes. Pratt & Whitney engines are also used on commercial airlines such as the Boeing 747 and the McDonnell Douglas DC-10. The company's Chemical Systems Division makes solid-fuel rocket boosters used to launch space probes such as the Voyager missions to Jupiter and Saturn.

Their Otis Elevator Company installs elevators and escalators around the world, from Atlanta's Peachtree Center to the subways of Hong Kong and Rio de Janeiro to the Abu Dhabi airport. Their Carrier Corporation supplies nearly one-third of the nation's commercial air conditioning and one-fourth of the residential market and also makes printing ink and automobile finishes. Their Essex division sells wires and cables to the Bell System and independent phone companies and makes electronic controls for Amana's microwave ovens.

History. United Aircraft was formed in the late 1920s, when an assortment of aviation companies came together through a series of mergers. Fred Rentschler had organized Pratt & Whitney, the airplane engine company, in 1925. Soon he got together with William Boeing, who was building airplanes and flying air mail and passengers, and Chance Vought, a leading airplane designer. Beginning in 1928, they formed the United Aircraft & Transport Corporation, encompassing their own companies along with Hamilton Aircraft and Standard Steel (propellers), Stearman (small planes), and several small airlines that were combined into United Air Lines. At the same time they picked up Sikorsky Aircraft to get the skills of Igor Sikorsky, who was then building amphibious planes and who had previously built the world's first four-engined military aircraft for the czar. Working for United, Sikorsky built the world's first helicopter.

The founders' idea was to build a single company that could make everything an airline needed and then run the airline. But they hit a snag in 1934 when Senator Hugo Black (later a Supreme Court justice) conducted an investigation of air-mail rates and the structure of the aviation industry in general. Fearing monopolization of the industry, Congress passed the Air Mail Act of 1934, which forced airplane builders out of the airline business. Boeing and United Air Lines were split off into separate compa-

Igor Sikorsky is at the controls of his VS-300 helicopter on September 14, 1939 on its first flight—it lifted inches off the ground. Sikorsky, who designed planes for the Russian czar, sold his company to United Aircraft in 1928.

nies. The rest of the operation remained as United Aircraft.

During World War II Pratt & Whitney made hundreds of thousands of airplane engines, supplying half the total power for U.S. planes. After the war United Aircraft moved into jet engines and then into space and missile work. For years their products had a reputation for high quality, but in the 1960s they began to run into turbulence. Their engines for the Boeing 747 jets developed problems, and they faced tough competition from General Electric. In 1971 they lost $43 million. To find a way out of their troubles, they brought in Harry Gray.

Gray was born Harry Gruson in Milledgeville Crossroads, Georgia, the son of a farmer and general storekeeper who deserted his family in the Depression. Gray's mother died when he was six, and he was about to be sent to an orphanage when an older sister who lived near Chicago agreed to take him in. He graduated from the University of Illinois, fought in the infantry and artillery in World War II, and returned to Illinois to get a master's degree in marketing. He became a supersalesman of Dodge trucks, then general manager of Greyhound's moving and storage operations, before winding up at newly founded Litton Industries in California in 1954. As Litton mushroomed into the first modern conglomerate, Gray rose quickly up the ladder from salesman to senior executive vice-president. He was the company's number 3 man when United Aircraft lured him away to become their president.

Gray was a controversial character from the time he set foot in United. It seems that six days before he accepted the job at United, Gray visited GE's Evendale, Ohio, plant where they make engines. He was a welcome visitor because Litton was a prime customer—and according to the GE folks, they gave him the red carpet treatment, showing him their long-range plans. When GE read a couple of weeks later that Gray had taken the top post at their arch competitor, they hit the ceiling, writing a letter to protest Gray's actions.

At United Aircraft Gray brushed off the GE criticism as unjustified (he had, he asserted, told GE not to reveal anything in their plans of a proprietary nature)—and began attacking the problems before him. He first smoothed out the problems with Boeing over the 747 engines and then set out to reduce the company's dependence on aerospace and the military by snapping up companies in other fields, such as Otis and Carrier. In 1974 he moved the company's headquarters from Pratt & Whitney's sprawling industrial complex in East Hartford, Connecticut, to a sleek highrise in downtown Hartford, and in 1975 he changed the company's name to United Technologies to reflect the new direction. In effect, he turned the company into a model of Litton Industries. They may not have as many divisions as Litton, but United now takes in more money.

Reputation. United Technologies is Harry Gray. He has transformed it into a company that's four times as large as the one he inherited—and in less than a decade. He's also made it quite clear that he's just beginning. He is ambition unbounded.

He's also not afraid to do things differently once in a while. In issuing the 1980 annual report, Harry Gray (remembering perhaps his Litton days) said it's time American business did something about fat, expensive annual reports, whereupon he confined the commentary in his annual report to a total of 116 words.

Who owns and runs the company. Institutional investors—banks, insurance companies, mutual funds—own about 40% of the stock. The largest holder, with 8.2%, is J. P. Morgan.

Chairman Harry Gray is well compensated for his efforts. A survey by *Business Week* and the management consultant firm of Booz, Allen & Hamilton found Gray the nation's highest-paid executive in 1976, earning $1.66 million in salary and benefits. He still earns more than $1 million a year. His capacity for hard work is legendary. In 1963, while motorcycling in the hills of California with his friend Keenan Wynn, the actor, he skidded into a guard rail, shattered his hip, and nearly lost his leg. Gray was bedridden for eight months, but he missed only two days' work: he imported files and a secretary and set up an office first in the hospital and then at his house.

In a surprise move at the end of 1979, Gray brought in a new president and chief operating officer, Alexander Haig, the former supreme allied commander of the NATO forces in Europe and the White House chief of staff in the declining days of Richard Nixon. Haig's last job in the "private sector" had been as a floorwalker in a Philadelphia department store.

In the public eye. Readers of the *Wall Street Journal* in 1979 and 1980 were treated to full-page presentations of Harry Gray's homespun philosophy. In a series of ads edited or rewritten by Gray himself, United Technologies eulogized John Wayne, urged business people to stop referring to women as "girls," pleaded for simple language and short meetings, argued against age discrimination, and defended office cut-ups who do good work. According to the company, they launched the ad campaign to make people more aware of United Technologies, whose main divisions are better known than the parent company.

Where they're going. Pratt & Whitney's share of the airplane engine market has been shrinking in recent years. As recently

General Alexander M. Haig, Jr., chief of staff in the White House in the last days of Richard M. Nixon, was installed as president of United Technologies in 1979.

as 1977 they made some 80% of all engines for commercial planes, but they have faced a stiff challenge from General Electric, and some observers think Pratt & Whitney's share will fall to 50% by 1985. Problems with their engines for the air force's F-15 and F-16 fighters led the Pentagon to give GE a contract to develop a possible alternative. Harry Gray has dismissed suggestions that GE poses a serious threat, but he replaced the head of Pratt & Whitney with an executive from Deere in 1979.

The way Gray sees it, it's GE that should be worried. He believes that by the time he retires in 1985 he will have finished laying the foundation to put United Technologies in the same league as GE or GM. After the old United Aircraft & Transport was split up in the 1930s, United people were disappointed for years that they had lost the chance to be "the General Motors of the air." Harry Gray thinks he's finally got the company back on the track. His stated goal for 1980 is sales of $20 billion.

Stock performance. United Technologies stock bought for $1,000 in 1970 sold for $2,191 on January 2, 1980.

Access. Hartford, Connecticut 06101; (203) 728-7000.

Consumer brands.

Carrier air conditioners.

16

STILL IN THE FAMILY

Sales: $6.8 billion
Profits: undisclosed
Rank in construction and engineering: 1
Founded: 1898
Employees: 31,000
Headquarters: San Francisco, California

What they do. Bechtel is America's secretive master builder. This San Francisco–based construction and engineering company, the nation's largest, has changed the face of the country. Alone or in concert with other companies they have built Hoover Dam, the San Francisco Bay Bridge, the subway systems for Washington, D.C., and the San Francisco Bay Area, and half of America's nuclear power plants. Their majestic projects are not confined to these shores. They built the 1,100-mile Trans-Arabian pipeline, the world's largest copper complex in New Guinea, and the world's largest hydroelectric project in

Labrador. But for all the grandeur of their works, Bechtel remains strangely shy. Family owned and run, Bechtel is not required to account to the Securities and Exchange Commission or to publish an annual report. The last time they disclosed their profits was in 1976, when they earned profits of $66.5 million on revenues of $4.5 billion. Within three years revenues had shot to a staggering $6.8 billion. (Although Bechtel is not required to disclose their figures, they provide some data in an annual report to employees they make available to the press.) They concentrate on becoming well known where it counts: in the corridors of power here and abroad, where governments hand out the billion-dollar contracts that are Bechtel's lifeblood.

Bechtel generally disdains such child's play as building skyscrapers and highways, preferring colossal projects, particularly in the energy field. About half their business comes from constructing power plants, nuclear and conventional, in the United States and in developing countries such as South Korea. Bechtel built the first commercial nuclear power plant in 1958 in Dresden, Illinois. They also have the distinction of being the first company to rehabilitate a nuclear power plant after an accident: they received the contract to clean up Three Mile Island at an estimated cost of $400 million over four years. In addition, Bechtel builds refineries, chemical plants, dams, mining complexes, and pipelines for oil, gas, and slurried coal.

But Bechtel has been turning to even bigger jobs. As the shrinking demand for energy has slowed the pace of power-plant construction in the United States, Bechtel has aggressively courted the leaders of oil-producing states, seeking not just to build a plant here or there but to plan and construct entire industrial complexes and cities. With a permanent engineering staff of 13,000, Bechtel is one of the few companies in the world capable of designing and overseeing the construction of Jubail—an entire city Bechtel is raising in Saudi Arabia. In the largest single construction project in history, they will create an industrial city of 300,000 persons where there are now no roads, water, power, or laborers, only the shifting sands of the Arabian desert. The eventual price tag on the project, which will take 20 years, is estimated at $55 billion.

History. Bechtel's success has been closely tied to the growth and power of big government in the United States. The company began in 1898, when Warren A. Bechtel left his Kansas ranch and hired out with his mule team to grade a stretch of railroad in Oklahoma. Bechtel followed the rails to Oakland, California, where he continued contracting for railroad construction and added new projects like irrigation canals, highways, and pipelines. Bechtel's three sons, Warren, Jr., Steve, and Kenneth, grew up among tractors and steam shovels; in their early twenties they were running field projects.

By the time they incorporated the company in 1925, Bechtel was one of the biggest construction outfits in the West. In 1931 a consortium of six companies organized by Bechtel won the contract to build Hoover Dam, the biggest in history. More huge projects followed: another dam on the Colorado River, Bonneville Dam on the Columbia, and the foundations for the San Francisco Bay Bridge. Warren Bechtel died in 1933, but his son Steve expanded the business and had it ready when World War II brought a flood of contracts. The most important jobs

Fratricide

Brothers who go into business together don't always remain each other's keepers. The following cases will sober the overconfident or sentimental.

The Dasslers

Adidas athletic shoes originated in a tiny Bavarian mill town, Herzogenaurach, not far from Nurnberg. Before World War II two brothers, Adolf and Rudolf Dassler, sons of a poor laundress, started a factory to make house slippers and then branched out to track shoes and soccer boots. They had a violent falling out and after the war went their separate ways—in the same small town. Rudolf Dassler started a rival athletic shoe company, Puma, and before long Adidas

and Puma were battling head-to-head all over the world. Both companies are still headquartered in Herzogenaurach. When Adolf died in 1978, the two brothers had not spoken to each other for 29 years. Adolf's only son, Horst Dassler, who had gone to France to run the French subsidiary 18 years earlier (after a family disagreement), returned to Adidas headquarters after his father's death.

The Revsons

Revlon, the cosmetics firm, was founded in 1932 by Charles Revson, his older brother, Joseph, and Charles Lachman. A younger brother, Martin Revson, later joined the firm. But it was Charles who led Revlon's drive to the

top. Joseph left the company in 1955 because he didn't think Revlon should go public; he sold all his stock to the company for $2.5 million. (Had he waited four years, the stock would have been worth $35 million.) Martin left in 1959 after bitter fights with his older brother. He sued the company, charging that his brother, Charles Revson, "engaged in a practice of mistreating executives and abusing them personally." The brothers didn't speak to one another for 13 years. "What brother?" Charles once said. "I don't have a brother."

The Mondavis

Cesar Mondavi bought the Charles Krug winery in California's Napa Valley in 1943.

The Bechtel boys: rancher Warren A. Bechtel, who started a railroad construction company in 1898, is shown here with his three sons—Steve, Kenneth and Warren Jr.

were building and operating huge shipyards in Los Angeles and Sausalito, California, where Bechtel turned out Liberty Ships. Between the two locations they turned out almost 600 ships for the war effort. According to one government document, the Los Angeles shipyards alone generated a profit of $44 million on an investment of $100,000.

After the war Bechtel followed the government into new areas. Benefiting from America's new role as the dominant power in the Middle East, Bechtel began an extensive involvement in that region when they landed the contract to build the Trans-Arabian pipeline. Bechtel also built the first

In the post–World War II years they became a leading maker of premium wines under the Krug label, and they also put out a line of popular wines under the C. K. Mondavi label. Cesar's two sons, Robert and Peter, went into the family wine business. After the death of Cesar the winery continued under the leadership of his widow, Rosa, and the two sons. But the brothers had a violent falling out that included fisticuffs. Robert Mondavi left and, under the sponsorship of the Rainier Brewing company, established his own winery down the road from Krug. After the death of Rosa Mondavi the feud continued, erupting into a court battle that threatened to undo the Charles Krug winery. The dispute was eventually settled out of court, with Robert now running his own winery, Robert Mondavi Vintners, and Peter running the Charles Krug winery.

The Johnsons

Three brothers—Robert Wood Johnson, Edward Mead Johnson, and James Johnson—started a drug firm in New Brunswick, New Jersey, in 1885. The company, Johnson & Johnson, grew to become one of the leaders of the pharmaceutical industry and the world's largest surgical dressing manufacturer, thanks in great part to their invention in 1920 of the Band-Aid adhesive bandage. But the brothers had a falling out. Edward Mead Johnson left the company before the turn of the century, and in 1900 he organized the American Ferment Company to make ferments from papaya juice in Jersey City. He then sold that company to Sterling Drug (the company that eventually made it big with Bayer aspirin) and started his own firm, Mead Johnson & Co., to make infant nutrition products, notably Pablum and a long line of baby vitamins. In 1914 he moved the company to Evansville, Indiana, where they remain today, although they were acquired in 1967 by the Bristol-Myers Company, which competes head-to-head with Johnson & Johnson with a number of products.

electricity-generating nuclear plant at Arco, Idaho, in 1951, and they constructed a nuclear fuel reprocessing plant at the same site. These jobs gave them a good head start when the federal government pushed the utility companies toward nuclear power in the 1950s.

Dependent on good relations with government, Bechtel has made sure that one of the revolving doors between government and business opens into their San Francisco headquarters. John McCone, head of the Atomic Energy Commission under Eisenhower and the CIA under Kennedy, was Bechtel's partner in the World War II Liberty Ship venture. In recent years Bechtel has hired George Shultz, Nixon's secretary of the treasury; Caspar Weinberger, Nixon's secretary of health, education and welfare; Parker Hart, former ambassador to Saudi Arabia; and Richard Helms, former CIA director and ambassador to Iran. Both Steve Bechtel and his son Steve, Jr., who now runs the company, have served on many top government committees, and they have easy access to important officials in Washington. Steve, Jr., also works hard developing ties with foreign leaders, whom he frequently visits as he circles the globe 10 times each year.

Reputation. The *Wall Street Journal* com-

pared Bechtel to Greta Garbo: "What especially excites public curiosity is its own penchant for secrecy." Though Steve Bechtel, Jr., denies that he has anything to hide, the fact that such a gigantic corporation remains privately owned, coupled with the astonishing influx of ex-cabinet members and U.S. agency heads, continues to stir excitement.

"I love them," said a Saudi magnate in 1977. "There is no question about their integrity and efficiency." Even competitors acknowledge Bechtel's ability to get awesome jobs done, usually well. But despite the stunning scale of their projects and scope of their activity (116 major projects in 21 countries in 1979), Bechtel doesn't always get high marks for performance; they have been widely criticized for poor design and cost overruns on the Washington, D.C., Metro subway and the San Francisco Bay Area Rapid Transit system; and in 1975 their role in the construction of the Alaskan pipeline was curtailed. *Newsweek* reported that the Aleyska Pipeline Service Company took over as construction manager, replacing Bechtel "after deciding that Bechtel was not doing a satisfactory job." But Bechtel engineers continued to work on the pipeline.

What they own. Bechtel's 31,000 engi-

Bechtel's Jubail complex in Saudi Arabia, with refineries, a port, and residential housing for 300,000 people.

neers, planners, procurement agents, and managers work out of their home office, a San Francisco skyscraper, and 21 permanent offices located around the world in Houston, Mexico City, London, Tokyo, Beirut, Jakarta, and other cities.

Who owns and runs the company. About 40% of Bechtel's stock is owned by a family trust controlled by the two Steve Bechtels. The rest belongs to about 60 top company managers. Although these managers must sell their stock back to the firm when they retire or die, all have probably become millionaires, making them the richest group of executives of any company anywhere. And Steve, Jr., an engineer with a Stanford business degree who took over the company in 1960 at the age of 35, stands a good chance of becoming the richest man in America when he inherits total control of the family fortune.

Bechtel's in-house publications have a warm, family tone: the founder is always "Dad Bechtel" and the son and grandson who inherited the realm are simply "Steve" and "Steve, Jr." But a *Mother Jones* reporter observed that secrecy prevails inside as well as outside, with long-time employees often knowing little about their company. And a young manager complained: "No one will listen to you around here unless you're 45 or older."

A unique telephone news service for employees offers company news every day. On a typical day a caller might learn of a visiting speaker on solar energy, a seminar on tax benefits for employees overseas, and space available on a weekend riverboat trip. The number is (415) 768-NEWS.

In the public eye. What is special about Bechtel is how much they are *not* in the public eye. In 1978 Mark Dowie of *Mother Jones* magazine was stonewalled by Bechtel's public relations department—meaning they refused to cooperate in any way with research for a major article on the company. Dowie emphasized the importance of subjecting such a company to public scrutiny: "If Bechtel manufactured musical instruments or beer, its complete lack of public accountability would not be so alarming. But a company that has designed or built almost half of our nuclear power plants, traded technological information with the Soviet Union and written three major sections of the Ford Administration's energy

plan must . . . be able to stand the light of day." Dowie offered his article as a stand-in for the company's nonexistent annual report. He compared Bechtel to a sovereign state whose annual sales often exceed the gross national products of the developing countries it contracts with: "Dealings on every level take on an ambassadorial tone: contracts sound like treaties, salesmen act like diplomats and meetings between Steve Bechtel, Jr., and the Chief of State resemble summit conferences." Bechtel issued a point-by-point rebuttal of the *Mother Jones* article to their employees, explaining that they refused to cooperate with the writer "because that magazine was clearly governed by its preconceptions."

Bechtel has recently been embarrassed by the display of some of their soiled laundry in court. In 1972 a female employee filed a class-action suit against Bechtel for sex discrimination in job assignments and promotion; the company settled out of court by paying $1.4 million in damages to 5,400 past and 2,300 current employees. Four hundred black employees subsequently filed a race discrimination suit. Bechtel was sued in 1978 by the directors of Consumer Power in Michigan when the Palisades nuclear power plant they had built broke down shortly after it opened. The company eventually settled this suit for $14 million. Bechtel was also charged in 1976 with refusing to deal with American subcontractors who were on the Arab blacklist of firms that do business with Israel. Bechtel denied the charge but the next year agreed with the government that they would not sign contracts with a boycott clause.

Where they're going. In the energy crisis Bechtel plans to play both sides of the street. While they help the oil-rich nations spend their loot by building cities and industrial complexes, Bechtel is eyeing the possibility of constructing synthetic-fuel plants in the United States and hydroelectric stations in Africa and Latin America, projects made necessary by the soaring cost of OPEC oil.

In 1979 Bechtel opened a Beijing office to accommodate "increasing activity" in relation to work prospects in China.

Access. 50 Beale Street, San Francisco, California 94105; (415) 768-1234.

♔ Hallmark Cards

Sales: $850 million
Profits: not public
Rank in greeting cards: 1
Founded: 1910
Employees: 10,000
Headquarters: Kansas City, Missouri

What they do. Hallmark is America's largest "social expression" company. That's their way of saying greeting cards, wrapping paper and ribbon, keepsake albums, crystal and pewter figurines, commemorative plates, diaries, novel bath products, party accessories, calendars, Christmas tree ornaments, gift books, and jewelry. What these products have in common, says a vice-president for creative services, is that "they all communicate special feelings."

Hallmark is best known for greeting cards, which provide 60% of their business. One out of every four times an American cares enough to send a card, she picks Hallmark. (An estimated 85% of the clientele are female.) The company turns out 10 million cards a day, in 17 languages. They have the largest force of artists (300–400) employed under one roof. Each year they produce Christmas cards in 1,700 designs (1,000 new and 700 "best-sellers").

A Hallmark Christmas card takes two years to prepare, in an intricate process that starts with sorting into price and "sending situation" (for example, "75 cents/wife"). The embryo greeting then gets a design selected from dozens constantly being roughed out by artists. An editor adds a "sentiment." Many more decisions and crisscrossing hierarchical consultations take place before the card is sent off for production and injected into the U.S. market, where 3 billion Christmas cards and 4 billion other greeting cards are sold each year. Nearly a billion of the total number sold bear the Hallmark five-pointed crown.

One of the few large privately owned companies in the United States, Hallmark doesn't have to disclose financial details, but a *TWA Ambassador* article in late 1979 said annual sales were "steadily approaching a billion dollars." Although they are the only card company most people know by name, they spend only about $15 million a year on

Joyce Hall, who founded his greeting card business at age 19 in 1910 and was still chairman of the company in 1980.

advertising. Most of that goes to sponsoring the five yearly "Hallmark Hall of Fame" TV shows. These 90-minute dramas, based on important literary works and featuring distinguished actors, have been praised as "an oasis in television's wasteland." The shows have gained only mediocre ratings (the figures that tell how many people are watching), but the company insists they will continue to sponsor them. The Hall of Fame is aimed less at selling cards than at promoting Hallmark as a name of quality.

Hallmark is engaged in a 20-year, $400 million real estate venture at their home base in Kansas City. Corporate headquarters is already located at Crown Center, but the project involves much more. When completed in the mid 1980s, Crown Center will occupy 21 square blocks and will include office buildings, apartment houses, a bank, a large plaza, 65 stores, and a 730-room hotel. The Center has won praise for its architectural design and is said to have provided the spark for a project to revive the city's decaying downtown area. "But most important," said the *Wall Street Journal*, "is the fact that Hallmark officials concede that Crown Center, with its attention to detail, will take twice as long to become profitable as most large real estate developments." A president of a large publicly owned company and a friend of the Hall family commented, "Everything is absolutely first class as you'd expect of Hallmark. But if I proposed anything like Crown Center to my directors, they'd probably fire me."

The Hallmark Gallery in New York is another monument to the Halls' almost aristocratic sense of pride, dignity, and beauty and their conviction that there should be more to business than making a profit. Designed by noted architect Edward Durell Stone, the elegant gallery has offered free to the public six exhibitions a year since its opening in 1963. These have included Carl Sandburg memorabilia, photography, kite making, and neon art. The

---

AMERICA'S 50 LARGEST PRIVATE COMPANIES*

Estimated Sales (1979)

CARGILL (grain wholesaling)	$12.7 billion
MOCATTA METALS (bullion dealers)	$12.0 billion
CONTINENTAL GRAIN (grain wholesaling)	$ 7.8 billion
BECHTEL GROUP (engineering services)	$ 6.8 billion
KOCH INDUSTRIES (crude oil)	$ 3.8 billion
INGRAM (petroleum marketing)	$ 3.5 billion
UNITED PARCEL SERVICE (package delivery)	$ 3.4 billion
KEN DAVIS INDUSTRIES	$ 2.0 billion
HUGHES AIRCRAFT (aerospace)	$ 2.0 billion
PUBLIX SUPER MARKETS (food retailing)	$ 1.9 billion
GARNAC GRAIN (grain exporting)	$ 1.7 billion
LOUIS DREYFUS (grain exporting)	$ 1.5 billion
THE AUSTIN CO. (engineering services)	$ 1.5 billion
MARS (candy)	$ 1.4 billion
DUBUQUE PACKING (meat packing)	$ 1.4 billion
CARLSON COMPANIES (trading stamps, hotels)	$ 1.4 billion
CITY TITLE INSURANCE (title insurance)	$ 1.4 billion
SUMMA (hotels, casinos)	$ 1.3 billion
MILLIKEN (textiles)	$ 1.3 billion
NEWHOUSE (publishing)	$ 1.2 billion
SC JOHNSON (polishes)	$ 1.2 billion
STEPHENS (department stores)	$ 1.2 billion
PEABODY COAL (coal)	$ 1.1 billion
TRIBUNE CO (communications)	$ 1.1 billion
PETER KIEWIT & SONS (heavy construction)	$ 1.0 billion
FARR MAN (commodity trading)	$ 1.0 billion
READER'S DIGEST ASSOCIATION (periodicals)	$ 1.0 billion
BELK BROTHERS (department stores)	$ 1.0 billion
GATES RUBBER (rubber products)	$962 million
MOBAY CHEMICAL (chemicals)	$955 million
SCURLOCK OIL (petroleum wholesaling)	$905 million
HE BUTT GROCERY (groceries)	$900 million
HALLMARK CARDS (greeting cards)	$850 million
TOPCO ASSOCIATED (retail groceries)	$802 million
GUY F. ATKINSON (engineering services)	$798 million
PEAT, MARWICK (accounting)	$775 million
THE ANDERSONS (agricultural commodities)	$774 million
GREENWICH MILLS (coffee)	$759 million
HUNT OIL (oil/gas production/refining)	$745 million
ROSEBURG LUMBER (softwood, veneers)	$719 million
COOPERS & LYBRAND (accounting)	$711 million
SPARTAN STORES (grocery wholesaling)	$702 million
MEIJER (grocery stores)	$695 million
HY-VEE FOOD STORES (groceries)	$683 million
ARTHUR YOUNG (accounting)	$650 million
ARTHUR ANDERSEN (accounting)	$645 million
PRICE WATERHOUSE (accounting)	$635 million
SOUTHWIRE (electrical wire)	$632 million
AMERICAN SECURITIES (securities)	$624 million
AMWAY (cleaning products)	$600 million

*Companies that do not sell their stock to the public. This table does not include privately owned financial companies (such as Morgan Stanley or Lazard Frères), cooperatives, or foreign-owned companies.

Source: Forbes, June 23, 1980, based on data compiled by Economic Information Systems.

gallery director, Walter Swartz, confesses to doubting that the 3 million visitors to the exhibits have contributed much to Hallmark sales.

But founder Joyce Hall says, "Good taste is good business." It was he who coined the famous slogan, "When you care enough to send the very best."

History. Joyce Hall (89 years old in 1980) started working at the age of 9 in a Norfolk, Nebraska, bookstore, to help support his mother, sister, and brothers. One of the things he sold was picture postcards. Imported from Germany and England, the cards had become a fad at the turn of the century. Greeting cards as we know them today didn't exist; there were only postcards and elaborate, prohibitively expensive valentines and engraved Christmas cards.

Joyce Hall quit school at 15 and a few years later went to Kansas City to seek his fortune. In 1910 he started a wholesale business in postcards, engraved Christmas cards, and valentines. His older brother, Rollie, joined him in 1911, and they began selling greeting cards made by another firm. Within five years they had bought an engraving company and were making their own greeting cards. The first two Hallmark cards went on the market in November 1915.

A third brother, William, joined the firm in 1921. They expanded their operations in Kansas, Oklahoma, Nebraska, and Missouri, and adopted the Hallmark brand name in 1923. In 1926 they introduced decorative gift wrap and ribbon to replace the brown wrapping paper and plain red and green tissue then commonly used.

After World War II Hallmark entered a period of explosive growth, largely based, according to the *Wall Street Journal,* on Joyce Hall's innovations and on "his near-obsession with promoting an image of quality." Besides developing a variety of gift products, Hall devised new display racks for greeting cards, which until the 1950s had been sold from drawers. The racks not only helped customers to choose but also helped stores to reorder.

In 1954 Hall Bros. became Hallmark, and in 1958 they went international. Hallmark products are now sold in 100 countries. There are 6,000 independent Hallmark shops, which account for nearly half of the company's sales. The rest come from 30,000

greeting card sections in department, grocery, and stationery stores.

Reputation. The "Hallmark Hall of Fame," Crown Center, and Hallmark Gallery have earned the company much praise and respect. Even Dugald Stermer—a leading graphic artist who has done covers for *Time* and who helped design muckraking *Ramparts* magazine—was impressed when he researched a story on the company for *Communications Arts* magazine in 1975. Because writers and artists usually speak of the greeting card industry with contempt, some employees hesitated to talk with Stermer, thinking he'd just write "another smart ass piece." But Stermer reported that he'd "caught" the contagious enthusiasm and enjoyment that he'd found at Hallmark, and he wasn't going to give it "smart ass" treatment.

Although Stermer's article (containing many reproductions of Hallmark cards through the years) is generally friendly, it does rap the company for "computerized cuteness and incredibly sanitized affection." An unabashed trafficker in sentiment, Hallmark says their job is to follow public taste, not prescribe it. "Our market," comments a vice-president (in a considerable understatement), "is not avant-garde. We are living in an age of pronounced sentimentalism."

What they own. Hallmark has three manufacturing centers in Kansas and one in Missouri. Of the 6,000 Hallmark retail outlets, they own only 18, which are used primarily for test-marketing.

Who owns and runs the company. In 1975 the Hall family began selling their stockholdings to the employee profit-sharing trust, explaining that they wanted all Hallmark people "to participate in the ownership of the company." By 1980 the trust held 25% of the stock; the rest was still in the hands of the Hall family members. Joyce Hall, still chairman but semiretired since 1966, has been described as shy and self-effacing. Far from fancying a corporate jet, he drove to the office during the 1970s in his 1963 Buick. Joyce Hall's only son, Donald, has taken on the presidency and the major responsibilities of running the company.

Access. 2501 McGee, Kansas City, Missouri 64108; (816) 274-5111. Tours can be arranged by writing, or by calling (816) 274-5672.

Consumer brands.

Greeting cards: Hallmark, Ambassador.
Costume jewelry: Trifari, Accents.
Crystal and pewter figurines, gifts: Little Gallery.

Sales: $1.2 billion
Profits: not public
Rank in floor-care products: 1
Rank in furniture-care products: 1
Rank in hair conditioners: 1
Employees: 11,800
Founded: 1886
Headquarters: Racine, Wisconsin

What they do. S. C. Johnson (better known as Johnson Wax) is a little like the well-intentioned but traditional suburban husband who one day finds that the "little woman" has gone off and enrolled at the local college or obtained a job. The country's top maker of nonlaundry household products—floor waxes, rug cleaners, furniture polishes, air fresheners, and insect repellents—learned the hard way that the modern woman is no longer wringing her hands about "waxy yellow build-up." The company notes stiffly that as women become more involved in activities outside the home, they become less concerned with "fastidious housekeeping."

As if the women's movement weren't bad enough news for this company that holds 60% of the household market, the new easy-to-care-for vinyl floors, synthetics like Corfam in shoes, super enamels on cars, and plastic surfaces on furniture just don't need much spit, polish, or elbow grease. Growth in household products has been sluggish.

Wisconsin-based Johnson Wax, by applying a generous coating of midwestern common sense and perseverance, is coping with the situation. In 1971 they created Johnson Diversified, which began buying small recreation-equipment companies. By 1979 the new division, now called Johnson Wax Associates, owned 15 firms making kayaks, scuba gear, tents, fishing rods, and other hiking and camping equipment. Johnson is now one of the top names in the outdoor recreation field.

But for the leading household products company, the venture into unknown territory hasn't always been easy. One of the largest privately owned companies in the country, Johnson has had their share of flops. First there was the paint business in the 1950s—never could turn a respectable profit. Then came the line of antifreeze, radiator cleaners, and car lubricants: a wipe-out. Next were industrial chemicals, a lawn-care enterprise, and finally, in the mid-1960s, an unsuccessful foray into the car-wash business. Those flings now over, it seems that Johnson Wax has found their proper place once more with the lady of the house—bringing her "personal care" items along with wax and rug cleaners.

Even here, Johnson has had trouble figuring out what women really want. Most at home in the lab mixing up pastes and waxes and concocting roach killers, the Johnson chemists were out of their element trying to come up with a perky fragrance or a jaunty little something to intrigue or delight the female buyer. After succeeding with Edge, the first shaving gel for men, Johnson tried a more fragrant version for women: Crazy Legs. Then they put out a unisex deodorant: Us. Both were miserable failures.

But Samuel C. Johnson, great-grandson of the founder, was not deterred by those bombs in the early 1970s. Johnson is a balding, easygoing man who has been known to stay up all night playing chess. He has a small-town, folksy way of talking, so that people are sometimes surprised to hear he's a Harvard Business School graduate. Johnson decided to do in the personal care field what they had traditionally done with household products: heavy market research. Agree, their successful creme rinse

and hair conditioner, was tested for 18 months with more than 2,000 women; the next stage was a nine-month test-marketing program in four cities. Finally Johnson figured they had something women really wanted: a conditioner that "helps stop the greasies," as the ads later said. The $14 million advertising campaign for Agree included TV, magazines, and 30 million samples. It was a stunning success: in its first year Agree became the number 1 hair conditioner.

In 1978, a year after they blitzed the market with Agree hair conditioner, Johnson brought out Agree shampoo. Again there were streamroller advertising and heavy free sampling (60% of the households in the country in an "initial mailing"). Hoping to capture 2% of the market in the first year, they climbed to 6%, only slightly behind Procter & Gamble's Head & Shoulders, Revlon's Flex, and Johnson & Johnson's Baby Shampoo.

History. It is fitting that Johnson's emer-

S.C. Johnson calls this their "Great Workroom," of their administration center in Racine, Wisconsin. The chairs and desks were designed by the architect, Frank Lloyd Wright. Employees call the pillars which support the building's roof "golf tees."

A rare look into the holdings of the Rockefeller family was provided in 1974 during congressional hearings on the nomination of Nelson Rockefeller as vice president of the United States. J. Richardson Dilworth, the family's financial adviser, disclosed then that the total value of the family's investments (both those owned outright and those held in trusts) came to a little over $1 billion. The following were the major stockholdings of the 84 members of the Rockefeller family:

	Total Number of Shares	Percentage of All Shares Outstanding	Market Value (1974)
EXXON	2,288,171	1.02	$156,700,000
IBM	384,042	0.26	$ 72,600,000
STANDARD OIL OF CALIFORNIA	3,410,148	2.01	$ 85,300,000
CHASE MANHATTAN BANK	429,959	1.34	$ 12,000,000
MOBIL	1,762,206	1.74	$ 63,600,000
EASTMAN KODAK	535,973	0.39	$ 38,400,000
AMERICAN TELEPHONE & TELEGRAPH	116,231	0.02	$ 5,400,000
GENERAL ELECTRIC	509,952	0.29	$ 19,400,000
STANDARD OIL OF INDIANA	134,652	0.20	$ 11,700,000
DOW CHEMICAL	70,491	0.08	$ 4,700,000
IBEC	2,460,407	78.60	$ 4,200,000
ALUMINUM COMPANY OF AMERICA	405,783	1.22	$ 13,400,000
TEXAS INSTRUMENTS	241,544	1.07	$ 17,700,000
INTERNATIONAL PAPER	63,470	0.14	$ 2,600,000
COHERENT RADIATION	316,805	19.08	$ 2,300,000
CATERPILLAR TRACTOR	213,979	0.37	$ 11,400,000
MARATHON OIL	194,217	0.65	$ 7,300,000
MOTOROLA	216,200	0.77	$ 9,700,000
THERMO ELECTRON	189,129	9.79	$ 2,100,000
ALLIED CHEMICAL	65,985	0.24	$ 2,100,000
SEARS, ROEBUCK	38,584	0.03	$ 2,000,000
DU PONT	17,533	0.04	$ 1,900,000
LUBRIZOL	39,283	0.19	$ 1,600,000
DANIEL INTERNATIONAL	102,125	1.46	$ 1,500,000
ARCHER DANIEL MIDLAND	89,404	0.59	$ 1,500,000
WEYERHAEUSER	180,414	0.14	$ 5,000,000
ROCKEFELLER CENTER	1,125,000	100.00	$ 98,300,000
MERCK	455,100	0.61	$ 30,000,000
3M	221,700	0.20	$ 13,700,000
MONSANTO	213,273	0.64	$ 10,900,000
XEROX	119,300	0.15	$ 8,700,000
KRESGE	336,800	0.12	$ 8,300,000
JOHNSON & JOHNSON	62,000	0.11	$ 5,400,000
HERCULES	130,000	0.31	$ 4,600,000
ALLIS-CHALMERS PFD.	430,000	3.45	$ 4,100,000
COCA-COLA	62,200	0.10	$ 3,900,000
UPJOHN	65,000	0.22	$ 3,000,000
CHESEBROUGH-POND'S	45,311	0.29	$ 2,000,000
J. C. PENNEY	40,596	0.07	$ 1,700,000
DUN & BRADSTREET	73,400	0.28	$ 1,400,000

gence as a big name in the personal care business has been based partly on giving out free samples. Johnson's Wax began as just that—a little extra something that great-grandfather Johnson gave his customers when they bought one of his parquet floors, back in the 1880s. Johnson, a carpenter, soon realized that there was more business in floor polishes than in floors, and the company developed a line of wax products.

Product development has been a prime focus for Johnson Wax. For many years they bragged that their research department was as big as their sales department. The Johnson chemists have brought out an impressive line of "firsts": Glo-Coat (1932), the first one-step floor polisher; Raid (1956), the first bug killer that could be used indoors and out; Off! (1957), the first aerosol insect repellent; Pledge (1958), the first aerosol furniture polish; Glade (1961), the first aerosol air freshener; and Glory (1968), the first home carpet cleaner.

But in recent years the sales department has assumed far more importance. With less than half of Johnson's business coming from floor polishing, and more and more coming from the personal care line, they have recognized that their new customers are often buying the pizzazz more than the product. And Johnson, still based in their hometown of Racine, Wisconsin, has shown that they can dish out the pizzazz just as lavishly as any New York outfit.

Even in the old days, Johnson knew the importance of advertising. For many years they sponsored "Fibber McGee & Molly"— the homespun, corny, ever popular radio show that somehow seemed to go very well with Johnson's wax. They were one of the biggest buyers of commercial time during the heyday of radio and a mainstay of the advertising agency business in Chicago. Today they divide their advertising among four major agencies, using their Chicago offices. According to *Advertising Age,* they invested nearly $44 million in advertising during 1978, ranking as the nation's 77th largest advertiser.

Reputation. Squeaky clean. They've never had a strike, and they seem to have been sensitive to their workers and to social change. In 1917 they introduced a profit-sharing plan for employees. They inaugurated a pension and hospitalization plan, and they laid off no workers during the Depression. Before the civil rights movement heated up in the 1960s, Johnson was spearheading programs in Racine to help blacks and Mexican-Americans get equal employment, housing, and education.

What they own. Waxdale is Johnson's 1.5 million–square foot factory complex in Racine. It is the company's only domestic manufacturing operation; the rest are located in 40 foreign countries.

Johnson's administrative headquarters in Racine, designed by Frank Lloyd Wright, is known as one of the Midwest's most dazzling architectural showpieces.

Who owns and runs the company. Since 1886 Johnson Wax has been family owned

and run, and chairman Sam Johnson insists it's going to stay that way. But in early 1979, following his father's death, Johnson turned the chief executive's post over to president William K. Eastham, who had been with the company since 1964. Sam Johnson said he needed a year off the job to take care of his father's estate. It is the first time a nonfamily member has been in charge of the corporation.

One of Johnson's seven directors is a woman: Dr. Helen Hilton, an emeritus dean of Iowa State University's College of Home Economics.

In the public eye. In 1975 Johnson Wax announced that they would no longer put fluorocarbons in their aerosol sprays because of suspected damage to the ozone layer in the atmosphere. (Ozone shields the earth from the sun's ultraviolet rays. More ultraviolet rays are believed to cause a higher incidence of skin cancer, genetic mutation, and damage to crops.) Johnson's quick and highly publicized action was not much appreciated by other aerosol manufacturers.

Where they're going. More expansion in the personal care market. With a number of new items already in the works, they plan to unveil one product a year through the mid-1980s. One analyst comments, "There is no fundamental reason why Johnson could not be one of the leading firms in the entire cosmetics-toiletry industry."

Access. 1525 Howe Street, Racine, Wisconsin 53403; (414) 554-2000.

Consumer brands.

Floor care: Future; Step Saver; Klear; Beautiflor; Klear Wood Floor Wax; Johnson's Paste Wax; Super Kleen Floor; Super Bravo.

Furniture care: Pledge; Favor; Klean 'n Shine; Jubilee; Regard.

Personal care: Agree shampoo, Agree creme rinse, and conditioner; Edge Protective Shave.

Laundry care: Shout soil and stain remover; Rain Barrel fabric softener.

Carpet care: Glory.

Air fresheners: Glade.

Specialty products: Scrunge scrubber sponge; Big Wally foam cleaner; Crew disinfectant bathroom cleaner.

Auto care: Johnson Wax line of auto-care products; Kit; Sprint; Supreme; Car-Plate.

Insecticides: Raid.

Insect repellents: Off!

Mars

Sales: $1.4 billion
Profits: $100 million
Rank in candy bars: 1
Rank in canned dog food: 2
Rank in canned cat food: 3
Founded: 1932
Employees: 12,000
Headquarters: McLean, Virginia

What they do. The figures listed above are all estimates. Mars is a privately held company whose owners—the Mars family—believe strongly in privacy and disclose nothing about their operations. More than one observer has noted the appropriateness of the company's headquarters location in McLean, just four miles from the home base of the Central Intelligence Agency. "They may *be* the CIA for all I know," joked one competitor.

Enough is known about Mars to rank them number 1 in the candy market. They passed Hershey in the early 1970s and now hold about 30% of a declining market (per capita consumption of candy plunged 25% in the past decade). Of the 10 top-selling candy bars 5 come from Mars: Snickers (number 1), M & M's peanut (number 3), M & M's plain (number 4), Three Musketeers (number 6), and Milky Way (number 9).

Mars is an odd three-legged corporate animal. Their two other product lines are rice and pet foods, each of which provides about one-sixth of the company's sales. Uncle Ben's rice, which they started from scratch in the early 1940s, ranks among the top five brands of rice. In 1978 they bought Kal Kan, a popular brand of canned dog and cat foods.

History. None of it is recorded (at least not for public view). Legend has it that Forrest Mars, Sr., went off to Britain in the early 1930s after quarreling with his father, who owned a candy company in Chicago. The father reportedly gave his son several thousand dollars, the recipe for Milky Way, and orders to get out of the country. The younger Mars built a formidable operation in England, where Milky Way and Mars bars were just right for the British sweet tooth. Mars also became a major pet food manufacturer in Britain—so major, in fact, that the British Office of Fair Trading alleged that the company commanded 55% of the pet food market in that country.

The British and American arms of Mars were merged in 1964 after bitter intrafamily squabbles. The British experience was crucial to Mars's success in the American market. The British are the world's biggest sweet eaters, and it was there that Forrest Mars saw Smarties, a sugar-coated candy with a chocolate center, made by the Rowntree Mackintosh firm. Mars got the rights to market Smarties in the United States, where it became M & M's (Mars and Mars) and sold so spectacularly on the strength of its television blasts at children—"Melts in your mouth, not in your hand"—that it propelled Mars to the top of the American candy industry.

Today Mars also markets candy in Australia, Belgium, the Netherlands, and West Germany. They probably do at least half their sales outside the United States.

Reputation. They're known for high-quality products and are said to make sure that at least 45% of a candy bar's selling price is the cost of ingredients. As the price of sugar and cocoa rise and fall, the bars shrink and

THE YEAR MONEY <u>DID</u> BUY THE BEST BASEBALL TEAMS

Order of Finish in the National League East 1977 Season

Player Payroll, 1977

1. PHILADELPHIA PHILLIES	$3.5 million
2. PITTSBURGH PIRATES	$2.5 million
3. ST. LOUIS CARDINALS	$1.8 million
4. CHICAGO CUBS	$1.7 million
5. MONTREAL EXPOS	$1.6 million
6. NEW YORK METS	$1.5 million

Source: *Sports Illustrated*, July 17, 1978.

expand—sometimes changing every two or three weeks.

What they own.   A rice plant in Houston; a pet food facility in Vernon, California; candy plants in Hackettstown, New Jersey; Chicago; Albany, Georgia; Waco, Texas; and Cleveland, Tennessee.

Who owns and runs the company.   The Mars family. The company is headed today by the two British-born sons of Forrest Mars: Forrest E., Jr., and John F. All the Mars family members appear to be recluses. Their photographs are not available; they do not submit to interviews; they do not attend industry conventions. But they run an extraordinary show, according to a rare profile of the company that *Business Week* pieced together in 1978. It was noted there that Mars:

was the first company in the candy industry to date their products and take back unsold items still on the shelves after four months;

insists on spotlessly clean conditions in their plants;

uses high-quality ingredients;

pays wages and salaries that are 10% higher than the industry standard;

offers unusually good fringe benefits;

practices an egalitarianism reflected in few special privileges for executives (hardly any private offices for top managers, no reserved parking slots).

Everyone at Mars, from the top down, punches a time clock. Bonuses are handed out to those who are never late.

In the public eye.   When the federal government banned the Red No. 2 food dye in the mid-1970s, Mars experimented with substitute red colorings but didn't like the results. So they just stopped making red M & Ms.

Where they're going.   More broadly into food products, notably cookies, as the prime candy-eating population (age 5–17) declines. Their new products in the American market include Twix, a chocolate-covered cookie introduced in Holland, and Summit, a cookie developed in Britain that features caramel and imitation chocolate.

Major employment centers: McLean, Vir-

ginia; Hackettstown, New Jersey; Houston, Texas; Vernon, California; London, England.

Access.   1651 Old Meadow Road, McLean, Virginia 22101; (703) 821-4900.

Consumer brands.

Candy: Snickers; M & M's; Three Musketeers; Milky Way; Mars bars; Forever Yours; Marathon; Bounty; Starburst; Twix; Summit; Lockets; Pacer's Punch Chews; Skittles Fruit Chews; Munch peanut bars.
Rice: Uncle Ben's.
Pet foods: Kal Kan; Mealtime; Crave; MPS Chunks; Whel-Pup; Thorofed.

Wm. **WRIGLEY** Jr. Company

Sales: $505 million
Profits: $36 million
Rank in chewing gum: 1
Founded: 1892
Employees: 5,800
Headquarters: Chicago, Illinois

What they do.   Wrigley has pretty much stuck to the basics—making chewing gum. There's been no thought of picking up a little hamburger chain here, or a kayak company there; no wild forays into the cosmetics industry. In fact, for over 75 years Wrigley limited itself to making three kinds of gum: the familiar Doublemint, Spearmint, and Juicy Fruit, all introduced before 1915. "It's not that we have a closed mind on diversification," says president William Wrigley, "but you're better off doing what you know how to do best."

For many years Wrigley refused to consider making other flavors, which they thought would only cut into their own markets. For a long time they had nearly two-thirds of gum sales wrapped up. In 1979 the figure was closer to 40%. Wrigley has been forced to come up with new gum flavors to compete. During the 1970s Wrigley introduced four new gums: Freedent, Big Red, Orbit, and Hubba Bubba; all this activity from a company that, prior to 1974, hadn't produced a single new gum in 59 years.

A company brochure called "Facts About Chewing Gum" will tell you all you ever wanted to know about the benefits of gum (natural, reduces tension, helps keep teeth clean, gives a pleasant little lift); some have called it simply an adult pacifier. The brochure also reports that although the United States leads the world in quantity of gum chewed, we are only second in number of gum companies (21). The leader is Turkey, with 62 companies. Wrigley has chosen not to become the 63rd company in Turkey, but they are playing a great role in spreading gum around the world, helping to fill the needs of gumchewers in nations like Kenya, Finland, and New Guinea.

History. William Wrigley, Jr., who gave gum away before he sold it, was a gregarious soap salesman. At 16 he started riding from town to town in Pennsylvania on a horse-drawn wagon, selling his father's soap to retailers and giving away a box of baking soda to go with it. Then he started selling baking soda. The gum was a gimmick, something he threw in with a baking soda sale. When he started selling gum, he kept up the gimmicks. Advertising was always a big item on the budget, and his oft-repeated dictum was, "Tell 'em quick and tell 'em often."

Wrigley was 29 in 1891, when he came to Chicago from Philadelphia with $32 in his pocket. Within a year his sales emphasis switched from soap to baking powder to gum. It didn't switch again. By 1910 Wrigley's Spearmint was America's biggest-selling gum. At the same time, Wrigley was setting up gum companies abroad—first in Canada (1910), then in Australia (1915) and Great Britain (1927). Today Wrigley has plants in over 20 countries on six continents, and international business accounts for 38% of sales.

William Wrigley relished people and activity. His idea of fun was seeing the Chicago Cubs play at Wrigley Field. In the afternoon sun, a beer in hand, Wrigley would watch the game, joke with friends, and hand out cigars when a Cub player hit a homer. He had a lot of friends, including Calvin Coolidge. Old pictures show a rosy-cheeked, round-faced man, always nattily dressed.

After Wrigley died in 1932, his son Philip took over. During World War II, when ingredients of the usual quality weren't available, Wrigley continued to make gum, using what they could get. But they refused to put their name on this inferior product. At the same time, as the company explains it, "to keep the name and quality of Wrigley's gum in people's minds," they published ads that featured pictures of an empty Spearmint wrapper with the caption: "Remember this Wrapper." Apparently people did, because two years after the war Wrigley's gums exceeded their prewar popularity.

Wrigley has their own way of doing things. Philip K. Wrigley, who ran the company for over 40 years until his death in 1977, could be singleminded and mistrustful of newfangled ideas. The owner of the Chicago Cubs and their stadium, Wrigley refused to allow home games at night; Wrigley Field is the only major league ballpark in the country that doesn't have night lighting. Although a Cub stockholder took him to court over the matter, Wrigley insisted, successfully, "Baseball is a daytime game, and the Cubs, so long as they play in Chicago, will play in daylight."

For several years Wrigley alone among the gum giants held out against the forces of inflation. While competitors raised their prices to a dime a pack, Wrigley stayed at a nickel. Finally, they grumpily went to 7¢ in 1971. Philip Wrigley commented: "My father, just as I did later with my son, hammered away at the idea that we are a five-

A Wrigley's delivery truck outside their Chicago factory garage at 35th Street and Ashland Avenue in Chicago in 1922.

cent business. Well, maybe today it's a seven-cent business. But we want our executives to keep a five-cent view of things." Apparently they now have a wider perspective: their gum now sells for 25¢.

During the 1970s Wrigley saw their leading position being rapidly chewed into by competitors—Squibb's Life Savers division (Beech-nut, Carefree) and especially Warner-Lambert's American Chicle (Trident, Dentyne, Chiclets). What was gumming up the works for Wrigley was sugarless.

When sugarless gum first went on the market in the early 1970s, Wrigley refused to make the stuff, just as they had refused to make bubble gum or anything else besides Doublemint, Spearmint, and Juicy Fruit. "Although we will remain flexible, we would not be stampeded into doing anything simply on the basis of a competitor," was the official statement. Stampeded, no. But nudged and finally budged by alarming inroads on their sales—yes.

In 1974 Wrigley come up with something new for the first time in 25 years. Something that wouldn't cut into existing markets but might capture a completely virgin market of 30 million Americans who weren't chewing gum at all. The market was denture wearers, and the gum was called Freedent. To introduce it, Wrigley veered from their traditional policy of advertising only one gum product at a time (a policy that continues to mystify ad agencies) and sank $5 million into TV and magazine ads for Freedent, which came out in two flavors.

Was Wrigley starting to play the game? Yes and no. The next year they introduced Big Red, a cinnamon flavored gum. But still no sugarless—not until 1977, when Wrigley finally brought out Orbit. The next year came Wrigley's soft bubble gum, Hubba Bubba, which followed the successful marketing of Squibb's soft bubble gum, Bubble Yum. Wrigley hopes to bring a liquid-center gum called Spurt, now being successfully sold in Australia, to the United States in 1981. Still, observers feel Wrigley's slowness has hurt them: one analyst estimates that they lost 10% of their market during the 1970s.

Reputation. The reliable chomp champ: a company with some rather backward ideas that still manages to stay out in front.

What they own. People get confused between what the Wrigley family owns and what the Wm. Wrigley Jr. Company (as the gum company is officially called) owns. It's the Wrigley family, not the company, that owns the Chicago Cubs and Catalina Island off Los Angeles. It's the Wrigley company that owns the double-towered French Renaissance–style Wrigley Building in Chicago. Founder William Wrigley, Jr., said he wanted a building that looked like a birthday cake. The tiered white structure, constantly lit by floodlights, is a Chicago landmark.

The company also owns Amurol Products, a maker of dietetic cookies and candies; 81,000 shares of AT&T (worth $4.3 million in mid-1980) and 125,000 shares of Texaco (worth $4.7 million in mid-1980).

Who owns and runs the company. William Wrigley, the third-generation heir, owns the largest block of stock, over 25%. Other major stockholders are American Home Products Corporation, with 9.6%; Dorothy Wrigley Offield, nearly 8%; and Wrigley Offield, 3.6%. Although an American Home Products executive said in 1974 that Wrigley is "the kind of business we would just love to make part of our business," there have been no signs of a takeover attempt—perhaps because three members of the Wrigley family own 40% of the stock.

William Wrigley, who became president in 1961, seems to have kept his father's "five-cent view of things." Wrigley executives, including the president, still answer their own calls and make their own appointments. Sounding a lot like the old man, Wrigley explains, "You can't get too 'uppity.' I went into our New York office one day and they asked me who was calling. I told them it didn't make a damn bit of difference. I might be some guy wanting to buy some gum—and that's all that mattered."

The do-it-yourself attitude has sometimes worked very well. The famous Doublemint Twins ad campaign, which they said doubled their sales, was a jingle cooked up by father and son one day in the office. But a management professor at Northwestern University said of William Wrigley, "He loses sight of the overall direction of the company. He should get past the attitude of 'This is my company and I'm going to do everything.'"

Doing it himself has been a passion for William Wrigley. Like his father, he is something of an introvert. He would rather watch the Cubs at home on TV than vacation at Catalina. The resort island doesn't appeal to him because it has "so damned many people."

In the public eye. Wrigley received some unwanted publicity in 1978 when xylitol, a natural sweetener, came under fire as a possible carcinogen. Wrigley was the only gum company to use the ingredient in sugarless gum. They voluntarily removed it from Orbit.

Stock performance. Wrigley stock bought for $1,000 in 1970 sold for $1,445 on January

Major employment centers. Chicago; Gainsville, Georgia; and Santa Cruz, California.

Access. Wrigley Building, 410 North Michigan Avenue, Chicago, Illinois 60611; (312) 644-2121.

Consumer brands.

Gum: Wrigley's Spearmint, Doublemint, and Juicy Fruit; Orbit; Freedent; Big Red; Hubba Bubba; Blammon Soft'n Sugarfree Bubble Gum; MVP Sports Gum; Zeno Bubble Gum; Amurol Sugarfree Gum.
Sugarless and dietetic products: Amurol.
Dental product: Xpose.

Part of Wrigley's "Mile Long" circus train advertising sign that ran along the Pennsylvania Railroad tracks in Atlantic City, New Jersey, from 1921-26.

CONSUMER BRAND INDEX: WHO MAKES WHAT

Note: The brand name is listed first, followed by the name of the company that owns the brand. The number refers to the first page of the profile of the parent company. When the company is not profiled in the book, the number refers to the page on which the company is mentioned.

Saginaw News Newhouse, 385
Saks Fifth Avenue B.A.T., 770
Salada Kellogg, 48
Salem R.J. Reynolds, 778
Salem Capitol Journal Gannett, 375
Salinas Californian Gannett, 375
Saluto General Mills, 32
Sam Lord's Castle Marriott, 724
Sam Snead PepsiCo, 64
Sam Wilson's Meat Market W.R. Grace, 816
Sambuca di Galliano Foremost-McKesson, 813
Samsonite Beatrice Foods, 1
San Antonio Light Hearst, 388
San Bernardino Sun Gannett, 375
San Francisco Examiner Hearst, 388
San Francisco Mint Foremost-McKesson, 813
San Giorgio Hershey, 41
San Jose Mercury and News Knight-Ridder,
  378
San Juan Star Scripps-Howard, 388
San Martin Norton Simon, 61
San Rafael Independent-Journal Gannett, 375
Sandcastle Gulf + Western, 819
Sandler IC Industries, 823
Sandoval Armstrong, 159
Sangrole Heublein, 794
Sani-Flush American Home Products, 213
Sani-foam American Home Products, 213
Sanka General Foods, 28
Sanna Beatrice Foods, 1
Sanson Beatrice Foods, 1
Santa Barbara Biltmore Marriott, 724
Santa Fe Heublein, 794
Sapporo Chrysler, 262
Sapulpa Green Sheet Park, 388
Sara Lee Consolidated Foods, 21
Saran Wrap Dow Chemical, 601
Saratogian Gannett, 375
Sardo Schering-Plough, 240
Satin Sheen Shaklee, 242
Saucettes Miles, 232
Sav-on Kroger, 112
Savoy Beatrice Foods, 1
Schick Warner-Lambert, 251
Schick Super II Warner-Lambert, 251
Schlitz Jos. Schlitz, 790
Schlitz Light Jos. Schlitz, 790
Schlitz Malt Liquor Jos. Schlitz, 790
School Weekly New York Times, 382
Schrader Scovill, 181
Schrafft's Gulf + Western, 819
Schwann ABC, 362
Schweppes Cadbury-Schweppes, 846
Science Fair Tandy, 331
Scooter Pie Quaker Oats, 70
Scope Procter & Gamble, 355
Scorches Mattel, 728
Scot Towels Scott, 583
ScotTissue Scott, 583
Scotch 3M, 837
Scotchguard 3M, 837
Scotkins Scott, 583
Scott Family Scott, 583
Scott Peterson-Saratoga United Brands, 78
Scott's Turf Builder ITT, 825
Scotties Scott, 583
Scout International Harvester, 624
Scrub 'n Sponge 3M, 837
Scrunge Johnson Wax, 865
Sculptured Touch Armstrong, 159
Sea & Ski SmithKline, 243
Sea World Harcourt Brace Jovanovich, 752
Seabrook Farms Springs, 135
Seagram's 7 Crown Seagram, 799
Sealtest Kraft, 51
Sears Sears, 308
Sears-O-Pedic Sears, 308
Seattle Post Intelligencer Hearst, 388
Seconal Lilly, 226
Secret Procter & Gamble, 355
Secretary 3M, 837
Sector General Mills, 32
Sedgefield Blue Bell, 142

See 'n Say Mattel, 728
Sego IC Industries, 67, 823
Seiberling Firestone, 284
SelectaVision RCA, 842
Selest Amfac, 809
Self Newhouse, 385
Selsun Blue Abbott, 211
Semicid American Home Products, 213
Sentry Genesco, 146
Sergeant's A. H. Robins, 339
Serutan Nabisco, 56
7-Eleven Southland, 118
Seven Seas Anderson, Clayton, 83
Seventeen Triangle, 400
7-Up Philip Morris, 774
Seven-Up Candy ITT, 22, 825
Seville General Motors, 271
Shainberg's Interco, 150
Shake 'n Bake General Foods, 28
Shaklee for Men Shaklee, 242
Sharon Herald Dow Jones, 371
Shasta Consolidated Foods, 21
Shedd's Beatrice Foods, 1
Sheer Indulgence IC Industries, 823
Shell Shell Oil, 525
Sheplers W.R. Grace, 816
Sheraton Hotels ITT, 825
Shillito's Federated, 324
Ship 'n Shore General Mills, 32
Shipstads & Johnston Ice Follies Mattel, 728
Shopko Super Valu, 122
Shout Johnson Wax, 865
Shower-To-Shower Johnson & Johnson, 223
Shreveport Times Gannett, 375
Sibley, Lindsay, & Curr Associated Dry Goods,
  318
Sierra Grande General Motors, 271
Signal Unilever, 846
Signet Times-Mirror, 397
Silk Crown Zellerbach, 572
Silkience Gillette, 203
Silva Thins American Brands, 765
Silver Springs ABC, 362
Silverado General Motors, 271
Silverado Country Club Amfac, 809
Silvertone Sears, 308
Similac Abbott, 211
Simon & Schuster Gulf + Western, 819
Simoniz Union Carbide, 614
Sine-Aid Johnson & Johnson, 223
Sine-Off Schering-Plough, 240
Singer Singer, 183
Sinutab Warner-Lambert, 251
Sioux Falls Argus-Leader Gannett, 375
Sir Galaxy Mattel, 728
Sir Robert Burnett's Seagram, 799
Sir Walter Raleigh B.A.T., 770
Sirena Consolidated Foods, 21
Sirloin Stockade Lucky, 113
Sizzlean Esmark, 26
Skaggs American Stores, 107
Ski Times-Mirror, 397
Ski Business Times-Mirror, 397
Skil-Craft Mattel, 728
Skinner Hershey, 41
Skinner Springs, 135
Skippy CPC International, 92
Skittles Fruit Chews Mars, 869
Skol Standard Brands, 76
Sky Chief Texaco, 539
Sky City Discount Center Interco, 150
Skyhawk General Motors, 271
Slaymaker American Home Products, 213
Sleep-Eze American Home Products, 213
Slender Carnation, 12
Slick-Kote Kraft, 51
Slim Jim General Mills, 32
Slo-Poke Beatrice Foods, 1
Smirnoff Heublein, 794
Snack Pack Norton Simon, 61
Snap-E-Tom Heublein, 794
Snarol American Home Products, 213
Snickers Mars, 869

Sno-Bol Staley, 99
Sno-balls ITT, 22, 825
Snow Crop Coca-Cola, 16
Snow's Borden, 5
Snow Crop Springs, 135
Snowmass Twentieth Century-Fox, 711
Society Brand Hart Schaffner & Marx, 148
Soft & Dri Gillette, 203
Soft Mate Revlon, 207
Soft'n Pretty Scott, 583
Soft-Weve Scott, 583
Softer Than Soft Shaklee, 242
Softuf Mattel, 728
Sohigro Standard Oil of Ohio, 536
Sohio Standard Oil of Ohio, 536
Solarcaine Schering-Plough, 240
Solarian Armstrong, 159
Sole di Roma Foremost-McKesson, 813
Sominex Nabisco, 56
Sommers Malone & Hyde, 114
Son of a Gun Bristol-Myers, 217
Son of a Gun! Esmark, 26
Sonnet Avon, 195
Sorry General Mills, 32
Souptime Nestle, 59
South Idaho Press Cowles, 388
South Macon Sun Park, 388
Southeast Oklahoma News Park, 388
Southern Bell Standard Brands, 76
Southern Comfort Brown-Forman, 802
Southern Queen Anderson, Clayton, 83
Southwestern Times-Mirror, 397
Souverain Standard Brands, 76
Sovereign Gulf + Western, 819
Spam Hormel, 44
Spanada Gallo, 803
Spark Plug Liggett, 772
Sparkletts Foremost-McKesson, 813
Spatini Unilever, 846
Speas Pillsbury, 68
Spec-T Squibb, 244
Special K Kellogg, 48
Speedy Muffler King Tenneco, 848
Spencer Gifts MCA, 708
Spey Royal Scotch American Brands, 765
Spic and Span Procter & Gamble, 355
Spill-Mate Crown Zellerbach, 572
Spin Blend CPC International, 92
Spinout 360 Mattel, 728
Spirit American Motors, 259
Spirograph General Mills, 32
Spoon-Up IC Industries, 67, 823
Sport Charter, 495
Sporting Goods Dealer Times-Mirror, 397
Sporting News Times-Mirror, 397
Sports Illustrated Time, 395
Sportsline Beatrice Foods, 1
Sportsman Chrysler, 262
Spotnails American Brands, 765
Spree Bar Colgate Palmolive, 201
Springfield Sunbeam, 187
Springfield Daily News Gannett, 375
Springfield Leader and Press Gannett, 375
Springfield News and Union Newhouse, 385
Springfield Sun and News Cox, 388
Springmaid Springs, 135
Sprinkle Sweet Pillsbury, 68
Sprint Johnson Wax, 865
Sprint Southern Pacific, 642
Sprite Coca-Cola, 16
Squibb Squibb, 244
St. Cloud Daily Times Gannett, 375
St. Francis United Airlines, 680
St. Joseph Schering-Plough, 240
St. Lawrence Plaindealer Park, 388
St. Louis Blues Ralston Purina, 72
St. Louis Globe-Democrat Newhouse, 385
St. Moritz Liggett, 772
St. Paul Pioneer Press and Dispatch
  Knight-Ridder, 378
St. Pauli Girl Foremost-McKesson, 813
St. Raphael Standard Brands, 76
St. Regis Chrysler, 262

St. Thomas Daily News Gannett, 375
Sta-Puf Staley, 99
Staff ITT, 22, 825
Staff PepsiCo, 64
Stag & Hound Ralston Purina, 72
Staley Staley, 99
Stamford Advocate Times Mirror, 397
Standard American Standard, 158
Standard Standard Oil of California, 528
Standard Standard Oil of Indiana, 532
Standard & Poor's McGraw-Hill, 758
Standard Sportswear Interco, 150
Star Jewell, 111
Star Liggett, 772
Star Wars General Mills, 32
Star-Kist Heinz, 39
Starburst Mars, 869
Start General Foods, 28
Startown Interco, 150
Staten Island Advance Newhouse, 385
Statesville Record & Landmark Park, 388
Statler City Investing, 811
StayLastic/Smith Scovill, 181
Stayfree Johnson & Johnson, 223
Ste. Roseline Standard Brands, 76
Steak & Ale Pillsbury, 68
Steak Supreme Heublein, 794
Steelcraft American Standard, 158
Steeler Uniroyal, 298
Steelmaster Uniroyal, 298
Steinway CBS, 366
Step Saver Johnson Wax, 865
Stepside General Motors, 271
Sterling Borden, 5
Sterling Coca-Cola, 16
Sterling Scovill, 181
Sterling & Hunt Hart Schaffner & Marx, 148
Stetson IC Industries, 823
Stewart & Co. Associated Dry Goods, 318
Stiffel Beatrice Foods, 1
Stix, Baer & Fuller Associated Dry Goods, 318
Stockbridge Armstrong, 159
Stockton Record Gannett, 375
Stomp American Cyanamid, 599
Storybrook Genesco, 146
Stouffer Nestle, 59
Stove Top General Foods, 28
Stratford Armstrong, 159
Stresstabs American Cyanamid, 599
Streusel Swirl Pillsbury, 68
Stri-Dex Sterling Drug, 246
Strongheart Esmark, 26
Stroudsburg Pocono Record Dow Jones, 371
Stuart News Scripps-Howard, 388
Stuckey's IC Industries, 823
Studio One by Campus Interco, 150
Stuffed Jeans Interco, 150
Stuffed Shirt Interco, 150
Sturgis Journal Gannett, 375
Stylistik Tile Armstrong, 159
Styrofoam Dow Chemical, 601
Suburban Virginia Times Park, 388
Sucaryl Abbott, 211
Success Colgate-Palmolive, 201
Success RCA, 842
Sucrets Beecham, 846
Sudden Tan Schering-Plough, 240
Sugar Corn Pops Kellogg, 48
Sugar Daddy Nabisco, 56
Sugar Frosted Flakes Kellogg, 48
Sugar Plum Esmark, 26
Sugar Smacks Kellogg, 48
Sugar Twin Alberto-Culver, 339
Summer-Time Liggett, 772
Summit Gulf + Western, 819
Summit Mars, 869
Sun Drop Procter & Gamble, 355
Sun Giant Tenneco, 848
Sun Gier Schering-Plough, 240
Sun Harvest United Brands, 78
Sun Line Marriott, 724
Sunbeam Sunbeam, 187
Sunbird General Motors, 271

Sunguard Miles, 232
Sunlite Norton Simon, 61
Sunmark Foremost-McKesson, 813
Sunoroid Gillette, 203
Sunrise ITT, 22, 825
Sunrise Nestle, 59
Sunset House Carter Hawley Hale Stores, 320
Sunset Sport Centers Malone & Hyde, 114
Sunshine American Brands, 765
SupeRx Kroger, 112
Super Bravo Johnson Wax, 865
Super Bubble General Mills, 32
Super Centers Supermarkets General, 122
Super D Malone & Hyde, 114
Super Dry Kimberly-Clark, 580
Super Kleen Floor Johnson Wax, 865
Super Links Miles, 232
Super Look Esmark, 26
Super Pop Liggett, 772
Super Saver American Stores, 107
Super Sugar Crisp General Foods, 28
Super Test Charter, 495
Superior IC Industries, 823
Superior Standard Brands, 76
Superman Spinball Pinball Mattel, 728
Superstar Liggett, 772
Supp-hose IC Industries, 823
Supreme Johnson Wax, 865
Sure Procter & Gamble, 355
Sure-Jell General Foods, 28
Sure-start Inco, 556
Sustagen Bristol-Myers, 217
Sutliff Private Stock Gulf + Western, 819
Suze Standard Brands, 76
Swans Down General Foods, 28
Swanson Campbell Soup, 9
Swedish Tanning Secret Pfizer, 234
Sweet Honesty Avon, 195
Sweeta Squibb, 244
Sweets Catalog Files McGraw-Hill, 758
Swift Esmark, 26
Swift 10 Pillsbury, 68
Swingline American Brands, 765
Swingster Beatrice Foods, 1
Swiss Cheese Snack Nabisco, 56
Swiss Miss Beatrice Foods, 1
Switzer Beatrice Foods, 1
Syracuse Herald-Journal and Post Standard
  Newhouse, 385

T.J. Socials Heublein, 794
T.J. Swann Heublein, 794
T.Y. Crowell Harper & Row, 754
TAB Coca-Cola, 16
TRS-80 Tandy, 331
TV Guide Triangle, 400
Tabac Original American Cyanamid, 599
Tack 'n Togs ABC, 362
Taco Bell PepsiCo, 64
Tailor's Bench Interco, 150
Talbots General Mills, 32
Tallahassee Democrat Knight-Ridder, 378
Tally Ho Diamond International, 574
Talwin Sterling Drug, 246
Tame Gillette, 203
Tampax Tampax, 209
Tan-Tan-A Resort Marriott, 724
Tang General Foods, 28
Tanqueray Norton Simon, 61
Tareyton American Brands, 765
Target B.A.T., 770
Target Dayton Hudson, 321
Tarrytown Daily News Gannett, 375
Tartan 3M, 837
Taru Heublein, 794
Tassel Gulf + Western, 819
Taster's Choice Nestle, 59
Tatum Bakers Beatrice Foods, 1
Taylor Coca-Cola, 16
Taylor California Cellars Coca-Cola, 16
Teaching Resources New York Times, 382
Team Nabisco, 56
Ted Lapidus Nestle, 59

Ted Williams Sears, 308
Teem PepsiCo, 64
Teflon Du Pont, 603
Tele-Ektra 1 Eastman Kodak, 407
Telfa Colgate Palmolive, 201
Tem-Cote Esmark, 26
Tempco Brown Group, 143
Temple Time, 395
Tempo Avon, 195
Tempos Brown Group, 143
Tender Leaf Standard Brands, 76
Tender Vittles Ralston Purina, 72
Tenneco Tenneco, 848
Tennessean Gannett, 375
Tennis New York Times, 382
Teri Kimberly-Clark, 580
Terramycin Pfizer, 234
Terry Gulf + Western, 819
Tes-Tender Greyhound, 652
Textile Products and Processes McGraw-Hill,
  758
Thalhimer's Carter Hawley Hale Stores, 320
Thayer McNeil Interco, 150
Theolair 3M, 837
Theragran Squibb, 244
Therapads Warner-Lambert, 251
Thick/Thirsty Kimberly-Clark, 580
Thiocal Hoffmann-LaRoche, 219
Thom McAn Melville, 156
Thomas E. Wilson Masterpiece LTV, 81
Thomas Wallace Interco, 150
Thomas' CPC International, 92
Thomasville's Founders Armstrong, 159
Thompson Interco, 150
Thorazine SmithKline, 243
Thornton's Interco, 150
Thorofed Mars, 869
3-in-One American Home Products, 213
3M 3M, 837
3-Minute Liggett, 772
Three Musketeers Mars, 869
Three-M-ite 3M, 837
Thrift J.C. Penney, 303
Thumsup Sears, 308
Thunderbird Ford, 265
Thunderbird Gallo, 803
Tickle Bristol-Myers, 217
Tide Procter & Gamble, 355
Tiffany's Avon, 195
Time Time, 395
Time Saver Dillon, 108
Time-Life Time, 395
Timeless Avon, 195
Times-Picayune and States-Item Newhouse,
  385
Timex Olsen, Lehmkul families, 846
Tinactin Schering-Plough, 240
Tinkertoys CBS, 366
Tinsley's Liggett, 772
Tipalet Gulf + Western, 819
Tipo Heublein, 794
Titan Revlon, 207
Titleist American Brands, 765
Tom Sawyer United Brands, 78
Tom Weiskopf Genesco, 146
Tom's General Mills, 32
Tone Greyhound, 652
Toni Gillette, 203
Top R.J. Reynolds, 778
Top Choice General Foods, 28
Top Drawer American Home Products, 213
Top Job Procter & Gamble, 355
Topaze Avon, 195
Topex Richardson-Merrell, 237
Torchbook Harper & Row, 754
Toronado General Motors, 271
Tortilla Flats Ralston Purina, 72
Tostitos PepsiCo, 64
Total General Mills, 32
Totino's Pillsbury, 68
Touch Up American Home Products, 213
Touchstone Gulf + Western, 819
Toughskins Sears, 308

Bradlee, Benjamin, 405
Bradlees discount stores, 122
Bradshaw, Thornton F., 491, 493, 494, 615
Brandeis University, 208
Brandino, Joseph, 814-815
Brando, Marlon, 702
Brandt, Joe, 703
brandy: top-selling brands, 795
Braniff International, 663-664, 373, 658, 665, 670, 671, 676, 682, food cost, 668; illegal political contributions, 620
Braniff, Paul, 663
Braniff, Thomas, 663
Brascan, 317
Brazil, 84, 460
Brazilian Coffee Institute, 60
Breaking Away (movie), 712
Bredin, J. Bruce, 605
Brennan, Edward A., 312
Brenninkmeyer Family, 846
Breslin, Jimmy, 793
Brewer, C., 810
Brewery Workers Union, 788
Brezhnev, Leonid, 618
Bridges, Harry, 15, 527
Bridges of Toko-Ri, The (Michener), 693
Brinckerhoff, Charles M., 550
Brinco, 467
Brinker, Norman, 69
Brisbane, Arthur, 269
Bristol, Henry, 217
Bristol, Lee, 217
Bristol, William Jr., 217
Bristol, William McClaren, 217
Bristol-Myers, 216-219, 197, 215, 234, 247, 359, 859
Britannia Beach Hotel, 737
Brite Industries, 773
British Airways, 670
British Columbia Forest Products, 467
British Market Research, 342
British Petroleum, 536, 846, in first oil cartel, 521; and Gulf, 506, 508; in Iraq 502, 507-8, 529
"British Poets" (Bell), 746
British-American Tobacco, see B.A.T
Broad, Eli, 166-167
Broadway, The, 320, 326, 328
Broadway-Hale, 320
Broder, David, 404
Brody, Herbert, 122
Broken Hill Proprietary Co., 549
Bromery, Randolph W., 504
Bromwell Wire Goods Company, 177
Bronco Wine, 805
Bronfman, Allan, 800, 803
Bronfman, Charles, 803
Bronfman, Edgar, 803, 730
Bronfman, Edward, 803
Bronfman, Peter, 803
Bronfman, Phyllis, 803
Bronfman, Samuel, 799-802
Bronfman, Yechiel, 800
Bronte, Emily, 750
Brooks, John, 152
Brooks, John, *Telephone*, 423, 425
Brooks, Joseph, 319
Brookside Vineyards, 804
Brophy, Hope, 289
Brophy, Theodore F., 428
Brosnan Forest, 647
Brosnan, D. William, 646
Brown & Root, 627
Brown & Williamson, 769, 776, 777
Brown Group, 143, 144, 152, 467
Brown University, 459
Brown, Charles L. 425
Brown, Colon, 621
Brown, David, 712
Brown, Francis Cabell, 240-241
Brown, Glenn, 538
Brown, Gov. Edmund G., Jr., 537-538
Brown, Harold G., 605

Brown, Harold, 441
Brown, Helen Gurley, 712, 734
Brown, John A., 328
Brown, John Y., 126
Brown, John, 596
Brown, R. Harper, 620
Brown, R. Manning, Jr., 467, 616
Brown, Stanley, 81
Brown, W. Melvin Jr., 227
Brown, W.F. Lyons Jr., 802
Brown-Forman distillery, 795, 802, 805
Brownie cameras, 408, 409
Browning, John Val, 620
Brownlee, Harold, 70
Brunet, Barrie K., 615
Bruns, Charles T., 227
Brunswick Corp., 147
Brush, Alvin George, 214
Brush, Alvin, 215
Bryan Brothers Packing, 22
Bryan, John H., Jr., 21-22
Bryan, William Jennings, 593
Bryant, Keith L., Jr., 642
Bryant, William Cullen, 755
bubblegum: invention of, 129
Buchan, Carl, 169
Buckeye Pipeline, 500
Buckingham Corp., 840
Buckley, William F., 213
Bucy, J. Fred, 445-446
Buddies supermarkets, 123
Buell, Margaret, 581
Buena Vista winery, 805
Buffet, Warren, 340
Buffett, Warren E., 597
Bugs Bunny, 715
Buick, 280, 293
Buick, David, 271
building: world's tallest, 308-309
Bulkeley, Eliphalet, 473
Bulkeley, Morgan, 473
bull semen: largest seller of, 817
Bullock's, 325, 328
Bundy, Mary Lothrop, 156
Bundy, McGeorge, 156
Burbank Studios, 704
Burdine's, 328
Burger King, 125, 128, 129, 132, 341, 345
Burger, Ralph, 104-105
Burgess, Carter L., 467, 471, 678
Burggraeve, Dr. Adolphe, 212
Burlington Industries, 133-135, 140, 152
Burlington Northern, 636-638, 32, 462, 645
Burnap, Williard H., 621
Burnett, Leo, 37
Burnett, Leo, ad agency, 345, 357
Burns, George, 347, 367-368
Burpee Seeds, 94
Burpee, W. Atlee (seeds), 29
Burr, Aaron, 454
Burroughs Wellcome, 215, 238
Burston-Marsteller, 348-349
Burton, Richard, 711
Bury My Heart at Wounded Knee, 746
Busch, Adolphus III, 786
Busch, Adolphus, 783-784
Busch, August A. III, 784-785
Busch, August A. Sr., 784, 786
Busch, Gussie, 785-786
Bush, A.G., 837
Business Week, 389, 758-759
business failures, 315
Butcher, Willard C., 455-456, 552
Butkus, Dick, 793
Butler International, 654
Butler, Kenneth, 227
Butler, Samuel, 750
Butt, H.E., Grocery, 120, 863
Butterfield, John, 482
Butz, A.M., 435
Butz, Earl, 74, 647
Buzick, William A., Jr., 21-22
Byars, J.B., 305

Byoir, Carl & Associates, 348-9, 559
Byoir, Carl, 104
Byrd, Admiral Richard, 186
Byrd, Robert (U.S. senator), 635
Byrne, Brendan, 226
Byron Jackson, 281

C.I.T. Financial, 842, 850
CBC Film Sales, 703
CBS, 366-370, 219, 454, 359, book sales, 745; magazines, 389
CF & I Steel, 162
CIA and the Cult of Intelligence (Marchetti), 763
CIA: and ITT, 828-829; and JWT, 351; in Iran, 503
CNA (insurance), 510
CNA Finance, 833-834
COPERSUCAR, 846
CPC International, 92-93, 82, 467, 818
CSR Limited, 549
CVS (Consumer Value Stores), 156
Cabell's dairies, 119
Cabot, 546
Cadbury-Schweppes, 846
Cadillac, 259, 263, 271
Caesar's Palace, 728
caffeine content in beverages, 18
Cafferty, Pastora San Juan, 581
Cahn, William, 57
Caidin, Martin, 685
calculator: first, 433
Calder, Alexander, 663-664
Caldwell, Phillip, 265
Califano, Joseph, 164, 227
California Air Resources Board, 261, 531
California Franchise Tax Board, 531
California Fruit Canners Association, 24
California Institute of Technology, 160
California Packing Corporation, 24
California Suite (movie), 702
California's Central Creamery, 815
California, U. of, 160, 574
Californians Against the Pollution Initiative, 531
Callahan, T.M., 304
Callaway Vineyards, 805
Callaway, Ely, 805
Caltex, 529, 539-540
Calvert Fire Insurance, 431
Calvert, Fred, 707
Cambridge Book Company, 383
Camel cigarettes, 567
Camera Art School Photographers, 13
cameras: ownership of, 411
Campbell Soup, 9-12, 23, 39, 82, 467, 471, 839
Campbell Taggart, 82
Campbell, Joseph, 9
Campbell, Rita Ricardo, 204
Campbell-Ewald ad agency, 336-337, 339
Canada Tungsten Mining, 548
Canadian Copper, 556
Canandaigua, 805
Candler, Asa Briggs, 17-18
candy bars, top 30, 42
Canfield, Cass, 755
Canfield, Cass, Jr., 756
Cannon Mills, 140, 348-9
Canon, 412-413
Canteen Corporation, 677
Canteen vending machines, 827
Capital Airlines, 658, 682
Capital Cities: newspapers owned by, 380-381
Capone, Al, 673, 715
Capote, Truman, 760
Capra, Frak, 702
"Captain Kangaroo" (TV series), 753-754
Capwell's, 320
Carborundum Co., 560-561
Carey, Edward, 495
Carey, Ron, 658
Cargill, 86-88, 863
Carlson Companies, 863
Carlson, Chester, 416-417

Goodyear, 297; and Gulf, 508; and *Los Angeles Times*, 399; and Marriott, 725-726; and McDonald's, 132; and 3M, 839; and Northrop, 696; and Pepsi-Cola, 65; and Phillips, 523-525; and *Reader's Digest*, 392; and Resorts International, 737; and Warner-Lambert, 252; enemies list, 778
Noble, Edward J., 363, 813
None of Your Business (Carroll), 347
Norden, 854
Norfolk and Western Railway, 639-640, 462, 645
Norge, 281
Norma Rae (movie), 712; and J.P. Stevens worker, 138
Normandin, Mary Anne, 810
Norris, Frank, 643, 749
Norris, William C., 429-431
North American Aviation, 667, 697
North American Coal, 564
North American Philips, 692
North Carolina Mutual, 517; and Pfizer board, 236
North Platte, Nebraska, 648-649
North, Phil, 333-334
Northeast Airlines, 666
Northern Pacific railroad, 636
Northern Telecom, 835-836
Northrop, 696-697, 685
Northrop: air force, 443; illegal political contributions, 621; military sales, 692
Northrop, Jack, 689
Northrop, John K., 696
Northrop-King seed company, 94
Northwest Airlines, 671-672, 462, 670, 676, 685, food cost, 668
Northwest Bancorp, 450, 469
Northwest Industries, 840-841, 835-836
Northwestern Mutual, 471
Northwestern National Bank, 32
Northwestern University, 160, 216
Norton Simon, 61-64, 82, 495, 831, as advertiser, 23, 359; purchase of wineries, 804; vs. ABC, 363
Norvell, Saunders, 814
Norway, Kingdom of: and Alcan, 543
Notre Dame, University of, 160
Novak, Kim, 702
November, Linda, 339
Now Shops, 157
Now, Barabbas (Jovanovich), 754
Noxell, 197; ad expenditures, 339
nuclear power: Bechtel plants, 861; General Electric plants, 181; Three Mile Island, 858; first plant, 857
nuclear war: false alarms, 435
nylon, invention of, 136-137
Nyrop, Donald, 671-677

O'Brien (Bryan), Jane, 813
O'Connell, Arthur, 356
O'Connor Moffat, 330
O'Donnell, John, 751
O'Donnell, William, 727-728
O'Dwyer Directory of Public Relations Firms, 348
O'Dwyer, Jack, 348
O'Flaherty, Terrence, 53
O'Green, Fred, 831
O'Hara, John, 761
O'Herron, Edward M., 253
O'Herron, Edward M., Jr., 254
O'Neil, John, 289
O'Neil, M.G., 822
O'Neil, Michael, 289-290
O'Neil, Thomas, 289
O'Neil, William, 289-290
O'Neill, Eugene, 760-761
O'Reilly, Anthony J.F., 40
O'okiep Copper, 548
O's Gold Seed Co., 94
OPEC, 506, 514, 520, 521, 528, 530
Oak Farms, 119

Oakland High School, 559
Oakland Motor Car, 271
Oakland Raiders, 559
Oberkotter, Harold, 657
Oberkotter, Paul, 657
Oberlin College, 160
Observer, The, 494
Occidental Life, 471
Occidental Petroleum, 517-521, and Mead, 582-583, 835-836; and Charter, 496; executive salaries, 505, 529; foreign sales, 818; illegal political contributions, 621; stockholders, 484; vs. Standard Oil (Indiana), 534
occupant mailing, birth of, 238
Occupational Health and Safety Administration (OSHA), 849
Ocean Club, 737
Ochs Trust, 384
Ochs, Adolph, 384
Octopus, The (Norris), 643
Odegard, Sigurd, 427
Odom, Guy, 171
Odyssey Records, 367
Oersted, H.C., 544
Offield, Dorothy Wrigley, 873
Off the Rax clothing, 122
Off-track betting: see New York City OTB
Ogden Foods, 726
Ogilvy & Mather, 340, 345, 597
Ohio Match, 62, 63
oil: consumption per second in U.S., 507
oil cartel: first, 502, 521
oil companies: officer salaries, 505, 529; oil reserves, 520; first involvement in Mid-East, 507; in Fortune 500, 536; in Standard Oil Trust, 500; rank in sales, production, reserves, 520
oil pipeline: world's first, 515
oil well, first offshore, 562; first successful, 500
Oil, Chemical & Atomic Workers (OCAW), 527, 563, 600, 609
Okefenokee Swamp (Georgia), 585
Old Ben Coal, 537, 564
Old Dominion University, 256
Old Masters of Retailing (Reilly), 322
Old Republic Life Insurance, 477
Olds, Ransom E., 271
Oldsmobile, 280, 293
Olinkraft, 163
Olin Mathieson Chemical, 245
Olins, Wally, 657
Olmsted, Frederick Law, 7, 167
Olshaker, Mark, 413
Olson, H. Everett, 620
Olson, James E., 425
Olympia Brewing, 798
Olympus camera, 413
Onassis, Jackie, 326
Ong, John D., 292
Opel, 265, 271, 293
Opel, John R., 441
Oppenheimer, Harry, 555
Opportunities Industrialization Centers, 276
Ordway, John G., 839
Ordway, Lucius P., 838
Ore-Ida, vs. Carnation, 13
Oreffice, Paul F., 602
Orford Copper, 556
Orion films, 852
Orlon, 137
Oscar Mayer, see Mayer, Oscar
Oscher, Max, 22
Osco stores, 116
Osfield, L. Rita, 171
Osgood, Colonel Samuel, 457
Oshkosh, truck sales, 260
Ostin, Mo., 716-717
Otis Elevator Co., 854-855
Otis, General Harrison Gray, 398
Ottaway newspapers, 374
Ottinger, Lawrence, 571
Ottinger, Richard, 571

Oursler, Fulton, 393
Oursler, Will, 478
Outstanding Young Farmer, 624
Overland Mail, 482
Owens-Illinois, 462, 587, 627
oyster crackers, 56

PBS (Public Broadcasting Service), 517, 789
PLATO (computer system), 429
PLUS stores, 106
PPG Industries, 348-349
PSA, 675-676
PUMA (robot), 430
Pabst Brewery, 783-784, 792; ads for, 340, 345; share of beer market, 785
Pace, Norma T., 839
Pacific Coast Condensed Milk Company, 12
Pacific Coast Oil Company, 528-529
Pacific Electric Heating Company, 179
Pacific Gas & Electric, 194, 665
Pacific Holding Corporation, 47
Pacific Lighting, 194
Pacific Mills, 134
Pacific Motor Trucking, 643
Pacific Power & Light, 564
Pacific Southwest Airlines, see PSA
Packaging Corp. of America, 848
Packard, David, 432-433, 531, 619, 686
Paddington, 773
Paepcke, Walter, 493, 516
Page, Fred, 60
Page, George, 59-60
Page, Jane, 471
Page, Walter H., 467, 471
pain killers, top ten, 215
Paine Webber, and GTE, 427
Paisley, David M., 245
Pakistan, 695
Palevsky, Max, 418
Paley, William, 366-369
Pall Mall cigarettes, 777
Palmer, Lowell M., 245
Palmer, Robert, 414
Palumbo, Art, 807
Pamplin, Robert E., 576-577
Pan American Grace Airlines (Panagra), 817
Pan American World Airways, 672-674, 462, 659, 661, 670, 676, 682, 685; foreign sales, 818; food cost, 668; and National Airlines, 669-676, 815, 835-836; vs. Gulf + Western, 821; and Iran, 496; Intercontinental Hotels, 723; PR staff, 348-349
Pan Handle line, 596
Pan-Alaska Fisheries, 14
Panasonic: dictation machines, 419
Panavision, 714
Panitt, Merrill, 402
Pantheon books, 762
paper bags: machine for, 585
"Paper Chase" (TV show), 712
paper companies: ten biggest, 584; price-fixing by, 587
Paperbacks for the People, 746-751
Parade, 389
Paradise Beach Hotel, 737
Paradise Island Casino, Hotel & Villas, 737
Paramount Pictures, 363, 703, 709, 740, 820-821
Pardee homebuilders, 587
Parfet, Ray T., 249
Parish, Preston, 250
Park Newspapers and Broadcasting Stations, 388-390, newspapers owned by, 380-381
Park Place casino, 728
Park, President Chung Hee (South Korea), 509
Park, Roy H., 358, 388, 390
Parke Davis, 235, 251-252
Parke-Bernet auctioneers, 811
Parker Bros. 32
Parker, Dorothy, 702, 750
Parks, Gordon, 794
Parks, Henry G., Jr., 819
Parr, Jeanne L., 243

Wheaties cereal, ads for, 530
Whirlpool, 189-191
whiskey: distilling of, 796-797; top-selling brands, 795
Whitcomb, Edgar D., 228
"White Christmas" (song), 721
White Consolidated Industries, 191-193, 261, 271
White Eagle Oil & Refining, 515
White Front discount stores, 325
White Motor Corp., 191-192, 260
White Spot restaurants, 30
White, Barry, 712
White, Captain Samuel, 135-136
White, Dan, 23
White, Edward II, 697
White, E. B., 755
White, Theodore, 754
White, Thomas H., 191
White-Westinghouse, 192
Whitehouse & Hardy, 147
Whitehouse, Alton G., 537
Whitin Machine Works, 192
Whitman, Marina von Neumann, 276, 634
"Whiz Kids," 268, 830
Wickes, 172-173
Wickes, Edward, 173
Wickes, Henry, 173
Wickes, Randall, 173
Wickman, Eric, 652
Wide World of Sports (ABC), 363
Wienstock's stores, 328
Wiggin, Albert H., 454
Wild, Claude, 508
Wildcat (Navy fighter), 687
Wilder, Thornton, 750
Wiley, Dr. Harvey W., 16
Wilkins, Beriah, 404
Wilkinson Sword, 204
Willamette Industries, 587
Willer, Thomas, 571
William Douglas McAdams ad agency, 235
Williamette Pulp & Paper Co., 573
Williams & Humbert sherry, 805
Williams Companies, 566
Williams, Andy, 717
Williams, Eugene F., Jr., 245
Williams, Franklin H., 7
Williams, Harold M., 62
Williams, Harold, 525, 815
Williams, J. B., toiletries, 58
Williams, Mary Lou, 716
Williams, Richard, 604
Williams, Winston, 679
Willis, Mrs. Verabelle, R.N., 36
Wills brothers, 770
Willys-Overland, 261, 263
Wilmington *News-Journal*, 608
Wilmington Trust Company, 608, 610
Wilson Foods, 81-82, 27, 47
Wilson Sporting Goods, 64, 81
Wilson, Charles E., 275
Wilson, Edward B., 350
Wilson, J. Tylee, 782
Wilson, Joseph C., 416-417
Wilson, Joseph R., Jr., 416
Wilson, Joseph R., Sr., 416
Wilson, Kemmons, 720-721, 722

Wilson, Lori, 377
Wilson, Margaret Push, 613
Wilson, Porterfield, 227
Wilson, Thornton, 685, 686
Wilson, Woodrow, 593, 631
Wiman, Colonel Charles Deere, 622-623
Wine Spectrum, 804
wine: expenditures on in U.S., 806; largest U.S. suppliers of, 804; produced in U.S., 806
Winegardner & Hammons, 723
Winegardner, Roy E., 722
wineries, bought by corporations, 804-805
winery, world's largest, 804
Wing, Daniel G., 79
Winkler, Henry, 363
Winn-Dixie, 123, 110, 120-1
Winnerman, Robert, 171
Winter, George F., 38
Winters, Jonathan, 514
Winthrop Chemical, 247
Winton, Alexander, 292
Witkin, Richard, 693
Wolfe, Dr. Sidney M., 227
Wolfe, Louis, 746
Wolfe, Paul J., 505
Wolfe, Tom, 733
Wolff, Kurt and Helen, 762
Wolff, Leon, 593-594, 596-597
Wolle, Francis, 585
Wolt, Irene, *Thinking Big*, 399
Wolverton, Marcine, 728
Women's Action Alliance, 735
Women's Right Project, 735
women: largest employers of, 313
Wonder Woman comic book, 714
Wood Bros. builders, 811
Wood, General Robert E., 516
Wood, Richard D., 226-227, 374
Wood, Robert Elkington, 311-312
Woodhull, Virginia, 649
Woodruff, Ernest, 18
Woodruff, Robert Winship, 18-20
Woodstock (movie), 716
Woodward, Harper, 669
Woodward/Lothrop, 306
Woolard, Paul P., 615
Woolco discount stores, 314, 317, 328
Woollcott, Alexander, 393
Woolman, C.E., 666
Woolsey, John (judge), 761
Woolworth's 314-319, 328, 348, employees, 628; foreign sales, 818
Woolworth, 628
Woolworth, Frank, 301, 315-6, 319
Worcester, Dr. Dorothy, 742
World Bank, first president of, 404
World Book Company, 753
World Color Press, 811
World Cruiser (airplane), 693
World Publishing, 399
World Wide Agency, 351
World Wildlife Fund, 616
Worth Ratliff, 306
Wrangler Wranch franchises, 143
Wrenn, Ann, 382
Wright J. Patrick, 272-273
Wright, Frank Lloyd, 866, 868
Wright, James S., 493

Wright, John W., 373
Wrigley Wm., Jr. Co.: expenditures, 339
Wrigley, Philip, 871
Wrigley, William Jr., 871, 873
Wrigley, William, 541
Wrigley, Wm., Jr., 870-873, 215, 865
Wriston, Henry, 459
Wriston, Kathryn D., 616
Wriston, Walter, 456, 458-459, 461, 616
Wuthering Heights (Bronte), 750
Wyeth, John, & Co., 214
Wyeth, N. C., 18, 625
Wyeth, Stuart, 214
Wyman, Thomas, 37-38, 69, 369
Wynn, Ed, 540
Wynn, Keenan, 856

Xerox, 415-419, 408, 410, 411, 781; charity, 535; foreign sales, 818; Rockefeller shares in, 867; and Citicorp, 460; and Time, 396; and public TV, 370; vs. Exxon, 505
xylitol (sweetener), 873

Yale University, 160, 439, 642, 672
Yankelovich, Skelly & White polling group, 613
Yellin, Harvey Z., 347
Yellin, Samuel, 347
Yellow Cab, 677
Yellow Freight System, 654
yellow journalism, 406
Yerxa, Thomas, 12
York, 281
Yosemite National Park, 708, 710
Young & Rubicam, 217, 345, 357
Young Men's Christian Association, 73
Young Quinlan (Minneapolis), 144
Young's Market Corp., 805
Young, C. C., 451
Young, James Harvey, 237
Young, James Webb, 342-343, 346-347
Young, John A., 433
Young, Margaret, 778
Young, Russell D., 621
Young, Whitney, 778

Zabriskie Point (movie), 730
Zaire, 695
Zanuck, Darryl F., 712-713
Zanuck, Richard, 712
Zellerbach, Anthony, 572-573
Zellerbach, Harold, 573-574
Zellerbach, Isadore (I.Z.), 573
Zellerbach, James David, 573
Zellerbach, William, 574
Zemurry, Samuel, 79
Zenith, 193-194
Zhizhin, Juri B., 65
Ziegler, Ron, 351
Ziff-Davis: 389
Zilg, Gerard C., 604-605
Zink, Jacqueline, 188
Zink, John, Company, 188
zipper, invention of, 153
Zornow, Gerald, 410
Zulu wars, 54
ZuZu ginger snaps, 56

CREDITS

We acknowledge permission granted for use of material on the following pages: (8) Reprinted with permission from the June 18, 1979, issue of *Advertising Age*. Copyright © 1979 by Crain Communications, Inc. (23) Reprinted with permission from the September 6, 1979, issue of *Advertising Age*. Copyright © 1979, Crain Communications, Inc. (29) Reprinted with permission from the April 30, 1979, issue of *Advertising Age*. Copyright © 1979 by Crain Communications, Inc. (31) Reprinted with permission from Simmons Market Research Bureau. (34) Reprinted with permission from the July 9, 1979, issue of *Advertising Age*. Copyright © 1979, Crain Communications, Inc. (42) Reprinted with permission from the September 17, 1979, issue of *Advertising Age*. Copyright © 1979 by Crain Communications, Inc. (65) Jingle is © 1940 PepsiCo, Inc. (152) Reprinted from *U.S. News & World Report*, © 1980, U.S. News & World Report, Inc. (160) Reprinted by permission of the National Association of College and University Business Officers, from the 1979 NACUBO Comparative Performance Study. (191) Reprinted by permission of the *Wall Street Journal*, Dow Jones & Company, Inc., © 1979. All rights reserved. (220) Reprinted with permission from the April 2, 1979, issue of *Advertising Age*. Copyright © 1979, Crain Communications, Inc. (272) Excerpts from J. Patrick Wright, *On a Clear Day You Can See General Motors*, reprinted by permission of J. Patrick Wright Enterprises, 917 Fisher Road, Grosse Point, Michigan 48230 (book available from that address, $12.95, plus postage). (339) Reprinted with permission from the September 6, 1979, issue of *Advertising Age*. Copyright © 1979, Crain Communications, Inc. (352) Reprinted with permission from the July 5, 1976, and the April 30, 1980, issues of *Advertising Age*. Copyright © Crain Communications, Inc. (359) Reprinted with permission from the September 6, 1979, issue of *Advertising Age*. Copyright © 1979, Crain Communications, Inc. (364) Article by Neil Hickey reprinted with permission from *TV Guide®* magazine, copyright © 1979 by Triangle Publications, Inc., Radnor, Pennsylvania. (366) Selection from *The Best Thing on TV* by Jonathan Price, copyright © 1978 by Jonathan Price. Reprinted by permission of Viking Penguin Inc. (369) Selection from *30 Seconds* by Michael Arlen. Copyright © 1979–80 by Michael Arlen. Reprinted by permission of Farrar Straus & Giroux. This material originally appeared in *The New Yorker*. (370) Reprinted courtesy *Mainliner* magazine, carried aboard United Airlines. © 1979 East/West Network, Inc. (389) Folio 400, Folio Magazine Publishing Corporation, New Canaan, Connecticut. (400) Copyright © 1977 by Samuel A. Schreiner, Jr., from *The Condensed World of Reader's Digest*. Reprinted with permission of Stein & Day, Publishers. (490) Copyright © 1980, The Earl G. Graves Publishing Co., 295 Madison Avenue, New York, New York 10017. All rights reserved. (697) Copyright © 1980, The New York Times Co. (701) Reprinted by permission of National Utility Service, Inc. (757) Copyright © 1980, The New York Times Co. (808) Copyright © 1980, The Earl G. Graves Publishing Co., 295 Madison Avenue, New York, New York 10017. All rights reserved. (826) Selections from *The Sovereign State of ITT* by Anthony Sampson. Copyright © 1973 by Anthony Sampson. Reprinted by permission of Stein & Day, Publishers, Inc. (863) Table reprinted by permission of *Forbes* magazine from the June 23, 1980, issue.

The individuals and corporations listed below granted permission to print the photographs that appear on the following pages: (2) Du Pont Company. (6) Borden's. (14, 15) Castle & Cook. (17) Reprinted with permission of The Coca-Cola Company. (24, 25) Del Monte. (33) General Mills. (35, 36) Gerber. (38) Green Giant. (49) Kellogg. (55) Oscar Mayer. (62) Norton Simon. (77) Standard Brands. (90) Doyle Dane Bernbach. (103) A&P. (115) Printed with permission of Safeway Stores, Incorporated © 1980. (126) Jolly Time. (134) Burlington Industries, Inc. (137) Du Pont Company. (138) Springs Mills, Inc. (145) Pictures from Cluett. (149) Hart Shaffner & Marx. (154) Levi Strauss & Co. (168) Kohler. (175) Black & Decker. (178, 180) General Electric. (182) Scovill. (187) Sunbeam Corporation. (189) Whirlpool Corporation. (196) Avon Products, Inc. (202) Colgate-Palmolive. (211) Abbott Laboratories. (250) The Upjohn Company. (266) Ford Motor Co. (286) Firestone Tire & Rubber Co. (288) Fruehauf Corp. (295) The BFGoodrich Co. (303) J.C. Penney. (309, 310, 311) Sears, Roebuck and Co. (332) NCR Corporation. (335) Montgomery Ward. (356, 361) Courtesy of the Procter & Gamble Company. (368) CBS, Inc. (391) Reader's Digest Association, Inc. (401) Copyright © Triangle Publications, Inc. (409) Eastman Kodak Company. (416) Xerox Corp. (424) AT&T. (432) Sperry Corp. (441) NCR Corporation. (452) United Press International. (457) St. Francis Hotel. (465) Reprinted with the permission of Continental Bank. (470) Morgan Guaranty Trust Co. (482) Wells Fargo. (492, 494) Atlantic Richfield Co. (510) Gulf Oil. (512) Carol Williams. (518) Occidental Petroleum Corp. (538) Kerr-McGee Corp. (548) AMAX Inc. (561) Kennecott Copper Corp. (595) Bethlehem Steel Corp. (606) Du Pont Company. (611) Monsanto Co. (622, 623) Deere & Co. (625) International Harvester. (627) Owens-Illinois, Inc. (630) Photos by Dick Frank, courtesy of The Continental Group, Inc. (637) Burlington Northern photo. (641) The Atchison, Topeka and Santa Fe Railway Co. (646) Southern Railway System. (651) The Bekins Co. (653) Greyhound and Hoefer-Amidei. (662) American Airlines. (663) Braniff International. (667) National Aeronautics and Space Administration. (678) Trans World Airlines. (681) United Airlines photo. (687) General Dynamics. (691) Lockheed Corp. (695) Los Angeles Times Syndicate. (711) 20th Century Fox. (719) Hilton Hotels Corp. (721) Holiday Inn. (725) Marriott. (749) Doubleday & Co. (769) American Brands Inc. (772) B.A.T Industries. (779, 781) R.J. Reynolds Industries. (786) Anheuser-Busch, Inc. (789) Adolph Coors Co. (792) Anheuser-Busch, Inc. (802) Brown-Forman Distillers Corp. (820) Gulf + Western. (838) 3M. (843) RCA. (852) Transamerica Corp. (855, 856) United Technologies Corp. (859, 860) Bechtel Power Corp. (862) Hallmark Cards, Inc. (866) S.C. Johnson. (871, 873) Wm. Wrigley Jr. Co.